The Domesday Book

England's Heritage, Then and Now

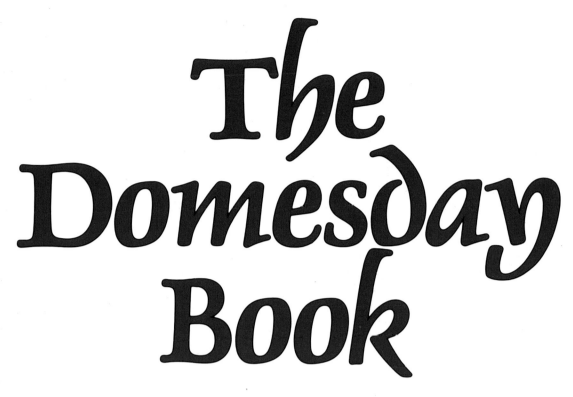

The Domesday Book

England's Heritage, Then and Now

Editor: Thomas Hinde

English Tourist Board

Guild Publishing London

THE DOMESDAY BOOK
England's Heritage, Then and Now

Created and Produced by
PHOEBE PHILLIPS EDITIONS

English translations of Domesday Book *entries:*
PHILLIMORE AND CO LTD

Specially commissioned photographs:
MARIANNE MAJERUS

Line drawings:
DENNIS AND SHEILA CURRAN

County maps:
JANET FAHY

Design:
Heather Kenmure
Geoffrey Marshall
Lucy McCrickard
Anthony Short

Phototypesetting:
Tradespools Ltd, Frome, Somerset

Origination:
Anglia Reproductions, Witham, Essex

Printed and bound in Italy by
Arnoldo Mondadori Editore, Verona.

Editorial:
Director: Tessa Clark
Jenny Barling
Ian Barritt
Tom Cain
Joanna Chapman
Andrew Chitty
DD Editorial Services
Bridget Daly
Louise Egerton
Neil Fairbairn
Fred Gill
R M Healey
Jonathan Hilton
Angela Jeffs
Penny Jones
Victoria Jones
Jane Kenrick
David Lorking
Henrietta March Phillips
Sheila Mortimer
M D Neal
David Neave
Martin Noble
Charlotte Plimmer
Redfern Publishing Services Ltd
Fiona St Aubyn
Rachel Stewart
Clive Unger Hamilton
Cecilia Walters

This edition published 1985
BOOK CLUB ASSOCIATES

by arrangement with Hutchinson
Century-Hutchinson Ltd
and
Phoebe Phillips Editions

First published in 1985
Reprinted 1986

Jacket photograph: FRAMLINGHAM CASTLE, *Suffolk.*

Frontispiece: THE TOWER OF LONDON. *Perhaps no single building in the country is more symbolic of William's conquest than the keep of the Tower. His first fortress-castle was thrown up hurriedly outside London's settlement and utilizing the old Roman walls for added protection. Soon after the great stone keep was begun, probably designed by Gundulf from the Abbey of Bec, who became Bishop of Rochester. Over the next two centuries various towers and buildings were added with two encircling walls, until by the 13th century the complex was much as we see it today.*

Pages 6 and 7: OLD ROMNEY, *Kent.*

Preface

There is nothing quite like *Domesday Book* – indeed, there is nothing remotely like it. This much historians agree about. There is no comparable 900-year-old inventory of a complete country, village by village, manor by manor. Alongside the Bible and the Koran, *Domesday* is probably one of the three best-known titles of the western world. What is more, the original book itself survives, preserved for centuries at Winchester, capital of the ancient Saxon kingdom of Wessex, now held in London at the Public Record Office. The irony is that something so well known has remained till recently, in every sense a closed book, except to a handful of medieval scholars.

The most obvious reason for this is that *Domesday* is not merely written in Latin, but in a highly abbreviated form of Latin. Another is that, even in translation, it describes a world which is so strange to us today that we need to be guided through its technicalities.

The Domesday Book: England's Heritage Then and Now aims to bring this world to life in all its fascinating detail; a world in which bishops were earls and earls were bishops, in which rents might be paid in 'sticks' of eels or sesters of honey, in which the pig, fattened on acorns, was by far the most important domestic animal, in which the south of the country was so prosperous that the king could collect his dues in the ancient way by settling with his court on a manor and living off it, while parts of the north had been so severely devastated by William I's scorched earth policy that a quarter of some counties were still waste.

As in the original survey, the book is divided into counties, based in our case on modern pre-1974 boundaries. And, following the example of William I, who allocated groups of counties to his Commissioners, we divided the country among seven writers and eight researchers in order to provide a twentieth-century view of the 13,000 settlements in *Domesday Book*.

Each county starts with a brief introduction describing the region as it was in 1086. This is followed by the major entries – an average of four or five to a county – chosen to reflect the area's geographical and social diversity. These begin with their *Domesday* entries, and go on to highlight aspects of the settlement's history – some grow into towns, some dwindle to farms, some actually fall into the sea, some remain remarkably unchanged through the centuries. Others are best known for people who lived there, battles that were fought nearby or their great houses.

The gazetteer entries that complete each county are listed alphabetically for easy reference, under the modern equivalent of their *Domesday* place-names. They give the names of leading landholders and key aspects of the settlements: churches, salt-houses, fisheries, – even vines and beehives.

Marianne Majerus travelled the country to take our specially commissioned photographs. Dennis and Sheila Curran contributed delightful line-drawings; Janet Fahy drew our county maps. Master maps show how the counties in which this book is arranged have changed, first from *Domesday* time, then after 1974. To make the technical terms understandable, we have provided a glossary, and to help with interpretation we have devised diagrammatic explanations of two sample entries. To bring to life the people, mainly Norman, who had so thoroughly taken charge of England that they became our native aristocracy, we have provided brief biographical notes on 200 of the most prominent. Dr Elizabeth Hallam who now has the original volumes in her charge as Assistant Keeper of the Medieval Records at the Public Record Office, has provided an authoritative introduction.

Domesday was commissioned by William I at his Christmas Court, 1085, and the whole enormous work of collecting the information and turning it into the book we have today was probably completed well before the end of 1086. Our book has taken rather longer. It would not have been possible without the help and enthusiasm of a great many people. I should like particularly to mention my fellow writers, Andrew Chitty, Neil Fairbairn, Clive Unger Hamilton, R.M. Healey, Michael Neal, and David Neave, as well as all the researchers and editors who worked tirelessly on the strange words and unusual names of our Anglo-Saxon and Norman ancestors.

For continuous enthusiasm and support I would like to thank particularly Phoebe Phillips, her staff, and especially Tessa Clark who became our *Domesday* scribe.

THOMAS HINDE

How this book was compiled

Major entries

Each of the main entries begins with the original *Domesday* information for that place. Names of English landholders are given as usual, while Norman names are in their French common usage of 'de' for 'of', and 'Fitz' for 'son of'. The complete entry is given except where we have omitted long lists of outlying manors. If a settlement is mentioned more than once in *Domesday* we give the other entries or indicate the number of landholders in the main text.

Gazetteer entries

The gazetteer place-names are listed alphabetically under the modern English equivalent of their 1086 place-names. Sometimes the original *Domesday* name has changed. Stanton in Huntingdonshire, for example, is now Fen Stanton. Or what was one settlement is now two modern places: Bardfield in Essex is now Great Bardfield and Little Bardfield. In both these cases, we have listed the places under their 'main' names – Stanton and Bardfield. When two 'similar' places are identified with two different *Domesday* settlements – Down Litherland and Up Litherland in Lancashire are examples – they are listed under the adjectives: Down, Up, Great, Little, Upper, Lower, etc.

The *Domesday* information, *in italic*, begins with the 1086 name, usually a Latinized version of the original English name. This is followed by the landholders, in the order in which they are listed in *Domesday Book* itself. It is sometimes interesting to see that before 1066 the land was held by Queen Edith, for example, or Earl Harold, indicated with the word 'formerly'. Earl Harold, as he is almost always called in *Domesday*, was King Harold, killed at the Battle of Hastings. Specific mentions of churches, mills, fisheries, etc. come next, as do details about beehives or vines and produce such as wheat or honey in which dues were paid.

Modern information, in ordinary type, shows how the settlement has developed since *Domesday*. We have highlighted anything that relates back to the *Domesday* entry – churches, mills, etc. – and artefacts such as ancient burial grounds or Roman roads that would have been visible in 1086. Information about notable events or people is also included.

On a number of occasions, *Domesday* places are described as 'lost', a term which, in medieval scholarship, is generally accepted to refer to a settlement which is no longer inhabited. We have described places as lost when they are not on the 1:50,000 Ordnance Survey map. In other cases, we have described houses, farms, etc. on the site. A 'lost' village is not one that cannot be identified. Places in *Domesday Book* that are now unidentifiable have not been included in our gazetteer.

Finally, the compilation of a book of this size requires constant updating and we hope that readers will feel free to write to us with specific additional information which we may be able to incorporate into future editions.

PHOEBE PHILLIPS EDITIONS

Contents

County boundary maps

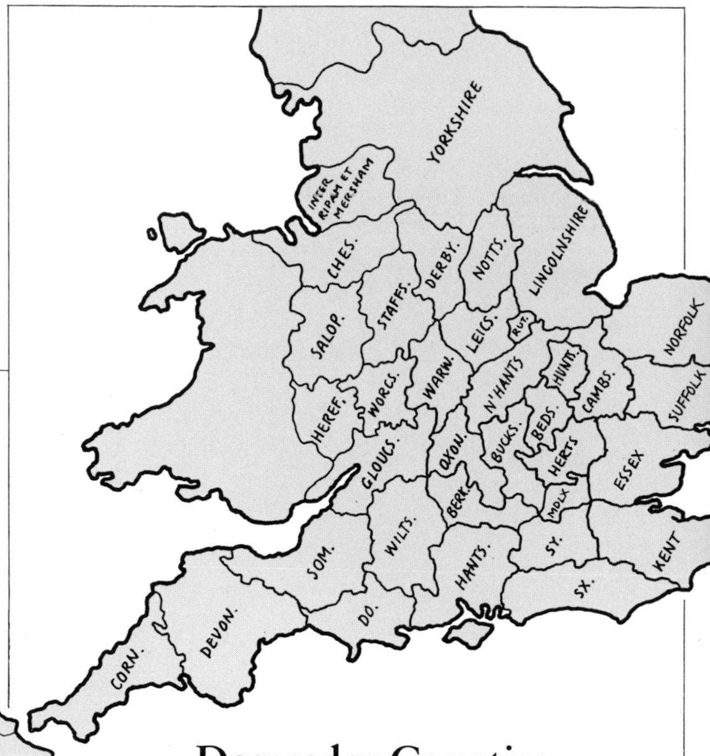

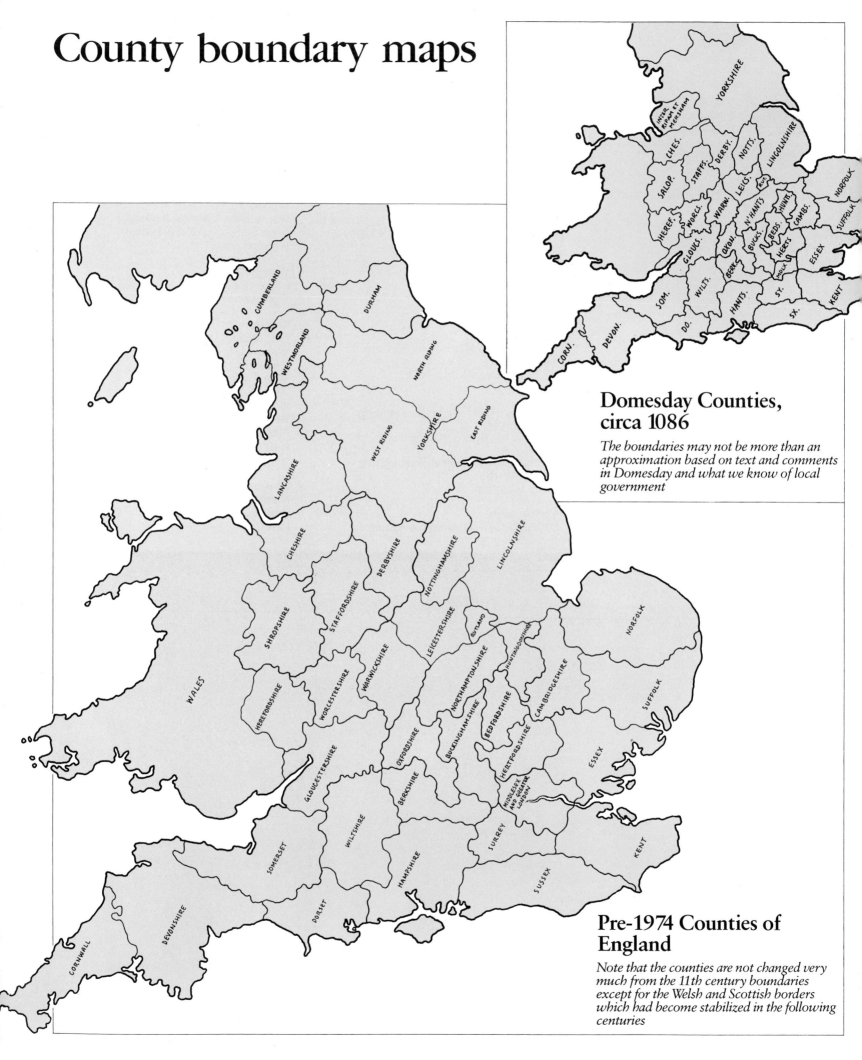

Domesday Counties, circa 1086

The boundaries may not be more than an approximation based on text and comments in Domesday and what we know of local government

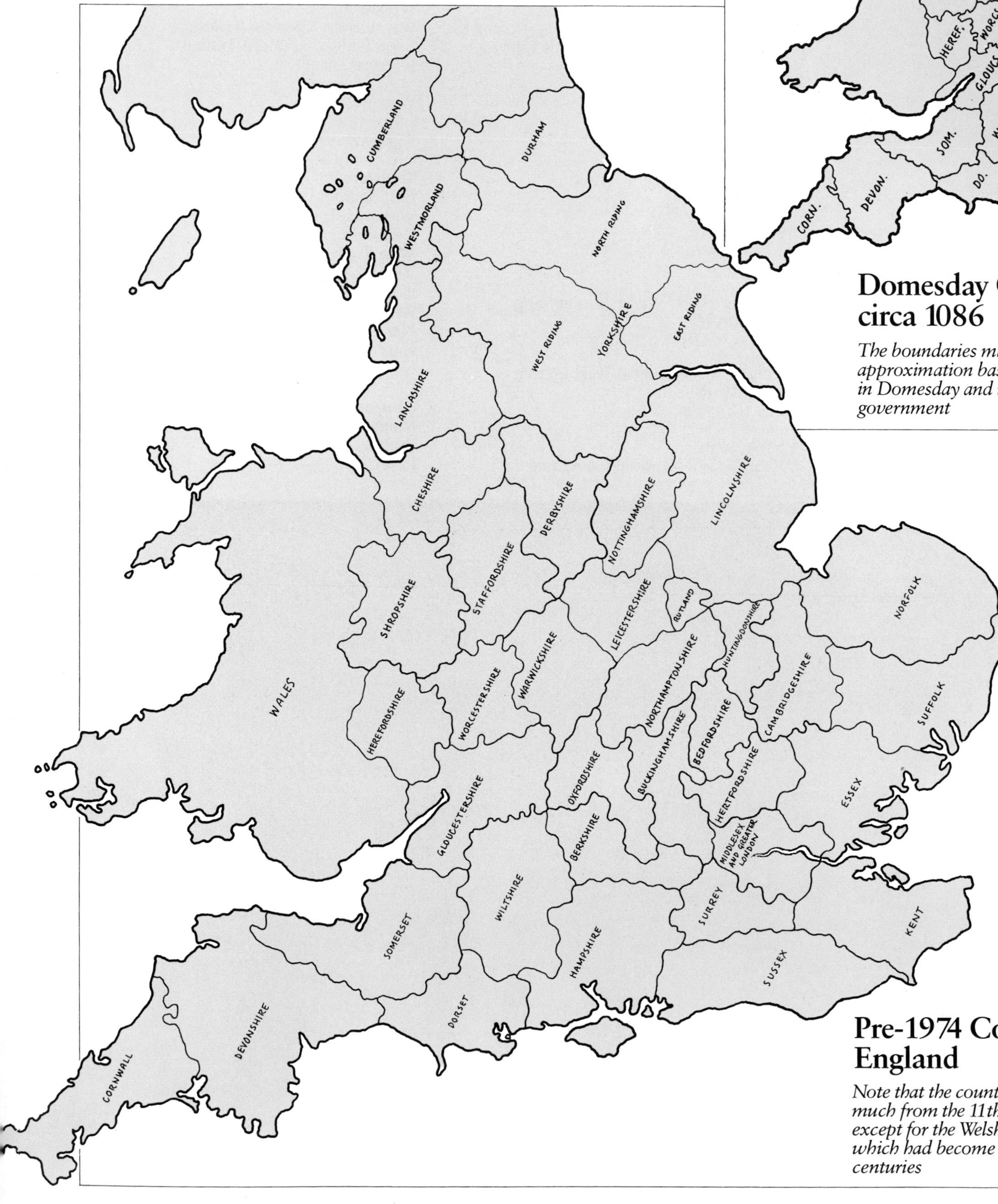

Pre-1974 Counties of England

Note that the counties are not changed very much from the 11th century boundaries except for the Welsh and Scottish borders which had become stabilized in the following centuries

Present Counties of England

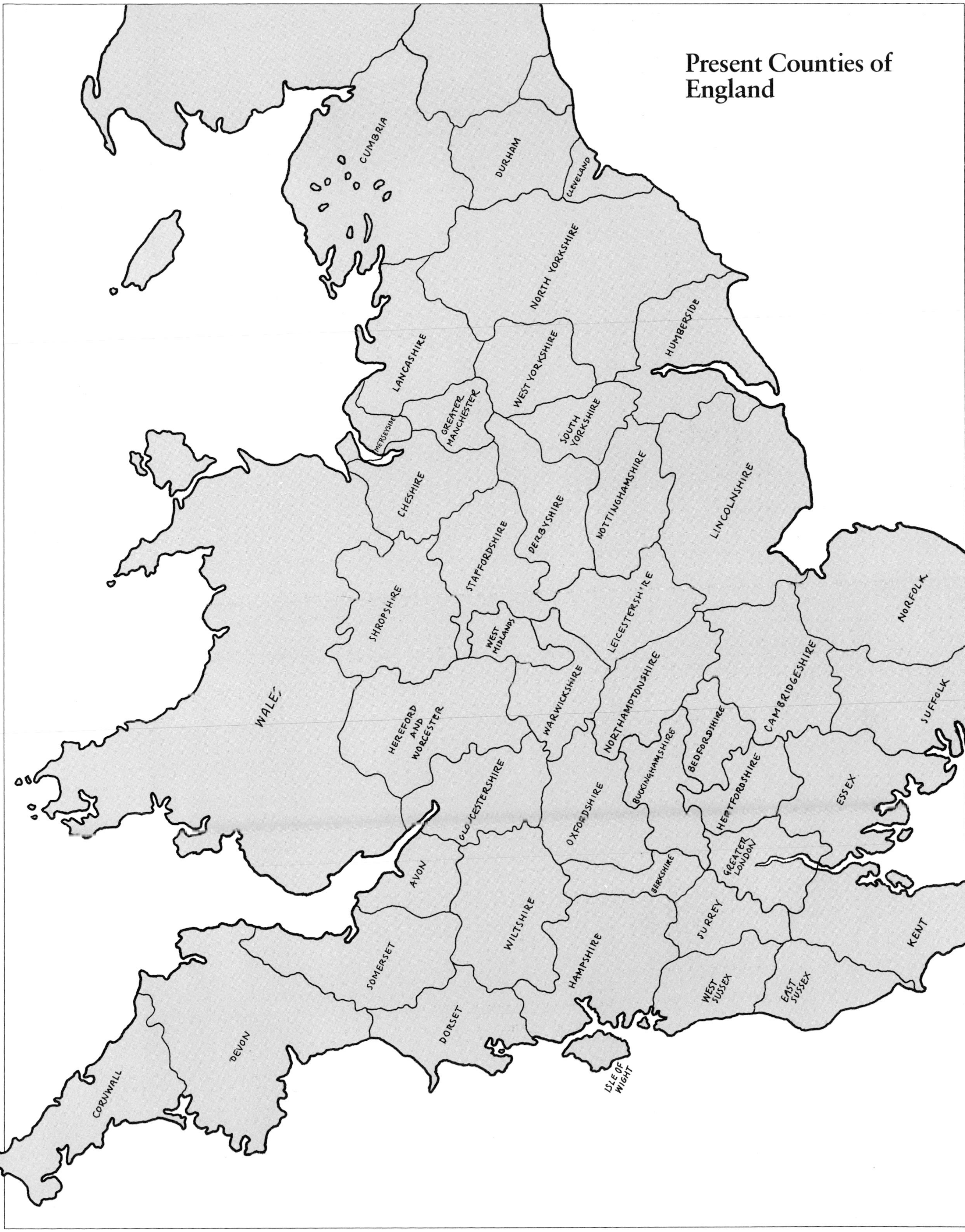

The Story of *Domesday Book*

Domesday Book, our earliest public record, is a rare and remarkable survey which details landholding and resources in late eleventh-century England. No other Western European state produced anything even broadly comparable in its scope until several centuries later. In its sophistication and in the comprehensiveness of its information, *Domesday Book* remained unequalled until the nineteenth century. Moreover, the wealth of information that it contains illuminates one of the most crucial times in our history: the conquest and settlement of England by William I and his Norman and northern French followers.

England in the eleventh century

The *Domesday* survey is essentially the product of the powerful will and relentless curiosity of William the Conqueror. Nevertheless, it could not have been made without the comparatively advanced administrative system that William inherited from his Anglo-Saxon predecessors. By the year AD1000 most of England was already divided into the network of shires that was to persist with relatively little alteration until the reorganization of the county boundaries in 1974. Medieval government was far from possessing all the centralized powers of the modern state, but the pre-Conquest English kings exercised considerable authority over most of the local magnates. This was true both in the Danelaw – those areas in East Anglia and other eastern and northern counties where Danish laws and customs had prevailed since the time of Alfred the Great – and in the other predominantly Anglo-Saxon regions. The English kings had been able to mint a coinage controlled from the centre. They were also powerful enough to gather substantial amounts of silver from the tax known as Danegeld, a name originally used in the 10th century for money raised to buy off marauding Danish armies. The silver was a sign of England's wealth, which was probably, even in this early period, founded in large measure upon its wool trade.

With such resources and with the means for a ruler to tap them, England was one of the greatest prizes in north-western Europe.

Edward the Confessor was childless, and although William, Duke of Normandy, was only related indirectly to him, Edward made him his heir in 1051. Powerful opposition came from Earl Godwin, the leading English noble, and his heir, Earl Harold.

In January 1066 Edward died and Harold at once seized the throne. The new king was soon called upon to defend his realm against King Harold Hadrada of Norway. The Norwegians were decisively defeated and Hadrada slain but less than three weeks later, Harold was again fighting for his kingdom, against William of Normandy at Hastings. Harold's army was annihilated by the superior tactics of William's cavalry. This, the most momentous military event of English history, resulted eventually in the large-scale destruction of the English aristocracy, the imposition of an alien nobility and a Norman reordering of society along feudal lines.

William the Conqueror was one of the most able monarchs ever to rule England. He succeeded to the ducal title in 1035 when still a child. He had been forced to struggle long and hard to bring his turbulent vassals to obedience, but by 1066 he had not only consolidated his power in the Duchy but extended its influence. After 1066 for two decades he dominated the politics of north-western Europe. William applied the lessons of political realism taught him in the course of winning control of Normandy to the process of subjugating England. When he thought it necessary, this included utter ruthlessness.

Why the *Domesday* survey was made

During the last years of his reign William's power was threatened from a number of quarters. The North was chronically rebellious, and in 1085, King Canute of Denmark and King Olaf of Norway gathered a great fleet of ships and made preparations for an invasion.

The invasion did not materialize, but such a large and costly exercise may have indicated to the Conqueror the need to reassess Danegeld in order to maximize the revenue, and the value of knowing, in as much detail as possible, precisely what his subjects possessed in England. A reassessment of geld was therefore set in motion and took place at about the same time as the *Domesday* survey (it only survives for the south-western counties), but this was not, as many Victorian historians believed, the principal object of the exercise. *Domesday* is far more than just a fiscal record. It is a detailed statement of lands held by the king and by his tenants and of the resources which went with those lands. It recorded which manors rightfully belonged to which estates, thus ending years of confusion resulting from the gradual and sometimes violent dispossession of the Anglo-Saxons by their Norman conquerors. It was moreover a 'feudal' statement, giving the identities of the tenants-in-chief (land holders) who held their lands directly from the Crown, and of their tenants and under-tenants. The importance attached by the king to exerting control over those on the lower rungs of the feudal ladder is demonstrated by the oaths of loyalty which he extracted from the important under-tenants at Salisbury in 1086. The compilation of such detailed information, however, required a survey wholly unprecedented in its scope and precision. The fact that the scheme was executed and brought almost to complete fruition within two years is a tribute to the political power and formidable will of William the Conqueror.

How *Domesday Book* was made

One of the most important near-contemporary accounts of the making of the *Domesday* survey is that of the Anglo-Saxon chronicler. He tells us that at his 1085 Christmas court at Gloucester William

had much thought and very deep discussion about this country – how it was occupied or with what sorts of people. Then he sent his men all over England into every shire and had them find out how many hundred hides there were in the shire, or what land and cattle the king himself had in the country, or what dues he ought to have in twelve months from the shire. Also he had a record made of how much land his archbishops had, and his bishops and his abbots and his earls, and . . . what or how much everybody had who was occupying land in England, in land or cattle, and how much money it was worth. So very narrowly did he have it investigated, that there was no single hide nor a yard of land, nor indeed (it is a shame to relate but it seemed no shame to him to do) one ox nor one cow nor one pig which was there left out, and not put down in his record: and all these records were brought to him afterwards.

This passage hints at the dismay and apprehension later expressed in the naming of the survey as *Domesday*, because of the association with the Day of Judgement, that terrible verdict against which there was no appeal.

Another important description of the survey was written within a few years of its completion by Robert, Bishop of Hereford, one of the ecclesiastics whom William had brought to England. The king's men, he wrote,

made a survey of all England; of the lands in each of the counties; of the possessions of each of the magnates, their lands, their habitations, their men both bond and free, living in huts or with their own houses and lands; of ploughs, horses and other animals; of the services and payments due from each and every estate. After these investigators came others who were sent to unfamiliar counties to check the first description and to denounce any wrongdoers to the king. And the land was troubled with many calamities arising from the gathering of the royal taxes.

Here we are given invaluable clues about when and how the inquiries were undertaken and in recent years most historians have come to agree on the general outlines of this vast operation.

As we have seen, the survey was launched at William's Christmas court in 1085. Initially each tenant-in-chief, whether bishop, abbot or baron, and each sheriff and other local official was required to send in a list of manors and men. There were already earlier lists of lands and taxes in existence, some dating from the Anglo-Saxon period, others from after 1066, which were kept both in the principal royal city of Winchester and locally in the shires. They too were drawn upon for the survey. All of England, apart from the northern counties, which were not yet firmly under Norman control, was divided into seven

SELBORNE, *Hampshire: Ancient yew tree, said to have been planted 100 years before* Domesday.

circuits. These circuits covered groupings of counties and to each of them were assigned three or four royal commissioners, high-ranking and trusted men whose task it was to test in the courts the accuracy of the information already provided. The Worcester circuit was travelled by Remigius, Bishop of Lincoln, with a clerk and two monks in attendance, and three important laymen: Henry de Ferrers, Walter Giffard and Adam FitzHubert, brother of Eudo the Steward. One of the commissioners in the south-west was probably William, Bishop of Durham. These are the only names to have survived, but in their rank and status they were almost certainly typical.

It was the king's will that the survey should proceed swiftly, and an annotation made in one of the volumes of *Domesday Book* soon after it was finished states that the intitial stages were completed in 1086. The commissioners visited each of the county courts in turn and cross-questioned all those with an interest in the land, from the barons to the villagers. In *The Ely Inquest*, a contemporary document, even the questions they asked are cited.

They inquired what the manor was called; who held it at the time of King Edward; who holds it now; how many hides there are; how many ploughs in demesne (i.e., held by the lord) and how many belonging to the men; how many villagers; how many cottagers; how many slaves; how many freemen; how many sokemen; how much woodland; how much meadow; how much pasture; how many mills; how many fisheries; how much had been added to or taken away from the estate; what it used to be worth altogether; what it is worth now; and how much each freeman and sokeman had and has. All this was to be recorded thrice, namely as it was in the time of King Edward, as it was when King William gave it and as it is now. And it was also to be noted whether more could be taken than is now being taken.

The Ely Inquest also records the names of the jurors for some 'hundreds'. In Flendish Hundred, Cambridgeshire, they represented both the Norman and English races: Robert of Histon, Osmund the small, Fulcold a man of the Abbot of Ely, Baldwin the cook, Edwin the priest, Wulfric of Tevresham, Silac, and Godwin of Fulbourn.

The mass of evidence thus produced was written down in Latin – as was the survey as a whole – and this material was then sorted and re-sorted until it reached its final format under counties, landholders, hundreds or wapentakes, and manors. It is not known how many drafts lay between the proceedings in the courts and the final circuit summaries as presented to the king, but there were probably variations betwen shires and circuits.

Certainly, one of the final circuit summaries has survived in the form of *Little Domesday* and perhaps a second in the Exeter (Exon) *Domesday*. The latter is something of a ragbag, containing records of the 1084–86 geld reassessment in the south-west, and the *Domesday* returns for Cornwall, Somerset, most of Devon, and parts of Wiltshire and Dorset, the rest having been lost. Arranged first by landholders and then by counties, it presents a great deal of information about the manors and boroughs that it lists. Thus details of the livestock and the names of tenants often appear which were left out when the entries were transferred to *Domesday Book* itself.

Little Domesday and *Great Domesday*

Little Domesday Book is undoubtedly the final summary for the Eastern circuit, which consisted of Essex, Norfolk and Suffolk, some of the most populous counties of England. It is arranged by counties first and then by tenants. The work of several scribes, it is neatly if hurriedly written, the haste emerging in the many minor errors which appear in the text. The material for the three counties which it covers was never incorporated into the final summarized volume of *Great Domesday*, and this other volume was therefore preserved by the royal administration as part of the final record. Its headings were later picked out in red ink in order to give it a more formal appearance and to make it easier to find individual items amongst the mass of detail.

All the other final circuit summaries were recast into the more concise pattern of *Great Domesday*, almost certainly by one scribe, most probably based at Winchester. His task could well have been cut short – before he had time to incorporate the returns for the Eastern circuit, for London and for Winchester – by the death of William the Conqueror in September 1087. He has been tentatively identified as Sampson, a royal chaplain, later to become Bishop of Winchester. As he was confronted with the awe-inspiring challenge not merely of copying but of summarizing an enormous quantity of material as quickly as possible, it is hardly surprising that minor errors crept in and produced inconsistencies which have exercised *Domesday* scholars ever since.

Each shire summary was inscribed in a quire, that is, a small booklet, with 44 lines of script to each carefully ruled folio. The headings were all written in red, often in capital letters. As the scribe progressed, however, the writing became more compressed and relatively less neat and some of the county sections overlapped between quires. The summary of the final circuit to be dealt with, which covered the West Midlands and the Welsh Marches, shows all the signs of having been dashed off extremely quickly.

Domesday is an impressive and agreeable document to consult and to handle. Throughout the centuries its custodians have treated it with great reverence, and its pages are for the most part in almost pristine condition. Because parchment benefits from the oil from human hands, the folios have remained soft and supple. The writing, which is in the Caroline minuscule style, is attractive and easy to read, although the Latin words are heavily abbreviated. In the early twelfth century the document was already known as a 'book', and it is probable that the quires were bound up at about that time. Recent research on the early covers of *Little Domesday* suggests that they date certainly from before 1220 and probably from far earlier than that.

Domesday's two volumes were widely used for many centuries for administrative purposes. They are of equal if different value to the historian, the geographer, the archaeologist and the demographer of today.

Domesday law and politics

Domesday Book can tell us a great deal about the political hierarchy of William's England. Feudal custom imposed by William on the English kingdom resulted in all land being deemed to be held from the king either directly or indirectly. The entries begin with the Crown lands, including those manors held directly by the monarch's tenants. The tenants-in-chief, great and small, were the next layer down in the feudal pryamid. In *Domesday Book* the ecclesiastics, the bishops and abbots, usually, but not invariably, come after the king. They are followed by the laymen; and the under-tenants of the tenants-in-chief, ecclesiastical and lay, are also named. Those who held the lands prior to the Norman seizure are always referred to as 'predecessors' of the current holders. King Harold is, except on two occasions which are clearly mistakes, consistently entitled 'Earl Harold'. Thus through these legal fictions was his reign consigned to oblivion.

The large-scale transfer of land had, not surprisingly, caused many problems, and there are numerous entries in *Domesday Book* that refer to disputes over rightful possession – indications that there was already much work for lawyers.

Domesday's contents: some manorial descriptions

The nature of the information which *Domesday* offers concerning manors and their inhabitants may be illustrated most clearly through a look at some individual entries. The first example, taken from *Great Domesday*, describes the royal manor of St Kew in Cornwall.

ST KEW. 5 h, but it paid tax for 2 h. Land for 22 ploughs; in lordship 1 h; 2 ploughs; 8 slaves. 59 villagers and 26 smallholders with 20 ploughs & 4 h. Meadow, 1 acre; pasture, 40 acres; woodland, 1 league long and 3 f. wide. It pays £6 weighed and assayed. 9 cattle; 120 sheep. Two manors, POUNDSTOCK and ST GENNYS, have been taken from this manor. 1½ h. Land for 12 ploughs. Iovin holds them from the Count of Mortain. Formerly 60s; value now 40s.

The second entry relates to the manor of Southwell in Thurgaton wapentake, held by the archbishop of York. The county, Nottinghamshire, was a former Danelaw area.

In SOUTHWELL with its outliers 22½ c. of land taxable. Land for 24 ploughs. Archbishop Thomas has 10 ploughs in lordship and 10 Freemen, 75 villagers and 23 smallholders who have 37 ploughs. 2 mills, 40s; a fishpond and a ferry 6s. 6 men-at-arms hold 4½ c. of this land. 3 clerics have 1½ c. of land, of which 2 b. are in prebend. 2 Englishmen have 3 c. and 5 b. of land. The men-at-arms have 7 ploughs in lordship and 35 villagers and 28 smallholders who have 21 ploughs. 1 mill, 8s. The clerics have 1½ ploughs in lordship and 7 villagers and 5 smallholders who have 3 ploughs. The Englishmen have 4 ploughs in lordship and 20 villagers and 6 smallholders who have 6½ ploughs. To Southwell belongs meadow, 188 acres; woodland

Domesday Decade *1080–1090*

1080
- Alliance between the Pope and the Normans in Sicily
- Building starts on St Sernin, Toulouse, a large pilgrim church
- Building, in Romanesque style, starts on Lund Cathedral, Sweden

1081
- El Cid (Rodrigo Diaz de Bivar) is expelled from Castile
- Robert Guiscard, the Norman, invades the Balkans
- Planning and building starts on old St Paul's in London; destroyed in the fire of 1666

1082
- Alexios I grants Venice extraordinary commercial privileges for its help against the Normans
- Building starts on Fécamp Abbey

1083
- Alexios defeats the Normans at Larissa
- Ely Cathedral is re-built
- St Etienne in Nevers is built as a Cluniac abbey, in the mature Romanesque style

1084
- Henry IV is crowned Holy Roman Emperor by the Pope
- Rome is sacked by the Normans
- Grande Chartreuse is founded by St Bruno
- Salerno Cathedral is built by Robert Guiscard
- Cloisters of the abbey at St Domingo de Silos with the finest Romanesque sculpture in Spain

1085
- Building starts on Mainz Cathedral
- Guiscard dies; Norman attacks on Byzantium cease and Alexios expels the Normans from the Balkans
- Umme, ruler of Bornu-Kanem, is converted to Islam and becomes sultan
- Mosque and mausoleum of Badr al-Jamali are built in Cairo
- Pope Gregory dies in Salerno
- Ssŭ-ma Kuang publishes his chronological history of China, considered a masterpiece of clear writing

1086
- William I collects information for *Domesday*
- Almoravid invades Spain and defeats Alfonso of Castile; 40,000 heads are sent to North Africa as a trophy
- Mi-Yuan, the Chinese painter, is born

1087
- William I dies; William Rufus becomes king of England
- Nizam al Mulk grants hereditary fiefdoms within the Caliphate

1088
- Odo of Bayeux rebels unsuccessfully, and is banished from England
- Bologna University is founded
- Urban II becomes Pope
- Cluny Abbey is rebuilt; considered the greatest of all Romanesque churches, it was largely destroyed in the French revolution
- Building starts on the Masiid-i-Jami mosque at Isphahan, a fine example of Seljuk architecture

1089
- Henry IV marries the Princess of Kiev
- Pope Urban takes Rome from Henry IV
- David the Restorer becomes King of Georgia (Russia)
- Hierarchy of state officials with 9 ranks is established in Vietnam
- Pope Urban II makes the re-conquest of the Holy Land the First Crusade
- Building starts on Gloucester Abbey, with its massive columns in the nave
- Cathedral of Assumption in Kiev is consecrated

1090
- Inge I becomes King of Sweden
- Henry IV campaigns in Italy and defeats the Pope
- Yusef born. Tashfin returns to Spain and takes Granada; the Almoravid dynasty begins in Spain, and lasts until 1147
- Building starts on Zurich Cathedral
- St Bernard of Clairvaux is born
- Chinese build a water-driven clock

pasture 8 leagues long and 2½ furlongs wide; arable land 5 leagues long and 3 wide. Value before 1066 £40; now £40 15s. In Southwell 12 outliers are enumerated.

The third entry, from *Little Domesday*, is for the manor of Ridgewell in Hinkford hundred, Essex, held by Eustace, Count of Boulogne.

1 free man, Godwin by name, held RIDGEWELL before 1066 as one manor, for 2 hides and 3 virgates. Then 5 ploughs in lordship, later and now 4. 14 villagers; 14 slaves; 3 smallholders. Woodland, 80 pigs; meadow, 36 acres. 22 cattle, 44 pigs, 102 sheep, 30 goats and 2 cobs. To this manor have always been attached 14 Freemen with 67½ acres, who have 1½ ploughs. Meadow, 6 acres. Value of the whole then £18; later and now [£]24. The Count holds it in lordship.

One of the most striking things about these entries is their diversity. Sometimes we learn what a manor was worth in the time of King Edward; just after the Conquest; and in 1086. Sometimes information for 1086 alone is given. The pre-Conquest landholders are often, but not always, mentioned. The social structures are also explained differently. In the old Danelaw there were many freemen, while in the West Midlands slaves abounded; but the words used in one part of the country did not necessarily correspond with those used elsewhere.

Even seemingly familiar terms which appear in *Domesday* can prove deceptive. Manors are the basic units. Some, however, are immense, taking in great areas of moorland and fen and with substantial outlying settlements attached. Others, on the other hand, accounted for a mere fraction of a village. County boundaries must also be treated with care. The tiny shire of Rutland was in the process of formation and in *Domesday Book* was largely apportioned between its neighbours. The Welsh Marches, a wild territory indeed, had very ill-defined edges. The Cheshire section took in parts of North Wales and of Lancashire as well. Gloucestershire, Warwickshire and Worcestershire were strangely intermingled on their borders, their shapes influenced by the landholdings of the bishopric of Worcester.

Domesday aristocracy

Of the land described in *Domesday*'s 35 counties the king and his family held about 17 per cent, the bishops and abbots about 26 per cent, and the 190-odd lay tenants-in-chief held about 54 per cent. Some of the holdings were huge and the dozen or so leading barons together controlled about a quarter of England. Such estates were often geographically scattered: 20 leading lay lords had lands in ten or more counties, and 14 had possessions both north of the Trent and south of the Thames. The dispersal was partly a matter of accident, but it did allow those whose possessions in the North were devastated to support themselves from the richer South. It is a situation which contrasts sharply with the great regional earldoms of the Anglo-Saxon period.

In border areas, certain barons were granted compact estates in order to defend England against attack. For example in 1071 the earldom of Chester was granted to Hugh 'the Fat' of Avranches, who was to dominate the region for three decades whilst he waged bloody wars against the Welsh. His Cheshire lands listed in *Domesday Book* were worth only about £200 annually, but he had other estates in 20 shires valued at about £700, which enabled him to finance his conflicts. He extended his authority into much of what was to become Flintshire and also into parts of the future Denbighshire.

The great majority of the *Domesday* landholders came from northern France, but there were still a few Anglo-Saxons and Danes. Only one member of the old nobility still possessed sizeable estates. He was Thorkill of Arden, who had lands in Warwickshire. He had co-operated with the Conqueror and had been permitted to inherit them from his father.

Many formerly independent Anglo-Saxon and Danish thanes and their descendants appear in *Domesday* as the under-tenants of Norman lords. One, a man called Toli, had retained a hold on his lands at Cowley in Oxfordshire which he had held freely before the Conquest. In 1086, however, he was the under-tenant of the

DOMESDAY BOOKS: *The volumes of* Domesday *were put together from folded quires or pages, then bound into substantial covers to protect them from damage.*

DOMESDAY MANUSCRIPT: *A page from the* Domesday Book*: the parchment has become slightly mottled here and there, and the ink has faded somewhat, but the neat lines of text and red underlining for emphasis are still clearly readable. Changes, erasures and marginal notes are all used by historians to provide added information.*

VIII. TERRA SCE MARIE GLASTINGBERIENSIS.

Eccla GLASTINGBERI habet in ipsa villa .xii. hid quae nunq
geldaveru. Tra. e. xx. car. De ea st in dnio .x. hidae. dimid virg
min. 7 ibi .v. car. 7 xvii. servi. 7 xxi. villi. 7 xxxiii. bord cu .v.
car. Ibi .viii. fabri. 7 iii. arpenz vineae. 7 lx. ac pti. 7 cc. ac pa
sturae. 7 xx. ac silvae. 7 ccc. ac silvae minutae. Valet .xx. lib.
Huic m adjacet insula quae vocat MERE. Ibi st .lx. ac trae. Tra
.i. car quae ibi. e. 7 x. piscatores. 7 iii. piscariae redd .xx. den. 7 vi.
ac pti. 7 vi. ac silvae. 7 ii. arpenz vineae. Valet .xx. solid.
Alia insula ptin ibi quae vocat PADENEBERIE. Ibi st .vi. ac trae.
7 iii. arpenz vineae. 7 un bord. Valet .iiii. solid.
Tercia insula adjacet ibi 7 vocat ESTERESIGE. In qua st .ii. hidae
quae nunq geldaveru. Ibi. e. i. car cu .i. bord. 7 ii. ac pti. 7 una ac
silvae minutae. Valet .xv. solid. Goduin ten de abbe.
Ipsa eccla ten WINESCOME. T.R.E. geldb p .xv. hid. Tra. e. xxx. car.
De ea st in dnio .v. hidae una v min. 7 ibi .ii. car. 7 iiii. servi. 7 xxviii.
villi 7 vi. bord cu .xx. car. Ibi molin redd .v. solid. 7 lx. ac pti.
7 una leu pasturae in lg 7 lat. Silva .ii. leu lg. 7 una leu lat.
De hac tra huj m ten de abbe Rogeri .ii. hid 7 dim. Radulf .i. hid.
7 una v. Pipe dim hid. Ibi st .v. car.
Hoc m valet abbi .viii. lib. hoib ej .lv. solid.
De tra huj m ten eps Constantiens de rege .i. hid. 7 val .xx. solid.
Brictric libe tenuit T.R.E. sed n poterat ab eccla separari.
Ipsa eccla ten MIDELTONE T.R.E. geldb p .vi. hid. Tra. e. vi. car.
De ea st in dnio .iiii. hidae. 7 vii. ac. 7 ibi .ii. car. 7 viii. villi 7 vi. bord
cu .iiii. car. Ibi .l. ac pti. 7 c. ac pasturae. Valuit 7 val .vi. lib.
Rogeri ten de eccla LIDEFORD. Aluuard tenuit T.R.E. nec pote
rat ab eccla separari. 7 geldb p .iiii. hid. Tra. e. v. car. De ea st
in dnio .iii. hidae 7 dimid v trae. 7 ibi .ii. car. 7 vi. servi. 7 vi. villi.
7 iii. bord cu .i. car 7 dim. Ibi molin redd .x. sol. 7 xl. ac pti.
Valuit 7 val .iiii. lib.
Ipsa eccla ten SAPESWICH T.R.E. geldb p .xxx. hid. Tra. e. xl.
car. Praeter hanc ht abb tra .xx. car. quae nunq geld. Ibi st .xii. car. villanor
7 alibi .iii. car in dnio. 7 vi. servi. 7 v. coliba. 7 xv. villi 7 xii. bord.
Ibi .lx. ac pti. 7 lx. ac pasturae. 7 lvii. ac silvae minutae.
De his .xxx. hid ten Rogeri de abbe .v. hid in SUTONE. 7 v. hid
in DUNINETONE. 7 v. hid in CEPTONE. 7 v. hid in CALDECOTE.
Has teneb .xiiii. taini T.R.E. 7 n poterant ab eccla separari.
Ibi st in dnio .x. car. 7 xi. servi. 7 xix. villi 7 xxiii. bord cu .viii.
car 7 dimid. Ibi .c. ac pti. una min. 7 xxxi. ac silvae minutae.
De eisd .xxx. hid ten Aluredus .v. hid in HUNLAUINTONE. 7 ibi ht
.ii. car. Ibi .v. servi. 7 xii. villi 7 viii. bord cu .vi. car. 7 Val .x. sol.
De ead tra ten Warmund dimid hid de abbe. 7 ibi ht .i. car 7 iiii. bord.
Hoc m valet abbi .xii. lib. Rogerio .xix. lib. Aluredo .vii. lib.
Ipsa eccla ten DOWI T.R.E. geldb p .xii. hid. Tra. e. xx. car.
De ea st in dnio .v. hidae. 7 ibi .ii. car. 7 ii. servi 7 viii. coliba. 7 xxviii.
villi. 7 xiii. bord. cu .xiiii. car. Ibi .xxx. ac pti. 7 xii. ac silvae
minutae. Valuit .x. lib. Modo .xxiiii. lib.
Walterus ten de abbe COSINSTONE. Aluuin tenuit de abbe pre
T.R.E. 7 geldb p .iii. hid. Tra. e. vi. car. De ea. e in dnio .i. hida
7 ibi .i. car. 7 iiii. servi. 7 ix. villi 7 ix. bord cu .v. car. Ibi .x. ac
pti. 7 ii. ac silvae minutae. Valuit 7 val .vi. lib.
Rogerius ten de abbe DEREBERGE. Osuuald tenuit de abbe
T.R.E. 7 geldb p .ii. hid. Tra. e. iii. car. Ibi st .iii. villi 7 iii. bord
cu .ii. car. 7 in dnio dimid car. 7 xi. ac pti. 7 xx. ac pasturae.
7 x. ac silvae. Val .xxx. solid. Cu recep .xl. solid valb.
Ailmuare ten de abbe BLACHEFORD. Alnod tenuit de abbe
T.R.E. 7 geldb p .iiii. hid. Tra. e. vi. car. In dnio st .iii. car. 7 v.
servi. 7 vii. villi 7 x. bord cu .iiii. car. Ibi .c.xv. ac pti. 7 xl. iii. ac
pasturae. 7 xl. vii. ac silvae. Valet .c. sol. Qdo recep .iii. lib.
Godescal ten de abbe STAWELLE. Aluuard tenuit T.R.E. 7 geldb
p .ii. hid 7 dimid. Tra. e. ii. car 7 dim. In dnio. e. i. car. 7 ii. servi.
7 iii. bord cu .i. car. 7 xx. ac pti. Valet .xl. sol. Qdo recep .v. solid.

Ipsa eccla ten WALTONE. T.R.E. geldb p .xxx. hid.
Tra. e. xl. car. De ea st in dnio .x. hidae. 7 ibi .iiii. car.
7 iiii. servi. 7 xxvii. villi 7 xii. bord cu .xviii. car.
Ibi .l. ac pti. Pastura .vii. qz lg. 7 una qz lat.
Silva .vii. qz lg. 7 iii. qz lat. Valet abbi .xv. lib.
De his .xxx. hid ten de abbe Rogerius .v. hid in CONTONE.
Walterus .iii. hid in ASSECOTE. 7 iii. hid in PEDEWELLE.
Qui teneb T.R.E. n poterant ab eccla separari.
In dnio st ibi .iii. car. 7 vi. servi. 7 xv. villi 7 xii.
bord cu .viii. car. Rogerius ht .xx. acs pti. 7 vi. qz
silvae in lg. 7 una qz lat. Walterus .xii. ac pti. 7 xl.
ac silvae minutae. Int eos valet .viii. lib.
Rogerius ten de abbe BODESLEGE. Wintegod tenuit
T.R.E. 7 geldb p .iii. v trae. Tra. e. i. car 7 dim. quae ibi st
cu .vii. bord. Ibi .vi. ac pti. 7 ii. ac silvae. Valet .x. solid.
Ide Ro. ten de abbe DONDEIGRE. Algar tenuit T.R.E.
7 geldb p .v. hid. Tra. e. iiii. car. De ea st in dnio .iii. hidae
7 dim v trae. 7 ibi .ii. car. 7 iiii. servi. 7 v. villi 7 x. bord
cu .iii. car. Ibi .xl. ac pti. 7 x. ac silvae. Valet .c. solid.
Ide Ro. ten de abbe ASSECOTE. 7 ptin ad WALTONE
m abbis. T.R.E. geldb p .ii. hid. Tra. e. iii. car. Ibi st
.ii. villi 7 iii. bord 7 ii. servi. cu .i. car. 7 iiii. ac pti.
Valuit 7 val .xl. solid.
Girard ten de abbe GRAINTONE. Uluiet tenuit T.R.E.
7 geldb p .ii. hid. 7 dim. Tra. e. ii. car. 7 dimid. In dnio
est .i. car. 7 v. servi. 7 ii. bord 7 ii. coliba. cu .i. car.
Ibi .xx. ac pti. 7 iii. ac silvae. Valet 7 valuit .l. solid.
Ipsa eccla ten LEGA. T.R.E. geldb p .iiii. hid. Tra. e. x.
car. De ea st in dnio .ii. hidae. Una ex his fuit teinland.
n tam poterat ab eccla separari. In dnio st .iiii. car.
cu .i. servo. 7 vii. villi 7 x. bord cu .v. car. Ibi .xxxv. ac
pti. 7 xxx. ac pasturae. 7 vi. ac silvae. Valet .viii. lib.
Ipsa eccla ten HAME. T.R.E. geldb p .xviii. hid.
Tra. e. xx. car. De ea st in dnio .v. hidae. 7 ii. v 7 dim.
7 ibi .iii. car. 7 v. servi. 7 xxii. villi 7 xxi. bord cu .viii.
car. Ibi .xxx. ac pti. 7 xvi. ac silvae. Valet .x. lib.
De hac tra huj m ten de abbe Robt .i. hid 7 una v.
7 Serlo .v. hid. Girard .iii. virg trae. Leuric 7 Aluuold
7 Almar tenuer T.R.E. nec poterant ab eccla separi.
In dnio st .ii. car. 7 iiii. servi. 7 ii. villi 7 xiiii. bord
cu .ii. car. Ibi .xxx. ac pti. 7 xx. ac pasturae.
Valet int tot .cx. solid.
Ipsa eccla ten BODECHELEI. T.R.E. geldb p .xx. hid.
Tra. e. xx. car. De ea st in dnio .v. hidae. 7 ibi .v. car. 7 vi.
servi. 7 xi. villi 7 vii. bord cu .vi. car. Ibi .l. ac pti.
7 c. ac silvae. Valet abbi .x. lib.
De hac tra huj m ten Tu. sub Ro. .iiii. hid. Rogerius .ii.
hid. Duo taini teneb de eccla T.R.E. 7 n poterant inde
separari. In dnio st ibi .iiii. car. 7 vi. servi. 7 xi. villi
7 vi. bord cu .iii. car. Ibi .xiiii. ac pti. 7 xii. ac silvae
minutae. Valuit 7 val .vii. lib int eos. 7 Valet .x. sol.
De ead tra ten Aleftan de abbe dimid hid. 7 ibi ht .i. car.
Hunfrid ten de rege .ii. hid in LODRETORD. 7 ptin huic m
Aluric teneb T.R.E. nec poterat ab eccla separari.
Tra. e. ii. car. Valet .xx. solid.
Ipsa eccla ten SIBTONE T.R.E. geldb p .xx. hid. Tra. e
xxx. car. Praeter hanc ht abb ibi tram .xx. car. quae nunq
geldav. In dnio st .x. car. 7 xv. servi. 7 xxi. villi 7 xl. ii.
bord cu .x. car sup tra n geldant. Ibi .ii. molini redd
.x. solid. 7 xl vi. ac pti. 7 xl. ac pasturae. Silva .i. leu
lg. 7 dim leu lat. De tra q n geld ten Alnod monach .i. hid
libaliter de abbe concessu regis. H teinland fuit. 7 nec potest
ab eccla separari. Tot valet .xxiiii. lib. Valuit .xvi. lib.
De hac tra huj m ten Rogeri in SEPTONE .vi. hid
7 dimid. 7 In CORISTONE .iii. hid. Uluiet 7 Elmer te
nuer T.R.E. 7 n poterant ab eccla separari.

Norman baron Miles Crispin. Another English under-tenant, Saewold, had kept property worth £10 in the same county, but it appears that he had problems in making ends meet, because he had mortgaged half of it to Robert d'Oilly. Such men were the sad remnant of a once proud and powerful aristocracy.

There was, however, one Englishman who occupied a place of the highest importance in 1086. He was the saintly Wulfstan, Bishop of Worcester. At first a monk, he rose to be schoolmaster, then prior, and in 1062, became bishop, an office he held until his death in 1095. Under him, the monks increased in numbers and zeal, and the cathedral school became and remained a centre of English learning. According to his biographer, Wulfstan was loved and respected by his community and by the people of his diocese alike. In Worcestershire alone the monks had more than a dozen valuable manors and lucrative legal powers. Their wealth had not gone unnoticed, however. Their taxation assessments were fixed at a high level, and were to cause them problems in future years.

Most of the high-ranking people cited in *Domesday* were men, but a few women do appear. Of these, the two most important were already dead in 1086. Queen Edith, Edward the Confessor's widow, had held estates worth £1600 each year, which after her death had reverted to the Crown. Matilda, William's queen, had similarly held valuable properties during her lifetime, and, although they appear in *Domesday* as Crown lands, their earlier ownership is made clear.

The most prominent living female in the survey was Judith, countess of Northumbria and Huntingdon, who possessed substantial holdings and a dramatic past. A niece of William I, she had been married off to Waltheof, Earl of Northumbria, after William's conquest of the North. Waltheof was not at first seriously implicated in the 1075 rebellion, but, when Judith testified of his treachery to the king, he was cast into prison and was executed in 1076. Ten years later Judith held not only her dower, consisting of lands in Huntingdonshire, but also other manors which William the Conqueror had given her.

Rents, tax and manorial values

The total value of the land in *Domesday* has been estimated at about £73,000 a year. Under-tenancies appear in abundance. Their holders generally owed military services to their lords, and those lords to the king. But there were also other ways by which land could be held. Most conspicuous in *Domesday Book* were leases or rents for money, and the figures for some of them were clearly exorbitant. The manor of Thaxted in Essex was worth £30 in 1066 and £50 in 1086, but its holder, Richard FitzGilbert, had leased it to an Englishman for an annual £60. His tenant had been unable to pay this inflated figure and had defaulted on at least £10 a year.

It used to be thought that the value which the *Domesday* Commissioners assigned to any particular manor had no more than a general connection with its size. However, the manorial entries for Essex have recently been analysed by computer, with interesting results. When the total values are compared with the resources – such as the pasture, plough teams, mills and livestock – it soon becomes clear that in many cases a mathematical equation links the two: the commissioners were evidently instructed to assign a set value to each resource.

In some instances the values of the manors and their geld assessments are also connected. (These are the figures expressed in hides, which could be subdivided into four virgates; or in carucates, containing eight bovates; or in sulungs subdivided into four yokes; or in leets – according to the area of the country.) But that correspondence is far from invariable, because some districts, such as parts of Cambridgeshire, were assessed at favourably low levels, and some places were let off lightly or escaped altogether.

Comparison of the values of some manors in 1066 and 1086 shows that certain areas, particularly in northern England, had suffered terrible devastation in the interim. Cradwell in Yorkshire had a pre-Conquest value of 20s, but by the time of *Domesday* was worth only 5s 4d and was uninhabited. It, like many others, had been ravaged by King William and his men, who had left a trail of devastation behind them. It was waste not in the sense of being uncultivable, but in that its value had been reduced. Harbury in Warwickshire had similarly been 'laid waste by the king's army' as it passed through.

But the Conqueror was not the only person to blame for such problems. Raiders from Ireland, for example, had cut the value of West Portlemouth, a settlement near the South Devon coast, to a mere quarter of its earlier level.

Justice was also valuable business in the Middle Ages, and part of the profits of some manors came from the courts that were attached to them. In these cases, *Domesday* records that the yields of the soke (i.e. the jurisdiction) of a hundred or wapentake went to the holder of the manor. The king usually reserved two-thirds of the money made from justice in the shire or hundred court. The earl kept the rest, the third penny, which was usually paid to a particular manor.

To sum up, the so-called value of a manor was an estimate of the total its lord would receive annually in money and kind from his peasants, and would include, for example, the annual dues paid by a mill or mine, a proportion of the eels caught or pigs kept, etc.

Manors and villages

The manors which appear were very diverse in size, and it is a great mistake to assume that in its boundaries a given manor necessarily corresponded to a village. Recently, archaeologists have raised another related problem. Many manorial entries look as though they describe the archetypal English village: compact, centred around hall and church, and separated from the next settlement by open land. But excavation work has shown that in 1086 such settlements were far from typical. Faxton in Northamptonshire is a case in point. Despite the impression created in *Domesday Book* of a tidy, planned village, archaeology has demonstrated that it did not attain such an arrangement for another century at least.

Habitations in most areas of late eleventh-century England followed a very ancient pattern of isolated farms, hamlets and tiny villages interspersed with fields and scattered over most of the cultivable land. As in the Iron Age and in the Roman and Anglo-Saxon periods, these settlements gradually but constantly shifted, changed their foci, were abandoned or reclaimed. Cornwall is one of the few places which still retains that pattern today.

Woodland accounted for a mere 15 per cent or so of the land, and only isolated areas such as the Weald corresponded to the traditional picture of virgin forest. The one relatively stable element in a countryside in constant flux was the boundary pattern of the parishes and larger manors, which may often have preserved the outlines of Roman estates. We must remember that the manorial name used in *Domesday* was probably that of the manor's principal settlement, which was perhaps one among many.

To compound the problem, many villages in a band running roughly from mid-Somerset to Northumberland were in the process of consolidation. This began in the tenth century and was substantially complete by 1300. Excavations at the *Domesday* settlement of Isham in Northamptonshire have demonstrated that this village already had a compact, planned form by the time of the Conquest, but we cannot tell how many others were like it.

Such changes in village layouts usually went hand in hand with the establishment of large, open fields subdivided into strips for arable farming. *Domesday* mentions such strips at Garsington in Oxfordshire, but it is very unlikely that there were many places where the fully fledged two- or three-field system of the later middle ages was in full operation at so early a date.

A high proportion of the places mentioned in *Domesday Book* still have much the same names today. Nevertheless, because so many settlements have moved in the interim, it is often hard to pinpoint their 1086 locations on a map. Some large places had already divided, such as Coxwell and 'the other' Coxwell in Berkshire or North Stoke and South Stoke in Lincolnshire. Others split apart later and we can rarely discern to which part the *Domesday* entry refers. There are now three Rissingtons in Gloucestershire and eight Rodings in Essex to choose from.

The people of the manor

The life of most villages centred on the hall, where the court was held and where the lord often lived. Some of the halls had minor fortifications for protection. When a manor had more than one lord, it often had more than one hall; conversely when it had been leased to the peasants, it was sometimes said to have no hall. The reeve was the chief organizer of the manorial lands, and either worked for the lord or was elected by the peasants to act on their behalf.

The other leading man of the village was the priest. About a thousand are mentioned in *Domesday Book*, a mere fraction of the real total. Some priests had fat livings attached to their churches, but others were virtually indistinguishable from the villagers and joined in with the communal labour. Many, like Aelemaer, the pre-Conquest holder of Blofield in Norfolk, were married. There had been fresh legislation against clerical marriage in 1076 but it was to prove difficult to enforce.

The free peasants of the manor were known either as 'freemen' or as 'Sokemen'. Distinctions between the two kinds are often very difficult to prove, and in many regions the two terms may have been used interchangeably. Free peasants were found all over England, but by far the highest proportion was in the former Danelaw. It was long believed that the sokemen represent the descendants of the rank and file of the old Danish armies which had ravaged England two centuries before the Normans came. Compared with 1066, the numbers of freemen and sokemen in 1086 show a marked decline, suggesting that the Conquest had an adverse effect on men's liberty. Such individuals were free in their persons, but generally had obligations to their lord, including the obligation to attend his court.

The great majority of the *Domesday* peasantry, the villagers (villans), the smallholders (bordars) and the cottagers (cottars), were personally unfree. They had to render labour services to their lord, and they were tied to their manor, but they had a stake in its resources. The villagers accounted for about one-third of the total recorded population. Most were obliged to plough their lord's land as well as their own. At Leominster in Herefordshire they had to cultivate 125 acres in their lord's demesne (i.e., holding) and to sow it with wheat seed. At Pagham in Sussex they paid him one pig for every six that grazed the herbage, and at Wraxall in Dorset they gave him a rent of £3 a year. However, they might have substantial holdings of their own, and at Alverstoke in Hampshire they even held land directly from the Bishop of Winchester. The smallholders and the cottagers were lower down in the social scale. Their services to their lord were correspondingly greater than those of the villagers. The entry for Stokesay in Shropshire includes an unusual mention of five female cottagers.

At the bottom of the heap were the slaves, who were wholly unfree, the chattels of their lord, and who had no land. They numbered about one-tenth of the total recorded population, and were found predominantly in the south and west of the country. In 1086 they worked entirely for their lord, but the lot of their descendants gradually improved as they merged with the great mass of villeins. The freedmen (coliberts) of the south-western counties were already on that path.

Other members of manorial communities appear sporadically, some only in certain regions. In counties bordering the Welsh Marches there are riders (radmen) and riding-men (radknights), who performed duties of escorting their lords, as at Ledbury in Herefordshire. *Drengs*, free peasants who held lands in return for military duties, are recorded in Lancashire and Yorkshire. Women are mentioned occasionally, such as the female slaves (*ancillae*) in West Midlands manors like Bishampton in Worcestershire. Dairymaids, nuns, widows and wives all make the occasional entrance, and at Barfreston in Kent there was one poor woman who paid 3¾d each year, for what is unknown.

England's population

Domesday Book is not a census. It records the heads of households but not necessarily the families which they supported. To attempt any calculation of the total population in England in 1086, therefore, some multiplier must be used, but slaves are probably recorded as individuals rather than as heads of families. Conversely, at least five per cent of the total population – such as retainers in castles, nuns and monks – is missing. Calculations for the missing areas in England must also be made and the Welsh areas excluded. A leading scholar has suggested that a multiplier of four would produce a total figure of a little under one and a quarter million, and a multiplier of five, about one and a half million. Other historians believe that two million would be more accurate.

All of these figures, however, show a marked decrease from the population estimates for Roman times. There may then have been as many as four million people, a figure not exceeded until about 1300.

The most densely populated areas, with more than ten people to the square mile, were parts of Lincolnshire, East Anglia and east Kent, with smaller concentrations in south Somerset and on parts of the South Coast. The whole of northern England, by contrast, together with the Weald, Dartmoor and the Welsh Marches, had less than three people to the square mile. Many places were not cultivable, others had been laid waste. For example, of 64 places which were attached to Preston in Lancashire, only 16 were inhabited, and those sparsely, but the actual number of people was unknown. The rest of the settlements were devastated.

The uses of the land: agriculture

In 1086, 80 per cent of the area cultivated in 1914 was already under the plough. About 35 per cent of the *Domesday* land was arable, 25 per cent was pasture and meadow, 15 per cent was woodland and the remaining area was occupied by settlements, by marginal land such as heath, moor and fen, and by devastated land. Such figures have been arrived at only by the most painstaking correlation of all available evidence.

The measurements for agricultural land are expressed in a variety of ways. The taxable units such as the hide and the carucate must originally have been linked to agricultural capabilities, but by 1086 were no more than arbitrary divisions. Another measurement given is that of ploughlands (land for x ploughs). On the face of it, this sounds like the amount of land which could support a given number of plough teams. However, there is frequently a puzzling discrepancy between the figures for ploughland and the – usually larger – actual number of ploughlands in a manor. The way in which figures for plough teams are recorded varies from region to region, and some authorities believe that these numbers, like the hide, represent units of fiscal assessment.

The figure giving the actual number of ploughs is the best guide to the agricultural capacity of the manor. A plough team consisted of eight oxen. Normally some teams were held by the lord and were worked for him, while others belonged to the peasants. Some areas, such as the Sussex coastal plain and parts of Herefordshire, were highly fertile and supported more than four plough teams to the square mile. At the opposite end of the scale were the poor lands, such as much of the North, the Somerset levels and Sherwood Forest, where there was on average one such team only to ever two square miles or more.

The arable land was used to grow wheat, barley, oats and beans. The grain once produced had next to be milled to make flour. Some was ground by hand, but the 6000 mills which appear in *Domesday* must have coped with a high proportion of this heavy work. They were driven by water power: windmills did not appear in England for another century. Some *Domesday* mills were very lucrative, but others produced no rents; fractions of mills, denoting multiple ownership, are not unusual. At Coleshill in Bedfordshire the three owners of the mill each took ten shillings from it. Sometimes a portion of a mill is missing from *Domesday Book*; at Leckford in Hampshire, half of one remains unaccounted for.

Gardens and orchards sometimes appear in the survey. Fruit, cabbages, peas, leeks, onions and herbs would have been grown in them. About 45 vineyards are also mentioned, and one at Wilcot in Wiltshire was said to be very productive.

Pasture, livestock and fisheries

Pasture was land where animals grazed all the year round. Meadow, which was much more valuable, was land bordering streams and rivers which was used both to produce hay and for grazing; the hay from Cogges in Oxfordshire produced a profit of 10s each year. Pasture was entered in *Domesday* less regularly than meadow, and, further to complicate matters, was measured in several different ways. In Essex, its size was estimated according to the number of sheep it could support, in Sussex and Surrey, sometimes according to the number of pigs. Linear dimensions or acreage are the units in the south-western counties.

Little Domesday and the Exeter (Exon) *Domesday* provide details of the livestock owned by the lord. We cannot, of course, know what proportion this was of the total. Sheep were then, as later in the Middle Ages, of great economic importance. At Puddletown in Dorset, a large and complex manor, 1600 sheep are mentioned. Other animals in the records are goats (used to produce milk), cows, oxen and horses – including packhorses, wild horses and forest mares. Bees, extremely important as the producers of honey and wax, were frequently mentioned, as at Methwold in Norfolk, where there were 27 hives. In some areas the total number of animals is given, in others only the proportion due to the manor, which was typically one pig in seven.

Inland and coastal fisheries recur throughout *Domesday Book*. Many of the references are to weirs along the main rivers, but fishponds, as at Sharnbrook in Bedfordshire, are also noted. A millpond at Stratford in Warwickshire is said to have produced 1000 eels each year. Petersham in Surrey rendered 1000 eels and 1000 lampreys.

Salt-making, mines and quarries

Not all the unfree people who appear in the *Domesday* survey worked on the land. There are some references to localized industrial activity, although these are far from comprehensive. Salt, which was essential for the preservation of food, was produced by the evaporation of brine from the sea and river estuaries or from inland saline springs. There were two inland centres, Droitwich in Worcestershire; and Northwich, Middlewich and Nantwich in Cheshire. Salt-making in Worcestershire was flourishing in the late eleventh century. Droitwich alone, it was said, had 263½ salt-pans and there were others nearby. Lead vats, furnaces and cartloads of wood for fuel also enjoy incidental mention. The Cheshire salt industry had by contrast apparently fallen on hard times. When Earl Hugh arrived in the area, only one salt-pan was still in operation. By 1086 a minor recovery seems to have occurred, but the value of the pans combined was only one-third of the 1066 total. On the coasts, salt-making was undertaken on a smaller scale. 27 salt-pans are mentioned at Lyme Regis in Dorset.

The extracting and forging of iron was widespread in eleventh-century England (though less so than in Roman times). Iron mines are mentioned in the Rhuddlan entry, and the city of Gloucester is said to render iron – presumably mined in the forest of Dean – for the king's ships. Lead-working is mentioned only in Derbyshire, where, for example, Wirksworth is said to have three mines and Matlock Bridge one. In 1066, the people of Bakewell, Ashford and Hope had rendered money, honey and five cartloads of lead, each of 50 slabs, but by 1086 a money rent alone was paid. Quarries appear in seven places – among them Limpsfield in Surrey and Whatton in Nottinghamshire – and there are three potteries, one of these at Westbury in Wiltshire. But such activities normally lie outside *Domesday's* terms of reference and are mentioned only incidentally.

Woods, forests and game-parks

Although large areas of woodland, were rare, smaller woods, used for timber, for brushwood and for pasturing swine, were a vital part of the manorial economy, and were scattered fairly widely throughout the country. In some regions they were measured according to the number of pigs which they could support, in others by their actual size. Underwood or coppice occurs frequently and sometimes the kinds of tree – alder, ash, oak, thorns and willow – are given. There are specific mentions of assarting (clearing the wood for agricultural purposes). Despite the tremendous effort involved it was probably a widespread practice.

Royal forests had since Anglo-Saxon times been areas used for the king's hunting. The Conqueror, whose attachment to the chase is well known, imposed harsh laws in his forests to protect the game, and particularly the deer and wild boar. Forests were not necessarily woodland areas, many having substantial proportions of open land within their boundaries. The New Forest, which occupies its own section of the Hampshire folios, is the only one specifically to be described in *Domesday Book*. Later chroniclers accused the king of having laid many villages waste to create it, but their assertions are not wholly borne out by the survey, which shows 40 settlements and even some agricultural activity within it. There are incidental references to land taken into the forest elsewhere, or to places devastated to make forest. Earl Hugh of Cheshire, like the king, had his own forest, later known as Delamere Forest. Such areas were administered by head foresters, who were trusted and sometimes powerful men. Waleran the forester had substantial estates in southern England. In the forest of Essex, Robert Gernon took a swineherd from Writtle and promoted him to the lofty office of royal forester, a classic example of a man being raised from the dust.

The king, like other lords, had a number of enclosed parks for his game. A total of 35 of these 'parks for wild beasts' is mentioned in *Domesday*. There are also references to 'hays' or hedged enclosures in many forests, into which game was driven. Another popular aristocratic activity was hawking, and in many areas, hawks are noted as being paid as dues from individual manors. These birds were highly priced creatures: the entry for Worcester reveals that the citizens were obliged to produce either a Norwegian hawk each year or an extra £10 in rent.

The *Domesday* boroughs

The treatment of boroughs is erratic. Many county sections begin with a description of the county town and other boroughs, but this is not a consistent pattern. London and Winchester are missing altogether, and, in some shire sections, the descriptions of boroughs come in the main body of the text. The entries vary from the long and disorganized to the brief and curt, suggesting that neither the commissioners nor the *Domesday* scribe were really sure how to incorporate them in the record. It is even possible that it was decided to include them only once the survey was already in progress. Nevertheless, there is much to learn from *Domesday Book* about urban life, customs and organization.

In a few cases there seems little obvious reason why a given place is called a borough. On the other hand, the descriptions of many show some or all of the characteristics which we would expect a borough to have in this period. These places first developed as fortified settlements.

Trade was a crucial element and there were markets in many boroughs. The urban court and administration of boroughs are also often mentioned; and for some towns, such as Shrewsbury, the legal customs are described. Before 1066 all boroughs had had one or more mints, and many still remained after the Norman Conquest. The moneyers who controlled them were wealthy and powerful people. In Lincoln they contributed £75 each year to the royal coffers.

The county towns were secure in their status as boroughs, but for others, particularly in parts of the south-west, their situation was less certain. Even in the largest towns, the burgesses often had interests in the fields outside and might well have taken part in their cultivation. Similarly, houses inside the town were frequently acquired by rural landholders, as well as by the Crown, which often had the controlling interest in urban property and affairs. The links between the towns and the countryside were thus very close.

Castles and churches

The few castles and churches built in the eleventh century but which still survive today are a tangible link between the England of 900 years ago and the England of today. The White Tower at the Tower of London, constructed of white stone, remains a vivid reminder of William's dominance and authority. Most of the other castles of his day were built of wood but had a similar motte and bailey plan, of the kind illustrated on the Bayeux tapestry. *Domesday Book* mentions 48, scattered from Okehampton to Richmond, although other evidence suggests that there were many more. Some, such as Ewias Harold in Herefordshire, had been built by the Norman favourites of the Confessor, but the majority were post-Conquest, symbols of the new military order.

Parish churches constructed immediately after the Conquest were probably indistinguishable from those raised just before. They are not recorded systematically in *Domesday*, which mentions only 147 churches in Kent where other sources note at least 400. It does, however, give details about some of them. At Bermondsey there was a 'new and beautiful church'; at Old Byland there was one made out of wood; Netheravon church in Wiltshire was on the point of collapse. They are treated as potentially lucrative manorial appurtenances, and sometimes divided into fractions – as small as one-twelfth at Freekingham in Lincolnshire.

Domesday Book in history

Most of the book's detailed information went rapidly out of date, and subsequently the survey was to baffle and perplex medieval judges quite as much as later historians. But *Domesday* remained as the proof of ancient landholding, rights and boundaries and this is a rôle which it has retained. It has been cited in court actions several times in the twentieth century and is still considered admissible legal evidence. Although until recently few have been appraised of its real contents, its reputation has remained resplendent down through the centuries. In the sixteenth century it began to be studied as a historical source, a process which still continues unabated. The Victorians, with their English translations, gave it a new use and historical relevance. Today *Domesday Book* is not just a relic of the past but a vital source book for understanding the origins of our modern institutions and society.

The English translation

Domesday Book was written in eleventh century clerical Latin, so stylised and abbreviated that it is beyond the scope of a graduate in Latin, without special training. English translations did not appear until the nineteenth century, when many county sections were tackled by different translators and published either in county record society volumes or Victoria County Histories. They varied greatly in reliability and, since no common editorial policy had been agreed, they differed in their choice of English equivalents for Latin words, which led to confusion among the students or historians who used them.

By the 1960s there was general agreement among *Domesday* scholars that a new, uniform translation was needed. There was much greater emphasis on original documents in schools and colleges and there was a growing army of local history enthusiasts for whom *Domesday* is a fundamental source. Dr. John Morris of University College, London, took the initiative in 1968 and, with a team of fellow 'medieval Latinists', produced a scheme and format for a completely new English text. The specialist local history publisher, Phillimore, agreed to back the project and work began in 1969.

The first county volumes appeared in print in 1975, warmly welcomed throughout the English-speaking world. Sadly, John Morris did not live to see his great work finished, but ten years and thousands of hours later the task is completed in 35 volumes, which correspond to the county divisions of the original. The English, the first complete translation in 900 years, is printed in parallel with the corresponding Latin (in the specially-designed type, cut at Government expense in 1783) and each volume contains a full explanation, notes, glossary, maps and indexes.

The Phillimore translation has been used throughout this book for all quotes and examples of the *Domesday* text and language. Anyone interested in having the complete text for a county – or the whole country – as it was originally compiled, and including all the details which must, of necessity, be excluded from our gazetteer, can obtain it easily; either in a durable library binding or a limp edition. Full details of the series can be obtained from the publishers: Phillimore & Co. Ltd., Shopwyke Hall, Chichester, West Sussex, PO20 6BQ, England.

THE PHILLIMORE EDITION: *the Latin text is a transcript from the 18th c, the English translation on the facing page is the first to encompass the entire* Domesday book.

Key to *Domesday* Entries

The photograph on page 15 is from *Domesday Book*; the script is remarkably clear, but the abbreviated Latin and the many Roman numerals make it almost impossible to read without special instruction. An entry, part of Robert de Watteville's holdings in Surrey, is shown here, with the same entry from Phillimore's edition. We have added the *Domesday* version of the place name, *Meldone*, and highlighted terms and phrases which need explanation.

Most of the phrases re-occur in the entries, although it must be remembered that *Domesday* is not consistent; the counties varied quite considerably in their use of technical terms and extra information. In addition, there is not always a consensus between historicans as to the exact meaning of eleventh century words; a hide, for example, is assumed to be an arbitrary amount of land, something like 120 modern acres. But, it was not a physically-measured amount; as far as we know, it was not surveyed or paced out, but was used simply to evaluate land for tax purposes. It may also have been an estimate of the amount of land a man needed to feed his family for a year; this would mean that a hide in a part of the country with poor and unproductive land would actually be much larger than a hide in the richer southern counties. Eventually this difference in productivity would have been handled by varying the tax value rather than the estimate of land area.

Then there are the differences in descriptive terms of class divisions. Villagers or villeins? Cottagers or slaves? We have made some arbitrary distinctions in our glossary and in these sample entries, but again, there are many disagreements among scholars, and without a dictionary from William's scribe, we will probably never know the exact truth.

Our second annotated diagram does not describe a real place, it was devised to include additional phrases. There are precise definitions in the glossary as well, but we hope these examples will make it easy to assimilate phrases used in the main text of the book.

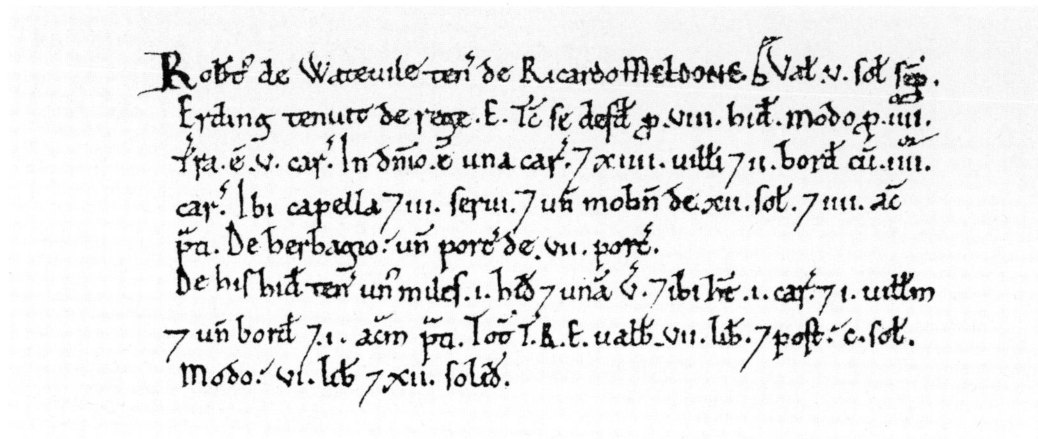
Robt' de Watevile ten' de Ricardo Meldone. Val' v. sol' sep.
Erding tenuit de rege. E. Tc se defd p viii. hid. modo p iiii.
Tra e v. car'. In dnio e una car' 7 xiiii. uilli 7 ii. bord cu iiii.
car'. Ibi capella 7 iii. serui. 7 un molin de xii. sol'. 7 iiii. ac
pa. De herbagio: un porc' de vii. porc.
De his hid ten' un miles. i. hid 7 una v. 7 ibi hr. i. car' 7 i. uillm
7 un bord 7 i. ac pa. Tot T.R.E. ualb vii. lib. 7 post: c. sol.
Modo: vi. lib 7 xii. solid.

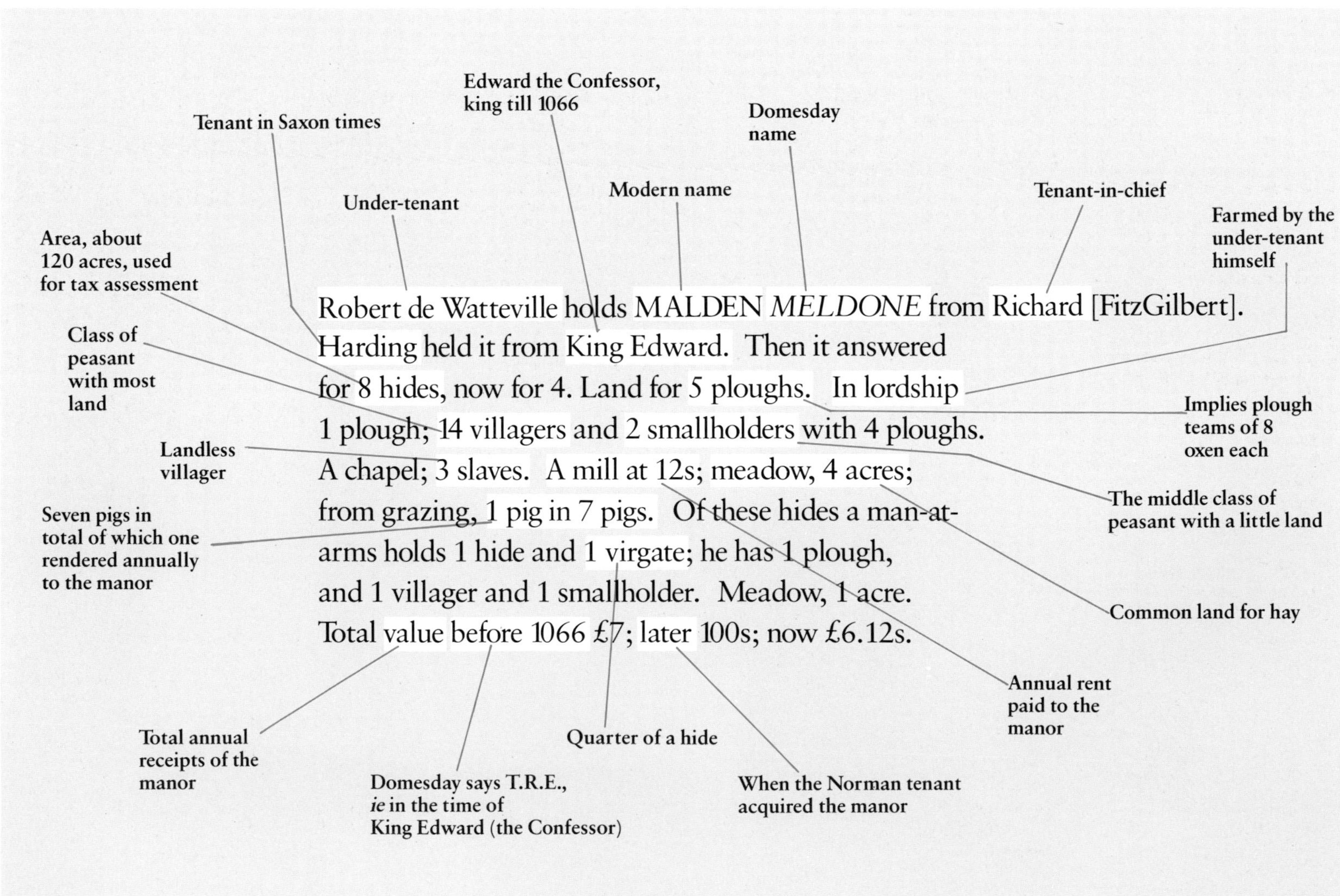
Edward the Confessor, king till 1066
Tenant in Saxon times
Domesday name
Under-tenant
Modern name
Tenant-in-chief
Farmed by the under-tenant himself
Area, about 120 acres, used for tax assessment
Robert de Watteville holds MALDEN MELDONE from Richard [FitzGilbert].
Harding held it from King Edward. Then it answered
for 8 hides, now for 4. Land for 5 ploughs. In lordship
1 plough; 14 villagers and 2 smallholders with 4 ploughs.
A chapel; 3 slaves. A mill at 12s; meadow, 4 acres;
from grazing, 1 pig in 7 pigs. Of these hides a man-at-
arms holds 1 hide and 1 virgate; he has 1 plough,
and 1 villager and 1 smallholder. Meadow, 1 acre.
Total value before 1066 £7; later 100s; now £6.12s.
Class of peasant with most land
Landless villager
Seven pigs in total of which one rendered annually to the manor
Implies plough teams of 8 oxen each
The middle class of peasant with a little land
Common land for hay
Annual rent paid to the manor
Total annual receipts of the manor
Quarter of a hide
Domesday says T.R.E., ie in the time of King Edward (the Confessor)
When the Norman tenant acquired the manor

The Domesday *volumes have been stored in this chest, to be carefully removed every few centuries or so when they need re-binding.*

In ASHBY *ASCBI* Edgar had 4 c. and 2 b. of land taxable. Land for 5 ploughs. Drogo has 2 ploughs there, and 2 Frenchmen and a man-at-arms have 2½ ploughs. 3 Freemen who render 2 sesters of honey. 2 cottagers. Vineyard, 1 arpent; pasture, 20 acres. 2 houses in the borough of Lincoln. Geoffrey has 60 acres of woodland for pannage there, for 10d of Warnod. Afric held it. He could go where he would. The value was £4, now 20s, found waste; tallage 10s. The full jurisdiction belongs to Botford.

Modern name

Domesday name

Assessment in carucates for periodic tax used in northern and eastern England. 1 carucate equals 120 acres

Saxon holder, pre-1066

Immigrant from France since the Conquest

1 bovate equals ⅛ carucate

Independent peasants who owed few dues to the manor, if any, but if called "sokeman", owed obligations, such as attendance at the manor court.

1 sester equals about 32 ounces

Tenant-in-chief

Peasant whose duties included military service (forerunner of a medieval knight)

About 1 acre

2 houses in Lincoln belong to the manor

Class of peasant with a cottage and little, or no, land

Rent which automatically increased if paid late

Autumn acorn and beech mast feed for pigs

Before 1066

He could transfer his land to another tenant-in-chief

Was either uncultivated or unusable when the Norman tenant acquired the manor

Law cases involving inhabitants of Ashby were tried at Botford, whose lord kept the fines

Common land for grazing

Tax due to the lord of the manor

Domesday Life

Although so much of the *Domesday* record seems to be land area, tax and assessment values, or disputes about ownership, there are many nuggets of information hidden in the texts which give us a picture of everyday people and their concerns. We have gathered some of them together under various headings – a vivid glimpse of what it was like to be living and working during 1086.

Due to the King

In the hierarchy of Norman England, the first consideration was King William. He owned land and dues in his own name, about 17 per cent of the total. In addition, customary dues and fines helped to pay for the court, the commissioners and clerks, the army, the defensive castles and their garrisons, and so forth.

Death duties, for example, were 40s, or the king took both the land and all the dead man's goods.

. . . anyone who defied the king's request to work on his buildings or to send harvesters for one day in August to cut the king's corn . . . was fined 2d
(Hampshire)

. . . at Southwark the king took the tolls on the shore or on the waterfront; a criminal charged there paid his fine to the king . . .
(Surrey)

. . . if a stranger lived and had a house in Oxford and died there, the king had whatever he left . . .
(Oxford)

. . . 'if anyone has concealed a sester of honey from the customary due and this is proved, he pays five sesters for the one sester – if he holds as much land as ought to produce them . . .'
(Herefordshire)

Not only was proof needed, but the fine was a practical one!

. . . it was customary for the royal burgesses to pay 2 marks of silver on the 15th day after Easter to the king's revenue . . .
(Colchester)

But then, as now, it wasn't always so easy to collect what was due, especially in some of the remoter parts of the country; there are a few plaintive remarks . . .

. . . The king has not had his customary due from every third animal on the moorland since he first arrived in England . . .
(Molland, Devon)

. . . 'To this manor has been added 1/2 virgate of land; it has been concealed so that the King has had no tax from it' . . .
(Eastleigh, Devon)

Previous page:
INGARSBY: *The shadows which show so much about our lost villages are most revealing in the early morning or late afternoon and evening.*

Law and order

William believed very strongly in law and order, exacting fines for all kind of civil disobedience and dishonesty:

. . . anyone giving false measure was fined 4d . . . making bad beer meant punishment with the dung stool . . . allowing a fire to spread meant a fine of 3 ora of pence with an extra 2d to the neighbours
(Huntingdonshire)

. . . the river Trent, the dyke and the road to York are so protected that if anyone hinders the passage of ships, or if anyone ploughs or makes a dyke within 2 perches of the king's road, he has to pay a fine of £8 . . .
(Nottingham)

However, for offences to property, there were no half-measures. Throughout the country there were carefully laid-down fines for anyone 'breaking the king's peace':

. . . 100s for highway robbery, for housebreaking, for violence to women . . .

Bloodshed was sometimes treated a little more ambiguously:

. . . 'whoever shed blood between Monday morning and Saturday noon was fined 10s, but from Saturday noon to Monday morning, the fine was 20s, as it was for the 12 days of Christmas, the first day of Easter . . . whoever killed a man on these holy days was fined £4, and on other days, 40s . . .'
(Worcestershire)

The customs 'before 1066' had also been carefully noted down:

. . . if a Welshman has killed a Welshman, the relatives of the slain man gather and despoil the killer and his relatives, and burn their houses, until the body of the dead man is buried the next day, about midday. The king has the third part of this plunder, but they have all the rest free . . .
(Archenfield, Herefordshire)

Welshmen obviously had had extra special attention from the law; in that same Hundred, if any Welshman stole a man, a woman, a horse, an ox or a cow, when he is convicted he first restored what he stole, and gave 20s in forfeiture, but *'for stealing a sheep or a bundle of sheaves, he paid a fine of 2s.'*

Sometimes they required a great deal of corroborative evidence . . . a man who has been accused of burning a house had to prove his innocence with 40 witnesses.

These customs were generally continued and approved under the Norman regime; William was anxious to show that he had succeeded rightfully to the throne.

War

Some cities and boroughs had special responsibilities laid down in their charter:

. . . 'When the King went on campaign by land 12 Burgesses from this city went with him but if he went against the enemy by sea, they sent him four horses from the Borough as far as London from bringing together weapons and anything else required . . .'
(Leicester)

The difference between land and sea was made more than once:

. . . 'When the king went on an expedition by land 10 Burgesses of Warwick went for all the others; whoever was notified but did not go paid a fine of 100s to the king. But if the king went against his enemies by sea they sent him either 4 boatmen or £4 of pence . . .'
(Warwick)

The king had given some boroughs rights to collect taxes and fines for themselves; Dover gave 20 ships for 15 days a year, Sandwich, also in Kent, gave a similar amount. Totnes, Barnstaple and Lydford, all in Devon, gave as much service for an expedition by land or sea as the city of Exeter.

And just occasionally there is the note of continuing depredations by marauding ships, though seldom now the Danes; in Devon, nine manors were *'laid waste by Irishmen . . .'*

Internal troubles

The land was still suffering from the effects of the Norman invasion, and William's policy of granting land to native barons over the heads of Anglo-Saxon holders. There were also disputes between Normans, arguments about inheritance, and judicial decisions of every kind:

. . . 'Those fleeing and others remaining have been utterly devastated, partly because of Earl Ralph's forfeitures, partly because of fines, partly because of the King's tax . . .'
(Norwich)

. . . 'very much is lacking from this manor which belonged to it in 1066, both in woodland and iron-working and in their payments . . .'
(Corby, Northamptonshire)

. . . 'Before 1066 this land was for the supplies of the monks; Ferron holds it by the king's order, against the Abbot's will . . .'
(Northamptonshire)

. . . 'before 1066 he held it himself; now he holds it from William (of Ansculf) harshly and wretchedly . . .'

. . . 'They were accustomed to fish in the River Trent, and now they make a complaint because they are forbidden to fish . . .'
(Nottingham)

Men also had obligations according to their status and rights:
... *'the owner of a horse went three times a year with the Sheriff to hear pleas and to meetings of the Hundreds at Wormelow'* ...
(City of Hereford, before and after 1066)

... *'Four free men held it from the Bishop before 1066, paying full jurisdiction, Church tax, burial, military service by land and sea, and pleas to [the] Hundred. The present holders do the same'* ...
(Bishampton, Worcestershire)

Trade and commerce
There were still a few arrangements for barter rather than money payments:
... *'for these [2 fisheries, 11 fishermen and 1 virgate of land] he gives pasture sufficient for 120 pigs, and if the pasture is inadequate he feeds and fattens 60 pigs with corn ...'*
(Whittlesey Mere, Huntingdonshire)

The Count of Mortain exchanged 2 manors (Benton and Haxton, in Devon) for a castle in Cornwall, a salt-boiler of Droitwich paid 10 loads of salt, and another manor gave fish every Friday for the village reeve's work. But more and more, barter was becoming a money economy;
... *'Then they paid 5 wagon-loads of 50 lead sheets; now they pay £10 ...'*

Houses were an important asset:
... *'he has 42 inhabited houses (in Oxford) which pay tax. The others cannot through poverty'*
(Oxford)

Markets were a valuable and prized source of revenue, bitterly disputed and eagerly applied for:
... *'in this manor there used to be a market on Saturdays. But William Malet made his castle at Eye, and he made another market in his castle on Saturdays and thereby the Bishops's market has been so far spoilt that it is of little value ...'*
(Thetford, Norfolk)

... *the Count of Mortain was very busy in his bartered Cornish castle, taking away the market from his manor and putting it in his own castle.*
(Cornwall)

There were all sorts of ways to raise money; a ferry paid tax in Weston upon Trent, and cargoes were eagerly awaited in most ports. Trade in fur was an enviable commodity, imported from abroad and sold almost at once to the richer merchants and nobility:
... *'if ships arrived ... or left ... without the King's permission, the King and the Earl had 40s from each man ... if it arrived against the King's peace ... the King and the Earl had both the ship and its cargo and everything in it. But if it came with the King's permission those in it sold what they had without interference, but when it left the King and the Earl had 4d from each cargo. If the King's reeve instructed those who had marten skins not to sell to anyone until they were first shown to him and he had made his purchase, whomsoever did not observe this was fined 40s ...'*
(Chester)

Crops and gardens
Only a few places actually mention gardens as part of the tax valuation; *8 cottagers* in Fulham and *23 men who have gardens* in Holywell; in Barnstaple (Devon), a garden paid 4d. Although 4d was not even then a great amount. Presumably this was more than a tiny plot for the family vegetables.

Main field crops and animals used for meat are commonly mentioned but there were some special notes: *arpents* of newly planted vineyards (in Middlesex especially), taxes from fishing nets and drag-nets in the Thames (Hampton), and Bloxham paying for its wool and cheese, and rather deliciously, a fishery in Cornworthy, (Devon) paid 30 salmon.

The People of *Domesday*
The rich landholders and senior churchmen are listed in our biographical section but throughout the records a few descriptive names stand out; Ralph the Haunted, and Alwin the Rat, are peculiarly direct. There are many names, too, which are based on the work or rank a man holds; Hervey the Commissioner, Richard the Artificer, Fulchere the Bowman. Just occasionally, a foreigner is singled out; a Frenchman, Fin the Dane (Cheddington).

For the rest, it became all too clear that the Normans were on the way up, and the Anglo-Saxons were watching their lands given away to a much smaller number of incoming families and soldiers.

Women in *Domesday*
Perhaps it is not surprising that women appear so seldom in the *Domesday* records; there are noble women who are major landholders in their own names, of course – the Countess Judith and the queen, for example, but there are many who are named only as wives or widows. Edeva the Fair held a number of manors in Lancashire; Golde and her son had 3 hides in Huntingdonshire, while 'Asgar's woman, a widow', held 2 hides as a manor in Hertfordshire. Hertfordshire had had many women owners, especially before 1066; there seem to be many fewer Norman women who are in control of their own land.
... *'On Alwin's death, King William gave his wife and land to Richard, a young man'* ... *'Bishop Aelmer annexed this land because the woman who held it married within a year of her husband's death ...'*
(Plumstead, Norfolk)

A wife or widow was normally protected in some way:
... *'if a thane should foreit his land, the King and the Earl between them have half his land and his money, but the lawful wife with his lawful heirs, if any have the other half ...'*
(Nottingham, and Chichester, Sussex)

... *'if anyone kills any man within his own court ... he ... shall be in the King's power, except for his wife's dowry, if he had her with a dowry ...'*
(Oxford)

There were stringent laws against rape and violence:
... *to draw blood, rape a woman or stay away from the Court when summoned all were fined 10s* ...
(Lancashire)

... and most counties added rape to the list of fines required by the king for conviction of robbery or housebreaking. However not all courts were as understanding:
... *'a man who committed highway robbery is fined 100s, a man who committed housebreaking 100s; a man who has committed rape pays no penalty other than corporal punishment ...'*
(Worcestershire)

A woman taken in adultery had to pay a fine in Kent to the archbishop, the man paid a fine to the king ...
... *'If a widow in Chester had intercourse with anyone unlawfully, she was fined 20s, but a girl 10s for such an offence ...'*
(Chester)

There are occasional stories, too:
... *'A man of Wihenoc's loved a certain woman on that land, and took her as his wife ...'*
(Pickenham, Norfolk)

... *Walter's wife gave a manor of 5 hides to St Pauls for her husband's soul* ...
(Gloucestershire)

Wulfin who lay ailing made sure that his friends and priest heard his wish that his wife should hold his land for as long as she lived, and only then would the land return to the church
(Selly Oak, Worcestershire)

Rare indeed is the mention of mothers:
... *'When he (Sigref) died, the Bishop gave his daughter, with this land, to one of his men-at-arms, so that he might maintain [her] mother and serve the Bishop from it'* ...
(Croome, Worcestershire)

But of all the women mentioned in Domesday, perhaps the pleasantest note of all is in the story of Aelgar, who had enough land to live on from the Sheriff of Trent, so that she might teach his daughter gold embroidery.

Bedfordshire

By the time of Domesday *Bedfordshire was already a well-settled model agricultural county. The remarkably even distribution of developed sites over its whole area is proof of its popularity. Villages were as frequent in the chalky southern hills as in the more fertile Vale of Bedford. The county was fortunate in its natural resources. The clay that covers two-thirds of Bedfordshire, and which is watered by the Ouse and the Ivel rivers, yields excellent wheat and barley, while the adjacent loamy tracts, rich mixes of clay, natural compost and sand, are even more fertile. The oxen that pulled the ploughs grazed on the lush meadows that abutted the main rivers, and sheep thrived on the chalky Chiltern downland. The county's central belt of rich greensand had the densest woodland, and thus on average the most pigs, although Luton, on the edge of the wooded Chilterns, had the greatest number of all – over 2000. Surprisingly, Luton also had the most mills, with seven on the infant Lea, but no eels were rendered here, as at 17 of the county's other mills, mainly on the Ouse.*

Bedford, though the county town and its only borough, was seemingly less important to the Domesday *compilers than Leighton Buzzard and Luton. Both were undoubtedly larger and, unlike Bedford, both had markets. So did Arlesley. Some modern places recorded in later medieval documents do not figure in* Domesday. *It is hard to understand why Dunstable, for instance, which lay at a busy crossroads, should have been omitted.*

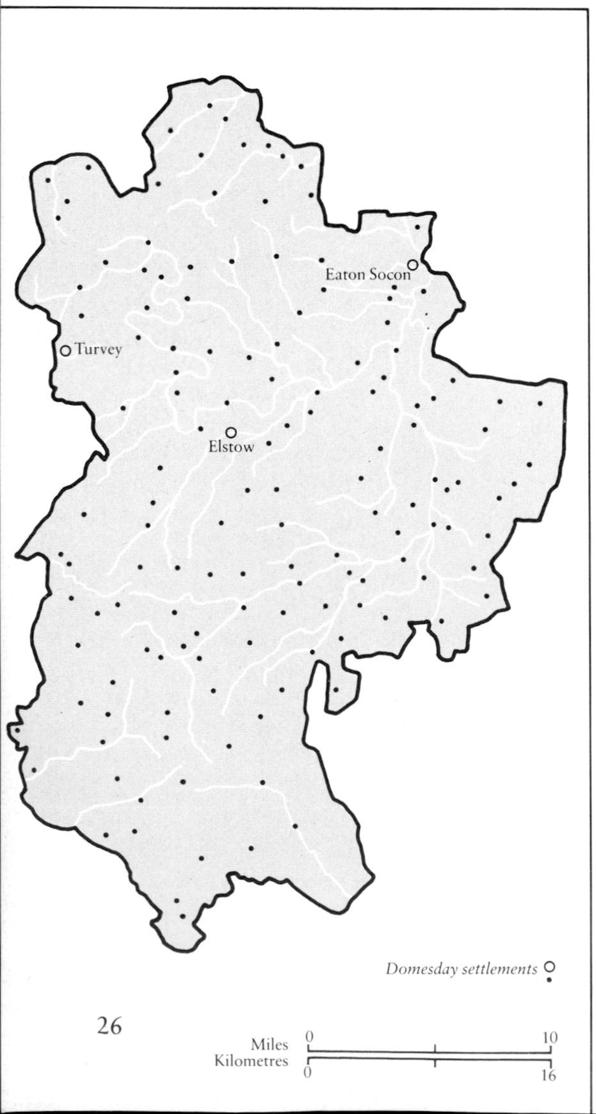

Eaton Socon

Eudo FitzHubert holds EATON (SOCON) *ETONE*. It answers for 20 hides. Land for 16 ploughs. In lordship 7½ hides; 4 ploughs there. 38 villagers have 12 ploughs. 7 smallholders and 8 slaves; 2 Freemen who could not grant or sell their land. 2 mills at 36s 6d and 100 eels; meadow for 12 ploughs; woodland, 400 pigs; vineyard, 2 acres. In total, value £15; when acquired £8; before 1066 £10. Wulfmer of Eaton, a thane of King Edward's, held this manor. In this manor were 2 Freemen who could sell and grant their land. Theodbald, Countess Judith's man, claims 1 hide of this land, of which Eudo dispossessed him after he came to this manor.

Eaton Socon, watered by the Ouse in the far east of the county, was once the largest parish in Bedfordshire. But boundary changes in the 1960s resulted in a portion's being incorporated into Huntingdonshire, which in turn (1974) was absorbed into Cambridgeshire. The major part, however, remains in Bedfordshire. This comprises a sizeable village on a main road and, to the west, a half-dozen isolated hamlets with their associated manors.

At the Conquest the great landowner, Eudo FitzHubert (the steward), took over what had become known as the barony of Eaton from Wulfmar, whose principal manor this had been. Eaton's 20 hides represented a third of Eudo's Bedfordshire holdings, the neighbouring Wyboston manor being another of them. Eaton is remarkable in having a vineyard – one of only 55 places recorded in *Domesday* where the Normans encouraged grapes to flourish; the most northerly of these was in Ely. Vines continued to be grown by the great lords and monasteries until the end of the fourteenth century, by which time the excellent imported wines from Gascony (20,000 tuns annually in the 1330s) were overwhelming English competition.

When Eudo died in about 1120 his land passed to the Crown which then granted it to a member of the house of Beauchamp. Hugh, the son of this tenant, bought the manor from his father for £23 1s 3d in 1156. It was he, no doubt, who improved the pre-Conquest castle, later dubbed the 'Hillings', which stands behind the church on the riverside. The Eaton barony passed through several families until a St Neots man bought it in 1847. The *Domesday* manor of Sudbury, in the northern corner of the modern parish, had, as its fourteenth-century manorial appurtenances, a 'broken-down dovecote, a garden and, an island in the Ouse from which the reeds were cut at the Feast of the Purification'. Other parish places that have survived from medieval times include Bushmead Priory (founded by Hugh de Beauchamp), Begwary and Basmead, all once manors. Sokes Manor gave its name to the present village.

Modern Eaton Socon, though it has expanded modestly, preserves much of its Georgian coaching-town character, but has unfortunately lost the medieval charm which in 1794 prompted Lord Torrington, the veteran traveller and amateur artist, to call it 'a spot of much beauty' which 'from a good pencil would furnish excellent drawings'.

Elstow

ELSTOW *ELNESTOV* answers for 3½ hides. The nuns of St Mary's hold it from Countess Judith. Land for 7 ploughs. In lordship 2 ploughs. 14 villagers have 5 ploughs. 11 smallholders and 4 slaves. 1 mill at 24s; meadow for 4 ploughs; woodland, 60 pigs. Value 100s; when acquired 40s; before 1066 £10. 4 Freemen held this manor. They were King Edward's men. They could grant and sell their land; but their jurisdiction always lay in Kempston.

Elstow, on the southern outskirts of Bedford, preserves its village identity despite encroaching suburbia. William the Conqueror gave the manor to his niece, Countess Judith, who

ELSTOW: *The Moot Hall dates from the 16th century and was used by John Bunyan's followers.*

founded a nunnery here in about 1075 and endowed it with the revenues from the village. Judith also gave the adjoining Wilshamstead Manor to the nuns, together with land in the manor of Maulden. Before the Conquest it seems that the holder of Kempston, a large and valuable manor to the west, had some jurisdiction over land transactions (and doubtless other matters) relating to Cardington, Harrowden, and Wilshamstead Manors, as well as Elstow.

The abbess and nuns of St Mary's held Elstow manor until the Dissolution, using their money and influence to help develop Elstow as a village. The convent church, which had an ambitious cruciform plan, was begun in the early twelfth century. In the thirteenth, a grand façade was built onto the west front, an indication of the manor's comparative wealth. The annual fair which Henry II had granted to the nuns was flourishing in those days. So popular was it with the people of nearby Bedford that the envious Bedford burgesses had to be restrained by writ from assaulting them on their way to Elstow! It was probably during the fourteenth century that the abbess ordered a gallows, pillory and ducking stool to be built on the village green so that offenders – mainly drunkards, scolds and sellers of substandard goods – could be publicly punished. According to a tantalizingly incomplete report, the nunnery itself was the object of attack by more dangerous criminals in 1408. Men carrying ladders and armed with axes, bows and arrows broke in and, after a struggle in which a servant was wounded, abducted a female named Crokebarrow.

At the Dissolution the nunnery was abandoned and the manor passed to the Crown. Subsequent lords of Elstow included the Radcliffes, the Chekes, and the Hillersdons. By the early seventeenth century, much of the nunnery lay in ruins, and Thomas Hillersdon used the fallen stones to build himself a splendid house. It stood on the south side of the church, which still survives, until 1759 and is now itself a ruin. In 1792 the daughters of Denis Hillersdon sold their rights in the manor to Samuel Whitbread of the brewing family. As MP for Bedford, he was already achieving a reputation as a determined and outspoken radical Whig – a bitter opponent of Pitt's war policies, and an 'unfaltering adherent' of Charles James Fox. The Whitbreads retained the manor throughout the nineteenth century.

Elstow is, however, best known as the birthplace and early home of Bedfordshire's most illustrious son, John Bunyan, the author of *The Pilgrim's Progress*. He was born in November 1628 at his parents' cottage near Harrowden hamlet, close to where his ancestor, William Boynon, lived in 1327. The Bunyan family (spelt 34 different ways over the centuries) had been associated with the district since the late twelfth century, a fact that John Bunyan preferred to ignore when describing his descent from 'the meanest and most despised of all the families of the land'. His father was, in fact, a tinker and John was not too proud to follow this trade himself.

He was sent to school (though he denied this too), probably in Elstow, and, by his own account, enjoyed a rumbustious childhood in which bell-ringing and dancing vied with 'cursing, swearing, lying, and blaspheming the name of God'. At 16 he enlisted in the Parliamentary army based at Newport Pagnell; a year later he narrowly escaped death when, during a siege, his last-minute replacement as sentinel was shot in the head. He married at 20 and returned to his home village and to the trade of tinker. It was his wife who introduced him to religious texts, stimulating the transformation of a ne'er-do-well and profaner into the fiery preacher who was to spend nearly 12 years in gaol for his puritan beliefs. He wrote *The Pilgrim's Progress* while in prison.

The cottage where he set up married life stood until 1958. Much of the village that he knew still remains, including the sixteenth-century Moot Hall which overlooks the green, the ancient church door that is probably the original of his 'wicket gate', and the nave's twelfth-century zigzag ornaments, which, with a tympanum, survive from Countess Judith's nunnery.

Turvey

In TURVEY *TORNAI* the Bishop [of Coutances] also holds 4 hides. Land for 6 ploughs. In lordship 2 hides; 3 ploughs there. 3 villagers have 3 ploughs; 8 smallholders and 1 slave. 1 mill, 20s; meadow for 2 ploughs; woodland, 40 pigs. Value £6; when acquired 40s; before 1066 £6. 3 Freemen, King Edward's men, held this manor; they could sell and grant. The Bishop has this land in exchange for Bleadon, as his men state.

Turvey, a picturesque golden limestone village, stands amid parkland beside the Ouse, which here forms the border with Buckinghamshire. There are no less than eight *Domesday* entries for Turvey, but the most significant is that which describes the holding of the Bishop of Coutances, whose manor was eventually to absorb most of the Turvey land held by others.

Although there is no mention of a tenant of the bishop in 1086, evidence exists to show that a family named de Alneto held the manor soon after the Conquest. At some time before 1221 two de Alneto heiresses, Alice and Sarah, married a Mordaunt and a Robert d'Ardres respectively, and it was their husbands who gave their names to the village's twin manors of Mordaunt and Ardres. Though a d'Ardres had held Turvey land in 1086, it was as Mordaunt Manor that the two were united in the late fourteenth century.

The Mordaunts were a colourful and eccentric family. The records show that Edward Mordaunt, on the Sunday before a religious feast in 1372, became frenzied, slaying his wife Ellen and drowning himself in a Turvey pool. Later Mordaunts achieved high rank in the Tudor courts.

Henry Mordaunt, a fervent Catholic, was suspected of being implicated in the Gunpowder Plot and long imprisoned. His son, the first Earl of Peterborough, was an ardent Parliamentarian in the Civil War, while the second Earl, a celebrated Royalist, lost his Turvey estates for his allegiance. The manor passed from the family in 1786.

Alwin, Turvey's priest in 1086, kept the small plot (valued at 3s) he had held before the Conquest in return for performing a weekly mass. This land was held from the king and on Alwin's death probably passed to Newnham Priory. The Priory of St Neots also benefited from gifts of Turvey land during the twelfth and thirteenth centuries and by 1278 had amassed 100 acres.

The village's most famous incumbent was Legh Richmond who, in 22 years as Rector from 1805, established himself as a sort of Regency Bunyan. Although he was a highly popular touring preacher and evangelist, eight volumes he compiled of selections from the Reformation divines proved unremunerative. He is buried in the churchyard.

Some masonry of the pre-Conquest church can still be seen in the upper parts of the north and south nave walls, but the Saxon chancel has been rebuilt. As in 1086, there is one mill, though there had been two in 1668. Turvey Abbey is partly Jacobean and Turvey House a fine Georgian building. Most of the rest of the village was rebuilt in stone during the mid-nineteenth century.

△ TURVEY: *The Abbey harks back to the days of the Mordaunts.*
▽ ELSTOW: *This tympanum survives from Judith's nunnery.*

AMPTHILL: *Market House on the corner of the square.*

Bedfordshire Gazetteer
Each entry starts with the modern place-name in **bold** type. The *Domesday* information is in *italic* type, beginning with the name or names by which the place was known in 1086. The main landholders and under-tenants follow, separated with semi-colons if a place was divided into more than one holding. A number of holdings were granted by the king to his reeves, almsmen, etc.; these are given with their office or described, at the end of a list of landholders, as holding land 'from the king'. More general information, including examples of dues such as wheat, eels, etc. rendered by tenants, completes the *Domesday* part of the entry. The modern or post-Domesday section is in normal type. ▣ represents a village, ⌂ a small village or hamlet.

Ampthill *Ammetelle: Nigel de le Vast from Nigel d'Aubigny.* Small Georgian town. Ampthill Park is now a Cheshire Home.

Arlesey *Alricesei(a)/eie: Bishop of Durham; Bernard from William d'Eu; Herfast from Nigel d'Aubigny; Wulfsi. 3 mills.* ▣ Large, straggling; brickworks.

Aspley Guise *Aspeleia: Acard d'Ivry from Hugh de Beauchamp. Mill.* ▣ 18th-century Guise House was a boys' school.

Astwick *Estuuiche: Bernard, Weneling and Ledmer from Hugh de Beauchamp; Hugh from Walter of Flanders. 2 mills.* ⌂

Barton-in-the-Clay *Bertone: St Benedict's of Ramsey before and after 1066.* ▣ Large.

Barwythe *Bereuuorde: Baldric from Robert de Tosny.* ⌂

Battlesden *Badelesdone/estone: Richard Talbot from Walter Giffard; Robert from William the Chamberlain; Azelina, Ralph Tailbois' wife.* ⌂ Only Battlesden Park remains of a large house demolished in 1885.

Bedford *Bedeford: Bishop of Lincoln. Church.* Prosperous county town. John Bunyan was imprisoned here for 12 years. Bedford Museum is on the site of the Norman castle. Cecil Higgins Art Gallery.

Beeston *Bistone: Roland, Norman and Pirot from Eudo FitzHubert; William Speke; Thurstan the Chamberlain; Godmund; Alwin from the king. Mill.* ▣

Biddenham *Bide(n)ham: Ernwin the priest from Bishop of Lincoln; Ordwy of Bedford from St Edmunds; St Pauls of Bedford; Serlo de Rots from Hugh de Beauchamp; Ralph and Serlo de Rots from William Speke; Burgesses of Bedford; Oscar of Bedford; Godwin; Ordwy; Wulfmer. 2 mills.* ▣ Outskirts of Bedford. A gallows stood at Gallows Corner until 1802.

Biggleswade *Bichelesuuade/ Pichelsuuade: Ralph de l'Isle. 2 mills.* Town which has had a market since 1227. Once an important coaching stop.

Biscot *Bissopescote: King's land.* Part of Luton.

Bletsoe *Bach/Blecheshou: Osbert de Breuil from Hugh de Beauchamp; Osbern from Countess Judith. Mill.* ⌂

Blunham *Blun(e)ham: St Edmund's; Dominic from Eudo FitzHubert; St Edmunds from Countess Judith. Mill.* ▣ On the Ivel; Blunham Mill House; South Mills, fertilizer works. The poet John Donne spent summers here.

Bolnhurst *Bole/Bulehestre: Tovi the priest and 2 freemen from Bishop of Bayeux; Bishop of Coutances; St Mary's of Thorney; Hugh from Countess Judith.* ▣ Scattered; timber-framed farmhouses.

Bromham *Brimeham/ Bruneham: Arnulf de Ardres from Count Eustace; Serlo de Rots from Hugh de Beauchamp; Hugh from Countess Judith; Osgeat from the king. 2 mills (225 eels).* ▣ Large; mill; 16th-century Bromham House. The medieval bridge with 26 arches is the county's longest. Bromham Hall is 16th century.

Broom *Brume: Nigel de le Vast from Nigel d'Aubigny.* ▣

Caddington *Cadendone: St Paul's of London.* ▣ Straw-plaiting was done here.

Cainhoe *Cainou/Chainehou: Nigel d'Aubigny; Thurstan from Avelina, Ralph Tailbois' wife. Mill.* Medieval Cainhoe Manor Farm; remains of a Norman motte and bailey castle.

Campton *Chambeltone: Ralph de Lanquetot from Walter Giffard; Fulbert from William d'Eu; Thurstan.* ▣

Cardington *Chernetone: Hugh de Beauchamp; Hugh from Countess Judith. Mill.* ▣ Cottages, owned by the Whitbread brewing family in the 18th century. The ill-fated R101 airship was built here.

Carlton *Carlehtone: Herbert FitzIvo from Bishop of Bayeux; Ketel and Bernard from Nigel d'Aubigny; Osbern Fisher and Ketelbert from the king. Mill.* ▣ Saxon church.

Chalgrave *Celgrave: Arnulf de Hesdin; Albert de Lorraine.* ⌂ Chalgrave Manor.

Chalton *Cerlentone: Adelaide, Hugh de Grandmesnil's wife. Mill.* ⌂

Chawston *Calnestorne/ Chauelestorne: Eudo FitzHubert; Rhiwallon from Hugh de Beauchamp; William FitzRainward and William Gross from William Speke. Mill.* ⌂ Market gardens.

Chicksands *Chichesana/e: William de Cairon from Bishop of Lincoln; 3 freemen and Walter from Azelina, Ralph Tailbois' wife (it is of her dowry). Mill.* US airforce base; medieval Chicksands Priory.

Clapham *Clopeham: Miles Crispin; claimed by Ramsey Abbey, which used it for supplies before 1066. Mill.* ▣ Large; 85ft-high Saxon tower; new housing.

Clifton *Cliftone/stone: William de Cairon from Bishop of Lincoln, Eudo FitzHubert and Nigel d'Aubigny; Leofwin from St Benedict's of Ramsey; Alwin from Countess Judith. 2 mills.* ▣ New housing estates.

Clophill *Clopelle: Nigel d'Aubigny.* ▣ Large; new housing.

Cockayne Hatley *Hatelai: Countess Judith; Azelina, Ralph Tailbois' wife. Mill.* ⌂

Colmworth *Colmeborde-worde/ Culmeuuorde: Wimund from Hugh de Beauchamp.* ▣ It was so poor in the 17th century that there were houses without even a hearth.

Cople *C(h)ochepol: Robert, Reginald, Gunfrid, Norman, Branting, Robert, Roger the Priest and Liboret from Hugh de Beauchamp; Hugh from Countess Judith.* ▣

Cranfield *Cranfelle: St Benedict's of Ramsey.* ▣ Large, scattered; Cranfield Institute of Technology. The country's first concrete runway was laid at Cranfield Airfield.

Dean *Dena/Dene: Bishop of Coutances; Godfrey from Bishop of Lincoln; William de Warenne; 11 freemen and Godwy Dear of Bedford, all before and after 1066.* Now 2 small villages, Upper and Lower Dean.

Dunton *Danitone/Donitone: Ralph de Lanquetot from Walter Giffard; Richard Poynant.* ▣

Easton *Estone: 4 freemen from Bishop of Coutances; William de Cairon from Bishop of Lincoln; William de Warenne and Theodoric from him; Wimund from Hugh de Beauchamp; Hugh Butler; Sigar de Chocques; Osbern FitzRichard.* ⌂

EATON BRAY: *Door of the 13th-century church.*

Eaton Bray *Eitone: Bishop of Bayeux.* ▣ Large, pretty; timber-framed buildings.

Eaton Socon *Etone:* See page 26

Edworth *Edeuuorde: 2 men-at-arms from William d'Eu; Alwin, the king's reeve.* ⌂

Elstow *Elnestou:* See page 26.

Elvedon *Eluendone:* Lost.

Eversholt *Evres(h)ot: Ansgot of Rochester from Bishop of Bayeux; Ralph from Hugh de Beauchamp; Herbert, the king's reeve.* ▣ Scattered. Tyrrels End is a 15th-century timber-framed house.

Everton *Evretone: Ranulf d'Ilger from Countess Judith.* ▣ 2 manor houses.

Eyeworth *Ai(ss)euuorde: William Speke; Brodo from Azelina, Ralph Tailbois' wife. Mill.* ⌂

Farndish *Fernadis/Farnedis: William; Henry FitzAzor; William Peverel.* ▣

Felmersham *Falmeresham/ Flammeresham: Gilbert FitzSolomon; Gilbert from Countess Judith. Mill.* ▣ Stone tithe barn.

Flitton *Flictha: Robert Fafiton.* ▣ Owned by the same family – the Greys – for 700 years; their mausoleum is in the churchyard.

Flitwick *Flicteuuiche: William Lovett. Mill.* Small town; mill on the River Flitt.

Goldington *Coldentone/ Goldentone: Ivo Tailbois from Bishop of Lincoln; Roger FitzTheodoric, Richard and Walter from Hugh de Beauchamp; Alric Wintermilk from the king.* Part of Bedford.

Goldington Highfields *Goldentone:* Lost.

Gravenhurst *Crauenhest: William from Hugh de Beauchamp.* ▣ Now 2 small villages, Upper and Lower Gravenhurst.

Great Barford *Bereford: Rhiwallon, Wimund of Tessel, Ansketel the priest and Theobold from Hugh de Beauchamp. Mill (80 eels).* ▣ Large; on the River Ouse; 17-arch, 15th-century bridge.

Harlington *Herlingdone: Nigel d'Aubigny. Packload of oats from woodland.* ▣ Large; on the Bedford-Luton railway line.

Harrold *Hareuuelle: Gilbert de Blosseville from Countess Judith. Mill (200 eels).* ▣ On the Great Ouse river; 14th-century 11-arch bridge; 18th-century market house; circular prison (1824).

Harrowden *Hergentone/ Herghetone: Ernwin the Priest; Nigel d'Aubigny; Canons of Bedford from Countess Judith.* ⌂ Adjoins Bedford.

Haynes *Hagenes: Hugh de Beauchamp.* Now Haynes Park (a school) and Haynes Church End, about a mile from the main village.

Henlow *Haneslau(ue)/ Hanslau(e): Herfast from Nigel d'Aubigny; Hugh from Walter of Flanders; Widder and Bernard from Azelina, Ralph Tailbois' wife; (Hugh de Beauchamp claims from her, stating it was never in her dowry); Alric. 2 mills.* ▣ Large; RAF station and airfield; Queen Anne grange; disused mill.

Higham Gobion *Echam: William de Loucelles from Hugh de Beauchamp.* ⌂ Part Tudor manor house.

Hinwick *Haneuuic(h)/ Heneuuic(h): Thurstan from Bishop of Coutances; Walter from William Speke; Hugh of Flanders; Gunfrid de Chocques and Theobald from him; Thurstan the Chamberlain, Edward.* ⌂ Tudor Hinwick Hall; 18th-century Hinwick House.

Hockliffe *Hocheleia: Azelina, Ralph Tailbois' wife.* ▣ On the Roman Watling Street. Georgian Hockliffe House incorporates part of a 13th-century hospital. The manor house is partly 18th century.

Hulcote *Holcot/Holecote: Ralph Passwater from William Speke. Mill.* ⌂

Holme *Holma/Holme: Wulfric from William d'Eu; Mordwing from Hugh de Beauchamp; Fulchere de Paris from Nigel d'Aubigny; Walter of Flanders, Ralph de L'Isle, Fulchere and 2 men from Countess Judith; Alwin, the king's reeve.* A few houses, part of Biggleswade.

Houghton Conquest *Houstone/ Oustone: Hugh de Beauchamp; Hugh from Countess Judith; Arnold from Adelaide, Hugh de Grandmesnil's wife.* ▣ Houghton House, now a ruin.

Houghton Regis *Houstone: King's land with William the Chamberlain holding the church. Wheat, honey.* A London overspill area; Iron Age earthwork at Maiden Bower; church with a Norman font.

Husborne Crawley *Crauelai/Crawelai: Thorgils from Nigel d'Aubigny; William Lovett. 2 mills.* Manor house.

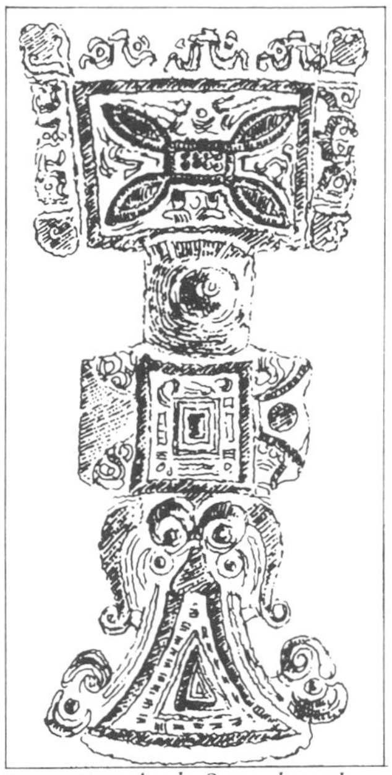

KEMPSTON: *Anglo-Saxon brooch.*

Kempston *Cameston(e): Countess Judith. Mill.* Bedford suburb. Site of Anglo-Saxon and Roman excavations. An old mill stands on the river.

Kensworth *Canesworde: St Paul's of London.*

Keysoe *C(h)aisot: Hugh de Beauchamp; Hugh Hubald from Osbern FitzRichard; William de Warenne; Alwin, the king's thane, the pre-Conquest holder.* Now 2 small villages, Keysoe and Keysoe Row.

Kinwick *Chenemondewiche:* Lost.

Knotting *Chenotinga: Bishop of Coutances.*

Langford *Langeford: Walter of Flanders. 2 mills.* Large; new housing; mill on the river.

Leighton Buzzard *Lestone: King's land with Bishop of Lincoln holding the church. 2 mills, market. Wheat, honey.* Market town; 15th-century market cross.

Lidlington *Litinclitone: Abbess of Barking.*

Little Barford *Bereforde: Eudo FitzHubert from St Benedict's of Ramsey and Osbern from him; Osbern Fitz Walter. Mill.*

Luton *Lintone/Loitone: King's land with William the Chamberlain holding the church. 6 mills, market, church. Wheat, honey.* Large industrial town with an airport; site of Iron Age, Roman and Saxon settlements. Luton Hoo is a vast Adam mansion with gardens by Capability Brown.

Marston Mortaine *Mer(e)stone: Hugh de Bolbec from Walter Giffard; Herfast from Nigel d'Aubigny.* Several Tudor half-timbered houses; brickmaking centre since the 16th century.

Maulden *Meldone: Hugh de Bolbec from Walter Giffard; Hugh de Beauchamp; Nigel d'Aubigny; Countess Judith and the nuns of Elstow from her; a reeve of the king. Mill.*

Melchbourne *Melceburne: Bishop of Coutances.* 17th-century manor house; thatched cottages.

Meppershall *Malpertesselle/Maperteshale: Gilbert FitzSolomon.* Market gardening. A 17th-century timber-framed manor house is built on the site of a Norman castle owned by William de Meppershall, the royal larderer.

Millbrook *Melebroc: Nigel de Le Vast from Nigel d'Aubigny. 2 mills.*

Millow *Melehou: Bishop of Durham; Ralph from Walter Giffard; William d'Eu.*

Milton Bryan *Middletone/Mildentone: Ansgot from Bishop of Bayeux; William Froissart from Hugh de Beauchamp.* 17th-century manor house.

Milton Ernest *Middletone/Mildentone: Miles Crispin and William Basset from Hugh de Beauchamp; Thorgils from Nigel d'Aubigny; Reginald from Walter of Flanders; Ivo, Hugh de Grandmesnil's steward from Adelaide, Hugh de Grandmesnil's wife; a beadle from the king. Mill.* Victorian manor house.

Nares Gladley *Gledelai: Jocelyn le Breton. Mill.* Part of Leighton Buzzard.

Northill *Nortigble/Nortgiue(le): Pirot and Ralph from Eudo FitzHubert; Walter from Hugh de Beauchamp; William Speke. 1½ mills.*

Oakley *Achelei(a): 2 men-at-arms from Robert de Tosny; Miles Crispin from Countess Judith. Mill.* Large. Rush mats were made here.

Odell *Wad(eh)elle: Arnulf d'Ardres from Count Eustace; Walter of Flanders. Mill (200 eels).* On the River Ouse. An old mill is now a house.

Old Warden *Wardone: William Speke; Ralph de l'Isle; Walter the monk from Azelina, Ralph Tailbois' wife (of her marriage portion). Mill.* Aircraft museum founded by the Shuttleworth family. A 1st-century bronze mirror and medieval floor tiles were unearthed here.

Pavenham *Pabeneham: Arnulf d'Adres from Count Eustace; Robert FitzNigel from Ranulf brother of Ilger; Thurstan the Chamberlain. Mill.* Pretty; stone houses. Once the centre of the rush-mat making industry.

Pegsdon *Pechesdone: St Benedict's of Ramsey. 2 mills.*

Pertenhall *Partenhale: William from Bishop of Lincoln.* Jacobean manor house.

Podington *Podintone/Potintone: Hugh from Walter of Flanders; Hugh of Flanders; William Peverel.*

Polehanger *Polehangre: Martell from Robert d'Oilly.*

Potsgrove *Potesgrava/grave: William the Chamberlain; Jocelyn le Breton; a groom of the king; Herbert, the king's reeve.*

Potton *Potone: Countess Judith and Hugh from her. Mill.* Small market town.

Priestley *Prestelei: Thorgils from Nigel d'Aubigny; a reeve of the king.* A few scattered farms.

Pulloxhill *Polochessele: Roger and Rhiwallon from Nigel d'Aubigny.* Fast-growing. Site of an 18th-century gold mine.

Putnoe *Putenehou: Hugh de Beauchamp. Mill.* Part of Bedford.

Radwell *Radeuuelle: Nigel de le Vast from Nigel d'Aubigny; Hugh from Countess Judith. Mill.*

Riseley *Riselai: 2 Frenchmen and 6 Englishmen from Bishop of Coutances; Godfrey from Bishop of Lincoln; Hugh de Beauchamp and Alric from him. Hugh Hubald from Osbern FitzRichard; David d'Argenton.* Straggling; one of the county's first brickmaking centres.

Roxton *Rochesdone/stone: Rhiwallon from Hugh de Beauchamp; William Speke. Mill (260 eels).* The countryman's linen smock was initiated here in 1714.

Salford *Saleford: Hugh de Beauchamp. Mill.*

Salph *Salchou: Hugh de Beauchamp.*

Sandy *Sandeia: Eudo FitzHubert. 2 mills.* Small town. Sandy Lodge is the headquarters of the Royal Society for Protection of Birds.

Segenhoe *Segenehou: Walter brother of Sihere.* Segenhoe manor farm.

Sewell *Sewelle: King's land.*

Sharnbrook *Sernebroc/Serneburg: Bishop of Coutances and Thorgils, 7 freemen and Humphrey from him; Robert FitzRozelin from Count Eustace; Osbert de Breuil from Hugh de Beauchamp; Robert from Hugh of Flanders; Osbern Fisher; Albert de Lorraine; Hugh from Countess Judith; Aelmer. 2 mills, fishpond.* Large, thriving. Tofte House is part 1613; Sharnbrook House is 18th century. The old tower windmill has been converted to a clock tower.

Shelton (in Marston Moretaine) *Es(s)eltone: Herfast and Stephen from Nigel d'Aubigny; Albert de Lorraine; Adelaide, Hugh de Grandmesnil's wife.* Now 2 small villages, Upper and Lower Shelton.

Shelton (near Swineshead) *Eseltone: 2 freemen from Bishop of Coutances.* The site of Shelton Hall dates from medieval times.

Shillington *Sethlindone: St Benedict's of Ramsey. Broken mill.* Hilltop, Danish earthworks nearby, half-timbered houses.

Shirdon *Segresdonet:* Lost.

Silsoe *Sewilessou/Siuuilessou: A concubine of Nigel d'Aubigny; Hugh from Walter brother of Sihere. Mill.* Wrest House in Wrest Park.

Southill *Sudgible/uele: William de Cairon from Eudo FitzHubert; Hugh de Beauchamp; 2 Frenchmen from William Speke; Walter of Flanders and Alric from him; Richard Poynant; Hugh from Countess Judith. 200 eels.* Its great house belonged to the Byng family (Admirals Sir George and John), then to Samuel Whitbread.

Stagsden *Stachesdene: Herbert FitzIvo from Bishop of Bayeux; Godwy from Count Eustace; Hugh de Beauchamp; Hugh from Countess Judith.* Bird gardens.

Stanford *Stanford(e): William de Cairon and 7 freemen from Eudo FitzHubert; Hugh de Beauchamp and Roger from him; Hugh from William Speke; Roger from Azelina, Ralph Tailbois' wife (of her marriage portion); Alric and Ordwy from the king. 2½ mills.*

Steppingley *Stepigelai: William FitzReginald from William Speke.*

Stevington *Stiuentone: Arnulf from Count Eustace.* Complete 18th-century postmill.

Stondon *Standone: St Benedict's of Ramsey; Engelhere from Azelina, Ralph Tailbois' wife.* Now 2 hamlets, Upper and Lower Stondon.

Stotfold *Stodfald/Stotfalt: Hugh de Beauchamp. 4 mills (400 eels).* Disused mill on the Ivel.

Stratton *Stratone: Fulchere de Paris from Walter Giffard; Walter of Flanders; Ralph de l'Isle; Fulchere de Paris from Countess Judith.* Part of Biggleswade.

Streatley *Stradl(e)i/Straillei: Walter from William d'Eu; William de Loucelles from Hugh de Beauchamp; Pirot from Nigel d'Aubigny; Hugh from William Speke; the reeve of the Hundred.* Georgian Streatley House.

Studham *Estodham: Baldric from Robert de Tosny.* Straw-plaiting was made here.

Sudbury *Subberie: Richard FitzGilbert.* Part of St Neots.

Sundon *Sonedone: William d'Eu.* Now Upper Sundon (site of cement works), Sundon Park (part of Luton) and Lower Sundon, a hamlet.

Sutton *Sudtone: Alwin from Eudo FitzHubert; Thorkell, Alwin, Leofgar, Robert, Sweeting and Robert, Thorbert, Godwin and Edric from Countess Judith; Alwin, the king's reeve.* Medieval packhorse bridge; ford.

Swineshead *Suineshefet: Eustace from William de Warenne; Ralph from Eustace the Sheriff.*

Tempsford *Tamiseforde: William de Cairon from Bishop of Lincoln; Eudo FitzHubert and William de Cairon from him; Robert from Richard Poynant; Alwin, the king's reeve. 2 mills.* Mill, now a sawmill.

Thurleigh *Lalega: Leofric from Miles Crispin; Leofgeat from Hugh de Beauchamp; Robert d'Oilly; Richard Basset and Solomon the priest from him; Hugh and Reginald from Walter of Flanders.* Airfield.

Tilsworth *Pileworde: Ambrose from William Peverel.* 15th-century gatehouse.

Tingrith *Tingrei: Thorgils from Nigel d'Aubigny.*

Toddington *Dodintone/Totingetone: Arnulf de Hesdin.* Large. Henrietta Wentworth, mistress of the Duke of Monmouth, lived here in the 17th century.

Totternhoe *Totenhou: Osbert from Walter of Flanders; William the Chamberlain. 4 mills.* Large; site of a Roman villa. Doo Little Mill is now a house.

Turvey *Tornei-nei(a)/Torue(e):* See page 28.

Westcotts *Wescote: Nigel d'Aubigny; Ordwy, the king's reeve.* Part of Wilstead.

Westoning *Westone: King's land, formerly Earl Harold.* New housing.

Wilden *Wildene: Herbert from Bishop of Bayeux and his nephew Hugh from him.* Scattered.

Willington *Wel(i)tone: Hugh de Beauchamp. Mill.* 2 Tudor buildings: a dovecote with 1400 openings; a stable.

Wilshamstead *Wescota: Countess Judith and the nuns of Elstow from her.* Growing; manor house now an hotel.

Woburn *Woberne/burne: Walter Giffard; Herbert, the king's reeve.* Mainly 18th-century houses. The park of Woburn Abbey, home of the dukes of Bedford since the 17th century, is now a wildlife safari park.

Wootton *Otone: Albert de Lorraine.* Once a brickmaking centre. Church bells were also made here.

Wyboston *Wiboldestone/tune: Eudo FitzHubert from St Benedict's of Ramsey; Eudo FitzHubert; Wimund from Hugh de Beauchamp; Pirot from Nigel d'Aubigny; monks of St Neot's from Richard FitzGilbert; Iudichael from Azelina, Ralph Tailbois' wife.* Market gardening.

Wymington *Wimentone: Walter from William Speke; Glew from Alfred of Lincoln; Osbert from Walter of Flanders; 5 brothers with their mother and Thorkell from the king.* Bronze Age axes were found here. A smockmill stood until the 20th century.

Yelden *Giveldene: Geoffrey de Trelly from Bishop of Coutances.* Site of a Norman motte and bailey castle; the mound remains.

Berkshire

In 1871 the historian Edward Freeman picked out Berkshire's Domesday *as of special interest. Compared with those of other counties its pages are rich in personal details which breathe life into the statistics. The customs of Berkshire, which it lists under the borough of Wallingford, add much to our picture of eleventh-century society (see page 24).* Domesday *records William's new castle at Windsor, built on half a hide taken from the manor of Clewer. It details the 22 holdings of Henry de Ferrers, forefather of the Earls of Derby (a surprise to find him holding so much land so far south), and the relatively small holdings of at least ten other Norman barons who held vast estates in other counties. Above all, it can be compared with the chronicle of the Abbey of Abingdon. This great Benedictine abbey had 47 Berkshire holdings, exactly as many as the king. The record of its dealings adds significance to* Domesday's *names and figures.*

Geographically the county was – and is – extremely varied. In the north from Lechlade to Old Windsor it was bounded for 100 miles by the Thames. Here there were extensive meadowlands and the opportunity for mills and fisheries. The Kennet in the south provided similar opportunities on a smaller scale.

But Berkshire's real agricultural wealth lay in the west, where its manors in the Vale of the White Horse were important producers of grain and cheese.

GOOSEY: *The view across the common towards the church. Today, as in 1086, dairy farming is its most important industry.*

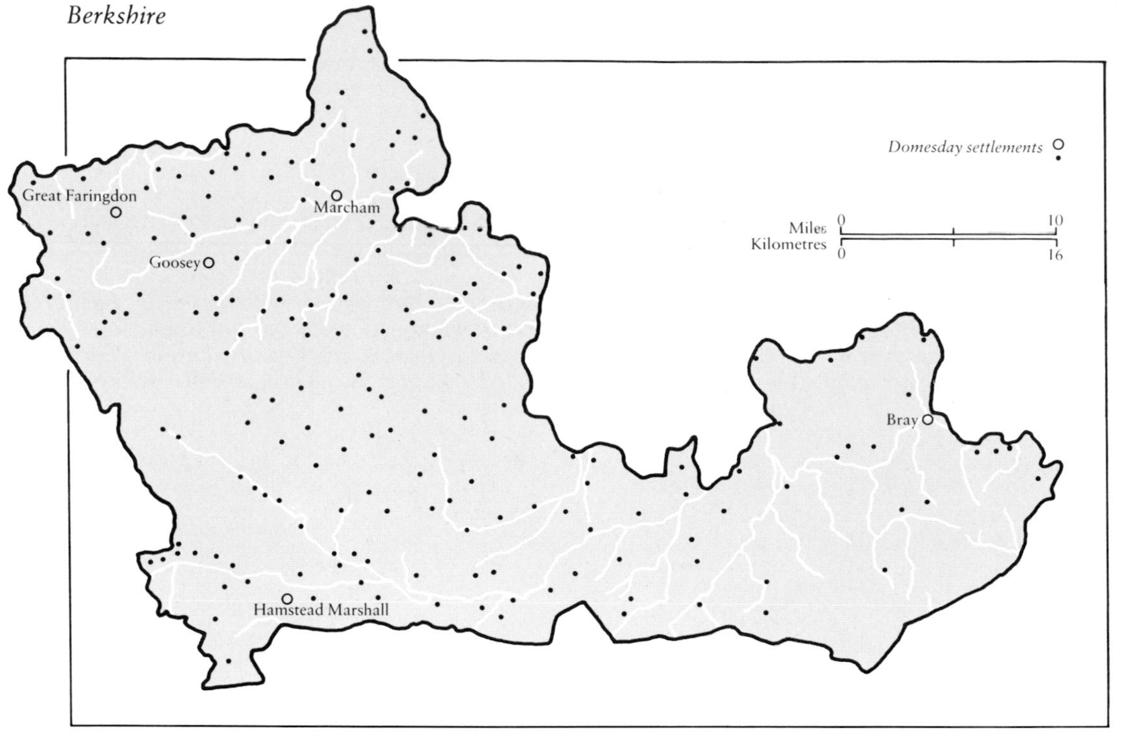

Goosey

The Abbey [Abingdon] holds GOOSEY *GOSEI* itself, and always held it. Before 1066 it answered for 17 hides, now for 11 hides. Land for 9 ploughs. In lordship 2 ploughs; 6 villagers and 3 smallholders with 2 ploughs; 1 riding man with his plough. Meadow 100 acres; from pastures, 16d. Hermer holds 7 hides of this land of this manor. It is for the monks' household supplies. He has 1 plough; 7 villagers with 1/2 plough. Meadow, 35 acres. Value of the whole before 1066 £9; later £10; now the same.

The hamlet of Goosey (pronounced by locals Goozy) in the Vale of the White Horse remains one of the county's most remote and peaceful, its houses scattered around a green so vast that those at the far side seem to dip beyond the earth's curve. In 1086 the manor of Goosey had already been held by Abingdon Abbey for three centuries; the abbey had been given it by King Offa of Mercia in exchange for the Island of Andersey in the Thames.

The monks valued Goosey for its dairy produce, in particular its cheeses; in the twelfth century its two dairies were supplying them with 28 *pondera* of cheese a year, each weighing 252 lb. Hermer, who in 1086 held seven of Goosey's 11 hides, was one of those Norman knights who frequently went abroad for military service. While crossing the channel he had been captured by pirates, who cut off his hands. Because he was now useless, the abbot had refused to give him any land; he relented only when Hermer appealed to the king.

Throughout the Middle Ages Goosey supported itself not only by dairy farming but by cultivating its three or four fields. These were split into strips each a furlong long and nine yards wide, and divided among the villagers. Centuries of such cultivation left deep pathways between the strips, and the undulations these produced are still clearly visible towards Charney Basset. Goosey's oldest architectural remains are at Abbey Farm, which incorporates parts of the cell of the monks of Abingdon.

Dairy farming is still Goosey's main business, and a huge herd of Friesians grazes its green. Only 50 years ago, when the present owner's family bought Church Farm, he remembers vast 'cheese trees' in its cheese room. Without doubt these were direct descendants of those used to dry the monks' cheeses at the time of *Domesday*.

Great Faringdon

[The King holds] (GREAT) FARINGDON *FERENDONE*. Harold held it. Then it answered for 30 hides; now it does not pay tax. Land for 15 ploughs. In lordship 3 ploughs; 17 villagers and 10 smallholders with 10 ploughs; 10 slaves; a mill with a fishery at 35s; 9 sites in this village at 40s; meadow, 130 acres; woodland for fencing. Of this manor, Bishop Osmund has 1 hide, with the church. Alfsi has 4 hides; in lordship 2 ploughs; 2 smallholders and 6 slaves. Value of the whole before 1066 £16; later £12; now £21 6s 8d; what the church or the priest (has) 40s; what Alfsi (has) 30s.

Domesday's entry for what is now the small market town of Great Faringdon seems at first a dry record, but on careful reading it becomes one of Berkshire's most interesting.

It reveals that before 1066 Faringdon had been King Harold's and that here as elsewhere William had taken possession of his defeated rival's manor as a natural consequence of his victory. It also shows that William sometimes used Englishmen to manage his new lands. Alfsi, an Englishman, now held four hides from William at Faringdon. As one of the king's thanes he also held Littleworth and Barcote (where he is called Alfsi of Faringdon). Both properties had been King Harold's, and at Littleworth Alfsi had previously held from him, so he obviously had no difficulty in switching loyalty.

In Oxfordshire Alfsi farmed Shipton-under-Wychwood for William. He also held land at Windrush in Gloucestershire, and farmed the next-door manor of Great Barrington for him as well. There is little doubt that he had become one of William's reeves.

Faringdon's fishery helps to confirm that fishing was an important Berkshire industry. Most of the county's 70 fisheries were on the Thames, where eels (caught in traps at weirs) were the usual fish. Fisheries were often valued by the number of eels a year they rendered (3000 at Wargrave). Abingdon Abbey received from its Berkshire manors large quantities, which were picturesquely numbered by 'sticks' of 25. Where Berkshire's fisheries are measured in money, it is easier to assess their status. Appleton, the most valuable, was worth 34s 2d out of a total of 60s for the entire manor. Even at Faringdon, where the fishery was valued with the mill, 35s out of £21 6s 8d suggests a useful contribution.

Faringdon's 135 acres of meadow show that it was also a dairy-farming manor. They were part of the fertile Thames-side acreage which made Berkshire so important at a time when cheese, bread, pulses and pork were the four basic foods. For Henry II's invasion of Ireland (1171–72), some 85 years after *Domesday*, 30 cart-loads of wheat and cheese were sent from Newbury and Abingdon to Bristol.

Another part of Faringdon's entry confirms what *Domesday* often left unsaid – that manors throughout England depended for their farming on a regular supply of fencing wood. This they would have cut at intervals of about 12 years from coppices of native trees – oak, ash, beech, thorn, etc.

Finally there are Faringdon's nine 'sites' (*hagae*). These were the shops of traders who had set up at this strategic gap in the hills where five roads met: from Oxford, Newbury, Chippenham, Cirencester and Burford. It was Faringdon's position here which led to its twice playing a part in the nation's history, both times in civil wars.

During the first, the supporters of Matilda, Stephen's rival for the throne, constructed a castle on a low hill, now called Folly Hill, to the east of the town, overlooking the Oxford and Newbury roads. In 1145 Stephen's troops took only four days to drive them out. Nothing remains of the castle, which would have been built of earth and timber.

It was last heard of in 1203, when King John gave it to the Cistercians of St Mary of Cîteaux for the founding of an abbey. Though they retained the manor till Henry VIII's dissolution of the monasteries, they seem not to have liked it here, for they moved the next year to Beaulieu, where they founded their influential New Forest abbey. No Cistercian buildings survive at Faringdon, but their large stone barn in the next-door village of Great Coxwell is one of the country's most remarkable.

There is more obvious evidence of Faringdon's second involvement with national affairs in its church of All Saints. This was hit by cannon fire during the Civil War, and though the south transept was rebuilt in the nineteenth century, the tower still looks oddly stunted. The Pye family, then the lords of the manor, were supporters of Parliament, but their residence, Faringdon House, was occupied by the Royalists. In 1644 Cromwell recaptured the town, but although he bombarded the house it held out. The following year, when 300 Royalists reoccupied the town, Robert Pye, eldest son and heir, was sent with his Parliamentary troop to attack his own family home. The Royalists fiercely defended Faringdon House and ultimately surrendered only when they also gave up Oxford.

The Pye family contributed in another way to history – by supplying George III with a poet laureate, Henry Pye, who was, unfortunately, a mediocre versifier. A writer who left a more visible mark was the 14th Baron Berners, who bought Faringdon House in 1919. Novelist, composer, painter and eccentric, he built the tower on Folly Hill which gives it its name. His workmen, when digging the foundations, found a man-made ditch filled with skeletons, doubtless those of Queen Matilda's defeated garrison.

Marcham

The Abbey [Abingdon] holds MARCHAM *MERCHA* itself. It always held it. Before 1066 it answered for 20 hides; now for 10 hides. Land for 10 ploughs. In lordship 3 ploughs; 18 villagers and 10 smallholders with 10 ploughs. A church; 6 slaves; a mill at 15s; meadow, 100 acres. Askell holds 1 hide of this land; Alwin held it from the Abbot; in lordship 1 plough. Value of the whole before 1066 £12 10s; now as much.

In the 1920s the low-lying village of Marcham was described as a 'very woebegone place', even though it had many good stone buildings, the sixteenth-century priory among them. Now Abingdon 2½ miles to the east and Harwell to the south-east have turned Marcham into something of a dormitory suburb.

In 1086 it was one of the manors of Abingdon Abbey, which had held it since at least 956 and continued to do so till the Dissolution. The abbey's chronicles tell how small parcels of Marcham land were allocated to its servants: four acres each to the cordwainer and the master cobbler. Marcham paid the abbey cook for carrying fish to the kitchen there.

Notable eccentrics have lived at Marcham. David Jones, an early eighteenth-century vicar, was notorious for 'the impetuousness of his voice, the fantasticalness of his actions, and the ridiculous meanness of his images and expressions'. He was sent to prison in about 1700 for contempt of court, when he brought an action against a man for mowing hay on Sunday, and again in 1709 when he got into 'more serious trouble'. At this time his 'coalblack hair was turned milkwhite of a night'.

Later in the same century the manor came into the hands of a notorious family of misers called Elwes. Amy Elwes inherited £100,000 but starved herself to death. Her brother, Sir Hervey Elwes, worth £250,000, lived on £100 a year and wore clothes which had belonged to his great-great-grandfather. Around Amy's son, Sir John, even weirder stories accumulated. When he badly cut both legs he left one untreated, but permitted the apothecary to treat the other, betting him his fee that the untreated leg would heal first. Sir John won by a fortnight. He died in bed in 1789, wearing worn-out shoes and a filthy old hat, grasping his walking stick – owning property worth £800,000.

The church which *Domesday* records had already been much altered by the time David Jones preached there, and today almost everything except the tower dates from an 1837 rebuilding. The charming white mill, on the other hand, which stands a mile from the village centre, where the River Ock forms the southern parish boundary, is in part ancient and occupies the site of the *Domesday* mill.

Bray

[The King holds] BRAY *BRAI*. King Edward held it. 18 hides; they did not pay tax. Land for... In lordship 3 ploughs; 56 villagers and 7 smallholders with 25 ploughs. 4 slaves; a church; 3 men-at-arms; meadow, 50 acres; woodland at 60 pigs. Reinbald holds 1 hide which belongs to the church; he has 1 plough there. Value of the whole before 1066 £25; later £18; now £17.

Today the Thames-side village of Bray is overshadowed by its northerly neighbour, Maidenhead. In 1086, however, Maidenhead, one of the manors of the minor Norman baron Giles of Ansculf, was assessed at a mere three hides, while Bray was a royal manor, assessed at 18. About 70 families farmed its 50 acres of meadow and had to pay 60 pigs a year from those they fattened in its woodlands.

Contemporary Bray, in spite of Maidenhead to the north and a complex of railways and motorways to the south, remains emphatically a village with a green, a pokey post office and timber-framed, white-painted cottages. It has two distinguished architectural features: the elegant seventeenth-century Jesus Hospital, and the sixteenth-century cottage built above the churchyard's lych-gate.

The priests who have served Bray's church have been its most curious characters. Reinbald, the earliest, appears in *Domesday* as the holder of a hide of church land. Like his notorious successors, he seems to have been an adroit politician, for he had been Edward the Confessor's chancellor. He still held 16 other livings, was a tenant-in-chief in five counties, and in Berkshire had not only kept his pre-Conquest manor of East Hagbourne but been granted another at Aston (now Aston Upthorpe).

In the mid-sixteenth century Simon Aleyn became Vicar of Bray. Thomas Fuller wrote of him in *Worthies of England* (1662): 'The vivacious Vicar living under King *Henry* the Eighth, King *Edward* the Sixth, Queen *Mary*, and Queen *Elizabeth*, was first a Papist, then a Protestant, then a Papist, then a Protestant again. He had seen some Martyrs burnt (two miles off) at Windsor, and found the fire too hot for his tender temper. This Vicar being taxed by one for being a *Turn-coat* and an unconstant Changeling, "Not so," said he; "for I alwaies kept my principle, which is this, to live and die the Vicar of Bray."' He succeeded in his ambition, and lies buried in the churchyard.

The well-known song, however, 'That whatsoever King shall reign, I'll be the Vicar of Bray, Sir!' was written in about 1720, and describes Dr Francis Carswell, who became vicar in 1667

BRAY: *Lychgate House, a 16th-c. cottage built above the lych-gate of the churchyard. Reinbald, the* Domesday *priest, was a predecessor of the celebrated vicar of Bray.*

and held the living during the reigns of Charles II, James II, William III, Anne and George I. The diarist, Thomas Hearne (1678–1735), called him 'an old rich stingy turncoat' and 'a curmudgeon of unsettled head'.

The ancient vicarages of Aleyn and Carswell have long since gone, but Bray's peaceful banks could well have formed part of the priest Reinbald's *Domesday* holding.

Hamstead Marshall

Hugolin the Steersman holds HAMSTEAD (MARSHALL) *HAMESTEDE* from the King. Edward held it as a manor from King Edward in freehold. Then it answered for 4 hides; now 1 hide. Land for 5 ploughs. In lordship 2; 4 villagers and 8 smallholders with 3 ploughs. 10 slaves; a mill at 20s; meadow, 6 acres; woodland at 10 pigs. The value is and was £4.

The widely scattered village of Hamstead Marshall lies in the south-west corner of Berkshire, in the picturesque valley of the Kennet. In 1086 it was held by Hugolin the Steersman, who also held the nearby manor of Irish Hill, now in Hamstead parish. But here all was not straightforward, and we get an insight into the sort of disputes which must often lie hidden below *Domesday's* bland surface. The men of the shire had testified to the *Domesday* Commissioners that Hugolin had no right to Irish Hill and even his own men had failed to support his claim. No doubt because he felt his holding to be insecure, Hugolin had removed not only its stock and buildings but even its hall.

'Marshall' was added to the village's name in the thirteenth century when it became the chief residence of William the Marshall, Earl of Pembroke, loyal supporter of Henry II, Richard and John, then regent for the young Henry III. Later it passed through many hands, including those of Jane Seymour and Catherine Parr, Henry VIII's third and sixth wives before it was bought by the Craven family in 1620.

William, later the Earl of Craven, built Hamstead's most splendid house after the Restoration, surrounding it with the sort of French-inspired geometric garden of clipped avenues and parterres which was then in fashion. Though an engraving of 1700 makes the house itself seem solidly English, it was said to have been an imitation of Heidelberg Castle, in honour of Elizabeth, Queen of Bohemia, to whom the earl was romantically attached; he died a bachelor at the age of 91.

The earl was an enthusiastic fire fighter. In London he regularly attended fires and gave advice. He was helped by a sensitive horse who could detect a fire and gallop him there before he had even heard of it. Ironically, in 1718, 21 years after his death, his own splendid house was entirely destroyed by fire.

All that can be seen today are the brick walls of its huge orchard/garden and six sets of gatepiers. There are however earlier remains at Hamstead, including some large overgrown mounds which once supported the Earl Marshall's defence works. And though the watermill on the Kennet is early nineteenth century, it probably stands on the site of the mill which once ground the corn of Hugolin the Steersman.

BRAY: *Still a village, despite encroaching traffic and its proximity to Maidenhead.*

Berkshire Gazetteer
Each entry starts with the modern place-name in **bold** type. The *Domesday* information that follows is in *italic* type, beginning with the name or names by which the place was known in 1086. The main landholders and undertenants are next, separated with semi-colons if a place was divided into more than one holding. A number of holdings were granted by the king to his thanes or reeves; these are given with their office or described, at the end of a list of landholders, as holding land 'from the king'. More general information completes the *Domesday* part of the entry, including examples of dues (eels, weys of cheese, etc.) rendered by tenants. The modern or post-Domesday section is in normal type. represents a village, a small village or hamlet.

Aldermaston *Ældermanestone/ Eldre-Heldremanestune: King's land. Mill, 2 fisheries, church.* Church with 3 Norman doorways; atomic research centre nearby.

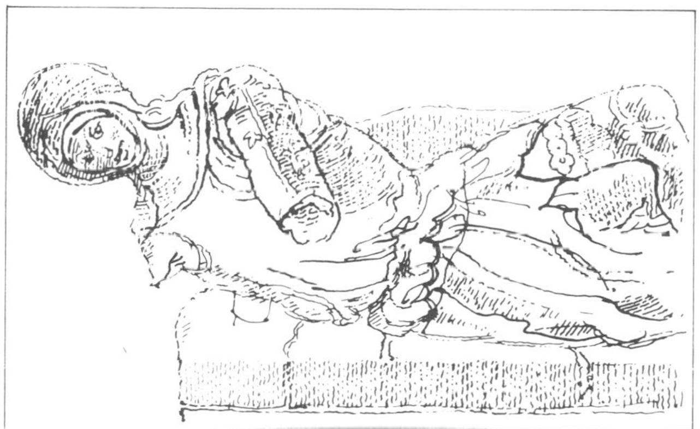

ALDWORTH: *One of 9 14th-c. effigies of the Norman de la Beche family.*

Aldworth *Elleorde: Theodoric the Goldsmith.* Once the seat of the Flemish de la Beche family, who came over with William I; the church contains their effigies.

Appleford *Apleford: Abingdon Abbey before and after 1066, and Robert from the Abbey. 2 mills, fishery.* Jockey John Faulkner, who rode his first winner at 8 and his last at 74, is buried here.

Appleton *Apletone/tune: Richard from Miles Crispin; Berner, the king's thane, from Bishop of Bayeaux. Fishery.* 12th-century manor house.

Ardington *Ardintone: Robert d'Oilly. 3 mills.* Lord Wantage, the first VC holder, is buried here.

Ashbury *Eissesberie: Glastonbury Abbey before and after 1066, and Robert d'Oilly, Alwin and Edward from the Abbey. 2 mills, church.* Church with Norman doorway. Wayland's Smithy, an Iron Age barrow, is nearby.

Aston Tirrold *Estone: King's land; Abbey of Preaux from Count of Mortain. Church.* Church with a Saxon doorway and a Norman font and windows. King Alfred is said to have won a battle against the Danes here.

Aston Upthorpe *Estone: Reinbald the Priest, formerly Aelfeva, a free woman.*

Avington *Avintone: Richard Poynant. Mill.* The church is a fine example of Norman architecture.

Bagnor *Bagenore: Humphrey the Chamberlain. Mill.* Stone Age axe-heads were found here.

Barcote *Lierecote: Alfsi of Faringdon from the king.* Barcote Manor House; Barcote Hill; Barcote Barn.

Barkham *Bercheham: King's land.* Memorial Cross to Edward Ball, an ancestor of George Washington; Barkham Manor; Barkham Square; Barkham Common.

Barton *Bertune:* Lost.

Basildon *Bastedene: King's land, formerly Aelfeva, a free woman, with 2 priests holding 2 churches before and after 1066. Mill.* Near the site of a Roman villa.

Bayworth *Baiorde: Askell and Gilbert from Abingdon Abbey.*

Beckett *Becote: Count of Evreux.* Beckett House. In the 14th century, the Beckett family paid 2 white capons to the king 'whenever he should pass'.

Beedon *Bedene: Walter de la Riviere from Abingdon Abbey.* Beedon House; Beedon Hill.

Benham *Ben(e)/Benneham: Walter de la Riviere from Abingdon Abbey, formerly Queen Edith; Humphrey Visdeloup; Wigar, the king's thane.* Benham Park.

Bessels Leigh *Leie: William from Abingdon Abbey before and after 1066.* William Lenthall, Speaker of the House of Commons during Charles I's reign, lived here.

Betterton *Bedretone: King's land; William from Miles Crispin. Mill.* Betterton House; Betterton Farm.

Bisham *Bistesham: Henry de Ferrers. Church, vines.* Church with Norman Tower. The abbey was originally a 14th-century priory.

Blewbury *Blid/Blitberie: King's land with William Beaufour holding the church; Count of Evreux. Mill.* A Saxon wattle-and-daub alleyway leads to the mill. An Iron Age hill-fort is on Blewburton Hill.

Bockhampton *Bochentone: Ralph the earl's son; Odo and Edward, the king's thanes. Mill.* Bockhampton Farm.

Boxford *Bochesorne/Bovsore: Berner from Abingdon Abbey; Humphrey Visdeloup and Aelfric and Aelmer from him. Mill, church.* On the River Lambourn; mill. Roman coins were found nearby.

Bradfield *Bradefelt: William FitzAnsculf. 3 mills.* Bradfield School.

Bray *Brai(o)/Bras:* See page 33.

Brightwalton *Bristoldestone: Battle Abbey, formerly Earl Harold. Church.* Skeletons of Roundheads and Royalists were found in the inn's garden.

Brightwell *Bricsteuuelle/ Bristowelle: Bishop of Winchester, formerly Bishop Stigand. Mill.* Brightwell Barrow nearby. Brightwell Manor is on the site of a castle built by King Stephen but destroyed in 1153.

Brimpton *Brintone: Robert FitzGerald; Ralph de Mortimer. 2 churches, 3 mills, dairy (10 weys of cheese).* The chapel, once owned by the Knights Templar, has a Norman doorway and tympanum.

Buckland *Bocheland(e): Bishop of Exeter; Abingdon Abbey; Count of Evreux. ½ fishery.* Buckland House, now a college.

Bucklebury *Boche/Borge/ Borche(l)deberie: King's land; Count of Evreux; Walter FitzOthere; Hugolin the Steersman. Mill, church.* Church with Norman carvings.

Burghfield *Borgefel(le): Henry de Ferrers; man-at-arms from Ralph de Mortimer. Mill, church, fishery.* Part-Norman church. The de Burghfield family held this land from Domesday until Roger de Burghfield's death in 1327.

Buscot *Boroardescote: Robert, Drogo and Randulf from Earl Hugh, formerly Earl Harold. Fishery.* On the River Thames; Buscot House. Church with a Norman chancel arch and a Burne-Jones window.

Calcot *Colecote: Lost.*

Carswell *Chersvelle: Lost.*

Catmore *Catmere: Henry from Henry de Ferrers.* Norman chapel.

Caversham *Caueres/Cavesham: Walter Giffard.* District of Reading (across the River Thames) linked by Caversham Bridge. A duel was fought here between Robert de Montfort and Henry of Essex before Henry II in the 12th century.

Chaddleworth *Cedeledorde/ neord: Winchester Abbey; Robert d'Oilly.* A farmhouse stands on the site of Poughley Priory, whose lands Cardinal Wolsey gave to the Abbot of Westminster in exchange for what is now St James's Park, London.

Charlton *Cerletone: King's land; Robert from Henry de Ferrers; Geoffrey from William FitzCorbucion; Drogo from Ralph de Tosny; Malmesbury Abbey. 2 mills.* Suburb of Wantage.

Charney Bassett *Cernei: Abingdon Abbey and Warin from the Abbey.* Attractive; Cherbury Camp, allegedly a stronghold of King Canute.

Chieveley *Civelei: Abingdon Abbey and William and Godfrey from the Abbey.* Cromwell's soldiers were quartered here on the eve of second battle of Newbury, 1644.

Childrey *Celrea: William FitzRichard and Godfrey from William; Roger de Lacy; Roger from Thurstan FitzRolf. Mill, church.* Near the site of a Roman villa; church with a Norman lead font.

Chilton *Cil(le)tone: Wynric from Abingdon Abbey; Walter FitzOthere.* Near atomic research centre.

Cholsey *Celsea/sei: King's land and Richard Poynant, Gilbert and Hervey from the king, with Abbey of Mont St Michel holding the church. 3 mills.* Partly Norman church. Ethelred II (the Unready) built an abbey here which was ravaged by the Vikings.

Clapcot *Clopecote:* Lost.

Clewer *Clivore: Ralph FitzSiegfried, formerly Earl Harold. Windsor Castle, mill.* It no longer includes the castle.

Coleshill *Coleselle/shalle: Abbess of Winchester (Walter de Lacy gave it to the Church so that his daughter might become a nun); William FitzRichard; Thurstan FitzRolf; Roger de Lacy; William Leofric. Mill.* 17th-century Coleshill House.

Compton *Contone: King's land with Henry de Ferrers holding the woodland; Bishop of Coutances.* Perborough Castle, an ancient British stronghold.

Compton Beauchamp *Contone: William FitzAnsculf. Church.* Once called Compton Regis, because it belonged to Edward the Confessor.

COOKHAM: *The tarry stone, a huge boulder that was used as a boundary mark.*

Cookham *Cocheham: King's land. 2 mills, 2 fisheries, market.* On the River Thames. The Saxon Witenagemot met here. The partly Norman church and the Stanley Spencer Gallery both contain work by the painter, who was born here in 1891.

BOXFORD

Crookham *Crocheham: Alfwy Chafersbeard, the king's thane, the pre-Conquest holder.* Crookham House.

Cumnor *Comenor: Abingdon Abbey before and after 1066, and Osbern and Reginald from the Abbey.* Cumnor Place.

Curridge *Coserige: St Pierre-sur-Dives Abbey; Edward, the king's thane.*

Dedworth *Dideorde: Albert from the king.* On the River Thames.

Denchworth *Dencheswordе: Jocelyn from William d'Eu; Rayner from Henry de Ferrers; Robert of Stafford and Lawrence from him, formerly Leofeva a free woman. Church.* The only copy of the *Golden Legend* printed by Caxton, in Oxford's Bodleian Library, is from the partly Norman church.

Denford *Daneford: William d'Eu. Church.* Denford Park. Iron Age axe-heads were found here.

Donnington *Deritone: William Lovett.* The ruins of 14th-century Donnington Castle, successfully defended by Royalist Sir John Boys during the Civil War, are nearby.

Draycott (Moor) *Draicote: Abingdon Abbey before and after 1066, and Gilbert from the Abbey. Fishery;* moor.

Drayton *Draitone/tune: William from Earl Hugh; Hascoit Musard.* Drayton Mill.

Dry Sanford *Sanford: Hugo Cook from Abingdon Abbey.*

Duxford *Dudochesforde: Odo of Winchester, the king's thane. Mill, fishery.* Duxford Farm; ford over the River Thames.

Earley *Er/Hur/Herlei: King's land; Osbern Giffard. 2 fisheries.* Suburb of Reading.

East Garston *Lamborne: Geoffrey de Mandeville. 2 mills.* Attractive; on the River Lambourn.

East Ginge *Acenge: Cola, the king's thane. Mill.* Near East Ginge Down, site of Scutchamer Knob, a barrow of unknown date where the Shire Moot met.

East Hagbourne *Hachebourne: Reinbald the Priest. Mill.* Attractive.

Easthampstead *Lachenestede: Westminster Abbey before and after 1066.* Caesar's Camp, an Iron Age fort. Sir William Trumbull, a 17th-century Secretary of State, was granted the land on condition he maintained a deer park for the royal chase.

East Hanney *Hanlei: Abingdon Abbey before and after 1066, and Nicolas and Wulfwin from the Abbey; Count of Evreux; Jocelyn from Gilbert de Bretteville. 2 mills.* Near Roman road.

East Hendred *Enrede/Henret: King's land; Cola the king's thane; Count of Evreux; Henry from Henry de Ferrers. Mill, church.* Former cloth centre; Hendred House, owned by the Eyston family for 500 years.

HARWELL: *15th-c. cruck cottage.*

East Ilsley *Eldeslei: Bishop of Salisbury; Roger from Henry de Ferrers; Stephen from William FitzAnsculf; Saswalo from Geoffrey de Mandeville.* On East Ilsley Down. A sheep market, originating in the 13th century, was held here until recently.

East Lockinge *Lachinge(s): Abingdon Abbey before and after 1066 and Gilbert from the Abbey. Mill, church.* Surrounded by stud farms; partly Norman church.

East Shefford *Siford: Aiulf, the Sheriff of Dorset. 2 mills.* On the site of a Saxon cemetery; mill; East Shefford House.

Eaton *Ed/Eltune: Richard and Alfred from Miles Crispin. 2 fisheries.* Eaton Heath.

Eaton Hastings *Etone: Walter FitzPoyntz. 2 fisheries.*

Eddington *Eddevetone: King's land. Mill.* Mill; trout farm.

Eling *Elinge: Roger d'Ivry.* Near the site of a Roman villa. Iron Age axe-heads were found here.

Enborne *Taneburne/Aneborne: William Lovett; William FitzCorbucion; Giles, brother of Ansculf; Roger de Lacy. Mill.* Near the site of the first battle of Newbury, in 1643.

Englefield *Englefel/Inglefelle: William FitzAnsculf and Gilbert and Stephen from him.* King Aethelwulf beat the Danes here prior to King Aethelred's victory at the Battle of Ashdown, 870.

Farnborough *Fermeberge: Abingdon Abbey.* On the downs.

Fawler *Spersold: Askell from Abingdon Abbey. Mill.*

Fawley *Farelli: Abbess of Amesbury.* Below Woolley Down.

Finchampstead *Finchamestede: King's land, formerly Earl Harold. Mill.* Near the course of a Roman road. The church font is probably pre-Conquest.

Frilford *Frieliford: Abingdon Abbey before and after 1066, and Reginald, Reinbald and Salvi from the Abbey.* Frilford Heath.

Frilsham *Frilesham: Roger from Henry de Ferrers. Mill.* The church is dedicated to St Frideswide, a Saxon princess who founded a convent in the forest; Frilsham House.

Fulscot *Follescote: Roger FitzSiegfried.* Fulscot Farm.

Fyfield *Fivehide: Henry from Henry de Ferrers, and another Henry from him. Church.* 14th-century manor house; partly Norman church.

Garford *Wareford: Abingdon Abbey before and after 1066, and Berner from the Abbey. Mill.* Near Garford Field, a prehistoric burial site; on the River Ock.

Goosey *Gosei:* See page 32.

Great Coxwell *Cocheswelle: King's land. Church.* Great Barn, shaped like a cross and built by the monks of Beaulieu in the 13th century has been restored, and is in use.

Great Faringdon *Ferendone:* See page 32.

Great Shefford *Siford: Robert d'Oilly and Roger d'Ivry from Bishop of Bayeaux; Hugh de Port; 1½ mills.*

Greenham *Greneham: Henry de Ferrers. Church, 1½ mills.* Once a centre of the milling industry. Mesolithic man-made tools were found nearby. Greenham Common, now an RAF airbase, is a famous centre of anti-nuclear protest.

Hampstead Norris *Hanstede: Theodoric the Goldsmith. Church.* Partly Norman church. Iron Age coins were found here.

Hamstead Marshall *Hamesteda/stede:* See page 34.

Hartley *Hurlei: Ralph de Mortimer.* Hartley Court.

Hartridge *Hurterige: Alfred from William FitzAnsculf.* Hartridge Farm.

Harwell *Hare-/Harowelle/Haruuelle: Bishop of Winchester; Roger d'Ivry. Mill, chapel.* Near atomic research centre.

Hatford *Heraford: Payne from Gilbert de Bretteville. Church.* 2 churches, one a partly Norman ruin.

Hinton Waldrist *Hentone: Odo, the king's thane, formerly Wulfwen, a woman. Church, 2 fisheries.* Elizabethan Hinton Manor, with moat; near a Roman earthwork, known as Hadchester or Adchester.

Hodcott *Hodicote: Stephen from William FitzAnsculf; Odelard from Ralph de Mortimer.* Hodcott Farm; Hodcott Down, site of a Bronze Age burial ground.

Hurley *Herlei: Geoffrey de Mandeville. Mill, church, 2 fisheries.* Editha, Edward the Confessor's sister, is allegedly buried in the Saxon/Norman church.

Inglewood *Ingl-/Ingheflot/Inglefol: Robert FitzGerald; Fulchard from William, the king's thane; Robert FitzRolf, the king's thane.* Inglewood House; Inglewood Farm.

Inkpen *Hinge/Ingepene: William FitzAnsculf; Ralph de Feugères, the king's thane. Mill.* Below Inkpen Beacon, with Combe Gibbet, last used in the 19th century for a public execution; Iron Age fort on Walbury Hill.

Irish Hill *Ebrige: Hugolin the Steersman. Mill.* Only a hill. 'Ebrige' means yew-covered ridge.

Kennington *Chenitun/Genetune: Berner and Alwin from Abingdon Abbey.* A 7th-century monastery was founded nearby by a nephew of the King of Wessex.

Kingston Bagpuize *Chingestune: Ralph de Bagpuize and Henry de Ferrers from him; Aethelhelm from William FitzAnsculf. Fishery.* Kingston Bagpuize House, possibly designed by Christopher Wren.

Kingston Lisle *Spersolt: King's land and Henry de Ferrers from the king. Dairy (6 weys of cheese).* Nearby is a sarsen stone, known as the Blowing Stone, allegedly used by King Alfred as a trumpet to assemble his soldiers.

Kintbury *Cheneteberie: King's land and Henry de Ferrers from the king; Abbess of Amesbury; Walter FitzOthere. 2 mills.* Old mill house; on the site of a Saxon burial ground.

Knighton *Nisteton: Odo, the king's thane.* Near the site of a Roman villa; Iron Age pottery found on Knighton Hill.

Lambourn *Lam/Lanborne: King's land; Hascoit Musard; Matthew de Mortagne. Church, 2 mills.* On Lambourn Downs. King Alfred allegedly had a palace at Lambourn Place.

Leckhampstead *Lecanestede: Abingdon Abbey, and Reinbald from the Abbey. Church.* A 17th-century red-brick building at Chapel Farm was once a church, possibly of Saxon origin.

Letcombe Bassett *Lede(n)cumbe: Robert d'Oilly. 2 mills.* Segsbury Camp, on Castle Hill, is an Iron Age fort.

Letcombe Regis *Lede(n)cumbe: King's land with Amesbury Abbey holding the church. 5 mills.* Partly 12th-century church. King John allegedly had a hunting lodge at Moat House.

Leverton *Lewartone: Hezelin from Abingdon Abbey. Mill.*

Little Coxwell *Alia Cocheswelle: King's land.* Tiny, partly Norman church.

Little Wittenham *Witeham: Abingdon Abbey before and after 1066. Church, mill.* Near Wittenham Clumps, one of which is ringed by a massive prehistoric moat; Saxon burial ground.

Littleworth *Ordia: King's land and Alfsi, the pre-Conquest holder, and Alfgeat from the king, formerly Harold.*

Lollingdon *Lolindone: Richard Poynant.* Lollingdon Farm; Lollingdon Hill.

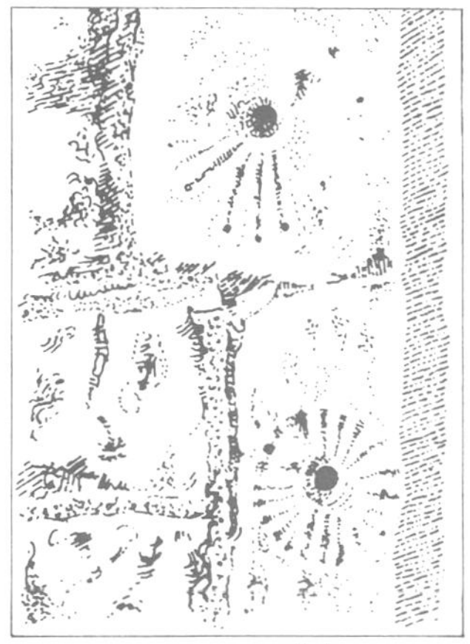

LONG WITTENHAM: *dials cut into the church window frame.*

Long Wittenham *Witeham: Walter Giffard, formerly Queen Edith.* Church on the site of an ancient barrow. Saxon skeletons and weapons were found here.

Longworth *Ordam: Abingdon Abbey before and after 1066. Church, fishery.* Partly Norman church. R. D. Blackmore, author of *Lorna Doone* (1869), was a rector here.

Losfield *Losfelle:* Lost.

Lyford *Linford: Walter Giffard and Reginald from Abingdon Abbey, before and after 1066.* Lyford Grange, a moated Elizabethan house, where the Jesuit Edmund Campion was captured in 1581.

Maidenhead *Elentone: Giles, brother of Ansculf, and Hugh and Landri from him.* Town on the River Thames. In 1647 the captive Charles I was permitted to see his children here. Maidenhead Thicket is the site of an ancient earthwork.

Marcham *Merceham:* See page 33.

Midgham *Migeham: Giles, brother of Ansculf, and Aelmer, Rayner and Gilbert from him. Mill.* Birthplace of the poet William Crowe (1745–1829).

Milton *Midde(l)tune: Abingdon Abbey before and after 1066, and Azelin and Reginald from the Abbey. 2 mills.* Partly 18th-century Milton Manor; Milton Mill on Milton Brook. Roman jewellery was found here.

Newbury *Ulvritone: Arnulf de Hesdin. 2 mills.* Town, first Roman, then Saxon, then Norman. 2 Civil War battles were fought over the Norman castle. Famous racecourse.

Newton *Niwetone: Payne from Gilbert de Bretteville.* Newton House.

North Moreton *Mortune: Ralph from William FitzCorbucion. Church, mill.*

Odstone *Ordegeston: William FitzRichard.* Odstone Farm; Odstone Barn. Odstone Down was a Romano-British settlement.

Padworth *Peteorde: Jocelyn from William d'Eu; Stephen FitzErhard from the king. 3 mills.* Padworth House.

PANGBOURNE: *Village sign.*

Pangbourne *Pande/Pangeborne: King's land; William from Miles Crispin. Mill.* On the River Thames; toll gate on bridge. Kenneth Grahame, author of *The Wind In The Willows* lived at Church Cottage.

Peasemore *Prax(e)mere: Count of Evreux; Richard from Gilbert de Bretteville; Odelard from Ralph de Mortimer.* Saxon settlement, with a church dedicated to St Peada. The manor house was once owned by Geoffrey Chaucer's son.

Purley *Porlai/lei: Roger FitzSiegfried; Theodoric the Goldsmith.* On the outskirts of Reading; Purley Park.

Pusey *Peise/Pesei: Gilbert from Abingdon Abbey; St Pierre-sur-Dives Abbey; Henry from Henry de Ferrers; Roger d'Ivry from Bishop of Bayeaux. Church.* Named after the Pewse family. William Pewse was allegedly given this land for saving King Canute from a Saxon ambush. Edward Bouverie Pusey, leader of the 19th-century High Anglican Oxford Movement, lived at Pusey House.

Reading *Radinges/Red(d)inges: King's land and Henry de Ferrers from the king; Battle Abbey holds the church. 6 mills, 5 ½ fisheries.* County town of Berkshire. Originally an Iron Age settlement, then Roman, then Saxon. St Mary's Church is partly 13th century. Oscar Wilde was imprisoned here 1895–97, inspiring his *Ballad of Reading Gaol.*

Remenham *Rameham: King's land; formerly Queen Edith. Mill (1000 eels).* Frederick, Prince of Wales and father of George III, lived at Park Place.

Seacourt *Seuacoorde: Askell from Abingdon Abbey.* Only Seacourt Stream.

Shaw *Essages: Hugh FitzBaldric. Mill.* Suburb of Newbury; Shaw House; Shaw Farm.

Sheffield *Sewelle: Count of Evreux. Mill.* Now Sheffield Bottom, by Kennet and Avon Canal.

Shellingford *Serengeford: Abingdon Abbey before and after 1066, and Gilbert and Wimund from the Abbey. Mill.*

Shinfield *Selingefelle: King's land. Mill (150 eels), 5 fisheries (550 eels).* Suburb of Reading; Shinfield Court; Shinfield Grange.

Shippon *Sipene: Reginald from Abingdon Abbey. Fishery.* Suburb of Abingdon.

Shottesbrook *Soteshroc: Alfward the Goldsmith, the king's thane, formerly his father from Queen Edith. Church.* Shottesbrook Park; Shottesbrook Farm.

Shrivenham *Seriveham: King's land. Church, 2 mills.*

Sonning *Soninges: Bishop of Salisbury; Roger the Priest holds a church. 2 mills, 5 fisheries.* 18th-century brick bridge over the River Thames; old mill; church with a Saxon coffin lid.

Sotwell *Sotwelle: Hugh de Port from Winchester Abbey. Mill.* Roman remains were found on Sotwell Hill.

Southcote *Sudcote: William de Braose. Mill, fishery.* Suburb of Reading.

South Denchworth Farm *Denchesworde: Rayner from Henry de Ferrers; Lawrence from Robert of Stafford. Church.* Farm in Denchworth.

South Fawley *Faleslei: King's land.* Fawley Manor.

South Moreton *Moretune: William Lovett; Humphrey Visdeloup. Church, mill.* On Mill Brook; moat; church with a Saxon doorway.

Sparsholt *Spersold/solt: King's land with Edred the Priest holding the church; Fulchard from Henry de Ferrers; Hascoit Musard; Roger from Thurstan FitzRolf. Church.* Sparsholt Field.

Speen *Spone: Humphrey Visdeloup. Church, mill.* Adjoining Newbury; Speen House.

Standen *Standene:* Lost.

Stanford Dingley *Stanworde: Gilbert from William FitzAnsculf. Mill.* Mill.

Stanford in the Vale *Stanford: Henry de Ferrers and Henry the Steward from him. 2 mills.* Once a market town. Stanford Park Farm, Stanford House Farm, and Mill Farm are all nearby.

Steventon *Stivetune: King's land, formerly Harold, with Robert d'Oilly holding 13 dwellings. Church, 3 mills.* On Mill Brook, near the remains of a Norman monastery.

Stratfield Mortimer *Stradfeld: Ralph de Mortimer. Church, mill.* Church with Saxon tomb of Aegelward, son of Kipping.

Streatley *Estralei: Geoffrey de Mandeville with Wibert the Priest holding the church. Mill, 2 fisheries.* On the prehistoric Ridgeway which ran from South Devon to the Wash; attractive Georgian houses; 19th-century gabled malt-house.

Sugworth *Sogoorde: Abingdon Abbey and Warin from the Abbey.* Sugworth Farm.

Sulham *Solcham. William de Cailly; William from Miles Crispin; Theodoric the Goldsmith. Church.* Sulham House.

Sunningwell *Soningeuuel: Abingdon Abbey and Warin from the Abbey.* Attractive.

Sutton Courtenay *Sud/Suttone/Sudtune: King's land and Henry de Ferrers from the king; Alwin the Priest from Abingdon Abbey.* Saxon huts were discovered here. Prime Minister Herbert Henry Asquith was buried here in 1928.

Swallowfield *Soanesfelt/Solafel: King's land; Aelfric from Stephen FitzErhard. Mill, 5 fisheries.* On the River Thames.

Thatcham *Taceham: King's land. Church, 2 mills.* One of Berkshire's oldest villages with traces of Mesolithic settlement. Markets have been held here since the reign of Henry I.

Tubney *Tobenie: Abingdon Abbey and Reinbald from the Abbey.* Wooded; Tubney Manor Farm.

Uffington *Offentone: Abingdon Abbey and Gilbert from the Abbey. 11 slaves, mill.* Below the White Horse, a huge Saxon hillside carving.

Ufton Nervet *Offetune: Giles, brother of Ansculf.* Ufton Court; Ufton Park.

Ufton Robert *Offetune: A man-at-arms from William FitzAnsculf.* Ufton Green; Ufton Bridge over the River Kennet.

Upton *Optone: Thurstan FitzRolf.* Partly Norman church; doorway possibly Saxon.

Wallingford *Walengeford/fort/Walingeford/Warengeford: King's land; Abingdon Church; Bishop of Salisbury; Bishop of Winchester; William FitzCorbucion; various king's thanes with Roger the Priest holding a church. Market.* Attractive town, strategically important since prehistoric times for its ford over the River Thames, crossed by the Conqueror on his way to take London.

Waltham St Lawrence *Waltham: King's land, formerly Queen Edith.* Now Waltham St Lawrence; site of a Roman temple nearby.

Wantage *Wanetinz: King's land with William the Deacon holding ⅓ of church. Mill.* Town; tiny Norman church. King Alfred was born here in 849.

Warfield *Warwelt: King's land, formerly Queen Edith.* Warfield Hall; Warfield House; Warfield Chase; Warfield Park.

Wargrave *Weregrave: King's land, formerly Queen Edith. Mill, 3 fisheries (3000 eels).* On the River Thames; Wargrave Manor.

Wasing *Walsince: Bernard the Falconer. Mill.* Flint axes and bones of prehistoric animals were found here.

Watchfield *Wachenesfeld: Abingdon Abbey, and Gilbert and Wimund from the Abbey.* Roman site nearby.

Welford *Waliford: Abingdon Abbey before and after 1066. 2 churches, 5 mills.* Partly Norman church. Roman coins were found here.

West Challow *Ceveslane: Abbess of Amesbury before and after 1066.* Near the site of a Roman villa. The church bell was made by Paul the Potter in 1282.

West Ginge *Gainz: Abingdon Abbey before and after 1066, and Reginald from the Abbey. Mill.* On Ginge Brook.

West Hagbourne *Hacheboume: Walter FitzOthere and Robert from Walter. Mill.* Hagbourne Hill, site of a Roman burial ground.

West Hanney *Hannei: Walter Giffard and Osbern and Theodoric from him. Mill.* Church with a Norman doorway.

West Hendred *Henret: St Alban's Abbey and Ernucion from the Abbey; Grimbald. Mill, church.* Mill.

West Ilsley *Hildeslei/Hisleleí/leu: Saswalo from Geoffrey de Mandeville.* Attractive; surrounded by racing stables.

West Lockinge *Lachinge(s): Hubert de Curzon from Henry de Ferrers.*

Weston *Westun: Abingdon Abbey and William from the Abbey. Church.*

Whatcombe *Watecumbe: Geoffrey de Mandeville.*

Whistley *Wiselei: Abingdon Abbey before and after 1066. Mill (250 eels), fishery (300 eels).* Now Whistley Green.

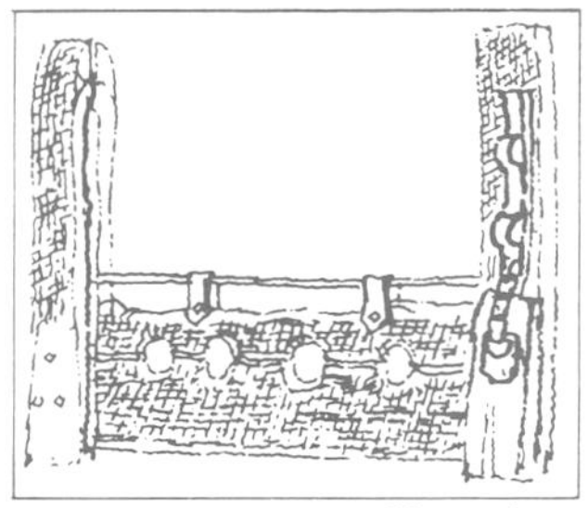

WHITE WALTHAM: *Double stocks made of oak.*

White Waltham *Waltham: Bishop of Durham, formerly Chertsey Abbey. Church.* Church with Norman carvings. Arthur Tudor, Henry VIII's son, lived at Waltham Place.

Whitley *Witelei: Theodoric the Goldsmith. Fishery.* Suburb of Reading.

Willington *Wibalditone: Nigel from Henry de Ferrers. Church.* Willington's Farm; Willington Down Farm.

Windsor *Windesores: King's land. Fishery, Windsor forest.* Town dominated by William I's impregnable moated castle, a royal residence since the 11th century; the Long Walk in Windsor Great Park was created by Charles II. A prehistoric site nearby was occupied by Romans then Saxons. Eton College is across the River Thames.

Winkfield *Wenesfelle: Abingdon Abbey before and after 1066.* Winkfield Manor.

Winterbourne *Wintreborne/burne: King's land, formerly Queen Edith, and Theodoric from the king; Ranulf Flambard from Bishop of Salisbury; Kenmarchuc and Norman from Hascoit Musard.* Winterbourne Manor.

Wokefield *Hocfelle/Offelle: King's land; a man-at-arms from Walter FitzOthere.* Wokefield Park, now a school.

Woolhampton *Ollavintone: Henry de Ferrers. Mill.* Woolhampton House; Old Mill House.

Woolley *Olvelei: William Peverel.* Woolley Home Farm; Woolley House; Woolley Down.

Woolstone *Olvricestone: Bishop of Winchester and Roger d'Ivry from him. 2 mills.* Near the site of a Roman villa.

Wyld *Wille: William from Gilbert de Bretteville.* Wyld Court Farm.

Wytham *Winteham: Abingdon Abbey and Hubert from the Abbey.* Near the ruins of Godstow nunnery, built in 1138. The Trout Inn, famous for the peacocks in its gardens, dates from the same year.

Yattendon *Etingedene: Godbald from William FitzAnsculf. Mill.* Once a market town; attractive cottages. Bronze Age implements (The Yattendon Hoard) were found here.

Buckinghamshire

The Buckinghamshire of Domesday *was probably a creation of tenth-century planners who wanted to provide territory for the newly created fortress town of Buckingham. They based it on the territory of the Danish borough, choosing an axis across central southern England that linked the Midland plain with the lower Thames valley. As a result, the county's long and irregular outline contained – and still contains – a broad cross-section of landscape, from clayey uplands and plain, through wooded Chiltern heights, to the water meadows of the far south.*

Not surprisingly it had been settled according to its terrain. The once well-wooded, but subsequently intensively farmed, north was heavily populated, with between five and ten persons a square mile (eleven in the Vale of Aylesbury). In the Chilterns the density varied from two to five per square mile, with eight in the Thames and Colne valleys. Domesday *also indicates that the Chilterns, although traditionally thought to be thickly wooded everywhere were, in some areas, as open as sections of northern Buckinghamshire, and thus well suited to arable farming. There may have been more acreage under the plough in the eleventh century than in the twentieth – a remarkable fact when one considers the smaller population.*

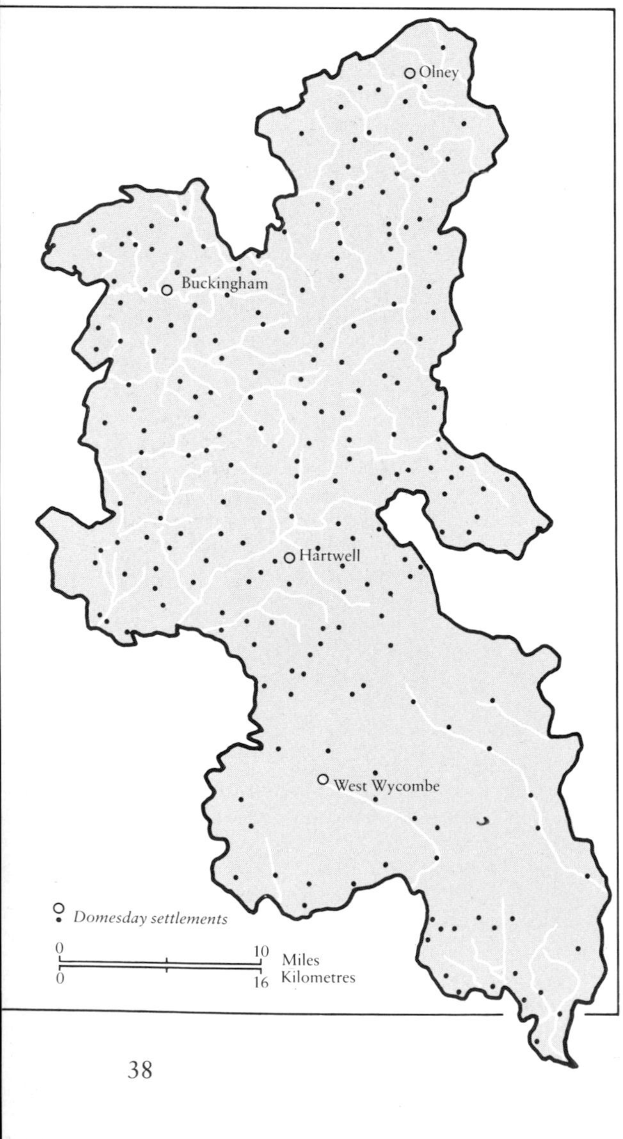

Olney

The Bishop [of Coutances] holds OLNEY *OLNEI* himself. It answers for 10 hides. Land for 10 ploughs; in lordship 3 hides; 3 ploughs there. 24 villagers with 5 smallholders have 7 ploughs. 5 slaves; 1 mill at 40s and 200 eels; meadow for 10 ploughs; woodland, 400 pigs. In total, value £12; when acquired £7; before 1066 £12. Burgred held this manor; 1 Freeman, his man, had 1 1/2 virgates; he could sell.

Olney is a small, quiet market town, on the Ouse in the northernmost tip of the county, close to the Northamptonshire border. Once celebrated for its manufacture of bone-lace it was more recently the centre of a boot and shoe industry. But it is undoubtedly best known for its Shrove Tuesday pancake race and for being the home of the eighteenth-century poet William Cowper.

The Bishop of Coutances held Olney manor from the Conquest, when the Buckinghamshire territory previously owned by Burgred (or Borret) was granted to him, until at some unknown date the Crown confiscated it. The mill at 40s was one of the largest in the district, equalling the combined value of those further down the Ouse at Newport Pagnell (which was a borough!). There were two manorial water mills in use by 1343, but only one recorded in 1411. The present mill is probably on the site of the *Domesday* original. The 200 eels demanded as part of the rent were no doubt caught in traps, as no fishery is mentioned. The manorial woodland in which the pigs rooted would have been part of Yardley Chase, an ancient tract that inevitably diminished in extent as time went on.

In 1194 Olney passed from the king to the Earl of Chester and thence to his four sisters and their descendants. The Daubeny, Basset and Beauchamp families afterwards held the manor in turn until, in 1492, it reverted to the Crown. By 1237 Olney had become a borough. Courts were held roughly every three weeks to hear pleas and for fines to be imposed. The Monday market, first mentioned in 1205/6, still exists. The town's hilarious Shrove Tuesday pancake race, said to be 500 years old, is heralded by the 'pancake bell'. The ladies, all Olney residents, must wear skirts and aprons with scarves or hats as they run the 400-yard course to the church porch, tossing their sizzling pancakes as they go. The pancakes that survive the race are given to the bellringer, who pays with a kiss. A similar custom is observed at Liberal in Kansas, USA, and there is keen competition between the two towns for the best running time.

In 1628/9 Olney Manor formed part of the grant made by Charles I to the citizens of London. Ten years later it was bought for the Nicholl family and in the mid-eighteenth century descended by marriage to Lord Dartmouth. It was this influential government minister who recommended the eccentric evangelist John Newton to the curacy at Olney in 1764, where he continued until 1779. Newton's 'awfully mad career', as he himself described it, began at the age of 11, when he went to sea on his father's ship. In due course he became a midshipman,

OLNEY: *View of the church across the River Ouse.*

but deserted, was flogged and degraded, and in the West Indies was starved and abused. Eventually he became a slave-trader, a profession he abandoned as religious convictions grew. He was Liverpool's tide surveyor, before studying for the ministry.

He convinced William Cowper to move (with his friend Mrs Unwin and her son) from Huntingdon to Olney in 1767. Newton evidently believed that practical evangelical work would help the young, emotionally unstable poet (he had attempted suicide several times and spent seven months in a madhouse) to put his melancholic thoughts into perspective. During nearly 20 years at Orchard Side, in the Market Place, Cowper taught in the Sunday school, attended Newton's prayer meetings, nurtured his greenhouse exotica, which included pineapples, and looked after three pet hares – Puss, Tiney and Bess – creatures of 'sagacity' and 'humour'.

With Newton, Cowper wrote the *Olney Hymns* (published in 1779), among which are 'Amazing Grace' and 'God Moves in a Mysterious Way'. When Newton left for a London parish Mrs Unwin encouraged a depressed Cowper to write more substantial verse, the result being 'Table Talk' and 'Expostulation', among other celebrated pieces collected in *Poems* (1782). In the garden of Orchard Side (now the Cowper and Newton Museum) the 'nutshell of a summerhouse' that served as the 'verse manufactory' survives. It was during this

period that the poet wrote the best of his many letters. He and Mrs Unwin moved to nearby Weston Underwood in 1786.

Doubtless today, as in Cowper's time, occurrences in Olney 'are as rare as cucumbers at Christmas'. The town has a quietly dignified character, with many modest Georgian stone façades (especially near the elegant stone bridge) and a magnificent church, which has one of only two medieval spires in Buckinghamshire.

Buckingham

BUCKINGHAM *BOCHINGHEHA* with BOURTON *BORTUNE* answered for 1 hide before 1066 and does the same now. Land for 8 ploughs; in lordship 2. The villagers have 3½ ploughs; a further 2½ possible. 26 burgesses, 11 smallholders and 2 slaves. 1 mill at 14s; meadow for 8 ploughs; pasture for the village livestock. In total value it paid £10 at face value before 1066; now it pays £16 in white silver.

Bishop Remigius [Bishop of Lincoln] holds the church of this Borough. Land for 4 ploughs, which belong to it. 4 ploughs there. 3 villagers, 3 smallholders and 10 cottages. 1 mill, 10s; meadow for 2 ploughs; wood for fencing. The value is and was £6; before 1066 £7. Bishop Wulfwy held this church from King Edward.

In this Borough the Bishop of Coutances has 3 burgesses, whom Wulfward son of Edeva held. They pay 6s 6d a year, and pay the King 11d.

Earl Hugh has 1 burgess who was Burghard of Shenley's man. He pays 26d a year, and 5d to the King.

Robert d'Oilly has 1 burgess who was Azor son of Toti's man. He pays 16d, and 5d to the King.

Roger d'Ivry has 4 burgesses who were also Azor's men. They pay 7s 6d, and 13d to the King.

Hugh de Bolbec has 4 burgesses who were Alric's men. They pay 28d, and 12d to the King.

Mainou le Breton has 4 burgesses who were men of Edeva, wife of Sired. They pay 29d; they owe nothing to the King.

Hascoit Musard has 1 burgess who was Azor son of Toti's man. He pays 16d, and 2d to the King.

Arnulf de Hesdin has 1 burgess who was Wiglaf's. He pays 2s a year, and 3d to the King.

William de Castellion has 2 burgesses, of the holding of the Bishop of Bayeux, who were Earl Leofwin's men. They pay 16d, and now nothing to the King; but before 1066 they paid 3d.

From Earl Aubrey's holding, 1 burgess pays 2d to the King.

Leofwin of Nuneham has 5 burgesses, and had them before 1066. They pay him 4s a year, and 12d to the King.

Buckingham had been made the capital of the newly formed shire in the tenth century, hence its appearance at the head of the *Domesday* entries for the county, and, indeed, the extent of these entries. Its borough status dates from the time of Edward the Elder, who fortified the River Ouse here against the Danes in 913. A mint was established by Ethelred II. After the Conquest the combined manors of Buckingham and Bourton (today, a suburb) were granted to the powerful Walter Giffard. His descendants built a castle above the river and held sway until 1164, although their headquarters were at Crendon, 12 miles away. The family's revenue of 'white silver' worth £16, mentioned in the *Domesday* entry, would have been in the form of coins, which first would have been melted, to remove the lead content, then weighed.

The Bishop of Lincoln took over the church and its land from his predecessor, the Saxon Wulfwy. Beginning in 1090, the living was appropriated by the Lincoln diocese for two and a half centuries, together with King's Sutton in Northants and Horley in Oxfordshire. A vicarage was instituted at Buckingham only in 1445.

Although Buckingham was the official county town, its geographical position made it unsatisfactory as an administrative centre. The medieval assizes, for instance, were held at Aylesbury, which is now the capital. If the wool trade at one time contributed to Buckingham's prosperity, there is evidence that by the 1470s this and other trades were on the decline. However, a new borough charter in 1550 probably revitalized the town. Certainly the borough was important enough to receive an ostentatious visit from Queen Elizabeth in 1578.

During the Civil War the town was stoutly Royalist. An incident in 1642, when Parliamentary soldiers ransacked the home of the lord of Bourton, Richard Minshull, in his absence is typical of the period:

'... they break open his library, they seize on all the Bills, Bonds, Deeds, Evidences, Writings, and Bookes ... they breake the Windowes, Doors, Wainscot, Seelings, Glasse, they take away all Iron Barres, Casements, Locks, Keys and Hinges ...' Moreover they emptied his wool-store, killed his pigeons and threatened his wife. Two years later Charles I came to town and promptly requisitioned cartloads of 'wine, groceries and tobacco' from the high road, all of which (recalled Clarendon, the indefagitable Cavalier historian) 'were very welcome to Buckingham'. The doorway of Maids Moreton church, just north of the town, is pierced by Civil War bullet holes.

Although the inadequate public facilities of the county capital were ameliorated somewhat by the construction of the present Town Hall in 1689, there was to be no gaol until 1748, when Lord Cobham of Stowe built one. He was chivvied into doing so by Dr Browne Willis, Buckingham's MP from 1705 to 1708, who, though celebrated for his eccentricities, was an ardent champion of his favourite town. He usually wore 'an old slouched hat . . . a weather-beaten large wig, three or four old-fashioned coats, all tied round by a leathern belt' over which he threw a cloak that he had had made when elected an MP. He was 'dirty' and 'disagreeable' to some, but most acknowledged his goodness of heart, and his lifelong devotion to antiquarianism. He wrote extensively on English topography, on abbeys and on cathedrals, losing money on every project but one – a book on Parliament – which earned him £15. But he gave this away, plus £20 more to build a new spire on Buckingham church tower, a replacement for an earlier one that had fallen in 1693. He was also instrumental in getting the summer assizes held in Buckingham and in persuading the archdeacon and the bishop to visit more often.

Although a fire in 1725 destroyed one-third of the town, Buckingham, with its market, busy streets and mainly Georgian and early Victorian buildings, preserves an air of importance. The old industries have declined, but there is now an independent university. New housing which will swell the population to 15,000 is beginning to cover the fields of the medieval manors.

West Wycombe

Walkelin, Bishop of Winchester holds (WEST) WYCOMBE *WICUMBE*. It answers for 19 hides. Land for 23 ploughs; in lordship 5 hides; 3 ploughs there. 27 villagers with 8 smallholders have 19 ploughs. 7 slaves; 3 mills at 20s; 1 fishery at 1000 eels; meadow for 7 ploughs; woodland, 1000 pigs. Total value £15; when acquired £10; before 1066 £12. This manor was and is for the supplies of the monks of the Church of Winchester. Stigand held it before 1066.

Straddling the Oxford road out of High Wycombe, with a wooded Chiltern ridge above, and the stream-like River Wye below, stands the National Trust village of West Wycombe. Ivinghoe, according to *Domesday*, was the only other Buckinghamshire manor always to have belonged to the diocese of Winchester, though several of Stigand's men had been tenants in the county before the Conquest. The Bishop of Bayeux and the Count of Mortain also held land in Wycombe, but their small pieces were eventually incorporated into that of the Bishop of Winchester, who kept his territory until 1551. The mills mentioned in 1086 continued to flourish, a Wythdich Mill being recorded in 1307, and a Margery Mill in 1550. The fishpond that fed the monks of Winchester may have been the 'Pitmill' listed in 1400.

The manor prospered throughout the middle ages, despite a visitation by the Black Death, which killed over 40 people. There were sheep on the hills; woodland pannage for pigs worth a useful 50s 5d in 1251, and a dovecote of 200 doves in 1324. The manor became divided into ten tythings, and in one of these, Haveringdon, a church was built, probably in the mid-thirteenth century. After the diocese of Winchester had relinquished its interest there were a succession of manorial lords until in 1698 the Dashwood family succeeded to the estate. A house was built by the first Sir Francis, but what we see today – the Palladian mansion; the park, with its splendid neoclassical temples, pavilions and bridges; the mausoleum on the hilltop, below a remodelled Haveringdon church (it has a rococo

WEST WYCOMBE: *Row of cottages, 15th to 18th c.*

interior), and the notorious caves of the Hell Fire Club – are the work of the second baronet (1708–81) and his team of architects and gardeners.

The second Sir Francis was a member of the Society of Dilettanti from its foundation in 1736, and the founder of the disreputable Knights of St Francis of Wycombe, commonly known as the 'Monks of Medmenham'. Its members included the radical politician John Wilkes; Lords Sandwich and Bute; the rascally George Bubb Dodington; the Grub Street poet Paul Whitehead, whose heart was later stolen from its resting place in the mausoleum, and Thomas Potter, the son of an Archbishop of Canterbury. Little is known of what exactly went on at Medmenham, or later at Wycombe, in the gloomy tunnels and chambers that Dashwood had hollowed out of the Chiltern chalk, but the *Essay on Woman*, a scurrilous parody of Pope by Wilkes and Potter, gives an indication of the Club's sexual preoccupations. Contemporary satirists like Charles Churchill ridiculed the set.

West Wycombe village was transferred to the National Trust in 1934, and the house with its gardens donated nine years later. The fifteenth-century Church Loft is probably the oldest village building. Much woodland has survived, but prehistoric Desborough Castle, after which the hundred is named, has been swallowed up by High Wycombe.

WEST WYCOMBE: *St Lawrence church with its gold sphere.*

Hartwell

William Peverel holds HARTWELL *HERDEWELLE*; 6 hides and 3 virgates. Teuthael holds from him. Land for 8 ploughs; in lordship 3. 16 villagers with 4 smallholders have 5 ploughs. 4 slaves; meadow for 8 ploughs. The total value is and was 100s; before 1066 £7. Alwin, a thane of King Edward's, held this manor; he could sell.

Hartwell is a mere handful of thatched and timbered cottages along a wooded lane off the main Aylesbury to Thame road. The church adjoins the manor house and its grounds. After the Conquest the manor was held by Peverel of Nottingham, who leased it to Teuthael (or Tekel). Bishop Odo, Bishop of Bayeux, also held land here, as did Walter de Vernon, Walter Giffard and William the Chamberlain. The bishop's territory, which was leased to Helto and Robert, the latter a prodigious county subtenant, appears to have been where the village of Bishopstone, 1½ miles south-east of Hartwell, later developed. *Domesday* records that Odo owned a mill worth 8s, but whether this stood on the River Thame or on its tributary at Bishopstone is not certain. Walter Giffard was one of Buckinghamshire's biggest landowners. As Earl of Buckingham he built a castle in his chief manor of Crendon (now Long Crendon) and his descendants wielded considerable influence, even bequeathing the family badge to the town of Buckingham, which in turn gave it to the shire.

The manor of Hartwell passed from the Peverels to Walter de Hertwell towards the end of the twelfth century, and in 1479 to the celebrated Hampdens of Great Kimble, immediately to the south. Sir Alexander Hampden, who lived at Hartwell until his death in 1617, left behind a fascinating inventory of his 'goodes and chattelles' which included, besides numerous 'fetherbedes, cubberds and chayres', a 'creeper', a 'payre of andirons, twelve spittes, fower drippinge pans, gredirons, one paire of Rackes, and all other iron-work'. All were tabulated with their values in most housewifely fashion. Sir Alexander was the guardian of the famous Parliamentarian, John Hampden, sworn opponent of Charles I, and a brilliant debater, who died tragically young of wounds received in a skirmish with Prince Rupert at Chalgrove Field in 1643.

The tenure of Hartwell had meanwhile moved on again, this time through marriage, to the Lee family. The most remarkable Lee to inhabit Hartwell House, however, was not a real Lee at all, but a Fiott. Born at Totteridge in Hertfordshire in 1783, John Fiott was orphaned in his teens and cared for by his uncle, William Lee Antonie, at Colworth in Bedfordshire. Lee Antonie was himself a dashing character, a passionate huntsman (he had a stable of 80 horses) and an equally impassioned parliamentary disciple of the great Whig politician Charles James Fox.

Fiott, after leaving Cambridge, where he read mathematics and graduated fifth wrangler, toured Scandinavia – a friend said he had a 'fervour for rambling' – then spent five years in Egypt, the Holy Land and Asia Minor. In 1815 he changed his name to Lee in order to inherit Colworth. By the time this onetime globetrotter inherited Hartwell 12 years later, he had become earthbound and was now a Doctor of Laws at Doctor's Commons, a country magistrate, a Fellow of the Royal Astronomical Society and also learned commentator on archaeological matters.

His inheritance was magnificent, a Jacobean mansion with eighteenth-century additions, its grounds traditionally laid out by Capability Brown. While Lee had been abroad, it had been occupied by the exiled Louis XVIII, his family and his advisers. Louis, who had claimed the title of king after the assumed death of his nephew, Louis XVII, in 1795, had been hounded through Europe until Sir George Lee offered him refuge at Hartwell in 1807. And there he remained for seven years. Other exiles joined the royal family and the huge house was full to the attics. Many principal rooms were partitioned; storage cupboards were transformed into bedrooms; nobles slept in servants' quarters, and servants slept under the stairs and on the kitchen floors. The Duc de Berri and his entourage took over the lodge. The Duchess of Angoulême, the only surviving child of the murdered Louis XVI, was assigned a woodman's cottage.

King Louis, a scholarly man with a gift for oratory, bore his exile with a philosophical dignity that earned him the title, 'The Sage of Hartwell'. The queen, however, grew frustrated: Aylesbury could not compare with the Russian court of her youth. She developed a hatred for some ancient carved figures that decorated Hartwell's grand staircase, and wantonly knocked all their heads off. She died in the house, probably of *ennui*, in 1810. Four years later, when Napoleon was deposed, the royal party returned to France. As a farewell gift the king donated £100 worth of consols (government securities) to the parishes of Hartwell and Stone, the dividends to be distributed at Christmas among widows and labourers.

The village of Hartwell prospered with John Lee as lord of the manor. He built cottages for his workers and provided allotments. He gave money for a new national school to be built in 1861 by his friend the architect Joseph Bonomi, to replace the modest affair of 1822. And he took a personal interest in the progress of young Hartwell emigrants to the Cape of Good Hope. As a scientist his major contribution was to astronomy, and in this he was helped by Admiral William Smyth, who had been responsible for 'the greatest scientific survey [it was of the Mediterranean] ever planned and completed by one individual'. Smyth progressed from having his own observatory at Bedford to taking charge of Lee's Hartwell observatory, then the largest of its kind in Britain.

On his eastern travels, Lee amassed treasures which today would be prohibited from export by the countries involved – Greek, Roman and Egyptian antiquities and manuscripts in Persian, Coptic and Sansckrit – for which he built a museum in Hartwell House.

Hartwell House is now an international women's college, a function that Lee, a progressive educationalist, would have applauded. The unusual Georgian Gothic church, built as part of the estate's improvements, also survives, as does an Egyptian-style pylon designed by Bonomi and placed over the spring that gave the village its name. The Victorian Peverel Court doubtless stands on the holding of the *Domesday* lord of the manor, William Peverel.

Buckinghamshire Gazetteer Each entry starts with the modern place-name in **bold** type. The *Domesday* information is in *italic* type, beginning with the name or names by which the place was known in 1086. The main landholders and under-tenants follow, separated with semi-colons if a place was divided into more than one holding. A number of holdings in Buckinghamshire were granted by the king to his thanes and almsmen; these are given with their office, or described as holding land 'from the king'. More general information, including examples of dues such as eels rendered by tenants, completes the *Domesday* part of the entry. The modern or post-Domesday section is in normal type. ▦ represents a village, ⌂ a small village or hamlet.

Addingrove *Eddingrave: Hugh from Walter Giffard.* Addingrove Farm.

Addington *Ed(d)intone: Robert of Romney from Bishop of Bayeux.* Secluded parkland; 2 manor houses.

Adstock *Edestoche: Ambrose from William Peverel.* ⌂ Some thatched, timber-framed houses.

Akeley *Achelei: Robert from Walter Giffard.* ▦ Attractive, tree-shaded; built round a square.

Amersham *Elm(n)odesham: Roger from Bishop of Bayeux; Aelmer from Count of Mortain; Geoffrey de Mandeville; Wulfgeat from Hugh de Bolbec; Thurstan Mantle; Jocelyn le Breton. 2 mills.* Town. 17th-century buildings; Mantles Green commemorates Thurstan Mantle.

Ashendon *Assedo(u)ne: Richard from Walter Giffard; Vicking from Miles Crispin.* ⌂

Aston Abbotts *Estone: St Albans Abbey.* ▦ The Abbey is a large house built on the site of what was once the abbot's country seat.

Aston Clinton *Estone: Edward of Salisbury. Mill.* ▦ Busy; Victorian and modern houses along a main road.

Aston Sandford *Estone: Robert from Bishop of Bayeux; Miles Crispin; Odo from Mainou le Breton.* ▦

Aylesbury *Eilesberia/e: King's land with the Bishop of Lincoln holding the church. 2 mills.* County town that spread rapidly in the 1960s from its medieval and Georgian centre. It was the home of John Wilkes, the radical 18th-century politician.

Barton Hartshorn *Bertone: Arnulf de Hesdin from Bishop of Bayeux.* ⌂ Tudor manor house.

Beachampton *Bec(h)entone: Hugh from Walter Giffard; Leofwin of Nuneham from the king and from Roger d'Ivry.* ▦ Beachampton Hall manor house; The Grange, a timber-framed farmhouse.

Beachendon *Bichedone: Bishop of Bayeux; Miles Crispin.* Beachendon Farm.

Bedgrove *Begraue: Roger from Bishop of Bayeux.* Bedgrove Farm.

Biddlesden *Bech(t)esdene: King's land; Count of Mortain. 2 mills.* ⌂ A large 18th-century house stands on the site of a Cistercian abbey.

Bierton *Bortone: Roger from Bishop of Bayeux.* ▦ Absorbed by Aylesbury.

Bledlow *Bledlai: Count of Mortain. Mill.* ▦ Built round a ravine of the River Lyde.

Bourton *Bo(u)rtune: King's land (assessed in Buckingham); Hugh from Walter Giffard. 2 mills.* ▦ On the outskirts of Buckingham.

Boveney *Boueni(a)e: Reinbald the Priest, the pre-Conquest holder, from the king; Gerard from Giles brother of Ansculf.* Ancient disused church near Boveney Court, a 15th-century timber-framed house.

Bow Brickhill *Brichelle: Robert from Bishop of Lisieux; Ralph and Robert from Walter Giffard. Mill.* ▦ Picturesque. It climbs the steep slope of a wooded hill crowned by Danesborough hill fort.

Boycott *Boicote: Reinbald.* ⌂ Boycott Manor.

Bradenham *Bradeham: Swarting and Harding from the king.* ▦ The childhood home of Benjamin Disraeli (1804–81), now owned by National Trust.

Bradwell *Bradew(uu)elle: Walter Hacket from Walter Giffard; William de Feugeres from William FitzAnsculf (who, as sheriff, wrongfully dispossessed William Cholsey).* ▦ Remains of a 12th-century Benedictine priory; earth works of a motte and bailey.

Brill *Brunhelle: King's land.* ▦ Hilltop; clay-working centre for 600 years; 17th-century post mill; mineral spring.

Brook *Broch:* Lost. Remembered only in the name of Brook's Copse.

Broughton (near Aylesbury) *Brotone: William de Warenne.* Broughton Manor Farm; traces of an ancient moat.

Broughton (near Moulsoe) *Brotone: Hugh from Walter Giffard; Morcar, the pre-Conquest holder, from Countess Judith. Mill.* ▦ Medieval wall paintings in church; manor farm with charming timber-framed buildings.

Buckingham *Bochingeham:* See page 39.

Buckland *Bocheland: Walter from Bishop of Lincoln.* ▦ Tree-shaded.

Burnham *Burneham: Walter FitzOthere.* ▦ Engulfed by Slough suburbs; site of a 12th-century Augustinian abbey which was restored by nuns as a convent in 1916.

Burston *Bricstoch: Alan from Count of Mortain; Thurstan from Walter Giffard; William from Miles Crispin.* The farms of Upper and Lower Burston recall the *Domesday* village name.

CHALFONT ST GILES: *Milton's cottage, partly a museum.*

Caldecote *Caldecote: Alfred from Count of Mortain; William FitzAnsculf; Swarting from the king. 2 mills.* ⌂

Calverton *Calvretone: Hugh de Bolbec. Mill.* ⌂ Old manor house.

Chalfont St Giles *Celfun(d)te: Mainou le Breton. 3 mills, a hawk's eyrie.* ▦ Pretty; home of poet John Milton (1608–74).

Chalfont St Peter *Celfun(d)te: Roger from Bishop of Bayeux. Mill, a hawk's eyrie.* ▦ Centre of Quakerism in 17th century; hawk's eyrie, source of young birds to train.

Charndon *Credendone: Ralph de Feugeres.* ▦ On a hill near Calvert brickworks.

Chearsley *Cerl(d)eslai: Arnulf and Geoffrey from Walter Giffard; Richard from Miles Crispin.* ▦ Unspoilt; timber-framed cottages on the banks of the River Thame.

Cheddington *Cete(n)done/Cetedene: Ralph and Ranulph from Count of Mortain; Swarting from the king and from William FitzAnsculf; Gilbert from Robert de Tosny; Ralph from Robert d'Oilly; Hugh de Bolbec.* ▦ Saxon cultivation terraces nearby. The Great Train Robbery took place here in 1962.

BRILL: *Old post-mill, 1689.*

Chesham *Cestreham: Bishop of Bayeux and Roger from him; Hugh de Bolbec; Thurstan Mantle; Alfsi. 4 mills.* Market town. Surviving tracts of woods which provided pastureland for 1650 pigs in 1086, still reach its outskirts.

Chetwode *Ceteode: Robert de Thaon from Bishop of Bayeux. Mill.* ⌂

Chicheley *Cicelai: Baldwin, the pre-Conquest holder, Andrew and Payne from William FitzAnsculf.* ▦ Chicheley Hall (1701).

Chilton *Ciltone: Walter Giffard.* ▦ Pretty, stonebuilt; 18th-century Chilton House.

Clifton Reynes *Clifton/Clis-Clystone: Morcar and Thorbert from Bishop of Coutances; William de Bosc-le-hard and his brother from Robert de Tosny; Roger d'Olney and Nigel from Countess Judith. 1½ mills, fishery (125 eels).* ⌂

Crafton *Croustone: Bishop of Lisieux; monks of St Nicholas from Count of Mortain.* ⌂

Creslow *Cresselai: Ranulf from Edward of Salisbury.* 300-acre Creslow Field, the county's largest enclosed pasture, provided meat for Elizabeth I. Creslow Manor, now a farmhouse, was built c.1300.

Cublington *Coblincote: Jocelyn le Breton. Mill.* ▦ The mound of a Norman castle, The Beacon, is to the west.

Dadford *Dodeforde: Haimard from Roger d'Ivry; Hugh FitzGozhere from the king.* ⌂

Datchet *Daceta: Giles brother of Ansculf. 2 fisheries (2000 eels).* Thames-side residential district, dominated by Windsor Castle across the river.

Denham *Daneham: St Peter's of Westminster. 2 mills, 3 fisheries.* Picturesque part of Greater London; a centre of the film industry.

Dilehurst *Dilehurst: Bishop of Lisieux from Bishop of Bayeux.* Lost in Taplow.

Dinton *Danitone: Helto from Bishop of Bayeux. Mill.* ⌂ Chestnut-shaded. 15th-century Dinton Hall was the home of Simon Mayne, who signed Charles I's death warrant in 1649.

Ditton *Ditone: Walter from William FitzAnsculf.* Parkland.

Dorney *Dornei: Miles Crispin. Fishery (500 eels).* ▦ Green Belt. England's first pineapple was grown here for Charles II in 1668. Dorney Court, c. 1500, has been the home of the Palmer family since 1624.

Dorton *Dortone: Walter Giffard.* ▦ Dorton House, set in parkland, is a private school.

Drayton Beauchamp *Draitone: William FitzNigel and Leofsi from Count of Mortain; Helgot from Mainou le Breton.* ▦ The Beauchamps held the manor in the 13th century.

Drayton Parslow *Drai(n)tone: Roger from Bishop of Bayeux; Nigel de Berville.* ▦ Remote. Once held by Ralph Passwater (*Passe l'eau*), who was dispossessed by Bishop of Coutances. The English name, Parslow, derives from *Passe l'eau*.

Dunton *Dodintone: Thurstan FitzGiron from Bishop of Bayeux.* ⌂ Isolated; manor farm.

Easington *Hesintone: Roger from Walter Giffard.* ⌂

East Burnham *Esburnham: St Peter's of Westminster.* ▦ Near Burnham Beeches.

East Claydon *Clai(n)done: Ralph from William Peverel; Geoffrey de Mandeville; 2 Englishmen and Geoffrey from Miles Crispin.* ⌂ Black-and-white cottages; traces of a moat.

Edgcott *Achecote: Ralph from Walter Giffard.* 18th-century manor farm.

Edlesborough *Ed(d)inberge: Gilbert de Ghent. 2 mills.*

Ellesborough *Esenberge/a: Ralph and Odbert from William FitzAnsculf, formerly Earl Harold; Mainou le Breton.* Sheltered by beechwoods; Cymbeline's Mount nearby.

Emberton *Ambre(i)tone: Godric and Wulfric, the pre-Conquest holders, from Bishop of Coutances; Roger from Countess Judith.* Manor farm; recreation ground; camp site; nature reserve.

Eton *Ettone: Walter FitzOthere, formerly Queen Edith. 2 mills, fisheries (1000 eels).* Town. Famous for its public school, founded by Henry VI in 1440.

Evershaw *Euressel: A cripple, the pre-Conquest holder, from the king.* Farm and copse.

Farnham Royal *Ferneham: Bertram de Verdun; Geoffrey de Mandeville (who dispossessed Bertram while he was overseas serving the king).* Suburb of Slough. Called 'royal' because William I granted the manor-holder the right to give a glove and support his right arm at his coronation.

Fawley *Falelie: Herbrand from Walter Giffard.* William of Orange was welcomed at Fawley Court in 1688 on his march from Torbay to claim the throne.

Fleet Marston *Merstone: Walter de Vernon.* Farms and cottages on Roman Akeman Street.

Foxcote *Foxescote: Thurstan from Bishop of Bayeux.* Foxcote Manor, partly Elizabethan, site of a Roman villa nearby.

Gawcott *Chauescote: Bishop of Lincoln.* Architect Sir Gilbert Scott was born here in 1811.

Gayhurst *Gateherst: Bishop of Lisieux from Bishop of Bayeux and Robert de Noyers from him.* Sir Francis Drake (1540–96) was given the manor house; the present Elizabethan mansion was built in 1597 after he sold it. Sir Everard Digby, Gunpowder conspirator, lived in the village.

Granborough *Grenesberga: St Albans Abbey.*

HAMBLEDEN: *Mill End Weir, c. 1338, on the Roman road.*

Great Brickhill *Brichella: William from Earl Hugh. 2 mills.* Attractive.

Great Horwood *Herewordè: William from Walter Giffard.*

Great Kimble *Chenebella: Hugh from Walter Giffard.* The name is thought to be a corruption of Cymbeline (Cunobelinus), the 1st-century British king. Pulpit Hill has an Iron Age fort.

Great Linford *Linforde: Ranulf from Count of Mortain; Hugh from Walter Giffard; Robert from William FitzAnsculf; Hugh de Bolbec.* Part of Milton Keynes New Town.

Great Marlow *Berlaue: Theodwald from Bishop of Bayeux; Ralph and Roger from Miles Crispin. Mill, fishery.* Town. Mary Shelley wrote *Frankenstein* here (1817–18). T. S. Eliot lived here.

Great Missenden *Missedene: Thurstan FitzRolf from Walter Giffard.* 19th-century Missenden Abbey stands on the site of a 12th-century Augustinian abbey.

Great Woolstone *Ulsiestone: St Peter's of La Couture from Walter Giffard.* Part of Milton Keynes New Town.

Grendon Underwood *Grennedone: Henry de Ferrers.* Shakespeare supposedly began *A Midsummer Night's Dream* while staying overnight at 16th-century Shakespeare Farm, then the New Inn.

Grove *Langraue: Robert from Jocelyn le Breton.* Beside a lock on the Grand Union Canal.

Haddenham *Nedreham: Archbishop Lanfranc. 2 mills.* Charming; noted for its medieval centre.

Halton *Haltone: Archbishop of Canterbury. Mill.* Iron Age fort on Boddington Hill. Baron Alfred de Rothschild built Halton House, now an RAF establishment, in 1841.

Hambleden *Hambledene: Queen Matilda. Mill, fishery (1000 eels).* Mill at Hambleden Mill End. The 17th-century manor house owned by Viscount Hambleden, was the birthplace of the 7th Earl Cardigan who commanded the Charge of the Light Brigade at Balaclava (1854).

Hampden *Hamdena: Odbert from William FitzAnsculf.* Now 2 villages, Great Hampden, with 14th-century Hampden House with parkland and a section of Iron Age Grim's Ditch earthwork, and Little Hampden.

Hanslope *Hamescle: Winemar the Fleming. Mill.* The 12th-century church has the grave of a prizefighter who died here in 1830 after an illegal 47-round bare-knuckle contest.

Hardmead *Herould/ Herulfmede: Hugh from Walter Giffard; Harvey, Payne and Baldwin from William FitzAnsculf; Hugh de Bolbec; Morcar from Countess Judith.* Some houses.

Hardwick *Harduic(h): Aelmer from Count of Mortain; William from Miles Crispin; Thurstan FitzRolf.* On a green; 17th-century manor house.

Hartwell *Herduuelle/ewelle:* See page 41.

Haseley *Haselie:* Lost.

Haversham *Havresham: William Peverel. Mill (75 eels).* Stone-built.

Helsthorpe *Helpestorp/trope: Helgot from Mainou le Breton; Aelmer from Count of Mortain.* Helsthorpe Farm.

High Wycombe *Wicumbe: Robert d'Oilly from his wife's holding. 6 mills.* Furniture manufacturing town; earthworks; Wycombe Abbey public school.

Hillesden *Ilesdone/Ulesdone: Ranulf from Count of Mortain; Hugh from Walter Giffard. Mill.* Remote, hilltop.

Hitcham *Hucheham: Ralph and Roger from Miles Crispin.* Near Maidenhead. Hitcham Park is the site of a manor house where Elizabeth I was entertained, 1602.

Hoggeston *Hochestone: Payne from William FitzAnsculf.* Remote; thatched cottages; Jacobean manor house.

Hogshaw *Hocsaga: William Peverel.* Traces of an ancient moat near Hogshaw Farm.

Hollingdon *Holedene/ Holendone: Payne from William FitzAnsculf; Nigel from Miles Crispin.*

Horsenden *Horsede(u)ne: Roger and Robert from Bishop of Bayeux; Ralph from Count of Mortain; Harding from the king. Mill.* Wooded.

Horton (in Ivinghoe) *Hortone: Alstan from Count of Mortain; Swarting from Gilbert de Ghent; Miles Crispin.* Moated hall.

Horton (near Slough) *Hortune: Walter FitzOthere. Mill.*

Hughenden *Huchedene: William FitzOger from Bishop of Bayeux.* Disraeli lived at Hughenden Manor, 1847–81.

Ibstone *Hibestanes/Ebestan/ Ypestan: Hervey the Commissioner from the king.* Its large common is on a Chiltern ridge.

Ickford *Iforde: The monks of Grestain from Count of Mortain; Richard from Miles Crispin.* Thatched cottages; traces of an ancient earthwork nearby.

Ilmer *Imere: Robert from Bishop of Bayeux. Mill.* Half-timbered cottages.

Iver *Evreham: Robert d'Oilly. 3 mills, 4 fisheries (1500 eels), vines.*

Ivinghoe *Evinghehou: Bishop of Winchester.* Fine 17th- and 18th-century houses; Iron Age hill fort nearby.

Ivinghoe Aston *Estone: Ralph from Count of Mortain; Germund from Geoffrey de Mandeville.*

Kingsey *Eie: Nigel de le Vast from Nigel d'Aubigny.* Between the River Thame and Cuttle Brook.

Lamport *Lan(d)port: Berner from Walter Giffard; Gerard from Mainou le Breton.*

Lathbury *Late(s)berie: Bishop of Lisieux from Bishop of Bayeux; William from Bishop of Coutances; William d'Orange from Hugh de Beauchamp.* 19th-century manor house.

Lavendon *Lauendene/ Lauue(n)dene: Bishop of Coutances and William, Ansketel and 3 freemen from him; Humphrey from Count of Mortain; Ralph from Walter Giffard; Roger and Ralph from Countess Judith; Ketel from the king. 1½ mills (250 eels), 1 mill (50 eels).* Lavendon Castle.

Leckhampstead *Lecham(e)stede: Gilbert Maminot from Bishop of Bayeux; Hugh from Walter Giffard; Osbert from Geoffrey de Mandeville. Mill.* Straggling; disused mill.

Lenborough *Edingeberge/ Ledingberge: Arnulf de Hesdin from Bishop of Bayeux; Ralph from Walter Giffard.*

Lillingstone Dayrell *Lelinchestane: Hugh from Walter Giffard.* Church with an 11th-century nave near the site of an old manor house.

Lillingstone Lovell *Lelinchestane: Benzelin; Richard the Artificer.*

Linslade *Lincelada: Hugh de Beauchamp. Mill.*

Little Brickhill *Brichelle: Thurstan from Bishop of Bayeux.* On Roman Watling Street. Buckinghamshire Assizes were held here for 200 years until 1638.

Littlecote *Litecota/e: Robert from Walter Giffard; Payne from William FitzAnsculf; Robert from Miles Crispin.*

Little Kimble *Parva Chenebelle: Albert from Thurstan FitzRolf. Mill.*

Little Linford *Linforde: Edeva, the pre-Conquest holder, from Bishop of Coutances. Mill.* Parkland, becoming a suburb of Milton Keynes New Town.

Little Marlow *Merlaue: Kings land, formerly Queen Matilda; Walter de Vernon. Mill, fishery (1000 eels).* Set round a green.

Little Missenden *Missedene: Count of Mortain; Wulfgeat from Hugh de Bolbec; Thurstan Mantle.* Unspoilt; church founded in Saxon times; Jacobean manor house.

Little Woolstone *Ulsiestone: Ralph from Walter Giffard; William FitzAnsculf. Mill.* Absorbed in Milton Keynes New Town.

Long Crendon *Credendone: Walter Giffard. Mill; park for woodland beasts.* Thatched cottages. Medieval buildings: 14th-century court house; 15th-century manor house owned by Catherine de Valois (1401–37), queen of Henry V.

LONG CRENDON: *Victorian sign.*

Loughton *Lochintone: Walter from Count of Mortain; Ivo from Walter Giffard; 2 men-at-arms from Mainou le Breton.* 16th-century manor house near a willow-shaded green.

Lower Winchendon *Winchendone: Walter Giffard. Mill (80 eels).* Picturesque; old cottages; 16th-century manor farm house; medieval Nether Winchendon House, formerly the manor house.

Lude *Lede: Walter from Bishop of Lincoln. 3 mills.* Lude Farm.

Ludgershall *Lotegarser: Bishop of Coutances; William FitzMann.* Scattered; 17th-century houses round a green.

Maids Moreton *Mortone: Thurstan from Walter Giffard; Leofwin, the pre-Conquest holder, from the king.* Buckingham suburb. The maids Moreton were sisters who founded the church in the 15th century.

Marsh Gibbon *Mersa/e: Monks of Grestain from Count of Mortain; Alric FitzAnsculf, the pre-Conquest holder, (under harsh conditions).* Sprawling.

Marsworth *Misseuorde: Ralph Basset from Robert d'Oilly. 3 mills.* Roman building site nearby.

Medmenham *Medemeham: Hugh de Bolbec. Fishery (1000 eels).* Iron Age fort called Bolbec's Castle.

Mentmore *Mentemore: Robert from Earl Hugh.* 19th-century Mentmore Park was built by the Rothschild family.

Middle Claydon *Clai(d)done: William Peverel.* Claydon House, where Florence Nightingale stayed with her sister, Lady Verney, is still the home of the Verney family.

Milton Keynes *Mid(d)eltone/ Midueltone: Hugh from Walter Giffard; Osbert from William FitzAnsculf; Godric Cratel from the king. Mill.* Near Milton Keynes New Town.

Monk's Risborough *Riseberge: Archbishop of Canterbury.* Close to Princes Risborough.

MONK'S RISBOROUGH: *Medieval dovecote behind the church.*

Moulsoe *Moleshou: Richard from Walter Giffard.*

Mursley *Muselai: Alfred from Count of Mortain; William from Walter Giffard; Leofwin, the pre-Conquest holder, from the king.* Market town in the 13th century; 17th-century manor house.

Nashway *Lesa: Picot from Roger d'Ivry.* Farm.

Newport Pagnell *Neuport: William FitzAnsculf. 2 mills.* Busy market town. The Great Ouse and River Lovat meet here.

Newton Longville *Neutone: Walter Giffard.*

North Marston *Merstone: Robert from Bishop of Bayeux; Ranulf from Bishop of Coutances; Ranulf and Bernard from William FitzAnsculf; Seric, the pre-Conquest holder, from Miles Crispin.* Famous for its rector, John Shorne, who worked miracles in the 13th century.

Oakley *Achelei: Robert FitzWalter from Robert d'Oilly. Before 1066 Aelfgeth, a girl, held 2 hides and was assigned ½ hide by Godric the Sheriff in exchange for teaching his daughter gold embroidery.*

Olney *Olnei:* See page 38.

Oving *Olvonge: 2 men-at-arms from Bishop of Coutances.* Quiet, hilltop; 17th-century inn.

Padbury *Pateberie: Mainou le Breton. Mill.* Norbury Camp, an ancient earthwork is nearby.

Pitstone *Pincelestorne/ Pincenestorne: Ralph, Bernard, Fulkhold and Thorgils from Count of Mortain; Ralph from Walter Giffard; Roger and Swarting from Miles Crispin.* Engulfed by cement works. Pitstone Windmill is one of England's oldest post-mills.

Pollicott *Policote: 2 men-at-arms from Walter Giffard.* Now 2 hilltop hamlets, Upper and Lower Pollicott.

Preston Bisset *Prestone: Ansgot de Rots from Bishop of Bayeux. Mill.*

Princes Risborough *Riseberge/ a: King's land, formerly Earl Harold. 2 mills.* Market town; earthworks nearby.

Quainton *Chentone: Miles Crispin; Hascoit Musard.*

Quarrendon *Querendone: Geoffrey de Mandeville, formerly Queen Edith.* Traces of Civil War earthworks near ruined parish church.

Radclive *Radeclive: Fulk from Roger d'Ivry. Mill.* 16th-century manor house.

Ravenstone *Ravenestone: Hugh from Walter Giffard. Mill.* All Saints' Church is on the site of an Augustinian priory.

Salden *Sceldene: Ralph from Count of Mortain; Leofwin of Nuneham, the pre-Conquest holder, from the king.* Remote farm.

Saunderton *Santesdo(u)ne: Roger from Bishop of Bayeux; Osbert from Miles Crispin. 3 mills.* 3rd-century Roman villa site.

Shabbington *Sobintone: Miles Crispin. Mill, fishery (100 eels).* Manor farm.

Shalstone *Celdestane/stone: Bishop of Bayeux; Robert from Robert d'Oilly.* Stone-built cottages; 18th-century manor house.

Shenley Brook End *Sen(e)lai: Richard the Artificer; Urse de Bercheres.*

Shenley Church End *Senelai: Hugh from Earl Hugh.* Medieval earthworks nearby.

Sherington *Serintone: Bishop of Coutances. Mill.* Large.

Shipton Lee *Sibdone: William Peverel; Henry de Ferrers; Alfsi with his wife, from the king.*

Shortley *Sortelai:* Lost.

Simpson *Sevinestone/ Siuuinestone: Bishop of Coutances, formerly Queen Edith; Leofwin Wavre, the pre-Conquest holder, from the king. Mill.*

Singleborough *Sincleberia: Walter de Bec from Walter Giffard.*

Slapton *Slapetone: Barking Church.*

Soulbury *Soleberie: Payne from William FitzAnsculf; Roger from Miles Crispin; Hugh de Beauchamp; Jocelyn le Breton; Azelina, Ralph Tailbois' wife; Godwin the Beadle.*

Southcote *Sudcote: Sweeting from William FitzConstantine.* Lost in Stone village.

Stantonbury *Stantone: Ralph from Miles Crispin. Mill (50 eels).* On the outskirts of Milton Keynes New Town.

Steeple Claydon *Claindone: Alric Cook from the king.* Camp Barn is said to have housed Cromwell's soldiers during the Civil War.

Stewkley *Stiuelai: William from Bishop of Coutances; Nigel from Miles Crispin.*

Stoke Goldington *Stoches: An Englishman from Bishop of Coutances; Drogo from William Peverel.*

Stoke Hammond *Stoches: Mainou le Breton. Mill.* Large.

Stoke Mandeville *Stoches: Bishop of Lincoln. Mill.* Famous for its paraplegics hospital. Earthworks mark the site of the old manor house.

Stoke Poges *Stoches: Walter from William FitzAnsculf. Mill.* Thomas Gray's poem 'Elegy in a Country Churchyard' immortalized this village.

Stone *Stanes: Helto from Bishop of Bayeux; Gilbert from Robert de Tosny.* A Roman pottery kiln was excavated nearby.

Stowe *Stou: Robert d'Oilly and Roger d'Ivry from Bishop of Bayeux.* Stowe House, public school, with 18th-century gardens landscaped by Capability Brown, James Gibbs and William Kent.

Swanbourne *Soeneberno/berie/ berne/borne: King's land, formerly Earl Harold; Ralph and Aelmer from Count of Mortain; William from Walter Giffard; Payne from William FitzAnsculf; Geoffrey de Mandeville.*

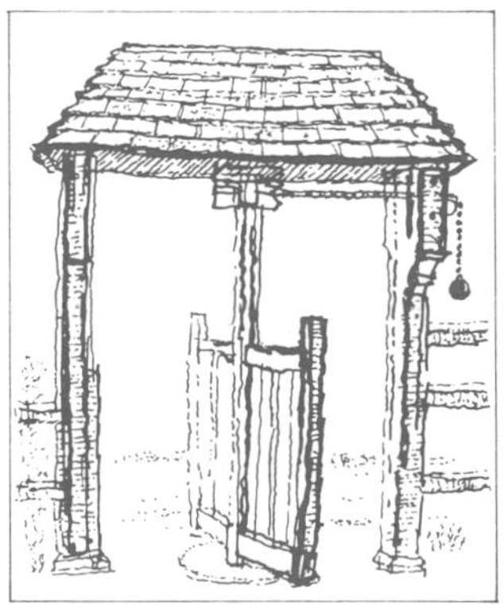

WESTON TURVILLE: *Double-entry lych-gate.*

Taplow *Thapeslau: Roger from Bishop of Bayeux. Fishery (1000 eels).* A Saxon burial-mound yielded a rich hoard in 1883.

Tetchwick *Tochingeuuiche: Payne from William Peverel.*

Thornborough *Torneberge: Berner from Mainou le Breton. Mill.* 2 Roman burial mounds near 14th-century Thornborough bridge.

Thornton *Ternitone: Godfrey from Roger d'Ivry. Mill.* Stone-built.

Tickford *Ticheforde: William FitzAnsculf.* Tickford Abbey.

Tingewick *Tedinwiche: Ilbert de Lacy from Bishop of Bayeux.* Roman villa nearby.

Turville *Tilleberie: Roger from Nigel d'Aubigny.* Pretty; windmill.

Turweston *Turvestone: William de Feugeres.*

Twyford *Tueverde/Tuiforde: Ralph de Feugeres.*

Tyringham *Te(d)lingham: Ansketel from Bishop of Coutances; Acard from William FitzAnsculf.* 18th-century Tyringham House in parkland.

Tythorp *Duchitorp: Ilbert de Lacy and Wadard from Bishop of Bayeux.* 17th-century mansion near Kingsey village.

Upper Winchendon *Winchendone: The Canons of Oxford before and after 1066.* Adjoins Waddesdon Manor.

Upton *Opetone: King's land, formerly Earl Harold; Robert from William Peverel; Alric from Miles Crispin. Mill, fishery (1000 eels).* Ancient; absorbed by Slough.

Waddesdon *Votesdone: Miles Crispin. Mill.* Ferdinand de Rothschild, owner of Waddesdon Manor, rebuilt the village in the 19th century.

Waldridge *Wa(l)druge: Helto from Bishop of Bayeux; Swarting from Geoffrey de Mandeville.* Waldridge Manor.

Wanden *Wandene:* Lost.

Water Eaton *Etone: Bishop of Coutances. Mill.*

Water Stratford *Stradford: Thurstan from Robert d'Oilly. Mill.*

Wavendon *Wau(u)endone: Ralph, Walter and Humphrey from Count of Mortain; Anselm from Hugh de Bolbec; Godwin the priest from Leofwin; Leofwin Cave from the king.*

Wendover *Wendoure/ovre: King's land; 3 men from the king. 2 mills.* Market town. Oliver Cromwell stayed at the Red Lion in 1642.

Westbury *Westberie: Roger from Bishop of Bayeux.* Grey stone.

Westbury (by Shenley) *Westberie: Payne from Roger d'Ivry. 2 mills.* Westbury Farm.

Weston Turville *Westone: Bishop of Lisieux and Roger from Bishop of Bayeux. 4 mills.* The 18th-century manor house is in the outer bailey of a Norman castle, near a moat and motte.

Weston Underwood *Westone: Bishop of Coutances; Ivo from Count of Mortain; Ansketel from Countess Judith.* Beautiful; golden stone cottages. 18th-century poet William Cowper stayed here.

West Wycombe *Wicumbe:* See page 40.

Whaddon *Wadone: Walter Giffard.* Hilltop; 19th-century Whaddon Hall.

Whaddon (in Slapton) *Wadone: Roger from Bishop of Bayeux; Hugh de Bolbec.* Whaddon Farm.

Whitchurch *Wicherce: Hugh de Bolbec from Walter Giffard.* Large; earthworks of Bolbec castle. The artist Rex Whistler lived at Bolbec House.

Wing *Witehunge: Count of Mortain.* Large; Anglo-Saxon church; Castle Hill; motte of a Norman castle.

Wingrave *Wit(h)ungraue: Alan from Count of Mortain; Nigel, Thurstan and Aelmer from Miles Crispin; Wibald from Gunfrid de Chocques.* Enlarged by Hannah Rothschild in the 19th century.

Winslow *Weneslai: St Albans Abbey.* Country town built round a market square.

Wolverton *Wluerintone: Mainou le Breton. 2 mills.* Railway town. The old village of Wolverton lies to the west.

Wooburn *Waborne: Walter from Bishop of Lincoln, formerly Earl Harold. 8 mills, fishery (300 eels).*

Worminghall *Wermelle: Bishop of Coutances, formerly Wulward's wife from Queen Edith.* Thatched cottages.

Wotton Underwood *Oltone: Walter Giffard.* 18th-century Wotton House, set in parkland.

Woughton *Ulchestone: Ralph from Count of Mortain; Martin.* Round a green; near Milton Keynes New Town.

Wraysbury *Wirecesberie: Robert Gernon. 2 mills, hay for the cattle of the court, 4 fisheries.* Thames-side; flanked by flooded gravel pits.

STOKE POGES: *'Bicycle' stained-glass window, 14th c., in St Giles Church.*

Cambridgeshire

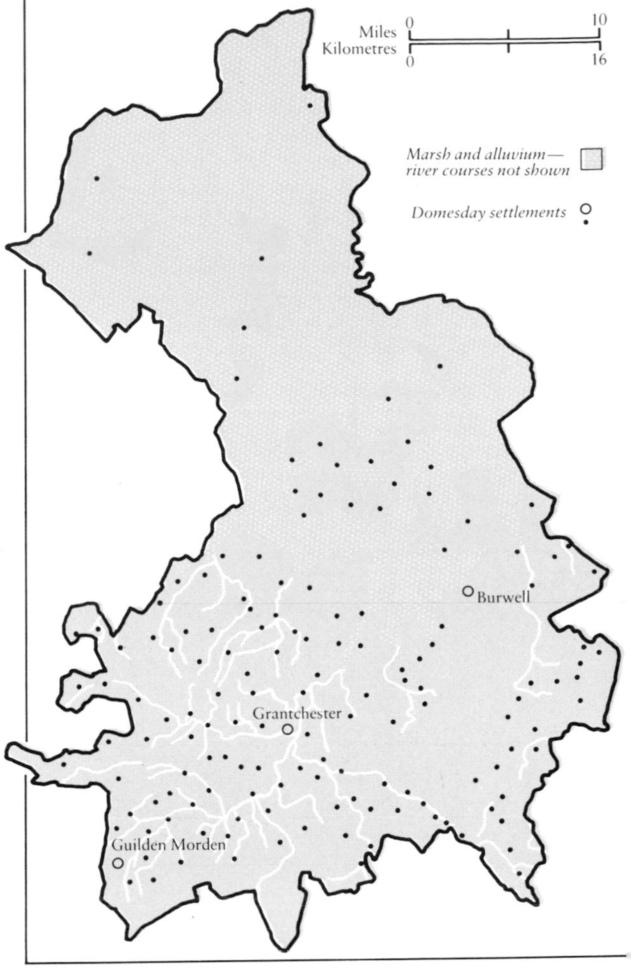

Cambridgeshire provides Domesday *scholars with a mountain of statistics. Not only is there* Domesday Book *itself, but there are two other contemporary manuscripts, their information apparently drawn from the same survey of 1086. These are the* Inquisitio Eliensis *and the* Inquisitio Comitatus Cantabrigiensis. *The first decribes the holdings of Ely Abbey, about one-fifth of the entire county. The second reads like an unabridged version of the Cambridgeshire* Domesday Book. *Although these three accounts are occasionally contradictory, they ultimately enrich our knowledge of* Domesday *England. Because this book is a reflection of* Domesday Book *itself, we have used only its entries on the following pages.*

Cambridgeshire in the eleventh century was only about two-thirds dry land. Much of the north of the county was fenland – half-sea, half-marsh and, except for its islands, entirely uninhabitable. The largest of these islands was Ely, where the wealthy abbey – the abbot was one of the greatest landholders in the region – nursed a grievance against the country's new Norman rulers, especially against Picot, Sheriff of Cambridge, 'a roving wolf, a crafty fox, a greedy hog'.

The city of Cambridge itself, near the southern edge of the fenland, was a simple agricultural community in 1086. Its population was nearly 2000, but nevertheless it remained, according to one scholar, 'as primitive as any county borough well could be'.

Grantchester

In GRANTCHESTER *GRANTESETA* Robert [Fafiton] holds 2 hides and 3 virgates. Land for 4 ploughs. In lordship 1 hide; 2 ploughs there. 4 villagers with 7 smallholders have 2 ploughs. 22 cottagers. 1 mill at 40s; from 1/2 weir 500 eels. In total the value is and was £7; before 1066 £10. 4 Freemen held this land. One of them, Earl Algar's man, held 3 virgates. The others, Earl Waltheof's men, held 2 hides; they could grant and sell their lands.

'The whole place is very lovely, with apple blossom now, later with roses. Will you come and stay here?' wrote the poet Rupert Brooke to a friend in 1910. 'I can promise you bathing and all manner of rustic delight.'

Another 75 years of the twentieth century have done some damage, but Grantchester retains at least a few delights that Brooke would recognize. It is still an easy walk across pleasant fields south from Cambridge. The River Cam (the 'yet unacademic stream', as Brooke called it) still flows neatly between grassy banks and pruned trees. The church is as snug as ever in its crowded graveyard. Its clock, however, is something of a disappointment. Immortalized by Brooke, in his poem 'The Old Vicarage Grantchester', as stopped perpetually at ten to three, it has kept excellent time for many years.

If medieval fables are to be believed, Grantchester was one of Britain's great cities when the Romans arrived. Even level-headed historians concede that until the Cam was bridged at Cambridge, Grantchester, with its two fords, lay on a busy east–west route. By the time of *Domesday* its land was in the hands of six nobles, by far the two largest holdings belonging to Count Eustace and Robert Fafiton. Each of these held equal areas of land and each owned a mill, of which there were many along the rivers Cam and Granta in the eleventh century. One difference was that Robert's holding included one-half of the weir at a rent of 500 eels. This form of payment was not at all unusual in Cambridgeshire. The county, and especially the fenland, was alive with eels in 1086. The fishery at Doddington paid 27,150 eels annually. Grantchester's 500 was a peppercorn rent in comparison.

The weir and both the mills are thought to have been where Byron's Pool is today. (The young Lord Byron had discovered the delights of Grantchester a century before Brooke, when he was an undergraduate at Cambridge.)

Until the learned men of Cambridge began to appreciate the countryside in the nineteenth century, Grantchester remained a rural backwater. Its population in 1801 was 294, almost certainly smaller than that of *Domesday's* time. An ordinance of 1802 forbade the owners of hogs to let their animals roam the street, but in spite of such attempts at modernization, it was not until 1834 that the main road to Cambridge was suitable for wheeled vehicles. Queen Elizabeth, it is true, had passed through the village in 1564, but on horseback, not in a coach.

'It does not appear that there have been any celebrated persons who have lived or been born here,' lamented a nineteenth-century local historian. That was before the doomed and handsome Rupert Brooke moved to Grantchester in 1909. Brooke's nostalgic celebration of his adopted home has made the village a symbol of a lost, innocent England. He himself is ironically celebrated in Grantchester's most unattractive building: a public house called the Rupert Brooke.

Guilden Morden

In (GUILDEN) MORDEN *MORDUNE* Picot [of Cambridge] holds 3 1/2 hides. Land for 7 ploughs. In lordship 1 hide; 1 plough there; another possible. 8 villagers with 11 smallholders and 18 cottagers have 3 1/2 ploughs; [another] 1 1/2 possible. 1 mill at 4s; meadow for 7 ploughs; pasture for the village livestock. In total, value £6 10s; when acquired £8; before 1066 £10.

Guilden Morden lies in the extreme south-west corner of Cambridgeshire, a mile from the borders of both Hertfordshire and Bedfordshire. It is a plain, shapeless village that halfheartedly straggles into the surrounding farmland. A few old houses near the centre help create a sense of community, but the scene here is dominated by the splendid parish church. St Mary's has a great square tower with a steep lead spire and a one-armed clock that stubbornly records the hours. The exterior is mostly fifteenth century; inside is the simpler style of a century or more earlier. It has a large, well-swept graveyard with a spare feeling about it, as if there were not yet enough occupants.

Domesday includes four separate entries for Guilden Morden, referring to it at one point as 'the other Morden' to distinguish it from Steeple Morden a mile to the south. By far the biggest landholder was Picot, the harsh and unpopular Sheriff of Cambridge. His estate, like nearly a third of those in the county, showed signs of having deteriorated during the 20 years since the Conquest, for although there was enough farmland for seven ploughs, only four and a half actually existed. And the value of the land reflects the same picture – from £10 to £8 to the £6 10s of 1086.

As if malignly inspired by this first public record, early accounts of Guilden Morden are a history of poverty and decay. One thirteenth-century vicar, Luke d'Abington, spent a lifetime arguing for an increase in his tiny income. But even when the archbishop interceded on his behalf, a frugal pope stepped in and crushed the rebellion. Poor Luke was buried in unconsecrated ground and only reinstated when his executors begged forgiveness of their overlords at the priory and convent of Barnwell.

More general deprivation awaited the village fifty years later. A survey of 1342 reported that 5000 acres of farmland lay unused in Cambridgeshire, including 'nearly the whole' of Guilden Morden. And in 1562 the church was reported to be in a derelict state, the glass completely broken and the chancel falling down.

Modern Guilden Morden has fully recovered from its medieval depression. The church of St Mary's, glazed and repaired, rises above a sea of prosperous farmland, where scarcely half an acre now remains unploughed.

Burwell

The Abbot of Ramsey holds BURWELL *BUREWELLE.* 10 hides and 1 virgate. Land for 16 ploughs. In lordship 3 hides and 40 acres; 4 ploughs there. 42½ villagers with 12 ploughs. 8 slaves; meadow for 10 ploughs; pasture for the village livestock; 2 mills at 6s 8d. The total value is and was £16; before 1066 £20. This manor lies and always lay in the lordship of St Benedict's Church.

Burwell is an attractive village four miles northwest of Newmarket. A number of distinguished buildings along its two main streets reflect a prosperous agricultural history, and its bright, graceful church has been called by Nikolaus Pevsner 'the most perfect example in the county of the Perpendicular ideal of the glasshouse'.

In the *Domesday* period Burwell was a coastal town – not on the coast of the sea, but on the edge of the marshy fenland that covered northern Cambridgeshire. Three-quarters of Burwell's land was owned by the Abbot of Ramsey. The village was prosperous then too. With 16 ploughs, the abbot apparently was able to use all his arable land, unlike owners of many other villages in Cambridgeshire. And four mills, two held by the abbot, two by Count Alan (another of Burwell's four landholders), made Burwell more than self-sufficient in the production of flour. (The half-villager who lived in the abbot's holding possibly served two masters, and was not a mere fragment.)

This early picture of Burwell is deceptively peaceful. Just 15 years before the *Domesday* survey, the village had been in the front line of Norman attempts to suppress Hereward the Wake, England's most successful rebel against William the Conqueror. Hereward used the Isle of Ely as his fortress and the fenland as his moat, emerging in sudden raids on the southern uplands. In the winter of 1070–71, according to the *Gesta Herewardi*, his men 'set fire to the town of Burwell and inflicted mischief in all directions'. Hereward was betrayed and defeated, but Burwell was not left in peace for long. In 1143 Geoffrey de Mandeville rebelled against King Stephen and also used the fenland as the base for a guerilla campaign. A year later, while besieging Burwell Castle, he removed his helmet and was shot in the head by an arrow. A grassy, rectangular ditch, to the west of the church, is all that remains of Burwell Castle.

Mayhem in more recent times occurred in 1727, when a barn burned down during the performance of a puppet show. Crushed against the tiny door and then engulfed by flaming thatch, more than 80 local people, many of them children, died in the blaze. 'In the morning what an hideous view of sculls, bones, carnage, etc...' wrote Thomas Gibbons D.D. in 1769. He concluded that puppet shows were 'an offence against God' and 'that if the persons that perished had not been sinners, they had not been sufferers'. A small memorial stone, decorated with a flaming heart, marks the spot where 78 of those sinners lie buried in Burwell churchyard.

BURWELL: *78 people who died in a fire in 1727 are buried in its churchyard.*

Cambridgeshire Gazetteer
Each entry starts with the modern place-name in **bold** type. The *Domesday* information that follows is in *italic* type, beginning with the name or names by which the place was known in 1086. The main landholders and undertenants follow, separated with semi-colons if a place was divided into more than one holding. More general information, including examples of dues such as eels rendered by tenants, completes the *Domesday* part of the entry. The modern or post-Domesday section is in normal type. represents a village, a small village or hamlet.

Abington *Abintone: Picot from the king; Count Alan; Aubrey de Vere and Firmatus from him. 2 mills.* Now 2 villages, Great Abington and Little Abington, on either side of Abington Hall Park.

Abington Pigotts *Abintone: King's land and Alwin Cock from the king; Hugh from Bishop of Winchester; Earl Roger; 2 men-at-arms from Hardwin of Scales; Picot of Cambridge.* Down Hall with moat and 15th-century gatehouse; 17th-century Manor Farm.

Arrington *Ernington: Earl Roger; Fulkwy from Count Alan.*

Ashley *Esselie: Evrard from Aubrey de Vere.*

Babraham *Badburgh/ Badbur(g)ham: Picot from the king; Hardwin from Abbot of Ely; Brian Ralph from Count Alan; Picot from Eudo FitzHubert; Hardwin of Scales and Durand from him; Firmatus from Aubrey de Vere; Robert Fafiton; Countess Judith.* 18th-century alms houses. 19th-century Babraham Hall is used by the Institute of Animal Physiology.

Badlingham *Bellingeham: Ordmer from Count Alan. 2 mills.* Badlingham Manor.

Balsham *Beles(s)ham: Abbot of Ely and Hardwin from him; Aelmer from Count Alan; Hardwin of Scales. Mill.*

Barham *Bercheham: A freeman from Abbot of Ely; Ansketel, Morin and a freeman from Count Alan. 2 mills.* Barham Hall.

Barrington *Barenton(e): Chatteris Church; Picot from Count Alan; Walter from Walter Giffard; Robert Gernon; Ralph from Picot of Cambridge. 2½ mills.* On the River Cam (also known as the River Rhee).

Barton *Bertone: Robert from Count of Mortain; Humphrey from Guy de Raimbeaucourt; William of Keynes.* Old and modern houses. The radio telescopes used by the University of Cambridge are to the south.

Bassingbourn *Basingborne: Bishop of Winchester; Count Alan; Leofing from Hardwin of Scales. 4 mills.*

Bottisham *Bodichessham: Walter Giffard, formerly Earl Harold. 4 mills. 400 eels.*

Bourn *Brone/Bruna/Brune: Ramsey church; Aelmer from Count Alan; Picot of Cambridge; Peter de Valognes.* Bourn Mill, the oldest-surviving postmill in the country (1636), is in working order.

Boxworth *Bochesuuorde: Ramsey church; 2 freemen from Count Alan; Picot from Robert Gernon; 6 freemen from Gilbert de Ghent; Payne from Hardwin of Scales.*

Burrough Green *Burch: Count Alan. Park for woodland beasts.* Large green; Tudor Burrough Green Hall.

Burwell *Burewelle/Buruuella/e:* See page 46.

Caldecote *Caldecote: Aelmer from Count Alan; 2 men-at-arms from Hardwin of Scales; David d'Argenton.* Straggling.

Cambridge *Grante/ Grentebridge: Count Alan; Count of Mortain from Judicael; Ralph Banks; Roger, Bishop Remigius's man; Erchenger; Picot of Cambridge. Castle, 5 mills.* Famous university city on the River Cam; Peterhouse, its oldest college, was founded in 1280. The Romans and Saxons had settlements here. The tower of St Benets Church is Saxon. Fine old buildings, museums and churches.

Carlton *Carle(n)tone: Wymarc from Count Alan; Walter de Grandcourt and the Abbot of Cluny from William de Warenne; 2 men-at-arms from Hardwin of Scales; Countess Judith, formerly Earl Harold.* Scattered.

Castle Camps *Canpas: Thurstan from Robert Gernon, Aubrey de Vere.* 2 villages, with Shudy Camps; some earthworks remain from de Vere's castle.

Caxton *Caustone: Hardwin of Scales.* On Roman Ermine Street; once a coaching village – 2 houses were coaching inns in Tudor times. A restored gibbet stands to the north.

Chatteris *Cetriz: Abbot of Ely before and after 1066; Ramsey Church. Fisheries (1500 eels).* Small fenland town, site of a pre-Conquest Benedictine monastery which was dissolved in 1538; a few stones remain.

Cherry Hinton *Hintone: Count Alan. 4 mills.* Suburb of Cambridge. The War Ditches are the remains of an Iron Age encampment where a massacre took place.

Chesterton *Cestretone: King's land. 1000 eels, honey, corn, malt.* Factory suburb of Cambridge.

Cheveley *Chavelai: King's land; Enisant from Count Alan. Honey, corn, malt.* Surrounded by Newmarket's stud farms.

Childerley *Cilderlai/Cildrelai: Bishop of Lincoln; Robert from Picot of Cambridge; Picot from Countess Judith.* Childerley Hall (now in Dry Drayton village) where Charles I was held for 14 days in 1647.

Chippenham *Chipeham: Geoffrey de Mandeville; fish pond.* Near one of the few undrained fens.

Chishill *Chishella/helle: Guy and Anselm from Count Eustace; Richard from William de Warenne; Roger d'Auberville; William Cardon from Geoffrey de Mandeville (who claimed back the land).* Now a village, Great Chishill, and Little Chishill, a small village.

Clopton *Cloptune:* Lost.

Comberton *Bertone: Kings land; 2 men from Picot of Cambridge; William of Keynes; Erchenger the baker.* 16th-, 17th- and 18th-century houses, thatched cottages and 2 dovecotes (now cottages); site of a Roman villa.

Conington *Con/Cunitone: Picot from Robert Gernon; 8 freemen from Gilbert de Ghent; Payne from Hardwin of Scales.* 17th-century Conington Hall.

Cottenham *Coteham: Abbot of Ely before and after 1066; Crowland Church; Roger from Picot of Cambridge; Picot from Church of Ely and from Church of St Guthlac. 1000 eels.* Many of Samuel Pepys' relatives lived here. A tower windmill is now a water tower.

Croxton *Crochestone: Aethelwulf from Hardwin of Scales; David d'Argenton. 500 eels.* In Croxton Park, which has a lake and Georgian house.

Croydon *Crauuedene: Earl Roger; Aelmer and Fulkwy from Count Alan; Humphrey from Eudo FitzHubert; 2 men-at-arms from Hardwin of Scales; Ansketel and Alfred from Picot of Cambridge.* Croydon Wilds Wood is famous for birds and butterflies.

Doddington *Dodinton: Abbot of Ely. Fisheries (27,150 eels).* On a large fen 'island'. It was the county's largest parish in medieval times and site of the Bishop of Ely's palace.

Downham *Duneham: Abbot of Ely. Fisheries (300 eels).* On a fen 'island'. Remains of the 15th-century palace of the bishops of Ely are now the outbuildings of Tower Farm.

Dry Drayton *Draitone: Crowland Church; monks of Swavesey from Count Alan; Payne from Hardwin of Scales; Asgot from Robert Fafiton; Roger from Countess Judith. Marsh.* Childerley Hall (see Childerley, below left).

Dullingham *Dulingham/ Dulling(e)ham: St Wandrille's; 2 men-at-arms from Count Alan; Hardwin of Scales; Roger from Picot of Cambridge.*

Duxford *Dochesuuorde/ Dodesuuorde: Gerard from Count Alan; Arnulf and Guy from Count Eustace; Robert de Tosny; Robert Gernon; Payne from Hardwin of Scales. 4 mills.* Chemical works.

East Hatley *Hatelai: Aelmer from Count Alan; Humphrey from Eudo FitzHubert; Picot of Cambridge.*

Elsworth *Elesuuorde: Ramsey Church; 2 freemen from Gilbert de Ghent; Payne from Hardwin of Scales.* Tudor Low Farm, formerly the Guildhall.

Eltisley *Hecteslei: Canons of Bayeux.* Thatched and timbered houses. A spring, St Pandiana's Well, is called after an Irish king's daughter who came to the pre-Conquest nunnery here.

Ely *Ely/i: Abbot of Ely. Fisheries, vines.* Small cathedral city on high fenland. The Saxons took their last stand against the Normans here. Etheldreda, daughter of the king of the East Angles, founded a monastery here in 673; sacked by the Danes in 870, it was rebuilt in the 12th century as an abbey and made a cathedral when the diocese of Ely was created in 1109. The famous octagonal tower was completed in 1342.

Eversden *Au(e)resdone: Robert and 2 Englishmen from Count Alan; Durand from Hardwin of Scales; Hugh de Bernières; Picot and Humphrey from Guy de Raimbeaucourt.* Now 2 small villages, Great and Little Eversden.

Fen Drayton *Draitone: 2 freemen from the king before and after 1066; Ramsey Church; 5 freemen from Count Alan (they held it from Edeva before 1066); Gilbert de Ghent; Roger from Picot of Cambridge.* Market-gardening. An 18th-century cottage with a Dutch inscription, 'Nothing Without Labour' is said to be home of Cornelius Vermuyden, famous fen drainer.

Fordham *Fordeham/Forham: Kings land and Bruman from the king; Wymarc from Count Alan. 2 mills. Honey, corn, malt.* On the River Snail; watermill.

Fowlmere *Fugelesmara/ Fuglemære: 2 men-at-arms from Count Alan; Robert Gernon. Mill.* Small ring of earthworks, Round Moats.

Foxton *Foxetune: Chatteris Church before and after 1066; Sigar from Geoffrey de Mandeville; Robert Gernon who appropriated ½ mill from Geoffrey. Mill.* Thatched houses.

Fulbourn *Fuleberne: Picot of Cambridge; Abbot of Ely; Count Alan; Geoffrey de Mandeville; John FitzWaleran. Mill.* Large. The sails of its 200-year-old smock mill are still intact.

Gamlingay *Gamelinge(i): Eudo FitzHubert; Ranulf brother of Ilger; 2 men from Robert Fafiton.* 17th-century almshouses.

Girton *Gretone: Morin from Count of Mortain; Ramsey Church; William from Picot of Cambridge.* Adjoins Girton College, the first Cambridge women's college (1873).

Grantchester *Granteseta/e: See page 45.*

Graveley *Gravelei: Ramsey Church.*

Guilden Morden *(Alia) Mordune:* See page 45.

Haddenham *Hadreham: 7 freemen from Abbot of Ely.* On a high fen 'island', 116 ft above sea-level.

Hainey *Haneia: Abbot of Ely.* Now Henny Farm.

Hardwick *Harduic: Abbot of Ely and Ralph from him.*

Harlton *Herletone: Walter FitzAubrey from Walter Giffard; Sigfrid from Picot of Cambridge. ½ mill. 100 eels.* Some recent development.

Harston *Herlestone: Picot of Cambridge from Abbot of Ely; Odo from Count Alan; Ranulf from Robert Gernon; Picot of Cambridge. Mill.* On the Upper Cam. A water mill is on the site of one from the 13th century.

Haslingfield *Haslingefeld(e): Kings land; Count Alan and Robert from him; Roger from Geoffrey de Mandeville; Sigfrid from Picot of Cambridge. Mill. Honey, corn, malt.* Beneath 215 ft high Chapel Hill, a medieval shrine.

Hatley St George *Hatelai: Aelmer from Count Alan; Eudo FitzHubert; Picot of Cambridge and Roger from him.* Hatley Park.

Hauxton *Hauochestone/tun: Abbot of Ely before and after 1066; Hardwin of Scales. 3 mills.*

Heydon *Haidenam: St Ethelreda's, Ely; Robert FitzRozelin. 10 bee-hives.*

Hildersham *Hildricesham: Aubrey de Vere. Mill.* Sail-less windmill nearby.

Hill Row *Helle: Abbot of Ely.* Near Haddenham.

Hinxton *Hestitone/Histetone: Kings land; Robert from Bishop of Lincoln; Durand from Hardwin of Scales; Picot of Cambridge. 3 mills.* Thatched and timber-framed houses.

Histon *Histone: Bishop of Lincoln and Picot from him; Abbot of Ely; Morin from Count of Mortain.* On the outskirts of Cambridge; old and new housing; factory.

Horningsea *Horningesie: Abbot of Ely before and after 1066. Mill. 1000 eels.* On a fen 'island'.

Horseheath *Horsei: Count Alan and Alwin from him; Wulfeva from Richard FitzGilbert; 5 villagers from Hardwin of Scales; Norman from Aubrey de Vere.* Near the Roman Via Devana.

Ickleton *Ichelintone/ Inchelintone: Count Eustace; Durand from Hardwin of Scales. 2 mills.* On the Roman Icknield Way; site of a Roman villa and basilica.

Impington *Epintone: Abbot of Ely before and after 1066; Walter from Picot of Cambridge.* Home of Samuel Pepys. The Village College, designed by Walter Gropius and Maxwell Fry, was opened in 1938.

Isleham *Gisleham: Kings land; Bishop of Rochester from Archbishop Lanfranc; Geoffrey from Count Alan; Hugh de Port. 4 mills. 1550 eels, honey, corn, malt.* Old windmill. The chapel of Isleham Priory, founded in the 11th century and dissolved in the 15th, remains.

Kennett *Chenet: Nicholas from William de Warenne. Mill.*

Kingston *Chingestone: Kings land; Earl Roger; Aelmer from Count Alan; Humphrey from Eudo FitzHubert; 2 men-at-arms and Robert the Bald from Hardwin of Scales; Ralph from Picot of Cambridge.* Market town in the Middle Ages.

Kirtling *Chertelinge: Countess Judith, formerly Earl Harold. Fishery (5500 eels), park for woodland beasts.* Scattered; Tudor gatehouse.

Knapwell *Chenepwelle: Abbot of Ely before and after 1066.* Its Red Well, so called because of the red-tinged water (due to iron), was the scene of 'miracles'.

Landbeach *Bece/Bech: Walter from Count Alan; Osmund from Picot of Cambridge. 1000 eels.*

Linden End *Lindone:* Lost.

Linton *Lintone: Count Alan. 2 mills.* Georgian and Queen Anne high street; windmill.

Litlington *Lidlin(g)tone/ Li(d)tingtone: William the Chamberlain and Otto the Goldsmith from the king; Aethelwulf from Hardwin of Scales.* A 30-room Romano-British house was found here in 1936.

Little Gransden *Gra(n)tedene: Abbot of Ely.*

Little Linton *Alia Lintone: Count Alan. Mill.* Small Tudor grange.

Littleport *Litelport: Abbot of Ely. Fisheries (17,000 eels).* Small town; light industry.

Little Thetford *Liteltedford: Abbot of Ely. Fisheries (3250 eels).*

Lolworth *Lolesuuorde: Robert from Picot of Cambridge. Mill.*

Longstanton *Stantone/tune: Picot from Count Alan; Hugh from Gilbert FitzThorold; Guy from Picot of Cambridge; William FitzAnsculf.* Formerly 2 villages; now 2 churches and an RAF base.

Longstowe *Stou: Guy from Ramsey Church; Aelmer from Count Alan; man-at-arms and 2 Englishmen from Hardwin of Scales.*

Madingley *Mading(e)lei: Picot from Bishop of Lincoln; Picot of Cambridge.* Thatched houses; on the edge of Madingley Hall park. Edward VII lodged in the Tudor hall when he was a Cambridge undergraduate.

March *Mercha/Merche: Abbot of Ely; St Edmund's.* A market town with large railway marshalling yard, it was a hamlet until the 19th century and the coming of the railway.

Melbourn *Melleborne/burne: Abbot of Ely; Abbot of St Evroul from Earl Roger; Colswein from Count Alan; Durand from Hardwin of Scales. Mill.* Surrounded by orchards; several moated houses.

Meldreth *Melrede: Abbot of Ely and Hardwin and Guy de Raimbeaucourt from him; Abbot of St Evroult from Earl Roger; Colswein from Count Alan; Hardwin of Scales and Hugh from him; Guy de Raimbeaucourt. 7½ mills, monastery.* Old stocks and whipping post.

Milton *Middletone: Ralph from Picot of Cambridge. 650 eels.* On the River Cam, close to Cambridge.

Oakington *Hochinton(e): Alfgeat the priest from Abbot of Ely before and after 1066; Abbot of Crowland; 3 men-at-arms from Picot of Cambridge; Roger from Countess Judith; the wife of Boselin de Dives.*

Orwell *Ord(e)uuelle/ Ore(d)uuelle: Chatteris nunnery before and after 1066; Earl Roger; Picot from Count Alan; Walter from Walter Giffard; Robert Gernon; Sigar from Geoffrey de Mandeville; Durand from Hardwin of Scales; Ralph from Guy de Raimbeaucourt. 2 mills.*

Over *Oure: Ramsey Church; Chatteris nunnery before and after 1066; Ralph from Hardwin of Scales; Sawin from Picot of Cambridge; Roger from Countess Judith.* 18th-century houses.

Pampisford *Pampesuuorde: Abbot of Ely and Hardwin from him; 2 men-at-arms from Count Alan; Pirot from Eudo FitzHubert; Hardwin of Scales; Ralph from Picot of Cambridge; a priest from Countess Judith. Mill.* Thatched cottages. Brent Ditch was a 4th-century rampart across the Roman Icknield Way.

Papworth *Papeuuorde/ Papeworde: Count Alan; William from Richard FitzGilbert; Gilbert de Ghent; Payne from Hardwin of Scales; Eustace of Huntingdon and Walter and Ordnoth, the pre-Conquest holder, from him; Picot of Cambridge.* Now 2 villages, Papworth Everard and Papworth St Agnes. Sir Thomas Malory, author of *Morte d'Arthur*, died in St Agnes in the 15th century.

Quy *Coeia: Picot from Abbot of Ely; Reginald from Aubrey de Vere; Picot of Cambridge. 3 mills.* Water mill on Quy Water. A mid-19th century hall stands on the site of the old village. The new village is Stow-cum-Quy.

Rampton *Rantone: Roger from Picot of Cambridge.*

Sawston *Salsiton(e): Abbot of Grestain from Count of Mortain; Roger from Geoffrey de Mandeville; Picot from Eudo FitzHubert. 4 mills.* Large; paper mills; leather industry. Tudor Sawston Hall, now a conference centre, was burnt down by the Protestants in 1553 because the owner had sheltered Mary Tudor, but it was subsequently rebuilt.

Saxon Street *Sextone: Aubrey de Vere.* Moated hall.

Shelford *Escelford(e)/Scelfort: Peter de Valognes from the king, formerly Earl Harold; Abbot of Ely and Hardwin and 7 freemen from him; Hardwin from Count Alan; Hardwin of Scales. 2 mills, monastery.* Now 2 villages, Great Shelford, joined to Stapleford, and Little Shelford, across the River Granta.

Shepreth *Escrepid(e): Hardwin of Scales; Chatteris nunnery; Reginald from Count Alan; Sigar from Geoffrey de Mandeville; Hardwin of Scales and Hugh from him. 4 mills.* Scattered; 3 manor houses; 2 mills (one a house).

Shingay *Scelgei: Earl Roger. Mill.*

Shudy Camps: See Castle Camps.

Silverley *Severlai:* Lost.

Snailwell *Snellewelle: Hugh de Port from Bishop of Bayeux.* The 'well' is the source of the River Snail.

Soham *Saham: Kings land; Abbot of Ely; St Edmund's; Adestan from Count Alan. 2 mills, Fisheries (3500 eels). Corn, malt, honey, fishing net.* Small town; 2 windmills. The mere is now orchards. A cathedral built in the 7th century was destroyed by the Danes in the 9th.

Stapleford *Stapleforde: Abbot of Ely.* Large; mostly modern houses. Joined to Great Shelford.

Steeple Morden *Mordune: Bishop of Winchester; Earl Roger; Hardwin of Scales. 5 mills.* Scattered; windmill.

Stetchworth *Sti(ui)cesuuorde/ Stuuicesworde: Abbot of Ely and Hardwin of Scales from him; Count Alan; Hardwin of Scales.* Once a town.

Stretham *Stradham: Abbot of Ely. Fisheries.* Large; site of a Roman villa.

Stuntney *Stuntenei: Abbot of Ely. Fisheries (24,000 eels).* Overlooks a main road built on a Bronze Age causeway. Cromwell's mother lived at the 17th-century Old Hall.

Sutton *Sudtone: Abbot of Ely. Fisheries.* Large. Burystead Farm, partly 14th century, is said to have been a priory.

Swaffham *Suaf(h)am: Abbot of Ely and Hardwin from him; Geoffrey and 3 men-at-arms from Count Alan; Hugh from Walter Giffard; Hardwin of Scales; Aubrey de Vere. 4 mills. 300 eels.* Now 2 villages, Swaffham Bulbeck with an 18th-century Abbey House containing the remains of a 12th-century nunnery, and Swaffham Prior with 2 derelict windmills.

Swavesey *Suavesy(e): Count Alan; Picot from Robert Gernon; Gilbert de Ghent. Mill, fisheries (3750 eels). 225 eels.* Thatched cottages.

Tadlow *Tadelai: Picot of Cambridge; Picot from Countess Judith; Azelina wife of Ralph Tailbois. Mill.*

Teversham *Teuersham/ Teuresham: Abbot of Ely; Count Alan and Robert from him; John FitzWaleran.*

Thriplow *Trepeslai/au: Abbot of Ely and Hardwin of Scales from him; Sigar from Geoffrey de Mandeville; Hardwin of Scales.* Near a spring, Nine Holes.

Toft *Tofth: Count Alan; 2 men-at-arms from Picot of Cambridge; Erchenger the baker.*

Trumpington *Trumpinton(e): Arnulf d'Ardres from Count Eustace; William de Warenne; Hervey from Picot of Cambridge; Robert Fafiton; Godlamb from Countess Judith. Mill.* Large; part of Cambridge.

Waterbeach *Vtbech: Mucel from Picot of Cambridge; 2 of the king's carpenters.* Large. Denny Abbey, originally a Benedictine monastery, later housed the Knights Templar; after them, Franciscan nuns.

Wendy *Wandei/Wandrie: Odo from Count Alan; Alfred from Hardwin of Scales. 2 mills.*

Wentworth *Winteworde: Abbot of Ely.*

Westley Waterless *Weslai: Abbot of Ely; 2 men-at-arms from Count Alan; Hardwin of Scales; Countess Judith.*

Weston Colville *Westone: Count Alan and Wymarc from him; William de Warenne and Walter from him; Hardwin of Scales and Durand from him.* Mostly modern.

Westwick *Westuuiche: Odo from Picot of Cambridge; Robert from David d'Argenton.* Westwick Hall.

West Wickham *Wicheham: Abbot of Ely; Count Alan; Lambert from William de Warenne; Wulfeva from Richard FitzGilbert; Hardwin of Scales.* Thatched barns.

SWAFFHAM PRIOR: *2 churches in one churchyard; the ruined tower is Norman and Early English.*

West Wratting *Waratinge: Abbot of Ely and Hardwin of Scales from him; Aelmer from Count Alan; Lambert from William de Warenne; Hardwin of Scales.*

Whaddon *Wadone/Wadune: Hardwin of Scales from Abbot of Ely; Colswein and Ralph from Count Alan; Hardwin from Richard FitzGilbert; Hardwin of Scales.* Now Whaddon Gap barracks; the village has moved to the north-east.

Whittlesey *Witesie: Abbot of Ely; Thorney Church. Weir.* Small brickmaking town on a fen 'island'.

Whittlesford *Witelesforde: Gerard from Count Alan; Hardwin of Scales; Countess Judith. 3 mills.* Large green; 18th-century mill house, now an extension of the Fitzwilliam Museum, Cambridge.

Whitwell *Watuuelle/Witeuuella: Earl Roger; Fulkwy from Count Alan; Robert the Bald from Hardwin of Scales; Ralph from Picot of Cambridge.* Whitwell Farm.

Wicken *Wicha: Count Alan. 3 mills. 4250 eels, 3 fishing nets.* Restored windmill. Wicken Fen is still natural fenland.

Wilbraham *Wiborgham/ Witborham: Kings land; Odo from Count Alan; Aubrey de Vere. 3 mills. Honey, corn, malt.* Now 2 villages, Great and Little Wilbraham; a former windmill is now a house.

Wilburton *Wilbertone: Abbot of Ely.* Timber-framed houses.

Willingham *Wiuelingham: Abbot of Ely; a freeman from Count Alan; Roger from Picot of Cambridge.* Large; 2 derelict windmills. Belsar Hill is a Bronze Age fort.

Wimpole *Winepol/e: Count Alan; Humphrey from Eudo FitzHubert.* Large stately home, Wimpole Hall (1640), with a park and folly.

Wisbech *Wisbece: Abbot of Ely and 2 fishermen from him; St Edmund's; Ramsey church; Crowland church; William de Warenne. Fisheries (3750 eels), vines.* Important town, centre for the fen country's fruit and flower industry; museum on the site of Wisbech Castle.

Witcham *Wiceham: Abbot of Ely.*

Witchford *Wiceford(e): Abbot of Ely.* Thurstan, Ely's last Saxon abbot, was born here, and the monks of Ely met the Conqueror here to make their submission.

Woodditton *Ditone: William de Noyers from the king; Wighen from Count Alan.* At one end of the Devil's Dyke ditch and bank across the Roman Icknield Way.

Wratworth *Warateuuorde/ Werateuuorde.* Lost.

Cheshire

At the time of Domesday *Cheshire was divided between two great landowners, the Bishop of Chester and Hugh d'Avranches, Earl of Chester. Earl Hugh, had two nicknames, 'the Wolf', for his ferocity against the Welsh, and 'the Fat', for his obesity. Bishop and earl presided over a long, densely wooded county which then included a narrow coastal strip of North Wales. Salt mining was Cheshire's principal industry.*

It was a land still partly devastated by warfare. Much of eastern Cheshire, an unproductive and sparsely populated area at the best of times, lay waste. Wasta est *is how* Domesday *describes such barren holdings. Conditions were better in the fertile west, but the city of Chester, Cheshire's only major town, contained many empty houses. It is tempting to blame King William for all this destruction. He marched through the region in 1069–70, bent upon subduing the rebellious north. But* Domesday *makes clear in a number of cases that some damage had been done even before the Normans arrived.* Wastam invenit, *'found waste', suggests that William's army was not the first at the scene, but that there had already been raiding and possibly outright invasion by the northern Welsh.*

There were indeed frequent changes of boundary between Wales and Cheshire during the eleventh century, and many places that are now in Wales were in Cheshire at the time of Domesday. *Hawarden, one of our main entries, is an example. Other identified settlements, now in Wales, are listed at the end of the gazetteer.*

Sandbach

[Bigot de Loges holds] SANDBACH *SANBEC.* Dunning held it; he was free. 1 hide paying tax; 1½ virgates likewise paying tax. Land for 2 ploughs. 1 Frenchman with ½ plough and 3 slaves. 2 villagers with ½ plough. A priest and a church. Woodland ½ league long and 40 perches wide. Value before 1066, 4s; now 8s.

There has been a market in Sandbach every Thursday since 1578, and its popularity shows no sign of diminishing. The two Saxon crosses in the market square rise above the parked cars of shoppers with an embattled dignity. They have survived worse than this since they were erected in the ninth century.

Sandbach has two entries in *Domesday*. Most of the land was held from Earl Hugh of Chester by Bigot de Loges, but another 2½ virgates formed part of a group of six manors about which *Domesday* merely records, 'It was and is all waste.' Although no date is given for the wasting, the implication is that William the Conqueror passed through in 1070, destroying part of Sandbach. The major holding gives an apparently contradictory picture. On the one hand there was land here for two ploughs, but only one existed, suggesting that half the arable land was unused. On the other, the total value had doubled in 20 years, from 4s to 8s. Perhaps the wasting occurred before William headed north, and Sandbach had prospered and not declined under Norman rule.

There was a church here in pre-Conquest days. The present building, St Mary's, is a fine Victorian reconstruction in late medieval style with little that dates from before the seventeenth century. The market crosses make up for any lack of antiquity in the church. It is remarkable that they have survived, for they were torn down in the seventeenth century, presumably by zealous puritans, who thought them idolatrous. Early in the nineteenth century fragments of the broken crosses were retrieved from throughout the town. One piece had been buried in a garden, one had served as a doorstep, another had formed part of the town well. These bits and pieces were painstakingly reassembled in 1816. It is said that if you stand on your head and look at the crosses, an inscription becomes legible, revealing the whereabouts of a vast treasure.

Neston

[William FitzNigel holds] NESTON *NESTONE.* Arni held it; he was a free man. 2 parts of 2 hides paying tax. Land for 4 ploughs. In lordship 2 ploughs; 1 slave. A priest, 4 villagers and 2 smallholders have 3 ploughs. Value before 1066, 20s; later as much; now 25s.

The Wirral is a square-nosed peninsula about fifteen miles long by six miles wide, which juts north-west into the Irish Sea between the estuaries of the Mersey and the Dee. Across the water on one side is Liverpool; on the other, the hills of Wales. Wallasey, Birkenhead and Ellesmere Port stretch along the Mersey side, together forming a city to rival Liverpool. On the Dee side there are still country towns, part village, part suburb, but closer in spirit to Chester than to Liverpool. One of the pleasantest is Neston.

Domesday suggests that Neston was a well-to-do settlement in 1086. It was divided into two separate holdings; St Werburgh's Church in Chester owned one ploughland, but the major portion, held by William FitzNigel from Earl Hugh, included four ploughlands and five teams to plough them. The exact significance of this imbalance is unclear, but it implies prosperity. The great majority of Cheshire holdings had fewer ploughs than ploughlands. In only 30, all in the west of the county, were there equal numbers of teams and lands, and in only five, including Neston, did the teams outnumber the lands. Added to this, the value of the major Neston holding had increased from 20s to 25s. It appears that Neston, along with most of the Wirral, had escaped both the revenge of King William's army and the fierce raids of their neighbours, the Welsh.

Neston's prosperity did not end in the eleventh century. When the port of Chester silted up in the Middle Ages, Neston became the principal point of departure for Ireland. John Wesley made the crossing more than 40 times and Handel, according to a disputed tradition, sailed from here to Ireland with the unperformed *Messiah* under his arm. But the River Dee was as faithless to Neston as it had been to Chester. As the relentless sand settled around the quay in the eighteenth century, the once thriving port found a new, brief life as a seaside resort. Young Emma Hart (later to become Lady Hamilton, Admiral Nelson's extravagant mistress) sought a cure for a skin complaint here, but found 2d for a bathing dress 'a great expense'.

Boats and bathers today go elsewhere. What was once the most fashionable coastal resort in the north of England is now a quiet and landlocked village.

Knutsford

[William FitzNigel holds] KNUTSFORD *CUNETESFORD.* Egbrand, who also held as a free man, holds from him. ½ hide paying tax. Land for 2 ploughs. It was and is waste. Woodland ½ league long and 2 acres wide. The value was 10s.

There is an apocryphal story that, in the eleventh century, King Canute (Cnut) forded a little stream in east-central Cheshire now called the Lily, and that the place where he crossed became known as Cnut's Ford, or Knutsford. Upon reaching the far bank, he sat down, just as a bridal procession was passing, and shook the sand from his shoes. From this coincidence, a quaint tradition developed: to celebrate a marriage the ladies of Knutsford sprinkled red and white sand on their doorsteps and pavements.

Whatever settlement it was that Canute discovered at this crossing seems to have disappeared within the next 50 years. Like several

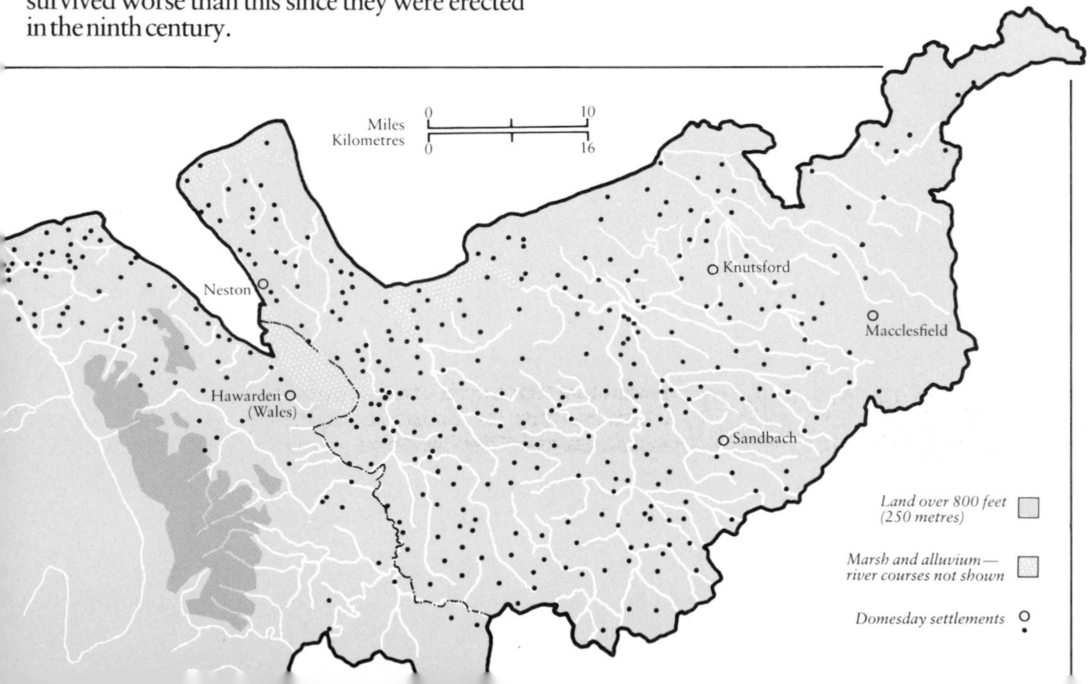

other holdings in this part of Cheshire, Knutsford was apparently deserted at the time of *Domesday*. Neither people nor animals were recorded. 'It was and is waste.' But when exactly had it become 'waste'? Possibly as early as 1070, one more victim of King William's destructive border wars in North Wales.

Knutsford came to life again in the early twelfth century. By the eighteenth century it was the fourth largest town in the county, the 'Metropolis of the Eastern Hundreds'. Yet it remained quietly provincial. It was this Knutsford which Elizabeth Gaskell (1810–65) immortalized in her second novel, *Cranford*, using it as the model for her fictional town, with all its intrigues, gossip and basic good nature. Several local characters were easily identified by contemporary readers.

The twentieth century has left its mark on Knutsford, with plate glass and car parks; and there is much that would surprise Mrs Gaskell, including her own extraordinary Moorish-style monument. But on the whole it is as though she had put a glass dome over Knutsford, for it is today almost as elegantly refined and enclosed as when it served as *Cranford's* prototype.

If Mrs Gaskell's Georgian spirit dominates the town, the legendary past is not entirely forgotten. During its May Day festivities, designs are wrought in multicoloured sand, a stylized memory of the day King Canute shook out his shoes after fording the Lily.

Macclesfield

[Earl Hugh holds] MACCLESFIELD *MACLESFELD*. Earl Edwin held it. 2 hides paying tax. Land for 10 ploughs. In lordship 1 plough; 4 slaves. A mill which serves the hall; woodland 6 leagues long and 4 wide; 7 enclosures; meadow for the oxen. The Third Penny of the Hundred belongs to this manor. Value before 1066, £8; now 20s; it was waste.

It is easy to miss old Macclesfield entirely, for the passing motorist is not encouraged into its narrow, unpredictable streets. It stands on a steep escarpment above the River Bollin, looking east towards the Pennines. The old market square is a hotchpotch of styles. The pretentious Town Hall – suggesting a rejected piece of the Parthenon – faces a brick and glass bank that appears to have been assembled overnight from a kit. 'Ye Old Shop', dated 1897, stands opposite St Michael's Church, which dates from the thirteenth century and which teeters at the top of 108 steep steps. All around is a history lesson in the industrial revolution and the story of a town that grew too quickly.

The English first settled near the site of the old market square in the tenth century and their community prospered: the pre-1066 value of £8 is high, especially for this poor region. But the prosperity seems short-lived, and for once the Normans do not appear to bear the guilt. They found the place waste – *wastam invenit* – and gradually began to reclaim it. Yet by 1086, with a population of about 20, there was still only one plough-team where there was land for ten. One natural asset that had not suffered was the large woodland area. This presumably stretched up into the eastern hills to form part of what was to become Macclesfield Forest, one of medieval England's great hunting reserves.

It was the silk industry that made a sow's ear out of Macclesfield. Silk manufacture had started in the seventeenth century; in 1756, after an energetic businessman named Charles Roe introduced machinery to his factory, mills began to spring up like mushrooms. The population in 1801 was 8743; in 1821 it was twice that, and by mid-century it had nearly doubled again. 'The neighbourhood has been spoiled by manufactures and is no longer fitted to be the residence of a gentleman', complained the Cheshire historian George Ormerod in 1819. Gentlemen are not what they used to be and many choose to live there today, for compared to its huge neighbour, Manchester, Macclesfield is still a pleasant country town.

HAWARDEN: *The circular keep of Hawarden Castle, in the park of its 19th-century successor.*

Hawarden (Wales)

[Earl Hugh holds] HAWARDEN *HAORDINE* in lordship. Earl Edwin held it. 3 hides paying tax. Land for 4½ ploughs. In lordship 2 ploughs; 4 slaves; a church, to which belongs ½ carucate of land. 4 villagers and 6 smallholders with 2 ploughs. Meadow, ½ acre; woodland 2 leagues long and 1 wide. Value 40s. 2 unoccupied dwellings in the City belong to there.

Hawarden lies in Clwyd in North Wales, just across the border from Cheshire. Motorists on the way from Chester to Conwy will scarcely notice this low, dark village. Yet a century ago its name was familiar to much of Britain. Tourists flocked to Hawarden Castle (the nineteenth-century version, not the ruin in the park) as they would to Windsor. And if they were lucky they would catch sight of the Grand Old Man himself, for William Ewart Gladstone, then the resident, did not like to disappoint his public. A wave from 'the greatest Englishman of the century' would send hundreds of tourists home exhilarated by their pilgrimage.

There was life in Hawarden before Mr Gladstone. *Domesday* mentions a church, St Deiniol's, one of only nine recorded for the entire county of Cheshire. It was here, according to a macabre legend, that a figure of the Virgin Mary fell from the roodloft and killed the wife of the castle's governor. The statue was put to trial by jury and condemned to death by drowning, but it floated up the River Dee and was washed ashore at Chester. This was in 946.

At the time of *Domesday*, Hawarden appears to have had a population of 60 to 70, a fair size for this lightly populated strip of North Wales that was then a part of Cheshire. The region's inaccessibility may have preserved it from the wrath of King William, who had laid waste much of the rest of the county in 1070. The number of working ploughs in Hawarden – four, where there was land for four and a half – also suggests that the village had not suffered too badly.

Like many settlements in *Domesday* Cheshire, Hawarden included substantial woodland. There were still plenty of trees in the nineteenth century, and Mr Gladstone took great pleasure in chopping them down. He was felling a tree in 1868 when the telegram arrived asking him to be Prime Minister. 'My mission is to pacify Ireland', he optimistically announced, and continued to chop until the tree had fallen. In the House he proposed Irish Home Rule, a suggestion which was as ruthlessly cut down as were his own trees.

Cheshire Gazetteer
Each entry starts with the modern place-name in **bold** type. The *Domesday* information that follows is in *italic* type, beginning with the name or names by which the place was known in 1086. The landholders and under-tenants are next, separated with semi-colons if the place was divided into more than one holding. In Cheshire, with the exception of land held by the Bishop of Cheshire or St Werburgh's Church, all land was held by Earl Hugh from the king. Similarly, in the Welsh settlements listed in the Cheshire *Domesday Book*, he held from the king all land except any granted to Robert of Rhuddlan. The earl is in the gazetteer only if *Domesday* lists him as tenant-in-chief, or if the under-tenants are his men. More general information completes the *Domesday* part of the entry. The modern or post-Domesday section is in normal type. ▣ represents a village, ⌂ a small village or hamlet.

Places now in Wales are listed at the end of the gazetteer.

ACTON: *Decorated Norman stones in St Mary's church.*

Acton *Acatone/une: William Malbank. Mill, hawk's eyrie; the manor has its assembly in the lord's hall.* ▣ Church with Saxon stonework.

Adlington *Edulvintune: Earl Hugh. 4 hawks' eyries.* ▣ Adlington Hall, *c.*1450.

Alpraham *Alburgham: Gilbert de Venables.* ⌂

Alsager *Eleacier: Earl Hugh.* Town. A mill, farm and hall mark the *Domesday* site on its outskirts.

Alvanley *Elveldelie: Leofric from Earl Hugh.* ▣

Antrobus *Entrebus: Earl Hugh.* ⌂ Antrobus Hall.

Appleton *Apletune: Osbern FitzTezzo.* Now Appleton Thorn village and Appleton Moss, a hamlet nearby.

Ashley *Ascelie: Hamo de Mascy.* ▣ Ashley Hall.

Ashton (near Tarvin) *Estone: Richard de Vernon.* ▣ 2 17th-century halls nearby; Ashton Hayes, a house with its own park.

Aston (near Budworth) *Estone: Payne from William FitzNigel.* Aston Park House.

Aston (near Sutton) *Estone: William from St Werburgh's Church; Odard from William FitzNigel. Mill.* ▣ Aston Lodge; Aston Grange.

Aston (in Newhall) *Estune: William Malbank.* ▣

Aston juxta Mondrum *Estone: William Malbank.* ▣ Aston Hall; Aston New Farm.

Audlem *Aldelime: Richard de Vernon. Hawk's eyrie.* ▣ 14th-century church. Audlem Mill (now a workshop) is on the Shropshire Union Canal.

Austerson *Essetune: William Malbank. Hawk's eyrie.* ⌂ Austerson Old Hall.

Baddiley *Bedelie: William Malbank.* ⌂ Now Baddiley Corner; farm.

Barnston *Bernestone: Ralph from William FitzNigel. 2 mills.* ▣ Manor house; hospital; on the Wirral Peninsula.

Barrow *Bero: William FitzNigel. 2 mills.* ▣ Now Great Barrow; hospital.

Barthomley *Bertemeleu: William Malbank. Hawk's eyrie.* ▣ Scene of a massacre by the Royalists in 1643.

Bartington *Bertintune: Mundret and Wulfgeat from Earl Hugh.* Bartington Hall Farm.

Basford *Berchesford: William Malbank.* Basford Hall.

Batherton *Berdeltune: William Malbank.* Batherton Hall.

Beeston *Buistane: Robert FitzHugh.* ⌂ The ruins of a 13th-century castle built by the Earl of Chester are on Beeston Rock.

Bickerton *Bicretone: Drogo from Robert FitzHugh.* ▣ Maiden Castle, an Iron Age fort.

Bickley *Bichelie: Fulk from Robert FitzHugh.* Now 2 small villages, Bickley Town and Bickley Moss; Bickley Hall Farm.

Blacon *Blachehol: Ranulf Mainwaring. Fishery.* Part of Chester.

Blakenhall *Blachenhale: Gilbert Hunter. Hawk's eyrie.* ⌂ Manor farm.

Bosley *Boselega: Hugh FitzNorman.* ⌂ On Bosley Reservoir.

Bostock *Botestoch: Richard de Vernon.* ▣ Now Bostock Green; Bostock Hall School.

Boughton *Bocstone: St Werburgh's Church.* Boughton Heath, part of Chester.

Bowdon *Bogedone: Hamo de Mascy. Church, mill.* Part of Altrincham and Hale. The church has fragments of Norman stonework.

Bramhall *Bramale: Hamo de Mascy.* On the outskirts of Stockport. The grounds of the old hall are now a museum and park.

Bredbury *Bretberie: Wulfric the pre-Conquest holder, from Richard de Vernon. Hawk's eyrie.* Former cotton town.

All land in Cheshire, with the exception of any held by the Bishop of Chester or St Werburgh's Church, was held by Earl Hugh from the king. He is in the gazetteer only if *Domesday* lists him as tenant-in-chief, or if the under-tenants are his men.

Brereton *Bretone: Gilbert Hunter and 2 of his men from him. Mill.* ▣ Now Brereton Green; 16th-century Brereton Hall.

Bridge Trafford *Tro(s)ford: St Werburgh's Church before and after 1066.* ⌂ Hall on the River Gowy.

Broomhall *Brunhala: William Malbank.* ⌂ Now Broomhall Green.

Broxton *Brosse: Roger and Picot from Robert FitzHugh.* ⌂ Broxton Old Hall.

Buerton (near Audlem) *Burtune: William Malbank. Hawk's eyrie.* ▣ Buerton Hall; Buerton Moss hamlet nearby.

Bunbury *Boleberie: Robert FitzHugh.* ▣ Pleasant; now merging with Lower Bunbury and Bunbury Heath hamlet.

Burton (near Tarvin) *Burtone: Bishop of Chester before and after 1066.* ⌂ Hall.

Burwardsley *Burwardeslei: Humphrey from Robert FitzHugh.* Now 2 villages, Burwardsley and Higher Burwardsley, at the foot of the Peckforton Hills.

Butley *Bote/Butelege: Robert FitzHugh; Wulfric from Earl Hugh.* ▣

Byley *Bevelei: Hugh FitzNorman.* ⌂

Caldecott *Caldecote: Hugh FitzOsbern. ½ fishery.* ⌂ Now Caldecott Green; Caldecott Hall.

Capenhurst *Capeles: David from William FitzNigel.* ▣ Hall.

Capesthorne *Copestor: Earl Hugh.* Capesthorne Hall.

Chapmonswiche *Cepmundewiche:* Lost.

Cheadle *Cedde: Gamel from Earl Hugh, formerly Gamel's father. Hawk's eyrie.* Urban area of Cheadle and Cheadle Hulme.

Cheaveley *Cavelea: St Werburgh's Church. Small boat and net.* Cheaveleyhall Farm, near the River Dee.

Chelford *Celeford: Earl Hugh.* ▣ Village with a Georgian church.

Chester *Cestre: Earl Hugh. The city had been devastated, but by 1086 many houses were rebuilt.* Walled city, once the Roman camp of Deva. A Roman amphitheatre and part of the original ramparts remain. It has medieval galleried streets, Tudor houses, a cathedral and a castle.

Cholmondeley *Calmundelei: Edwin and Drogo from Robert FitzHugh.* 18th-century castle, with a church, in a deer park.

Cholmondeston *Chelmundestone: William Malbank, formerly Wulfeva, a free woman.* Cholmondeston Hall.

Chorley *Cerlere: William Malbank.* ⌂

Chorlton (near Nantwich) *Cerletune: William Malbank.* ⌂

Chowley *Celelea: Mundret from Robert FitzHugh, formerly Wulfeva, a free woman.* ⌂

Christleton *Cristetone: Robert FitzHugh. Mill.* ▣ Large. It was a Royalist outpost in the Civil War, near Rowton Moor, where Charles I was defeated in 1645.

Church Minshull *Maneshale/Manessele: William Malbank. Hawk's eyrie.* ▣ Attractive. Minshull Hall is a farm on an old moated site.

Claverton *Cleventone: Hugh FitzOsbern.* ▣

Clifton *Clistune: William from St Werburgh's Church.* Part of Runcorn.

Clive *Clive: Earl Hugh.* ⌂ Now Clive Green; Clive House.

Clotton *Clotone: Ilbert.* ▣ Clotton Common.

Clutton *Clutone: William FitzNigel.* ⌂ Clutton Hall Farm.

Coddington *Cotintone: Earl Hugh. Mill.* ▣ Attractive farm-houses; duckpond.

Cogshall *Cocheshalle: Payne from Richard de Vernon; Ranulf Mainwaring.* Cogshall Hall.

Conersley *Kenardeslie:* Lost.

Congleton *Cogeltone: Bigot de Loges.* Town on the River Dane. The borough charter dates from the 13th century.

Coppenhall *Copehale: William Malbank.* Part of Crewe; the parishes of Church Coppenhall and Monks Coppenhall developed with the railway in the 19th century.

Cranage *Croeneche: Robert FitzHugh.* ▣ Manor farm.

Crewe (by Nantwich) *Creu: Richard de Vernon.* Town, developed in the 19th century with the railway. Crewe Green, a hamlet, nearby.

Crewe (near Farndon) *Creuhalle: Eli, the pre-Conquest holder, from Robert FitzHugh. ½ fishery.* ▣

Croughton *Crostone: St Werburgh's Church before and after 1066.* Croughton Cottage.

Croxton *Crostune: Jocelyn.* Croxton Hall Farm.

Cuddington *Cuntitone: Robert FitzHugh.* ⌂ Cuddington Green; Cuddington Hall.

Davenham *Deveneham: Richard de Vernon.* ▣ On the outskirts of Northwich.

Davenport *Deneport: Gilbert Hunter.* Davenport Hall Farm.

Dodleston *Dodestune: Osbern FitzTezzo.* ▣ Earthworks of a castle; Dodleston Hall, on a moated site.

Duckington *Dochintone: Edwin, the pre-Conquest holder, from Robert FitzHugh.* ⌂

Dunham on the Hill *Doneham: Earl Hugh.* ▣

Dunham Massey *Doneham: Hamo de Mascy.* ▣ Now Dunham Town on the outskirts of Greater Manchester.

Dutton *Duntune: William FitzNigel; Edward, the pre-Conquest holder, from Osbern FitzTezzo; Odard from Earl Hugh. Hawk's eyrie.* ⌂ 2 farms and a hall nearby; also Dutton Hollow hamlet.

Eanley *Enelelei: William FitzNigel.* Eanleywood Farm, near an artificial ski slope on the outskirts of Runcorn.

Eastham *Estham: Earl Hugh. Mill.* Part of Bebington; once a resort with a ferry to Liverpool.

Eaton *Etone: Earl Hugh. Fishery (1000 salmon).* Eaton Hall, part of the Grosvenor Estate.

Eccleston *Eclestone: Gilbert de Venables. Boat and net.* ▣ On the Roman road to Chester.

Eddisbury *Edesberie: Earl Hugh.* Eddisbury Hill. An Iron Age fort near Delamere Forest is all that remains of the Norman forests Mara and Mondrem.

Edge *Eghe: Edwin, the pre-Conquest holder, from Robert FitzHugh.* ⌂ Now Edge Green; Edge Hall and a manor house farm.

Elton *Eltone: Earl Hugh.* ▣ On the outskirts of Ellesmere Port.

Farndon *Ferentone: Bishop of Chester; Bigot de Loges. Mill.* ▣

FARNDON: *Memorial to Roger Barnston, a 19th-c. military hero.*

Frith *Tereth: William Malbank.* Frith-hall Farm.

Frodsham *Frotesham: Earl Hugh. Church, winter mill, 2½ fisheries, ½ salt-house for the hall.* Town, once a major port at the mouth of the River Weaver. The church has 12th-century arcades and fragments of Norman carving.

Gawsworth *Gouesurde: Earl Hugh.* Attractive; Georgian New Hall and rectory; 16th-century Old Hall.

Gayton *Gaitone: William from Robert of Rhuddlan. 2 fisheries.* Part of Heswall.

Golborne *Colborne/burne: William Malbank; Osbern FitzTezzo. Winter mill.* Golborne Hall on Golborne Brook.

Goostrey *Gostrel: Ralph from William FitzNigel; Hugh FitzNorman.* Large.

Grappenhall *Gropenhale: Edward from Osbern FitzTezzo.* Suburb of Warrington. A Georgian hall is now a school.

Greasby *Gravesberie: Nigel de Burcy.* Built up.

Great Budworth *Budewrde: Payne from William FitzNigel. Mill for the hall.* 17th-century houses.

Great Caldy *Calders: Hugh de la Mere.* Part of Hoylake. Caldy Hill is National Trust.

Guilden Sutton *Sudtone: Bishop of Chester; Robert FitzHugh.*

Hadlow *Edelaue:* Lost.

Hale *Hale: Hamo de Mascy. Hawk's eyrie.* Town with Altrincham.

Halton *Heletune: William FitzNigel.*

Hampton *Hantone: Edwin and Drogo from Robert FitzHugh. Sparrow-hawk.* Now Hampton Heath; hall.

Handbridge *Bruge: William FitzNigel; Hugh de la Mere; Hugh FitzOsbern.* Part of Chester; once an industrial suburb.

Handley *Hanlei: Osbern FitzTezzo.*

Hargrave *Haregrave: Robert Cook.* Hargrave Hall; Hargrave House Farm.

Hartford *Herford: Gilbert de Venables. Salt-house, ½ derelict salt-house.* Town; a railway viaduct crosses the Weaver valley.

Hassall *Eteshale: William Malbank. Hawk's eyrie.* Now 2 hamlets, Hassall (with a hall) and Hassall Moss.

Hatherton *Haretone: William Malbank.* 2 farms; lodge; manor house.

Hatton *Etune: Ilbert.* Hatton Heath; moated hall; 2 farms; lodge.

Helsby *Helesbe: Earl Hugh.* Town between Helsby Marshes and Helsby Hill; traces of an Iron Age camp.

Henbury *Hamede/Hameteberie: Earl Hugh.* Henbury Hall.

Heswall *Eswelle: Herbert from Robert of Rhuddlan.* Recently developed town; long sea-front.

High Legh *Lege: Gilbert de Venables. Church.* 18th-century High Legh Hall has a 16th-century chapel in its park.

Hollingworth *Holisurde: Earl Hugh.* Large.

Hooton *Hotone: Richard de Vernon.*

Huntington *Hunditone: St Werburgh's Church. Small boat and net.* Huntington Hall.

Iddinshall *Etingehalle: St Werburgh's Church.* Iddenshall Grange.

Ince *Inise: St Werburgh's Church.* Partly ruined manor house, *c.*1500, of the Abbots of Chester.

MALPAS: *Iron-bound chest in St Oswald's church.*

Kermincham *Cerdingham: Hugh FitzNorman.* Kermincham Hall.

Kinderton *Cinbretune: Gilbert Hunter.* Kinderton Lodge.

Kingsley *Chingeslie: Dunning from Earl Hugh. 1½ fisheries, hawk's eyrie, 4 deer parks.* Church designed by Gilbert Scott.

Kinnerton *Edritone: Richard from Hugh FitzOsbern.*

Knutsford: See page 49.

Lach Dennis *Lece: William FitzNigel; Moran from Earl Hugh.*

Lache *Leche: St Werburgh's Church.* Part of Chester.

Landican *Landechene: William Malbank.* Part of Chester.

Larkton *Lavorchedone: Edwin and Drogo from Robert FitzHugh.*

Lawton *Lautune: Hugh FitzNorman.* Now the village of Church Lawton, and Buglawton, part of Congleton.

Lea near Backford *Wisdelea: St Werburgh's Church.* Lea Manor Farm; Lea Hall; Lea Farm.

Lea Newbold *Lai: Earl Hugh; Bigot de Loges.* Lea Newbold Farm; Lea Hall with a moat.

Ledsham *Levetesham: Walter de Vernon.*

Leftwich *Wice: Richard de Vernon.* Large; on the River Dane; Lea Grange Farm.

Leighton *Lestone: William from Robert of Rhuddlan. 2 fisheries.* Leighton Hall Farm.

Little Budworth *Bodeurde: Earl Hugh.* Budworth Common, a country park; Budworth Pool.

All land in Cheshire, with the exception of any held by the Bishop of Chester or St Werburgh's Church, was held by Earl Hugh from the king. He is in the gazetteer only if *Domesday* lists him as tenant-in-chief, or if the under-tenants are his men.

Little Caldy *Calders:* Lost.

Little Leigh *Lege: William FitzNigel; Earl Hugh.* Near the Trent and Mersey Canal.

Little Nestone *Nestone: Robert Cook.* Area near Neston.

Lower Withington *Hungrewenitune: Earl Hugh.* The village of Withington is north of the *Domesday* site.

Ludworth *Lodeuorde: King's land.*

Lymm *Lime: Gilbert de Venables; Edward from Osbern FitzTezzo. Church.* Town on the Bridgewater Canal. Lymm Hall was the home of the Norman Domville family; the present house is part Elizabethan.

Macclesfield *Maclesfeld:* See page 51.

Malpas *Depenbech: Robert FitzHugh.* Small, attractive town with half-timbered cottages; Malpas Castle, now earthworks.

Manley *Menlie: Earl Hugh.* Manley Old Hall.

Marbury *Merberie: William Malbank, formerly Earl Harold.* Hall; timbered cottages; 13th-century church.

Marlston *Merlestone: Asgar from William FitzNigel.* Marlston Heyes Farm.

Marton *Meretone/utune: Earl Hugh and Hugh FitzNorman from him.* 14th-century timber chapel.

Meols *Melas: Robert of Rhuddlan.* Coastal area. Roman and Saxon coins and jewellery were found at nearby Dove Point.

Mere *Mera: Gilbert de Venables.* Mere Hall; lake.

Mickle Trafford *Traford: Earl Hugh.* Large.

Middle Aston *Midestune:* Lost; a moat and Old Moat Wood remain.

Middlewich *Wich: Earl Hugh. Salt pans rendering 2 cartloads of salt.* Town, with a 13th-century borough charter; still produces salt.

Millington *Mulintune: William FitzNigel.* Millington Hall.

Minshull Vernon *Maneshale/sele: William Malbank. Hawk's eyrie.* Part of Church Minshull.

Mobberley *Motburlege: Bigot de Loges.* Manor house.

Mollington *Molintone: Robert of Rhuddlan and Lambert from him.* Mollington Grange.

Mottram *Motre: Gamel (whose father held it) from Earl Hugh. Hawk's eyrie.* Now 2 villages, Mottram St Andrew and Mottram Cross; Mottram Old Hall.

Moulton *Moletune: Richard de Vernon.* Large.

Nantwich *Wich: William Malbank. Salt-pit, salt-pans.* Town, largely rebuilt (with the help of Elizabeth I) after a fire in 1583. Still has many black-and-white houses. Salt production from the *Domesday* pit continued until 1856.

Ness *Nesse: Walter de Vernon.* Part of Neston; birthplace of Lady Hamilton (1761–1815).

Neston *Nestone:* see page 49.

Nether Alderley *Aldredelie: Bigot de Loges.* 16th-century watermill.

Netherleigh *Lee:* Lost.

Nether Tabley *Stablei: Jocelyn.* Lake; ruined hall on island.

Newbold Astbury *Neubold: Gilbert Hunter from Earl Hugh.* Now Astbury. The church was granted to St Werburgh in the 11th century and rebuilt in the 13th and 16th centuries. The remains of Astbury Yew are possibly pre-1066. Nearby is Newbold, on the edge of Congleton.

Newton by Chester *Neutone/Newentone: William FitzNigel.* Part of Chester.

Newton in Middlewich *Neutone: Jocelyn.* Newtonia, part of Middlewich.

Noctorum *Chenoterie: Richard from William Malbank.* Part of Birkenhead.

Norbury near Marbury *Norberie: William Malbank, formerly Earl Harold.* Norbury Common.

Norbury near Stockport *Nordberie: Bigot de Loges.* Norbury Moor, part of Hazel Grove.

North Rode *Rodo: Bigot de Loges.* Manor house; grange; Rode Hall Farm.

Northwich *Norwich/Wich: Earl Hugh. Salt house.* Town that still produces salt; damaged by subsidence from salt mining. There is a medieval motte and bailey on Castle Hill.

Norton *Nortune: Ansfrid from William FitzNigel.* Wooded area on the outskirts of Runcorn; remains of Norton Priory.

Occleston *Aculvestune: Earl Hugh.* Now Occleston Green; manor farm.

Odd Rode *Rode: Hugh and William from Earl Hugh. Hawk's eyrie.* Rode Heath; Rode Hall.

Ollerton *Alretune: Earl Hugh; Ranulf Mainwaring; Wulfric from Earl Hugh.* Ollerton Grange; manor farm; Ollerton Hall nearby.

Oulton *Alretone: Nigel de Burcy.* Oulton Park car-racing circuit.

Over *Ovre: Earl Hugh.* Part of Winsford; formerly a borough with its own mayor.

Over Alderley *Aldredelie: William.*

Overleigh *Lee: Hugh de la Mere.* Overleigh Road, Chester.

Over Tabley *Stab(e)lei: William FitzNigel.*

Overton *Ovretune: Robert FitzHugh.* Overton Hall; hamlet of Overton Heath nearby.

Peckforton *Pevretone: Robert FitzHugh.* At the foot of Peckforton Hills. Peckforton Castle was built in 1840.

Peover *Pevre: William FitzNigel; Gilbert de Venables; Ranulf Mainwaring. Hawk's eyrie.* Now Lower Peover; mainly 14th-century church. Peover Hall nearby.

Picton *Pichetone: Richard de Vernon.* Picton Hall.

NORTON: *12th-c. doorway from the Augustinian priory.*

Pool *Pol: William Malbank.* Now Overpool, part of Ellesmere Port.

Poole *Pol: William Malbank, formerly Wulfeva, a free woman.* 2 halls; 2 farms.

Poulton *Pontone: Richard Butler.* Poultonhall Farm.

Poulton Lancelyn *Pontone: Roger from Osbern FitzTezzo.* Poulton Hall.

Prenton *Prestune: Walter de Vernon. Mill.* Part of Birkenhead.

Puddington *Potitone: Hamo de Mascy.* 2 halls; home farm.

Pulford *Pulford: St Werburgh's Church; Hugh FitzOsbern.* Earthworks of Pulford Castle; gateway to the Grosvenor Estate.

Raby *Rabie: St Werburgh's Church and William from the church; Hardwin from William FitzNigel.* Flower farm.

Redcliff *Rade/Redeclive:* Lost.

Romiley *Rumilie: Earl Hugh.* Former cotton town close to Stockton.

Rostherne *Rodestorne: Gilbert de Venables.* Rostherne Mere, a nature reserve; Cicely Mill, *c.*1650, nearby.

Rushton *Rusitone: Earl Hugh.*

SAIGHTON: *The grange gatehouse, built in 1490.*

Saighton *Saltone: St Werburgh's Church.* Saighton Grange with a 15th-century gatehouse.

Sandbach *Sanbec(o):* See page 49.

Saughall *Salhale: St Werburgh's Church; William Malbank. Fishery.* Large.

Shavington *Santune: William Malbank.* Large; Shavington House; Shavington Hall; Shavington Green Farm.

Shipbrook *Sibroc: Richard de Vernon.* Shipbrookhill.

Shocklach *Socheliche: Drogo from Robert FitzHugh.* Church with 12th-century chapel; remains of Shocklach Castle.

Shotwick *Sotowiche: St Werburgh's Church.* 17th-century hall.

Shurlach *Survelec: Richard de Vernon. Fishery.* Higher Shurlach, an area on the outskirts of Northwich.

Siddington *Sudendune: Bigot de Loges.* Sailing club at Redes Mere; Siddington Hall.

Snelson *Senelestune: Ranulf Mainwaring.* Snelson House.

Somerford *Sumreford: Hugh FitzNorman.* Somerford Hall Farm; Somerford Park Farm.

Somerford Booths *Sumreford: Tesselin from Earl Hugh.* Somerford Booths Hall.

Sproston *Sprostune: William Malbank.* Now Sproston Green; Sproston Hall.

Spurstow *Spuretone: Robert FitzHugh.* 2 halls; Spurstow Spa nearby.

Stanney *Stanei: Restald from Earl Hugh. Fishery.* Now Little Stanney.

Stapeley *Steple: William Malbank.* Stapeley Hall; Stapeley House.

Stapleford *Stapleford: Ralph Hunter. Mill.* Stapleford Hall.

Stoneley *Stanleu: William Malbank, formerly Earl Harold.* Now Stoneley Green.

Storeton *Stortone: Nigel de Burcy.*

Sunderland *Sundreland: Gilbert, Ranulf and Hamo from Earl Hugh.* Area of Sinderland.

Sutton (near Middlewich) *Sud/Sutone: Earl Hugh; Bigot de Loges.* Sutton Hall Farm.

Sutton *Sudtone: St Werburgh's Church.* Now Great and Little Sutton, in Ellesmere Port; Sutton New Hall; Sutton Lodge.

Tarporley *Torpelei: Gilbert de Venables.* Oldest hunting club in England.

Tarvin *Terve: Bishop of Chester.* Georgian and half-timbered houses.

Tattenhall *Tatenale: William Malbank.* Tudor cottages; Jacobean hall.

Tatton *Tatune: William FitzNigel; Ranulf Mainwaring.* Tatton Hall 1788–1815; part 15th-century hall in a large park.

Tetton *Tadetune: Ranulf Mainwaring.* Tetton Hall.

Thingwall *Tuigvelle: Durand from William Malbank.* Part of Heswall.

Thornton Hough *Torintone: William from Robert of Rhuddlan.* Thornton Farm; manor house.

Thornton le Moors *Torentune: Bigot de Loges. Church.* Attractive; 14th-century church; moated site of an old hall.

Thurstaston *Turstanetone: William from Robert of Rhuddlan.* Church; part 14th-, part 17th-century hall; Thurstaston Hill, a National Trust park.

Tilston *Tillestone: Robert FitzHugh. Mill.*

Tilstone Fearnall *Tidulstane: William from Robert FitzHugh.* Tilston Hall; Tilston Lodge.

Tintwistle *Tengestvisie: Earl Hugh.* Also Tintwistle Low Moor on the Cheshire–Derbyshire border.

Tiverton *Tevretone: Robert FitzHugh.* On the River Gowy.

STAPELEY: *Half-timbering set off by water gardens.*

Tushingham *Tusigeham: Humphrey from Robert FitzHugh.* Tushingham House; Tushingham Hall.

Upton *Optone: Colbert from William Malbank.* Part of Birkenhead. A runic stone was found here.

Upton by Chester *Op(e)tone: Hamo, Herbert and Mundret from Earl Hugh.* Part of Chester; also Upton Heath.

Walgherton *Walcretune: William Malbank.* Manor farm.

Wallasey *Walea: Robert of Rhuddlan.* Town whose centre is still called Wallasey Village.

Warburton *Warburgetone/tune: William FitzNigel; Osbern FitzTezzo.* 14th-century half-timbered church of St Werburgh.

WINNINGTON: *Tirley Garth, a 'medieval' house begun by C. E. Mallows in 1906.*

Wardle *Warhelle: Hugh FitzOsbern.* Wardle Hall; Wardle Bridge Farm.

Warford *Wareford: Godgyth a free woman, the pre-Conquest holder, from Ranulf Mainwaring.* Warford House.

Waverton *Wavretone: Ilbert.* Large; Jacobean farm beside the church.

Weaver *Wevre: Earl Hugh; Bigot de Loges.* Weaver Hall.

Weaverham *Wivreham: Earl Hugh. Church, mill, 2 deer enclosures.* Town with timbered houses; 15th–16th-century church.

Werneth *Warnet: Earl Hugh.* Werneth Hall Farm.

Wervin *Wivevrene/revene: St Werburgh's Church; William Malbank.* Hall; ruins of a Norman chapel.

Weston *Westone: Odard and Brictric from William Malbank.* Part of Runcorn; Weston Point docks on the Manchester Ship Canal.

Wettenhall *Watenhale: Gilbert de Venables.* Wettenhall Hall; manor farm.

Wharton *Wanetune: Richard de Vernon.* Part of Winsford in the Weaver valley; centre of 19th-century salt production.

Wheelock *Hoiloch: Ranulf Mainwaring.* Wheelock Hall; Wheelock Heath nearby.

Whitley *Witelei: Payne and Orde from William FitzNigel.* Now 2 villages, Higher and Lower Whitley; moated Whitley Hall; Whitley House Farm.

Wilkesley *Wivelesde: William Malbank. Hawk's eyrie.*

Willaston *Wilavestune: William Malbank.* Large; on the outskirts of Crewe.

Willington *Winfletone: Walter de Vernon.* Now Willington Corner; manor farm; Willington Hall.

Wimboldsley *Wibaldelai: Earl Hugh; Bigot de Loges.* Wimboldsley Hall on the Shropshire Union Canal.

Wimbolds Trafford *Tro(s)ford: Earl Hugh.* Trafford Hall.

Wincham *Wimundisham: Gilbert de Venables. Hawk's eyrie.* On Wincham Brook.

Winnington *Wenitone: Ranulf Mainwaring; Osbern FitzTezzo.* Industrial area with a large chemical works. Scene of the Parliamentarian victory in 1659 that marked the end of the Cheshire Rising.

Wirswall *Wiresuelle/swelle: William Malbank, formerly Earl Harold.* Wirswall Hall.

Wistaston *Wistanestune: William Malbank.* Suburb of Crewe.

Wisterson *Wistetestune:* Lost.

Witton *Witune: Gilbert Hunter. Mill.* Witton Mill Bridge on Witton Brook in Northwich.

Worleston *Werelestune: William Malbank.*

Wrenbury *Wareneberie: William Malbank. Hawk's eyrie.* On the Shropshire Union Canal; Wrenbury Mill, now a boatyard; Wrenbury Hall, mainly Victorian.

Wybunbury *Wimeberie: Bishop of Chester and William from him. Priest.* Moated site of an old hall.

RHUDDLAN: *Ruins of the 13th-c. castle.*

Wales Gazetteer

Allington *Allentune: Hugh FitzOsbern.* Allington Farm.

Aston *Estone: Hamo de Mascy.* Suburb of Shotton.

Axton *Asketone: Marchiud from Earl Hugh.*

Bagillt *Bachelie: Robert of Rhuddlan and Roger from him.* Industrial area on the Dee Estuary; centre of lead-ore smelting in the 18th and 19th centuries.

Bettisfield *Bed(d)esfeld: Robert FitzHugh.* Bettisfield Hall Farm; Bettisfield Park.

Bistre *Biscopestreu: Hugh FitzNorman and Odin from Earl Hugh.* Bistre Farm.

Blorant *Blorat:* Lost.

Bodeugan *Bodugan: Earl Hugh.*

Broughton *Brochetone/tune: Robert of Rhuddlan; Hugh FitzOsbern; Ralph Hunter.*

Bryn *Bren: Earl Hugh; Robert of Rhuddlan.* Bryn Cwnin Farm.

Bryncoed *Bruncot: Warmund Hunter from Earl Hugh.* Now Broncoed-isaf; Bryn Coch Hall and Farm nearby.

Brynford *Brunfor(d): Earl Hugh; Robert of Rhuddlan. Church, mill.*

Bryngwyn *Brenuuen: Earl Hugh.* Bryngwyn Hall.

Brynhedydd *Brennehedui:* Lost.

Bychton *Putecain: Robert of Rhuddlan. Fishery.*

Caerwys *Cairos: Robert of Rhuddlan.* Quiet; important medieval market town. Eisteddfodau have been held here since the 12th century.

Calcot *Caldecote: Earl Hugh. Priest, church.* Now Calcoed; small.

Carn-y-chain *Cancarnacan: Robert of Rhuddlan. Derelict church.*

Cefn Du *Keund: Earl Hugh; Robert of Rhuddlan.*

Cilowen *Chiluen:* Lost.

Clayton: Lost; possibly represented by Clay Hill.

Coleshill *Coleselt: Edwin, the pre-Conquest holder, from Robert of Rhuddlan.* On the edge of Flint Marsh.

Cwybr *Cauber: Earl Hugh.*

Cwybr Bach *Parva Cauber:* Lost.

Cyrchynean *Charcan: Robert of Rhuddlan.*

Dincolyn *Dicolin: Robert of Rhuddlan.* Area near Dyserth.

Dyserth *Dissard: Earl Hugh; Robert of Rhuddlan. Church, mill, hawk's eyrie.* Limestone gorge; Bodrhyddan Hall, 17th century with later additions.

Erbistock *Erpestoch: Reginald Balliol.* Attractive; Erbistock Hall on the River Dee.

Eyton *Eitune: St Chad's of Lichfield, the pre-Conquest holder, from Bishop of Chester; Hugh FitzOsbern. Mill, 2½ fisheries.* Eyton Hall; Eyton Grange; 2 farms.

Fulbrook *Folebroc: Earl Hugh.* Lost near Holywell.

Gellilyfdy *Cheslilaued: Marchiud from Earl Hugh.* Only a house remains.

Golden Grove *Uluesgraue: Robert of Rhuddlan.* 17th-century Golden Grove House.

Golftyn *Ulfemiltone: Ascelin from Robert of Rhuddlan.* Golftyn Cemetery in Connah's Quay.

Gop *Rahop: Robert of Rhuddlan.* Gop Hill; cairn, possibly Bronze Age; caves, in use *c.*4000–2000 BC, in which the bones of humans and the woolly rhino where found.

Gresford *Gretford: Reginald Balliol; Hugh, Osbern and Reginald from Earl Hugh. Church, 2 hawks' eyries, mill.* Mainly 15th-century church, with 2 bells of 1623; Gresford Lodge, *c.*1790.

Gronant *Gronant: Robert of Rhuddlan.* Large; holiday camp.

Gwaenysgor *Wenescol: Robert of Rhuddlan. Derelict church.* Hill-top. A walled Neolithic village was found at Bryn Llwyn nearby.

Gwespyr *Wesberie: Robert of Rhuddlan. Church.* Henblas, a 17th-century stone house, nearby.

Gwysaney *Quisnan: William from Earl Hugh.* Gwysaney Hall.

Halkyn *Alchene: Earl Hugh; Robert of Rhuddlan. Church; mill.* 19th-century Halkyn Castle. Halkyn Mountain has been a lead-mining area since Roman times.

Hawarden *Haordine:* See page 51.

Hendrebiffa *Hendred:* Lost.

Hiraddug *Raduch: Robert of Rhuddlan.* Moel Hiradugg, a hill with an Iron Age fort.

Hope *Hope: Gilbert de Venables.* On the River Alyn; Hope Hall; 1085ft Hope Mountain.

Hoseley *Odeslei: St Werburgh's Church.* Hoseley House; Hoseley Bank.

Iscoyd *Burwardestone: Robert FitzHugh. Salt-house.* Now Iscoed.

Kelston *Calstan: Robert of Rhuddlan. Church.* Kelston Farm.

Leadbrook *Latbroc: Robert of Rhuddlan.* Leadbrook Hall.

Llewerllyd *Lauarludon/Leuuarludae: Earl Hugh; Robert of Rhuddlan. Mill.*

Llys Edwin *Castreetone: Hamo de Mascy and Osmund from him.* Now 2 hamlets, Coed Llys and Bryn Edwin.

Llystyn Hunydd *Lesthunied:* Lost.

Llys y Coed *Lessecoit: Earl Hugh.* Moel Llys-y-Coed, a hill with an Iron Age fort.

Maen Efa *Maineual: Earl Hugh.* Moel Maenefa, a hill with tumuli.

Mechlas *Moclitone:* Lost.

Meliden *Ruestoch: Robert of Rhuddlan. Church.* Suburb of Prestatyn.

Mertyn *Meretone: Odin from Earl Hugh. Church.*

Mostyn *Mostone: Robert of Rhuddlan.* On the Dee Estuary; Mostyn Quay.

Pentre *Peintret: Earl Hugh.*

Pen y Gors *Penegors:* Lost.

Picton *Pichetone: Robert of Rhuddlan.*

Prestatyn *Prestetone: Robert of Rhuddlan. Church.* Resort at the northern end of Offa's Dyke.

Radington *Radintone:* Lost.

Radnor *Radenoure:* Lost.

Rhiwargor *Ruargor:* Lost.

Rhos Ithel *Risteselle: Ralph from Earl Hugh.*

Rhuddlan *Roelend/lent: Earl Hugh; Robert of Rhuddlan. Church, castle, mint, iron mines, mills, fisheries, forests; toll.* Large; on the River Clywd. Strategically important since the Dark Ages it has the motte of a Norman castle, Twthill, and the ruins of a 13th-century castle.

Rhyd Orddwy *Reuuordui: Robert of Rhuddlan from Earl Hugh. Mill.* Now Rhydorddwy Fawr.

Soughton *Sutone: Ralph Hunter.* Soughton Hall was built c.1720 by Bishop Wynne of St Asaph and rebuilt 1868.

St Asaph (Llanelwy) *Lannuuile: Robert of Rhuddlan.* Town on the River Clwyd, founded in 560. Its cathedral was restored in the 19th century by Gilbert Scott.

Sutton *Sutone: Hugh FitzOsbern.* Now Sutton Green.

Trefraith *Treueri: Robert of Rhuddlan.* Wood.

Trelawnyd *Riuelenoit: Robert of Rhuddlan.*

Trellyniau *Treuelesneu: Earl Hugh.* Now Trellyniau Fawr.

Tremeirchion *Dinmersch: Earl Hugh.* Hillside. Nearby Brynbella was built by Dr Johnson's friend, Mrs Thrale.

Wepre *Wepre: St Werburgh's Church and William from the church; William Malbank.* Area close to Connan's Quay.

Whitford *Widford: Earl Hugh; Robert of Rhuddlan. Fishery.* Nearby is Maen Achwyfan, a carved Celtic cross, *c.*1000.

Worthenbury *Hurdingberie: Robert FitzHugh. New mill.* On Worthenbury Brook; fine 18th-century church.

Ysceifiog *Schiuian: Earl Hugh.*

All land in Wales, with the exception of any held granted to Robert of Rhuddlan, was held by Earl Hugh from the king. He is in the gazetteer only if *Domesday* lists him as tenant-in-chief, or if the under-tenants are his men.

DYSERTH: *A spectacular waterfall.*

Cornwall

Robert, Count of Mortain, was the biggest landholder in England after his half-brother King William, and Cornwall was above all his province. There he was lord of many more manors than the king himself; the Exchequer Domesday *lists 248 manors, and the Exon version nearly 40 more, while the latter held a mere 19.*

Most of the county was poor and sparsely populated: for each man recorded by Domesday *there were 160 acres of land. The manors tended to be small, and no less than ten are assessed at as little as one acre. Cornwall's maritime importance did not assert itself until well after the Norman Conquest: Penzance, for example, is not mentioned until the middle of the fourteenth century, and Bude is first recorded in 1400.*

Cornwall was divided into seven 'Hundreds', and that of Connerton – known today as Penwith – had only 14 manors. Only six mills are listed, two of these at Launceston on the county's eastern border. The reason, it has been suggested, was that the technology of harnessing water-power was only gradually spreading from the east; both Dorset and Somerset had more mills than Devon, which in turn had more than Cornwall.

In Cornwall, many of the old place names were mistranslated by the Domesday *scribes. Thus, identification is often tentative – even speculative.*

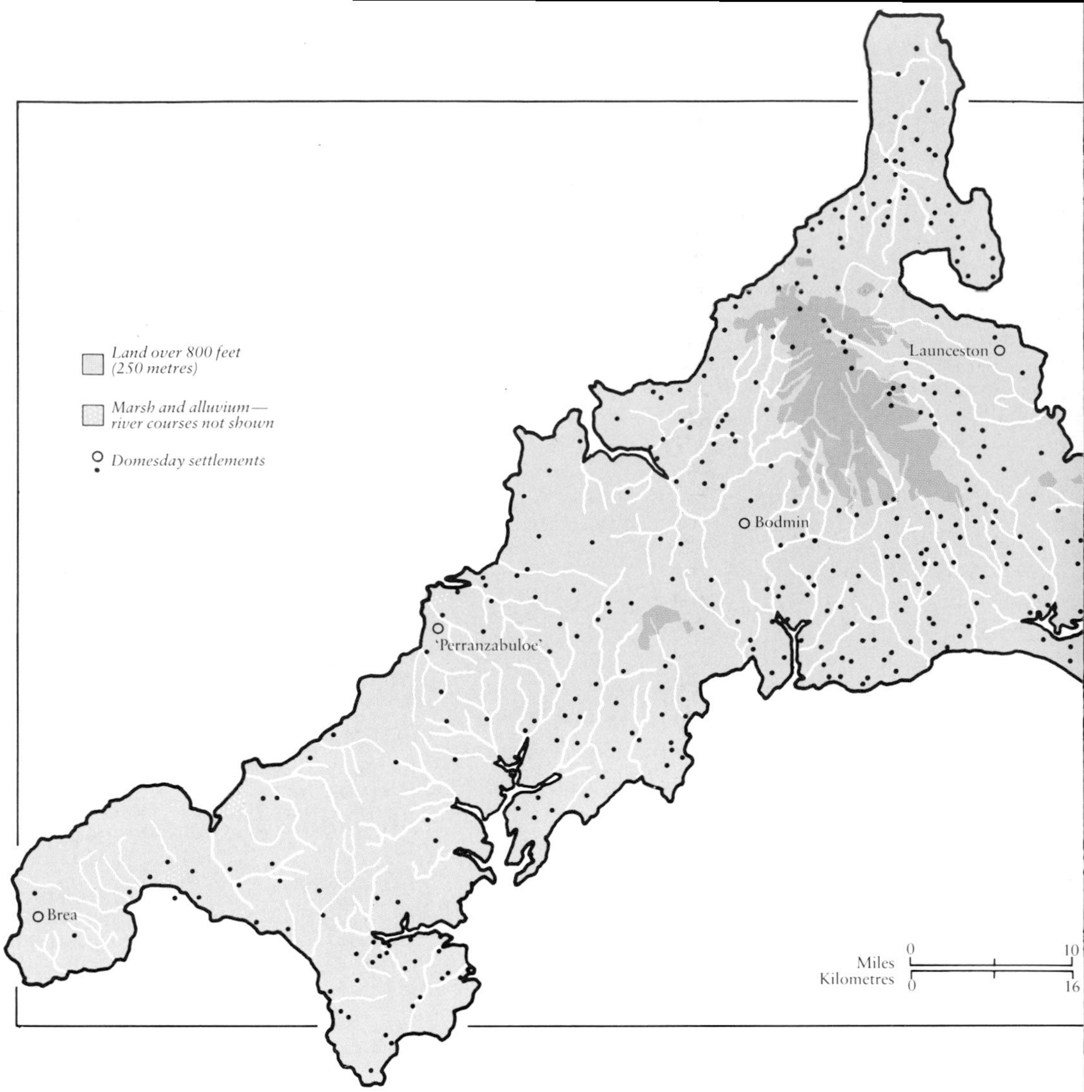

Perranzabuloe

The Canons of St Piran's hold PERRANZABULOE *LANPIRAN*; before 1066 it was always free. 3 h[ides]. Land for 8 ploughs; 2 ploughs there; 2 slaves. 4 villagers and 8 smallholders. Pasture, 10 acres. 8 cattle; 30 sheep. Value 12s; value when the Count received it, 40s. Two lands have been taken from this manor which before 1066 paid four weeks' revenue to the Canons and 20s. to the Dean by custom. Berner holds one of them from the Count of Mortain; the Count has taken away all the stock from the other hide, which Odo holds from St Piran's.

Perranzabuloe was held by the collegiate church of St Piran, but as *Domesday* shows, the acquisitive Count of Mortain never missed an opportunity to enlarge his territory. Perranzabuloe has moved twice, and the reason is given in its name, which means Piran-in-the-sand. The Celtic missionary Piran apparently came from Ireland early in the sixth century and founded a monastery on the coast some two miles from the site of the present church. Legend has it that he floated across on a millstone, which may be a reference to the small stone altars such missionaries often carried.

The earliest church we can precisely locate – a building only about 25 feet by 12 – dates from the ninth century. The place where it stood can still be seen on the beach. It was excavated by a Truro antiquarian named Mitchell in 1835, who found all four walls intact and a highly ornamented doorway embellished with stone heads.

'The masonry of the building', he wrote, 'is of the rudest kind, and evidently of remote antiquity. There is not the slightest attempt at regular courses, but the stones, consisting of granite, quartz, sandstone, porphyry, etc., appear to have been thrown together almost at random – horizontally, perpendicularly, and at every angle of inclination – just as the hand, not the eye, of the workman happened to direct him. To render the church as perfect as when it was erected, nothing seemed wanting but its doors and roof.'

He recorded that many bodies lay buried within the chancel and the nave, and that several skeletons were discovered with their feet under the altar. One was a giant – some seven feet six inches tall.

'On the southern and western sides of this venerable ruin', he went on, 'is the ancient burying-ground, strewed over tens of thousands of human bones and teeth as white as snow . . .'.

Unfortunately, nothing was done to protect the site. Local children knocked down the walls; souvenir hunters filched the stones, and the carved heads were carted off to be exhibited in the Truro Museum. Worst of all, according to the renowned antiquarian, the Rev. Sabine Baring-Gould, was 'the mischievous meddlesomeness of the curate-in-charge, Rev. William Haslam, who turned the altar stones about, as he had got a theory into his head that they had formed a tomb, and rebuilt them in this fashion, pointing east and west, and cut upon the altar-slab the words *S. Piranus*.' Haslam also had the temerity to claim Mitchell's discoveries for his own.

The little church had been abandoned in the twelfth century because of the encroaching sand, and a new one was built some quarter of a mile inland beyond a stream. It stood safe for some 400 years. Then tin-miners in the area diverted the stream's flow for their own uses and the sand poured in once more. Some repairs were made early in the eighteenth century, but they didn't last, and in 1804 a third (or perhaps fourth) church was built. It stands at Lambourne on the main road, on land given by the local member of Parliament.

This, the present St Piran, incorporates fragments of its predecessor: the font; some wood carvings and window tracery, and parts of the tower. But nothing remains of the little church of Piran-in-the-Sands. For 750 years after *Domesday* it survived intact, most of it embalmed in sand; but when once more it saw the light of day, it was torn to pieces.

Brea

[Erchenbald] also holds BREA *BRET.* Doda held it before 1066, and paid tax for 1 f; 1/2 h [ide] there, however. Land for 3 ploughs; 1 1/2 ploughs there; 3 slaves, with 1 villager and 5 smallholders. Pasture, 40 acres. Formerly 20s; value now 12s 6d. 4 cattle; 4 pigs; 25 sheep.

The lonely farmhouse called Brea is a low, squat building on a minor road between Sennen Cove and Land's End. It was held by Count Robert of Mortain, and at the time of *Domesday* one Erchenbald was his under-tenant. Erchenbald seems to have come to England from the Low Countries. He had two other Cornish holdings besides Brea.

The land has changed little over the last 900 years. Behind the stone-built farm, flat pasture, broken by low dry-stone walls, comes to an end less than a mile away; beyond lies the Atlantic Ocean. The farm was never large – in the year 1284 it amounted to only eight acres – but the house was once dignified with its own chapel, which survived until the eighteenth century. The Cornish word *bre* means hill, and facing Brea Farm is Chapel Carn Brea, a bald, rocky eminence ringed at its base by gorse and scrub. Present-day Druids light a bonfire on its summit each Midsummer's Eve.

Also on the summit of Chapel Carn Brea is a large neolithic chamber tumulus, excavated in the nineteenth century. In the Middle Ages a chapel was built above this, though, like the farm's chapel, it was demolished in the eighteenth century. It was dedicated, as were so many hill top chapels, to St Michael, and it is believed at one time to have been inhabited by a hermit, who kept a fire permanently alight to guide ships safely past the nearby rocks. But finding sufficient fire-wood must have been a formidable task; in the words of a nineteenth-century guidebook, 'not a twig will be found wherewith to whip a sorry horse, nor a bush to hide the nest of the singing bird'.

Bodmin

St Petroc's Church holds BODMIN *BODMINE*. 1 h. [ide] of land which never paid tax. Land for 4 ploughs. 5 villagers have 2 ploughs, with 6 smallholders. Pasture, 30 acres; underwood, 6 acres. St Petroc's has 68 houses and a market. Total value 25s.

The town's name derives from *Bod-minachau* (The Home of Monks), indicating that it was originally a religious settlement. The manor was not large, but the church which held it was wealthy. St Petroc's estates included land for 146 ploughs in 18 manors – though seven of these had been seized by the Count of Mortain and another by the king. All lay either around Bodmin itself or in the estuary of the River Camel, and had come originally from land gifts or from land the monks had themselves enclosed. St Petroc's holdings survived more or less intact until the Reformation.

The founding father of Bodmin was not Petroc but a hermit called St Guron, after whom the parish of Gorran, near Mevagissey, is named. In about 530, he surrendered his hermitage to Petroc, the most impassioned of all the Cornish saints. He was a Welsh prince, the son of Glwys, king of Gwent or Monmouthshire. As a young man he gathered together a band of nobly born companions with whom he went to Ireland to study sacred and profane literature. They stayed for 20 years, possibly as disciples of St Eugenius. According to tradition, when Petroc found that he knew as much as his master, he led his group to Cornwall to spread the Gospel. The county, though already partly converted to Christianity, was still predominantly pagan.

They travelled in the same boat (miraculously preserved) which had brought them to Ireland – a large wicker-built craft with a leather sail. The winds were against them, but their ship 'was borne along by the fear of God with great rapidity'. They landed on the salt flats in the Camel estuary close to the settlement of Lanwethinoc, later to be renamed Padstow (Petrocstow). The north Cornishmen had no love for the Irish, who had caused them a deal of trouble in the past, and the story goes that, on arrival, they were refused water by a party of reapers they met working in the fields. Petroc thereupon struck the ground with his staff, and a spring appeared.

The missionaries founded a monastery at Padstow, where they led a life of strict asceticism. Petroc fasted assiduously, but on Sundays, 'out of reverence for the Lord's Resurrection he tasted sparingly of a little pulse, so as not to become so enfeebled in body as to be unfit for the Lord's service'. He also regularly immersed himself in cold water, a form of penance which originated in the Orient, where, according to legend, he had spent some time. There is a fable associated with his period there. Standing on the beach one day, he saw a great silver bowl floating on the sea. He stepped into it and was carried swiftly away to an island where he remained for seven years. His diet consisted of one fish: he ate it every day, and every day it miraculously returned to be eaten again.

The reason put forward for his leaving Padstow is equally fanciful: there had been a period of torrential rain, and one day he assured his followers that on the morrow the bad weather would cease. He was so exasperated when it did not, that he set out on a journey. His real reason for moving from Padstow to Bodmin may have been to escape attack from Danish seaborne war parties. At Bodmin he and his followers founded a great priory, where he died, 'ceasing at once to work and live', probably in the year 564.

His fame spread after his death, and, in a perverse sort of compliment, his body was stolen in the twelfth century. The events were described by Benedictus Abbas, a contemporary ecclesiastical historian: 'In 1177 ... a certain canon of the abbey of Bodmin in Cornwall, by name Martinus, secretly took away the body of St Petroc; fleeing with it, he passed beyond the seas, and carried the body to the Abbey of St Maen, in the lesser Britain [Brittany] ... Roger, Prior of Bodmin ... went to Henry [II], King of England ... that by his powerful aid they might again get possession of the body of St Petroc, of which they had been fraudulently deprived. The king ... commanded ... the Justiciary of Brittainy that without any delay he should cause the body to be restored. ... [The Justiciary] came with a powerful and armed band to the abbey and ordered that the body should be given up. And when the Abbot and Monks were unwilling to comply, he added threats, that unless the body were yielded immediately, he would use force and take it; which when they heard, they feared to incur the displeasure of the King of England, and therefore restored that blessed body to the before-named Roger ... The Prior of Bodmin, returning with joy to England, brought the body of the blessed Petroc, closed in an ivory shell, to the city of Winchester. And when it was brought into the King's presence, the King having seen and adored it, permitted the Prior to return in peace with his holy charge to the Abbey of Bodmin.'

Though the saint's remains are now lost, the priceless ivory casket in which Prior Roger brought them back to England can be seen in Bodmin's parish church of St Petroc. The story of the recovery of the saint's remains may have given Bodmin something of a reputation for security: more than 700 years later, during World War I, the Crown Jewels of England and the *Domesday Book* itself were put for safe keeping into Bodmin gaol.

Only a few fragments of Norman work and a fishpond survive of Bodmin's great abbey. And though the tower of St Petroc's church is Norman up to the third storey, it was largely rebuilt in 1469–91 and 'sweepingly restored' in 1869–85.

BODMIN: *This fishpond and some Norman fragments are all that remain of the abbey. The town was originally a religious settlement.*

Launceston

The same count [Robert of Mortain] holds LAUNCESTON *DUNHEUET*. Before 1066 it paid tax for 1 v.[irgate] of land; 1 h. [ide] there, however. Land for 10 ploughs; in lordship 1 plough; 3 slaves; 1 villager and 13 smallholders with 4 ploughs. 2 mills which pay 40s; pasture, 40 acres. Formerly £20; value now £4. 5 cattle; 50 sheep. The Count's castle is there.

Even before the Conquest Launceston was a Cornish place of significance. It had both a Saxon mint and an ecclesiastical college. The name Launceston, however, derives from Lan Stephen, the Church of Stephen and the pre-Norman town was sited around St Stephen's on the opposite side of the River Kensey from where it is today. In 1086, the canons of St Stephen still had a manor here, known as 'Lanscauestone' (now St Stephen's by Launceston), with a large pasture. But the Count of Mortain had meanwhile obtained the manor of Dunheut, where he built his castle. It was around this that the medieval and modern towns grew up.

Military commanders placed great importance on Launceston. It is Cornwall's only walled town, and the castle (Castle Terrible, as Malory called it in *Morte d'Arthur*) that crowns the hill above the Tamar valley is splendidly placed to guard the border between Cornwall and Devon. The castle is now in ruins, but enough remains to indicate its impregnable strength. Across the castle green (until the last century the scene of public executions) a steep flight of steps leads to the massive circular keep, from which the view extends as far as Bodmin Moor to the west and Dartmoor in the east.

Though ruined castles fill the imagination with thoughts of gallant deeds and romantic sieges, their more important function was to subdue and terrify the local population, and Launceston Castle, grimly dominating its surroundings, obviously deserved the nickname that Malory gave it.

By way of contrast, Launceston and its environs seems to have been well populated with fairies, even as late as the nineteenth century. According to a guidebook published in 1865, they were useful folk: 'An old woman, the wife of a respectable farmer in the parish of Werrington, near Launceston, has frequently told . . . of a piskey which often made its appearance in the form of a small child, in the kitchen of the farmhouse, where the inmates were accustomed to set a little stool for it. It would do a good deal of household work; but if the hearth and the chimney were not kept neatly swept, it would pinch the maid . . it was a familiar guest in the house for many months. At last, with a sudden start from its stool, exclaiming

Piskey fine, and piskey gay,
Piskey now must run away,

it vanished, after which it never appeared again.'

Launceston is a market town, as it has been since Norman times. *Domesday* records that the Count of Mortain had already seized the market which used to belong to the manor of the canons of St Stephen and removed it to his new castle across the river.

LAUNCESTON: *The ruins of the castle mentioned in* Domesday; *a circular tower and the shell of the keep remain.*

Cornwall Gazetteer
Each entry starts with the modern place name in **bold** type. The *Domesday* information that follows is in *italic* type, beginning with the name or names by which the place was known in 1086. The main landholders and under-tenants are next, separated with semi-colons if a place was divided into more than one holding. More general information completes the *Domesday* part of the entry, including animals given in the *Domesday* entries when the totals reach or exceed: 160 sheep, 15 goats, 40 wild mares, 240 castrated rams, 33 unbroken mares, 50 cattle, 14 pigs, and 2 oxen. The modern or post-Domesday section is in normal type. ▦ represents a village, ⌂ a small village or hamlet.

BOSSINEY: *The view down to the cove.*

Alvacott *Alvevacote/a: Berner from Count of Mortain.* Farm.

Alverton *Alwareton:* Lost.

Amble *Amal: Thurstan from Count of Mortain.* ▦ Now Chapel Amble; slate cottages; stone bridge.

Antony *Antone/a: Ermenhald from Tavistock Church.* ▦ Antony House, designed by James Gibbs in 1721.

APPLEDORE: *Georgian cottages slope down to the quay.*

Appledore *Pedeleforda: Reginald from Count of Mortain.* ⌂ Iron Age hill-fort.

Arrallas *Arganlis: Thurstan from Count of Mortain.* ⌂

Ashton *Aissetone/a: Reginald from Count of Mortain.* ⌂

Balsdon *Bellesdone/a: Iovin from Count of Mortain.* Now 2 moorland hamlets, East and West Balsdon.

Barnacott *Betnecote: Hamelin from Count of Mortain.* ⌂

Bicton *Bichetone/a: Reginald from Count of Mortain.* ⌂ Manor house; Bicton Wood.

Binnerton *Bennartone/a: King's land.* Manor house.

Blisland *Glustone/a: King's land, formerly Earl Harold.* ▦ Manor house with a Norman archway and windows.

Boconnoc *Bochenod/Botchonod: Osferth, the pre-Conquest holder, from Count of Mortain.* The original boundary ditch of a medieval deer park. William Pitt the Elder grew up in Boconnoc House.

Bodardle *Botharder:* Lost.

Bodbrane *Bodbran: Erchenbald from Count of Mortain.* ⌂

Boden *Boten: King's land.* Higher Boden, a farm.

Bodigga *Botchatwo/uwe: Canons of St Stephen's of Launceston from Count of Mortain.* ⌂ National Trust area of Bodigga Cliff; nearby is Murrayton Monkey Sanctuary, breeding place for Amazon monkeys.

Bodiggo *Bodenwitghi: Richard from Count of Mortain.* ⌂ Near Luxulyan, famous for granite quarries.

Bodmin *Bodmine:* See page 57.

Bodrugan *Bodeworgoin/wrgoin: Richard from Count of Mortain. 20 goats.* ⌂ Now Bodrugan Barton.

Boduel *Botiual: Awta, the pre-Conquest holder, from Count of Mortain. 15 goats.* ⌂ Cornish cross.

Bojorrow *Bodeworwei/ruei/owrueu:* Lost.

Bonyalva *Pennadelwan: Canons of St Stephen's of Launceston from Count of Mortain.* ⌂ In Lydcott Wood.

Bosent *Buchant/Bocent: Richard from Count of Mortain.* ⌂

Bossiney *Botcinii/cinnu: Count of Mortain from St Petroc's Church.* ▦ Near Tintagel, the legendary stronghold of King Arthur; a castle mound survives. It returned Sir Francis Drake to Parliament.

Bosvisack *Beveshoc:* Lost.

Botelet *Botiled: Odo from Count of Mortain.* ⌂

Bowithick *Bowidoc: Osferth, the pre-Conquest holder, from Count of Mortain.* ⌂ On Bodmin Moor.

Boyton *Boieton/atona/etonai: Count of Mortain from Tavistock Church; Hamelin from Count of Mortain.* ▦

Braddock *Brodehoc: Reginald from Count of Mortain.* Only a beautiful, isolated church.

Brannel *Bernel: Count of Mortain. 20 unbroken mares.* ⌂

Brea *Bret:* See page 56.

Bucklawren *Botconoan/chonoam: Canons of St Stephen's of Launceston from Count of Mortain.* ⌂

Burniere *Bernerh/Berner: Richard FitzThorold from Bishop of Exeter.* ⌂

Burthy *Brethei: Richard from Count of Mortain.* 2 farms.

Buttsbear *Brecelesbeorge/Bretelesbeorge: Alfred from Count of Mortain.* ⌂ Now Buttsbear Cross.

Cabilla *Cabulian: Aelmer, the pre-Conquest holder, from Count of Mortain.* ▦ Cabilla moorland.

Callestick *Calestoc(h): Count of Mortain from St Petroc's Church.* ⌂ Farm near Chyverton; Georgian house with park.

Callington *Calwetone/a: King's land, formerly Earl Harold. 180 sheep.* Quiet market town with Dunpath Well in a 15th-century chapel.

Calstock *Calestoch/Kalestoc: Reginald from Count of Mortain.* Small town. Cotehele House is a fine Tudor mansion with 16th-century furnishings.

Cann Orchard *Orcet: Alfred from Count of Mortain. 20 goats.* ⌂

Caradon *Carneton/e: King's land, formerly Earl Harold; Thurstan from Count of Mortain. 180 sheep.* Town, near Caradon Hill where copper was mined.

Cargoll *Cargau: Count of Mortain from St Petroc's Church.* ⌂

Carsella *Karsalan: Doda, the pre-Conquest holder, from Count of Mortain.* Farm near the china claypit area of St Austell, centre of Cornwall's most important industry.

Cartuther *Croftededor: Richard from Count of Mortain.* ⌂ Now Cartuther Barton.

Carvean *Carbihan: Andrew from Count of Mortain.* ⌂

Carworgie *Carewrge/reu(u)rga: Aiulf from the king, formerly Queen Mathilda.* ⌂

Climsom *Clismestone/a: King's land, formerly Earl Harold. 187 sheep.* ⌂

Clinnick *Clunewic/Gluinwit:* Lost.

Colquite *Chilcoit: Richard from Count of Mortain.* ⌂ Also Colquite Wood.

Connerton *Conarditone/a:* Lost.

Constantine *Sanctus Constantinus: St Constantine's from Count of Mortain.* ▦ Slate and granite; 15th-century church with a fine 16th-century palimpsest brass.

Cosawes *Cudawoid/t:* Lost.

Coswarth *Cudiford/Gudiford: King's land, formerly St Petroc's Church.* ⌂

Crackington *Crachenwe: Berner from Count of Mortain.* ⌂ Now Crackington Haven; Crackington Cove. Near the highest cliff in Cornwall, described by Thomas Hardy in *A Pair of Blue Eyes.*

Crantock *Langoroch/orroc: Canons of St Carantoc from Count of Mortain.* ▦

Crawle *Cariahoil:* Lost.

Curry *Chori: Iovin from Count of Mortain.* Now 2 hamlets, East and West Curry; Curry Lane.

Dannonchapel *Duuenant: Blohin from Count of Mortain.* ⌂

Dawna *Douenot: Hamelin from Count of Mortain.* ⌂

Delabole *Deliau/iou: Roger from Count of Mortain.* ▦ Delabole slate quarries; the largest is up to 500ft deep and 1½ miles in circumference.

Delamere *Deliau: Blohin from Count of Mortain.* ⌂ Near Delabole slate quarries.

Dizzard *Disart/Lisart: Iovin and Alnoth from Count of Mortain.* ⌂ Near 500ft high Dizzard Point.

Domellick *Dimelihoc: Gunnar from Count of Mortain.* ⌂

Downinney *Donecheniv/Donnechenif: Richard from Count of Mortain.* ⌂ Near Warbstow Bury; impressive Iron Age hill-fort nearby, with a double rampart.

Draynes *Drainos: Alric and Wulfsi, the pre-Conquest holders, from Count of Mortain.* ▦ Remote; granite cottages and a farm.

Ellbridge *Telbrig/bricg: Reginald from Count of Mortain.* ⌂

Ellenglaze *Elhil/Elil: St Petroc's Church.* ⌂ On the edge of Penhale Sands.

Fawton *Fawintone: Count of Mortain. 287 sheep, 33 unbroken mares.* ⌂

Froxton *Forchetestane/a: Thurstan from Iudhael of Totnes.* ⌂ Camping and caravan sites nearby.

Fursnewth *Fosnewit: Maccus, the pre-Conquest holder, from St Petroc's Church.* ⌂

Galowras *Gloeret: Nigel from Count of Mortain.* ⌂

Garah *Garuerot/ruro:* Lost.

Gear *Caer: Reginald from Count of Mortain.* The *Domesday* name survives in the settlement of Caer Vallack and in the hamlet of Caervallack.

Genver *Tregebri:* Lost.

Glynn *Glin: Osferth, the pre-Conquest holder, from Count of Mortain.* Glynn Mill on the River Fowey.

Goodern *Woderon: Richard from Count of Mortain.* Manor farm near Wheal Jane, a recently opened tin mine.

Gothers *Widewot: Sheerwold, the pre-Conquest holder, from Count of Mortain.* Near Restormel china clay pits.

Goviley *Ghivaile: Richard from Count of Mortain. 232 sheep.* Now 2 hamlets, Goviley Major and Goviley Dean.

Gurlyn *Worselin: Thurstan from Count of Mortain.*

Halliggye *Heligin/ighi: King's land, part of Winnianton Manor; Thurstan.* Halliggye Fougou, an underground chamber with a long main passage similar to those found near Iron Age settlements.

Halton *Haltone/a: Reginald from Count of Mortain, formerly Earl Harold.* Now Halton Barton; Halton Quay.

Halvana *Ermenheu/Hirmeneu: Leofnoth, the pre-Conquest holder, from Count of Mortain.* Halvana Plantation.

Halwyn *Elhil:* Lost.

Hamatethy *Hamotedi: Richard from Count of Mortain.*

Hammett *Hamet: Roger from Count of Mortain.* Near Hammett Down.

Hele *Hela: Cola, the pre-Conquest holder, from Count of Mortain.*

Helland (in Probus) *Henland/t: Sibert from Count of Mortain.* Now Helland Barton.

Helston *Henlistone/a: King's land, formerly Earl Harold. 14 unbroken mares, 200 sheep, 40 ale-men, who probably paid their dues in beer.* Market town, celebrated for its annual Furry (Floral) dance.

Helstone *Henliston/a: Count of Mortain. 18 unbroken mares.*

Hennett *Hesland: Count of Mortain.* On the River Valency.

Hilton *Hiltone/a: Alfred from Count of Mortain.* Overlooks Widemouth Bay.

Hornacott *Norniecote/a: Berner from Count of Mortain.* Now Lower Hornacott, near the River Tamar.

Idless *Edelet: Algar from Count of Mortain.*

Illand *Elent/Heli: Count of Mortain wrongfully from Tavistock Church; the Abbot claims it back.* Near the River Inny.

Kelynack *Chelenoc/h: Richard*

HELSTON: *Memorial to the inventor of shore-to-ship rockets.*

from Count of Mortain. Near Land's End aerodrome.

Kilkhampton *Chilchetone/a: King's land, formerly Earl Harold. 600 sheep, 50 cattle, 40 goats.* Large; 15th-century church with Norman doorway. 17th-century Stowe Barton nearby was once the home of the Grenville family.

Killigorrick *Chilorgoret: Reginald from Count of Mortain.*

Kilmarth *Chenmerch/ Chienmerc:* Lost.

Lamellen *Landmanuel/ Lantmanuel: Berner from Count of Mortain.*

Lametton *Lantmatin: Iovin from Count of Mortain.* Farm, Lametton Mill and Museum on the East Looe River.

Lancarffe *Lancharet/ Nan(t)chert: Nigel from Count of Mortain; taken from St Petroc's Church by the Count.*

Landinner *Landiner/Lan(i)liner: Count of Mortain, formerly Queen Edith.*

Landreyne *Lander: Reginald from Count of Mortain.*

Landulph *Landelech: Richard from Count Mortain.* A flourishing 15th-century port. Centre of population is now at Cargreen.

Lanescot *Lisnestoch: Richard from Count of Mortain.*

Langunnett *Langenewit/ Langunuit: Reginald from Count of Mortain.* Nearby is the 'Giant's Hedge', once 7 miles long; origin unknown.

Lanhadron *Lanlaron: Reginald from Count of Mortain.* Farm.

Lanherne *Lanherwen/ Lanherueu: Fulchard from Bishop of Exeter.* Now 2 hamlets, Higher and Lower Lanherne.

Lanreath *Lauredoch/Lanredoch: Richard from Count of Mortain.* Picturesque cottages.

Lansallos *Lansalhus/saluus: Richard from Count of Mortain.* Lansallos Beach has a smuggler's cove.

Lantivet *Nantuat/Namtiuat:* Lost; Lantivet Bay remains.

Lantyan *Lanthien/Lantien: Osferth, the pre-Conquest holder, and Reginald from Count of Mortain.* Also Lantyan Wood.

Lanwarnick *Lanawernec: Alric, the pre-Conquest holder, from Count of Mortain. 15 goats.*

Launcells *Landseu: Alfred from Count of Mortain. 50 goats.* On Bude Canal; Georgian manor; old cottages.

LANHERNE: *Saxon cross.*

Launceston *Dunheuet/d:* See page 58.

Lawhitton *Languitetone/a: Bishop of Exeter.* 13th-century church with granite pillars hewn from single stone blocks.

Lee *Lege/Lega: Hamelin from Count of Mortain.* Now Lee Barton; Lee Wood, part of a nature trail through National Trust Coombe Valley.

Leigh *Legea: Roger from Count of Mortain.* Farm.

Lesnewth *Lisniwen: Brictric, the pre-Conquest holder, from Count of Mortain.* In a wooded valley.

Levalsa *Avalde: Erchenbald from Count of Mortain.*

Lewarne *Languer:* Lost.

Liskeard *Liscarret: Count of Mortain. Market, mill. 250 sheep.* Market town; tin was tested and sold here in the Middle Ages.

Lizard *Lusart/Lisart: Richard from the king.* Tourist town on Lizard Point; its name means 'high place' in Cornish.

Ludgvan *Luduham/Luduam: Richard from Count of Mortain. 27 unbroken mares.* Nearby is Chysauster, England's oldest village street, *c.*100 BC to 3rd century AD.

Maker *Macretone: Reginald from Count of Mortain.* From Maker Heights, Mount Edgecumbe House (rebuilt in original Tudor style) looks across to Plymouth Sound.

Manely *Mingeli: Osferth from Count of Mortain.*

Marhamchurch *Maronecirche/ Maroncirca: Hamelin from Count of Mortain.* Thatch and slate houses.

Mawgen (in Meneage) *Mawan/ Maiuian/Mawant: Brictric from the king.* Nearby Trelowarren House is 16th–17th century.

Methleigh *Matele/a/Mathela: Bishop of Exeter. Count of Mortain took the fair, previously held by the Bishop.*

Milton *Mideltone/a: Hamelin from Count of Mortain.*

Minster *Talcar:* Lost.

Moresk *Moirieis:* Lost.

Moreton *Mortune: Iovin from Count of Mortain.* Now Great Moreton; Moreton Pound Farm; Moreton Mill.

Muchlarnick *Lanher: Reginald from Count of Mortain.* On the West Looe river; St Nonna's Well.

Nancekuke *Lanchehoc/ Lancichuc: Berner from St Petroc's Church.* Nancekuke Common, a disused airfield; hamlet of Nance.

Newton Ferrers *Neweton/ Niwetona/Niwetone: Reginald from Count of Mortain.* On the River Lynher near a clapper bridge; probably medieval.

Norton *Nortone/a: Iovin from Count of Mortain.* Now Norton Barton.

Old Kea *Landighe: Godwin from Count of Mortain.* Norman font in the church.

Otterham *Otrham/Ottram: Richard from Count of Mortain.*

PADSTOW: *Abbey House, possibly once part of a nunnery.*

Padstow *Lanwenehoc/ Languienoc: St Petroc's Church from St Michael's Church.* Fishing town with narrow slate alleys and quays. Padstow is named for St Petroc, who founded a monastery here in the 6th century.

Patrieda *Peret/Pedret: Count of Mortain.* Now Patrieda Barton.

Pawton *Pautone: Bishop of Exeter.* Farm; Neolithic burial mounds on the downs.

Pelynt *Plunent: Algar from Count of Mortain.* Attractive. 14th–15th century church with arcade of Tuscan columns.

Pencarrow *Penguare/Penquaro: Thurstan from Count of Mortain.* Now Pencarrow Cross; 17th century manor house.

Pendavey *Pendavid: Boia the priest from Count of Mortain.*

Pendrim *Paindran/dram:* Lost.

Penfound *Penfou: Brian from Count of Mortain.* Penfound Manor on one of Cornwall's oldest inhabited sites.

Pengelly *Pengelle/i: Ednoth, the pre-Conquest holder, from Count of Mortain.*

Pengold *Panguol: Rabel from Count of Mortain.*

Penhallym *Penhal/Pennalum: Richard from Count of Mortain. 20 goats.* Farm.

Penhalt *Pennalt: Osferth, the pre-Conquest holder, from Count of Mortain.* Penhalt Cliff overlooks Bude Bay.

Penharget *Pennehalgar: Tavistock Church.*

Penhawgar *Pennhalgar/ahalgar: Reginald from Count of Mortain.* Farm.

Penheale *Pennehel: King's land, formerly Earl Harold.* Manor house.

Penhole *Polhal: Wulfsi from Count of Mortain.*

Penpell *Penpel:* Lost.

Penpoll *Paenpau/Penpau: Reginald from Count of Mortain.*

Penpont *Penponte/a: Osferth, the pre-Conquest holder, from Count of Mortain.* Only Penpont Water, a tributary of the River Inny, remains.

Pentewan *Bentewoin: Algar from Count of Mortain.* On Mevagissey Bay. Tin from Pentewan Valley was once shipped from the harbour; there were tin works 50 feet below sea level.

Penventinue *Penfontenio: Hamelin from Count of Mortain.*

Perranuthnoe *Odenol: Brictric, the pre-Conquest holder, from Count of Mortain.* Church with 15th-century tower and a Norman font.

Perranzabuloe *Lanpiran:* See page 56.

Philleigh *Egleshos/Eglossos: Thurstan from Count of Mortain, formerly Earl Harold.* 'Cob' cottages made of straw and clay.

Pigsdon *Pigesdone/Pighesdona: Gotshelm.* Farm.

Pillaton *Piletone/a: Reginald from Count of Mortain.* Clapper bridge near Pentille Castle.

Polroad *Polrode/a:* Lost.

Polscoe *Polescat/Polschat/Polscat: Richard and Andrew from Count of Mortain. 20 unbroken mares, 240 castrated rams.* Near Restormel Castle, originally Norman and rebuilt by the Dukes of Cornwall, the first of whom was the Black Prince.

Polsue *Polduh/Poldu: Richard from Count of Mortain.* Manor farm.

Polyphant *Polefand/t: Nigel from Count of Mortain.* On the edge of Bodmin Moor. Norman stone quarries are still being worked.

Porthallow *Portatlant: Odo from Count of Mortain.* Holiday resort; formerly a fishing village.

Poughill *Pochehelle/Poccahetilla: William from Count of Mortain.* Near the site of the Royalist victory at Stamford Hill.

Poundstock *Podestot/Pondestoch: Iowin from Count of Mortain.* Norman church, rebuilt in the 15th century.

Probus *Lanbrebois/brabois: Canons of St Probus from St Michael's Church. 160 sheep.* Georgian houses. Church, with Cornwall's highest tower, is dedicated to Saints Probus and Grace, a married couple.

Rame *Rame: Ermenhald from Tavistock Church. 18 goats.* Rame Head is the site of the ruined 14th-century chapel of St Michael's once a landmark for sailors entering Sutton Pool.

Raphael *Raswale: Reginald from Count of Mortain, formerly Aelfeva.*

Rialton *Rieltone/a: St Michael's Church.* The Old Hall the summer residence of the last Prior of Bodmin (*c.* 1542) has a wagon roof and holy well.

Rillaton *Risleston/Rislestona: Count of Mortain.* On the River Lynher, opposite Rilla Mill.

Rinsey *Renti/s: Count of Mortain and Wulfward from him.* Rinsey Head, overlooking Praa Sands; remains of medieval Pengersick Castle nearby.

Roscarnon *Roscarnau:* Lost.

Roscarrock *Roscaret: Nigel and Alfred from Count of Mortain.* Ruins of a manor house; 17th-century farm buildings; chapel; holy well.

Rosebenault *Rosminuet:* Lost.

Rosecare *Roschel: Berner from Count of Mortain.*

Rosecraddoc *Recharedoc/Rekaradoc: Hamelin from Count of Mortain.* Manor house.

Roseworthy *Ritwore/i: King's land, formerly Earl Harold.* Now Roseworthy Barton; 18th-century Methodist chapel of thatch and whitewash.

St Buryan *Eglosberrie/a: Canons of St Buryan's.* Surrounded by Bronze and Iron Age relics including a stone circle, the Merry Maidens.

St Enoder *Heglosenuder/Heglosenuda. Count of Mortain from St Petroc's Church.* 14th–15th-century church with Norman font.

St Gennys *Sainguinas/Sanwinas: Iovin from Count of Mortain.* Holy well.

St Germans *St Germani/Scs German: Canons of St German's Church; Bishop of Exeter.* Town. St Germans was the seat of the Bishops of Cornwall, 926–1043. Church has a fine Norman west end and doorway.

St Juliot *Sanguiland/t: Thurstan from Count of Mortain.* Only a church still bears the name; restored by Thomas Hardy as a young architect (his wife, Emma, was the vicar's sister-in-law).

St Keverne *Lannachebran: Canons of St Achebran's from St Michael's Church.* Church with a tower-cum-spire which warns ships of a dangerous reef, The Manacles.

St Kew *Lanehoc/Lantloho: King's land. Iovin from Count of Mortain, formerly Earl Harold.* A Georgian rectory; slate cottages; Tregeare Rounds. Nearby is an Iron Age fort, with double ramparts.

St Michael's Mount *Scs Michael/Michahel: Count of Mortain, formerly Brismar the priest.* Island, castle and village named after St Michael. The castle, built as a monastery, dates from 1135.

St Neot *Neot/Nietes(s)tou: St Neot's Church; Odo from Count of Mortain.* Church with magnificent 16th–17th-century stained glass; holy well of St Neot.

POLSCOE: *Restormel Castle with a motte and bailey and parapet walk.*

St Stephen's (by Launceston) *Lanscauestone/a: St Stephen's Church; Count of Mortain took a market from this manor and put it in his castle.* District of Launceston; St Stephen's Church.

St Winnow *Sanwinuec/San Winnuc: Godfrey from Bishop of Exeter.* Church with beautiful 15th-century stained glass.

Sheviock *Savioch: Ermenhald from Tavistock Church.* Slate cottages; medieval dovecote.

Skewes *Schewit/Eschewit:* Lost.

Stratton *Stratone/a: Count of Mortain, formerly Bishop Osbern and Alfred the Marshal. 10 salt-houses, 300 sheep.* Almost a suburb of Poughill; inn with medieval timbering and a Tudor fireplace.

Tehidy *Tedintone/a: Count of Mortain.* Now Tehidy Barton; 18th-century stable block; near Tehidy Park estate.

Thorne *Torne/a: Hamelin from Count of Mortain.*

Thurlibeer *Tirlebere/a: Alfred from Count of Mortain.*

Tinten *T(h)inten: Richard from Bishop of Exeter.* Typical Cornish squire's manor, built of slate and granite.

ST KEVERNE: *Memorial window to shipwreck victims.*

Tolcarne (in Newquay) *Talcarn/Tarcharn: Count of Mortain.* Now Higher Tolcarne.

Tolcarne (North Hill) *Talgar: Ermenhald from Tavistock Church.* Tolcarne Tor on Bodmin Moor.

Tolgullow *Talgolle/o: Alnoth, the pre-Conquest holder, from Count of Mortain.* Part of the built-up area near Redruth.

Towan *Bewintone/Dewintona: King's land, formerly Earl Harold. 200 sheep, 17 cattle.*

Treal *Tragol: Thurstan from Count of Mortain.* In Poltesco Valley.

Trebarfoot *Treuerbet: Thurstan from Count of Mortain.* On Millook Common.

Trebartha *Tribertha/bertan: Thurstan from Count of Mortain.* Trebartha Barton, a farm.

Trebeigh *Trebichen/Tre-Tribicen/Trebihan/au: Count of Mortain.* Trebeigh Wood.

Trecan *Richan/Ricann:* Lost.

Tredaul/e *Tredaual: Nigel from Count of Mortain.* On Bodmin Moor; hotel; camping sites.

Tredinnick *Trehinoch/hynoc: Reginald from Count of Mortain. 2 cows.*

Tredower *Tretdeword/t/ch:* Lost.

Tredwen *Riguen: Heldric from Count of Mortain.* On Bodmin Moor.

Trefreock (in St Endellion) *Trefrioc: Blohin from Count of Mortain.* The village of St Endellion has a 15th-century church with a shrine said to be that of St Endelienta, a Celtic virgin saint.

Trefrize *Treverim: Reginald from Count of Mortain.*

Tregaire *Tregel: Lost.*

Tregamellyn *Tregemelin: Hamelin from Count of Mortain.*

Tregantle *Argentel: Reginald from Count of Mortain.* Farm. Tregantle Fort, now dismantled, was built by French prisoners-of-war during the Napoleonic wars.

Tregardock *Tragaraduc: Alfward, the pre-Conquest holder, from Count of Mortain.* Tregardock Beach, on a bleak coast, is accessible only by foot.

Tregarland *Gargalle/a: Reginald from Count of Mortain, formerly Brictric.*

Tregavethan *Treganmedan: Hamelin from Count of Mortain.* Manor house.

Tregeagle *Tregingale/a: Brictric, the pre-Conquest holder, from Count of Mortain.*

Treglasta *Teglaston/Treglastan: Count of Mortain, formerly Earl Harold.* Farm.

Tregole *Tregal: Richard from St Petroc's Church.*

Tregona *Tregon/a. Count of Mortain from St Petroc's Church.* On cliffs near Bedruthan Steps, named after a giant.

Tregony *Trelingan: Frawin from Count of Mortain.*

Tregoose *Tricoi/Trecut: Wihomarch from Count of Mortain.*

Tregrill *Tregril: Osferth from Count of Mortain.* Near Menheniot, famous in the 15th century for its stone quarries.

Tregrenna *Tregrunon/nou: Tavistock Church.* Near Tregune hut circles.

Tregunnick *Trevocarwinoc:* Lost.

Trehaverne *Tregauran:* Lost.

Trehawke *Trehauoc: Reginald from Count of Mortain.*

Trehundreth *Trewderet: Alnoth from Count of Mortain.* Trehundreth Downs.

Treknow *Tretdeno: St Petroc's church.* In a valley, once a centre of the slate trade; Treknow was the chief port.

Trelan *Treland/t: Thurstan and Doda from Count of Mortain.* Near Goonhilly Downs, an area of rare wild flowers, prehistoric remains and, now, a satellite-tracking station.

Trelaske *Trelosch/sca: Osferth, the pre-Conquest holder, from Count of Mortain.* Trelaske House, a large manor with a park.

Trelawne *Trewellogan/Trevelloien: Reginald from Count of Mortain.* Manor house, home of the Trelawney family, who settled here before the Conquest.

Treliever *Trewel/Trelivel: Bishop of Exeter.* Adjoins Penryn.

Treligga *Treluge: Odo from Count of Mortain.*

Trelowarren *Trellewaret/Trelweren: Thurstan from Count of Mortain.* 16th-17th century Trelowarren House.

Trelowia *Treoloen: Hamelin from Count of Mortain.*

Trelowth *Trel(u)wi: Thurstan from Count of Mortain.* In mining country.

Treloy *Trelloi: Count of Mortain from St Petroc's Church. 20 goats.*

Tremadart *Tremeteret/Tremethereht: Osferth from Count of Mortain. 15 goats.* Tremadart Wood, near the West Looe River.

Tremail *Tremail: Count of Mortain from St Petroc's Church. 15 cattle.* Farm.

Trematon *Tremetone/a: Reginald from Count of Mortain.* Site of the count's castle and market; Norman keep and medieval gatehouse of Trematon Castle; Regency house inside the bailey walls.

Tremblary *Trebleri: Iovin from Count of Mortain.*

Trembraze *Trenbras: Brictsi from Count of Mortain.* Prehistoric standing stones at nearby St Keverne.

TRERICE: *Manor house with extravagantly curled gables, built by Sir John Arundell in the 1570s.*

Tremoan *Tremor: Reginald from Count of Mortain.* Possibly Tremear, lost in St Ive Parish, or Tremoan, a hamlet near St Mellion.

Tremoddrett *Tremodret:* Lost.

Tremore *Tremhor/mor: Count of Mortain.* Also Tremorebridge on a tributary of the River Camel.

Trenance (in Mullion) *Trenant: King's land, part of Winnianton manor; Blectu.* Farm near Mullion Cove, once a smugglers' haunt.

Trenance (in St Austell) *Tremarustel/Tremar/wstel: Hamelin from Count of Mortain.* Trenance Downs in the china clay pit area.

Trenance *Trenant: Algar from Count of Mortain.* Near Pencra Head.

Trenant *Trenand: Osferth, the pre-Conquest holder, from Count of Mortain.* Now Trenant Cross; Trenant Park, a large house with a landscaped park on East Looe River.

TRETHEVY: *Ancient burial chamber known as the 'Trethevy Quoit'.*

Trenant in Fowey *Trenant:* Lost.

Trenderway *Trewinedoi/Treuiunadoi:* Lost.

Trenewean *Chenowen: Thurstan from Count of Mortain.*

Trenhale *Trenhal:* Lost.

Treninnick *Trinnonec/Trincnonet/Trinnonech: Count of Mortain (taken from St Petroc's Church).* Absorbed in Newquay, a holiday resort.

Trenowth *Trenwit/Trenuwit: Count of Mortain. 21 unbroken mares, 200 sheep.* Trenowth House with a ruined chapel.

Trenuth *Trevoet: Nigel from Count of Mortain.* Farm.

Trerice *Treuret: Iovin, the pre-Conquest holder, from Count of Mortain.* Elizabethan manor house with magnificent plaster ceilings and a hall window composed of 576 glass panes.

Treroosel *Tremarustel/Tremarwestel: Wihomarch from Count of Mortain.* On the outskirts of St Teath, whose church is dedicated to one of St Brychan's 24 saintly children.

Trescowe *Trescau: Alnoth, the pre-Conquest holder, from Count of Mortain.* In tin-mining country.

Treslay *Roslech/let: Berner from Count of Mortain.*

Tresparrett *Rosperuet/paruet: Iovin from Count of Mortain.* Also Tresparrett Down.

Trethake *Tredhac/Trethac: Hamelin from Count of Mortain.* Farm near Pont Pill, an attractive inlet of the River Fowey.

Tretheake *Trethac: Thurstan from Count of Mortain.* Manor house.

Trethevy *Tewardevi: Richard from Count of Mortain.*

Trevague *Trevagau/gan: Nigel from Count of Mortain.* On the edge of East Bodmin Moor.

Trevalga *Melledham: King's land.* Slate-built; church with a 13th-century tower.

Treval *Trewale: Oswulf from Count of Mortain.* Lost.

Trevedor *Travider:* Lost.

Trevell *Trewille/villa: Count of Mortain.* On Penpont Water.

Trevelyan *Trewillan/Trevillein: Reginald from Count of Mortain.* Near wooded Penpoll Creek.

Treveniel *Treviniel:* Lost.

Treverbyn *Treverbin: Richard from Count of Mortain.*

Treverres *Tretweret: Brictric from Count of Mortain.* On the east side of the River Fal.

Trevesson *Trefitent:* Lost.

Trevigue *Trerihoc: Berner from Count of Mortain.*

Trevillis *Trefilies: Humphrey from Count of Mortain.* Trevillis Wood.

Trevillyn *Trevelien: Count of Mortain.* Trevilliln Farm.

Trevisquite *Trawiscoit/Trauiscoit: Richard from Count of Mortain. Mill.* Manor house on the River Alten.

Trevornick *Trefornoc/Trefoznoc: Count of Mortain (taken from St Petroc's Church).* Tiny. Nearby are the Nine Maidens and the Fiddler, Iron Age standing stones.

Trewanta *Treiswantel/Trewant: Count of Mortain.* Farm.

Trewarnevas *Treurnivet/Trewrnivet: King's land, part of Winnianton manor; Alwin from Count of Mortain.* Near Nare Head.

Trewen *Trewin/Treguin: Berner from Count of Mortain.* Farm.

Trewethart *Treveheret/Trewehret: Blohin from Count of Mortain.* Lost; a hamlet called Trewetha remains.

Trewidland *Treviliad: Reginald from Count of Mortain.* On the East Looe River.

Trewince *Trewent: Algar from Count of Mortain.* Near the Satellite Earth Station on Goonhilly Downs.

Trewint *Trawint: Roger from Count of Mortain.* John Wesley's Cottage.

Trewirgie *Trewitghi: Count of Mortain. 180 sheep.*

Trewolland *Trewallen:* Lost.

Trewoon *Tregoin: Hamelin from Count of Mortain.* On the outskirts of St Austell.

Treworder *Trewode/wda:* Lost.

Treworrick *Treworoc: Thurstan from Count of Mortain.*

Treworyan *Treurgen: Iovin from Count of Mortain.* Treworyan farms.

Trezance *Thersent: Richard from Count of Mortain.* Near Cardinham with its fine Celtic cross and the remains of a castle belonging to the Earls of Cornwall.

Truthall *Trouthel/Treuithal: King's land, part of Winnianton Manor; Thurstan.*

Truthwall *Treiwal/Treuthal: St Michael's Church; Blohin from Count of Mortain.*

Tucoyse (St Ewe) *Ticoit(h): Richard from Count of Mortain.* Near St Ewe.

Tucoyse (in Constantine) *Tucowit: Wihomarch from Count of Mortain.* Lost in Constantine Village.

Tybesta *Tibesteu:* Lost.

Tywardreath *Tiwardrai: Richard from Count of Mortain. 200 sheep.* Large. Nearby is the Du Maurier home, Menabilly.

Tywarnehayle *Tiwarthal: Count of Mortain from St Petroc's Church. 250 sheep.* Lost; on the site of Perranporth, a village with a famous surfing beach.

Veryan *Elerchi: Leofnoth from Count of Mortain.* Some circular Regency cottages with Gothic windows.

Wadfast *Wadefeste/Wadefeste: Hamelin from Count of Mortain.*

Week Orchard *Orcert: Hamelin from Count of Mortain.*

Week St Mary *Wich/Wihc: Richard from Count of Mortain.* Market square.

Westcott *Wescote/a: Berner from Count of Mortain. 10 cattle.*

Whalesborough *Walesbrau: Brian from Count of Mortain.* Overlooks Bude Bay.

Whitstone *Witestan: Ralph from Count of Mortain. 40 goats.*

Widemouth *Widemot: Brian from Count of Mortain.* In a built-up area on Widemouth Bay.

Wilsworthy *Wilewrde/eurda: Thurstan from Count of Mortain.* Farm; Wilsworthy Cross, a T-junction.

Winnianton *Winetone/Uingetona/Uinnetona/Winnetona: King's land, formerly Earl Harold; Count of Mortain.* Farm overlooking Church Cove.

Withiel *Widie: St Petroc's Church.* Attractive; Georgian rectory; granite cottages.

Woolston *Ullavestone: Alnoth from Count of Mortain.*

Woolstone *Ulnodestone/Ulnotetestona: Nigel from Count of Mortain.*

Worthyvale *Gu(e)rdevalan: Nigel from Count of Mortain. 180 sheep.* Manor house.

Cumberland

The borders of England's most north-western territory were first defined in the twelfth century. The new county was called Cumberland, after its Welsh-speaking inhabitants, the Cymri. In 1086 there was no such place. The forbidding mountains of the Lake District were then a part of Scotland, and William I had to content himself with four isolated settlements along the Irish Sea: Millom, Whicham, Kirksanton and Bootle. These had previously belonged to Tosti, or Tostig, Earl of Northumbria, who had fallen in battle against his brother Harold shortly before the Norman invasion.

It is unlikely that William grew any richer through these frontier communities. Domesday *includes them as a part of Yorkshire, giving only their names and the amount of land (measured in carucates) at which they were taxed. Whether or not they ever paid these taxes is unknown, and it is possible that their value existed on paper alone. Being so out of the way, perhaps they escaped the march of William's army in 1069–70, when much of northern England was laid to waste. If not, they may have been reduced to medieval ghost towns and remained, more than 15 years later, four empty villages on a sand-swept coast.*

MILLOM: *The remains of Millom Castle now incorporated into a farm.*

Millom

Land of the King...
In MILLOM (HOUGUN) Earl Tosti had 4 c[arucates] of land taxable. In Killerwick 3c., Sowerby 3c., Heaton 4c., Dalton 2c., Wart 2c., Newton 6c., Walton 6c., Suntun 2c., Fordbootle 2c., Roose 6c., Hart 2c., Leece 6c., another Leece 6c., Gleaston 2c., Stainton 2c., Crivelton 4c., Orgrave 3c., Martin 4c., Pennington 2c., Kirkby Ireleth 2c., Broughton 6c., Bardsea 4c., Whicham [Westmorland] 4c., BOOTLE [Cumberland] 4c., Kirksanton [C] 1c., MILLOM (CASTLE?) (HOUGENAI) [C] 6c. (BODELE). All these villages belong to Millom.

The Lake District, like the moon, has a side to it that is not often seen. On the sandy estuary of the River Duddon, within sight of Scafell Pike, is the town of Millom. It is a place that courts both tourists and industry but fails to attract quite enough of either. Industry is still trying to pick itself up after the collapse of the iron works in the 1920s. New businesses have established themselves, encouraged by the incentives of a Special Development Area, but the industrial debris of the last century, when Millom was Cumberland's boom town, is a reminder of prosperous times that have not returned. As for the tourists, they do not come to the Lake District for broad empty beaches or bowls or miniature golf. There's gold in them thar hills, but not much of it spills down into Millom.

In 1086 Millom was on the very edge of England, the principal settlement in a group of north-western holdings that King William had taken over from Tosti, Earl of Northumbria. Only four of these are in the county that became Cumberland; the other 22 were later included in Lancashire. The *Domesday* surveyors recorded nothing but the amount of land taxable for these holdings, perhaps because more detailed information was physically difficult to obtain from such remote parts, or perhaps because there was, in truth, nothing at all to record, men and animals having fled from the rampaging armies of William the Conqueror.

It was called Hougun in *Domesday* and was assessed at four carucates of land. A holding known as Hougenai, and taxed at six carucates, is generally assumed to have been part of the same community, possibly Millom Castle. It is believed that there was a church here before the Conquest, possibly on the same site as the Church of the Holy Trinity, built by the de Boyvilles in the twelfth century. This Old Church, as it is known, was enlarged in the fourteenth century and then restored by the Victorians, but still retains an air of the embattled frontier settlement. It is a low building standing amid dry-stone walls and pastureland half a mile or so outside the modern town. Beside it is Millom Castle, now part of a working farm. Its square tower, tamed by Georgian sash windows, serves as the farmhouse; its ruined walls rise among the outbuildings. This domestic scene was once a stronghold for the Lords of Millom, who ruled the district with an authority that any tyrant would envy. Perhaps because of their distance from central authority, they were granted *Jura Regalia*, the right to hang their subjects without time-wasting trials or interfering bureaucracy. The Sheriff of Cumberland, it was said, could not enter their domain without permission.

Two powerful families, first the de Boyvilles and then, for 500 years, the Hudlestons, ruled over this little kingdom. Geographical isolation gave them scant security. Like the rest of Cumberland, Millom was plagued by the Scots after their victory at Bannockburn. In 1460 the castle was partially destroyed by the Lancastrians during the Wars of the Roses. And it was besieged again in the Civil War, when Sir William Hudleston and eight of his brothers fought for Charles I. Throughout these wild centuries Millom remained no more than a village, its population only exceeding 1000 in the nineteenth century, when iron-rich ore was discovered beneath the waters of the Duddon estuary.

Two of the other Norman holdings in Cumberland are along the coast road within five miles of Millom. Whicham, known as Witingham to the *Domesday* surveyors, has a church but little more. Kirksanton (Santacherche) is a tiny village with a row of cottages, a public house, a post office and a solid little bus stop – everything, in fact, except the church which the name implies. According to legend, Kirksanton's church sank to the bottom of a lake in ancient times, together with its minister and congregation. The fate of a modern church at Kirksanton suggests that this preposterous tale might have in it a grain of truth. Christ Church, consecrated in 1891, was torn down only 60 years later because of subsidence. Since then the villagers have taken the bus to church.

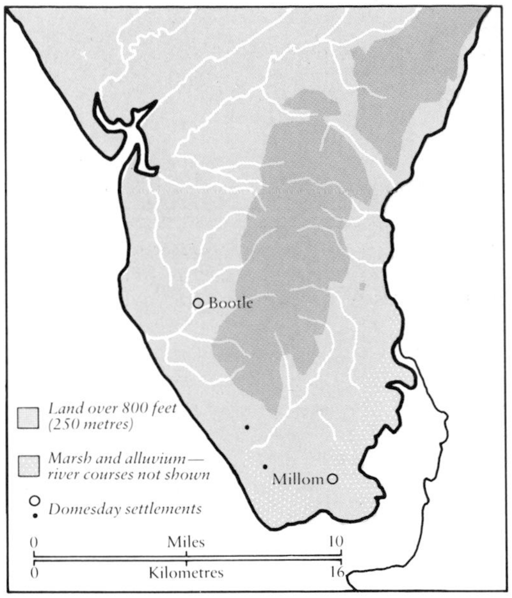

Bootle

'Bootle is a small but neat market town consisting principally of one short street of good houses, pleasantly situated about two miles from the ocean.' This description, from the *Cumberland and Westmorland Directory of 1829*, needs little alteration today. There are, of course, new houses, and a small community has sprung up around Bootle Station, which misses the town itself by about a mile. But the population, which was 656 in 1829, is still less than 1000. At heart Bootle remains a one-street town.

At the time of *Domesday*, Bootle (which is mentioned only in the entry for Millom) was the farthest that the Normans had penetrated into Cumberland. They had not yet attempted to tame the Celtic people who inhabited the mountains of the Lake District. They merely inherited those former Saxon lands that safely hugged the coast, and it is not at all certain how they held them. The property was assessed at four carucates of land, but this figure may have been completely academic. Was the community inhabited at all? The coastal plain thereabouts is fertile. It can be inferred that a settlement at Bootle in 1086 would have survived if left alone, but the *Domesday* surveyors neither knew nor, possibly, cared.

It was known as Bodele to the Normans, a name which probably derives from the Anglo-Saxon *buthl*, meaning buildings. A more colourful, local explanation has it that Bootle is a corruption of Booth-hill. At some point in Bootle's history a regular watch was kept for marauders on the Irish Sea. The watchmen were paid from a communal fund called the sea-wake. They sheltered in 'booths' on a hill above the town and lit a beacon fire when threatening ships approached. Today the British army occupies much of Bootle's sandy shore. Its guns practise firing regularly across the water, as if to warn off any lingering Viking or Scottish fleet.

'It is a matter of great surprise that tourists do not visit the town,' continued the *Directory* of 1829. Not really. The mountains, although no longer a barrier, keep most visitors for themselves; the sea here is not a great enough attraction.

Bootle's most famous tourist was William Wordsworth, who gave the town a bad press. The weather was inclement and the ocean, he complained, made too much noise.

Cumberland Gazetteer
Each entry starts with the modern place name in **bold** type. The *Domesday* information that follows is in *italic* type, beginning with the name or names by which the place was known in 1086. The main landholder – the king – is next. The modern or post-Domesday section is in normal type. represents a village, a small village or hamlet.

Bootle *Bodele:* See left.

Kirksanton *Santacherche: King's land.* 2 prehistoric burial stones.

Millom *Hougenai/Hougun:* See far left.

Whicham *Witingham: King's land.* Whicham Hall is nearby.

Derbyshire

Derbyshire was the most westerly of England's Northern Danelaw counties. Here, as in the other four, holdings were assessed for tax in carucates and bovates, rather than in the hides and virgates of the south, and the county was subdivided into wapentakes rather than hundreds. Here, oo, the tax assessments of particular settlements or groups of settlements often made totals of 3, 6 or 12, suggesting that the duodecimal system typical of the Northern Danelaw was being used.

The county was dramatically divided into two: the steep north-western corner, the Peak District, where the Pennines begin and where the recorded population was a mere 0.4 per square mile, and all the rest, where normal agriculture was possible.

In 1086, 43 settlements lay waste, and another 25 were partly waste. In the main, these settlements lay in the less fertile upland areas of the Peaks where economic expansion such as clearing and reclamation of less arable land was taking place. Most of these settlements were 'waste' or 'partly waste' to the geld or the royal taxation system. As usual William I had taken for himself large parts of the county – 38 holdings. The church, on the other hand, had a remarkably small share, divided between the Bishop of Chester and the Abbey of Burton. The largest lay tenant-in-chief was Henry de Ferrers, whose son became the first Earl of Derby.

Wirksworth

[Land of the King...] In WIRKSWORTH *WERCHESVORDE* 3 c. of land taxable. Land for 4 ploughs. A priest and a church; 16 villagers and 9 smallholders who have 4 ploughs. 3 lead mines; meadow, 26 acres; woodland pasture 2 leagues long and 2 leagues wide. Outliers of this Manor. In CROMFORD 2 c; MIDDLETON 2 c; HOPTON 4 c; WELLEDENE 2 c; CARSINGTON 2 c; CALLOW 2 c; (KIRK)IRETON 4 c.

In 1563 the town of Wirksworth, set prettily in hilly countryside on the southern edge of the Peak District, was the second most populous in the county. Today it has been left far behind, but in the steep lanes which rise and fall in all directions from its market place there is ample evidence of 800 years of prosperity.

In 1086 it was certainly prosperous; a royal manor, it was assessed at three carucates, had 27 families, a priest and a church. It gave its name to the wapentake in which it lay, and had seven outlying manors, each assessed as highly as most other individual Derbyshire manors. But the real clue to its prosperity lies in a two-word phrase: '*III plubariae*' (three lead mines). No other place in Derbyshire had more than one.

Wirksworth is mentioned again, twice, by *Domesday*, the first time in a unique way. It is included with four other large royal manors – Darley, Matlock Bridge, Ashbourne and Parwich – which, in Edward the Confessor's time, had paid £32 and 6½ sesters of honey, but now paid £40 of pure silver. There is no similar entry, and it seems likely that some silver as well as lead was being extracted from the ore. The second of these mentions describes land held by Ralph FitzHubert.

Lead mining was by no means new in Derbyshire. Twenty-seven pigs of lead with Roman inscriptions have been found in the county. Wirksworth and Matlock were the main centres of Roman mining. From AD 874, when the Danes destroyed Renton Abbey and took the manor of Wirksworth, it became the more important – the centre of what was to be known as the King's Field. There were other mining 'liberties' in the county, but the King's Field, extending over 115 square miles of limestone country, was the largest.

Domesday makes no mention of the elaborate customary laws which governed mining here. These were not formalized till 1288, and even then were difficult to remember. For the benefit of miners, Edward Manlove, steward of the Wirksworth Barmote, put them into verse. Many were stern:

> For stealing oar twice from the minery,
> The Thief that's taken fined twice shall be,
> But the third time, that he commits such theft
> Shall have a knife, stuck through his hand to th' Haft
> Into the Stow, and there till death shall stand,
> Or loose himself by cutting loose his hand;

The 'stow' was the wooden windlass built over the mine for lifting the ore. The barmaster would cut a nick in the stowes if the mine was not being worked. After the third nick a rival claimant could have the mine – hence perhaps the colloquial verb, to nick.

Wirksworth's lead mines were administered by the Barmote Council, and in 1814 lead mining was still sufficiently important for a new Moot Hall to be built for its meetings. Today this is a Christian Assembly hall and no lead has been mined since the beginning of the century. Already cotton spinning had come to the town – Arkwright's Haarlem Mill stands nearby to the south – and once the railway arrived, limestone quarrying gradually supplanted mining.

At the start of the 1970s, Wirksworth was decaying. Today it is being given a face-lift organized by the Civic Trust. Stone cottages have been repaired and an educational 'Stone Centre' created in its Colehill quarries. The town deserves it, if only for its pleasant Georgian houses. Climb up behind the town to get a wider picture of its history. Deep below on one side machines still grind out limestone. On the other side lies the vast grey-sided canyon of the lead mines. In 1086 they had already been making Wirksworth important for 1000 years.

Peak Cavern

[Land of William Peverel...] In PEAK CAVERN *PECHEFERS* Arnbern and Hunding held the land of William Peverel's castle. They had 2 c. of land taxable. Land for 2 ploughs. Now in lordship 4 ploughs; 3 villagers with 1 plough. Meadow, 8 acres. Value before 1066 40s; now 50s.

Peak Cavern is a vast limestone cave, lying close to the village of Castleton. The *Domesday* name, 'Pechefers', is also translated as 'Peak's Arse', so perhaps it was from modesty that nineteenth-century scholars mistakenly identified the place as Peak Forest, a hamlet about three miles away. From the cave a cliff rises almost vertically to the land on which the remains of Peverel's castle still stand.

William Peverel is said to have been one of William I's bastards, but this story was invented by a seventeenth-century antiquary. With a dozen holdings, he was by no means the county's greatest lay tenant-in-chief, but he also acted as the king's bailiff for the manors of Hope, Bakewell and Ashford, each of which had several outlying manors; within 22 years all these became his.

More important perhaps than his lands was his position as Steward of the Royal Forest of the Peak, which included 40½ square miles, mainly north of Castleton, and was bounded by the rivers Wye, Goyt, Etherow and Derwent. It was a hunting reserve, with a full range of officials of whom Peverel had charge; he was also responsible for bringing to justice offenders against forest law.

His stronghold, because of its position 300 feet above the village of Castleton, is England's most spectacular surviving Norman castle. It has been attracting sightseers since the eighteenth century, and there were even more after Walter Scott made it famous in his novel *Peveril of the Peak* in 1823. It is protected on the west by the unscalable precipice which falls into Peak Cavern, and on the south-east by a descent into Cave Dale, which is only a little less vertical. Even the relatively easy approach from the village demands a long zigzag path.

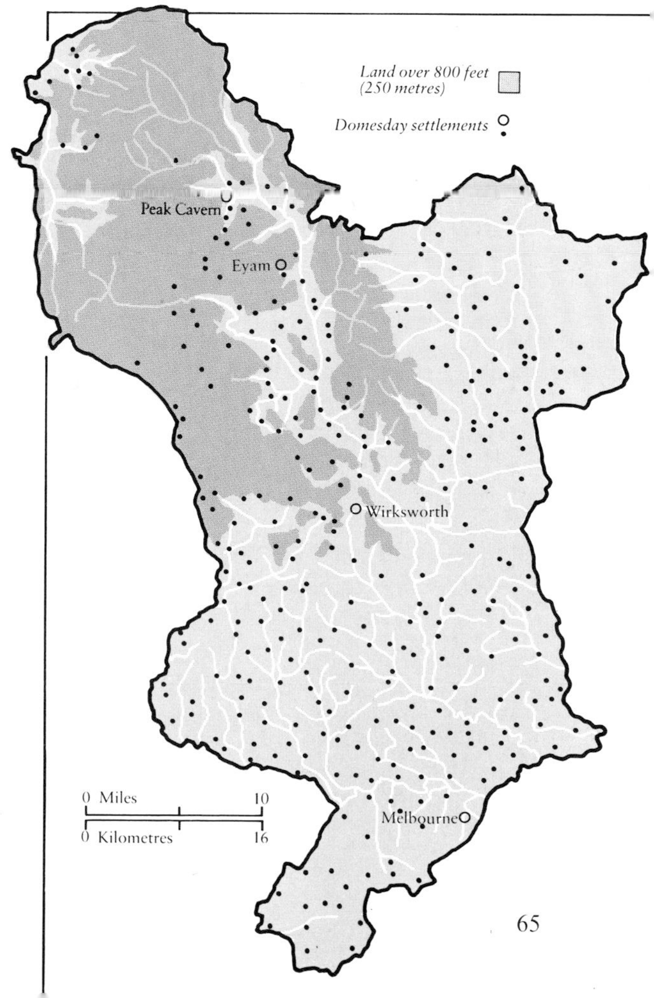

EYAM: *Detail from the Saxon cross, weather-worn but still-powerful carvings.*

Peverel erected a curtain wall, enclosing a parallelogram roughly 220 feet by 160 feet, but he built no other buildings; so it seems certain that even if his knights sometimes lived up there, their camp followers did not. They had their own settlement of Castleton, with its own defensive work. Known as the Town Ditch, this circled the village to the north, east and west; small lengths can still be seen.

The Peverel family fought on the wrong side in the civil war during Stephen's reign (1135–1154) and though they briefly returned to favour under Henry II (1154–1189) they were finally dispossessed when the second William Peverel poisoned his mistress's husband, the Earl of Chester. It was after this that Henry II added the castle keep, today its most picturesque feature. The walls, eight feet thick at the bottom, formed a hall 22 feet by 19 feet. A small additional room, built partly in one wall and partly projecting over Peak Cavern, was a latrine.

Eventually the castle fell into disrepair and much of its stone was taken to build local houses. By 1561 the curtain wall formed a pound for animals illegally grazing the forest. On one occasion foresters impounded 800 ewes without water; according to their owners, many died, though the foresters denied this.

As if the castle were not enough to draw visitors, the village contains some of England's most remarkable limestone caves of which Peak Cavern is the finest. Its mouth is 40 feet high, 100 feet wide and 300 feet deep, and it stretches back for some 2000 feet in the form of gradually lower chambers, with pools of water. To reach the last, it was once necessary to lie flat on your back in a small boat and be floated below a rock barrier two feet above your head; but Queen Victoria, who visited Castleton when a child, suggested that the barrier be raised. Her advice was unfortunately taken. Byron came here to spend a romantic day with his love, Mary Chawton, daughter of the man his great uncle had killed in a London tavern. In the nineteenth century visitors could arrange with the parish clerk to have Castleton's choir sing to them 'from a high ledge near the roof'.

To the west of Castleton, up a narrow gorge known as Winnats, the most interesting of the other local caves produces 'Blue John', a semi-precious variety of fluorspar found nowhere else in the world.

But these underground wonders are mere sideshows to the castle. The crowds who come to be awed by it partly spoil what they came to experience. Castleton, however, perhaps because it never got a railway and has remained a village, survives better than most such places. Turn your back on the tearooms and souvenir stalls, and look up at the castle. Subtract Henry II's keep, and it is easy to catch the unpleasantly threatening flavour of William Peverel's impregnable bastion of 900 years ago.

Eyam

[Land of the King. . .] In (EYAM) *AIVNE* Kaskin had 2 c. of land taxable. Land for 2 ploughs. 12 villagers and 7 smallholders have 5 ploughs. Woodland pasture 1 league long and 1 wide. Value before 1066 and now 20s.

Eyam is a bosky place, compared to the nearby uplands of the Peak District, with their treeless stone-walled fields. The well-wooded length of Eyam Edge protects it to the north, there are beech clumps among its stone houses, and the church is surrounded by tall limes. In a nearby sycamore there is even a rookery.

Here in the churchyard stands one of the features which make Eyam somewhat self-conscious: its superb eighth-century cross. Its existence suggests that Christianity had reached Eyam two hundred years or more before the Conquest, so it is strange that *Domesday* mentions no church.

Eyam, one of the king's manors, supporting 19 families, was then also bosky, with a large area of wood pasture. Like many other places in the county, it is credited with more plough teams than land for them to plough, but *Domesday* scholars now remind us that figures given for plough lands, like figures given for carucates, may have been for tax purposes and do not necessarily reflect the real facts.

As late as the eighteenth century Eyam's cross lay neglected in a corner of the churchyard. By the beginning of the present century it was well known enough to be endangered by 'those who think it sport to climb up and sit on the arms'. But it survived, and is almost as perfect today as when it was carved some 1250 years ago.

Eyam is justly proud of the way it behaved in 1665, the year of the Plague of London. That August, George Vicars, a tailor lodging in a cottage near the church, received a box of cloth from London. Two days later he was ill with 'swellings and a rose-red rash'. On 7 September he died.

Soon there were more cases of plague, and some villagers, including Squire Bradshaw and his family, fled. But the rector, William Mompesson, helped by his nonconformist predecessor, Thomas Stanley, persuaded the rest to put the village into voluntary isolation. Food was left for them a mile away at Mompesson's well and the money they left in return was disinfected with vinegar before it was taken. Gallant though they were, the villagers may not have had much choice. Derbyshire had had outbreaks of plague before and knew the danger. Visitors to Sheffield who were suspected of coming from Eyam were driven away with sticks and stones.

Some 350 villagers out of about 850 died, including Mrs Mompresson, whose tomb (with her name spelt Mompesson) is in the churchyard. The epidemic seemed to end when winter came, but raged again all next summer. A certain Mrs Hancock buried seven of her family, who all died in one week. But thanks to Mompresson, the plague was confined to Eyam.

Today George Vicars' cottage is known as Plague Cottage. Beside its door, and the doors of many other village houses, wooden plaques list the victims of Eyam's great disaster.

Melbourne

[Land of the King. . .] In MELBOURNE *MILEBVRNE* King Edward had 6 c. of land taxable. Land for 6 ploughs. The King has 1 plough and 20 villagers and 6 smallholders who have 5 ploughs. A priest and a church; 1 mill, 3s; meadow, 24 acres; woodland pasture 1 league long and 1/2 league wide. Value before 1066 £10; now £6; however it pays [£]10 . . .

The small town of Melbourne lies eight miles south of Derby, close to the Leicestershire border. In 1086 this was the most heavily populated part of the county. Melbourne was a large royal manor, with a mill, a priest, a church, meadows for hay and a large area of wood pasture to support its 26 families. It had six outlying manors. Unlike many villages that lay to its north, mining did not contribute to its prosperity.

Today Melbourne has a busy upper town, with shops and traffic, and a quiet lower village. Here the great pool, the castle ruins, the twelfth-century tithe barn, the Hall with its formal gardens and the Norman church of St Michael-with-St-Mary make it one of the most interesting places in Derbyshire.

The church is so grand for so small a place because it was the Bishop of Carlisle's. When the Scottish borders became too fierce for comfort, he would take refuge at Melbourne. It had probably replaced the Saxon church of *Domesday* before 1152. Though the great west door is impressive, it is the interior – the nave with its dog-toothed arches, second storey of arches and ambulatory – which gives the church its breathtaking magnificence.

The garden of the Hall (once the bishop's palace) is in its way as remarkable. It was laid out for Thomas Coke around 1700 by the famous designers London and Wise in the style of André le Nôtre, gardener to Louis XIV. Many English gardens were then created in his style. Melbourne Hall's is remarkable because it is one of the very few which were not swept away later by Capability Brown and his imitators.

Thomas Coke's son-in-law, Matthew Lamb, a successful solicitor, went into Parliament and bought Brocket in Hertfordshire. From then on this was the main family residence, and remained so even when they were made peers, though they took the title of Melbourne. The second Viscount Melbourne became Queen Victoria's prime minister, and his sister, to whom the estates passed, married Lord Palmerston. As a result, few changes were made to the Melbourne gardens. Today, with their clipped beech avenues, round ponds and outgrown yew hedges, they seem a fossilized if shaggy miniature Versailles.

All that survives of Melbourne's fourteenth-century castle is a great chunk of wall, supporting Castle Farm's outbuildings. Nearby there was a mill – possibly that listed in *Domesday* – though another lay closer to the Hall, where its millpool was enlarged in the eighteenth century to form Melbourne's great pool. Interesting as these things are, there is nothing medieval at Melbourne that can be compared with its magnificent church.

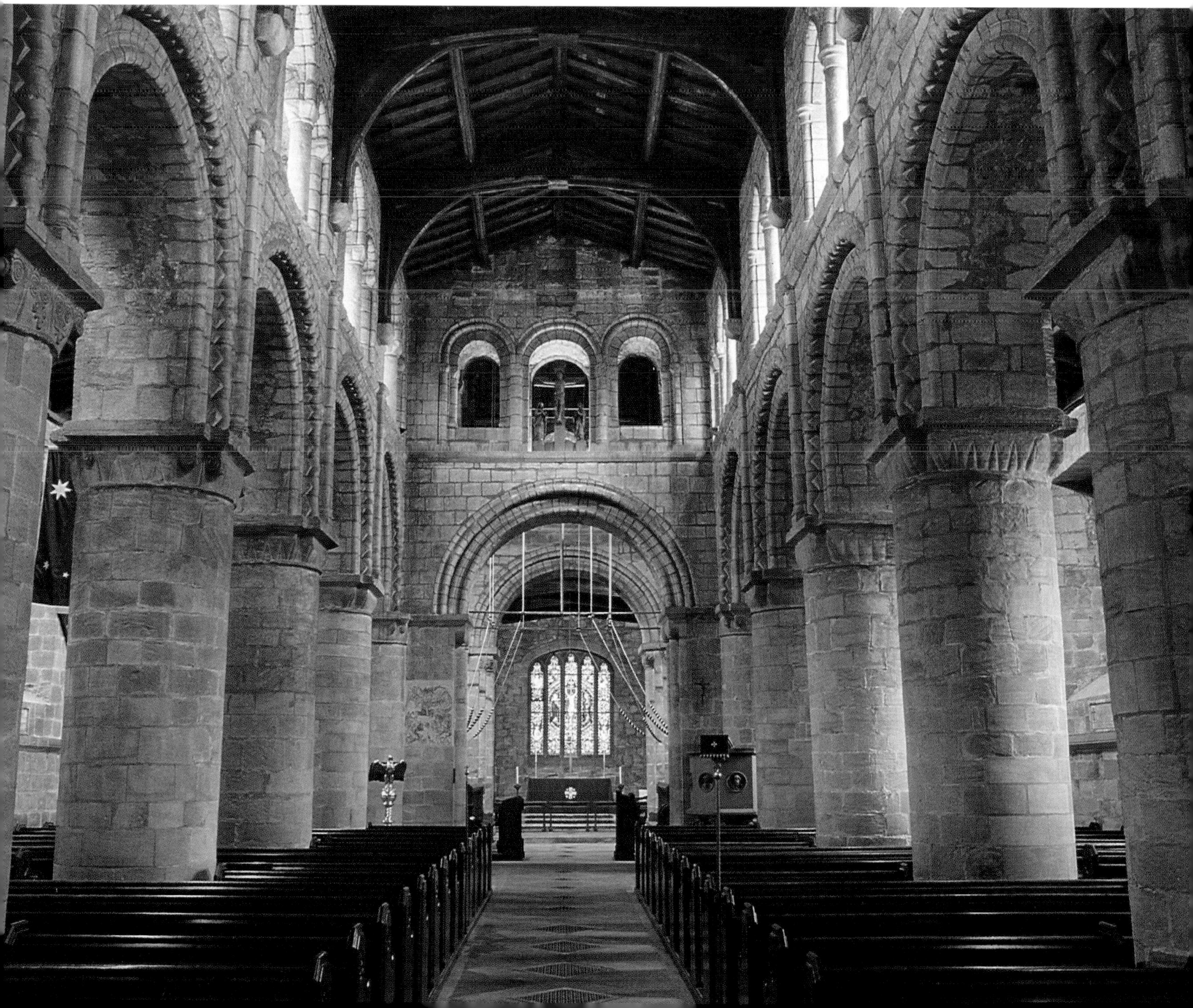

MELBOURNE: *The imposing nave of St Michael-with-St-Mary, with its 2 storeys of Norman arches. It probably stands on the site of the* Domesday *church.*

Derbyshire Gazetteer
Each entry starts with the modern place-name in **bold** type. The *Domesday* information is in *italic* type, beginning with the name or names by which the place was known in 1086. The main landholders and under-tenants follow, separated with semi-colons if a place was divided into more than one holding. The king's thanes, always the last in a list, are described as holding land 'from the king'. More general information, including examples of dues such as honey rendered by tenants, completes the *Domesday* part of the entry. The modern or post-Domesday section is in normal type. ▦ represents a village, ⌂ a small village or hamlet.

Abney *Habenai: William Peverel.* ▦ Abney Grange. William Newton, the minstrel, was born at Cockey Farm.

Alfreton *Elstretune: Ingran from Roger de Bully.* ▦ Industrialized Market town; Alfreton Park.

Alkmonton *Alchementune: Ralph from Henry de Ferrers.* ▦

Allestree *Adelardestreu: Earl Hugh.* ▦

Alsop (en) le Dale *Elleshope: Coln from the king.* ▦

Alvaston *Aleuuoldestune: Geoffrey d'Alselin. Church, mill.* ▦ On the River Derwent. St Michael's Church has a Saxon coffin lid.

Ambaston *Emboldestune: Geoffrey d'Alselin. Church, mill.* ⌂

Arleston *Erlestune: Henry de Ferrers.* ▦

Ash *Eisse: Robert from Henry de Ferrers.* ⌂

Ashbourne *Esseburne: King's land. Church. £40 of pure silver.* Market town on the Henmore Brook. Wesley preached here; Thomas Moore and Rousseau both lived here; Dr Johnson stayed at the Green Man Inn.

Ashford (in the Water) *Aisseford: King's land. Mill, mill site, lead mine.* ▦ Remains of a moat from the 14th-century fortified house that belonged to Edward II's brother.

Ashover *Essorre: Serlo from Ralph FitzHubert. Church, mill.* ▦ Lead-mining. All Saints' Church has an important Norman font. Dorothy Mately of Ashover was immortalized in Bunyan's *The Life and Death of Mr Badman (1680).*

Aston (near Hope) *Estune: King's land, in the charge of William Peverel.* ⌂ Aston Hall (1578) is probably the first Renaissance building in the Peak District.

Aston (near Sudbury) *Estune: Alchere from Henry de Ferrers.* ⌂

Aston-upon-Trent *Estune: Uhtbrand from the king; Henry de Ferrers.* ▦ Aston Hall.

Atlow *Etelauue: Henry de Ferrers.* ⌂

Bakewell *Badequella: King's land. Church, mill, lead mine. Outliers: Burton, Conkesbury, Haddon, Holme, Monyash, One Ash, Rowsley.* ⌂ Central town of the Peak District, where the famous Bakewell tart originated; Roman and Saxon well sites. Chatsworth and Haddon Hall are nearby.

Ballidon *Betidene: Ralph FitzHubert.* ⌂ Prehistoric burial chambers on the crest of Minning Low hill; partly Norman chapel.

Bamford *Banford: Ralph FitzHubert.* ▦ It has had an association with cotton spinning ever since the original corn mill was converted 200 years ago.

Barlborough *Barleburg: Robert from Ralph FitzHubert. Church, 2 mills.* ▦ Barlborough Hall; Barlborough House.

Barlow *Barleie: Hascoit Musard; the king's thanes.* ▦

Barrow-upon-Trent *Bar(e)uue: King's land; Henry de Ferrers; Ralph FitzHubert, the pre-Conquest holder.* ▦

Barton Blount *Barctune: Ralph from Henry de Ferrers. Church, 2 mills.* ▦

Baslow *Basselau: King's land.* ▦ Old packhorse toll bridge. Eagle Stone at Baslow Edge is a great gritstone boulder.

Bearwardcote *Bereuuardescote: Burton Abbey; Henry de Ferrers.* ▦

Beeley *Begelie: King's land.* ▦ Scattered, with a brook running through it.

Beighton *Bectune: Roger de Poitou, the pre-Conquest holder; Ralph FitzHubert; Leofwin from Roger de Bully.* ▦

Birchill *Berceles: King's land.* Birchill Bank Wood; Birchill Bank Farm.

Birchover *Barcovere: Henry de Ferrers, the pre-Conquest holder.* ▦ Museum of Bronze Age finds from Stanton Moor.

Blackwell (near Tideswell) *Blacheuuelle: King's land.* ⌂ Jedediah Strutt, who with Arkwright invented the spinning jenny, had a farm here.

Blingsby *Blanghesbi: King's land, formerly Roger de Poitou.*

Bolsover *Belesovre: Robert from William Peverel.* Town. Bolsover Castle is Jacobean with a Norman keep. Charles I was entertained here with a masque by Ben Jonson.

Bonsall *Bunteshale: King's land.* ▦ Lead-mining; evidence of population in *c.*2000 BC. In the 19th century, it was a centre for framework knitting.

Boulton *Boletune: Ralph FitzHubert.* ▦ With Alvaston.

Boyleston *Boilestun: Roger from Henry de Ferrers. Mill.* ▦ 200 Cavaliers were captured in Boylestone Church by Roundheads.

Boythorpe *Buitorp: King's land.* ⌂

Bradbourne *Bradeburne: Henry de Ferrers. Church.* ⌂ The shaft of an 8th-century Saxon cross remains in its churchyard.

Bradley (in Belper) *Bradelei: Henry de Ferrers. Church, 2 mills.* ⌂

Bradley (near Ashbourne) *Braidelei: Henry de Ferrers.* ▦ Dr Johnson often visited Bradley Hall.

Bradwell *Bradewelle: William Peverel.* ▦ Plain quarrying; formerly lead-mining. A well-dressing festival is held in August. Bagshaw Cavern is in Bradwell Dale.

Brailsford *Brailesford: Elfin from Henry de Ferrers. ½ church, mill.* ▦ There is a circular Saxon cross at All Saints Church.

Bramley *Branlege: Roger de Bully.* ⌂

Brampton *Brandune/tune: Walter d'Aincourt; Hascoit Musard.* ▦

Brassington *Branzinctun: Henry de Ferrers.* ▦ Quarrying; formerly a lead-mining centre. It is set among limestone caves in which prehistoric animal bones were found.

Breadsall *Braideshale: Henry de Ferrers and Robert from him. Church, mill.* ▦ Norman All Saints Church was set on fire by suffragettes (1914). Erasmus Darwin spent his last years at Breadsall Priory.

Breaston *Bradestune/ Braidestone/-tune: Herbert from Henry de Ferrers; Geoffrey d'Alselin and Gilbert de Ghent, the pre-Conquest holders; Mauger from Gilbert de Ghent; Fulk from Roger de Bully.* Suburb of Long Eaton.

Bretby *Bretebi: King's land.* ▦ Attractive; Bretby Park; earthworks in Castle Field.

Brimington *Brimintune: King's land.* ▦

Broadlowash *Bredelauue: King's land.* ⌂

Bubnell *Bubenenli: King's land.* ⌂ Attractive 17th-century hall.

Bupton *Bubedene/dune: Bishop of Chester before and after 1066; Elfin from Henry de Ferrers. Church, mill.* ⌂

Burley *Berleie: King's land. Church.* Burley Fields Farm in Darley Dale; Burley Hill; Burley Grange.

Burnaston *Burnulfestune: Henry de Ferrers.* ▦

Burton *Burtune: King's land.* Burton Close; Burton Moor.

Caldwell *Caldewelle: Burton Abbey.* ▦ Caldwell Hall, now a school.

Callow *Caldelauue: King's land.* Farm.

Calow *Calehale: Dolfin claims it from Steinulf and Dunning, the king's thanes.* ▦

Calver *Caluoure: King's land.* ▦ Calver Mill was used as the background in the television series on Colditz.

Carsington *Ghersintune: King's land. Outlier of Wirksworth.* ⌂ Defoe is said to have discovered a mining family who were born and lived in a cave at Carsington Pasture.

Catton *Chetun: Nigel from Henry de Ferrers.* ▦

Chaddesden *Cedesdene: Henry de Ferrers, the pre-Conquest holder.* ⌂

Charlesworth *Cheuenesuurde: King's land.* ▦ Medieval market town.

Chatsworth *Chetesuorde: King's land in the charge of William Peverel.* Chatsworth House, home of the Cavendish family and the Dukes of Devonshire, is one of Britain's greatest and most beautiful houses.

Chellaston *Cele/Celardestune: King's land; Amalric from Henry de Ferrers.* ▦ Famous in the Middle Ages for its alabaster quarries used for figure carving by Nottingham and Burton artists.

Chelton *Cellesdene. Lost.*

CHESTERFIELD: *Remarkable 15th c. twisted spire.*

Chesterfield *Cestrefeld: King's land.* Large industrial town; the first town to be lighted by gas lamps.

Chisworth *Chiseuurde: King's land.* ⌂

Chunal(l) *Ceolhal: King's land.* ⌂

Church Broughton *Broctune: Henry de Ferrers.* ▦

Clifton *Cliptune: Ralph FitzHubert.* ▦

Clowne *Clune: Robert from Ralph FitzHubert; Ernwy from the king.* ▦ Markland Grips is an earthwork with a 600ft long, 7ft wide rampart.

Coal Aston *Estune: Leofwin, from the king.* ▦

Codnor *Cotenoure: Warner from William Peverel. Church, mill.* Town; 13th-century Codnor Castle ruins.

Coldeaton *Eitune: Coln from the king.* ▦ Site of a pagan cremation ground.

Conk(e)sbury *Cranchesberie: King's land.* ▦ Old packhorse bridge.

Cotes in Darley *Cotes: King's land. Church.* Cotes Park in Alfreton district.

Coton-in-the-Elms *Cotes/ Cotune: Burton Abbey from the king.* ▦

Cottons *Codetune: King's land. Henry de Ferrers.* Cottons Farm.

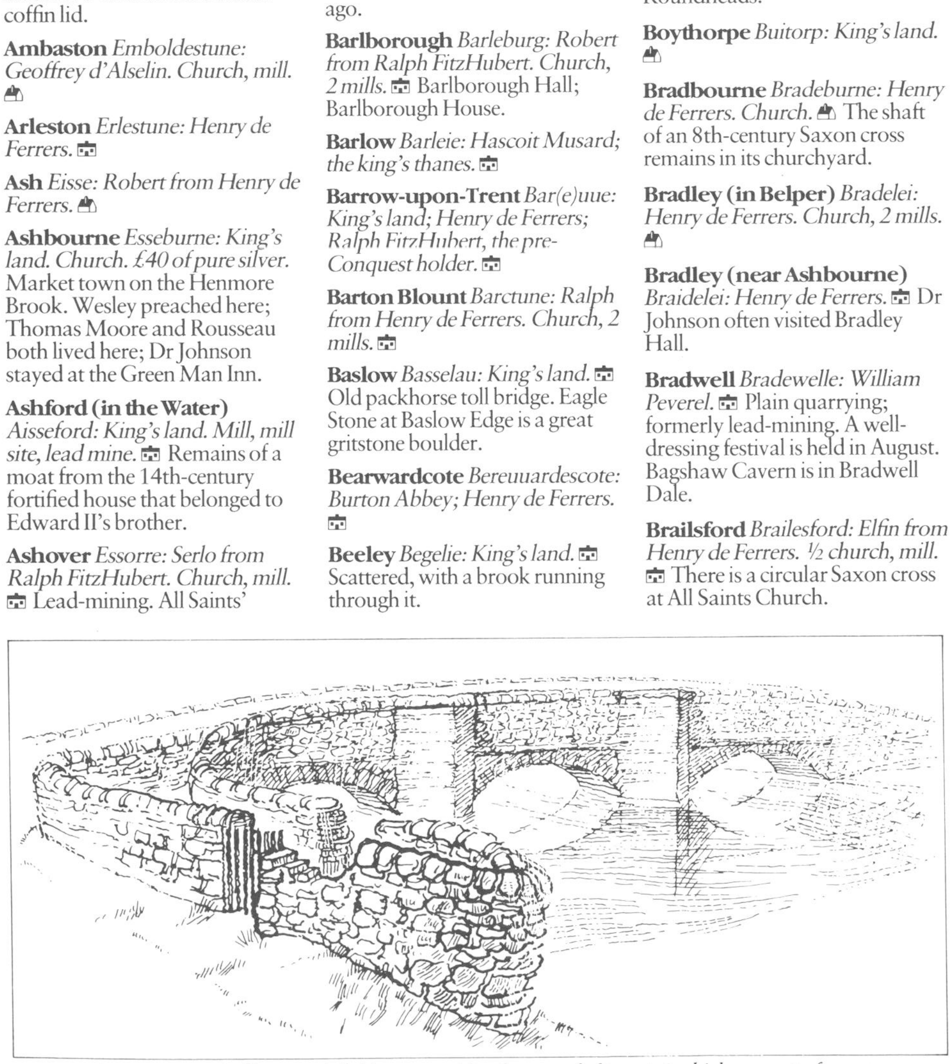

ASHFORD (IN THE WATER): *Sheepwash Bridge, named for the extended parapet which curves to form an enclosure for sheep waiting to be driven across the river.*

Cowley *Collei: Swein from Henry de Ferrers.*

Coxbench *Herdebi: Henry de Ferrers; Ralph de Buron. Church, 2 mills.*

Crich *Crice: Ralph FitzHubert. Lead mine.* Mining; Crich Cliff quarry. Crich Stand war memorial is 950ft above sea level on a limestone cliff.

Cromford *Crunforde: King's land. Church.* Market town with an old mill (1771) where Richard Arkwright first used water power for a cotton mill.

Cubley *Cobelei: Ralph from Henry de Ferrers. Church, mill.* Now 2 hamlets, Little and Great Cubley, the latter on a Roman road.

Dalbury *Delbebi/Dellingeberie: Burton Abbey. Robert from Henry de Ferrers. Church.*

Darley *Derelei(e): King's land formerly King Edward. Church. 2 sesters of honey, £40 of pure silver.* Church with a Norman font and Burne Jones window. A world-famous yew tree, allegedly England's oldest (2000 years), is in Darley Dale churchyard.

Denby *Denebi: Ralph de Buron. Mill site.* Denby Old Hall, an Elizabethan manor house.

Drakelow *Drachelauue: Nigel of Stafford. Mill site.* Drakelow House.

Draycott *Draicott: Bishop of Chester before and after 1066. 2 churches, mill, fishery.*

Dronfield *Dranefeld: King's land.* Small town. In 1643 Dronfielders complained to their bishop that they had not heard a sermon for a year, or received the sacrament for 10 years.

Duckmanton *Dochemaneston: Geoffrey from Ralph FitzHubert.* Now Long Duckmanton.

Duffield *Duuelle: Henry de Ferrers. Church, 2 mills.* Small town. The mound of Duffield Castle, a formidable Norman fortress built by Henry de Ferrers, is at the bottom of Castle Hill.

Eaton Dovedale *Aitun: Alchere from Henry de Ferrers. Mill.*

Eckington *Echintune: King's land; Ralph FitzHubert. Mill.* Town.

Edale *Aidele: King's land in the charge of William Peverel.* Marks the beginning of the Pennine Way.

Edensor *Ednesoure: Henry de Ferrers.* Near Chatsworth; a 19th-century architectural fantasy with houses incorporating Swiss, Italian, Tudor and Jacobean elements; built by the Duke of Devonshire and designed by John Robertson of Derby.

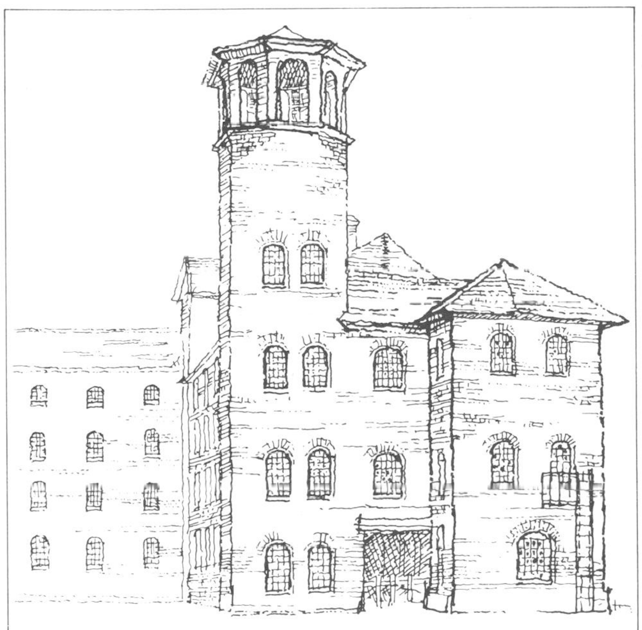

DERBY: *Lumbe's Silk mill, 1717, on an island in the Derwent River.*

Derby *Derby: King's land and the Abbot of Burton, Osmer the priest and Godwin the priest from the king; Earl Hugh; Geoffrey d'Alselin; Ralph FitzHubert; Norman of Lincoln; Edric; Henry de Ferrers. 4 churches, 4 residences, fishery.* County town with mainly 18th-century centre. England's first silk mill was built here in 1717; engineering is its main industry.

Dinting *Dentinc: King's land.* Now Dinting Vale. Railway Centre is a railway museum.

Doveridge *Dubrige: St Pierre sur Dives Abbey from Henry de Ferrers. Church, mill.* Ancient yew tree in St Cuthbert's churchyard.

Edlaston *Duluestune: Orm from Henry de Ferrers.*

Ednaston *Ednodestun(e): Jocelyn from Earl Hugh; Geoffrey d'Alselin. ½ church.*

Egginton *Eghintune: Azelin from Geoffrey d'Alselin. Church, mill.* Attractive. St Wilfrid's Church is *c.*1300.

Egstow *Tegestou: Robert from Ralph FitzHubert.*

Elmton *Helmetune: Walter d'Aincourt. Church.* Church.

Elton *Eltune: Henry de Ferrers.* Its high street runs between limestone and gritstone.

Elvaston *Aluuoldestun: Geoffrey d'Alselin. Church, mill.* Elvaston Castle, partly 17th century, is the seat of the Earl of Harrington.

Etwall *Etewelle: Saswalo from Henry de Ferrers; Azelin from Geoffrey d'Alselin. Church.* Norman St Helen's Church.

Eyam *Aiune.* See page 66.

Farley *Farleie: King's land. Church.* In mining district.

Fenny Bentley *Benedlege: King's land.* Church contains effigies of Thomas Beresford, whose 21 children provided Henry V with a complete troop of horsemen at Agincourt.

Fenton *Faitune: Henry de Ferrers. Mill.*

Findern *Findre: Burton Abbey. 2 mill sites.*

Flagg *Flagun: King's land.* Bleak, mining. Dry-stone wall-building contests and Easter point-to-point steeplechases are held here.

Foremark *Forneuuerche: Nigel of Stafford. Mill.* Foremark Hall.

Foston *Faruluestun: Henry de Ferrers.*

Glapwell *Glapewell: Serlo from William Peverel.* Glapwell Hall.

Glossop *Glosop: King's land.* Town. Old Glossop was a Roman settlement and from 1290 a market town. Its importance was reinforced by the Industrial Revolution.

Gratton *Gratune: Henry de Ferrers.* Gratton Moor.

Great Rowsley *Reuslege: King's land.* Stanton Moor is nearby, with a stone circle and Bronze Age (1000 BC) burial ground.

Greyhurst *Greherst:* Lost.

Hadfield *Hetfelt: King's land.* Town.

Hallam *Halen/lun: Ralph de Buron; Mauger from Gilbert de Ghent. Mill site.* Now 2 villages, Kirk and West Hallam.

Handley near Stavely *Henlege: Robert from Ralph FitzHubert; Leofwin and Sidred from the king.* Now 2 hamlets, Middle and Nether Handley.

Handley near Stretton *Henlege: Robert from Ralph FitzHubert.* Handley Lodge.

Hanson Grange *Hanzedone: Coln from the king.* Old farmstead, site of an ancient burial ground.

Hardstoft *Hertestaf: King's land.*

Harthill *Hortle/til: Henry de Ferrers, the pre-Conquest holder; Colle from Ralph FitzHubert.* Harthill Hall. Stone sites on Harthill Moor include Nine Stones, the remains of an Iron Age fort and a hermit's cave.

Hartington *Hortedun: Henry de Ferrers.* Town with lead and copper mines and a market since the 13th century.

Hartshorne *Heorteshorne: Henry de Ferrers.*

Hassop *Hetesope: King's land.* Hassop Hall was a royalist garrison in 1643 during the Civil War.

Hathersage *Hereseige: Ralph FitzHubert.* According to tradition, the grave of Little John, Robin Hood's follower, is in the churchyard.

Hatton *Hatun(e): Henry de Ferrers and Saswalo from him.*

Hayfield *Hedfelt: King's land.* Famous for its old fair with sheepdog trials. Joseph Hague (Dick Whittington) was born here.

Hazlebadge *Hegelebec: William Peverel.* Hazlebadge Hall (1549), the earliest example of the vernacular style of manor houses in the Peak District.

Heanor *Hainoure: Warner from William Peverel. Church.* Town.

Hearthcote *Hedcote: Nigel of Stafford. Mill site.*

Heath *Lunt: Roger de Poitou.*

Hilton *Hiltune: Burton Abbey, Robert from Henry de Ferrers. 2 mills.*

Hognaston/eston *Ochenauestun: King's land.*

Holbrook *Holebroc: Henry de Ferrers.* Holbrook Hall.

Hollington *Holintune: Henry de Ferrers; Geoffrey d'Alselin.*

Holme *Holun: King's land; Hascoit Musard.* 17th-century Holme Hall.

Holme (in Chesterfield) *Holun: Hascoit Musard.* Holme Hall Farm.

Holmesfield *Holmesfelt: Walter d'Aincourt.* 17th-century Holmesfield Hall.

Hoon *Hougen: Burton Abbey.* Hoon Ridge; Hoon Mount.

Hope *Hope: King's land, in the charge of William Peverel. Church, mill.* Attractive; 9th-century Saxon cross in the churchyard.

Hopton *Opetune: King's land.*

Hopwell *Opeuuelle: Bishop of Chester before and after 1066 and Ralph FitzHubert from him. 2 churches, mill, fishery.*

Horsley *Hosselei: Ralph de Buron.* Horsley Hall.

Hough *Hoge: Saswalo from Henry de Ferrers. Mill.*

Hucklow *Hochelai: William Peverel.* 2 hamlets, Great and Little Hucklow. Grindlow, an ancient settlement with a prehistoric barrow, and 1300ft Burrs Mount, now a landing area for gliders, are on either side of Great Hucklow.

Hulland *Hoilant: Geoffrey d'Alselin. ½ church.* Hulland Hall.

Hungry Bentley *Benelene: Ralph from Henry de Ferrers.* Jacobean farm house, all that remains of a lost village.

Ible *Ibeholon: King's land..*

Ilkeston *Tilchestune: Mauger from Gilbert de Ghent; Osmund Bent and Toli, from the king. Mill site.* Market town.

Ingleby *Englebi: King's land. Ralph FitzHubert and Nigel of Stafford, the pre-Conquest holders from the king. Mill site.* Pagan cemetery (AD 800–950) with over 50 burial mounds, in Heath Wood.

Ivonbrook *Winbroc: Henry de Ferrers.* Ivonbrook Grange.

Kedleston *Chetelestune: Wulfbert from Henry de Ferrers. Mill.* Ancient seat of the Curzons. Kedleston Hall is a superb Georgian house with work by Robert Adam.

Kidsley *Chiteslei: King's land.* Kidsley Park Farm.

Killamarsh *Chinewoldemaresc: Hascoit Musard; the king's thanes.* On Chesterfield Canal.

Kinder *Chendre: King's land.* Near the Kinder Scout, the highest (2088ft) summit in the Peak District, often called 'the Peak'.

Kirk Ireton *Hiretune: King's land.*

Kirk Langley *Lengelei: Ralph FitzHubert.*

Kniveton *Cheniuetun: Earl Hugh.* Ancient yew outside an 11th-century church.

Langley *Langelei: Warner from William Peverel. Church, mill.* Langley Mill.

Lea *Lede: Ralph FitzHubert, the pre-Conquest holder.* Lea Hurst in nearby Holloway was the home of Florence Nightingale.

Linton *Linctune: Henry de Ferrers.* Manor house.

Litchurch *Ludecerce: King's land.* Part of Derby.

Little Chester *Cestre: King's land. Church.* Part of Derby; Roman Camp of Derwent, the largest in Derby.

Little Eaton *Detton: King's land.* On the River Derwent. Nearby Peckwash Mills, important for paper in the 19th century, are on the site of a 13th-century corn mill.

Little Ireton *Iretune: Orm from Henry de Ferrers.* Mill. Ireton Farm.

Littleover *Parva Ufra: Burton Abbey. 2 mill sites.*

Litton *Litun: William Peverel.* Site of a flourishing stocking-making industry in 18th century. A well-dressing festival is held here in summer.

Longdendale *Langenedele: William Peverel from the king.* In the old Royal Forest.

Long Eaton *Aitone: Bishop of Chester before and after 1066. 2 mill sites.* Part of Derby.

Longstone *Lang/Longesdune: King's land; Henry de Ferrers.* Now 2 villages, Little Longstone, and Great Longstone, previously a shoemaking centre with 18th-century houses.

Lowne *Lunt: Roger de Poitou.* Lowne Heath.

Ludwell *Ledouuelle:* Lost.

Lullington *Lullitune: Edmund from the king. Mill.*

Mackworth *Macheuorde: Earl Hugh.* Ruined castle.

Makeney *Machenie: Henry de Ferrers.*

Mapperley *Maperlie: King's land in the charge of William Peverel.* Mapperley Park.

Mappleton *Mappletune: King's land.* Quiet.

Markeaton *Marcheto(u)ne: Earl Hugh; Henry de Ferrers. Church, mill, fishery.* Markeaton Hall.

Marsh *Mers.* Lost.

Marston-upon-Dove *Merstun: St Pierre-sur-Dives Abbey from Henry de Ferrers. Church, mill.* Part of the original foundation of Tutbury Priory, founded 1080. St Mary's Church has Derbyshire's oldest bell (1366).

Matlock *Maslach: King's land.* Spa and beauty spot known as 'Little Switzerland', written of by Byron and D. H. Lawrence; caverns and spring at High Tor.

Matlock Bridge *Mestesforde: King's land. Lead mine. £40 of pure silver.* Part of Matlock; 19th-century church; 13th-century bridge.

Melbourne *Mileburne.* See page 67.

Mercaston *Merchenestune: Robert and Roger from Henry de Ferrers.* Mercaston Hall.

Mickleover *Overe/Ufre: Burton Abbey. 2 mill sites.*

Middleton *Middeltune: Henry de Ferrers.* Spectacular Hopton Wood quarries. The writer. D. H. Lawrence lived at Mountain Cottage (1918–19).

Middleton by Youlgr(e)ave *Middeltune: King's land.* Charming. Featured in the television series, *Country Matters.*

Milford *Muleforde: Henry de Ferrers.* Jedediah Strutt founded the mill in 1780 and lived at Milford House.

Milton *Middeltune: King's land. Church, 2 mills.*

Monyash *Mareis: King's land. Lead mine.* A market fair has been held here since 1340; long a lead-mining centre.

Morley *Morelei/eia: Henry de Ferrers.* St Matthew's Church is Norman with a moated mound.

Morton *Mortune: Walter d'Aincourt. Church, mill.*

Mosborough *Moresburg: Ralph FitzHubert, the pre-Conquest holder.* Mosborough Hall.

MUGGINGTON: *Halter Devil Chapel, early 18th c.*

Mugginton *Mogintun: Ketel from Henry de Ferrers. Church, mill.* Norman All Saints Church. Halter Devil Chapel was built by a farmer who swore to ride to Derby even if he had to halter the Devil.

Nether Haddon *Hadune/un/una: King's land.* Haddon Hall, built on the foundations of a Norman stronghold; Norman font in the chapel.

Nether Seal *Scella: Robert from Henry de Ferrers. Mill.*

Newbold *Neuuebold: King's land.* Part of Chesterfield. Its Norman church was sacked by a Protestant mob in 1688.

Newton (near Alfreton) *Neutone: Ralph FitzHubert.* Tibshelf nearby is the site of Newton Old Hall (1690).

Newton *Neutune: Henry de Ferrers.* Newton Grange. It was a sheep farm in the Middle Ages, owned by Combermere Abbey.

Newton Solney *Newetun: King's land.*

Norbury *Nordberie/Nortberie: Henry de Ferrers. Church, mill.* St Mary's Church has 2 Saxon cross shafts. Norbury Hall, now a farmhouse, was the home of the powerful Fitzherbert family.

Normanton by Derby *Norman(es)tune: King's land; Henry de Ferrers. Church, 2 mills.*

North Wingfield *Winnefelt: Walter d'Aincourt. Church.* Chantry House; Norman St Lawrence Church.

Ockbrook *Ochebroc: Geoffrey d'Alselin.* Moravian settlement.

Offcote *Ophidecotes: King's land.* Offcote House.

Offerton *Offretune: King's land in the charge of William Peverel; Ralph FitzHubert.* Offerton Hall; Offerton Moor. Little John, Robin Hood's follower, is said to have been born here.

Ogston *Ougedestun/ghedestune: Walter d'Aincourt; Ralph FitzHubert, the pre-Conquest holder. Church, mill.* Ogston Hall.

One Ash *Aneise: King's land.* Medieval Ash Grange farmstead where the Liberal statesman John Bright spent his honeymoon.

Osleston *Osmund/Oslavestune: John from Henry de Ferrers.* Osleston Hall is near the site of a lost village.

Osmaston *Osmundestune: Elfin and Orm from Henry de Ferrers.*

Osmaston by Derby *Osmundestune: King's land; Henry de Ferrers.* Part of Derby.

Over Haddon *Hadune/un/una: King's land.*

Over Seal *Alia Scela: Robert from Henry de Ferrers.*

Owlcotes *Caldecotes: Walter d'Aincourt.*

Padfield *Padefeld: King's land.*

Palterton *Paltretune: Rainward from Ralph FitzHubert. Mill.*

Parwich *Pevrewic: Coln from the king. £40 of pure silver.* 18th-century Parwich Hall. Mesolithic tools prove the existence of an Anglo-Saxon community.

Peak Cavern *Pechefers:* See page 65.

Pentrich *Pentric: Ralph FitzHubert.*

Pilsbury *Pilesberie: Henry de Ferrers.* Grassy mounds known as Pilsbury Castle mark a Norman castle on a Saxon or Iron Age earthwork.

Pilsley (near Bakewell) *Pirelaie: Henry de Ferrers.*

Pilsley *Pinneslei: Walter d'Aincourt.*

Potlock *Potlac: Burton Abbey.* Potlocks Farm House.

Potter Somersale *Alia Summersale: Aelfric from Henry de Ferrers.*

Priestcliffe *Presteclive: King's land.* Scene of the legend of Talcen, who lived with a holy hermit in a cave near here after his love, Ethelfleda, was killed during battle against the Danes.

Quarndon *Cornun: King's land. Church.* Medicinal spring; ivy-covered tower wall from the old church.

Radbourne *Radburne/Rabburne: Henry de Ferrers.* Radbourne Hall.

Ravensholme *Rauenef:* Lost.

Repton *Rapendun(e): King's land. Church, 2 mills.* Mercian capital in the 7th century. Repton public school, founded *c.*1556, incorporates the remains of a 12th-century priory.

Ripley *Ripelie: Ralph FitzHubert.* Mining and market town.

Risley *Riselie: Ernwin claimed it from Fulk who held it from Roger de Bully; Leofwin's son from the king.* Risley Hall.

Rodsley *Redeslei/Redlesleie: Burton Abbey; John from Henry de Ferrers.*

Rosliston *Redlauestun: King's land. Church, mill.*

Roston *Roschintone/tun: Henry de Ferrers. Church, mill.* With Norbury.

Rowland *Ralunt: King's land.* Old mining settlement.

Rowthorn *Rugetorn: Roger de Bully.*

Sandiacre *Sandiacre: Toli, the pre-Conquest holder, from the king. Church, mill.* Norman St Giles Church.

Sapperton *Sapertune: Roger from Henry de Ferrers.*

Sawley *Salle: Bishop of Chester before and after 1066. 2 churches, mill, fishery.*

Scarcliffe *Scardeclif: Rainward from Ralph FitzHubert. Mill.* Norman St Leonard's Church; Scarcliffe Park is nearby.

Scropton *Scroftun/Scrotun(e): Henry de Ferrers, claimed by Geoffrey d'Alselin. Church, mill, mill site.*

Sedsall *Segessale: Alchere from Henry de Ferrers. Mill.*

Shardlow *Serdelau: Uhtbrand from the king.* Fine 18th-century canal port; 17th-century Shandlow Hall.

Shatton *Scetune: King's land in the charge of William Peverel.* The model for Jane Eyre lived at Shatton Hall.

Sheldon *Scelhadun: King's land.* Manor house; well-preserved lead-mining buildings at Magpie Mine.

Shipley *Scipelie: Mauger from Gilbert de Ghent.* Shipley Hall.

Shirland *Sirelunt: Warner from William Peverel.*

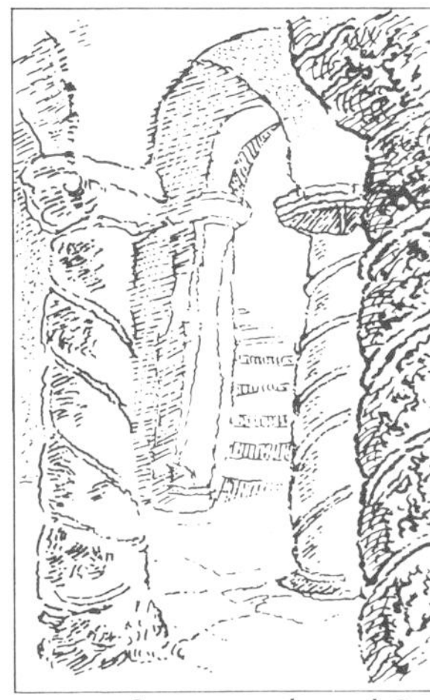

REPTON: *Saxon crypt beneath St Wystan Church.*

Shirley *Sirelei(e): Henry de Ferrers. Church, mill.* The church contains tombs of the Ferrers family.

Shottle *Sothelle: Godric from Henry de Ferrers.* Shottle Hall.

Shuckstonfield *Scochetorp: Ralph FitzHubert. Lead mine.*

Sinfin *Sedenfeld: William from Henry de Ferrers.* Part of Derby.

Smalley *Smalei: King's land.*

Smisby (Smithsby) *Smidesbi: Nigel of Stafford.*

Snelston *Snellestune: Burton Abbey; Ralph from Henry de Ferrers.*

Snitterton *Sinetretone: King's land.* Snitterton Hall (1590), an outstanding example of Peakland vernacular architecture.

Snodeswick *Estrotrewic:* Lost.

Soham *Salham.* Lost.

Somersal Herbert *Sommersale: Alchere from Henry de Ferrers.* Elizabethan Somershall Hall.

South Normanton *Normentune: Edwin from William Peverel.* Birthplace of Jedediah Strutt (1726–97), whose spinning machine revolutionized the cotton industry.

South Wingfield *Winefeld: William Peverel from Count Alan and Robert from him.* Wingfield Manor House where Mary Queen of Scots stayed.

Spondon *Spondune: Henry de Ferrers. Church, mill.*

Stainsby *Steinesbi: Roger de Poitou.*

Stanley *Stanlei: Robert FitzWilliam.*

Stanton (near Newhall) *Stantun: Henry de Ferrers.* Close to collieries and pottery manufacturers.

Stanton by Bridge *Stantun: Ernwy from the king. Mill.*

Stanton by Dale *Stantone: Gilbert de Ghent. Mill site.* Stanton Hall.

Stanton in the Peak *Stantune: Henry de Ferrers.* Stanton Moor has many prehistoric sites marking cremation burials.

Stavely *Stavelie: Hascoit Musard. Church, mill.* Mining town.

Stenson *Steintune: Henry de Ferrers.*

Stoke *Stoche: King's land in the charge of William Peverel.* Stoke Ford.

Stoney Houghton *Holtune: Walter d'Aincourt.*

Stony Middleton *Middeltu(o)ne: King's land. Ralph FitzHubert.* A summer well-dressing festival is held here.

Stretton *Stratune: Robert from Ralph FitzHubert.* Stretton House.

Stretton Hall *Stratune alia: Robert from Ralph FitzHubert.* Stretton Hall Farm.

Sturston *Stertune: Henry de Ferrers. Mill.* Sturston Grove.

Sudbury *Sudberie: Alchere from Henry de Ferrers. Church, mill. 100 eels.* 17th-century Sudbury Hall, home of Queen Adelaide, wife of William IV for 3 years, has Grinling Gibbons carvings.

Sutton on the Hill *Sudtun(e): Burton Abbey; Wazelin from Henry de Ferrers. Church, mill.*

Sutton Scarsdale *Sudtune: Roger de Poitou. Mill.* Sutton Hall (1724), now a ruin, was the county's grandest mansion.

Swadlincote *Sivardingescotes: Nigel of Stafford.* Town.

Swarkeston *Sorchestun/ Suerchestune: King's land; Henry de Ferrers. Mill site.* Spectacular; Swarkeston Bridge spans the Trent and runs ¾ mile across meadows.

Taddington *Tadintune: King's land.* Mining. Five Wells tumulus, a Bronze Age chambered tomb, the highest in England (over 1400ft), is on Taddington Moor.

Tansley *Taneslege/Teneslege: King's land; Ralph FitzHubert, the pre-Conquest holder.* Pretty; mill.

Tapton *Tapetune: King's land; Dolfin from the king.* Tapton House was the home of George Stephenson, the engineer.

Temple Normanton *Normantune: King's land.*

Thornsett *Tornesete: King's land.*

Thorpe *Torp: King's land.*

Thulston *Torulfestune/ulvestun: Geoffrey d'Alselin from Henry de Ferrers. Church, mill.*

Thurvaston *Tor/Turverdestune: Elfin and Robert from Henry de Ferrers.*

Tibshelf *Tibecel: King's land in the charge of William Peverel.*

Ticknall *Tichenhalle: King's land; Burton Abbey; Nigel of Stafford, the pre-Conquest holder.*

Tideswell *Tidesuuelle: King's land in the charge of William Peverel.* Market town, 1000ft above sea level.

Tissington *Tizinctun: Henry de Ferrers. Mill.* Possibly the Peak District's prettiest; famous well-dressing festival.

Trusley *Toxenai: Hugh from Henry de Ferrers.*

Tunstal *Tunestalle:* Lost.

Tupton *Top(e)tune: King's land; Walter d'Aincourt; the king's thanes.* Parish.

Twyford *Tuiforde: Henry de Ferrers. Mill.*

Uftonfields *Upetun: Warner from William Peverel; Nigel from Ralph FitzHubert, the pre-Conquest holder.*

Unstone *Honestune/Onestune: King's land. Church, 2 mills.*

(Upper) Hurst *Herct: Ralph FitzHubert.*

Upton *Upetune:* Lost.

YOULGREAVE: *The village well, 'dressed' with flowers in gratitude for an abundant supply of water.*

Wadshelf *Wadescel: Walter d'Aincourt; Hascoit Musard.*

Wallstone *Walestune: Godric from Henry de Ferrers.* Wallstone Farm.

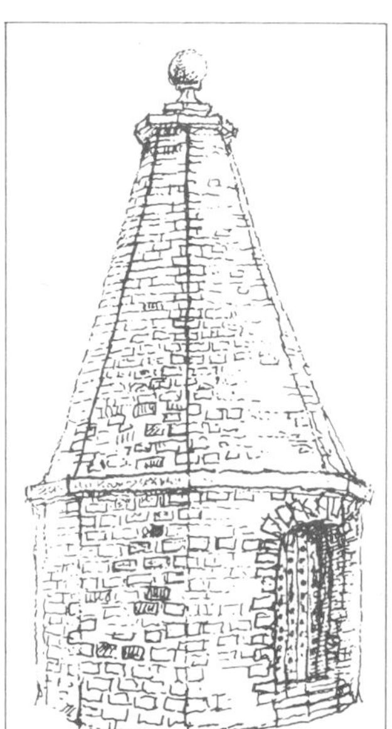

TICKNALL: *17th c. village lock-up.*

Walton *Waletune: King's land.*

Walton-upon-Trent *Waletune: King's land. Church, mill.*

Waterfield *Watrefold.* Lost.

Wensley *Wodnesleie: King's land.* Attractive, with one street; probably a pre-Christian settlement.

Wessington *Wistanestune: Walter d'Aincourt; Leofing from Ralph FitzHubert, the pre-Conquest holder. Church, mill.*

Weston Underwood *Westune: Gilbert from Ralph de Buron.*

Weston upon Trent *Westune: King's land. 2 churches, mill, fishpond, ferry.* Weston Grange; mainly 13th-century church; old mill wheels.

Whitfield *Witfeld: King's land.* Part of Glossop.

Whittington *Witintune: King's land.* Now 2 towns, Old and New Whittington. The plan to replace James II with William of Orange was plotted in Revolution House.

Whitwell *Witeuuelle: Robert from Ralph FitzHubert. Church, 2 mills.* Whitwell Hall; Norman St Lawrence Church.

WINSTER: *Market Hall with 17th c. arches.*

Willesley *Wiuesleie/Wiuleslei: King's land; Henry de Ferrers.* Area near Ashby de la Zouch.

Williamthorpe *Wilelmestorp: Walter d'Aincourt.* Williamthorpe Lane; Williamthorpe Colliery.

Willington *Willetune: Ralph FitzHubert.*

Wingerworth *Wingreurde: King's land.* Wingerworth Hall was a Roundhead garrison.

Winster *Winsterne: Cola from Henry de Ferrers.* Market since 1640; lead-mining in the 18th century. A Pancake Race takes place every Shrove Tuesday.

Wirksworth *Werchesu(u)orde.* See page 65.

Wormhill *Wruenele: Henry de Ferrers.* Trappers hunted wolves in the nearby royal forest. William Bagshawe, 'the Apostle of the Peak', preached his first sermon here.

Wyaston *Widerdestune: Orm from Henry de Ferrers.*

Yeaveley *Ghiveli: Alfsi from Henry de Ferrers.* Remains of a Preceptory of the Knights Hospitallers: Stydd Hall, *c.*1190.

Yeldersely *Geldeslei: Cola from Henry de Ferrers.* Yeldersley Hall; Yeldersley Farm.

Youlgreave *Giolgrave: Henry de Ferrers. Mill.* Name is a corruption of the Saxon 'auldgroove', meaning old mine. Well-dressing displays and a carnival are held in July.

Devonshire

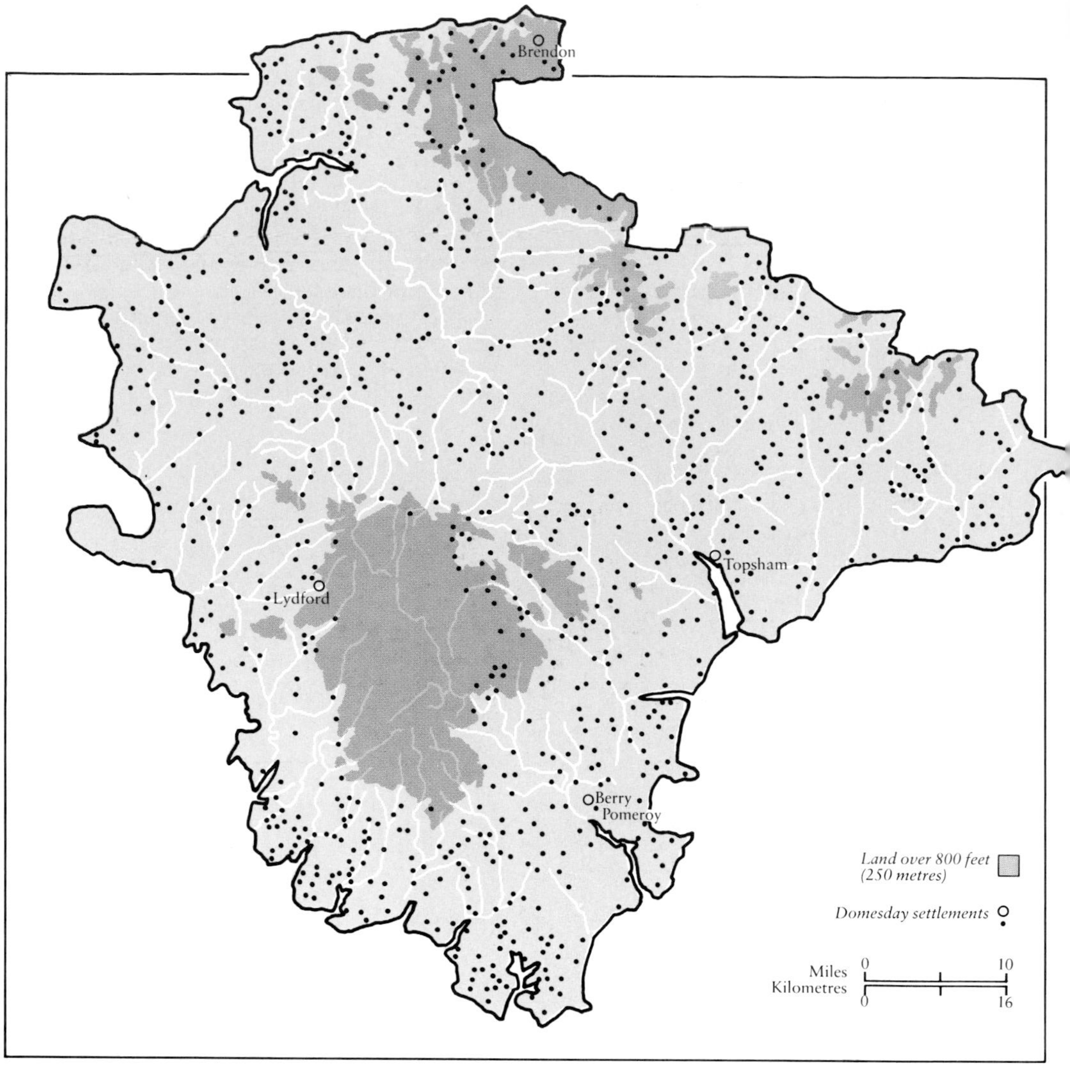

Devonshire is England's third largest county, and one of only three to have both a north and south coast. The Anglo-Saxon Chronicle *in 823 referred to the inhabitants as* Defnas, *a name derived from the Celtic Dumnonii, who settled in the south-west of England.*

The county is bordered to the north-east by Somerset (with which it shares the national park of Exmoor) and by Dorset to the south-east. Its western border is the River Tamar, a boundary that was probably fixed during Athelstan's reign, 150 years before Domesday. *Its most prominent feature is Dartmoor, a great granite mass that rises to more than 2000 feet. The population was probably between 60,000 and 80,000, scattered in small hamlets over the lower, more hospitable areas. The only place of any size was Exeter, with about 1500 inhabitants. The four boroughs of Totnes, Barnstaple, Okehampton and Lydford would all be no more than small villages by today's reckoning.*

Another set of entries known as the Exeter (Exon) Domesday *covered Cornwall, Somerset and Devon. Information from these is included in the translations used here.*

Brendon

Ralph [de Pomeroy] himself holds BRENDON *BRANDONE.* Alward son of Toki held it before 1066. It paid tax for 1 hide. Land for 8 ploughs. In lordship 2 ploughs; 5 slaves; 1/2 hide. 7 villagers and 6 smallholders with 6 ploughs and 1/2 hide. Woodland, 30 acres; pasture, 2 leagues. 1 cob; 104 unbroken mares; 25 cattle; 8 pigs; 100 sheep; 30 goats. Formerly 30s; value now 100s. 'LANK COMBE' has been added to this manor. Edwin held it before 1066. It paid tax for 1 furlong. Land for 1 plough. 1 villager who pays 3s. This Edwin could go where he would.

The little village of Brendon, just across the Devon border from Somerset, near the northern coastal edge of Exmoor, was part of a large parish. This embraced three other *Domesday* manors that no longer exist: Cheriton, Badgworthy and Lank Combe. They were all held by Ralph de Pomeroy, who with his brother, William Cheever ruled over a large slice of north-west Exmoor. Judging by the inventory of their animals and the increase in the value of their land, they seem to have been expert livestock farmers in areas that were then poorly cultivated and climatically inhospitable. The Exeter (Exon) *Domesday* lists Ralph as having at Brendon one packhorse, 104 unbroken mares, 25 head of cattle, eight swine, 100 sheep and 30 goats; there were comparable lists in many of their other holdings.

The moor around Brendon has been a romantic place of pilgrimage ever since 1869, when R. D. Blackmore's novel *Lorna Doone*, appeared. More than a century later, there is still speculation about whether or not his Doone family were real, and if so, which was the valley in which they lived. There were certainly legends in Blackmore's day of a long-gone band of brigands named Doone. A local guidebook of 1853 says, 'The Doones of Badgworthy were a gang of bloodthirsty robbers who haunted ... Exmoor about the reign of Charles I, and ravaged the whole country around. Many tales are still extant of their daring and ferocity.'

They were reputed to have been a noble Scottish family who had fled from their native land to the south-west after their claim to the lands of the Earl of Moray was frustrated. Settling in a remote valley of the East Lyn, they survived and prospered by plundering the local populace. There is a quantity of circumstantial evidence in support not only of them having existed, but of their bloodthirstiness. A lady who signed herself Audrie Doon wrote in 1901 to the *West Somerset Free Press* claiming to be a descendant of Sir Ensor Doone, the original head of the family who settled on Exmoor. She owned relics, she said, including a pistol dated 1681 bearing the name C. Doone (Carver?) and a portrait of Sir Ensor. But, alas, they were all lost in a fire before they could be examined.

The most likely valley for Blackmore to have chosen for the ruffians' hideout is Hoccombe Combe which runs into Badgworthy from below Brendon and where there were ruined medieval dwellings which the gang could have used. Some enthusiasts, however, favour nearby Lank Combe, which has better natural fortifications and also boasts the Water Slide that plays such an important part in the story. Up to a point both may be true, for Blackmore later said, 'If I had dreamed that it ever would be more than a book of the moment, the descriptions of scenery ... would have been kept nearer to their fact. I romanced therein, not to mislead any other, but solely for the uses of my story.'

No matter what the tourists seek, what they find is some of the finest landscape in the West Country. The Exmoor ponies, with their mealy-coloured muzzles, are probably indigenous and truly wild, unlike other so-called 'wild' British breeds. They are sturdy little beasts, highly valued, and capable of carrying heavy men over considerable distances. It will have been a herd of these ponies that Ralph de Pomeroy kept, and which was noted down so carefully by the *Domesday* surveyors.

Berry Pomeroy

Ralph [de Pomeroy] himself holds BERRY (POMEROY) *BERIE.* Alric held it before 1066. It paid tax for 2 hides. Land for 25 ploughs. 16 slaves. R(alph) has 1 hide and 4 ploughs in lordship. 45 villagers and 17 smallholders with 17 ploughs and 1 hide. Meadow, 10 acres; woodland, 100 acres; pasture, 40 acres. 8 cattle; 17 pigs; 560 sheep. Formerly £16; value now £12.

The ownership of Berry Pomeroy Castle has changed only once in over 900 years. Soon after the Conquest King William granted the manor of Berry to the Norman Ralph. With his brother, William Cheever, he controlled more than 60 manors in Devonshire, including over 45,000 acres under cultivation.

Although the more important part of their lands was in the north-west of the county, Ralph chose a magnificent site at the other end of Devon for his residence. He was a successful and committed farmer: the Exon entry for Berry lists cattle and swine as well as 560 sheep, and the decrease in the value of the manor shown in

Domesday may reflect the sale of some assets to pay for the building of his extremely grand stronghold.

Berry Pomeroy stands upon a rocky prominence some two and a half miles north-east of Totnes. Thick woods of beech and oak cover the sides of its hill, while on the only exposed flank the ground drops away to Gatcombe Brook, some 200 feet below. The original Norman castle was probably square with only one entrance, on the south side. The present ruin dates chiefly from the fourteenth century, and while the entrance is still in the same place, it now consists of a heavy gatehouse set into a huge curtain wall.

The Pomeroys held Berry for almost 500 years, until the middle of the sixteenth century. The last of the family to live there, Sir Thomas Pomeroy, was rumoured to have been heavily implicated in the rebellion of 1549, and he may have made the castle over to Edward Seymour, Lord Protector and Duke of Somerset, to escape persecution. It is more likely, however, that the property was simply sold to the Seymour's whose descendants still own it and who lived there until late in the seventeenth century.

Berry Pomeroy is a ruined castle with a difference, for inside the broken medieval fortifications are the ruins of a great mansion, built by the Seymours. They were immensely wealthy, and were reputed to have spent more than £20,000 to build this house, which, even so, was never completed to their satisfaction. A writer who went there in the late seventeenth century, not long after the fourth baronet, Sir Edward Seymour, had finally abandoned the place, wrote: 'Before the door of the Great Hall was a noble work, whose length was the full breadth of the court, arched over with curiously carved freestone, supported in the fore part by several stately pillars of the Corinthian order, standing on pedestals having cornices and friezes finely wrought. The apartments within were very splendid . . . well adorned with mouldings and fretwork, some of whose marble clavils were so delicately fine that they would reflect an object from a great distance.'

It was splendidly conceived, and it is still unique: the shell of an opulent aristocratic mansion set among the ruins of a grim medieval fortress of the lords of Pomeroy.

Lydford

The King has the Borough of LYDFORD *LYDFORDE*. King Edward held it in lordship. 28 Burgesses within the Borough, 41 outside. Between them they pay 60s by weight to the King. They have 2 carucates of land outside the Borough. 40 houses destroyed since the King has come to England. But if an expedition goes out by land or by sea, (the Borough) pays as much service as Barnstaple or Totnes.

Towards the end of the ninth century, King Alfred created four fortified *burhs* for defence against the Danish marauders, and Lydford was an obvious choice for one. Standing on Dartmoor's western foothills, it is surrounded on three sides by deep valleys, including the profound gorge of the River Lyd. Alfred built a massive earth rampart across the exposed approach from the north-east, much of which remains. The wealthy Ralph de Pomeroy, as well as the king, held some of the land, and if the town was somewhat desolate at the time of the survey, as *Domesday* implies, it did not remain so for long. It became significant in the administration of Dartmoor Forest and was the juridical centre of the immensely valuable tin-mining (stannary) industry. At the end of the twelfth century, a castle was built on the site of an earlier Norman stronghold to hold prisoners, and it remained in use as an occasional prison for over 500 years; the present tower was rebuilt in the thirteenth century.

This was a dreadful gaol, infamous for its cruelty. Since the Crown derived a substantial income from Dartmoor tin, it encouraged production by permitting the tin miners to run their own Stannary courts in which they alone could try and be tried for all offences except murder, bodily injury and the theft of land. Accordingly, they behaved much as they wished, and retribution to any who opposed them was swift and terrible.

In the words of an old local rhyme:

They have a castle on a hill;
I took it for some old wind-mill,
The vanes blown off by weather.
To lie therein one night 'tis guessed
'Twere better to be ston'd or press'd
Or hang'd, ere you come thither . . .
I oft have heard of Lydford Law,
How in the morn they hang and draw
And sit in judgement after . . .

During the reign of Henry VIII, a miner named Richard Strode tried to get a bill through

PRINCETOWN. *The prison churchyard reflects the town's gloomy history.*

LYDFORD: *A village on Dartmoor's foothills.*

Parliament restricting mining operations near the coastal ports, in order to prevent the harbours from becoming blocked with silt washed down from the mines. Stannary law fined him for this, and when he refused to pay he was thrown into the castle dungeon, 'which prison,' he wrote with impassioned loathing, 'is one of the most annoious, contagious and detestable places wythin this realme.'

The extraordinary privilege granted to the tin-miners to exert such rough justice was at last withdrawn in Elizabeth I's reign, but Lydford Castle continued to attract those with a taste for blood. During the Civil War the Royalists summarily executed most of the prisoners they held here. After the Monmouth rebellion Judge Jeffreys lit on it with alacrity as the perfect place for a sitting of his Bloody Assizes; his ghost is said to haunt the prison tower.

Lydford Castle's decline as a prison was thanks to Sir Thomas Tyrwhitt, secretary to the Prince of Wales (later George IV) and Lord Warden of the Stannaries. The Prince, as Duke of Cornwall, was Dartmoor's landlord, and it was one of Tyrwhitt's many successful ideas early in the nineteenth century, to build a prison on the moor to hold Frenchmen captured during the Napoleonic Wars. It could house as many as 9000 prisoners. A small town – Prince's Town (later Princetown) – grew up beside the prison to provide services, and although ten miles away, this fell within the parish of Lydford. Princetown, over 1400 feet above sea level, is the highest town in England, and one of the bleakest. 'Here are good walks to get a stomach, but small means to satisfy hunger,' remarked a nineteenth-century guidebook. The prison also held Americans taken during the War of 1812. For sixpence a day, they helped build Princetown's parish church, a large, dark building in a depressingly dilapidated condition – soggy from the damp. Inside, there is a memorial to Thomas Tyrwhitt, and in the churchyard are rows of little square granite headstones, carved only with initials and dates, to mark the graves of convicts who have died within the prison walls. The prison was closed at the end of the Napoleonic Wars and the town sank into a decline, but it was reopened in 1850 for long-term prisoners and has since been greatly extended.

There is at least one cheerful building in Lydford – the lovely granite church of St Petrock which stands next to the castle. It was built in the thirteenth century and enlarged 200 years later, but much of its elegant decoration dates from the beginning of this century. Petrock, who spent many years as a missionary in this area in the sixth century, has some 30 churches in Devon and Cornwall dedicated to him.

The church contains a gravestone whose inscription is a remarkable example of a metaphor stretched to the limits of endurance:

Here lies in horizontal position the outsize case of GEORGE ROUTLEDGE, Watchmaker Whose abilities in that line were an honour To his profession Integrity was the mainspring, And prudence the regulator Of all the actions of his

life. Human, generous and liberal His hand never stopped Till he had relieved distress. So much regulated were all his motions That he never went wrong Except when set agoing By people Who did not know His key. Even then he was easily Set right again. He had the art of disposing his time So well That his hours glided away In one continual round Of pleasure and delight Till an unlucky minute put a period to His existence. He departed this life Nov. 14 1802 Aged 57 Wound up In hopes of being taken in hand By his Maker And of being thoroughly cleaned, repaired And set-going In the world to come.

Lydford was already old at the time of *Domesday*. There had probably been a Celtic settlement here before the Saxons built their fortifications. That it has changed so little over the centuries must be at least partly due to its isolated position. It is a forgotten place, long overtaken in stature by its *Domesday* fellow boroughs, Totnes, Okehampton, Barnstaple and Exeter.

Topsham

[The King holds...] TOPSHAM *TOPESHANT*. Before 1066 it paid tax for 1 hide. Land for 12 ploughs. In lordship 1 plough; 5 slaves; 1/2 hide. 16 villagers and 12 smallholders with 12 ploughs. Meadow, 10 acres; pasture, 60 acres. 1 cob; 5 cattle; 50 sheep. It pays £6 by weight.

Although the manor of Topsham had been granted in 937 by Athelstan to the Church of St Peter's, Exeter, it was held after the Conquest by King William himself. The little town lies about half-way between Exmouth and Exeter, on the eastern bank of the Exe estuary where the River Clyst joins it. There is no *Domesday* reference to Topsham's coastal situation; until some 200 years later it was merely an unremarkable farming settlement, boats for Exeter passing it on their way upriver.

Then in 1284 the Countess of Devon had a petty disagreement with the Exeter authorities. She was Isabella de Fortibus, daughter of Baldwin de Redvers, Earl of Devon, and so grievously insulted did she feel that she built a weir across the Exe below the city, forcing all incoming merchant ships to unload their cargo at Topsham. Her heir, Hugh Courtenay, built a customs house and collected substantial tolls on incoming goods. Topsham flourished as a port, to the cost of its outraged neighbour.

Exeter had no redress until the middle of the sixteenth century, when technological advances made it possible to build a canal that bypassed 'Countess Weir'. The Exeter Ship Canal, the first in England with a lock system, was constructed between 1564 and 1567. In the seventeenth century it was extended to Topsham, although on the opposite – west – bank of the estuary, and in 1829 it was extended even further to Turf, a total distance of five miles.

Topsham had traded vigorously with the Dutch, the local merchants finding ready markets for their woollen goods in Amsterdam and Rotterdam. They brought back sail-cloth and linen from Haarlem, and, as ballast, small Dutch bricks with which the prospering merchants built gabled houses in imitation of those in Holland; several still stand along the quays. Once the canal was opened, however, their wool monopoly came to an end, and they gradually evolved in its stead a substantial shipbuilding and repair industry.

Topsham's shipbuilders boasted that they 'turned out their ships complete', and the town housed scores of little factories and warehouses making nails, rope, chain and other chandlers' necessaries. The leading shipbuilding family were the Holmans, who owned three separate yards and a large pond where the timber for building was moored to posts and floated.

But like the wool trade before it, the shipbuilding industry declined, leaving behind a pretty little quayside town whose old inns – the 'Passage House', the 'Lighter' and the 'Steam Packet' – are the only working reminders of its busy heyday. Its maritime potential meant nothing to the Norman invaders, and now it has dwindled away again to nothing. Even at the end of the last century, when the writer George Gissing used to come here, he found it a place of peace and quiet: 'A whole day's walk yesterday ... ended at Topsham, where I sat on the little churchyard terrace, and watched the evening tide coming up the broad estuary. I have a great liking for Topsham, and that churchyard, overlooking what is not quite sea, yet more than river, is one of the most restful spots I know.'

TOPSHAM: *View towards the sea.*

Devonshire Gazetteer
Each entry starts with the modern place name in **bold** type. The *Domesday* information that follows is in *italic* type, beginning with the name or names by which the place was known in 1086. The main landholders and under-tenants are next, separated with semi-colons if a place was divided into more than one holding. A number of holdings were granted by the king to his thanes; these holders, always the last in a list, are described as holding land 'from the king'. More general information completes the *Domesday* part of the entry, including examples of dues such as salmon rendered by tenants, and animals where totals reach or exceed 10 cattle, 20 goats, 20 pigs, 100 sheep and all mares, wethers and cobs. The modern or post-Domesday section is in normal type. represents a village, a small village or hamlet. The word Barton, widely used in Devonshire, means a farm – which can develop into a hamlet.

Abbots Bickington *Bichetone/Bicatona: Gerald the Chaplain. 20 cattle.*

Abbotsham *Hame/Hama: Tavistock Church. 118 sheep.*

Abbotskerswell *Carsuelle/ella: Horton Church. 30 goats.* Tudor and Georgian centre.

Adworthy *Odeordi: William from Ralph de Feugeres.* Also the nearby hamlets of Higher and Lower Adworthy.

Afton *Afetone/tona: Ralph de Feugeres. 231 sheep.* Afton Down nearby.

Aller (in Abbotskerswell) *Alre/Alra: Nicholas the Bowman. 24 goats.* On Aller Brook, adjoining Kingskerswell.

Aller (in Kentisbeare) *Alre/Alra/Avra/Avvra: Baldwin the Sheriff; Ralph Pagnell.* Also Aller Barton nearby.

Aller (in South Molton) *Alre/Alra: Bishop of Coutances; Odo FitzGamelin.* Now 2 hamlets, North and South Aller.

Allisland *Alelsland/lant: King's thanes.*

Almiston *Almerescote/cota: Colwin from Odo FitzGamelin. 20 goats.* Now Almiston Cross.

Alphington *Alfintone/tona: King's land, formerly Earl Harold. 1 cob.* Part of Exeter; 17th-century rectory.

Alston *Alwinestone/tona: Fulk from Iudhael of Totnes.* Alston Farm.

Alverdiscott *Alveredescote/cota: Erchenbald from Count of Mortain.* Church with Norman work and a 16th-century barrel roof.

Alwington *Alwinetone/tona: Hamelin from Count of Mortain. 120 sheep.* Some houses.

Anstey *Anestinge: Bishop of Coutances; Earl Hugh; Ansger from Baldwin the Sheriff. 25 cattle, 46 goats.* Now 2 villages, East and West Anstey, on the edge of Exmoor.

ASHBURTON: *View of the village across the moors.*

Appledore (in Burlescombe) *Suraple: Walter de Claville. 1 cob, 121 sheep, 6 wild mares.*

Appledore (in Clannaborough) *Apledore/dora: Ralph de Bruyere from Baldwin the Sheriff.* Appledore Farm.

Arlington *Alferdintone/tona: Alfred d'Epaignes. 100 sheep.* Arlington Court, built c.1820, with watercolours by William Blake.

Ash (in Bradworthy) *Aisse/Aissa/Eissa: Ralph de Pomeroy.* Now 2 hamlets, East and West Ash.

Ash (in Petrockstow) *Aisse/Aissa: Buckfast Church. 10 cattle.*

Ash (in South Tawton) *Aisse/Aissa: King's land.* Now East Ash.

Ash Barton (in Braunton) *Essa: Ralph from William Cheever.* Ash Barton.

Ashburton *Essebretone/tona: Bishop of Exeter.* Market town with a grammar school founded in 1314; 17–18th-century houses and inns.

Ashbury *Esseberie: Wihenoc from Alfred d'Epaignes.*

Ashclyst *Clist: Canons of St Mary's from Baldwin the Sheriff. 20 cattle.* Ashclyst Farm near Ashclyst Forest.

Ashcombe *Aissecome/coma: Ralph de Pomeroy. 42 cattle, 150 sheep, 50 goats.* 14th-century church; rectory; a few farms.

Ashford (near Barnstaple) *Aisseford/Aiseforda: Robert from Baldwin the Sheriff.*

Ashleigh *Aisselie/Assileia: Ralph from Iudhael of Totnes. Alder grove.*

Ashmansworthy *Essemundehord/horda: Gilbert from Baldwin the Sheriff. Wild mare, 100 sheep.*

Ashprington *Aisbertone/tona: King's land. 2 fisheries, salt-house. Cob, 100 sheep.* Church chalice has been in use since 1275.

Ashreigney *Aisse/Aissa: Gotshelm from the king. 17 cattle, 35 goats.*

Ash Thomas *Aisa: Godfrey from Gotshelm, formerly Aelfeva, a free woman.*

Ashton *Essestone/Essetona: Buckfast Church; the wife of Hervey de Hellean.* Now 2 hamlets, Lower Ashton with a 17th-century stone bridge, and Upper Ashton.

Ashwater *Aisse/Aissa: Bishop of Coutances. 42 cattle, 161 sheep.* Church with richly carved 13th-century wagon roof.

Aunk *Hanc/Hanche: Ralph de Pomeroy. Cob, 11 cattle, 100 sheep.* Tiny.

Aveton Gifford *Avetone: Roald Dubbed.* At the head of the Avon estuary with a medieval causeway across water meadows.

Awliscombe *Aulescome/coma: William Cheever and Ralph and Hamo from him; Gotshelm; Ralph de Pomeroy and Helgot from him. Mill, 16 cattle, 287 sheep, 97 goats.*

Axminster *Alseminstre/menistra/ministra/Axeministra/tre: King's land; Edwulf from William Cheever. 2 mills.* Small town where Aethelstan founded a college in the 10th century; famous for carpet-making. Nearby are the ruins of Newnham Abbey, founded by Reginald de Mohun in the 13th century.

Axmouth *Alsemude/muda: King's land.* Resort; an important port until the 14th century when the River Axe silted up.

Aylesbeare *Eilesberge/Ailesberga: Baldwin the Sheriff. 12 cattle, 100 sheep.*

Aylescott *Eileuses/Ailesuescote/Aileuescota: Bishop of Countances.* Now 2 hamlets, Lower and Higher Aylescott.

Ayshford *Aisseford/Aiseforda: Walter the Steward from Walter de Claville. Cob, 14 cattle, 33 goats, 2 wild mares.* 17th-century Ayshford House.

Baccamoor *Bachemore/mora: Ralph from Iudhael of Totnes.* Baccamoor Waste, on heathland.

Backstone *Bachestane: Robert Bastard.* Now West Backstone.

Badgworthy *Bicheordin: Fulcwold from William Cheever.* Badgeworthy Hill.

Bagton *Bachedone/dona: Osbern from Iudhael of Totnes.*

Bagtor *Bagetore/Bagathora: Roger from Nicholas the Bowman.* Bagtor House near Bag Tor.

Bampton *Baden/Baen/Bentone/Badendone/entone/Baentona: Walter de Douai and Rademar and Gerard from him. Mill. 2 cobs, 50 goats.* Small market town. The church has the base of a Saxon cross.

Barlington *Baldrintone/tona: King's land.* Now 2 hamlets, Middle and Great Barlington.

Barnstaple *Barnestapla/staple/Bardestapla/Barnestabla: Royal borough; Bishop of Coutances; Baldwin the Sheriff; Robert d'Aumale; Robert de Beaumont. Mill.* Main market town of north Devon, it received its town charter from King Aethelstan in 930. Birthplace of John Gay (1685–1732), who wrote *The Beggars Opera.*

AXMOUTH: *Stedcombe House, built in 1695.*

Batson *Badestane/tana: Hugh from Count of Mortain.* Some houses.

Battisborough *Bachetesberia/Bacetesberia: Alfred le Breton.* Now Battisborough Cross.

Battisford *Botesforde/forda: William de Poilley.* Tiny.

Battleford *Bacheleford: William from Alfred le Breton.* Tiny.

Beaford *Baverdone/dona: King's land. 14 cattle, 28 goats.*

Beara Charter *Bera: Bishop of Coutances. 10 goats.* Now Beara Charter Barton.

Beaworthy *Begeurde/eurda: William de Poilley. 20 cattle.* St Alban's Church with carved Norman capitals.

Beenleigh *Beuleie/Benleia:* Lost.

Beer (in Offwell) *Collebere:* Lost.

Beer (near Seaton) *: Horton Church. 100 sheep; 4 salt-houses, taken from the church were held by Drogo from Count of Mortain.* Stone quarries in use since Roman times.

Beetor *Begatore/tora: Ansger from Baldwin the Sheriff.* Beetor Farm.

Belstone *Belestham/Bellestam: Richard from Baldwin the Sheriff. 10 goats.* Prehistoric stone circle, the Nine Maidens, nearby.

Benton *Botintone/tona/Bontintona: Bishop of Exeter, given to him by Count of Mortain in exchange for a castle in Cornwall.*

Bere Ferrers *Birland/landa: Reginald from Count of Mortain. 11 goats.* At the meeting of the rivers Tavy and Tamar.

Berrynarbor *Hurtesberie/beria: Walter de Douai. 200 sheep, 83 goats.* Near the church, manor house, c.1480, of the Berry family.

Berry Pomeroy *Berie/Beri:* See page 72.

Bickford *Bicheford/forda: Robert Bastard; Aldred the pre-Conquest holder, from the king.* Bickfordtown Hall.

Bickham *Bichecome/coma: Robert of Hereford from Robert d'Aumale. 10 goats.* Bickham Barton near Bickham Moor.

Bickleigh (near Plymouth) *Bichelie/leia: William de Poilley. Fishery. 146 sheep.* 13th-century church with a Norman font.

Bickleigh (near Silverton) *Bichelie/lia: Alward from Count of Mortain. Mill.* Bickleigh Castle, rebuilt in Tudor times, with a Norman gatehouse and chapel opposite.

Bickleton *Picaltone/tona: Bernard from Theobald FitzBerner.*

Bicton *Bechetone/Bechatona: William the Porter, the king's servant. Cob.* Bicton House, c.1730, now the Devon School of Agriculture.

Bideford *Bedeford/Bediforda: King's land. 18 cattle, 300 sheep.* Small port and market town, granted its market charter in 1272. Timber of the original 13th-century bridge was rediscovered in 1925.

Bigbury *Bicheberie/beria: Reginald de Vautortes from Count of Mortain. Salt-house. 107 sheep.*

Bishop's Nympton *Nimetone/tona: Bishop of Exeter. Mill.* First granted to Aelfhane in 974, when it was called Nymet, the old name for the River Yeo.

Bishop's Tawton *Tautone/Taintona: Bishop of Exeter. 15 cattle, 153 sheep.* Turreted farm-house, once part of a palace of the Bishops of Exeter.

Bishopsteignton *Tantone/Taintona: Bishop of Exeter. 24 salt-houses. 37 cattle, 410 sheep, 40 goats.* Ruins of Bishop Grandisson's summer palace, 1332, nearby.

Bittadon *Bededone/dona: Bishop of Coutances. 135 sheep, 48 goats.*

Blachford *Blacheurde/eorde: Iudhael of Totnes; Robert Bastard.* Below Hanger Down.

Blackawton *Avetone/tona: King's land, formerly Asgar the Cramped. Salt-house. 120 sheep.* 14th-century church with a Norman font.

Blackborough *Blacheberge/beria/berie/Blacaberga: Baldwin the Sheriff; Ralph de Pomeroy; Ralph Botin from William the Usher, the king's servant. 15 cattle, 38 goats.*

Blackpool *Blachepole/Blacapola: King's land, formerly Earl Harold.* Higher Blackpool Farm.

Blackslade *Blachestach/tac/Bacheslac: Ralph de Pomeroy.* Below Blackslade Down.

Black Torrington *Torintone/tona: King's land, formerly Earl Harold. 10 pigs, 200 sheep, 50 goats.*

Blagrove *Blachegrave/Blacagrava/Blachagava: William de Poilley. 27 cattle.*

Blakewell *Blachewelle/willa: Robert de Pont-Chardon from Baldwin the Sheriff.*

Blaxton *Blachestane: Alfred le Breton. Salt-house.* On the Tavy Estuary, with Blaxton Wood.

Boasley *Boslie/a: Rolf from Baldwin the Sheriff. 12 cattle.* Now 2 hamlets, Boasley and Boasley Cross.

Boehill *Bihede/heda: Walter de Claville.*

Bolberry *Boltesberie/beria/Boteberie/Botestesberia: Hugh and Richard from Count of Mortain.* Some houses.

Bolham (in Tiverton) *Boleham: William the Usher, the king's servant. Mill. Cob.*

Bolham Water (in Clayhidon) *Boleham: Otelin from Baldwin the Sheriff. 10 cattle.*

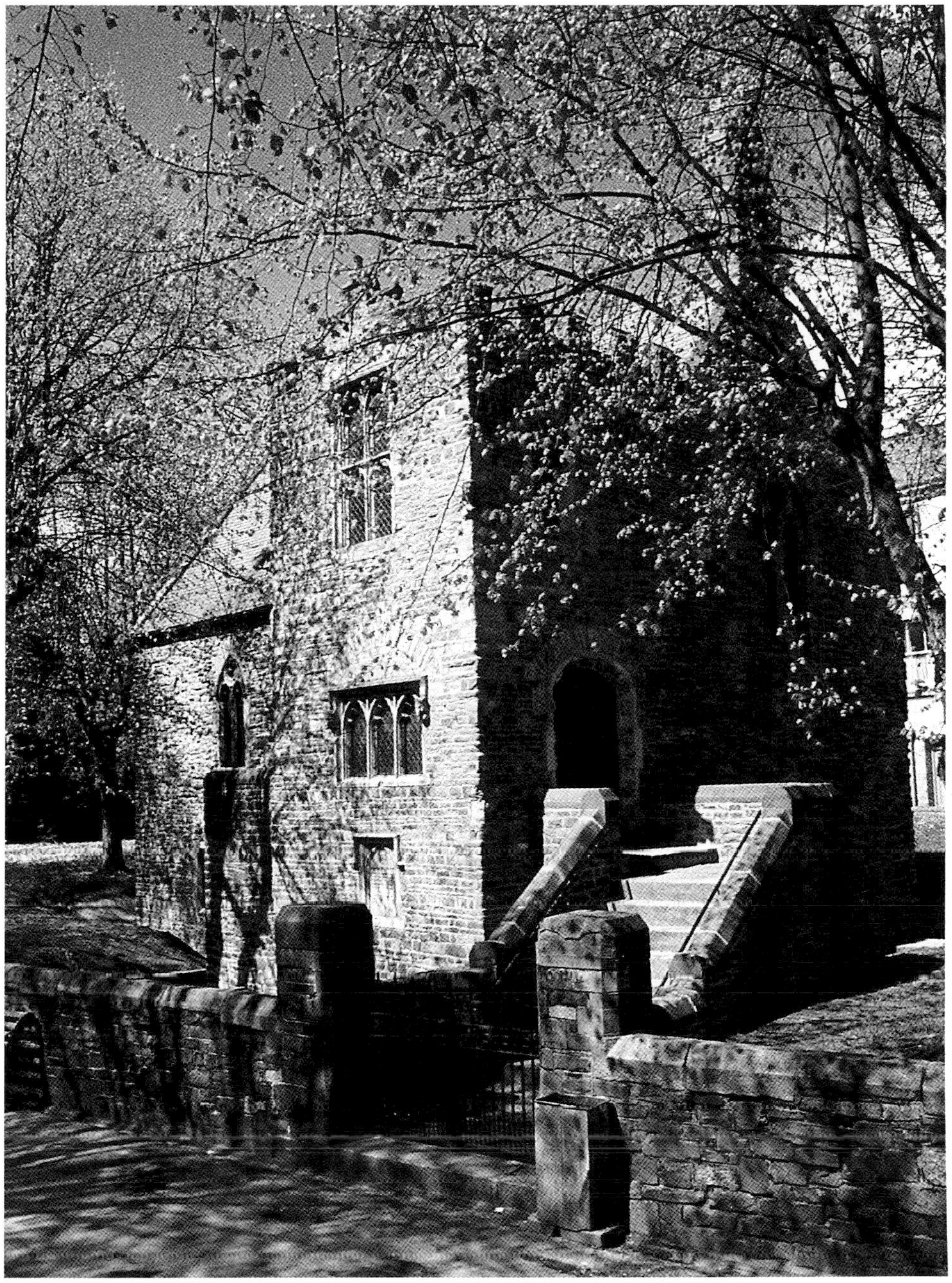

BARNSTAPLE: *The Chapel of St Anne also houses a local museum.*

Bondleigh *Bolenei(a): Bishop of Coutances.* Church with a Norman tympanum.

Borough (in Bridgerule) *Borge: Count of Mortain.*

Bovey Tracey *Bovi: Bishop of Coutances. Mill. 30 cattle.* Small town named after the Tracey family. The original church is said to have been built by Sir William de Tracey in penance for his part in the murder of Thomas à Becket.

Bowcombe *Cume/Coma: Reginald from Count of Mortain.*

Bowley *Bovelie/lia: William de Poilley.* Now 2 hamlets, Great and Little Bowley.

Bradaford *Bradeforde/forda: Iudhael of Totnes.*

Bradford (near Cookbury) *Bradeford/fort: Baldwin the Sheriff.*

Bradford (in Pyworthy) *Bradeford/fort: William from Iudhael of Totnes.* Bradford Manor.

Bradford (in Witheridge) *Bradeford/forda: Beatrix, William's sister, from William Cheever.* Bradford Mill on the Little Dart River; also Bradford Barton near the hamlet of Bradford Tracy.

Bradley *Bradelie: Bishop of Coutances; Haimeric.* Now 2 hamlets, Middle and Great Bradley.

Bradninch *Bradenese/nesa: Alfred le Breton. Mill. 324 sheep.* Small town.

Bradstone *Bradestone/tana: King's land, formerly Earl Harold.* Partly Tudor manor house.

Bradwell *Bradewelle/Bradeuilla: Ralph de Limesy.* Some houses.

Bradworthy *Brawordine/Braor/Bravordina: Ralph de Pomeroy. 40 cattle, 30 unbroken mares, 120 sheep.* Remote; a large central square.

Bramford Speke *Branford/fortune/fort/fortuna: Bishop of Coutances; Walter from Baldwin the Sheriff; Vitalis of Colyton from Baldwin the Sheriff, Walter de Claville. 35 cattle, 204 sheep.* Thatched 18th-century cottages.

Branscombe *Branchescome/coma: Bishop of Exeter, for the canons' supplies. 150 sheep.* Belonged to Alfred in the 9th century and then given by Aethelstan to the Benedictine monks of Exeter in the 10th century.

BRANSCOMBE: *The church has a mainly Norman transept.*

BROADHEMBURY: *A lovely Devon village near the tranquil Hembury hill-fort, c. 4200–3900 BC.*

Bratton Clovelly *Bratone/tona: Baldwin the Sheriff. 8 wild mares, 18 cattle.* Church dates from the 13th century and has wall paintings and a Norman font.

Bratton Fleming *Bratone/ Brotone: Erchenbald from Count of Mortain. 40 pigs, 100 sheep.*

Braunton *Bracton/tona/ Brantone/tona: King's land and Robert de Pont Chardon from the King; Algar the priest. 200 sheep.* Town. Braunton Great Field is an example of the Saxon open strip system.

Bray (in South Molton) *Brai: Bishop of Coutances; Alnoth from the king. Garden in Barnstaple.* Now South Bray; also Bray Mill Cross; Bray Bridge.

Brayley *Bredelie/lia: Reginald from Odo FitzGamelin.* Brayley Barton near Brayley Hill.

Bremridge *Bremerige: Bishop of Coutances. 22 goats.* Near Bremridge Wood.

Brendon *Brandone/done:* See page 72.

Brexworthy *Bristelesworde/ shorda: Colwin from the king.*

Bridestowe *Bridestou: Ralph de Pomeroy from Baldwin the Sheriff. 135 sheep.* Norman arch from the church was used as a gateway on the main road.

Bridford *Bredford/fort/ Brideford/forda: Emma from her husband Baldwin the Sheriff; Iudhael of Totnes. 180 sheep, 38 goats.*

Bridgerule *Brige: Roald Dubbed. Mill.*

Bridwick *Bredviche: Bishop of Coutances. 13 cattle.* Bridwick Farm.

Brimblecome *Bremelcome: Ansger de Montacute.* Brimblecombe Wood nearby.

Brixham *Briseham: Iudhael of Totnes. 2 cobs, 200 sheep.* Town, once a Roman settlement, with an Iron Age fort at Berry Head.

Brixton (in Broadwood Kelly) *Bristanestone/tona: Richard from Baldwin the Sheriff. 14 cattle.* Brixton Barton.

Brixton (in Shaugh Prior) *Brictricestone/Bristrichestona: Ralph from Iudhael of Totnes.*

Brixton (near Yealmpton) *Brisestone/tona: Iudhael of Totnes.* Brixton Barton.

Broadaford *Bradeford/forda: Reginald from Count of Mortain.* Tiny.

Broad Clyst *Clistone/tona: King's land. Mill. 100 sheep.* Broad Clyst House is Georgian. Killerton Park is a botanical garden with Killerton Clump, an Iron Age earthwork.

Broadhembury *Ham-/Han-/ Henberie/-beria/Hain-/Hemberia: Odo FitzGamelin. Mill. 100 sheep.* 15th-century Drewe Arms. Hembury Fort, largest Iron Age earthwork in Devon, nearby.

Broadhempston *Hamestone/ Hamistona: Hamelin from Count of Mortain.*

Broadley *Bradelie/leia: Ralph from Iudhael of Totnes.* Tiny.

Broadnymet *Limet/Limete: Ralph de Bruyere from Baldwin the Sheriff.* Ruined 13th-century chael.

Broadwood Kelly *Bradehode/ hoda: Modbert from Baldwin the Sheriff. 13 cattle.* Church, 16th-century stained-glass windows.

Broadwoodwidger *Bradewode/ e(w)oda: Nigel from Iudhael of Totnes. 31 cattle, 200 sheep.* Named after the Wyger family, who acquired the manor in 1273. Nearby, Wortham Manor is 15th century.

Bruckland *Brocheland/lande/ landa: Geoffrey from Ralph de Pomeroy, formerly Aethelhard the monk.* Now Higher Bruckland Farm and Lower Bruckland, a tiny hamlet.

Brushford *Brigeford(a)/ Brisforde/forda: Godfrey the Chamberlain from Baldwin the Sheriff; Godfrey from Gotshelm; Godbold.* Brushford Barton.

Buckfast *Bucfestra/Bulfestra: Buckfast Church.* Benedictine monks settled here in 1018; in 1147 abbey became Cistercian. The present building is mainly early 20th century; a stone block in the churchyard may be the Norman altar.

Buckland (in Braunton) *Bocheland/lant: Godfrey from William Cheever. 26 goats.* Buckland Manor.

Buckland (in Dolton) *Bocheland/Bocchelanda: Aelmer from Odo FitzGamelin. 14 Cattle.* Buckland Farm.

Buckland (in Haccombe) *Bocheland/landa: Robert from William Cheever. 25 goats.* Part of Newton Abbot.

Buckland (in Thurlestone) *Bocheland/landa: Hugh from Count of Mortain.*

Buckland Brewer *Bocheland/ landa: Ansger le Breton from Count of Mortain. 19 cattle, 150 sheep, 50 goats.* Partly Tudor Orleigh Court nearby.

Buckland Filleigh *Bochelan(d): Bishop of Coutances. 16 cattle, 15 goats.*

Buckland in the Moor *Bochelande/landa: Nicholas the Bowman. 20 goats.* Moorland site; Georgian Buckland Court.

Buckland Monachorum *Bocheland(a): William de Poilley. Salt-house, fishery. 20 cattle, 10 pigs, 130 sheep.* Named after a Cistercian abbey founded in 1278, later Sir Francis Drake's home and now a museum.

Buckland Tout Saints *Bocheland(e)/landa: Walter de Claville; Baldwin from Gotshelm. 26 goats.*

Bucks Cross *Bochewis/ Bochewys/Bochiywis: Theobald FitzBerner.*

Budshead *Bucheside: Alfred le Breton.* Budshtad Creek in Plymouth.

Bulkworthy *Bucheswordel- surda/Bochesorda/-surda: Ansger le Breton from Count of Mortain. 100 sheep.* Old farms; superb tithe barn. The church was built by Sir William Hankford, who imprisoned Prince Hal and later became his Chief Justice.

Bulworthy *Boleborde/ Bolehorda: Godric from the king. 40 goats.* Bulworthy Farms.

Burlescombe *Berlescome/coma: Walter de Claville. 22 cattle.*

Burn (in Silverton) *Burne/ Borna: Godbold.* Part of Tarrant Rushton hamlet.

Burrington (near Chulmleigh) *Bernintone/- intona/Bernurtona: Tavistock Church and William Cheever and Geoffrey from the Abbot. 28 goats.* 15th-century church with a fine wooden screen.

Burrington (in Weston Peverel) *Buretone/tona: Iudhael of Totnes.* Burrington Way in Plymouth.

Burston *Limet/Limete/Limeta: Otelin from Baldwin the Sheriff.*

Bury *Berie/Beria: Bishop of Exeter.* Bury Barton, with a chapel.

Buscombe *Burietescome/ Buriestescoma: Bishop of Coutances.*

Butterford *Botre-/Butreforde/ Botreforda: Thorgils from Iudhael of Totnes.* Tiny.

Butterleigh *Buterlei(a): Edwin, the pre-Conquest holder, from the king.* Hamlet of East Butterleigh nearby.

Bywood *Biude/Biuda: Walter de Claville, formerly Mathilda.* Bywood Farm near Bywood Copse.

Cadbury (near Thorverton) *Cadebirie/Cadabiria: William de Poilley. Cob.* Cadbury Castle, an Iron Age fort where Roman coins have been found.

Cadeleigh *Cadelie/lia: William Cheever; William the king's servant. Mill. 130 sheep.*

Caffyns Heanton *Hantone/tona: Ralph de Pomeroy. 13 cattle, 20 goats.* Caffyns Heanton Farm near Caffyns Heanton Down.

Calverleigh *Calodelie/leia: Godric from the king.*

Canonsleigh *Leige/Leiga: Walter de Claville.* Canonsleigh Farm with the ruins of a 12th-century priory.

Canonteign *Teigne/Teigna: Geoffrey de Trelly from Bishop of Coutances. Cob.* Canonteign Barton; Canonteign House.

Chagford *Cage-/Chageford/ Cage-/Kagefort: Bishop of Coutances; Ralph Pagnell.* Old stannary town for assessing and stamping tin. On the edge of Dartmoor and surrounded by prehistoric hut circles and standing stones.

Challacombe *Celdecome/ comba: Bishop of Coutances. 11 cattle, 19 goats.* On the edge of Exmoor, with Chapman Barrows, grave mounds with a standing stone.

Challonsleigh *Lege/Lega: William de Poilley. 110 sheep.*

Chardstock *Cerdestoche: Sherborne Church.* Chardstock Court, dating from the 14th century.

Charford *Chereford(a): Buckfast Church.* Charford Manor, now a hotel.

Charles *Carmes: Robert from Baldwin the Sheriff.* Richard Blackmore wrote much of *Lorna Doone* (1864) here.

Charleton *Cheletone/tona: Iudhael of Totnes. 2 cobs.* Now 2 villages, East and West Charleton.

Chawleigh *Calvelie/leia: Baldwin the Sheriff. 20 cattle, 200 sheep.*

Cheldon *Cadel/Cheledone/ Cha(d)eledona: Walter from Baldwin the Sheriff; Ansger, formerly Mathilda.*

Cheriton (in Brendon) *Ciretone/tona: Ralph de Pomeroy. 27 cattle.* Some houses.

Cheriton (in Payhembury) *Cherletone/tona: Bretel from Count of Mortain.* Now 2 hamlets, Lower and Higher Cheriton.

Cheriton Bishop *Ceritone/tona: Godwin from the king.* Church with a Norman font shaped like a sheaf of corn.

Cheriton Fitzpaine *Cerintone/ tona: Theobald FitzBerner.* Thatched Tudor and Georgian cottages; 16th-century almshouses.

Chettiscombe *Chetelescome/ Chettelescoma: Ansger from Baldwin the Sheriff. Mill.* Some houses.

Chevithorne *Chenetorne/ Chevetorna/Chiveorne/-orna: Rogo from Baldwin the Sheriff; Beatrix from Ralph de Pomeroy. 15 cattle.* Elizabethan Chevithorne Barton nearby.

Chichacott *Cicecote/cota: Roger from Baldwin the Sheriff.* Some houses.

Chillington *Cedelintone/tona: King's land. 157 sheep.* Mill Farm.

Chilsworthy *Chelesworde/ sorda: Colwin from the king. 15 cattle.*

Chilton (in Cheriton Fitzpaine) *Cilletone/-tona/ Cillitone: Odo FitzGamelin. Cob.* Some houses.

Chitterley *Chiderlie/Chederlia: Alfred from Count of Mortain.* On the River Exe.

Chittleburn *Chichelesberie/ beria: William from Iudhael of Totnes.* Tiny; Chittleburn Wood.

Chittlehampton *Curem'tone/ Citremetona: Godwin from the king.* Church, named after St Heiritha, a Celtic martyr.

Chivelstone *Cheveletone/tona: Ralph from Iudhael of Totnes.*

Chudleigh Knighton *Chenistetone/tona: Roger from Bishop of Exeter. Cob.*

Chulmleigh *Calmonleuge/ Chalmonleuga: Baldwin the Sheriff. 60 cattle, 400 sheep.* Small town, mainly Georgian. Colleton Barton nearby has the gatehouse and chapel from the medieval house.

Churchill *Cercelle/Cercilla: Norman from William de Falaise. 100 sheep.* Some houses.

Churston Ferrers *Cercetone/ Cercitona: Iudhael of Totnes. Cob, 120 sheep.* On the outskirts of Brixham. Churston Court is 17th century with a walled garden.

Clannaborough *Cloenesberg(a): Ralph de Pomeroy from Baldwin the Sheriff.* Clannaborough Barton; tiny church.

Clawton *Clavetone/tona: Iudhael of Totnes. 47 cattle, 200 sheep.* Church with a Norman font with cable decoration and carved heads.

Clayhanger *Clehangre/hangra: Robert from William de Mohun.*

Clayhidon *Hidone/dona: Otelin from Baldwin the Sheriff. Mill. 22 cattle, 27 goats.* View of the Vale of Taunton; memorial obelisk to the Duke of Wellington.

Clifford *Cliford(e)/forda/fort: Stephen from Baldwin the Sheriff; Godbold. 142 sheep.* Clifford Barton, an old farm; 17th-century Clifford Bridge.

Clovelly *Clovelie/leia: King's land. 45 cattle, 100 sheep.* Clovelly Dykes, Iron Age earthworks.

Clyst Gerred *Clist: Osbern de Sacey. 27 goats.* Clyst Gerred Farm.

Clyst Hydon *Clist: Otelin from Baldwin the Sheriff.* 18th-century Chelves Hayes, house with Georgian plaster-work.

Clyst St George *Chisewic/ Clisewic: Roger from Ralph de Pomeroy, formerly Viking.* Traditionally Devonian, with red brick and red earth.

Clyst St Lawrence *Clist: Alward, the pre-Conquest holder; from Count of Mortain. 38 goats.*

Clyst St Mary *Cliste/Clista: Bishop of Coutances. Cob, 10 cattle.* 14th-century bridge. Winslade House was the site of the insurrection when the first English Prayer Book was introduced in 1549.

Clyst William *Clist: Edwin from the king.*

Cockington *Cochintone/ Chochintona: William de Falaise. Cob, 159 sheep, 42 goats.* Thatched cottages; watermill; forge.

Coddiford *Codeford/aforda: Odo from the king.* Tiny.

Coffinswell *Welle/Willa: Grenta, a man-at-arms, from Tavistock Church.* Large prehistoric camp on Milber Down.

Colaton Raleigh *Coletone/tona: King's land, formerly Earl Harold. Mill. 5 wild mares.* Place Court, a medieval manor house, owned by Sir Walter Raleigh's family.

Coldridge *Colrige/riga: Bishop of Coutances.* On a hilltop north of Dartmoor.

Coldstone *Coltrestan: Thorgils from Iudhael of Totnes. 22 goats.* Coldstone Farm.

Colebrook (in Cullompton) *Colebroch(e)/broca: Manfred from William Cheever. 25 goats.* Some houses.

Coleridge (in Egg Buckland) *Colrige: Odo from Iudhael of Totnes.* Part of Plymouth.

Coleridge (in Stokenham) *Colrige/riga: Alric and Aelfeva from Walter de Douai.* Coleridge House.

Coleton *Coletone/-tona: Warin from Iudhael of Totnes.* Some houses.

Collacombe *Colecome/ Colacoma: Robert d'Aumale. 14 cattle, 20 goats (with Ottery and Willestrew).* Collacombe Barton near Collacombe Down.

Collaton (in Marlborough) *Coletone/-tona: Thorgils from Iudhael of Totnes.*

Colscott *Colsovenescote/cota: Alward, the pre-Conquest holder, from the king.* Some houses.

Columbjohn *Colum: Fulchere. Mill.* On the River Culm.

Colwell *Colewille/willa: Roger from Baldwin the Sheriff. 20 goats.* Colwell Barton. The hamlet of West Colwell is nearby.

Colyton *Culitone: King's land. Mill, church.* Saxon settlement c. AD 700. Pieces of a Saxon cross were found in the church. During the reign of Henry VIII, a group of Colyton men, the Feoffees, founded the grammar school and built the town hall.

Combe (in south Pool) *Cumbe/ Conba: William from Iudhael of Totnes.* Some houses near Prawle Point.

Combe Fishacre *Cumbe/ Comba: Ralph de Pomeroy from Iudhael of Totnes.* Combefishacre House.

Combeinteignhead *Cumbe/ Comba: William Cheever.* In a combe leading to the Teign Estuary; Bourchier Almshouses, built in 1620.

Combe Martin *Cumbe/Comba: William de Falaise. 21 cattle, 140 sheep.* Once known for lead and silver mines.

Combe Raleigh *Otri: Hubert from Walter de Douai. 38 cattle, 28 pigs, 200 sheep, 50 goats, 4 wild mares.* Chantry House, built in 1498 probably for village priest.

Combe Royal *Cumbe: Osbern from Robert Bastard.* Tudor house.

Combe Sackville *Colun/Colum/ Colunp:* Lost.

Comboyne *Come/Coma: Odo from Baldwin the Sheriff.* 13th-century church with Saxon foundations.

Compton Gifford *Contone: Stephen from Iudhael of Totnes.* Part of Plymouth.

Cookbury Wick *Wiche/Wicha: Robert d'Aumale, formerly Wulfrun, a free woman. 20 cattle.*

CHAGFORD: *The church with a typical barrel-shaped roof.*

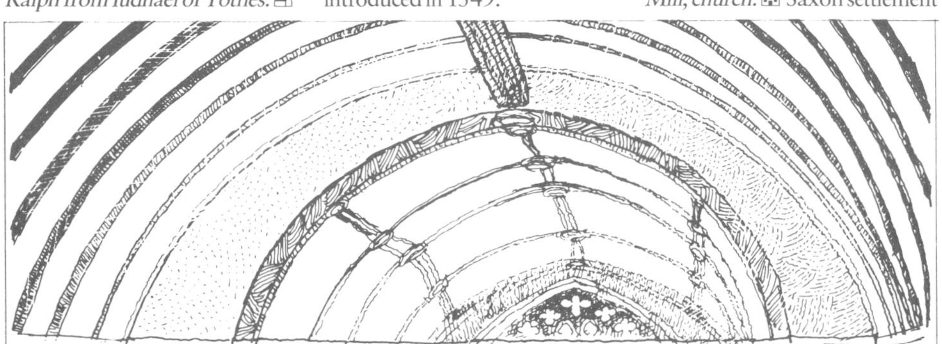

EXETER: *Carved decoration on the west front of Exeter Cathedral.*

CLOVELLY: *One of England's prettiest villages.*

Coombe (in Cheriton Fitzpaine) *Cumbe/Comba: Jagelin from Theobald FitzBerner.* Tiny.

Coombe (in Cruwys Morchard) *Cumbe/Conba: Haimeric.* Tiny.

Coombe (in Drewsteignton) *Cume/Cuma: Godwin from the king.* Coombe Hall.

Coombe (in Templeton) *Come/Coma: Bishop of Coutances. 20 cattle.* Now 2 hamlets, North and South Combe.

Coombe (in Uplowman) *Come/Coma/Conma: Walter the Wild from Walter de Claville; Gotshelm. Mill.*

Cornwood *Cornehode/huda: Reginald from Count of Mortain. 3 unbroken mares, 10 cattle, 22 goats.* On Dartmoor, surrounded by prehistoric remains.

Cornworthy *Corneorde/orda: Iudhael of Totnes. Mill, fishery (30 salmon). 140 sheep.* 14th-century gatehouse remains from an Augustinian priory.

Coryton *Coriton/tona: Drogo from Bishop of Coutances.*

Cotleigh *Cotelie/leia: Richard from Count of Mortain.*

Countisbury *Contesberie/beria: William Cheever. Cob, 24 pigs, 300 sheep, 35 goats.* Roman signal station on Old Barrow Hill; earthwork on Wind Hill, where a battle with the Danes was fought in 873.

Cowick *Coic:* Lost.

Craze Loman *Lonmele/-mela/ Lonnela/Lonmine/mina: Walter de Claville. Cob, 20 cattle.* On the River Lowman.

Creacombe (in Newton Ferrers) *Crawecome/coma: Alfred le Breton.* Creacombe Farm.

Creacombe (near Witheridge) *Crawecome/Crabecoma/ Crahecome/Crawecoma: Ansger from Baldwin the Sheriff.*

Crealy *Cravelech/lec: Edmer from the Bishop of Coutances.* Crealy Barton.

Crediton *Critetone/Chritetona/ Chrietona: Bishop of Exeter. Mill. 64 cattle, 57 pigs, 400 sheep, 125 goats.* Mainly Georgian and Victorian market town. St Boniface, missionary to the Germans, born here (680). 10th-century Crediton was the seat of the Devon bishopric, which then moved to Exeter because of the Danish threat. The church dates from 1150.

Crockernwell *Crochewelle/ wella: Reginald from Roald Dubbed.*

Crooke Burnell *Cruc: William, the king's servant.*

Croyde *Crideholde/holda: Erchenbald from Count of Mortain. 11 cattle, 100 sheep.* Also Croyde Bay, a hamlet on the coast.

Cruwys Morchard *Morceth/cet/ ceta/Morchet: Bishop of Coutances; William Cheever. 13 cattle, 200 sheep.* Some houses. Estate farmed by the Cruwys family since the 13th century.

Culleigh *Colelie/leia: Erchenbald from Count of Mortain.*

Cullompton *Colitone/tona: Battle Church. Church.* Small town with houses built by wool merchants. The Church has a Golgotha wood-carving of skulls, bones and rocks.

Culm Davy *Cumbe/Comba: Oliver from Theobald FitzBerner. Mill. 20 cattle.*

Culm Pyne *Colun: Otelin from Baldwin the Sheriff. Mill. 20 goats.* Culm Pyne Barton.

Culmstock *Clumestoche/stocha: Bishop of Exeter. Mill.* Quaker Meeting House founded in 1650 and rebuilt in 1815.

Culm Vale *Colun: Fulchere.* Area on the River Exe.

Culsworthy *Colteswordel shorda: Colwin, the pre-Conquest holder, from the king.* Tiny.

Curscombe *Cochalescome/ coma: Drogo from Count of Mortain.* Curscombe Farms.

Curtisknowle *Cortescanole/ola: Ralph de Pomeroy from Iudhael of Totnes.*

Curworthy *Corneurde/ Corneorda: 3 thanes, the pre-Conquest holders, from Alfred le Breton.* Curworthy Farm.

Dart (in Cadeleigh) *Derte/ Derta: Ralph from William de Poilley. Mill.* Dart Cottages on the River Dart.

Dartington *Dertrintone/tona: William de Falaise. 2 fishermen paying 80 salmon. 11 cattle.* Dartington Hall, the ruined palace of the Duke of Exeter, established in 1931 as a self-supporting community.

Dart Raffe *Derte/Derta: Ralph from William de Poilley.* Dart Raffe Farm.

Dawlish *Doules/Douelis: Bishop of Exeter, for the canons' supplies. 100 sheep.* Resort town with 5 railway tunnels by Brunel. Nearby is Luscombe Castle by John Nash.

Dean Prior *Dene/Dena: 4 men-at-arms from William de Falaise. 16 cattle, 50 goats.* Robert Herrick (1591–1674) was vicar here.

Delley *Dalilei/lea: Odo FitzGamelin. Cob.*

Denbury *Deveneberie/ Devenaberia: Tavistock Church.* 17th-century manor house with a Georgian façade.

Dennington (in Yarcombe) *Donitone/tona: Mont St Michel Church, formerly Earl Harold. 16 cattle, 200 sheep, 23 goats.* Tiny; Dennington Lane.

Densham *Dimewoldesham/ Donevoldehame/hamma: Alfred from Count of Mortain; an Englishman from William de Falaise.* Now 2 hamlets, Higher and East Densham.

Dinnaton (in Cornwood) *Dunintone/Dinintona/Dunitone/ tona: Reginald from Count of Mortain. 20 goats.* Tiny; on the edge of Dartmoor.

Dipford *Depeforde/Deppaforda: Wulfric from Walter de Douai. Mill. 2 asses, 109 sheep, 54 goats.* Tiny; remains of a chapel.

Diptford *Depeforde/forda: King's land.* Gara Bridge, a medieval packhorse bridge.

Dittisham *Didasham/sam: Baldwin from Bishop of Exeter. Cob, 20 pigs, 40 goats.* On the Dart Estuary.

Dockworthy *Docheorde/ Dochorda: Walter from Roald Dubbed.* Now 2 tiny hamlets, Little and West Dockworthy, and Dockworthy Cross.

Dodbrooke *Dodebroch/broca: Godiva. 16 cattle, 108 sheep, 27 goats.* Part of Kingsbridge. St Thomas's Church has a much restored 15th-century wall painting and Norman font.

Doddiscombsleigh *Leuge/ Leuga: Godbold. 15 cattle, 120 sheep, 50 goats.* Church with 5 windows of 15th-century stained glass.

Dodscott *Dodecote/cota: Walter de Burgundy from Gotshelm. 20 cattle.* Some houses.

Dolton *Duveltone/-tona/ Oueltone/Dueltona: Walter FitzWimund from Baldwin the Sheriff. 30 cattle, 25 goats.* Church with a font made from a carved Saxon cross.

Donningstone *Donicestone/ tona:* Lost.

Dotton *Otrit: Rainer from Baldwin the Sheriff. Mill.* Dotton Farm near Dotton Warren, a wood.

Dowland *Duvelande/landa: Walter de Claville. 2 cobs, 33 cattle, 106 sheep.* Church.

Downicary *Kari: Waldin from Iudhael of Totnes. 20 goats.* Also known as Downacarey.

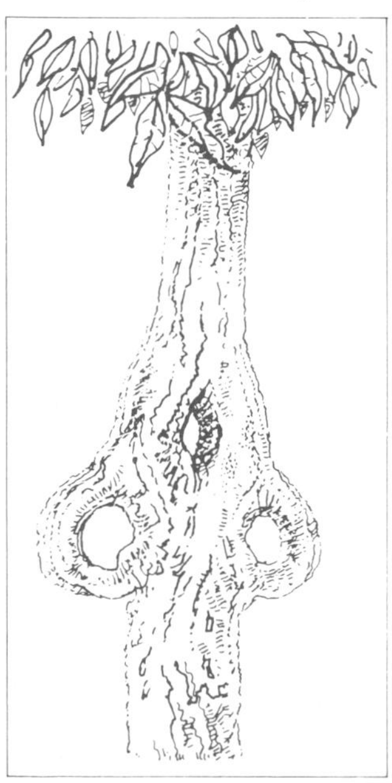

DAWLISH: *Unusual bay tree known locally as the "Scissors Tree".*

Down St Mary *Done/Dona: Adolf from the king; Buckfast Church. 11 cattle.* Church with an unusual Norman tympanum carved with grotesque animals.

Down Thomas *Done/Dona: Iudhael of Totnes.*

Drayford *Draheford/forda: Walter de Claville.* Some houses.

Drewsteignton *Taintone/tona: Baldwin the Sheriff. 14 cattle, 100 sheep, 31 goats.* Above Teign gorge with a narrow packhorse bridge over the river.

Dunchideock *Dunsedoc/ Donsedoc: Ralph Pagnell.* Iron Age fort at Cotley Castle nearby; late 14th-century church with a restored medieval priest's house.

Dunkeswell *Doduchleswelle/ Duduceswilla: Ralph de Pomeroy.* Gatehouse of Dunkeswell Abbey, founded in 1201. The church has documents from the abbey, and a Norman font with a carving of an elephant.

Dunsbear *Denesberge/berga: Colwin from the king.*

Dunscombe *Danescome/coma:* Lost.

Dunsdon *Dunewinesdone/- winnusdona/Denewynesdone: Ralph de Pomeroy; Count of Mortain. 35 cattle.* Tiny.

Dunsford *Dunesford/forda: Gerard from Walter de Douai; Saewulf, the pre-Conquest holder, from the king.*

Dunsland *Donesland/landa: Cadio from Baldwin the Sheriff. 15 cattle.* Now Dunsland Cross.

Dunstone (in Widecombe in the Moor) *Dunestanetune/ Dunestanaetuna: Roger from Ralph de Pomeroy.*

Dunstone (in Yealmpton) *Donestanestone/stanestona: Ranulf from Robert Bastard; Algar, the pre-Conquest holder, from the king.*

Dunterton *Dondritone/tona: Ralph de Bruyere from Baldwin the Sheriff. 11 cattle, 33 pigs, 100 sheep, 30 goats.* On a hill above the River Tamar.

East Allington *Alintone: Richard FitzThorold.* Home of the Fortescue family, one of whom is said to have saved the Conqueror's life at the battle of Hastings.

East Buckland *Bocheland/landa/ lant: Bishop of Coutances.*

East Budleigh *Bodelie/leia: King's land.* Sir Walter Raleigh (1552–1618) was born at Hayes Barton nearby.

East Down *Dune/Duna: Ralph de Limesy. 110 sheep.* East Down House, c. 1700.

Eastleigh *Lei/Leia: Ansketel from William Cheever.*

East Manley *Maenelege: Gotshelm.*

East Putford *Potiforde/forda: Ansger le Breton from Count of Mortain. 23 cattle, 150 sheep.*

Edginswell *Wille/Willa: Ralph Pagnell. 30 cattle.* Part of Torquay.

Efford *Elforde: Robert Bastard. Fishery.* Part of Plymouth.

Eggbeer *Eigebere/Eighebera: Modbert from Baldwin the Sheriff.* Lower Eggbeer Farm.

Eggbuckland *Bocheland/landa: Iudhael of Totnes. Salt house.* Part of Plymouth.

Elfordleigh *Lege/Lega: Ralph from Iudhael of Totnes.* Elfordleigh Hotel; Elfordleigh Farm, Elfordleigh Wood.

Elsford *Eilavesford/Ailavesfort: Bishop of Coutances.* Elsford Farm; 2 tiny hamlets, Elford Rock and Lower Elford.

Englebourne *Engleborne/ borna: Baldwin the Sheriff; Reginald from William de Falaise. Cob.* Now 2 hamlets, Key's and Great Englebourne.

Ermington *Ermentone/-tona/ Hermentona: King's land, formerly Asgar the Cramped. Salt-house.* On the Saxon plan; church with a leaning spire.

Essebeare *Labere/bera: Hubert from Odo FitzGamelin.*

Exbourne *Echeburne/ Etcheborna/Hechesburne: Roger from Baldwin the Sheriff; Alfred le Breton. 18 cattle.*

Exeter *Execestre/Essecestra/ Exonia: 300 king's houses (48 destroyed since the king came to England); various landholders own houses; churches held by Bishop of Exeter, Battle Church (St Olaf's), Count of Mortain (who also holds an orchard).* City and county capital, dating from Roman times and an important port until the 13th century. The Bishop's Palace contains the Exeter Book of 950 and the Exon Domesday Book.

Exminster *Aise-/Axe-/ Esseminstre/Aexe-/Aise-/Axe-/ Esseministra: King's land and William d'Eu and Battle Church from the king; William Cheever, formerly Viking. Fishery. 220 sheep.* Church with an unusual 17th-century plaster ceiling.

Exwick *Essoic: Baldwin the Sheriff. Mill.* Part of Exeter.

Fardel *Ferdendel/delle/della: Reginald from Count of Mortain. Cob, 11 cattle, 30 goats.* Fardel Mill Farm; Fardel, a tiny hamlet.

Farleigh *Ferlei/leia: King's land.*

Farringdon *Ferentone/-tona/ Ferhendone/-dona: Bretel from Count of Mortain; Fulchere. 6 cows.*

Farway *Farewei/weia: Bishop of Coutances; Ludo from Gotshelm. 12 cattle, 30 goats.* Named after the old ridgeway above the village.

Farwood *Forhode/Forohoda: Herbert from William de Poilley.* Farwood Barton.

Fenacre *Wennacre/Vennacra: Osmund from Gotshelm.* Fenacre Farm.

Feniton *Finetone/Finatona: Drogo from Count of Mortain.*

Fernhill (in Shaugh) *Fernehelle/hella: Thorgils from Iudhael of Totnes.* Tiny, and the site of an old manor house.

Filleigh *Filelei/-leia/Filileia: Baldwin the Sheriff. 14 cattle.* Castle Hill, a 17th-century house with a park designed by William Kent.

Flete *Flutes: Robert d'Aumale.* Flete House, a Victorian Tudor mansion by Norman Shaw.

Follaton *Foletone/tona: St Mary of Totnes from Iudhael of Totnes.* Follaton House, now council offices.

Ford (in Chivelstone) *Forde/Forda: Ralph from Iudhael of Totnes.* Tiny.

Fremington *Framintone/tona: Bishop of Coutances, formerly Earl Harold. 150 sheep.* Church with a carved Norman water stoup and fragments of medieval wall painting.

Frithelstock *Fredelestoch/Fredeletestoc: Robert FitzIvo from Count of Mortain. 20 cattle.* 18th-century houses round the village green; ruins of an Augustinian priory founded 1220.

Frizenham *Friseham: Alfred the Butler from Count of Mortain.*

Fursham *Fierseham: Monks of Mont St Michel from Baldwin the Sheriff.* Tiny.

Furze (in West Buckland) *Ferse: William de Falaise.* Tiny.

Galmpton (in Churston Ferrers) *Galmentone/tona: Ralph de Feugeres. Cob, 100 sheep.* Some houses.

Galmpton (in South Huish) *Walementone/Walementona: Ralph from Iudhael of Totnes.*

Galsworthy *Galeshore/hora: Ansger le Breton from Count of Mortain.*

Gappah *Gatepade/pada: Roger from Ralph de Pomeroy. 12 cattle, 100 sheep, 60 goats.* Some houses.

Gatcombe *Gatccumbe/Gatcumba: Ansger, the king's servant. 100 sheep.* Gatcombe Farm.

Georgeham *Hamel-Hama: Theobald FitzBerner.* Thatched cottages; 13th-century church, much restored.

George Nympton *Limet/Nimete/Nimet/Nimeta: Odo FitzGamelin. Cob, 12 cattle.*

George Teign *Teigne/Teigna: Roger de Meulles from Baldwin the Sheriff.* George Teign Barton.

Germansweek *Wiche/Wica/Wyca: Rainer from Baldwin the Sheriff.*

Gidcott *Gildescote/cota: Gilbert from Robert d'Aumale. 15 cattle.* Now Higher Gidcott.

Gidleigh *Chiderleia/Ghiderleia: Godwin the Priest, the pre-Conquest holder, from Count of Mortain.* Gidleigh Castle, built by Baldwin de Brionne, possibly on Saxon foundations.

Gittisham *Gidesham/sam: Gotshelm. Mill. 2 cobs.* Bronze Age barrows. The Rolling Stone, said to be the site of human sacrifices, is nearby; when the moon is full, it rolls down to the River Sid to cleanse itself of blood.

Goodcott *Godevecote/vacota: Easthelm, formerly Godive.* Tiny.

Goodleigh *Godelege/lega: Robert d'Aumale.* Old mill, now part of a school.

Goodrington *Godrintone/tona: Ralph, a man-at-arms, from Walter de Douai. Cob, 16 cattle, 166 sheep.* Part of Paignton; Goodrington Sands.

Goosewell *Gosewelle/wella: Robert from William de Poilley. Cow.* Part of Plymouth.

Gorhuish *Gohewis: Bernard from Baldwin the Sheriff. 22 cattle.* Now 2 hamlets, Higher and Lower Gorhuish.

Gorwell *Gerwille/Gorwilla: Oliver from Theobald FitzBerner.* Gorwell Farm.

Gratton (in High Bray) *Gretedone/dona: Bishop of Coutances.* On the edge of Exmoor.

Great Beere *Bera: Walter from Baldwin the Sheriff. 10 cattle, 27 goats.* Great Beere Farm near Great Beere Moor.

Great Fulford *Foleford: Modbert from Baldwin the Sheriff.* House.

Great Torrington *Toritone/tona: Roger from Ralph de Pomeroy; Ansger de Montacute; Odo FitzGamelin and 3 Frenchmen from him. 12 cattle, 146 sheep.* Town and market centre since Saxon times, with a park on the site of a Norman castle. The church was blown up in 1645 with 200 Royalists inside.

Greenslade *Ghernesle te/leta: Rainer the Steward from Baldwin the Sheriff.*

Greenslinch *Grennelize/liza: Nicholas the Bowman.*

Greenway *Grenowei/weia: Walter de Douai. 40 cattle, 40 goats.* Greenway Farm.

Grimpstone *Grismetone: William from Alfred le Breton.* Tiny.

Grimpstonleigh *Lege/Lega: William from Alfred le Breton.*

Hacche *Achie/Achia: Alwy from Odo FitzGamelin. 14 cattle, 25 goats.* Now Hacche Barton; Hacche Moor.

Haccombe *Hacome/coma: Stephen from Baldwin the Sheriff; Robert from William Cheever. 50 goats.* Some houses.

Hackworthy *Hacheurde: Hervey de Hellean's wife.* Tiny; Hackworthy Brakes, a wood.

Hagginton *Haintone/Hagintona/Hagetone/Hagitona: Bishop of Coutances; Robert from Baldwin the Sheriff; Wulfric from Walter de Douai. 150 sheep, 37 goats.* Hagginton Hill.

Halberton *Als-/Halsbretone/-tona: King's land and Gotshelm from the king. 2 mills. 11 cattle, 150 sheep.*

EXETER: *Carved decoration on the west front of Exeter Cathedral.*

Halse *Hax: Modbert son of Lambert from Baldwin the Sheriff.* Tiny.

Halstow (in Dunsford) *Alestou/Halestou: Godbold.* Tiny.

Halwell *Hagewile/Hagowila: William from Iudhael of Totnes.* Tiny.

Halwill *Halgewelle/willa: King's land. 33 cattle. 20 pigs.* Name comes from a holy well, still in existence; Halwill Forest nearby.

Hampson *Nimet: Hermer from Gotshelm.* Tiny.

Hamsworthy *Hermodesword/Hermondesworda: Drogo from Bishop of Coutances.* Tiny.

Hankford *Hancheford/Hanecheforda: Reginald from Roald Dubbed.* Hankford Barton.

Harbourneford *Erberneford/Herberneforda: Reginald from William de Falaise.* White-Oxen Manor nearby.

Hareston *Harestane/tana: Reginald from Count of Mortain.* Hareston Farm.

Harford (near Cornwood) *Hereford/forda: Reginald from Count of Mortain.* On the edge of Dartmoor, surrounded by prehistoric remains and fine old farm houses.

Hartland *Hertitone/tona: King's land, formerly Gytha mother of Earl Harold. 137 cattle, 50 pigs, 700 sheep, 100 goats.* On one of the finest coastal stretches in Britain. Hartland Quay is a 15th-century harbour built by the monks of Hartland Abbey, founded by Gytha, Harold's mother – now an 18th-century Gothic house.

Hartleigh *Herlege/Hierlega: Bishop of Coutances.* Harleigh Wood.

Hatherleigh (in Bovey Tracey) *Harlei/leia: Bishop of Coutances.* Tiny.

Hatherleigh (near Okehampton) *Adrelei/Hadreleia: Tavistock Church and Nigel, Walter, Geoffrey and Ralph from the Church. Mill. 15 cattle, 24 goats.* 15th-century George Inn. Hatherleigh Moor was granted as common land by John of Gaunt in the 14th century; St John's Well was believed to cure eye troubles.

Hawkmoor *Hauocmore/mora: Bishop of Coutances.* Hawkmoor Cottages.

Haxton *Haustone/tona: Bishop of Exeter.* Now 2 hamlets, Haxton and Haxton Down.

Hazard *Haroldesore: Robert Bastard.* Tiny.

Heanton Punchardon *Hantone/tona: Robert de Pont-Chardon from Baldwin the Sheriff. Mill, fishery. 11 cattle, 163 sheep.* Burial place of the postman poet, Edward Capern (1819–94), whose handbell hangs by his tomb.

Heanton Stachville *Hantone/tona: Ralph de Bruyere from Baldwin the Sheriff.* Heanton Satchville estate.

Heathfield *Hetfeld/felt: Buckfast Church. 11 cattle, 16 goats.* Heathfield Manor.

Heavitree *Hevetrove/trowa: Roger from Ralph de Pomeroy, formerly Viking.* Part of Exeter.

Hele (in Ilfracombe) *Hela: Bishop of Coutances.*

Hele *Helescaue/Helecaue/Hela: Erchenbald from Count of Mortain; Wihenoc from Alfred le Breton; Godbold.* Hele Barton; Hele Bridge over the River Torridge; also the hamlets of Crockers, Friars and Giffords Hele.

Hemerdon *Hainemardun: Walter from Roald Dubbed.*

Hemyock *Hamihoch/hoc: King's land.* Castle ruins. Nearby Whitehall was the home of the de Brewer family who founded Dunkeswell Abbey in 1201.

Henford *Hindeford/fort: Ralph de Pomeroy from Iudhael of Totnes.* Some houses; Henford Water.

HATHERLEIGH: *Church of John the Baptist noted for its 9th c. Saxon font.*

ILSINGTON: *The church from the gate.*

Hennock *Hanoch/Hainoc: Roger FitzPayne from Baldwin the Sheriff. Cob.* Originally Saxon, it belonged to Torre Abbey in the 13th century; the vicarage dates from that time.

Henscott *Engestecote/-cota/ Hainghestecota: Drogo from Bishop of Coutances. 20 cattle, 20 goats.* Tiny; Henscott Bridge over the River Waldon.

Highampton *Hanitone/ Hantona: Roger from Baldwin the Sheriff. 17 cattle.*

High Bickington *Bichentone/ tona: King's land. 12 cattle.* Church with fine old bench ends; Norman arch and font.

High Bray *Brai/Braia: Bishop of Coutances.*

Highleigh *Henlei/leia: Ralph de Pomeroy.* Some houses.

Hill (in Cruwys Morchard) *Hille/Hilla: Haimeric.* Hill Farm.

Hillersdon *Hilesdone/ Hillesdona: Reginald from Odo FitzGamelin.* Hillersdon House.

Hittisleigh *Hiteneslei/leia: Ralph de Pomeroy from Baldwin the Sheriff.* Hittisleigh Barton; Hittisleigh Cross, a tiny hamlet.

Hockworthy *Hocoorde/rda: Rogo from Baldwin the Sheriff; Walter de Douai.*

Holbeam *Holebeme/bema: Roger Goad from Nicholas the Bowman.*

Holbrook *Holebroch/broca: Bretel from Count of Mortain; Alstan, the pre-Conquest holder, from the king.* Holbrook Farm.

Holcombe (in East Dawlish) *Holecome/Holcomma: Ralph de Pomeroy.*

Holcombe Burnell *Holecumbe/ cumba: King's land. 50 goats.* Some houses.

Holcombe Rogus *Holecome/ coma: Rogo from Baldwin the Sheriff. 2 mills. 22 pigs.* Holcombe House is 16th century with a 3-storey tower, Great Hall and Long Gallery.

Hole (in Clayhidon) *Holne/ Holna: Otelin from Baldwin the Sheriff.* Some houses.

Hole (in Georgeham) *Hole/ Hola: Theobald FitzBerner.* South Hole Farm.

Hole (in Hartland) *Hola: Gosbert from Theobald FitzBerner.* Now South Hole.

Hollacombe (near Holsworthy) *Holecome/coma: Priests of Bodmin, the pre-Conquest holders. 12 cattle.*

Hollacombe (in Kentisbury) *Holecome/coma: Walter de Douai.* Tiny.

Hollam *Holnham: Gilbert from Roald Dubbed.*

Holland *Hovelande/Honelanda: Ralph from Iudhael of Totnes.* Tiny.

Hollowcombe (in Ermington) *Holescome/coma: Ralph de Pomeroy from Count of Mortain. 4 salt-houses.* Hollowcombe Farm.

Hollowcombe (in Fremington) *Holecome/ Holcomma: Theobald FitzBerner. 3 salt-workers paying 5 packloads of salt, 1 packload of fish.* On the edge of Bickington.

Holne *Holle/Holla: William de Falaise. Cob.* Birthplace of Charles Kingsley (1819–75); 2 15th-century stone bridges.

Holsworthy *Haldeword/eurdi: King's land, formerly Earl Harold. 100 cattle, 30 pigs, 300 sheep, 20 goats.* Town where fairs have been held since the 12th century.

Honeychurch *Honecherde/ chercha: Walter from Baldwin the Sheriff. 30 cattle.* Name comes from the Saxon for Huna's church.

Honicknowle *Hanechelole/ Hanenchelola: Reginald from Count of Mortain.* Part of Plymouth.

Honiton (near Axminster) *Honetone/tona: Drogo from Count of Mortain. Mill. 100 sheep.* Mainly Georgian town, an important posting stage on the London-Exeter road. Famous for Honiton lace, probably introduced by Huguenots in the 16th century.

Honiton (in South Molton) *Hunitone/tona: Odo FitzGamelin.* Honiton Barton.

Hooe *Ho: Stephen from Iudhael of Totnes.* Part of Plymouth.

Hook (in Ashreigney) *Hocha/ Hoca: Godbold.* Hook Farm.

Horton *Hortone/tona: Bishop of Coutances.* Horton Farm.

Horwood *Horewod/-wode/ Horewda/-woda: Bishop of Coutances; Ralph de Pomeroy. Cow, 90 sheep.* Overlooking the Taw and Torridge Estuary.

Houndtor *Hundatore/tora: Reginald from Tavistock Church.* Now Great Houndtor. Hound Tor, with a stone circle and cairn, is nearby.

Huish (near Dolton) *Hiwis/ Hywis/Iwis/Ywis: Gotshelm; Ralph Vitalis from Odo FitzGamelin. 24 cattle, 102 sheep, 35 goats.*

Huish (in Instow) *Torsewis: Bishop of Coutances, formerly Wulfeva.*

Huish (in Tedburn St Mary) *Chiwartiwis: Fulchere the Bowman, the king's servant.* Great Huish Farm; East Huish Farm.

Huntsham *Honesham/ssam: Odo FitzGamelin. 10 cattle.* Huntsham Barton.

Huntshaw *Huneseue/eua: William Cheever. 10 cattle, 100 sheep, 30 goats.* Mainly 15th-century church with a 12th-century chancel; all who helped rebuild it in 1439 were granted indulgences.

Huxham *Hochesham/sam: Roger from Ralph de Pomeroy. Mill.*

Huxhill *Hochesile/sila: Roald Dubbed.* Tiny; Great Huxhill; Higher Huxhill.

Iddesleigh *Edeslege/-lega/ Iweslei/Ywesleia: King's land. Walter de Claville, formerly Aelfeva Thief. 35 cattle, 100 sheep.*

Ide *Ide/Ida: Bishop of Exeter. Cob.* 13th-century bridge; group of 17th-century cottages called 'The College'.

Ideford *Yudeford/Yudaforda: Nicholas the Bowman. 120 sheep.* Attractive; thatched cottages.

Ilfracombe *Alfreincome/coma: Robert from Baldwin the Sheriff. Cob, 133 sheep.* Seaside resort with an important harbour since the 13th century, when St Nicholas's Chapel on Lantern Hill was the cell of a hermit who kept a light to guide shipping.

Ilkerton *Crintone/Incrintona: William Cheever. 58 cattle, 200 sheep, 75 goats, 72 wild mares (with Lynton).* Now 2 tiny hamlets, East and West Ilkerton.

Ilsham *Ilesham/sam: Roger from William the Usher, the king's servant.* Absorbed in Wellswood.

Ilsington *Lestintone/Ilestintona: Ralph Pagnell. 23 goats.* Near Haytor Rocks.

Ilton *Eddetone/Edetona: Fulk from Iudhael of Totnes.* Tiny.

Ingleigh *Genelie: Alfred le Breton.* Now Ingleigh Green.

Ingsdon *Ainech-/Ainichesdone/ Ainechesdona: Ralph Pagnell; Osbern de Sacey. 125 wethers.* Ingsdon Hill.

Instaple *Essastaple/Esas-/ Esestapla: Ansketel from William Cheever.* Instaple Farm.

Instow *Johannestou/sto: Walter de Claville. Priest.* On the Torridge Estuary.

Inwardleigh *Lege/Lega: Otelin from Baldwin the Sheriff.*

Ipplepen *Iplepene/pena: Ralph de Feugeres. Cob, 250 sheep.* Name comes from the Celtic for upland enclosure.

Irishcombe *Eruescome/coma: King's land.* Irishcombe Farm.

Ivedon *Otri: Warin and Ralph FitzPayne from William Cheever; Ralph de Pomeroy and Rozelin from him.* Ivedon Farm.

Kelly *Chenleie/leia: Modbert from Baldwin the Sheriff. 11 cattle.* Partly Tudor and partly Georgian manor house.

IDE: *A thatched cottage with unusual windows.*

Kenn *Chent: Baldwin the Sheriff. Mill. 150 sheep.* Church with a Norman table-top and font.

Kentisbeare *Chentesbere/bera: Baldwin the Sheriff.* Medieval priest's house; remains of Kerswell Priory.

Kentisbury *Chentesberie/beria: Baldwin the Sheriff.* Barton built in 1674.

Kenton *Chentone/tona: King's land, formerly Queen Edith. Mill. 20 cattle, 200 sheep, 20 goats.* Church, c.1400, with a fine 15th-century screen, pulpit and rood-loft.

Kerswell (in Broadhembury) *Carsewelle/euilla: Gunter from Ralph Pagnell. Mill.*

Kerswell (in Hockworthy) *Cressewalde/walla: Gerard from Walter de Douai.* Kerswell Barton.

Keynedon *Chenigedone/ Chenighedona/-irghedona: Roger from Ralph de Pomeroy. 106 sheep.* Keynedon Barton, partly Tudor.

Kidwell *Cadewile/wila:* Lost.

Kigbeare *Cacheberge: Rainer from Baldwin the Sheriff.* Tiny.

Killington *Cheneoltone/tona: Bishop of Coutances. 30 goats.* Some houses.

Kilmington *Chenemetone/ Chienemetona: King's land, formerly Earl Leofwin. Mill.*

Kimber *Chempebere/ Chiempabera: Roger of Flanders from Roald Dubbed.* Now Kimber West, some houses.

Kimworthy *Chemeworde/ worda: Bishop of Coutance's niece from him. 15 cattle.* Tiny.

Kingsford *Chinnesford/fort: Baldwin the Sheriff.* Now 2 tiny hamlets, Higher and Lower Kingsford.

Kingskerswell *Careswelle/willa: King's land. Church. 120 sheep.* Residential district between Newton Abbot and Torquay.

King's Nympton *Nimetone/ tona: King's land, formerly Earl Harold. 16 cattle, 100 sheep.* Named after the old name for the River Yeo – Nymet.

King's Tamerton *Tanbretone/ tona: King's land.* Part of Plymouth.

Kingsteignton *Teintone/tona: King's land.* Small industrial town.

Knowstone *Chenudestane/ Chenutdestana: Rolf from Walter de Douai; Algar and Alfhild, a woman, the pre-Conquest holders, from the king. 24 cattle, 142 sheep, 45 goats, 28 pigs.*

Lambert *Lanford/forda/ Lantfort: Osbern de Sacey; Godwin from the king.* Tiny.

Lambside *Lamesete/Lammaseta: Iudhael of Totnes.* Tiny.

Lamerton *Lanbretone/ Lanbretona: Roald Dubbed. 2 mills. 20 pigs.* Tudor manor house.

Landcross *Lanchers: Robert from Baldwin the Sheriff. 30 goats.*

Langage *Langehewis:* Lost.

Langdon *Langedone/gadona: Waldin from Iudhael of Totnes.* 16th-century Langdon Court; Langdon Lodge.

Langford (in Cullompton) *Langeford/gafort: Rainer from Baldwin the Sheriff. Cob.*

Langford (in Ugborough) *Langeford/forda: Baldwin from the king.* Langford Barton.

Langley (in Yarnscombe & Atherington) *Bichenelie: King's land.* Now Langley Cross; tiny.

Langstone *Langestan/ Langhestan: Hugh from Baldwin the Sheriff.* Clapper bridge nearby.

Langtree *Langetreu/trewa: King's land.*

Lank Combe *Lacome/Lancoma: Ralph de Pomeroy.* Downland.

Lapford *Slapeford/Eslapa-/ Slapeforda: King's land. 30 cattle, 180 sheep.* Bury Barton, nearby, with a private chapel, licensed in 1434, and now a farm building.

Larkbeare *Laurochebere/bera: Alfred le Breton from Baldwin the Sheriff; Alfred le Breton.* With Larkbeare Court.

Lashbrook *Lochebroc/ Lachebroc: Roger from Baldwin the Sheriff. 17 cattle, 21 goats.* Now Little Lashbrook.

Leigh (in Churchstow) *Lega/ Lega: Walter de Claville. Cob.* 16th-century farmhouse, once part of Buckland Abbey with a dormitory, refectory and 15th-century gatehouse.

Leigh (in Coldridge) *Bera: Walter from Baldwin the Sheriff.* Now 3 hamlets, East Leigh, Leigh Cross and Trinity Leigh.

Leigh (in Harberton) *Lege/ Lega: William from Iudhael from Totnes.* Now 2 hamlets, East and West Leigh.

Leigh (in Loxbeare) *Lege/Lega: Roger from Fulchere.* Tiny; Leigh Barton.

Leigh (in Milton Abbot) *Lege/ Lega: Tavistock Church.* Leigh Barton Farm; Leigh Wood.

Leigh (in Modbury) *Lege/Lega: Iudhael of Totnes.* Now 2 hamlets, East and West Leigh.

Leonard *Lannor/Limor/Linor: Walter de Claville; Morin, the king's servant.* Leonard Farm.

Lewtrenchard *Lewe/Leuya: Roger de Meulles from Baldwin the Sheriff. 18 cattle.* Home of the Gould family for 400 years. The Reverend Sabine Baring-Gould plundered various Tudor houses to decorate his own.

Liddaton *Lidel-/Liteltone/ Lideltona: Tavistock Church and Geoffrey from the Church. 24 cattle, 100 sheep, 50 goats.* Liddaton Green, some houses.

Lifton *Listone/tona: Colwin from the king, formerly Queen Edith. 55 cattle, 250 sheep, 50 goats.*

LEWTRENCHARD: *The church has a richly carved oak interior.*

Early Tudor Wortham Manor nearby.

Lincombe *-Lincome/coma: Robert from Baldwin the Sheriff. Cob, 100 sheep.*

Lipson *Lisistone/-tona/Lisitona: Reginald from Count of Mortain. 30 goats.* Part of Plymouth.

Little Bovey *Adonebovi: Bishop of Coutances.*

Littleham (near Bideford) *Liteham: Gotshelm from the king. 100 sheep.* Church with an old muniment chest carved from a single tree trunk.

Littleham (near Exmouth) *Liteham: Horton Church. 139 sheep.* Church with a Saxon scratch dial; burial place of Nelson's wife, Frances.

Littlehempston *Hamestone/ Hamistone/Hamistona: King's land, formerly Earl Harold. Ralph de Pomeroy from Iudhael of Totnes. 40 goats.* Old Manor, c.1400 with a 15th-century fresco.

Little Marland *Mer-/Mirland/- landa: Gosbert from Theobald FitzBerner.* Some houses.

Little Rackenford *Litel Rachenford/forda: Ludo from Walter de Douai.* Little Rackenford Farm.

Little Torrington *Torintone/ Toritone/-tona: King's land, formerly Gytha, mother of Earl Harold; Alfred the Butler from Count of Mortain; Richard from Baldwin the Sheriff. 16 cattle, 65 goats.*

Little Weare *Litelwere/wera: Odo FitzGamelin.* Little Weare Barton.

Lobb *Loba/Lobe: Reginald from Roald Dubbed. Salt-house.* Now 2 hamlets, Lobb and North Lobb.

Loddiswell *Lodeswille/willa: Iudhael of Totnes. Fishery (30 salmon).*

Loosebeare *Losbere/bera: Cranbourne Church.* Some houses.

Loosedon *Lollardesdone/estone/ esdona: Walter de Claville.* Loosedon Barton.

Loughtor *Lochetore/tora:* Lost.

Lovacott (in Shebbear) *Lovecote/cota: Roald Dubbed.*

Loventor *Lovenetorne/torna: Iudhael of Totnes.* Loventor Manor Farm, now a hotel.

Lower Creedy *Credie/Cridie/ Creda/Cridia: Bishop of Coutances; William from Ralph de Pomeroy.* Some houses.

Lowley *Levelege/Levaliga: Godbold. 160 sheep, 20 goats.*

Lowton *Lewendone/dona: Rainer from Godbold.* Tiny.

Loxbeare *Lochesbere/bera: Bishop of Coutances.*

Loxhore *Locheshore/sore/sora/ ssora: Robert de Beaumont from Baldwin the Sheriff. Alder-grove. 20 cattle, 100 sheep.* Old farms with stone barns and granaries.

Ludbrook *Lodebroc/Lodrebroc/ Ludebroch/-broca: Reginald from Count of Mortain. Mill.*

Luppitt *Lovapit: Walter de Douai. 26 cattle, 30 goats.* Church with a Norman font carved with centaurs and a fine waggon roof.

Lupridge *Loperige/Olperiga/ Luperige/-riga/Kluperiga: Reginald from Count of Mortain; Walter de Claville; Baldwin from Gotshelm.* Tiny.

Lupton *Lochetone/tona: Iudhael of Totnes.* Lupton House, now a school; Lupton Park.

Luscombe (in Rattery) *Luscome/cumma: Ansketel from William de Falaise.* Tiny.

Lydford *Lideford/-forde/-forda/- fort/Tideford:* See page 73.

Lympstone *Levestone/tona: William Cheever from Richard FitzGilbert.*

ILFRACOMBE: *Built among the hills; 14th c. Chambercombe Manor and a local botanic museum.*

Lyn *Line/Lina: William Cheever. New mill. 34 cattle.* East Lyn, some houses.

Lynton *Lintone/tona: William Cheever. 58 cattle, 22 pigs, 200 sheep, 75 goats, 72 wild mares (with Ilkerton).* New town on the cliffs; below is the old fishing village of Lynmouth, scene of a disastrous flood in 1952.

Mackham *Madescame: Hamo from William Cheever.*

Maidencombe *Medenecome/coma: Bernard from Baldwin the Sheriff.* Some houses.

Malston *Mellestone/tona: Ralph from Iudhael of Totnes.* Malston Barton.

Mamhead *Mammeheua/-hetua/ Manneheua: Ralph de Pomeroy from Baldwin the Sheriff; Saewulf, the pre-Conquest holder, from the king. Cob, 27 goats.* Mamhead House, rebuilt in Tudor style in the 19th century on the site of a medieval castle.

Manadon *Manedone/dona: Odo from Iudhael of Totnes.* Part of Plymouth.

Manaton *Manitone/tona: Edwy from Baldwin the Sheriff; Aldred, the pre-Conquest holder, from the king. 25 goats.* On the edge of Dartmoor; old stone cottages round the village green; home of John Galsworthy. Nearby Grimspound is a Bronze Age village with 24 hut circles.

Mariansleigh *Lege/Liege/Liega/ Leiga: William the Usher, the king's servant.*

Martin *Mertone/tona: Richard FitzThorulf from Baldwin the Sheriff.*

Martinhoe *Matingeho: Bishop of Coutances.* Restored 11th-century church.

Marwood *Merehode/-hoda/ Mereude/-uda/Merode/-oda: Robert from Baldwin the Sheriff; 2 men-at-arms from Robert d'Aumale; Oliver from Theobald FitzBerner. 20 cattle, 128 sheep, 20 goats.*

Mary Tavy *Tavi: Iudhael of Totnes. 16 cattle, 120 sheep.* Once a prosperous mining area. Tavy Cleave, nearby, is a dramatic gorge with many prehistoric sites.

Matford *Madford/-fort/Matford/ -forda: Alfred the Butler from Count of Mortain; Ralph from William Cheever.* Matford Barton; Matford Home Farm; Matford Bridge.

Meavy *Mewi: William and Nigel from Iudhael of Totnes; Robert Bastard.*

Meddon *Madone/dona: Ansgot, the pre-Conquest holder, from the king.* Some houses.

Medland *Mideland/landa: Godwin from the king.* Medland Manor.

Meeth *Meda: Bernard from Baldwin the Sheriff.* Thatched 14th-century inn; church with a Norman nave and font.

Melbury *Meleberie/beria: William de Poilley.* Some houses.

Melhuish *Melewis: Hugh de Rennes from Baldwin the Sheriff. 24 goats.* Melhuish Barton.

Membland *Mimidlande/landa: Waldin from Iudhael of Totnes.*

Membury *Maiberie/Maaberia/ Maneberie/Manberia: Warin from William Cheever.* Nearby is the Iron Age hill-fort after which the village was named.

Merton *Mertone/tona: Bishop of Coutances. Cob, 12 cattle.* Birthplace of Walter de Merton (*d.* 1277), founder of Merton College, Oxford.

Meshaw *Mauessart: Gilbert from Baldwin the Sheriff. 11 cattle.*

Metcombe *Metcome/coma: Bishop of Coutances.*

Middlecott (in Broadwood Kelly) *Mildecote/Mildelcote(a): Ranulf and Richard from Baldwin the Sheriff.*

Middlecott (in Chagford) *Midelcote/cota: Alwin, the pre-Conquest holder, from the king.*

Middleton *Middeltone/ Mideltona: Bishop of Coutances. 15 pigs.* Now West Middleton.

Middlewick *Wiche/Wica/Wicca: Bishop of Coutances.*

Mildon *Mildedone/dona: William Cheever, formerly Edith.*

Milford (in Hartland) *Meleforde/forda: Gosbert from Theobald FitzBerner.* Some houses.

Milford (in Stowford) *Meleford/ fort: Engelbald's wife from Bishop of Coutances.* Tiny.

Milton Abbot *Middeltone/ Midel-/Mildeltona: Tavistock Church. 22 cattle, 170 sheep, 30 goats.* Early 19th-century Gothic buildings; Endsleigh Cottage, with garden and grotto.

Milton Damerel *Mideltone/ tona: Robert d'Aumale, formerly Wulfeva. 30 cattle, 25 goats.* 14th-century church with a Tudor arcade. The list of rectors goes back to 1276.

Mockham *Mogescome/coma: Robert de Pont-Chardon from Baldwin the Sheriff. 12 cattle.* Mockham Barton near Mockham Down.

Modbury *Mortberie/Motberia/ Motbilie/-lia: Richard and Reginald from Count of Mortain. 30 goats.* 16th-century Exeter Inn.

Mohun's Ottery *Otri: Walter de Douai. Mill. 26 cattle, 30 pigs, 100 sheep, 50 goats, 20 wild mares.* Gatehouse of a house built by Sir Reginald Mohun in the 13th century.

Molland (in North Molton) *Molland/landa: Bernard from Theobald FitzBerner. 3 oxen.* Molland Cross, some houses.

Molland (in West Anstey) *Mollande/landa: King's land, formerly Earl Harold; Bishop of Coutances.* On Exmoor.

Monkleigh *Lege/Lega: Alfred from Count of Mortain. 100 sheep.* Thatched cottages; old lime kilns.

Monkokehampton *Monuchementone/ Monacochamentona: Baldwin the Sheriff. Cob, 18 cattle.*

Monkswell *Reginald from Roald Dubbed.* Tiny Monkswell House.

Moor (in Broadwoodwidger) *More/Mora: Nigel from udhael of Totnes.*

Morchard Bishop *Morchet: King's land.* Views of Dartmoor and Exmoor.

Morebath *Morbade/batha: King's land, formerly Earl Harold.*

Moreleigh *Morlei/Morleia: William from Alfred le Breton.*

MORETONHAMPSTEAD: *The almshouses with arcades.*

Moretonhampstead *Mortone/ tona: Baldwin from the king, formerly Earl Harold. 20 cattle, 130 sheep.* Small market town on Dartmoor with 17th-century almshouses, old wayside crosses nearby include Horspit Cross. The church has tombstones of Napoleonic prisoners of war.

Mortehoe *Mortehou/ho: Aelfric from Ralph de Limesy.* Morte Point looks across to Lundy Island; Tudor farmhouse nearby.

Mowlish *Milchewis/Milehyuis: Richard from Ralph de Pomeroy; Saewulf, the pre-Conquest holder, from the king. Cow.* Mowlish Manor.

Mullacott *Molecote/Molacota: Godbold.* Now 2 tiny hamlets, Higher and Lower Mullacott; Mullacott Farm.

Murley *Morlei/leia: Walter the Wild from Walter de Claville.*

Musbury *Musberie/beria: Baldwin the Sheriff. Mill. 18 unbroken mares, 16 cattle, 100 sheep. 30 goats.* 15th-century Ashe House with a 14th-century tiltyard; church with monuments to the Drake family.

Mutley *Modlei/leia: Odo from Iudhael of Totnes.* Part of Plymouth.

Muxbere *Mochelesberie/beria: Ansger de Montacute. Mill.* Tiny.

Natson *Nimet: Godwin from the king.*

Natsworthy *Noteswrde: Richard FitzThorold.* Natsworthy Manor.

Neadon *Benedone/Beneadona: Hervey's wife from Baldwin the Sheriff.* Now Neadon Cleave.

Nether Exe *Niresse/essa: Bishop of Coutances. Cow.* On the River Exe; chapel.

Newton (in Chittlehampton) *Neutone/Neuetona: Ansger from Baldwin the Sheriff.* Now 2 tiny hamlets, North and South Newton.

Newton (in Zeal Monachorum) *Newentone/ tona: Osmund from Gotshelm; Godbold.* Now Man's Newton.

Newton Ferrers *Niwetone/tona: Reginald from Count of Mortain.* Town with old fishermen's cottages; Puslinch House, nearby, built 1720.

Newton St Cyres *Niwetone/ Newen-/Niwentona: Dunn from Bishop of Exeter; Dunn, the pre-Conquest holder, from the king.* Church of St Cyrica and St Julitta with a boss of a piglets suckling a sow. Inspired by the tradition that the church should be built where a sow farrowed.

Newton St Petrock *Newetone/ Nietona: Priests of Bodmin.*

Newton Tracey *Newentone/ tona: Walter de Burgundy from Gotshelm.*

Nichol's Nymet *Limet/Limete: Osmund from Gotshelm.* Nichol's Nymet House, now a hotel; Nichol's Nymet Cross.

Northam *Northam: St Stephen's Church, Caen. 2 salt-houses, fishery. 345 sheep.* Town with Georgian houses. Nearby Westward Ho is the only town to be named after a novel (by Charles Kingsley, 1855).

North Bovey *Bovi: Thorgils from Iudhael of Totnes.* 18th-century thatched cottages; village green; old cross; pump.

North Buckland *Bocheland/ lant: William Cheever. Cob, 12 cattle, 100 sheep, 20 goats.*

Northcote (in East Down) *Norcote/cota: Bishop of Coutances. 15 cattle, 17 pigs.* Tiny.

North Huish *Hewis: Ralph from Iudhael of Totnes.*

Northleigh *Lege-/Lega: Alward from Count of Mortain; Nicholas the Bowman. 16 cattle.*

Northlew *Leuia: King's land. 10 wild mares, 50 cattle, 100 sheep.* On the Saxon plan with a large square; old preaching cross by the church gate.

North Molton *Nortmoltone/ tona: King's land. 30 cattle, 170 sheep, 30 goats.* 16th-century court house; Georgian Court Hall.

North Tawton *Taue-/Tawetone/- tona: King's land.* Once a flourishing market town with an Elizabethan manor house nearby.

Norton (in Broadwoodwidger) *Nortone/tona: William from Iudhael of Totnes. 17 cattle.* Norton Barton Manor.

Norton (in Churchstow) *Notone/tona: Buckfast Abbey.*

Nutcott *Nochecote: Gerard.* Tiny.

Nutwell *Notewille/willa: Dunn, the pre-Conquest holder, from the King. 100 sheep.* Nutwell Court on the Exe Estuary.

Nymet Rowland *Limet: Walter from Baldwin the Sheriff. Mill.*

Nymet Tracey *Limeta: Bishop of Coutances. Cob.*

Oak *Acha: Richard from Baldwin the Sheriff.* Now Oak Cross.

Oakford *Alforde/forda: William Cheever. Mill. 200 sheep, 100 goats.* Oak Bridge with an old mill, nearby.

Offwell *Offewille/Offawilla: Reginald from Baldwin the Sheriff.* Church with fine Jacobean carving.

Okehampton *Ochementone/ Ochenemitona: Baldwin the Sheriff. Castle, market, mill.* Market town, originally a Saxon settlement. The ruins of Okehampton Castle include a Norman keep.

Okenbury *Ocheneberie/beria: Iudhael of Totnes.*

Oldridge *Walderige: Jocelyn Bernwin from Baldwin the Sheriff. 62 goats.* Some houses.

Orcheton *Orcartone/tona: Reginald from Count of Mortain. Salt-house.* Great Orcheton Farm.

Orway *Orrewai/Orrawia: Alfred d'Epaignes.*

Oussaborough *Aseberge: Theobald FitzBerner.* Tiny.

Otterton *Otritone/tona: Mont St Michel Church, formerly Countess Gytha. Market on Sundays. 3 mills. 60 pigs, 18 cattle, 300 sheep, 22 goats.* Nearby is Ladram Bay with rock stacks and large caves.

Ottery (in Lamerton) *Odetreu/ trewa: Robert d'Aumale. 14 cattle, 20 goats (with Collacombe and Willestrew).* Tiny; Ottery Cottages; Ottery Park.

Ottery St Mary *Otrei/Otri: St Mary's Church, Rouen, before and after 1066. 3 mills, garden. 24 cattle, 130 sheep, 18 wild mares.* Town given to Rouen Cathedral by Edward the Confessor and bought back by Bishop Grandisson of Exeter who rebuilt the church in the 14th century. Restored by William Butterfield in the 19th century, it is now one of the county's finest churches.

Owlacombe *Olecumbe/ Ulacumba: Gotshelm from Theobald FitzBerner.*

Paignton *Peintone/tona: Bishop of Exeter. Salt-house. 20 cattle, 350 sheep.* Town. A Bronze Age, then Saxon, settlement, it developed as a resort in the 19th century. The church, on a Bronze Age site, has Saxon foundations. Coverdale Tower was part of a palace of the Bishops of Exeter.

Panson *Panestan: Alfred le Breton from Roald Dubbed.* West Panson, some houses.

Parford *Patford/forda: Osbern de Sacey.*

Parkham *Percheham: Richard from Baldwin the Sheriff.* Church with a Norman door, font and holy water stoup.

Parracombe *Pedrecumbe/ Pedracomba: William de Falaise. 27 goats.* Stone-built; named after St Petroc's combe; Georgian church saved by John Ruskin. Prehistoric sites include Holwell Castle, a hill fort.

Patchole *Patsole/sola: Bishop of Coutances.* Some houses.

Payhembury *Ham-/Han-/ Henberie/Hain-/Ham-/Han-/ Hemberia: Rainer from Baldwin the Sheriff; Odo from the king. Mill. 2 cobs.* Thatched cottages.

Peadhill *Pedehel/hael: Bishop of Coutances.* Tiny.

Peamore *Peumere/mera: Roger FitzPayne from Ralph de Pomeroy.* Peamore House.

Pedley *Pidelige/Peideliga/ Pidaliga/Piedelege: Ralph from William de Poilley.* Pedley Barton.

Peek (in Ugborough) *Pech: Reginald from Count of Mortain. 20 goats.* Now East Peekes.

Peeke (in Luffincott) *Pech: Walter d'Omonville from Roald Dubbed.* Now West Peeke.

Peters Marland *Mer-/Mirland/- landa: Reginald from Roald Dubbed.*

Peter Tavy *Tawi: Alfred le Breton.* Former mining area.

Pethill *Pidehel, Thorgils from Iudhael of Totnes.* Pithill Farm.

Petrockstowe *Petrochestou: Buckfast Church.* Hillside site.

Pickwell *Wedicheswelle/ Pediccheswella: Bishop of Coutances.* Some houses.

Pilland *Pillande/Welland/ Pillanda: Bishop of Coutances. 147 sheep.* Tiny.

Pilton *Wiltone/Pi(lto)na: Bishop of Coutances. Cob.* Part of Barnstaple.

Pinhoe *Pinnoch/Pinnoc: King's land with Battle Church holding the church.* Part of Exeter.

Pirzwell *Pissewelle/willa: Hamo from William Cheever.*

Plaistow *Pleistou/Pleiestou: Bishop of Coutances.* Plaistow Mill, Plaistow Barton; East Plaistow, a tiny hamlet, nearby.

Plympton *Plintone/tona: King's land.* District of Plymouth. Plympton St Mary, a 9th-century religious community, became an Augustinian priory in 1121, owning Sutton Prior, the nucleus of Plymouth.

Plymstock *Plemestoch/stocha: Tavistock Church. 34 goats.* Part of Plymouth.

Plymtree *Plumtrei: Odo FitzGamelin. 13 sheep.* Church with fine 15th-century woodwork.

Polsloe *Polesleuge/leuia: Ansger from Bishop of Coutances; Canons of St Mary's from Baldwin the Sheriff.* Part of Exeter.

Poltimore *Pontimore/-mora/ Pultimore/-mora: Canons of St Mary's from Baldwin the Sheriff; Haimeric. 112 sheep, 20 cattle.* Thatched cottages.

Ponsford *Pantesford/fort: William from Baldwin the Sheriff.* Tiny.

Pool *Pole/Pola: William from Iudhael of Totnes; Ansfrid from Walter de Claville; Roger from Ralph de Pomeroy.* Now South Pool, at the head of Southpool Creek.

Potheridge *Porrige: Aubrey from Baldwin the Sheriff. Mare.* 3 clusters of houses, Great and Little Potheridge and Potheridge Gate.

Poughill *Pocheelle/-eella/ Pochehille/-hilla: Alfred the Butler from Count of Mortain; Roald Dubbed.*

Poulston *Polochestone/tona: Robert from Iudhael of Totnes. 122 sheep, 33 goats.*

Powderham *Poldreham: Ranulf from William d'Eu. Mill. 150 sheep, 40 goats.* Partly 14th-century Powderham Castle, home of the Earls of Devon.

Praunsley *Plantelie/-leia/ Plateleia: Reginald from Roald Dubbed.* Tiny.

Puddington *Potitone/tona: Ralph from William Cheever.*

Pulham *Polham: Reginald from Roald Dubbed.* Tiny.

Pullabrook *Polebroch/broc: Bishop of Coutances.* Pullabrook Farm.

Pyworthy *Paorde/Paorda: Iudhael of Totnes. 35 cattle, 200 sheep.*

Rackenford *Rachenetode/toda: Jocelyn from Baldwin the Sheriff. 12 cattle, 25 goats.* Partly Georgian manor house.

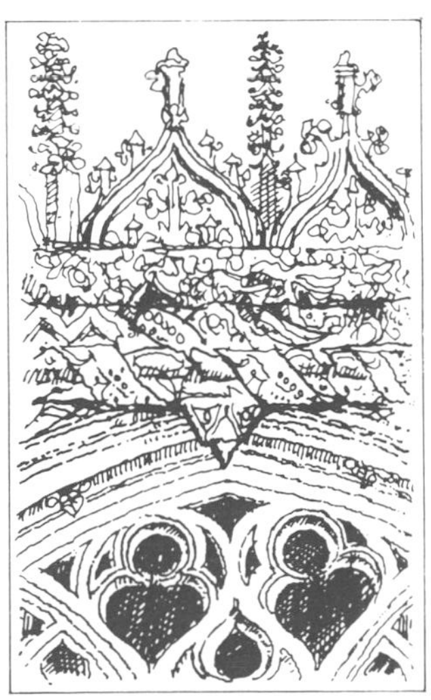

PILTON: *Church screen with tracery unique in Devon.*

Raddon (in Marystowe) *Ratdone/dona: Nigel from Iudhael of Totnes. 20 cattle, 140 sheep.*

SALCOMBE: *Sheltered beach near a steep yachting town.*

Raddon (in Thorverton) *Radone/Redone/Raddona/ Reddona: William the Usher from Tavistock Church; William the Usher, the king's servant. Cob, 11 cattle.* West Raddon; Raddon Court.

Radish *Redic/Red(d)ix/Radix/ Radiz:* Lost.

Radworthy (in Challacombe) *Radeode/euda: Reginald from William de Poilley.* Area near Challacombe.

Radworthy (in North Molton) *Raordin: William Cheever.* Now North Raddon; on Exmoor.

Raleigh *Radelie/leia: Bishop of Coutances.* Raleigh House on the edge of Barnstaple.

Rapshays *Otri/Oteri: Warin from William Cheever; Rozelin from Ralph de Pomeroy.* Rapshayes Farm.

Rattery *Ratreu: William de Falaise.* Church House Inn, said to date from the 13th century.

Rawridge *Rouerige/Rourige: St Mary's Church, Rouen, formerly Wulfeva. 20 cattle, 30 goats.*

Rewe *Rewe/Reuwa: Bishop of Coutances.* Packhorse bridge; village cross.

Riddlecombe *Ridelcome/coma: Gotshelm. 20 cattle, 114 sheep.*

Rifton *Restone/tona: Aubrey from Theobald FitzBerner.* Tiny; Rifton Moor.

Ringcombe *Ringedone: Ansger from Baldwin the Sheriff.* Tiny.

Ringmore (near Bigbury) *Reimore/mora: Iudhael of Totnes.* Castle Farm, a Victorian Gothic ruin.

Ringmore (in St Nicholas) *Rumor: Stephen from Baldwin the Sheriff. Cob, 100 sheep.* Part of St Nicholas on the Teign Estuary.

Roadway *Radehide/hida: Ralph Pagnell.* Tiny.

Roborough (near Great Torrington) *Raweberge/berga: Bishop of Coutances, formerly Wulfeva.* Old thatched cottages.

Rockbeare *Rochebere/Roce-/ Rochebera: Alward from Count of Mortain; Rainer and Gotshelm from Baldwin the Sheriff. 110 sheep.* Georgian Rockbeare Court.

Rocombe *Rachun/Racum/ Racome/-coma: Bernard from Baldwin the Sheriff; William Cheever; Ralph from Nicholas the Bowman. 23 cattle, 140 sheep.* Now Middle Rocombe; tiny. Lower Rocombe Farm; Higher Rocombe Barton.

Romansleigh *Lege/Liege/Leiga/ Liega: Nigel and Robert from Tavistock Church.* Named after the Celtic St Ruman.

Rose Ash *Aisse/Aissa: Ansger from Baldwin the Sheriff. 30 cattle.* Manor house, church and school around the village green.

Rousdon *Done/Dune/Dona/ Duna: Odo from the king, formerly Mathilda.* Victorian mansion imitating a variety of styles from Renaissance to Louis XIV, built for the Peek Frean family.

Rowley *Rodelie: Bishop of Coutances. 24 goats.* Little Rowley; Rowley Down, with tumuli, Holwell Barrow is nearby.

Ruckham *Rouecome/coma: Haimeric.* Now tiny hamlets, East and West Ruckham.

Rushford *Risford/fort: Edwy, the pre-Conquest holder, from Baldwin the Sheriff.* Rushford Barton; Rushford Mill Farm; Rushford Wood.

Ruston *Rinestandedone/dona: Edhild from Bishop of Coutances.* Tiny.

Rutleigh *Radeclive/cliva: Roger de Flanders from Roald Dubbed. 20 sheep.* Now Great Rutleigh; tiny. Rutleigh Ball Farm.

St James's Church *Jacobescherche: Aelfeva, the pre-Conquest holder.* Site of St James's Priory in Exeter.

St Mary Church *Ecclesia Sanctae Mariae: Bishop of Exeter; Richard FitzThorulf from Count of Mortain. 174 sheep.* St Marychurch, a coastal area of Torquay; fine cliffs and combes.

Salcombe Regis *Secome/coma: Bishop of Exeter.* Given by King Aethelstan to the monks of Exeter, who worked the salt-pans after which the village is named. The church dates from 1150.

Sampford Courtenay *Sanford/ fort: Baldwin the Sheriff. 28 cattle, 200 sheep, 40 goats.* Attractive village street with thatched cottages.

Sampford Peverell *Sanforde/ forda: Roger de Bully (given to him by Queen Mathilda on his marriage). 50 goats.* Home of the Peverell family and site of their castle, demolished in 1775. Probable effigy of Hugh Peverel, a crusader, in the church.

Sampford Spiney *Sandford/ forda: Robert from William de Poilley.* Farmhouse, 1617.

Satterleigh *Saterlei/leia: Godbold.*

Saunton *Santone/tona: Theobald FitzBerner. Salt house.* Saunton Sands, one of Devon's finest beaches.

Scobitor *Scabatore/tora: Bishop of Coutances.* Tiny.

Seaton *Flueta/Fluta: Horton Church. 11 salt-houses.* Seaton Junction. Nearby Seaton, a small resort on the River Axe with a largely Norman church, was an important medieval port until the harbour silted up.

Sedborough *Sedeborge/-borga/ Seteberge/Setleberga: Ansgot from the king.* Tiny.

Sellake *Selac: Gotshelm from Baldwin the Sheriff.*

Shapcombe *Cobecume/ Scobacoma/Scobecome/ Escobecoma: Walter de Douai; Ludo (wrongfully).* Tiny.

Shapley (in Chagford) *Scapelie/ Escapeliea: Robert and Godwin from Baldwin the Sheriff; Gerald the Chaplain.* Tiny; on Dartmoor, with prehistoric sites nearby.

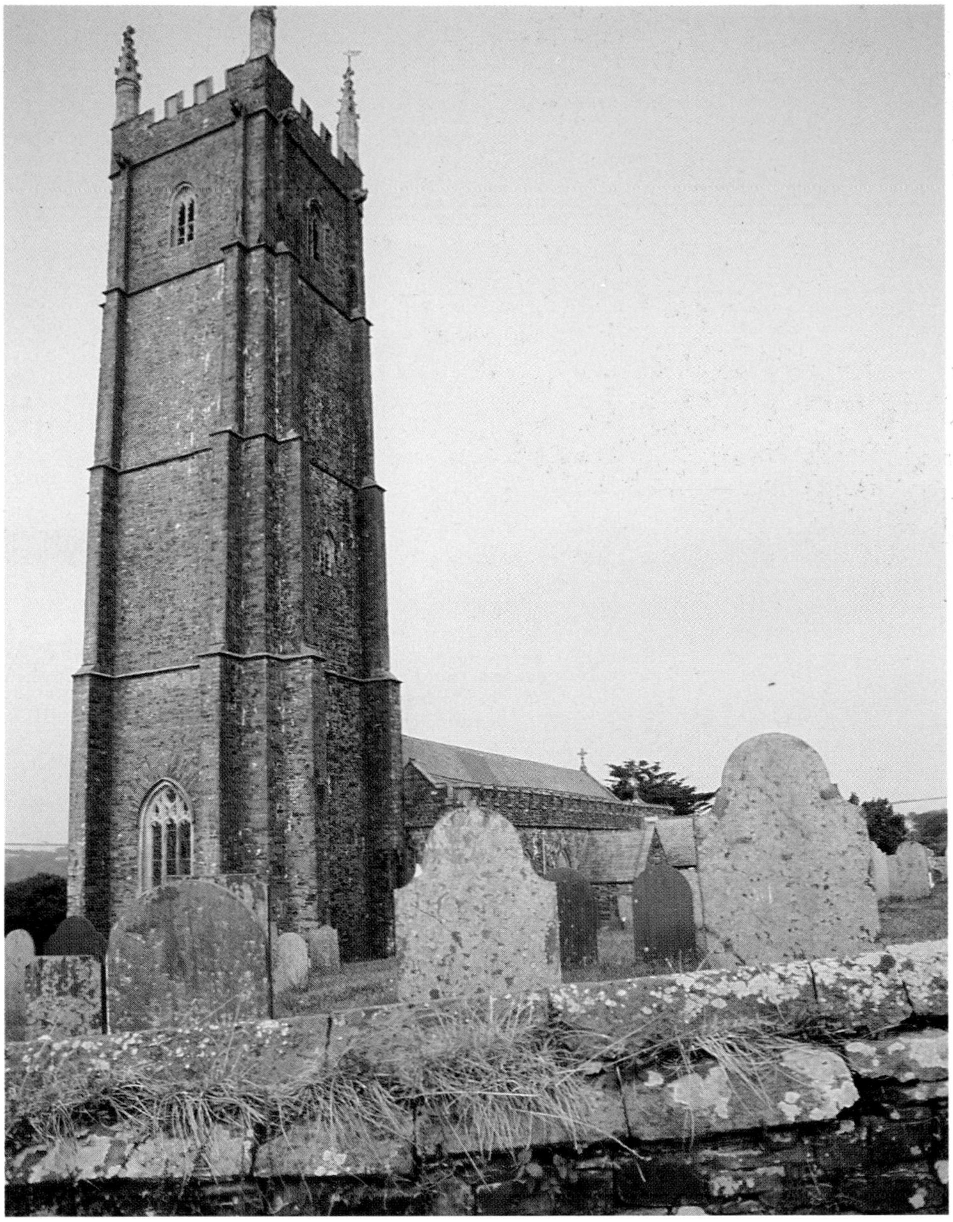

STOKE: *The remarkable tower of Stoke church rises above the neighbouring houses.*

Shapley (in North Bovey) *Essaple/-apla/Scapelie/Escapeleia: Aelfric, the pre-Conquest holder, from the king.* Tiny. Shapley Common; Shapley Tor.

Shaugh Prior *Scage/Escaga: Iudhael of Totnes and Thorgils from him.*

Shebbear *Sepesberie/beria: King's land, formerly Earl Harold. 30 pigs, 100 cattle, 500 sheep, 50 goats.* Devil's Stone marks an early sacred site.

Sheldon *Sildene/denna: Ralph de Pomeroy. 10 cattle.*

Sherford (in Brixton) *Sireford/fort: William from Iudhael of Totnes.* Now 2 tiny hamlets, East and West Shaugh.

Sherford (near Kingsbridge) *Sireford/-fort/forda: Battle Church from the king.* Mainly 14th-century church with medieval paintings.

Shillingford *Esselingeforde/-aforda/Selingeforde/-forda: William Cheever; Fulchere. 11 cattle.* Now Shillingford St George; also Shillingford Abbot.

Shilston *Silvestene/Silfestana: Richard from Count of Mortain.* Shilston Barton and Shilston Bridge on Shilston Brook.

Shilston *Selvestan: Osbern de Sacey.* Now Shilston Bridge; tiny. Shilston Barton.

Shiphay Collaton *Coletone/tona: Iudhael of Totnes.* Now Shiphay, part of Torbay.

Shirwell *Ascerewelle/Aiscirewilla/Sirewelle/-willa: Robert de Beaumont from Baldwin the Sheriff; William de Poilley; Gilbert from Odo FitzGamelin. 130 cattle, 28 goats.*

Shobrooke (near Crediton) *Sotebroch/broca: Count of Mortain.*

Shobrooke (in Morchard Bishop) *Schipebroc/Eschipabroca/-pebrocha: Walter de Claville.* Shobrooke Farm.

Sidbury *Sideberie/beria: Bishop of Exeter. 10 cattle, 140 sheep.* Church with a partly Saxon crypt (670); Sidbury Castle, a large prehistoric fort.

Sidmouth *Sedemude/muda: St Mary's Church, Rouen. Salt-house.* Resort and old fishing port; Regency architecture.

Sigford *Sigeford/forda: Solomon from Roald Dubbed. Cow.* Some houses.

Silverton *Sulfretona/tona: King's land. 3 mills.* Silverton Park, a decayed Georgian house, once belonged to the Earls of Egremont.

Skerraton *Siredone/dona: Aelfric, the pre-Conquest holder from the king.* Tiny.

SIDMOUTH: *A toll-house of classical design.*

Slapton *Sladone/dona: Baldwin the Sheriff from Bishop of Exeter. 100 sheep.* Ruined tower of a chantry founded by Sir Guy de Brien, 1372. Slapton Ley, a lagoon is a nature reserve.

Smallicombe *Smelecome/Hesmalacoma: Roger from Baldwin the Sheriff.* Smallicombe Farm.

Smallridge *Smarige/Smaurige/Esmarige/Esmaurige: Ralph de Pomeroy. Mill. 15 cattle, 32 goats.*

Smytham *Smitheham/Esmite-/Esmitteham: Ansger le Breton from Count of Mortain.*

Snydles *Smidelie/Esnideleia: Gilbert from Baldwin the Sheriff.* Snydles Farm.

Soar *Sure/Sura: Odo from Iudhael of Totnes. 15 cattle, 240 sheep and goats.*

Sorley *Surlei/leia: Fulk from Iudhael of Totnes. 18 cattle, 125 sheep.*

Sourton *Surintone/tona: Engelbald's wife from Bishop of Coutances. 18 cattle, 100 sheep, 50 goats.* According to legend, the devil died of cold on Sourton Moor. Bronze spearheads were found at Sourton Tor.

South Allington *Alintone/tona: Thorgils from Iudhael of Totnes.*

South Brent *Brenta/Brente: Buckfast Church. 25 cattle, 95 sheep, 30 goats.* Old village centre with a priest's house and toll-house.

South Huish *Hewis/Heuis: Ralph from Iudhael of Totnes. 143 sheep.* Some houses near the boast; ruins of a 15th-century chapel.

Southleigh *Lege/Lega: Beatrix from her brother William Cheever. 10 cattle.* Blackberry Castle is a large Iron Age hill-fort.

South Milton *Mideltone/Miltitona: Tovi from Alfred le Breton.* A bronze crucifix, c.1150, was discovered at Trendwell Farm in 1961.

South Molton *Sudmoltone/Sut Moltona: King's land and 4 clergy from the king.* Market town with Georgian and Victorian houses and 3 old mills.

South Tawton *Tauestone/-etone/Tauetona: King's land, formerly Countess Gytha. 100 cattle, 400 sheep, 70 goats.* Church House, built in 1572.

Southweek *Wicha/Wica/Wyca: Ralph de Pomeroy. 30 cattle.* Tiny; Southweek Wood.

Sowton (formerly Clyst Fomison) *Clis: Geoffrey from Bishop of Coutances. 2 cobs, 100 sheep.* Bishop's Court, in 1863, is said to have been the home of one of the builders of Exeter Cathedral.

Sparkwell *Sperchewelle/willa: Richard from Baldwin the Sheriff.* Tiny.

Speccott *Spececote/cota: Gosbert from Theobald FitzBerner.*

Spitchwick *Spicewite/Espicewita: King's land, formerly Earl Harold.* Spitchwick Manor.

Spreacombe *Sprecome/Esprecoma: Theobald FitzBerner.* Spreacombe Manor with a chapel. Now Higher Spreacombe.

Spreyton *Spreitone/Espreitona: Baldwin the Sheriff. 11 cattle, 35 goats.* Church with Saxon and Norman fonts and an inscription to Henry le Maygue, a native of Normandy, 'who caused me to be built 1451'.

Spriddlescombe *Combe/Comba: Dunn from Count of Mortain.* Now Higher Spriddlescombe; tiny.

Spriddlestone *Spredelestone/Espredelestona/-eletona: Reginald from Count of Mortain.*

Sprytown *Sprei: Wihenoc from Alfred le Breton.*

Spurway *Esprewei/Espreuweia: Bishop of Coutances; Hermer from Walter de Douai. 16 cattle.* Spurway and Spurway Mill, near West Spurway, a tiny hamlet.

Stadbury *Stotberie/beria: Ralph from Iudhael of Totnes.* Stadbury Farm.

Staddiscombe *Stotescome/coma: Iudhael of Totnes.* Part of Plymouth.

Staddon (in Plymstock) *Stotdone/Estotdona: William from Iudhael of Totnes.* Staddon Heights.

Stafford *Staford/-fort/Stadforda: Ansger de Montacute.* Stafford Barton; Stafford Moor Fishery.

Stallenge Thorne *Stanlinz: Odo FitzGamelin.* Stallenge Thorne Farm.

Stancombe *Stancome/coma: Thorgils from Iudhael of Totnes.* Now Stancombe Cross; tiny.

Staplehill *Stapelie/Estapeleia: Nicholas the Bowman.* Tiny.

Staverton *Sovretone/Stovretona: Bishop of Exeter. 101 sheep.* 15th-century Staverton Bridge.

Stedcombe *Stotecome/Estotacoma: Morin from Baldwin the Sheriff.* Stedcombe House.

Stockland *Ertacomestoche/stoca: Hervey FitzAnsger from Milton Abbey. 3 mills.* Near Stockton Great Castle, an Iron Age hillfort.

Stockleigh (in Highampton) *Tochelie/Estocheleia: Alward from Count of Mortain. 24 goats.* Stockleigh Farm.

Stockleigh (in Meeth) *Stochelie/Estocheleia/-lia: Erchenbald from Count of Mortain; Aubrey from Baldwin the Sheriff.* Stockleigh Barton.

Stockleigh English *Stochelie/Estocheleia: Reginald from Count of Mortain.*

Stockleigh Pomeroy *Stochelie/Estocheleia: Ralph de Pomeroy. Cob, 103 sheep, 23 goats.* Belonged to the Pomeroy family until the Catholic Rising of 1549.

Stoke (in Devonport) *Stoghes: Robert d'Aumale. 15 cattle, 160 sheep, 40 goats.* Part of Plymouth.

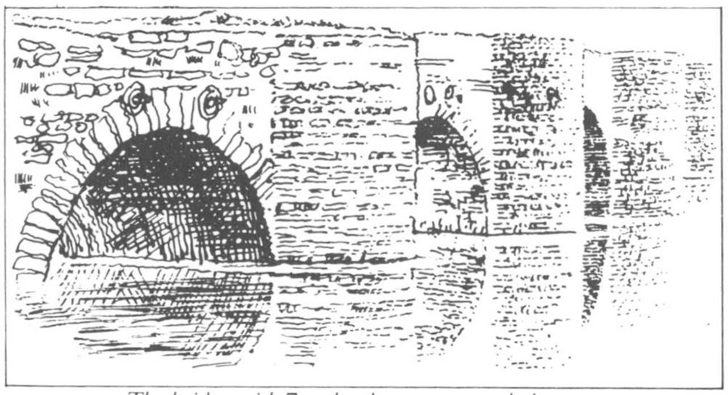

STAVERTON: *The bridge with 7 arches between rounded supports was built in 1413.*

Stoke (in Hartland) *Nistenestoch: Canons, the pre-Conquest holders, from Gerald the Chaplain.* 14th-century St Nectan's Church with a richly carved Norman font and painted waggon roof.

Stoke (in Holne) *Stoche/Estocha: Winemar from William de Falaise. 1 animal.* Tiny; on Dartmoor.

Stoke Canon *Stoche/Stocha: Bishop of Exeter. 2 mills.* Bridge dating from the 13th century over the River Culm.

Stoke Fleming *Stoch/Stoc: Ludo, Ralph and a woman from Walter de Douai.* Church with a 13th-century effigy of Elinor Mohun.

Stokeinteignhead *Stoches: Nicholas the Bowman.* Church with a 1375 brass, the earliest in Devon.

Stoke Rivers *Stoche/Estocha: William de Poilley. 100 sheep.*

Stonehouse *Stanehus: Robert Bastard.* Part of Plymouth.

Stoodleigh (near Oakford) *Stodlei/Estodleia: Bishop of Coutances; Robert from Ralph de Pomeroy. 18 cattle, 33 goats, 100 sheep.* East Stoodleigh Barton nearby.

Stoodleigh (in West Buckland) *Stodlei/Estotleia: Bishop of Coutances; Arnold from Walter de Douai.* Some houses.

Stowford (in Colaton Raleigh) *Staford/Estaforda: Earl Hugh.* Tiny.

Stowford (near Lifton) *Staford/Estatforda: Ralph Vitalis from Odo FitzGamelin. 10 cattle, 20 goats.* Romano-British stone in the churchyard.

Stowford (in West Down) *Staveford/Estaveforda: Bishop of Coutances.* West Stowford Barton.

Strete Ralegh *Estrete/eta: Thurstan from Ralph de Pomeroy. 60 goats.* Houses in a park.

Sutcombe *Sutecome/coma: Edric, the pre-Conquest holder, from Bishop of Coutances. 18 cattle.*

Sutton (in Halberton) *Suetetone/Suetatona/Suetetona:* Lost.

Sutton (in Plymouth) *Sudtone/Sutona: King's land.* Part of Plymouth.

Sutton (in Widworthy) *Sutone/Sutuna: Richard from William the Usher, the king's servant.* Sutton Barton.

Swimbridge *Birige: Saewin the priest, formerly Brictferth his uncle.*

Sydeham *Sideham: Osbern from Walter de Claville.* Sydeham Farm.

Sydenham (in Marystowe) *Sidreham: William from Iudhael of Totnes.* Sydenham House; Sydenham Wood.

Sydenham Damerel *Sidelham/Sidreham: Iudhael of Totnes.* On the wooded slopes of the River Tamar; packhorse bridge.

Tackbear *Tacabere/beara: Bernard the priest from Count of Mortain. 14 cattle.* Tiny.

Talaton *Taletone/tona: Robert from Bishop of Exeter. Mill.*

Tale *Tale/Tala: Ralph de Pomeroy. Mill. 15 cattle, 50 goats.* Lower Tale, some houses.

Tamerton Foliot *Tambretone: Alfred le Breton. Salt-house.* Part of Plymouth.

Tapeley *Tapelie/leia: Osbern from Bishop of Coutances. 10 cattle, 20 goats.* House once owned by John Christie, who founded Glyndebourne just after World War II.

Tapps *Ause/Ausa: Roger from Baldwin the Sheriff.* Now 2 tiny hamlets, East and West Tapps.

Tattiscombe *Totescome/coma: William de Lestre from Count of Mortain. 10 cattle, 20 pigs, 100 sheep, 25 goats.* Tiny.

Tavistock *Tavestoc/stocha: Tavistock Church; Ermenald, Ralph, another Ralph, Robert, Geoffrey and Hugh from the Church. Mill. Cob, 26 cattle, 200 sheep, 30 goats.* Market town, originally a prehistoric settlement, then a Saxon site with an abbey in the 10th century; one of the 4 stannary towns after tin was discovered in the 13th century.

Taw Green *Tavelande/landa: Robert from William the Usher, the king's servant. 12 cattle.* Lost in Ivybridge.

Tawstock *Tauestoch/-stoche/-stoca/-stocha: King's land, formerly Earl Harold. 67 cattle, 28 pigs, 500 sheep.* Gateway of the old Tudor manor; church with monuments to the 3 families who owned Tawstock – the Martins, Bourchiers and Wrays.

Tedburn St Mary *Teteborne/burne/borna: Rainer and Ralph de Pomeroy from Baldwin the Sheriff; William Cheever. Cob, 12 cattle, 162 sheep.*

Teigncombe *Taincome/coma: Bishop of Coutances.* Tiny.

Teigngrace *Taigne/Taigna: Ralph de Bruyere from Baldwin the Sheriff. Cob, 12 cattle, 35 goats.* 18th-century Stover House nearby.

Teignharvey *Taine/Taigna:* Lost.

Tetcott *Tetecote/cota: Iudhael of Totnes.* Tetcott House, built in 1603 with later additions.

Thelbridge *Talebrige/breia/brua: Bishop of Coutances. 29 goats.* Consists of Thelbridge Barton and Thelbridge Cross.

Thornbury (in Drewsteignton) *Torneberie/beria: Alfred from Count of Mortain.* Tiny.

Thornbury (near Holsworthy) *Torneberie/beria: Ralph from Tavistock Church. 14 cattle, 30 goats.*

Thorne (in Holsworthy Hamlets) *Torne: Engelbald's wife from Bishop of Coutances. 3 cows.* Thornemoor; tiny. Thorne Farm.

Throwleigh *Trule/Trula: Ralph Pagnell.* Old church house; Throwleigh Common with prehistoric hut circles.

Thrushelton *Tresetone: Iudhael of Totnes. 17 cattle.*

Thuborough *Teweberie/beria: Frank from Robert d'Aumale. 30 cattle, 23 pigs, 100 sheep.* Thuborough Barton, a Georgian house.

Thurlestone *Torlestan: Iudhael of Totnes. 150 sheep.* Overlooking Bigbury Bay; a 'thurled', or pierced rock, after which the village is named.

Tillislow *Tornelowe/lowa: Iudhael of Totnes.*

Tiverton *Tovretone/tona: King's land; Gerard from Ralph Pagnell. 2 mills.* Market and manufacturing town. Cranmere Castle, an earthwork, was the first settlement. The parish church contains Norman work; the original building was consecrated in 1073.

Topsham *Topeshant:* See page 75.

Torbryan *Torre/Torra: Godiva, formerly Brictric, her man. 120 sheep.* 15th-century church has its original box pews; Church House Inn was the old priest's house.

Tormoham *Torre/Torra: William the Usher, the King's servant. 2 cobs, 145 sheep.* Part of Torquay. Tor Abbey was founded in 1196; a 14th-century gatehouse, a tithe barn and the Abbot's tower remain.

TOTNES: *The castle, owned by a friend of William I, was mentioned in 1080, and restored in the 13th c.*

Torridge *Tori/Torix: Reginald from Count of Mortain; Ralph from Iudhael of Totnes. 18 goats.* Administrative district of Devon.

Totnes *Totenais/-neis/Totheneis/Thotonensium: Iudhael of Totnes.* Town, once a Saxon market centre with a mint; Saxon walls are still traceable and the ruins of a castle built by Iudhael remain.

Townstal *Dunestal: Ralph from Walter de Douai. 15 goats.* Part of Dartmouth.

Train *Alfelmestone: Reginald from Roald Dubbed. Salt-house.* Now Higher Train; tiny.

Trentishoe *Trendesholt: Bishop of Coutances. 22 goats.* Old smuggling centre; Heddon's Mouth, combe with old lime kiln on the beach, relic of trade with Wales.

Trusham *Trisma: Buckfast Church. 103 sheep, 22 goats.*

Twigbear *Tuche-/Tuichebere/Tuca-/Tuicabera: Roald Dubbed. 20 goats.* Tiny.

Twinyeo *Betunie/tunia: Leofric, the pre-Conquest holder, from the king.* Twinyeo Farm.

Twitchen (in Arlington) *Tuichel/Tuchel: Alfred d'Epaignes.* Tiny.

Uffculme *Offecome/coma: Walter de Douai. 2 mills. 14 cattle, 220 sheep.*

Ugborough *Ulgeberge: Alfred le Breton.* Church on the site of an ancient earthwork.

Umberleigh *Umberlie/leia: Holy Trinity Church, Caen. 16 cattle.* On the River Taw.

Undercleave *Odesclive/cliva: Edward from the king, formerly his father Edric the Cripple in alms from King Edward. Church.* Undercleave Farm.

Up Exe *Ulpesse/Olpessa: Drogo from Bishop of Coutances and Humphrey from him. Mill.* On the River Exe.

Uplowman *Oplomie/-ia/Oppelaume/Oppaluma: Gotshelm; Aelmer the Priest from Gotshelm; Alwin from Ralph de Pomeroy. Cob, 14 cattle.* 14th-century church built by Henry VIII's mother.

Uplyme *Lim: Glastonbury Church.* In the hills behind Lyme Regis.

Upottery *Otri: Ralph de Pomeroy. Mill.* On the River Otter.

Uppacott (in Tedburn St Mary) *Opecote: Modbert from Baldwin the Sheriff.* Now Great Uppacott.

Varley (in Marwood) *Fallei/Falleia: Bishop of Coutances.* Varley Farm.

Varleys (in Petrockstowe) *Ferlie/leia: Ansgot from the king. 10 cattle, 30 goats.* Tiny.

Venn (in Ugborough) *Fen: Reginald from Count of Mortain.* Venn House.

Villavin *Fedaven: Walter de Burgundy from Gotshelm, formerly Edlufu Thief and Edeva. 20 cattle, 16 wild mares.* Tiny.

WOOLACOMBE: *The rocky cliffs and sandy beaches of Devon make most coastal towns into resorts.*

Virworthy *Fereodin/Fereurde/-urdi: William Cheever; Riculf from Walter de Claville and Gotshelm. 31 cattle.*

Wadham *Wadeham: Ulf, the pre-Conquest holder, from the king. 8 wild mares, 12 cattle.* Tiny. Home of the Wadham family; Sir Nicholas Wadham founded Wadham College in 1610.

Walkhampton *Wachetone/tona: King's land.*

Wallover *Waleurde/urda: Bishop of Coutances.* Wallover Barton.

Walson *Nimet/Nimeth: Ralph de Pomeroy from Baldwin the Sheriff.* Walson Barton.

Warcombe *Warcome/coma: Bishop of Coutances.* Now Higher Warcombe.

Waringstone *Otri/Otrie/Oteri/Otria: Warin from William Cheever. 10 cattle, 20 pigs.* Now Weston.

Warmhill *Wermehel: King's land.* Warmhill Farm.

Warson *Wadelescote: Roger de Meulles from Baldwin the Sheriff.* Tiny.

Washbourne *Waseborne/borna: Hermer from Gotshelm. 1 animal.*

Washfield *Wasfelle/felte/fella/felta: Ralph de Pomeroy.* Church with a Norman font.

Washford Pyne *Waford/fort: Peter from William de Falaise; Walter from Walter de Claville; Theobald FitzBerner. Cob, 30 cattle.* Records of rectors date back to 1257.

Waspley *Wasberlege: Alric, the pre-Conquest holder, from the king.* Waspley Farm.

Weare Gifford *Were/-Wera: Roald Dubbed and Count of Mortain from him. ½ fishery.* 15th-century Weare Gifford Hall.

Webbery *Wiberie/Wibeberia: Roger Goad from Nicholas the Bowman.* Tiny.

Wedfield *Widefelle/fella: Alfred the Butler from Count of Mortain.* Tiny.

Week (in Thornbury) *Wiche:* Lost.

Welcombe *Walcome/coma: Wulfrun from Bishop of Coutances. 25 pigs, 100 sheep.* Tudor cottages; small Georgian houses; holy well.

Wembworthy *Mameorde/orda: Richard de Néville from Baldwin the Sheriff. 12 cattle, 30 goats.*

Werrington *Uluredintone/tona: King's land, formerly Earl Harold; Count of Mortain.*

West Alvington *Alvintone/tona: King's land.*

West Buckland *Bocheland/landa/lant: Ansger from Baldwin the Sheriff. 12 cattle, 36 goats.*

West Clyst *Cliste/Clista: Canons of St Mary's from Baldwin the Sheriff.* Tiny.

West Down (near Ilfracombe) *Dune/Duna: Bishop of Coutances.* Elizabethan manor house.

West Heanton *Hantone/tona: Colwin from the king.* Tiny.

Westleigh (near Bideford) *Weslege: Robert d'Aumale.*

Westleigh (near Burlescombe) *Lege: William from Aiulf. Mill. 30 goats.*

West Manley *Manelie: Gerard.* Site of an old chapel.

Weston Peverel *Westone/tona: Odo from Iudhael of Totnes. 15 cattle, 180 sheep, 60 goats.* Part of Plymouth.

West Portlemouth *Portemute: Fulk from Iudhael of Totnes.* Portlemouth Barton.

West Prawle *Prenla: Otelin from Baldwin the Sheriff.* Tiny. The village of East Prawle is nearby.

West Putford *Podiford/-forda/Poteford/-forde/Potaforda/-fort/Peteforda/Pudeforde/-forda: Ansketel from William Cheever; Roger from Ralph de Pomeroy; Reginald from Roald Dubbed. 38 cattle.*

West Raddon *Ratdone/dona: Count of Mortain. 40 goats.* Near Raddon Hills.

West Whitnole *Withechenolle/Witechenolla: Jagelin from Godbold. 15 cattle.* Tiny.

Weycroft *Wigegroste/Wigacrosta/Willecroste/-crosta/-crostra: Roger from Ralph de Pomeroy. 2 mills. 25 goats.* On the River Axe.

Whiddon *Willeden/denna: Ralph from Odo FitzGamelin.* Some houses.

Whimple *Winple/Winpla: Baldwin's wife from Baldwin the Sheriff; Ralph from William Cheever; 18 cattle, 24 goats.* Cider factory.

Whipton *Wipletone/tona: William Cheever. Cob, 12 cattle.* Part of Exeter.

Whitchurch *Wicerce: Roald Dubbed.* 2 old crosses mark the Abbot's Way from Tavistock. Honour Oak, on the Tavistock road, was the parole boundary for French prisoners of war from Princetown, during the Napoleonic wars.

Whitefield (in Challacombe) *Witefelle/fella: Bishop of Coutances.* Whitefield Barton.

Whitefield (in High Bray) *Witefelle/fella: Bishop of Coutances.* Near Whitefield Down.

Whitefield (in Marwood) *Whitefelle/fella: 2 men-at-arms from Robert d'Aumale. 100 sheep.* Whitefield Barton.

Whitestone (near Exeter) *Witestan/tani: Bernard Nap(e)eless(?) and Robert de Beaumont from Baldwin the Sheriff; Ranulf from William d'Eu.*

Whiteway *Witewei/weia: Ranulf from Baldwin the Sheriff. Salt-house.* Whiteway Barton.

Whitford *Witeford/fort: King's land, formerly Earl Leofwin. Mill.*

Whitleigh *Witelie/leia: Odo from Iudhael of Totnes; Robert d'Aumale.* Part of Plymouth.

Whitnage *Witenes: Gotshelm.*

Whitstone *Wadestan: Ansger from Baldwin the Sheriff. 10 cattle.* Tiny; Whitstone House.

Widey *Wide/Wida:* Lost.

Widworthy *Wideworde/worda: Oliver from Theobald FitzBerner. Mill. 12 cattle.* 14th-century church; manor house with a plaster fireplace dated 1591.

Willand *Willelande/landa: Vitalis from Odo FitzGamelin. Mill.*

Willestrew *Wilavestreu: Robert d'Aumale. 14 cattle, 20 goats (with Ottery and Collacombe).* Tiny.

Willsworthy *Wifleurde: Alfred le Breton.* 16th-century farmhouse on the site of a Saxon farm.

Wilmington *Wilelmitone/tona: Morin from Baldwin the Sheriff; Oliver from Theobald FitzBerner.*

Wilson (in Witheridge) *Welingedinge/Welisedinga: William from Baldwin the Sheriff.* Wilson Farm.

Winscott (in Peters Marland) *Winescote/cota: Roald Dubbed.* Winscott Farm.

Winsham *Wenneham: Bishop of Coutances.*

Winston *Winestane/tona: Reginald from Count of Mortain.* Tiny.

Winswell *Wifelswille/Wivleswilla: Roald Dubbed.*

Witheridge *Wirige/riga: King's land, formerly Countess Gytha.* Large market-place, the site of fairs since the 13th century.

Withycombe Raleigh *Widecome/coma: Walter de Claville. 16 cattle.* Suburb of Exmouth, once owned by the Raleigh family.

Wolborough *Ulveberie/Olveberia: Ralph de Bruyere from Baldwin the Sheriff. Mill. 12 cattle, 100 sheep.* Part of Newton Abbot.

Wolfin *Nimet: Walter de Claville. Cob, 18 cattle.* Wolfin Farm.

Wollaton *Ulvevtone/Olvievetona: Iudhael of Totnes.* Tiny.

Wonford (in Heavitree) *Wenford/fort: King's land, formerly Queen Edith.* Part of Exeter.

Wonford (in Thornbury) *Wenford/forda: Walter d'Omonville from Roald Dubbed. 20 cattle.* Tiny; also the hamlet of South Wonford.

Woodbeare *Widebere: Godfrey from Gotshelm. 30 goats.* Woodbeer Court nearby.

Woodburn *Odeburne/borna: Oswy from Baldwin the Sheriff.* Tiny.

Woodbury *Wodeberie/beria: King's land with Church of Mont St Michel holding the church. Mill. 15 cattle.* Woodbury Castle, an Iron Age hillfort overlooking the Exe Estuary.

Woodcombe *Wodicome: Alric from Walter de Douai.* Tiny; on a combe running down to the sea.

Woodford *Odeford/forda: Ralph from Iudhael of Totnes. Salt-house, fishery.* Part of Plymouth.

Woodhuish *Odehiwis: Richard FitzThorold.* Woodhuish Farm.

Woodleigh *Odelie: Robert d'Aumale, formerly Aelfric Pike. Fishery. 15 cattle, 100 sheep.* Above Kingsbridge Estuary.

Woolacombe *Wellecome/coma: William Cheever; Jocelyn from Theobald FitzBerner. 21 cattle, 330 sheep.* Resort on Morte Bay; Woolacombe Sands.

Woolfardisworthy (near Hartland) *Olvereword/Olfereordi: Colwin from the king. 20 cattle.*

Woolfardisworthy (near Witheridge) *Ulfaldeshodes/Olfaldeshodes: William de Poilley.*

Woolladon *Oladone/dona: Aubrey from Baldwin the Sheriff.* Tiny.

Woolleigh (in Bovey Tracey) *Bovi: King's land.* Tiny.

Woolleigh (in Beaford) *Uluelie: Colwin from Baldwin the Sheriff.*

Woolston (in Staverton) *Ulestanecota/Wolestanecota: Colbert from Iudhael of Totnes.* Some houses.

Worlington (in Instow) *Ulvretone/Ulwritona: Bishop of Coutances.*

Worlington (near Witheridge) *Uluredintune: Bishop of Coutances; Hugh de Dol from William de Falaise; Alwy from Odo FitzGamelin. 27 cattle.* Now 2 hamlets, East and West Worlington.

Worth *Worde/Wrda: Ralph from William de Falaise.* Worth House on the River Exe.

Worthele *Ordihelle/hella: Iudhael of Totnes.* Now 2 tiny hamlets, East and West Worthele.

Worthy (in Rackenford) *Ordie/Ordia: Ansketel from Baldwin the Sheriff.* Worthy Farm.

Worthygate *Wrdiete/ieta: Tavistock Church.* Now 2 hamlets, Higher and Lower Worthygate; Worthygate Wood overlooking Clovelly Bay.

Wray *Wergi/Wereia: Godwin from the king.* Wray Barton.

Wyke (in Shobrooke) *Wiche/Wica: Count of Mortain.*

Wyke Green (in Axminster) *Wiche/Wicca: Odo from the king.*

Yarcombe *Herticome/Erticoma: Mont St Michel Church, formerly Earl Harold. Mill.* Elizabethan Sheafhayne House.

Yard (in Rose Ash) *Hierde/Hierda: Ansger from Baldwin the Sheriff. 12 cattle.* Now 2 tiny hamlets, South Yard and Yard Wood.

Yard (in Silverton) *Heierde/Heierda: Godbold.* Absorbed in Kingston Lacy Park; Roman road.

Yarde (in Ilfracombe) *Laierda: Robert from Baldwin the Sheriff.* Yarde Farm.

Yarnscombe *Herlescome/-coma/Hernescome/-coma: Robert from Baldwin the Sheriff; Theobald FitzBerner.*

Yeadbury *Addeberie: William from Ralph de Pomeroy.* Tiny.

Yealmpton *Elintone/tona: King's land and the clergy of this village from the king.* Sarah Martin wrote 'Old Mother Hubbard', based on the housekeeper, in Kitley House. Bones of prehistoric animals were found in a cave at Yealmbridge.

Yowlestone *Aedelstan/Aeidestan: Ralph from William Cheever.* Yowlestone House.

Zeal Monachorum *Nimet/Nimeth: Buckfast Church.* Given by King Canute to the monks of Buckfast Church. A block of stone in the churchyard is possibly the altar of the Norman church.

Dorset

Dorset has always been agricultural, with large landowners and small villages. At the time of Domesday, *more than one-third of its land was held by the Church: even before William I set foot in England there were nine monasteries.*

About one-half the total acreage was forest and waste land, which suggests that it was a centre for hunting; Waleran the hunter held nine manors. The rest of the land was pasture and, to a lesser extent, woodland. Dorset was divided into 39 Hundreds, though only three of these could boast more than 100 hides.

Hamlets, often with fewer than a dozen inhabitants, are characteristic of Dorset. Another feature was the proliferation of settlements along the county's rivers – hence the numerous Winterbournes, Wimbournes, Piddles or Puddles, Tarrants, Cernes, Chars and Weys that exist today. In Domesday, *many were merely referred to by their river names, leaving them not only unidentified, but unidentifiable. Although there is evidence that most of the Winterbournes, for example, existed in 1086 the identification of which 'wintreburne' was which is at best speculative.*

The population in 1086 probably numbered between 35,000 and 50,000, mostly farmers. But along the Channel coast, there was also a thriving fishing industry; and in Norman times there was no busier port than Wareham, in the east of the county.

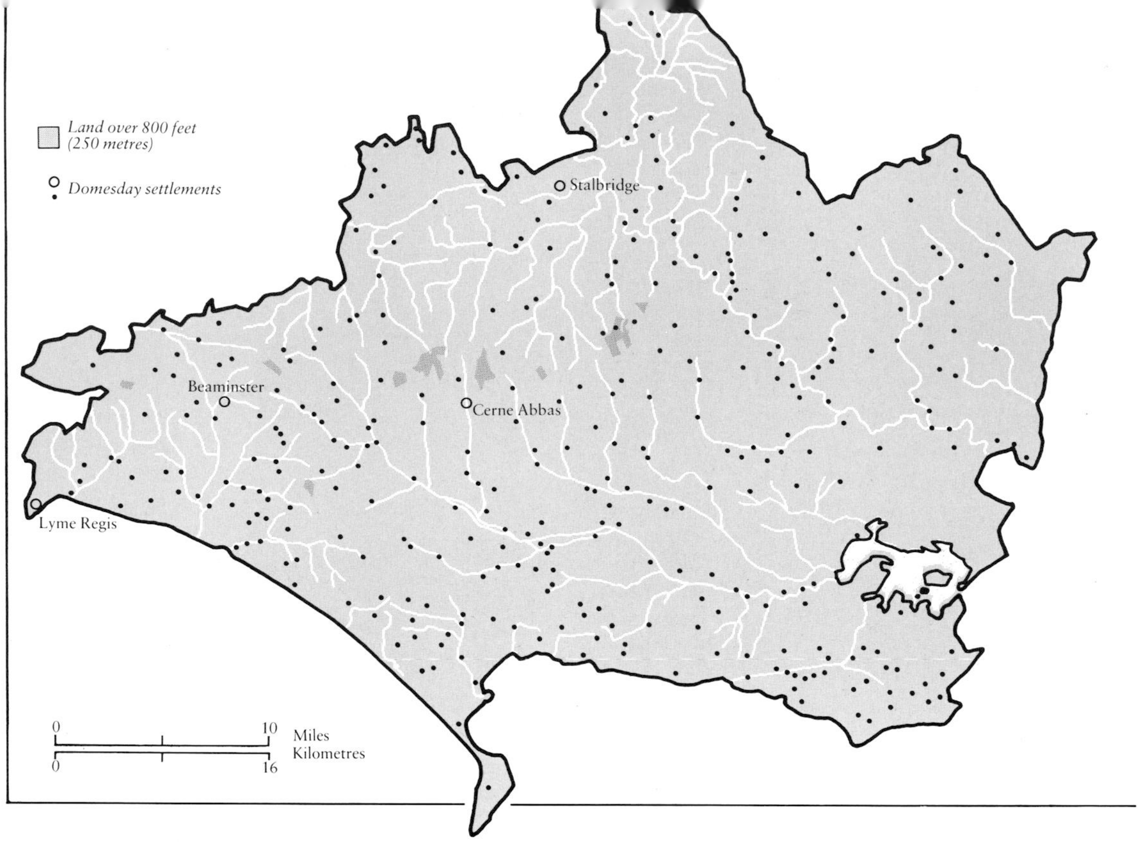

Beaminster

[The Bishop of Salisbury holds, for the supplies of the monks of Sherborne] BEAMINSTER *BEIMINSTRE.* Before 1066 it paid tax for 16 hides and 1 virgate of land. Land for 20 ploughs. Besides this land he has in lordship 2 carucates of land which have never paid tax; he has 2 ploughs there; a mill which pays 20d. Under the Bishop are 19 villagers, 20 smallholders and 5 slaves. Meadow, 33 acres; pasture 1 league long and 1/2 league wide; woodland 1 1/2 leagues long and 1/2 league wide. Also of this land Algar holds 2 hides from the Bishop, H(umphrey) of Carteret 2 hides less 1 virgate, Sinoth 5 hides, Brictwin 1 1/2 hides. 9 ploughs there; 11 slaves. 19 smallholders, 2 villagers and 2 Cottagers. 2 mills which pay 28d; meadow, 40 acres; pasture 4 furlongs long and 2 furlongs wide; a further 32 acres of pasture; woodland 13 furlongs long and 9 furlongs wide. Value of the Bishop's lordship £16; of the men's, £7.

Domesday's statistics show that medieval Beaminster was what estate agents today would call a 'much sought-after area'. It was a market town, formed one of the county's hundreds, and was held by Dorset's richest ecclesiastical landowner, the Bishop of Salisbury. He was Osmund of Seez in Normandy, member of the Privy Council, sometime Chancellor to the king, and believed to have been earl of both Dorset and Somerset.

Beaminster lies at the bottom of a shallow basin in what was once – as the *Domesday* entry implies – thickly-wooded country, well supplied with enough streams to work many more mills than the three *Domesday* lists, and, indeed, over the years, there were at least eight. The name probably comes from Beam Ministre, a church in a wood, and there must have been a Saxon church there, though nothing remains of it. The little river that now runs underground through the town was ideal for the establishment of a tanning industry as well as for numerous woollen and sail-cloth workshops. These declined only with the harnessing of steam power in the nineteenth century. There was also clay, for manufacturing pottery, tiles and bricks, and, in the eighteenth century, clay pipes.

Beaminster's size has hardly changed over the centuries. There have been several reasons, chief of which is its geography. The only natural access is up the valley of the little River Brit from Bridport. More dramatically, progress was checked by a series of disastrous fires. The first occurred during the Civil War, on Palm Sunday, 1644, while Prince Maurice (brother of Prince Rupert) and his troops were billeted in the town on their way to Lyme Regis. Beaminster was disaffected with the Royalist cause, and the fire may have been started deliberately; at any rate a musket ball was discharged into the thatched roof of a cottage in North Street. It was a windy day and within two hours 144 houses were destroyed, almost the entire town. The following year General Fairfax and the Parliamentary army stayed one night and found Beaminster 'a place of the pittyfullest spectacle that Man can behold, hardly an House left not consumed with fire'. Even six years later, when Charles II intended to stop there on his flight inland from Charmouth, he 'was so struck by the melancholy aspect of the place that he would not halt there as he intended'.

Such rebuilding as had been done was undone on 28 June 1684, when 'about the hour of Four in the Afternoon, there happen'd a most Sudden and Dreadful Fire in the Town ... which in the space of Three hours ... Burnt down and consumed the Dwelling-Houses of George Martyn, John Stevens ... and of above Fourscore other inhabitants of the said Town ... The loss sustained amounting to Thirteen Thousand Six Hundred Eighty Four Pounds, and upwards.' So stated a Parliamentary broadsheet issued by Charles II, ordering collections to be made all over England. Many of the present buildings were constructed with the money raised by this appeal.

Less than a hundred years later it happened again. Between four and five in the morning of 31 March 1781, a blaze that started in the stables or brew-house of the King's Arms (the leading inn, one of ten on the tiny market-place) destroyed more than 50 houses. 'The Greater part of the Goods belonging to the Inhabitants was saved. A Daughter of Mr Paviott, Master of the Free School was burnt to Death.' Since then, tiles have been used for roofing.

In 1832, Beaminster reached outward with the opening of a tunnel that gave free access to Crewkerne and the whole of Somerset. It is 115 yards long, took more than two years to dig and is still in use today.

> In swelling streams may cheering wealth
> To Beaminster descend;
> And ever joy-inspiring health
> Her social sons attend...

A local poet hymned at the opening ceremony.

Soon after this there was talk of a railway to link Crewkerne with Bridport by way of Beaminster, but though discussions continued intermittently for nearly half a century, nothing ever came of them. This is another reason why Beaminster has stood still.

In 1848 the population was over 3000 (it is now 2600) and included eight bakers, four barbers, and twelve each of bootmakers and dressmakers. An imposing workhouse stood – and still stands – one mile to the south-west, where in 1842 John Palmer received ten lashes for deserting over the wall and where George Minter, for fighting in school, was sentenced to 'no cheese for a week'. The workhouse has now been converted to luxury flats.

BEAMINSTER: *The valley of the River Brit reflects the town's ancient name, 'church in a wood'.* →

Lyme Regis

[The Bishop of Salisbury holds] LYME (REGIS) LYM. Land for 1 plough. It has never paid tax. Fishermen hold it; they pay 15s to the monks [of Sherborne] for fish. Meadow, 4 acres. The Bishop has 1 house there which pays 6d.

The Church [of St Mary's, Glastonbury] holds LYME (REGIS) itself. Before 1066 it paid tax for 3 hides. Land for 4 ploughs. Wulfgeat held and holds it from the Abbot. He has 2 ploughs and 9 villagers and 6 smallholders and meadow, 4 acres; pasture 4 furlongs long and 2 furlongs wide; woodland, 10 acres. 13 saltworkers who pay 13s. Value of the whole 60s.

William Bellett also holds LYME (REGIS). Aelfeva held it before 1066. It paid tax for 1 hide. Land for 1 plough. 1 villager with 1/2 plough; 14 salt-workers. A mill which pays 39d; meadow, 3 acres; pasture 4 furlongs long and 1 furlong wide; woodland, 1 furlong in length and width. Value 60s.

Three separate manors formed this curious little fishing port clustered at the foot of the cliffs at the far western end of Dorset – cliffs so steep that there was no descent for wheeled vehicles until 1759. The town is mentioned as far back as the eighth century, since when the sea has probably claimed a fair portion of its southern reaches. But its curved stone jetty, The Cobb, is believed to have stood for more than one thousand years and must surely have been used by the fishermen mentioned in the first *Domesday* entry; it achieved a measure of immortality when Jane Austen set Louisa Musgrove's dramatic accident there in *Persuasion*. By the time Jane Austen saw Lyme Regis, in 1804, tourism had long overtaken agriculture, fishing and maritime trade as the chief industry. The little harbour had proved too shallow in the eighteenth century to cope with the new large merchant vessels.

Prince Maurice had marched here from Beaminster with his army in 1644, intending to rout the Parliamentary forces. But though the Royalists greatly outnumbered the Cromwellians, the siege failed, partly because enemy supplies arrived by sea, and partly because of the bravery of the town's women. Dressed as soldiers to confuse the enemy, they fought valiantly beside their men.

Lyme's most dramatic day was 11 June 1685 when the foolish and ill-starred Duke of Monmouth landed west of The Cobb, to begin his hopeless attempt to usurp the English throne from his Catholic uncle James II. Monmouth, the natural son of Charles II, had deluded himself into believing that he could rally an army to follow his Protestant leadership in a victorious march on the capital. He chose Lyme for his landing because he had had a personal success in a tour of the west country five years earlier, and he picked this particular beach because The Cobb was guarded by a fort with five cannon which he hoped to capture. That there was no powder for them, he was not to know.

After his frigate and its two tenders grounded on the beach, Monmouth and his men knelt in prayer. Then with townsmen cheering him on, he marched up the steep hill to the market-place. His notorious Declaration was there proclaimed, a foolish statement which he should have known would cost him his life, as it did little more than a month later. Among other fantastic aberrations it accused King James of having started the Great Fire of London and of poisoning Charles II to secure the Crown. But the townsfolk, openly anti-Catholic, were smitten by the handsome, romantic Monmouth. When he marched north from Lyme Regis, he had amassed more than 2000 followers, all badly armed and without military discipline.

At the Battle of Sedgemoor on 6 July, the king's forces crushed Monmouth's men in about 100 minutes. Two days later 'The little Duke' was captured hiding in a ditch; in his pocket was the insignia of the Garter his father had given him. A week later, he was beheaded at the Tower. The headsman, Jack Ketch, had had 20 years' experience, but needed five strokes of the axe to despatch his prisoner and still had to finish his bloody work with a knife.

And there was more blood to be spilled. The sadistic Judge Jeffreys extracted a high price for the West Country's folly; that September alone 800 men were transported and 300 hanged. It was a nightmare landscape after the Lord Chief Justice had passed, with human heads and dismembered bodies adorning all the highways and cross-roads. Twelve men were hanged at the Duke's landing-place.

With tourism its major industry Lyme has lost a lot of its personality in self-conscious attempts to preserve it. But still the little fishing boats leave from The Cobb in pursuit of mackerel, prawns and conger-eel, keeping alive a way of life that *Domesday* recorded 900 years ago.

LYME REGIS: *The view from The Cobb; the jetty was probably used by the* Domesday *fishermen.*

Cerne Abbas

Cerne Abbey holds CERNE (ABBAS) *CERNELI.* Before 1066 it paid tax for 22 hides. Land for 20 ploughs, of which 3 hides are in lordship; 3 ploughs there; 5 slaves; 26 villagers and 32 smallholders with 14 ploughs and 15 hides. A mill which pays 20s; meadow, 20 acres; pasture 2 leagues long and 8 furlongs wide; woodland 1 league long and 8 furlongs wide. 3 cobs; 6 cattle; 14 pigs; 500 sheep. Brictwin holds four hides of this land from the Abbot; he has 4 ploughs there. He held them likewise before 1066; he could not withdraw from the church, nor can he. The value of the Church's lordship was and is £21; of Brictwin's, 100s.

The holdings of the Benedictine Abbey of Cerne were considerable, comprising 16 other manors in Dorset, two of which (Symondsbury and Long Bredy) were both reckoned at the same high value as Cerne Abbas. The abbey was founded in 987, but an account written by William of Malmesbury in 1125 would date it much earlier. He tells how St Augustine himself had a hostile reception in Cerne; the villagers tied cows' tails to his clothes and threw mud at him. Then, while washing in a spring, he looked up and 'saw God': '*Cerno Deum*', he said.

The god he saw was probably the Cerne Abbas giant which had already been there some hundreds of years and is still there today, standing naked, 180 feet tall and wielding an enormous club. Cut into the chalk slopes of Giant Hill overlooking the village, he was long thought to represent the celtic god Nodens. But more recent scholarship suggests that he is a Hercules, carved in the first century AD. Other authorities date the giant 150 years earlier, and believe that it depicts one of the Druids' brutal wicker men, mentioned by Julius Caesar – colossal covered framework figures – into which human sacrifices were placed and set on fire.

The giant, with his 30-foot phallus, was long the scene of fertility rites, not only organized Maypole dancing, but pilgrimages by childless couples or barren women who would walk the length or lie upon the awe-inspiring organ.

What remains of the abbey is fifteenth century, privately owned and in a deplorable state. The ruins of an embattled tower and gatehouse stand forlorn in a muddy farmyard. In a romantic graveyard nearby is a spring known as St Augustine's Well, where the saint is supposed to have commanded the water to come forth. Of the rich manor described by *Domesday*, there is little evidence. The prosperity of Cerne has shifted to the village itself, whose pretty streets and cottages have an undeniably well-fed air.

CERNE ABBAS: *Splendid 15th c. window, one of the few remaining buildings of the Benedictine Abbey.*

Stalbridge

[The Bishop of Salisbury holds] STALBRIDGE *STAPLEBRIGE.* Before 1066 it paid tax for 20 hides. Land for 16 ploughs, of which 6 hides are in lordship; 2 ploughs there, with 1 slave; 19 villagers and 2 smallholders with 11 ploughs. A mill which pays 15s; meadow, 25 acres; pasture 4 furlongs long and 2 furlongs wide; woodland 1 league long and 3 furlongs wide. Value £12. Lambert holds 2 hides also of this land. He has 1 plough there, with 6 smallholders. Value 20s. Also of this land Manasseh holds 3 virgates which W(illiam) son of the King took from the church without the agreement of the Bishop and monks. 1 plough there.

The substantial settlement of Stalbridge was, like part of Lyme Regis, leased by the Bishop of Salisbury to the monks of Sherborne. William was William Rufus and Manasseh was the king's head cook. The village lies at the northern end of the Blackmore Forest, and around the parish was 'waste or common covered with forest or pasture'. From the middle ages Stalbridge boasted a market and a fair and had a thriving textile industry; but Defoe in his *Tour* of 1722–23 comments that it was 'once famous for making the finest, best and highest prized knit stockings in England, but that the trade is now much decayed by the increase of the knitting-stocking engine or frame'.

Stalbridge's most famous son was the great scientist and writer Robert Boyle (1627–91). Though born in Ireland he inherited the manor of Stalbridge Park while young. He spent his holidays from Eton here, as well as a four-year period before he left England for study abroad. He is best remembered for his law on the relationship between the pressure and volume of gases, said to have been discovered at Stalbridge. His experiments in pneumatics made possible a host of applied inventions, from steam-engines to diving equipment. He wrote a religious romance, *The Martyrdom of Theodora and Didymus*, and works on natural philosophy, colour, blood, cold and a *Discourse of Things above Reason*. One of his moral essays is supposed to have inspired Swift to write *Gulliver's Travels*. He helped to found both the Royal Society and the Society for the Propagation of the Gospel.

Because of its situation on a busy main road, Stalbridge has suffered from ribbon development and lost much of its charm. Only the view from this once-favoured possession of the monks of Sherborne, over the lovely Blackmoor Vale, retains any quality of timelessness.

Dorset Gazetteer

Each entry starts with the modern place name in **bold** type. The *Domesday* information that follows is in *italic* type, beginning with the name or names by which the place was known in 1086. The main landholders and undertenants are next, separated with semi-colons if a place was divided into more than one holding. Thanes hold land 'from the king'. More general information completes the *Domesday* part of the entry, including examples of dues (wheat, honey, etc.) rendered by tenants, and animals when the totals reach or exceed: 160 sheep, 15 goats, 40 wild mares, 240 castrated rams, 33 unbroken mares, 50 cattle, 14 pigs and 2 oxen. The modern or post-Domesday section is in normal type. ⊞ represents a village, ⌂ a small village or hamlet.

Abbotsbury *Abedesberie/ Abodesberie: Abbotsbury Abbey; Wife of Hugh FitzGrip. 2 mills. 600 sheep, 23 cattle, 4 cows.* ⊞ Stone-built; famous swannery; tithe barn; remains of an 11th-century Benedictine abbey.

Abbotts Wootton *Widetone: Abbotsbury Abbey. 20 goats.* Abbotts Wootton Farms.

Acton *Tacatone/a: Wife of Hugh FitzGrip. Mill.* ⌂

Adber *Ateberie/a, Etesberie/ Ettebere: Drogo from Count of Mortain; Ralph de Conteville from Walter de Douai.* Part of Sherborne rural district.

Afflington *Alfrunetone/-a/ Alvretone, Alvronetone: Roger de Beaumont; Walter from William de Braose; Walter de Claville and Durand the Carpenter from the king.* Afflington Farm near Corfe Castle.

Affpuddle *Affapidele/a: Cerne Abbey. 2 mills. 9 oxen.* ⊞ The arms in the church, of the Lawrence family, ancestors of George Washington, are thought to have inspired the United States flag.

Ailwood *Aleoude: Swein from the king, and Hugh's wife from him.* Ailwood Farm.

Allington *Adelingtone: Thurstan FitzRolf. Mill.* Suburb of Bridport.

Alton Pancras *Altone: Bishop of Salisbury. Mill.* ⊞ Ancient field systems.

Ash *Aisse: David from William de Braose.* ⌂ Site of a Roman camp.

Ashmore *Aisemare/a: King's land. 826 sheep, 50 goats.* ⊞ Highest in Dorset; thatched cottages; Georgian houses; ancient burial mounds.

Askerswell *Oscherwille/a: Tavistock Abbey.* ⊞ Secluded.

Athelhampton *Pidele: Ohdold from Bishop of Salisbury. Mill.* ⌂ Water meadows; 15th-century Athelhampton Hall.

Atrim *Atrem/um: Bolle the priest and a widow from Abbotsbury Abbey.* ⌂

Bardolfeston *Pidele: Monks of Sherborne.* Near Bardolf manor house

Beaminster *Beiminstre:* See page 89.

Bere Regis *Bere/a: King's land and Brictward the priest from the king; William de Moutiers from the wife of Hugh FitzGrip. Mill.* Ancient town; Iron Age fort nearby.

Bestwall *Beastewell: Count of Mortain.* Part of Wareham.

Bexington *Bessintone/Bessinton: Roger of Arundel. 2 cows.* ⌂

Bhompston *Frome:* Lost.

Bincombe *Beincome: St Stephen's of Caen, formerly Earl Harold.* ⊞ Near Chalbury Iron Age hill fort.

Blackmanston *Blachemanestone: Aelfric from the king.* Blackmanston Farm.

Blandford St Mary *Bleneford/(e) Blaneford/(e): Bretel from Count of Mortain; Auilf and Edwin from the king; William from William d'Eu.* ⊞

Bloxworth *Blocheshorde/a: Cerne Abbey.* ⊞ Pretty. The partly Norman church originally belonged to Cerne Abbey.

Bockhampton *Bochehamtone/ tona: Countess of Boulogne.* ⌂ Now Higher Bockhampton. Birthplace of the novelist Thomas Hardy (1840–1928).

Boveridge *Boverhic: St Mary's, Cranborne. Mill.* ⌂

Bovington *Bovintone: Aelfric, the king's thane, the pre-Conquest holder.* Bovington Farm. T. E. Lawrence (Lawrence of Arabia) served in the Tank Corps at nearby Bovington Camp.

Bowood *Bovewode: 3-men-at-arms from Bishop of Salisbury.* Now the localities of North and South Bowood.

Bradford Abbas *Bradeford: Monks of Sherborne. Mill.* ⊞ Ancient, stone-built. King Alfred gave the land to Sherborne Abbey in AD 933. Nearby Wyke Farm, a moated manor house, belonged to the monks of Sherborne until the Dissolution.

Bradford Peverell *Bradeford: William d'Eu. 2 mills.* ⊞ On high, wooded ground.

Bradle *Bradelege: Aiulf the Chamberlain.* Bradle Farm.

Bradpole *Bratepolle: King's land.* ⊞ On the outskirts of Bridport.

Bredy (in Burton Bradstock) *Bridie: Berengar Giffard from the king.* Bredy Farm.

Brenscombe *Brunescume: Wife of Hugh FitzGrip.* Brenscombe Farm.

Briantspuddle *Pidele: Godric the priest.* ⊞ White-walled, thatched cottages; also known as Prestes Puddle.

Bridge *Brige/a: Aiulf the Chamberlain from the king; Hugh from the wife of Hugh FitzGrip; Edric from the king. 20 oxen.* ⊞ Probably Bridge Farm.

Bridport *Brideport/Brideporta: Bishop of Salisbury; St Wandrille's Abbey.* Town; rope and net-making centre for 1000 years. Parliamentary soldiers almost captured Charles II here in 1651.

Broadmayne *Maine: Earl Hugh.* ⊞ Large.

Broadwindsor *Windesore: Hundger FitzOdin from the king.* ⊞ 17th-century cottages. Charles II fled here after the Battle of Worcester (1651).

Brockington *Brochemtune: Count of Mortain; Wulfgeat. Mill.* Brockington Farm.

CHARMOUTH: *The George, a well-known coaching inn, a waiting-room above the porch.*

Bryanston Blaneford *Blaneford. Count of Mortain; Wulfgeat from the king. Mill.* ⊞ Bryanston public school, set in parkland.

Buckham *Bochenham: Walter from Bishop of Salisbury.* ⌂ Remote.

Buckhorn Weston *Westone: Hamo from Count of Mortain.* ⊞

Buckland Newton *Bochelande: St Mary's, Glastonbury.* ⊞ 17th-century manor house; church with a slate figure, thought to be Saxon.

Buckland Ripers *Bocheland/t: Wife of Hugh FitzGrip. Mill. 200 sheep.* ⌂ Manor house.

Burleston *Pidele: Milton Abbey. Mill.* ⊞

Burstock *Bureuuinestoch: Earl Hugh.* ⊞ Tudor manor farm.

Burton Bradstock *Bridetone/a: King's land with St Wandrille's Abbey holding the church.* ⊞ Thatched stone cottages.

Canford Magna *Cheneford: Edward of Salisbury. 2 mills..* Parish; Canford Manor, a public school.

Catherston Leweston *Cerneli: Count of Mortain.* ⊞ Almost absorbed by Charmouth; 19th-century manor house.

Catsley *Catesclive: William from Earl Hugh.* Catsley Farm.

Cattistock *Stoche Estocha: Milton Abbey. Mill.* ⊞ Victorian church with work by Gilbert Scott and William Morris.

Cerne Abbas *Cerneli/um:* See page 92.

Chaldon *Calvedone/a: King's land; Bolle the priest from the king; Hugh from the wife of Hugh FitzGrip. 500 sheep.* ⊞ Now Chaldon Herring; also known as East Chaldon; Bronze Age barrows.

Charborough *Cereberie/a: King's land.* Charborough House. It was blown up during the Civil War and rebuilt in 1661 by Parliamentarian Sir Walter Erle whose descendants still own it.

Charlton Marshall *Cerletone/a: King's land. 2 mills.* ⊞

Charminster *Cerminstre: Bishop of Salisbury.* ⊞

Charmourth *Cernemude: Count of Mortain.* ⊞ Regency houses; thatched cottages.

Chelborough (West) *Celberge/ a: Ranulf from William de Mohun (claimed by the son of Odo the Chamberlain); Roger of Arundel.* ⊞ Remote; an ancient manor farm.

Cheselbourne *Ceseburne: Shaftesbury Abbey. Mill.* ⊞ Remote.

Chettle *Ceotel: Aiulf the Chamberlain.* ⊞ Chettle House, a Queen Anne mansion.

Chickerell *Cicherelle: Bolle the priest frhe king.* ⊞

Chideock *Cidi(o)hoc: King's land.* ⊞ Chideock Castle. The Chideock Martyrs, 4 Roman Catholics executed during Elizabeth I's reign, were tried in Chideock House.

Chilcombe *Ciltecome: Brictwin from the king.* ⌂

Child Okeford *Acford/a: King's land; Count of Mortain. 2 mills.* ⊞ Ruined mill-race; Iron Age fort.

Chilfrome *Frome/a: William de Mohun.* ⊞

Church Knowle *Glole/-ua/ Chenolle: Roger de Beaumont; William de Braose; Waleran; Walter de Claville.* ⊞

Clifton Maybank *Clistone: William Malbank from Earl Hugh.* ⊞

Clyffe *Clive: Milton Abbey.* Clyffe Farm.

Colber *Colesberie: King's land.* Colber Crib House.

Compton (near Sherborne) *Contone: Monks of Sherborne. Mill.* Now 2 villages, Nether and Over Compton. Nearby Compton House is a farm where butterflies and moths are bred.

Compton Abbas *Cuntone: Shaftesbury Abbey.* ⊞

Compton Valence *Contone: Hugh de Port.* ⊞ Near a Roman road; 17th-century manor house.

Coombe *Come:* Lost.

Coombe Keynes *Come: Bishop of Lisieux; Walter de Claville.* ⌂ Green; 13th-century church.

Corfe Castle *Castellum Warham: King's land.* ⊞ Ruins of a castle originally built by William I on a fortified Saxon site and blown up by Cromwell's Roundheads in 1646.

Corfe Mullen *Corf: Robert FitzGerald. Mill.* ⊞ Suburban.

Corscombe *Coriescumbe/ Corscumbe/Coriscumbe: Bishop of Sherborne; William from Count of Mortain; Godwin from the king.* ⊞ Expanding.

Corton *Corfetone: Roger de Coursteulles.* Corton Farm.

Cranborne *Creneburne/borna: King's land. 4 mills, 10 cows, 4 cattle, 1037 sheep, 40 goats.* ⊞ Jacobean and Georgian houses; Cranborne Chase, a medieval royal hunting ground; 13th-century manor house, possibly King John's hunting lodge.

Creech *Cric/Crist/Criz: Count of Mortain; Roger de Beaumont; William de Braose; wife of Hugh FitzGrip.* ⌂ East Creech nearby.

Cruxton *Frome: William de Mohun. Mill.* ⌂

Dewlish *Devenis: Count Alan.* ⊞ Dewlish House, an 18th-century manor house, is on the site of a Roman villa.

Didlington *Dedilintone: Wilton Abbey.* ⌂

Dorchester *Dorecestre/a: King's land with Brictward the priest holding the church.* County town on a prehistoric site. Once the Roman town of *Durnovaria*. Judge Jeffreys held his Bloody Assize here after Monmouth's Rebellion.

Dudsbury *Dodesberie: Waleran.* ⌂ Traces of ancient earthworks.

Durweston *Dervinestone/ Derwinestone: Aiulf the Chamberlain; the wife of Hugh FitzGrip. Mill, vines.* ⊞

Durweston Knighton *Dervinestone: Count of Mortain.* Knighton House.

East Holme *Holne/a: Walter de Claville; Edric from the king.* Holme priory is on the site of Montacute priory.

East Stoke *Stoches: Count of Mortain. Mill.*

Edmondsham *Amedesham/ Medesham/Medessan: King's land; Humphrey the Chamberlain. 2 mills.* Edmonsham House.

Elworth *Aleurde: Ansfrid from William d'Eu.*

Farnham *Ferneham, Fernham: Shaftesbury Abbey; Aiulf the Chamberlain; Odo FitzEverbold; wife of Hugh FitzGrip. Cow.* Thatched cottages.

Fifehead Magdalen *Fifhide: Earl Hugh. 2 mills.*

Fifehead Neville *Fifhide: Ingolmann from Waleran. Mill.* Water-meadows; arched packhorse bridge.

Fifehead St Quintin *Fifhide: Vietel from Shaftesbury Abbey.*

Fleet *Flete/-a/Flote/-a: King's land with Bolle the priest holding the church.*

Fontmell Magna *Fontemale: Shaftesbury Abbey. 3 mills.* Thatched cottages.

Fordington *Fortitone: King's land.* Fordington Fields; Fordington High Street.

Frampton *Frantone: St Stephen's of Caen. 2 mills.* Thatched, stone cottages; near the site of a Roman villa.

Frome Billet *Frome/a: William Bellett from the king. Mill.* Stafford House, possibly including Everard's Farm.

Frome St Quintin *Litelfrome/a: King's land. Mill. 50 goats, 400 sheep.*

Frome Vauchurch *Frome: Roger de Beaumont; William de Braose; Waleran; Walter de Claville.*

Frome Whitfield *Frome: Wife of Hugh FitzGrip. 250 sheep, 1 ass.*

Galton *Galtone/Gaveltone: Brictwin; Osmund the Baker from the king.*

Gillingham *Gelingeham/eha: King's land; St Mary's, Cranborne; Bernard from Thurstan FitzRolf; Edwin, Wulfwin, Edward Hunter and Fulcred from the king.* Light industry; fine Georgian houses.

Glanvilles Wootton *Widetone: William de Braose.* Manor house.

Goathill *Gatelme: Humphrey from Count of Mortain. Mill.*

Gold Hill *Hille: Osbern from the king.*

Graston *Graustan: William from the wife of Hugh FitzGrip.*

Great Crawford *Graveford: Aelfric from the king.* Part of Spetisbury.

Gussage All Saints *Gessic: Count of Mortain. Mill.* Gussage House.

Gussage St Michael *Gessic: King's land.* Manor farm.

Hammoon *Hame: William de Mohun.* Ancient; 15th-century thatched manor house.

Hampreston *Ham/a/e: King's land; Aiulf the Chamberlain; William Chernet from the wife of Hugh FitzGrip; Thorkel from the king.* Parish on the outskirts of Bournemouth.

Hanford *Hanford: Count of Mortain.*

Hawcombe *Havocumbe: King's land; St Stephen's of Caen.* Part of Frampton.

Hemsworth *Hemedesworde/ wrde: Humphrey the Chamberlain; Hubert from Count of Mortain.* On the site of a Roman villa.

Herston *Herestune/a: Roger Arundel; Godfrey Scullion.*

Hethfelton *Aelfatune Hafeltone: William de Braose.*

Hilton *Eltone: Abbotsbury Abbey. Mill. 400 sheep, 25 goats.*

Hinton Martell *Hinetone: King's land, formerly Countess Goda. 2 mills.* Much developed.

Hinton St Mary *Haintone: Shaftesbury Abbey. Mill.* Ancient manor house.

LITTLE BRADY: *The church in its rural setting.*

Holton *Holtone: William de Braose.* East Hilton Farm near Holton Heath.

Holwell (in Radipole) *Halegewelle: Count of Mortain.* Holwell Farm.

Holworth *Holverde/a: Milton Abbey. 4 cows, 224 sheep. Sester of honey.* Remote.

Hooke *Lahoc: Count of Mortain.* Ruins of ancient Hooke Court.

Horton *Hortune: Horton Abbey.* 18th-century folly, Horton Tower. The Duke of Monmouth was captured in a ditch nearby.

Hurpston *Herpere/a: Wife of Hugh FitzGrip.* Locality; ancient Harp Stone.

Ibberton *Abristetone/a: King's land. 4 cows.* 17th-century manor house.

Ilsington *Elsangtone: Earl Hugh. Mill.*

Iwerne Courtney (or Shroton) *Werne: Baldwin the Sheriff. 2 mills.* At the foot of 600ft Hambledon Hill (with its Iron Age fort), where General Wolfe trained his troops before scaling the Heights of Abraham to attack Quebec in 1759.

Iwerne Minster *Euneminstre: Shaftesbury Abbey. 3 mills.*

Iwerne Stepleton *Werne/ Iwerna: William de Mohun. 282 sheep.* 17th-century Stepleton House.

Kimmeridge *Cameric: Cerne Abbey; Richard from William de Braose. 2 cows. 250 sheep.* Pretty; oil well at Kimmeridge Bay.

Kingcombe *Chimedecome: Arnulf de Hesdin; the king's thanes, the pre-Conquest holders.* Possibly Higher Kingcombe.

Kingston (in Corfe Castle) *Chingestone: Shaftesbury Abbey.*

Kington *Chintone: Ketel from the king; Ranulf from Waleran; Arnulf de Hesdin.* Now Kington Magna.

Knowlton *Chenoltone/una: King's land; Ansger from Count of Mortain. Mill.* The Knowlton Circles, a sacred neolithic henge. The ruins of a 12th century church lie inside one circle, Knowlton Farm is circled by another.

Langford *Langeford: St Mary's Cranborne.* Possibly Langford in West Farley.

Langton Herring *Langetone/a/ uetona: King's land; the wife of Hugh FitzGrip. 170 sheep.* A 16th-century pub.

Langton Long *Blandford Blaneford/Bleneford: Dodman from Count of Mortain; Roger Tilly from Roger Arundel; Edwin from the king. Mill.*

Lazerton *Werne: Edwin the king's thane. Mill.* Lazerton Farm.

Leftisford *Levetesford:* Lost.

Leigh (Colehill) *Lege: Robert FitzGerald.* 15th-century cross.

Remains of a turf maze nearby, said to have been the haunt of witches.

Lewell *Lewelle/Liwelle: Brictwin and Hugh from the king.* Lewell Lodge.

Littelton *Liteltone: Bretel from Count of Mortain. Mill.*

Little Bredy *Litelbride/a: Cerne Abbey. 550 sheep.* Bronze Age burial chambers.

Little Puddle *Litelpidele/idre:* Lost.

Littlewindsor *Windresorie/a: William de Mohun.* Remote.

Loders *Lodres: King's land; Count of Mortain; the wife of Hugh FitzGrip; Aelfric and Brictric from the king. 2 mills.* Saxon field systems nearby.

Long Bredy *Langebride/ia: Cerne Abbey. Mill. 353 sheep, 20 goats.* Prehistoric earthworks nearby.

MILTON ABBAS: *Possibly England's prettiest village.*

Long Crichel *Circel: William d'Eu; Aiulf the Chamberlain. Mill.* Isolated, at foot of Crichel Down.

Lulworth (East and West) *Luluorde/worde: King's land. Count of Mortain; Aiulf the Chamberlain. 4 mills.* Ruined castle. The first post-Reformation Roman Catholic church was built here.

Lyme Regis *Lym/Lime:* See page 91.

Lyscombe *Liscome/a: Milton Abbey.* Lyscombe Farm. A nearby ruined 12th-century chapel and priest's house were associated with Milton Abbey.

Lytchett Matravers *Lichet: William d'Eu.* Ancient. Becoming a suburb of Bournemouth and Poole. Sir John Matravers, buried in the 13th-century church, was Edward III's gaoler and probable murderer.

Maiden Newton *Newetone: Waleran. 2 mills.* Carpet mill.

Mannington *Manitone: Count of Mortain.*

Manston *Manestone: Waleran from the king. 2 mills.* Georgian manor house.

Mapperton (in Almer) *Mapledretone: Shaftesbury Abbey. 30 goats.*

Mapperton (near Beaminster) *Malperetone/Malperretona: Arnulf de Hesdin; William de Mohun. Mill.* Mapperton House, a 16th-century manor house. The original village was wiped out during the plague of 1665.

Mappowder *Mapledre: King's land; Count of Mortain; Hugh from William d'Eu; Bolle the priest from the king.*

Martinstown *Wintreburne: Wife of Hugh FitzGrip. 380 sheep.* Stone, thatched houses.

Melbury Abbas *Meleberie: Shaftesbury Abbey. 4 mills.*

Melbury Bubb, *Melesberie/ leberie: Dodman from Count of Mortain; Roger Arundel; Urse from Arnulf de Hesdin; Brictwin from the king.* Also Melbury Osmond.

Melcombe Horsey *Melcome: King's land.*

Milborne St Andrew *Meleburne: Matthew de Mortagne.* On a Roman road.

Milborne Stileham *Meleburne/ orne:* Lost.

Milton Abbas *Mideltune/ona: Milton Abbey. Mill. 50 goats, 450 sheep.* Demolished and rebuilt a mile from its original site by the Earl of Dorchester in the 18th century. He turned the medieval Milton Abbey into a grand house, now a public school.

Milton on Stour *Miltetone/ Mideltone: Godmund the king's thane, the pre-Conquest holder; Roger from William de Falaise.* Nearby Purns Mill was painted by Constable.

Moorbath *Mordaat: Fulcred from the king.* Isolated.

Moor Crichel *Chirce: King's land.* Moved here in the 18th century when Crichel House was landscaped.

Morden *Mordone/-a/Mordune: Robert from Count of Mortain; Aiulf the Chamberlain; William Chernet from the wife of Hugh FitzGrip; Wulfric from the king. 2 mills.* Thatched cottages.

Moreton *Mourtune: Robert from Count of Mortain; Brictwin from the king. Mill.* T. E. Lawrence (Lawrence of Arabia) is buried here.

POXWELL: *Manor house, built in the 17th c., it has hardly changed over the centuries.*

Mosterton *Mortestorne: Richard de Reviers. Mill.*

Moulham *Moleham: Durand Carpenter, the king's servant.* Lost in Swanage.

Netherbury *Niderberie: Monks of Sherborne. 2 mills.* Stone-built; mill-see on the River Brit; once a centre for flax milling.

Nettlecombe *Netelcome/a: Cerne Abbey.* Near Powerstock Castle.

Nutford *Nortforde/Nodford/-a: King's land; William Bellette from the king.* France farm.

Nyland *Iland/Inlande: Count of Mortain; Thurstan FitzRolf.*

Oborne *Wocburne: Monks of Sherborne. Mill.* The ruined church was a chapel for the monks of Sherborne.

Odenham *Odeham:* Lost.

Okeford Fitzpaine *Adford: St Mary's Glastonbury. Mill.*

Orchard *Hocerd: Wife of Hugh FitzGrip.* West Orchard Farm.

Osmington *Osmentone: Milton Abbey. Mill.* Stone, thatched cottages; manor house. The figure of George III is cut into the chalk down above the village.

Ower *Ora: Milton Abbey. 13 salt workers.*

Ower Moigne *Ogre: Matthew de Mortagne. Mill.* 13th-century Court House, scene of a treacherous murder in the 16th century.

Pentridge *Pentric: King's land.* Remote; the Trantridge of Thomas Hardy's *Tess of the d'Urbevilles.*

Petersham *Petrishesham: Odo FitzEverbold; Isolde. Mill.* Petersham Farm.

Piddle *Pidele:* Lost.

Piddlehinton *Pidele: Abbey of Marmoutier; Count of Mortain.* Stone-built, thatched houses.

Piddletrenthide *Pidrie: St Peter's, Winchester. 3 mills.* Straggling.

Pilsdon *Pilesdone: Edric the king's thane.* Tudor manor house.

Pimperne *Pinpre/a: King's land.* Neolithic barrow nearby.

Plumber *Plumbere: Swein, the king's thane, and Ralph from him.* Plumber Manor.

Poorton *Povertone/-a/Povrtone/ Powrtone/-a/Bovetone: Abbotsbury Abbey; Tavistock Abbey; Arnulf de Hesdin; Roger Arundel; David the Interpreter. Mill. 1 mare, 32 goats.* Now North Poorton; thatched cottages.

Portesham *Portesham: Abbotsbury Abbey; the wife of Hugh FitzGrip.* 17th-century manor house, home of Admiral Hardy who fought with Nelson at the battle of Trafalgar.

Portland *Porland: King's land. 900 sheep.* The Isle of Portland, famous for stone quarrying and its naval base.

Povington *Povintone: Robert FitzGerald. Mill.* In the danger area of the Lulworth army firing ranges.

Powerstock *Povrestoch/a: Hugh from Roger Arundel. 16 goats.* Earthwork of Norman Powerstock Castle; Iron Age fort nearby.

Poxwell *Pocheswelle/a: Cerne Abbey and Hugh's wife from the abbey.* 17th-century manor house.

Poytington *Ponditone/a: William from Count of Mortain. Mill.*

PRESTON: *An ancient footbridge across the Jordan.*

Preston (in Tarrant Rushton) *Prestetune: Bishop of Lisieux.* Preston Farm.

Puddletown *Piretone: King's land; Bolle the Priest. 2 mills.*

Pulham *Poleham: Reinbald the priest from the king; William de Mohun. 15 goats, 170 sheep.*

Puncknowle *Pomaconole/a: William de Moutiers from the wife of Huge FitzGrip. Mill.* 16th-century manor house.

Purbeck *Porbi: King's land.* Possibly Purbeck Hill, or land in vanished Purbeck Hundred.

Purse Caundle *Candel/e: Saeward from the king; Athelney Abbey; Alfred the butler.* 15th-century Purse Caundle Manor. An earlier house was given by King John to John Alleyn who looked after sick or injured royal hounds.

Radipole *Retpole/a: Cerne Abbey.*

Rampisham *Ramesham: Bishop of Bayeux.* Jacobean manor house.

Ranston *Iwerne: Robert from Robert FitzGerald.* Ranston House in Shroton village.

Renscombe *Romescumbe/ Romescumba: Cerne Abbey. 2 cows, 250 wethers.* Rensombe Farm.

Ringstead *Ringestede/hestede/-a: Hugh de St Quentin; Hugh and Ralph from the wife of Hugh FitzGrip; Brictwin from the king. ½ mill.* Deserted, medieval village.

Rollington *Ragintone/a: Robert Tilly from Roger Arundel.* Rollington Farm.

Rushton *Ristone/a: William de Braose; Odo FitzEverbold; 2 men-at-arms from the wife of Hugh FitzGrip; Alward and Edric from the king. 4 sesters of honey.*

Sandford Orcas *Sanford/a: Humphrey the Chamberlain.* Early Tudor church; haunted manor house.

Seaborough *Seveberge/-a/ Sewebeorga/Sewoberga: Bishop of Salisbury and Walton Tirrell from him. ½ mill.* Ancient manor farm.

Shaftesbury *Sceptesberie: King's land, Shaftsbury Abbey before and after 1066.* Ancient hill town, with the foundations of the abbey, originally endowed by King Alfred.

Shapwick *Scapcwic: King's land. 3 mills.* Remote.

Sherborne *Scireburne: Bishop of Salisbury, formerly Queen Edith.* 1000 year old town, dominated by Sherborne Abbey.

Shilvinghampton *Silfemetone, Scilfemetone/Sevenetone/ Sefemetona: Edwin, the king's thane.* Remote.

Shipton Gorge *Sepetone/a: King's land.* Stone-built; modern housing.

Silton *Seltone: William de Falaise. 3 mills.* Remote.

Sixpenny Handley *Hanlege: Shaftesbury Abbey.* Scattered; manor farm nearby; once a smuggling centre.

Smedmore *Metmore: Richard from William de Braose.* 17th-century Smedmore House, near Kimmeridge.

South Perrott *Pedret: William from Earl Hugh.* Stone-built. Charles I stayed here after his victory at Lostwithiel.

SHERBORNE: *Edward I's coat-of-arms. He founded the boys' school that now occupies part of the abbey buildings.*

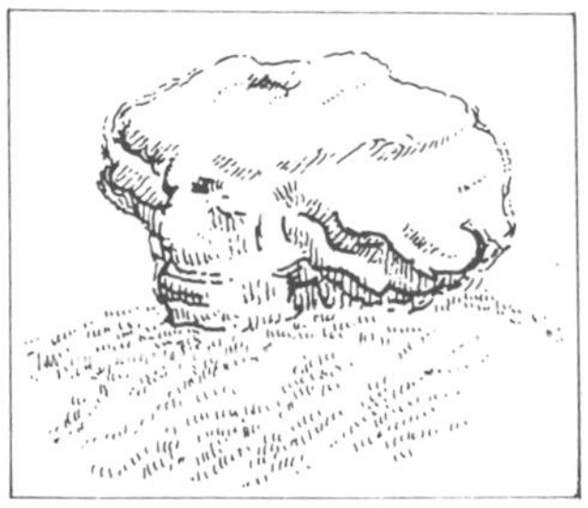

STUDLAND: *The agglestone, a huge mass of ironstone.*

Spetisbury *Spesteberie/ Spehtesberie/Spestesberia: William de Mohun.* Fine thatched houses; near Spetisbury Rings, an Iron Age earthwork.

Stafford *Staford/Stafort: Robert from Count of Mortain; Hugh and William from the wife of Hugh FitzGrip.* Now the village of West Stafford.

Stalbridge *Staplebrige:* See page 92.

Stalbridge Weston *Westone: Bishop of Salisbury.* Manor farm nearby.

Stanton St Gabriel *Stantone: Alfred from Count of Mortain.* Ruined 13th-century chapel, once a smugglers' hiding place.

Steeple *Stiple: Roger de Beaumont.* Farmhouse; manor house.

Stinsford *Stincteford, Stiteford: Hugh de St Quentin; Brictwin from the king and Aiulf from him.* Poet laureate C. Day Lewis and novelist Thomas Hardy's heart are buried in the churchyard. The village is Mellstock of Hardy's writings.

Stoborough *Stanberge: Count of Mortain. Mill.*

Stock Gaylard *Stoches: William d'Eu.* 18th-century Stock House, with deer park.

Stoke Abbot *Stoche: Monks of Sherborne. Mill.* Stone, thatched houses.

Stoke Wake *Stoche: Shaftesbury Abbey.* Partly Elizabethan manor house.

Stoke Wallis *Stoche: Edric, the king's thane; Ranulf from Thurstan FitzRolf.*

Stour *Stur/Sture: Shaftesbury Abbey; Roger de Beaumont. 4 mills.* Now 2 villages, East and West Stour. Novelist Henry Fielding lived in East Stour manor house, now replaced by a farmhouse.

Stourpaine *Sture: Humphrey the Chamberlain; William Bellett from the king.* At the foot of Hod Hill, which is crowned with an Iron Age and Roman hill-fort.

Stourton Caundle *Candel/e/lle: Count of Mortain and Alwin from him; Hugh from William d'Eu; William d'Ecouis; Wimer from Walscin de Donai; Hugh Silvester; Godric from the king.* The manor farm chapel was part of the Stourton family's fortified house.

Stubhampton *Stibemetune: Aiulf the Chamberlain.*

Studland *Stollant: Hamo from Count of Mortain. 32 salt-houses.* Harbour was used by 16th-century pirates.

Studley *Slitlege/Stodlege: Edric from the king.* Lost in Ryall village.

Sturminster Marshall *Sturminstre: Roger de Beaumont. 2 mills.* Scattered.

Sturminster Newton *Newentone: St Mary's, Glastonbury; Waleran, Roger, Ketel and Gotshelm Cook from the king. 4 mills.* Small town with a working 17th-century corn mill that replaced a medieval one.

Sturthill *Sterte(a): William de Daumeray from the wife of Hugh FitzGrip.* Lower Sturthill Farm.

Sutton Poyntz *Sutone: King's land.* Near Chalbury Iron Age hill-fort.

Sutton Waldron *Sudtone: Waleran.*

Swanage *Sonwic/Sonwich/ Swanwic: Walter Thunder from Countess of Boulogne; wife of Hugh FitzGrip.* Seaside resort.

Swyre *Svere: William from William d'Eu. Mill.* Stone-built.

Sydling *Sidelince: Milton Abbey; Ansger and Amund from Count of Mortain. 3 mills.* Attractive, unspoilt; working smithy. Yew trees in the vicarage garden are said to be 1000 years old.

Symondsbury *Simondesberge: Cerne Abbey.* Pretty; stone and thatch; 17th-century manor house.

Tarrant Crawford *Tarente: Bishop of Lisieux.* Manor farm.

Tarrant Hinton *Tarente: Shaftesbury Abbey.* Thatched cottages.

Tarrant Keyneston *Tarente: Bishop of Lisieux. 2 mills.*

Tarrant Launceston *Tarente: Holy Trinity, Caen.*

Tarrant Monkton *Tarente: St Mary's, Cranborne.* Thatched cottages; ford.

Tatton *Tatentone/Tatetun: Aiulf the Chamberlain; wife of Hugh FitzGrip.* Tatton Farm.

Thorncombe *Tornecome: Baldwin the Sheriff.* Forde Abbey, founded in 1148, is nearby.

Thorne *Torne: Walter Thunder and Robert from the wife of Hugh FitzGrip.*

Thornford *Torneford: Monks of Sherborne. Mill.* Much developed.

Thorn Hill *Tornehelle: Wulfric from the king.* Possibly Thornhill House.

Thornicombe *Tornecome: Alward from the king.*

Thornton *Torentone: William from William d'Eu.* Thornton Farm.

Tincleton *Tincladene: William from Earl Hugh.*

Todber *Todeberie/a: Geoffrey Mallory from William de Mohun.* Part-Saxon cross in churchyard.

Toller Fratrum, *Tolre: Oger from Waleran. Mill.* Remote, mainly Tudor settlement, connected with the Knights Hospitallers of St John of Jerusalem. St Basil Church has pre-*Domesday* carvings. Also Toller Porcorum with a church font thought to be part of a Roman altar.

Toller Whelme *Tolre: Count of Mortain.* Tudor manor house.

Tolpuddle *Pidele: Abbotsbury Abbey. 2 mills. 300 sheep..* Home of the Tolpuddle Martyrs, who formed the first trade union and were sentenced to transportation to Australia (1834).

Trent *Trente/a: Ansger from Count of Mortain.* Manor house with a hiding place for Charles II after the battle of Worcester (1651).

Trill *Trelle: Earl Hugh.* Trill Farm.

Turners Puddle *Pidele: Walter Thunder from the wife of Hugh FitzGrip. Mill. 40 goats, 12 mares with their foals.*

Turnworth *Torneworde: Alfred d'Epaignes.*

Tyneham *Tigeham/Tingeham: Count of Mortain; Edric from the king.* Derelict. In the danger area of army firing ranges near Lulworth.

Up Cerne *Obcerne: Bishop of Salisbury.* 17th-century manor house.

Waddon *Wadone: St Mary's, Montivilliers.* Waddon Manor.

Walditch *Waldic: William de Daumeray from the king. Mill.* Traces of ancient field systems.

Walford *Walteford: Godwin Hunter from the king.* Part of Wimborne Minster.

Wareham *Warham: Bishop of Salisbury; St Wandrilles Abbey; William d'Eu.* Town settled by Britons, Romans and Saxons and fought over by Danes and during the Civil War. It was rebuilt in Georgian style in 1762.

Warmwell *Warmemoille/ Warmwelle: Robert from Count of Mortain; Earl Hugh; Thorold from the wife of Hugh FitzGrip. 2 mills. 200 sheep.* 17th-century manor house, home of John Sadler who predicted the Great Plague, the Fire of London and Monmouth's Rebellion.

Watercombe *Watrecome/ Watrecoma: King's land. ½ mill.*

Waterston *Pidere: Serlo de Burcy, formerly Earl Harold. Mill. 393 sheep.* Waterston House, home of Bathsheba Everdene in Thomas Hardy's *Far from the Madding Crowd.*

Weathergrove *Weregrave/a: Ralph from Bishop of Coutances. Mill.* Weathergrove Farm.

Wellwood *Welle: Monks of Sherborne.*

West Compton *Contone: Milton Abbey.* Remote.

West Knighton *Chenistetone: William d'Ecouis. 2 mills.*

West Milton *Mideltone/a: Cerne Abbey. Mill.* Unspoilt; watermill, now a private house.

West Parley *Perlai: Ralph of Cranborne.* On the outskirts of Bournemouth.

Whitchurch Canonicorum *Witcerce: St Wandrille's Abbey holds the church.* Norman church with relics of St Wite, the village's patron saint.

Whitcombe *Widecome/a: Milton Abbey.* 12th–16th-century church where the Dorset poet, William Barnes, preached his last sermon.

Whitecliff *Witeclive/a: Serlo de Burcy.* Whitecliff Farm.

Wilkswood *Wilceswde/-a/ Wilchesode/a: Wife of Hugh FitzGrip and Durand Carpenter from her. 2 oxen.* Wilkswood Farm.

Wilksworth *Wedecheswordе: Aethelrun, the king's thane.* Wilksworth Farm.

Wimborne Minster *Winborne/ burne: King's land; Edward of Salisbury. 377 sheep, 2 cattle, 74 goats.* Market town. Ethelred, king of the West Saxons and brother of Alfred the Great, is said to be buried here.

Wimborne St Giles *Winburne: King's land; St Mary's, Cranborne; Wilton Abbey; William Chernet from the wife of Hugh FitzGrip; Wulfgeat from the king; Hervey the Chamberlain. 1⅓ mills.* St Giles House, seat of the Shaftesbury family; 17th century mill house.

Winfrith Newburgh *Winfrode/ a: King's land with Bolle holding the church. 4 mills.* Overshadowed by a nuclear power station.

Winterborne Abbas *Winterborna/Wintreburne: Cerne Abbey. 18 goats.* Near the Bronze Age Nine Stones Circle.

Winterborne Belet *Wintreburne:* Lost.

Winterborne Houghton *Wintreborne/burne: Ogis from William de Mohun; Hugh from the wife of Hugh FitzGrip; Swein from the king and Robert from him. 300 sheep.* Remote.

Winterborne Monkton *Wintreburn: Countess of Boulogne.* Below the Neolithic and Iron Age hill fort of Maiden Castle.

Winterborne Stickland *Wintreburne: Canons of Coutances.*

Winterborne Whitechurch *Wintreborne: Milton Abbey.* Thatched cottages.

Witchampton *Wichemetune, Wichamatuna: King's land; Hubert from Count of Mortain, formerly Queen Matilda.* Old Mill, once a 13th-century manor house.

WOODSFORD: *England's only thatched castle.*

Woodsford *Wardesford/ Werdesford/Werdesfort: Cerne Abbey; William from the king. Mill.* 14th-century Woodsford Castle.

Woodstreet *Windestorte: Osmund, the king's servant.* Woodstreet Farm.

Woodyates *Odiete: St Mary's, Glastonbury.*

Wool *Welle, Wille: Count of Mortain; Alward from the king; Aelmer.* Elizabethan Woolbridge Manor, now an hotel.

Woolcombe (in Melbury Bubb) *Wellecome: Hugh from William d'Eu.*

Woolcombe (in Toller Porcorum) *Wellacome/ Wilecome: Hugh Gosbert, the king's servant; Doda, the king's thane.* Woolcombe Farm.

Woolgarston *Orgarestone: Humphrey from William de Braose.*

Woolland *Winlande/a: Milton Abbey. 16 goats.* Fine Victorian buildings.

Wootton Fitzpaine *Odetun: Bretel from Count of Mortain; Aiulf the Chamberlain. 3 mills, vines.* Tudor-style Victorian manor house.

Worgret *Vergroh/Weregrote/ Wiregrote: Cerne Abbey; Walter from William de Braose; Hugh from the king.* Part of Wareham.

Worth Matravers *Orde/Wirde/ Wode: Roger Arundel. 250 sheep.* Stone-built; early Norman, part-Saxon church.

Wraxhall *Brocheshale/ Brochessala: Roger Arundel. 2 cows.* Scattered; Jacobean manor house.

Wyndlam *Windelham: Roger Arundel.*

Wynford Eagle *Wenfrot: William d'Eu. Mill.* Manor house, with a 17th-century porch, owned by the Sydenham family for 200 years.

Yetminster *Etiminstre: Bishop of Salisbury. Mill.* Stone-built.

Essex

Domesday Essex was probably not the happiest place to live. The county is included with Norfolk and Suffolk in the so-called 'Little Domesday Book', *which compares conditions in 1086 with those at the time of the Conquest. From this we see evidence of what one historian has called 'obscure little revolutions', and of an increase of the unfree population at the expense of the relatively free. By 1086 only seven per cent of the residents were freemen, while the subservient smallholders* (bordarii) *had grown to nearly half the total, superseding villagers and slaves. This increase may represent a Norman attempt to simplify the social order. Many of the new smallholders would have been expected to undertake slaves' work. In the process of Norman colonization, the Saxon men of Essex lost not only their lands but also much of their liberty.*

Life may have been better for the nearly 50,000 sheep recorded in 1086. Many were put out to pasture near the salt-pans in the marshes along the low-lying coast. To the west the great woodlands of Essex (within a century almost the entire county was to become royal forest) helped to sustain the 13,171 pigs that one scholar has counted.

Colchester, a town with a population of about 2000, and Maldon, a semi-agricultural community with about 1000, were the largest settlements in an otherwise rural county.

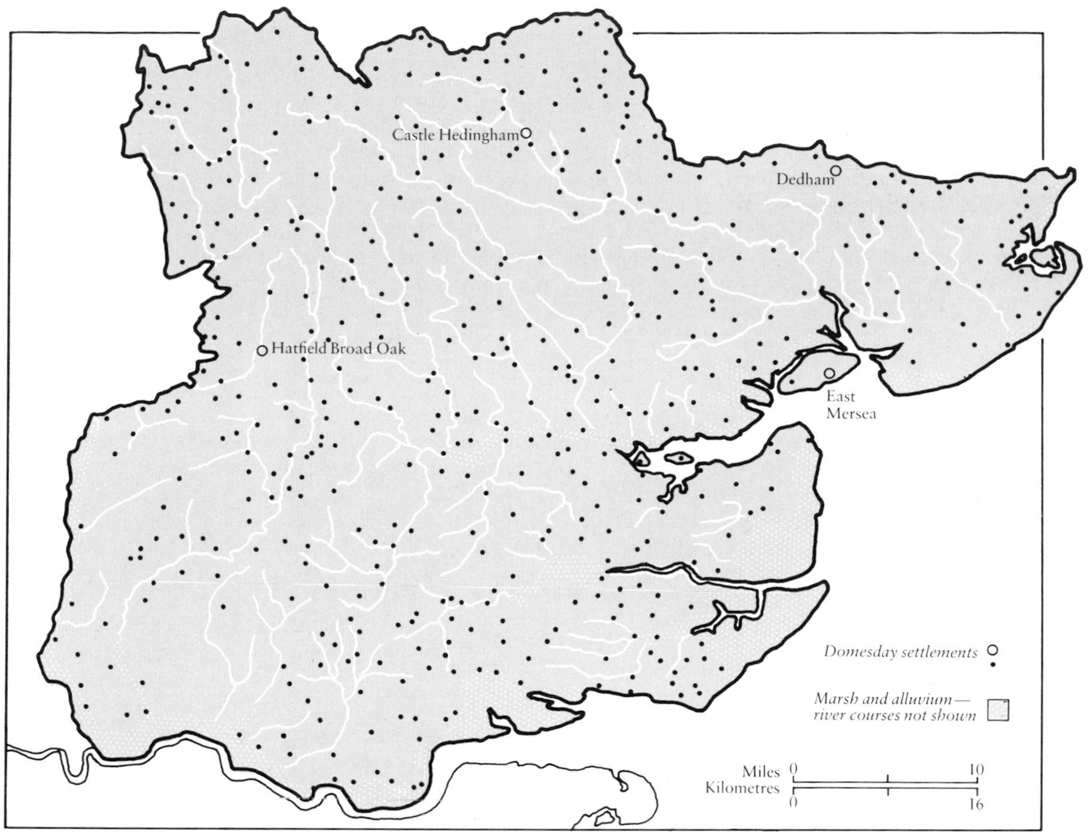

Hatfield Broad Oak

Harold held HATFIELD (BROAD OAK) *HADFELDA* before 1066 as 1 manor, for 20 hides. Then 51 villagers, now 60; then 19 smallholders, now 30; then 20 slaves, now 22. Then 9 ploughs in lordship, now 8. 3 cobs, 40 cattle, 195 pigs and 200 sheep less 7. Then 40 men's ploughs, now 31½; this loss was in the time of all of the sheriffs and through the cattle plague. Woodland, 800 pigs; meadow, 120 acres; pasture which pays 9 wethers in the manor; 41 acres of ploughland. To the church of this manor belonged 1 hide and 30 acres, which Swein took away after he lost the Sheriffdom; this land paid the customary due to this manor. Before 1066, there also belonged to this manor 1 Freeman with ½ hide, whom G(eoffrey) de Mandeville took away; attached to this land is 1 villager with 1 acre which Count E(ustace) holds, value 4d. Also 30 acres which a smith, who was put to death on account of robbery, held before 1066, and the King's reeve added that land to this manor; also 40 acres of woodland which King Edward's reeve held; of which land and woodland Osmund of Anjou dispossessed the King's reeve and the manor. Robert Gernon now holds it. ½ hide which 1 Freeman held before 1066; Robert Gernon also holds this. Apart from this, 3 outliers were attached to this manor before 1066, HERTFORD, AMWELL and HODDESDON, which lie in Hertfordshire, (and) which Ralph of Limésy now holds. Also 1 freeman with 30 acres who always belonged to this manor. Value of the manor then £36; now £60, but the Sheriff receives £80 from it, and 100s in gifts. Also the value then of the 3 outliers £12, the Freemen's land 45s. Woodland, 40 pigs. Later on we recovered ½ hide which 1 Freeman of Harold's held before 1066; now Ralph of Marcy holds it in Hamo's Holding. Value then 10s; now 7[s].

It is easy to overlook the village of Hatfield Broad Oak. The modern tourist, like the kings of England, from Harold to Henry VIII, visits the parish chiefly to see Hatfield Forest.

What he finds is a Forest with a capital F – not an area densely overgrown with tall trees, but a Forest in the ancient legal sense, a place of mixed and carefully managed grassland and woods. Now owned by the National Trust, the land is used for much the same purposes as it was in the eleventh century. Deer still thrive among the coppices; cattle graze beneath the grotesque stumps of pollarded hornbeams. 'Hatfield is the only place where one can step back into the Middle Ages to see, with only a small effort of the imagination, what a Forest looked like in use,' wrote Oliver Rackham, an authority on British woodlands. It is as close as one can ever get to 1000 acres of *Domesday* England.

Close to the forest lies the village – two neat streets with attractive seventeenth- and eighteenth-century buildings. Above it rises an imposing, flint-towered parish church, St Mary the Virgin, more church than the few houses would seem to require. Yet this is only a fragment of the ecclesiastical complex that once stood here. From the twelfth century until the dissolution of the monasteries, a Benedictine priory shared the church's hilltop site. Walled and moated, it had an uneasy relationship with the local residents. In 1378 King Richard II was obliged to mediate after enraged parishioners, led by their vicar, threw out the monks and destroyed much of the cloisters.

It had had its troubles, too, in William I's time. Although its population rose slightly after the Conquest, it was stricken with cattle plague, which swept away one-quarter of its plough oxen.

Hatfield Broad Oak has always stood figuratively as well as literally in the forest's shadow. Daniel Defoe, in his *Tour through the Whole Island of Great Britain* (1724–7), dismisses the town and several of its neighbours. These villages are renowned, he wrote, 'for husbandry and good malt, but of no other note'.

William the Conqueror had recognized the property's value, for he personally took over Hatfield from the defeated Harold, making it a royal manor. Early in the twelfth century it became known as Hatfield Regis. This is not to suggest that Norman and Plantagenet kings were frequent visitors. In those venison-eating days, the royal forests served principally as official larders. Ordinary people who had the misfortune to live within their boundaries were shackled with regulations regarding grazing, hunting, tree felling and the gathering of wood.

Popular resistance to such exclusive use of potentially good farmland eventually whittled away the royal forests. Hatfield passed out of royal hands in the reign of Henry VIII, and there followed 250 years of bitter feuds between those with hunting rights and those who wished to graze their animals. Despite occasional violence, the forest survived, and it was only in this century that it nearly met its end. In 1924 a number of the finest trees had been cut down for timber before Edward Buxton, already the saviour of Epping Forest, bought Hatfield as he lay dying. That same year his son presented the property to the National Trust.

Those searching for the stately shade trees of an imagined Sherwood Forest will be disappointed by the enclosed and businesslike coppices. Twelve have survived from at least the seventeenth century and many of their names remain unchanged: Hangman's, Beggar's Hall, Spittlemore. In Elgin Coppice the National Trust has reintroduced a traditional system of coppicing, cutting the stools below the standard trees in the sort of managed sequence already well established when the *Domesday* agents made their visit. Today the fallow deer, unmolested by horses and hounds, are regularly stalked by marksmen to prevent their becoming a nuisance to local farms and gardens.

The forest is not entirely medieval. In the centre is a lake, created in the eighteenth century by the pleasure-loving Houblon family and now a rich fishing ground for pike and tench. On its banks, the Houblons built a bizarre tea house, its walls encrusted in sea shells like a petrified *fruit de mer*. Nor are the trees quite up to eleventh-century size. Many of the great oaks were cut down in the nineteenth century. The largest of all, the Doodle Oak, died a natural death in 1859. Its trunk measured 60 feet in circumference, and it is from this tree, so legend goes, that Hatfield Broad Oak derived its name.

Old and picturesque as parts of the village may be, it is to the forest that a visitor must go for the true flavour of the eleventh century; there is no place in England where he will find it more successfully.

Dedham

Roger [de Raismes] holds DEDHAM *DELHAM* in lordship, which Aelfric Kemp held as a manor, for 2½ hides. Then 7 villagers, now 5; always 24 smallholders. Then 4 slaves, now 3. Then 2 ploughs in lordship, now 3. Then among the men 10 ploughs, now 5. Woodland, 250 pigs; meadow, 40 acres; then 1 mill, now 2. Then 2 cobs, now 10; then 5 cows, now 3; then 40 sheep, now 100; then 25 pigs, now 30. Value always £12. Of this manor, Gerald holds 30 acres. Value 10s in the same assessment.

The little High Street of Dedham makes such a pretty picture that it is easy to imagine that it was purpose-built by some millionaire of rare good taste. Architecture of at least four centuries mingles discreetly, from the sixteenth-century Marlborough Head Inn to the neo-Georgian Great House of 1936. And complementing this lovely collection is the Tudor church of St Mary the Virgin in a yard of close-cropped yew trees and erect, unshowy gravestones. 'Dedham is easily the most attractive small town in Essex,' wrote Nikolaus Pevsner in *The Buildings of England*.

There is an inkling of this future prosperity in *Domesday*'s description of Dedham. While the numbers of Essex farm animals often declined in the unhappy 20 years between the Conquest and the survey, flocks of sheep frequently increased, in this case, more than doubling. This was eventually to have a profound influence upon the British economy. It was also to be the making of wool towns like Dedham, which was, in its prime, intellectually and industrially vigorous.

Another point of interest in Dedham's *Domesday* entry is the building of a second mill, believed to be the Shirburn mill on the township's eastern boundary. A mill on the earlier site, at the confluence of Black Brook and the River Stour, still dominates the northern approach to Dedham. In the eleventh century it ground corn, but by the Middle Ages it was playing a part in the wool trade. It is in association with this mill, in one of its later incarnations, that we encounter Sir John Fastolf, Lord of Dedham Manor, and the model for Shakespeare's fat old coward, Sir John Falstaff. In 1450 the real Sir John wrote angrily to his agent, instructing him to begin proceedings against the parson of neighbouring Stratford, who had destroyed his new mill and stolen 24 swans and cygnets. Unlike Shakespeare's Sir John, Fastolf was a celebrated soldier, elected to the Order of the Garter for his valour against the French. His reputation came to grief at the battle of Patay, where, according to Hall's *Chronicle*, he retreated from the field 'without any stroke stricken'. But then, so did a lot of others; the opposing general was Joan of Arc.

Another mill stood upon this spot when the artist John Constable, who was born in nearby East Bergholt in 1776, was a schoolboy in Dedham. The village became the centre of his artistic soul, and the tower of St Mary's church figures in several of his landscapes, even where it shouldn't. He sometimes used artistic licence to move it for a better composition.

'These scenes made me a painter,' he wrote, and he in turn made Dedham Vale a part of English cultural experience. He did not think of his work as 'pretty', but he saw in the local countryside what he called 'an amenity and elegance hardly anywhere else to be found'. The public, at first hostile to his aims, gradually began to realize that rural elegance was fast disappearing. A wave of nostalgia eventually influenced official thinking, and in the 1960s Dedham Vale was designated an 'area of outstanding natural beauty'.

Castle Hedingham

Aubrey [de Vere] holds (CASTLE) HEDINGHAM *HAINGHEHAM in lordship, which Wulfwin held as a manor, for 2 hides. Always 4 ploughs in lordship; 6 men's ploughs; 15 villagers, 7 smallholders; 8 slaves. Woodland, 200 pigs; meadow, 30 acres; then 1 mill, now none; now 6 arpents* of vines. Then 11 cattle, 140 sheep, 80 pigs, 4 cobs; now 160 sheep, 100 pigs, 1 cob, 100 goats. 13 Freemen who could not withdraw (and) who held 1 hide and 10 acres. Always 7 ploughs. Then 15 villagers, now 18; now 22 smallholders; then 6 slaves, now 2; who have 3 ploughs. Woodland, 60 pigs; meadow, 43 acres; always 1 mill. Value then £13; now [£]20. To this manor are attached 15 burgesses in Sudbury; they are assessed in the £20. Of this manor, Robert Blunt holds 35 acres, Warin 25 acres, Pinson 15 acres, Godwin 15 acres; who have 5 ploughs. Value £7 in the same assessment.

The village of Castle Hedingham retains a medieval appearance. On a steep hill stands the castle keep, its great square tower more than a hundred feet high. Far below, clustered around the church of St Nicholas, lies the village. The general effect is of two communities – high and low, lord and liegemen.

The *Domesday* entry reflects this division. At the top of the hill lived Aubrey de Vere, a Norman lord of many holdings, who chose Hedingham (later Castle Hedingham) as his principal residence. The village consisted of 13 freemen and their underlings (their freedom did not include leaving Castle Hedingham for another lord) on land assessed at only one hide and ten acres.

In most *Domesday* descriptions there is little to indicate that Normans and Saxons were of different cultures, but Hedingham is an exception.

DEDHAM VALE: *The River Stour, in 'Constable' country.*

EAST MERSEA: *The Colne estuary in winter.*

The de Veres settled in with a touch of class, bringing their own grape vines with them. It is likely that in 1086 these vines had not yet begun to crop, for the description of another Essex vineyard, also owned by de Vere, states that only one of the 11 'arpents of vines' bore fruit. Aubrey had to wait some years for his first English table wine.

The de Veres dominated life in Hedingham just as their castle, built at the end of the eleventh century, dominated the Colne Valley. John de Vere, thirteenth Earl of Oxford, brought the family its greatest glory with his exploits on behalf of Richmond (Henry VII) at the Battle of Bosworth in 1485. Only 100 years later, the seventeenth Earl, Edward de Vere, plunged the name into disrepute, dismantling much of the castle to pay for his extravagances. Yet this poet, soldier and darling of Queen Elizabeth I was one of the most talented men of his age. Among his many activities, he found time to write the complete works of William Shakespeare – or so a determined minority believe.

The de Veres died out in the eighteenth century. Their vines lingered on; wild red grapes grew for a while near the ruins of their ancestral home. 'Hedingham Castle,' wrote Horace Walpole in about 1770, 'is now shrunk to one vast curious tower.'

East Mersea

Swein [of Essex] holds (EAST) MERSEA *MERESAILA* in lordship, which Robert son of Wymarc held before 1066 as a manor, for 6 hides. Always 2 ploughs in lordship. Then 8 [men's] ploughs, now 6. Then 9 villagers, now 8; then 12 smallholders, now 14; then 3 slaves, now none. Woodland, then 40 pigs; meadow, 5 acres; 4 fisheries. Then 1 cob, 9 cattle, 25 pigs, 107 sheep; now 3 cobs, 12 cattle, 10 pigs, 100 sheep, 1 beehive. Value £10.

East Mersea has always played second fiddle to its neighbour in the west. In 1086, West Mersea was assessed for three times more land than East Mersea and, with a population of around 500, had five times the number of inhabitants. Only in its fisheries could East Mersea claim superiority. Despite equally good opportunities for sea fishing in the Blackwater and Colne estuaries, West Mersea appears to have lost its one fishery in the 20 years after the Conquest, while East Mersea boasted four in 1086. It is not clear precisely what these fisheries caught – perhaps shellfish. Since Roman days, Colchester oysters have been the speciality of Mersea Island. And in Victorian times, women scooped up winkles at low tide for the London market.

The village continues to lag behind. While the population of West Mersea has quadrupled in this century (from 1306 in 1901, to an estimated 5733 in 1980), in East Mersea it has fallen from 218 to 217.

'I cannot say that I either liked the place or became attached to the people,' wrote Sabine Baring-Gould, East Mersea's outspoken vicar, and the author of *Onward Christian Soldiers*, who lived there from 1871 to 1881. He had little doubt what was wrong with the place: 'the intolerable stench that pervades the air when the tide goes out . . . ; the smell when a field was fertilized with sprats . . . ; the myriads of mosquitoes . . . ; the incessant 'piping of the wind'. And, as if that were not enough, described his parishioners as 'dull, shy, reserved and suspicious'.

He would still recognize the place. East Mersea church, dedicated to St Edmund, is a weather-beaten building with a rough, pock-marked tower. Together with East Mersea Hall, it huddles behind a few tall trees in a featureless plain of farmland. This is the centre of East Mersea, but it is not the centre of much – a scattered row of cottages along the one main road, a pub, a post office and a shanty town of holiday caravans on the shore nearby.

Yet, because of its position, East Mersea has always been militarily significant. The eastern shore of Mersea Island overlooks the mouth of the Colne estuary; and about ten miles upriver is the city of Colchester, within easy reach of Europe and a tempting first footing for any invading army. It thus became one of the routine measures of any war to fortify East Mersea. Nervous about a French invasion, Henry VIII built an enormous triangular blockhouse here. It saw no action then, but during the Civil War, first the Royalists and then the Roundheads occupied it. It was refortified against the Dutch before it was demolished in the eighteenth century. Napoleon's non-invasion of England sent soldiers scrambling again to Mersea Island, where they occupied the church. A more serious threat from Hitler turned the beaches into a mined tangle of barbed wire, and clusters of fortified gun emplacements sprang up along the shore.

A few of these concrete pill boxes still remain, their slit eyes staring out over the mud flats of the Colne. But this eastern part of the island is now a nature reserve and a popular spot for hikers and sunbathers, a development that would have astonished the Reverend Baring-Gould.

Essex Gazetteer
Each entry starts with the modern place-name in **bold** type. The *Domesday* information that follows is in *italic* type, beginning with the name or names by which the place was known in 1086. The landholders and under-tenants are next, separated with semi-colons if the place was divided into more than one holding. More general information, including examples of dues rendered, completes the *Domesday* part of the entry. The modern or post-Domesday section is in normal type. represents a village, a small village or hamlet.

A number of villages, hamlets, etc., that are now 2 or more separate places are indistinguishable in the *Domesday* records. In these cases, the places are listed, alphabetically, under their main names. Great Easton and Little Easton, for example, both come under Easton.

Numbers of animals are given when they reach or exceed: 150 sheep, 50 pigs, 15 cattle, 10 goats, 3 cobs. All cows, wethers, foals and unbroken mares are mentioned.

Abberton *Edburg(h)etuna: Ralph de Marcy from Count Eustace; Odo from Swein of Essex; Ranulf Peverel.* Reservoir; Stone Age remains; Abberton Hall, with moat, ancient barns.

Abbess Roding *Roinges: Eudo the Steward; Geoffrey Martel from Geoffrey de Mandeville.* Once owned by the Abbess of Barking.

Alderford *Alreforde: 2 men-at-arms from Richard FitzGilbert.*

Alderton *Aluertuna: Canons of Waltham before and after 1066.* Alderton Hall.

Aldham *Aldeham: Aubrey's wife from Bishop of Bayeux.* Philip Morant, 18th-century rector of the church, edited Parliament's 1st records (1278–1413).

Alphamstone *Alfelmestuna: St Edmund's Abbey; 15 freemen, Derwulf and Hold from Richard FitzGilbert.* Norman church on Roman site and Bronze Age burial place.

Alresford *Aleforda/E(i)lesforda: Humphrey from Bishop of London; Hato from Count Eustace; Algar from Richard FitzGilbert.* Roman villa sites.

Amberden Hall *Amberdena: Ely Abbey claims from Ranulf Peverel. 1 beehive, 3 cobs.* Amberden Hall Farmhouse.

Ardleigh *Erlega/-eia/-iga/Herlega: William from Geoffrey de Mandeville; William from Robert Gernon; Roger de Raismes; Agnes from Hugh de Gournai. 2 mills, 3 beehives. 10 goats.* Middle Bronze Age finds.

Arkesden *Archesdana: Eudo the Steward; Roger d'Auberville; Picot from Robert Gernon; the King claims from Geoffrey de Mandeville. 2 beehives. Foal.* Bronze Age remains.

Ashdon *Ascenduna: Ralph Baynard, formerly Aethelgyth, a free woman. Vines, 3 beehives.* Roman burial mounds in nearby Bartlow Hills.

Asheldham *Hain(c)tuna: Warner and Ralph from Swein of Essex. 11 goats.* Formerly an Iron Age camp and Roman settlement.

Ashen *Asce: Richard FitzGilbert. Mill.* Ashen Hall Farmhouse.

ASHINGDON: *Church overlooking the 1016 battleground.*

Ashingdon *Nesenduna: Roger from Swein of Essex.* Canute fought Edmund Ironside here (1016).

Ashwell Hall *Asseuuella: Walter Cook.*

Aveley *Aluielea/-thelea/Auileia: Mauger from Bishop of Bayeux; John FitzWaleran; Ansger Cook.* Roman road called Bredle Street; church with Roman tiles.

Bardfield *Berdefelda/Birdefella/Byrdefelda: Adelulf from Count Eustace; Richard FitzGilbert and Widelard from him. 3 mills, 2 beehives, fishpond. 107 pigs, 200 sheep, 30 goats, 5 cobs, 41 cattle.* Now 2 villages: Great Bardfield has a tower windmill; Little Bardfield has a Saxon church.

Barking *Berchingas/ingu: Barking Abbey before and after 1066. 2 mills, fishery, 10 beehives. 150 pigs, 24 goats, 34 cattle.* London borough; 7th-century Barking Abbey.

Barling *Berlinga: Canons of St Paul's before and after 1066; Bishop of Bayeux.* Wooden mill; Norman prison wall at Jail Farm.

Barn Hall *Borooldituna: Modbert from Ralph Baynard.* House in Devil's Wood, reputedly built by a watchman on the Devil's instructions.

Barnston *Bernestuna: Hugh de Bernières from Geoffrey de Mandeville.* Elizabethan Barnston Hall.

Barrow Hall *Berreuuera: Richard FitzGilbert.* Manor house.

Barstable Hall *Berdestestapla: FitzThorold from Bishop of Bayeux.* Part of Basildon.

Basildon *Be(r)lesduna: Thorold and 'W' from Swein of Essex.* New town; formerly a hamlet.

Bassetts *Mildermet: Ralph FitzBrian from Bishop of London.* The Bassetts were 13th-century lords of the manor.

Baythorn End *Babiterna: Ranulf, brother of Ilger. Mill.* Part of Birdbrook; Baythorn Hall; Baythorn Park.

Beauchamp Roding *Roinges: Aubrey de Vere from Count Alan.*

Beaumont *Fulepet: Edward from Aubrey de Vere. 2 salt-houses, 3 beehives.*

Beckney *Bacheneia: Bishop of Bayeux.*

Belchamp *Belcamp/Belcham: Canons of St Paul's before and after 1066; Wulfmer and Bernard from Count Eustace; Aubrey de Vere; Robert de Vaux from Roger Bigot. Vines. 28 cattle, 200 sheep, 100 pigs.* Now 3 villages, Belchamp Otten, Belchamp Walter and Belchamp St Paul which has a church on a Roman site. Athelstan, 1st King of All England gave it to St Paul's Cathedral in the 10th century.

Belstead Hall *Belesteda: Richard from William de Warenne; Robert FitzGobert.* Manor house.

Bendysh Hall *Benedisc: Count Eustace; Engelric claims from Richard FitzGilbert.* Bendysh Hall.

Benfleet *Benflet: Ranulf brother of Ilger and Theodoric Pointel from the King; Westminster Abbey; Swein of Essex. Mill.* Now the village of North Benfleet and town of South Benfleet.

Bensted *Bedenesteda: Robert from Hugh de Montfort; claimed by monks of Ely; Nigel from Robert FitzCorbucion.*

Bentfield Bury *Benedfelda: Robert Gernon. Mill. 3 cobs.*

Benton *Breddinchon: William FitzGross; St Edmund's Abbey. Mill.* Benton Hall, a manor house.

Berden *Berdane: Alfred from Swein of Essex. Beehive. 3 cobs, 2 foals.* 16th-century Berden Hall and Priory.

Berners Roding *Rodinges/-ingis: Hugh de Bernières from Geoffrey de Mandeville. Mill.*

Bigods, formerly Alfriston *Alferestuna: Martel from Geoffrey de Mandeville. Mill. 350 pigs.* Takes its name from Norman warlords who lived here.

Binsley *Bineslea: Widelard from Richard FitzGilbert; Peter de Valognes.*

Birch *Bricceia/Bricia/Parva Bricceia: Hugh from Count Eustace; Robert from Robert Gernon; Hugh de St Quentin. Mill. 3 cobs, 53 goats.* Previously 2 villages, Great and Little Birch; a ruined church built with Roman bricks.

Birchanger *Becangra/Bilichangra/Blichangra: Tascelin the priest from the king; St Valery; Germund from Geoffrey de Mandeville. 2 mills. 36 goats.* Birchanger Place, a mansion.

Birch Hall *Birichou: Robert from Count Eustace.* Birch Hall, near Colchester. Only the outbuildings and kitchen wing remain of this country house.

Birdbrook *Bridebroc: Ranulf brother of Ilger.* Church with Roman tiles; a tablet proclaims that Martha Blewitt (died 1681) had 9 husbands.

Blatchams *Blacham: Count Eustace.*

Blunt's Hall *Blundeshala: Count Eustace, formerly a free woman; Humphrey from Ranulf Peverel. Mill. 4 cows, 4 calves.* Manor house.

Bobbingworth *Bubingeordea: Richard from Ranulf, brother of Ilger.* Small green; Blake Hall.

Bocking *Bochinges: Holy Trinity, Canterbury. Mill.* Samuel Courtauld began his silk business here. The old mills remain on the factory site.

Bockingham *Botingham: William FitzGross from Hugh de Montfort.*

Bollington Hall *Boli(n)tuna: Robert Gernon; Alfred claims from Swein of Essex. 1 freeman.* In Ugley, a London suburb.

Bonhunt *Banhunta: Sasselin.* Bonhunt Farm.

Boreham *Borham: Lambert from Count Eustace; Ranulf Peverel claims from the Count; William de Warenne; Osbert from Swein of Essex. Mill, church.* New Hall, palace built by Henry VIII and granted to Thomas Radcliffe by Elizabeth I.

Borley *Barlea: Countess of Aumâle; Grim and Godwin claim from Ansketel, who holds from Richard FitzGilbert. 2 beehives.* Churchyard with 15 yews.

Bowers Gifford *Bura: Westminster Abbey; Serlo from Ranulf Peverel; a man-at-arms from Walter the Deacon; Grim the Reeve. 4 calves.* Tudor church.

Boxted *Bocche-/Bucchesteda/Bocstede: Count Eustace; Arthur from Eudo the Steward; St Benedict's claims from Aubrey de Vere. 2 beehives. 16 cattle.*

Boyton Hall *Boituna: Richard FitzGilbert.*

Bradfield *Bradefelda: Roger de Raismes; Roger de Poitou. Salt-house.* Bradfield Hall, home of Sir Harbottle Grimston, leading Essex Parliamentarian during the Civil War.

Bradwell Quay (or Waterside) formerly Hackfleet *Hacflet: Bishop of Bayeux. Fishery.* The church is on the site of a Roman fort; nuclear power station nearby.

Braintree *Branchetreu: Ledmer of Hempstead, who claims it for Richard FitzGilbert.* Part of Bocking; 19th-century centre of Courtauld's rayon industry. Nicholas Udell, vicar of Braintree (1537), wrote the first English comedy, *Ralph Roister Doister*.

Brightlingsea *Brictricseia/Brictesceseia: Peter de Valognes from the king. Mill, church. 16 cattle, 5 cobs, 166 sheep.* Town; member of the Cinque Ports of Sandwich; Norman church.

Broomfield *Brumfelda: Walter from Geoffrey de Mandeville. Mill.* Stone Age and Saxon remains; Norman church built of Roman bricks.

Broxted *Broc(c)hesteuot: Ely Abbey before and after 1066; Richard from Eudo the Steward. 2 beehives.* Windmill; Roman-tiled church.

Bulmer *Bulenemera: Mascerel from Richard FitzGilbert.* Roman-bricked church.

Bulphan *Bulgeuen: Barking Abbey.*

Bures *Bura/Buro: Richard FitzGilbert, formerly Leofeva, a free woman; Hugh from John FitzWaleran.* Mostly situated in Suffolk, across the county border. The 16th-century Eight Bells Inn is on the Essex side.

BURNHAM: *Typical 18th and 19th c. weather-boarded cottages.*

Burnham *Burn(e)ham: Ralph Baynard; the king claims from Theodoric Pointel. Mill. 6 cobs, 336 sheep.* Small town. Yachting centre.

Buttsbury *Cinga: The steward of Henry de Ferrers.* Now merged with Stock and Ingatestone.

Byrton *Bertuna: Roger Marshal.*

Canewdon *Carenduna: Swein of Essex. 3 cobs, 342 sheep.* Model, built 1960; church with Roman bricks. Canute fought his last fight here against Edmund Ironside.

Canfield *Cane(d)felda/Chenefelda: Aubrey de Vere from Count Alan; William de Warenne; Richard from Geoffrey de Mandeville; Aubrey de Vere; the king claims from Richard, who held it from Geoffrey de Mandeville. 2 mills, 3 beehives. 50 pigs, 3 cobs.* Now 2 hamlets,

Great Canfield and Canfield End. Earthworks of de Vere's Castle at Great Canfield, one of England's best preserved sites.

Castle Hedingham. See page 98.

Chadwell *Celdewella: Hugolin from Bishop of London; FitzThorold from Bishop of Bayeux; Grim the Reeve.* Now Chadwell St Mary, originally 'Cold-well'. Extensive ancient chalk workings. St Cedd, an East Saxon missionary reputedly baptised his converts in a well near the church.

Chardwell, formerly Ainsworth *Einesuurda: Richard from William de Warenne. 3 beehives.*

Chatham *Cetham: Walter from Geoffrey de Mandeville.* Now Chatham Green.

Chaureth *Ceauride: Warner from Richard FitzGilbert; 2 freemen claim from Aelmer who held it from Richard FitzGilbert.*

Chelmsford *Celmeresfort: Bishop of London before and after 1066. Mill.* Saxon settlement, and a county town since the 13th century. The world's first radio factory (Marconi) started production here in 1899.

Chickney *Cicchenai: Warin from Ranulf Peverel.* Saxon church. Tudor Sibleys Farm has one of Essex's oldest dovecotes.

Chignall *Cingehala: Richard, Richard Garnet, Ralph, Leofson, Leofric, Leofwin, Alstan from Geoffrey de Mandeville; Ansketel from Robert Gernon.* Originally Chignall St James's and Smealy, joined 1888. St James Church has Roman bricks.

Chigwell *Cingheuuella: Ralph de Limesy. Mill.* William Penn, founder of Pennsylvania, studied in the 16th/17th-century grammar school.

Childerditch *Ciltedic/-endis: Sheriff of Surrey from the king; formerly Queen Edith; Osbern from Swein of Essex, formerly Alwen, a free woman; Sasselin.* Celebrated by Edward Thomas ('If I should ever by chance grow rich/I'll buy Codham, Cockridden and Childerditch').

Chingford *Cing(h)efort: Canons of St Paul's before and after 1066; Ordgar from Robert Gernon. 6 fisheries, mill.* London borough, near Epping Forest; Forest Museum. Queen Elizabeth I's hunting lodge is nearby.

Chipping Ongar *Angra (Ongar): Count Eustace.* Small town. Livingstone lived here before going to Africa.

Chiswick *Ceseuuic: Robert de Tosny.*

Chrishall *Cristeshala: Count Eustace. 4 beehives. 24 goats.* Highest village in Essex; moated earthwork.

Clacton *Clachintuna: Bishop of London before and after 1066. Fishery, mills.* Now 2 villages, Great and Little Clacton. Great Clacton had medieval market; Saxon graves; Roman-tiled Norman church. There is a Norman church in Little Clacton.

Claret Hall *Clare: Count Eustace. Mill. 3 cobs, 239 sheep.* Manor house.

Clavering *Clauelinga: Swein of Essex; Ansgot, Wicard, Robert and Ralph from Swein of Essex. Mill, 5 beehives. Foal, 23 goats.* Sail-less windmill. Robert FitzWinarc, a Frenchman, built his pre-Conquest castle here; the moats survive.

Cliff *Cliva: Roger de Raismes.*

Coggeshall *Cogheshale/-essala: Holy Trinity; Count Eustace; Theodoric Pontel. 2 mills, 4 beehives. 4 cobs.* Probably Roman; famous for cloth making in the Middle Ages; Roman-bricked Norman church. There is a watermill near Little Coggeshall Abbey.

Colchester *Colecastro/-cestra: Bishop of London; King's land; Count Eustace; John FitzWaleran; king's burgesses; the Abbot of St Edmund's; Eudo the Steward; Hugh de Montfort; Roger de Poitou; Count Eustace; Abbot of Westminster; Geoffrey de Mandeville; Swein of Essex; Abbess of Barking; Aubrey de Vere; Bishop Walkelin. 400 houses, 2 churches (including St Peter's), 4 mills, court. 4 sesters of honey.* Britain's oldest recorded town. Roman High Street; keep of a Norman Castle; University of Essex. From the fortified Iron Age settlement here Cunobelin (Shakespeare's Cymbeline) ruled the whole of southwest Britain.

Cold Norton *Nortuna: Ralph Baynard. Mill. 6 cobs.*

Colne, Earls, Wakes and White *Coles/Colun: St Edmund's Abbey; Robert from Count Eustace; Wulfwin, 2 of his nephews and Leofric from Richard FitzGilbert; Aubrey de Vere; Robert Malet; Lutting; Wulfric claims from Richard FitzGilbert; Thorbern, 5 mills, 3 beehives. 45 cattle, 160 sheep, 80 goats, 4 cobs, 6 asses, 20 mares.* Now 2 villages, Earls and Wakes Colne, and White Colne hamlet. The de Veres founded a Benedictine priory in Earls Colne in about 1100.

Colne Engaine *Parva Colun: Man-at-arms from Walter the Deacon; Walter from Robert Malet. 2 mills, 3 beehives. 13 goats.* Roman-tiled church.

Copford *Copeforda: Bishop of London.* Roman ford, 800-year-old wall paintings in Roman-tiled Norman church.

Cornish Hall, formerly Norton *Nortuna: Brictric claims from Mascerel.*

Corringham *Currincham: William from Bishop of London. Mill.* Norman church.

Coupals, formerly Chelveston *Celeuestuna: 5 freemen from Richard FitzGilbert; 6 freemen claim from Baynard.* Coupal's Farm.

Cowbridge *Cubrigea: William from Ranulf, brother of Ilger.*

Cranham, formerly Bishop's Ockenden *Craohu: Hugh from Bishop of London; Hugh from Bishop of Bayeux.*

Crawley(bury) *Crauuelaea: Roger from Count Eustace.* Also called Crawley End, in the rural district of Saffron Walden.

Cray's Hill *Winthelle: Sasselin.* Part of Billericay; formerly Ramsden Crays.

Creeksea *Criccheseia: Swein, Pointel and Modwin from Bishop of Bayeux.* Also called Cricksea, or Crixeth, meaning landing place in the creek. Elizabethan house; caravan camp.

Crepping *Crepinga/-inges: Modwin; Alfward claims from Richard FitzGilbert.* Crepping Hall, a manor house.

Culverts *Richeham: Azo from Robert Gernon. Mill.* Culverts Farm.

Curling Tye Green *Curlai: Pointel from Ralph Baynard.*

Cuton *Keuentuna: Osbert from Geoffrey de Mandeville. Mill, 5 beehives. 14 goats.* Cuton Hall, a manor house.

Danbury *Danengeberia: William from Geoffrey de Mandeville.* Originally Daningbury, a fortified Danish settlement; Tudor house.

Debden (near Newport) *Deppedana: Ranulf Peverel. Mill, vines, 3 beehives. 7 cobs, 2 foals, 168 sheep, 1000 pigs..* Idyllic; old houses, farms; Peverel wood.

Debden (Green) (in Loughton) *Tippedana: Canons of Waltham before and after 1066.* In Chigwell.

Dedham: See page 98.

Dengie *Daneseia: St Valery; Bishop of Bayeux.* Church with Roman bricks. The peninsula between the Blackwater and Crouch rivers is called the 'Island of Dene's people'.

'Derleigh' *Der(e)leia: Roger from Ranulf, brother of Ilger; Modwin.*

Dickley *Dicheleia: Nigel from Robert Gernon.*

Doddinghurst *Doddenhenc: Gerard from Robert FitzCorbucion.* Old stocks on the common; tiny Tudor house.

DUNMOW: *Carved chair for the winner of the 'Flitch'.*

Dovercourt *Druvrecurt: Aubrey de Vere.* Port (with Harwich) for Continent.

Down (Hall) *Dona/Duna: Richard from Eudo the Steward; Ranulf Peverel and Ascelin from him. 159 sheep.* Downham, originally the home of the Selwins, now a girls' boarding school. Matthew Prior, diplomat and poet, lived here in the 18th century.

Dunmow *Dommauua: Adelulf de Marck from Count Eustace; Wulfbert from William de Warenne; Edmer from Swein of Essex; Ralph from Eudo the Steward; Serlo from Hamo the Steward; Ralph Baynard; Geoffrey de Mandeville and Martel and William from him, formerly Aethelgyth a free woman. 3 mills, 20 beehives. 65 goats, 11 cobs, 21 cattle.* Great Dunmow, a town, and Little Dunmow, a village nearby. Little Dunmow is famous for presenting a 'flitch of bacon' to any married couple who swear they have not regretted their marriage within the past year.

Dunton *Dantuna: Bishop of Bayeux.* Disused Victorian church in Basildon.

East Donyland *Dunilanda/Dunulanda: Count Eustace; Robert from Count Eustace; Modwin; Ilbod; Hagebern.* Old; includes hamlet of Rowhedge; attractive, neglected fishermen's quayside.

East Ham *Hame: St Peter's Westminster; Robert Gernon. 4 cobs.* Part of Greater London.

Easthorpe *Estorp: Hugh from Count Eustace.* Now joined with Copford; small, Norman Roman-tiled church.

East Mersea: See page 99.

Easton *E(i)stanes: William de Warenne, formerly Dove, a free woman; Richard from Geoffrey de Mandeville; Walter the Deacon; Matthew de Mortagne. 2 mills, 9 beehives. 23 cattle, 24 goats.* Now 2 villages, Great and Little Easton. Remains of a motte and bailey castle at Great Easton; Easton Lodge in Little Easton.

Eastwood *Estuuda/Nestuda: Swein of Essex and Robert from him. Mill. 2 foals.* On the edge of Stansted airport; Norman church.

Eiland *Eiland: Swein of Essex. 2 mills.*

Elmdon *Elmerduna: Roger de Sommery from Count Eustace. 288 sheep.* On a hillside. The moated mound of Roger de Sommery's castle is in the adjoining wood.

Elmdon Lee, formerly Leebury *Lea: Roger from Count Eustace.*

Elmstead *Almesteda/Elmesteda: Siric from Swein of Essex. Mill, salt-house, 2 beehives. 80 goats, 5 cobs, 190 sheep.* Medieval hall; Roman-tiled Norman church.

Elsenham *Alenham/Elsenham: Peter from Robert Gernon; John, nephew of Waleran. Mill. Calf.* Roman-tiled Norman church.

Emanuel Wood *Monehala/Munehala: Hervey from Count Alan; Germund from Geoffrey de Mandeville.*

Epping *Ep(p)inga/inges: Canons of Waltham before and after 1066; Osbern from Count Alan; 2 free men from Ranulf, brother of Ilger.* Market town; its name means 'the people on the upland'. The old church lies in rural Epping Upland. Epping Forest was originally called Waltham Forest.

Fairstead *Fairsteda: Thorold from Ranulf Peverel. Mill, 3 beehives.* Remote; Roman-bricked Norman church.

Fanton *Fantune/Phantuna: Westminster Abbey before and after 1066; Barking Abbey.* Fanton Hall.

Farnham *Phern(e)ham: Serlo from Hamo the Steward; Robert Gernon; 4 freemen claim from 4 men-at-arms who held from Geoffrey de Mandeville: 1 freeman claims from Ralph Latimer. 3 beehives. 39 goats, 150 pigs.* Walker's Farmhouse.

Faulkbourne *Falcheburna: Ralph from Hamo the Steward.* Norman church; famous castellated brick house beside the 'falcon stream'.

Feering *Ferigens/-ingas/Pheringas: Westminster Abbey and Roger de Raismes from the Abbey; Westminster Abbey claims from Hugh de Montfort. 3 mills, 2 houses in Colchester. 5 cobs, 16 cattle.* Rye Mill; gabled rectory where the painter John Constable stayed.

Felste(a)d *Felesteda/-stede/Phensteda: Holy Trinity Abbey, Caen; Roger God-save-Ladies; Gilbert FitzSolomon. 2 mills. 21 cattle, 200 pigs, 30 goats.* Large Norman church. Cromwell's sons studied in the public school here.

Finchingfield *Fincing(h)efelda/Phincing(h)efelda: Otto the Goldsmith, formerly Queen Edith; Guy from Count Eustace; Count Alan and Hervey from him; Elinant, Arnold, 2 men-at-arms and 11 freemen from Richard FitzGilbert. 2 mills. 25 cattle.* Pond; windmill. Wethersfield air base is nearby.

Fingrith *Phingheria: King's land. 1000 pigs.* Fingrith Hall.

Fobbing *Phobinge: Count Eustace. Fishery.* On hill overlooking marshes; Saxon church; 15th-century Lion Inn.

Fordham *For(de)ham: William de Warenne; Wulmer from Richard FitzGilbert; Tovild claims from Richard FitzGilbert; Geoffrey from Hugh de Gournai. Mill, 6 beehives. 25 goats.* Roman-bricked church; medieval Hall.

Fouchers *Ginga: 'W' from Ranulf, brother of Ilger; formerly 2 girls.*

Foulton *Fuletuna: Odard from Swein of Essex; Gerard from Robert FitzCorbucion. 2 beehives.*

GREAT STAMBRIDGE: *Stained glass window in the Saxon church.*

Foxearth *Foscearde: 19 freemen from Richard FitzGilbert.* Moated 15th-century hall, now a farmhouse; 16th-century cottage, now a post office.

Frating *Frat-/Fretinga: Count Eustace; Thorold from Ranulf Peverel. 6 beehives. 2 cows.* Anglo-Saxon church.

Frinton *Frie(n)tuna: Ralph de Marcy from Count Eustace; Rainalm from Geoffrey de Mandeville.* Seaside resort. First telephone cable to a lighthouse at sea was laid here in 1893.

Fristling *Festinges: Barking Abbey.*

Frowick *Froruuica: Count Eustace.*

Fryerning and Ingatestone *Inga: Robert Gernon and Ilger and William from him; Battle Abbey. 2 beehives. 5 cobs, 2 calves.* Town. Off London–Chelmsford Roman road; magnificent red-towered, Roman-tiled Norman church.

Fyfield *Altera Fifhida/Fifhida: Iwain from Count Eustace; Roger from John FitzWaleran. Mill, beehive.* Winding, with willow-shaded River Roding; 13th-century hall; Roman-tiled Norman church.

Gestingthorpe *Ghestingetorp/ Glestingethorp: William Peche from Richard FitzGilbert; Otto the Goldsmith.* Roman-bricked Norman church. Captain Oates, who died trying to save others in Scott's 1912 Antarctic expedition, was born here.

Goldhanger *Goldhangra: Adelulf from Count Eustace; Hugh FitzMauger from Hugh de Montford; Richard from Ranulf Peverel. 1½ salt-houses. Cow.* Norman, Roman-bricked church. A wheel-turned pump is still in use.

Goldingham *Goldingham: Hubert from Robert Malet. 5 beehives. 260 sheep.* Goldingham Hall, a manor house.

Good Easter *Estra: Canons of St Martins, London. Mill.*

Great Baddow *Baduuen: Holy Trinity Abbey, Caen; Roger God-save-ladies. Foal, 13 goats.* Stone Age and Bronze Age remains; Roman tiles in the church.

Great Bentley *Benetle(i)a: Aubrey de Vere. Salt-house. 100 sheep, 3 cows, 26 cattle.*

Great Braxted *Brac(c)hesteda/ eda: Richard from Eudo the Steward; Guthmund from Hamo the Steward. ½ mill, 4 beehives.* Park.

Great Bromley *Brumhele(i)a: Ralph Pinel.*

Great Burstead *Burghesteda: Bishop of Bayeux.* Attractive.

GREAT CHESTERFORD: *An ancient timbered cottage.*

Great Chesterford *Cestreforde: Picot the Sheriff in the king's hand. 2 mills.* Remains of Belgic settlement; Roman fort and town.

Great Maplestead *Maplesteda/ Mappesteda: Ilger from Robert Gernon. 2 beehives. 23 goats.* Church, probably Saxon.

Great Oakley *Accleia/Adem: Robert Gernon; Mill, 2 salt-houses. 4 cobs.*

Great Saling *Salinges: Thurstan from John FitzWaleran; Algar from Richard FitzGilbert.*

Great Sampford *Sanforda: Godric the Steward in the king's hand. Mill.* Separated from Little Sampford by a row of pylons.

Great Slam(p)seys *Slamonesheia: Roger from Bishop of London.*

Great Stambridge *Stanbruge: Swein from Bishop of Bayeux and Wicard from him. Mill.* Saxon church. The ancient tide mill was burned down in 1965.

Great Wakering *Wachelinga: Swein of Essex. 4 cobs.* Farming.

Great Whitmans *Witham: Ansketel from Robert Gernon.*

Greenstead (near Colchester) *Grenesteda: King's land; Count Eustace; John FitzWaleran. 2 houses, mill. 40 goats.* In the Borough of Colchester. The church was in the centre of the Parliamentarian fort during the siege of 1648.

Greensted-juxta-Ongar *Gernesteda: Hamo the Steward. Mill.* Famous wooden Saxon church in which King Edmund's body rested (1013) en route to Bury St Edmunds.

Hadstock *Cadenham: Ely Abbey before and after 1066.* Late Saxon church; timber-framed manor house.

Hallingbury *Halingeb(er)ia/-heberia/Hallingeberia: Bishop of London; Walter from Swein of Essex; Roger d'Auberville; Martel and Hugh from Geoffrey de Mandeville. 2 mills, 10 beehives. 2 foals, 32 goats.* Now 2 villages, Great and Little Hallingbury. Hallingbury Place, a thatched cottage in Great Hallingbury, was the home of William Parker, Baron Morley, who discovered the Gunpowder Plot. Wallbury Camp, an Iron Age settlement is in Little Hallingbury.

Halstead *Hal(te)steda: William de Warenne; 22 freemen from Richard FitzGilbert; Wulfwin claims from Waleran; a freeman claims from Alfred who held it from Richard FitzGilbert. 3 mills, 2 beehives.* Town. Remains of a 'smock' windmill on the site of 13th-century 'Cheeping' market. Stansted Hall was the home of the Bourchier family, including Thomas, the 15th-century cardinal who crowned Edward IV, Richard III and Henry VII.

Hanningfield *Haningefelda: Ralph FitzThorold from Bishop of Bayeux; Wulfbert and Ranulf from William de Warenne; Berengar from Ralph Baynard; Ranulf from Robert FitzCorbucion.* Now 3 villages, East, South and West Hanningfield.

Harlow *Herlaua: St Edmund's Abbey before and after 1066; Geoffrey from Count Eustace; Thorgils from Eudo the Steward; Richard from Ranulf, brother of Ilger. Mill, 7 beehives. 8 cobs, 43 cattle, 3 foals.* New Town, adjacent to the medieval clothing-town. Market; sports centre.

Hassenbrook *Hasing(h)ebroc: FitzThorold from Bishop of Bayeux; Thorold from Swein of Essex.* Hassenbrook Hall.

Hatfield Broad Oak: See page 97.

Hatfield Peverel *Ha(d)felda: Bishop of Bayeux; Ranulf Peverel and Serlo, Arnulf and Richard from him. 5 men-at-arms. 2 mills. 5 cobs, 4 foals, 5 cows, 7 calves, 20 goats.* The church is the nave of an ancient priory church founded by Ranulf Peverel.

Havering-atte-Bower *Hauelingas/Haueringas: King's land; Westminster Abbey. Mill. 160 pigs, 269 sheep.* Havering Park; manor house.

Hawkwell *Hac(he)uuella/ Hechuuella: Godfrey from Swein of Essex; Pirot from Eudo the Steward; Eudo the Steward. 4 beehives. 6 cobs.*

Hazeleigh *Halesheia/Halesleia: Serlo and Godric from Ranulf Peverel. 4 cows.*

Helions Bumpstead *Bumesteda/ Bunsteda: Aethelhelm from Aubrey de Vere; Edwy a freeman, claims from Robert Blunt. 5 beehives. Foal, 5 cobs, 40 goats.* Elizabethan manor house, Boblow Hall.

Hempstead *Hansteda: Robert de Vatteville from Richard FitzGilbert.* Dick Turpin, highwayman, was born at the 17th-century inn. William Harvey, discoverer of blood circulation, is buried in the church.

Henham *Henham: Ralph Baynard; formerly Aethelgyth, a free woman; 2 freemen claim from Ralph Baynard. 10 beehives. 8 cobs.* Broad green; long, moat-like pond.

Henny *Hanies/Heni(es): Thorold from Ranulf Peverel; Roger from John FitzWaleran; Robert de Vaux from Roger Bigot. Mill, 3 beehives, 5 cobs, 9 cows with calves.* Now the hamlet of Great Henny, and locality of Little Henny.

Heybridge (formerly Tidwoldington) *Tidwoldituna: Canons of St Paul's before and after 1066. Mill, salt-house, 3 beehives, 150 sheep.* Part of the borough of Maldon; Roman-bricked Norman church.

Higham (Hill) *Hecham: Peter de Valognes. 2 beehives, 15 cattle, 1 ox.*

High Easter *Estre: Geoffrey de Mandeville. 17 beehives.* Roman-bricked church.

Hockley *Hacheleia/Hocheleia: Barking Abbey before and after 1066; Goldbold, Odo and Payne from Swein of Essex. 3 mills, 10 beehives. 4 cobs, 300 sheep, 53 goats.* London suburb; church where Roman coins were found.

Holland *Ho(i)landa: Adelulf from Count Eustace; Leofstan from Walter de Douai.* Now the village of Great Holland, and Holland-on-Sea, part of Clacton.

Horndon *Tor(n)induna: Bishop of Bayeux; Siric from Swein of Essex; Drogo from William Peverel. 5 cows.* Now the hamlet of East Horndon, and West Horndon, absorbed in Ingrave. Anne Boleyn's head is said to lie in East Horndon church.

Horndon-on-the-Hill *Hornindune: William from Bishop of London; Warner from Count Eustace; Payne from Swein of Essex; Hugh de St Quentin; Edmund son of Algot; Godwin Woodhen holds land Hugh de St Quentin held from the king; the king claims from Godwin Woodhen.* Overlooking the Thames estuary.

Horseham *Ersham, Hers(h)am: Battle Abbey; Aethelhelm from Aubrey de Vere; Widelard from Richard FitzGilbert; Widelard from the king. 3 beehives.* Horseham Hall.

Housham *Ouesham: Richard from William de Warenne; Roger from Ralph de Tosny. 3 beehives. Calf.* Now Housham Tye.

Howbridge *Hobruge: FitzBrian from Bishop of London; Richard from Robert Gernon. Mill. 24 goats.*

Howe *Weninchou/Weninghou: Germund from Richard FitzGilbert. 32 goats.* The Howe, a manor house near Halsted.

Hunt's Hall, formerly Pooley *Polheia: William de Warenne. Mill, 2 beehives.* Manor house.

Hutton *Atahoi: Battle Abbey. 4 beehives. 3 cobs, 19 cattle, 92 pigs.* Suburb of Brentwood.

Ilford *Ilefort: Jocelyn Lorimer. Mill, fishery.* London borough; photographic industry; paper mill.

Iltney *Altenai/Eltenai: Count Eustace; Ralph from Swein of Essex.* Iltney Farm.

Ingrave *Inga: FitzThorold from Bishop of Bayeux; Serlo from Ranulf Peverel; 'W' from Ranulf, brother of Ilger. 3 beehives.* Merged with West Horndon. Thorndon Hall was the home of the 9th Earl of Petre.

Jacques Hall, formerly Manston *Manestuna: Roger de Raismes. Salt-house.* Ja(c)ques Bay, near Wrabness.

Kelvedon *Chelleuadana/-euedana: Westminster Abbey; William FitzGross from Hugh de Montfort. 2 mills. 140 sheep.* Large; on the site of a Belgic village and Roman settlement; Norman church with Roman bricks.

Kelvedon Hatch *Kal-/ Kelenduna: Westminster Abbey; Herbert's nephew from Bishop of Bayeux; Ralph from Hamo the Steward. Mill.* Woodland area; 3 old parks including Kelvedon Hall's. 'Hatch' means 'forest gate'.

Kenningtons *Helituna/ Kelituna: Wulfbert from William de Warenne; Leofstan from Swein of Essex.*

Laindon *Legendunda/Leiendina: Bishop of London, formerly Aelfthryth, a woman; Ralph from Bishop of London.* Part of Basildon.

Lamarsh *Lamers: Ranulf Peverel and Thorold from him; 8 freemen from Thorold. 6 beehives. 7 cobs, 5 foals, 10 cows, 8 calves, 60 goats.* Church with round towers, one of only 3 known to have been built by Normans.

Lambourne *Lamburna: David from Count Eustace.* At edge of ancient forest of Hainault. Elizabethan Lambourne Hall.

Langdon *Langenduna: Walter from Swein of Essex.* Langdon Hills, above Basildon.

Langenhoe *Langhou: Count Eustace. Mill, salt-house.* Merged with the village of Abberton in 1962.

Langford *Langefort/ Langheforda: Geoffrey from Ralph Baynard. Mill.* Mill; Saxon church.

Langham *Laianhagam: Walter Tirel from Richard FitzGilbert. 2 mills. 200 sheep, 80 goats, 22 cattle, 80 pigs.* Constable painted here.

Lashley *Lacelea: Grim claims from Arnold who holds from Richard FitzGilbert.* Lashley Hall.

Latchingdon *Lac(h)enduna/ Lachentuna/Lessenduna: King's land; Holy Trinity, Canterbury; Humphrey and Wulmer from Hugh de Montfort; Wulfeva wife of Finn. 245 sheep.*

Latton *Lattuna: St Edmund's Hall; Adelulf from Count Eustace; Thorgils from Peter de Valognes. Church.* Part of Harlow New Town; medieval church with Roman, Saxon and Norman bricks.

Laver *Laghefara: Count Eustace and Richard from him; Roger from Ralph de Tosny.* Now 3 hamlets, High, Little and Magdalen Laver. John Locke the publisher had a library of 4000 books at High Laver in the late 17th century; Roman remains were found at Little Laver.

Lawford *Laleforda/Leleforda: King's land; Peter de Valognes; Roger de Raismes; Richard FitzGilbert; Waleran from the king, and Bishop of Bayeux and Ralph FitzThorold from him; Ranulf, Hugh de Montfort, Ralph Baynard, Eudo the Steward, Roger, Walter the Deacon and Adelulf from Count Eustace. 2 mills.* Merged with Manningtree; Lawford Hall, an Elizabethan mansion.

Lawling *Lalinga/inge: Holy Trinity, Canterbury; Richard from Eudo the Steward; Ranulf Peverel; 'W' from Robert FitzCorbucion; 3 freemen claim from Monks of Canterbury. Mill, fishery.*

Lawn Hall *Laghenberia: Ralph from Bishop of Bayeux.* Manor house.

Layer *Legra: King's land; Roger from Bishop of London, formerly a free woman; Count Eustace; Hugh de Montfort; Thorold from Ranulf Peverel; Sasselin; Modwin. 2 mills, salt-house, 10 beehives. 7 cows, 5 calves, 3 cobs.* Now 2 villages, Breton and de la Haye Layer, and a hamlet, Marnay Layer. Marney Hall was the home of the Marney family, of whom the 1st Lord was Keeper of the Privy Seal to Henry VIII.

Lee (Chapel) *Lea: Canons of St Paul's.* Name derives from long-gone medieval chapel.

Leigh *Legra: Ranulf Peverel. 4 cows, 5 calves.* Leigh-on-Sea. Fishing; coastal resort.

Leighs *Leg(r)a: Richard from Eudo the Steward; 'W' from Geoffrey de Mandeville. 2 mills. 11 goats.* Now Great Leighs village and Little Leighs hamlet. Great Leighs church is one of 6 in Essex with a round tower. Little Leighs Priory, now ruined, was given to Lord Rich after the Dissolution in 1536.

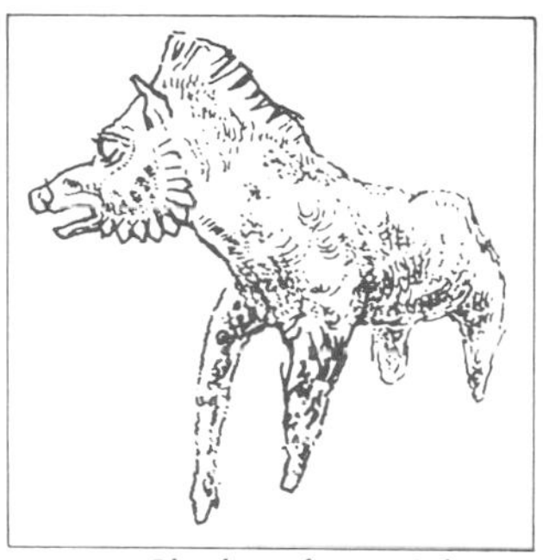

LEXDEN: *Clay boar from a Celtic burial mound, c.* AD *100.*

Lexden *Lessendena/Lexsendena: King's land; burgesses of Colchester claim from the Colchester holders.* Colchester suburb; gravegoods found here might derive from Cunobelin (Cymbeline).

Lindsell *Linesela/-seles; St Valery; Eudo the Steward. Mill, 5 beehives.* Secluded; delightful small church.

Liston *Listuna: Geoffrey Talbot from Hugh de Gournai; Ilbod. Mill, 8 beehives. 3 cows with calves.* White-boarded mill house near Milford Roman villa site.

Little Baddow *Baduuer: Lambert from Count Eustace; Germund from Ralph Baynard. Mill. 10 cobs, 53 cattle, 163 sheep.*

Little Bentley *Benetle(i)a: Hervey of Spain from Count Alan; Roger from Richard FitzGilbert.* Ruins of Little Bentley Hall.

Little Braxted *Brac(c)hesteda/ teda: Hugolin from Bishop of London. Mill.* Tudor Braxted Hall with watermill.

Little Bromley *Brumbele(i)a: Roger from Richard FitzGilbert; man-at-arms from Walter the Deacon. 2 beehives.*

Little Burstead *Burghesteda: Walter from Bishop of London.*

Littlebury *Litelbyria: Ely Abbey before and after 1066. 5 mills, 5 beehives.* Nestles in ancient Granta valley route; mill house.

MALDEN: *Boat basin at the head of Blackwater estuary. Beeliegh Abbey is nearby.*

Little Chesterford *Cestreforda/-e, Cestrefort: Man-at-arms from Walter the Deacon; formerly Queen Edith. Mill. 23 goats.* 13th-century manor house.

Little Maplestead *Maple/ Mappesteda: Osmund from John FitzWaleran. Mill. 2 cows.* Church, one of 5 round churches built in England by the Knights Hospitalers.

Little Oakley *Accleia/Aclem: Germund from Ralph Baynard. Fishery.*

Little Sampford *Sanforda: Richard FitzGilbert. Beehive.*

Little Stambridge *Stanbruge: Ralph Barnard from Holy Trinity, Canterbury.* Tudor hall on the site of a lost village.

Littlethorpe *Torpeia: Odo from Swein of Essex. 2 beehives. 160 sheep.*

Little Thurrock *T(h)urrucca: Ansketel from Bishop of London; in the king's hand. Fishery.* Nearby Hangman's Wood contains 72 pits known as Dane holes.

Little Wakering *Wachelinga: Swein of Essex. Beehive.* Church with pillory.

Loughton *Lochetuna/-intuna: Canons of Waltham before and after 1066; 'W' Corbun from Robert Gernon; Ralph from Peter de Valognes; Peter de Valognes. Mill.* Suburban town on the edge of Epping Forest. Made famous by the 19th-century fight of Thomas Willingale for the people's rights to the freedom of the forest.

Maldon *Malduna/Meldona/-una: Ranulf Peverel; Hugh de Montfort from the king; King's land; Canons of St Martin's, London from Count Eustace; Gunner from Swein of Essex: Ranulf Peverel. 180 houses, mill. 336 sheep, 12 cobs, 140 cattle, 103 pigs, 3 cows, 4 calves.* Ancient town. *The Battle of Maldon*, a 10th-century Anglo-Saxon poem, records the heroic stand here in 991 by Essex militia against Viking invaders.

Manuden *Magellana/ Magghedana/Menghedana. Robert Gernon and 4 men-at-arms from him; Amalfrid from Ralph Baynard; Aubrey de Vere. Foal.* Saxon church where Sir William Waad, 17th-century diplomat and Raleigh's jailer, is buried.

Margaretting and Mountnessing *Ginga: King's land; Ranulf, brother of Ilger, William de Bosc from Ranulf, brother of Ilger; Matthew de Montagne.* Killigrews, a moated Tudor house.

Markshall *Mercheshala: Nigel from Hugh de Montfort. 3 beehives.*

Marks Tey *Teia: Geoffrey de Mandeville. 2 beehives. 6 calves.* Church built of Roman bricks.

Mashbury *Masceberia, Massebirig: Edwin from Geoffrey de Mandeville; Geoffrey de Mandeville, formerly Aelfeva, a free woman.* Lonely; Norman church built of Roman bricks.

Matching *Matcinga/-inge/ Metcinga: St Valery; Geoffrey de Mandeville; Hugh from Robert Gernon; Edmund son of Algot. 2 beehives.* Regency fishing-lodge.

Messing *Metcinges: Bernard from Ralph Baynard; Roger de Raismes. Mill. 35 goats, 2 cows with calves.* Roman-tiled Norman church.

Michaelstow *Michelestou: Bernard from Ralph Baynard.* Michaelstow Hall, a Georgian mansion, in Ramsey.

Middleton *Milde(l)tuna: 13 freemen from Richard FitzGilbert; Gilbert the Priest; Robert Malet.* Delightful, wooded slopes.

Milton *Mildentuna: Holy Trinity, Canterbury.*

Mistley *Mitteslea: Henry's wife from Roger de Raismes.* A memorial tablet in the church to Richard Rigby, Paymaster of the Forces 1768–84, does not mention that he died leaving 'nearly half a million pounds of public money' that he had stolen.

Moreton *Mortuna: William d'Ecouis. 60 goats.* Gravel quarrying.

Moulsham (in Chelmsford) *Molesham: Westminster Abbey. Mill.* Part of Chelmsford.

Moulsham (in Great Leighs) *Alia Molesham/Melesham: Ralph from Bishop of Bayeux. Mill. 4 foals.* Moulsham Hall.

Mount Bures *Bura: Roger de Raismes; Roger de Poitou. Mill.* Belgic tomb found near church with Norman moated castle-mound.

Mountnessing *Ginga: Ranulf, brother of Ilger, and William de Bosc from him.*

Moze *Mosa: Geoffrey de Mandeville. 3 salt-houses, 3 beehives, 1 dwelling in Ipswich.* With Beaumont.

Mucking *Muc(h)inga: Barking Abbey and William from the abbey. Mill, fishery. 250 sheep.* Quaint old farms and cottages.

Mundon *Munduna. Eudo the Steward. Vines, 4 beehives.* Moated hall.

Napsted *Nepsteda: Aubrey's wife from Bishop of Bayeux.*

Navestock *Alia Nessetocha, Astoca, Nas(s)estoca: Canons of St Paul's; Ralph from Hamo the Steward. 4 beehives.* Norman church with memorials to Waldegrave family; James Waldegrave was Prime Minister for 5 days (8–12 June 1757).

Nazeing *Nasinga: Canons of Waltham before and after 1066; Odo from Ranulf, brother of Ilger, and 2 freemen from him. ½ fishery.*

Nevendon *Nezendena: Roger Marshal; Hagebern.* Nevendon Hall.

Newland *Neuuelanda: Mauger from Count Eustace.* Newland Hall, an outlying moated manor house with Tudor brick-nogging.

Newnham *Neuuham: Count Eustace.* Newnham Hall.

Newport *Neuport: King's land. 2 mills. 79 pigs.* On the Roman road to Cambridge; church with 700-year-old portable altar on which are the earliest-known English oil paintings on wood.

Newton *Niuuetuna: Hugh de Bernières from Geoffrey de Mandeville.* Newton Hall Park, in Great Dunmow.

Northey Island *Car(e)seia: Richard from Hamo the Steward; Hamo the Steward.* Island in estuary from which Viking invaders successfully fought Byrhtnoth's Anglo-Danish defence force.

North Fambridge *Fanbruge: Theodoric Pointel. 5 asses, 200 sheep.* 2 cottages beside ancient ferry; one of the county's best-kept villages.

North Weald Bassett *Walda/Walla: Ralph from Peter de Valognes; Ralph the Haunted; Richard from Ranulf, brother of Ilger. 5 beehives. 17 cattle.* Scattered between Ongar and Epping; RAF Station.

Norton Mandeville *Nortuna: Canons of St Paul's, formerly Godith, a woman; Winund from Hamo the Steward.* One of Essex's smallest (Norman) churches; Norton Manor House, near Norton Heath.

Notley *Nut(h)lea: Aelfric from Count Eustace; Godbold from Swein of Essex; Ralph from Hamo the Steward; Walter from Geoffrey de Mandeville; John FitzErmicion from John FitzWaleran; Sasselin; Roger Marshal. 4 mills, 10 beehives. 5 cows.* Now Black Notley, a suburb of Braintree, and White Notley, a small village, with a Roman/Saxon/Norman church.

Ockendon, North and South *Wochanduna/-e(n)duna: King's land; Westminster Abbey and William the Chamberlain from the abbey; Thorold from Geoffrey de Mandeville. Mill, beehive.* Now North Ockendon, part of London, and South Ockendon, a London suburb. One of Essex's most interesting moated hall-sites near South Ockendon church; smock windmill.

Old Hall, formerly **Sheldon** or **Sharing** *Sciddinchon: Countess Aumale.* Old Hall Marshes and Old Hall Cottages.

Ongar *Angra: Count Eustace; Roger from John FitzWaleran; Berengar from Count Eustace.* Now the town of Chipping Ongar and village of High Ongar. The moated castle in Chipping Ongar was Count Eustace's local headquarters. Henry Livingstone lived here.

Orsett *Dorseda/Orseda: Bishop of London before and after 1066; Count Eustace.* Small green and pond. Bishop Bonner's Palace, a ring-and-bailey earthwork, is the site of a former castle.

Osea Island *Vueseia: Richard from Hamo the Steward. Fishery.* Part of Great Totham.

Ovington *O(l)uituna: Roger Bigot; Brictwulf from Richard FitzGilbert.* Absorbed Blechamp St Ethelbert in 1473.

Paglesham *Pachesham: Westminster Abbey; William de Warenne; Theodoric Pointel from Ralph Baynard; Gerard from Robert FitzCorbucion; in the king's hand.* Yachting resort; Norman church with Roman bricks.

Panfield *Penfelda: St Stephen's Abbey, Caen, formerly a free woman; Robert from Richard FitzGilbert.* 17th-century Great Priory Farm is on the site of a priory belonging to St Stephen's Abbey, Caen.

Parndon *Perenduna/-induna: Barking Abbey before and after 1066; Iwain from Count Eustace; Roger from Peter de Valognes; Alfred from Ranulf, brother of Ilger. Mill, 3 beehives.* Now Great Parndon and Little Parndon, part of Harlow.

Paslow *Passefelda: Canons of Waltham before and after 1066.* Paslow Wood Common, in the rural district of Ongar.

Patching *Pacingas/-inges: Ralph from Bishop of Bayeux; Walter from Geoffrey de Mandeville; Picot from Robert Gernon. 2 mills.* Patching Hall, a mansion near Chelmsford.

Pebmarsh *Bebenhers/Peben(h)ers: 18 freemen from Richard FitzGilbert; Warengar from Roger Bigot; Leofcild from Richard FitzGilbert; Aubrey de Vere's wife.* Courtauld's 1st silk mill started here (1798). Sir Ronald Storr, Governor of Jerusalem and Judea from 1917 is buried in the church.

Peldon *Peltenduna: Odo from Swein of Essex; Thorkell from William the Deacon. Salt-house, church.* Scattered, between Colchester and Mersey Island; Norman/Tudor church.

Pentlow *Pentelauua: Ralph Baynard, formerly a free woman. Mill, 8 beehives. 3 cobs, 24 cattle.* Church with 1 of Essex's 6 round towers; mill.

Peyton *Pachenhau: Simond from William de Warenne.* Peyton House, near Bishop's Stortford.

Pinchpools *Pincepo: Sasselin.* Elizabethan Pinchpools farmhouse, in Manuden.

Pitsea *Piceseia: Wulfeva wife of Finn. Mill.* On hills above Thames marshlands.

Pledgdon Hall *Plicedana: Richard from Endo the Steward (claimed by Geoffrey de Mandeville); Richard from Geoffrey de Mandeville. 6 beehives. 200 sheep.*

Plesingho *Plesingho: Bernard from Count Eustace; the king claims from Humphrey 'Goldenbollocks'.*

PAGLESHAM: *The Sail and Plough, a weatherboarded inn.*

SAFFRON WALDEN: *Town Hall, with black and white timbering.*

Plumberow *Plumberga: Ranulf from William de Warenne; Ascelin from Swein of Essex. Mill. Foal, 23 goats.* Oak-clad.

Plunker's Green *Plumtuna: Ravenot from Ranulf Peverel.*

Prested *Peresteda: Ranulf Peverel. 2 beehives. Mare, foal.* Prested Hall.

Prittlewell *Pritteuuella: Swein of Essex. 9 beehives. 3 foals, 196 sheep, 66 goats.* Part of Southend; Roman/Saxon/Norman church; remains of a Cluniac priory.

Pudsey *Pueseia: Ascelin, John, Aelmer and Hugh from Swein of Essex. Foal.* Pudsey Hall.

Purleigh *Purlai: Count Eustace; Hugh de Montfort; Richard from Robert Gernon; Walter the Deacon. 7 cobs, 306 sheep, 23 goats.* Hilltop. Lawrence Washington, great-great-grandfather of George Washington, preached in its church.

Quendon *Kuenadana: Richard from Eudo the Steward. 17 beehives. 44 goats.* With Rickling; 100-acre deer park.

Quick(s)bury *Cuica: Richard from William de Warenne. Mill. 2 foals.* Quicksbury Farm.

Radwinter *Redeuuintra: Richard from Eudo the Steward; Demiblanc from Aubrey de Vere; Guthred from Tihel le Breton; Frodo, brother of Abbot Baldwin. 8 beehives. 18 cattle, 30 goats.* Its Old Rectory was the home of William Harrison (rector 1559–93), commentator on 16th-century morals and mores.

Rainham *Raineham/Reineham/Renaham/Reneham: Hugh from Bishop of Bayeux; Robert from Robert Gernon; Walter de Douai; Hagebern. 12 beehives.*

Ramsden Bellhouse *Ramesdana/-duna: William from Bishop of London; 2 men-at-arms from Bishop of Bayeux; Osbern from Hugh de Montfort; Robert Gernon and Ansketel from him; Humphrey from Ranulf, brother of Ilger. Mill, 4 beehives.* Called after its 13th-century holder, Richard de Belhui.

Ramsey *Rameseia: Roger from Ralph Baynard. Mill, salt-house, 8 beehives. 309 sheep.* Elegant but dilapidated post-windmill.

Rayleigh *Ragewneia/eleia: Swein of Essex; Vines, Swein's Castle.* Town with a magnificent earthwork, the motte-and-bailey castle built by Swein.

Rayne *Raines: Bishop of London before and after 1066; Alchere from Hugh de Montfort; Ralph from Hamo the Steward; Roger de Raismes. 3 mills. 10 goats.* The hall was built by Sir William Capel, ancestor of the Earls of Essex.

Rettendon *Radenduna/Ratenduna: Ely Abbey before and after 1066; Ely Abbey claims from Richard, who holds from Eudo the Steward and from Ralph FitzBrian, who holds from Ranulf Peverel.* Includes Battlesbridge.

Rickling *Richelinga: King's land.* With Quendon.

Ridgewell *Rideuuella: Count Eustace.* Granted a market in 1318 and a fair for St Lawrence, whose church still stands. The Hall, now a farmhouse, is on the site of a Norman castle.

Ridley *Retleia: Walter from Geoffrey de Mandeville.* Ridley Hall.

Rivenhall *Riuuehala/Ruenhala/-hale/Ruuuenhala: Count Eustace; formerly Queen Edith; Clarenbold from Swein of Essex; Ascelin from Robert Gernon; Roger God-save-ladies. ½ mill, 4 beehives.* Rivenhall Place (16th and 18th centuries), was the home of Kitty O'Shea, whose husband named Charles Parnell as co-respondent when he filed for divorce.

Rochford *Rochefort: Alfred from Swein of Essex. Mill. 3 cobs, 2 foals, 160 sheep.* Market town. Rochford Hall was built for Sir Robert Rich, the 2nd Earl of Warwick, in the 17th century.

Rockells, formerly **Wyggepet** *Wigghepet: Geoffrey de Mandeville. Mill.* Rockells Wood, described by Morant in 1768 as 'the joy of fox-hunters'; Rockells Farm.

Roding *Rodinges/-is/Roinges/-chinges: King's land; Ely Abbey before and after 1066; William de Vatteville and Walter from William de Warenne, formerly a free woman; Richard FitzGilbert; Thorgil from Eudo the Steward; Roger d'Auberville; Serlo from Hamo the Steward; Hugh de Bernières, Martel, Rainam and William from Geoffrey de Mandeville. Mill, beehive.* Now The Rodings (as in 'loathing'): the parish of Aylthorpe Roding, the hamlet of Berners Roding, and 4 villages, High, Leaden, Margaret and White Roding. Also Abbess Roding (page 100) and Beauchamp Roding (page 100). White Roding has a Roman-bricked Norman church.

Roth(end) *Roda: Count Alan.*

Roydon *Ruindune: Ranulf, brother of Ilger. Mill.* Nether Hall, where Sir Thomas More courted Jane Colte, his 1st wife.

Runwell *Runewella: Canons of St Paul's before and after 1066; Lambert from Count Eustace.*

Ryes, The *Sireceslea: Ralph from Hamo the Steward.* Regency house.

Saffron Walden *Waledana: Geoffrey de Mandeville. Mill, 30 beehives.* Delightful town which specialized in growing saffron crocuses in the Middle Ages. Audley End, now a magnificent example of 17th-century architecture, was built on the ruins of a monastery founded by the Mandeville family.

St Lawrence, formerly **Newland** *Niuuelanda, Niwelant: Holy Trinity, Canterbury; 'W' from Ranulf, brother of Ilger.* Sometimes called St Lawrence Newland; two ancient farms.

St Osyth *Cice/Cita: Bishop of London; Count Eustace; Thorold from Ranulf Peverel. Mill. 4 cobs, 18 goats.* Ruins of 12th-century priory.

St Peter's Chapel *Effecestra/cestre: St Valery; Wulfmer from Hugh de Montfort. Fishery, 216 sheep.* Isolated Saxon church.

ST PETER: *The Chapel, built c. 654.*

Sampsons *Samartuna: Ralph FitzThorold from Bishop of Bayeux.* Sampsons Farm.

Shalford *Celdeforda/ Esceldeforde/Scaldefort: Otto the Goldsmith from the king; formerly Queen Edith; William the Deacon; Walter Cook. Mill, 5 beehives. 20 goats, 4 cobs.* Ancient ford.

Sheering *Seeringa: Peter de Valognes. Mill, 3 beehives. Mule, ass.*

Shelley *Senleia: Reginald from Geoffrey de Mandeville.*

Shellow Bowells *Scelda/Scelga: King's land; Eudo the Steward; Lambert from Geoffrey de Mandeville; Geoffrey de Mandeville; Ely Abbey claims from William, who held it from Geoffrey de Mandeville. Beehive.*

Shenfield *Scenefelda: Roger from Count Eustace.* With Hutton in Brentwood suburbs; church in wooded arcade.

Shoebury, North and South *Essoberiam Soberia: Bishop of Bayeux; Swein of Essex and Walter from him.* Now the hamlet of North Shoebury and Shoeburyness, both part of Southend-on-Sea.

Shopland *Scopelanda: Count Eustace. 3 cobs.* Farm; row of cottages.

Shortgrove *Scortegrava/ Sortegrana: Adelulf from Count Eustace; Robert Gernon. Mill, 11 beehives.* Shortgrove Hall.

Sible Hedingham *Haingheham/ Hedingham/Hidingham: Warengar from Roger de Raismes; Roger Bigot. Mill.* Watermill; Hawkwoods Manor House.

Smallands *Sonalelant: Nigel from Robert FitzCorbucion. 2 parts of fishery. 2 foals.*

Smalton *Smaltuna: Aubrey de Vere.*

Smeetham *Smedetuna: Raines from Count Eustace.* Smeetham Hall.

Sokens, The *Aelduluesnasa: Canons of St Paul's before and after 1066. 2 mills, 2 salt-houses, 4 beehives. 22 cattle, 200 Sheep.* Now 2 villages, Kirby and Thorpe-le-Soken, and seaside town of Walton-on-the-Naze.

Southchurch *Sudcerca: Holy Trinity, Canterbury. 2 fisheries. 4 cobs, 150 sheep, 16 goats.* Satellite of Southend; 14th-century moated hall.

South Fambridge *Phenbruge: Ely Abbey claims from Reginald the Crossbowman.* Part of Ashingdon.

South Hanningfield *Haningfelda: Thorold from Bishop of Bayeux.*

Southminster *Sudmunstra: Bishop of London. 1700 sheep.*

South Weald *Walda/Welda: Canons of Waltham before and after 1066; Ralph from Robert Gernon.* Large; woods and valleys. Rochetts was the home of Nelson's Admiral Jervis, Lord St Vincent.

Springfield *Springafelda/- inghefelda: Corp from Robert Gernon; Robert from Ranulf Peverel. Mill, beehive. 2 asses, 14 cobs, 5 foals, 26 cattle.* Part of Chelmsford; Roman-bricked Norman church. Oliver Goldsmith lived here.

Stambourne *Stanburna: Hamo the Steward; Geoffrey de Mandeville; Alstran, a freeman, and 12 freemen from Hamo the Steward. Vines, 4 beehives.* Roman-bricked Norman church.

Stan(e)sgate *Stanesgata: Ralph FitzBrian from Ranulf Peverel.* Stanesgate Priory, a Cluniac monastery, of which only 1 wall remains.

Stanford Rivers *Parva Stanfort/ Stanfort: Count Eustace. Mill. 40 cattle, 233 sheep, 4 cobs.* Large church in farmyard.

Stanmer *Stantmere: Sasselin.*

Stanstead *Stanesteda: Hubert from Robert Malet. 2 mills, 8 beehives. 26 goats.* Stanstead Hall, the surviving wing of mansion probably built by Lord Parr, Earl of Essex, in the 16th century.

Stansted Mountfitchet *Stanesteda: Robert Gernon. Mill. 16 cattle, 24 goats, 5 asses.* Town. Earmarked as London's 3rd airport; ancient windmill.

Stanway *Stanewega: King's land. 3 mills. 260 sheep, 11 cobs.* Called after the 'stone-way', used by the Romans *en route* from Colchester. The Roman-bricked Norman church was a wayside chapel for pilgrims.

Stapleford Abbots *Stapleforda/- fort: St Edmunds Abbey before and after 1066; Robert Gernon and Nigel from him.*

Stapleford Tawney *Stapleforda/ -fort: Siric from Swein of Essex. Mill, 2 beehives.* Locality.

Stebbing *Stab-/Stibinga: Henry de Ferrers; Ranulf Peverel. 2 mills, vines, 5 beehives.* Traces of a Roman building beneath the green; enormous castle mound built by Ranulf Peverel.

Stebbingford *Horstedafort: Adam son of Durand Malzor.* Stebbingford House.

Steeple *Stepla: King's land; Richard from Eudo the Steward; Henry de Ferrers. 160 sheep.* In the Blackwater estuary.

Steeple Bumpstead *Bum(m)esteda: Adelulf de Marck from Count Eustace; 1 man-at-arms from Count Alan; Wulfbert from William de Warenne; 3 freemen from Richard FitzGilbert; Tihel de Breton; Leofwin and Leofmer from Richard FitzGilbert. 4 beehives, mill.* Entrenchments of ancient stronghold.

Stevington *Stauintuna/ Staumtuna/Steintuna: Hervey from Count Alan; Reginald from Aubrey de Vere; Tihel le Breton; Frodo the Abbot; Baldwin's brother. Beehives. 5 cows.* Stevington End.

Stifford *Estinfort/Stiforda/-fort: Barking Abbey; Hugh and FitzThorold from Bishop of Bayeux; Ansger Cook. Church.* Roman Samian ware was found here.

Stisted *Stiesteda: Holy Trinity, Canterbury. Mill.* The overlordship was the subject of an 11th-century trial between the monks of Canterbury and Bishop Odo, half-brother of the Conqueror.

Stow Maries *Fenna/Fenne/ Phenna: Hugh from Geoffrey de Mandeville and Hugh de Verly from him; man-at-arms from Walter the Deacon.*

Strethall *Strathala: Hugh from Ely Abbey. Mill, 2 beehives.* Saxon church.

Studley *Estoleia: King's land; Hugh de Montfort.*

Sturmer *Sturmere: Tihel de Breton. 3 beehives, mill. Foal.*

Sutton *Suttuna: Ascelin, Alfith and Roger from Swein of Essex; Theodoric Pointel. 6 beehives. 160 sheep.*

Takeley *Tacheleia: St Valéry; Eudo the Steward; Robert Gernon. ½ mill, 5 beehives. 90 goats, 600 pigs, 3 cows, 20 cattle, 103 sheep.*

Tendring *Tenderinge/-inga/-: Roger from Bishop of London; Count Eustace and Richard from him; Walter from Robert Gernon, Ranulf Peverel; Modwin. 3 beehives.*

Terling *Terlinga(s): Richard from Ranulf Peverel; Ranulf Peverel. 2 mills, 2 Colchester houses. 2 foals, 16 goats.* Working smock mill. Henry VIII had a palace here, now vanished. Terling Place is set in magnificent parkland.

Tey *Teia: Count Eustace. Mill.* Now the village of Great Tey and hamlet of Little Tey; 12th-century church at Great Tey.

Thaxted *Tachesteda: Richard FitzGilbert. Mill, 16 beehives. 4 cobs, 128 pigs, 36 cattle, 320 sheep.* Town, the original source of thatch. Known for its cutlery in the 14th and 15th centuries. Old tower mill.

Theydon Bois, Garnon and Mount *Taindena/Teidana: Robert from Swein of Essex; Eudo the Steward; Peter de Valognes; William FitzConstantine. 18 beehives, 2 mills. 3 cobs, 3 foals, 92 pigs, 157 sheep, 15 goats.* Now the 2 hamlets of Theydon Garnon and Mount, and the village of Theydon Bois with modern housing. Theydon Garnon was granted a market and fair in 1305 and Theydon Mount has a park and church.

Thorpe(hall) *Thorp: Odo from Ranulf, brother of Ilger. 4 beehives.*

Thorrington *Torinduna: Ralph from Bishop of Bayeux. Mill, salt-house.* The church is approached through a farmyard.

TOLLESBURY: *Boathouses with sail lofts.*

Thunderley *Tunreslea: Ralph from Aubrey de Vere. 5 beehives.* Thunderley Hall in Wimbish.

Thundersley *Thunreslea: Swein of Essex. 2 beehives.* The heathen God Thunor's clearing, on a precipitous hill, screened by trees.

Thurrock *Turoc(ha)/Turroc/ Turruc: Hugh and Ansketel from Bishop of Bayeux; Count d'Eu; William Peverel. 2 fisheries. 3 cobs, 683 sheep, 10 cows, 4 calves, 2 cattle.* Now the town of Grays Thurrock (sometimes called Grays) and West Thurrock an industrial area.

Tilbury *Tiliberia/Tilibiam: Ranulf from William de Warenne; Osbern and Ralph from Swein of Essex; Hunwald from Theodoric Pointel. 12 foals, 31 cattle, 260 sheep, fishery.* Now 2 villages, East and West Tilbury near the port of Tilbury.

Tilbury juxta Clare *Tiliberia: Tihel le Breton.*

Tillingham *Tillingham: Canons of St Paul's. Mill, fishery.* Belongs to the Dean and Chapter of St Paul's, possibly since the foundation of St Paul's (*c.* 604) as cathedral of East Saxons.

Tilty *Tileteia: Henry de Ferrers.* Cistercian abbey-site.

Tollesbury *Tolesberia: Barking Abbey before and after 1066; Amalfid from Count Eustace. Fishery, 3 salt-houses. 2 cobs, 10 cattle, 300 sheep.* Centre of oyster fishing, near the Blackwater estuary; Saxon/Norman church on a Roman site.

TILLINGHAM: *Town pump on the village green.*

WALTHAM ABBEY: *The Denny family tomb,* c. 16th.

Tolleshunt *Toleshunta, Tollensumte: Bishop of Bayeux; Count Eustace and Adelulf and St Martin's from him; Odo from Swein of Essex; Humphrey from Hugh de Montfort; Robert de Verly from Robert Gernon; Bernard from Ralph Baynard; Humphrey from Ranulf Peverel; Mauger from Robert FitzCorbucion; Gundwin. 13 salt-houses, 8 beehives. 560 sheep, 38 goats, 3 cobs, 2 cows, calf, 20 cattle.* Now 2 villages, Tolleshunt D'Arcy and Tolleshunt Major and hamlet of Tolleshunt Knight. The church of D'Arcy contains D'Arcy family treasure; a knight is carved in effigy in Tolleshunt Knights church. Tolleshunt Major takes its name from Mauger, the *Domesday* tenant.

Toppersfield *Topesfelda/-felde: Bernard from Count Eustace; Hamo the Steward; Ralph and 'G' from Richard FitzGilbert. 4 beehives, vines.* Old houses.

Totham *Tot(e)ham: William FitzBrian and William Bold from Bishop of London; Gunner, the pre-Conquest holder from Swein of Essex; Hugh FitzMauger from Hugh de Montfort; Richard from Hamo the Steward. 5 salt-houses. 18 goats.* Now 2 villages of Great and Little Totham.

Twinstead *Turnesteda: 18 freemen from Richard FitzGilbert.*

Ugley *Ugghelea: Ralph from Aubrey de Vere. 2 beehives. 4 cobs, 20 goats.* Charming, belying its name; original name may have been Oakley.

Uleham *Uleham: Hugh from Bishop of London.* Uleham's Farm, near Latchingdon.

Ulting *Ultinga: Gerard from Ralph Baynard. 2 mills, 2 beehives. 4 cobs.*

Upminster *Upmonstra/ Upmunstra/tre: Canons of Waltham; Mauger from Bishop of Bayeux; Walter de Douai.*

Vange *Phenge: FitzThorold from Bishop of Bayeux; Serlo from Ranulf Peverel. Fishery, mill. 270 sheep.* Until the 17th century flooding was a perennial problem; in 1620 the Government employed Dutchmen to set up stout walls.

Virley *Salcota: Robert de Verly from Robert Gernon.* With Salcott.

Wallbury *Walla: Richard FitzGilbert.* Wallbury Camp, on early Iron Age settlement, in Little Hallingbury.

Walter *Wal(c)fara: Canons of Waltham; Ralph from Bishop of Bayeux; Thorkell the Reeve. 2 beehives.* Walter Hall.

Waltham *Waldham/Waltham: Albert from St Edmund's Abbey; Lambert from Count Eustace; Geoffrey de Mandeville and Roger from him; 'W' and Ranulf from Robert FitzCorbucion. 4 mills, vines, 20 beehives. 3 cobs, 11 cows, 7 goats.* Now 2 villages. Great Waltham contains 8 hamlets, and includes the Black Chapel, a leading Essex sight; Little Waltham is across the Chelmer.

Waltham Holy Cross *Wal(t)ham: Bishop of Durham. 3 mills, 5 fisheries, 12 London houses, gate.* London district, including Waltham Abbey. Possibly the best of the 12 Eleanor crosses that marked the route of Queen Eleanor's funeral procession from Nottingham to London was built here.

Wanstead *Wenesteda: Ralph FitzBrian from Bishop of London; Mill, salt-house.* Town; includes Wanstead Flats.

Warley *War(e)leia: Humphrey from Bishop of London; Barking Abbey before and after 1066; Swein of Essex. Beehive.* Now the hamlet of Little Warley and village of Great Warley. Its ruined medieval church has been annexed by Greater London. Little Warley contains Essex Regimental Museum.

WILLINGALE: *2 Norman churches in one churchyard.*

Weeley *Wileia: Eudo the Steward. 12 beehives. 240 sheep.*

Well *Wella: Ralph and Thorold from Bishop of London.* Well Farm.

Wendens *Wendena: Richard from William de Warenne; Hugh from Robert Gernon; Amalfrid from Ralph Baynard; a freeman from Geoffrey de Mandeville. Mill. 3 foals.* Now 2 villages: Wenden Lofts, part of Elmdon, and Wendens Ambo, with a Roman-bricked Norman church.

Wennington *Wemtuna: Westminster Abbey before and after 1066.*

West Bergholt *Bercolt(a): Goding from Richard FitzGilbert; Roger de Poitou; Richard FitzGilbert. Mill.* Stone Age and Roman remains.

Westend *Westuna: Adeluf from Count Eustace; Hugh de Houdain from Roger Bigot. Mill.*

West Ham *Hame: Robert Gernon; Ranulf Peverel. 9 mills. 3 cobs, 6 cows with calves, 30 goats.* Part of Greater London; famous football club.

West Mersea *Meresai(a): St Ouen's Abbey before and after 1066. 11 cobs, 2 foals, 300 sheep.* Resort on Mersea Island.

Wethersfield *Westrefelda/ Witheresfelda: Picot from the king; Stanhard. 2 mills. 40 goats.*

Wheatley *Watele(a)a: Pointel and Osbern from Bishop of Bayeux; Walter from Swein of Essex; Swein of Essex. 2 fisheries. Cob, foal.*

Wicken (in Wicken Bonhunt) *Wica: Gilbert FitzThorold. 30 goats.*

Wickford *Wi(n)cfort: Pointel Osbern, Teher and FitzThorold from Bishop of Bayeux; William FitzOdo and Maynard from Swein of Essex; Modwin; Ilbod. 3 beehives. 3 cobs, 2 foals.*

Wickham Bishops *Wicham: Bishop of London before and after 1066. Mill.* Roman-bricked Norman church. 15th-century, moated Wickham Hall.

Wickham St Paul's *Wica, Wicham: Canons of St Paul's before and after 1066; Arnold from Richard FitzGilbert. 2 beehives.*

Widdington *Widi(n)tuna: St Valery Abbey; Robert from Robert Gernon; Ranulf Peverel.* Secluded farmlands.

Wigborough *Wi(c)gheberga: Barking Abbey before and after 1066; Vitalis from Hamo the Steward; Algar from Ranulf Peverel; Hugh de St Quentin; the king claims from Hamo the Steward. 6 salt-houses. 490 sheep, 3 cobs, 4 foals, 16 cattle.* Now the village of Great Wigborough and the area of Little Wigborough, where a Zeppelin raider crashed in 1916.

Willingale Doe and Spain *Ulinghehala/Willing(h)ehala: Hervey from Count Alan; Warner from Swein of Essex; Ravenot from Ranulf Peverel; Adam son of Durand Malzor. 5 beehives.* Once 2 villages, Willingale Doe and Willingale Spain, named after Norman lords d'Eu and d'Epaignes. Their churches stand side by side.

Wimbish *Wimbeis: Ralph Baynard, formerly a free woman. 4 beehives.* Tiptofts Farm, with its famous 14th century open hall, is still working.

Witham *Witham: Peter the Sheriff from the king; Richard from Count Eustace; Hugh from Robert Gernon; Modwin. 2 mills, 3 beehives. 150 pigs.*

Wivenhoe *Wiunhou: Nigel from Robert Gernon. Mill. 20 goats.* Quay on River Colne opposite Fingrinhoe, to which the ferry plies. Restored church.

Wix *Wica: Roger from Hugh de Montfort, formerly Queen Edith; Walter the Deacon, formerly Queen Edith. 10 beehives.* Pre-Conquest dairy farms existed here. The priory, founded in Henry I's reign was dissolved by Cardinal Wolsey.

Woodford *Wdefort: Canons of Waltham before and after 1066. Mill.*

Woodham Ferrers *Udeham: Henry de Ferrers. Mill. 28 cattle, 15 cobs, 300 sheep, 100 pigs, 35 goats.* Edwin's Hall, home of Edwin Sandys, Archbishop of York, 1619.

Woodham Mortimer *Odeham: Ranulf Peverel.* Hall where Dr Peter Chamberlain, Physician in Ordinary to James I, Charles I and Charles II, lived.

Woodham Walter *Wdeham: Pointel from Ralph Baynard, formerly Leofeva, a woman. 2 mills. 13 beehives, 6 asses.* Hoe Mill.

Woolston *Ulfelmestune: King's land.* Woolston Hall, c.1600, in Chigwell.

Wormingford *Widemondefort: Ilger from Robert Gernon. Mill, fishery, 7 beehives. 33 cattle, 200 sheep, 47 goats.* Hundreds of Roman urns were discovered here in the 19th century.

Wrabness *Wrabenasa: St Edmund's Abbey before and after 1066. Mill, salt-house, 5 beehives. 2 foals, 200 sheep.*

Writtle *Wiretala/-tela/Writa/-tela: King's land; Bishop of Hereford. 2 mills. 318 sheep, 172 pigs, 9 cobs, 5 foals, 40 cattle.* Excavations at its moated site, 'King John's Castle', revealed traces of 13th-14th- and 15th-century buildings.

Yardley *Gerdelai: Serlo from Tihel le Breton. 3 beehives.*

Yeldham *Geld(e)ham/Gerham: Count Eustace; Count Alan; Goismer from Richard FitzGilbert; Walter from Ranulf, brother of Ilger; Bernard from Richard from Richard FitzGilbert.* Now 2 villages, Great and Little Yeldham.

Gloucestershire

It was at Gloucester that King William, 'after deep speech with his wise men', ordered the Domesday *survey to be made.*

From the heavily wooded uplands of Dean, across the Vale of Severn, and thence to the Cotswolds and the upper waters of the Thames, Gloucestershire was as varied a county as any to be surveyed: the folios would also provide a unique glimpse into Wales's social system.

Economically the county ranged from iron smelting and charcoal burning in the west – the Abbot of Glastonbury's tenants at Pucklechurch rendered 90 pigs (lumps) of iron – to sheep farming on the limestone wolds in the east. By the end of the thirteenth century one-third of Winchcombe Abbey's revenue came from the sale of wool; there is documentary evidence for a fulling mill at Temple Guiting by 1185, and (in a letter from Offa to Charlemagne) for cloth manufacture much earlier.

Judging from the number of plough teams and strip terraces in the valleys, it seems certain that Gloucestershire's arable regions were even more extensive than today. Apart from the wooded Cotswold Edge and the land between the Severn and the Wye, the population was evenly spread, which suggests that most of the county was well tilled.

DEERHURST: *The square tower of one of England's few Saxon buildings rises in this tiny village.*

DEERHURST: *Remarkable stone carved capitals inside the church.*

Deerhurst

[Westminster Abbey] holds DEERHURST *DERHEST*. 59 hides. Before 1066 5 hides in the head of the manor. 3 ploughs there. 20 villagers and 8 smallholders with 10 ploughs. 6 slaves; meadow, 60 acres; woodland 2 leagues long and 1/2 league wide. The value is and was £10. These outliers belong to this manor: HARDWICKE, 5 hides; BOURTON (on the Hill), 8 hides; TODENHAM, 7 hides; SUTTON (under Brailes), 5 hides; in total 25 hides. In lordship 13 ploughs; 45 villagers and 27 smallholders with 21 ploughs. 37 slaves; 4 mills at 20s; meadow, 20 acres; woodland 1 league long and 1/2 wide; water-meadows 3 furlongs long and 1 wide. Riding men, that is, free men, held of this manor's land before 1066, who all, however, ploughed, harrowed, scythed and reaped for the lord's work. [A further list of 15 holdings follows.] Besides these (lands) Gerard the Chamberlain holds 8 hides in KEMERTON and 3 hides in BODDINGTON which have always paid tax and rendered other services in Deerhurst Hundred. But after Gerard had them, they rendered neither tax nor service. Before 1066 the whole manor gave in revenue £41 and 8 sesters of honey by the King's measure; value now £40, of which £26 belongs to the lord's manor and £14 to the men.

Deerhurst is not easy to find; there are signposts to Deerhurst Walton – in an opposite direction – and nothing that points directly to the village. Fortunately, the silver-grey tower of the church reaches above the trees and leads one to the edge of its water meadows.

The present priory was built in the fourteenth century and the path across the churchyard overlooks its rose-laden garden.

The windows in the church's south wall are filled-in doorways that led to long-vanished cloisters. These included, it has 17 doorways, no two of the same date, and few at the same level.

A pair of windows high above the west door give onto the one-time chapel in the tower. These are said to be similar to windows in the monastery of Debra Damo, in Abyssinia. In the north-west corner stands a font (rescued from a farm yard) alive with Celtic trumpet spirals; it is said to be the finest of all surviving Saxon fonts.

This is a church much treasured and cared for. Founded in the seventh century, probably the mausoleum of the rulers of Hwicce (a sub-kingdom of Mercia), Deerhurst once ruled 30,000 acres of Gloucestershire.

The priory was almost certainly past its prime when St Alphege – Bishop of Winchester at the age of 30, slaughtered by the Danes as Archbishop of Canterbury in 1012 – was a monk there. At some time after that it became two separate entities, the priory and the manor. This paved the way for Edward the Confessor to give the priory to the great house of St Denis in Paris, and the manor to his new foundation of St Peter's Westminster.

Domesday, surprisingly, does not mention the church. Though it had declined since the days when Canute and Edmund Ironside signed a peace treaty here, it was still important. Perhaps the explanation lies in the Conqueror's Ordinance of 1069: 'Let this Monastery and all belonging to it, be free from all earthly service.' Tewkesbury Abbey, which was finally to devour Deerhurst, was not so fortunate; *Domesday* itemizes all the land for which Tewkesbury Church paid tax before 1066. Whatever advantage Deerhurst Priory may have had, however, it lost once the French wars began. It was then alien, and that meant periodic reversion to the Crown and a series of levies. Although the priory had a fleeting moment of independence in the reign of Henry V, but by 1469 it had been absorbed by Tewkesbury and shared its fate at the Dissolution.

So the Norman Conquest, in confirming the division Edward the Confessor had made, foreshadowed an end and not a beginning for Deerhurst. Even by 1125 William of Malmesbury was reporting that the church was '*antiquitatis inane simulacrum*' ('an empty monument of antiquity'). Judging by the twelfth-century work in the church, he must have been referring to the priory as a whole. Two centuries later the church was still attracting fine monuments. The brasses of Sir John Cassey of Wightfield Court, Chief Baron of the Exchequer to Richard II, together with Lady Cassey and her dog, Cherry, are magnificent.

But in 1530 the village was described as 'poor and shrunken'. And Samuel Rudder, in the eighteenth century, in his *History of Gloucestershire* wrote, 'Upon the whole the church is a good figure but kept in a miserable and filthy condition. Services performed in it once every 4, 5, or 6 weeks, at uncertain times; and hence also the greater part of the inhabitants of this large parish either frequent ale houses on Sunday, idle or lie, like swine in the lanes and public highways for want of a minister to teach them their duty.'

The village has remained a backwater in more senses than one. The vagaries of the River Severn have probably kept the developers at bay; in 1947, for instance, there was a serious flood. There were fewer houses in Deerhurst in 1964 (15) than there were in 1811 (26). As for the church, its fame will help it to survive, but it is a groomed and emasculated thing compared with Saxon days, when it had multiple storeys, because the liturgies required different levels for their full performance. Reminders of these former wonders are few: sculpture like the Angel of Deerhurst in the apse belonged to a world the Normans were out to eradicate. But fortunately, Deerhurst, hidden away among its ditches and dykes, was spared.

Tetbury

Roger [d'Ivry] also holds TETBURY *TETBERIE*. 23 hides which pay tax. Siward held it before 1066. In lordship 8 ploughs; 32 villagers, 2 smallholders and 2 riding men with a priest, who between them have 14 ploughs. 19 slaves; a mill at 15d; pasture at 10s; meadow, 10 acres. Roger also holds (Tetbury) UPTON . . . Value of these two manors before 1066 £33; now they are at a revenue of £50.

Domesday gives no hint that Tetbury, today a spacious town in the southern Cotswolds, would grow to fame for its wool staple. The long seven-bay Market House standing on squat round pillars is a reminder of this. The funeral effigies of a wool stapler and his wife have been stood upright to preside over the north ambulatory of the sleek Gothic-revival church. They look rather awkward in such smart surroundings, but it was their efforts that made the town rich.

The demand for finer cloth and the absence of a good water supply led to Tetbury's decline, and by 1829 it was being described as 'uncommonly dull in consequence of the desertion of trade'. Cheese and bacon took the place of wool for a time, but because the railway arrived so late the town survived only as a county mart. Brewing, its last industry, had disappeared by the 1930s.

By then the two riding men of *Domesday* seem to have been reincarnated as two Guards officers: the Duke of Beaufort and George Whyte Melville. The Duke, in spite of his military commitments in London, never missed a hunt; and Whyte Melville, after commanding the Turkish irregular cavalry in the Crimean War, settled in Tetbury and spent the rest of his life writing and hunting. His books were immensely popular amongst those who shared his sort of life – or wished they did. He met his death when his horse, Shah, fell on him after stumbling over the plough.

Prince Charles and Princess Anne, who both have homes within a few miles of Tetbury, will no doubt help to maintain the town's equestrian reputation. Meanwhile its Snooty Fox, after a brief period as the White Hart, is now the Snooty Fox again.

Since 1970 the growth of an industrial estate has helped Tetbury come to terms with rural unemployment. Firms manufacturing earth-moving equipment, electrical circuits and automatic vending machines have put its economy on a sounder footing than at any time since the eighteenth century. It remains a town and not merely an antiques fair.

Dymock

King Edward held DYMOCK *DIMOCH*. There were 20 hides. 2 ploughs in lordship; 42 villagers, 10 smallholders and 11 freedmen who have 41 ploughs. A priest who holds 12 acres. 4 riding men with 4 ploughs. Woodland 3 leagues long and 1 wide. Before 1066 the Sheriff paid what he wished from this manor. King William held it in his lordship for 4 years. Later Earl William and his son Roger had it; the men of the County do not know how. Now it pays £21.

A moated grange selling Jøtul stoves; a bakery selling bread through the night, and an old-style garage that looks like an aircraft hangar, cruck-truss timber frames jostling with stucco for a place on the Forest road – this is today's Dymock. Newent, a few miles off, grew into a town, having been granted a market; Dymock 'attended to the living seasons', brewed its cider (Red strake), raised its sheep (Ryelands) and, when the parish register started to fall apart, bound it up with what came to hand – a sheet of eighth-century Vulgate. It is not surprising that the place bewitched the American poet Robert Frost and, in the years before 1914, the Georgian poets Rupert Brooke, Lascelles Abercrombie, Edward Thomas and Wilfred Gibson, who lived here till the war swept them away.

'King Edward held Dymock', so it was 'ancient demesne', and successfully pleaded so in 1433, when the freeholders escaped the sheriff's demand for the expenses of the knights of the shire. *Domesday*, as translated above, says that the sheriff paid what he wished for this manor, but this was not necessarily the 'open till' it appears. The *Domesday* clerk, pressed for space and time, used a shorthand that can be confusing. In this case he wrote no endings on the words for 'pay', 'sheriff' and 'wish' ('*reddeb*...' '*vicecomu*...' and '*voleb*...'). With the verbs in the plural and the sheriff in the dative, the entry would read, 'they paid the sheriff what they wished'. This makes more sense and may be an early example of tax relief for the inhabitants of ancient demesne. The sheriffs generally seem to have been a rapacious lot.

The name Dymock (or Dymoke) is probably best known in the College of Heralds, for the family have been hereditary King's Champion and Standard Bearer of England since Sir John Dymoke beat off his rival in 1377. The Champion throws down the gauntlet at the coronation, ready to do combat with any who challenge the monarch's right to ascend the throne. A Dymoke has done this at every coronation since that of Richard II, claiming for their service the horse, the saddle, the armour, the 'furniture' and 20 yards of crimson satin. When the family took the name Dymoke no one can say. It is possible that they once lived at Knight's Green, a mile from Dymock Church, and only adopted the surname when they moved away.

The Dymokes have survived splendidly; the FitzOsberns (the family name of Earl William and his son, Roger) have disappeared. William was killed in 1071 and his son was locked up for life after his rebellion against the king in 1075. Ordericus Vitalis, the Norman chronicler, says the family were lost without trace, adding 'Truly the world's glory droops and withers like the flowers of grass. It is spent and scattered like smoke.'

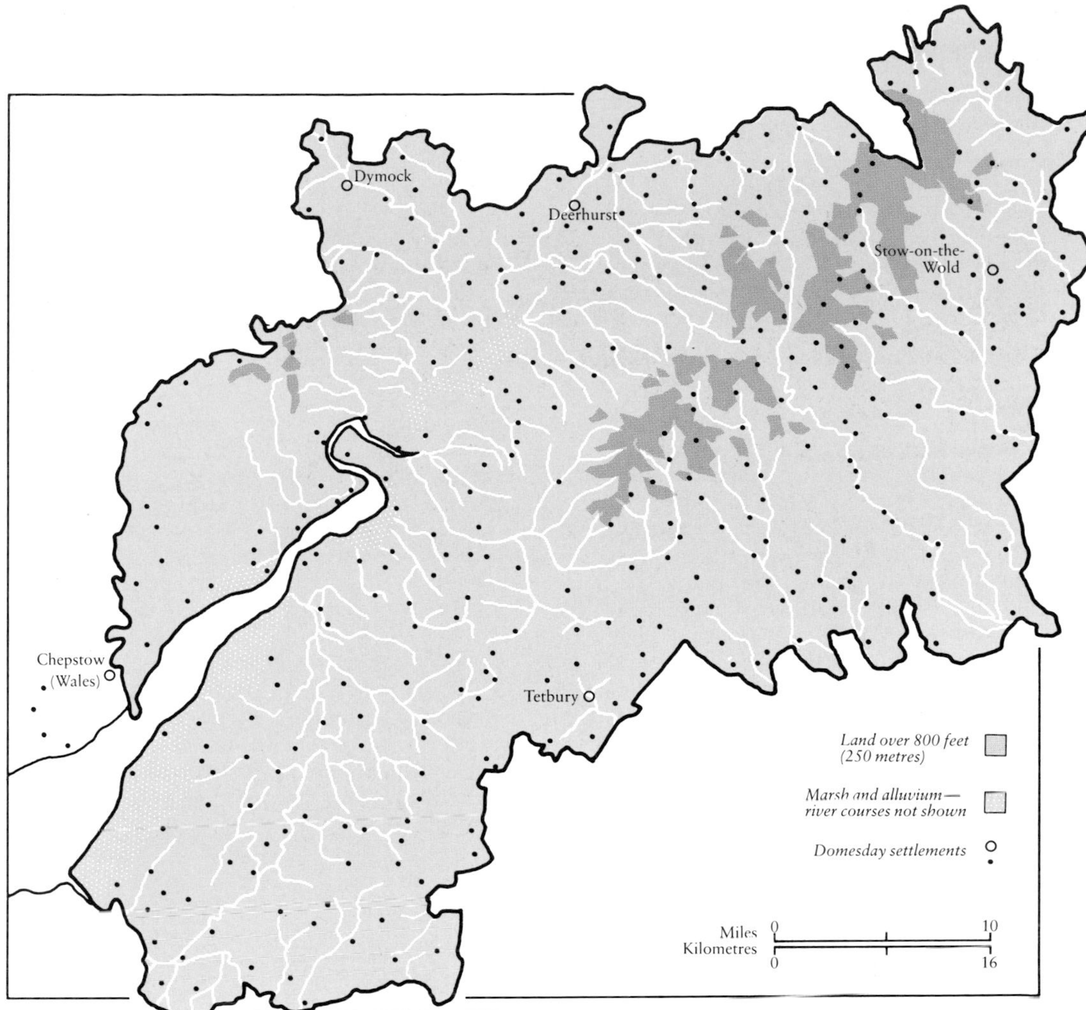

Stow-on-the-Wold

[Evesham Abbey] holds MAUGERSBURY near STOWE (ON THE WOLD) *EDUUARDESTOU*. Before 1066 there were 8 hides and a ninth hide lies near St Edward's Church. King Aethelred gave it, exempt. In lordship 3 ploughs; 12 villagers, 1 free man and a priest, who between them have 7 ploughs. 6 slaves; a mill at 8s; some meadow. Value before 1066, 100s; now £7.

Stow-on-the-Wold
Where the wind blows cold
and the cooks can't roast their dinners.

Stow-on-the-Wold has a good deal in common with Shaftesbury in Dorset, another Saxon hill-top town. Though Stow was never defended as a hill-top site, the link between the two is close. The Edward of 'Eduuardstou' is almost certainly Edward the Martyr, King of the English, whose final resting place was with the nuns at Shaftesbury. He was murdered at Corfe Castle in 978 by those who wished to see his half brother, Aethelred, made king. Whilst Aethelred cannot be held responsible for the murder, his reign suffered from its stigma and he probably granted land to the monks of Evesham for the same reason that he gave Bradford-on-Avon to the nuns of Shaftesbury: as an act of reparation.

As time went on, a market developed round the church, on the hill where the road from Tewkesbury to Oxford crosses Fosse Way, rather than at Maugersbury, just south of the town, which remains a village. The Abbot of Evesham, whose upland property this was, applied for and got, from Henry I in 1107, recognition of 'a port and market at Stow St Edwards'. Permission to hold two annual fairs followed in the reign of Edward III. By that time the canonization of Edward the Confessor had taken place and St Edward the Martyr was eased out.

Stow prospered by being at a crossroads in the Cotswolds, but what was an advantage in peace became a liability in war, and when King and Parliament took up arms, Stow was caught between them. If Parliament was to relieve Gloucester from London they were bound to go through Stow. Later in the war, Sir Jacob Astley could lead the garrison of Worcester to reinforce the king at Oxford only by moving through Stow. The ensuing battle left 200 dead in the square. Forced to surrender to the Parliamentary colonels, Astley is reputed to have said, 'You may now sit and play for you have done all your work if you fall not out amongst yourselves.'

The Chamberlaynes (of Maugersbury) and the Leighs (of Addlestrop, three miles to the east of Stow) recovered their estates after the war and remained Stow's patrons and benefactors until the twentieth century. They were distinguished families: the Leighs produced a Master of Balliol and Jane Austen, whose mother was a Leigh; and the Chamberlaynes produced John Chamberlayne, one of the first Fellows of the Royal Society (1702) and 200 years of naval officers, four of whom lost their lives in the Napoleonic wars. 'Make way for the Weights and Measures of Maugersbury', Admiral Chamberlayne shouted as he ran up the aisle at the coronation of William IV, determined to secure a seat – an appropriate cry for a town of shopkeepers.

If you board a coach anywhere in Britain, it is almost certain (as it is said of Cheltenham Spa) that you will sooner or later pass through Stow-on-the-Wold. The turnpike acts of the eighteenth century made sure that Stow never lacks visitors. At the latest count it had 34 antique shops and a delicatessen where they sell 70 different kinds of cheese.

Chepstow (Wales)

Earl William built the Castle of CHEPSTOW *ESTRIGHOIEL* and in his time paid only 40s from the ships going into the woodland. In the time of his son, Earl Roger, this town paid £16 and Ralph de Limesy had half. Now the King has £12 from it.

Roger de Berkeley holds 2 carucates of land at Chepstow and has 6 smallholders with 1 plough. Value 20s.

Roger de Lacy holds in the Chepstow holding as much populated land with 1 mill as is worth 36s.

Chepstow lay in the Welsh commote of Is Coed, but appears, with five other places later in Monmouthshire, in the *Domesday* folios for Gloucestershire. The town has none of the spaciousness of Ludlow or Monmouth, and the closing of the Aust-Chepstow ferry when the Severn Bridge opened in 1966 has left it cut off. In spite of a fine town wall, its character has been spoilt by clumsy redevelopment. But its castle, on one of Britain's most dramatic sites, remains superb. The great square keep rises from the limestone cliff above the muddy arc of the River Wye, flanked by a long and massive curtain wall. Chepstow (Old English '*ceap-stow*' = market place) is a rather feeble name for it; '*Castellu de Estrighoiel*' of *Domesday* suits it better.

The entries for Chepstow and the lands between the Usk and the Wye lack the accustomed order and fullness of the other Gloucestershire folios. Barely assimilated territory and a frequently hostile population made for a patchy survey. Welsh customs, too, were different and we read of reeves and villages rather than ploughteams and villagers. Only when carucates (not the usual hides) are mentioned do we get any idea of acreage. Even then, the carucates granted by Earl William to Ralph de Limesy in the Chepstow holding were, for want of a clear local system of measurement, '*sic fit in Normannia*' ('as is done in Normandy'); and Roger de Lacy's holding of 'as much populated land with 1 mill as is worth 36s' was vague, given the systematic measurements of most of *Domesday*. The entry for Roger de Berkeley is more in tune with other *Domesday* entries. The emphasis on river tolls – 'ships going into the woodland' – suggests that they were already worth holding.

Chepstow was to become one of the largest and most successful of the Norman boroughs on the Welsh March. It lay on the ancient road from Gloucester to Caerleon, on the right bank of one of the Wye's meanders. As both castle and town could be supplied by sea from Bristol it was a place of great strength. Its rising prosperity is reflected in the increased toll yields between the time of Earl William and his son, and in the attempts to cash in on them by William d'Eu, the successor to Ralph de Limesy. Chepstow became the property successively of the Clares (who conquered Leinster and built Tintern Abbey), the Bigods (who several times enlarged the castle), and the Herberts (whose seat was at Raglan to the north of Chepstow).

In the Civil War the Marquis of Worcester, a Herbert, held Chepstow for the king until October 1645; later Sir Nicholas Kemeys, Member of Parliament for Monmouthshire, paid for his part in its defence with his life. The castle next became a political prison. It held the saintly Jeremy Taylor, author of *Holy Living and Dying*, before the Restoration, and afterwards, Henry Marten, the unrepentant regicide, who died in the prison after 20 years, still insisting that Charles I got what he deserved.

Chepstow declined in the seventeenth century,

but became fashionable in the eighteenth with the vogue for 'doing the Wye'. Dr Egerton, the future bishop of Durham, started things when, as Rector of Ross, he had a pleasure boat built to take his friends sightseeing on the river. Thomas Gray, the poet, and William Gilpin, the painter, found nameless beauties in craggy nature on their journey down the Wye in 1770, and Gilpin's *Observations on the River Wye*, published in 1782, accelerated the craze.

In 1852 a Brunel bridge was built, and the land inside the town wall, long derelict, started to attract industry – grindstone manufacture, ship repair – but Chepstow never boomed.

The town mattered most when the FitzOsberns were thrusting into South Wales and when the Clares were taming Leinster. If it seems ineffective now, the castle still creates a fearsome atmosphere of armed might.

CHEPSTOW: *FitzOsbern's stone ruins still command the skyline, and the border Chepstow Castle was built to control.*

Gloucestershire Gazetteer
Each entry starts with the modern place name in **bold** type. The *Domesday* information that follows is in *italic* type, beginning with the name or names by which the place was known in 1086. The main landholders and undertenants are next, separated with semi-colons if a place was divided into more than one holding. A number of holdings were granted by the king to his thanes; these holders, always the last in a list, are described as holding land 'from the king'. More general information completes the *Domesday* part of the entry, including examples of dues (iron, honey, etc.) rendered by tenants. The modern or post-Domesday section is in normal type. ▦ represents a village, ▲ a small village or hamlet.

Places that were in the Gloucestershire *Domesday Book* and are now in Wales are listed at the end of the gazetteer.

Abbots Barton *Bertune: Gloucester Abbey.* Part of Gloucester.

Acton (Ilger) *Actune:* Lost.

Acton Turville *Achetone: Arnulf de Hesdin.* ▦

Adlestrop *Tedestrop: Evesham Abbey.* ▦ Humphrey Repton designed the gardens of Adlestrop Park (c.1750).

Alderley *Alrelie: Miles Crispin. Mill.* ▦

Alderton *Aldritone: Dunning from the king; a man-at-arms from Winchcombe Abbey.* ▦ Church with a broken Saxon font.

Aldsworth *Aldesorde/wrde: Gloucester Abbey, Alfward FitzReinbald from the king.* ▦ Last surviving flock of pedigree Cotswold sheep.

Alkerton *Alcrintone: Edric FitzKetel from the king. Mill.* ▦

Alkington *Almintune: King's land.* Farm.

Almondsbury *Almondesberie: King's land.* ▦ Roman entrenchments; 2 Elizabethan houses: Knole Park and Over Court.

Alveston *Alwestan: King's land, formerly Earl Harold.* ▦ Ruined church with a Saxon tympanum; Roman tumulus.

Alvington *Alwintune: Thurstan FitzRolf. Mill. 20 blooms of iron, 8 sesters of honey.* ▦

Ampney *Omenie:* Lost.

Ampney Crucis *Omenel: Thurstan FitzRolf and Baldwin from the king; Humphrey the Chamberlain. Church, mill.* ▦ Saxon church; cornmill; 15th-century cross.

Ampney St Mary *Omenie: Reinbald from the king. 2 mills.* ▦

Ampney ('St Nicholas'): *Arnulf de Hesdin.* Part of Ampney St Peter.

Ampney St Peter *Omenie: Gloucester Abbey. Mill.* ▦ Saxon church.

Arlingham *Erlingeham: King's land.* ▦

Arlington *Alvredintune: King's land. 2 mills.* Arlington Row cottages, part of Bibury. Mill, now a museum.

Ashbrook *Esbroc/Estbroce:* Lost.

Ashleworth *Esceleuuorde: King's land.* ▦ Tithe barn; 2 half-timbered houses of 1460.

Ashley *Esselie: Durand the Sheriff.* ▦

Aston Blank (Cold Aston) *Estone: Drogo from Bishop of Worcester.* ▦

Aston on Carrant *Estone: King's land; Gerard from the king.* ▦

Aston Subedge *Estune: Lambeth Church.* ▦ 17th-century manor. Famous Cotswold Games were held here.

Aust *Austreclive: Thurstan FitzRolf from Bishop of Worcester.* ▦ The start of the Severn Bridge. Important dinosaur fossils were found at Rhacklin Bed and Aust Passage.

Avening *Aveninge: King's land. 5 mills, hawk's eyrie.* ▦ Stone Age long barrows. Pubs serve 'pigs face' on 'Pigs Face Sunday' in mid-September, to commemorate a wild boar killing.

Awre *Avre: King's land. Salt-house, church, mill.* ▦ Church with Saxon mortuary chest.

Aylworth *Ailewrde/Elewrde: William Goizenboded; Walter from Gilbert FitzThorold.* ▲

Badgeworth *Beiewrde: William d'Eu. Mill.* ▦

Badminton *Madmintune: Arnulf de Hesdin.* ▦ Home of the Dukes of Beaufort since the 17th century; gave its name to a hunt and a game brought from India.

Bagendon *Benwedene: Gilbert from Hugh de Lasne. Mill.* ▦ Trinity Mill, on a Saxon site, still has machinery *in situ*. Coins were minted here in the Early Iron Age.

BARNSLEY: *Turned oak staircase in Barnsley House.*

Barnsley *Bernesleis: Durand and Eudo from Bishop of Worcester.* Barnsley Park, a 17th-century house, once housed Isaac Newton's library. In the park are the remains of a Roman villa.

Barnwood *Berneuude: Gloucester Abbey before and after 1066.* Part of Gloucester; Birthplace of Sir Edmund Saunders, beggar turned judge (17th century) and inventor Charles Wheatstone (b.1802).

'Barton Regis' *Bertune: King's land. 2 mills.* Part of Bristol.

Batsford *Beceshore: Ansfrid de Cormeilles.* Batsford Park and Lord Redesdale's Arboretum.

Baunton *Baudintone/tune: Geoffrey Orlateile; Edric FitzKetel from the king.* ▲

Bedminster *Beiminstre: King's land and Bishop of Coutances from the king. Mill.* Part of Bristol.

Berkeley *Berchelai: King's land. 2 mills, 1 market.* Small town where Double Gloucester cheese is made; birthplace of Edward Jenner (1749–1823), discoverer of vaccination. Edward II was murdered in the 11th-century castle.

Beverston *Beurestane: King's land.* ▦ 13th-century castle; 2 stone medieval barns.

Bibury *Begeberie: Bishop of Worcester. 2 mills.* ▦ Church with Saxon features; famous group of cottages: Arlington Row; 17th-century mill. Bibury Court (1635) is now an hotel.

Bishops Cleeve *Clive: Bishop of Worcester.* ▦ The old rectory (13th century) is the oldest parsonage in England.

Bishop's Norton *Nortune: Archbishop of York. Mill.* ▲

Bisley *Biselege: Robert from Earl Hugh. 5 mills. 2 sesters of honey.* ▦

Bitton *Betone: Dunn from the king.* ▦

Bledington *Bladinton: Winchcombe Abbey. Mill.* ▦

Bledisloe *Bliteslau:* Lost.

Blockley *Blochelei: Bishop of Worcester.* ▦ Northwick House.

Boddington *Botingtune/intone: Gerard the Chamberlain from Westminster Abbey and the king. Mill.* ▦ Tudor manor house.

Bourton-on-the-Hill *Bortune: Westminster Abbey.* ▲ Tithe barn; home of Sir Thomas Overbury, poisoned in the 16th century in the Tower of London.

Bourton-on-the-Water *Bortune: Robert FitzAlfred from Evesham Abbey.* ▦ On Saxon site; model village and Birdland.

Boxwell *Boxewelle: Gloucester Abbey. Mill.* ▲ Charles II came to its manor house after the Battle of Worcester.

Brawn *Brewere: Miles Crispin from the king.* Farm.

Brimpsfield *Brimesfelde: Osbern Giffard. 2 mills.* ▦

Bristol *Bristou: King's land; Bishop of Coutances. 2 mills.* Famous seaport, manufacturing centre and University city with many fine Regency buildings. The Clifton Suspension Bridge was designed in 1830.

Broadwell *Bradewelle: Evesham Abbey.* Georgian manor.

Brockworth *Brocowardinge: Hugh de Lasne. Mill.* Suburb of Gloucester; a Norman church and 15th-century barn remain.

Bromsberrow *Brunmeberge: Ralph de Tosny, formerly Earl Harold.*

Brookthorpe *Brostorp: King's land.*

Buckland *Bochelande: Gloucester Abbey.* Manor; church with a medieval mazer bowl.

Bulley *Bulelege: Walter Balistarius.*

Burnt Norton *Nortune: Ansfrid de Cormeilles.*

Calcot *Caldecot: St Denis' Church, Paris.*

Caldicot *Caldecote:* Lost.

Cam *Camma: King's land.* Part of Dursley town. A cloth mill, founded here in 1815, is still working.

Carswall *Crasowel: Odo from Roger de Lacy.* Manor house.

Cassey Compton*: Bishop of Worcester.*

Castlett *Cateslat: William Goizenboded. Mill.* Farm.

Charfield *Cirvelde: Jocelyn le Breton. Mill.* Light industry.

Charingworth *Cheuringaurde: Roger from Ralph de Tosny.* Several manor houses nearby.

Charlton Abbots *Cerletone: Winchcombe Abbey. Mill.* Stone Age grave (Belas Knap); 2 excavated Roman villas; 2 springs; Tudor manor house.

Chedworth *Cedeorde: King's land. 3 mills, a salt toll.* Straggling. A Long Barrow and Chedworth Roman Villa and Museum are in the woods.

Cheltenham *Chinteneham: King's land; Reinbald from Cirencester Church. 5 mills. 20 cows, 20 pigs, 16s for bread, formerly 3000 loaves for dogs.* Town, Saxon in origin and made famous as a spa by George III. Now a prosperous commercial centre with fine Regency buildings.

Cherington *Cerintone: Geoffrey from Miles Crispin. Mill.* Georgian cottages.

Chesterton *: Hugh from William FitzBaderon.* Suburb of Cirencester.

Chipping Campden *Campedene: Earl Hugh, formerly Earl Harold. 2 mills.* Small town, a 'wool' town in the middle ages; 17th-century arcaded Market Hall; 14th-century Grevel's House; the remains of Campden House, burnt in 1645.

Churcham *Hamme: Gloucester Abbey. The Church had a hunt here both before and after 1066.* Churcham Court, now a farmhouse.

Churchdown *Circesdune: Archbishop of York.* Suburb of Gloucester.

Church Icomb *Iacumbe: Bishop of Worcester; for the supply of the monks.* Now Icomb; Icomb Place, a 15th-century manor house.

Cirencester *Cirecestre: King's land (before 1066 the Queen had the sheeps' wool). Hugh from William FitzBaderon; Cirencester Church. 3 mills.* Town based on light industry and agriculture. As *Corinium* it was the second largest Roman town in the British Isles; many Roman remains. An important medieval 'wool' town, it declined in the 19th century.

Clifton *Clistone: Roger FitzRalph.* Part of Bristol; Georgian spa with fine Regency buildings; Bristol University Buildings; Clifton Suspension Bridge.

Clingre *Claenhangare: King's land; Roger from the king. 2* farms; manor house.

Coaley *Covelege: King's land.*

Coberley *Coberleie/Culberlege: Roger de Berkeley.*

Cold Ashton *Ecestone: Bath Church. Mill.* Battlefields House named after the Battle of Lansdown (1643).

Coln Rogers *: King's lad.* Saxon church with nave and chancel intact.

Coln St Aldwyns *Culne: Gloucester Abbey. 2 mills.* Between large estates; Elizabethan manor.

Coln St Dennis *Colne: St Denis' Church, Paris.*

Combe Baskerville *Icubee:* Lost.

Compton Abdale *Contone/ Cuntune: Archbishop of York. Mill.*

Compton Greenfield *Contone: Gilbert FitzTurold from Bishop of Worcester.*

Condicote *Condicote/Cornicote: Archbishop of York; Osbern from Bishop of Worcester; William Breakwolf; Osbern from Durand the Sheriff.* Surrounded by prehistoric earthworks and burial mounds.

Cowley *Kulege: Pershore Abbey. Mill.* Manor house.

Cromhall Abbots *Cromale/ Cromhal: King's land.* Abbotside Farm.

Cromhall Lygon *Cromale/ Cromhal:* Lost.

Culkerton *Culcorto(r)ne: Herbert from William d'Eu; Ansketel from Roger d'Ivry; Roger d'Ivry from Durand the Sheriff.*

Cutsdean *Codestune: Archdeacon Alric from Bishop of Worcester.*

Daylesford *Eilesford: Stephen FitzFulcred from Bishop of Worcester; Bishop of Bayeux.* Daylesford House, home of Warren Hastings, 1st governor-general of British India, 1774–84.

Deerhurst *Derheste:* See page 108.

Deerhurst Walton *Valton: St Denis' Church, Paris.*

Didmarton *Dedmertone: Ansketel from Durand the Sheriff.* At source of the River Avon; site of a camp for French POWs during the Napoleonic wars.

Ditchford *Dicford: Richard from Evesham Abbey; Ansgot from Bishop of Worcester.* Now Ditchford Hill.

DODINGTON: *The Round Lodge, at the south end of the park.*

Dixton *Dricledene: Humphrey from the king.*

Dodington *Dodintone: Roger from Bishop of Coutances; Roger of Berkeley.* Dodington Park, built by James Wyatt and landscaped by Capability Brown.

Dowdeswell *Dodesuuelle: Robert from Bishop of Worcester.* Several manor houses.

Down Ampney *Omenie: King's land.* Birthplace of the composer Ralph Vaughan-Williams (1872–1958).

Down Hatherley *Athelai: King's land.* Straggling.

Doynton *Didintone: Bishop of Coutances. 2 mills.* Mill.

Driffield *Drifelle: Reinbald the Priest.*

Dumbleton *Dubentone/ Dunbentune: Abingdon Abbey; William Goizenboded; William Breakwolf; Ralph from Durand the Sheriff. Mill.* Dumbleton Hall, designed by George S. Repton (1830).

Duntisbourne *Duntes/ Dantesborne:* Lost.

Duntisbourne Abbots *Duntesborne/Tantesborne: Gloucester Abbey Ansfrid de Cormeilles.* Cotswold Farm has a window by Sir Edward Burne-Jones.

Duntisbourne Hotat*: Bernard from Ansfrid de Cormeilles; Gilbert from Roger de Lacy.* Now Middle Duntisbourne.

Duntisbourne Leer*: Lyre Abbey.* Ford.

Duntisbourne Rouse *Duntesborne/Tantesborne: Ralph from Durand the Sheriff.* Church with Saxon nave. Pinbury Park with its Nuns Walk was the home of furniture-maker Ernest Gimson before his death in 1919.

Dursley *Dersilege: King's land.* Market town.

Dymock *Dimoch:* See page 109.

Dyrham *Dirham: William FitzGuy. 3 mills.* 17th-century mansion and deer park.

Eastleach Martin *Lec(c)e: Walter FitzPoyntz; Drogo FitzPoyntz. 2 mills.* Divided from Eastleach Turville by the river, but connected by a footbridge of flat paving stones called Keble's Bridge.

Eastleach Turville *Lec(c)e: William from Roger de Lacy.* John Keble preached here for 8 years.

Ebrington *Bristentune: William Goizenboded. 2 mills.* Thatched cottages; manor.

Edgeworth *Egeisuurde/ Egesworde: Roger de Lacy claims from Earl Hugh; Roger de Lacy. Mill.* Remains of Saxon church; manor house; Edgeworth Mill Farm.

Elberton *Elbertone: King's land.* Remains of a Roman camp; Jacobean manor house.

Elkstone *Elchestane: Ansfrid de Cormeilles.*

Ellings *Telinge:* Lost.

Elmstone *Almundestan: Reinbald from Westminster Abbey.* Now Elmstone Hardwicke.

English Bicknor *Bicanofre: William FitzNorman.* Remains of a motte and bailey castle.

Etloe *Ete(s)lau: Roger de Berkeley from the king.*

Evenlode *Eunilade: Hereward from Bishop of Worcester. Mill.* Tudor manor house.

Evington *Giuingtune:* Lost.

Eycot *Aicote: Ordric from Bishop of Worcester. Mill.* Now Eycotfield.

Eyford *Aiforde: Hascoit Musard.* Eyford Park manor house where Milton wrote some of *Paradise Lost.*

Fairford *Fareforde: King's land. 3 mills.* Small town with a mill, the birthplace of John Keble (1792–1866).

Farmcote *Fernecote: Geoffrey from William Goizenboded.*

Farmington *Tormentone: Walter FitzPoyntz from Archbishop of York.* Gabled pump house; its roof was donated by Farmington USA in 1935.

Fiddington *Fitentone: King's land; Tewkesbury Abbey.*

Forthampton *Fortemeltone/ Forhelmentone: King's land; Ansgot from the king; Lyre Abbey. Hawk's eyrie.* 17th-century timber-framed cottages; Forthampton Court.

Foxcote *Fuscote: Morin from Bishop of Worcester.*

Frampton *Freolintune: Winchcombe Abbey.* Frampton Farm.

Frampton Cotterell *Frantone: Walter Balistarius.* Adjacent to Bristol; famous for making felt hats.

Frampton Mansell *Frantone: Robert de Tosny. Mill.* William and Mary farmhouse almost under the railway arches.

Frampton-on-Severn *Frantone: Drogo FitzPoyntz (Roger de Lacy wrongfully holds 1 hide). Mill.* On a canal; half-timbered houses; large village green. Frampton Court is a Georgian manor house.

FRAMPTON-ON-SEVERN: *A house on the Sharpness Canal.*

Fretherne *Fridorne: Thurstan FitzRolf.*

Frocester *Frowcestre: Gloucester Abbey.* Fine old tithe barn. Elizabeth I visited Frocester Court, built on the site of a Roman villa.

Gaunts Earthcott *Herdicote: Robert from Bishop of Coutances.*

Gloucester *Glouuecestre: King's land; Gloucester Abbey both before and after 1066. 5 fisheries, mill.* Cathedral city, formerly Roman; 18th-century and older houses. The 'New' Inn is a 15th-century Pilgrims' Hostel. William I commissioned the *Domesday* survey here at his Christmas council in 1085.

Gossington *Gosintune: King's land.*

Gotherington *Godrinton: Thurstan FitzRolf from Bishop of Worcester.* Expanding.

Great Barrington *Berni(n)tone: King's land; Walter FitzRoger from the king. 3 mills.* Barrington Park House is a mid-18th-century mansion with a deer park.

Great Colesbourne *Colesborne/burne: Swein, Walter FitzRoger and Ansfrid de Cormeilles from Bishop of Worcester. 2 mills.* Remains of a mansion; great park with beautiful trees.

Great Rissington *Risedune: Robert de Tosny. Mill.* Tudor manor house, near a disused RAF airfield.

Great Washbourne *Waseburne: Tewkesbury Church from the king.*

Guiting Power *Getinge: William Goizenboded. 2 mills, 5 salt-houses (20 packloads of salt).*

Hailes *Heile: William Leofric. Mill.* Remains of a great Cistercian abbey founded in 1246.

Hambrook *Hanbroc:* Lost.

Hampen *Hagenepene/Hagepinc: Ansgar from Archbishop of York.*

Hampnett *Hantone: Roger d'Ivry.*

Hanham *Hanun: Hunbald from Arnulf de Hesdin.* Suburb of Bristol.

Hardwicke *Herdeuuic: Westminster Abbey.* The first 'Borstal', opened in 1852, was in the grounds of Hardwicke Court.

Harescombe *Hersecome: King's land.*

Haresfield *Hersefel(d): King's land.* Bisected by a railway line; 3000 Roman coins were found here in 1837.

Harford *Hurford: Gilbert FitzTurold. Mill.* Lower Harford Farm.

Harnhill *Harehille: Roger from Ralph de Tosny.* 16th-century manor house.

Harry Stoke *Estoch: Theobald from Bishop of Coutances.*

Hasfield *Hasfelde: Thurstan FitzRolf from Westminster Abbey.* Much altered medieval manor house, home of the Pauncefoote family till 1598.

Hatherop *Etherope/Hetrope: William from Roger de Lacy; Arnulf de Hesdin. Mill.* Manor house with park and model village (1860s).

Hawksbury *Havochesberie: Pershore Abbey. 3 mills.* Scattered; imposing monument to Lord Rupert Somerset, 1846.

Hawling *Hallinge: Sigar de Chocques, formerly Countess Goda.* Manor house.

Hayes *Hege:* Lost.

Hazleton (near Northleach) *Hasedene: Sigar de Chocques, formerly Countess Goda.*

Hazleton (in Rodmarton) *Hasedene: Roger d'Ivry. ½ mill.* Hazelton Manor Farm.

Hempsted *Hechanestede: King's land. ½ fishery.* Gloucester. Newark House was built in 1501; behind it is the site of a Roman camp.

Henbury *Henberie: Bishop of Worcester.* Within Bristol city's boundary; Blaise Castle House, a Folk Museum; 18th-century Blaise Castle.

Hentage *: Humphrey from the king.* In Alderton village.

Hewelsfield *Hiwoldestone: William FitzBaderon; this land is by the King's order, in the Forest.* Between two stretches of the Forest of Dean.

Hidcote Bartrim *Hidi/Hedecote: 2 men-at-arms from Evesham Abbey.* Hidcote Manor's gardens were created by Lawrence Johnston in 1905.

Hidcote Boyce *Winchcombe Abbey.*

Highnam *Hamme: Gloucester Abbey.* Cromwellian manor house.

Hilcot *Willecote: Ansketel from Bishop of Worcester.*

Hill *Hilla: King's land; Roger holds the land of Bernard the priest.* Manor house. Sir Francis Fust built the Great Sewer at Hill Pill in 1750.

Hillsley *Hildeslei: Bernard from Thurston FitzRolf. 3 mills.*

Hinton (in Sharpness) *: King's land.*

Horfield *Horefelle: King's land.* Part of Bristol.

Horsley *Horselei: Troarn Church, formerly Goda. Mill.*

Horton *Horedone: Robert de Tosny. Mill.* Norman and Tudor manor house, The Court.

Hucclecote *Hochilicote: Archbishop of York. Mill.* Suburb of Gloucester, on a prehistoric and Roman site.

Hullasey *Hunlafesed: King's land.* Hullasey House in Tarlton.

Huntley *Huntelei: William FitzBaderon.* Manor house.

Hurst *Hirslege: Roger from the king.* Hurst Farm; Old Hurst Farm.

Icomb *Ic(c)umb: Walter from Durand the Sheriff.*

Icomb Place *Ic(c)umb: Ralph from Roger de Lacy.* Medieval manor house in Icomb hamlet.

Idleberg *Ildeberga: Evesham Abbey:* Lost. The Four Shire Stone, marking the meeting-place of Gloucestershire, Warwickshire and Oxfordshire is all that remains.

Iron Acton *Actune: Humphrey the Chamberlain. 1½ mills.* Several old manor houses.

Itchington *Icetune: Constantine from Bishop of Worcester.*

Kemble *Chemele: Malmesbury Abbey. 2 mills.*

KEMPLEY: *An ornate headstone in the churchyard.*

Kempley *Chenepelei: Roger de Lacy.* St Mary's Church has unique 12th-century frescoes.

Kempsford *Chenemeresforde: Arnulf de Hesdin. 4 mills.* The church tower is all that remains of a castle built by John of Gaunt for his wife Blanche in 1359.

Ketford *Chitiford: Ansfrid de Cormeilles.*

Kilcot *Chilecot: Ansfrid de Cormeilles.*

'Kings Barton' *Bertune: King's land. Mill. 20 cows, 20 pigs, 16s for bread, formerly 3000 loaves for dogs.* Part of Gloucester.

Kingscote *Chingescote: King's land.* Given as a dowry to William I's niece on her marriage to the king of Denmark's grandson.

King's Stanley *Stantone: Thurstan FitzRolf; Tovi. 2 mills.* Small town. Stanley Mills, c.1812, is the largest of the Stroud Valley cloth mills.

Kingsweston *Westone: King's land.* Part of Bristol.

Knowle *Canole: Osbern Giffard.* Part of Bristol.

Lasborough *Lesseberge: Hugh from Gilbert Bishop of Lisieux.* Manor house; ancient barn.

Lassington *Lesedune: Roger from Archbishop of York.* Part Saxon church; famous 600-year-old Lassington Oak.

Lechlade *Lecelade: Henry de Ferrers. 3 mills. A fishery.* Near 3 rivers; 2 mills on the Leach; several fine old Georgian houses.

Leckhampton *Lechametone/antone: William Leofric; Britric from the king.* Adjacent to Cheltenham. Stone for Regency Cheltenham came from the precipitous cliff called Devil's Chimney.

Lee *Lega:* Lost.

Leigh *Lalege: St Denis' Church, Paris.*

Leonard Stanley *Stanlege: Ralph de Berkeley.* Small town adjoining Kings Stanley; remains of a Saxon church; tithe barn; site of an old priory.

Little Barrington *Berni(n)tone: Ralph from William Goizenboded. Mill.*

Little Colesbourne *Colesborne/burne: Ansketel from Bishop of Worcester.*

Little Lydney *Ledenei: William FitzBaderon. Mill, ½ fishery in the Wye.* Remains of 13th-century castle.

Little Rissington *Risendone/dune: Robert d'Oilly. 2 mills.*

Little Sodbury *Sopeberie: Hugh from Gilbert, Bishop of Lisieux.* 15th-century manor house.

Little Taynton *Tatinton: William FitzNorman.* Possibly Taynton Pound Farm.

Littleton *Litentune:* Lost.

Littleton-on-Severn *Liteltone: Malmesbury Abbey. Church.*

Little Washbourne *Waseburne: Urso of Worcester.*

Longborough *Langeberge: Count of Mortain; Humphrey the Chamberlain.*

Longhope *Hope: William FitzBaderon. Mill.*

Long Newnton *Newentone: Malmesbury Abbey and Osbern, William and a man-at-arms from the abbey. 2 mills.* Scattered.

Lower Hampen *Hagenepene:* Lost.

Lower Lemington *Lemingtune/Limentone: Tewkesbury Church from the king.* On a Saxon site.

Lower Slaughter *Sclostre: King's land. 2 mills.* 19th-century corn mill; manor (1640) with a dovecote.

Lower Swell *Su(u)elle: William d'Eu; Drogo from Ralph de Tosny. Mill.* Roman and Saxon remains; odd-looking 1810 Spa House by a mineral spring; Hyde Mill on the River Dikler.

Lower Turkdean *Turchedene/Turghedene: Geoffrey from William Leofric.* Separated from Upper Turkdean by a bank.

Lydney *Lindenee: King's land. Mill.* Small industrial town on a Saxon site. Roman remains were found in Lydney Park.

Madgett *Modiete: King's land with Roger de Lacy and Malmesbury Abbey each holding a fishery; William d'Eu from the king. 4 fisheries (claimed by William d'Eu) in the Wye.* Madgetts Farm.

Mangotsfield *Manegodesfelle: Bristol Church from the king.* Suburb of Bristol. W.G. Grace was born in Downend House, 1848.

Marshfield *Meresfelde: King's land, formerly Queen Edith.* Small town of Georgian and earlier houses; Nicholas Crispe's almshouses date from 1625. The Three Shire Stone is near a fine mansion called The Rocks.

Maugersbury *Malgeresberiae: Evesham Abbey. Mill.* Manor.

Meysey Hampton *Hantone: Thorold, Wigot's nephew from Earl Roger.* Old farms, cottages; 16th-century rectory.

Mickleton *Mucletude: Eynsham Abbey.* Large; part Saxon church; Queen Anne manor house.

Minchinhampton *Hantone: Holy Trinity Church, Caen, formerly Countess Goda. 8 mills.* Small 'wool' town. Gatcombe Park and Lammas Park houses. It has a 17th-century market house.

Miserden *Grenhamstede: Hascoit Musard.* Late Saxon church. Miserden Park is Elizabethan, enlarged by Sir Edward Lutyens.

Mitcheldean *Dene: William FitzNorman.* Small town; much new housing; old timbered houses.

Mitton *: Bishop of Worcester.* Suburb of Tewkesbury.

Moorcroft *Morcote: William FitzNorman.* Moorcroft House.

Moreton-in-Marsh *Mortune: Altrith from Westminster Abbey before and after 1066.* Small town with the Roman Fosse Way forming its main street; medieval Curfew Tower; 17th-century Creswyke House.

Moreton Valence *Mortune: Durand the Sheriff.* On a busy road.

Morton *Mortune:* Lost.

Morwents End *Mereuuent: Gloucester Abbey before and after 1066.* Possibly part of the small village of Murrells End.

Murrells End *: Nigel the Doctor from the king.*

Nass *Nest: King's land, formerly Earl Harold. Fishery.* Naas Court and Naas House in Lydney.

Natton *Ætone/Natone: King's land; Tewkesbury Church.*

Naunton *Niwetone: Robert D'Oilly, Cwenhild the nun from the king. Mill.* Just one long street; 15th-century dovecote with 1000 openings.

Naunton (in Toddington) *Niwetone: 2 men-at-arms from Winchcombe Abbey.* Naunton Farm in Toddington.

Newent *Noent: Cormeilles Abbey; Durand from the Abbot; William FitzBaderon (by force); King's land held by the Abbot and William and Osbern FitzRichard. Mill.* Small town; much new housing; Bronze Age and Roman finds; gabled Tudor market-house.

Newington Bagpath *Neueton: Roger from the king.* The last 2 men hanged for highway robbery are buried here.

Newnham *Neuneham: William FitzBaderon.* Little town on the River Severn; mostly Georgian houses, some with old rope-walks down to the river.

Norcote *Nor(t)cote: Reinbald the Priest; Humphrey the Chamberlain.*

North Cerney *Cernei: St Oswald's of Gloucester from Archbishop of York before and after 1066; Gilbert FitzThorold. 2 mills.* North Cerney House, c.1780.

Northleach *Lecce: Archbishop of York. 2 mills.* Large, formerly an important wool town; 17th-century manor house; 16th-century almshouses.

Notgrove *Nategraue: Azelin from Bishop of Worcester.* Excavated Long Barrow nearby.

Nympsfield *Nimdesfelle: King's land.* Long Barrow known as Hetty Peglers Tump.

Oakley *Achelie: Gerard from Roger de Lacy; Oswulf from Gilbert FitzTurold; Thurstan FitzRolf.* Oakley Wood.

PAINSWICK: *Typical of the Cotswolds: stone walls, stone-tiled roofs, steep-pitched gables.*

Oddington *Otintune: Archbishop of York.* Oddington House.

Oldbury *Aldeberie:* Lost.

Oldbury on the Hill *Aldeberie: Arnulf de Hesdin.* Church, used once a year.

Oldland *Aldelande: Osbern Giffard.* Town with much new housing.

Old Sodbury *Sopeberie: King's land. Park, 2 mills.* Ancient 12-acre British and Roman camp.

Olveston *Alvestone: Bath Church.*

Oridge Street *Tereige: William FitzBaderon from Westminster Abbey.*

Oxenhall *Horsenehal: Roger de Lacy.*

Oxenton *Oxendone: King's land.*

Ozleworth *Osleuuorde: King's land.* Church with a unique 6-sided tower; Mansion House built on the site of an old mill; farms; 16th-century Newark Park.

SAINTBURY: *Village church in a rich Cotswold landscape.*

Painswick *Wiche: Roger de Lacy and Cirencester Church. 4 mills.* Small 'wool' town with many fine 17th-century and Georgian houses; mill; a hill called Paradise; Adam and Eve inn.

Pamington *Pamintonie: King's land.*

Pauntley *Pantelie: Ansfrid de Cormeilles.* Said to be the birthplace of Dick Whittington.

Pegglesworth *Peclesurde: Robert from Bishop of Worcester.* On the Cotswold Way.

Pinbury *Penneberie: Holy Trinity Church, Caen. Mill.* Pinbury Park.

Pinnock *Pignocsire: Alfwold from the king. Mill.* Pinnock Farm.

Poole Keynes *Pole: Azelin from Edward of Salisbury. Mill.*

Postlip *Poteslepe: Ansfrid de Cormeilles. 2 mills.* Restored medieval manor; mill on the River Isbourne.

Poulton (in Awre) *Pontune: King's land.* Poulton Court.

Poulton (near Cirencester) *Pontune: Earl Roger.* Remains of 14th-century Poulton Priory. A house called Ready Token was once the haunt of highwaymen.

Prestbury *Presteberie: Bishop of Hereford.* Joined to Cheltenham by new housing; near Cheltenham racecourse.

Preston (near Cirencester) *Prestetune/itune: Reinbald the Priest; Humphrey the Chamberlain.*

Preston (in Dymock) *Prestetune: Gloucester Abbey.* 17th-century manor house.

SAPPERTON: *The Queen Anne church with fine monuments, including Sir Robert Atkyns who waits for Judgement Day.*

Pucklechurch *Pulcrecerce: Glastonbury Abbey. 2 mills. 6 men pay 90 lumps of iron.* Much new development; 17th-century houses.

Purton *Peritone/tune: Earl William.* On the Gloucester and Sharpness Canal and bisected by the River Severn.

Quenington *Quenintone: Roger de Lacy. 2 mills.* 2 former mills at each end. The gatehouse of Quenington Court belonged to the Knights Hospitallers.

Redmarley d'Abitot *Ridmerlege: Urse from Bishop of Worcester and William from him.* Many Tudor cottages. Site of a Civil War battle, won by the Roundheads.

Redwick *Reduuiche: Bishop of Worcester.*

Rendcomb *Rindecome/cumbe: Walter from Gilbert FitzTurold. Mill.* Mansion built in 1863 is now a school.

Rockhampton *Rochemtune: Osbern Giffard. Salt-house.*

Rodmarton *Redmertone: Hugh Maminot from Gilbert, Bishop of Lisieux; Osward.* Large manor, 1900; remains of a Roman villa, found in 1636.

Roel *Rawelle: St Evroul's Church.* 2 farms.

Ruardean *Ruuirdin: Solomon from William FitzBaderon.*

Ruddle *Rodele: Walter Balistarius.*

Rudford *Rudeford: Madog, the pre-Conquest holder, from the king. Mill.* A 20ft high obelisk was erected last century to mark where Welsh soldiers fell in the Civil War in 1643.

Rye *Trinleie:* Lost.

Saintbury *Suineberie: Hascoit Musard. Mill.* Part Saxon church.

Salperton *Salpretune: Hugh de Lasne.* Manor house and park.

Sandhurst *Sanher: King's land.* Scattered; timber-framed cottages; originally Saxon church.

Sapperton *Sapletorne: Robert de Tosny. Mill.* Partly 14th-century Daneway House.

Sevenhampton *Sevenhamtone: Durand from Bishop of Hereford.* Jacobean manor house.

Sezincote *Cheisnecot(e)/Chi(i)esnecote: Walter from Durand the Sheriff; Walter the Deacon; Urso of Worcester; Hascoit Musard; Humphrey of Maidenhall.* Sezincote House is in the Indian style (1803–5).

Sharpness *Nesse: King's land (claimed by Roger).* Small town with docks, on the River Severn and Gloucester to Berkeley Canal.

Sherborne *Scireburne: Winchcombe Abbey. 4 mills.* Birthplace of Astronomer-Royal James Bradley (1693–1762); 16th-century house, deer park.

Sheriff's Haresfield *: Durand the Sheriff.* Part of Haresfield.

Shipton Chamflurs *Sciptune:* Lost.

Shipton Dovel *Sciptone: Hugh from William d'Eu.* Shipton Wood.

Shipton Moyne *Scip(e)tone: Matthew de Mortagne from the king; Rumbald from Matthew. 2 mills.* An inn called the Cat and Custard Pot.

Shipton Oliffe *Scip(e)tune: Geoffrey from William Leofric; Ansfrid de Cormeilles. Mill.* Adjacent to Shipton Solers.

Shipton Solers *Scip(e)tune: Gundulf from Archbishop of York.* Adjacent to Shipton Oliffe; Celtic cross in the churchyard.

Shorncote *Shernecote: Humphrey the Chamberlain.* Area near Cirencester.

Siddington *Sudintone/Suintone: Roger de Lacy with his mother holds it as her dowry; Hascoit Musard; Ansketel from Humphrey the Chamberlain. 2 mills.*

Siddington House *Suditone: William FitzBaderon.* Siddington Roman. An inscribed stone from a Roman tomb, found in the 18th century, is in its grounds.

Siston *Sistone: Roger de Berkeley, formerly Anna.* Elizabethan manor, Siston Court.

Slimbridge *Heslinbruge: Roger from the king.* The old parsonage garden, with a moat, is the site of the old manor house. New Grounds by the river belongs to the Severn Wildfowl Trust.

Snowshill *Snawesville: Winchcombe Abbey.* Bronze Age and Stone Age finds; 16th-century manor house, with a fine collection of musical instruments.

Somerford Keynes *Summreford: Gilbert, Bishop of Lisieux. Mill.*

Southam *Surham: Durand the Sheriff from Bishop of Worcester.* Much new housing; large Tudor manor, Southam de la Bere.

South Cerney *Cernei: Walter FitzRoger; Roger from Ralph de Tosny. 3 mills.* Gravel pits; Cotswold Water Park; street called Bow-wow.

Southwick *Sudwicham: King's land.* Southwick Park, Southwick Farm.

Standish *Stanedis: Archbishop of York and Abbot of Gloucester, Durand the Sheriff and Earl Hugh (wrongfully) from him. ½ fishery.* Chest hospital in the grounds of former Standish House.

Stanley Pontlarge *Stanlege: Tewkesbury Church from the king.* Two Tudor farmhouses.

Stanton *Stantone: Winchcombe Abbey.* Perfectly preserved Cotswold village; Tudor cottages.

Stanway *Stanwege: Tewkesbury Church from the king. Monastery, salt-house in Droitwich.* Aristocratic twin of Stanton; Cotswold cottages, barns. Tudor Stanway House has a Jacobean gatehouse.

Staunton *Stantun: King's land.* Two giant stones, Suckstone and Buckstone.

Staverton *Staruenton: St Denis' Church, Paris.* Manor house.

Stears *Staure: William FitzBaderon.* House near Newnham.

Stoke Bishop *Stoche: Bishop of Worcester.* Suburb of Bristol.

Stoke Gifford *Estoch/Stoche: Osbern Giffard.* Stoke Park, a great 16th-century mansion, is now a hospital.

Stoke Orchard *Stoches: Bernard and Reginald who refuse to do service to Bishop of Worcester.* Timbered houses.

Stonehouse *Stanhus: William d'Eu. 2 mills, vines.* Small industrial town with 19th-century mills; Tudor Stonehouse Court; Wycliffe College, 1882.

Stow on the Wold *Eduuardestou:* See page 109.

Stowell *Stanuuelle: Archbishop of York. Mill.* Some houses.

Stratton *Stratune: Roger de Lacy. 2 mills.* Small town near Cirencester; mill on the River Churn.

Sudeley *Sudlege: Harold FitzRalph. 6 mills.* Sudeley Castle, once the property of Richard III, was bought and restored by the Dent family in 1837.

Swindon *Suindone: Archbishop of York from St Oswald's Church.* Now a suburb of Cheltenham; new housing estates.

Syde *Side: Thurstan from Ansfrid de Cormeilles.*

Symonds Hall *Simondeshale: King's land.* Now Symonds Hall Farm.

Taddington *Tatintone: Tewkesbury Church.*

Tarlton *Torentone/Torentune: Herbert from William d'Eu; Ralph from Ralph Pagnell.*

TAYNTON: *Hown Hall, 18th c. brick building.*

Taynton *Tatinton/Tetinton: William Goizenboded.* Scattered. Taynton House has a 1695 barn, cider-mill and oxhouse. Taynton stone was used to build Blenheim Palace.

Teddington *Teotintone: Bishop of Worcester.*

Temple Guiting *Getinge: Roger de Lacy; Gerwy de Loges' wife. 3 mills, salt-house.* Land here was given to the Knights Templar by Gilbert de Lacy, a descendant of Roger de Lacy. The Tudor house was the summer house of the Bishops of Oxford.

Tetbury *Teteberie.* See page 108.

Tetbury Upton *Uptone: Roger d'Ivry.* 18th-century house, The Grove, in a park.

Tewkesbury *Tedechesberie/ Teodechesberie/-kesberie: King's land. 2 mills, salt-house, fishery, market.* Town with a great Norman abbey church, 13th-century King John's Bridge, an old mill and many fine buildings made famous in Mrs Craik's *John Halifax Gentleman.* The Battle of Tewkesbury was fought in 1471, during the Wars of the Roses.

Thornbury *Turneberie: King's land.* Small town. Thornbury Castle was built by the Duke of Buckingham, who was executed in 1521.

Througham *Troham: Earl Hugh.*

Tibberton *Tebriston: William FitzBaderon.* Tibberton Court.

Tidenham *Tede(ne)ham: King's land. Mill, William d'Eu; Roger de Lacy, fisheries.* Scattered.

Tockington *Tochintune: King's land. Mill.*

Toddington *Todintun: Harold FitzRalph. 2 mills, salt-house.* Gothic revival house, now a college.

Todenham *Teodeham/ Toteham: Westminster Abbey.*

Tormarton *Tormentone: Richard the Commissioner.* Georgian houses.

Tortworth *Torteword: Thurstan FitzRolf. 3 mills.* 19th-century mansion; church; ancient chestnut tree.

Tredington *Trotintune: King's land.*

Trewsbury *Tursberie: Osward from Gilbert FitzTurold.* Trewsbury House and outbuildings.

Tuffley *Tuffelege: Gloucester Abbey.* Suburb of Gloucester.

Twyning *Tu(e)ninge: King's land; Winchcombe Abbey.* New housing.

Tytherington *Tidrentune: Osbern Giffard.* Many Roman artefacts.

Uckington *Hochinton: St Denis' Church, Paris.*

Uley *Euuelege: King's land.* Fine prehistoric camp; Neolithic Long Barrow. Broadcloth was made here.

Upleadon *Ledene: Gloucester Abbey. Mill.* Scattered.

Upper Lemington *Lemingtune/ Limentone: Gilbert FitzTurold from Westminster Abbey.* A few cottages, part of Lower Lemington.

Upper Slaughter *Sclostre: Roger de Lacy and his mother. Mill.* Cottages remodelled by Sir Edwin Lutyens; Tudor manor house.

Upper Swell *Su(u)elle: Evesham Abbey. 3 mills.* Mill on the River Dikler; Abbotswood House, designed by Sir Edwin Lutyens.

Upper Turkdean *Turchedene/ Turghedene: Robert d'Oilly.* Separated from Lower Turkdean by a bank.

Upton St Leonards *Optune: Humphrey of Maidenhill from the king.* Adjacent to Gloucester; Bowden Hall, now an hotel; Prinknash Abbey, a Benedictine monastery.

Walton Cardiff *Waltone: King's land.* Part of Tewkesbury.

Wapley *Wapelei/lie: King's land; Ralph de Berkeley from the king.*

Wapley Rectory *Waperlie: Aldred from the Bishop of Coutances.* Part of Wapley.

Westbury on Severn *Wes(t)berie: King's land.* Westbury Court Gardens are England's earliest Dutch-style water gardens (c.1700).

Westbury on Trym *Huesberie: Bishop of Worcester.* Part of Bristol. Its church is said to stand on a 1200-year-old site.

Westonbirt *Westone: Earl Hugh.* Famous arboretum; mansion by Vulliamy (1863–70).

Weston Dovel *Westone: William FitzBaderon.* Part of Westonbirt.

Weston Subedge *Westone: Ansfrid de Cormeilles.*

Whaddon *Wadune: Durand the Sheriff.*

Wheatenhurst *Witenhert: Harding in pledge from Britric, the pre-Conquest holder. Mill.* Part of Whitminster village. Whitminster House is nearby.

Whippington *Wilboldingtune: Bishop of Hereford. Fishery.* Possibly part of Hillersland hamlet.

WINCHCOMBE: *A gargoyle in the 15th c. church.*

TEWKESBURY: *The 11th-c. Benedictine abbey.*

Whittington *Witentune: William Leofric. Mill.* Tudor Whittington Court; Sandywell Park.

Wickwar *Wichen: The Queen gave it to Humphrey the Chamberlain.* Georgian houses.

Wightfield *Wicfeld: Walter Ponther from Westminster Abbey.* Wightfield Manor.

Willersey *Willersei: Evesham Abbey.* Large village green.

Winchcombe *Wicecombe/ Wicelcumbe/Wincelcumbe: Gloucester Abbey. 3 mills.* Small town, once an Anglo-Saxon walled city, that was prosperous from wool, then tobacco, then paper. Mill at Postlip; row of 19th-century almshouses by Sir Gilbert Scott; fine houses.

Windrush *Wenric: Alfsi of Faringdon from Winchcombe Abbey; Ralph and Hugh from Roger de Lacy; Alfsi of Farringdon and Ketel, from the king. 4½ mills.* Built of oolitic limestone; mill on the River Windrush.

Winson *Winestune: Ansfrid de Cormeilles. Mill.*

Winstone *Winestan(e): Ansfrid de Cormeilles. Mill.* Saxon church.

Winterbourne *Wintreborne: King's land.* Residential area adjacent to Bristol.

Withington *Widindune: Bishop of Worcester.* Manor; dovecote; mill; foundations of a Roman villa.

Woodchester *Udecestre/ Widecestre: King's land; Britric from the king. Mill.* Old mills; fine clothiers' houses; Roman mosaic pavement in the churchyard.

Woolaston *Odelaveston: William d'Eu. Fishery in the Severn, mill.*

Woolstone *Olsendone: St Denis' Church, Paris.*

Wormington *Wermentun: Walter FitzArcold from Roger de Lacy. Mill.* Late Georgian Grange; Saxon cross.

Wotton St Mary *Utone: William Breakwolf.* Part of Gloucester.

Wotton under Edge *Vatune: King's land.* Market town, an important wool town in the 17th–19th centuries. Isaac Pitman developed his shorthand system here.

Wyck Rissington *Risendone/ dune: Hugh from Roger de Lacy. Mill.*

Wyegate *Wigheiete: William d'Eu. Fishery.* Now Wyegate Green.

Yanworth *Teneurde: Sigar de Chocques. Mill.*

Yate *Giete: Bishop of Worcester.* Overspill town for Bristol and Bath. A stone called Celestine, used in purifying sugar, is found here.

Wales Gazetteer

Caerleon *Carleion: Thurstan from William d'Ecouis. 4 sesters of honey.* Small town, sometimes identified with Camelot; remains of a Roman fortress and amphitheatre.

Caerwent *Caroen: Jocelyn le Breton.* On the site of one of South Wales' most important Roman towns. Parts of the original walls still stand.

Caldicot *Caldecote: Durand the Sheriff.* Town. The castle keep dates from the 13th century.

Chepstow *Estrighoiel, Strigoielg:* See page 110.

Llanvair-Discoed *Lamecare.*

Portskewett *Poteschivet.*

Hampshire

Hampshire is intimately connected with Domesday Book*: the earliest name for it was* Liber Wintoniensis *– Book of Winchester – because it was kept in the king's treasury in Winchester, the county capital which had been the capital of the Anglo-Saxon kingdom.*

It was here that the returns, now lost, from the different hundreds all over the country were gathered, rearranged for each county under the names of the tenants-in-chief and copied, probably by a single scribe, into the book that survives.

Domesday's *treatment of Hampshire is unusual. Surprisingly, Winchester is not included. The reason may well be that, as a result of its royal connections, the city enjoyed tax exemptions. Entries for the Isle of Wight and the New Forest are both separate from the main county account. For the Isle of Wight the reason is obvious, detached as it is from the mainland. It is harder to be certain about the New Forest. The forest itself, like the law that governed it, were innovations of King William. Although not technically King's Land, the forest was subject to forest law and few people, even the tenants-in-chief, had any rights outside its courts. This may explain why the New Forest was seen by the* Domesday *scribe as a separate entity.*

Canterton

The King holds CANTERTON *CANTORTUN* in his Forest. Kenna held it from King Edward, and is still there. Then it paid tax for 1/2 virgate; now for a quarter; the other quarter lies in the King's Forest. In lordship 1/2 plough with 4 smallholders. The woodland and meadow lie in the Forest. Value before 1066, 20s; now Kenna, 4s; the King, 16s.

Upper and Lower Canterton lie just outside today's New Forest, with Canterton Manor a few hundred yards to the north. Canterton Glen, said to have been the scene of one of history's most baffling assassinations, is inside the forest. The famous Rufus Stone marks the spot. It was here, so the story goes, that in the year 1100, William the Conqueror's son, the rapacious King William Rufus, was killed by an arrow while out on a hunting expedition. There have been at least half a dozen explanations of his death. The earliest is that the Norman Sir Walter Tyrrell shot him by mistake; the most far-fetched is that William Rufus offered himself as a sacrifice in an ancient fertility rite; the most recent is that Henry I arranged to have him killed because he was frustrating his (Henry's) plan to marry Eadgyth, daughter of the king of Scotland. Two facts are certain: that the church refused Christian burial to the old king; and that Henry wasted no time in making himself the next king. Although his elder brother, Robert Duke of Normandy, should have inherited, Henry rushed to Winchester, seized the keys of the treasury and rode on to London where, within three days, he had himself crowned.

Whoever killed Rufus, there was general agreement that he was killed in Canterton Glen, based on John Leland's 16th-century report that local tradition named the place Thorougham. This he identified as Fritham, just west of Canterton. In 1745 the Rufus Stone was erected in Canterton Glen and in 1841 cased in iron, because it was being chipped away by souvenir hunters. Alas for tradition, it has now been realized that Park Farm, 10 miles south-west of Canterton, was originally called Thorougham and historians favour this as the murder site.

Canterton has altered little in the last 900 years. True, the cottages are now 19th-century, but the groves of oak which surround them retain the character of the forest's Ancient and Ornamental Woodlands, and deer still emerge at twilight among the oak and birch of Canterton Glen.

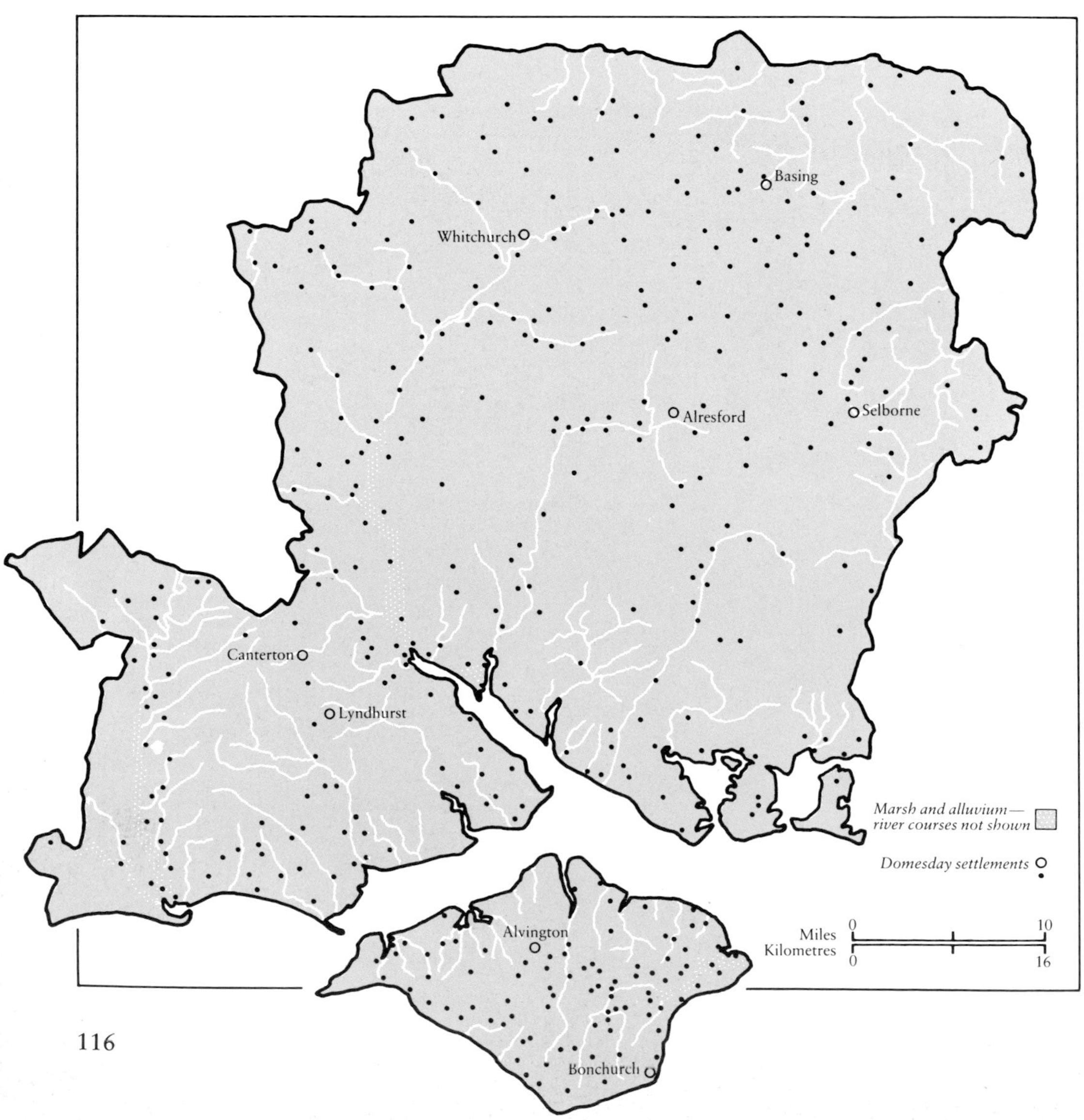

Whitchurch

[The Bishop of Winchester holds] WHITCHURCH *WITCERCE.* It was always in the (lands of the) Monastery. Before 1066 there were 50 hides. Then it answered for 38 hides; now for 33. Land for 33 ploughs. In lordship 5 ploughs; 42 villagers and 50 smallholders with 28 ploughs. 10 slaves; 3 mills at 40s; meadow, 15 acres; woodland at 40 pigs. Value before 1066 and later £30; now £35. ... Aelfric the priest holds this manor's church with 1 hide. He has in lordship 1 plough with 3 smallholders; meadow, 3 acres. Value 20s.

The small market town of Whitchurch lies about 12 miles north of Winchester. Thanks to a by-pass, its little central square, where five roads converge, still has the flavour of a meeting place for country folk.

It may have developed as a settlement because the Winchester to Newbury route crossed the River Test here. The river was certainly important in its economy, as the mills recorded in *Domesday* prove. Its name comes from its church – a white church, built from the hard local chalk – which was probably already in existence in AD 800.

Nothing of this church survives, but during a rebuilding in 1868 an ancient carved stone with a Saxon inscription was discovered. Bellringers had been using it as a stand. The carving was at first thought to represent Frithburga, possibly a local nun, because it was inscribed with her name but it is in fact Christ, and more Roman than Saxon in style. Possibly the Saxons took this stone, meant for a Roman church, and adapted it to set above Frithburga's grave.

In 1086 the manor was among the Bishop of Winchester's largest. The *Domesday* commissioners noted, however, that it was 'always in (the lands of) the Monastery'. They were probably referring to a charter of 909 which had granted Whitchurch to the monks of Winchester, though making no attempt to reverse the bishop's land grab. Whitchurch's entry is interesting for another reason. It is one of only a few which make a clear distinction between the real area of the manor's land – 50 hides – and its nominal area for tax purposes – 38 hides reduced to 33.

For most of the last 900 years, Whitchurch has remained a sleepy backwater. In 1863 the writer Charles Kingsley came here to fish. In a letter to his wife from the White Hart Inn he gives a vivid impression of the place: 'There are . . . two gutters down which are running now gallons, ay, tons, of true London milk – chalk and water, with a slight tinge of animal matter . . . there was a Methodist parson walked up to the station an hour ago, and came back again worse luck for the place . . . a shepherd came and stood in the exact centre of the town, of course with an umbrella (all Chalk shepherds have umbrellas), and has been doing nothing in particular, certainly for an hour, in pouring rain. Also a groom boy went by, who looked as if he had been expelled from Lord Portland's stables for dirt. And there you have the Whitchurch news.

Just the same Whitchurch has had an interesting history, largely connected with its five mills. The one which stands on an island in the river became a silk mill and remains one of only about three operating in England. Two others were still grinding grain in 1911, and the last two became connected with the making of fine paper. Henri de Portal, a Huguenot who fled religious persecution in France in the early 1700s, set up a paper-making business at Bere Mill, a mile east of the town centre.

By 1724, when he had moved upriver to another mill at Laverstoke, he had already obtained a contract to provide paper to the Bank of England. The business has now transferred to Overton, where it makes bank-note paper for over 100 countries. Portal built tiled cottages for his workers which were replaced by thatched ones in the 1930s. They still stand at Freefolk, a name which he might well have invented to celebrate his own escape to England. But it actually occurs in *Domesday*, where 3 hides with assets including a mill are recorded at FRIGFOLC, a part of Whitchurch.

WHITCHURCH: *The busy* Domesday *village is now a small country town.*

BASING: *The coat-of-arms; almost all that survives of Basing House.*

Basing

Hugh [de Port] holds BASING *BASINGES*. Altei held it from King Edward; he could go whither he would. Then it answered for 11 hides; now for 6½. Land for 10 ploughs. In lordship 3 ploughs; 20 villagers and 41 smallholders with 11 ploughs. 7 slaves; 3 mills at 50s; meadow, 19 acres; woodland at 25 pigs. Value before 1066 £12; later £8; now £16.

Basing lies on the River Lodden, barely two miles east of the large bustling town of Basingstoke, yet miraculously it retains its village character. In 1086 it was one of 55 Hampshire manors held by Hugh de Port, by far the largest landholder in Hampshire, who was probably also the county's sheriff. Unlike other great Norman barons whose holdings were spread about the country, he held little land elsewhere.

He seems to have been a vassal of Odo, Bishop of Bayeux, and was under-tenant of 13 more Hampshire manors. Elsewhere in Hampshire, he was also under-tenant to five other tenants-in-chief. Among his own under-tenants, he had two other Hampshire tenants-in-chief, an example of the complications of *Domesday* land-holding.

His family owned Basing for many centuries, and built a motte and bailey here, but in the fifteenth century this passed to the Paulets, who demolished it and built Basing House in its place. In 1531 Sir William Paulet, the first Marquis of Winchester obtained permission to fortify the house, and in 1643, just after the start of the Civil War, John Paulet, the fifth Marquis, declared that he would defend it for the king to the end.

The siege which followed was the most prolonged of the war. After two years and three months, Cromwell at last stormed the house. Among Royalists inside were the architect Inigo Jones and the historian Thomas Fuller, who had continued to work in its fine library, but complained that the cannon of 'those howling wolves' disturbed his concentration.

Only ruins of the house survive. The church on its hill half a mile away was also badly battered. It was described in 1644 as 'demolished, the seats and pulpit burned, the bells and other ornaments taken away, the window ledges used as breastworks with firing platforms beneath them'. It was rebuilt by public subscription, largely in brick. Although *Domesday* doesn't mention one, there was probably a church here in 1086, and Basingstoke's earliest church was its dependent chapel.

Lyndhurst

The King himself holds LYNDHURST *LINHEST*. It lay in (the lands of) Amesbury, of the King's revenue. Then it answered for 2 hides; now Herbert the Forester has 1 virgate of these 2 hides and pays tax for as much; the others are in the Forest. Now there is nothing except 2 smallholders there. Value 10s; before 1066 the value was £6.

The small town of Lyndhurst lies near the centre of the New Forest, one of the royal forests created by William the Conqueror. The forest's verderers (forest officials who have protected the game since Norman times) still hold court here every two months, in the ancient Verderers' Hall. The same building, also known as the Queen's House, is the official New Forest headquarters of the Forestry Commission, which today manages the forest. Two miles away stands the Knightwood Oak, one of the forest's largest trees.

Lyndhurst does not appear in *Domesday's* separate New Forest section, for it belonged to the royal manor of Amesbury, 22 miles to the north in Wiltshire. Its land-owning forester, however, is one of only three in Hampshire mentioned by *Domesday* and his holding was considered to lie partly in the forest. To have been included in this or any other royal forest was no blessing.

William I had turned vast tracts of England's land into royal forests, defined their boundaries and applied to them their own system of law. They were hunting reserves, but not necessarily wooded and by no means always uninhabited. Whole towns as well as small settlements could lie within them. And the imposed law was highly unpopular, not only because it decreed such drastic punishments as death and mutilation for poachers, but because it even forbade forest landowners from cutting their own trees or turning their own woodland into arable land. It also forbade dogs from entering the forests unless they had been 'lawed' – had the claws of their front feet cut off to prevent them from chasing the game. (The operation was carried out with a wide chisel on a wooden chopping block.) Small dogs were exempt and the strange 'stirrup of Rufus' in the Verderers' Hall is said to have been the object through which dogs had to pass to qualify as 'small'.

The law was enforced by three courts; in ascending order of importance there were the woodmote or court of inquisition, the swainmote or court of attachment, and the court of eyre, or high court, which in theory visited the forest every three years. The New Forest's swainmote may have been held at Lyndhurst from the time of the forest's creation, and definitely was from 1388 on, with the verderers sitting as judges. But their powers were severely limited and they had to refer all verdicts except those on minor offences to the visiting justices of eyre for confirmation.

Accounts of William I's creation of the New Forest by the chroniclers of the twelfth century were hostile; he destroyed churches and emptied villages of inhabitants for more than 30 miles, wrote William of Malmesbury. He laid waste more than 60 parishes, wrote Ordericus Vitalis. The land of the forest before William took over had been full of habitations of men and thick set with churches, wrote Florence of

Worcester. For hundreds of years, these criticisms were taken as gospel.

Towards the end of the eighteenth century, however, Richard Warner, historian of Hampshire, among others, began to question them; by the 1820s the politician and essayist William Cobbett, applying typical common sense, estimated that if they had been true it would have meant that this infertile countryside had once had a church every 1960 yards! At the end of the century the great *Domesday* historian, J. Horace Round, wrote, 'The evidence not only of geology and agriculture, but also . . . of Domesday itself, is absolutely irreconcilable with the statements of the Chroniclers'.

Today historians continue to ask more questions than they answer. Certainly many settlements in the forest are given no value by *Domesday*. But equally certainly, the very fact that they are in *Domesday* shows that they survived. If they were depopulated, then who was it who used the meadows which *Domeday* records? Who gave evidence to the *Domesday* surveyors? Where did the previous inhabitants go? Is it possible that, for some unknown reason, valuing places in the forest was not part of the *Domesday* surveyors' brief?

Acts of Parliament have gradually changed the New Forest from a royal hunting reserve to a nature reserve, with recreation areas and a commercial forest. The best known of these was the Deer Removal Act of 1851. Its purpose was to get rid of the deer because they 'demoralized' local people by tempting them to poach. They were never entirely eliminated and red, fallow and roe deer can all be seen on the heaths and woodland around Lyndhurst.

Other acts have gradually changed the functions of the verderers and their court until today, ironically, instead of acting always for the Crown, they often take the part of the public against the Crown's modern representative, the Forestry Commission.

On a hilltop close to the Queen's House stands Lyndhurst's Victorian Gothic church (1860). Though a fine example of its period, with windows by Sir Edward Burne-Jones and William Morris, it does not compare for interest or charm with the Queen's House itself, a substantial brick building which dates largely from Stuart times.

Its history goes back much further; the manor house, first mentioned in 980, probably stood here. So did the hunting lodge and royal residence, first mentioned in 1297 when 20 oaks were cut to build, or possibly to repair it. The Verderers' Hall itself was added within the lodge in 1388. The Stuarts started to rebuild in 1635 when Charles I added stables for 40 horses. James I, Charles I and Charles II all hunted from the King's House (as it was then), and George III, the last king to stay here, allowed the citizens of Lyndhurst to watch him at meals through its windows.

Whether *Domesday's* Herbert the Forester ever used a building on the site of the Queen's House is uncertain. Perhaps so, if, as seems likely, his family rose to some standing in the forest. One Herbert Lyndhurst, who may have been a descendant, was the forester of the bailiwick of Lyndhurst in 1265, as were Lyndhursts for the next hundred years. The hunting lodge which then stood here would have been their headquarters, just as it is of today's forest officers.

SELBORNE: *The garden of Gilbert White's house, The Wakes.*

Selborne

[The King holds . . .] SELBORNE *SELESBURNE*. Queen Edith held it. It never paid tax. The King gave 1/2 hide of this manor with the church to Radfred the priest. Value before 1066 and later 12s 6d; now 8s 4d.

The small village of Selborne, made famous by its eighteenth-century curate, the naturalist Gilbert White, has changed little in the last 200 years. Despite its tarred roads, it remains the secluded village that White knew. Although it stands at 400 feet, the hills around it give it the feel of being in a dell.

The above *Domesday* entry shows Selborne to have been a royal manor which once belonged to Edward the Confessor's queen, Edith. A second entry states that at Selborne, Walter FitzRoger held land assessed at four hides. It was possibly also here that the Bishop of Winchester founded Selborne Priory in 1232; but the land which Henry III gave to the priory the following year had probably belonged to Radfred the priest.

The priory stood close behind the present Priory Farm. Nothing remains above ground, but Gilbert White thought that blocks of 'chalk stone' in the hedges and ditches between the site and the village had probably been taken from the priory. During this time labourers found a large Doric capital, and in a more systematic excavation begun in 1953 many discoveries were made, including the tomb of an unknown lady in a place of honour near the high altar.

Two-thirds of the royal Forest of Woolmer lay in today's parish of Selborne, but it was probably outside the *Domesday* manor lands since these were assessed at a mere three pigs. By White's time the forest had become a sandy, treeless waste. It supported a herd of red deer which never mixed with the fallow deer of Alice Holt Forest to the north, even though there was no barrier. The Normans had introduced fallow deer into England soon after the Conquest, to be pursued as quarry in the royal forests and to be eaten as the only fresh meat during winter.

White's grandfather was the vicar of Selborne, and White was born in 1720 in the vicarage. He died 73 years later, 100 yards away, at a house called The Wakes. The family had moved here when he was seven and although he studied at Oxford and held curacies in other parts of the country, he returned to The Wakes when he was 41 and never left Selborne again. He was curate for 24 years of the village of Farringdon, two miles away, and for the rest of his life was curate of Selborne itself.

His book, *Natural History of Selborne*, which made the village one of the best known in the land, is in the form of letters written to two friends, the explorer Daines Barrington and the zoologist Thomas Pennant. In these White described the plants, animals and birds he saw around him.

He differed from earlier naturalists in his attempts to verify his theories by careful and detached observation. To prove his contention, for instance, that swallows hibernated in England in winter, he employed men to beat the bushes around Selborne in search of them.

The types of birds and plants that he recorded can still be seen at Selborne, and the paths that he walked still followed. The Wakes survives, though much enlarged. So do many of the other places he mentions, and even some of his trees, including the limes in front of the butcher's shop which he planted to hide the 'blood and filfth'. When he measured Selborne's famous ancient yew, its trunk had a circumference of 23 feet. The politician and essayist William Cobbett journeyed to Selborne to measure it again in the 1820s, and said that its girth had increased by eight inches. Today it measures 26ft 4in at three feet from the ground. It is believed to be 1000 years old; if so Radfred the priest would have seen it outside his church as a flourishing tree already a century old.

Alresford

Walkelin Bishop of Winchester holds ALRESFORD *ALRESFORDE* in lordship. It is and always was in the Bishopric. Before 1066 it answered for 51 hides; now for 42 hides. Land for 40 ploughs. In lordship 10 ploughs; 48 villagers and 36 smallholders with 13 ploughs. 31 slaves; 9 mills at £9 30d. Meadow, 8 acres; woodland at 10 pigs pasturage; from grazing, 50d; 3 churches at £4. They paid £6 a year, but they could not bear it.... Robert holds 3½ hides of the land of this manor; Walter 2 hides; Durand 4 hides in SOBERTON and 6 hides in BEAUWORTH; an Englishman 1½ hides. They have in lordship 6 ploughs; 17 villagers, 6 smallholders and 19 slaves with 6 ploughs. A mill at 20s; meadow, 6 acres. Wulfric Chipp, Robert's predecessor, could not go whither he would, nor could Osbern, Walter's predecessor; nor Edward and Alric, Durand's predecessors. Value of the whole manor before 1066 £40; later £20; now, the Bishop's lordship £40, Robert's £4, Walter's 40s, Durand's £11.

Alresford comes first in *Domesday's* list of the Bishop of Winchester's holdings in Hampshire. It was also his most highly assessed, though Overton, 12 miles to the north, was close behind. It had always been the bishop's, granted in the seventh century to his remote predecessor by Kinewald, king of the West Saxons, when Kinewald was converted to Christianity. Although the bishopric temporarily lost Alresford during the religious upheavals in both Tudor and Commonwealth days, it finally passed from Winchester's control only when the Ecclesiastical Commissioners took it over in 1869.

From the start it almost certainly included what are now parishes of New Alresford and Medstead, and their churches would have been two of the three *Domesday* mentions. Its nine mills – an unusually large number – were no doubt powered by the tributaries of the Itchen which rose nearby. Godfrey de Lucy, Bishop of Winchester from 1189 to 1204, used these tributaries to create the lake now known as Old Alresford Pond, holding them up by a great dyke. This pond made the Itchen navigable to Winchester and it made him rich. Though he paid for the damming himself, King John granted him the right to take all fines, tolls, taxes and customs from goods transported up and down the Itchen.

John also permitted him to hold a market at New Alresford, which as a result, quickly superseded Old Alresford. By the fourteenth century it was one of England's ten largest wool markets. But its importance declined, and over the centuries it was struck by a number of disasters, from fires to plague. One of the most remarkable occurred in 1689 when, according to one Mary Collins, 67 Irishmen and six Irishwomen arrived claiming to be distressed Protestants forced out of Ireland. But their real purpose was to wreak devastation in England. All were well armed and the women carried fireballs. They had already set houses alight near Sherborne and were on their way to Winchester. Almost the whole town of New Arlesford was destroyed including the church, the market house and the council house.

Old Alresford meanwhile remained a small agricultural settlement. But in the nineteenth century it was suddenly at the centre of a notorious church scandal, when Brownlow North, Bishop of Winchester, gave its living, together with those of New Alresford and Medstead to his own son Francis North, Earl of Guildford.

The three together were worth £1410 a year, a nice addition to the £2000 a year the earl already earned from a living he held at Southampton. But it was the way in which he exploited his mastership of St Cross at Winchester that finally caused his downfall. By selling the tenancies of its lands, he was said to have netted some £305,700! He and his countess lived with their five children in the greatest splendour at Old Alresford Place, tended by 17 servants. When he was compelled to resign, the forced sale of his belongings included 62 dozen bottles of assorted fine wines. Nor did the Reverend George Sumner who succeeded him at Old Alresford, seem to want for much: his wife Mary distinguished though she was as founder of the Mothers' Union, claimed never in her life to have put on her own stockings.

Old Alresford today remains a village. And New Alresford has never regained its one-time prosperity. As a result, it is a delightful small town, and although its wide central street is lined with Georgian houses, there can be few places where it is so easy to picture a medieval market.

Isle of Wight

Domesday *separates the Isle of Wight from the rest of Hampshire, but, strangely, more than half the king's island holdings appear in the mainland section. His holdings, here as elsewhere, were extensive – almost 40 manors. The religious tenants-in-chief, on the other hand, held surprisingly little: only one manor each for the Bishop of Winchester, the Chapel of Carisbrooke Castle (called the Church of St Nicholas) and the Abbey of Wilton. As for the Abbey of Lyre, the monastery of William FitzOsbern, the extensive lands it held before his son Robert was disgraced in 1075 for rebellion had been reduced to six unnamed churches.*

The island's three lay tenants-in-chief were William FitzStur and the brothers Jocelyn and William FitzAzor. The great baron of mainland Hampshire, Hugh de Port, held nothing on the island.

Administratively, it was divided into three 'hundreds', of which Bowecombe was by far the largest. But less than 100 years later it was split more evenly by a north–south boundary into East and West Mendine Hundreds. Geographically it was divided the opposite way, into the heavy clay lands of the north with only one person recorded per square mile, and the fertile southern half with about ten times as many.

Bonchurch

William FitzAzor holds BONCHURCH *BONECERCE* from the King. Estan held it from Earl Godwin in freehold as a manor. Then it paid tax for 1 virgate; now for nothing. Land for ½ plough. 3 smallholders. Value before 1066, 30s; later and now 20s.

About the seaside village of Bonchurch now overshadowed by its neighbouring resort, Ventnor – in the nineteenth century, Elizabeth Sewell wrote: 'Sometimes it has seemed to me that Heaven itself can scarcely be more beautiful,' a comment which a 1920s guide to the island suggests 'rather lowers one's anticipation of the future'. Others, however, including the poet Alfred Lord Tennyson, admired it. Algernon Swinburne, whose home was nearby in the parish of East Dene, lies in the yard of its nineteenth-century church.

The small Norman church is more interesting. Though not mentioned by *Domesday*, there was almost certainly one on this site at the time, and parts of the surviving church are twelfth century. Below, in Monks Bay, the monks of the Abbey of Lyre are said to have landed to collect dues from their island lands. The Abbey held six churches on the island in 1086, and Bonchurch's may well have been one of them. The manor of Bonchurch, however, was held by William FitzAzor, the powerful tenant-in-chief of 16 other manors, all but one in the east of the island.

Although Bonchurch is today a settlement of villas, they have fortunately not yet risen onto the downs above, and they are kept from the shore by its cliffs. They are also to some extent hidden by the subtropical vegetation of this south coast, most dense at Bonchurch's famous Landslip a little to the east. Arriving here a thousand years ago, the monks of Lyre must have found a more familiar climate than they expected in so northern a country.

Alvington

The King also holds ALVINGTON *ALWINESTUNE*. Dunn held it. Then (it answered) for 2½ hides; now for 2 hides, because a castle stands on one virgate. Land for 6 ploughs. 8 villagers and 2 smallholders with 4 ploughs. 2 mills at 5s; meadow, 6 acres. The value is and was £3; however, it pays £4.

The manor of Alvington lay near the centre of the island, just to the west of its capital, Newport. It was never large, assessed in 1086 at only two hides, but on one virgate of its land, in the island's most formidable defensive position, stood Carisbrooke, castle of the Lord of the island.

In the years immediately after 1066 this castle belonged to William FitzOsbern, the great baron who had been William I's 'dearest friend', and who had 'done more than any other man to bring about the invasion of England'. According to tradition, he had conquered the Isle of Wight himself in a separate expedition. True or not, there is no doubt of his early power over the island. Yet *Domesday's* Isle of Wight pages mention him only once. After his death (on an expedition to Flanders in 1071) and the disgrace of his son in 1078, he seems either to have been forgotten or intentionally removed from the records. Though he almost certainly once held Alvington Manor, there is no direct evidence which says so.

The same would be true of the nearby, much larger manor of Bowecombe, which was probably his home manor but for a reference in Wiltshire's *Domesday*. Here, under Amesbury, he is reported to have obtained Bowecombe by surrendering Wiltshire land in exchange. In its only mention of him on the island, *Domesday* records that his bakery was a mile and a half

further south at Cheverton, and that Reginald, his baker, had been given one and a half acres here.

Although Carisbrooke Castle existed in 1086, there was undoubtedly little stonework until about 1100, when the king, who had taken it over after the disgrace of the FitzOsberns, granted it to Richard de Redvers. The great keep, described today as 'the most perfect specimen of a Norman shell in existence' was not built until the time of his son, Earl Baldwin.

Thereafter, although the fortifications were frequently repaired, they were not radically changed. In the years before the Armada, however, local gentry, yeomen and labourers combined to dig temporary trenches, and ten years later the Italian military engineer Gianibelli added an outer line of defence.

The castle has seen little military action. It successfully survived its only siege in 1377, when the French attacked after landing in the north of the island burning Yarmouth and Newtown. It has, however, appeared memorably in history, for it was here that Charles I was imprisoned for 12 months before his execution. He made several attempts to escape, and during the second got stuck in the bars of his window, believing that 'where his head would pass his body would follow'. His page Firebrace reported, 'Whilst he stuck I heard him groan, but could not come to help him, which (you may imagine) was no small affliction to me.'

CARISBROOKE: *The impressive ruins of the castle stand on the site of a Roman fort; Charles I was imprisoned here.*

The castle today is a magnificently preserved ruin, where a donkey demonstrates how water was drawn up 161 feet from the twelfth-century well. To the west, Alvington Farm probably occupies the site of Alvington Manor. Amazingly, Reginald the baker's one and a half acres at Cheverton may still be identifiable. They are said to lie on Idlecombe Down, where a small wild area known as 'no man's land' was neither claimed by the Forestry Commission when they planted up here, nor by Cheverton Farm.

Hampshire Gazetteer
Each entry starts with the modern place name in **bold** type. The *Domesday* information that follows is in *italic* type, beginning with the name or names by which the place was known in 1086. The main landholders and under-tenants are next, separated with semi-colons if a place was divided into more than one holding. A number of holdings were granted by the king to his thanes; these holders, always the last in a list, are described as holding land 'from the king'. More general information completes the *Domesday* part of the entry, including examples of dues (such as honey) rendered by tenants. The modern or post-Domesday section is in normal type. ▦ represents a village, ⌂ a small village or hamlet.

Places on the Isle of Wight are listed at the end of the gazetteer.

Abbotstone *Abedestune: Hugh de Port from Bishop of Winchester (who held it before and after 1066).* ⌂ Mill.

Abbotts Ann *Anna: St Peter's, Winchester before and after 1066.* ▦ Finds from a Roman villa, including a mosaic pavement, were discovered in 1854.

Abbot's Worthy *Ordie: St Peter's, Winchester before and after 1066.* ⌂ Held by the abbey until Henry VIII gave it to his Venetian physician.

Allington *Ellatune: William Alis. Church, 2 mills.* Allington Manor Farm.

Allum *Alwinetune: In the New Forest. Robert from Edward of Salisbury.* Allum Green House.

Alresford *Alresforde.* See page 120.

ALTON: *Originally Norman church.*

Alton *Aultone: St Peter's, Winchester, formerly Queen Edith.* An old cloth making and brewery town.

Alverstoke *Alwarestoch: The villagers from Bishop of Winchester's monks before and after 1066; a man-at-arms from St Peters, Winchester.* A 13th-century agreement made the villagers practically free tenants. Part of Gosport.

Amport *Anne: Hugh de Port; Ingelrann from Ralph de Mortimer. 2 mills.* ▦ Amport House.

ABBOTTS ANN: *Re-thatching is necessary at regular intervals.*

Andover *Andovere: King's land. 6 mills.* Market town, and London overspill.

Anstey *Hanstige: King's land, formerly Queen Edith.* Part of Alton.

Arnewood *Ernemude: In the New Forest. Hugh Latimer, formerly Earl Tosti.* ▦ Arnewood Manor.

Ashe *Esse: Eudo FitzHerbert. Church.* ▦ Jane Austen often stayed at 17th-century Ashe House.

Ashley *Esselei/lie: In the New Forest. The sons of Godric Malf, the pre-Conquest holders. Nigel from Earl Roger.* ⌂ King John hunted in Ashley Wood.

Avington *Avintune: Monks of Winchester before and after 1066.*

Avon *Avere: In the New Forest. William d'Anneville from Earl Roger; William, Ralph and another tenant from Hugh de Port.* ⌂ Sir Walter Tyrrell, reputed killer of William Rufus, is said to have crossed the River Avon at Tyrrell's Ford after shooting the king.

Awbridge *Abedric: Heldred from Hugh de Port; Bernard Pancevolt.* ⌂ Awbridge House.

Badley *Beddeleie: William from Bishop of Winchester's monks (who held it before and after 1066).* Clare Park and farm. Part of a Roman villa was excavated nearby.

Bartley *Berchelei: Godwin from the king. Mill.* Bartley Heath, the site of Odiham racecourse from 1760 to 1875.

Barton *Ber/Burmintune: In the New Forest. Durand from Earl Roger.* Now Barton-on-Sea.

Barton Stacey *Bertune: King's land; Hugh de Port from William FitzRoger; St Victor's Church from Ralph de Mortimer.* ▦

Bashley *Bailocheslei: Alfsi the Priest from Canons of Twynham.* ▦ Manor farm; lodge.

Basing *Basinges.* See page 118.

Basingstoke *Basingstoches: King's land; Mont St Michel Church. 3 mills, market.* Expanding industrial town.

Battramsley *Bertramelei: In the New Forest.* Now 2 hamlets, Battramsley and Battramsley Cross.

Beckley *Beceslei: In the New Forest. Nigel from Earl Roger.* Farm.

Bedhampton *Betametone: Hugh de Port from St Peter's, Winchester, the pre-Conquest holder. Church, 2 mills, 2 salt-houses.* Part of Havant; partly Norman church.

Bentley *Beneclege/Benedlei: Bishop of Winchester; William the Archer; Osmund from the king.* Bentley Farms.

Bickton *Bichetone: Hugh Maci from Earl Hugh. Mill.* ▦ On the River Avon; water mill.

Bighton *Bighetone: St Peter's, Winchester. Church.* ▦ Church with a Norman font.

Binstead *Benestede: Hugh de Port from Bishop of Winchester's monks (who held it before and after 1066).* ▦ Roman finds.

Bishop's Sutton *Sudtone: Count Eustace, formerly Earl Harold. Church, mill.* ⌂ The Bishops of Winchester kept hounds here; kennel foundations are still in a field near the church.

Bishopstoke *Stoches: Bishop of Winchester before and after 1066. Church, mill.* Town.

Bishop's Waltham *Waltham: Bishop of Winchester before and after 1066. Park for wild animals.* ▦ Ruined 12th-century palace, once part of Winchester See.

Bisterne *Betestre: In the New Forest. Sons of Godric Malf, the pre-Conquest holders.* ⌂ Manor house; 2 farms.

Boarhunt *Borehunt: The Bishop of Winchester's monks; Earl Roger; Tesselin from Hugh de Port. 2 mills, 2 salt-houses.* ▦ Church with a Saxon chancel, arch and font.

Bolderford *Bovreford: In the New Forest.* Lost.

Boldre *Bovre: In the New Forest. Hugh de St Quentin.* ▦ Robert Southey married Caroline Bowles here.

Bosley *Bortel:* Lost; name survives in Bosley Road.

Bossington *Bosintone: Robert FitzGerald.* Bossington House and a mill on the River Test.

Botley *Botelie: Ralph de Mortimer. 2 mills.* Town on the River Hamble. The remains of a Danish war galley were found in the mud.

Boyatt *Boviete: Herbrand de Pont Audemar.* Farm; Boyatt Wood.

Bradley *Bradelie: Geoffrey from Bishop of Winchester (who held it before and after 1066).* ⌂

Bramdean *Biondene/Brondene: Odo of Winchester from the king; Miles the Porter, the King's servant.* ⌂ Elizabethan manor house.

Bramley *Brumelai: Hugh de Port. Woodland for 80 pigs.* ⌂ Church with 13th-century paintings, one of which shows Thomas à Becket's martyrdom.

Bramshaw *Bramessage: Edmund from the king.* ⌂ Bramshaw Wood.

Bramshill *Bromselle: Gilbert de Breteuill; Hugh de Port.* ⌂ 17th-century Bramshill House is now a police college.

Bransbury *Brandesberee: Richere the Clerk claimed from Bishop of Winchester.* ▦

Breamore *Brumore: King's land.* ▦ Tudor; medieval maze.

Brockenhurst *Brocestre: In the New Forest. Aelfric (formerly his father and uncle). Church.* ▦ Early English church.

Brockham *Brocheseve: Nigel the Doctor. Mill.* Part of Lascham.

Brockhampton *Brochem: St Peter's, Winchester before and after 1066; Herbert the Chamberlain from Hugh de Port. Mill.* Part of Havant.

Brookley *Brochelie:* Lost.

Broughton *Brestone: King's land. 3 mills.* ▦ A Saxon warrior's grave was found nearby.

Brown Candover *Candevre: Hugh de Port from St Peter's, Winchester.* ⌂ Manor farm.

Brownwich *Burnewic: Bishop of Winchester.* Farm.

Buckland *Bocheland: Heldred from Hugh de Port.* Part of Portsmouth.

Bullington *Bolende: Wherwell Abbey. Mill.* ⌂ Elizabethan house.

Burgate *Borgate: King's land; Picot from the king. 2 mills. 1000 eels.* Now 2 hamlets, Upper and Lower Burgate.

Canterton *Cantortun:* See page 116.

Chalton *Ceptune: Earl Roger. Churches.* ▦ 13th-century church.

Chawton *Celtone: Hugh de Port.* ▦ Jane Austen, whose house is now a museum, died here in 1817.

Chilbolton *Cilbodetune: Bishop of Winchester's monks before and after 1066; Richard Sturmy. Church, 2 mills.* ▦ Thatched cottages; Tudor house; 13th-century church.

Chilcomb *Ciltecumbe: Ralph de Mortimer from Bishop of Winchester's monks. 9 churches, 4 mills.* ⌂ Norman church.

Chiltley *Ciltelei:* Lost.

Chilton Candover *Candevre: Richere from Bishop of Winchester.* ⌂

Chilworth *Celeorde: Bernard Pancevolt.* ▦ Church with a Norman font.

Chineham *Chineham: Agemund, the pre-Conquest holder, from Hugh de Port.* ▦ Moated farm.

CHILBOLTON: *The ancient Quarley Bells.*

Clanville *Clavesville: Herbert from Hugh de Port.* Near 2 Roman sites.

Cliddesden *Cleresden: Ralph from Durand of Gloucester. Church.* Manor farm.

Colemore *Colemere: Humphrey the Chamberlain.*

Compton *Cuntune: William the Archer. Mill.* 17th-century manor house.

Copnor *Copenore: Robert FitzGerald. Salt-house.* Part of Portsmouth.

Corhampton *Quedementune: Hugh de Port. Church, 2 mills.* Saxon church with its original stone altar.

Cosham *Cos(s)eham: King's land; Geoffrey from Hugh de Port; Ansketel. Salt-house.* Part of Portsmouth.

Cove *Cove:* Lost.

Coxlease *Cocherlei: In the new Forest. Aelfric and Agemund.* High Coxlease House.

Cranborne *Gramborne: Hugh de Port from St Peter's, Winchester.* Manor house.

Crawley *Crauuelie: Hugh from Bishop of Winchester.* Largely 16th century; the inspiration for Queen's Crawley in Thackeray's *Vanity Fair.*

Crofton *Croftone/une:* Lost.

Crondall *Crundele: Bishop of Winchester's monks. Church.* Impressive Norman church.

Crow *Crone: Sons of Godfric Malf.* Now 3 scattered hamlets, Crow, Crow Hill and Crow Hill Top.

Crux Easton *Estune: Croc Hunter. Church.*

Damerham *Dobreham: Serlo and Hugh's wife from Glastonbury Abbey; Cranborne Abbey. 4 mills.*

Deane *Dene: William d'Eu.*

Dibden *Depedene: In the New Forest. Odo from the king. Salt-house, fishery.* 2 manor houses and Depdene hamlet.

Dogmersfield *Ormeresfelt: Hugh Beard from the king. Church, mill.* 18th-century Dogmersfield House is on the site of an earlier house where Henry VIII and Catherine of Aragon first met.

Drayton *Draiton:* Lost.

Droxford *Drochenford: Bishop of Winchester's monks; Ralph de Mortain holds part by force. Church, 2 mills.* Norman church.

Dummer *Dummere: Hugh de Port from the king.*

Dunbridge *Denebridge: Gilbert de Breteuil.*

Durley (in Colbury) *Derleie: Edmund FitzPayne from the king.* Durley Farm.

East Cholderton *Cerewartone: Ralph from Hugh de Port; Gilbert de Breteuil; William FitzBaderon; Robert FitzMurdoch from the king.* Scattered houses.

East Dean *Dena: King's land with Archbishop Thomas holding a chapel; Waleran Hunter; Walter FitzRoger.* Adjoins West Dean village.

Eastleigh *Estleie: Henry the Treasurer.* Town near Southampton.

East Meon *Mene/s: King's land; Bishop of Winchester. 7 mills, church.* 14th-century Court House.

Easton *Estune: Bishop of Winchester; Thurstan; Geoffrey; Alwin. 2 churches, 2 mills.* Norman church.

Eastrop *Estrope:* Lost.

East Tytherley *Tiderlai/ Tederlec: Archbishop Thomas (a chapel); Papald from Gilbert de Breteuil; Alfwy FitzSaewulf from the king. 2 mills.*

East Wellow *Weleue: Agemund from the king.* Mill. Florence Nightingale is buried in the church.

East Worldham *Wardham: Geoffrey the Marshall. Mill.*

Ecchinswell *Eccleswelle: Monks of Winchester.*

Efford *Einforde: In the New Forest. Aelfric. Mill.* Manor house.

Eling *Edlinges: King's land. 2 mills, fishery, salt-house, church. In the Forest . . . 3 sesters of honey . . . now missing.* Outskirts of Totton; mill; 15th-century inn.

Ellingham *Adelingeham: Cola the Hunter from the king. Mill.* Nearby Moyle Court was the home of Dame Alice Lisle, put to death for harbouring rebels during Monmouth's rebellion, 1685.

Ellisfield *Esewelle: Hugh de Port. Church.* Manor house.

Elvetham *Elveteham: Hugh de Port from Chertsey Church.* Church; modern Elvetham House. The Earl of Hertford entertained Queen Elizabeth I at the old house.

Embley *Emelei: Bernard Pancevolt.* Embley Park School; wood.

Empshott *Hibesete: Geoffrey the Marshall. Mill.*

Enham *Etham: Seric from the king; Alfsi the valet. Mill.* Now Enham-Alamein.

Eversley *Evreslei: St Peter's, Westminster. 2 mills.* Sprawling; 17th-century Bramshill House and deer park.

Ewhurst *Werste: Hugh de Port.*

Exton *Essessentune: Bishop of Winchester's monks before and after 1066; Leofwin. Church, 3 mills.* Picturesque cottages; church.

Eyeworth *Jvare: King's land.* Eyeworth Manor.

Faccombe *Facumbe: Roger de Poitou from the king.*

Fareham *Fernham: Ralph, Geoffrey and William from Bishop of Winchester. Church, 5 mills.* Dormitory town.

Farleigh Wallop *Ferlege: Siric the Chamberlain from the king.* Farleigh House has been the Wallop family's home since 1414.

Farley Chamberlain *Ferlege: Herbert FitzRemigius.* Manor farm; Saxon grave nearby.

Farnborough *Ferneberga: Odin of Windsor from Bishop of Winchester. Mill.* Town. St Michael's Church has a Norman fresco.

Farringdon *Ferendone: Bishop Osbern of Exeter.* Now 2 villages, Upper and Lower Farringdon.

Fawley *Falegia/Falelie: Bishop of Winchester's monks. Church.* Partly Norman church; Calshot Castle ruins nearby.

Fernhill *Fernehelle: In the New Forest. Earl Roger.* Part of New Milton.

Fordingbridge *Forde: Robert from Robert FitzGerald. Church, 2 mills.* Attractive town with a medieval church.

Foxcotte *Fulsescote: Ralph from Waleran Hunter.*

Fratton *Frodintone: Osmelin from William de Warenne.* Part of Portsmouth.

Freefolk *Frigefole: Ralph FitzSifrid from Bishop of Winchester. Mill.*

Froyle *Froli: St Mary's Winchester. Church, 2 mills.* Now 2 hamlets, Upper and Lower Froyle.

Fullerton *Fugelerestune: St Peter's, Winchester. Mill.* Manor house; Roman site close by.

FORDINGBRIDGE: *The River Avon, famous for its chub.*

BROCKENHURST: *Grave of Brusher Mills.*

Funtley *Funtelei: Count Alan; Robert FitzGerald; Ranulf Flambard. 2 mills.* On the outskirts of Farnham.

Fyfield *Fifhide: William Mauduit. Church.* Roman villa nearby.

Gatewood *Gatingeorde: In the New Forest.* Now Gatewood Hill.

Goodworth Clatford *Godorde: Wherwell Abbey.*

Gorley *Gerlei: Osbern the Falconer from the king.* Now 2 villages, North and South Gorley.

Greatham *Greteham: King's land, formerly Queen Edith.*

Gritnam *Greteham: In the New Forest. Waleran Hunter.* Gritnam Wood.

Hambledon *Ambledune/ Hambledune: Edward from Earl Roger; William de Percy. Mill.* 15th-century Benedictine priory; Hambledon Cricket Club, founded 1760.

Hanger *Hangre: Sons of Godric Malf, from the king, formerly their father, the king's thane.* Farm.

Hannington *Hanitune: Bishop of Winchester's monks; Leofwin from the king.* Church with Saxon stonework.

Harbridge *Herdebrige: In the New Forest. Bernard the Chamberlain.*

Hardley *Hardelie: Bernard Pancevolt; Saewin.*

Hartford *Hariforde: In the New Forest.* Harford House; Hartford Copse.

Hartley Mauditt *Ha(e)rlege: William Mauduit.*

Hartley Wespall *Ha(e)rlei: Aubrey the Chamberlain and Aelfric from the king. Mill.*

Hatch Warren *Heche: Geoffrey, the Chamberlain of the king's daughter, claimed by Odo of Winchester. Church.* Farm.

Havant *Havehunte: Bishop of Winchester. 2 mills, 3 salt-houses.* Town. Parchment has been made here for nearly 1000 years.

Hayling Island *Halingei/gey/hei: King's land; Bishop of Winchester's monks; St Peter's, Jumièges (claimed by the monks of Winchester). Salt-house, 2 fisheries.* Now 2 villages, North and South Hayling.

Headbourne Worthy *Ordie: Ralph de Mortimer; Bernard Pancevolt. Church, 3 mills.* Church, one of Hampshire's oldest, with a Saxon crucifix.

Headley *Hallege: Count Eustace.* Headley Mill Farm.

Heckfield *Effelle: Hugh de Port. Church, mill, fishery (100 eels).*

Herriard *Henert: Walter from Hugh de Port.* Herriard House; manor farm and church.

Highclere *Clere: St Mary's, Winchester and Aelfric the priest from Bishop of Winchester's monks. Mill, church.* Nearby Highclere Castle belonged to the Bishops of Winchester until 1550. It was rebuilt in 1842.

Hinchelsea *Hincelveslei: In the New Forest.* Hinchelsea Moor.

Hinton Admiral *Hentune: In the New Forest. Earl Roger and Fulkwin and Nigel from him.* Hinton Park.

HINTON ADMIRAL: *The Cat and the Fiddle, a thatched pub.*

Hinton Ampner *Hentune: Bishop of Winchester's monks.* Hinton Ampner House.

Hoburne *Hoburne: In the New Forest. Saewulf's wife.* Absorbed by Christchurch.

Hoddington *Odingetone: Bishop of Winchester's monks.* Hoddington House.

Hoe *Hou: Hugh de Port.* East Hoe Manor.

Holdenhurst *Hole(h)est: King's land. Church, mill, 3 fisheries serving the hall.*

Holybourne *Haliborne: King's land.* Writer Mrs Gaskell lived here.

Hook *Houch: Germanus from Hugh de Port.* Hook Park.

Hordle *Herdel: In the New Forest. Odilard from Ralph de Mortimer. Mill, 6 salt-houses.* Hordle Grange.

Houghton *Holstune: Bishop of Winchester; Thorold from Earl Roger; Heldred from Hugh de Port; Thurstan the Chamberlain; Ansketel FitzOsmund from the king. 4 mills, fishery, 2 churches.* Manor house; ford; 2 mills.

Hound *Hune: Hugh de Port.* Part of Warnford.

Hurn *Herne: Hugh from Hugh de Port. ½ fishery.*

Hurstbourne Priors *Eisseburne: Bishop of Winchester's monks; Geoffrey, Richere, William and Leofwin from Bishop of Winchester. 6 mills.* Manor house; park; partly Norman church; prehistoric finds.

Hurstbourne Tarrant *Esseborne: King's land; Vitalis the Priest from the king. Church.* Church with 13th-century wall paintings.

Ibsley *Tibeslei: Ralph from Hugh de Port. Mill. 700 eels.* Weir.

Itchell *Ticelle: Bishop of Winchester. Mill.* Farm.

Itchen Abbas *Icene: Hugh FitzBaldric (claimed by St Mary's, Winchester).* Remains of a Roman villa.

Itchen Stoke *Stoche: Romsey Abbey. 1½ mills.*

Kempshott *Campessete: Walter from Hugh de Port.* Outlying district of Basingstoke.

Kilmeston *Chelmestune: Aldred from Bishop of Winchester.* Manor; green; dovecote.

Kimpton *Chementune: Hugh de Port.* Manor house.

Kingsclere *Clere: King's land; St Peter's, Winchester; Fatherling from Hugh de Port; Ravelin and Leofwin from the king; 5 mills, church.* Small town with a largely Norman restored church.

King's Somborne *Sumburne: King's land; Roger from Waleran Hunter. 2 churches, 3 mills.* The remains of John of Gaunt's deerpark are nearby.

King's Worthy *Ordie: King's land.*

Kinson *Chinestanestone: Edward of Salisbury. Mill.* District of Bournemouth.

Knapp *Chenep: Hugh from Hugh de Port. Mill, fishery.* Absorbed in Christchurch.

Knowl *Chenol: Odilard from Ralph de Mortimer; Fatherling from Hugh de Port. 2 mills.* Now Great Knowl Hill.

Langley *Langelie: Cola Hunter from his father Wulfgeat; Hugh de St Quentin from Bishop of Bayeux in exchange for a mill.*

Lasham *Esseham: King's land.* Lascham Wood.

Laverstoke *Lavrochestoche: St Peter's, Winchester, formerly Wulfeva Beteslau, a woman who held it until her death when the king returned it to the church for the sake of his soul and that of his wife.* Laverstoke House and park. Paper for bank notes has been made here since the 18th century.

Leckford *Lecford/Lechtford: St Peter's, Winchester. 1½ mills.*

Linkenholt *Linchehou: St Peters, Gloucester.* Tudor manor house.

Liss *Lis: St Mary's, Winchester before and after 1066. Mill.* Small town.

Litchfield *Liveselle: Fatherling from Hugh de Port.* The Seven Barrows, Bronze Age burial mounds are to the north.

Little Ann *Anna: Wherwell Abbey before and after 1066. 2 mills.* Prehistoric fort on nearby Bury Hill.

Little Somborne *Sumburne: Bernard Pancevolt.* Manor house in parkland.

Littleton (in Kimpton) *Liteltone: Hugh de Port.* Littleton Copse.

Lockerley *Locherlega/ Locherslei: Hugh de Port; Archbishop Thomas (a chapel); Wulfric and Alfwy from the king. Mill.* Manor house; mill; farm.

Lomer *Lammere: Roald from St Peter's, Winchester.*

Longstock *Stoches: St Mary's, Winchester. Mill.* Single main street lined with period houses.

Long Sutton *Sudtune: Thurstan from Bishop of Winchester.* Partly Tudor farmhouse.

Ludshott *Lidessette: Hugh de Port. Mill.* Manor; Ludshott Common.

Lychpit *Lichepet: Hugh from St Peter's, Winchester.* 2 burial mounds in Little Basing.

Lymington *Lentune: In the New Forest. Earl Roger.* Small town; tidal harbour.

Lyndhurst *Linhest.* See page 118.

Mapledurham *Malpedresham: King's land, formerly Queen Matilda, and Albold Cook and Theobald from the king. Church, 3 mills.* Mapledurham Farm.

Mapledurwell *Mapledrewelle: Hubert de Port. 2 mills.*

Marchwood *Merceode: Alwin from the king, formerly Wulfgeat his father.* Scattered; farm.

Martyr Worthy *Ordie: Bishop of Winchester's monks before and after 1066. Church, mill.* Partly Norman church.

Mattingley *Matingelege: Alfsi son of Brictsi from the king. Mill.*

Meon *Mene: Bishop of Winchester.* Farm.

Meonstoke *Menestoche/s: King's land; Bishop of Winchester. 2 mills.* Attractive.

Micheldever *Miceldevre: Herbert the Chamberlain, Odo the Steward, Alfsi, Aldred, Waleran Hunter and Siward Hunter, the pre-Conquest holder, from St Peter's, Winchester.* Saxon burial ground at Norsbury Ring.

Michelton *Mulceltone:* Lost.

Middleton *Middletune: Wherwell Abbey. 2 mills, fishery for the hall.* Farm; Lower Mill.

MOTTISFONT: *Mottisfont Abbey, set in lovely gardens.*

Midgham *Mingeham: Alfwy from the king; Picot from Edeva, the king's thane.* Farm; some houses.

Milford *Melleford: In the New Forest. Wulfgar and Aelfric from the king. Mill.* Now the town of Milford-on-Sea.

Millbrook *Melebroc: Bishop of Winchester's monks.* District of Southampton.

Milton *Mildetune: William de Chernet from Hugh de Port.* Now the towns of Old and New Milton.

Minley *Mindeslei: Alfsi from the king.* Manor house near Minley Wood.

Minstead *Mintestede: In the New Forest. Sons of Godric Malf.* The Rufus Stone marks the spot where William II was killed.

Monk Sherbourne *Sireborne: Hugh de Port from Bishop of Bayeux.*

Monxton (Anne) *Anne: King's land. Mill.*

Mottisfont *Mortelhunte/ Mortesfunde: Archbishop Thomas (church); Edwulf (a dwelling) from the king.* 18th-century Mottisfont Abbey incorporates the remains of a 12th-century Augustinian priory.

Nateley *Nataleie: Ansketel from Hugh de Port. Mill.* Now 2 villages, Up Nately and Nately Scures.

Neatham *Neteham: King's land. 8½ mills.*

Nether Wallop *Alia Wallope: King's land; Alfsi son of Brictsi from the king. 3 mills, salt-house, 2 churches. 10s worth of honey in the king's forest.* Mill; 14th-century church; Iron Age Fort on Danebury Hill.

Netley *Latelie: Richard Poynant. Church.* Small town with the ruins of Cistercian Netley Abbey.

Newton Stacey *Niwetone: William FitzManni with his wife.* Close to a Roman road.

Newton Valence *Newentone: Thurstan FitzRolf. Church, 2 mills.* 13th-century church; manor house.

North Baddesley *Bedeslei: Ralph de Mortimer. Church.* Church. The manor house walls contain part of a Knights' Hospitallers building.

North Charford *Cerdeford: Ranulf from Edward of Salisbury; Alfwy son of Thurber from the king. 2 mills. 1250 eels.* Site of a Saxon settlement.

North Stoneham *Stan(e)ham: St Peter's, Winchester. Church, 2 mills.* North Stoneham Park.

Norton (in Selbourne) *Nortone: Robert from Hugh de Port; Ralph de Mortimer.* Farm.

Norton (in Wonston) *Nortune: Odo from the king. Church, mill.* 18th-century Norton Manor; lake.

Nursling *Notesselinge: Bishop of Winchester's monks. Church, mill.* Nursling mill; 14th-century church.

Nutley *Noclei: Henry the Treasurer; Geoffrey the Marshall.*

Oakhanger *Acangre: Richard from Edwin, the king's thane.*

Odiham *Odiham: King's land, formerly Earl Harold. 8 mills, 4 churches.* Country town with a 14th-century church.

Otterbourne *Otreburne: Ralph de Mortimer. Church, fishery.*

Otterwood *Otreorde: In the New Forest. Thorbert Hunter; Aelfric.* Includes Otterwood Gate.

Outwick *Otoiche: Jocelyn from Waleran Hunter.*

Overton *Ovretune: Robert the Clerk and Gilbert from Bishop of Winchester. 2 churches, 4 mills.* Medieval church; old inn.

Over Wallop *Wallope: King's land, formerly Earl Harold; Hugh de Port and Boda from him; four Englishmen from the king. 3 mills.* Attractive.

Ower *Hore: Gilbert de Breteuil from Glastonbury Abbey.*

Penton Grafton *Penitone: Grestain Church, formerly Queen Edith. Church.*

Penton Mewsey *Penitone: Thorold from Earl Roger. Church.* Penton Lodge; park.

Pilley *Pistelei/Pistesla(e)i: In the New Forest. Hugh de Port from Hugh de St Quentin.* 15th-century inn.

Pittleworth *Puteorde/Puteleorde: Archbishop Thomas (chapel); Humphrey the Chamberlain.* Farm.

Plaitford *Pleiteford: Edmund from the king. Mill.*

Polhampton *Polemetune: Ralph FitzSifrid from Bishop of Winchester's monks; William Bertram. 2 mills, church.* Farm.

Popham *Popeham: Hugh de Port from St Peter's, Winchester.* Manor house.

Porchester *Porcestre/Portcestre: King's land; Durand and Fulkhold from William Mauduit. Fishery for the hall, 3 mills.* Part of Portsmouth with the ruins of Henry II's castle, built within a Roman fort.

Preston Candover *Candevre/ Candovre: Clerks from Earl Roger; Ansketel from Hugh de Port; Odilard from Ralph de Mortimer; William Mauduit; Chipping and Edwin the Priest from the king.*

Quarley *Ferlei: King's land, formerly Earl Harold. Church.* Largely 12th-century church, on the *Domesday* site, with a Saxon doorway.

Redbridge *Rodbrice: Hugh de Port. 2 mills.* Part of Southampton.

Ringwood *Rincvede: King's land. Church, 2 mills.* Busy market town. The Duke of Monmouth was captured here in 1685.

Ripley *Riple: Hugh from Hugh de Port; Wulfgeat Hunter from the king.* Farm.

Rockbourne *Rocheborne: King's land; Alfwy and Saewin from the king.* A large farm incorporates a 13th-century manor house.

Rockford *Rocheforde: Hugh de St Quentin from Hugh de Port.* Also Rockford Common.

Rockstead *Rochesire: Hugh de Port. Mill.* Farm, near the remains of a Roman villa.

Rollstone *Rowestre: In the New Forest. Godric and Agemund.* Farm.

Romsey *Romesy: Romsey Abbey; Hundger. Church, 4 mills.* 13th-century house; 12th-century church.

Rowner *Ruenore: William Mauduit.* Part of Gosport.

Segensworth *Sugion.* Segensworth House; near the ruined abbey of St Mary and St John.

Selborne *Lesborne/Selesburne.* See page 119.

Shalden *Seldene: William Mauduit.* Shalden Park; wood; farm.

Sherborne St John *Sireburne: Hugh de Port. Church, 3 mills.* The Vyne is a manor house built for Henry VIII's chancellor Lord Sandys.

Sherfield English *Sirefelle: Robert FitzGerald; Reginald from Alfred of Marlborough. Church.*

Shipton Bellinger *Scepto(u)ne: Robert FitzGerald; Reginald from Alfred of Marlborough. Church.*

Shirley *Sirelei: Ralph de Mortimer. Church, mill, fishery.* Part of Southampton.

Shoddesden *Sotesdene: Agemund from the king.* Now 2 hamlets, Great and Little Shoddesden.

Silchester *Silcestre: Ralph de Mortimer; Ralph Bloiet from William d'Eu.* Near Calleva Atrebatum, an excavated Roman town.

Snoddington *Snodintone: Hugh de Port.* Manor farm.

Soberton *Sudbertune: King's land; Herbert the Chamberlain; Henry the Treasurer; Earl Roger.*

Sopley *Sopelie: William FitzStur. Mill. 875 eels.*

South Baddesley *Bedeslei: Earl Roger.*

South Charford *Cerdeford/Cerdi: Hugh de Port.* Farm.

Southampton *Hantone/tune: King's land. 65 Frenchmen and 31 Englishmen from 1066. The king granted property to churchmen, nobles, a doctor, an engineer, a naval officer and the Abbess of Wherwell who received a fishery and a little land.* Important industrial port with a history dating back to Roman times; the ancient town walls are still visible.

South Stoneham *Stan(e)ham:* Lost.

South Tidworth *Todeorde: Hugh from Robert FitzGerald; Croc Hunter. Church.* Manor farm.

South Warnborough *Wergeborne: Guy and his daughter from Hugh FitzBaldric. Church, mill.* Timbered cottages; church with a rood loft.

Stanpit *Stanpeta: Hugh de Port.* Part of Christchurch.

Stanswood *Staneude: King's land. Mill, 2 fisheries.* Farm near Stanswood Bay; prolific oyster bed.

Steventon *Stivetune: Alfsi the Valet from the king.* Birthplace of writer Jane Austen (1775–1817).

Stockbridge *Stoche: William d'Eu. Mill.* Small town. Neighbouring Marsh Court School, built of chalk, was designed by Sir Edwin Lutyens.

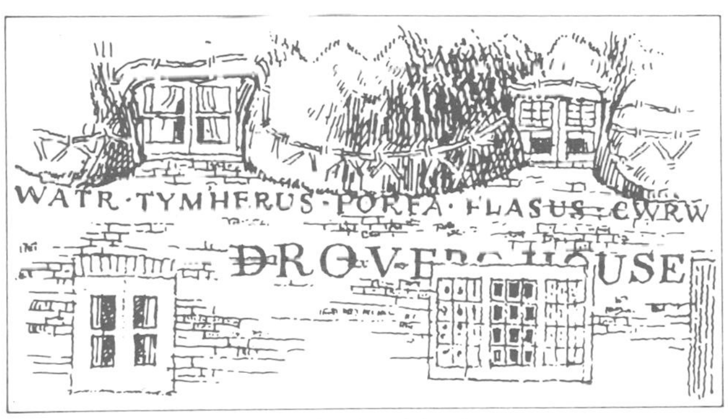

STOCKBRIDGE: *Drovers House, brick and thatch.*

Stone *Stanes: Edmund from the king.* Stone Farm.

Stratfield Saye *Stradfelle: Hugh from Gilbert de Breteuil; Hugh FitzBaldric; Aelfric from the king. Church, 2 mills.* The Duke of Wellington's house.

Stratfield Turgis *Stradfelle: Aelfric from Hugh de Port. Forge, mill.* Farm.

Stubbington *Stubitone: Hugh de Port.* Town on the Solent.

Sunwood *Seneorde: Walter from Earl Roger. Church. Mostly destroyed by the wind.* Farm.

Sutton Scotney *Sudtune: Robert FitzGerald; Odo from the king. 2 churches, 2 mills.*

Swampton *Suantune: Ralph de Mortimer. Mill.* Adjoins St Mary Bourne.

Sway *Suie: In the New Forest. Romsey Abbey; Fulkwin and Nigel from Earl Roger; Edmund from the king. 3 mills.* Town.

Sydmonton *Sidemanestone: Romsey Abbey.*

Tatchbury *Taceberie/Teocreberie: St Peter's, Winchester.* On the outskirts of Totton.

Througham *Tru(c)han:* Lost.

Thruxton (Anne) *Anne: Jocelyn de Cormeilles with Cormeilles Abbey holding the church.* Aerodrome; motor-racing circuit.

Tidgrove *Titegrave: Fatherling from Hugh de Port. Mill.* Farm.

Timsbury *Timbreberie: St Mary's Winchester. Mill.* Manor house.

Titchfield *Ticefelle: King's land. Mill, market, toll.* Small town; Saxon church; ruin of Place House where Charles I spend his last night before imprisonment.

Totton *Dodintune: Romsey Abbey; Agemund from the king. Mill, salt-house.* Town.

Tufton *Trochiton: Wherwell Abbey. 2 mills.*

Tunworth *Tuneworde: Hugh de Port, formerly Queen Edith.* Remote.

Twyford *Tuiforde: Bishop of Winchester. Church, 6 mills.* Benjamin Franklin lived at Twyford House in the late 18th century; Alexander Pope was expelled from the village school.

Twynham *T(h)uinam: King's land; the Canons of Twynham. Mill.* Part of Christchurch.

Upper Clatford *Cladford: King's land; the Abbot of Lyre; Adelina the Jester. 3 mills.*

Upton (in Hurstbourne Tarrant) *Optune: King's land, formerly Queen Edith.* Roman earthworks were found nearby on the site of a Celtic field system.

Walhampton *Wolnetune: In the New Forest. Fulkwin from Earl Roger.*

Warblington *Warblitone: Earl Roger. 2 churches, mill.* Remains of 16th-century castle.

Warnford *Warneford: St Peter's, Winchester; Hugh de Port. 2 mills.* Church with a Saxon sundial.

Westbury *Wesberie: Jocelyn from Hugh de Port.* Westbury House and park.

West Meon *Menes: Bishop of Winchester. Church, 2 mills.* The church is the burial place of Thomas Lord of Lord's Cricket Ground.

Weston Patrick *Westone: Wherwell Abbey. 3 mills.* Built on a Saxon site; bridge with a Saxon cross; remains of a Saxon priory.

West Tisted *Tistede: Ranulf from Bishop of Winchester. Church.* Old manor house; church.

West Tytherley *Tiderlai/Tederlec: Archbishop Thomas (chapel); Roger from Waleran Hunter; Alfwy son of Thurber from the king (Alwin the Rat may have been the pre-Conquest holder, 2 previous holders were killed in the Battle of Hastings); Alfwy son of Saewulf and Wulfric from the king.* Manor farm.

Whitchurch *Witcere:* See page 116.

Whitnal *Windenaie: William de Fecamp from Bishop of Winchester's monks. Mill, church.* Farmhouse and buildings.

Wickham *Wicheham: Hugh de Port. 2 mills.* Small town, the birthplace of William Wykeham (1324–1404), Bishop of Winchester, Chancellor of England and founder of New College, Oxford.

Wield *Walde: Durand from Bishop of Winchester.* Remote.

Will Hall *Wildehel: Walter FitzOthere. Church.* Farm.

Winchfield *Winsefiet: Walter FitzOthere from Chertsey Abbey.* Court Farm, on the site of the old manor house.

Winkton *Weringetone: Robert from Waleran Hunter. 2 mills for the hall. 450 eels.* On a stretch of the River Avon where there are 2 weirs.

Winslade *Winesflot: Walter from Hugh de Port.* Hackwood Park nearby, rebuilt by the Dukes of Bolton in the 18th century.

Wolverton *Ulvretune: Alfred the Priest, formerly Aelfeva, a woman.* Wolverton House.

Wonston *Wenesistune: Bishop of Winchester's monks. Church, mill.* Medieval rectory; farm.

Woodcott *Odecote: Fatherling and his daughter from William Bellett.* Manor farm.

WARNFORD: *Norman church contains 15th-c. benches.*

Woodmancott *Udemanecote: Alfsi son of Brictsi from St Peter's, Winchester.*

Woolston *Olvestune: Reginald FitzCroc.* Part of Southampton.

Wootton (in Milton) *Odetune: In the New Forest. Godric.*

Wootton St Lawrence *Odetone: In the New Forest. Bishop of Winchester's monks; Hugh de Port.* Part-14th century Manydown House.

Worting *Wortinges: St Peter's, Winchester. Church.* Near the site of a Roman villa.

Wymering *Wimeringes: King's land.* Part of Portsmouth.

Yavington *Eb/Edintune: Bishop of Winchester; St Mary's, Winchester. 2½ mills.* Estate with Avington house.

Isle of Wight Gazetteer

Adgestone *Abedestone: William FitzAzor; Edric from the king.* Near a Roman villa site.

Afton *Affetune: King's land.*

Alvington *Alwinestune.* See page 120.

Appleford *Apledeforde/Apleford: Robert from William FitzStur; Edwin and Bolla from the king.* Now 2 hamlets, North and Upper Appleford.

Arreton *Adrintone: King's land; Abbey of Lyre. Church.* 17th-century manor house; museum.

Atherfield *Avrefel/Egrafel: King's land; William FitzStur.* Now 2 hamlets, Little Atherfield and Atherfield Green.

Bagwich *Abaginge: Alfsi from the king.* Farm.

Barnsley *Benverdeslei/Benveslei: King's land; Roger from William FitzAzor.* Farm.

Bathingbourne *Bedingeborne: King's land.*

Binstead *Benestede: William FitzStur.* District in Ryde near Quarry Abbey, the ruins of a 12th-century Cistercian monastery.

Blackpan *Bochepone: William FitzAzor.*

Bonchurch *Bonecerce.* See page 120.

Borthwood *Bordourde: William FitzAzor.* Farm.

Bowcombe *Bouecome: King's land and William FitzStur, Jocelyn and William from the king, with the monks of Lyre holding a church. 2 mills, salt-house.*

Brading *Berardinz: William FitzAzor.* Remains of a Roman villa. It was an important Norman trading centre.

Branstone *Brandestone: William FitzAzor.*

Briddlesford *Breilesforde: Nigel from William FitzAzor.* Farm; manor house; near the Steam Railway Centre.

Brook *Broc: King's land. Mill.* Manor house; nature trail.

Calbourne *Cauborne: Robert, Herpolf, Alfsi and Mauger from Bishop of Winchester; William FitzStur. 3 mills, church.* Calbourne Water Mill.

Chale *Cela: William FitzStur; Wulfsi from the king.*

Cheverton *Chevredone: William FitzStur; Humphrey from William FitzStur, formerly Reginald the Baker from Earl William (whose oven was here).*

Chillerton *Celertune: Geoffrey from William FitzAzor; Geoffrey from Jocelyn FitzAzor.*

Chilton *Celatune: William the Forester from William FitzAzor; Jocelyn FitzAzor.* Chilton Farm.

Compton *Cantune: King's land.* Compton Farm.

Coombe *Seutecombe: William FitzAzor.* Coombe Farm.

Dungewood *Dunniorde: King's land.* Farm.

Durton *Drodintone: Swarting from the king.* Farm.

East Standen *Standone: Humphrey from William FitzStur.* Farm.

Freshwater *Frescewatre: King's land and the Abbey of Lyre and William FitzAzor from the king with Roger holding from William FitzAzor.* Tennyson lived near here.

Gatcombe *Gatecombe: William FitzStur. Mill.* Gatecombe House; mill.

Gotten *Gadetune: William FitzStur.* Manor Farm.

Great Pan *Lepene: Herbrand from the king.* Great Pan farm, overlooking Pan, a district of Newport.

Hale *Atehalle: William FitzStur.* Hale Common.

Hamstead *Hamestede: Jocelyn FitzAzor; Nigel from William FitzAzor.*

Hardley *Hardelei:* Lost.

Heasley *Haselie: King's land, formerly Earl Harold.* Manor farm.

Huffingford *Huncheford: Godric from the king. Mill.* Lost; previously the name of a mill in Blackwater.

Kern *Lacherne: King's land, formerly Earl Harold.* Farm.

Kingston *Chingestune: King's land.*

Knighton *Chenistone: King's land; Tovi from the king.* Farm.

Lessland *Lisceland/Litesland: King's land; William FitzAzor.* Farm.

Little Whitefield *Alia Witesfel: William FitzStur. 3 mills.* Farm.

Luccombe *Lovecumbe: King's land.* Luccombe Bay, Luccombe Chine where smugglers stored their goods.

Luton *Levintun: King's land; Alnoth from the king.* Farm.

Merstone *Merestone/Messetone: Humphrey from William FitzStur.* Manor house.

Moor *Lamore: Ansketel from William FitzAzor.* Farm on Stenbury Trail.

Mottistone *Modrestan: William FitzAzor.* Attractive; Tudor manor. The Long Stone, part of a barrow dating from 2000–3000 BC is nearby.

Nettlestone *Hotelstone(e): King's land; Alric, his nephew and Humphrey from the king.*

Ningwood *Lenimcode: Gerin from the king.*

NITON: *Buddle Inn.*

Niton *Neeton: King's land.* Smuggling centre in the 19th century.

Nunwell *Nonoelle: King's land.* Parkland; Nunwell Farm and Trail. A skeleton of one of the Beaker people was found here.

Pan *Lepene: Herbrand from the king.* Part of Newport.

Preston *Prestetone: William FitzStur. Fishery.* Part of St Helens.

Puckpool *Chochepon: King's land.* Puckpool Point.

Roud *Rode: Jocelyn FitzAzor.*

Rowborough *Rodeberge: William FitzAzor.* Farm.

Sandford *Sandford: King's land. 2 mills.* French Mill on the River Yar.

Sandown *Sande: King's land.* Popular holiday resort with Sandown Bay.

Shalcombe *Eseldecome: St Nicholas Church.* Pottery.

Shalfleet *Seldeflet: Jocelyn FitzAzor. Mill, church.* Part-Norman church; mill nearby.

Shanklin *Sencliz: William FitzAzor; Jocelyn FitzAzor.* Modern town adjoining Sandown.

Shate *Soete: Wulfnoth and Browning from the King. Mill.* Lost; possibly Shate Farm in Brightstone.

Sheat *Essuete: Alric from the king.* Sheat Manor in Gatcombe.

Shide *Sida/Side: King's land; William FitzAzor; Jocelyn FitzAzor. 7 mills.* Part of Newport; Roman villa with an elaborate heating system. An earthquake observatory was established here in 1895.

Shorwell *Sorewelle: King's land; Jocelyn FitzAzor. Mill.*

Sofleet *Soflet/Shoflet: King's land.* Part of Whippingham.

MOTTISTONE: *The Longstone, a sandstone block.*

Stenbury *Staneberie: King's land.* Stenbury Manor Farm.

Thorley *Torlei: Alfsi son of Brictsi from the king.* On Thorley Brook.

Walpan *Valpenne: King's land.*

Watchingwell *Watingewelle: St Mary's, Wilton. Salt-house.* Now 2 hamlets, Upper and Lower Watchingwell.

Week *Wica: King's land. 2 mills.* Week Farm at the foot of Week Down and its earthworks.

Wellow *Welige: King's land.*

West Standen *Standone: William FitzAzor.* Standen House.

Whippingham *Wipingeham: King's land; William FitzStur; Wulfward from the king.* Osborne House and park, one of Queen Victoria's homes; Prince Albert designed the church.

Whitcombe *Witecome: William FitzStur.* Manor house.

Whitefield *Witesfel: William FitzStur. Salt-house.* Farm.

Wilmingham *Wilmingeham: King's land.*

Wolverton *Ulwartone: William FitzStur; Thorold from Jocelyn FitzAzor.* Wolverton Manor in Shorwell.

Woolverton *Ulvredestune: King's land.* Lost area around Longlands Farm which lies between earthworks and Bembridge Fort.

Wootton *Odetone: King's land.* On Wootton Creek; mill pond.

Wroxall *Warochesselle: King's land, formerly Countess Gytha from Earl Godwin. 2 mills.* Manor farm.

Yafford *Heceford: Aelfric and Wihtlac from the king.*

Yarmouth *Ermud: Aelfric and Wihtlac from the king.* Remains of a castle built by Henry VIII; Georgian town hall.

Yaverland *Everlant/Evreland: King's land; William FitzAzor. Mill.*

SHORWELL: *A 15th-c. painting of St Christopher, in the church.*

Herefordshire

Normans had already been attracted to Herefordshire while Edward the Confessor still reigned. Among them, for instance, was Alfred of Marlborough who appears in Domesday *as a leading landholder. They liked the county's mild climate, its fertile soil and the opportunities to grab land from the Welsh.*

It was, however, a newcomer, William FitzOsbern, who, as Earl of Hereford, played the chief role after the Conquest in making the western frontier militarily secure. He built a castle at Clifford and rebuilt those at Ewyas Harold and Wigmore. He also acted for King William in assigning land grants. He died in 1071 and before Domesday *his own holdings had had to be redistributed because his son joined the uprising of 1075 known as the 'revolt of the three earls'. Those who remained loyal to the king reaped their reward, and the county came under the control of Ralph de Mortimer and Roger de Lacy.*

Hereford was the only town of any significance, although Leominster Priory, with its huge agricultural estate in the middle of the county, had been important since Mercian times. Neither, however, had been safe from Welsh attacks; Hereford was sacked in 1055.

Ewyas, in the Black Mountains, and Archenfield, between the Monnow and the Wye, were predominantly Welsh. Domesday *shows this by including Welsh customs for Archenfield – payment of a fine of 20s for example, for stealing a man or woman, horse or cow, and 2s for stealing a sheep or a bundle of sheaves. It also shows that some settlements west of Offa's Dyke were English; they are assessed in hides.*

LEDBURY: *Church lane.*

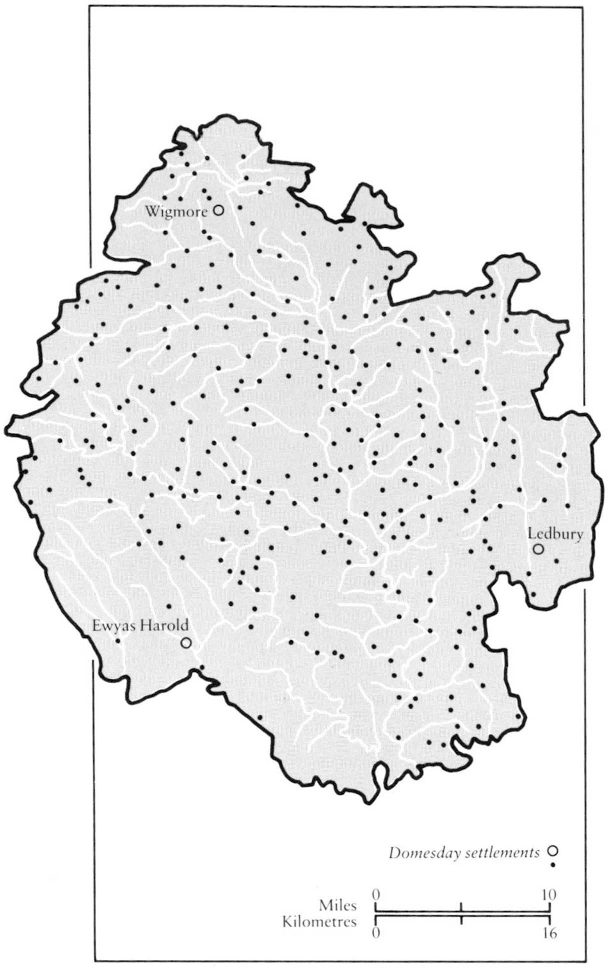

Ledbury

In LEDBURY *LIEDEBERGE* 5 hides. In lordship 2 ploughs; 10 villagers and 1 boor with 11 ploughs. A mill at 32d; meadow, 7 acres; woodland ½ league long and ½ wide: it pays nothing. Of this manor a priest holds 2½ hides; 2 men-at-arms 1 hide; a rider 3 virgates. They have 10 ploughs in lordship; 7 smallholders with other men who have 8 ploughs. Part of a salt-house in Droitwich. Value before 1066 £10; later and now £8. Value of what the priest holds, 50s. Of this manor Earl Harold wrongfully held 1 hide, HAZLE, and Godric from him. King William restored it to Bishop Walter. In lordship 3 ploughs; 4 villagers with 3 ploughs. A mill at 2s; meadow, 7 acres. Value before 1066, later and now, 25s.

'A country of Gardens and Orchards, the whole country being very full of fruit trees etc it looks like nothing else, the apples and pear trees etc are so thick even in their cornfields and hedgerows.' So wrote the early travel writer, Celia Fiennes (1662–1741), as she viewed 'Herrefordshire' from the top of the Malverns. Ledbury, the principal market for all that fruit, lay at her feet.

With its huge minster church rivalling Hereford's cathedral at the time of the Conquest, Ledbury may once have been the capital of the See. That a priest owned half the hides while the knights owned only one-fifth, points to a stronger and more local ecclesiastical dominion than that of the Canons of Hereford. The bishop's accounts testify to the part Ledbury played in feeding his retinue: Easter Sunday 1281 up at Colwall saw 60 gallons of wine (from the vineyards at Wall Hills) – and probably much verjuice made from crab apples – downed, together with '5 pigs, 4½ calves, 22 kids, 3 fat deer, 12 capon, 88 pigeon and 1400 eggs.' No wonder Bishop Cantilupe wrestled so persistently with Gilbert de Clare, the eighth Earl of Gloucester, in the thirteenth century over the hunting rights on Malvern Chase. On one occasion he issued from the woods in full canonicals, accompanied by priests with lighted candles, to pronounce anathemas against those who encroached on the church of Hereford's rights in its woods and forests.

Today those who oppose a by-pass for Ledbury (lorries have actually knocked pieces off the first storey of the county's finest black and white house) do so because they fear that it could revert to being 'just a market town'. This anxiety is not new. In the late 18th century, the magnificent viaduct built to bring the railway across the Leadon to Ledbury, and the 2000-yard tunnel dug to bring the canal from Gloucester were both intended to forestall such a fate. Although the canal halved the price of coal in the town, the company had difficulty in remaining solvent. That the canal continued as far as Hereford owed everything to the tenacity of Stephen Ballard, a nineteenth-century engineer, and one of Ledbury's most enterprising sons. Tunnels that leaked, bridges that subsided and grasping farmers who held out for huge way-leaves, would have defeated most people. But Ballard was undaunted. After six years of literally living on the job, he had to admit that he shed a tear when not a single person turned out to see the filling of the canal basin.

Despite his efforts Ledbury, set amidst the fields where William Langland conceived the vision of *Piers Plowman* on a May morning 'when softe was the sone', still keeps the industrial world at a distance, as it did in 1086, with no more than a share in a salt-house at distant Droitwich.

LEDBURY: *Detail of a Norman doorway in the minster.*

Ewyas Harold

Alfred of Marlborough holds the castle of EWYAS (HAROLD) *EWIAS* from King William. The King himself granted him the lands which Earl William, who had refortified the castle, had given him; that is, 5 carucates of land in that place and 5 other carucates at MONNINGTON. The King also granted him the land of Ralph of Bernay which belonged to the castle. He has 2 ploughs in lordship; 9 Welshmen with 6 ploughs who pay 7 sesters of honey; 12 small holders who work 1 day a week. 4 ploughmen; 1 man who pays 6d. Five men-at-arms of his, Richard, Gilbert, William, William, and Arnold, have 5 ploughs in lordship; 12 smallholders and 3 fisheries; meadow, 22 acres. Two others, William and Ralph, hold land for 2 ploughs. Thurstan holds land which pays 19d; Warner land at 5s. They have 5 smallholders. Value of this castle of Ewyas (Harold) £10.

In the castlery of EWYAS (HAROLD) Earl William gave 4 carucates of waste land to Walter de Lacy. Roger de Lacy his son holds them, and William and Osbern from him . . . 4 Welshmen who pay 2 sesters of honey . . . Value of this land 20s.

In the castlery of EWYAS (HAROLD) Roger holds from Henry [de Ferrers] 3 churches, a priest and 32 acres of land; they pay 2 sesters of honey. In the castle he has 2 dwellings.

Ewyas Harold is not a graceful village; somehow an awkward name seems to have spawned an awkward place. A modern Catholic church surfaces like the conning tower of a submarine from the valley floor, and the castle mound is without a stone, too hidden in the dense undergrowth to give the village a focus. The modern cul-de-sac housing is no more than an extended residential lay-by, off the Hereford–Abergavenny trunk road.

Situated at the junction of the Monnow and the Dore Rivers, Ewyas Harold was designed to command the routes through the Black Mountains. Welshmen rendering sesters of honey sounds benign enough, but the area was by no means stable in the eleventh century, and the atmosphere must have been taut. The Norman military network stretched at its westerly end as far as Roger de Lacy's castle at Ewyas Lacy (Longtown) higher up the valley of the Monnow within the Welsh 'commote' called Ewyas. Osbern Pentecost had built Ewyas Harold castle before 1066, when the Normans were beginning to settle in Herefordshire. He was banished by Edward the Confessor and died with Macbeth at Dunsinane. The *Domesday* landholder, Alfred of Marlborough, was his nephew. The carucates, or ploughands, at Monnington, in more settled country down the Wye, were the sort of economic back-up which a border holding needed; the men-at-arms (*milites*) were there for obvious reasons.

The castle at Ewyas Harold remained of some strategic value until the death of the Welsh rebel Owen Glendower in 1416. In the antiquarian John Leland's day (1550) some stones were still standing, but a later antiquary, Richard Symonds, who visited it with Charles I after the battle of Naseby, found it 'all ruined and gone'. Like the great Cistercian abbey at Dore, it had been picked to pieces by stone scavengers.

Compared with its medieval excitements, the village's later history is dull. Self-sufficiency broke down during the depression of the nineteenth century and the links of today's families with Canadian relatives are reminders of depopulation by emigration. The building of the Golden Valley railway line gave the village a brief revival, but cars have pulled the focus back in the direction of nearby Pontrilas.

Today, only the common, 120 acres of upland

scrub, gives Ewyas Harold any distinctiveness. The long hold of a military society seems to have discouraged the development of a great house: the Marquess of Abergavenny, an absentee landlord, sold up his Herefordshire estates in 1920. With no manor to serve and with a common on which to graze and to burn lime, the villagers have remained an independent lot.

Wigmore

Ralph de Mortimer holds WIGMORE *WIGEMORE* Castle. Earl William built it on waste land which is called MERESTUN, which Gunfrid held before 1066. 2 hides which pay tax, Ralph has 2 ploughs in lordship and 4 slaves. The Borough which is there pays £7.

The River Teme winds its way through the north of the Vale of Wigmore, a saucer-shaped depression on the border between Shropshire and Herefordshire. The south of the vale, called Leinthall Moor, is poorly drained and occasionally flooded. The village of Wigmore lies on its edge; the castle is perched on a bluff above it. Because the bluff is heavily eroded on its west side, making this approach very steep, it is a position of great natural strength. William FitzOsbern was using a well-tried site when he rebuilt a castle here to hold down the Middle March.

Domesday aptly describes the castle as set in wasteland called Merestun – farm on the lake. The main Roman route south from Viriconium to Blestium keeps to the western side of the vale, in full view of the castle until it dips down to follow the valley of the Lugg. Since the tracks from Wales followed the Teme and the Lugg, Wigmore, set between the two, was a key border stronghold.

Unlike those other border strongholds, Ewyas and Clifford, Wigmore was long associated with a single family – the Mortimers. It was they who founded the Augustinian abbey here and used it as their mausoleum; the prior's house is now Wigmore Grange Farm. Some of the Mortimers, Roger, the first Earl of March, for instance, were brought back here in disgrace. He was hanged for his part in the breaking of Edward II. Some came from abroad like Roger, the second Earl (1327–60), who died commanding the English troops at Rouvray, or like Roger, the fourth Earl, who was brought back hewn in pieces, from the Battle of Kells in 1398.

The fateful marriage of Anne Mortimer to Richard Earl of Cambridge brought the family to its most illustrious decades. It was her grandson, Edward Duke of York, who defeated the Lancastrians at the battle of Mortimer's Cross (three miles south of Wigmore), and thus became Edward IV. As a result, Wigmore became royal demesne and remained so until Elizabeth granted it away.

Long before that the Welsh had been tamed and the castle had become a place of confinement for prisoners of the Council of the Marches who deserved more rigorous treatment than the castle at Ludlow could provide. It was dismantled by the Parliamentarians in 1643 and eighteenth-century prints show it as a stylish ruin.

Today Wigmore is an unpretentious village with an efficient old-fashioned garage and a modern secondary school. It is hard to imagine it as the dominating medieval borough which the castle of the Mortimers once made it.

Herefordshire Gazetteer
Each entry starts with the modern place-name in **bold** type. The *Domesday* information that follows is in *italic* type, beginning with the name or names by which the place was known in 1086. The main landholders and under-tenants are next, separated with semi-colons if a place was divided into more than one holding. More general information completes the *Domesday* part of the entry, including examples of dues (eels, honey, etc.) rendered by tenants. The modern or post-Domesday section is in normal type. represents a village, a small village or hamlet.

Places now in Wales are listed at the end of the gazetteer.

Acton Beauchamp *Actune: Urso from Bishop of Bayeux.* Isolated; church with Saxon remains.

Adforton *Alfertintune: Ralph de Mortimer.* Near Wigmore Abbey.

Adley *Adelestune/Edelactune: Earl Roger; Ralph de Mortimer.* Lost. Only Adley Moor and Common remain.

Ailey *Walelege: Gilbert FitzTurold, formerly Earl Harold. Fortified house.*

Almeley *Elmelie: Roger de Lacy.* Castle mound; manor house. Possibly the birthplace of the Lollard martyr, Sir John Oldcastle (d. 1417).

Amberley *Amburlege: Richard from Ansfrid de Cormeilles.* 15th-century Amberley Court.

Ashe Ingen *Ascis: King's land; Alfred of Marlborough.* Ashe Ingen Court.

Ashperton *Spertune: Brictwold the Priest from Ralph de Tosny; William FitzBaderon; Ralph from Durand of Gloucester; Madoc from the king.* Along the Roman road; park; site of a castle, once the seat of the Grandison family. The first Viscount Grandison (of Limerick) was created in 1623.

Ashton *Estune: Manor of Leominster, formerly Queen Edith.* Earthworks.

Aston *Hesintune: Ralph de Mortimer.* Site of a castle.

Aston Ingham *Estune: Godfrey from Ansfrid de Cormeilles, formerly King Edward. Mill.* Church with rare lead font.

Avenbury *Aweneburi: Nigel the Doctor. Mill.* Farm; ruined church.

Aymestry *Elmodestreu: Manor of Leominster; Ralph de Mortimer from the king, formerly Queen Edith.* On Roman road. At nearby Mortimer's Cross, Edward Duke of York defeated Owen Tudor to become Edward IV.

Bach *Becce:* Lost.

Bacton *Bachetune: Gilbert from Roger de Lacy.* Monument to Blanche Parry, lady-in-waiting to Elizabeth I.

Bagbarrow *Bageberg:* Lost.

Bartestree *Bertoldestreu: Nigel the Doctor.* 19th-century convent.

Barton *Bertune: Hereford Church.* Lost in Hereford.

Barton (in Kington) *Beuretune: King's land, formerly Earl Harold.* On the outskirts of Kington.

Baysham *Baissan: William FitzNorman from the king.*

Bickerton *Bicretune: Geoffrey from William FitzBaderon.* Bickerton Court Farm.

Birley *Burlei: Richard from Ralph de Mortimer; Godmund from Roger de Lacy.* Partly 14th-century house.

Bishop's Frome *Frome: Hereford Church; Hugh from Roger de Lacy. 3 mills.*

Bodenham *Bodeham: Herbert from Roger de Lacy; Osbern FitzRichard, the pre-Conquest holder. Mill.*

Bollingham *Burardestune: Kings land.*

Bosbury *Boseberge: Hereford Church. Mill.* Medieval church, the burial-place of the Victorian novelist Edna Lyall.

BOSBURY: *Detached belfry.*

Bowley *Bolelei: Ralph from Nigel the Doctor.* Scattered.

Bradley *Bradelege:* Lost.

Brampton Abbotts *Bruntune: Gloucester Church; St Guthlac's Church.* On the outskirts of Ross-on-Wye. The church was given to the Abbots of Gloucester in Norman times.

Brampton Bryan *Brantune: Ralph de Mortimer.* Ruined castle named after a 13th-century knight, Bryan de Brampton.

Breadward *Brudeford: King's land.*

Bredenbury *Bridenberie: Herman from Roger de Lacy.*

Bredwardine *Brocheurdie: Alfred of Marlborough.* Remains of a castle.

Bridge Sollers *Bricge/Brigge: Hereford Church, formerly Earl Harold who held it wrongfully.* Traces of Offa's Dyke nearby.

Brierley *Bretlege: king's land, formerly Queen Edith.*

Brimfield *Brome/Brumefelde: king's land, formerly Queen Edith; Ralph de Mortimer from the king.*

Brinsop *Hope: Richard from Alfred of Marlborough.*

Broadfield *Bradefelde: Manor of Leominster, the pre-Conquest holder; Ralph de Tosny from the king.* Lower Broadfield.

Broadward *Bradeford: William FitzNorman from the king; Stephen from William d'Ecouis. Mill, fishery (500 eels).* Hall.

Brobury *Brocheberie: Robert from Roger de Lacy.* Ancient camp on nearby Scar Hill.

Brockhampton *Caplefore: Hereford Church.* Morrisite church; ancient Capler Camp nearby.

Brockmanton *Brochementone: Roger de Lacy from the king; Hereford Church.* Hall.

Bromyard *Bromgerbe: Hereford Church. Mill.* Small market town. Charles I led his army through here in 1645.

Buckton *Buctone: Ralph de Mortimer.*

Bullinghope *Boninhope: Roger de Lacy; Ansfrid de Cormeilles; Gilbert FitzTurold. 2 mills.*

Bunshill *Bunesulle: Gruffydd of Maredudd.*

Burghill *Burgelle: Alfred of Marlborough. Mill. 25 sticks of eels.*

Burrington *Boritune: Ralph de Mortimer.* Hilltop; Victorian school.

Butterley *Buterlei: Urse d'Abetot from the king; Alwin from Roger de Lacy. Mill.* Court.

Byford *Buiford: Walter from Roger de Lacy. Mill.* Cotterell family church and Court; Garnon's hill, with traces of Offa's Dyke.

Byton *Boitune: Osbern FitzRichard.* Timber-framed, Tudor Combe Farm.

Canon Frome *Frome: Gerard from Roger de Lacy. Mill.* Georgian house.

Canon Pyon *Peune: Hereford Church. Mill.*

Castle Frome *Brismerfrum: Roger de Lacy, formerly Earl Harold. Mill.* Castle remains.

Chadnor *Chabenore: Ralph de Tosny.* Now Lower Chadnor; Chadnor Court.

Chickward *Cicwrdine/Stiuingeurdin: King's land; Hugh de Lasne.*

Cholstrey *Cerlestreu: King's land.* Cholstrey Court.

Cleeve *Clive: King's land, formerly Earl Harold. Fishery. 10½ sesters of honey.* Lost in Ross-on-Wye.

Clehonger *Cleunge: Ansfrid de Cormeilles, formerly Earl Harold; Ilbert FitzTurold. Mill.*

Clifford Castle *Cliford: Ralph de Tosny; Roger de Lacy. Mill.* Ruined castle, the region's westernmost English fortress. It belonged first to the Clifford family and later to the Mortimers.

EARDISLAND: *Peaceful village with a 13th-c. church, on the River Arrow.*

Cobhall *Cobewelle: Gerard from Roger de Lacy.* 17th-century house; 15th-century hall.

Coddington *Cotingtune: Hereford Church, formerly held wrongfully by Earl Harold.*

Coldborough *Calcheberge: Bernard from Durand of Gloucester.* Coldborough Park; Coldborough Park Farm.

Collington *Col(l)intune: Hereford Church, formerly held wrongfully by Earl Harold; Hugh from Roger de Lacy.* Large house; church.

Colwall *Colewelle: Hereford Church, formerly held wrongfully by Earl Harold. Mill.* Collection of villages surrounded by an Iron Age hill-fort; several barrows. Elizabeth Barrett Browning spent her childhood in Colwall.

Covenhope *Camehop: Ralph de Mortimer.*

Cradley *Credelaie: Hereford Church, formerly held wrongfully by Earl Harold. Mill.* Church with Saxon remains.

Credenhill *Cradenhill/ Credenhelle: Hereford Church; Hugh de Lasne.* Hereford suburb; RAF base; on a Roman road. Thomas Traherne, the poet, was vicar of the church, 1661–69.

Croft *Crofta: Bernard from William d'Ecouis.* Lost; a church, parts of a castle and an Iron Age settlement remain at Croft Ambrey.

Cuple *Chipelai:* Lost.

Cusop *Cheweshope: Roger de Lacy from the king.* Castle remains.

Didley *Dodelegie/lige: Hereford Church.*

Dilwyn *Dilge/Dilven: William d'Ecouis and Ilbert from the king; William d'Ecouis.*

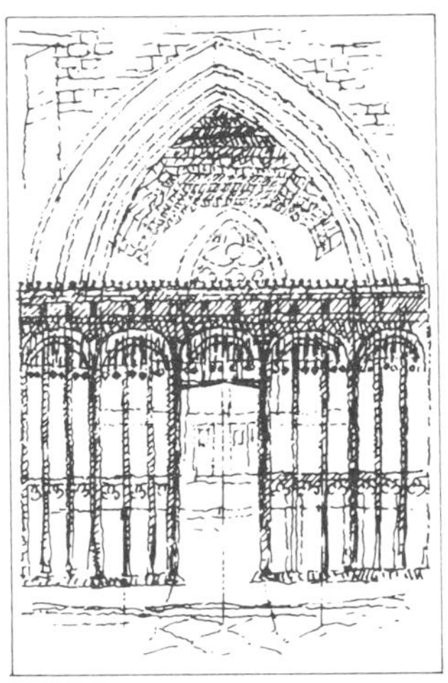

DILWYN: *15th-c. church screen.*

Dinedor *Dunre: William and Ilbert from Ralph de Tosny. Mill.* On the outskirts of Hereford below Dinedor Hill, an Iron Age fort.

Donnington *Dunninctune: Hereford Church.* Church; farm; hall. A Roman kiln and building were found here in the 19th century.

Dormington *Dermentune: Walter from St Guthlac's Church.* Below Backbury Hill, where Ethelbert is said to have camped in 794 before setting out for Offa's palace and his death.

Dorstone *Dodintune: Drogo FitzPoyntz, formerly Earl Harold.* Large; at the top of the Golden Valley; castle remains. Nearby are Arthur's Stone, a megalithic burial chamber, and Scotland Bank, where Charles I met the Scots in 1645.

Downton on the Rock *Duntune: Odilard from Ralph de Mortimer. Fishery.* 18th-century 'medieval' mansion of Richard Knight, MP for Hereford (1780–84), poet and archaeologist.

Fardisland *Lene: King's land. 2 mills. Wheat, barley.* Large; fine houses; mill; earthworks.

Eardisley *Herdeslege: King's land; Robert from Roger de Lacy; Hugh de Lasne. Fortified house.* Mill. The castle motte belonged to Roger de Lacy and was ruined in the Civil War.

Eastnor *Astenofre: Hereford Church. Part of a salt-house in Droitwich.* Ruins of Bronsil Castle; Iron Age fort nearby.

Eaton *Edtune: Alfred of Marlborough, formerly Earl Harold.* Near the Hill of Eaton.

Eaton *Etone: Ralph de Tosny from the king.* Locality near Leominster.

Eaton Bishop *Etune: Hereford Church. Mill, market.* Large; on the outskirts of Hereford. A hill-fort nearby, probably Iron Age.

Edvin Loach *Edevent: Cormeilles Church; Osbern and William FitzRichard from the king; Herbert from Osbern FitzRichard.*

Edwyn Ralph *Gedeuen: King's land, formerly Queen Edith; Urse d'Abetot from the king.* Deserted medieval moated homestead.

Elton *Elintune: Ralph de Mortimer.* Thomas Knight conducted fruit-raising experiments here in the 19th century.

Evesbatch *Sbech: Odo from Roger de Lacy, formerly Earl Harold.* Farm house; tiny church.

Ewyas Harold *Ewias:* See page 128.

Eyton *Ettone: William FitzNorman from the king.* Probably the birthplace of Richard Hakluyt, 16th-century travel writer.

Felton *Feltone: St Guthlac's Church.* Shakespeare plays are staged annually in the church.

Fencote *Fencote: Abbess of Fencote from the king.* Fencote Abbey.

Fernhill *Fernhalle:* Lost.

Ford *Forne: Ralph de Tosny from the king and Drogo from him.* Chapel.

Fownhope *Hope: Richard from Ansfrid de Cormeilles; Hugh de Lasne; 2 mills, 3 fisheries (300 eels). Church.* Now 2 villages, Fownhope and nearby Sollens Hope, each with a church; close to Iron Age camps.

Garway *Lagademar: Herman from the king.* Scattered; round church founded by the Knights Templars in the 12th century.

Gattertop *Gadredehope: Roger de Lacy from the king.*

Grendon Bishop *Grenedene: William from Roger de Lacy.* Scattered; prehistoric camp.

Halmond's Frome *Nerefrum: Roger de Lacy, formerly Queen Edith. Mill (5 sticks of eels).* Scattered.

Hamnish *Hamenes: Drogo FitzPoyntz from the king.* Hamnish House.

Hampton *Hantone: Manor of Leominster; Roger de Lacy and Drogo FitzPoyntz from the king. Mill.* Part of Hope under Dinmore.

Hampton Bishop *Hantune: Hereford Church. 2½ mills.*

Hampton Wafre *Hantone: Roger de Lacy from the king.* Locality near Leominster.

Hanley's End *Hanlie:* Lost.

Harewood *Harewde:* Lost.

Hatfield *Hetfelde: Hugh de Lasne from the king; William d'Ecouis.*

Hazle *Hasles: Hereford Church, formerly held wrongfully by Earl Harold. Mill.* Hazle Farm.

Heath *Hed: Gerard from Roger de Lacy.* Now Great Heath.

Hereford *Hereford: King's land; Hereford Church.* City. Roman and Saxon settlement; burial place of St Ethelbert; meeting place of King Athelstan and the Welsh princes in 926. Harold Godwinson (King Harold) built a castle here, which has not survived. Norman cathedral with later additions.

Hergest *Hergest(h): King's land, formerly Earl Harold.* Now 2 hamlets, Upper and Lower

HEREFORD: *The See was established in 676, and the Gothic front (1904) hides much fine medieval architecture.*

Hergest. Hergest Court belonged to the Vaughan family, who owned the *Red Book of Hergest* containing the ancient Welsh *Mabinogion* stories.

Hinton *Hinetune: St Guthlac's Church. Mill.* Farm.

Holme Lacy *Hamne: Hereford Church, formerly held wrongfully by Earl Harold. Church.* Church; Holme Lacy House.

Holmer *Holemere: Hereford Church.* Suburb of Hereford.

Hope Mansell *Hope: William FitzBaderon.* Parkfields House.

Hope under Dinmore *Hope: Hereford Church.* Large.

Hopley's Green *Hope: Roger de Lacy from the king and Walter from him.*

Hopton Sollers *Hopetune: Richere from William FitzNorman.*

How Caple *Capel: Hereford Church. Mill.*

Howle *Hulla: Godric Mapson from the king. Fishery.*

Humber *Humbre: Roger de Lacy from the king.* Nearby is the Iron Age Risbury Camp; Roman finds have been made in the area.

Huntington *Huntenetune: Hereford Church.* Within the boundaries of the city of Hereford.

Huntington (near Kington) : *King's land, formerly Earl Harold.* Large; earthworks of a castle which belonged first to King Harold and later to Owen Glendower.

Ivington *Ivintune: King's land, formerly Queen Edith.* Iron Age camp nearby.

Kenchester *Chenecestre: Godric and Gruffydd of Maredudd from Hugh de Lasne. Mill.* Major Roman site, Magna Castra.

Kilpeck *Chipeete: William FitzNorman from the king. 15 sesters of honey.* Church with Saxon remains. The ruined castle belonged to William FitzNorman.

King's Caple *Cape: William FitzNorman from the king.* Mound of a Norman castle.

Kingsland *Lene: King's land. 2 mills. 500 eels.* Large; ruined castle, the reputed burial place of Merewald, 7th-century Mercian king. At Mortimer's Cross nearby, Edward Mortimer defeated Owen Tudor in 1461 to become Edward IV.

King's Pyon *Pionie: Roger de Lacy.*

Kingstone (near Hereford) *Chingestone: King's land; Ilbert FitzTurold from the king.* Near a Roman road.

Kingstone (in Weston under Penyard) *Chingestune: Cormeilles Church.*

Kington *Chingtune: King's land, formerly Earl Harold.* Market town; remains of Lyonshall Castle.

Kinnersley *Elburgelega: Richard from Ralph de Mortimer.* Elizabethan House, now an old people's home.

Knill *Chenille: Osbern FitzRichard.* The birthplace of Anne Garbett, wife of the 19th-century scholar Sir Samuel Romilly.

Lawton *Lautone/tune: Roger de Lacy from the king and an Englishman from him.* Locality near Leominster.

Laysters *Last: Roger de Mussegros; Bernard from Durand of Gloucester and his nephew Walter; Edric, the pre-Conquest holder.* Scattered; castle mound. One of Wordsworth's favourite haunts.

Lea *Lecce: Gloucester Church.* Castle End House.

Ledbury *Liedeberge:* See page 128.

Ledicot *L(e)idecote: Ralph de Mortimer; Gilbert from Roger de Lacy, formerly Aelfled, a woman.*

Leinthall *Len/Le(n)te/Lintehale: King's land; Ralph de Mortimer, formerly Queen Edith. Mill.* Now 2 villages, Leinthall Earls and Leinthall Starkes.

Leintwardine *Lenteurde: Earl Roger; Ralph de Mortimer.* Large; on a Roman road.

Leominster *Leo(f)minstre: King's land, formerly Queen Edith; Urse d'Abetot; Roger de Lacy; Ralph de Mortimer; William FitzNorman; Widard. 10 mills, hawk's eyrie. 90 sticks of eels. 20 outliers.* Small town which grew up around a Saxon priory and was once famous for its wool. Daniel Bourn invented the first wool-carding machine here in 1748.

Letton (near Clifford) *Letune: Tesselin from Roger de Lacy. Mill.*

Letton (near Wigmore) *Lectune: Ralph de Mortimer.*

Lingen *Lingham: Ralph de Mortimer.* Ruined castle; priory.

Linton *Lintone/une: King's land; William FitzBalderon with St Mary's of Cormeilles holding the church. Mill. 6 sesters of honey.* Castle remains; prehistoric earthworks.

Litley *Lutelei: Widard from Durand of Gloucester.* Litley Court (in a Hereford suburb), a large building belonging to the Ministry of Agriculture, Fisheries and Food.

Little Brampton *Bruntune: Osbern FitzRichard.* Medieval farmhouse.

Little Cowarne *Colgre: Nigel the Doctor.* Humphry Smith, the 17th-century Quaker preacher, was born here.

Little Hereford *Lutelonhereford: Hereford Church. Mill.* Easton Court.

Little Marcle *Merchelai: Odo from Roger de Lacy, formerly Earl Harold; Thurstan from Thurstan FitzRolf. Mill.*

KILPECK: *Norman church, 1135, with red sandstone carvings.*

Llanwarne *Ladgvern: Hereford Church, formerly wrongfully held by Earl Harold. Church.* Ruined medieval church.

Longtown *Ewias: Roger de Lacy.* Formerly known as Ewias Lacy. Dominated by the 12th-century castle, possibly built on the site of King Harold's castle.

Lower Harpton *Hercope:* Lost near Kington.

Lugwardine *Lucuordne: King's land. 4 mills.* Large.

Lulham *Lulleham: Hereford Church.*

Luntley *Lutelei: Ilbert from the king.* Jacobean Luntley Court.

Luston *Lustone: King's land, formerly Queen Edith.* Tudor house.

Lyde *Leode/Lude: Hereford Church; Ralph from Roger de Lacy, formerly Earl Harold; Roger de Lacy from Osbern FitzRichard.* Part of the village of Pipe and Lyde.

Lye *Lecwe/Lega/Lege: William FitzNorman, Ralph de Mortimer, Osbern FitzRichard and Gruffydd of Maredudd from the king.* Now 2 hamlets, Upper and Lower Lye, separated by Sned Wood.

Lyonshall *Lenehalle: Walter from Roger de Lacy, formerly Earl Harold.* Castle remains; section of Offa's Dyke nearby.

Madley *Medelagie. Hereford Church.*

Mansell Gamage *Malveselle: Roger de Lacy, formerly Aelfled, a woman.*

Mansell Lacy *Malveselle: Gruffydd of Maredudd.*

Marden *Maurdine: King's land; Roger de Lacy; Stephen. Mill, fishery.* St Ethelbert's well.

Marston *Merstune: Herman de Dreux.*

Marston Stannett *Merstune: King's land, formerly Queen Edith; Godmund from Roger de Lacy; William d'Ecouis; Rayner Carpenter.*

MIDDLETON: *Carved oak bench end.*

Mathon *Matma/e: Odo from Roger de Lacy; Aethelhelm from Drogo FitzPoyntz; Urso and Walter Ponther from Pershore Church. Mill.* Scattered.

Maund Bryan *Mage(ne)/Magga/-e: Nigel the Doctor; Roger de Lacy and William from him; William d'Ecouis.* Maund Court and Common nearby.

Mawfield *Malfelle: Ingelrann from Roger de Lacy.* Farms.

Middleton on the Hill *Miceltune: King's land held by Bernard from Durand the Sheriff.* Scattered. Moor Abbey, a moated house, once belonged to the monks of Leominster.

Middlewood *Midewde: Gilbert FitzThorold, formerly Earl Harold.*

Middlewood *Mideurde:* Lost.

Miles Hope *Hope: King's land.*

Milton *Mildetune: Osbern FitzRichard.*

Moccas *Moches: St Guthlac's Church; Ansfrid from Nigel the Doctor.* Castle site.

Monkland *Leine: St Peter's of Castellion from Ralph de Tosny. Mill (25 sticks of eels).* The 19th-century compiler of hymns, Sir Henry Baker, was vicar here.

Monnington *Manetune/itone: Alfred of Marlborough, formerly Earl Harold.* Monnington Court.

Monnington on Wye *Manitune: Roger from Ralph de Tosny, formerly Earl Harold.*

Moor *More:* Lost.

Moreton Jeffreys *Mortune: Hereford Church.* Isolated.

Moreton on Lugg *Mortune: Hereford Church. Mill.* Large; Moreton Hall.

Much Cowarne *Cuure: Alfred of Marlborough, formerly Earl Harold.* Scattered; Leighton Court.

Much Marcle *Merchelai: King's land, formerly Earl Harold; Lyre Church; William FitzBaderon. Mill.* Castle mound.

Munsley *Moneslai/Muleslage/Muneslai: Ralph from Roger de Lacy; William FitzBaderon; William FitzNorman; Humphrey de Bouville.* Remote.

Nash *Hech: Osbern FitzRichard.* Ford.

Newton *Neutone: Osbern FitzRichard.* Newton Court.

Newton *Newentone/Niwetune: King's land held by William d'Ecouis and Bernard from him.* Scattered.

Norton Canon *Nortune: Hereford Church.*

Ocle Pychard *Acle: Roger de Lacy.*

Orleton *Alretune: Ralph de Mortimer, formerly Edith.* Large. The 13th-century Adam of Orleton became bishop of Worcester, Hereford and Winchester.

Pembridge *Penebruge: Alfred of Marlborough, formerly Earl Harold. Mill.* Small town with a Tudor market hall.

Pedwardine *Pedewrde: Ralph de Mortimer.*

Pipe *Pipe: Hereford Church.*

Pixley *Picheslei: Ansfrid de Cormeilles; Humphrey de Bouville.*

Pontrilas (formerly Elvastone) *Elwistone: Alfred of Marlborough from the king.*

Pontshill *Panchille: Durand of Gloucester.*

Poston *Poscetenetune: Ralph from William d'Ecouis.* Poston House, outside Vowchurch. An Iron Age fort is nearby.

Preston on Wye *Prestretune: Hereford Church. Mill.*

Preston Wynne *Prestretune: Hereford Church.* Court Farm.

Priors Frome *Frome: St Peter's of Hereford; Henry de Ferrers; Ilbert FitzThorold.*

Puddleston *Pillesdune: Roger de Lacy.* Scattered; Ford Abbey; Puddleston Court, now a school.

Putley *Poteslepe: William from Roger de Lacy.* Putley Court.

Richard's Castle *Auretone: Robert Gernon; Osbern FitzRichard. Mill (15 sticks of eels).* Remains of a castle built by Richard FitzScrob before the Conquest and later rebuilt by the Mortimers.

Risbury *Riseberie: William d'Ecouis from the king. Mill.* Iron Age fort nearby.

Ross *Rosse: Hereford Church. Mill.* A market town and 19th-century resort.

Rotherwas *Retrowas: Gilbert FitzThorold.* Suburb of Hereford.

Rowden *Ruedene: King's land; Ralph the chaplain's wife and her son Walter.* Abbey.

Rushock *Ruiscop: King's land and William d'Ecouis, formerly Earl Harold.*

Sarnesfield *Sarnesfelde: King's land; Roger de Lacy; Ralph de Tosny. Fishery (600 eels).* John Abel, 17th-century architect of timber-framed houses, is buried in the church.

Sawbury *Salberga/Sargeberie:* Lost.

Shelwick *Scelwiche: Hereford Church. Mill.*

Shirley *Sirelei: Ralph de Mortimer.* Farm.

Shobdon *Scepedune: Ralph de Mortimer, formerly Edith.* Castle mound; church founded as a priory in 1140 by Hugh Mortimer's chief steward.

Soller's Hope *Hope: Richard from Ansfrid de Cormeilles.*

Stanford Bishop *Stanford: King's land, formerly Queen Edith; Thurstan from Roger de Lacy. Mill.*

Stanway *Stanewei:* Lost.

Staunton on Arrow *Stantune: Ralph de Mortimer; Drogo from Osbern FitzRichard.* The court of Noke Manor House; mill.

Staunton on Wye *Standune/tune: Leofric and William from Roger de Lacy.*

Stockton *Stoctune: King's land, formerly Queen Edith.* House built on the site of a Dark Ages settlement.

Stoke Edith *Stoches: Ralph de Tosny, formerly Queen Edith. Mill.* Remains of an estate belonging to the Foley family.

Stoke Lacy *Stoches: Roger de Lacy. Mill.*

Stoke Prior *Stoca: King's land, formerly Queen Edith.* Once a Roman settlement.

Strangford *Etone: Hugh de Lasne. 2 sesters of honey.*

Street *Lestret/Strete: King's land; Roger de Lacy.* Street Court.

Stretford *Stratford: Thurstan from Alfred of Marlborough, formerly Earl Harold.* Ancient ford; Roman road.

Stretton *Stratone: Robert from Roger de Lacy; Vitalis from Hugh de Lasne.* Stretton Court.

Stretton Grandison *Stratune: William FitzBaderon, formerly Earl Harold.* New House; once a Roman settlement.

Sugwas *Sucwessen: Hereford Church, formerly wrongfully held by Earl Harold.* Part of Stretton Sugwas.

Sutton St Michael *St Nicholas Su(d)tune: Nigel the Doctor; Hugh de Lasne. 2 mills (8 and 7 sticks of eels).* Now 2 villages, Sutton St Michael and St Nicholas. Nearby Sutton Walls is said to have been the site of King Offa's palace, where Ethelbert was murdered.

Swanstone *Suenestun: Godmund from Roger de Lacy.* Swanston Court.

Tarrington *Tatintune: Ansfrid from Roger de Lacy; Ansfrid de Cormeilles.* The 19th-century geologist Sir Roderick Murchison studied local strata here, as described in his *Silurian System.*

Tedstone *Tedesthorne/Tetistorp: Hereford Church; Roger de Lacy.* Now the hamlet of Tedstone Delamere (whose church has Saxon remains) and village of Tedstone Wafre, both named after medieval knights; Roman fort nearby.

Thinghill *Tingehalle/hele: St Guthlac's Church; Geoffrey from Nigel the Doctor.* 14th-century Thinghill Grange.

Thornbury *Torneberie: Alfred d'Epagne.* Scattered. Birthplace of Roger Mortimer and Robert, Earl of Essex, Elizabeth I's last lover. Wall Hills, an Iron Age fort, is nearby.

Thruxton *Torchestone: Bernard from Durand of Gloucester.* Round barrow, possibly Bronze Age.

Titley *Titel(l)ege: Osbern FitzRichard, formerly Earl Harold.* Titley Court; a section of Offa's Dyke nearby.

Treville *Trieuline: King's land. Wood.* Treville Wood.

Tupsley *Topeslage: Hereford Church. Mill.* Suburb of Hereford.

Tyberton *Tibrintintune: Hereford Church.*

Ullingswick *Ullingwic: Hereford Church.*

Upleadon *Lede(n): St Peter's from Roger de Lacy; Albert de Lorraine, formerly Edith, sister of Earl Oda. Mill.* Upleadon Court Farm.

Upton *Up(e)tone: King's land; Roger de Mussegros.* Part of Brimfield.

Upton Bishop *Uptune: Hereford Church; Upton Court.*

Venn's Green *Fenne: William FitzNorman.*

The Vern *Ferne: William FitzNorman.*

Walford *Waliford/e: Ralph de Mortimer.* Castle mound; Court House.

Walford (near Ross) *Walecford: Hereford Church.* Watford Court.

Walsopthorne *Walesapeldor: Gerald from William FitzBaderon.* House.

Wapley *Wapletone: King's land; Osbern FitzRichard.* Site of an Iron Age fort associated by legend with the Ancient British King Caractacus.

Warham *Werham: Hereford Church.* On the outskirts of Hereford.

Webton *Webetone: Bernard and Gerald from Roger de Lacy.*

Wellington *Walintone: Hugh de Lasne and Ralph from him. 2 mills.* Large.

Welson *Ulfelmestune: King's land, formerly Earl Harold.* Now 2 small villages, Upper and Lower Welson.

Weobley *Wibelai: Roger de Lacy. Park.* Large. The ruined castle was the scene of King John's surrender to William de Braose.

Westhide *Hide: Ralph de Tosny, formerly Edith; Tesselin from Roger de Lacy.*

Weston *Westune:* Lost.

Weston Beggard *Westune: Roger de Lacy. Mill.*

Weston under Penyard*: Bernard from Durand of Gloucester.* Stone-built; castle remains. The site of the Roman settlement of *Ariconium* is nearby.

Wharton *Wavertune: King's land: William d'Ecouis. Mill.*

Whitney *Witenie: King's land; Harold from St Guthlac's Church.* On the edge of the Wye flood plain; the poet Christopher Harvey was vicar here in the early 17th century.

Whitwick *Witewiche: William FitzBaderon, formerly Earl Harold.* Manor.

Whyle *Huilech: Osbern FitzRichard.*

Wicton *Wigetune: Ursc d'Abetot and Roger de Lacy by exchange from him.* Farm.

Wigmore *Wig(h)emore:* See page 129.

Willersley *Willaveslege: Ralph de Tosny, formerly Earl Harold; a Welshman.* Willersley Court.

Wilmastone *Wilmestune: Hugh de Lasne. Mill.* Farm.

Wilton *Wiltone: King's land, formerly Earl Harold; William FitzBaderon.* Elizabethan bridge over the River Wye; ruined castle.

Winforton *Widferdestune: Ralph de Tosny formerly Earl Harold and a Welshman from him.* Winforton Court.

Winnall *Wilehalle: Picot from Gilbert FitzThorold.*

Withington *Widingtune: Hereford Church. Mill.* Large; on a Roman road; famous for its tile works in 19th century.

Wolferlow *Ulferlau: Ralph de Mortimer; Hugh and Walter from Roger de Lacy.* Scattered; Roman fort nearby.

Woolhope *Hope: Hereford Church.* The church is thought to have been given to Hereford Cathedral by Wulviva, sister of Godiva.

Woonton *Wennetune: King's land; Roger de Lacy.*

Woonton *Wenetone: Gerald from Roger de Lacy.*

Wormsley *Wermeslai/Wrmesleu: Hereford Church; Leofric from Roger de Lacy.* Scattered; Wormsley Grange.

Yarkhill *Achel: Roger de Lacy, formerly a thane of Earl Harold. Mill.*

YARPOLE: *The old bakehouse.*

Yarpole *Iarpol(e): King's land; Leofwin Latimer; Robert Gernon.*

Yarsop *Ardes/Edreshope/Erdeshop/sope: Hereford Church; Robert from Roger de Lacy; William d'Ecouis; Ralph the chaplain's wife.*

Yatton *Getune: King's land.* Scattered.

Yazor *Iavesoure: Robert from Roger de Lacy.* House of Sir Uvedale Price, 19th-century theorist of the English Picturesque.

Wales Gazetteer

Burlingjobb *Berchelincon: King's land.* Limestone quarry nearby.

Cascob *Cascope: Osbern FitzRichard.*

Clatterbrune *Clatretune:* Lost.

Discoed *Discote: Osbern FitzRichard.* Castle mound; a section of Offa's Dyke nearby.

Harpton *Hertune: Ralph de Mortimer; Osbern FitzRichard.*

Monmouth *Monemude: King's land; William FitzBaderon. 3 mills, church belonging to St Florent's of Saumur. 33 sesters of honey.* Market town with the remains of 2 castles, one built by Roger de Montgomery c.1070. Iron Age and Roman settlement; birthplace of the 17th-century poet George Herbert.

Old Radnor *Raddrenoue: King's land, formerly Earl Harold.* Castle remains; once a base for king Harold.

Pilleth on Lugg *Pelelei: Ralph de Mortimer.* Castle remains. Nant-y-Groes was the house of Dr John Dee, 16th-century mathematician and astrologer.

Weston *Westune: Ralph de Mortimer.* Part of Llangunllo.

Hertfordshire

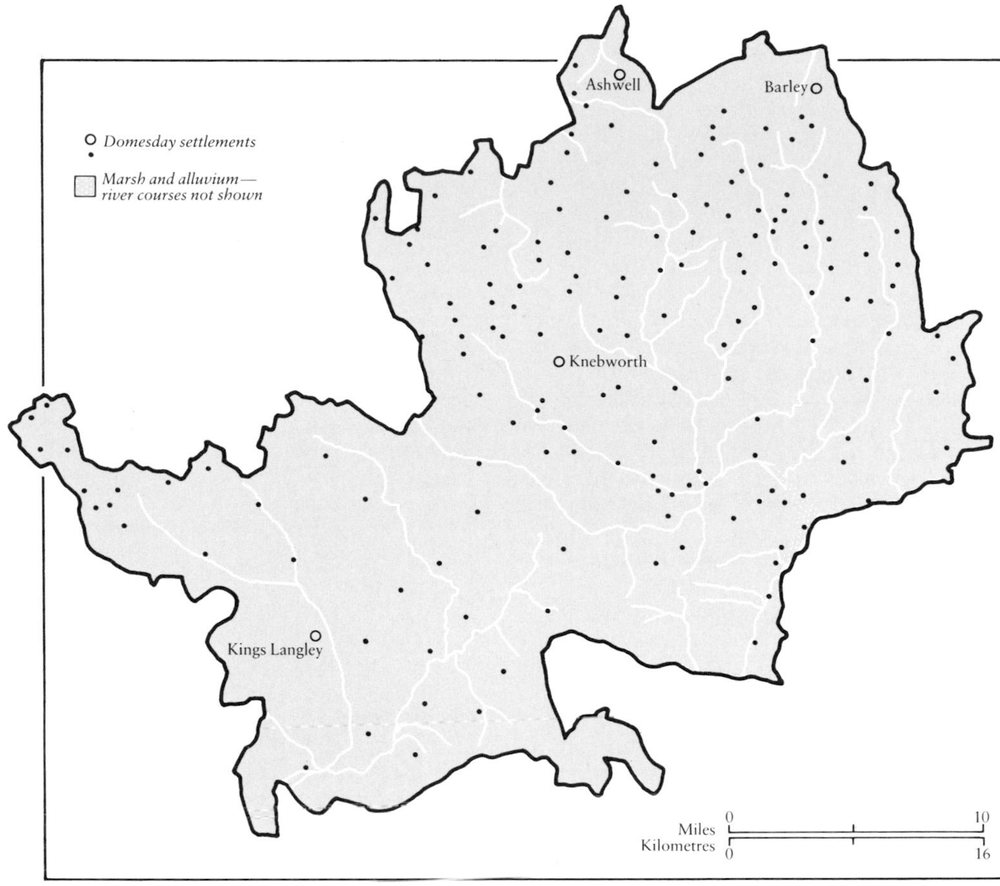

A map of Domesday *Hertfordshire shows a striking concentration of settlements in the north and east of the county. It is as if a magnet had drawn them there, at the expense of the south and west, which, except for the peninsula 'Hundred' of Tring, are thinly populated.*

The key lies in the great claylands just north of the River Lee and west of the Stort. They provide what is still some of England's best cereal-growing soil, whose fertile qualities had been recognized for centuries. It is no wonder that powerful men like Bishop Odo, Hardwin of Scales and Geoffrey de Bec held land here. In contrast, the territory to the south consisted either of intractable woodland or of heath and scrub on poor sandy soil. Settlements in the western Chiltern districts were most common in river valleys, notably the Gade, and where there were plentiful supplies of woodland for timber and for the keeping of pigs.

Of Hertfordshire's five Domesday *boroughs, Hertford, with its 146 burgesses, was by far the most important. Although St Albans had a large abbey, it was not yet a significant town. Stanstead and Ashwell were more modest boroughs, as was Berkhamsted in the far west. Watford, now Hertfordshire's largest town, does not even figure in* Domesday!

Barley

In BARLEY *BERLAI* Theobald holds 4 hides and 10 acres from Hardwin. Land for 3½ ploughs. In lordship 2. 3 villagers with a priest and 8 smallholders have 1½ ploughs. 4 cottagers; 2 slaves. In total, value 45s; when acquired 15s; before 1066, 60s. 5 Freemen held this manor. Three of them, Earl Algar's men, had 1 hide and 10 acres; the fourth, Earl Gyrth's man, had 2 hides; the fifth, Earl Harold's man, had 1 hide. All of them could sell.

Barley is a small farming community crowning a hilltop in the north-eastern corner of Hertfordshire. Viewed from a distance in high summer it seems an island in a golden sea of the grain that gave it its name. In *Domesday*, each of the four manors into which the village was divided had a different holder. William d'Odburgville held one, Eudo another, the Abbess of Chatteris (religious houses were usually permitted to keep their property after the Conquest) still another and Hardwin of Scales, one of William's right-hand men, the manor of Greenbury, in which the present-day village stands.

All told, 59 men including ten landless serfs worked land assessed at 1,910 acres. Yet in neighbouring Newsells (now a hamlet) only 21 serfs worked 615 acres – a proportion unmatched anywhere else in the county. Most of these slaves must have been used to clear the substantial Newsells woodland and thus increase its value from £12 before 1066 to £18 in 1086. In contrast the value of the combined Barley manors dropped from £16 to £12 in the same period.

The five freemen *Domesday* mentions were probably the founders of Barley's first church. Nothing is known of the priest, but he would have worked his glebe land himself in strips intermingled with those of his fellow landholders. The oldest part of the present church dates from the twelfth century and is very likely the work of a descendant of Hardwin, inspired by his experiences in the first Crusade.

Another descendant, Henry de Stikewand, sold Greenbury Manor to Anglesey Priory at Bottisham and donated the advowson – the gift of living – of the church to the Abbess of Chatteris, who already held one Barley manor. Possibly as a result, there was established a long and almost unbroken line of learned incumbents, including two rectors, Warham (1495–1503) and Herring (1722–31), who went on to become archbishops of Canterbury. Many of the clerics were college fellows and masters, and a few were canons of Ely.

The most intellectually distinguished of them all started his working life as a jobbing carpenter. Dr Samuel Lee (1783–1853) taught himself Latin, Greek, Hebrew and Persian, among other languages, and having been forced to abandon his trade when a fire destroyed his tools, arrived as the only student in Cambridge with a knowledge of Hindustani. Academically brilliant, he was elected to the chair of Arabic two years after graduation. By the time he arrived in Barley in 1838, he was widely regarded as one of Europe's greatest Orientalists. He had already been appointed Cambridge's Regius Professor of Hebrew.

Another illustrious Barley resident was R.N. Salaman, a physician from a wealthy family of ostrich-feather importers, who settled here in 1906. A geneticist, he specialized in the study of the potato, and in 1949 published *The History and Social Influence of the Potato*, the culmination of his life's work. His friend James Parkes, a world authority on Judaeo-Christian relationships, lived in The Old Granary for some years.

Barley today seems a rather ordinary village of brick, flint and plastered cottages, with a few grander houses, and the odd picturesque vista, notably around the church. The early Tudor Town House, formerly a school and almshouses, now the village hall, is Barley's most striking building. Of the four original manors the names of two – Mincinbury and Abbotsbury – live on as farm names on the eastern borders of the parish. Interestingly, about 100 acres of Barley are still farmed from neighbouring Newsells, just as they were by Eudo, their tenant, in 1086.

Knebworth

Eudo FitzHubert holds KNEBWORTH *CHENEPEWORDE* and Humphrey from him. It answers for 8 hides and 1 virgate. Land for 12 ploughs. In lordship 2 ploughs; another 2 possible. 20 villagers with 2 men-at-arms and 2 smallholders have 8 ploughs. 3 cottagers; 4 slaves; 2 countrymen. 1 mill at 12s; meadow for ½ plough; pasture for the village livestock; woodland, 1000 pigs. Total value £10; when acquired 100s; before 1066 £12. Askell, a thane of King Edward's, held this manor; one of his men had 1 hide and 1 virgate; he could sell. He found 1 cartage in customary dues, when the King came into the Shire; if not, he paid 5d.

In well wooded country south of Stevenage New Town, Old Knebworth, clustered on the edge of parkland, and new Knebworth, centred on the railway station, lie half a mile apart, separated by the busy motorway. Eudo FitzHubert, the King's Steward was granted land in little pockets, particularly in north Hertfordshire. His Knebworth property was by far his largest. The huge number of pigs tallied in *Domesday* indicates the extent of woodland, which has remained fairly constant throughout the centuries.

Humphrey d'Anneville was Eudo's under-tenant and it is from his line that Knebworth descended to the famous Lyttons. The connection began in 1492, when William, son of Robert Lytton, inherited two-thirds of the manor on the death of Thomas Bourghchier (the other one-third went to his widow). In about 1500 Robert began to build a grand two-storied courtyard house, one of whose four ranges survived the drastic reconstruction of 1811 undertaken by the wife of William Earle Bulwer Lytton. She died in 1843 leaving her neo-Tudor palace of stuccoed turrets and parapets to her third son Edward, the fashionable novelist and poet, who continued the transformation in his own high Gothic vein. The state drawing room by John Crace is a stunning monument to Lytton's taste for the extravagantly theatrical. Amateur drama, indeed, was one of the pleasures Lytton shared with Charles Dickens who, with Mark Lemon, John Forster, Douglas Jerrold and other actors *manqué*, spent some memorable days in 1850 taking part in a 'Dramatic Festival' at Knebworth House. From this event was born the Guild of Literature and Art – a sort of early Arts Council which would reward both established and rising artists and writers with endowments and rent-free accomodation in Knebworth Park. The scheme was to be financed by profits from countrywide dramatic performances by Dickens and his amateur theatrical troupe. After a promising start, however, support dwindled and the Guild was eventually dissolved.

The novelist (who became Lord Lytton in 1866) wrote much of his fiction at Knebworth House, but his verse was often composed in a cottage by the lake. The surroundings of this retreat he evocatively described in 1835: '... its venerable avenues, which slope from the house down to the declivity of the park, giving wide views of the opposite hills, crowded with cottages and spires, impart to the scene that peculiarly English, half stately and wholly cultivated character'.

Today house and park may have lost some of their dignity, but the vistas have altered little. The ancient Newton Wood blots out a view of Stevenage's industrial quarter, thereby preserving the pastoral effect.

Kings Langley

Ralph holds LANGLEY *LANGELEI* from the Count [of Mortain]. It answers for 1½ hides. Land for 16 ploughs. In lordship none, but 2 possible. 1 Frenchman with 4 villagers and 5 smallholders have 2 ploughs; 12 ploughs possible. 2 mills at 16s; 2 slaves; meadow for 3 ploughs; pasture for the livestock; woodland, 240 pigs. Total value 40s; when acquired £4; before 1066 £8. Thorir and Seric, two of Earl Leofwin's men, held this manor.

The village of Kings Langley lies in a valley on the western bank of the River Gade, a jumbled patchwork of old timber and brick, randomly sited Georgian houses, Victorian and Edwardian villas and pleasant modern estates. Arable land still touches the village on all sides. One mile to the west is the site of the former royal palace of Langley, much favoured by generations of kings and queens. Beside it lie the remains of a Dominican friary, once the richest in the kingdom.

Robert de Mortain, the tenant-in-chief of the *Domesday* entry, was half-brother to William I. He gave the manor of Langelei to Ralph, a sergeant-of-arms at Berkhamsted Castle. When the Mortain family was dispossessed for rebellion in 1104, Ralph's family, the Chenduits, became true overlords of the manor.

Domesday records that there were extensive areas of woodland – enough to support 240 pigs. The River Gade with its two mills was also of value to the community. But in 1086 the village was not prosperous. Although there was enough arable land for 16 plough teams – perhaps some 1700 acres – only two ploughs were operating. One explanation may be that the manor had some 20 years earlier lain across the direct Norman line of march between London and Berkhamsted, and had been ravaged by William's soldiers in his scorched-earth tactics to isolate London.

The Chenduits quarrelled acrimoniously with the monks of St Albans who continually pressed their claim as owners in Anglo-Saxon times. As late as 1247 William Chenduit still paid 20s a year rent to the abbot. Although facts from this period are scarce, it is known that Richard, Earl of Cornwall, and an heir to the Holy Roman Empire (there were many such heirs, all of whose claims were based on a mythological game), became the next overlord.

A closer royal association began in 1276 when Queen Eleanor of Castile, a keen business-woman, bought the moated manor house for £20, and re-created it as a royal palace. Skilled masons and carpenters, famous craftsmen and artists were brought from London to rebuild and to decorate. These included Alexander of Abingdon who later carved many of the Eleanor Crosses erected after the queen's death by her husband, Edward I, to commemorate the places where her body rested on its way from the Midlands to Westminster for burial.

A new vineyard was laid out, and the Constable of Windsor brought 30 live doe to stock the 128-acre park. Cain's field, near what is now the village centre, even boasted a camel and a lion cub, possibly imported by a Crusader wishing to ingratiate himself with the queen. By 1290 this was a thriving village. A market was held every Thursday and a fair during Whit week.

The Prince of Wales, later Edward II, was the only member of the royal family to disrupt the harmony that prevailed between palace and village. His agents periodically raided markets and bullied farmers out of their produce, '... for as much as 200 dishes of meat were not sufficient for his kitchen'. As king, Edward spent his time at Langley with the sinister Piers Gaveston, an allegedly homosexual friendship which brought the country to the edge of civil war. Gaveston was eventually beheaded by zealously loyal barons, and Edward brought his bones from Warwick for re-burial at the friary. No less than 23 tuns of wine came from London to ease the occasion.

Edmund Langley, the fifth son of Edward III and the first Duke of York, was born at Langley Palace in 1341, and died there in 1401. His tomb, which was transferred from the friary to the parish church at the Dissolution, was opened in 1877, and was found to contain three skeletons: Edmund's, his wife's and, lying on the top in a mummy-shaped lead wrapping, that of a woman of about 30, with long auburn hair. Sarah Holt, in her novel of 1875, *The White Maid of Langley*, identified her as Constance, the duke's only daughter.

Henry V bestowed Langley Palace on Queen Joan of Navarre in 1415. During her day, rabbits were so abundant that they were used as currency, and a warren was established to provide the villagers legally with what they had previously poached. After Joan's death, the palace was owned by a succession of queens, none of whom lived here. Henry VIII gave it to three of his wives in succession, Katherine of Aragon, Anne Boleyn and Jane Seymour. Finally he annexed it to the Duchy of Lancaster.

Over the centuries Lords of the Manor at Kings Langley included Sir Francis Bacon and John Russell, Earl of Bedford, who, after being fined for rent arrears, departed to settle at Woburn. In 1628 the manor briefly belonged to the Ditchfield Grant, set up to guarantee Charles I's debts to City of London financiers. It passed eventually to a local man, a Mr Betts, who in 1831 demolished the building.

The village thrived over many generations, while rents remained at medieval rates. Agriculture was its lifeblood, but it also supported a wide range of trades. In the early nineteenth century a farming boom, stimulated by the Napoleonic Wars, combined with the opening of the Grand Junction Canal – now Grand Union – to set the local economy booming, a boom which stopped abruptly when gigantic imports from Canada and the United States coincided with a fall in the local water table that made the mills inoperable. E.M. Forster, in *Howard's End* (1910) described the sort of quiet Hertfordshire landscape in which Kings Langley lies as 'England meditative'.

Farming is still, although barely, the major economic activity, but light manufacturing is catching up. Despite Kings Langley's royal heritage, its ancient agricultural landscape and its pleasant understated nature, travellers might today – as they speed by on main-line trains, pick out the Ovaltine factory as its symbol.

Ashwell

Westminster Abbey holds ASHWELL *ESCEWELLE.* It answers for 6 hides. Land for 12 ploughs. In lordship 2½ hides; 2 ploughs there. A priest with 16 villagers and 9 smallholders have 5 ploughs; another 5 ploughs possible. 14 burgesses; 9 cottagers. From tolls and other customary dues of the Borough, 49s 4d. 4 slaves. 2 mills at 14s; meadow for 6 ploughs; pasture for the livestock; woodland, 100 pigs. The total value is and was £20; before 1066 £22. Peter the Sheriff holds ½ hide of this land from the Abbot; Geoffrey de Mandeville, 1 virgate, and 1 mill at 10s. This manor lay and lies in the lordship of St Peter's Church, Westminster.

Ashwell is a large, prosperous-looking village huddled under a spur of the Hertfordshire Chilterns in the far north of the county, with wide, uninterrupted views over neighbouring Bedfordshire and Cambridgeshire. The manor was granted by Edward the Confessor to Westminster Abbey in 1066 and remained under its control until 1539 when, as part of the Dissolution, it was transferred to the newly formed bishopric of Westminster. This in turn was dissolved by Edward VI in 1550 and the manor then granted to Dr Nicholas Ridley, Bishop of London. On the arrest of this zealous Protestant in 1553, Ashwell passed to the equally fervent Bishop Bonner, who was to become the Catholic Queen Mary's stalwart. The manor was sold privately for £416 9s 2d during the Civil War, but was returned at the Restoration to the see of London, where it remained until 1868, when the Ecclesiastical Commissioners took it over.

ASHWELL: *The mellow oak of a timbered lime-washed house in its natural colours.*

Peter de Valognes ('the Sheriff'), who had a great deal of Hertfordshire land, chiefly that confiscated from Aelred of Benington, held one of the mills mentioned in 1086. In 1198 a man and a woman were 'drowned in the pool of the mill at Ashwell'. According to thirteenth- and fourteenth-century Minister's Accounts (of revenue from Crown lands), there were by then only one water mill and one 'horse mill'. Today the tiny River Rhee, which rises here, still drives one mill-wheel, that of the Mill House, now a private residence.

Ashwell's 14 burgesses in 1086 sound impressive, but *Domesday* does not distinguish between categories of borough. Unlike Hertford (which had 146 burgesses in 1066) Ashwell could hardly be called a town, although it undoubtedly became one later. It was Peter de Valognes' duty, as sheriff, to ensure that the king received all that was due to him in the way of revenue and services from Ashwell borough. As a major figure in the village, Valogne presumably had a strong influence on its government. Although there is no mention of any corporate governing body in later medieval records, it is likely that the Guild of St John, a sort of early trade union composed of merchants and craftsmen, became involved in running Ashwell. Their Guild Hall still stands in the High Street.

Medieval Ashwell's prosperity was due mainly to its proximity to the ancient Icknield Way, a trading route that linked Salisbury Plain with the Wash, and the Roman Ashwell Street. In time, however, the success of Hertford, Ware and Stortford, all malting centres on navigable rivers, began to eclipse Ashwell's. Eventually, because of the absence of a main road, neighbouring Hitchin, Baldock and Royston all prospered while Ashwell languished. Nevertheless, brewing, with agriculture, remained its chief industries long after the market (first mentioned in 1211) and annual fair (abolished in 1872) had gone.

A magnificent monument to Ashwell's medieval prosperity is its 176ft church tower which was begun early in the fourteenth century and is built entirely of clunch, a local material midway between chalk and stone. Not long after its completion the Black Death decimated the population; one witness in 1361 recorded his feelings in Latin graffiti cut deep onto a wall inside the tower: 'Miserable, wild and distracted, the dregs of the people alone survive...' Below this is scratched a small, remarkably accurate view of old St Paul's Cathedral, complete with spire, then England's highest. Elsewhere in the church are other graffiti, including a lover's complaint about his mistress – 'Barbara is barbarous' – also in Latin.

Ashwell is charming today for the same reasons that it failed to grow and eventually declined. Country roads may arrive from all directions to tangle in a picturesque knot of streets and lanes, but there is no major highway bringing heavy traffic. Even the railway station is two miles away. The little industry apart from agriculture is unobtrusive – a bakery, a bottling plant. New private housing is well-mannered, the older council property pushed on to the periphery. With its wealth of timber-framed buildings, many with overhangs and plaster pargeting, its old inns and old-fashioned shops, Ashwell is strongly rooted in its past; but it is in and around the church that a sense of the medieval is most powerfully evoked.

Hertfordshire Gazetteer
Each entry starts with the modern place name in **bold** type. The *Domesday* information that follows is in *italic* type, beginning with the name or names by which the place was known in 1086. The main landholders and under-tenants are next, separated with semi-colons if a place was divided into more than one holding. A number of holdings in Hertfordshire were granted by the king to his thanes; these holders, always the last in a list, are given with their office, or described as holding land 'from the king'. More general information completes the *Domesday* part of the entry, including examples of dues (eels, etc.) rendered by tenants. The modern or post-Domesday section is in normal type. [village symbol] represents a village, [hamlet symbol] a small village or hamlet.

Abbots Langley *Langelai: St. Albans Church. 2 mills.* Nicholas Breakspear (*d.*1159), only Englishman to become pope (Adrian IV), was born here.

Albury *Eldeberie: Ralph from Bishop of London.* Albury Hall; Albury Lodge.

Aldbury *Aldberie: Count of Mortain.* Picturesque; pond; stocks; whipping post.

Aldenham *Eldeham: Westminster Abbey before and after 1066; Geoffrey de Bec from St Albans Church.* The sculptor, Sir Alfred Gilbert, who created Piccadilly Circus's Eros, lived here. The gardens at Aldenham House are famous.

Almshoe *Almeshou: Adam from Bishop of Bayeux, formerly Earl Harold.* Now Little Almshoe.

Alswick *Alsieswiche: William from Ralph Baynard.* Alswick Hall.

Amwell *Emmewelle: Ralph de Limesy, formerly Earl Harold. Mill.* Now 2 villages, Great and Little Amwell, on the New River. Lord Allenby, World War I general who captured Jerusalem, was educated at Haileybury College near Little Amwell.

Anstey *Anestei/stige: Count Eustace, formerly Earl Harold; Payne from Hardwin of Scales.* Birthplace of poet and musician, Thomas Campion (1543–1620). Henry VIII gave Anstey Castle to his first 3 wives.

Ardeley *Erdelei: St Paul's, London before and after 1066.* Birthplace of Charles Chauncy, President of Harvard College (1654–72). Sir Henry Chauncy instigated England's last trial for witchcraft (1712).

Ashwell *Asceuuelle/Escewelle:* See page 135.

Aspenden *Absesdene: Richard de Sackville from Eudo FitzHubert.* The historian, Thomas Macaulay, was educated at Aspenden Hall (1814–18).

Aston *Estone: Bishop of Bayeux.*

Ayot St Lawrence *Aiete: Geoffrey from Westminster Abbey; the reeve of Broadwater Hundred from the king. Mill.* George Bernard Shaw lived the last 44 years of his life at the Old Rectory.

Ayot St Peter *Aiete: William from Robert Gernon.* On hilltop, surrounded by woods.

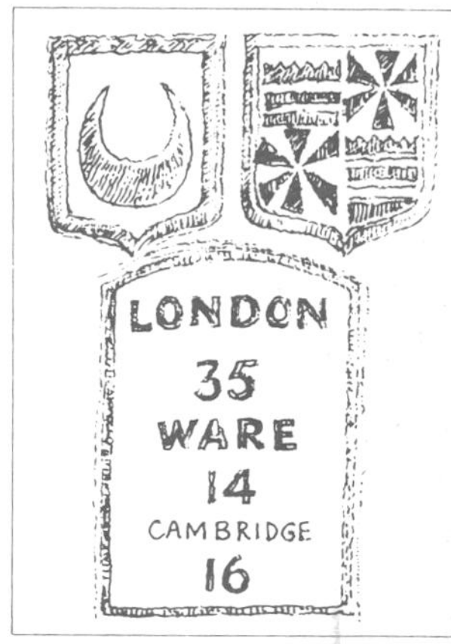

BARKWAY: *1725 milestone, with the arms of Trinity Hall, Cambridge.*

Barkway *Bercheuuei(g): Hugh from Geoffrey de Mandeville; 2 men from Hardwin of Scales; Godwin from Prince Edgar.* A Roman statue of Mars was found in a nearby wood.

Barley *Berlai:* See page 133.

Bayford *Begesford: King's land. 2 mills.* The early 19th-century zoologist, William Yarrell, is buried here.

Beauchamps (formerly Affledwick) *Alfledauuicha: Rumold from Count Eustace. Mill.* Ancient moat.

Bendish *Benedis: St Albans Church before and after 1066.*

Bengeo *Belingehou: Count Alan; 2 men-at-arms from Hugh de Beauchamp; Howard from Geoffrey de Mandeville; Geoffrey de Bec and 3 men-at-arms, Roger, a priest and a Frenchman from him; Peter de Valognes. 2 mills.* Now Bengeo Rural, a village and Bengeo Christchurch, an ecclesiastical district.

Bennington *Belintone: Peter de Valognes. Park for woodland beasts.* Hertfordshire's only Norman castle keep, home of the kings of Mercia.

Berkesden *Berchedene: Robert from Count Eustace, formerly Earl Harold; Peter and Theobald from Hardwin of Scales. Mill.* Berkesdon Green, an ancient site.

Berkhamsted *Berch(eh)amstede: Count of Mortain, formerly Earl Harold. 2 mills. 2 vines.* Market town with the ruins of the 11th-century castle where Edgar Atheling submitted to William I. The High Street is on the line of the Roman Akeman Street.

Bishop's Stortford *Storteford: Bishop of London. 2 mills.* Market town; Birthplace of Cecil Rhodes (1853–1902), after whom Rhodesia (now Zimbabwe) was named.

Boarscroft *Bure: Leofwin from Count of Mortain.*

Box *Boxe: Osbern from Bishop of Bayeux; Peter from William d'Eu; Peter de Valognes.* Now Box Lane.

Bozen *Bordesdene: Count Eustace; William from Robert Gernon; Thorold from Geoffrey de Mandeville.* Bozen Green, in Hadham.

Bramfield *Brandefelle: Hardwin of Scales, formerly Earl Harold.* Thomas à Becket was rector at the church; the rectory garden pond is known as Becket's pond.

Braughing *Brachinges: Count Eustace. Mill.* On the River Quin; Roman remains.

Brickendon *Briche(n)done: Canons of Waltham before and after 1066; Walter from Geoffrey de Mandeville; Isambard from Geoffrey de Bec; Baldwin from the king. Mill.* Now Brickendon Rural, in the borough of Hertford.

Broadfield *Bradefella/felle: Bishop of Chester; Earl Roger, formerly Queen Edith; Theobald from Hardwin of Scales; Sigar de Chocques.*

Broxbourne *Brochesborne: Adelaide, Hugh de Grandmesnil's wife. Mill.* Norman church; priest's house; giant yew on the River Lea.

Buckland *Bochelande: Osbern from Bishop of Bayeux.* Roman Ermine Street climbs to the church.

Buntingford (Eckington) *Ichetone: Osbern from Bishop of Bayeux; Rumold and 2 men-at-arms from Count Eustace; Walter from Eudo FitzHubert; Humphrey from Peter de Valognes; Theobald from Hardwin of Scales.* Small town with a Roman High Street. Seth Ward, the 17th-century astronomer and divine, went to school here. Hilltop church with Roman bricks.

Bushey *Bissei: Geoffrey de Mandeville, formerly Queen Edith. 2 mills.* Town. The roundhead turned royalist, Silius Titus, who plotted to kill Cromwell, is buried here.

Bygrave *Bigrave: Bishop of Chester. Mill.* On the Chilterns; manor farm surrounded by pre-Roman ditches and banks.

Caldecote *Caldecota: Ralph de Limesy.* Once a Roman settlement.

Cassio *C(h)aissou: St Alban's Church; Thorold from Geoffrey de Mandeville, formerly Queen Edith. 4 mills.* Cassiobury Park, once the home of the Earls of Essex.

Chaldean *Celgdene: Rodhere from Bishop of London.*

Charlton *Cerletone: King's land. Mill.*

Chells *Esceluela/Scelua/Scelue: William from Robert Gernon; Aelfric Bush from Geoffrey of Bec; Godfrey from Peter de Valognes.* Part of Stevenage.

Cheshunt *Cestrehont/hunt: Count Alan, before and after 1066. Mill.* Town with the Waltham Cross, one of the 'Eleanor' crosses erected by Edward I to mark the places where his wife's body rested on its way to London. Cheshunt Great House was the home of Cardinal Wolsey.

Clothall *Cladhele: Osbern from Bishop of Bayeux; Theobald from Hardwin of Scales; Leofgeat from Count Alan; William d'Eu.* Prehistoric terraces in the wheat fields; the Roman way passes through the village.

Cockhampstead *Cochehammestede: Count Eustace.*

Codicote *Codicote: St Alban's Church. 2 mills.*

Cokenach *Cochenac: Ansfrid from Geoffrey de Bec.*

Corney(bury) *Cornei: Robert from Count Eustace.*

Cottered *Chodrei: Bishop of Winchester.* 500-year-old farmhouse, 'The Lordship'. The surgeon who founded the Royal Society of Tropical Medicine, Sir James Cantlie, died here (1926).

Datchworth *Daceuuorde: Ansketel from Archbishop of Canterbury; Westminster Abbey; 2 men-at-arms from Geoffrey de Bec; Robert from Peter de Valognes.* The 18th-century poet, Edward Young, wrote his most famous work, *Night Thoughts*, under its yew trees.

Digswell *Dichelesuuelle: Thorkell from Geoffrey de Mandeville; Roger from Peter de Valognes. 2 mills.* Also Digswell Water, a hamlet.

Dunsley Dan *Deneslai: A widow from Count of Mortain; Mainou le Breton.*

Eastwick *Esteuuiche: Reginald from Geoffrey de Bec. Mill.*

Epcombs *Thepecampe: A priest from the king. Mill.*

Flamstead *Flammestede: Ralph de Tosny.* On the River Ver.

Flexmore *Fles/Flexmere: A freeman, the pre-Conquest holder (from Earl Harold), from the king; Peter de Valognes.*

Graveley *Grauelai: Adam from Bishop of Bayeux; William from Robert Gernon; Peter from William d'Eu; Gosbert de Beauvais; Godfrey from Peter de Valognes.* 17th-century farmhouse.

Great Gaddesden *Gatesdene: Edward of Salisbury. Mill.* On the River Gade; Whipsnade Zoo nearby; Norman church with Roman bricks. Stone Age flints, tools and hunting weapons were found in Gaddesden Row.

Great Hormead *Horemede: 2 Englishmen from Count Eustace; William from Ralph Baynard.* Old post-mill sails near the stump of a small smock-hill.

Great Munden *Mundene: Count Alan. Mill.* Near Munden Furnival, a hamlet, now called Nasty.

Great Offley *Offelei: 5 freemen and Edward of Pirton from the king; William Delamere from William d'Eu.* Reputedly named after Offa, king of Mercia, who is said to have died in his palace here.

Great Wymondley *Wimundeslai: King's land; Adam from Bishop of Bayeux; Gosbert de Beauvais.* Motte and bailey.

Gubblecote *Bublecote: Fulcwold from Count of Mortain. Mill.*

Hailey *Hailet: Geoffrey de Bec. 50 eels.* Part of Ware.

Hanstead *Henammesteda: St Albans Church. 2 mills.*

Hare Street (formerly **Langport**) *Langeport: Roger from Count Alan; Saeward from Geoffrey de Mandeville.*

Hatfield (Bishops Hatfield) *Hetfelle: Abbot of Ely. 4 mills.* Market town with Hatfield House (the seat of the Marquess of Salisbury), one of England's greatest houses.

Hazelhanger *Haslehangra/gre:* Lost.

HEMEL HEMPSTEAD: *Formerly a street pump, dated 1848.*

Hemel Hempstead *Hamelamestede: Count of Mortain. 4 mills. 300 eels.* Market town, one of the first New Towns; Norman church with Roman bricks.

Hertford *Hertforde: King's land; Count Alan and Eudo FitzHubert from him; Geoffrey de Bec; Humphrey d'Anneville from Eudo FitzHubert; Peter de Valognes; Geoffrey de Mandeville; Ralph Baynard; Hardwin of Scales; Peter the Sheriff. 2 churches, 3 mills.* Town, capital of Hertfordshire, where the first national Synod of the Church in England took place (673). It was burnt down by the Danes and rebuilt by Edward the Elder and the Normans.

Hertingfordbury *Herefordingberie: Ralph Baynard. 2 mills.* 300-year-old school; Panshanger Park.

Hexton *Heg(a)estanestone: A freeman from the king; St Albans Church; Ralph from Geoffrey de Bec. 3 mills.* Pretty; beneath the Barton Hills, site of the earthwork fort of Ravensburgh Castle.

Hinxworth *Hain(ge)steuuorde/Hamsteuuorde: 2 men-at-arms from William d'Eu; Peter de Valognes; Theobald from Hardwin of Scales.* The 15th-century historian Robert Clutterbuck lived at Hinxworth Place. A Roman Venus was found here, and a pre-Roman gravel pit revealed traces of 4 British tribes.

Hitchin *Hiz: King's land, formerly Earl Harold. 4 mills, monastery.* Market town; birthplace of the poet George Chapman (1559–1634) and the inventor Sir Henry Bessemer (1813–98). The Norman church, the biggest in Hertfordshire, contains Roman bricks.

Hixham *Tedricesham: William and Ranulf from Bishop of London.* Hixham Hall.

Hoddesdon *Dodesdone/Hodesdone/Odesdone/Hodesduna: Count Alan; Canons of St Martin's, London from Count Eustace; Edward the Sheriff, formerly Queen Edith; Ralph from Geoffrey de Mandeville; Peter from the king. Fishery (300 eels), weirs (143 eels).* Remains of Rye House, where a plot was hatched to assassinate Charles II and his brother James; the River Lea fills the moat.

Hodenhoe *Odenhou: Osbern from Bishop of Bayeux; Theobald from Hardwin of Scales.*

Holwell *Holewella/welle: Abbot of Romsey; Westminster Abbey. 2 mills.* Mineral spring.

Hunsdon *Hodesdone/Honesdone: Ralph Taillebois' daughter. Mill.* Hunsdon House; Henry VIII's daughter Mary (later Mary Tudor) set out from here on the 12-day ride that took her to the throne.

Hyde Hall (formerly **Somersale)** *Summersele: William from Robert Gernon.* House near Sawbridgeworth.

Kelshall *Cheleselle: Abbot of Ely.*

Kimpton *Kamintone: Ralph from Bishop of Bayeux. Mill.*

Kings Langley *Langelei:* See page 130.

King's Walden *Waldenei: King's land; Asgar's widow, the pre-Conquest holder, from the king.*

Knebworth *Chenepeworde:* See page 129.

Langley (near Stevenage) *Langelei: Osbert from Geoffrey de Bec.*

Letchworth *Leceworde: William from Robert Gernon.* Garden city (founded 1903 by Ebenezer Howard as a pioneering example of urban planning). The central highway is the prehistoric Icknield Way.

Leverage *Leuuareuuiche: William from Bishop of London, formerly Leofwara, a woman.* In Much Hadham.

Leygreen (Ley Green) *Leglega: King's land.*

Libury *Stuterehela/hele, Sutrehella, Sutreshele: An Englishman from Archbishop of Canterbury before and after 1066; Bishop of Bayeux and Peter and Thurstan from him; Walter the Fleming; Peter de Valognes and 2 freemen and Alfward from him; Derman from the king. 2 mills.* Libury Hall.

Lilley *Linlei(a): Geoffrey de Bec.* John Janeway, first scholar of King's College, Cambridge, was baptised in the Norman church where his father was a curate.

Little Berkhamsted *Berchehamstede: Hardwin of Scales.*

Little Gaddesden *Gatesdene: Humphrey from Count of Mortain.* In Ashridge Park.

Little Hadham *Parva Hadam: William from Bishop of London; Abbot of Ely.* Hadham Hall, built for the Capel family. Lord Arthur Capel, loyal to Charles I, had his heart placed in a silver casket in the church vault.

Little Hormead *Horemede: Godwin from Prince Edgar.*

Little Munden *Mundane: Walter the Fleming.* Scattered houses, also called Munden Freville.

Little Offley *Altera Offelei: A freeman, the pre-Conquest holder, from the king.*

Little Wymondley *Wimundelai: William from Robert Gernon.* Priory remains; moat.

Luffenhall *Lufenel(le), Lufenhate: Osbern from Bishop of Bayeux; Canons of St Paul's, London; Theobald from Hardwin of Scales.*

Mardley(bury) *Merdelai: Alfward from Robert Gernon.*

Meesden *Mesdone: Payne from Bishop of London.* Meesden Green; Meesden Manor.

Minsden *Menlesdene: King's land, formerly Earl Harold.* Minsden Chapel, an ivy-covered ruin.

Miswell *Mascewelle/Misseuuelle: Ralph from Count of Mortain; Ralph from Robert de Tosny.*

Much Hadham *Hadam: Bishop of London and William and Osbern from him; Abbot of Ely. Mill.* Hadham Palace, now a farmhouse, was the country home of the bishops of London for 800 years. Henry V's widow Catherine gave birth here to Edmund Tudor, father of Henry VI.

Napsbury *Absa: St Albans Church. Mill.*

Newnham *Newham: St Albans Church.*

Newsells *Neusela/selle: Eudo FitzHubert.* Scattered houses.

North Mimms *Mimmine: Bishop of Chester.*

Norton *Nortone: St Albans Church; Frenchman. 2 mills.*

Orwell *Orduuelle: Osbern from Bishop of Bayeux; Withgar from Hardwin of Scales.*

Patmore *Patemere: Baldwin from Bishop of London.* Now Patmore Heath.

Panshanger *Blachemene: Geoffrey de Runesville from Geoffrey de Bec.*. District near Welwyn Garden City.

Pelham *Peleham: Bishop of London and Ralph, Payne, Ranulf, Gilbert, 2 men-at-arms, Aldred and Riculf from him.* Now 3 villages, Furneaux and Stocking Pelham, and Brent Pelham.

Pendley *Pentlai: Count of Mortain.* Pendley Manor.

Pirton *Peritone: Ralph de Limesy. 4 mills.* Once fortified, it clusters around Toots Hill, on top of which the ramparts of a Norman castle remain.

Puttenham *Puteham: Roger from Bishop of Bayeux. 2 mills.*

Radwell *Radeuuelle: Adam from Bishop of Bayeux; Roger from Peter de Valogues. Mill.* Mill on the River Ivel.

Redbourn *Redborne: Wigot from Bishop of Lisieux; St Albans Church and Amalgar from the church; Ranulf from Count of Mortain. 2 mills.* An Ancient British plateau fort above the valley. The Roman Watling Street runs through the new Redbourn.

Reed *Rete/Retth: Osbern from Bishop of Bayeux; Hardwin and Alfward from Count Alan; Robert FitzRozelin from Count Eustace; Eudo FitzHubert; Hardwin of Scales.* Traces of 6 moats; Saxon church.

Rickmansworth *Prichemareworde: St Albans Church. Mill.* Small town.

Rodhanger *Rode(ne)hangre:*Lost.

Roxford *Rochesforde: Guy from Geoffrey de Bec. Mill.*

Rushden *Risendene: Sigar de Chocques.*

Rye *Eia: Peter from Bishop of Bayeux. Mill, weirs (200 eels).* Rye House.

Sacomb(e) *Seuechampe/champa, Sueuecampe/champ: Ansketel from Archbishop of Canterbury; Peter de Valognes; Hardwin of Scales; Derman and a freeman from the king. Mill.*

St Albans *Villa Sancti Albani: St Albans Church. Park for woodland beasts, fishpond.* Cathedral city, originally Verulamium, a key Roman settlement, destroyed by Boadicea. It was rebuilt and named after the first British martyr, the Roman soldier, Alban.

St Paul's Walden *Waldene: St Albans Church. 2 mills.*

Sandon *Sandone: Canons of St Paul's, London.* The foundations of England's earliest known windmill were behind the church.

ST ALBANS: *The Norman abbey church, begun in 1077 on a Saxon site. The Tower was built with Roman bricks from Verulamium.*

Sandridge *Sandrige: St Albans Church. Mill.* Pre-Saxon entrenchments at Devil's Dyke and the Slad. Sarah Jennings of Sandridge married John Churchill, 1st Duke of Marlborough.

Sawbridgeworth *Sabrixteworde: Geoffrey de Mandeville. Mill.* Town.

Sele *Sele: Godwin from Geoffrey de Bec. Mill.* House.

Shenley *Scenlai/lei-Senlai: St Albans Church; Ranulf from Count of Mortain; Geoffrey de Mandeville.* Burial place of Nicholas Hawksmoor, architect and Wren's assistant on St Paul's. Charles II visited frequently.

SHENLEY: *The Cage, an 18th c folly.*

Shephall *Escepehala/hale: Ansketel from Archbishop of Canterbury; St Albans Church.*

Stagenhoe *Stagnehou: William from Ranulf, brother of Ilger.* Stagenhoe Park is in nearby St Paul's Walden.

Standon *Standone: Rothais, Richard FitzGilbert's wife. 5 mills, vines.* Sir Ralph Sadler, Henry VIII's Secretary of State for Scotland, who taught and eventually gaoled Mary Stuart, is buried in the church.

Stanstead Abbots *Stanestede: Ranulf brother of Ilger; a freeman from Geoffrey de Mandeville; Geoffrey from Geoffrey de Bec; Godmund from the king.* Roman pavement (5th century).

Stevenage *Stigenace: Westminster Abbey.* Town. The name derives from the Saxon, meaning 'hills by the highway'; 6 little hills near the Great North Road are possibly burial mounds.

Stone(bury) *Stanes: Peter de Valognes.*

WESTMILL: *Peaceful village; the church was originally Saxon.*

Temple Dinsley *Deneslai: King's land. 2 mills.*

Tewin *Theunge: Westminster Abbey.* Queen Hoo Hall.

Theobald Street *Titeberst(h): Adam from Bishop of Bayeux; Westminster Abbey and Geoffrey de Mandeville from the Abbey; Geoffrey de Bec from St Albans Church; Ralph from Geoffrey de Mandeville; Lovett from Geoffrey de Bec.* Temple Bar, originally in London, was erected here in 1888.

Therfield *Dereuelde, Furreuuelde: St Benedict's of Ramsey; Withgar from Hardwin of Scales.* On the last spur of the Chilterns. Birthplace of John Bourchier (1467–1533), 2nd Baron Berners, deputy of Calais and translator of Froissart's *Chronicles*.

Thorley *Torlei: Rodhere from Bishop of London; Geoffrey de Mandeville. Mill.* Samuel Horsley, the eccentric, powerful preacher who had a bitter controversy on the Incarnation with Joseph Priestley, discoverer of oxygen, in the 1780s was rector of the Norman church.

Throcking *Trochinge: Humphrey from Bishop of London; Osbern from Bishop of Bayeux; Rumold from Count Eustace; Theobald from Hardwin of Scales.*

Thundridge *Tonrinch: Hugh de Grandmesnil from Bishop of Bayeux. Mill.*

Tiscott *Theisescote: Ralph Bassett from Robert Gernon. Mill.*

Tring *Tredung(a), Tredwye: Count Eustace. 2 mills.* Market town. Nell Gwynn stayed at the house in Tring Park, later owned and rebuilt by the Rothschilds.

Wain Wood *Wi/Welei: King's land and 2 freemen from the king.* John Bunyan often preached here in the 17th century.

Wakeley *Wachelei: Ralph from Count Alan; Robert from Count Eustace; Theobald from Hardwin of Scales.*

Walkern *Wakchra: Derman and others of the King's Englishmen from the king.* Saxon church. Jane Wenham, the last woman condemned for witchcraft in England (1710) lived here and was ducked in the pond.

Wallington *Wallingtone: Wimund from Count Alan; William from Robert Gernon; Siward from Geoffrey de Mandeville; Fulk from Gosbert de Beauvais; Siward from Hardwin of Scales.*

Wandon *Wavedene: King's land, formerly Earl Harold.* Now Wandon End.

Ware *Wara(s), War(r)es: Hugh de Grandmesnil. 5 mills, park for woodland beasts, vines. 375 eels.* Town, known to the Danes who brought their ships up the River Lea. The Great Bed of Ware (alluded to in *Twelfth Night*) was in Ware Park (now a sanatorium).

Watton *Watone: Ansketel from Archbishop of Canterbury; Westminster Abbey, Godwin from Count Alan; Derman and Alfward from the king.* Now Watton at Stone. Watton Hall was rebuilt in 1636; an inscription reads: 'Watton Hall alias Watkins Hall'.

Wellbury *Welle: a freeman from the king.* Now 2 hamlets, New and Old Wellbury.

Welwyn *Welga, Welge, Wilga, Wilge: Bishop of Chester; Robert de Pont-Chardon from Robert Gernon; William d'Eu and William Delamere from him; Roger from Geoffrey de Bec, formerly Queen Edith; a priest from the king. Mill.* Small town close to Welwyn Garden City, on the site of a Roman villa and probably a temple; Norman church with Roman bricks.

Westmill *We(t)mele: Ansketel from Robert Gernon; Roger from Ralph de Tosny. 4 mills.* Thatched cottage belonged to Charles Lamb; museum of Westmill relics dating back to Roman times.

Weston *Westone: William d'Eu. Mill.* The Norman church was given to the Knights Templars by Gilbert Strongbow whose son captured most of Ireland for Henry II in the late 12th century. Jack O'Legs, a gigantic highwayman, is buried here.

Wheathampstead *Watamestede: Westminster Abbey. 4 mills.* On the River Lea. The Heath of No Man's Land was the dividing line between the domains of St Albans Church and of Westminster Abbey.

Wickham *Wicheham: Bishop of London and Humphrey and 2 men-at-arms from him; Geoffrey de Mandeville and a freeman and 2 men-at-arms from him; Roger and Osbert from Geoffrey de Bec.* Wickham Field.

Widford *Wideford(e): Bishop of London and Theodbert from him. Mill.* John Elliot of Widford preached the Gospel to the Red Indians. His psalm book was the first book printed in America.

Wigginton *Wigentone: Humphrey from Count of Mortain, formerly Queen Edith. Mill.* Pre-Saxon Grim's Dyke nearby. James Osborne, who won the VC in the Zulu Wars, is buried here.

Willian *Wilie: Geoffrey de Bec.* Within the green belt of Letchworth Garden City.

Windridge *Wenriga/rige: Geoffrey de Bec from St Albans Church; Ralph from Geoffrey de Bec.*

Woolwicks *Wluueneuuiche:* Lost.

Wormley *Wermelai: Canons of Waltham; Widmund from Count Alan; Alwin Dodson from the king. 50 eels.* Norman church on Roman Ermine Street; last home of the topographist, Richard Gough (d. 1809).

Wyddial *Widihale: Hardwin of Scales.*

Huntingdonshire

A Domesday survey of Britain in 1986 would include no return for Huntingdonshire. The little county is now officially a part of Cambridgeshire, but until it amalgamated with Peterborough in 1965 and then finally 'disappeared', its boundaries were much the same as they had been in 1086.

Domesday divided Huntingdonshire into four 'hundreds', each of roughly equal size. Throughout the county the distribution of population and of settlements was fairly even except in the north-east corner. Here was the marshy fenland, which stretched east into Cambridgeshire and north to the Wash. It was land fit only for eels and, on patches of higher ground, for abbeys. Ely Abbey in Cambridgeshire was the pre-eminent monastic house of the fens, but Huntingdonshire claimed Ramsey, whose abbot was one of the county's leading landholders. To the south and the west were the clay uplands, attractive both to farmers and to huntsmen. By 1086 William had already claimed part of Huntingdonshire as a royal forest. A century later Henry II turned the entire county into a private hunting preserve.

Huntingdonshire was of great strategic value to the Norman conquerors. Ermine Street, the Roman road from London to York, crossed the River Ouse at Huntingdon, its principal town, and William I was quick to build a castle defending this spot. Now only its earthworks remain.

LITTLE GIDDING: *The tiny 17th-c. church has been restored, and contains a unique brass font.*

Little Gidding

In GIDDING *REDINGES* 6 Freemen, that is Alfwold and his five brothers, had 4½ hides taxable. Land for 6 ploughs. Jurisdiction in the King's manor of Alconbury. Now Eustace has it, and Ingelrann from him. Now 2 ploughs in lordship. 16 villagers and 4 smallholders with 6 ploughs. Meadow, 22 acres. Value before 1066 and now £4. Alfwold and his brothers claim that Eustace took this land from them unjustly. William the Artificer claims ½ virgate and 18 acres of land. This is the witness of the whole Hundred.

There are three Giddings now, clustered together ten miles north-west of Huntingdon, but only one, Great Gidding, is large enough to be called a village. A mile to the south-east along a narrow lane is Steeple Gidding, merely a church and a few houses set in farmland. Little Gidding, so small it is easily overlooked, lies between the two. A tiny church and an ungainly farmhouse are its only buildings, yet it is Little Gidding which has become famous, one of the holy places of the Anglican church – an island of sanctity, like a landlocked Iona.

At the time of *Domesday* Gidding was in the hands of three men. The biggest landlord was the Abbot of Ramsey, who held much of the south of the parish, including what is now Steeple Gidding. To the north the land was divided equally between Eustace the Sheriff of Huntingdon and a man called William the Artificer; but all of Eustace's property was disputed, partly by William, partly by six Anglo-Saxon brothers who had previously owned it. They claimed, and the *Domesday* commissioners seem to have believed them, that Eustace had no right to their land. Justice was not done: Eustace defied popular opinion and clung to his manor.

By 1279 the population of Little Gidding was nearly 150, and it might have become a thriving town had not the plague of 1348 struck the area with unusual fury. The tiny surviving population was further diminished by the change in land use, from crops to sheep farming, that occurred later in the Middle Ages.

The fortunes of Little Gidding were transformed in 1625, when the manor was bought by Nicholas Ferrar, then 33. He was a former high official with the Virginia Company and a recently elected Member of Parliament, but his ambitions were now entirely spiritual. With his mother and the families of his brother and sister (who had a total of 16 children), he established a semi-monastic community at Little Gidding. In 1626 he was ordained in Westminster Abbey.

The devout community held three daily services in the little church beside the manor; hourly prayers (attended on a shift system), and a night watch. They also gave generously to the poor and became masters of decorative bookbinding.

Charles I visited Little Gidding three times, and it paid dearly for his attentions; in 1646 the manor and church were ruthlessly plundered by Parliamentarian soldiers. By then Nicholas had been dead nine years, buried in his own church.

A new religious community has recently arisen here, the manor farm is crowded with residents and pilgrims. But the little church, beautifully restored in the eighteenth and nineteenth centuries, remains a place of great tranquillity.

Kimbolton

In KIMBOLTON *CHENEBALTONE* Earl Harold had 10 hides taxable. Land for 20 ploughs. Now William de Warenne holds it. He had 5 ploughs in lordship on 5 hides; 84 villagers and 36 smallholders with 25 ploughs. A priest and a church. Meadow, 70 acres; woodland pasture 1 league long and 1 league wide; 1 mill, 5s. Value before 1066 £7; now £16 4s. 2 men-at-arms have 1 hide of this land. They have 1 plough and 5 oxen. Value 20s.

A motorist approaching Kimbolton from St Neots finds that the road swings suddenly to the left and then equally abruptly to the right. In front of him is the broad and gracious High Street, lined with elegant eighteenth-century shops and houses. This was once Kimbolton market-place, and it is because of the market that the road developed its extraordinary course. In the middle ages all traffic was diverted into the town centre, and travellers forced to pay a toll for passing through the market. Poor Kimbolton now pays in wracked nerves for its medieval avarice as articulated lorries thunder down the High Street.

It was a thriving village of about 500 inhabitants in 1086. The only manor in Huntingdonshire that had belonged to King Harold, it was one of the few to have increased in value in the 20 years since the Conquest. Kimbolton was blessed abundantly with both arable land and forest. A century after *Domesday* Richard Russell was able to fell 222 oaks from a patch of Kimbolton woodland to build himself a court in Leicestershire.

The present church dates from the thirteenth and fourteenth centuries, but it almost certainly stands on the site of the *Domesday* church, at the north-west end of the High Street. At the other end, massive and threatening, is Kimbolton Castle. All that can be seen from the outside is the work of Sir John Vanbrugh, who was called in around 1707 to buttress an earlier building that had begun to collapse. Sir John did more; he enveloped the old building wih a classical façade that somewhat overwhelms its intimate setting.

It was in Kimbolton Castle that Katherine of Aragon spent her last unhappy years, in virtual imprisonment. Although her marriage to Henry VIII had been unofficially annulled in 1533, she insisted on retaining the title of Queen, thus embarrassing the newly re-wed Henry. In the twentieth century Kimbolton Castle became a school for boys, a transformation that may finally have exorcised Katherine's melancholy spirit.

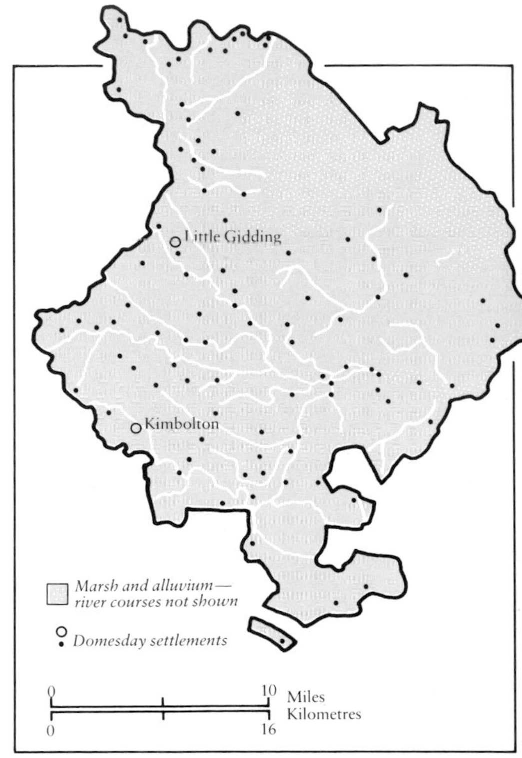

Huntingdonshire Gazetteer
Each entry starts with the modern place-name in **bold** type. The *Domesday* information that follows is in *italic* type, beginning with the name or names by which the place was known in 1086. The main landholders and undertenants are next, separated with semi-colons if a place was divided into more than one holding. A number of holdings in Huntingdonshire were granted by the king to his thanes; these holders, always the last in a list, are given with their office, or described as holding land 'from the king'. More general information completes the *Domesday* part of the entry, including examples of dues (eels, etc.) rendered by tenants. The modern or post-Domesday section is in normal type. represents a village, a small village or hamlet.

Alconbury *Acumesberie, Almundeberie: Ranulf, brother of Ilger from the king.* Maypole square was the site of a 14th-century market.

Alwalton *Alwoltune: Peterborough Abbey. 2 mills, fishery. 500 eels.* Known for limestone 'Alwalton marble'. The 17th-century Dryden family house, formerly at Chesterton, was rebuilt here.

Bluntisham *Bluntesham: Ely Abbey; Ramsey Abbey. Church.* Much new building.

Botolph Bridge *Botulvesbrige: Ranulf brother of Ilger from the king; the priests Burgred and Thorkell from Eustace the Sheriff. Church.* Now in Peterborough. Only one tombstone is left of the church.

Boughton *Buchetone: Eustace the Sheriff.* Farm on the Great Ouse river; traces of a moated manor house and village.

Brampton *Brantune: Ranulf brother of Ilger from the king; Alric, the king's thane. Church, 2 mills.* Racecourse. Pepys' House was owned by the diarist's family.

Brington *Breninctune: Ramsey Abbey.*

Broughton *Broctone/tune: Ramsey Abbey/(Eustace the Sheriff claimed part of the land). Church, mill.* Traces of a moat in a field outside the village mark the site of a manor house belonging to the Abbots of Ramsey.

Buckden *Bugedene: Bishop of Lincoln. Church, mill.* Site of the Bishop of Lincoln's palace, established in the 12th century; a fine 15th-century tower and gatehouses remain.

Buckworth *Bucheswoorde: Count of Eu and a man-at-arms from him. Church.* Isolated.

Bythorn *Bierne: Ramsey Abbey and 2 men-at-arms from the Abbey.* Near Old Tollbar Hill, one of the highest in the country.

Caldecote *Caldecote: Man-at-arms from Eustace the Sheriff.* Remote. Remains of a moat mark the site of a manor house.

Catworth *Cateworde: Eustace the Sheriff from William de Warenne; Eustace the Sheriff in the king's hand; Eric from the king. Mill.* Quiet, attractive.

Chesterton *Cestretune: Lunen and 2 men-at-arms from Eustace the Sheriff. Church, 4 shillings to Peterborough Abbey.* Roman town of Durobrivae nearby. In the church is a monument to the famous 17th-century poet John Dryden, whose family home was rebuilt at Alwalton.

Colne *Colne: Ely Abbey.* Nearby is the site of a fen fishermen settlement.

Conington *Coninctune: Countess Judith. Church.* The church's monuments were erected by Sir Robert Cotton (born 1571), who lived at Conington Castle.

Coppingford *Copemaneforde: Humphrey from Earl Hugh. Church.* Cottages; farm. A moat marks the manor house visited by Charles I on his way to join the Scots at Newark in 1646.

Cotton *Cotes: Thursten from Bishop of Lincoln; Countess Judith and Gilbert the Priest from her.* Farm.

Covington *Covintune: Roger d'Ivry and 2 men-at-arms from him.* Hilltop; timbered houses.

Denton *Dentone: Thursten from Bishop of Lincoln. Church.* Ruined church.

Diddington *Dodinctun, Dodintone: William from Bishop of Lincoln; Alan from Countess Judith. Church.* Church in the grounds of Diddington Park.

Dillington *Dellinctune: Ramsey Abbey.*

Easton *Estone: Eustace the Sheriff.* Thatched cottages. A tributary of Ellington Brook runs down the main street.

Ellington *Elintune: Ramsey Abbey and 2 men-at-arms from the abbey (part in royal woodland and not cultivated). Church.* Thatched cottages.

Elton *Adelintune/tone: Ramsey Abbey. Church, 2 mills.* Attractive. Elton Hall dates from the 15th century.

Everton *Evretune: Ranulph brother of Ilger. Church.*

Eynesbury *Einuluesberia/ie: Countess Judith and St Helen's of Elstow, Gilbert the Priest and Alan, the Countess's steward from her; Rohais wife of Richard FitzGilbert and St Neot's Abbey and William le Breton from her. Church, 3 mills, sheepfold, fishery.* Part of St Neot's. The old centre remains.

Fenstanton *Stantone: Gilbert de Ghent. Church.* The tomb of Capability Brown, 18th-century landscape gardener, is in the church.

Fletton *Fletone/tun: Peterborough Abbey.* Now Old Fletton, part of Peterborough; church with Saxon carvings.

Folksworth *Folchesworde: Walter Giffard.* Dormitory town to Peterborough.

Gidding *Geddinge/Gedelinge/Redinges:* See page 140.

Glatton *Glatune: Lunen from Count Eustace. Church.* Attractive; many old houses. John Hausted, cartographer, mapped it in detail in 1613.

Godmanchester *Godmundcestre: King's land. Church, 3 mills.* Part of Huntingdon. Originally Roman; its medieval inhabitants had privileges of self-government.

Grafham *Grafham: King's land; Odilard the Larderer from Eustace the Sheriff.* Isolated; Grafham Water, nearby.

Gransden *Grantesdene: Ranulf from the king. Church.* Now 2 villages, Great Gransden with timber and plaster houses and thatched cottages, and Little Gransden.

Haddon *Adone: Thorney Abbey. Church.* Church with Saxon walls and a Norman chancel arch.

Hail Weston *Westone/tune: Eustace the Sheriff; Robert FitzFafiton.* Near saline springs described by the chronicler Holinshead in 1577.

Hamerton *Hambertune: Eudo FitzHubert and 2 men-at-arms from him.*

Hartford *Hereforde: Ranulf brother of Ilger from the king. 2 churches, 2 mills.* Part of Huntingdon. Its name means 'ford of the invading army'. There is still a fordway near the church.

Hemingford *Emingeforde: Ramsey Abbey; Eustace the Sheriff; Ralph FitzOsmund from Aubrey de Vere; Ralph FitzOsmund. Church, 3 mills, fishpond.* Now Hemingford Abbots by the Great Ouse river.

Hemingford Grey *Alia Emingeforde: Aubrey de Vere from Ramsey Abbey and a man-at-arms from him.* On the Great Ouse river; Norman house, c.1160.

Holywell *Haleiwelle: Ramsey Abbey and Alfwold from the abbey. Church.* Named after its spring (said to effect cures).

Houghton *Hoctune: Ramsey Abbey. Church, mill.* Attractive; 17th-century watermill on the site of a mill given by the 10th-century founder of Ramsey Abbey to the abbot.

and fine Georgian houses; earthworks of a castle built by William I. Oliver Cromwell was born here in 1599, and the Cromwell Museum is in what remains of the Hospital of St John, founded 1160. St Mary's Church, originally Norman, was rebuilt in the 13th century.

Keyston *Chetelestan, Ketelestan: Ranulf brother of Ilger from the king.* Named after Ketil's stone, probably a Saxon boundary mark.

Kimbolton *Chene/Kenebaltone:* see page 140.

Leighton Bromswold *Lectone: Bishop of Lincoln. Mill.* Moated gatehouse.

Little Catworth *Alia/Parva Cateworde: Ely Abbey; Thored from William de Warenne.*

Molesworth *Molesworde: Eustace the Sheriff from Countess Judith.* Site of US Cruise Missile base.

Morborne *Morburne: Crowland Abbey. Church.* 17th-century manor house; Norman chancel arch in church.

Offord Cluny *Opeforde, Upeforde: Monks of Cluny from Arnulf de Hesdin. Church, 2 mills.* Attractive; 13th-century church.

Offord Darcy *Up/Opeforde: Ramsey Abbey; Odo from Eustace the Sheriff, Hugh from Countess Judith.*

Old Weston *Westune: Ramsey Abbey; Wulfbert from Eustace the Sheriff. Church.* Isolated in the wolds.

Orton Longueville *Ovretone/tune: John from Bishop of Lincoln; Eustace the Sheriff and John and Roger from him. Church.* Part of Peterborough; named after a Norman family.

HOUGHTON: *Tenants of Ramsey Abbey were heavily fined if they did not use the abbey mill on this site.*

Huntingdon *Huntedone-/dun: Ramsey Abbey; Gilbert de Ghent; Ely Abbey; Bishop of Lincoln; Countess Judith; Bishop of Coutances; Eustace the Sheriff. Castle, market, mint, at least 1 mill, over 100 unoccupied residences, 2 churches.* Town, now linked with Godmanchester, with a 14th-century stone bridge

Orton Waterville *Ovretone/tune: Ansgered from Peterborough Abbey for the supply of the monks and in the king's jurisdiction.* Part of Peterborough; named after the Waltreville family.

Paxton *Pachstone, Parchestune: Countess Judith. 3 mills.* Now 2 villages, Great and Little Paxton.

Ripton *Riptune: Ramsey Abbey; Church.* Now Abbots Ripton; attractive. The Moat House was once the main manor; nearby is Monks Wood, given to Sawtry Abbey in 1147, and now a nature reserve.

St Ives *Slepe: Ramsey Abbey and Everard, Ingelrann and Pleines from the Abbey. Church.* Town.

Sawtry *Saltrede: Ramsey Abbey; Walter from Eustace the Sheriff; Countess Judith; Alwin's wife. 3 churches.* Large; recent building; earthworks and fishponds of a Cistercian Abbey, founded 1147.

Sibson *Sibestune: Thorney Abbey; Lunen from Count Eustace. 2 ½ churches, 2 ½ mills.* Manor house; Sibson Aerodrome.

Somersham *Summersham: Ely Abbey; 3 fishponds.* Large; traces of a moated palace of the bishops of Ely.

Southoe *Sutham: Eustace the Sheriff; Robert FitzFafiton. Fishery. 1000 eels.* Manor farm; sites of 3 moated manor houses nearby.

Spaldwick *Spalduic: Ely Abbey. Mill.* On Ellinton Brook. The George Inn, c.1500, has medieval wall paintings.

Stanground *Stangrun: Thorney Abbey. Church.* Part of Peterborough; Cromwellian fortress nearby on Horsey Hill.

Staughton *Tochestone: Eustace the Sheriff from Bishop of Lincoln. Church.* Now an aggregate of 3 villages, Great Staughton and Staughton Green and Highway; site of a 13th-century fortified manor house, formerly a castle.

Stibbington *Stebintone/tune: Thorney Abbey; Lunen from Count Eustace. Church.* 17th-century hall and manor house; partly Norman church.

Stilton *Stic(h)iltone: The king's freemen of Normancross from the king; John from bishop of Lincoln; Eustace the Sheriff.* Home of Stilton cheese.

Stukeley *Stivecle: Ramsey Abbey; Richard and Hugh, the Abbot's men-at-arms, from the abbey; Herbert from Eustace the Sheriff; Countess Judith. 2 churches.* Now 2 villages, Great and Little Stukeley.

Tilbrooke *Tilebroc: William de Warrenne.*

Upton *Opetune: Fulk from Earl Hugh. Church, mill.* Moated manor house; 17th-century manor farm.

Upwood *Upehude: Ramsey Abbey; Church.* Attractive; old windmill.

Warboys *Wardebusc: Ramsey Abbey. Church.* Fenland. After the deaths of the witches of Warboys in 1593, Henry Cromwell, Oliver's son, paid a Cambridge lecturer to preach against witchcraft each year in Huntingdon, a custom that continued until 1814.

Waresley *Wederesle, Wedreslei(e): Thorold from Swein of Essex; Roger from Eustace the Sheriff; Ranulf brother of Ilger from William FitzAnsculf.* On a wooded ridge; Waresley Park.

Washingley *Wasingelei(a):* Lost.

Water Newton *Newetone: Thorney Abbey. Church, 2 mills.* 17th-century Water Newton House.

West Perry *Pirie: Eustace the Sheriff. Church.* Now 2 villages, East and West Perry, on Grafham Water; sailing club; ornithological centre.

Winwick *Winewiche/wincle: Odilard the Larderer from Eustace the Sheriff.*

Wistow *Wistou: Ramsey Abbey. Church, mill.* Timber-framed, pargetted houses; 16th-century farm.

Wood Walton *Waltune: Hugh de Bolbec from Earl William. Church.* Ruins of a castle, possibly built by Geoffrey de Mandeville.

Woodstone *Wodestun: Thorney Abbey. Church.* Part of Peterborough.

Woolley *Cilvelai: Eustace the Sheriff. Golde and her son Wulfric, the pre-Conquest holders.* Manor house; rectory; cottages.

Wyton *Witune: Ramsey Abbey. Church, mill.* 17th-century houses.

Yaxley *Iacheslei: Thorney Abbey. Church.* Large; important brickworks.

Yelling *Gel(l)inge, Ghellinge: Swein from Ramsey Abbey. Aubrey de Vere. Church.* Quiet. Italian paintings in the late Norman church were part of Napoleon's loot, and bought by a private collector.

WARBOYS: *Mid-13th-c. church.*

Kent

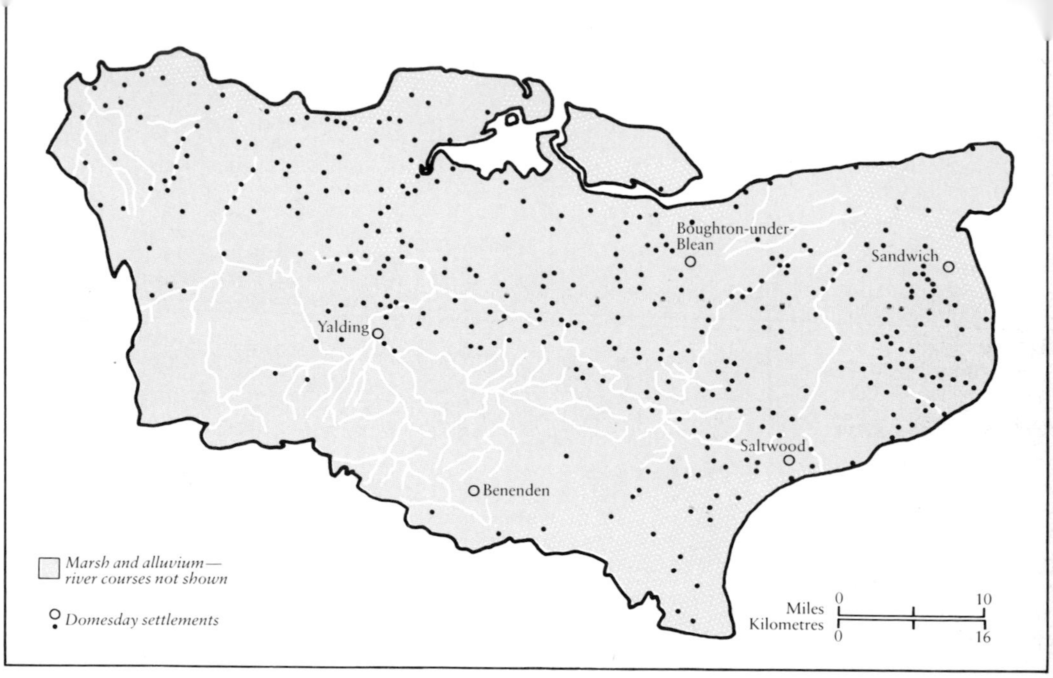

Although William I's landing at Pevensey Bay and his victory at Battle both occurred in Sussex, he instantly marched east into Kent, where at Dover his troops, against his orders, burned the town. Kent was as good a route as Sussex from the continent, as the events of the following year showed. In 1067 Eustace of Boulogne unsuccessfully attacked Dover, hoping to raise the men of Kent against William in support of his son's claim to the throne. Kent's Domesday *provides clear evidence that William took the continental threat into account when allocating the county's land. Over a third he gave to his half brother, Odo, Bishop of Bayeux, whom he made Earl of Kent. Two other baronial holdings were designed to provide barriers between the coast and London: Richard FitzGilbert, with his castle at Tonbridge, and Hugh de Montfort, at Saltwood Castle overlooking Romney Marshes.*

The Domesday *account of Kent contains peculiarities. Only in Kent is the sulung (divided into four yokes) the unit of land assessment. It is usually assumed that the sulung was larger than the more common hide, but it probably also represented the amount of land on which one family could live for one year. Administratively the shire was divided into hundreds as were most English shires. But in Kent the hundreds were grouped into seven lathes. West Kent had Aylesford and the half-lathes of Milton and Sutton. East Kent had the lathes of Wye, Borough, Lympne and Eastry. The lathes continued to be the basis of Kentish local government until the 1974 Local Government Reorganization.*

Sandwich

SANDWICH *SANDWIC* lies in its own Hundred. The Archbishop [of Canterbury] holds this Borough. It is for the clothing of the monks. It pays the same service to the King as Dover. The men of this borough testify this, that before King Edward gave it to Holy Trinity, it paid £15 to the King. In 1066 it was not in the revenue. When the Archbishop acquired it, it paid £40 in revenue and 40,000 herrings for the supplies of the monks. In the year in which this Survey was made Sandwich paid £50 in revenue and herrings as before. Before 1066 there were 307 habitable dwellings; now there are 76 more; that is, 383 altogether.

In SANDWICH the Archbishop has 32 dwellings which belong to this manor and pay 42s 8d; Aethelwold has 1 yoke, value 10s . . .

. . . the King has a body-guard for 6 days at Canterbury or at Sandwich. They have food and drink from the King; if they have not had it they withdraw without penalty.

The ancient Cinque Port of Sandwich lies on Kent's east coast, immediately to the south of the River Stour, which divides the Isle of Thanet from the mainland. Further south along the coast, beyond a cluster of golf courses, lies Deal. North are the muddy expanses of Pegwell Bay with its hoverport, then the cliffs of Ramsgate. It was in Pegwell Bay that three of the most significant foreign landings in England occurred: the Roman landing of AD 43, led by the Emperor Claudius, the landing of the legendary Anglo-Saxon leaders Hengist and Horsa in 449 and the arrival of the Christian mission from Rome in 597, led by St Augustine. The vast ditches and flint walls of Richborough Castle, which the Romans built, survive, as do the foundations of their triumphal arch (AD 85) which stood at the start of Watling Street and celebrated the conquest of Rome's new colony.

Sandwich did not then exist, for the sandbank on which it stands had not yet emerged from the sea. It is first mentioned when St Wilfrid returned here from France in 661 on his way to his diocese at York. In 850 it was the landing place for one of the first Danish attacks on England, which led ultimately to Canute becoming king in 1016.

By then Sandwich was a borough. It had been granted by King Edgar (959–975) to the monks of Christchurch, Canterbury. Ethelred the Unready (979–1016) and Canute (1016–1035) both confirmed this, Canute's charter granting land as far inland 'as the taper axe can be thrown from a vessel afloat at high water'.

Sandwich was one of the many holdings of William I's half brother, Odo, Bishop of Bayeux, Earl of Kent. Though he heaped favours on him, William respected him little. 'Odo, my brother,' he said, 'is light minded and ambitious, cleaving to carnal desires and of boundless harshness, and will never be changed from his dissolute and noxious vanities.' Nevertheless he remained in favour until 1072, when Lanfranc, the new Norman Archbishop of Canterbury, charged him with unlawfully holding church lands. The great case against Odo was held at Penenden Heath. It was important enough not only to require the attendance of such powerful barons as Richard FitzGilbert and Hugh de Montfort but for the king to have the deposed Anglo-Saxon Bishop of Selsey, Ethelric, 'most ancient and learned in the law', brought in a cart all the way from Chichester.

Odo lost his case, and Sandwich among other places was returned to the monks of Christchurch, but he retained a toehold here; *Domesday* records that his nearby manor of Woodnesborough had 32 burgesses at Sandwich. He fell into further disgrace in 1082 and his lands were sequestered – a fact which *Domesday* nowhere mentions, though it does omit his title, referring to him only as a bishop.

Domesday confirms that Sandwich, although not a royal borough, had naval arrangements with the king similar to those at Dover. In return for sac and sock – the right to administer its own justice and keep the profits – it supplied the king with 20 ships, each manned by 21 men, for 15 days a year.

Sandwich was sacked by the French early in the thirteenth century during King John's war with the barons. In the reign of his son Henry III, however, its ships defeated the French, though they were outnumbered by 80 to 16. This battle included an early example of chemical warfare: the English won by throwing 'great pots' of powdered quicklime on to their enemies' decks which burned and blinded whoever came in contact with it. The battle was fought on St Bartholomew's Day (24 August) and its spoils used to found a chapel and hospital in his honour for the housing of the poor and old of Sandwich. St Barts survives and the saint's day is celebrated by a children's race for the Bartholomew Bun.

Most dramatic of all attacks was that by the French in 1457. They landed in three parties and fought their way to the town centre, which they largely destroyed, killing the mayor, before reinforcements drove them out.

During the sixteenth and seventeenth centuries the Cinque Ports lost trade to the ports of the West Country. Sandwich also lost its sea. At one time Fordwich, 15 miles up the River Stour, had been able to send ships to contribute to those 20 supplied to the king. But the Stour became so silted that even Sandwich's ships were able to use it only at high tide. As early as 1495, the port was said to be 'sore decayed'.

There was eventually one compensation. In 1755 the Stour was bridged at Sandwich and the town granted the following tolls: 'Coach, chariot, landau, berlin, chaise, chair, calash or other vehicle, drawn by six or more horses or other beasts, 2s 6d; by four horses, 2s; by two horses 1s 6d; by one horse 9d . . .' These revenues (to which horseless carriages at 2s were added) were not abandoned till the 1970s.

The collapse of Sandwich as a port preserved it as a small town with many old houses and great charm. Small boats still tie up near its bridge, though for the last 30 years none has brought home any herrings, let alone the vast catches which allowed them to send 40,000 in 1086 to the monks of Christchurch.

SANDWICH: *A narrow 16 c. gatehouse.*

Benenden

Robert of Romney also holds BENENDEN *BENINDENE* from the Bishop of Bayeux. It answers for 1/2 sulung. Land for 2 ploughs. In lordship 1 plough. 4 villagers with 9 smallholders have 2 ploughs. Woodland, 5 pigs; a church. Value before 1066 and later 40s; now 50s. Osgeard held it from King Edward.

On a sunny summer afternoon no village better epitomizes the fabled peace of rural England than Benenden. Though the church no longer chimes '*All Through the Night*' every three hours, as it did before 1939, it still looks down on the prettiest of village greens, where cricket is played dangerously close to the surrounding houses. Benenden lies on the Kentish Weald, an expanse of hilly country with clay soil which forms most of the south-west of the county. In 1086, according to *Domesday*, the Weald's population was less than one person to the square mile.

Manors of the better populated parts of Kent had rights to pig pastures in the Weald, known as denes. Though many are recorded unnamed by *Domesday*, others like Benenden had become sufficiently permanent by 1086 to have both a name and a church.

The same church may have been standing in 1323, when the earliest of Benenden's vicars was appointed by the religious House of Combwell. But little survives today. In 1672 it was destroyed by a phenomenal thunderstorm, described in a pamphlet entitled *This Winter's Wonders:* or *A True Relation of a Calamitous Accident at Bennenden*:

'On December the twenty-nineth at about eleven p.m. the parishioners saw on the East Side of the Town a very great Light... It being Winter they little dreamt of Lightning, but after a little Observation of the Elements, were convinced that it was nothing else...; but that so terrible, the Flashes so long, that the Beholders were afraid not onely their Houses, but themselves should be consumed...

'The devouring Flames and Impetuous Thunder found no great resistance from this stony pile [the church]. The steeple... what with the Fiery Flashes and Mighty Thunder-claps was quickly forced to resign it self to that earth... The very walls of the Church were demolished, that it is onely now a Ruinous heap.'

The village's peace was again disturbed in 1830 when rioting labourers destroyed agricultural machinery all over the county. At Benenden they became so threatening that troops were called out and the Riot Act read on the green.

There was so little work at Benenden in the early nineteenth century that 'able-bodied men were playing cricket in the midst of haying and harvest'. Perhaps as a result, Benenden became famous for its cricketers, in particular Edward Gower Wenman and Richard Mills. In 1834 this pair defeated an eleven of the Isle of Oxney before a crowd of 2000 to win a wager of £20.

Great houses surround Benenden, and for centuries it was dominated by Hemsted House, which was owned by the Guldeford family from 1388 to 1718. In the mid-sixteenth century Jane Guldeford became the wife of John Dudley, Duke of Northumberland.

It was their son, Lord Guldeford Dudley, who married Lady Jane Grey in 1553 and was executed with her a year later. As she was about to be beheaded Lady Jane, who was only 17, told her husband that their separation would be only for a few minutes.

Since 1924 Hemsted House has been occupied by the exclusive Benenden School for Girls.

The Forest of Hemsted north of the village still suggests the wild rolling country in which villagers of 1086 pastured their pigs.

Boughton-under-Blean

[The Archbishop of Canterbury holds] BOUGHTON *BOLTUNE* in lordship. It answers for 5 sulungs. Land for... In lordship 2 ploughs, and 31 villagers with 31 smallholders who have 15 ploughs. Meadow, 4 acres; a fishery at 10d; a salt-house at 16d; woodland, 45 pigs. Total value before 1066 and later £15 16s 3 1/2d; value now £30 16s 3 1/2d.

For over 1900 years the main road from Canterbury to London ran through Boughton-under-Blean – or Boughton Street as it is called today. The village's main street was part of the Roman Watling Street. Armies, kings and queens all passed this way. So did Canterbury pilgrims, and in the reign of Richard II a hospital was built here for them.

The fishery and salt-house of 1086 must have used one or other of the two streams which rise near Boughton and flow north.

A tradition of unruliness at Boughton goes back at least to 1450, when it was one of the Kent villages where murders were committed and houses wrecked during Jack Cade's rebellion. Four centuries later, in 1838, it was the setting for one of the most pathetic incidents in British agricultural history, less famous than the events of 1834 at Tolpuddle, Dorset, but far bloodier. It centred on a charismatic lunatic from Cornwall, John Tom, who called himself Sir William Percy Honeywood Courtenay, Knight of Malta.

Six years earlier, Courtenay had stood at Canterbury during the election which followed the Great Reform Bill, promising a return to 'the good old days of roast beef and mutton, and plenty of prime, nut brown ale'. He first called himself Count Moses Rothschild, before awarding himself his Malta knighthood to which he added, 'King of the Gypsies, King of Jerusalem'. On a show of hands he seemed elected, but was defeated on a count.

In 1838, after also failing at the county election, where he got three votes and a period in the lunatic asylum, he settled in Boughton, where he aroused passionate support among the small farmers. On 27 May he urged 200 supporters to forsake all and follow him. Two days later, blowing a bugle, he led 30 men, singing hymns, around the countryside, and ended up at Bossenden Farm. Here on 31 May, when the High Constable of Boughton and his brother tried to arrest him, he shot the brother and drove his sword into the body many times, shouting that he was the saviour of the world.

Soon afterwards 100 troops defeated Courtenay and his supporters in Bossenden Wood, killing him and seven more. Fragments of his hair, bloody smock and the bark of the tree against which he died became valued relics.

In the eighteenth and nineteenth centuries coaches passing through Boughton day and night destroyed its peace; so did motor traffic until a bypass created a peaceful village again.

Saltwood

Hugh de Montfort holds SALTWOOD *SALTEODE* from the Archbishop [of Canterbury]. Before 1066 it answered for 7 sulungs; now for 3 sulungs. Land for 15 ploughs. In lordship 2 ploughs, and 33 villagers, with 12 smallholders who have 9 1/2 ploughs. A church; 2 slaves; 9 mills at 20s; meadow, 33 acres; woodland, 80 pigs. To this manor belong 225 burgesses in the Borough of Hythe. Between the borough and manor, value before 1066 £16; when acquired, £8; in total, now £29 6s 4d.

Suburbia today connects the hilltop village and moated castle of Saltwood with its southerly neighbour, the port of Hythe. But Saltwood, whose name is said to derive from the seaside woods at the base of its promontory, was important when the land on which Hythe stands was still below the sea. A stronghold was built here in 488 by Aesc, son of Hengist of Kent.

In 1026 Canute granted it to Canterbury Cathedral. It was held briefly after the Conquest by Odo, Bishop of Bayeux, then returned to Canterbury by the decision of the great court at Penenden Heath in 1072. But it was Hugh de Montfort, the lay tenant, who really controlled Saltwood, defending a long stretch of coastline, including the Romney Marshes, from its castle.

The de Montfort family lost Saltwood early in the twelfth century, when they opposed Henry I (who had grabbed the throne from his brother, Count Robert of Normandy) and it passed to the d'Essex family. When Becket became archbishop, in Henry II's reign, he recovered control of the castle, which he called 'the most pleasant house in Kent'.

Becket's quarrels with Henry II are well known, and soon after Becket went into voluntary exile in 1164, the king transferred Saltwood to Becket's enemy, Ranulf de Broc. When, six years later, four knights attending on Henry in France decided to rid him of 'this turbulent priest', they came to Saltwood.

According to tradition, on the night of 28 December 1170, they plotted in the castle's great hall before riding to Canterbury Cathedral next day. The knights sat down after dinner with the archbishop's household, brawling drunkenly until Becket left for the cathedral. They followed and attacked. According to his clerk, Becket refused to defend himself. It is said that Fitzurse struck Becket first, and William de Tracy struck next, bringing the archbishop to his knees. Then Richard le Breton struck him so violently that he broke his own sword on the ground. One of the escort provided by de Broc spread Becket's brains about the cathedral floor.

In spite of Henry's public remorse at Becket's murder, he kept Saltwood, and, as part of a policy of neutralizing the power of his nobles, pulled parts down. His son John, however, returned it to Canterbury, and in the fourteenth century the Lollard, William Thorpe, was imprisoned here for sixteen years before, in 1389, he escaped in the confusion caused by an earthquake.

The following year William Courtenay became archbishop. He enlarged the keep and added two watch towers tall enough to give a view of pilgrims on their way to Canterbury. Cranmer, some 150 years later, was the last archbishop to occupy Saltwood, before surrendering it to Henry VIII. It has since had many owners. Although it fell into decay in the nineteenth century, it was conscientiously restored by Lady Conway of Alington in the 1930s, and finally became the residence of a high priest of the arts, Lord Clark.

The best-preserved parts of today's castle date from William Courtenay's time, the oldest from the rebuilding in about 1160 by the d'Essex faily. It appears at its finest when seen from the east, across the Saltwood valley. From here the strength of its hilltop position is clear – though the castle from which Hugh de Montfort once controlled the Romney Marshes was, like most early Norman castles in England, mainly wood.

Yalding

Richard FitzGilbert holds YALDING *HALLINGES*. Aethelred held it from King Edward. It answered for 2 sul ngs then and now. Land for 16 ploughs. In lordship 1 1/2. 16 villagers with 12 smallholders have 6 ploughs. 2 churches; 15 slaves; 2 mills at 25s; 4 fisheries at 1700 eels less 20. Meadow, 5 acres; woodland, 150 pigs. Value before 1066 and later £30; now £20, because the land has been despoiled of livestock.

Kent has been famous for its hop gardens ever since the Puritans insisted on adding hops to ale to make it bitter. Yalding, at the centre of Kent's hop-growing district, is one of the county's prettiest villages. Here the River Beult (pronounced Belt) is crossed by a long medieval bridge. Picturesque as this is, the river is also a problem since it periodically floods its valley, hence the steps which lead up to the front doors of many of the cottages. Perhaps some recent disastrous flood explains *Domesday*'s otherwise surprising note that Yalding had no livestock.

It was one of only two manors which Richard FitzGilbert (alias Richard of Tonbridge), held as tenant-in-chief in Kent. Of two others he was under-tenant. But he held land in 25 more, all lying north of Tonbridge; together these formed the largeholding which *Domesday* calls his *leuua* or lowy. Still more importantly, he held the formidable Tonbridge Castle, which had almost certainly been granted to him to enable him to defend the south-eastern approaches to London.

Richard was a political opportunist, but insufficiently astute always to back the winning side. When William I died he joined Odo, Bishop of Bayeux, in support of Robert of Normandy's claim to succeed instead of William Rufus. They lost and Richard was imprisoned in France, where he died.

Throughout the Middle Ages Yalding remained a small and unimportant rustic settlement until hops brought it prosperity. Then each summer ever-increasing numbers of pickers from the east end of London would arrive for their annual working holiday, frightening the respectable villagers. In the 1870s a great fight was staged between one of these, known as 'The Booster' and a gypsy, 'Billy Slit Nose'. When four policemen forced their way through the crowd of 2000, the fighters knocked them to the ground and this began a general fight between pickers and gypsies which left the road looking 'more like a slaughter house than a village street'.

Eels are still caught at Yalding, as they were in 1086, though not in such quantity, and none to compare with the monster landed in 1757. It was 5feet 9 inches long, 18 inches in girth, and weighed 40 pounds – a worthy dish for Richard FitzGilbert.

YALDING: *One of Kent's most picturesque villages, it has been a hop-growing centre since the 17th century. This old hop barn was in use until recently.*

Kent Gazetteer
Each entry starts with the modern place-name in **bold** type. The *Domesday* information that follows is in *italic* type, beginning with the name or names by which the place was known in 1086, then the main landholders and under-tenants, separated with semi-colons if a place was divided into more than one holding. More general information completes the *Domesday* part of the entry, including examples of dues rendered by tenants.
The modern or post-Domesday section is in normal type. represents a village, a small village or hamlet.

Acrise *Acers: Ansketel de Rots from Bishop of Bayeux. Church.* Deserted. Acrise Place, a Tudor mansion was owned by Papillon family.

Addington *Ralph son of Thorold from Bishop of Bayeux. Church, 2 mills.* 2 Neolithic tombs are nearby.

Adisham *Edesham: Archbishop of Canterbury's monks.* Sprawling.

Aldglose *Aldelose: Bishop of Bayeux, but outside his territory.* Outskirts of Brabourne.

Aldington (near Hythe) *Aldintone: Archbishop of Canterbury. Church, 3 mills, 3 fisheries.* Home of Elizabeth Barton, Holy Maid of Kent, a servant who claimed to see visions. She was hanged in 1534 after denouncing Henry VIII's marriage to Anne Boleyn.

Aldington (in Thurnham) *Audintone: Ansgot of Rochester from Bishop of Bayeux. Church, mill.* Part of Thurnham village.

Allington (in Hollingbourne) *Alnoitone: Hugh de Port from Bishop of Bayeux. Church, 2½ mills.* Allington Farm.

Allington (near Maidstone) *Elentun: Ansketel from Bishop of Bayeux. Church, ½ mill.* Moated Allington Castle, founded soon after the Conquest and restored this century, belongs to the Carmelite Fathers. Sir Thomas Wyatt, Tudor poet and courtier, was born here.

Appledore *Apeldres: Archbishop of Canterbury's monks. Church, 6 fisheries.* On the edge of Romney Marsh. Danish stronghold in the Saxon Andred forest, and a busy port until the River Rother changed course in 1287.

Appleton *Apletone: Ralph from Bishop of Bayeux.* Appleton Manor.

Arnolton *Ernoltun/ultone: Ansfrid from Bishop of Bayeux; Ranulf. 2 salt-houses, with 1 dwelling in the City of Canterbury.* Lost.

Ash *Eisse: Hugh de Port from Bishop of Bayeux.* On downland; 17th-century manor house.

Ashenfield *Esmerefel: Ansketel from St Augustine's abbey.* Ashenfield Farm.

Ashford *Allia Essetesford: Maino from Hugh de Montfort. Church, 2 mills.* London dormitory town with busy market and industry.

Atterton *Etretone: Hugh de Montfort, but part claimed by Canons of St Martins of Dover. Mill.* Part of Dover.

Aylesford *Elesford: King's land. Mill.* Picturesque. Hengist and Horsa defeated the British here in 455. The first Carmelite Friary was founded here in 1292 and restored in 1949.

Badlesmere *Badelesmore/ Bedenesmere: Bishop of Bayeux, claimed by St Augustine's Abbey before 1066. Church, fishery.* Tiny church.

Barfreston *Berfrestone: Ralph de Courbépine from Bishop of Bayeux; a poor woman paid 3½d.* Isolated on hilltop. The Norman church, built of flint and Caen stone at time of *Domesday*, is noted for its carved-stone decorations.

Barham *Berham: Fulbert from Bishop of Bayeux. Church, 3 mills, 25 fisheries.* Prehistoric earthwork, Roman burial mounds and Saxon cemetery on Barham Downs.

Beamonston *Betmontestun:* Lost.

Beauxfield *Bevesfel:* Lost.

Beckenham *Bacheham: Ansgot of Rochester from Bishop of Bayeux. Mill.* Residential London suburb.

Beckley *Bichelei: Adam from Bishop of Bayeux. Mill.* Beckley Hill in industrial marshland.

Bekesbourne *Burnes/Borne: Bishop of Bayeux; St Augustine's Abbey. Church, mill, salt-house, 1½ fisheries.* Archbishop Cranmer lived here.

Benenden: See page 140.

Bensted *Benedestede:* Lost.

Berwick *Berewic: William of Adisham from Archbishop of Canterbury.* .

Betteshanger *Bedesham: Osbern son of Ledhard from Bishop of Bayeux.* Site of lost medieval village; mansion in parkland.

Bexley *Bix: Archbishop of Canterbury. Church, 3 mills.* Thames-side London borough.

Bilsington *Bilsuitone: Bishop of Bayeux. Church, 10 salt-houses, 2 fisheries.* On the edge of Romney Marsh.

Birling *Berlinge: Ralph de Courbépine from Bishop of Bayeux. Church, mill, fishery (60 eels). 330 eels.* Attractive.

Bishopsbourne *Burnes: Archbihop of Canterbury. Church, 2 mills.* Writer Joseph Conrad lived in what is now the rectory for 5 years before his death in 1924.

Blackmanstone *Blachemenestone: Harvey from Hugh de Montfort. Church; named after Blackman, who held it formerly.* Deserted.

The decorated doorway of a Norman church, typical of many in Kent.

BARFRESTON: *An example of the carvings on its church.*

Blean *Bleham: Hamo the Sheriff. Church, fishery.* Once in the royal forest of Blean; Blean Woods and Dunkirk Woods nearby (now a nature reserve) are all that remain.

Bodsham *Bodesham: Geoffrey from St Augustine's Abbey.* Now Bodsham Green.

Bonnington *Bonintone: William son of Gross from Hugh de Montfort. Church.* The church, of Norman foundations, is dedicated to St Rumbold, who, legend has it, professed Christianity and preached a sermon before he died aged 3 days.

Borstal *Borchetelle/Borcstele: Bishop of Rochester 2 mills.* The first Borstal institution for young offenders was established here in 1901.

Boswell Banks *Brochestele:*. Lost.

Boughton Aluph *Boltune: Count Eustace. Church, 2 mills.* Boughton Court manor house. A fireplace in the church porch may have been used by medieval pilgrims.

Boughton Malherbe *Boltone: Ralph son of Thorold from Archbishop of Canterbury; Hugh nephew of Herbert from Bishop of Bayeux. 2 churches.* Fine views across the Weald. Sir Henry Wotton, the Elizabethan poet and diplomat, lived in the manor house behind the church.

Boughton-under-Blean: See page 144.

Bowley *Bogelei: Bishop of Bayeux. Church, mill.* Bowley Farm.

Boxley *Boseleu: Robert Latimer from Bishop of Bayeux. 3 mills.* At the foot of the Downs. Boxley Abbey, founded in 1146, was famous for its Rood of Grace on which Christ's figure miraculously moved; exposed as a mechanical fraud in 1539. The abbey's 13th-century tithe barn still stands.

Brabourne *Brade/Breburne: Hugh de Montfort, Church, 2 mills.* .

Brasted *Briestede: Hamo the Sheriff from Archbishop of Canterbury. Church, 2 mills.* Napoleon III lived at Brasted Place in 1840 before returning to France, eventually to become Emperor.

Brenzett *Brand(et)/Brensete: Canons of St Martin's of Dover.* In Romney Marsh on the line of the ancient Rhee Wall.

Bromley *Bronlei: Bishop of Rochester. Mill.* Founded 862; the Bishops were Lords of the Manor until 1845; the market, granted in 1205, is still there. H. G. Wells was born here.

Broomfield *Brunfelle: Robert Latimer from Bishop of Bayeux. Mill.* .

Buckland (near Dover) *Bocheland/e: Alwin from Canons of St Martin's of Dover.* Part of Dover.

Buckland (in Luddenham) *Alius Bocheland/Bocheland/ Tercius Bocheland: Osbern and Thurstan de Gironde from Bishop of Bayeux.* Parish with Roman villa site.

Buckwell *Berchuelle: Wadard from Bishop of Bayeux. Mill.* Buckwell Farm.

Burham *Borham: Ralph de Courbépine from Bishop of Bayeux. Church, mill.* The manor, church and part of the old village lie adjacent to modern Burnham. A Roman villa site is nearby.

Burmarsh *Borchemeres/ Burwarmaresc: St Augustine's Abbey.* Isolated.

Canterbury *Cantuaria/iensis: Under the king's jurisdiction; Ralph de Courbépine held 4 houses which Harold's concubine had held. 3 mills.* Cathedral city with Norman walls. Building of the cathedral started in 1070.

Chalk *Celca: Adam from Bishop of Bayeux. Church, mill.* Part of Gravesend, where Charles Dickens spent his honeymoon.

Charing *Cheringes: Archbishop of Canterbury. Mill.* Attractive; part of 14th-century archbishop's palace (now a farmhouse), where Henry VIII stayed on his way to Field of the Cloth of Gold.

Charlton (near Dover) *Cerlentone: Ralph of St Samson and William FitzOdger from Canons of St Martin's of Dover.* Part of Dover.

Charlton (near Greenwich) *Cerletone: Sutton, Greenwich; William FitzOdger from Bishop of Bayeux.* Absorbed by Greenwich.

Chart Sutton *Certh: Adam FitzHubert from Bishop of Bayeux. Church, vines, park of wild beasts.* Surrounded by orchards.

Chartham *Certeham: Archbishop of Canterbury's monks. Church, 5½ mills.* In the Stour valley; paper mill; angling centre.

Chatham *Ceteham: Robert Latimer from Bishop of Bayeux. Church, mill, 6 fisheries.* Elizabeth I established the dockyards (now closed), where the ships that sank the Spanish Armada were built. Sir Francis Drake and Lord Nelson sailed from here and Charles Dickens spent part of his childhood here when his father was a dockyard pay clerk.

Chelsfield *Ciresfel: Arnulf de Hesdin from Bishop of Bayeux. Mill.* On high ground.

Chilham *Cilleham: Fulbert from Bishop of Bayeux. Church, 2 fisheries, 6½ mills.* Famed for its beauty. The castle combines a 12th-century keep with a 17th-century Jacobean mansion, containing a Battle of Britain museum; traces of a Roman camp in the grounds.

Chillenden *Cilledene: Osbern FitzLedhard from Bishop of Bayeux.* Near coalfields; century-old windmill on the Downs above.

Chislet *Cistelet: St Augustine's Abbey. 4 French men-at-arms held what was valued at £12 a year. Church, 47 salt-houses (50 packloads of salt), vines.* Scattered.

Cliffe *Clive: Land of Archbishop of Canterbury's monks; Arnulf de Hesdin from Bishop of Bayeux.* Fine Norman church.

Coldred *Colret: Ralph de Courbépine from Bishop of Bayeux.* Saxon church, possibly built on a Roman earthwork.

Cooling *Colinge/s: Adam and Odo from Bishop of Bayeux.* Marsh; setting for Charles Dickens' novel *Great Expectations*. 14th-century Cooling Castle was the home of Sir John Oldcastle, the Lollard leader hanged and burned as a heretic in 1417, on whom Shakespeare is said to have modelled his character Falstaff.

Coombegrove *Cumbe: Wadard from Bishop of Bayeux.* Big Coombe Manor.

Court-at-Street *Estraites: Hugh de Mandeville from Hugh de Montfort. Church.*

Crayford *Erhede: Archbishop of Canterbury. Church, 3 mills.* Industrial area of Greater London; site of large Iron Age settlement and the Roman town of Noviomagus.

Crofton *Croctune: Ansketel from Bishop of Bayeux.* Part of Bromley.

Cudham *Codeham: Gilbert Maminot from Bishop of Bayeux. Church, 2 mills.* Surrounded by orchards.

Cuxton *Coclestane: Bishop of Rochester. Church, mill.* Dormitory for London; cement works.

Darenth *Tarent: Archbishop of Canterbury; Ansketel de Rots from Bishop of Bayeux. 4 mills.* Partly Saxon church; site of a large Roman villa; mill on the River Darent.

Dartford *Tarentefort: King's land. Mill, 3 churches, 2 harbours.* Industrial town on the River Darent with a 2000-year history. Locally born Wat Tyler started his revolt against poll tax here in 1381.

Deal *Addela: Archdeacon Ansketel, Aethelwold, St Augustine's Abbey and William FitzThorold from Canons of St Martin's of Dover.* One of the Cinque Ports, nowa resort town. Julius Caesar landed near here in 55 BC.

Dean *Dena/ne: Aethelwold from Bishop of Bayeux.* Now Dean Court, off the Pilgrims' Way.

Dengemarsh *Maresc: Robert of Romney from Bishop of Bayeux. Fishery.* Tract of land and coastguard station near Dungeness.

Denton (near Barham) *Danetone: Bishop of Bayeux and Ralph de Courbépine from him. Church.* Half-timbered cottages round a green.

Denton (near Gravesend) *Danitone: Bishop of Rochester. Church.* Suburb of Gravesend, with a wharf on the River Thames.

Dernedale *Darenden:*. Lost.

Ditton *Dictune: Hamo the Sheriff from Bishop of Bayeux. Church, mill.* Round a green, now much extended; near paper mills.

Dover *Dovera/e: King William burnt the town when he invaded England so its value could not be fairly reckoned when Bishop of Bayeux acquired it. 2 mills, 3 churches. The king received fines from men who committed adultery in most parts of Kent; women's fines were paid to the archbishop. The king also received half the goods of anyone condemned to death.* Busy Channel port with Saxon church of St Mary in Castro; 40ft-high remains of Roman lighthouse. 12th-century Dover Castle is built on the site of an early Norman castle.

Each *Ece: Osbern FitzLedhard from Bishop of Bayeux. Church, mill.* Manor farm.

Easole *Essewelle/Eswalt: Ralph de Courbépine from Bishop of Bayeux.*

East Barming *Bermelinge: Richard FitzGilbert. Mill.* Absorbed by Maidstone.

Eastbridge *Estbrie:*. Lost in Romney Marsh; ruined church.

East Farleigh *Ferlaga: Archbishop of Canterbury's monks. 4 mills, 6 fisheries (1200 eels).* Fine medieval bridge, over which General Fairfax marched in 1648 to the Battle of Maidstone.

East Lenham *Ler(t)ham: Godfrey the Steward from Archbishop of Canterbury. Mill.*

Eastling *Eslinges: Roger FitzAnsketel and Fulbert from Bishop of Bayeux. 2 churches, 2 mills.*

East Malling *Mellingetes: Archbishop of Canterbury. Church, 2 mills.* Large.

East Peckham *Pecheham: Archbishop of Canterbury before and after 1066. Church, mill.* Large.

Eastry *Estrei: Archbishop of Canterbury's monks. 1½ mills, 3 salt-houses.* Eastry Court is said to stand on the site of an ancient royal hall.

Eastwell *Estwelle: Hugh de Montfort.* Eastwell Park. The ruined church has a tomb reputed to be that of Richard Plantagenet, son of Richard III. He is said to have escaped after the Battle of Bosworth to the Eastwell estate, where he became a bricklayer.

Eccles *Aiglessa: Ralph FitzThorold from Bishop of Bayeux.*

Elham *Alham: Bishop of Bayeux. Church, 2 mills.* Large; houses set round a market square; royal charter granted in 1251. The Duke of Wellington made 17th-century Abbot's Fireside his temporary headquarters during the Napoleonic Wars.

Elmstone *Aelvetone: Ansfrid from St Augustine's Abbey.*

Elmton *Esmetone:* Lost.

DOVER: *The ancient church of St Mary in Castro and the remains of the Roman lighthouse, in the castle grounds.*

KESTON: *View of Keston Ponds, a cluster of small lakes close to the remains of the Roman settlement.*

Eltham *Alteham: Hamo the Sheriff from Bishop of Bayeux.* London Suburb. Once the site of one of the largest medieval royal palaces. The 15th-century Great Hall still stands. William Roper, son-in-law and biographer of Sir Thomas More, lived at the now vanished Well Hall. In the 19th century the hall was owned by Hubert Bland, founder member of the Fabian Society.

Evegate *Tevegate: Hugh de Montfort.* Evegate Manor Farm.

Eynsford *Elesford: Ralph son of Ospak from Archbishop of Canterbury. 2 churches, 2 mills.* Pretty; moated castle dating from 1100; ford.

Fairbourne *Fereburne: Hugh nephew of Herbert and Ralph de Courbépine from Bishop of Bayeux. 2 mills.* Manor farm.

Fanscombe *Fane/nne: Adam from Bishop of Bayeux. Church.* Possibly Fanscoombe Wood.

Farningham *Ferligeham/Fe(o)rningeham: Ansgot from Archbishop of Canterbury; Mauger, Wadard and Arnulf de Hesdin from Bishop of Bayeux. 1½ mills.* Attractive; on River Darent with a water flour-mill. Captain Bligh of the *Bounty* lived in the Manor House.

Farthingloe *Ferlingelai: William FitzGeoffrey from Canons of St Martin's of Dover.*

Faversham *Favreshant: King's land. 2 salt-houses, mill, market.* Market town and small port. Richard Arden, a 16th-century mayor, was murdered here by his wife and her lover. An early domestic drama, *Arden of Faversham*, is based on this story.

Fawkham *Fachesham: Bishop of Rochester. Church, 2 mills.* Manor house.

Finglesham *Flenguessam: William Follet from Archbishop of Canterbury.*

Fleet *Fletes: William de Arques from Archbishop of Canterbury. Fishery, salt-house.* Fleet Farm.

Folkestone *Fulchestan: William de Arques from Bishop of Bayeux. 5 churches, 11½ mills, salt-house.* Seaside resort and fishing port; birthplace of William Harvey, the physician who discovered blood circulation. East Cliff has remains of a Roman villa, but Caesar's Camp is Norman. The 13th-century parish church stands on the site of a 7th-century Saxon nunnery.

Foots Cray *Crai/ie: William FitzOdger frm Bishop of Bayeux. Mill.* Urban district of Greater London.

Fordwich *Forewic: St Augustine's Abbey.* Once the port for Canterbury and a member of the Cinque Port Confederation. A tomb in the part-Norman church is said to be St Augustine's.

Frindsbury *Frandesberie: Bishop of Rochester. Church, mill.* Church founded in 1075 still stands; cement-works.

Frinsted *Fredenestede: Hugh nephew of Herbert and Aethelwold the Chamberlain from Bishop of Bayeux. Church.* Wooded country.

Garrington *Warwintone: St Augustine's Abbey.* Garrington Farm.

Giddinge *Getinge: Archbishop of Canterbury's monks.* Part of Dover.

Gillingham *Gelingeham: Archbishop of Canterbury; Odo from Bishop of Bayeux. Church, 2 mills, 3 fisheries.* Town on the River Medway, site of much of Chatham Royal Dockyard (now closed).

Godmersham *Gomersham: Archbishop of Canterbury. Church, mill.* On River Stow. Jane Austen visited her brother at Godmersham Park and based her novel *Mansfield Park* there.

Graveney *Gravenel: Richard the Constable from Archbishop of Canterbury. 4 salt-houses.* On the edge of marshland.

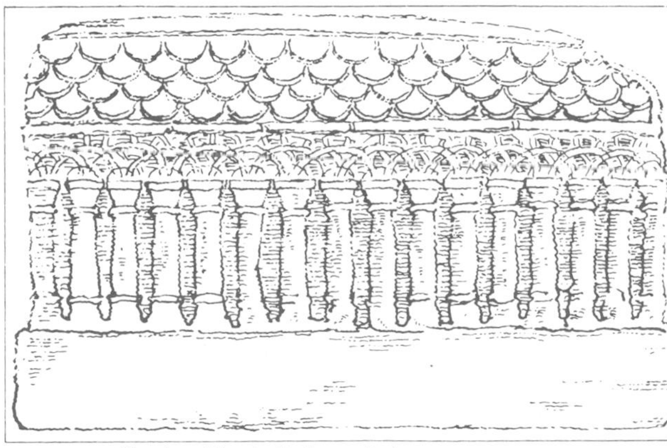

FORDWICH: *Tomb, said to be St Augustine's.*

Gravesend *Gravesham: Herbert FitzIvo from Bishop of Bayeux.* Part of industrial development on the Thames. The Red Indian princess Pocohontas died here in 1616.

Great Chart *Certh: Archbishop of Canterbury's monks. 2 mills, salt-house.* Half-timbered houses; moated house.

Great Delce *Delce: Ansgot of Rochester from Bishop of Bayeux.* Part of Chatham.

Greenwich *Grenviz: Bishop of Lisieux from Bishop of Bayeux.* Thames-side London borough; developed by the Stuart kings. The royal palace was the birthplace of Henry VIII, Queen Mary and Elizabeth I.

Guston *Gocistone: Wulfric from Canons of St Martin's of Dover.* Louis Blériot landed the first cross-Channel aeroplane here in 1909.

Hadlow *Haslow: Richard FitzGilbert from Bishop of Bayeux. Church, 2 mills, 12 fisheries.* Settled since Roman times.

Halling *Hallinges: Bishop of Rochester. Church.* Surrounded by industry and quarries.

Ham *Hama: Osbern son of Ledhard from Bishop of Bayeux.* Thatched cottages.

Hammil *Ai/Hamolde: Bishop of Bayeux.* Remote.

Hampton *Haintone: Hugh de Montfort.*

Harbilton *Herbretitou:* Lost.

Harrietsham *Hariardesham: Hugh nephew of Herbert from Bishop of Bayeux. Church, 2 mills.*

Hartanger *Hertange:* Lost.

Hartley *Erelei: Ralph son of Thorold from Bishop of Bayeux; formerly a woman.* Dormitory suburb of Gravesend.

Harty *Herte: King received part of fines for house-breaking, breach of the peace and highway robbery.* Isle of Harty. Remote; traces of ancient salt-workings. 15th-century Sayes Court was built by first Lord Saye and Sele, Warden of the Cinque Ports.

Hastingleigh *Hastingelai/lei: Roger FitzAnsketel from Bishop of Bayeux; Hugh de Montfort.*

Haven *Hadone:* Lost.

Hawkhurst *Hauochesten: Robert of Romney but claimed by Canons of St Martin's of Dover.* Once the hub of the Wealden iron industry.

Hawley *Hagelei: Hugh de Port from Bishop of Bayeux. Mill.* Suburb of Dartford.

Hemsted *Hamestede: Ranulf de Vaubadon from Bishop of Bayeux.*

Henhurst *Hanehest: Ansgot of Rochester from Bishop of Bayeux.*

Higham *Hecham: Adam from Bishop of Bayeux. Church, mill, fishery.* At Gads Hill, notorious in the 17th and 18th centuries for highwaymen. Charles Dickens bought Gads Hill Place in 1856.

Hollingbourne *Hoilinegeborde/Holingeborne: Archbishop of Canterbury's monks. Church, 2 mills.* Tudor manor house on the Pilgrims' Way.

Hoo *Hou: Bishop of Bayeux. 6 churches.*

Horton *Hortone: Ansfrid from Bishop of Bayeux. 2 mills. King received fines for house-breaking, breach of the peace and highway robbery.* On the Great Stour river.

Hougham *Hi(u)cham/Huham: Baldwin from Canons of St Martin's of Dover.*

Howbury *Hou:* Lost in Crayford, a London suburb.

Hurst (in Chilham) *Herste: Hugh de Port from Bishop of Bayeux. King received penalties for house-breaking, breach of the peace and highway robbery.* Hurst Farm near Chilham.

Hythe *Heda/ae: Archbishop of Canterbury.* Ancient market town; one of the original Cinque Ports; resort.

Ickham *Gecham: Archbishop of Canterbury's monks. Church, 4 mills.*

Idleigh *Didele: Hugh de Port from Bishop of Bayeux.* Idleigh Court.

Kennington *Chenetone: St Augustine's Abbey, formerly the villagers'. Church.* On a Roman road.

Keston *Chestan: Gilbert Maminot from Bishop of Bayeux.* Suburban; Roman villa, temple and cemetery nearby.

Kirby Horton *Hortune: Ansketel de Rots from Bishop of Bayeux. Mill, church.* On the River Darent.

Knowlton *Chenoltone: Thurstan from Bishop of Bayeux.*

Langley *Languelei: Bishop of Bayeux. Church.* Surrounded by orchards.

Langport (near Romney) *Lamport:* Lost in Denge Marsh.

Langport (in Canterbury) *Lanport: St Augustine's Abbey.* Now a street in Canterbury just outside city wall.

Leaveland *Levelant: Richard from Archbishop of Canterbury.* Tudor farmhouse; Leaveland Court.

Lee *Lee: Walter de Douai from Bishop of Bayeux.* London suburb.

Leeds *Esledes: Aethelwold from Bishop of Bayeux. Vines, 5 mills, church.* Church has a massive 11th-century tower. Normans rebuilt the wooden Saxon castle, Leeds Castle, in stone in 1120.

Lenham *Ler(t)ham: St Augustine's Abbey. 2 mills.* Picturesque. 3 6th-century skeletons with swords, daggers and spearheads were discovered in the foundations of the Saxon Warriors chemist shop.

Lessness *Loisnes: Robert Latimer from Bishop of Bayeux. 3 fisheries.* District of London.

Lewisham *Levesham: Ghent Abbey. 11 mills.* London borough.

Leybourne *Leleburne: Adam from Bishop of Bayeux. Church, mill.* Remains of Norman castle.

Littlebourne *Liteburne: St Augustine's Abbey. Church.* Oast-house; tithe barn; mill on the Little Stour river.

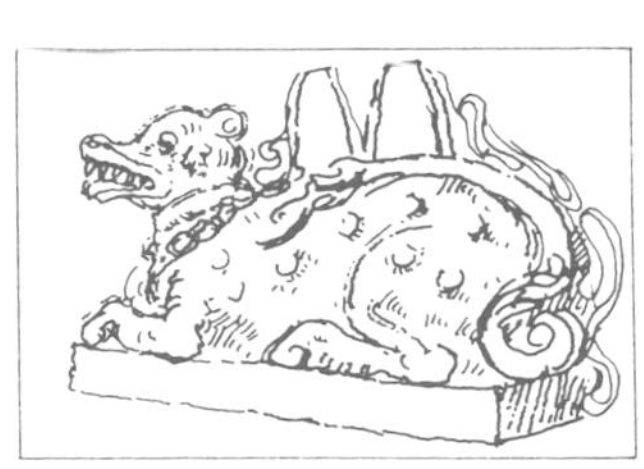

HOLLINGBOURNE: *Effigy at the base of Lady Culpepper's tombstone; she lived at the manor house.*

Little Chart *Litelcert: Archbishop of Canterbury's monks. 2 mills.* Hop-growing; Roman villa site; mill.

Little Delce *Delce: William Thaon's son from Bishop of Bayeux.* Part of Chatham.

Longfield *Langafel: Ansketel the priest from Bishop of Rochester.* Suburban.

Loose *Abel the Monk from Archbishop of Canterbury's monks.* On the River Loose. Quarry Wood, which surrounds it, contains an Iron Age camp.

Lower Hardres *Hardes: Ranulf de Colombières from Bishop of Bayeux. Church.* Parish named after Hardres family,who were associated with the district from the Conquest to the 17th century, and lived at Upper Hardres Court.

Luddenham *Dodeham: Fulbert from Bishop of Bayeux. Church, ½ fishery (300 herrings).* Luddenham Court and church on the edge of Luddenham Marshes.

Luddesdown *Ledesdune: Ralph from Bishop of Bayeux. Church.* The manor house, of Saxon, Norman and Tudor workmanship, is said to be one of the oldest inhabited houses in England.

Lullingstone *Lolingestone: Geoffrey de Rots, Manger and Osbern Paisforiere from Bishop of Bayeux. Mill (150 eels).* 4th century Roman villa site; Christian chapel; Lullingstone Castle.

Lyminge *Leminges: Archbishop of Canterbury. Church, mill, fishery (40 eels).* Norman church built from the ruins of a Saxon priory founded in 633.

Lympne *Limes: Archbishop of Canterbury. Church, mill.* Once a Roman port; walls of Roman fort at Stutfall Castle; Norman church.

Macknade *Macheheve/t: Ansfrid from Bishop of Bayeux. King had the fines for house-breaking, breach of the peace and highway robbery.* Lost, near South Preston.

Maidstone *Meddestane: Archbishop of Canterbury. Church, 6 mills, 4½ fisheries (450 eels), 2 salt-houses.* County town of Kent on the River Medway. The archbishop's palace is a manor house dating from the 14th century. During the Civil War (1642–48) General Fairfax took the town after a 5-hour siege.

Maplescombe *Maplescamp/ Mapledescam: Ansgot of Rochester and Wadard from Bishop of Bayeux.*

Marley *Merlea: Adam from Bishop of Bayeux. Church.* Marley Court Farm.

Marshborough *Masseberge: Bishop of Bayeux.*

Mederclive *Medredive:* Lost, near Abbot's Cliff.

Meopham *Mepeham: Archbishop of Canterbury.* Famous for cricket; birthplace of John Tradescant (1608–62), who introduced the acacia, plane and lilac to England.

Mereworth *Marourde: Hamo the Sheriff. Church, 2 mills, 2 fisheries.* 18th-century model village built by the 7th Earl of Westmorland on the old village site around his Palladian castle.

Mersham *Merseham: Archbishop of Canterbury. Church, 2 mills, 2 salt-houses.*

Merston *Melestun:* Lost, but in 1957 the foundations of a Norman church were discovered at Green Farm.

Midley *Midelea: Bishop of Bayeux. Church.* Midley House.

Milton *Meletune: Bishop of Bayeux. Church, mill.* Thames-side district of Gravesend.

Milton Regis *Milde(n)tone/ Middeltun: King's land. 6 mills, 27 salt-houses, 32 fisheries. A due of 56½ weys of cheese was paid in Newington.* Suburb of Pittingbourne; church has some Saxon masonry.

Minster (in Thanet) *Tanet: St Augustine's Abbey. Church, salt-house, 2 fisheries, mill.* Church still stands. Benedictine nuns live in the 12th-century grange, Minster Abbey.

Mongeham (Great and Little) *Mundingeham: St Augustine's Abbey. Mill, church.*

Monk's Horton *Hortone/un: Alnoth and Ralph from Hugh de Montfort. 2 mills, church.* Parish. 12th-century Cluniac priory forms part of a farmhouse. Tudor Kite Cottage was once the manor house.

Monkton *Monocstune: Archbishop of Canterbury's monks. 2 churches, fishery, salt-house.*

Nackington *Latintone: Hamo the Sheriff from Bishop of Bayeux.* Canterbury suburb.

Nashenden *Essedene: Ranulf de Colombières from Bishop of Bayeux.* Nashenden Farm.

Nettlestead *Nedestede: Hamo the Sheriff from Bishop of Bayeux. Church, 2 mills, fishery.* Vines; Iron Age fort.

New Shelve *Westselve: William FitzRobert from Bishop of Bayeux.* New Shelve Farm.

Newenden *Newedene: Archbishop of Canterbury.*

Newington (near Folkestone) *Neuentone: Hugh de Montfort from Bishop of Bayeux; Hugh de Montfort and a freeman, the pre-Conquest owner, from him. Church, 3½ mills.* Attractive; 17th- and 18th-century houses.

Newington (near Milton Regis) *Neutone/Newetone: Albert the Chaplain. Fishery.* On Watling Street; Newington Manor.

Northbourne *Norborne: St Augustine's Abbey.* Seaside. Northbourne Court is on the site of a grange built by St Augustine's monks.

Northfleet *Norfluet: Archbishop of Canterbury. Church, mill, fishery.* Industrial district.

North Cray *Crai/ie: Ansketel de Rots from Bishop of Bayeux.*

Church. Part of Greater London on the River Cray.

North Eastling *Nordeslinge: Bishop of Bayeux.* Near Eastling.

Northgate *Norduede: Archbishop of Canterbury's monks.* Now a street just outside Canterbury's city wall.

Norton *Nortone: Hugh de Port from Bishop of Bayeux. 3 churches, 3 mills, 2 fisheries.* Norton Court was built by Inigo Jones in 1625.

Northwood *Nordeu(uo)de: Canons of St Martin's of Dover.*

Nurstead *Notestede: Wadard from Bishop of Bayeux.* Nurstead Court is surrounded by parkland.

Oakleigh *Arclei: Ralph son of Thorold from Bishop of Bayeux.* Near a ruined priory.

Oare *Ora/e: Adam from Bishop of Bayeux. 1½ churches, mill, 2 fisheries, salt-house.*

Offham *Ofeham: Hugh de Port and Ansketel from Bishop of Bayeux. 2 mills.*

Old Romney *Romenel: Archbishop of Canterbury. 3 fisheries, mill, church.* Outskirts of New Romney.

Old Shelve *Estselve: Bishop of Bayeux.* Old Shelve Farm.

Orlestone *Orlavestone: William from Hugh de Montfort.*

Orpington *Orpinton/tun: Mauger from Archbishop of Canterbury; Archbishop of Canterbury's monks. 3 mills, 2 churches.* Suburb of Greater London.

Ospringe *Ospringes: Hugh from Bishop of Bayeux. King received penalties for house-breaking, breach of the peace, highway robbery. Church, mill, fishery, salt-house.*

MONKTON: *Brass-rubbing, a reminder of the time when the village was held by the Church.*

Otford *Otefort: Archbishop of Canterbury. 8 mills.* Ruins of Otford Castle, the Archbishop of Canterbury's manor, where Thomas à Becket stayed. The castle was given to Henry VIII by Archbishop Cranmer.

Otham *Oteham: Geoffrey de Rots from Bishop of Bayeux.* Picturesque; 15th-century yeoman's house.

Otterden *Otringedene: Bishop of Bayeux.* Otterden Place, a Tudor mansion in parkland.

Otterpool *Obtrepole: Harvey from Hugh de Montfort.* Otterpool Manor.

Paddlesworth *Pellesorde: Hugh de Port from Bishop of Bayeux. Church.* Norman church, now a barn.

Palstre *Palestrei: Osbern Paisforiere from Bishop of Bayeux. Church, 5 fisheries.* Palstre Court, a manor house.

Patrixbourne *Borne: Richard FitzWilliam from Bishop of Bayeux. Fishery.*

Penenden *Pinnedenna: King's land.* Penenden Heath.

Perry (in Faversham) *Perie/Alia Piria: Ansfrid from Bishop of Bayeux. King received penalties for house-breaking, breach of the peace and highway robbery.* Perry Court on the outskirts of Faversham.

Petham *Piteham: Archbishop of Canterbury. 2 churches.*

Pett *part of manor of Little Chart held by William from Archbishop of Canterbury.* Pett Place.

Pimp's Court *Pinpa/e: Adam from Bishop of Bayeux. ½ fishery.* Pimp's Court house and cottages; Pympe's Court nearby.

Pinden *Pinnedene: Mauger from Bishop of Bayeux.* Remote.

Pineham *Piham: Hugh de Port from Bishop of Bayeux.* On Roman road.

Pising *Pesinges:* Lost.

Pivington *Piventone: Ralph de Courbépine from Bishop of Bayeux. Church, mill.* Mill; moat.

Pluckley *Pluchelei: Archbishop of Canterbury.* Said to be one of Englands' most haunted villages.

Plumstead *Plum(e)stede: St Augustine's Abbey from Bishop of Bayeux.* London suburb.

Ponshall *Popeselle/ssale: Bishop of Bayeux.* Ponshall House in Coldred.

Postling *Pist/Postinges: Ralph from Bishop of Bayeaux; Roger from Hugh de Montfort. 2 churches, 2 mills.* Pretty; black-and-white-timbering. Writer Joseph Conrad lived here for 30 years.

Poulton *Poltone: Herfrid from Hugh de Montfort. Church.* Poulton Farm near the ruins of 12th-century St Radegund's Abbey.

Preston (in Faversham) *Prestetone: Archbishop of Canterbury. Church, mill, fishery. (250 eels).* Suburb of Faversham.

OTHAM: *15th-century doorway with carved stone decoration.*

Preston (near Fordwich) *Prestetune: St Augustine's Abbey.*

Reculver *Roculf: Archbishop of Canterbury. Church, mill, 5 salt-houses, fishery.* Seaside town; site of the Roman fortress Regulbium. The twin towers of ruined St Mary's Church were built by the Normans on the site of a 7th-century Saxon church and are used as a landmark by ships.

Ridley *Redlege: Adam FitzHubert from Bishop of Bayeux.* Remote, wooded.

Ringlestone *Rongostone: Richard from Bishop of Bayeux.*

Ringleton *Ringetone: Herbert for the king from Bishop of Bayeux. Mill.* Ringleton Manor.

Ripe *Ripa/e: Canons of St Martin's of Dover.* Area in the Ministry of Defence Ranges.

Ripton *Rapentone: Ansered from St Augustine's Abbey. ¼ mill.*

Rochester *Rou(e)cestre: Bishop of Bayeux from Bishop of Rochester.* Ancient city now a major port and an industrial and commercial centre. Rochester Cathedral, begun in 1077, was completed in the 13th century. Rochester Castle, built in 1127, has the tallest keep in Britain.

Rooting *Rotinge: St Augustine's Abbey.* Now Rooting Manor.

Ruckinge *Rochinges: Ralph FitzRichard from Hugh de Montfort.*

Ruxley *Rochelei: Mauger from Bishop of Bayeux. Mill.* Part of Sidcup.

Ryarsh *Riesce: Hugh from Bishop of Bayeux. Church, mill.*

St Margaret's (at Cliffe) *Sancta Margarita: Ralph, Alfred, Robert Black, Walter Thorbert, Edwin, Wulfric of Oxford and Nigel the Doctor from Canons of St Martin's of Dover.* Holiday camp above St Margaret's Bay.

St Martin's *Sanctus Martinus: Archbishop of Canterbury. Mill, church.*

St Mary Cray *Sudcrai: Adam FitzHubert from Bishop of Bayeux. Church.* Industrial, in Greater London.

St Pauls Cray *Alia Craie: Ansketel de Rots from Bishop of Bayeux. Mill.* Industrial, now part of Greater London. The 13th-century church is dedicated to St Paulinus, one of St Augustine's missionaries.

Saltwood: See page 144.

Sandlings *Sentlinge: Hugh nephew of Herbert from Bishop of Bayeux. Church.* Part of Bromley.

Sandwich: See page 142.

Seal *Lasela: Geoffrey de Rots from Bishop of Bayeux. Fishery. (90 eels).* Suburban.

Seasalter *Seseltre: Archbishop of Canterbury's monks. Church, 8 fisheries.* Low-lying land with chalets and caravans.

Sellindge *Sedlinges: Harvey from Hugh de Montfort. 2 churches, mill.* Expanding.

Selling *Setlinges: St Augustine's Abbey.* Pretty; surrounded by orchards.

Sevington *Seivetone: Maino from Hugh de Montfort. Church, mill.*

Shalmsford (Street) *Essamelsford: Herfrid from Bishop of Bayeux.* Manor house.

Shelborough *Selesburne:* Lost.

Shelving *Selinge:* Lost.

Sheppey *Scape. Godfrey from Archbishop of Canterbury.* Near Queensborough.

Shepherdswell *Sibertessuald/suualt: William de Poitou, Wulfstan son of Wulfwin and Sigar from Canons of St Martin's of Dover; St Augustine's Abbey.* Green; previously known as Sibertswold.

Siffleton *Sifletone: Vitalis (a knight depicted in the Bayeux tapestry) from Bishop of Bayeux.* Lost, near Ditton.

Snodland *Esnoiland: Bishop of Rochester. 3 mills, church.* Industrial parish.

Soles (Court) *Soles: Ansfrid from Bishop of Bayeux.* Soles Farm.

Solton *Soltone: Hugh from Bishop of Bayeux.* Solton Manor Farm.

"Sonnings" *Soninges: Hugh de Port from Bishop of Bayeux.* Name of a field in Horton parish.

South Ashford *Estefort: Maino from Hugh de Montfort.* Ashford suburb.

Southfleet *Sudfleta: Bishop of Rochester. Church.* Green belt.

Stalisfield *Stanefelle: Adam from Bishop of Bayeux. Church.* Unspoilt; in wooded downland.

Stansted *Stanestede/Stanetdeste: Canons of St Martin's of Dover.*

Statenborough *Estenberge: William from Archbishop of Canterbury.*

Stelling *Stellinges: Bishop of Bayeux.*

Stockbury *Stotchingeberge: Ansgot from Bishop of Bayeux.* Earthworks of a Norman castle surrounded by orchards.

Stoke *(E)Stoches: Part claimed by Bishop of Rochester from Bishop of Bayeux; Ansgot from Bishop of Bayeux. Church, fishery.* On the River Medway.

Stone *Estanes: Bishop of Rochester. Church, mill, fishery. Porpoise, ounce of gold.* Ancient; engulfed by Thames-side industry and the Kent entrance to the Dartford Tunnel.

Stourmouth *Ezilamerth: Vitalis from Archbishop of Canterbury.* Rural. The church was founded before the Norman Conquest.

Stowting *Estotinghes: Count d'Eu from Archbishop of Canterbury. Mill, church.* Quiet; Bronze Age barrows nearby; remains of a Norman motte and bailey castle.

Stuppington *Stepedone: Hugh from Bishop of Bayeux.* Stuppington Farm.

Sturry *Esturai: St Augustine's Abbey. Church, 10 mills, 7 fisheries.* Largely rebuilt after World War II bombing. It has a 16th-century manor house and medieval tithe barn once owned by St Augustine's Abbey, now owned by King's School, Canterbury.

Sunridge *Sondresse: Archbishop of Canterbury. 3½ mills, church.* Birthplace of Cardinal Manning, 19th-century preacher and ecclesiastical statesman.

Sutton (Valence) and **East Sutton** *Sudtone: Adam FitzHubert from Bishop of Bayeux.*

Swalecliffe *Soaneclive: Vitalis from Bishop of Bayeux.* Coastal.

Swanscombe *Suinescamp: Helto from Bishop of Bayeux. 6 fisheries.* Industrial district and site of Barnsfield Pit, which yielded the earliest fossilized human remains found in Britain. The old parish church has a Saxon tower.

Swanton (in Bilsington) *Suanetone: Hugh de Montfort.* Swanton Farm.

Swanton (in Lydden) *Suanetone: Ralph from Bishop of Bayeux.* Swanton Court Farm.

Swarling *Archbishop of Canterbury.* Now Swarling Farm.

Temple Ewell *Etwelle/Ewelle: Hugh and Ralph from Bishop of Bayeux; Hugh de ontfort. Church, 6½ mills.* Dover suburb, once owned by the Knights Templar.

Teston *Testan: (Aylesford, Twyford; Aethelwold from Bishop of Bayeux.* Famous for making cricket balls.

Throwley *Brulege: Herfrid from Bishop of Bayeux. Church. King had penalties for house-breaking, breach of the peace, highway robbery.* Remote; half-timbered.

ROCHESTER *The castle keep is 120ft. high, the tallest in England.*

Thurnham *Turneham: Ralph de Courbépine from Bishop of Bayeux. Church, mill.* On the Pilgrims' Way. Earthworks of early Norman Thurnham Castle are half a mile away.

Tickenhurst *Tichetestc: Thurstan from Bishop of Bayeux.*

Tiffenden *Tipindene: Hugh de Montfort.* On the track of a Roman road.

Tilmanstone *Tilemanestone: William from Archbishop of Canterbury.* In the Kent coalfields. An ancient yew in the churchyard may be older than the Domesday Survey.

Tinton *Tintentone:* Lost.

Tonbridge *Tonebridge: Bishop of Rochester.* Busy market town with the ruins of a Norman castle captured by William Rufus in 1088.

Tonge *Tangas: Hugh de Port from Bishop of Bayeux. Church, mill.* Mill beside the ruins of 12th-century Tonge Castle.

Tottington *Totintune: Robert Latimer from Bishop of Bayeux at a revenue from the king.* Tottington Farm.

Trimworth *Hamo the Sheriff. Church, mill.* Trimworth Manor.

Trottiscliffe *Totesclive: Bishop of Rochester. Church.* Artist Graham Sutherland lived here. Bishop Gundulph built the chancel of the church in 1100 on Saxon foundations.

Tudeley *Tivedele: Richard FitzGilbert from Bishop of Bayeux, formerly Edeva from the king.* Parish church with window by Marc Chagall.

Tunstall *Tunestelle: Hugh de Port from Bishop of Bayeux. Salt-house.* Attractive.

Ulcombe *Olecumbe: Count d'Eu from Archbishop of Canterbury.* Ancient moat.

Upchurch *Cerce: Hugh de Port from Bishop of Bayeux.* The Romans had a large pottery here. Sir Francis Drake's father was vicar from 1560 to 1566.

Upper Hardres *Hardes: Bishop of Bayeux. Church.* Parish named after Hardres family.

Wadholt *Platenout: St Augustine's Abbey.* Wadholt Wood near Coldred.

Waldershare *Walwalesere: Ralph de Courbépine from Bishop of Bayeux.* Waldershare Park, seat of the Earl of Guilford.

Warehorne *Werahorne: Archbishop of Canterbury's monks.* Set round a green.

Wateringbury *Otrinberge/ Otringe: Ralph FitzThorold and Hugh de Breboeuf from Bishop of Bayeux. Church, 3 mills, fishery. (30 eels).* On River Medway.

West Barming *Bermelie:* Lost. Barham Court is built on the site of the original manor house.

West Cliffe *Westclive: Hugh de Montfort from Bishop of Bayeux. 2 mills.*

Westerham *Oistreham: Count Eustace.* Market town; home of Sir Winston Churchill.

West Farleigh *Ferlaga: Ranulf de Colombières from Bishop of Bayeux. Church, mill.* In hopfields and orchards.

Westgate (in Canterbury) *Estursete: Archbishop of Canterbury. Church, 12 mills.* District of Canterbury, outside city walls.

West Malling *Metlinges: Bishop of Rochester. Church, mill.* Large. St Mary's Abbey incorporates parts of a Benedictine nunnery founded in 1090 by Gundulph, Bishop of Rochester.

West Peckham *Pecheham: Corbin from Bishop of Bayeux.* Quiet.

Westwell *Welle: Archbishop of Canterbury's monks.* On the Pilgrims' Way.

West Wickham *Wicheham: Adam FitzHubert from Bishop of Bayeux. Church, mill.* London suburb.

Whitstable *Nortone: Archbishop of Canterbury. 7 salt-houses, 2 churches.* Holiday resort and yachting centre, famous for oysters.

Wichling *Winchelesmere: Bishop of Bayeux. Church.* Downland.

Wickhambreux *Wicheham: Bishop of Bayeux. Church, park, 2 mills, 2 salt-houses, 3 fisheries.* Unspoilt; Green; mill.

Wilderton *Wirentone: St Augustine's Abbey.*

Wingham *Wingheham: Archbishop of Canterbury. 2 mills, fishery, salt-house.* Set among woodland. Next to the medieval Old Canonry is an 18th-century house built on the site of the archbishop's manor house.

Woodnesborough *Gollesberge/ Wanesberge: Ansfrid and Thurstan from Bishop of Bayeux.* On a hill.

Woolwich *Hulviz: Hamo the Sheriff.* London borough.

Wormshill *Godeselle: Hugh nephew of Herbert from Bishop of Bayeux. Church.* Remote; manor house.

Wouldham *Oldeham: Bishop of Rochester. Fishery, church.* Industrial.

Wricklesmarsh *Witenemers: The son of Thorold of Rochester from Bishop of Bayeux.* Area between Blackheath and Woolwich Common; the name survives in Wricklemarsh Road, Kidbrooke.

Wrotham *Broteham: Archbishop of Canterbury. Church, 3 mills.* On the Pilgrims' Way; ruins of an ancient archbishop's palace; Wrotham Place manor house.

Wrotham Heath *Litelbroteham: Ralph FitzThorold from Bishop of Bayeux.* Orchards.

Wye *Wi: Battle Abbey. Church, 4 mills. 300 eels.* Pleasant market town, once a royal Saxon manor. Wye College, the agriculture college of London University, is here.

Yalding: See page 141.

WYE: *Grotesque corbels on a 17th-century doorway.*

Lancashire

Lancashire did not become a county until 1182, more than a century after the Norman Conquest. Domesday *treated it as two separate entities: everything north of the River Ribble was bundled in with Yorkshire, while the southern area, 'between the Ribble and the Mersey', was considered a poor relation of Cheshire. Very little information is given about either section, although the one to the south at least includes the names of tenants and a few statistics. Generally, the picture that emerges is of a poor, sparsely populated land where moor, marsh, forest and mountains kept the villages small and scattered. Roger de Poitou had once owned most of the area, and although he had mysteriously lost possession to the king by 1086, he was repossessed shortly afterwards. The inhabitants probably included both Scandinavians and Anglo-Saxons, for the land is sometimes measured in a curious mixture of carucate (Scandinavian) and hide (English).*

For the northern section Domesday *does little more than list the names of settlements. The Lancashire historian William Farrer has suggested that the commissioners of 1086 may not even have visited the region. In the 'Hundred' known as Amounderness, 62 settlements are mentioned. Of these, says* Domesday, *16 'have a few inhabitants ... The rest are waste.' The armies of King William, or the marauding Danes or Celts – or all three – had made the north-west of England scarcely worth considering.*

HEYSHAM: *View through an Anglo-Saxon arch; Ireland lies straight across the sea.*

Heysham

Land of the King in Yorkshire . . . In Halton Earl Tosti had 6c. of land taxable. In Aldcliffe 2c., Thurnham 2c., Hillam 1c., Lancaster 6c., Kirk Lancaster 2c., Hutton 2c., Newton 2c., Overton 4c., Middleton 4c., Heaton 2c., HEYSHAM *HESSAM* 4c., Oxcliffe 2c., Poulton (le Sands) 2c., Torrisholme 2c., Skerton 6c., Bare 2c., Slyne 6c., Bolton (le Sands) 4c., Kellet 6c., Stapleton Terne 2c., Newsham 2c., Carnforth 2c. All these villages belong to Halton.

There is now no way of telling exactly where the brash resort of Morecambe ends and the town of Heysham begins, but they were once two distinct places. Holiday-makers who grow tired of Morecambe's sand and slot machines can drive a couple of miles south and suddenly find themselves in a corner of old England almost too quaint to be true. Old Heysham is not entirely untouched by modern Morecambe, however. There is Heysham rock, candy floss and a shop that claims to sell the Largest Selection of Fudges in Lancashire. But the eighteenth- and nineteenth-century buildings along the little main street are genuine, and the two churches which stand side by side on the rocks above the beach are more venerable than donkey rides and even than *Domesday* itself.

In 1086 there was already an ancient Christian tradition at Heysham. Just how ancient is a matter of dispute. A stubborn local tale insists that St Patrick (389–461) was shipwrecked in Morecambe Bay and brought Christianity to this shore. The little chapel of St Patrick, dating perhaps from the eighth century, is now a ruin. A simple Anglo-Saxon arch frames the western sea, where straight across lies Ireland. Just below St Patrick's is the parish church of St Peter, which, although much restored, also dates from pre-Norman days.

Little is known about *Domesday* Heysham. The Normans considered it a part of Yorkshire, one of 22 settlements belonging to the manor of Halton. They were tiny villages then and, with the notable exception of Lancaster, they still are. Heysham remained for a long time a place of religious significance. Two holy wells kept the pilgrims coming until the wells dried up. In about 1800 a Dr Whitaker wrote of it gloomily: 'no market, no shop, no butcher, no doctor or attorney or school, no seaworthy boat and no manufacturing because there was no good water'. By the end of the century things had taken a turn for the better. 'A most picturesque little village situated on a wooded rocky promontory', said a guide book of 1880. A nuclear power station, a ferry port and a holiday entertainment centre complete the picture of modern Heysham. St Patrick would have a job finding a quiet place to worship today.

Argarmeles

Roger de Poitou held the undermentioned land. Between the Ribble and the Mersey. In (West) Derby Hundred [a list follows, naming 45 holdings, including:] Wigbert held ARGARMELES *ERENGERMELES*. 2 carucates of land. The value was 8s. This land was exempt apart from tax.

HEYSHAM: *Near St Patrick's is a strange graveyard hewn out of the rock.*

'The country about Southport has as few charms as it is possible for any region to have,' wrote the disgruntled Nathaniel Hawthorne, forced to spend the winter of 1856–7 on the Lancashire coast. 'In the close neighbourhood of the shore, it is nothing but sand hillocks, covered with coarse grass.'

This coastal area was much the same in 1086, long before there was a resort called Southport. To the north of the present town was North Meols; to the south was Argarmeles; the common suffix (pronounced mels) is an Old Norse word meaning sand dune. There was little except dunes when the Norsemen arrived. A few miles inland lay the great marshy lake that became known as Martin Mere. This strip of coast was poor land in a poor region at the time of *Domesday*.

Argarmeles, listed as Erengermeles in *Domesday*, was presumably named after a Scandinavian settler called Erenger. It was probably poverty that exempted it from all payments to the king except tax. *Domesday*, so reticent about most Lancashire holdings, gives an interesting description of feudal law as it related to West Derby Hundred, in which Argarmeles was included. For theft or highway robbery, a free man would be fined 40s; for 'drawing blood' or rape he would pay a mere 10s.

Argarmeles was an early victim of the sea. In 1346 there is reference to 'Argarmeles, which is now annihilate by the sea and there is no habitation there'. But 150 years later the king's officials were stubbornly trying to prove that there was indeed an Argarmeles and that it must pay up like any other village. In 1503 Sir Henry Halsall, th nominal holder, proved that no such place existed by calling as witnesses three old men. One, an 80-year-old named John Shirlock, who had lived locally all his life, may have clinched matters when he testified that he had 'hard say that suche londes there were, and drowned in the sea, but where ne in what parte he never hard tell'. After that Argarmeles disappeared even from the tax man's gazetteer.

Exactly where it stood is unknown, but its south-eastern corner is believed to have been in what is now the town of Birkdale, the southern extension of Southport. Until the mid-nineteenth century, this area consisted mainly of 'sand hills and rabbit warrens', but by then sand and sea were becoming fashionable. In 1848 the *Liverpool Mercury* advertised the land for development. 'We do not despair of shortly seeing the healthy locality covered with beautiful residences suitable for the habitation of the most respectable parties.' This is more or less what happened. The once barren dunes have become Royal Birkdale, one of Britain's great golf links. All that remains of impoverished Argarmeles is a playground for the wealthy.

Warrington

Roger de Poitou held the undermentioned land. Between the Ribble and the Mersey ... In Warrington Hundred. King Edward held WARRINGTON *WALINTUNE* with 3 outliers. 1 hide. To the manor itself belonged 34 *drengs* and they had as many manors, in which there were 42 carucates of land and 1½ hides. St Elfin's held 1 carucate of land exempt from all customary dues except tax. The whole manor with the Hundred paid £15 less 2s in revenue to the King. Now 2 ploughs in Lordship; 8 men with 1 plough. These men hold land there: Roger 1 carucate of land; Theobald 1½ carucates; Warin 1 carucate; Ralph 5 carucates; William 2 hides and 4 carucates of land; Aethelhard 1 hide and ½ carucate; Osmund 1 carucate of land. Total value £4 10s; value of the lordship £3 10s.

Warrington now belongs to Cheshire, but in spirit it remains Lancastrian, part of that great industrial belt which spans the south of the county from Liverpool to Oldham. It is a businesslike town, not the place for a long family weekend. The city centre is difficult to recognize even when you have found it, and one of its most striking buildings is a high-rise car park. Yet, even though there are few architectural treasures, the whole winding, patched-up city has an air of antiquity. Below the formidable disguises of industry and urban development lies a very ancient town.

It was ancient even at the time of the Conquest. The Romans established a settlement here in the first century, which they called *Veratinum*, or ford town, borrowing the Celtic word *werid*, meaning ford. It was strategically important, the place nearest the sea where the River Mersey could be crossed by a marching army. Roman roads led from here to Chester, Kinderton, Wigan and Manchester. In time the Saxons arrived, but moved the town from the south to the north of the river, where St Elphin founded a church in the seventh century. It was still there in 1086, one of the rare churches that *Domesday* actually identifies by name.

Warrington was known to the Normans as Walintune and was the chief town in the Hundred. Its *Domesday* entry tells us everything we know about the whole of Warrington Hundred. This is typical of the entire frustrating survey of South Lancashire. The area defined as *'inter Ripam et Mersham'* (between the Ribble and the Mersey) is divided into six Hundreds, in only one of which, West Derby, are the villages identified by name. In the others the holdings are summarized and lumped together under the principal manor. The Warrington entry reveals that there were 34 subsidiary settlements which had belonged to 34 'drengs' at the time of the Conquest. Dreng was a Scandinavian term, roughly equivalent to the Anglo-Saxon thegn (thane) or freeman, which crops up only rarely in *Domesday*. It appears here because this north-west corner of England was largely settled by Norsemen. Except for land and its value, little else is recorded – neither livestock nor woodland nor number of inhabitants. One local historian reckoned that the eleventh-century population was around 120, but this is only an educated guess.

In 1086 Warrington belonged to King William. He had taken it back from the first Norman lord, Roger de Poitou, together with all of Roger's other Lancashire holdings, because of some obscure dispute. By the end of the century Roger had just as obscurely regained them all. He gave Warrington to one Paganus de Vilars, whose descendants remained Lords of Warrington until 1586. By then it was a thriving town with a population of about 2500, paved roads, a prosperous market and a bridge over the Mersey.

The most extraordinary chapter in its history was its sudden cultural flowering in the eighteenth century. From 1757 until 1786 the Warrington Academy was one of Europe's

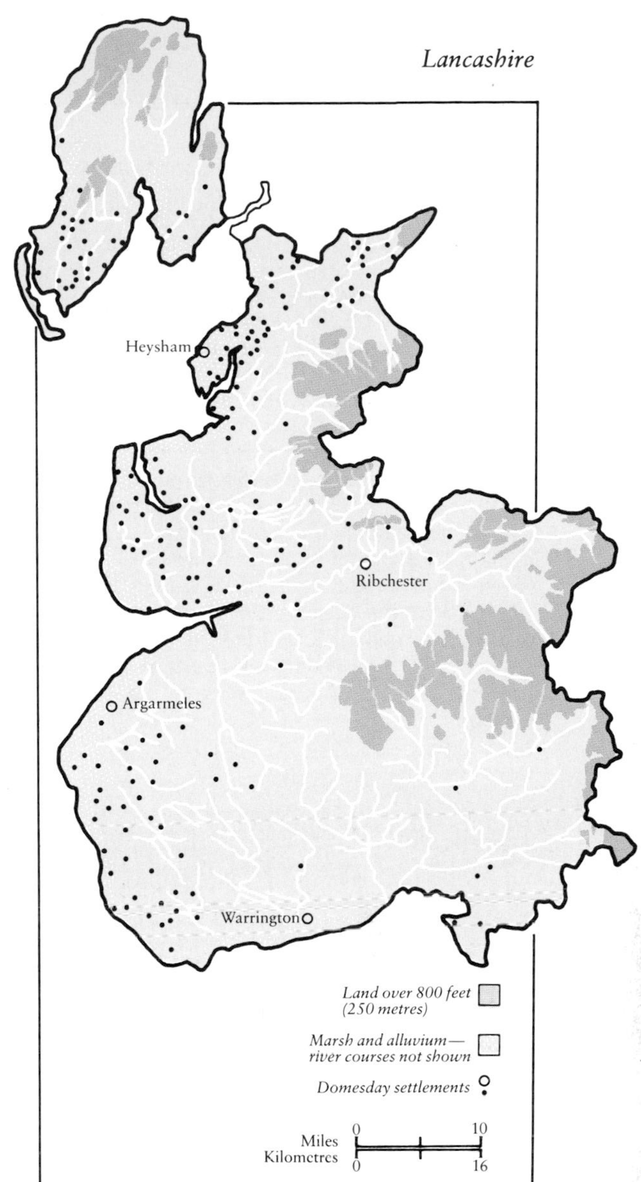

principal seats of learning. It was founded for the education of religious dissenters, who were denied admission to Oxford or Cambridge. Its tutors, also dissenters, were remarkably distinguished. They included the French revolutionary, Jean Paul Marat, and Joseph Priestley, who taught languages and *belles lettres*. By way of a side-line, he wrote his *History and Present State of Electricity*, and it was here that he attended his first chemistry lectures which led to his discovery of oxygen.

It is not for culture but for industry that Warrington is renowned today. The Romans manufactured iron, bronze and pottery here, and established what may have been Britain's earliest glass furnace. In the seventeenth and eighteenth centuries there were clock-making, pin-heading and the making of sail cloth. But industry on a large scale began only after Richard Arkwright, a barber from Bolton, employed a Warrington clockmaker to 'bend him some wires and turn him some pieces of brass', thus creating a machine which he patented in 1769 for spinning raw cotton into finished thread. His invention transformed southern Lancashire into a land of factories, railways, slums and canals, the scars of which survive. Within 50 years of Arkwright's arrival the ancient town had become a victim of new money. Even the *Domesday* church of St Elphin's was given a substantial face-lift in the nineteenth century. Very few ploughlands now lie within sight of its narrow spire – just hide upon hide upon carucate of concrete, brick, muck and brass.

Ribchester

Land of the King in Yorkshire . . .
Amounderness.
In Preston, Earl Tosti, 6c. taxable. These lands belong there.
Ashton 2c., Lea 1c. [a list of 59 towns follows, including RIBCHESTER *RIBELCASTRE* 2c.] All these villages and 3 churches belong to Preston. 16 of them have a few inhabitants, but how many is not known. The rest are waste. Roger de Poitou had them.

Nine miles north-east of Preston the River Ribble has worn a broad bed through which it meanders unhurriedly to its meeting with the Irish Sea. Here the town of Ribchester is poised on the north bank, a relaxed and pleasant spot.

The Normans knew it as Ribelcastre and entered it as such in *Domesday*, but it was clearly a place of little significance. It belonged to that sad region called Amounderness, where 46 of 62 settlements were deserted and waste. The 16 with 'a few inhabitants' are unspecified, but there is no reason to believe that Ribchester was a living community in 1086. The exact cause of the devastation in this area will probably never be discovered. Two historians, J. Beddoe and J. H. Rowe, place the blame on King William. After brutally suppressing rebellions in the East and West Ridings of Yorkshire in 1069–70, he moved south-west 'through the hills in a broad front by many paths, so as to overrun the entire county and to debauch upon Amounderness, which was treated with almost as great severity as Yorkshire'. Ribchester, which lay on a major route to the west coast, was unlikely to have escaped his attentions.

In Roman days this had been *Bremetennacum Veteranorum*, the largest fort in Lancashire, standing at the junction of roads that led to Chester, York and Carlisle. Five hundred cavalrymen were stationed here in a walled enclosure, outside which there was a substantial community of veterans, men for whom Rome could find no further purpose and who ended their days as farmers or horse breeders in this remote outpost of the empire.

In the fourth century, after 300 years of occupation, the Romans withdrew. A lengthy Dark Age followed, and next to nothing is known about Ribchester's history for 1000 years. The few remains that have been discovered show that the Saxons eventually arrived and probably lived within the abandoned shell of the Roman town.

Ribchester was again reduced to ruins by the Scots in 1323, but signs of its Roman past still remained. 'Great squarid stones, voultes and antique coins be found ther', wrote John Leland, Henry VIII's travelling antiquary. Almost nothing is left above ground from those days, although a Roman museum displays many small items uncovered by successive excavations. Of the fort itself there remain only the foundations of two garrison granaries and a western defensive ditch. There is little to confirm a wistful local saying:

It is written upon a wall in Rome:
Ribchester was as rich as any town in
Christendom.

RIBCHESTER: *The River Ribble flows as peacefully now as it did when the Romans were stationed here.*

Lancashire Gazetteer
Each entry starts with the modern place name in **bold** type. The *Domesday* information that follows is in *italic* type, beginning with the name or names by which the place was known in 1086. The main landholders and undertenants are next, separated with semi-colons if a place was divided into more than one holding. Although Roger de Poitou had lost possession of his lands at the time of *Domesday*, he is nevertheless considered to be the holder and is listed as such in the gazetteer. More general information completes the *Domesday* part of the entry. The modern or post-Domesday section is in normal type. ⊞ represents a village, ⌂ a small village or hamlet.

Aighton *Actun:* . Lost.

Ainsdale *Einuluesdel: Roger de Poitou.* Seaside district of Southport; holiday camp; Aighton Sands.

Aldcliffe *Aldeclif: King's land.* ⊞ On the outskirts of Lancaster.

Aldingham *Aldingham: Arnulf from the king.* ⊞ On Morecambe Bay; Norman castle site at The Moa.

Allerton *Alretune: Roger de Poitou.* Part of Liverpool; Allerton Hall.

Altcar *Acrer: Roger de Poitou.* ⊞ Now Great Altcar; hall.

Argarmeles *Erengermeles:* . See page 152.

Arkholme *Ergune: King's land.* ⊞ Earthworks of a possibly Norman castle.

Ashton *Estun: Roger de Poitou.* Ashton Hall; remains of a tower and fishpond.

Ashton-on-Ribble *Estun: King's land.* Ashton Park in Preston.

Aughton *Achetun: Roger de Poitou. 2 hawk's eyries.* ⊞ Church with a Norman doorway.

Baguley *Bagelei: Gilbert, Ranulf and Hamo.* In the urban district of Altrincham–Sale. Bowden church has a 13th-century monument to the de Baggiley family.

Bardsea *Berretseige: King's land.* ⊞ On Morecambe Bay. Nearby Conishead Priory was founded in the 12th century.

Bare *Bare: King's land.* Part of Morecambe.

Barton *Bartune: Roger de Poitou.* ⌂

Barton (near Preston) *Bartun: King's land.* ⊞ Barton House; hall; farm.

Birkby *Bretebi: Orm from the king.* Birkby Hall.

Bispham *Biscopham: King's land.* Locality, with Little Bispham, on the coast between Blackpool and Clevelys.

Blackburn *Blacheburne: Roger de Poitou.* Large, spreading town with much modern development, a cotton weaving centre since the 14th century.

CARNFORTH: *The crest of the Lancashire and Yorkshire Railway Company.*

Bolton-le-Moors : *King's land.* Bolton Heads near Little Urswick.

Bolton-le-Sands *Bodeltone: King's land.* ⊞ 17th- and 18th-century stone houses; recently much developed.

Bootle *Boltelai: Roger de Poitou.* Industrial town with Merseyside docks, adjoining Liverpool.

Borwick *Berewic: Ernwin the Priest from Roger de Poitou.* ⊞ Tudor hall.

Broughton *Broctun: King's land.* ⊞ Broughton House.

Broughton-in-Furness *Borch: King's land.* Small market town.

Burn *Brune: King's land.* Burn Hall and Burn Naze on the outskirts of Clevelys.

Cantsfield *Cantesfelt: King's land.* ⊞ Hall.

Carleton *Carlentun: King's land.* Locality on the outskirts of Poulton le-Fylde.

Carnforth *Chreneforde: King's land.* Town; railway museum.

Cartmel *Cherchebi: Dwan from the king.* Town; beautiful priory church founded in 1188; 14th-century gatehouse.

Caton *Catun: King's land.* ⊞ On a stretch of the River Lune painted by Turner.

Catterall *Catrehala: King's land.* ⊞ Catterall Lodge.

Childwall *Cildeuuelle: Roger de Poitou.* Part of Liverpool. The Calder Stones are from a prehistoric burial mound.

Chipping *Chipinden: King's land.* ⊞ Pretty.

Claughton *Clactune: King's land.* ⊞ Hall.

Claughton (near Lancaster) *Clactun: King's land.* ⊞ Tudor Claughton Hall.

Clifton *Clistun: King's land.* ⊞ Hall; Clifton Farm.

Cockerham *Cochreham: Roger de Poitou.* ⊞ Cockersand Abbey Farm and the ruins of an abbey are nearby.

Crimbles *Crimeles:* Lost.

Crivelton *Clivertun:* Lost.

Crosby *Crosebi: Roger de Poitou.* Now Great Crosby, part of the town of Crosby, and Little Crosby, a village with a Tudor hall, partly rebuilt in the 18th century.

Dalton (near Wigan) *Daltone: Roger de Poitou.* ⌂ Ashurst Hall has a 17th-century gatehouse.

Dalton-in-Furness *Daltune: King's land.* Once the capital of the Furness district and a market centre for Furness Abbey, founded in 1127; birthplace of George Romney (1734–1802).

Dendron *Dene: King's land.* ⌂

Dilworth *Bileuurde: King's land.* Dilworth House.

Downholland Cross *Holand: Roger de Poitou.* ⊞

Down Litherland *Liderlant/ Literlant: Roger de Poitou.* Part of Liverpool.

Ellel *Ellhale: Roger de Poitou.* ⊞ Ellel Moor.

Elswick *Edelesuuic: King's land.* ⊞ Elswick Manor; Elswick Grange Farm.

Farleton *Fareltun: Ernwin the priest from Roger de Poitou.* ⊞ Moated site.

Field Plumpton *Pluntun: King's land.* Now 2 villages, Great and Little Plumpton.

Fishwick *Fiscuic:* Lost.

Fordbootle *Fordebodele:* Lost.

Formby *Fornebei: Roger de Poitou.* Resort town, once threatened by encroaching sand as the sea receded. An 18th-century law enforced the planting of trees and grass to form a barrier.

Forton *Fortune: King's land.* ⊞ Forton Hall.

Freckleton *Frecheltun: King's land.* ⊞

Garstang *Cherestanc: King's land.* Town; ruins of Greenhalgh Castle built by the first Earl of Derby in 1490.

Gleaston *Glassertun: King's land.* ⊞ Ruins of 14th-century Gleaston Castle.

Goosnargh *Gusansarghe: King's land.* ⊞

Great Eccleston *Eglestun: King's land.* ⊞ Toll bridge over the River Wyre.

Greenhalgh *Greneholf: King's land.* ⌂

Gressingham *Ghersinctune: King's land.* ⊞ Church with fragments of Saxon carvings.

Grimsargh *Grimesarge: King's land.* ⊞ Grimsargh House; Grimsargh Hall.

Haighton Green *Halctun: King's land.* ⊞ Haighton Hall; Haighton House.

Halsall *Heleshale/Herleshala: Roger de Poitou.* ⊞

Halton *Haltun(e): King's land.* ⊞ Recently developed church with a Roman altar and a Danish cross in the churchyard.

Hambleton *Hameltune: King's land.* ⊞ Known for its pearl mussels.

Hart *Hert:* Lost.

Heaton *Hietun:* Lost.

Heaton Bridge *Hietune: King's land.* ⊞ On the Leeds and Liverpool Canal.

Heysham *Hessam:* See page 152.

Hillam *Hillun: King's land.* ⌂

LANCASTER: *Williamson's Park, a setting for a folly built by Lord Ashton.*

Holker *Holecher: Orm from the king.* ⊞ Holker Hall, rebuilt in 1873, is in a large deer park.

HORNBY: *The Castle was demolished in 1643, and its walls rebuilt later.*

Hornby *Hornebi: Orm and Ulf from the king.* ⊞ Rebuilt but romantic-looking castle described by Scott in *Marmion*; Castle Stede, a Norman earthwork, nearby.

Huncoat *Hunnicot: Roger de Bully and Albert Grelley.* ⊞ Hall; castle remains.

Hurlston *Hir(l)etun: Roger de Poitou.* Now 2 small hamlets, Hurlston and Hurlston Green.

Hutton *Hotun:* Lost.

Huyton *Hitune: Roger de Poitou.* Now Huyton-with-Roby, part of Liverpool.

Ince Blundell *Hinne: Roger de Poitou.* ⊞ 18th-century hall whose artworks include Roman sculpture.

Inskip *Inscip: King's land.* ⊞

Ireby *Irebi: King's land.* ⊞ Ireby Hall Farm.

Kellet *Chellet: King's land.* ⊞ Now Nether Kellet. Dunald Mill Hole is a stalactite cave.

Killerwick *Chilvestreuic:* Lost.

Kirby *Cherchebi: Roger de Poitou.* Dormitory town for Liverpool; large housing estates.

Kirk Lancaster *Chercaloncastre:* Lost. Probably on the site of Lancaster Castle and Priory.

Kirkby Ireleth *Gerleworde: King's land.* ⊞ Church dedicated to St Cuthbert, whose body was possibly brought here.

Kirkdale *Chirchedele: Roger de Poitou.* Part of Liverpool.

Kirkham *Chicheham: King's land.* Town.

Knowlsey *Chenulueslei: Roger de Poitou.* On the edge of Liverpool. Knowlsey Hall was built *c.*1490 by the Earl of Derby.

Lancaster *Loncastre: King's land.* County town and city on the River Lune, once a large port, named after a Roman camp, and dominated by its castle with a Norman keep. The priory church of St Mary's, on a Roman site, has Anglo-Saxon work and 14th-century choirstalls.

Lathom *Latune:* Lost.

Layton *Latun: King's land.* Part of Blackpool, with Little Layton.

Lea *Lea: King's land.* ⊞ Now Lea Town.

Leck *Lech: King's land.* ⊞ On Leck Beck.

Leece *Lies/Alia Lies: King's land.* ⊞ Surrounds Leece Tarn.

Leyland *Lailand: Gerard, Robert, Ralph, Roger and Walter from Roger de Poitou. 5 hawk's eyries.* Town; Tudor hall.

LYTHAM: *Windmill on the seafront, an ideal position to catch the prevailing winds.*

Little Eccleston *Alia Eglestun: King's land.*

Little Woolton *Ulventune:* Lost.

Lonsdale *Lanesdale:* Lost.

Lydiate *Leiate: Roger de Poitou.* Adjoins Maghull.

Lytham *Lidun: King's land.* Combined with St Anne's; both towns developed as 19th-century seaside resorts. Lytham Hall is 18th century.

Maghull *Magele: Roger de Poitou.* Town adjoining Lydiate; moated site.

Manchester *Mamecestre: St Mary's Church and St Michael's Church.* City with a textile tradition dating back to 14th-century Flemish weavers. Transformed by the Industrial Revolution, it became an inland port on the 1894 Manchester Ship Canal. It is also the home of the Halle Orchestra and Old Trafford cricket ground.

Martin *Merretun: Roger de Poitou.* Martin Hall; Martin Mere, with a Wildfowl Centre.

Marton *Meretun: King's land.* Now Great Marton, part of Blackpool, which was named after the peat-coloured water of Marton Mere; and the adjoining locality of Little Marton.

Melling *Mellinge: King's land.* Overlooking the Lune valley; castle earthworks.

Melling (near Liverpool) *Melinge: Roger de Poitou.* Melling House. Nearby is the hamlet of Melling Mount.

Middleton *Middeltun: King's land.* Middleton Sands.

Much Woolton *Uuetone: Roger de Poitou.* Part of Liverpool.

Mythop *Midehope: King's land.*

Nether Burrow *Borch.*

Newsham *Neuhuse: King's land.* Newsham Hall; Newsham Lodge.

Newsham (in Skerton) *Neuhuse: King's land.*

Newton *Neutun: King's land.*

Newton (in Cartmel) *Neutun: King's land.* Now 2 villages, High and Low Newton; on the edge of Newton Fell.

Newton (near Preston) *Neutune: King's land.* Hall.

SPEKE: *Hall with remarkable black-and-white timbering.*

Newton (in Whittington) *Neutune: King's land.*

Newton-le-Willows *Neweton: Roger de Poitou; St Oswald's of Winwick.* Town on Sankey Brook; Sankey Valley Park.

Northenden *Norwardine: Ranulf and Bigot from Earl Hugh. Church.* Part of Altrincham–Sale conurbation.

North Meols *Otegrimele/ Otringemele: Roger de Poitou.* Meols Hall in Southport.

Orgrave *Ouregrave: King's land.* Orgrave Villa.

Over Burrow *Borch: King's land.* Site of a Roman fort.

Overton *Ouretun: King's land.* Church with Anglo-Saxon cornerstones, a Norman doorway and Norman walls.

Oxcliffe *Oxeneclif: King's land.* Oxcliffe Hill.

Pendleton *Peniltune: Roger de Bully; Albert Grelley.* On the edge of Pendle Moor. Pendle Hill was famous for its witches in the 17th century.

Pennington *Pennigetun: King's land.* The church, founded by Gamel de Pennington in the 12th century, has a tympanum with a Scandinavian inscription.

Penwortham *Peneverdant: Roger de Poitou. Castle, ½ fishery, woodland and hawk's eyries.* Now 2 villages adjoining Preston: Higher Penwortham, with the site of a Norman castle, and Lower Penwortham.

Poulton le Fylde *Poltun: King's land.* Town; attractive market-place with a tithe barn.

Poulton le Sands *Poltune: King's land.* Once a tiny fishing village, now absorbed by Morecambe.

Preesall *Pressouede: King's land.* Brine wells nearby on the Wyre estuary.

Preese *Pres: King's land.* Preese Hall.

Preston *Prestune: Roger de Poitou.* County administrative centre and inland seaport at the head of the Ribble Estuary.

Priest Hutton *Hotune: King's land.*

Radcliffe *Radeclive: Roger de Poitou.* Town on the River Irwell; only the tower is left of the 15th-century house belonging to the Radcliffes.

Raven Meols *Mele: Roger de Poitou.* Raven Meols Hills.

Rawcliffe *Rodeclif: King's land.* Road and parish name.

Ribby *Rigbi: King's land.* Adjoining Wrea Green.

Ribchester *Ribelcastre:* See page 154.

Roby *Rabil: Roger de Poitou.* Huyton-with-Roby, part of Liverpool.

Rochdale *Recedham: Roger de Poitou.* Important cotton manufacturing town where the Co-operative Movement began in 1844.

Roose *Rosse: King's land.* Part of Barrow-in-Furness.

Rossall *Rushdale:* Lost.

St Michael's on Wyre *Michelescherche: King's land.* Hall; museum of local history.

Salford *Salford: Roger de Poitou.* Industrial town in the Manchester conurbation. Peel Park was the first free municipal library; the art gallery has paintings by L.S. Lowry (1887–1976).

Salwick *Saleuuic:* Lost.

Scotforth *Scozforde: Roger de Poitou.* Part of Lancaster.

Sefton *Sextone: Roger de Poitou.* Mill; Old Hall Farm.

Singleton *Singletun: King's land.* Also Little Singleton with Singleton Hall.

Skelmersdale *Schelmeresdele: Roger de Poitou.* Town with large housing estates and a modern town centre; formerly a mining village.

Skerton *Schertune: King's land.* Part of Lancaster.

Slyne *Sline: King's land.* Adjoining Hest Bank; Slyne Hall; manor house.

Smithdown *Esmedune:* Lost.

Sowerby *Sourebi:* Lost.

Sowerby (near Preston) *Sorbi: King's land.* Sowerby Hall Farm.

Speke *Spec: Roger de Poitou.* Part of Liverpool. Speke Hall is a fine 16th-century half-timbered house in a wooded park.

Staining *Staininghe: King's land.*

Stainton *Steintun: King's land.* 2 farms near limestone quarries.

Stalmine *Stalmine: King's land.*

Stapleton Terne *Stopeltierne:* Lost.

Swainseat *Suenesat:* Lost.

Tarbock *Torboc: Roger de Poitou.* Now Tarbock Green; Tarbock Hall Farm.

Tatham *Tathaim: King's land.* On the River Wenning. Tatham Hall is on the opposite bank.

Thirnby *Tiernebi:* Lost.

Thornton (near Fleetwood) *Torentun: King's land.* Town.

Thornton (near Liverpool) *Torentun: Roger de Poitou.* Part of Crosby.

Threlfall *Trelefelt:* Lost.

Thurnham *Tiernun: King's land.* Now 2 villages, Upper Thurnham, with a partly 16th-century hall, and Lower Thurnham.

Torrisholme *Toredholme: King's land.* Part of Morecambe.

Toxteth *Stochestede: Roger de Poitou.* Part of Liverpool.

Treales *Treueles:* Lost.

Tunstall *Tunestalle: King's land.* Thurland Castle; moated hall; school attended by the Brontës, now a cottage.

Ulverston *Ulvrestun: Thorulf from the king.* Town with a Tudor church and many Quaker associations. The tower on Hoad Hill, a copy of the Eddystone Lighthouse, is a memorial to the founder of the Royal Geographical Society, Sir John Barrow (1764–1848).

Up Holland *Hoiland: Roger de Poitou.* Part of Skelmersdale; ruins of a priory founded by Robert de Holland.

Up Litherland *Literland: Roger de Poitou.* Part of Liverpool.

Walton *Walletun: King's land.* Walton Hall.

Walton-le-Dale *Waletune: Roger de Bully and Albert Grelley.* Town on the site of a Roman ford over the River Ribble.

Walton on the Hill *Waletone: Roger de Poitou.* Part of Liverpool.

Warrington *Walintune:* . See page 153.

Wart *Warte:* Lost.

Warton (near Carnforth) *Wartun: King's land.* Parsonage dating from the 14th century. The first grammar school was founded here in 1594 by Archbishop Hutton.

Warton (near Preston) *Wartun: King's land.*

Wavertree *Wauretreu: Roger de Poitou.* Part of Liverpool.

Weeton *Widetun: King's land.* Also hamlet of Weeton Lane Heads.

Wennington *Wennigetun: King's land.* Hall.

West Derby *Derbei/berie: Roger de Poitou. Hawk's eyrie.* On the edge of Liverpool; 18th-century Croxteth Hall in a large park.

Westby *Westbi: King's land.* Hall.

Whalley *Wallei: Roger de Poitou.* Attractive small town with the ruins of a 13th-century Cistercian abbey and a mainly 13th-century church.

Wheatley *Watelei: King's land.* Wheatley Farm.

Whittingham *Witingheha: King's land.* Whittingham House.

Whittington *Witetune: King's land.*

Woodplumpton *Pluntun: King's land.*

Yealand *Jalant: Ernwin the priest from Roger de Poitou.* Yealand Manor.

Leicestershire

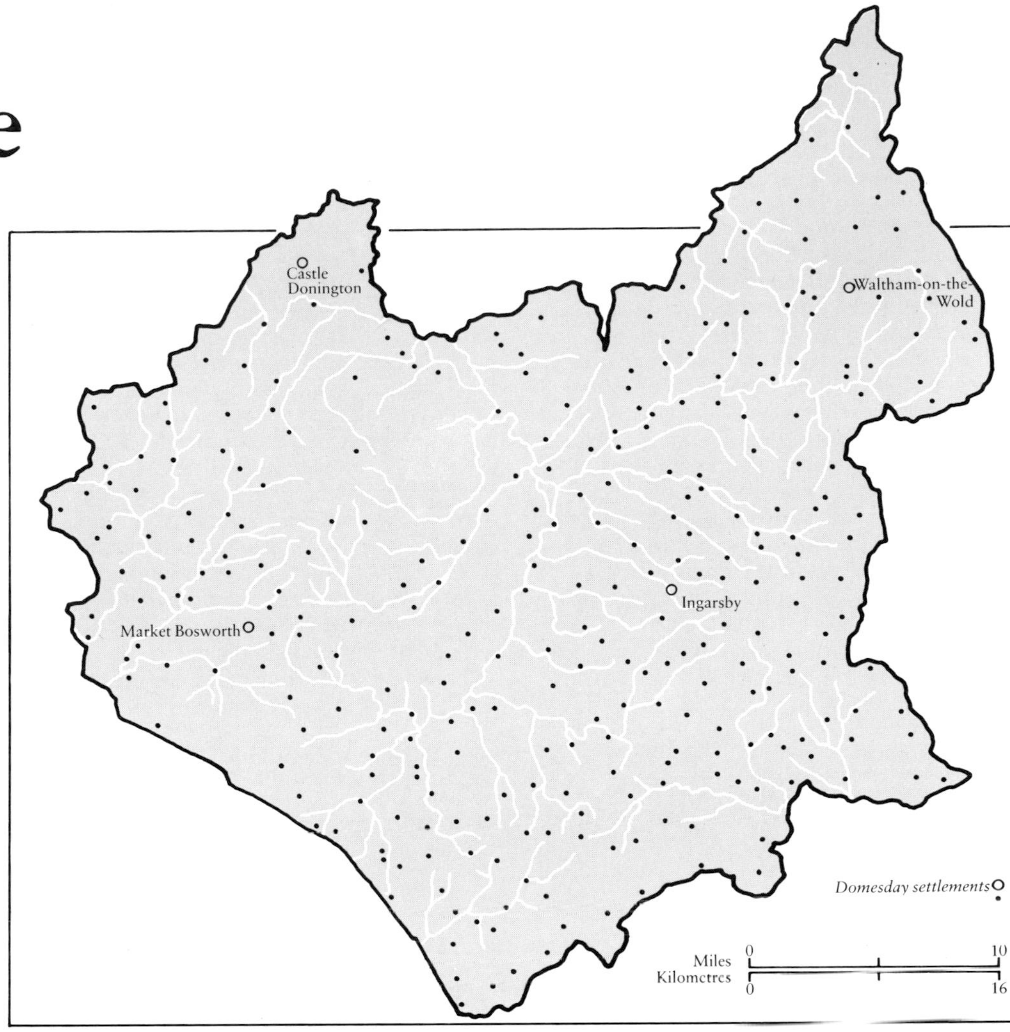

Domesday Leicestershire belonged to the Northern Danelaw, the central section of England occupied by the Vikings in the ninth century. It is a typical Danelaw county: carucates instead of hides, wapentakes instead of hundreds, and a tendency for assessments to add up in multiples of 6 instead of 5, as in English England. But English units do occasionally creep in, indicating that the county was not entirely Danish, The proportion of freemen, typical of Danish areas, is high only in the eastern half of the county, as are place names with Scandinavian endings.

Except for Charnwood Forest in the west, which was apparently unsettled, the county was one of England's more densely populated. Yet the values given for its manors are on the whole very low. This, with other clues, suggests that Leicestershire may have been devastated by William during his suppression of the post-Conquest revolts.

The county's greatest landholder was Hugh de Grandmesnil, who was probably Sheriff in 1086 and who held 180 houses and four churches in Leicester itself, and land in 67 villages scattered across the entire southern half of the county. Earl Aubrey, listed as one of the landholders in Domesday, *had in fact returned to Normandy in the early 1080s. As his holdings in Leicestershire and elsewhere had not been granted to anyone else in 1086, they are customarily regarded as being the king's land. Countess Godiva, who had three holdings in Leicestershire, is said to have ridden naked through Coventry so that her husband Leofric, Earl of Mercia, would remit the heavy taxation on its people.*

Castle Donington

The Countess [Aelfeva] held (CASTLE) DONINGTON *DUNI(N)TONE* herself. 22½ c. of land. Before 1066, 20 ploughs. Now in lordship 3. 30 villagers with a priest, 5 Freemen and 11 smallholders have 12 ploughs. A mill at 10s 8d; woodland 12 furlongs long and 8 wide. The value was 100s; now £11.

Castle Donington is a steep, genteel, slightly decayed red-brick market town that straggles across a couple of little hills overlooking the Trent, the border with Derbyshire. Its castle was built in medieval days because of its strategic position commanding the nearby Trent crossings. But although the *Domesday* entry shows that it was already a sizeable settlement, there is no evidence of a castle this early.

The *Domesday* entry is one of many in Leicestershire which give the number of ploughs on the land before 1066, instead of the more prevalent system which recorded the number of ploughs for which there was land. The implication is that the number of pre-1066 working ploughs was taken to indicate the land's 'normal' capacity, against which to contrast those at work in 1086. Twenty years after the Conquest, William still continued to treat as the norm conditions as they had been in the time of Edward the Confessor, despite the transformations in English society he was producing. One sign of the upheavals is that although the current number of ploughs (15) was lower than before 1066 (20), the value had increased from £5 to £11. This apparent contradiction – common to many Leicestershire entries – has been explained by supposing that the figure for earlier values (unlike that for ploughs) referred to a period *after* the Conquest, when much of the county had been devastated by William's suppression of revolts. Certainly the line of his march in 1068 through Leicestershire from Warwick to Nottingham to put down the first of these is marked by a series of villages entered as 'waste' in *Domesday*.

Countess Aelfeva, the wife of Earl Aelfeva of Mercia, was probably an indirect victim of these revolts and their aftermath. However, the fact that no successor for her is named may mean that she had only recently lost her lands. Possibly her holdings were in the process of reverting to the king. But *Domesday's* brief reference to Donington states that Earl Hugh of Chester held five carucates, a foothold he seems to have used effectively, for a document of 40 years later, the Leicestershire survey, shows that the Earl of Chester held all of the Countess's former lands.

The Countess was the first of many holders of Castle Donington whose careers ended badly. Eustace, Baron of Haulton, built the first castle on the site, only for it to be demolished at the king's order in 1216. Henry de Lacy, Earl of Lincoln, who rebuilt it, was beheaded in 1322. His successor, Edmund Earl of Kent, was also beheaded seven years later. After a period in the Duke of Lancaster's hands the castle was granted to Sir William Hastings in 1461, and he too was subsequently beheaded, by Richard III. After the Battle of Bosworth Henry VII restored the family's lands and titles to Hasting's grandson, and created him the first Earl of Huntingdon.

Things began to go badly again with the nephew of the tenth Earl, who was the first Marquis of Hastings. By this time the castle had been demolished and the stones used to build a great house in Donington Park. In 1793 the Marquis pulled this down to build the present Donington Hall, which he filled with paintings by Old Masters. But 15 years later a visitor lamented the collapse of his fortunes: 'that hopeless pond! in endeavouring to fill which Lady Moira expended so much trouble and money without success: the water still escaping like his own wealth, through some invisible and unaccountable outlets ... *O curas hominem!* Poor Lord Hastings!'

The sister of the second Marquis, Lady Flora Hastings, who was a Lady of the Bedchamber to Queen Victoria's mother, became the victim of a malicious Court rumour. Gossips insisted that a complaint for which she consulted a doctor was in fact an illegitimate pregnancy. She had to submit to a medical examination to clear herself. 'The court is plunged in shame and mortification,' wrote Charles Greville in his diary '... the palace is full of bickerings and heart-burnings, while the whole proceeding is looked upon by society at large as to the last degree disgusting and disgraceful.' Lady Flora, distraught, died a few months later. The fourth Marquis was the family's greatest disaster. A drunken gambler with a 'narrow, care-worn, devil-driven face', he quickly dissipated his inherited wealth. As the final blow, he lost £140,000 on the Derby in 1866, and was dead within the year. *The Times* obituary commented, '... the bearer of a dozen peerages, the descendant of a family which dates from the Conqueror, the owner of a princely fortune, the possessor, in a word, of everything that rank, family, wealth and marriage can bestow has died at the age of twenty-six, ruined alike in health, in honour, and in estate.'

It was the end of Donington Hall as a great house, although the family held on to it for another thirty years. It was sold in 1902 and has since been a prisoner-of-war camp (during World War I), a country club hotel, an Army officer's training camp, a Hungarian refugee reception centre, an Ockenden Venture refugee camp, a computer company's office and, since 1980, the head office of British Midland Airways. The park is now the site of Britain's first man-made racing circuit, the pennants of the track waving over the brow of the hill opposite Donington Hall's front door. Nothing is left of the castle except for a slight depression where the moat once was, and a few stones in the wall of a private garden. But there is one survival of *Domesday* Donington a few hundred yards from the hall – the Ancient King's Mills on the Trent which are the remains of a watermill complex that began with the 'mill at 10s 8d' listed in the survey. It was used for centuries for grinding corn, fulling, milling paper and plaster. It was burned down in 1927, but three huge rusting wheels remain in the midst of a jumble of overgrown stone ruins. The way back to Castle Donington takes one past its successor, an enormous power station.

Ingarsby

[Ivo] also holds 12 c. of land in INGARSBY *GERBERIE* from Hugh [de Grandmesnil]. Land for 8 ploughs. In lordship 2; 4 male and 1 female slaves. 16 villagers with 7 smallholders and 1 man-at-arms with 3 Frenchmen have 5 ploughs. A mill at 4s. The value was 40s; now £4.

Ingarsby is now only a series of mounds and depressions spreading over two sloping meadows in the countryside near Hungerton, a few miles east of Leicester. But *Domesday* shows that in 1086 it was a larger than average settlement, with no signs of decay.

The village was granted to Leicester Abbey in 1352, except for a few bits which it bought up over the next hundred years. There were five major outbreaks of bubonic plague in Leicestershire between 1349 and 1400, depleting the population by up to a half and bringing about an agricultural depression. As a result, the abbey enclosed the estate with hedges and ditches in 1469 and converted it into a sheep and cattle ranch. This appears to have caused the complete desertion of the village, says a plaque on the site.

Ingarsby was one of perhaps 1000 villages which were cleared for sheep between 1450 and 1600. 'Thirty persons departed in tears and have perished', wrote a contemporary of the clearance of nearby Willowes in 1495. Dispossessed peasants wandered the roads, robbing travellers or poaching to stay alive, while Parliament passed a series of Acts in a vain attempt to halt the 'Pulling Down of Towns'. The peasant uprisings of 1607 in Leicestershire, Northamptonshire and Warwickshire were a direct reaction to these clearances. Protesting 'diggers' cut down hedges and filled in ditches used to enclose old arable land, while sympathizers supplied them with spades and food. They warned

anyone against trying to stop them by force: '... better it were in such a case we manfully die than hereafter to be pined to death for want of that which these devouring encroachers do serve their fat hogs and sheep withal ... They have depopulated and overthrown whole towns and made thereof sheep pastures, nothing profitable for our commonwealth.'

Civil order was restored without too much trouble, and today Ingarsby and much of the land around it is still pasture. From low on the opposite slopes, it is easy to see the irregular rectangular pattern of banks and shallow ditches where ancient houses once stood, each with its own garden and orchard. The pond at the bottom, now overgrown by trees, was probably dug by the abbey as a fishpond. Large earth ramparts enclose the whole area, which villagers would have patrolled, keeping a night watch against marauders.

INGARSBY: *Mysterious and evocative pastureland, once a thriving* Domesday *village.*

A deeply hollowed main street runs down the middle of the settlement, still marked by a couple of old thorn trees. An extension of this continues on to the stream at the bottom of the little valley, where there is another remnant of *Domesday* Ingarsby: the stone foundations either of the 'mill at 4s', or of its successor.

Market Bosworth

The Count [of Meulan] also holds 6 c. of land in (MARKET) BOSWORTH *BOSEWORDE*. In lordship 3 ploughs; 2 slaves. 7 Freemen with 10 villagers and 7 smallholders have 2 ploughs. Woodland 1 league long and 1/2 league wide. The value was £4, now 50s. Saxi held all these lands and could go where he would.

Hugh holds 2 c. of land in MARKET BOSWORTH from Hugh [de Grandmesnil]. Land for 1 plough. A priest with a deacon, 4 smallholders and 2 slaves have it. Meadow, 12 acres; woodland 1 furlong long and 1/2 furlong wide. The value was 10s; now 20s.

The town of Market Bosworth feels like a peaceful village with its low cottages and wide, quiet square, but it has a dramatic history. Its name was made famous by the Battle of Bosworth Field, a historical landmark, which took place two miles to the south near the village of Shenton, on 22 August 1485. Here, an invading army under Henry Tudor defeated Richard III, killing him and thus bringing to an end the Wars of the Roses and initiating the Tudor dynasty.

Richard's vanguard was drawn up at the top of Ambion Hill, the site of a medieval hamlet too tiny to have been listed separately in *Domesday*. From here, the king attacked Henry's smaller army below. Henry's men resisted stubbornly, and the fighting was vicious and steady. Henry, recognizing his danger, set off with a bodyguard of some 50 knights to appeal for support to Lord Stanley and Sir William Stanley, who had thus far taken no side, and whose troops were drawn up noncommitally, watching the fight.

Richard, gambling on the Stanleys' continued indecisiveness, seized his opportunity to attack. With 1000 or more knights in full armour he charged straight down the slopes of the hill, nearly overwhelming Henry's bodyguard. He would have succeeded had not Sir William Stanley suddenly made up his mind and thrown his 4000 men against Richard's flank. The king, though now hopelessly outnumbered, fought on, crying 'Treason!', until he was cut down: 'They hewed the crown of gold from his head with dowtful dents; his death was dyghte.'

Bosworth Field is no longer a field, but a large formless area of countryside criss-crossed by hedges and woods. Even so, it is a self-conscious tourist attraction, with panels describing the battle and a striking black stone at the spot where Richard is said to have fallen.

A more poignant piece of landscape history lies in the faint undulations on Ambion Hill, the unremarked remains of tiny Ambion which had already been long abandoned and forgotten before Richard marshalled his army there. It may have been an outlying section of the Bosworth *Domesday* holding at a time almost as distant from that of the Battle of Bosworth as the battle is from our own.

Waltham on the Wolds

Walter holds 16 1/2 c. of land in WALTHAM (ON THE WOLDS) *WALTHA* from Hugh [de Grandmesnil]. Land for 11 ploughs. In lordship 2 ploughs. 24 Freemen with 1 villager and 1 smallholder have 6 ploughs. 1 man-ar-arms with 7 smallholders and 3 male and 1 female slaves has 1 1/2 ploughs. Meadow, 100 acres. The value was £3, now £6.

Waltham on the Wolds is a solid stone village in the north-east uplands of Leicestershire that could belong to the Cotswolds. Its landholder, Hugh de Grandmesnil, was the effective overlord of all of Leicestershire. He was a military man almost to the end of his long life. In the crucial first years after the Battle of Hastings, when the whole country was in a virtual state of rebellion, William put him in command of the old Saxon capital of Winchester. He then fell out of favour with the king, and after William's death he joined Bishop Odo's unsuccessful rebellion against William II in favour of William's brother Robert. In 1091 however, he found himself defending his castle at Courcy in Normandy, this time *against* Robert and for William II. He died in 1094, having renounced the world and become a monk a few days earlier.

Waltham rose to the status of a market town early in the nineteenth century, with an annual horse and cattle fair. Today it seems the idealized sleepy English village, down to its ivy-drenched pub. The only reminder of *Domesday* is its magnificent Norman font.

WALTHAM ON THE WOLDS: *The Norman carved stone font.*

Leicestershire Gazetteer
Each entry starts with the modern place name in **bold** type. The *Domesday* information that follows is in *italic* type, beginning with the name or names by which the place was known in 1086. The main landholders and under-tenants are next, separated with semi-colons if a place was divided into more than one holding. Earl Harold, listed as a former (pre-Conquest) landholder is King Harold. More general information completes the *Domesday* part of the entry. A number of holdings were granted by the king to his thanes; these holders, always at the end of a list, are described as holding land 'from the king'. The modern or post-Domesday section is in normal type. 🏘 represents a village, 🏠 a small village or hamlet.

Ab Kettleby *Chetelbi: Gerard from Robert de Bucy.* 🏠

Allexton *Adelachestone: King's land; Grimbald from Countess Judith. 2 mills.* 🏘 Hall.

Alton *Heletone: Arnold from Hugh de Grandmesnil. Mill.* Alton Grange.

Anstey *Anstige/Hanstigie: Hugh de Grandmesnil.* 🏘 Traditionally the birthplace of Ned Ludd, a mythical figure who gave his name to the Luddite riots (1811–16).

Appleby *Apleberie/bi: King's land; Countess Godiva; Robert from Henry de Ferrers.* Now 2 villages, Appleby Parva, with an impressive school designed by Sir Christopher Wren, and Appleby Magna.

Arnesby *Erendesberie/bi: Wulfric from Bishop of Coutances; William Peverel.* 🏘 Birthplace of Robert Hall (1764–1831), the Nonconformist preacher.

Asfordby *Esserberie/Osferdebie: King's land; Ralph Framen from the king. 2 mills.* 🏘 Church with Saxon cross.

Ashby-de-la-Zouch *Ascebi: Ivo from Hugh de Grandmesnil.* Small town, a spa resort in the 19th century. Home of Selina, Countess of Huntingdon, a member of the first Methodist society in Fetter Lane, in 1739.

Ashby Folville *Ascbi: Hugh from Henry de Ferrers; Ralph from Countess Judith. Mill.* 🏘

Ashby Magna *Essebi: Saxfrid from William Peverel; Gerbert from the king.* 🏘

Ashby Parva *Parva Essebi: Robert de Bucy.* 🏘

Aylestone *Aileston(e): Count of Meulan and Thorold and Wulfnoth from him; Countess Aelfeva. 4 mills.* Part of Leicester.

Baggrave *Badegrave: King's land.* 🏘 Deserted; Baggrave Hall survives.

Bagworth *Bageworde: Ralph from Count of Meulan.* 🏘 Coal mines nearby.

Barkby *Barcheberie/ebi: William from Robert de Tosny; Leofric from Adelaide wife of Hugh de Grandmesnil. Mill.* 🏘 Barkby Hall and Park. William Pochin, the 18th-century Saxon scholar, was born here.

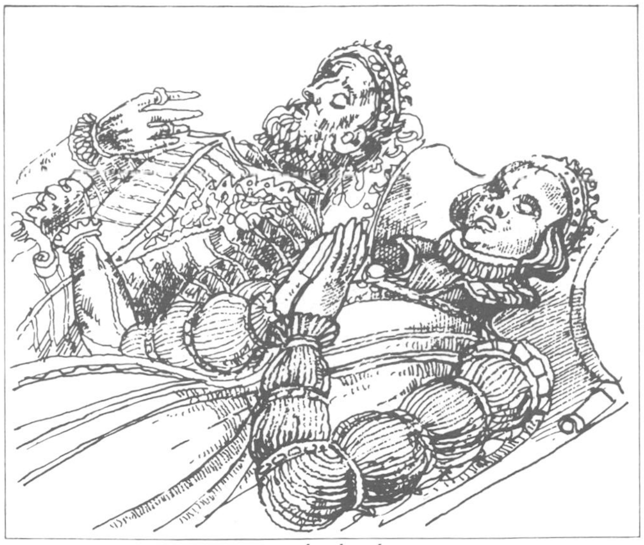

BOTTESFORD: *Fine monuments in the church.*

Barkestone *Barchestone: Robert de Tosny.* 🏘

Barlestone *Berulvestone: Ralph and Arnold from Hugh de Grandmesnil; Geoffrey from Robert de Bucy.* 🏘 3 churches.

Barrow upon Soar *Barhou: Earl Hugh, formerly Earl Harold. 3 mills.* Part of Greater Leicester; Roman settlement; limestone quarries.

Barsby *Barnesbie: King's land.* 🏠

Barton in the Beans *Bartone: Hugh from Hugh de Grandmesnil.* 🏘

Barwell *Barewelle: Coventry Abbey.* 🏘 Romano-British finds.

Beeby *Bebi: Crowland Abbey.* 🏘 Birthplace of Robert Catlin, a judge under Elizabeth I.

Belgrave *Merdegrave: Hugh de Grandmesnil; his wife Adelaide. Mill.* Part of Leicester. It was the site of the city's only suburban railway station when the Great Central Railway was built in the 1890s.

Billesdon *Billesdone: Norman from Geoffrey Alselin.* 🏘 Site of Bronze and Iron Age settlements; Saxon settlement. George Fox, founder of the Society of Friends in the mid-17th century, went to school here.

Bilstone *Bildestone: Countess Godiva.* 🏠

Birstall *Burstel(l)e: Hugh de Grandmesnil and Widhard from him. Mill.* 🏘 Part of Greater Leicester.

Bittesby *Bichesbie: King's land. Mill.* Bittesby House.

Bitteswell *Betmeswel(le): Robert from the king and Geoffrey de La Guerche.* 🏘

Blaby *Bladi: William from Count of Meulan. Mill.* 🏘 In Greater Leicester.

Blaston *Blade/Bla(ue)stone: Robert de Tosny from the king and Countess Judith.* 🏘

Boothorpe *Bortrod: Robert from Henry de Ferrers.* 🏠

Bottesford *Bot(h)es/Holesford: Robert de Tosny and Odard, Baldric, Clarebald, Robert, Heldwin, Gilbert and 4 Frenchmen from him. 6½ mills.* 🏘 The county's biggest village church, containing the tombs of the Earls (later Dukes) of Rutland.

Branston *Brantestone: Ralph from Bishop of Lincoln. 2 mills.* 🏘

Brascote *Brocardescote: Hugh de Grandmesnil.* 🏠 Brascote House.

Braunstone *Brantestone: Robert Burdet's son from Hugh de Grandmesnil.* Part of Leicester.

Bromkinsthorpe *Brandesthorp/dinestor, Brunechinestorp: Hugh de Grandmesnil; Payne from William Peverel.* Absorbed in Leicester.

Brooksby *Brochesbi: Wulfsi from Countess Judith; Earl Hugh, formerly Earl Harold. Mill.* 🏘 Deserted; Tudor Manor House, the home of Lord Cardigan in the 19th century.

Broughton Astley *Broc/Broh/Bros(s)tone: Ralph from the king; Osbern from Hugh de Grandmesnil; Hugh de Grandmesnil from Countess Judith.* 🏘 Part of Greater Leicester. The Quaker George Fox addressed his first large outdoor meeting here in the mid-17th century.

Bruntingthorpe *Brunestan/Brunestinestorp: Hugh de Grandmesnil; Robert from Count of Meulan. Mill.* 🏠 Manor house.

Buckminster *Bucheminstre: Son of Walter from Bishop of Lincoln.* 🏘 The church is probably one of the sites where missionaries baptized Anglo-Saxon converts.

Burbage *Burbece: Coventry Abbey.* 🏘 On the outskirts of Hinckley. Fine common; handsome old houses. Roger Cotes, the first Professor of Astronomy at Cambridge in 1706, lived here.

The 'Burgh' *Burgo:* Lost.

Burrough on the Hill *Burc/Burg: Robert from Henry de Ferrers; Geoffrey de la Guerche; Herbert from the king.* 🏘 Site of a prehistoric hill fort.

Burton Lazars *Burtone: Robert from Henry de Ferrers; Richard from Roger de Bully; Geoffrey de La Guerche.* 🏘 Hall and park. Its name comes from a leper hospital founded by a Crusader.

Burton on the Wolds *Bor/Burtone: William from Geoffrey de La Guerche; Durand Malet, Leofwin, Godric and Hugh from Earl Hugh.* 🏘 Late Georgian hall.

Burton Overy *Burtone: Hugh de Grandmesnil.* 🏘 Near Roman road; birthplace of Hugh Weston (1505–58) who presided over Cranmer's trial. The Banks nearby are earthworks, possibly the site of a deserted village.

Cadeby *Catebi: Ivo from Hugh de Grandmesnil.* 🏘 Early 18th-century manor farm.

Carlton Curlieu *Carle/Carlintone: King's land; Hugh de Grandmesnil.* 🏘 Jacobean hall.

Castle Donington *Duni(n)tone:* See page 157.

Catthorpe *Torp: Mainou le Breton. Mill.* 🏠 Church, c.1300, where the poet John Dyer was rector in the mid-18th century.

Chadwell *Caldeuuelle: King's land. 2 mills.* 🏠

Charley *Cernelega: Earl Hugh, formerly Earl Harold.* Hall; Charley Mill Farm.

Chilcote *Cildecote: King's land.* 🏠

Claybrooke *Claibroc: Fulk from Count of Meulan.* Now 2 villages, Claybrooke. Magna and Parva. Nearby High Cross was the site of Venonae, a major Roman settlement, and the junction of Watling Street and the Fosse Way.

Cold Newton *Niwetone: Aubrey from Geoffrey de La Guerche; Herbert from the king.* 🏘 Deserted; only a few houses remain.

DONINGTON-LE-HEATH: *Manor house, built c. 1280.*

Cold Overton *Ovretone: Fulk from Drogo de La Beuvriere.* 🏘 Associated with the Mowbray family until the 15th century, when Anne de Mowbray, aged 6, was married to one of the Princes in the Tower.

Coleorton *Ovretone: Meginta from Henry de Ferrers; Warin and Roger from Robert de Bucy.* 🏘 Coal has been mined here since the 15th century.

Congerstone *Cuningestone: Roger from Henry de Ferrers; Robert the Bursar. Mill.* 🏠

Cosby *Cos(se)bi: Count of Meulan; Robert from Robert de Bucy; Countess Judith.* 🏘 In Greater Leicester; Tudor hall. A stream runs down the main street.

Cossington *Cosintone: Earl Hugh, formerly Earl Harold.* 🏘

Coston *Castone: Henry de Ferrers. Mill.* 🏘 Enclosed in the 1630s.

Cotesbach *Cotesbece: Walter and Edwin from Hugh de Grandmesnil. Mill.* 🏠

Cotes-de-Val *Toniscote:* Lost.

Cranoe *Crau/Craweho: King's land; Azor from Countess Judith.* 🏠

Croft *Crec/Crebre: Ralph from the king; Robert de Bucy from Hugh de Grandmesnil. Mill.* 🏘 Large; at the foot of the hill where Wiglaf, King of Mercia, held council in 836; quarry.

Croxton Kerrial *Crohtone: King's land. 2 mills.* Croxton Park originally belonged to the Abbey of Croxton (founded 1160); the house, built c.1730, was formerly the hunting seat of the Dukes of Rutland.

Desford *Deres/Diresford: Hugh de Grandmesnil.* 🏘 Large; manor houses; 2 churches.

Diseworth *Diwort: William Lovett.* 🏘 William Lilley the 17th-century astrologer was born nearby. Langley Priory was built on the site of a nunnery founded soon after the Conquest.

Dishley *Dexleia/Dislea: King's land, formerly Queen Edith; Robert from Earl Hugh. 2 mills.* Farmhouse; watermill.

Donington le Heath *Duntone: Thorkell from Nigel d'Aubigny.* 🏘 County's oldest medieval house. Coal has been mined here since the 1290s.

Donisthorpe *Durandestorp: Carl from Nigel of Stafford; Roger from Henry de Ferrers.* 🏘

Dunton Bassett *Donitone: Robert de Bucy.* 🏘 On high ground; centre of framework knitters in the 19th century. The church was used as a beacon during the Napoleonic wars.

Earl Shilton *Sceltone: Hugh de Grandmesnil. Mill.* Industrial; remains of a 12th century castle.

East Langton *Lagintone/ Lang(e)tone: Walkelin from Archbishop of York; Peterborough Abbey.*

East Norton *Nortone: Robert the Bursar; Geoffrey de La Guerche. 2 mills.*

Eastwell *Est(e)welle: Geoffrey de La Guerche; Askel from the king.* On a prehistoric road.

Edmondthorpe *Edmerestorp: Henry de Ferrers.* Ruined hall.

Enderby *Andretesbie/Endrebie: Ulf from Hugh de Grandmesnil. Mill.* Large, industrial; quarries; mill; well within Greater Leicester.

Evington *Avintone: Ivo from Hugh de Grandmesnil; Robert de Bucy. Mill.* Part of Leicester; dry moat and fish pond; remains of the manor house of the Greys, lords of Evington from the 13th century.

Eye Kettleby *Chitebie: Geoffrey de La Guerche.* Deserted; only the hall remains.

Fenny Drayton *Draitone: Aelmer from the king.* Commuter suburb of Nuneaton, beside the Roman road to Watling Street. Birthplace of George Fox, the Quaker (1624-91).

Fleckney *Flechenie/nio: Robert the Bursar.* Large; industrial.

Foston *Fostone: William Peverel.* Church with Saxon and Norman remains; Foston Hall Farm.

Foxton *Fox(es)tone: King's land; Robert de Bucy from Countess Judith.* Large; church on pre-Conquest site with Saxon and Norman remains. 10 locks carry the Grand Union Canal to its highest point.

Freeby *Fredebi: Geoffrey de La Guerche.*

Frisby *Frisebi: Fulk from Hugh de Grandmesnil.* Deserted village, on Frisby Hall farm land.

Frisby on the Wreake *Frisebi(e): King's land; Earl Hugh, formerly Earl Harold. Part of a mill.* Large.

Frolesworth *Frel(l)esworde: Count of Meulan; Hugh de Grandmesnil; Robert de Bucy; Countess Judith.* 18th-century almshouses.

Gaddesby *Gadesbi(e): King's land; Feggi and Odincar from Countess Judith; Earl Hugh, formerly Earl Harold. Mill.*

Galby *Galbi: King's land; Robert Burdet's son from Hugh de Grandmesnil. Mill.*

Gilmorton *Mortone: Godfrey from Robert de Vessey.* Large; earthworks, probably the remains of a moated manor house.

Glenfield *Clanefelde: Hugh de Grandmesnil and Erneis from him. Mill.* Suburb of Leicester, where the 1-mile railway tunnel, built by George Stephenson, begins.

Glooston *Glorstone: Hugh de Grandmesnil from Countess Judith.* On a Roman site; remains of Roman villa.

Goadby *Goutebi: Norman from Geoffrey Alselin.*

Goadby Marwood *Golt/ Goutebi: Ralph Pippin from Robert de Bucy; Geoffrey de La Guerche.* Jacobean hall; hall farm. Edwin Cartwright, reputed inventor of the first power loom in *c.*1785, was rector here.

Gopsall *Gopeshille: Roald from Henry de Ferrers.* Gopsall Hall Farm.

Great Bowden *Bugedone: King's land; William Lovett; Robert de Bucy from the Countess Judith.* Suburb of Market Harborough; large green.

Great Dalby *Dalbi: Godfrey from Bishop of Lincoln; Ansfrid from Robert de Bucy; Humphrey the Chamberlain.* Attractive.

Great Easton *Estone: Peterborough Abbey.* Large; Romano-British remains.

Great Glen *Glen: Lovett and Alwin from Hugh de Grandmesnil. Mill.* Large; church with Saxon and Norman remains. A royal charter was issued in 849.

Grimston *Grimestone: King's land; Gerard from Robert de Bucy.*

Groby *Grobi: Hugh de Grandmesnil.* Part of Greater Leicester; largest natural pool in the county.

Gumley *Godmundelai/ Gutmundeslea: Geoffrey from Robert de Vessey; Robert de Bucy from Countess Judith.* Park; words. Mercian King Aethelbald held council here in 749.

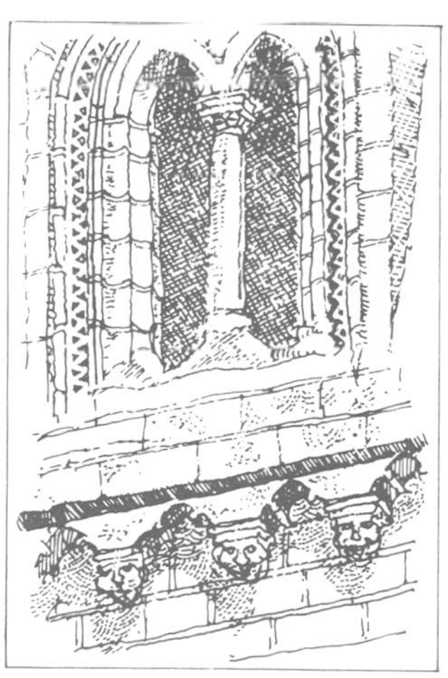

HALLATON: *12th-c. window in St Michael's tower.*

Hallaton *Alctone: Norman from Geoffrey Alselin.* Large; fine 17th to 19th-century cottages.

Halstead *Elstede: King's land.*

Harby *Herd/Hertebi: Robert de Tosny; Gerard from Robert de Bucy.* Large; once with a wharf on the Nottingham–Grantham Canal.

Harston *Herstan: King's land.* Near Iron Age pits and the site of Anglo-Saxon dwellings; church with Saxon stone.

Hathern *Avederne: Robert from Earl Hugh.* Large. John Heathcote invented his lace-making machine here *c.*1808.

Heather *Hadre: Countess Judith.*

Hinckley *Hinchelie: King's land.* Industrial town. Castle Hill is on the site of Roman earthworks.

Hoby *Hobie: Aethelhelm from Drogo de La Beuvriere.* Ancient cross.

Holwell *Holewelle: Ketelbern from Bishop of Lincoln; Gerard from Robert de Bucy.* Ironstone has been worked here since the 1870s.

Holyoaks *Haliach: Ranulf from Bishop of Lincoln. Mill.* Farm.

Horninghold *Horniwale: Robert de Tosny.*

Hose *Hoches/Howes: Gilbert from Robert de Tosny; Robert the Usher from the king and Thurstan from him.* Once with a wharf on the Nottingham-Grantham Canal.

Hoton *Hoh/Holetone: Robert de Jort (who occupied it by force); Earl Hugh, formerly Earl Harold.*

Houghton on the Hill *Hohtone: Godric from Henry de Ferrers.* Possibly on a pre-Conquest site; ancestral home of the Herrick family.

Humberstone *Humerstane: Hugh de Grandmesnil.* Part of Leicester. Home of Thomas Paget, MP for Leicester at the time of the Reform Act, 1832.

Huncote *Hunecote: Count of Meulan. Mill.* Large.

Hungerton *Hungretone: William from Robert de Tosny.* Jacobean hall.

Husbands Bosworth *Baresworde/worde: Abbot Benedict from Guy de Raimbeaucourt; Laurence from Robert de Vessey. Mill.*

Ibstock *Ibestoche: Ingenwulf from Count of Meulan.* Large; mining. The 14th-century church was Archbishop Laud's living for 9 years early in the 17th century.

Illston on the Hill *Elve/ Nelvestone: King's land; Hugh de Grandmesnil; Ingold from Robert de Bucy.* Manor house.

Ingarsby *Gerberie/Inuuaresbie:* See page 158.

Kegworth *Cacheuuorde/ Cogeworde: Robert from Earl Hugh, formerly Earl Harold.* Prosperous small town, centre of the knitting trade, in the 19th century.

Keyham *Caiham: King's land.*

Keythorpe *Cai/Cheitorp: Osbern from Archbishop of York; Norman from Geoffrey Alselin.* Hall Farm; grange.

GREAT EASTON: *Ironstone house.*

Kibworth Beauchamp *Chiburde: Robert the Bursar.* Belonged to Merton College, Oxford, since the 13th century.

Kibworth Harcourt *Chiborne/ Cliborne: Robert de Vessey.* 12th-century castle mound. Philip Doddridge, the Nonconformist divine, preached here 1723–25.

Kilby *Cilebi: Oger Le Breton. Mill.* Medieval manor house.

Kimcote *Chenemundescote: Ralph from Bishop of Lincoln.* 18th-century Free School.

King's Norton *Nortone: King's land.* Manor house.

Kirby Bellars *Cher/Chirchebi: Geoffrey de La Guerche and Ralph from him.*

Kirby Muxloe *Carbi/Chirchebi: Riculf from William Peverel.* Suburb of Leicester; brick castle, built for William Lord Hastings in the 15th century. Nearby Kirby Moats are said to be of Saxon origin.

Kirkby Mallory *Cher(ch)ebi: Hugh from Coventry Abbey; Hugh de Grandmesnil and Serlo from him.* Suburb of Leicester; hall with park and lake; motor racing course nearby.

Knaptoft *Cnapetot: King's land.* Depopulated by 17th-century change from arable to sheep farming; Hall Farm; moated site of an earlier hall; fishponds.

Knighton *Cnihtetone: Bishop of Lincoln.* Part of Leicester; hall, now the residence of the Vice-Chancellor of the University.

Knipton *Cnipe/Gniptone: King's land; Robert de Tosny. 7 mills.* Wooded; near Knipton reservoir.

Knossington *Closin/Nossitone: King's land; Roger de Bully.* On high ground which belonged to Owston Abbey and passed to the son of Thomas Cromwell at the Dissolution.

Laughton *Lachestone: Walter from Robert de Tosny.*

Leesthorpe *Luvestorp: Buterus from Geoffrey de La Guerche.* Hall; grange.

Leicester *Ledecestre: King's land; Hugh de Grandmesnil; Countess Judith; Bishop of Lincoln. 6 churches, 2 mills.* Town. Iron Age settlement; established as 'Civitas' by the Romans; Cathedral see of the Bishop of Leicester until the 9th century when it became a Danish borough. It was the site of the first Parliament called by Simon de Montfort, in 1265, and an early centre of the dissenting tradition; from the 18th century it was dependent on the hosiery and boot and shoe trades for its wealth.

Leire *Legre: Bishop of Lincoln; Robert de Bucy; Robert the Bursar; Hugh de Grandmesnil.*

Little Bowden *Bugedone: Count of Mortain. Mill.* In the suburbs of Market Harborough.

Little Dalby *Dalbi: Roger from Henry de Ferrers; Robert from Geoffrey de La Guerche.* Hartopp Hall, now flats, produced the first widely known Stilton cheese, *c.*1730.

Little Thorpe *Torp:* Lost.

Loddington *Ludintone: Robert from Robert de Bucy. Mill.* In hilly, wooded countryside; hall.

Long Clawson *Clachestone: Ivo from Robert de Tosny; Thurstan and Theobald from Robert Usher.* Large; in the Vale of Belvoir; manor house.

Loughborough *Locte/ Lucteburne: Roger, Ralph, Hugh, Godric and Roger from Earl Hugh. 2 mills.* Town; a centre of the hosiery trade, past and present, and of Luddite riots. Its November Fair dates from the 13th century.

Lowesby *Glowesbi: Hugh Burdet from Countess Judith. Mill.* Depopulated in 15th cenury; site of famous pottery in 19th century. Church hall and fishponds remain.

Lubbesthorpe *Lupestorp:* Lost.

Lubenham *Lobenho/Luban/ Lubeham: Walkelin from Archbishop of York; Osbern from Robert de Tosny; Robert de Bucy from Countess Judith.* Hall; pond; green.

OLD DALBY: *Typical Leicestershire village.*

Lutterworth *Lutresurde: Mainou le Breton.* Small town. Reformer and theologian John Wycliffe was rector here in the late 14th century.

Market Bosworth *Boseworde:* See page 159.

Markfield *Merchenefeld: Hugh de Grandmesnil from Countess Judith.* On the edge of Charnwood forest; Home of framework knitters in the 19th century.

Measham *Messeham: King's land.* Mining; brick-making; on the Ashby Canal.

Medbourne *Medburne/ Metorne: King's land; Robert de Tosny.* Probably inhabited since Roman times; granted a weekly market in 1266; manor house; hall; medieval bridge.

Melton Mowbray *Medeltone: Geoffrey de La Guerche and William and Roger from him. 2 mills.* Market town; the hunting capital of England in the early 19th century. The market dates from Saxon times, ancient British cemetery.

Misterton *Menstre/Minis/ Minstretone: Ralph from Bishop of Lincoln; Abbot Benedict from Guy de Raimbeaucourt; Mainou Le Breton.* Church; hall.

Mowsley *Muselai: Gunfrid de Chocques; Gerbert.* Fishponds.

Nether Broughton *Broctone: King's land.* Large; overlooking Vale of Belvoir; site of a Roman villa.

Newbold Folville *Niwebold:* Lost.

Newbold Saucey *Neubold: Hugh from Henry de Ferrers. Mill.* Farm.

Newbold Verdon *Niwebold: Hugh de Grandmesnil.* Ancient earthworks; hall, home of Lady Mary Wortley Montagu, the 18th-century blue stocking.

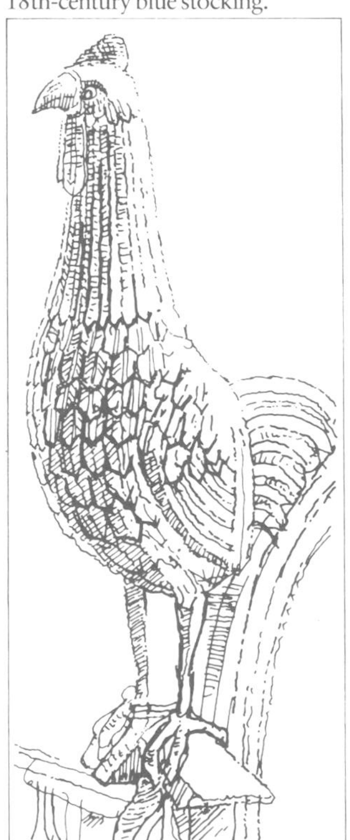

NOSELEY: *Ornate stalls in the church.*

Newton Burgoland *Neutone: Gladwin and Roger from Henry de Ferrers.*

Newton Harcourt *Neu/ Niwetone: Robert de Vessey. Mill.* On the Grand Union Canal; 17th-century manor.

North Kilworth *Chivelesworde: Ralph from Count of Meulan. Mill.* 13th-century church, where Archbishop Laud was rector for one year in the early 17th century.

North Marefield *Merdefelde: King's land.* Deserted.

Norton juxta Twycross *Nortone: Countess Godiva.* Birthplace of William Whiston (1667–1752) who succeeded Sir Isaac Newton as Lucasian professor at Cambridge.

Noseley *Noveslei: Hugh de Grandmesnil.* 13th-century church; hall; park.

Oadby *Oldebi: Roger from Hugh de Grandmesnil; Countess Judith and Robert from her.* Part of Leicester; site of a pagan Anglo-Saxon cemetery.

Oakthorpe *Achetorp: Erwin from Nigel of Stafford.*

Odstone *Odestone: Robert the Bursar.* Hall.

Old Dalby *Dalbi: Robert from Ralph FitzHubert.*

Orton on the Hill *Wortone: Henry de Ferrers.* Hall.

Osbaston *Sbernestun: Roger from Ralph de Mortimer.* Hall.

Osgathorpe *Osgodtorp: Ardwulf from Henry de Ferrers.* 17th-century school.

Othorpe *Actorp: Robert de Bucy from Countess Judith.* Hall.

Owston *Osulvestone: Grimbald from Countess Judith.* Remote.

Packington *Pachintone: Coventry Abbey. Mill.* Site of a weekly market in the Middle Ages.

Peatling Magna *Petlinge: Godwin the priest; Robert de Bucy; Countess Judith; Robert from Count of Meulan.* Large; ancient cross.

Peatling Parva *Alia Petlinge: Howard from Hugh de Grandmesnil; Leofric from Adelaide wife of Hugh de Grandmesnil. 2 mills.*

Peckleton *Pechintone: Hugh de Grandmesnil.* On the Roman road from Leicester to Watling Street; possibly an Old English settlement.

Pickwell *Pichewelle: Buterus from Geoffrey de La Guerche. Mill.* Iron Age hill-fort; manor house.

Potters Marston *Mersitone:* Lost; once a pottery-making centre.

Poultney *Pontenei: Ralph from Bishop of Lincoln.* Farms.

Prestgrave *Abegrave:* Lost.

Prestwold *Prestewalde/wolde: Durand Malet; Earl Hugh, formerly Earl Harold.* 14th-century church; big house. The estate still belongs to the Packe family, who bought it in the 17th century.

Primethorpe *Torp:* Lost.

Quenby *Quenberie: William from Robert de Tosny.* Depopulated in the late 15th century. The site of the village is in Quenby Hall park.

Queniborough *Cuinburg: William from Geoffrey de La Guerche. Mill.*

Ragdale *Ragendel(e): Hugh from Robert de Bucy.* 18th-century hall.

Ratby *Rotebie: Hugh de Grandmesnil. Mill.* Large. On the edge of Charnwood Forest; Old Hayes, a moated homestead site.

Ratcliffe Culey *Redeclive: Robert the Bursar.* Moated site of a manor house.

Ratcliffe on the Wreak *Radeclive: Robert Burdet's wife from Robert de Bucy. Mill.* Hall; old mill; birthplace of Richard Kilbye (1561–1620), one of the translators of the authorized version of the Bible.

Ravenstone *Ravenestorp: Ingold from Robert de Bucy; Hugh Burdet from Countess Judith; Earl Hugh. 2 mills.* Suburb of Leicester; medieval bridge.

Rearsby *Re(d)resbi: Ingold from Robert de Bucy; Hugh Burdet from Countess Judith; Earl Hugh, formerly Earl Harold. 1 ½ mills.* Suburb of Leicester; medieval bridge.

Redmile *Redmelde: Robert de Tosny.* Once on the Nottingham-Grantham Canal.

Ringlethorpe *Ricoltorp: Hugh de Grandmesnil from Countess Judith; Raven from the king. Mill.* Goldsmith Grange, named after John Goldsmith, a wealthy 15th-century merchant.

Rollestone *Rovestone: Norman from Geoffrey Alselin.* Modern hall on old site; ancient cross.

Rotherby *Redebi: Earl Hugh, formerly Earl Harold.*

Rothley *Rodolei: King's land. Mill.* Large, site of a Roman villa, church with Norman remains and a Saxon cross. Rothley Temple, home of the Babington family from the 15th to 19th century, was the birthplace of the poet and historian Lord Macaulay (1800–59).

Saddington *Sadin/Setintone: King's land. Mill.*

Saltby *Saltebi: Roger de Bully. 2 mills.* Site of a Roman pavement. Nearby earthworks, King Lud's Entrenchments, are thought to date from 9th century.

Sapcote *Sape/Scepecote: King's land; Hugh de Grandmesnil and Fulbert from him. Mill.*

Saxby *Saxebi: Henry de Ferrers; Hugh Musard from Countess Judith. 2 mills.* The church is the site of an Anglo-Saxon cemetery.

Saxelby *Saxelbie: King's land.*

Scalford *Scaldeford: Ralph Pippin from Robert de Bucy; Robert from Countess Judith.* Site of a 14th-century weekly market.

Scraptoft *Scrapentot: Coventry Abbey.* Part of Leicester.

Seagrave *Satgrave: King's land; Henry de Ferrers; Robert de Bucy; Earl Hugh, formerly Earl Harold.* Robert Burton, author of the *Anatomy of Melancholy*, was rector here, 1630–40.

Sewstern *Sewesten: William Lovett.* Old drove road nearby.

Shackerstone *Sacrestone: Robert the Bursar.* Saxon jewellery was here.

Shangton *San(c)tone: King's land; Hugh from Hugh de Grandmesnil; Geoffrey from Robert de Vessey.*

Sharnford *Scene/Scerneford: Robert from Bishop of Lincoln; Hugh de Grandmesnil; Countess Judith; Thorkell from the king.*

Shawell *Sawelle Robert from Count of Meulan. Mill.*

Shearsby *Seuesbi/Sue(ue)sbi: Quentin's wife, Norman and Howard from the king.* Yeoman's house.

Sheepy Magna *Scepa: Henry de Ferrers. Mill.* Mill; mill pond.

Sheepy Parva *Scepehe: Walter from Hugh de Grandmesnil. Mill.*

Shenton *Scentone: King's land; Roger from Henry de Ferrers; Norman from Robert de Vessey.* 17th-century hall.

Shepshed *Scepe(s)hefde: King's land. Mill.* Large; market place.

Shoby *Seoldesberie:* Lost.

Sibson *Sibetesdone: King's land.* Inn was a 13th-century tithe barn.

Sileby *Seg/Siglebi/Siglesbie: King's land; Arnold from Hugh de Grandmesnil; Earl Hugh, formerly Earl Harold. 2 mills.* Industrial; medieval church.

Skeffington *Sciftitone: King's land. Mill.* The hall was the home of the Skeffington family from the late 13th century.

Slawston *Slaches/Slagestone: Ingold, Godric and Fran from Robert de Bucy.* Secluded.

Smeeton Westerby *Esmeditone/Smi(te)tone: King's land; Hugh de Grandmesnil and Robert from Hugh; Robert the Bursar.*

Smockington *Snochantone: Wazelin from Henry de Ferrers.*

Snarestone *Snarchetone: Robert the Bursar.*

Somerby *Sumerdeberie/lidebie/Summerdebi(e): King's land; Roger from Henry de Ferrers; Robert the Bursar.* Birthplace of the surgeon William Cheselden (1688–1752).

South Croxton *Crochestone/Croptone: Roger from Bishop of Lincoln; William from Robert de Tosny. Mill.*

South Kilworth *Cleveliorde: Robert de Vessey; Robert from Guy de Raimbeaucourt.* Large; Tudor house; medieval moated site; fishponds. William Peason, the astronomer, was rector here from 1817 and built an observatory.

South Marefield *Alia Merdefelde: King's land.* Marefield near Melton Mowbray.

Sproxton *Sprotone: Warin from Guy de Craon; Godfrey de Cambrai; Hugh Musard from Countess Judith. 3 mills.* Saxon cross.

STAPLEFORD: *The house, Stapleford Park, is a curious amalgam of every style from c. 1500 to late Victorian.*

Stanton under Bardon *Stantone: Geoffrey de La Guerche.*

Stapleford *Stapeford: Henry de Ferrers. 2 mills.* Church; hall; safari park; once a Roman and Saxon settlement.

Stapleton *Stapletone: Coventry Abbey; Crowland Abbey.* Richard III camped south of here before the Battle of Bosworth Field.

Stathern *Stachedirne/tone: William from Robert de Tosny; William and Roger from Geoffrey de La Guerche.* Red and white cottages; formerly a lace-manufacturing centre.

Staunton Harold *Stantone: Arnolf from Hugh de Grandmesnil.* Hall with park and lakes.

Stockerston *Stoctone/tun: Hugh de Grandmesnil. Mill.*

Stonesby *Stovenebi: Guy de Craon.* On old drovers' road.

Stoney Stanton *Stantone: Robert the Bursar.* Quarries.

Stonton Wyville *Stantone: Hugh from Hugh de Grandmesnil; Osbern from Countess Judith. 2 mills.* Fishponds.

Stormesworth *Stormeorde/mode:* Lost.

Stoughton *Sto(c)tone: Howard and Erneis from Hugh de Grandmesnil.* On outskirts of Leicester.

Stretton *Stratone: King's land.* Now the village of Little Stretton, and a church, all that remains of Great Stretton.

Stretton en le Field *Stretone/Streitun: Roger from Henry de Ferrers. Mill.*

Sutton Cheney *Sutone: Crowland Abbey; Arnold from Hugh de Grandmesnil.* Overlooking Bosworth Field.

Sutton in the Elms *Sutone: Quentin's wife and Ralph from the king.* The county's oldest Nonconformist chapel.

Swepstone *Scopestone: Nigel from Henry de Ferrers.*

Swinford *Suin/Suinc(s)ford: Ralph from Bishop of Lincoln; Arnbern the priest; Robert from the king; Hugh de Grandmesnil; Hugh and Warin from Robert de Bucy; Alwin from Geoffrey de La Guerche. Mill.*

Sysonby *Sist/Sixtenebi: Geoffrey de La Guerche and Rainer from him; Hugh Burdet from Countess Judith.* Part of Melton Mowbray.

Syston *Sitestone: Swein from Hugh de Grandmesnil. Mill.* Large; industrial.

Theddingworth *Dedigworde/Tedi(nges)worde: Norman from the king; William Lovett; Gundwin from Countess Judith; Roger from Earl Hugh, formerly Earl Harold. Mill.*

Thorpe Acre *Torp: King's land.* Part of Loughborough.

Thorpe Arnold *Torp: Walter from Hugh de Grandmesnil.* On the outskirts of Melton Mowbray; ancient cross and earthworks.

Thorpe Langton *Torp: Hugh de Grandmesnil and Osbern from him; Moriland from Robert de Vessey; Roger from Robert de Bucy. Mill.*

Thringstone *Trangesbi: King's land; Nigel of Stafford.*

Thrussington *Turstanestone: Guy de Raimbeaucourt. Mill.*

Thurcaston *Turchi(te)lestone: Hugh de Grandmesnil. Mill.* Birthplace of Hugh Latimer, the reforming divine (1485–1555).

Thurlaston *Lestone/Letitone: Robert de Bucy from Hugh de Grandmesnil.*

Thurmaston *Turmodestone: Hugh de Grandmesnil and William from him. Mill.* Part of Leicester; site of an Anglo-Saxon cemetery.

Tilton *Tile/Tillintone: King's land; Hugh from Archbishop of York; Robert the Bursar.* The highest in the county.

Tonge *Tunge: Henry de Ferrers.*

Tugby *Tochebi: King's land.*

Tur Langton *Cher/Terlintone: Walkelin from Archbishop of York.* Manor house.

Twycross *Tuicros: Nigel from Henry de Ferrers.* Small zoo. The medieval stained glass in the church was brought from France at the time of the Revolution.

Twyford *Taiworde/Tuiuorde: King's land; Robert from Hugh de Grandmesnil.* In the valley below Burrough Hill.

Ullesthorpe *Ulestorp: Walter from Geoffrey de La Guerche. Mill.* Large; once a centre of the framework knitting trade.

Walcote *Walecote: Ralph from Bishop of Lincoln; Hugh from Robert de Bucy. Mill.*

Waltham on the Wolds *Waltham:* See page 159.

Walton *Waltone: Norman from the king.*

Walton on the Wolds *Waletone: Ralph de Chartres from the king.*

Wanlip *Anelepe: Ralph de Chartres from the king. Mill.* Within Greater Leicester; site of a Roman villa.

Wartnaby *Worcnodebie: King's land.* Hall.

Welby *Alebi(e): Geoffrey de La Guerche; Hugh Burdet, Godwin and Ralph from Countess Judith. Part of a mill.* A few houses; fishponds; church.

SUTTON CHENEY: *Bosworth battlefield.*

Welham *Wale/Weleham/Walendeham: Osbern from Archbishop of York; Gilbert from Robert de Bucy and Countess Judith. Mill.*

Weston *Westone:* Lost.

Whatborough *Wetberga:* Lost.

Whetstone *Westham: Ralph from Count of Meulan. Mill.* Part of Leicester.

Whitwick *Witewic: Hugh from Hugh de Grandmesnil.* Mining; granted weekly market in the 13th century. Nearby is Mount St Bernard Abbey, the first Cistercian Abbey to be built after the Reformation.

WITHCOTE: *15th-c. stained glass window in a contemporary church (c. 1500).*

Wigston Magna *Wichingestone: Hugh de Grandmesnil; Robert from Countess Judith.* Part of Leicester; the county's second largest town in the Middle Ages.

Wigston Parva *Wicestan: Aelfric the priest.* Hall farm; manor house; church.

Willesley *Wiuleslei(e): King's land; Aelfric from Henry de Ferrers.*

Willoughby Waterless *Wil(ech)ebi: Ivo and Ulf from Hugh de Grandmesnil.* Many fine 17th- to 19th-century houses.

Willows *Wilges:* Lost.

Wistow *Wistanestou/Witenesto: Robert the Bursar. Mill.* Church with Norman remains. Jacobean hall where Charles I took refuge after Naseby.

Withcote *Wicoc/Wicote: Robert the Bursar; Alfwold from Geoffrey de La Guerche.* Hall; church.

Woodcote *Udecote: John from Henry de Ferrers.*

Worthington *Werditone: Henry de Ferrers.*

Wycomb *Wiche: King's land. 2 mills.*

Wyfordby *Werdebi/Wivordebie/Wordebi: Henry de Ferrers; Richard from Roger de Bully; Geoffrey de La Guerche. 2 mills.* Moated medieval homestead.

Wymeswold *Wimundeswald: Robert and Serlo from Hugh de Grandmesnil; Durand Malet; Robert de Jort from the king.* Large; weekly market granted 1338; 2 old drovers' roads.

Wymondham *Wimundesham: Henry de Ferrers; Ansfrid from Robert de Bucy.* Large; Roman remains. It was once a small town, with a weekly market granted in 1303.

Lincolnshire

Lincolnshire in 1086 must sometimes have felt like a separate nation from the rest of England. It was the second most populated county in the kingdom, after Norfolk; and its county town was one of the four largest, with London, York and Norwich. Yet it was isolated from these other centres by the vast undrained fenlands in the south and north-west, which made it virtually a peninsula.

It must have felt isolated too by its Danish inheritance: if any one county could be called the heart of the Danelaw it was Lincolnshire. Place names, language, units of measurement and legal customs were all strongly Danish in flavour. And the proportion of free peasants – almost certainly descendants of the Scandinavian armies who settled eastern England in the ninth century – was higher, 51 per cent, than in any other county.

The concentration of these freemen here may have been partly due to the fact that the county also had an unusually large number of tenants-in-chief from outside Normandy, especially from Brittany, where the feudal system was weaker and less centralized. This may have helped the free peasants to hold on to their independence longer than in other counties, against the forces that were making for their absorption into the large manors of the feudal system proper.

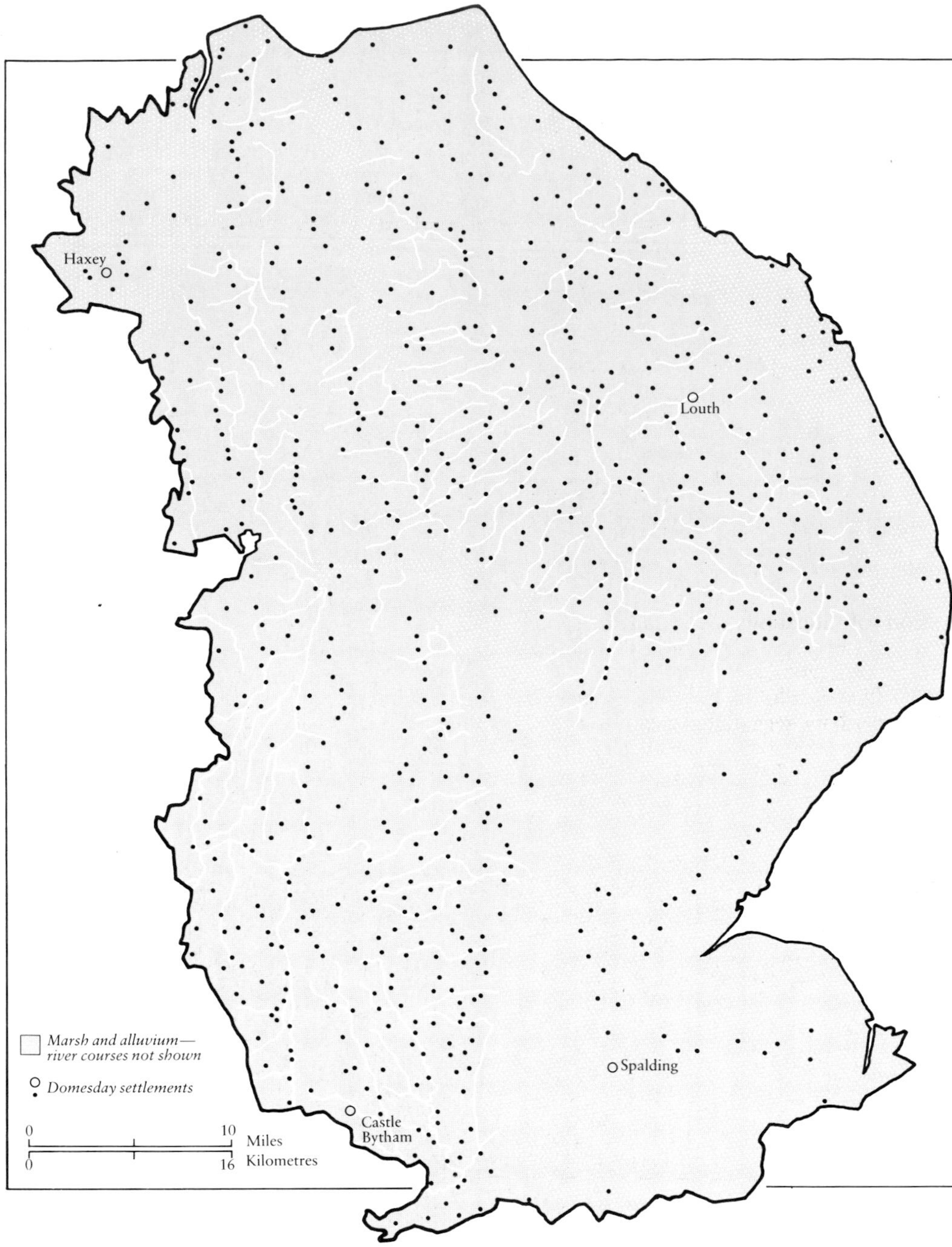

Spalding

In SPALDING *SPALLINGE* Earl Algar had 9 carucates of land taxable. Land for as many ploughs. Ivo [Tailbois] has 4 ploughs in lordship; 40 villagers and 33 smallholders who have 13 ploughs. A market, 40s; 6 fisheries, 30s; from salt-houses, 20s; a wood of alders, 8s. Value before 1066 £23 2s 8d; now £30, Exactions £30.

Spalding today is a prosperous Georgian town near the Wash surrounded by fertile plains of reclaimed fenland. It is the capital of the district of South Holland, the 'centre of tulipland'. There was nothing in 1086 to presage the area's future prosperity. Spalding was the largest of a string of villages along a belt of silt running beside what was then the coastline of the Wash. On one side was the sea, on the other the empty expanse of the marshy fens, unsettled because the peaty soil was too soft to build on. Its limited economy is evident from its *Domesday* entry, with its references to fishing and saltmaking, and the absence of watermills or of almost any woodland. Land held by Guy de Craon is similarly described.

The entries also reflect a conflict of interests that was to preoccupy Spalding's population for many centuries. In its original form this was between Ivo Tailbois, the lord of Spalding, and the Abbey of St Guthlac's at Croyland (now Crowland), nine miles to the east. Ivo was King William's nephew and had been his standard bearer at the Battle of Hastings, but is known best – thanks largely to Charles Kingsley's nineteenth-century novel, *Hereward the Wake* – for the unhappy role he is said to have played in the rebellion of 1070–71, when Hereward was making his last stand against the Normans on the Isle of Ely. Ivo allegedly blundered so badly in attempting to flush a raiding party out of the woods that Hereward made off with the Abbot of Peterborough, whom Ivo was supposed to be defending. Later, when the rebels were being besieged on the island, so the story goes, Ivo persuaded the king to build a movable wooden tower with a sorceress at its top, to cast spells on the English defenders while his own soldiers built a wooden bridge across the marshes to the island. Hereward succeeded in outflanking the entire operation and in burning down both tower and bridge.

Nevertheless, after the revolt had been crushed, William granted the manor of Spalding to Ivo. It was the most important of his 100 Lincolnshire holdings, making him the county's largest landholder. Why he almost immediately made an enemy of the monks of Croyland Abbey and Ingulph, their abbot, is not clear. Perhaps he associated them with his humiliation at Ely, where the local monks had supported the other side. In any case, within a year he had given the priory at Spalding to the abbey of his home town, Angers.

In the interim, according to what was known as Abbot Ingulph's *Croyland History*, Ivo, besides tormenting and harassing his own men, 'raged with such tyrannical and frantic fury,' against the monks 'that he would many a time lame their cattle, oxen, as well as horses, would daily impound their sheep and poultry, and frequently strike down, kill and destroy their swine and pigs; while at the same time, the servants of the prior were often assaulted in the highways with swords and staves, and sometimes killed.' Eventually the monks retired to Croyland, and Ivo brought six monks over from Angers to replace them.

When William died in 1087, Ivo seized all the lands in his area belonging to Croyland, including the two carucates in Spalding mentioned by *Domesday*. Ingulph produced a charter from Earl Algar, Ivo's Saxon predecessor, proving Croyland's rights to the lands, and succeeded in having them restored by the new king, William II. Four years later, however, a fire destroyed the monastery and Ivo, assuming that all the charters had been burnt, again challenged the monks' title. But some charters had survived, providing the monks with the necessary evidence in court. Ivo next tried to belittle the charters because they were in Saxon characters.

That, too, had no effect, and he then had the monks' clerk ambushed on his way home from court, in an attempt to steal the papers. But this tactic also failed, for another monk, anticipating trouble, had already taken the charters back to the monastery.

Ivo's attacks on Croyland were at last brought to an end by his involvement in Bishop Odo's attempt to overthrow William II and replace him by his brother Robert. He was banished to Anjou, and permitted back only when Henry I became king in 1100. He died soon afterwards of a paralytic stroke, leaving no heirs. 'Thus,' wrote Ingulph, 'in order that his bastard slips might not take deep root in the world, did the accursed line of this wicked man perish, the axe of the Lord hewing down all his offspring.'

This entire story, however, must be treated with some scepticism, since Ingulph's history is now thought not to have been written by him, but probably to have been a medieval forgery which argued Croyland's case in a bitter succession of litigations over land disputes between Spalding and Croyland which lasted into the fifteenth century.

Henry VIII's dissolution of the monasteries should finally have terminated the dispute, but antagonism between the two towns smouldered on, erupting briefly again during the Civil War. Although the area was in the heart of Parliamentary territory, the men of Crowland in 1643 declared themselves Royalists, fortified the town, and raided Spalding, carrying off a few prisoners. When Parliamentarians attacked the town they resisted, and pinioned their prisoners in the firing line of the attackers. The town fell only after a much larger force directed by Cromwell himself attacked it from three sides.

Today Spalding is the undisputed centre of the region, with Crowland no more than a satellite. But the priory itself has disappeared, except for a small octagonal building called the Prior's Oven in the town centre. Once the monastic prison, it is now a cakeshop. The only remnant of the Spalding-Croyland rivalry is the quite unnecessary opulence of the nearby village churches in which it expressed itself: Pinchbeck, Moulton, Whaplode and Gedney. They are as a group unrivalled in the whole of Britain. All traces of Ivo's great castle have disappeared. The sea that fed the salt-pans has retreated ten miles to the East. But the *Domesday* market still functions on Saturday morning, although it now deals in irline bags and jeans rather than in sheep and cattle as it did 900 years ago.

Louth

In LOUTH *LUDES* the Bishop of Lincoln had 12 carucates of land taxable. Land for 12 ploughs. The bishop now has in lordship 3 ploughs; 80 burgesses; 1 market at 29s, 40 Freemen and 2 villagers; between them they have 13 ploughs. 13 mills pay 60s. 2 men-at-arms have 2 ploughs and meadow, 21 acres; woodland, pasture in places, 400 acres. 1 league 8 furlongs long and 10 furlongs wide. Value before 1066 £12; now £22. Exactions £3.

Louth stands at the foot of a stream valley that makes a natural gateway into the Lincolnshire Wolds from the flat coastal strip of land to its east: an obvious place for a market town. Its *Domesday* entry, one of five in Lincolnshire which mention burgesses, also shows that the population would have been about 600. In addition to its market, its economic life must have revolved around the milling of grain from the flat lands nearby in its 13 mills.

An unusual feature of Louth's entry is that it records an almost entirely free peasantry: 40 freemen against only two villagers. The area surrounding Louth had the highest concentration of free peasants in all Lincolnshire – about 70 per cent of the recorded population; there is evidence that a large independent peasantry persisted here into the thirteenth century. An independent yet conservative spirit has been characteristic of Louth's history since. The only time it has entered into national history was as the ignition point in the clergy-inspired rebellion of 1536 against Henry VIII's dissolution of the monasteries.

When the rebellion broke out 37 minor Lincolnshire monasteries had already been dismantled, their monks turned out, and their valuables removed or sold. There were rumours that the king was not only going to seize all the jewels and ornaments in the parish churches as well, but also to ban holy days. The people of Louth would have been particularly incensed, because they had devoted over a century to a magnificent rebuilding of their churches. When the Bishop of Lincoln's registrar arrived to read a commission from Thomas Cromwell, Henry's chief tool in the suppression, the crowd burnt his books, and he barely escaped with his life.

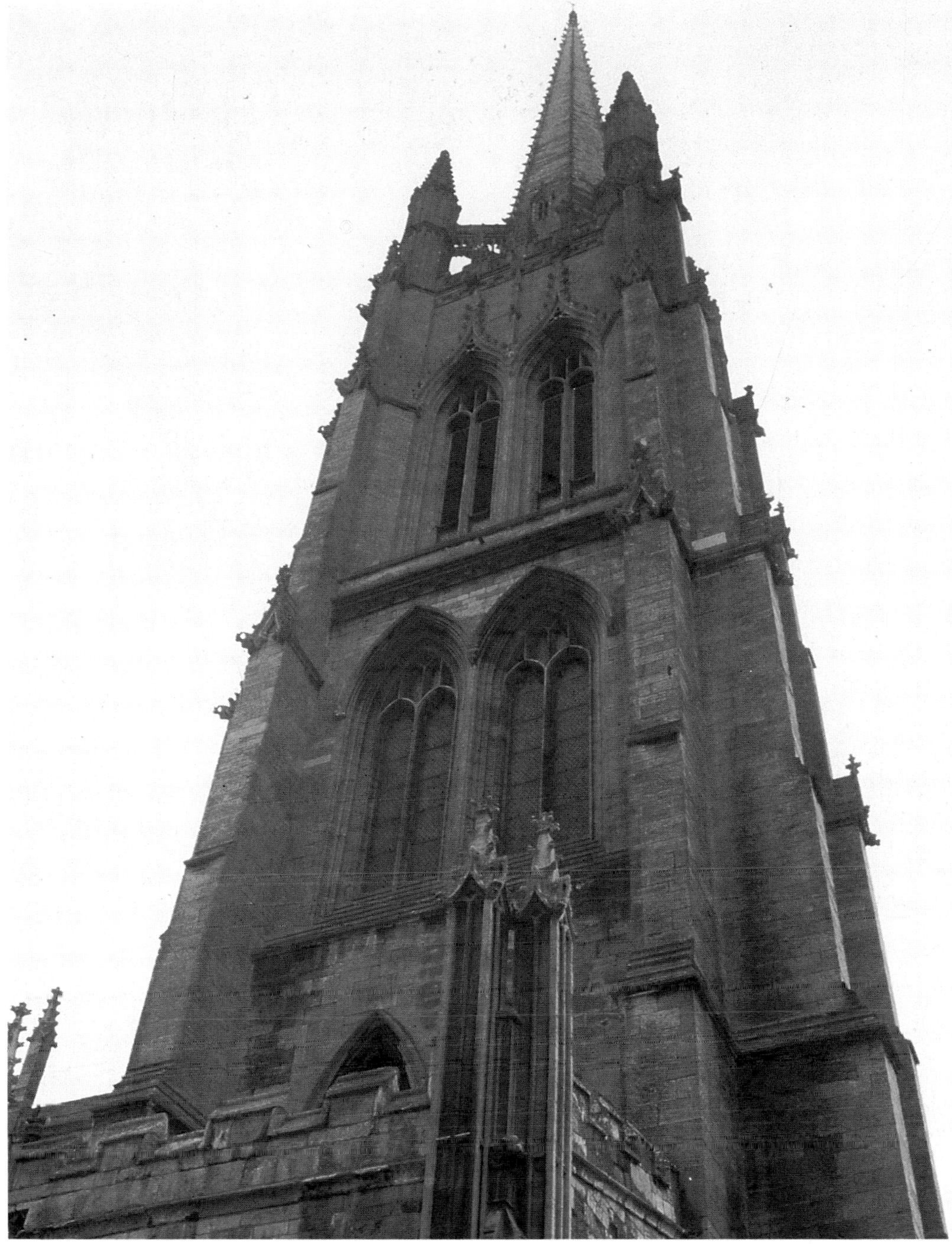

LOUTH: *Flying buttresses support the church spire.*

This and a subsequent raid on Caistor nearby, where the king's commissioners were sitting, inspired uprisings at Horncastle and elsewhere. When the rebels converged in Lincoln they were said to be 40,000 strong, including 16,000 'in harness' and 700 or 800 monks and nuns. The local gentry, however, although they had been dragooned into the rebellion, successfully delayed action until the king should send a reply to the rebels' demands, and the movement lost momentum. By the time an answer came, in the form of a royal proclamation ordering everyone to go home, the rebels were ready to oblige. Their leaders were routinely executed in the following months.

In later centuries Louth demonstrated its conservatism by resisting economic change. It was a modest-sized agricultural market town in 1086, and, after the failure of seventeenth-century attempts to industralize it, this is exactly how it could be described today. In that sense it is still close to its *Domesday* past, even if nothing tangible remains from those times.

Haxey

In HAXEY *ACHESEIA* Siward Barn had 3 carucates of land taxable. Land for 6 ploughs. Wazelin, Geoffrey [de La Guerche]'s man, has 2½ ploughs. 16 villagers and 8 smallholders with 3½ ploughs. 9 fisheries, 7s; meadow, 3 acres; woodland, pasture in places, 5 furlongs long and 1 furlong wide. Value before 1066 and now, 100s. Exactions 20s.

Most of Haxey now appears to be a plush suburb of well-kept private houses. But, looking out from the edge of the village it is easy to imagine what a wild and remote place it must once have been. It stands on a low ridge of clay a few miles long called the Isle of Axholme, surrounded in every direction by miles of flat land which was so waterlogged in *Domesday* times that it supported a fishing industry. 'Water putrid and muddy, yea full of loathsome vermin,' ran a seventeenth-century description, 'earth spongey and boggy, fire noisome by the stink of noisome [peat] hassocks.'

The Isle of Axholme's isolation may have contributed to the fierce independence of its people, who resisted the drainage of the fens for almost a century with riots and legal actions. It is perhaps this same isolation that has preserved the old folk custom of 'Haxey Hood', in which every year on January 6 a procession of local men arrives in Haxey dressed in red coats and wearing top hats decorated with red flowers. Of these, 12 are known as 'Boggins'. They are led by the 'Lord of the Hood', who carries a staff made of 13 willow switches and the famous hood itself, a sausage-shaped object about two feet long and two inches thick, tightly bound in leather.

With them is the 'Fool', who wears a battered hat trimmed with flowers and a goose's wing. He carries a bladder full of bran on a string attached to a stick, and has the right to kiss any woman in sight. He tries to break away from the Boggins, who bring him to the mounting stone in front of the church where he makes a speech. Straw scattered around him is set alight as he finishes, and he then leads the crowd up a low ridge to the boundary line with the next village, Westwoodside. Here, sackcloth replicas of the hood are tossed into the air. Whoever catches one races with it to his favourite pub on either side of the boundary, where the landlord will redeem it with a drink if he arrives before a Boggins catches him. If he is caught, the hood is 'boggined' and must be thrown up again. The result is a succession of free-for-alls in what is often freezing mud.

As darkness falls, the leather hood itself is brought out and tossed into the air. One man catches it, and the others lock their arms around him or each other until he is at the centre of a heaving, steaming mass of as many as 200 bodies. This is called 'the Sway'. Everyone tries to push the Sway towards his own local pub, but it has a life of its own. Anyone in its path gets pulled into it, and it tramples crops and smashes through hedges as it slews across the countryside, sometimes breaking arms or legs when it collapses. Whatever pub it finally reaches will keep the hood for the rest of the year.

According to local tradition the custom began in the Middle Ages, when Lady de Mowbray's silk hood blew off while she was out riding. Thirteen labourers working on the land ran after it, but the one who caught it was too shy to return it. She christened him the 'Fool', addressed the man who handed it to her as 'My Lord' and called the others 'Boggins'. But this is probably apocryphal. It is easier to believe that the ritual stems from some early pagan fertility rite. The proceedings are rich with sexual, as well as sacrificial, symbolism: red flowers, willow, drooping bladder.

The hood itself, hanging behind a public bar, in Haxey or Westwoodside, looks almost shockingly phallic. It is in startling contrast to the modern comfort of the village around it, as is the high ground where the game is played. Here the land is almost completely open, and still cultivated in strips that go back to 1086. It is easy to imagine the peasants of *Domesday* Haxey ploughing and sowing – and gathering once a year for a strange celebration whose origins even then were lost in the past.

HAXEY: *Strip farming is a form of cultivation that goes back to* Domesday.

Castle Bytham

In CASTLE BYTHAM *WESTBITHAM* Morcar had 9 carucates of land taxable. Land for as many ploughs. Drogo [de Beuvriere] has 3 ploughs in lordship; 24 Freemen on half of this land; 7 villagers with 8 ploughs. 7 Frenchmen have 2 ploughs and 3 iron – works at 40s 8d. Woodland, pasture in places, 1½ leagues long and as wide; meadow, 60 acres. Value before 1066 £19 10s; now £10.

Castle Bytham is now merely a largish grey stone village spreading down a low hillside in south-east Lincolnshire, but it was important in 1086. Its three iron-works (apparently run by immigrants from France) made it one of the nation's major iron-working centres. Since there are no local deposits of iron ore, it may be that the industry was established here because the extensive woodland nearby would have provided charcoal for the forges.

Castle Bytham's lords were men of power and influence. Its last Saxon holder, Earl Morcar, and his brother Edwin were part of the family which was the chief rival to that of Harold and his father Godwin in the internal power struggle that so seriously weakened the country before the Norman invasion. When Morcar was made Earl of Northumberland after a local uprising in 1065, the two brothers, who now controlled all of the north of England, marched with armies to Oxford in what appeared to be an attempt to establish an independent northern kingdom. King Edward was so enraged that he fell into the illness from which he died two months later. Harold negotiated a peace on his behalf, but from then on it was never certain where the brothers' loyalties lay. In 1066 they gallantly held off the invading Norwegian army outside York for most of a day's fighting, and their resistance probably weakened the Norwegians enough to enable Harold to rout them at the Battle of Stamford Bridge five days later. But they failed to follow Harold to the Battle of Hastings.

Under William they alternated between attendance at his court as semi-captive guests, and half-hearted attempts at rebellion from the north. They were bystanders in the major northern insurrection of 1069, but in 1071 they finally turned against William. Edwin was killed by his own followers, but Morcar joined the last defence of the Isle of Ely under Hereward the Wake. After it fell he was imprisoned for life.

CASTLE BYTHAM: *The castle built by Drogo de Beuvriere, the* Domesday *landholder, is now a huge earthwork that looms over the village.*

Drogo de Beuvriere, the main landholder at the time of *Domesday* (others were the Abbot of Peterborough, Godfrey de Cambrai and Robert of Stafford), is said to have married a kinswoman of King William and then to have poisoned her. He was bold enough to ask the king for money so that he could visit his home in Flanders 'with his wife'. When his request was granted he fled the country. William never tracked him down.

In the eleventh century the undoubted proof of Castle Bytham's importance must have been the great Norman castle which, now a huge green earthwork, still towers menacingly over the village. It was built by Drogo and destroyed by fire in the Wars of the Roses. Today cows graze over the enormous banks at its top, but it is easy to discern the classic motte and bailey structure.

Two miles to the west, on the road to South Witham, a remnant of Saxon Bytham remains: Morkery Woods, named after Earl Morcar, whose ambivalent loyalties exemplified the failings of the last Saxons, just as Drogo's castle exemplified the indomitability of the Normans.

Lincolnshire Gazetteer
Each entry starts with the modern place name in **bold** type. The *Domesday* information that follows is in *italic* type, beginning with the name or names by which the place was known in 1086. The main landholders and under-tenants are next, separated with semi-colons if a place was divided into more than one holding. A number of holdings were granted by the king to his thanes; these holders are described as holding land 'from the king'. More general information completes the *Domesday* part of the entry, including examples of dues such as eels rendered by tenants. The modern or post-Domesday section is in normal type. ▦ represents a village, ⌂ a small village or hamlet.

Aby *Abi: Bishop of Bayeux and Wadward from him; Earl Hugh.* ▦

Addlethorpe *Ardulvetorp/ Hardetorp/Herde(r)torp/ Heretorp: Archbishop of York; Gilbert de Ghent; Eudo FitzSpirwic; Robert the Steward and Robert from him; Chetelbern from the king. 2 churches.* ⌂

Ailby *Alebe/Halebi: Archbishop of York; Bishop of Bayeux.* ⌂

Aisby (in Corringham) *Asebi/ by: King's land.* ⌂

Aisby (in Heydour) *Asebi: William from Colsuan.* ⌂

Aisthorpe *Aestorp/Estorp: Gilbert de Ghent; Uluuiet and Alden the priest from the king. Church (with Thorpe in the Fallows).* ⌂

Alford *Alforde: Gilbert de Ghent; William Tailbois.* Small market town.

Algarkirk *Alfgare: Colegrim from Abbot of Croyland; Count Alan.* ⌂ Abandoned woad mill, operated until 1930.

Alkborough *Alchebarge: Archbishop of Peterborough; Ivo Tailbois.* ▦ Roman camp site known as Countess Close after Countess Lucy, wife of Ivo Tailbois.

Allington *Adelinctune/ Adelingetone: Robert de Tosny and Warin from him; Berengar de Tosny; Godric from Robert Malet. 2 churches.* ▦ Church with Norman features.

Althorpe *Aletorp: Geoffrey de La Guerche.* ▦

Alvingham *Alivng(e)ham: King's land; Bishop of Bayeux; Alfred of Lincoln and Gocelin from him; Rayner de Brimou.* ▦ Watermill.

Amcotts *Amecotes: Geoffrey de La Guerche.* ▦

Anwick *Amuinc/Haniuuic: Drogo de Beuvriere; Geoffrey Alselin and Drogo from him.* ▦

Apley *Apelei(a): William de Percy.* ▦

Appleby *Aplebi: Ralph from Abbot of Peterborough; Gilbert de Ghent and Robert from him; Roger de Bully. Church (with Risby and Sawcliffe).* ▦

Asgarby (near Spilsby) *Asgerebi: Ivo Tailbois.* ▦ Pond.

Ashby (in Bottesford) *Aschebi: King's land; the Abbot of Peterborough.* Part of Scunthorpe.

Ashby (near Fenby) *Aschebi: Bishop of Bayeux and Ilbert from him; Count Alan; Alfred from Guy de Craon. Mill.* ▦

Ashby by Partney *Aschebi: Bishop of Durham; Earl Hugh. 3 churches (with Fordington, Bratoft and another holding lost in Irby in the Marsh).* ▦

Ashby de la Launde *Aschebi: Colsuan; Ralph Pagnell.* ▦ Roman building nearby.

Ashby Puerorum *Aschebi: Bishop of Bayeux; Gocelin FitzLanbert. 2 mills.* ⌂ Its revenues went to Lincoln Cathedral choirboys.

Aslackby *Aslachebi: Robert de Tosny; Gilbert de Ghent; Oger le Breton. ½ church, part of the church in Sempringham.* ▦ Fragments of a preceptory of the Knights Templar.

Asterby *Estrebi: Ivo Tailbois.* ⌂

Aswarby *Asuuardebi/Wardebi: Gilbert de Ghent; Guy de Craon. Church, 2 parts of another church.* ▦

Aubourn *Adburne: Robert de Tosny and Berengar from him. Church, mill, fishery (1000 eels).* ▦ Mill.

Audleby *Aldulvebi: Bishop of Bayeux; Blancard from Roger de Poitou.* ⌂ By Vikings Way.

Aunsby *Ounesbi: Inglerann from his father Guy de Raimbeaucourt.* ▦

Autby *Adulve(s)bi/Alwolde(s)bi: Bishop of Durham and Ilbert from him; Hugh FitzBaldric; Alfred of Lincoln; Durand Malet. 23 salt-pans (with North Thoresby).* House.

Authorpe *Agetorp: Ansgot.* ▦

Avethorpe *Avetorp:* Lost.

Aylesby *Alesbi: Nigel from Bishop of Durham; Picot from Count Alan; Alfred of Lincoln. 1½ mills, mill-site, church.* ▦

Bag Enderby *Adredebi/Andrebi: Bishop of Bayeux; Baldric and Lanbert from Gocelin FitzLanbert. Mill.* ▦ A Saxon shield boss was found nearby.

Banthorpe *Barnetone/torp: Robert de Tosny; Gilbert de Ghent; Robert of Stafford. 2 mills, ⅓ church (with Braceborough).* Banthorpe Wood.

Bardney *Bardenai: Gilbert de Ghent. Mill, 5 fisheries.* Small town, site of a great Saxon abbey.

Barholm *Bercaham/ Berc(he)ham: Abbot of Peterborough and Robert from him; Gilbert de Ghent; Godfrey de Cambrai.* ⌂ Church with a Saxon/Norman doorway.

Barkston *Barcheston(e)/tune: King's land; Ivo Tailbois; Osbern the Priest and Ralph the Sewer; Colegrim. 4 mills.* ▦ Roman camp nearby.

Barkwith *Ba(r)cwrde/Barcourde: Archbishop of York; Bishop of Bayeux; Ernis de Burun; Rayner de Brimou and Girard from him.* Now 2 villages, East and West Barkwith.

Barlings *Berlinga/linge: Bishop of Durham; William de Percy; Colsuan.* ▦

Barnetby le Wold *Bernedebi/ Bernetebi/Bernodebi: Earl Hugh and William from him, formerly Earl Harold; William de Percy; Ernis de Burun and Ulric from him. ½ church.* ▦ Old, originally Saxon, church.

Barnoldby le Beck *Bernulfbi: Count Alan.* ▦

Barrowby *Berbegi: Ivo Tailbois; Robert Malet. Church, mill.* ▦ Developing; church with fragments of Anglo-Saxon sculpture.

Barrow upon Humber *Barewe: Drogo de Beuvriere and Tetbald from him. Mill.* Small town with the site of a Norman motte and bailey castle.

Barton upon Humber *Bertone/ tune: Earl Hugh; Gilbert de Ghent. Church, 2 mills, market, ferry.* Town opposite Hull. Some boatbuilding and a Saxon church tower.

Bassingham *Basingeham: King's land. 2 mills, church.* ▦ Church with a Norman nave and Anglo-Saxon carved stones.

Bassingthorpe *Torp: Azor from Ivo Tailbois.* ⌂

Baston *Ba(c)stune: Abbot of Croyland; Gilbert de Ghent and Ivo from him. Church, ½ mill, marsh.* ▦ Roman road and canal; Saxon pottery remains.

Baumber *Badeburg: Gilbert de Ghent. Mill.* ▦

Beckering *Bechelinge: Archbishop of York; Roger de Poitou; Robert from William de Percy; Gocelin FitzLanbert; Norman d'Arci and Herbert from him.* ⌂

Beelsby *Belesbi/Bilesbi: Count Alan; Waldin the Engineer and William from him; Odo the Arblaster; Godric from the king. 3 mills.* ▦

Beesby (in Hawerby) *Basebi: Count Alan.* Some houses round a church near the ancient site of Beesby village.

BARHOLM: *Saxon/Norman church doorway.*

Beesby in the Marsh *Besebi/ Bizebi: Eudo from Count Alan; Gilbert de Ghent; Gocelin FitzLanbert and Eurold from him. Church.* ⌂

Belchford *Badesford/Beltesford: Abbot of Croyland, given to him by Thorald for his soul; Ivo Tailbois. 2 mills.* ▦

Belleau *Elgelo: Earl Hugh. 6 mills (with Swaby, South Thoresby, Claythorpe and Tothill).* ⌂ Named after a spring which rises here; dovecote; moated manor ruins.

Beltoft *Beltot: Geoffrey de La Guerche.* ⌂

Belton (near Epworth) *Beltone: Geoffrey de La Guerche. 11 fisheries.* ▦

Belton (near Grantham) *Beltone: King's land; Walter d'Aincourt; Guy de Craon; Ingelrann from his father Guy de Raimbeaucourt; Colegrim. Church, 5 mills.* ⌂ Church with Norman font. Belton Hall's garden has 2 apple trees said to be descendants of Newton's tree.

Benniworth *Beningurde: Archbishop of York and Godwin and Osbern the priest from him; Ivo Tailbois and Odo from him. Church, mill-site.* ▦ Partly Norman church.

Bicker *Bichere: Archbishop of York; Count Alan; Countess Judith; Guy de Craon; Godric. 23 salt-pans, church.* ▦ Norman and medieval church with Anglo-Saxon stones.

Bigby *Bechebi: Bishop of Lincoln and Ranulf from him; Earl Hugh; Hugh FitzBaldric. Church.* ▦

Billingborough *Bellingeburg/ Bil(l)ingeburg/Bolinburg: Walter d'Aincourt from Archbishop of York; Count Alan and Colegrim from him; Colsuan and Brunel from him; Alfred of Lincoln and Gocelin from him. Mill, mill-site, ½ church.* ▦ Near Roman Carr Dyke.

Billinghay *Belingei: Archbishop of York and Walchelin and 2 sons of Swen from him. 3 sites of fisheries.* ▦ Billingham Skirth dyke.

Bilsby *Billesbi: Earl Hugh.* ▦ Moated sites.

Binbrook *Binnibroc: Robert de Tosny and Berengar from him; Osbern the Priest; Guy de Craon and Alfred from him. 2 churches, 3 mills, another mill (with Orford).* Small market town with priory earthworks nearby; World War II airfield.

Birthorpe *Berchetorp: Gilbert de Ghent.* ⌂

Biscathorpe *Biscopetorp: Bishop of Durham. 2 mills.* ▦ Tumulus; remains of ancient Biscathorpe village.

Bishop Norton *Nortune: Bishop of Lincoln. Mill-site.* ▦

Bitchfield *Billesfelt: Bishop of Lincoln and Walter from him; Colsuan and William from him; Robert of Stafford and Basuin from him. Church, mill.* ▦ Church with a Norman doorway.

Blankney *Blachene: Walter d'Aincourt and his knights. Church.* ▦

Bleasby *Belesbi/Blasebi/Blesebi: Roger de Poitou; Gocelin FitzLanbert and Herman from him; Odo the Arblaster and Herbert from him.* ⌂

Bloxham *Blochesham: Roger de Poitou; Alfred of Lincoln.* ⌂

Blythborough *Bliburg: Bishop of Durham; Ivo Tailbois and Neal from him; Gocelin FitzLanbert; Geoffrey de La Guerche and Robert from him. Church, 2 mills.* ▦ Church with Norman fragments.

Blyton *Blit(t)one: King's land; Roger de Poitou; Guy de Craon.* ▦

Bolingbroke *Bolinbroc: Ivo Tailbois. Church, new market.* ▦ Now Old Bolingbroke; remains of a Norman castle, where Henry IV was born in 1367.

Bonby *Bundebi: Hugh FitzBaldric; Ralph de Mortimer and William from him. Possibly ½ mill (with Thornton Curtis, etc.).* ▦ Church with 2 late Saxon doorways.

Bonthorpe *Brunetorp: Bishop of Durham and Nigel from him.* ⌂ Tumuli.

Boothby (in Welton le March) *Bodebi: Ivo Tailbois; Gilbert de Ghent; Gocelin FitzLanbert and Rayner from him. Mill.* Boothby Hall and Grange.

Boothby Graffoe *Bodebi: King's land; Gocelin from Alfred of Lincoln. Church, mill.* ⌂

Boothby Pagnall *Bodebi: Gilbert de Ghent and Roger from him; Guy de Craon and Godwin from him. Church.* ▦ Partly Norman church.

Bottesford *Bu(d)lesforde: King's land; Gocelin FitzLanbert.* Part of Scunthorpe. Some of the old village remains; 2 Saxon sundials.

Boultham *Buletham: Robert of Stafford.* Part of Lincoln.

Bourne *Brune: Odo from Ivo Tailbois; Alfred of Lincoln and Dodin from him; Oger le Breton; Robert of Stafford and Geoffrey from him; Sven from the king. 6 mills, 24 fisheries, church.* Small town, the source of Bourne Eau. Church with Norman features; traces of a moated Norman castle. Once a Saxon stronghold.

Braceborough *Braseborg/ Breseburc/-burg: Robert de Tosny; Gilbert de Ghent; Robert of Stafford and Geoffrey from him. 2 mills, ⅓ church (with Banthorpe).* ▦ Norman church font.

Bracebridge *Brachebrige/ Bragebruge: Bishop of Coutances; Roger de Poitou and Ernuin from him. Church, 5 fisheries (with Canwick).* Part of Lincoln; church with a Saxon chancel arch.

Braceby *Bre(i)zbi: King's land; Bishop of Durham; Ivo Tailbois. Church (with Sapperton).* ▦

Brackenborough *Brachenberg: Alfred of Lincoln and Ranulf from him. Mill.* Brackenborough Hall and moat.

Bradley *Bredelou: Bishop of Bayeux. 3 churches, 2 mills (with Laceby and Scartho).* On the outskirts of Grimsby; originally Norman church.

Brampton *Brantune: Bishop of Lincoln.*

Brandon *Brandune: Derinc from Gilbert de Ghent; Robert de Vessey.*

Bransby *Branzbi: Robert de Tosny and Berengar from him.*

Branston *Branztone/tune: Walter d'Aincourt. 2 churches, 4 mills, 3 fisheries.* Developing; church with Saxon masonry and a Norman tower.

Brant Broughton *Burtune: Count Alan. Church, mill.* Medieval church with fine 19th-century glass windows.

Bratoft *Bre(ie)toft: Earl Hugh; Sortebrand from the king. 3 churches (with Ashby by Partney, etc.).*

Brattleby *Brotulbi: Bishop of Durham; Gilbert de Ghent; Colsuan.*

Brauncewell *Branzewelle: Alfred of Lincoln; Geoffrey Alselin. Church.* Some houses.

Brigsley *Brige(s)lai: Bishop of Bayeux; Count Alan; Guy de Craon.*

Brinkhill *Brincle: Earl Hugh. 9 mills (with Langton by Spilsby, Hagworthingham, Salmonby, Tetford, Winceby and Claxby Pluckacre).*

BROCKLESBY: *Memorial arch to the 2nd Earl of Marlborough.*

Brocklesby *Brachelesbi/Brochelesbi: Nigel from Bishop of Durham; Ivo Tailbois and Neal from him; Norman d'Arci; Ernis de Burun and Ranulf from him.* Area of scientific forestry management; Brocklesby Park art collection; ancient burial mound in the park.

Broughton *Bertone/Brocktone: Ralph Pagnell; Durand Malet. Church, mill.* Near Roman Ermine Street; Saxon and Norman work in the church.

Broxholme *Broxholme: Robert de Tosny. Church.* Scattered.

Brumby *Brunebi: King's land.* Part of Scunthorpe; Brumby Common and Grove.

Buckland *Torp:* Lost; formerly Langton Thorpe.

Bucknall *Buchehale: Abbot of Croyland; Earl Hugh; Hugh FitzBaldric.* Ancient moated site nearby.

Bulby *Bolebi: Alfred of Lincoln; Guy de Craon.*

Bullington *Bolintone: Bishop of Durham and Nigel from him; Earl Hugh and Colsuan from him; Ivo Tailbois and Odo from him.* Some houses; hall.

Burgh (in Evedon) *Burg:* Lost.

Burgh in the Marsh *Burch/Burg: Count Alan; Gilbert de Ghent; Eudo FitzSpirwic. Church.* Small market town near a Roman road with an Anglo-Saxon burial mound nearby.

Burg on Bain *Burg: Ernis de Burun.* Neolithic long barrow.

Burnham Altera *Brune/Brune: Geoffrey de La Guerche.* Now 2 hamlets, High and Low Burnham.

Burnham (in Thornton Curtis) *Brune: Ernis de Burun and Ulric from him.*

Burreth *Burgrede:* Lost.

Burtoft *Brutoft: Abbot of Croyland before and after 1066.*

Burton (near Lincoln) *Burton(e): Bishop of Lincoln; Robert de Tosny; Gilbert de Ghent; Peter de Valognes; Sortebrand from the king.* On the outskirts of Lincoln; a Roman villa.

Burton Coggles *Bertone/tune: Ivo Tailbois and Azor from him; Colsuan; Walter d'Aincourt; Ralph Pagnell and Oger from him.*

Burton Pedwardine *Berton/tun: Gilbert de Ghent; Guy de Craon. Church, mill.* Towerless church with Saxon and Norman traces.

Burton upon Stather *Burtone: King's land. ½ market (with Thealby and Darby).*

Burwell *Buruelle: Ansgot. Church, mill.* Once a market town, its church has a Norman chancel arch.

Buslingthorpe *Esetorp: Robert de Tosny. Church.* Moated site; Manor Farm.

Butterwick (near Freiston) *Butuic: Guy de Craon. 2 churches.* Old Brew House.

Butyate *Butiate:* Lost.

Cabourne *Caburne: Ivo Tailbois and Roger from him; William de Percy and Norman from him; Hugh FitzBaldric; Alfred of Lincoln; Durand Malet.* The church tower is believed to be pre-Conquest.

Cadney *Catenai: King's land; Count Alan; Roger de Poitou.*

Caenby *Couenebi: Bishop of Lincoln. Church, mill.* Caenby Corner crossroad, inn, church and farmhouse.

Caistor *Castre: King's land; William de Percy. Church (with Hundon), 4 mills.* Roman-walled town. The church has Saxon and Norman traces. Mounds may mark the site of King Egbert's victory over the Mercians in 829.

Calceby *Calesbi: Bishop of Durham and William from him; Earl Hugh. 20 salt-pans (with Wainfleet, Haugh, Theddlethorpe and Mablethorpe).* Georgian farmhouse; ruined church.

Calcethorpe *Torp: Alfred of Lincoln.* Ancient village site; manor; farm; duckpond.

Cammeringham *Came(s)lingeham: Colsuan; Durand Malet.* Church with pre-Conquest work.

Candlesby *Calnodesbi: Count Alan; Gilbert de Ghent; Eudo FitzSpirwic; Chetelbern from the king. 2 churches.*

Canwick *Can(eu)uic: Bishop of Bayeux and Ilbert from him; Bishop of Coutances; Bishop of Lincoln; Roger de Poitou and Ernuin from him; Norman Crassus; Colegrim. Church, 5 fisheries (with Bracebridge).* Adjoining Lincoln; manor farm; church with Norman features.

Carlby *Carlebi: Bishop of Lincoln and Erchenold from him; Berewold from Ivo and Ivo from Gilbert de Ghent; Robert of Stafford and Geoffrey from him.*

Carlton le Moorland *Casletune: Drogo de Beuvriere. Church.* Anglo-Saxon towered church.

Carlton Scroop *Carlentun(e): Count Alan; William de Warenne and Adelin from him, formerly Earl Harold. Church.* Church with Norman features.

Casewick *Casuic: Alfred of Lincoln and Boso from him; Gunfrid de Chocques. ½ mill.* Casewick Hall.

Castle Bytham *Bi(n)tham/Westbitham:* See page 167.

Castlethorpe *Castorp: Durand Malet.* Hall; Castlethorpe Bridge over Wen Dyke.

Cawkwell *Calchewelle: Ivo Tailbois; Norman d'Arci and Roger from him. Church.*

Cawthorpe *Calctorp: Oger le Breton.* Pond.

Caythorpe *Ca(ri)torp: Robert de Vessey. 2 churches, ½ mill.* Hall and park.

Cheal *Ceila: Bishop of Lincoln and Malger from him. Salt-pan.* Now Gosberton Cheal.

Cherry Willingham *Gullingham/Ulingeham/Wilingeham: Bishop of Lincoln and Osbern from him; Gilbert de Ghent. Church, 2 fisheries.* Dormitory of Lincoln.

Claxby (near Normanby le Wold) *Clachesbi: Ivo Tailbois and Hugh and Godfrey from him; Gocelin FitzLanbert; Drogo de Beuvriere and Colsuan from him; Durand Malet; Norman d'Arci and Geoffrey from him. Mill, 2 churches and ¼ mill (with Normanby le Wold).*

Claxby (near Welton le Marsh) *Clachesbi: Count Alan; Gilbert de Ghent and Rademer from him; Hugh FitzBaldric and Guy his son-in-law from him. Church, mill.* Medieval earthworks.

Claxby Pluckacre *Calchesbi/Clasbi: Earl Hugh; Gocelin FitzLanbert and Walter and Rayner from him. 9 mills (with Brinkhill, etc.).* Some houses.

Claypole *Claipol: Bishop of Bayeux; Geoffrey Alselin and Elduin from him. Church, mill.*

Claythorpe *Clactorp: Earl Hugh. 6 mills (with Belleau, etc.).* Mill.

Cleatham *Cletham: Bishop of Bayeux and Ilbert from him; Abbot of Peterborough and Roger from him; Gocelin FitzLanbert; Aldene from the king. 2 mills.*

Clee *Cleia: Archbishop of York; Bishop of Bayeux and Ilbert from him; Wimund from Ivo Tailbois.* Now Old Clee, traces of the original village; church with a Saxon font.

Clixby *Clisbi: King's land.* Farmland; near Vikings Way.

Coates (near Stow) *Cotes: Bishop of Bayeux and Ilbert from him; Bishop of Lincoln and Erchenold from him; Roger de Poitou; Colsuan; Gocelin FitzLanbert. Mill.*

Cockerington *Cocrinton(e)/Crochinton: Bishop of Durham; Bishop of Bayeux and Ilbert from him; Colsuan and Mathew from him; Alfred of Lincoln and Gocelin from him; Rayner de Brimou. Mill, mill-site.* Now 2 hamlets, North and South Cockerington near Monks Dyke.

Cold Hanworth *Haneurde/Haneworde: Roger de Poitou; Gocelin FitzLanbert. Thorald the priest from Colsuan. Mill.* Small farming community.

Coleby (near Boothby Graffoe) *Colebi/by: King's land; Norman d'Arci; Countess Judith. Church.* Church with a Saxon or early Norman tower.

Coleby (in West Halton) *Colebi: Earl Hugh; Ernis de Burun and John from him.*

Colsterworth *Colsteuorde/Colstewrde: Archbishop of York; a thane, the pre-Conquest holder. 2 mills.*

Collow (formerly Calcote) *Caldecote: Ernis de Burun. 2 mill-sites.* Moated site; Collow Holt and Grange.

Conesby *Cunesbi:* Once 2 hamlets, North and South Conesby. Now lost.

Coningsby *Cuningesbi: King's land; Earl Hugh; Drogo de Beuvriere; Robert the Steward; Chetelbern from the king. 15 fisheries.* Airfield.

Corby *Corbi/by: Bishop of Lincoln and Walter from him; Bricteua, the pre-Conquest holder, from the king.* Small town with an ancient market cross.

Corringham *Coring(e)ham: King's land; Berengar from Robert de Tosny. Church (with Springthorpe).* Anglo-Saxon church tower.

Coteland *Coteland:* Lost.

Coton *Cotes:* Lost.

Counthorpe *Cudetorp: Drogo de Beuvriere and Ulric and Walter from him; Robert of Stafford.* Counthorpe and Creeton parish; Counthorpe Lodge.

Covenham *Covenham: Monastery of St Calais from Bishop of Durham; William de ercy. Church, 7 salt-pans.* Now 2 adjoining villages Covenham St Bartholomew and St Mary, each with a church.

Craiselound *Altera Lund: Geoffrey de La Guerche. Fishery.* Also Eastlound.

Cranwell *Cranewelle: Abbot of Ramsey; Gilbert de Ghent and Geoffrey from him.* Suburban; remains of an ancient cross. At Bayard's Leap, 2 huge horseshoes are embedded in the ground in memory of a legendary horse.

Creeton *Cretone/tun(e): Ralph from Alfred of Lincoln; Godfrey de Cambrai; Basuin from Robert of Stafford.*

Croft *Croft: Gilbert de Ghent and Ralph from him. Salt-pan.* Fenland.

Crosby *Cropesbi: Earl Hugh; Norman d'Arci.* Suburb of Scunthorpe.

Crowle *Crul(e): Selby Abbey from Geoffrey de La Guerche. 31 fisheries, church.* Fenland market town, a brickmaking and agricultural centre. Crowle Stone, in the church, is believed to be part of an Anglo-Saxon carved cross.

Croxby *Cro(c)sbi: Odo from Ivo Tailbois; Robert de Tosny; Norman d'Arci and Odo from him; William Blunt. Mill.* Area near Binbrook.

Croxton *Crocestone/Crochestone/tune: King's land; Gocelin from Bishop of Lincoln; Anschitil from Roger de Poitou; Hugh FitzBaldric and Hamelin from him.*

Culverthorpe *Torp: Gilbert de Ghent. Church.*

Cumberworth *Combreuorde: Rayner de Brimou.*

Cuxwold *Cucualt: Archbishop of York and William from him; Gocelin from Ivo Tailbois; William de Percy; Hugh FitzBaldric; Alfred of Lincoln and Gleu from him; Durand Malet; Seward from the king.* Long barrow.

Dalby *Dalbi: Earl Hugh. 2 churches.*

Darby *Derbi:* Lost.

Deeping St James *Depinge/Estdeping(e): Alfred of Lincoln; Godfrey de Cambrai. Fishery.* Tithe barn.

Dembleby *Delbebi/Dembelbi/Denbelbi: Gilbert de Ghent; Colsuan and Rainard from him; Guy de Craon.*

Denton *Dentone/tune: King's land; Robert de Tosny; Geoffrey from Robert of Stafford.*

Dexthorpe *Dr(e)istorp: Earl Hugh; Eudo FitzSpirwic and Ivo from him. 2 churches.*

GAINSBOROUGH: *The Old Hall, rebuilt in the 15th c.*

Digby *Dicbi: Geoffrey Alselin.* Church with traces of Saxon work; ancient village cross.

Donnington *Donninctune/ Duninctune: Abbot of Peterborough before and after 1066; Count Alan. 22 salt-pans.* Market town.

Donnington on Bain *Duninctune: Ivo Tailbois. 2 mills.*

Dorrington *Derintone: Geoffrey Alselin.* Village cross.

Dowdyke *Dwedic: Abbot of Croyland and Colegrim from him.* Dowdyke Grange; old sea bank.

Dowsby *Dusebi: Archbishop of York and Hugh from him; Guy de Craon; Offram, the pre-Conquest holder. Mill.*

Drayton *Draitone: Abbot of Croyland; Count Alan and Toli from him; Guy de Craon. 4 salt-pans.* Part of Swineshead.

Driby *Dribi: Gilbert de Ghent and Ivo from him. Mill.* Remote; earthworks; moated manor site.

Dry Doddington *Dodintone/ tune: Bishop of Bayeux and Baldric from him; Geoffrey Alselin; Colsuan. Mill.* Green.

Dunholme *Duneham: King's land and Odo the Arblaster from the king; Ilbert de Lacy and his knight from him; Ralph Pagnell and his knight from him; Odo the Arblaster.*

Dunsby (in Brauncewell) *Dunnesbi: Abbot of Ramsey; Geoffrey Alselin.* Dunsby House; mounds of a vanished village and manor house.

Dunsby (near Hacconby) *Dunesbe: Bishop of Lincoln and Ralph from him. Church.*

Dunstall *Tonestale/tele: Ivo Tailbois; Roger de Poitou. Church, mill.* Earthworks.

Dunsthorpe *Dunetorp: King's land.* Part of Old Somerby.

Dunston *Dunestuna: Norman d'Arci. Church, 6 mills.* Former haunt of highwaymen.

Dyke *Dic: Oger le Breton; Heppo the Arblaster. Church, mill.*

Eagle *Ac(he)lei/Acley/Akeley/ Aycle: Roger de Poitou; Durand Malet; Odo the Arblaster; Countess Judith. Church.*

East Halton *Haltune: Probably Ivo Tailbois.*

East Keal *Estrecale: Bishop of Durham; Ivo Tailbois; Eudo FitzSpirwic. ½ church.*

East Kirkby *Cherchebi: Ivo Tailbois. 2 churches (with Revesby).* Manor house.

Eastlound *Lund: Geoffrey de La Guerche. Fishery.* Also Craiselound.

Easton *Estone: Archbishop of York and Osbern from him. ½ church, mill.*

Edenham *Ed(en)eham: Gilbert de Ghent.*

Edlington *Ellingetone: Walter from Ivo Tailbois; Gilbert de Ghent and Egbert from him. 2 mills, church.*

Elkington *Alchinton/ Archintone: Ivo Tailbois and Geoffrey from him; William de Percy and Fulk from him. 1½ churches, mill, mill-site.* Now 2 hamlets, North and South Elkington.

Elsham *Ele(s)ham: Bishop of Bayeux and Ilbert from him; Bishop of Lincoln and Gocelin from him; Roger de Poitou and Ernui from him; Geoffrey Alselin. Mill-site.*

Elsthorpe *Aig(he)lestorp: Alfred of Lincoln; Guy de Craon.* Elsthorpe Grange.

Epworth *Epeurde: Geoffrey de La Guerche. 11 fisheries.* Small town, the birthplace of John Wesley (1703), whose father was rector here.

Eresby *Iresbi: Bishop of Durham. 2 mills (with Spilsby and Thorpe St Peter).* Eresby House, on the outskirts of Spilsby.

Evedon *Evedune: King's land; Bishop of Durham; Bishop of Lincoln and Osmund from him; Colsuan; Geoffrey Alselin; Colegrim. 2 mills, mill-site, church.*

Ewerby *Geresbi/Grene(s)bi/ Ieresbi: Bishop of Lincoln; Gilbert de Ghent; Colegrim, the pre-Conquest holder and Rold from him. Church (with Ewerby Thorpe).* Saxon gravestone.

Ewerby Thorpe *Oustorp: King's land; Gilbert de Ghent; Colsuan; Martin. Church (with Ewerby), mill (with Howell, Heckington and Quarrington).*

Faldingworth *Falding(e)urde/ Falingeurde: Colsuan; William Blunt; Osbern the Priest.*

Farforth *Farforde: Earl Hugh and Baldwin from him. Church, mill.*

Fenby *Fendebi: Count Alan.* Now Ashby-cum-Fenby.

Fillingham *Felingeham/ Fi(ge)lingeham: Roger de Poitou and Anschitil from him; Colsuan; Anschitil from the king. Church.* Roman site. John Wycliffe was rector here, 1361–68.

Firsby *Frisebi: Bishop of Bayeux and Ilbert from him. Church.* Now 2 hamlets, East and West Firsby.

Fishtoft *Toft: Count Alan; Guy de Craon. Church, mill.* Vegetable growing; statue of the Saxon St Guthlac in the church.

Fiskerton *Fiscartone/tune: Abbot of Peterborough. Church, 3½ fisheries.* Church with Norman arches. Bronze Age axes have been found.

Fleet *Flec/Fleot: King's land. 2 salt-pans, fishery.* Originally on the sea shore.

Flixborough *Flichesburg: Norman d'Arci. 2 mill-sites.* Birthplace of Sir Edmund Anderson (1530–1605) who tried Mary Queen of Scots and Sir Walter Raleigh.

Folkingham *Folching(e)ham/ Fulchingeham: Gilbert de Ghent. Church, mill.* Remains of Gilbert de Ghent's castle; market square; church with Norman work.

Fonaby *Fuldenebi: King's land.* Now Fonaby Top; Fonaby House Farm.

Fordington *Fotintone: Earl Hugh. 3 churches (with Ashby by Partney, etc.).* Ancient village site nearby; Giants Hill; long barrow.

Foston *Foztune(e): Count Alan.*

Fotherby *Fo(d)rebi: Bishop of Durham and Turstin from him; Robert de Tosny and Berengar from him; Fulk from William de Percy. 4 salt-pans.*

Frampton *Franetone/tune: Count Alan; Guy de Craon. Church, 15 salt-pans.*

Freiston *Fristune: Guy de Craon.* Once on the coast, now 2 miles inland. Called after a colony of Frieslanders who invaded and settled here.

Friesthorpe *Frisetorp: Colsuan.*

Frieston *Fristun: Robert de Vessey.* Adjacent to Caythorpe.

Friskney *Frischenei: Chetelbern from the king.* Moated site; mill mound; ancient fishpond site.

Fulbeck *Fulebec: Count Alan and Colegrim and Derinc from him. 2 churches, ½ mill (with Leadenham).* Fine village cross; church with a Norman font.

Fulletby *Fullobi: Bishop of Durham and William from him; Earl Hugh and Baldric from him, formerly Earl Harold.* Manor house by Viking Way; Roman urns discovered nearby.

Fulnetby *Fulnedebi: Ernis de Burun.* Hall

Fulsby *Folesbi: King's land.* Fulsby Wood.

Fulstow *Fugelestou: Bishop of Durham and Walbert from him; Picot from Count Alan; Earl Hugh and Rozelin from him; Robert the Steward. 14 salt-pans.* Moated grange.

Gainsborough *Gainesburg: Geoffrey de La Guerche and Rainald from him.* Large industrial town.

Gainsthorpe *Camelstorp: Ivo Tailbois.* Gainsthorpe Farm.

Ganthorpe *Germuntorp:* Lost; also called Ganthrops.

Garthorpe *Gerulftorp: Geoffrey de La Guerche.*

Gate Burton *Borotona/Bortone: Count Alan.*

Gayton le Wold *Gedtune/ Gettune: King's land, formerly Queen Edith. Church.*

Gedney *Gadenai/nay: King's land. Fishery.* Straggling.

Gelston *Chevelestune: Count Alan. Warren for hares.* Remains of an ancient cross.

Girsby *Griseby: Archbishop of York and William from him; Ernis de Burun.* Girsby Grange.

Glentham *Glandham/Glantham/ Glentham: Bishop of Bayeux and Wadard from him; Bishop of Lincoln; Ivo Tailbois and Rainfrid from him.* Moated house.

Glentworth *Glenteu(u)rde: King's land; Bishop of Bayeux and Wadard from him; Gocelin FitzLanbert and Anschitil from him; Martin; Restold.* Bulb growing.

Gosberton *Gosebertcherche/ techirche/Gozeberdecherca: Bishop of Lincoln and Malger from him; Count Alan and Ulbert from him. 3 salt-pans.* Town.

Goulceby *Colchesbi: Ivo Tailbois. Church, mill.*

Goxhill *Golsa/Golse: Bishop of Lincoln and Roger from him; Alfred of Lincoln and Ralph from him; Drogo de Beuvriere; Hugh, the pre-Conquest holder, from the king.* Remains of Goxhill Priory nearby, in a farm building.

Graby *Greibi: Archbishop of York; Robert de Tosny and Gunfrid from him.* Remote.

Grainsby *Grenesbi: Count Alan and Wimund from him.*

Grainthorpe *Germund(s)torp: King's land; Bishop of Durham; William de Percy. 6 salt-pans.* Once a port; salt-pan traces on the coast.

Grantham *Graham/ Gran(d)ham/Gran(t)ham: King's land, and Colegrim, Ivo and Ernuin the priest from the king. Church, 4 mills, 111 burgesses.* Town with St Wulfran church containing Norman pillars and a splendid library. The Angel and Royal is one of the rare medieval hostels established by the Knights Templar.

Grasby *Gros(e)bi: King's land; Bishop of Bayeux; a thane. Church, mill.*

Grayingham *Gra(i)ngeham: King's land; Bishop of Lincoln and Malger from him; Ernis de Burun.* Manor house.

Great Coates *Cotes: Bishop of Bayeux; Count Alan; Alfred of Lincoln and Bernard from him; Norman d'Arci and Richard from him; Durand Malet and Richard from him.* Part of Grimsby.

Greatford *Greteford/ Griteford(e): Berengar from Robert de Tosny; Gilbert de Ghent; Godfrey de Cambrai and Euremar from him. 2 mills.*

Great Gonerby *Gouerdebi/ Gunfordebi/Gunnewordebi: King's land; Bishop of Durham and Lanbert from him; Bishop Osmund of Salisbury; Walter d'Aincourt and Elwi from him; Guy de Craon. 5 mills.*

Great Limber *Limberge/ Linberge: King's land; Archbishop of York; Ivo Tailbois; Hugh FitzBaldric; Drogo de Beuvriere; Rayner de Brimou. ½ slaughter-house.* Mausoleum built by James Wyatt, 1787.

GLENTWORTH: *Memorial to Elizabeth I's Chief Justice*

Great Ponton *Magna Panptune/ Magna Pantone/Pamptune/ Pantone: King's land; Drogo de Beuvriere; Countess Judith and Nigel from her.* Ancient manor; Roman building.

Great Steeping *Stepi(nge): Gilbert de Ghent; Robert the Steward. 2 churches.* .

Great Sturton *Stratone: Bishop of Bayeux and Ilbert from him; Ranulf de St Valery. Church, mill.*

Greetwell *Grentewelle: Roger de Bully and Thorald from him. Church, 2 fisheries, mill.* Greetwell Hall; Roman villa.

Greetham *Granham/Gretham: Earl Hugh, formerly Earl Harold.* Cluster of houses with a pond, grange and church.

Grimoldby *Grimalbi/Grimoldbi: King's land; Alfred of Lincoln and William from him.* Expanding; adjoining Marby.

Grimsby *Grimesbi: Bishop of Bayeux; Drogo de Beuvriere; Ralph de Mortimer and Richard from him. Customs and ferry rendering 40s, another ferry rendering 5s, church, mill.* Large and famous fishing port. The Church of St James was originally built in 1110.

Gunby (near North Witham) *Gunnebi: Ralf FitzHubert with William leasing part. Mill.*

Gunnerby *Gunresbi: Count Alan. Mill.*

Habrough *Aburne/Haburne: King's land; Earl Hugh; Ivo Tailbois; William de Percy and Norman from him; Alfred of Lincoln and Ralph from him; Norman d'Arci; Ernis de Burun. Salt-pans (with Newsham), mill.*

Hacconby *Hacone(s)bi/ Hacunesbi: Bishop of Lincoln; Oger le Breton; Robert of Stafford and Gulfar from him; Heppo the Arblaster. Church.* Hacconby Fen; church with a Norman font.

Haceby *Hazebi: Gilbert de Ghent; Waldin le Breton and Godwin and Guy de Craon from him; Odo the Arblaster.* Roman villa ruins.

Hackthorn *Agetorne/Hagetorne/ torn/e: Archbishop of York and William from him; Roger de Poitou; Colsuan; Gocelin FitzLanbert; Martin; Waldin the engineer. Church, 4 mills.* Near Roman Ermine Street.

Haddington *Hadinctone/tune: Robert de Tosny and Warin from him; Baldwin the Fleming. Church.* Moated site.

Hagnaby *Hagenebi: Ivo Tailbois; Eudo FitzSpirwic.*

Hagworthingham *Haberdingham/Hacberdincham/ Hacberdingham/ Hacberding(e)ham: Count Alan and Eudo from him; Earl Hugh; Gilbert de Ghent; Gocelin FitzLanbert; Drogo de Beuvriere and Robert from him. Church, 3 mills, 9 mills (with Brinkhill, etc.).* Mill Mound; church with a Norman pillar; early barrow.

Hainton *Gaintone/Haintone/- tune(e): Archbishop of York and William from him; Bishop of Bayeux and Ilbert from him; Roger de Poitou and Hacon and Albert from him; Gocelin from Alfred of Lincoln; Rayner de Brimou.* Hainton Hall and Park, landscaped by Capability Brown in the 18th century.

Hale *Hale: Gilbert de Ghent and Ralph from him.* Now 2 villages, Great and Little Hale.

Hallington *Halintun: Earl Hugh.*

Haltham *Holtham: King's land; Robert the Steward. 2 mills.* Fine thatched Elizabethan inn.

Halton Holegate *Haltun: Count Alan and Eudo from him; Ivo Tailbois. Church, 4 mills.*

Hanthorpe *Hermodestorp: Gilbert de Ghent; Oger le Breton; Heppo the Arblaster and Simund from him.* Windmill.

Hardwick (in Panton) *Harduic/ Hardwic:* Lost.

Hardwick (near Torksey) *Harduic: King's land and Berengar de Tosny, Roger de Bully and Bishop of Lincoln from the king. 11 fisheries (with Torksey).* On Fosdyke Navigation Canal; manor farm.

Hareby *Harebi: Ivo Tailbois.*

Harlaxton *Herlavestune: King's land. 2 mills.* Restored cross on the green; Harlaxton Manor.

Harmston *Hermestune/ Hermodestone/tune: Earl Hugh; Norman d'Arci; Ralph de Mortimer. Church, fishery (50 score eels and 5).* Church with an early tower and an Anglo-Saxon cross shaft and crucifixion.

Harpswell *Herpeswelle: King's land; Archbishop of York and William from him; Gocelin FitzLanbert. ½ church.* Church with an Anglo-Saxon tower and Norman font.

Harrowby *Herigerbi: King's land; Count Alan and Godric from him; Algar, the pre-Conquest holder, from Guy de Craon. 2 mills (with Horbling).* Part of Grantham.

Hasthorpe *Havoldestorp: Gilbert de Ghent and Roger from him. Marsh.*

Hatcliffe *Hadeclive: Count Alan. 2 mills.*

Hatton *Hatune: Ernis de Burun.*

Haugh *Hag(h)e: Bishop of Durham and William from him; Earl Hugh. 20 salt-pans (with Calceby, etc.).* Church with an 11th-century chancel arch.

Haugham *Hecham: Earl Hugh and the Monks of St Sever from him.*

Hawerby *Hawardebi: Count Alan.* Some cottages; hall; vicarage.

Hawthorpe *Awartorp: Alfred of Lincoln.*

Haxey *Acheseia:* See page 166.

Haythby *Hedebi:* Lost.

Healing *Hechelinge/ Heg(h)elinge: Archbishop of York; Bishop of Bayeux and Wadward from him; Alfred of Lincoln and Bernard from him. ½ mill.* On the outskirts of Grimsby, named after a nearby spring, Healing Wells.

Heapham *Iopham: King's land; Count Alan.* Ancient cross; church with a Saxon doorway.

Heckington *Echintune: King's land; Bishop of Lincoln; Gilbert de Ghent; Colsuan and Conded from him; Robert de Vessey; Guy de Craon. Church, 3 fisheries and a mill (with Ewerby Thorpe, etc.).* Working tower windmill.

Helpringham *Helperi(n)cham: Ivo Tailbois; Gilbert de Ghent; Colsuan; Robert de Vessey; Godfrey de Cambrai.* Large.

Hemingby *Hamingebi: Earl Hugh and Baldric from him; Ivo Tailbois; Hugh FitzBaldric. ½ mill.* Manor house.

Hemswell *Helmeswelle: King's land; Bishop of Bayeux and Leosard from him; Martin.* Maypole.

Hibaldstow *Hiboldeston(e)/ Hi(l)boldestou: King's land; Abbot of Peterborough; Colsuan; Outi from the king. Mill.* Farmland.

Holbeach *Holebech/ben/ Holobec/h: King's land; Abbot of Croyland; Count Alan and Landric from him; Guy de Craon.* Little market town with evidence of Roman occupation.

Holme (in Beckingham) *Holm:* Lost.

Holme (in Sudbrooke) *Holme: Abbot of Peterborough; Colsuan. Mill.* Modern Sudbrooke Holme.

Holme (near Bottesford) *Holm: Abbot of Peterborough. Mill.* On the outskirts of Scunthorpe; Holme Hall.

Holtham *Houten:* Lost.

Holton (near Beckering) *Houtone/tune: Archbishop of York; Gocelin FitzLanbert.*

Holton le Clay *Holtone/tun: Count Alan and Wimund from him; Ivo Tailbois and Hermer from him; Rayner de Brimou and Roger from him.* Expanding; 11th-century church tower.

Holton le Moor *Hoctun/(e): King's land; Ivo Tailbois and Odo from him; Roger de Poitou and Roger from him.*

Honington *Hondintone/ Hundindune/Hundinton/(e): Ivo Tailbois; Gilbert de Ghent and Fulbert from him. Church, mill-site.* Iron Age camp on the heath; church with Norman work.

Horbling *Horbelinge/Orbelinge: Walter from Archbishop of York; Count Alan and Stefan from him; Colsuan and Matthew from him; Waldin le Breton. Church and 2 mills (with Harrowby).* Church with a Norman tower.

Horkstow *Horchetou: Gilbert de Ghent.* Site of a Roman pavement, now in the British Museum. George Stubbs is said to have done his engravings for 'Anatomy of a Horse', 1766, in a nearby farmhouse.

Horncastle *Hornecastre: King's land. 2 mills.* Market town. Parts of the wall and bastions of the original Roman town of *Banovallum* remain.

Horsington *Horsi(n)tone: Earl Hugh; Ivo Tailbois; Hugh FitzBaldric.* Moated site.

Houflet *Wenflet:* Lost.

Hougham *Hac(h)am: Bishop of Lincoln; Colsuan and William from him; Bishop Remigus from Countess Judith. Church, 3 mills, mill-site.* Church with pre-Conquest work; Anglo-Saxon cross; moated manor house.

Hough on the Hill *Hach(e)/ Hag: Count Alan; Derinc from Gilbert de Ghent. Church, 4 mills.* Castle Hill mound; a pagan Saxon cemetery site; church with a Saxon tower and circular outside staircase.

Houghton *Hoc(h)tune/ Hog(e)tone: Colegrim from Abbot of Peterborough; Walter d'Aincourt; Fredgis and Abbot Thorold from Colegrim. 4 mills.* Houghton Farm.

Howell *Huuelle/Welle: King's land; Bishop of Lincoln; Gilbert de Ghent; Colsuan; Colegrim. Church, and a mill (with Ewerby Thorpe, etc.).* Partly Norman church with an Anglo-Saxon slab.

Howsham *Usun: King's land; Count Alan.*

Humberston *Humbrestone: Ivo Tailbois.* Small seaside town.

Humby *Humbi: Walter d'Aincourt.*

Hundleby *Hundelbi: Bishop of Durham; Ivo Tailbois. Church, mill.* Adjoining Spilsby.

Hundon *Humendone/ Hunidune:* Lost.

Hungerton *Hungretune: Robert de Tosny.*

HUTTOFT: *Church font; the decoration shows the 12 apostles.*

Huttoft *Hoto(f)t: Earl Hugh; Alfred of Lincoln and Dodo and Bernard from him; Chetelbern from the king.* Evidence of a submerged prehistoric forest on the beach.

Immingham *Imungeham/ Mingeham: William de Percy; Norman d'Arci.* Port.

Ingham *Ingeham/Lagerham: Bishop of Bayeux and Ilbert from him; Bishop of Lincoln and Erchenold from him; Mainard from Roger de Poitou; Colsuan and Roger and Anschitil from him; Gocelin FitzLanbert; Rayner de Brimou; Ernuin from the king and queen.*

Ingleby *Englebi: Bishop of Bayeux and Colsuan and Wadard from him; Berengar from Robert de Tosny; William de Percy.*

Ingoldsby *Goldesbi/Ingoldesbi: Gilbert de Ghent; Walter d'Aincourt; Robert Malet; Colegrim, the pre-Conquest holder; Aschil from the king in alms. Church.* Church with Norman arches.

HORNCASTLE: *Ironwork against sober brown brick.*

Irby upon Humber *Irebi/Iribi: Earl Hugh; Ivo Tailbois and Odo from him; Durand Malet. Church.* Church with Norman arcades and font, and an engraved 15th-century floorstone showing John Malet and his wife.

Irnham *Gerneham/Greneham: Alfred of Lincoln; Ralph Pagnell. Church.*

Itterby *Itrebi: Bishop of Bayeux and Ilbert from him; Waldin the Engineer and William from him.*

Keddington *Cadinton(e)/Caditon: Bishop of Durham and Turstin from him; Rayner de Brimou and Baldwin from him. Church, 5½ mills.* Church with late Norman work.

Keelby *Chelebi/Chilebi: King's land; Archbishop of York and William from him; Bishop of Bayeux and Wadard from him; Ranulf from Bishop of Lincoln; Ivo Tailbois and Neal from him; Drogo de Beuvriere and Robert from him; Norman d'Arci and Geoffrey from him; Waldin the Engineer and William from him. 1½ mills, salt-pan.*

Keisby *Chisebi: Gilbert de Ghent; Guy de Craon; Sortebrand.*

Kelby *Chelebi/Chillebi: Bishop of Durham and Almod from him; Bishop of Lincoln and Colegrim from him; Guy de Craon and Aschil the priest from him.*

Kelstern *Cheilestorne/Chelestorne/turne: Earl Hugh; Alfred of Lincoln; Waldin the Engineer.* Bronze Age barrows.

Ketsby *Chetelesbi: Earl Hugh and Hugh from him. Mill.*

Kettleby *Chetelbi: Drogo de Beuvriere and Rayner from him; Ernis de Burun and Turstin from him; Geoffrey Alselin.* Kettleby House.

Kettleby Thorpe *Torp: Hugh FitzBaldric and Gilber from him.* Kettleby Thorpe Farm.

Kexby *Cheftesbi: Bishop of Lincoln, Colsuen and Adeleln from him; Leduin from the king. Mill.*

Killingholme *Chelvingeholm(e)/Chelvingehou: Count Alan and Landric from him; Ivo Tailbois and Odo from him; Drogo de Beuvriere, Norman d'Arci. ½ mill.* Now 2 villages, North and South Killingholme.

Kingerby *Chenebi: Bishop of Bayeux; Gocelin from Bishop of Lincoln. Church, mill.* Hall; church with circular windows, possibly Saxon.

Kingthorpe *Chinetorp: Ivo Tailbois and Odo from him; Ernis de Burun; Rayner de Brimou.*

Kirkby Green *Cherchebi: Walter d'Aincourt; Norman d'Arci; Heppo the Arblaster. Church, 6½ mills (with Scopwick).*

Kirkby la Thorpe *Cherchebi/Chirchebi: King's land; Bishop of Durham and Alnod from him; Gilbert de Ghent. ½ church (with Silk Willoughby).* Church with Anglo-Saxon interlace work.

Kirkby on Bain *Cherchebi/Chirchebi: Bishop of Durham; Bishop of Bayeux and Ilbert from him; Eudo FitzSpirwic. Mill-site.*

Kirkby Underwood *Cherchebi: Count Alan and Godric from him; Robert de Tosny; Alfred of Lincoln and Offram, the pre-Conquest holder, from him.* Anglo-Saxon work in the church.

Kirmington *Chernitone: King's land; Count Alan; Hugh FitzBaldric; Drogo de Beuvriere and Robert from him.* Humberside airport.

Kirmond le Mire *Cheuremont: William de Percy. Church, mill.*

Kirton (in Holland) *Cher/Chirchetune: Count Alan and Toli from him; Guy de Craon. Church, 2 salt-pans.* Fine church.

Kirton in Lindsey *Chircheton(e)/Circeton: King's land. Mill.* Small town.

Knaith *Cheneide: Bishop of Lincoln. Priory.* Birthplace of Thomas Sutton (1532–1611), founder of Charterhouse School.

Laceby *Lenesbi/Levesbi: Bishop of Bayeux; William de Percy; Drogo de Beuvriere. 3 churches, 2 mills.* Church with Norman work.

Langtoft *Langetof: Abbot of Croyland. Marsh.* Between Roman Carr Dyke and a Roman road.

Langton (near Horncastle) *Langetone: King's land; Bishop of Bayeux; Drogo de Beuvriere and Geoffrey from him. Mill (with Langton Thorpe, later Buckland).*

Langton (near Spilsby) *Langetune: Earl Hugh. 9 mills (with Brinkhill, etc.).*

Langton by Wragby *Langetone: Bishop of Durham; Gilbert de Ghent; Ernis de Burun; Robert the Steward; Waldrin the Engineer.*

Laughton (near Avethorpe) *Loctune: Robert de Tosny; Gilbert de Ghent; Oger le Breton; Guy de Craon and Warner from him. Church.*

Laughton (near Blyton) *Lac(es)tone/Tastone/Leston: Roger de Poitou and Blancard from him; Guy de Craon and Alfred from him. ½ mill.*

Laythorpe *Ledulvethorpe: Bishop of Lincoln; Colsuan and Conded and Anchitil from him. ½ church.* Some houses.

Lea *Lea: Count Alan and Robert from him. Fishery, ferry.*

Leadenham *Ledeneham: Count Alan and Colegrim and Derinc from him. 2 churches, ½ mill (with Fulbeck).* Church with Renaissance glass.

Leasingham *Lessingham/Leuesingham: Bishop of Lincoln and Adam from him; Geoffrey Alselin.* Expanding.

Legbourne *Lecheburne: Earl Hugh; Roger de Poitou and Gerard from him.*

Legsby *Lagesbi: William de Percy and Evrard from him. Mill.*

Lenton *Lavintone: Archbishop of York and Ranulf, the archbishop's clerk, from him; Guy de Craon; Gilbert de Ghent and Azelin from him.* Formerly Lavington.

Leverton *Levretune: Count Alan. Church.*

Lincoln *Lincolia(e): King's land; main landholders include: Bishop Remigius; Ralph Pagnell; Earl Hugh; Countess Judith; Gilbert de Ghent. Colsuan. At least 3 churches; 166 dwellings destroyed to clear a site for the castle.* County town and cathedral city built on Roman site; castle built by William I.

Linwood *Lindude: Alfred of Lincoln; Durand Malet. ⅓ church, mill.*

Lissington *Lessintone: Archbishop of York and Herbert from him.*

Little Carlton *Carleton(e): William de Percy and Osbern from him. Church, 2 mills.* Mill.

Little Coates *Sudcotes: Bishop of Bayeux; Drogo de Beuvriere.* Part of Grimsby.

Little Gonerby *Gunfordebi:* Lost.

Little Grimsby *Grimesby: Bishop of Durham; Ivo Tailbois and Geoffrey from him; William de Percy and Fulk from him. Church, salt-pan.*

Little Lavington *Parva Lavintune:* Lost.

Little Limber *Linbergham: King's land; Norman d'Arci.*

Little Ponton *Alia Pamtone/Pamptune/Parva Pantone: Drogo de Beuvriere; Countess Judith and Nigel from her. 4 mills.* Towerless church, possibly of Saxon origin.

Little Steeping *Stepi(nge): Count Alan and Eudo from him; Ivo Tailbois. Church, 4 mills.*

Little Sturton *Stratone:* Lost.

LINCOLN: *One of England's most magnificent cathedrals.*

Lobingham *Lobingeham:* Lost.

Lobthorpe *Lopintorp: Bishop of Lincoln; Algar, the pre-Conquest holder, from the king.*

Londonthorpe *Lunde(r)torp: King's land; Bishop Osmund of Salisbury; Colegrim. Mill.* Tower mill.

Long Bennington *Beninctun/Beningtone: Count Alan and Hervey from him; William de Warenne. Church, 4 mills.* Church with some Norman work.

Long Sutton *Sudtone: King's land.* Small market town.

Lound (in Toft) *Lund: Gilbert de Ghent and Berewold from him. Church, 2 mills (with Witham on the Hill, Manthorpe and Toft).*

Louth *Lude(s):* See page 165.

Ludborough *Ludeburg: Robert de Tosny and Berengar from him.*

Luddington *Ludintone: Geoffrey de La Guerche.*

Ludford Magna *Lude(s)forde: Ivo Tailbois and Odo from him; William de Percy; Hugh FitzBaldric; Rayner de Brimou. Mill.*

Lusby *Luzebi: Gilbert de Ghent and William from him. Church, mill.* Water mill; Anglo-Saxon and Norman work in the church.

Lutton *Luctone: King's land. Fishery.* Once a market town.

Mablethorpe *Malbertorp/Mal(te)torp: Earl Hugh; Gilbert de Ghent; Rayner de Brimou. 20 salt-pans (with Calceby, etc.).* Holiday resort.

Maidenwell *Welle: Earl Hugh. Salt-pan.*

Maltby (in Raithby) *Maltebi: Earl Hugh.*

Maltby le Marsh *Maltebi/-by/Maltesbi: Eudo from Count Alan; Gilbert de Ghent; Hugh FitzBaldric; Gocelin FitzLanbert and Eurold from him.*

Manby (in Broughton) *Mannebi: Durand Malet.* Manby Wood.

Manby (near Stewton) *Mannebi: King's land.* Late Anglo-Saxon slab in the church.

Manthorpe (near Witham on the Hill) *Mannetor(p): Abbot of Peterborough and Ansfrid and Asfort from him; Gilbert de Ghent and Berewold from him. Church, 2 mills (with Lound, etc.).*

Manton *Malmetune/Mameltune: Abbot of Peterborough and Ralph from him.* Manor farm.

Mareham (in Burton) *Marram: Guy de Craon.* Lost; village site marked by a 9-acre moated enclosure and Mareham Lane.

Mareham le Fen *Marun: King's land. Church.* Manor house; thatched church.

Mareham on the Hill *Meringhe: Robert the Steward.*

Markby *Marche(s)bi: Bishop of Bayeux; Earl Hugh; Gocelin FitzLanbert.* Scattered.

Market Rasen *Altera Rase: Alfred of Lincoln. Mill (with Osgodby, etc.).* Town.

Market Stainton *Staintone: Ranulf de St Valery. 2 mills.*

Marston *Heveston(e)/tune: Count Alan; Colsuan; Alfred of Lincoln; Osbern the Priest and Ralph the Sewer; Guy de Craon and Osbert from him. 4 mills, mill-site.* Tudor Marston Hall owned by the Thorold family since the 14th century.

Martin (near Horncastle) *Martune: Bishop of Durham; Eudo FitzSpirwic.*

Marton *Martone: Count Alan.* Church with Saxon and Norman work.

Mavis Enderby *Endrebi: Bishop of Durham; Ivo Tailbois; Eudo FitzSpirwic. ½ mill-site (with Raisby near Hundleby).*

Melton Ross *Medeltone: Ernis de Burun. Church.* Moated site.

Messingham *Messingeham: Bishop of Lincoln and Malger from him; Abbot of Peterborough and William from him; Ernis de Burun and Turstin from him. 2 mills.* On the outskirts of Scunthorpe.

Metheringham *Medric(h)esham: Earl Hugh; Walter d'Aincourt and Wintrehad from him; Robert of Stafford and Enelo from him; Sortebrand from the king. Church, 3 mills.* Church with a Norman tower.

Middle Rasen *Rasa: Bishop of Bayeux and Wadard the bishop's man from him; Roger de Poitou; Alfred of Lincoln; Gocelin FitzLanbert; Ralph Pagnell; Durand Malet. Church.* Partly Norman church.

Miningsby *Melingesbi: Ivo Tailbois.*

Minting *Mentinghes/Duo Mentinghes: Ivo Tailbois; William the Priest from Countess Judith.*

Moorby *Morebi: King's land. Church.* Manor farm.

Morton (near Gainsborough) *Mortum/Mottune: King's land; Ivo Tailbois. Moors.* Adjoining Gainsborough.

Morton (near Hanthorpe) *Mortun(e): Gilbert de Ghent; Oger le Breton; Heppo the Arblaster. Church.*

Moulton *Multune: Ivo Tailbois; Guy de Craon.* Green.

Muckton *Machetone: Ansgot. Church.* Manor farm.

Mumby *Mund(e)bi: Count Alan and Eudo from him; Gilbert de Ghent; Eudo FitzSpirwic.* Manor house.

Navenby *Navenebi: Durand Malet.* Near Roman Ermine Street; evidence of the original Roman settlement.

Nettleham *Eteleham/Netelham: King's land, formerly Queen Edith; Gilbert de Ghent.* Expanding small town. The bishops of Lincoln had a palace here until the 17th century; the mounds remain.

Nettleton *Neteltone: Bishop of Bayeux and Ernegis and Wadard from him; Roger de Poitou and Blancard from him; Ernis de Burun; Durand Malet; Leueva, a woman, the pre-Conquest holder, from the king. Church, 9 mills.* Manor farm; ironstone church with Saxon tower and Norman work.

Newball *Neuberie: Earl Hugh and Osbern from him.*

Newsham *Neuhuse: King's land; Ivo Tailbois and Roger from him; Ernis de Burun. Mill, salt-pan (with Habrough).* Newsham Lodge and Bridge.

Newton (near Folkingham) *Neutone: Bishop of Durham; Ulviet and his wife from the king; Colsuan and Ralph from him; Odo the Arblaster. Church.* With Norman work.

Newton (near Toft) *Neutone: Bishop of Bayeux and Ilbert from him; Rayner de Brimou; Justen, the pre-Conquest holder, from the king.*

Newton upon Trent *Neutone: Archbishop of York.* Cast-iron toll bridge, 1832, across the River Trent.

Nocton *Nochetune: Norman d'Arci. Church.* In Nocton Wood is the site of a priory founded by Norman's son, Robert.

Normanby (in Burton upon Stather) *Normanebi: Drogo de Beuvriere and Gocelin from him; Guy de Craon and Alfred from him. Mill-site.*

Normanby (near Fillingham) *Normanebi/Normanestou: Bishop of Bayeux and Ilbert from him; Ivo Tailbois; Gocelin FitzLanbert and Colsuan from him. Church, 2 mills.* Church with Norman work.

Normanby (in Stow) *Normanebi: Bishop of Lincoln.*

Normanby le Wold *Normane(s)bi: Ivo Tailbois and Hugh from him; Gocelin FitzLanbert; Drogo de Beuvriere and Colsuan from him. 2 churches, ¼ mill (with Claxby).*

Normanton *Normenton: Robert de Vessey.*

North Cadeby *Cadebi: Count Alan.* Remains of Cadby Hall; site of ancient Cadby village.

North Carlton *Nortcarletone: Sortebrand from the king. Church.*

North Hykeham *Northicam/Northniche: Count Alan and Colegrim from him; Baldwin the Fleming from the king. Mill.* Suburb of Lincoln.

North Kelsey *Chelsi/Norchelsei/Nortchelesei: King's land; Count Alan; Norman from William de Percy. Mill.*

North Kyme *Nortchime: Robert de Tosny and Ivo from him; Colsuan. Fishery.* Fenland.

North Ormsby *Ormesbi: Bishop of Lincoln; Ivo Tailbois and Wimund from him; Drogo de Beuvriere and Geoffrey from him.*

North Stoke *Notrstoches: King's land; Colegrim from Drogo de Beuvriere. 2 mills (with South Stoke).* Stoke Rochford.

North Thoresby *Toresbi: Bishop of Bayeux and Ilbert from him; Count Alan; Hugh FitzBaldric; Alfred of Lincoln and Durand Malet (a salt-pan each). 2 salt-pans, 23 salt-pans (with Authby).* Medieval church with one of the county's oldest Anglo-Saxon carved stones.

Northorpe *Torp: King's land; Bishop of Bayeux and Ilbert from him; Abbot of Peterborough; Roger de Poitou and Roger from him.*

North Willingham *Wifilingham/Wivilingeham: Ivo Tailbois; Gocelin FitzLanbert; Ralph Pagnell.*

North Witham *Nortwine: Archbishop of York and Walchelin, the archbishop's man, from him; Countess Judith. Church, mill-site.*

Norton Disney *Nortune: Countess Judith.* Fortified Roman villa site.

Oasby *Asedebi: Gilbert de Ghent.*

Obthorpe *Ope(s)torp: Ivo Tailbois; Gilbert de Ghent.*

Old Leake *Leche: Count Alan. 41 salt-pans.* Market gardening and potato growing.

Old Sleaford *Eslaforde: Bishop of Lincoln; Abbot of Ramsey. Church, 8 mills.* Sleaford Lodge.

Old Somerby *Sum(m)erdebi: King's land; Walter d'Aincourt and Reynald from him; Guy de Craon and Godwin from him; Torchil from the king. Church.* Church with a Norman chancel arch.

Orford *Erforde: Guy de Craon and Alfred from him. Mill (with Binbrook).* Orford House.

Osbournby *Esbernebi/Osbern(ed)bi: Gilbert de Ghent; Guy de Craon and Vitalis from him. Church (with Willoughby in the Marsh).* Flat-topped church steeple; Norman font.

Osgodby (in Bardney): Lost.

Osgodby (near West Rasen) *Osgote(s)bi/Summerlede: Bishop of Bayeux; Ivo Tailbois; Roger de Poitou and Geoffrey from him; Gocelin FitzLanbert; Ralph Pagnell; Seward and Siward the priest from the king. Mill, another mill (with Tealby), another mill (with Market Rasen, Walesby and Otby).* Osgodby Moor.

Osgodby (in Lenton) *Osgotebi: Abbot of Peterborough before and after 1066 and Anschitil from him; Sortebrand.* Manor farm.

Otby *Ote(s)bi: Ivo Tailbois and Geoffrey from him; Roger de Poitou. Mill (with Osgodby near West Rasen).* Farm.

Ouseby *Ulvesbi/Uuesbi*: Lost.

Owersby *Aresbi/Oresbi: Bishop of Bayeux and Wadard from him; Bishop of Lincoln and Gocelin from him; Roger de Poitou; William de Percy; Norman d'Arci and Geoffrey from him; Siward the priest from the king. Church, 3 mills.* Now 2 hamlets, North and South Owersby.

Owmby (near Fillingham) *Dunebi/Dune(s)bi: Bishop of Bayeux and Ilbert and Wadward from him; Bishop of Lincoln; Ivo Tailbois and Peter from him; Gocelin FitzLanbert and Colsuan from him.* Roman coins were found nearby.

Owmby (in Searby) *Odenebi: King's land; Count Alan; William de Percy and William from him. Mill.*

Owston *Ostone: Geoffrey de La Guerche. 3 fisheries.* Earthworks of Kinnards Castle, destroyed in 1173.

Oxcombe *Oxecume/Oxetune: Bishop of Durham; Earl Hugh.*

Panton *Pantone: Archbishop of York and Gilbert from him; Ernis de Burun. Church.* Roman road nearby.

Partney *Partenai/Partene: Gilbert de Ghent; Robert the Steward. Market.* Anglo-Saxon barrow nearby.

Pickworth *Picheu(o)rde/Pichewordé: Bishop of Durham and Gocelin from him; Gilbert de Ghent; Colsuan and William from him. Church.* Church with medieval wall paintings.

Pilham *Pileham: King's land.*

Pinchbeck *Picebech/Pincebec: Ivo Tailbois; Guy de Craon. 4 fisheries (1500 eels).* Small town in a bulb-growing area.

Pointon *Pochinton(e)/Podintone: Count Alan; Gilbert de Ghent; Colsuan and Conded from him; Gunfrid de Chocques; Guy de Craon and Warner from him.*

Potter Hanworth *Haneworde: Walter d'Aincourt and a knight from him. Church.*

NORTH KYME: *Fenland dykes keep peat dry with sluices and pumps to provide agricultural land.*

Quadring *Quadheueringe/Ouedhaueringe: Bishop of Lincoln; Guert from Count Alan. 2 salt-pans.*

Quarrington *Corninctone/-tune/Cornintone: King's land; Bishop of Lincoln and Osmund and Hugh Rufus from him; Abbot of Ramsey. 2 churches, and a mill (with Ewerby Thorpe, etc.).*

Raithby (near Hundleby) *Radebi: Bishop of Durham; Ivo Tailbois; Eudo FitzSpirwic. Church, mill. Mill-site and ½ mill site (with Mavis Enderby).*

Raithby (near Louth) *Radresbi: Earl Hugh.*

Ranby *Randebi: Bishop of Bayeux; Ranulf de St Valery. 2 churches, mill.* Church with a Norman chancel arch.

Rand *Rande: Ernis de Burun.* Site of an ancient village.

Rauceby Altera *Rosbi/Rosbi/Roscebi: Robert de Vessey; Robert of Stafford and Edelo from him; Bishop of Durham and Almod from him; Geoffrey Alselin. Church.* Now 2 villages, North and South Rauceby.

Ravendale Altera *Ravendale/Ravendal/Raven(e)dale: Bishop of Durham and Walbert from him; Bishop of Bayeux; Waldin the Engineer; Guy de Craon.* Now the hamlet of West Ravendale and the village of East Ravendale.

Raventhorpe *Ragenaltorp/Rageneltorp: Abbot of Peterborough and Ralph from him.* Raventhorpe Farm.

Reasby *Revesbi: King's land; Earl Hugh; William de Percy and Norman from him; Gocelin FitzLanbert.* Hall; moated site.

Redbourne *Radburne/Reburne: King's land; Bishop of Lincoln and the Canons of St Mary; Ivo Tailboirs; Colsuan; Gocelin FitzLanbert; Osbern d'Arcis; Odo the Arblaster; Heppo the Arblaster. Mill.* Hall once the home of the Dukes of St Albans, descendants of Nell Gwynn.

Reepham *Refa(i)m/Refam: Abbot of Peterborough; Colsuan; Ranulf de St Valery.*

Reston *Ristone: William de Percy and Osbern from him. Church, 2 mills.* Now 2 villages, North and South Reston.

Revesby *Resuesbi: Ivo Tailbois. 2 churches (with East Kirkby).* Round barrows; Revesby Abbey, built on the site of the 12th-century abbey, was the home of the naturalist Sir Joseph Banks, who accompanied Captain Cook on his voyage around the world, 1768–71.

Rigby *Ribi: Earl Hugh; Ralf, and Azelin from him; Roger de Poitou and Ernuin from him.*

Rigsby *Richesbi/Rig(h)esbi: Archbishop of York; Bishop of Bayeux and Losoard from him. Church.* Some houses; church with Norman features.

Ringstone *Ringesdene/dune*: Lost.

Rippingale *Reping(h)ale: Alfred of Lincoln and Dodin from him; Oger le Breton; Guy de Craon and Widwald from him. ⅓ church.* Traces of Ringstone village, now lost, nearby.

Risby (in Roxby) *Risebi: Abbot of Peterborough and Ralph from him; Roger de Bully; Gilbert de Ghent and Robert from him. Church (with Appleby, etc.).* Now 2 hamlets, High and Low Risby.

Risby (in Walesby) *Risebi: Bishop of Bayeux.* Scattered houses.

Riseholme *Risun: Colsuan from Abbot of Peterborough; Gilbert de Ghent; Colsuan and Mathew from him; Church of St Michael from the king. 2 mills.* Romano-British burial barrow nearby.

Ropsley *Ripeslai/Ropeslai: Robert de Tosny and Ivo from him. Church.* Sailless windmill; partly Norman church with Anglo-Saxon traces.

Rothwell *Rodewelle/Rodowelle: Bishop of Bayeux; Alfred of Lincoln and Gleu from him; Durand Malet. Church, salt-pan, 2 mills.* A stream runs through the main street; church with a Saxon tower and Norman arcades.

Roughton *Rocstune: king's land; Robert the Steward. Fishery.*

Rowston *Rouestune: Geoffrey Alselin.*

Roxby *Roscebi/Roxebi: Gilbert de Ghent: Norman d'Arci; Ralph Pagnell.* Roman pavement; church with a Saxon window.

Roxholm *Rochesham: Alfred of Lincoln; Geoffrey Alselin.* Some houses and 2 halls.

Ruckland *Rocheland: Earl Hugh and Brisard from him. Church, mill.*

Ruskington *Reschintone/Rischintone: Drogo de Beuvriere; Geoffrey Alselin and Ralph from him. Church, 3 mills.* Church with Norman work.

Saleby *Salebi/by: Gilbert de Ghent; Hugh FitzBaldric.* Moated Saleby Manor, now a farm.

Salmonby *Salmundebi: Earl Hugh. 9 mills (with Brinkhill, etc.).*

Saltfleetby *Salflatebi: King's land; Bishop of Durham; Alfred of Lincoln and William from him; Rayner de Brimou; William Blunt. Ship toll.* Now 3 villages, Saltfleetby All Saints, St Clements and St Peter.

Santon *San(c)tone: Roger de Bully; Gilbert de Ghent; Guy de Craon and Alfred from him.* Farmsteads of High and Low Stanton.

Sapperton *Sapretone: King's land; Ivo Tailbois. Church (with Braceby).*

Sawcliffe *Saleclif: Abbot of Peterborough and Ralph from him; Roger de Bully; Gilbert de Ghent and Robert from him. Church (with Appleby, etc.), another church.* Sawcliffe Farm.

Saxby All Saints *Saxebi: Ivo Tailbois and Roger from him. 3 fisheries.*

Saxby (near Fillingham) *Sassebi: King's land; Eudo FitzSpirwic. 2 mills.*

Scamblesby *Scamelesbi: Ivo Tailbois.*

Scampton *Scanton(e)/tune: Gilbert de Ghent; Church, mill.*

Scartho *Scarhou: Bishop of Bayeux. 3 churches, 2 mills (with Bradley and Laceby).* Suburb of Grimsby; church with a Saxon tower.

Scawby *Scal(l)ebi: Ivo Tailbois; Colsuan and Alfred from him; Gocelin FitzLanbert and Baldric from him; Ralph Pagnell; Osbern d'Arcis; Durand Malet; Odo the Arblaster.*

Scopwick *Scap(e)uic/Scapewic: Walter d'Aincourt; Norman d'Arci; Heppo the Arblaster. Church, 6½ mills (with Kirkby Green).*

Scothern *Sco(l)torne/Scotstorne: Abbot of Peterborough; Ilbert de Lacy; Colsuan; Norman d'Arci; Ranulf de St Valery. Church, mill.*

Scotter *Scot(e)re: Abbot of Peterborough, formerly Aschil from King Edward. Mill and part of 2 mills, 2 fisheries.* Once a market town. Its church was given to Peterborough Abbey by the King of Mercia in the 7th century; some Saxon work remains.

Scotterthorpe *Scaltorp: Abbot of Peterborough.*

Scottlethorpe *Scache(r)torp: Robert de Tosny; Guy de Craon.*

Scotton *Scotone/tune: Abbot of Peterborough and Richard from him; Ivo Tailbois and Gocelin from him; Roger de Poitou; Guy de Craon. Mill-site.*

Scott Willoughby *Wilgebi: Gilbert de Ghent; Guy de Raimbeaucourt; Guy de Craon. Church.*

Scredington *Scredinctun/intune: Gilbert de Ghent; Robert of Stafford and Gulfered from him. Church.* 5 moated sites, 3 with water; 2-arched packhorse bridge.

Scrivelsby *Scriv(v)elesbi: King's land; Robert the Steward. Church, mill.* Deer park. The lord of the manor has the right, granted by William the Conqueror, to act as Grand Champion of England; a standard bearer at coronations.

Scremby *Screnbi: Bishop of Durham and Fenchel, the pre-Conquest holder, from him; Gilbert de Ghent; Eudo FitzSpirwic. Church.*

Scunthorpe *Escumetorp: King's land; Abbot of Peterborough.* Large industrial town.

Searby *Seurebi/Sourebi: King's land; Count Alan; Durand Malet. Church, mill.*

Sedgebrook *Sechebroc: Robert Malet. 3 mills.*

Sempringham *S(e)pingeham/Stepingeham: Robert de Tosny; Gilbert de Ghent; Alfred of Lincoln and Gocelin from him. Church (with Aslackby).* Fishponds; well. St. Gilbert, son of a Norman knight called Jocelin, was born here in 1083 and founded a priory in 1131; traces of the foundations remain.

SCARTHO: *The Saxon tower with double windows and simple but elegant proportions.*

Sibsey *Sibolci: Ivo Tailbois. Church.* Church with a Norman nave and doorway.

Silk Willoughby *Wilgebi: Bishop of Durham and Almod from him; Bishop of Lincoln and Ralph from him; Gilbert de Ghent; Waldin le Breton; Odo the Arblaster and Colegrim from him; Robert of Stafford and Godwin from him. Church, and ½ church (with Kirkby la Thorpe.* Manor House Farm; Bull mound; church with a Norman font.

Sixhills *Sisse: Bishop of Bayeux and Ilbert from him; Roger de Poitou; Rayner de Brimou. Church.*

Skegness *Tric: Count Alan; Eudo FitzSpirwic; Robert the steward.* Large seaside resort.

Skellingthorpe *Scheldingchope/Schellingop: Baldwin the Fleming.*

Skendleby *Scheueldebi: Gilbert de Ghent. Church, 2 mills.* Giant's Barrow, built 1800 BC, nearby.

Skidbrooke *Sc(h)itebroc: King's land; Bishop of Durham and St Calais from him; William Blunt.* Once a thriving port, now a mile from the sea.

Skillington *Schellintune/Schillintone/tune: King's land; Archbishop of York and Walchelin and Osbern from him; Guy de Craon; Carle, the pre-Conquest holder, from the king. ½ church, mill.* Green; Saxon masonry and Norman columns in the church.

Skinnand *Schinende: Robert of Stafford and Colegrim from him.* House; manor farm.

Skirbeck *Sc(h)irebec: Count Alan; Eudo FitzSpirwic. 2 churches, 2 fisheries.* Part of Boston.

Sloothby *Lodeby/Slodebi: Bishop of Durham; Ivo Tailbois; Gilbert de Ghent; Hugh FitzBaldric and Guy his son-in-law from him.*

Snarford *Snardesforde/Sner(t)eforde/Suardesforde: Bishop of Durham and Colsuan from him; Mainard and Thorald from Roger de Poitou; Ralph Pagnell.* Farm.

Snelland *Esnelent/Snelesunt: Archbishop of York; William de Percy and Waldin from him; Gocelin FitzLanbert and Rayner from him.* Farmland.

Snitterby *Esnetrebi/Snetrebi: King's land; Ivo Tailbois; Gocelin FitzLanbert; Heppo the Arblaster.*

Somerby (in Corringham) *Sum(m)erdebi/Summertebi: King's land; Count Alan; Ivo Tailbois; Geoffrey de La Guerche.*

Somerby (near Howsham) *Sum(m)ertebi: Earl Hugh; William de Percy.*

Somercotes *Summercotes: King's land; Roger de Poitou; Rayner de Brimou; Ilbert de Lacey from Bishop of Bayeux. Mill.* Now 2 villages, North and South Somercotes.

Somersby *Summerdebi: Gocelin FitzLanbert. ½ mill.* Birthplace of Alfred, Lord Tennyson (1809–92).

Somerton *Summertune: Alfred of Lincoln and Gocelin from him.* Ruined Somerton Castle.

Sotby *Sotebi: Bishop of Bayeux and Ralph from him. Church.* Norman chancel arch in the church.

South Cadeby *Catebi: Bishop of Durham and Turstin from him; Roger de Poitou; Alfred of Lincoln and William from him; William Blunt.* Cadeby Hall.

South Carlton *Carletone/tune: Bishop of Bayeux and Ralph the Sewer and Gilbert de Ghent from him; Colsuan and Mathew, Colsuan's man, from him; Sortebrand from the king.*

South Ferriby *Berebi: Gilbert Tison and Anschitil from him. Church, mill.* Small busy town. Chalk and limestone cliffs provide material for its cement and tile industry.

South Hykeham *Hicham: Baldwin the Fleming. 3 fisheries.*

South Kelsey *Colesi: King's land; Roger de Poitou and Roger from him.*

South Kyme *Chime: King's land; Gilbert de Ghent and Egbriht from him. 2 churches, 6 fishponds, 3 fisheries.* Church with some Saxon work.

South Ormsby *Ormesbi: Archbishop of York; Earl Hugh; Norman d'Arcis and Herbert from him. Mill.*

Southorpe (in Edenham) *Sudtorp:* Lost.

Southorpe (in Northorne) *Altera Torp: King's land; Roger de Poitou.* Some houses.

Southrey *Sudtrie/Sutrei(e): Bishop of Bayeux; Bishop of Lincoln and Osbern his clerk from him; Roger de Poitou; Gilbert de Ghent. 2 fisheries.*

South Stoke *Sudstoches: King's land. 2 mills (with North Stoke).* Laid out by William Burn in Tudor style in the mid-19th century.

South Thoresby *Toresby: Earl Hugh. 6 mills (with Belleau, etc.).*

Southwell *Sudwelle:* Lost.

South Willingham *Archbishop of York and William from him; Bishop of Bayeux; Rayner de Brimou.*

South Witham *Widme Wim(m)e: Alfred of Lincoln and Gleu, Alfred's man, from him; Countess Judith; Ernuin the priest from the king in alms. 1½ churches.*

Spalding *Spallinge:* See page 160.

Spanby *Spane(s)bi: Colsuan; Oger le Breton.*

Spilsby *Spilesbi: Bishop of Durham. 2 mills (with Eresby, etc.).* Town.

Spittlegate *Nongetune/Nongtone: King's land; St Wlfrann of Grantham from Bishop Osmund of Salisbury. Mill.* Part of Grantham; Spittlegate Farm.

Spridlington *Sperlin(c)tone/Spredelintone: Count Alan; Colsuan.*

Springthorpe *Springetorp: King's land. Church (with Corringham).* Church with a Saxon tower.

Stainby *Stigandebi: Alfred of Lincoln.*

Stainfield (in Hacconby) *Steintone/Stentuith: Oger le Breton; Heppo the Arblaster. Church, mill.* Site of a Roman settlement.

Stainfield (near Lincoln) *Stain/Steinfelde: William de Percy.*

Stainton (near Lincoln) *Staintune: Earl Hugh and Osbern from him. Mill.* Roman road nearby.

Stainton (in Waddingham) *Sta(i)ntone:* Lost.

Stainton le Vale *Stainton(e): William de Percy and Alulf from him; Hugh FitzBaldric; Drogo de Beuvriere and Geoffrey from him; Rayner de Brimou. Mill, 2 mill-sites.* Manor farm.

Stallingborough *Stalin(ge)burg/Stanlingeburg: Archbishop of York and Herbert from him; Bishop of Bayeux; Hugh FitzBaldric; Norman d'Arci. ½ church, 3½ mills, 2 sites, 4½ salt-pans, ½ slaughter-house.* The Mercian King Offa is thought to have held his court here 12 centuries ago. The church has a monument to Anne Askew, martyred at the stake in 1546 for nonconformity; she wanted a divorce.

Stamford *Stanford: King's land, formerly Queen Edith; Brand; Ulchetel FitzMerwine; Hugh Musard; Eudo the Sewer; Gunfrid de Chocques; Countess Judith; Abbot of Peterborough; Alfred; Guy de Raimbeaucourt. 4 churches, 3½ mills.* Town that became rich from the wool trade and was once the capital of the Fens. It has a fine market place, medieval gateway and a ruined Norman castle.

STAMFORD: *Stained glass in a medieval almshouse.*

Stapleford *Stapleforde: Bishop of Bayeux and Tor from him; Osbern from Countess Judith. Church.* Norman work in the church.

Steeping *Stepi(nge): Gilbert de Ghent; Count Alan; Ivo Tailbois; Robert the steward. 3 churches, 4 mills.* Now 2 villages, Great and Little Steeping.

Stenigot *Stangehou: Ivo Tailbois.*

Stenning *Stevenige: Count Alan and Geoffrey from him; Robert de Vessey. 8 salt-pans, fishery (200 eels).* Part of Swineshead; Estovening Hall.

Stenwith *Stanwald/walt: Robert Malet. Mill.* Lock on the Grantham Canal.

Stewton *Stiveton(e): Ilbert from Bishop of Bayeux; Alfred of Lincoln.*

Stickford *Stichesforde: Ivo Tailbois. Church.*

Stickney *Stichenai: Ivo Tailbois. Church.* Vegetable growing area.

Stixwold *Stigeswald(e)/walt: Ivo Tailbois; Alfred of Lincoln; Waldin le Breton. 2 fisheries.*

Stoke Rochford *Stoche(s): Count Alan and Colegrim from him; Drogo de Beuvriere. 4 mills.*

Stow (near Torksey) *Stou: Bishop of Lincoln and William de Percy from him; Count Alan; Ilbert de Lacey; Gilbert de Ghent, Gocelin FitzLanbert; Ralph de Mortimer (3 mansions). Church, 3 iron works.* Anglo-Saxon and Norman church; Stow Park. St Etheldreda is said to have stayed here.

Stow (in Threekingham) *Stou: Gilbert de Ghent and Robert from him. Church.*

Stowe *Estou:* Lost.

Stroxton *Stroustune: Drogo de Beuvriere and Guy, Archbishop Thomas, and Hugh de Grandmesnil from him. Church.* Manor farm; church with a Norman arch.

Strubby (in Langton by Wragby) *Strubi: Bishop of Bayeux; Ivo Tailbois; Roger de Poitou; Rainer de Brimou.* Strubby Hall.

Strubby (near Maltby le Marsh) *Strobi: Bishop of Bayeux; Count Alan; Gilbert de Ghent; Hugh FitzBaldric.* RAF station nearby.

Stubton *Stobetun/Stubetune: Norman d'Arci and Gamelin from him; Geoffrey Alselin. Church.*

Sturton (in Scawby) *Str(i)tone: Ivo Tailbois; Colsuan and Alfred from him; Ralph Pagnell; Osbern d'Arcis and Alfred his man from him; Durand Malet and Alfred his man from him.*

Sturton (near Torksey) *Stratone: Ilbert from Bishop of Bayeux.* Roman road.

Sudbrooke *Sudbroc/Sutbroc: Abbot of Peterborough; Colsuan; Colsuan from the king. Mill.* Suburb of Lincoln.

Surfleet *Suerefelt: Heppo the Arblaster. 2 salt-pans.*

Sutterby *Sutrebi: Earl Hugh.*

Sutton (in Great Sturton) *Sudtone: Lost.*

Sutton le Moor *Sudtone/Su(d)tune: Archbishop of York; Count Alan; Earl Hugh; Eudo FitzSpirwic; Chetelbern from the king.* Now Sutton on Sea, a seaside resort. Traces of Iron Age salt workings and other medieval traces by the sea shore indicate that the early village was submerged.

Swaby *Suabi: Earl Hugh. 6 mills (with Bellau, etc.).*

Swallow *Sualun: Archbishop of York; Bishop of Bayeux; Count Alan and Picot from him; Roger de Poitou and Wimund from him; Alfred of Lincoln.*

Swarby *Suarrebi: Odo the Arblaster; Guy de Craon and Vitalis from him. ½ church.* Green.

Swaton *Suavetone/Suavi(n)tone: Colsuan; Robert de Vessey; Guy de Craon and Warner from him.* Swaton Fen; moated site.

Swayfield *Suafeld: Bishop of Lincoln.*

Swinderby *Suindrebi/Sunderby: Countess Judith; Colegrim.* RAF station nearby.

Swine *Suine:* Lost.

Swinhope *Suinhope: Count Alan; Norman d'Arci; Odo the Arblaster. Mill.* Neolithic long barrows nearby.

Swinstead *Suamestede/Suinham/stede: Bishop of Lincoln, Walter d'Aincourt and Odo from him; Ralph Pagnell; Countess Judith; Ragenald, the pre-Conquest holder, from the king.*

Swinthorpe (in Snelland) *Sonetorp: King's land; Archbishop of York; Gocelin FitzLanbert.* Remote.

Syston *Sidestan/Sidestham: Ivo Tailbois; Guy de Raimbeaucourt. Church, 6 mills.* Park; church with a Norman tower.

Tallington *Talintone/tune: Robert de Tosny and William and Roger from him; Alfred of Lincoln. Mill.* Originally Saxon church.

Tathwell *Tadeswelle: Earl Hugh, formerly Earl Harold; Robert the Steward. Church, 3 mills.* Bronze Age barrows and a Neolithic long barrow nearby; originally Norman church.

Tattershall Thorpe *Torp: Bishop of Durham; Bishop of Bayeux; Eudo FitzSpirwic. 2¼ mills, 12 fisheries.*

Tealby *Tavele(s)bi: Bishop of Bayeux and Leosard from him; Ivo Tailbois; Roger de Poitou; Alfred of Lincoln; Gocelin FitzLanbert and Godard from him; Ralph Pagnell; Rayner de Brimou. 12 mills, another mill (with Osgodby), 3 mill-sites.*

Tetford *Tedforde/Tesforde: Archbishop of York and Gilbert from him; Earl Hugh; Gocelin FitzLanbert and Walter from him. Church, mill, 9 mills (with Brinkhill, etc.).* By Double Dyke.

TATTERSHALL THORPE: *The nearby castle was built by Lord Cromwell in the 15th c. as a fine residence, with magnificent fireplaces.*

Tetney *Tatenai: Ivo Tailbois. Mill, 13 salt-pans.* Artesian wells. An urn of Anglo-Saxon silver was unearthed here.

Thealby *Tedul(f)bi: King's land; Earl Hugh; Drogo de Beuvriere; Norman d'Arci. Market (with Burton on Stather, etc.).* Hall, quay.

Theddlethorpe *Te(d)lagestorp: Count Alan; Earl Hugh; Alfred of Lincoln; Chetelbern from the king. 20 salt-pans (with Calceby, etc.).* Now Theddle all Saints.

Thimbleby *Stimblebi/Stinblebi: King's land; Bishop of Bayeux; Drogo de Beuvriere and Geoffrey from him. Mill.* Conservation area.

Thonock *Tunec: Roger de Poitou.* Scattered. Large earthwork nearby, possibly a motte and bailey.

Thoresthorpe *Thuorestorp: Hugh FitzBaldric.*

Thoresway *Toreswe: Ivo Tailbois and Odo from him; Alfred of Lincoln. 2 mills.*

Thorganby *Togre(m)bi/Turgrebi/Turgrimbi: Bishop of Durham; Bishop of Bayeux; Ivo Tailbois and Odo from him; Robert de Tosny and Berengar from him; Norman d'Arci; Waldin the Engineer and William from him; Odo the Arblaster and Herbert from him; William Blunt. 5 mills, hall, 4 salt-pans.*

Thorley *Turlai:* Lost.

Thornton (near Horncastle) *Torintune: Robert the Steward. 2 mills.*

Thornton Curtis *Torentone/tune: Ernis de Burun and Ulric from him; Ralph de Mortimer. ½ mill (with Wooton and possibly Bonby).*

Thornton le Moor *Torentone/tun(e): Roger de Poitou; William de Percy.* Part of an Anglo-Saxon cross in the church.

Thorpe in the Fallows *Torp: Gilbert de Ghent; Uluiet and Alden the priest from the king. Church (with Aisthorpe).*

Thorpe on the Hill *Torp: King's land; Abbot of Westminster.* Near the Roman Fosse Way.

Thorpe St Peter *Torp: Bishop of Durham; Ivo Tailbois. Church, 2 mills (with Eresby, etc.).*

Threekingham *Triching(e)ham/heham: Bishop of Durham; Uluiet from the king; Abbot of Ramsey; Gilbert de Ghent and Guy de*

Craon from him; Colsuan. ½ mill, market. Named after a legendary 9th-century battle when 3 Danish kings were slain.

Thrunscoe *Ternesco(e)/Ternesc(r)ou: Archbishop of York; Bishop of Bayeux; Ivo Tailbois and Wimund from him.* Part of Cleethorpes.

Thurlby (near Norton Disney) *Turolfbi/Turolve(s)bi/Turulfbi: Odo the Arblaster; Countess Judith.* Church with some Saxon work.

Thurlby (near Bourne) *Torulfbi/Turolvebi: Abbot of Peterborough and Geoffrey from him; Alfred of Lincoln; Robert of Stafford.* On the Roman Carr Dyke.

Thurlby (near Cumberworth) *Torulvesbi: Earl Hugh.*

Timberland *Timberlunt/Timbrelund: Earl Hugh; Walter d'Aincourt; Norman d'Arci; Heppo the Arblaster and Simund from him.* By the Roman Carr Dyke.

Toft (near Bourne) *Toft: Ansfrid from Abbot of Peterborough; Gilbert de Ghent and Berewold from him. Church, 2 mills (with Lound, etc.).*

Toft next Newton *Tofte: Bishop of Bayeux and Wadard from him.* Tiny church with fragments of Saxon carving.

Torksey *Dorchesyg/Torchesey/-seyg/-sig/-siy/-syg: King's land, formerly Queen Edith; Berengar de Tosny; Roger de Bully. 11 fisheries (with Hardwick).* Once a Roman port. The canal has operated for more than 1000 years.

Torrington *Terintone: Alfred of Lincoln and Gocelin from him; Ernis de Burun; Roger de Poitou.* Now 2 hamlets, East and West Torrington.

Tothby *Touedibei: Bishop of Bayeux.* Tothby Manor, c.1565, with a plague stone on its lawn.

Tothill *Totele: Earl Hugh. 6 mills (with Belleau, etc.).*

Towthorpe *Tode/Tudetorp:* Lost.

Toynton *Tedintone/Tedlintune/Todintune: King's land; Earl Hugh.* Now 2 small villages, High and Low Toynton; manor farm.

Toynton *Totintun(e): Ivo Tailbois; Bishop of Durham. 2 churches.* Now 2 villages, Toynton All Saints and St Peter.

Trusthorpe *Dr(e)uistorp: Archbishop of York; Earl Hugh.* Seaside town with caravan sites.

Tumby *Tunbi: Eudo FitzSpirwic. 2 mills, 1½ fisheries.* Tumby Lawn, a house; the hamlet of Tumby Woodside.

Twyford *Tuiforde/Tuiuorde: Archbishop of York; Countess Judith.* Twyford Wood.

Tydd St Mary *Stith/Tid/Tite: King's land; Ivo Tailbois; Guy de Craon. Fishery, church.*

Uffington *Offinton(e)tune: Abbot of Peterborough and Geoffrey from him; Alfred of Lincoln and 9 burgesses of Stamford from him; Countess Judith. Church.*

Ulceby (near Well) *Ulesbi: Gilbert de Ghent; Rayner de Brimou.*

Ulceby (near Wooton) *Ulvesbi: Bishop of Lincoln and Ranulf from him; Odo from Norman d'Arci; Ernis de Burun; Hugh, the pre-Conquest holder, from the king. Church, ½ mill (500 eels).*

Upton *Opetune: Bishop of Lincoln.* Windmill.

Waddingham *Wading(e)ham: King's land; Bishop of Bayeux and Ilbert from him; Gocelin FitzLanbert; Heppo the Arblaster; Alden and Elfain from the king. Mill.* Green.

Waddington *Wadintone/tune: Earl Hugh, formerly Earl Harold. Church, 2 mills.* Town on the outskirts of Lincoln.

Waddingworth *Wa(l)dingurde: Bishop of Durham; Eudo FitzSpirwic.* Farmhouse. The church bell fell on the last Sunday before World War I, and again in 1939.

Wainfleet *Wenflet/Wemflet: Bishop of Durham; Earl Hugh; Gilbert de Ghent; Gocelin FitzLanbert; Eudo FitzSpirwic. 7 salt-pans, 20 salt-pans (with Calceby, etc.).* Market town of Wainfleet All Saints, once a port but now 5 miles from the sea; also the village of Wainfleet St Mary, with ancient salt-works.

Waithe *Wade: Bishop of Bayeux; Count Alan; Ivo Tailbois; Guy de Craon.* Church with an Anglo-Saxon central tower.

Walcot (near Folkingham) *Walecote: Abbot of Peterborough; Gilbert de Ghent. 1½ churches.* Church with Norman work.

Walcote (in Billinghay) *Walecote: Archbishop of York; Walter d'Aincourt.*

Walcote on Trent *Walecote: Ivo from Abbot of Peterborough; Earl Hugh; Norman d'Arci and Robert from him; Ernis de Burun.*

Walesby *Walesbi: Ivo Tailbois; Roger de Poitou; Rayner de Brimou and Baldwin from him. Mill (with Osgodby, etc.).* Roman villa site.

Walmsgate *Walmesgar: Earl Hugh.* A few farms; large barrows nearby.

Waltham *Waltham: Count Alan. Church, 2 salt-pans.* Town.

Washingborough *Washingburg: King's land.*

Waterton *Watretone: Geoffrey de La Guerche.* Waterton Hall.

Weelsby *Wivelesbi: Drogo de Beuvriere and Robert from him.* District of Grimsby.

Welbourn *Wellebrune: Robert Malet. Church, mill.*

Welby *Wellebi: King's land; Guy de Craon. Church.* Near the Roman Ermine Street.

Well *Welle: Bishop of Bayeux; Gilbert de Ghent and Ravemer from him. Mill.*

Wellingore *Wel(l)ingoure: King's land; Durand Malet. Church.* Expanding.

Welton (near Lincoln) *Welletone: Bishop of Lincoln and 6 canons from him.*

Welton le Marsh *Waletone/tune: Ivo Tailbois; Gilbert de Ghent; Gocelin FitzLanbert and Rayner from him.*

Welton le Wold *Welletone/tune: King's land; Bishop of Durham; Landric from Count Alan; Roger de Poitou; Ansgot. 2 mill-sites, mill, ¼ church.*

West Ashby *Aschebi: King's land; Gilbert de Ghent and Roger from him; William Tailbois; Chetelbern from the king. Mill.*

Westborough *Westburg: Geoffrey Alselin and Ralph. Church, 2 mills.* Site of a Roman settlement; church with Norman features and circular, possibly Anglo-Saxon, windows.

West Butterwick *Butrewic: Geoffrey de La Guerche. Mill.*

Westby *Westbi: Count Alan and Colegrim from him; Colsuan; Robert of Stafford and Basuin from him.*

West Deeping *Westdepinge: Godfrey de Cambrai. 4 mills.* Watermill.

West Halton *Haltone: Earl Hugh and William FitzNeal from him, formerly Earl Harold.*

West Keal *Cale/Westrecale: Ivo Tailbois; Eudo FitzSpirwic; Chetelbern from the king. Church, mill.*

Westlaby *Westledebi: Ivo Tailbois and Odo from him; William de Percy and Ralph from him.*

Westhorpe *Wes(t)orp: Walter d'Aincourt and Raynald from him. 3 mills.* Part of Old Somerby.

Weston *Westune: Ivo Tailbois; Guy de Craon.*

West Rasen *Rase: Bishop of Bayeux and Wimund from him; Ralph Pagnell. 2 mills.*

West Willoughby *Wilgebi: Robert de Vessey.* Willoughby Hall; Willoughby Heath.

Westwood *Westude: Geoffrey de La Guerche.* Now Westwoodside.

Whaplode *Copelade/Copolade: King's land; Abbot of Croyland; Count Alan and Landric from him; Guy de Craon.*

Wharton *Warton: Roger de Poitou.* Hall.

Whisby *Wizebi: Baldwin the Fleming.*

Whitton *Witenai: Henry de Ferrers and Saswolo from him.*

Wickenby *Wichingebi/Wighingesbi: King's land; William de Percy and Osbern and Robert from him; Gocelin FitzLanbert.*

Wilksby *Wilchesbi/Wilgesbi: King's land; Robert the Steward.*

WOOLSTHORPE MANOR: *Sir Isaac Newton's birthplace (1642).*

Willingham (near Torksey) *Welingeham/Wilingeham: Bishop of Bayeux and Ilbert from him; Bishop of Lincoln; Count Alan; Ilbert de Lacy; Gocelin FitzLanbert and Walo from him.* Now Willingham by Stow.

Willoughby in the Marsh *Wilgebi: Gilbert de Ghent and Rayner from him. Church (with Osbournby).* Bronze Age barrows; church with Saxon stones; birthplace of John Smith (1580–1631), founder of Virginia.

Willoughton *Wilchetone: Waldin the Engineer; Odo the Arblaster.* Roman and Anglo-Saxon relics. Old moats mark the site of an ancient priory.

Wilsford *Wivelesforde: Godfrey de Cambrai; Robert Malet. Church, mill.* Stone quarries on the Heath; Anglo-Saxon church nave.

Wilsthorpe *Wivelestorp: Ivo Tailbois and Odo from him. 2 mills.*

Winceby *Wi(n)zebi: Earl Hugh; Gocelin FitzLanbert and Walter from him. 9 mills (with Brinkhill, etc.).* Nature reserve.

Winteringham *Wintringeham: Gilbert de Ghent and Robert from him. Church, 3 mills, ferry, fishery site.* The remains of a possible Roman jetty lie under the river bed.

Winterton *Wintretune/Wintrintone/tune: King's land; Earl Hugh; Henry de Ferrers; Norman d'Arci; Ernis de Burun; Ralph Pagnell; Durand Malet; Seward the priest from the king.* Small market town. The church has a partly Saxon tower.

Wispington *Wispinctune: Bishop of Durham; Eudo FitzSpirwic.*

Witham on the Hill *Witham: Anstrid and Asfort from Abbot of Peterborough; Colegrim from Drogo de Beuvriere; Gilbert de Ghent and Berewold from him; Ralph Pagnell and Hacon from him. Church, 2 mills (with Lound, etc.).* Stocks.

Withcall *Wichale/Widcale: Bishop of Bayeux and Ilbert from him; Rayner de Brimou; William Blunt. Church, 2 mills.* Ancient village site nearby.

Withern *Widerne: Earl Hugh; Gilbert de Ghent and Raveman from him; Hugh FitzBaldric. Church, mill.*

Wold Newton *Neutone: Bishop of Durham and Walbert from him; Count Alan.*

Wood Enderby *Endrebi: King's land; Robert the Steward.*

Woodthorpe *Endretorp: Hugh FitzBaldric.*

Woolsthorpe *Ulestane(s)torp: Robert de Tosny. Church, 4½ mills.* Birthplace of Sir Isaac Newton (1642–1727). An inn in the village is named after him.

Wooton *Udetone: Bishop of Lincoln and Roger from him; Norman d'Arci; Ralph de Mortimer. ½ mill (with Thornton Curtis. etc.).* Pond; green.

Worlaby *Uluricebi/Wirchebi: Bishop of Lincoln and Gocelin from him; Earl Hugh; Hugh FitzBaldric and Ralph from him.* Church with an Anglo-Saxon tower.

Worlaby (near Tetford) *Wlurice(s)bi: Archbishop of York; Bishop of Durham.*

Wragby *Waragebi: Ernis de Burun, formerly Countess Gudeta; Waldin the Engineer. Church, ½ mill, mill-site.* Once a market town; Norman work in the church.

Wrangle *Weranghe/Werangle: Count Alan; Guy de Craon.* Expanding.

Wrawby *Waragebi: Ralph from Geoffrey Alselin. Church.* Expanding.

Wyberton *Wibertone/tune: Count Alan; Guy de Craon. Church.* Small town on the outskirts of Boston.

Wyham *Widun: Bishop of Lincoln and Malger from him; Ivo Tailbois and Wimund from him.*

Wykeham (in Nettleton) *Wiham:* Lost.

Wykeham *Wicham: Roger de Poitou; Alfred of Lincoln; Hugh FitzBaldric; Rainer de Brimou.* Wykeham Hall; ancient village site.

Wyville *Muuelle: Robert de Tosny.*

Yaddlethorpe *Iadulf(es)torp: King's land.* Part of Scunthorpe.

Yarburgh *Gereburg: King's land.*

Yawthorpe *Iole(s)torp: Abbot of Peterborough; Roger de Poitou; Geoffrey de La Guerche.*

Middlesex

The old county of Middlesex was bounded by the Thames to the south and by its tributaries the Lea to the east and the Colne to the west. To the north its border with Hertfordshire was thickly wooded. Today almost the whole county is built up, but in 1086 the northern wooded area which lay on clay was only thinly settled, while the river valleys with their gravels and loamy soils were better populated.

The great disappointment about Middlesex Domesday *is that London is omitted. Two pages at the start may have been left blank for it. On the other hand it contains more details about the peasant landholders and gives a better idea of the class structure than any other county's pages.*

In Middlesex half the recorded population were villagers (villani)*, who were often assessed for as much as a hide of land. Below them came* bordarii, *best translated as smallholders, who mostly held up to an eighth of a hide, although some held more and others were landless. Below again were the cottagers* (cotarii) *who held up to five acres, although half held no land.* Domesday *records that some of all these classes paid rent. Most, however, would have paid in kind, or with work, the lower the class the more work. Finally came landless slaves.*

Into this pattern must be fitted the Frenchmen and knights. The majority of Frenchmen are referred to as 'milites'*, a loose term indicating military service and roughly translated as 'man-at-arms' or 'knight' (knighthood as we know it today is far removed from this hardened semi-professional warrior). These men, mercenary soldiers, in a sense held their land as a stipend from the man they served in return for filling the tenant-in-chief's quota in the king's army.*

Edmonton

Geoffrey de Mandeville holds EDMONTON *ADELMENTONE*. It answers for 35 hides. Land for 26 ploughs. In lordship 16 hides; 4 ploughs. The villagers have 22 ploughs. 1 villager with 1 hide; 3 others, 1/2 hide each; 20 villagers with 1 virgate each; 24 others, 1/2 virgate each; 9 smallholders with 3 virgates; 4 smallholders with 5 acres each; 4 smallholders with 4 acres each; 4 cottagers with 4 acres; 10 cottagers; 4 villagers with 1 hide and 1 virgate; 4 slaves. 1 mill, 10s; meadow for 26 ploughs, and 25s over and above; pasture for the livestock; woodland, 2000 pigs; from the payments of the woodland and pasture, 12s. Total value £40; when acquired £20; before 1066 £40. Asgar, King Edward's Constable, held this manor. An outlier called (South) Mimms lay and lies in (the lands of) this manor: it is assessed with the manor.

Geoffrey de Mandeville, who held the large manor of Edmonton, was among the most powerful Norman barons of the south-east, with manors in 11 counties. In Middlesex he held seven, including Islington. He is a good example of the way in which William I gave his barons the estates of particular Englishmen; in all but one county some of de Mandeville's land had been held, like Edmonton, by Asgar, Master of Edward the Confessor's stud and leader of the London contingent at the Battle of Hastings.

As Edmonton's 2000 pigs show, it was well wooded although it lay just to the south of the land which became Enfield Chase. Places like Southgate along its north-western boundary were the old southern entrances to the chase. To the east Edmonton was bounded by the River Lea and a wide belt of swamp. This was still undrained in the late eighteenth century when John Gilpin rode through Edmonton in an attempt to celebrate his wedding anniversary at the Bell Inn. William Cowper wrote,

'And there he threw the wash about
On both sides of the way,
Just like unto a trundling mop,
Or a wild goose at play.'

Edmonton had achieved a form of fame early in the seventeenth century when the story of Elizabeth Sawyer, who had witched her neighbour's 'nurse children' to death, was made into two plays. Three 'grave matrons, laying niceness aside' stripped Elizabeth and found the devil's mark just above the base of her spine. She was duly hanged. Edmonton was better known later for its three-day fair. This was nominally for hiring servants, but was also used for recruiting. In 1813 a newspaper reported that a number of fine fellows were picked up while the drum and fife played 'How happy is the soldier who lives on his pay, and spends half a crown out of sixpence a day.'

By then Edmonton was ceasing to be a desirable residential suburb. In 1800 its inhabitants were described as 'retired embroidered weavers, their crummy wives and tightly laced daughters'. Its decline accelerated around the middle of the nineteenth century when many of the old estates were sold for building.

Nothing of *Domesday* Edmonton can be seen today. Its woods are cut down, its river a reservoir and even the Bell Inn, later the Angel, has been replaced by a traffic roundabout.

Chelsea

Edward of Salisbury holds CHELSEA *CHELCHED* for 2 hides. Land for 5 ploughs. In lordship 1 hide; 2 ploughs there now. The villagers, 1 plough; a further 2 ploughs possible. 2 villagers with 2 virgates; 4 villagers with 1/2 virgate each; 3 smallholders with 5 acres each; 3 slaves. Meadow for 2 ploughs; pasture for the village livestock; woodland, 60 pigs, and 52d too. Total value £9; when acquired and always the same. Wulfwen, King Edward's man, held this manor; she could sell to whom she would.

For over 450 years Chelsea has been fashionable. As far as it was ever a district for impoverished Bohemians it was so only briefly. More typically the smart and rich have settled here for centuries, conveniently close to London on a picturesque reach of the Thames. But there is no evidence that they did so before Tudor times, and for the previous 400 years Chelsea seems to have remained the simple riverside settlement of 1086.

It was Edward of Salisbury's only Middlesex manor. Although he held extensive lands in Wiltshire, where he was sheriff, and manors in six other southern counties, he was not one of the great barons of *Domesday* and there was nothing to suggest that his grandson, Patrick, would become the first Earl of Salisbury. He may possibly have been an Englishman. Since no previous holders are named for his first three Wiltshire manors, it is likely that he had held them in Saxon times. But he took over many, including Chelsea, from a woman named Wulfwen, about whom nothing is known. (The term *homo* is used in the original to mean 'woman'.)

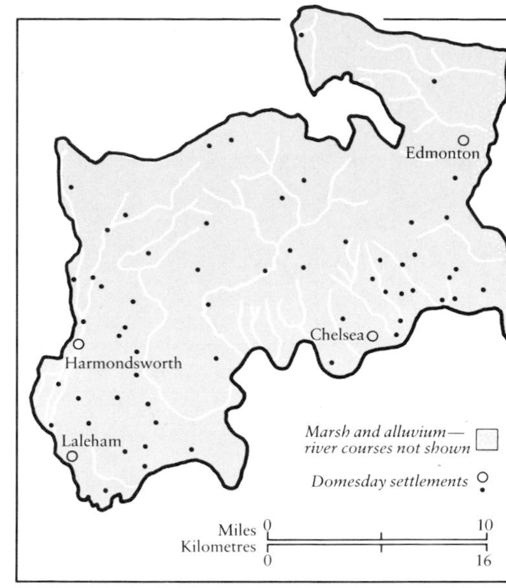

Chelsea Manor's lands lay at the western end of the present parish. Here a sandy ridge, 25 feet above sea level, extended south from Campden Hill (120 feet) to the Thames near today's Albert Bridge. Its height is not obvious now because of infilling, but then it fell to the west to the swampy lands of Fulham, and to the east to marshes, now the grounds of the Royal Military Hospital, and to the West Bourne.

There were Tudor mansions at Chelsea before Sir Thomas More's, but it was his, built in 1523, which did most to make the village fashionable. Later it became the Duke of Beaufort's; it stood near the junction of today's Beaufort Street and the King's Road.

According to More's friend Erasmus it was 'not mean nor invidiously grand but comfortable'. Here More lived for 11 years, and here he detained suspect heretics, before sending them on for racking in the tower. He became increasingly fanatical, wore a hair shirt and beat himself till he bled. From Chelsea he set out by boat in 1534 for Lambeth, where he refused to take the Oath of Supremacy, an act of defiance which led to his execution a year later.

The year after More's execution, Henry VIII acquired the manor of Chelsea, and soon built a new house. It stood close to today's Embankment, near Manor Street, on what may have been the site of *Domesday*'s manor. The house was intimately involved in the power struggle which followed Henry's death.

It was occupied by his widow, Catherine Parr,

and here she secretly married Admiral Thomas Seymour, the uncle of Jane Seymour, Henry's third wife. Here in 1548 Catherine Parr discovered Seymour with Princess Elizabeth in his arms. Seymour had already tried to marry Elizabeth before he married Catherine, and tried again when Catherine died that year. He was soon arrested for piracy and treason and executed, the death warrant signed by his brother, the Lord Protector.

Meanwhile Chelsea Manor had passed to John Dudley, later Duke of Northumberland, whose attempt to make his daughter-in-law, Lady Jane Grey, queen in succession to Edward VI ended in his, his son's and her executions. Lady Jane had lived at Chelsea Manor during Catherine Parr's time there.

Chelsea's finest surviving building, the Royal Military Hospital, had its origins in a theological college which was founded during James I's reign, but never prospered. After the Restoration it was used for Dutch prisoners, under the charge of the diarist John Evelyn, but the derelict building was eventually knocked down and on its site, in 1682, Charles II laid the foundation stone of Wren's new hospital.

Early in the next century, the royal physician and naturalist, Sir Hans Sloane, bought Chelsea Manor. He later bought and demolished More's house to extend his own estate. He occupied the manor from 1741, bringing to it his vast and varied natural history and manuscript collections. By the time he died in 1753 he owned half Chelsea. He bequeathed his collections to the nation (in exchange for £20,000 for his two married daughters) and they formed the basis for the British Museum's collections. By 1780 the manor had been pulled down.

Ranelagh Gardens – now part of the Royal Hospital grounds – were then at the height of their popularity. They were named after Lord Ranelagh, a corrupt paymaster general who built a fine riverside house here where he entertained royalty. But the central attraction of Ranelagh Gardens when they were opened to the public in 1742 was a great wooden rotunda, modelled on the Pantheon at Rome. For 60 years the gardens flourished, providing masques, firework displays, balls and, in their final year, an ascent by Monsieur Garnerin in a hot-air balloon.

Nothing – except the river – remains of *Domesday* Chelsea. Even Oswulf's stone, which probably marked the meeting place of Ossulston hundred of which Chelsea was a part, where its jurors would have given evidence to the *Domesday* Commissioners, has long since gone. Until at least 1614 it was in what is now Park Lane, near the junction with South Street, and as late as 1890 at Marble Arch.

Laleham

Robert Blunt holds 8 hides in LALEHAM *LELEHA* from the King. Estrild, a nun, holds from him. Land for 5 ploughs. In lordship 4 hides; 1 plough there. The villagers have 4 ploughs. 1 villager with 1 virgate; 7 villagers, 1/2 hide each; 3 smallholders with 1 virgate; 3 cottagers. Meadow for 5 ploughs; pasture for the village livestock. Total value 60s; when acquired 40s; before 1066 £6. Aki, one of King Edward's Guards, held this manor; he could sell to whom he would; the jurisdiction lay in Staines.

The Thames-side village of Laleham, which lies opposite Chertsey, was probably one of the four outliers of Westminster Abbey's manor of Staines. Besides the abbey's land, which *Domesday* does not separate from Staines's, it included Robert Blunt's holding described above, and two hides held by the Abbot of Fecamp from the Count of Mortain.

Blunt is one of the few *Domesday* characters of whom we can get any physical picture. The Latin reads *Blundus*, and in other places he is called *Albus* or *Blancardus*. Clearly his name derived from his unusually blond hair. Most of the Blunt family land was in Suffolk, where they were barons of Ixworth.

The greater part of Laleham remained Westminster Abbey's until the Dissolution. Soon afterwards Henry VIII, trying to create a belt of hunting land to connect Hampton Court with Windsor Forest, added it to the honour of Hampton Court, but the project collapsed when Henry died.

Three well-known nineteenth-century figures had connections with Laleham. Thomas Arnold lived here for nine years before he became headmaster of Rugby. His son Matthew was born here and is buried in the churchyard. And the third Earl of Lucan, notorious as the commander of the British cavalry during the Crimean War, which made the disastrous Charge of the Light Brigade, owned the 23-acre family riverside estate just south of the village. At Laleham he quarrelled with the vicar, demanding that a clean sweep be made of the church so that it would not be 'obstructed by Norman pillars'; and with the Lord Chamberlain whose swans fouled his fields, threatening to shoot six every Friday until they were reduced to six. He did not succeed: pillars and swans survive.

CHELSEA: *A 'village' street of small houses; it has been a prosperous area for centuries.*

LALEHAM: *Looking across the peaceful River Thames; the village was surrounded by fields until* c. 1911.

The western boundary of Laleham parish is formed by the Thames. At one time there was a ferry connecting it to Surrey, but no bridge, and as a result as late as 1911 it was still a quiet village surrounded by fields growing 'wheat, barley, oats, turnips and mangoldwurzel'. During the previous 40 years its population had actually declined by 20 per cent. Although today gravel pits have turned one part of the parish into an artificial lake, its pretty riverside grasslands, once the villagers' meadow and animal pasture, are delightfully preserved.

Harmondsworth

Holy Trinity Abbey, Rouen holds HARMONDSWORTH *HERMODESWORDE* from the King. It answers for 30 hides. Land for 20 ploughs. 8 hides belong to the lordship; 3 ploughs there. There are 10 ploughs between the Frenchmen and the villagers; a further 7 possible. A man-at-arms has 2 hides; 2 villagers, 1 hide each; 2 villagers with 1 hide; 14 villagers with 1 virgate each; 6 villagers with 1/2 virgate each; 6 smallholders, 5 acres each; 7 cottagers; 6 slaves. 3 mills at 60s, and 500 eels; from the fishponds, 1000 eels; meadow for 20 ploughs; pasture for the village livestock; woodland, 500 pigs; 1 *arpent* of vines. Total value £20; when acquired £12; before 1066 £25. Earl Harold held this manor. In this manor there was a Freeman who held 2 of these 30 hides; he could not grant or sell them outside Harmondsworth before 1066.

Sandwiched between motorway and trunk road, disturbed by the constant roar of Heathrow's jets, the small core of Harmondsworth village remains remarkably picturesque. Less so the wrecked fields around. But it was these flat once-fertile fields in the Colne valley on the western border of Middlesex that made Harmondsworth valuable in 1086.

The manor had, in fact, more cultivatable land than plough teams. Perhaps it was not fully exploited because it was held by an abbey with little experience of foreign management. While other Norman abbeys held extensive lands in England, Holy Trinity at Rouen held only Harmondsworth.

Typically for Middlesex, *Domesday* gives details of the lands held by the various classes of peasants, from villagers (*villani*) at the top to cottagers (*cotarii*) at the bottom. Earl Roger held one hide. Harmondsworth's 500 pigs were probably the total kept. The Middlesex commissioners seem always to have given this figure and not, as in Surrey and Sussex, the number paid annually to the manor. Its mills would have been on the River Colne, which forms several channels near the village. But it also had fishponds which are recorded only at two other manors in the county. Its vines were less unusual – seven other Middlesex manors had them. Two had been 'newly planted', and this suggests that the

Normans had reintroduced vines to England. So does the ancient Gallic *arpent* by which they were usually measured.

Some time before 1211 the abbey established a priory and from then on the prior was in effect lord of the manor. He soon had trouble with his tenants, which persisted for 230 years, indicating that the villagers were a rebellious lot. In 1275 they stole the priory's records, felled its trees and killed a number of its workmen. In 1281 12 villagers were in prison for burning down the priory buildings.

The villagers' case was that since Harmondsworth had been a royal manor they should not pay customs to the priory. The priory successfully used its *Domesday* entry to prove the opposite. It valued this entry so highly that in 1341 it had a copy made, and 50 years later, when William of Wykeham took over the manor, this passed to Winchester College, which still preserves it.

South of the Bath Road, which ran through the parish, the Fairey Aviation Company in 1930 established its Great West Aerodrome. This became an RAF station in 1944 and today's international civil airport in 1946.

Harmondsworth's church, on the site of the *Domesday* church, is its oldest building, but its earliest parts are only twelfth century. Even newer but more unusual is its great tithe barn, probably built by Winchester College in 1426. This astonishing 190-foot barn with its massive posts separating the 'nave' from the side aisles, is the more impressive for being slightly dilapidated and not yet a museum.

HARMONDSWORTH: *The interior of the great tithe barn, built in 1426, recalls the impressive solemnity of a church or abbey.*

Middlesex Gazetteer
Each entry starts with the modern place-name in **bold** type. The *Domesday* information that follows is in *italic* type, beginning with the name or names by which the place was known in 1086. The main landholders and under-tenants are next, separated with semi-colons if a place was divided into more than one holding. 2 women, Aelfeva and Edeva, were given land 'in alms' by the king, and are listed as holding land 'from the king'. More general information completes the *Domesday* part of the entry, including examples of dues such as eels rendered by tenants. The modern or post-Domesday section is in normal type. ⌂ represents a village, △ a small village or hamlet.

Ashford *Exeforde: Count of Mortain.* ⌂ Heathrow airport nearby.

Bishopsgate *Porta Episcopi: Canons of St Paul's before and after 1066.* Part of London. The street called Bishopsgate was the main Roman route.

Camden Town *Rugemere: Canon Ralph from Bishop of London.* Part of London.

Charlton *Cerdentone: Roger de Raismes.* △ Squeezed between reservoir and motorway.

Chelsea *Chelched:* See page 177.

Colham *Coleham: Earl Roger. 2½ mills, vines.* London suburb.

Cowley *Covelie: Westminster Abbey. Mill.* ⌂ Dr William Dodd, clergyman and forger, was buried here in 1777.

Cranford *Cranforde: William FitzAnsculf and Hugh from him.* Extension of Hounslow; 18th-century park.

Dawley *Dallega: Alnoth from Earl Roger.* Hayes housing estates.

East Bedfont *Bedefunde/funt: Count of Mortain; Richard from Walter FitzOthere.* ⌂ Green; overlooks Heathrow airport.

Ebury *Eia: Geoffrey de Mandeville.* Part of London. Ebury Street and Square are named after Ebury Farm, leased by Queen Elizabeth I. Mozart stayed here in 1764.

Edmonton *Adelmentone:* See page 177.

Enfield *Enefelde: Geoffrey de Mandeville. Mill, fishponds, park.* Sprawling London suburb.

Feltham *Felteham: Count of Mortain.* Huge dormitory suburb; 17th-century manor house.

Fulham *Fuleham: Bishop of London and Fulcred from him; Canons of St Paul's before and after 1066. Gardens, weir.* London borough; 16th-century Fulham Palace, past residence of the bishops of London; once famous for its market gardens.

Greenford *Greneforde: Westminster Abbey before and after 1066; Arnulf and Ansgot from Geoffrey de Mandeville; Aelfeva from the king.* Part of London.

Haggerston *Hergotestane: Robert Gernon.* Depressed area of East London near Shoreditch.

Hampstead *Hamestede: Westminster Abbey and Ranulf Peverel from the abbey.* Part of London.

Hampton *Hamnetone: Walter de St Valery. 3s from fishing nets and drag-nets in the River Thames.* ⌂ Magnificent 16th-century palace built by Cardinal Wolsey. In the 1870s, the Thames Conservancy hatched and reared fish here to release them into the Thames.

Hanwell *Hanewelle: Westminster Abbey before and after 1066.* ⌂ Modern housing estates nearby.

Hanworth *Haneworde: Robert from Earl Roger.* London suburb. Henry VIII had a shooting seat here; there is an old people's home on the site.

Harefield *Herefelle: Richard FitzGilbert. 2 mills, 4 fishponds (1000 eels).* ⌂ Country character; Breakspears manor house.

Harlesden *Herulvestune: Canons of St Paul's before and after 1066.* Part of London.

Harlington *Herdintone: Alfred and Olaf from Earl Roger.* ⌂ Straggling; squeezed between Heathrow and the M4.

Harmondsworth *Hermodesworde:* See page 179.

Harrow *Herges: Archbishop Lanfranc.* Town with a famous public school.

Hatton *Ha(i)tone: Walter de Mucedent from Walter FitzOthere.* △ Enlarged as a result of the development of Heathrow airport.

HAYES: *The Tapsel gate at St Mary's church.*

Hayes *Hesa: Archbishop Lanfranc. Mill.* Town engulfed by modern housing; remains of 11th-century manor house; moat.

Hendon *Handone: Westminster Abbey before and after 1066.* London borough with the (much altered) remains of a house built by the actor David Garrick in the 18th century.

Hillingdon *Hillendone: Earl Roger. Weir.* London borough.

Holborn *Holeburne: King's land.* London district so-called because a road in medieval times followed the course of a bourne (or burn). St Etheldreda's church and Gray's Inn were both established by the 15th century.

Hoxton *Hochestone: Canons of St Paul's before and after 1066.* Absorbed by Shoreditch.

Ickenham *Ticheham: 3 men-at-arms and an Englishman from Earl Roger; 2 Englishmen from Geoffrey de Mandeville; Robert FitzFafiton.* ⌂

Isleworth *Gisteleswordе: Walter de St Valery. 2 mills, 1½ weirs.* ⌂ Thames-side; Syon House, begun after the Dissolution from the ruins of a Bridgettine convent.

Islington *Iseldone/Isendone: Canons of St Paul's before and after 1066; Wulfbert from Geoffrey de Mandeville; Derman of London.* Part of London; 16th-century Canonbury House. Henry VIII hawked here.

Kempton *Chenetone: Count of Mortain. Vines.* Famous race course. Remains of a Henry I palace probably lie beneath it.

Kensington *Chenesit: Aubrey de Vere from Bishop of Coutances. 3 vines.* Part of London (combined with Chelsea as a borough). A. de Vere gave land to the Abbey of St Mary, Abingdon; the present parish church named St Mary Abbots recalls this.

Kingsbury *Chingesberie: William the Chamberlain from Westminster Abbey; Albold from Arnulf de Hesdin. Mill.* Part of London; modern housing.

Laleham *Leleha:* See page 178.

Lisson *Lilestone: Edeva from the king.* Lisson Grove and Lisson Street in London. In medieval times, a settlement between the hamlets of Tyburne (now Marylebone) and Paddington.

Northolt *Northala: Geoffrey de Mandeville.* ⌂ Overrun by metropolis; airport.

Ruislip *Rislepe: Arnulf de Hesdin. Park for woodland beasts.* ⌂ Part of London; manor Farm, on the site of the motte and bailey castle built by de Hesdin; Park Wood, a fragment of the *Domesday* hunting ground.

St Pancras *Sanctus Pancratius: Canons of St Paul's before and after 1066; Canon Walter of St Paul's.* Part of London; Norman church, built c.1180, possibly on the site of a Roman camp.

Shepperton *Scepertone: Westminster Abbey before and after 1066. Weir.* Thames-side village. Manor house; several weirs.

South Mimms *Mimes: Geoffrey de Mandeville.* ⌂ Site of a motte and bailey castle nearby, probably that of the de Mandevilles.

Staines *Stanes: Westminster Abbey. 6 mills, 2 weirs, vines.* Town; weirs.

Stanmore *Stanmera/mere: Count of Mortain; Roger de Raismes.* Part of London. Handel was organist at the church.

HAMPSTEAD: *George Romney's house in London's artistic and literary quarter.*

Stanwell *Stanwelle: Walter FitzOthere. 4 mills (400 eels less 75), 3 weirs (1000 eels).* ⌂ Much expanded; Stanwell Place, Georgian manor house.

Stepney *Stibenhed(e): Bishop of London; Hugh de Bernieres; Brian's wife; Ranulf Flambard; William de Vere; Canon Engelbert before and after 1066; Bishop of Lisieux before and after 1066; William the Chamberlain; Aelfric Catchpoll; Edmund son of Algot and Alwin son of Brictmer from him; Robert FitzFafiton; Robert FitzRozelin. 7 mills. Wood for fences.* London borough; green with Georgian houses.

Stoke Newington *Neutone: Canons of St Paul's before and after 1066.* Part of London; a rural village until the 1870s.

Sunbury *Suneberie: Westminster Abbey.* ⌂ Large; Thames-side.

Tollington *Tolentone: Ranulf brother of Ilger.* Tollington Park.

Tottenham *Toteham: Countess Judith. Weir.* Part of London.

Tottenham (Court) *Totehele: Canons of St Paul's before and after 1066.* Part of London.

Twyford *Tueverde: Durand and Gyrth, Canons of St Paul's.* Part of London.

Tyburn *Tiburne: Barking Abbey before and after 1066.* Part of London. Criminals were executed here as early as 1196. Number 49 Connaught Square is said to be the site of the 17th-century gallows where the bodies of Cromwell, Ireton and Bradshaw were hung after disinterment.

West Bedfont *Westbedefund: Walter de Mucedent from Walter FitzOthere.* Merged with Stanwell.

(West) Drayton *Draitone: Canons of St Paul's. Mill, weir.* ⌂ Fine green; weir; Tudor gatehouse.

Westminster *Aecclesia Sancti Petri Westmonasterii: Westminster Abbey and Baynard from the abbot. Gardens, houses, newly planted vines.* City of Westminster, in London. Westminster Abbey dates from 1245 and is on the site of the Saxon church.

Willesden *Wellesdone: Villagers from the Canons of St Paul's (who before 1066 held the manor for their household supplies).* Part of London. Medieval church; from the 13th century to the Reformation the pilgrimage to Our Lady of Willesden rivalled the one to Walsingham.

WESTMINSTER: *William I was crowned in the original abbey.*

Norfolk

Eleventh-century Norfolk was a county much influenced by water. In mills and fresh-water fisheries it easily outnumbered any of its eastern neighbours. And in the wet areas to the east and west, where broadland and fenland both made agriculture difficult, salt pans and sheep held sway. There was almost no woodland in these low-lying coastal regions, and therefore few pigs, but sheep thrived on the marshy land that was fit for little else. Central Norfolk occupied higher, forested ground, while the most prosperous agricultural region lay to the south of Norwich, near the border with Suffolk.

A good deal is known about the county in 1086, thanks to detailed accounts provided by the Little Domesday Book. *As in Suffolk, there was a large free population of men who made their living on small farms, relatively unbeholden to a great landowner. It has been suggested that this independent peasantry survived in areas settled by the Scandinavians where they had never been fully assimilated into the rigid Saxon pecking order.*

Norwich, with a population of around 5000, was the largest city. Surprisingly, it was rivalled in size and exceeded in importance by Thetford, the county's ecclesiastical capital, whose bishop was one of Norfolk's major landlords. Although Yarmouth, on the North Sea, also numbered burgesses among its inhabitants, it had a population of only about 500 and was little more than a fishing village.

Castle Rising

Further [the Bishop of Bayeux holds] 1 outlier, (CASTLE) RISING *RISINGA*, 3 c. of land. Always 12 villagers; 38 smallholders. Then 4 slaves, now 3. Meadow, 14 acres. Always 2 ploughs in lordship; 2 men's ploughs. Also 7 Freemen, 24 acres of land. Always 1 plough; 3 mills; 12 salt-houses; 1 fishery. Also 3 Freemen, 60 acres of land; always 1 plough. Also 1 Freeman, 60 acres; 1 plough. 26 smallholders. 1 plough; meadow, 8 acres; 1 mill; 1 salt-house.

Rising was a sea port
When Lynn was but a marsh

runs an old verse;

Now Lynn it is the sea port
And Rising fares the worse.

Castle Rising was never more than a village in size, but it once aspired to much grander things. The great square keep of its castle is among the most elegant Norman remains in Britain, as much a mansion as a fortification. It stands in the middle of a circular earthwork, 12 acres in area, with a surrounding ditch more than 100 feet deep. In the village is the church of St Lawrence, rich in late Norman decoration and, across the road, the Jacobean almshouses, the Hospital of the Holy and Undivided Trinity, where ten spinsters have traditionally found accommodation.

As if to keep pace with these architectural splendours, Castle Rising became a borough in the early thirteenth century and was subsequently permitted to elect its own mayor, a privilege that was not accorded to its arch-rival King's Lynn until some years later. Even more surprisingly, from 1558 it was represented by two Members of Parliament, among them Sir Robert Walpole, before the Reform Bill of 1832 abolished this most rotten of boroughs. It had twice-weekly markets and an annual autumn fair. And yet Castle Rising never grew to match these distinctions. Left high and dry by the retreating sea in the Middle Ages, it remained a Norman village, as if petrified by the great castle in its midst.

At the time of *Domesday*, Castle Rising stood on the edge of the fenland, with easy access to the sea. In common with several other western villages it was a major salt-producing centre. Forty-five manors in Norfolk had salt-houses, where salt was produced from seawater, by evaporation – making the industry an important one. Castle Rising owed its four mills to the Babingley river and had no woodland worth recording. The holder in 1086 was Odo, Bishop of Bayeux. When he rebelled against his half brother, William the Conqueror, the estate passed to William d'Albini, the king's butler, whose family built the castle and whose descendants, by the maternal line, continued to preside over local affairs into the twentieth century. For generations, the noble Howard family lent the village a political lustre that was quite out of proportion to its size.

As aristocratic privileges declined, so did Castle Rising's importance. By the mid-nineteenth century the castle was an overgrown ruin and the first tourists were coming to picnic within its huge ditches. A guidebook of 1858 pompously reflects this new order: 'To the intellectual visitor, a day spent at Castle Rising will assuredly rank among the sunny memories of the past.'

Blakeney

[Land of the King] ... Further 1 outlier, in BLAKENEY *ESNUTERLE* at 1 c. of land. Always 7 villagers; 1 smallholder. Always 1 men's plough. Value then £20, 1 night's honey and 100s in customary dues; now £50 at face value. Holt and Cley have 2 leagues in length and 1 in width, 2s 4[d] in tax. Before 1066, 8 free men belonged to this manor, at 3 1/2 c. of land; now Walter Giffard holds them by livery of the King, so his men state. Further, there belonged to this manor 1 free man, 23 acres; now Earl Hugh holds them.

Those for whom Noel Coward's 'very flat, Norfolk' is an article of faith are continually surprised to find themselves panting up the steep, narrow streets of villages like Blakeney. In parts this picturesque northern coast feels more like Devon than East Anglia, although the flint-walled cottages and the flat expanses of mud and sand are proof of where you are.

Blakeney, formerly Snitterley, first officially appears in a document of 1340; in that same period Edward III's Queen Philippa is said to have dined upon Blakeney fish. From then until the sixteenth century Blakeney and Snitterley seem to have been alternative names for the same town. Although the name Blakeney prevailed, its early history must be sought under the name of Snitterley. This, many historians believe, was an English corruption of the *Domesday* Esnuterle.

Other scholars disagree, arguing that the ancient Snitterley/Esnuterle was once a separate village, a few miles to the north of the present Blakeney. During the early Middle Ages, they maintain, the treacherous coastline caved away from under Snitterley, it was engulfed by the sea, and its name taken over by neighbouring Blakeney. There is no evidence for this theory, but the *Domesday* village of Shipden, not far to the east, suffered precisely this fate.

In 1086, by far the most valuable part of the settlement formed an outlier of the royal manor

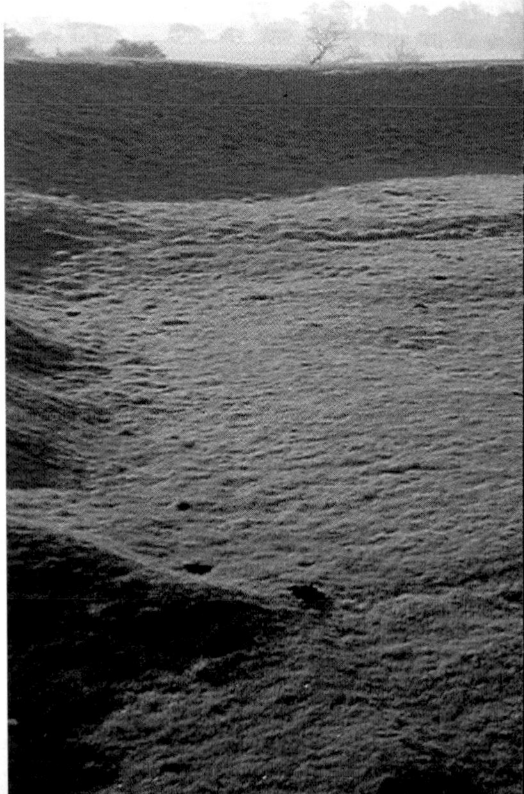

of Holt. It rendered, as well as 100s, a night's honey, meaning ironically a complete day's production, evening, night and morning. The Walter Giffard to whom the king had transferred the holdings of eight freemen was the same powerful landholder who was a tenant-in-chief in nine counties in the south and east. He held these holdings from the king by livery, meaning by the king's gift. A third landholder was William de Noyers.

Whether or not the true Blakeney is now below the sea, the shifting coastal sands have played an important part in its history. The estuary of the River Glaven on which it stands provided a safe harbour, but could not be relied upon to remain the same even from one generation to the next. The fortunes of the villages along this stretch of coast – Cley, Wiveton and Blakeney – rose and fell as the Haven moved slowly westward. In the fourteenth century Blakeney was predominant – a major port for the export of corn and wool to the Low Countries. It increased its revenue with open acts of piracy. In 1328–50 men of Blakeney boarded two vessels from Flanders, sailed them back to the Haven and stripped them of their cargoes. The merchant captain who sought shelter from a storm at Blakeney might well leave with an empty ship. It may have been this spirit of lawless independence that prompted Blakeney to refuse to supply a ship to fight against the Spanish Armada.

Both the sea and society conspired against Blakeney in the seventeenth century. An embankment built across the River Glaven in 1637 made the harbour silt up, and trade came to a halt. Although this barrier was torn down two years later, landowners who wanted to extend their farmland kept building new ones, forcing the eventual collapse of the once thriving port.

By the mid-nineteenth century only one merchant remained, and property values had plummeted by 50 per cent. Because of this depression, the railway never reached the town. Some of the locals survived by trading in oysters and mussels, a few made a hard living digging lugworms.

In the twentieth century Blakeney, like many coastal towns, has suffered the mixed blessing of becoming fashionable. As early as 1907 *Country Life* had discovered its charms: it offered 'a simple inn where the wayfarer may lodge' and 'many a hearty welcome to be received from the rough but honest people'.

Today Blakeney leads a double life. In the winter it remains embalmed in half-deserted solitude. In the summer it comes alive with trippers, yachtsmen and seasonal residents. There remain only a few reminders of its former importance: the fourteenth-century Guildhall near the quay and the east tower of the parish church, where a lantern once guided sailors into the quiet waters of Blakeney Haven.

CASTLE RISING: *Built by the son of William I's butler, d'Albini, c. 1150, the keep is second only to that of Norwich Castle in size and importance.*

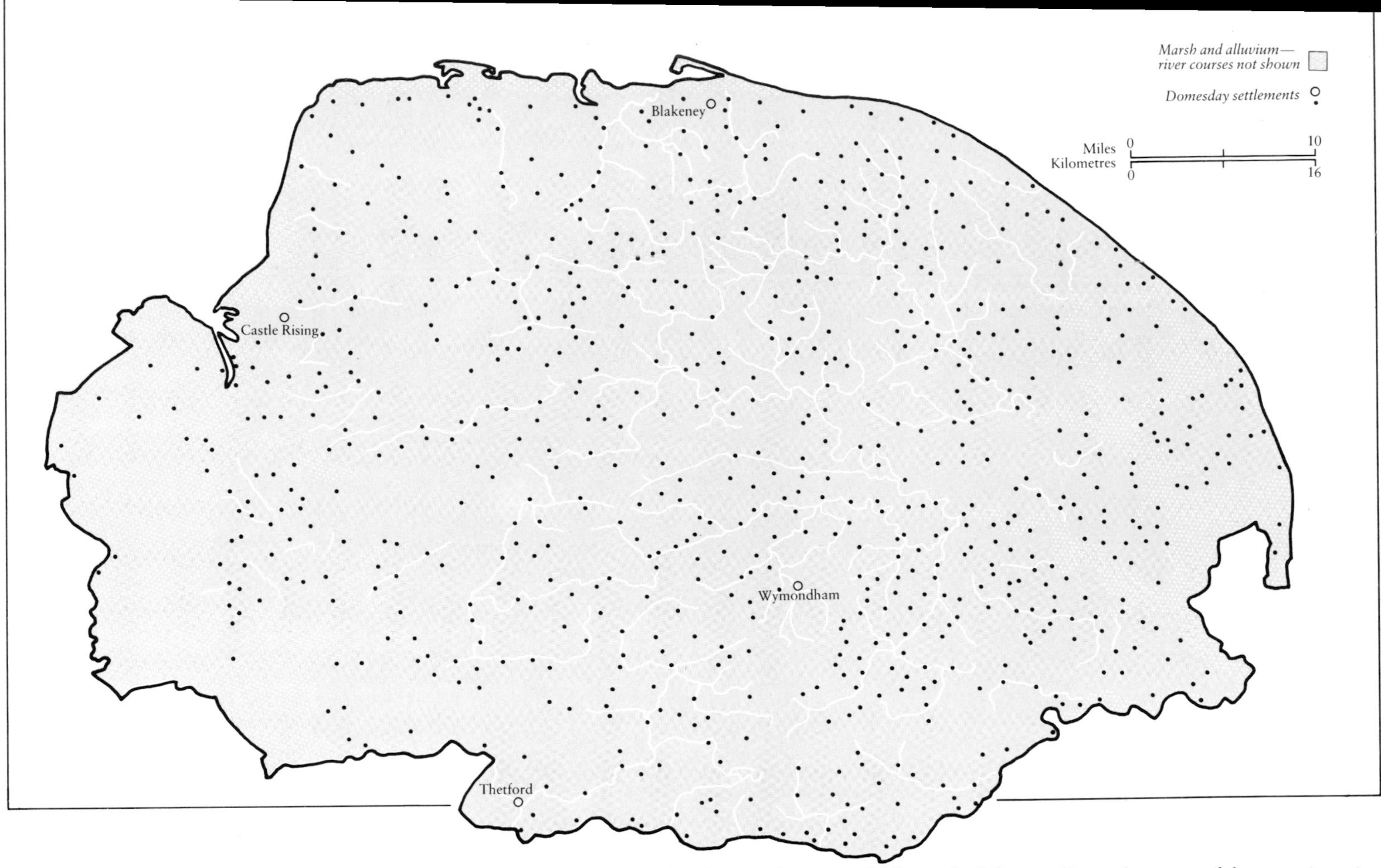

Thetford

Of the King's land in THETFORD *TETFORD* beyond the water towards Norfolk there is 1 league of land in length and 1/2 in width of which the King has 2 parts moreover the third part of these two parts lies in the Earldom. Roger Bigot (has) the third part of the above-mentioned league; all this land is half arable, the other (half) in pasture. On this land the King has 1 plough, 3 smallholders, 1 slave and 1 horse. Also of 2 mills the King has 2 parts and the Earl the third (part). The King also has 2 parts of a third mill and of these 2 parts the Earl has a third. Of the other part towards Suffolk there is 1/2 a league of land in length and 1/2 in width; a third part of this land belongs to the Earldom; meadow, 4 acres. All this land is arable; 4 ploughs can plough it. Moreover in the Borough there were 943 burgesses before 1066; of these the King has all the customary dues. 36 of these same men belonged to King Edward, their lord, to such an extent that they could not be anyone else's men without the King's permission. All the others could be anyone else's men but always the customary dues remained the King's except for heriot. Now there are 720 burgesses and 224 empty dwellings; 21 of these burgesses have 6 c. and 60 acres which they hold from the King. It is in St Edmund's Jurisdiction. Besides this 2 burgesses have 1 mill. Value of all the above-mentioned before 1066 £20 at face value and for the Earl's use £10 at face value; now it pays £50 by weight to the King and to the Earl £20 blanched and £6 at face value. Now it also pays to the King £40 from the mint; always 16s to 2 pensioners. Before 1066 it also paid 4 sesters of honey and 40d, 10 goat skins and 4 ox hides. The Abbot of St Edmund's has 1 church in the city and 1 house (which are) free. The Abbot of Ely (has) 3 churches and 1 house (which are) free and 2 dwellings by custom in one (of which) is his house. The Bishop also (has) 20 houses (which are) free, 1 mill and 1/2 church; Roger Bigot (has) 1 house (which is) free, 1 monastery and 2 smallholders (belonging) to the monastery.

Until this century Thetford was a border city, one foot in Norfolk, the other in Suffolk. Now it lies entirely in Norfolk, 31 miles south-west of Norwich, where the River Thet joins the Little Ouse on its way north to the Wash. It is an unsettling mixture of old and new, picturesque and plain, bustling city and provincial back-water. It has been at times a political and military capital, an ecclesiastical centre, a health resort and an overspill town for London's surplus population.

By 1086 Thetford was already on the political decline. As capital of the Anglo-Saxon kingdom of East Anglia, it had suffered some of the earliest and fiercest assaults by the invading Danes. It was here in 870 that King Edmund (Saint and Martyr, as he became known) was forced to flee after a battle lasting three days. The city was burned down in 1004 and again within ten years. Between disasters Thetford rose with astonishing vitality. Although its population had dropped considerably during the 20 years following the Conquest (from 943 burgesses to 720), it still had over 4000 inhabitants at the time of *Domesday*, making it second in size in East Anglia only to Norwich.

Domesday includes four separte entries for Thetford. The king had the major holding using William de Noyers to manage the part of it which had once been held by Stigand, the ejected Archbishop of Canterbury, as he did some 13 other manors in the county; Roger Bigot held the rest. He was a trusted supporter of the king, appointed Constable of Norwich Castle when the Earl of East Anglia rebelled in 1077. Their holdings between them amounted to a city of considerable resources, with more than a dozen churches and seven and two-thirds mills. Mill buildings still stand on two of these ancient sites along the Little Ouse, although they have undergone many changes of shape and use in 900 years.

There is no mention of woodland. In 1086, as for centuries, the city stood in a great expanse of sandy heath, known today as Breckland. 'Scarce a tree to be seen for miles, or a house', wrote a traveller in 1745. One historian went so far as to describe it as 'a miniature Sahara'. Rabbits, burrowing and nibbling, had as much to do with its condition as geology, for Thetford was England's rabbit centre, sending some 20,000 annually to London. On a good morning, with his ferrets and lurchers working efficiently, a warrener could return with more than 200. But woe to the man, who poached even one. In 1813, Robert Plum, who removed 'one coney' from a trap, was deported for seven years.

By the end of the nineteenth century the Breckland was beginning an irreversible change. Landowners had discovered that pine forests prospered on the sandy soil. 'What a few years ago resembled the sea from a distance, is now losing its distintive character', lamented a contemporary historian. In the 1920s the Forestry Commission initiated a policy of planting up the Breckland. Today little open heath remains.

Although Thetford lost much of its political importance early in the Middle Ages, it remained well fortified. On its eastern outskirts stands Castle Hill, a precipitous man-made earthwork 81 feet high and nearly 1000 feet around at the base, the largest such mound in East Anglia. Little is known about this curiosity except that the Normans had a castle here which was allegedly torn down in 1173. A popular local legend maintains that an entire castle once lay within the mound, buried by a nervous king who wanted to preserve his riches.

Under the Normans Thetford became a major religious centre. For a time in the eleventh century it was the seat of the bishops of East

Anglia, and the flint-studded stubble of its Cluniac priory was once a place of pilgrimage. In the reign of Edward III there were 20 churches. Descendants of only three of these survive. St Cuthbert's, the sole medieval church still in full-time use, looks down upon the modern shopping precinct of a secular city.

For centuries Thetford was a royal retreat. The King's House, where Thetford Council now sits, was once a hunting lodge, last used in the seventeenth century. It is said that James I, rebuked by a local farmer for hunting across his land, took such offence that he never returned; nor did any of his successors.

The departure of royalty, coming so hard upon the Dissolution plunged Thetford into decline and there has been relatively little incident since. One commercial enterprise in the early 19th century did, however, leave an agreeable permanent mark. In 1819 an attempt was made to turn Thetford into a spa, like Bath or Tunbridge Wells, exploiting the medicinal properties of its mineral springs to cure 'low spirits and green sickness' among other ailments. The waters are now forgotten, but Spring Walk along the Little Ouse, where invalids once took the air, is still a secluded and pleasant promenade.

The birth in 1737 of Thomas Paine, Thetford's most famous son, went uncelebrated until the present century. A modern statue of this great revolutionary now stands in gold-plated bronze before the King's House. He seems strangely disordered, poised as if to throw his quill pen, while holding a copy of *The Rights of Man* upside down in his other hand. His surprise may come from finding himself welcomed back to a city where for so long he was reviled as a traitor.

Wymondham

[Lands of Bishop Stigand of which William de Noyers has charge in the King's hand. . . .] Stigand held WYMONDHAM *WIMUNDHAM* before 1066. 4 c. of land. Always 60 villagers; 50 smallholders; 8 slaves. Always 4 ploughs in lordship. Then 60 men's ploughs, now 24; Ralph Wader made this undoing before he forfeited, and they could all be restored. Then woodland 100 pigs, now 60. Meadow, 60 acres. Always 2 mills; 1 fishery. Always 2 cobs; 16 head of cattle; 50 pigs; 24 sheep. 87 Freemen appertained to this manor before 1066, now only 18. They have 30 acres of land. Always 1 plough. Further 1 Freeman, 1 c. of land. Always 4 villagers; 10 smallholders; 1 mill; woodland, 16 pigs; meadow, 4 acres. Value of this manor with all jurisdiction before 1066 [£.], with (the) jurisdiction (worth) £20; now 60. It has 2 leagues in length and 1 in width, tax of 6s 8d. Among these Freemen who have been taken away William de Warenne has 55. They have under them 57 smallholders. In all they have 5 c. of land. Meadow, 12 acres. Before 1066 they had 20 ploughs, now 13. 1/2 mill. Value always £10. Also Ralph of Beaufour has 10 Freemen, 2 c. of land. 32 smallholders. Always 7 ploughs; meadow, 12 acres; 1 1/2 mills. Also Count Alan (has) 1 Freeman, 1 1/2 c. of land. 13 smallholders. 3 ploughs; meadow, 9 acres; 1 mill. Value 30s. Also Roger Bigot (has) 2 Freemen, 45 acres of land. 6 smallholders. 2 ploughs; meadow, 2 acres. Woodland, then 60 pigs, now 16. Value 7s 6d.

Wymondham is confusingly still pronounced Windham, as once it was spelled. It is an attractive, bustling town, mercifully preserved from the fierce traffic which runs between Thetford and Norwich. The sloping market square, with its fine half-timbered cross is the heart of modern Wymondham. The earliest visible evidence of its history however, lies in a quiet spot at the bottom of the hill, among the twisted pines and a ruined churchyard where in 1207 the Benedictines of St Albans established their priory.

Wymondham had already been the centre of some disorder. *'Confusionem'* is how the *Domesday* surveyors chose to describe the events that resulted in the dramatic decline in plough teams from 60 to 24. As the figures suggest, 'Wimundham' was a populous community in 1086, supporting nearly 700 inhabitants. But not so prosperous as it had once been. Its misfortune was to have been allocated after the Conquest to Ralph de Wader, Earl of East Anglia, who joined his brother-in-law Roger, Earl of Hereford, in rebellion against King William. This insurrection was quickly suppressed, and Earl Ralph was forced to escape abroad. One *Domesday* scholar has suggested that on his retreat eastward from Cambridge to Norwich, Ralph passed through his thriving holding at Wymondham and licensed his Breton soldiers to slaughter the livestock belonging to his innocent subjects. If this were so, Ralph's soldiers had a splendid barbecue, as Wymondham's loss of 36 plough teams represents 288 oxen. Eventually they paid for their dinner. When Ralph fled the country, his army remained under the generalship of his wife Emma. For a while they held out at Norwich, before King William's forces overwhelmed the city.

The manor, together with its outlier at Talconeston, then passed to the king, and was among the 14 in Norfolk which he put into the charge of William de Noyers. But by 1086 all except 18 of its freemen had transferred their holdings to other tenants-in-chief: 55 to William de Warenne and others to Ralph de Beaufour, Count Alan, Roger Bigot and (listed in a separate entry) to Ralph Baynard at Dykebeck. A further entry for William de Warenne suggests that these freemen did not all change allegiance at once but followed each other over a period of years. In spite of its reduced condition, Wymondham kept the right to administer justice in William de Warenne's prospering manor of Barnham.

The monks of Wymondham created a different kind of disorder. Their attitude to the townspeople with whom they shared the church of St Mary and St Thomas of Canterbury was distinctly unchristian. This church has a magnificent early twelfth-century nave, but is even more remarkable for having two towers, the solid western one, still a part of the main edifice, and the eastern one, an octagonal shell. It is only poetic justice that it is this tower that suffered, for the monks, who wrangled constantly with the Wymondhamites, built a six-foot-thick wall across the middle of the church, dividing it into two places of worship. The local parishioners riposted by building their own grander west tower. There might have been no end of towers had Henry VIII not thrown in his weight on the side of the parishioners. In 1539 the townspeople took complete possession of what was left of the church buildings.

It was while they were attending church that much of the town burned down in 1615. Over 300 houses were lost, including that of the vicar, Edward Agas. The Bishop of Norwich asked the clergy to help relieve the poor man, 'who lost all whatsoever he had . . . save only the cloathes of his back and the Bible in his hand in the time of the sermon.' The town was quickly rebuilt and the then new seventeenth-century houses and shops contribute greatly to Wymondham's charm.

WYMONDHAM: *In winter the abbey's tall towers suggest something of its violent history.*

Norfolk Gazetteer
Each entry starts with the modern place name in **bold** type. The *Domesday* information that follows is in *italic* type, beginning with the name or names by which the place was known in 1086. The tenants-in-chief and main undertenants are next, separated with semi-colons if a place was divided into more than one holding. More general information completes the *Domesday* part of the entry, including examples of dues such as honey rendered by tenants and animals when the totals reach or exceed: 150 sheep, 30 goats, 8 cattle, 15 pigs, 3 cobs and 3 oxen. The modern or post-Domesday section is in normal type. ▣ represents a village, ⌂ a small village or hamlet.

Acle *Acle: King's land, formerly Harold, in the custody of Godric. Mill, 15 beehives.* Small market town on the broads.

Acre *Acre/a: William de Warenne; Abbot of Ely before and after 1066; Ralph de Tosny. 6½ mills, 2 fisheries, 5½ salt-houses, church. 18 pigs, 11 cattle, 540 sheep.* Now 2 villages, Castle Acre, with the remains of William de Warenne's castle, and a church with Norman features; and West Acre.

Alburgh *Aldeberga: King's land, in the custody of Godric and in the charge of William de Noyers; Count Alan.* ⌂ Once a linen-weaving centre.

Alby *Alabei/ebei: Roger Bigot. Mill.* ⌂ Now Alby Hill.

Aldborough *Aldebur(c)/burg: William de Warenne; Roger Bigot. 1½ mills.* ▣

Aldeby *Aldebury: Ralph de Beaufour. Church.* ⌂ Church with a Norman doorway.

Alethorpe *Alatorp: King's land and Stibbard from the king.* Alethorpe Hall. The village was depopulated during the 16th-century enclosures.

Alpington *Appletona/tuna: Godric the Steward; Roger Bigot. Horse.* ⌂ Alpington Hall.

Anmer *Anamere/Anemere: Count Eustace; William de Warenne. Fishery, 1½ salt-houses.* ⌂ On the Sandringham estate.

Antingham *Antigeham/Antingham/Attinga: Roger Bigot and Thurston FitzGuy from him; Abbot of Holme.* ▣ The source of the River Ant is at Antingham Common.

Appleton *Ap(p)letuna/tona: Roger Bigot; Thorgils from Peter de Valognes. Church. 2 oxen.* Appleton House and Farm; remains of St Mary's church; Roman villa site nearby.

Arminghall *Hameringahala: King's land, in the charge of William de Noyers.* ⌂ Site of a now covered neolithic temple.

Ashby *Essebei: King's land, in the custody of Godric.* Ashby Mere, a small lake near Snetterton.

Ashby (near Acle) *Aschebei/Asseby: Bishop William; Abbot of Holme; William d'Écouis. 8 beehives.* Ashby Hall.

ACLE: *The River Bure – a typical scene on the Broads.*

Ashby St Mary *Ascebei/As(s)ebei: Roger Bigot; Godric the steward.* ▣ Straggling.

Ashill *Asscelea/Essalai: Reynald FitzIvo; Abbot of Ely.* ▣ Green.

Ashwellthorpe *Torp: Count Eustace. 8 beehives. 40 goats.* ▣ Moated site; Lord Berners, chancellor to Henry VIII and translator of Froissart's Chronicles, lived here.

Ashwicken *Wica/Wiche: Count Alan; Reynald FitzIvo. ½ salt-house.* ▣ Fenland.

Aslacton *Aslactuna/Aslaktuna/Oslactuna: Count Alan; Roger Bigot and Hugh from him.* ▣

Attleborough *Alia Atleburc/Atlebur(c): Roger FitzRainard; Alfred. Fishery. ⅔ mill, ½ mill. Cow, 8 cattle.* Small town famous for cider and turkeys. The church has Saxon foundations, a Norman tower, and a pulpit possibly carved by Grinling Gibbons.

Attlebridge *At(l)ebruge/Attebruge: Count Alan; Geoffrey from Bishop William; William d'Écouis; Walter Giffard. Church.* ⌂

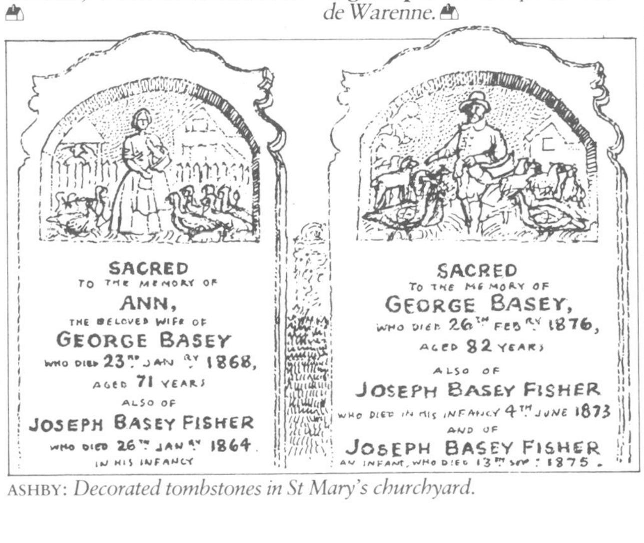

ASHBY: *Decorated tombstones in St Mary's churchyard.*

Aylmerton *Almartune/Almertuna: Frederic from William de Warenne; Roger Bigot. ½ church.* ▣ Near the coast; church with a round tower and priest's room; Roman camp and Saxon iron ore workings on nearby Aylmerton Heath.

Aylsham *Aelsaham/Ailesham/Ailessam: King's land, in the custody of Godric. 2 mills.* Small market town on the River Bure; mid-Victorian mill.

Bablingley *Babin/ghelea/keleia: Geoffrey from Eudo FitzSpirwic; William from Peter de Valognes. Moiety of 2 mills, 5 salt-houses, another mill. 8 cattle, 177 sheep.* ⌂ Moated Hall Farm.

Baconsthorpe (in Attleborough) *Baconstorp: Thurstan from Count Alan.* ▣

Baconsthorpe (near Holt) *Torp: Thorold from Roger Bigot; Osbert from Robert Gernon. ½ mill, 100 pigs.* ▣ Fortified 15th-century manor house; mainly ruined gatehouse.

Bacton *Baketuna: Robert Malet. 2 mills.* ▣ On the coast; remains of Bromholm priory nearby.

Bagthorpe *Bachestorp: William de Warenne.* ⌂

Bale *Bathele: King's land; Harold from Count Alan.* ⌂ Moated site; Bale Oaks, a stand of 18th-century evergreen oaks.

Banham *Benham: William de Warenne; Berard from Roger Bigot; Bishop Osbern; William d'Ecouis from Abbot of Ely, who held before and after 1066; William d'Ecouis. Church. 30 goats.* ▣ Zoo; orchards; a cider-making industry.

Banningham *Banincham/Hamingeham: William de Warenne; Abbot of Holme; Roger from Reynald FitzIvo.* ▣

Barford *Bereforda/fort: Count Alan; Abbot of Holme; Richard from Ralph de Beaufour. ½ mill.* ▣

Barmer *Benemara: Ralph from William de Warenne. ½ church.* ⌂

Barney *Berlei/Berneia: William from Peter de Valognes. 2 beehives. 14 wild mares, 14 cattle, 38 goats.* ⌂ Church with Saxon work and some Roman bricks; 3 moated medieval sites nearby.

Barnham Broom *Ber(n)ham: William de Warenne; Godwin Haldane; Starculf before and after 1066. 2½ mills.* ▣ 16th-century manor house. The church has a 16th-century screen with a rare portrait of St Walstan.

Barsham *Barfham/saham/seham: King's land; Hugh from William de Warenne. 4 mills, church. 200 sheep.* Now 2 villages, East and West Barsham.

Barton Bendish *Bertuna: William from Hermer de Ferrers; Reynald FitzIvo; Ralph Baynard, formerly Aethelgyth, a free woman. 2 churches. 4 cobs.* ⌂ 2 churches, one with a late Norman doorway.

Barton Turf *Bertuna: Abbot of Holme before and after 1066; Geoffrey from Ralph Baynard. 2 churches.* ▣ On the edge of Barton Broad; nature reserve; church with a rare portrait of Henry VI.

Barwick *Bereuuica: Simon from William de Warenne. ½ church. 160 sheep.* Now 2 hamlets, Little and Great Barwick; also the site of the medieval village of Great Barwick.

Bastwick *Bastu(u)ic/Bastuuuic: Count Alan; 2 free women, the pre-Conquest holders, from Roger Bigot; Bishop William; Abbot of Holme; Aelmer.* ⌂

Bawburgh *Bauenbu(r)c: Count Alan. Mill.* ▣ Church with a round tower, possibly Saxon. It was the birthplace of St Walstan in 965 and a place of pilgrimage until the Reformation.

Bawdeswell *Baldereswella: Count Alan.* ▣

Bawsey *Boweseia/Heuseda: Count Alan; Robert Malet. 1½ salt-houses. 50 goats.* ⌂

Bayfield *Baiafelda: King's land; Walter Giffard. 1¼ mills.* Part Jacobean Bayfield Hall; Bayfield Brecks, scattered cottages.

Beck *Bec: Count Alan.* Beck Hall, formerly Beck Hostel for travellers to Walsingham.

Bedingham *Bedingaham: King's land, in the custody of Godric; Roger Bigot.* ⌂ Now Bedingham Green; several medieval moated sites.

Beechamwell *Bechersuuella/Bicham/Bycham/Hekesuuella: Ribald, the pre-Conquest holder, from Count Alan; Robert de Vaux from Roger Bigot; Reynald FitzIvo; Ralph Baynard. Church. Ass.* ⌂ Church with a Saxon tower.

Beeston Regis *Besentuna/Besetuna/tune: Ingulf from William d'Écouis; Hugh de Montfort.* Seaside suburb of Sheringham.

Beeston St. Andrew *Boefetuna/Bes(e)tuna: King's land, in the custody of Godric; Robert Malet; Godric the steward; Ralph de Beaufour. 2 mills, church.* Beeston Hall.

Beeston St Lawrence *Besetuna: Abbot of Holme.* Some houses.

Beotley *Betellea: Bishop William. Church.* ▣ Scattered.

Beighton *Begetona/tuna: Bishop William. Church.* ⌂ Manor house; church with a 13th-century font.

Belaugh *Belaga: King's land, in the custody of Godric and in the charge of William de Noyers; Abbot of Holme; Ralph de Beaufour.* ▣ Belaugh Broad.

Bergh Apton *Berc: Godric the steward from Abbot of Ely. Mill. 203 cattle.* ▣ Manor house; 6th–7th-century barrows and ring ditches.

Bessingham *Basingeham: Drogo de Beuvrière.* ▣ Manor house; moated site.

Besthorpe *Besthorp: Roger Bigot.* ▣ Saxon earthworks.

Bexwell *Beches/Bekes/uuella: Ralph FitzHerlwin from Roger Bigot; Abbot of Ely. Church, ½ fishery.* ▣ Church with Norman windows.

Bickerston *: Under dispute.* Bickerston Bridge and Farm.

Billingford (near Diss) *P(re)lestuna: King's land, in the charge of William de Noyers; Roger de Raismes from Abbot of Ely; Roger de Raismes and Warenger from him.* Tower windmill.

Billingford (near East Dereham) *Billingeforda/ Belingesfort: Humphrey and Count Alan from Ranulf Peverel; Humphrey FitzAubrey. 2 mills, 4 beehives.* Mill nearby.

Billockby *Bit(h)lakebei: Roger Bigot; Ketel and Bernard from Bishop William. ⅔ church.*

Binham *Benincham/Bin(n)eham: Peter de Valognes. 2 mills.* Remains of a Benedictine priory founded c.1091 by Peter de Valognes.

Bintree *Binctre/Binnetra: Godric the steward; Walter Giffard; Hagni the King's reeve.* Manor house; mill.

Bircham Newton *Niwetuna: Ralph de Beaufour. Church.*

Bircham Tofts *Stofsta: Bishop of Bayeux.*

Bittering *Britringa: King's land, in the custody of Godric and in the charge of William de Noyers.* Site of the medieval village of Little Bittering.

Bixley *Bichesle/Biskele/Bischelai/ Fiskele: Roger Bigot.* Bixleybottom Plantation; remains of a moated hall.

Blakeney *Esnuterle(a)/Snuterlea:* see page 182.

Blickling *Bliclinga/Blikelinga/ inges: Godric and Walter Giffard from the king, formerly Harold. Bishop William. 3½ mills.* Jacobean Hall.

Blofield *Bla(uue)felda: Bishop William.* Broadland.

Blo Norton *Nortuna: Fulcher from William de Warenne; Alfred an Englishman from Roger Bigot; St Edmund's; Abbot of Ely. 1½ mills, church.* Church; Blo Norton Hall.

Bodham *Bod(en)ham/Botham: Ralph from Hugh de Montfort; Walter Giffard.*

Bodney *Bod/Budeneia: William de Warenne; Ralph de Tosny; Hugh de Montfort. 3¼ mills.* Flint church with Saxon carvings; tumuli nearby.

Booton *Botuna: Tihel le Breton.* Booton Manor.

Boughton *Bucbetuna: Ranulf from Reynald FitzIvo; Ralph Baynard. Church, 3 beehives. Cow.* 18th-century houses round a green; pond; church.

Bowthorpe *Bo(w)ethorp: King's land, in the custody of Godric. Mill.* Recent suburban development near Norwich.

Boyland *Boielund:* Lost.

Bracon Ash *Braccas/Braccles: Roger Bigot.* Birthplace of Edward Thurlow (1731–1806), Lord Chancellor.

Bradenham *Brade(n)ham/ Brehendam: William de Cailli from William de Warenne; Ralph de Tosny; Ralph Baynard.* Now 2 villages, East and West Bradenham.

Bradeston *Bregestuna/ Breiestuna: William de Noyers and Edric, a steersman of King Edward's, from Bishop William.* Bradeston church on high ground overlooking Bradeston Marsh.

Bramerton *Bramb(r)etuna: Aitard de Vaux from the king; Bishop of Bayeux; Roger Bigot and Ranulf Fitz Walter from him; Godric the steward. Church.* Mostly 14th-century church.

Brampton *Brantuna: William de Warenne; Ralph de Beaufour.* Home of the Brampton family from 1066 to the 17th century.

Brancaster *Broncestra: St Benedict's of Ramsey before and after 1066. Mill, 600 sheep.* On the coast; adjacent to the site of the Roman fort, *Branodunum.*

BLICKLING: *The Hall, 1620, of red brick with Dutch gables, is one of the loveliest homes in England.*

Brandiston *Brantestuna: King's land.* Stump cross.

Brandon Parva *Brandim: Count Alan.* Scene of 19th-century agricultural workers riots.

Breckles *Brecc(h)les/Brec(l)es: King's land; Roger Bigot; Ralph de Tosny. Customary honey.* Church with a Norman and Saxon tower, and a memorial stone to Ursula Webb who was, at her own request, buried upright in the 17th century.

Bressingham *Brasincham/ Bresing(a)ham: King's land, in the custody of Godric; St Edmund's and Roger Bigot from the abbey. Church.*

Brettenham *Bre(t)ham: William de Bourneville from Roger Bigot; Abbot of Ely; Eudo the steward; William from John nephew of Waleran. 2 mills, 5 beehives.*

Bridgham *Brugam: Abbot of Ely before and after 1066. Church, 4 mills, 5 beehives. 180 sheep.* Church with a Norman font.

Briningham *Bruningaham/ Burningaham: Geoffrey from Count Alan; Roger Longsword from Bishop William. Church, mill, 5 beehives.* Circular lookout post nearby, was used at the time of the Armada.

Brinton *Bruntuna: Bishop William.* Georgian hall.

Briston *Burstuna: King's land; William de Warenne.* Adjoining Melton Constable.

Brockdish *Brodise/Brodiso: King's land, in the charge of William de Noyers; St Edmund's. Church.* Church with Saxon and Norman windows.

Brooke *Broc: St Edmund's. 5 cobs, 14 cattle.* Reed mere; the birthplace of Sir Astley Cooper, famous 18th-century surgeon.

Broome *Brom/Bron: Roger Bigot; Frodo from St Edmund's, who held before and after 1066; Humphrey from Robert FitzCorbucion. Church, mill, ½ fishery, 2 beehives.* On marshes near the River Waveney.

Broomsthorpe *Bruneston: Abbot of Ely. Mill.*

Brumstead *Brume/Brunestada: Robert from Roger Bigot. Church, mill. 30 goats.* Some houses; church with a thatched nave.

Brundall *Brundala: King's land, in the custody of Godric; Gilbert the Crossbowman.* Yacht centre.

Buckenham (near Acle) *Bucanaham/Buc(hana): King's land, in the custody of Godric; Eli from Bishop William; Roger Bigot from St Edmund's, who held before and after 1066. 4 cattle.* Near the Broads.

Buckenham (near Attleborough) *Buccham/ Buc(he)ham: King's land, in the custody of Godric; William de Warenne; St Edmund's before and after 1066; Roger d'Evreux from William d'Ecouis. 2 mills.* Now 2 villages, Old and New Buckenham. Old Buckenham castle was moved to New Buckenham c.1136.

Buckenham Tofts *Buch/ Buckenham: Hugh de Montfort; Roger FitzRainard. ½ mill.* Buckenham Tofts Park; ancient flint mine nearby; Saxon earthworks.

Burgh (next Aylsham) *Bu(r)c: Roger Bigot; Drogo de Beuvrière. 1½ mills.* On the River Bure; Oxhead's Mill nearby.

Burgh St Margaret *Burc/Burh: King's land, in the custody of Godric; Roger Bigot and Stanard from him; Bishop William; Abbot of Holme. 2 salt-houses.* Broadland.

Burnham *Brunaham/Bruneham: Humphrey de Culey from Roger Bigot; St Benedict's of Ramsey before and after 1066; Hugh de Montfort. 1⅔ mills.* Now Burnham Norton; Burnham Sutton, Burnham Ulph and Burnham Westgate adjoin Burnham Market village.

Burnham Deepdale *Depedala: Thurstan FitzGuy from Roger Bigot.* On the coast by Peddars Way, a Roman road.

Burnham Overy *Brumeham: King's land, in the custody of Godric. 2½ mills.* Watermill on the River Bure; picturesque miller's house.

Burnham Thorpe *Brunehamtorp: Walter from William de Warenne; Robert de Verley. Mill, church. 345 sheep, ass, 6 cobs.* Moated manor house. Birthplace of Horatio Nelson (1758–1805), whose father was rector here, 1755–1802.

Burston *Borstuna: King's land, in the custody of Godric; Robert Malet (holding of the queen's gift) and his mother and Walter from him.* Mill at Mill Green nearby.

Buxton *Buk/Buchestuna: Ralph de Beaufour. Mill, church. 18 pigs.* Watermill on the River Bure. It was the birthplace of Thomas Cubitt (1788–1855), founder of the first modern builders' firm.

Bylaugh *Belega: Wigwin from Count Alan. Mill, 3 beehives. 12 cattle.* Mill at Mill Street nearby; tiny church with painted box pews and fireplaces, and a 3-tier pulpit.

Caister-on-Sea *Castre/o/a: King's land, in the custody of Godric; Abbot of Holme. ½ mill, 45 salt-houses. 8 cattle.* Seaside town with the remains of Caister Castle built by Sir John Fastoff, (Falstaff) in the mid-15th century nearby.

Caistor St Edmunds *Castra/u: St Edmund's; Ralph de Beaufour. Church. 1½ mills. 5 cattle.* Site of Venta, Norfolk's most important Roman fortress, containing a tiny church with Saxon windows.

Caldecote *Calda(n)chota: Reynald FitzIvo; Ralph de Tosny. Mill.* Caldecote Farm and Fen; remains of Old St Mary's Church.

Calthorpe *Calatorp/Caletorp: Roger Bigot; Abbot of Holme; Guerri and Osbert from Tihel le Breton. 2½ mills, church, 2 beehives.*

Calvely *Cavelea: Berner the Crossbowman from Abbot of Ely who held it before and after 1066.* Calveley Hall.

Cantley *Cantelai: King's land, in the custody of Godric. Salt-house. 400 sheep.* Broadland; sugar beet refinery.

Carbrooke *Cherebroc: Ralph de Tosny; John nephew of Waleran. Mill, ½ fishery. 700 pigs.* Site of a religious house of the Knights Templars, founded in the mid-12th century by Roger de Clare. The church has two 13th-century sepulchral slabs commemmorating the Countess of Clare.

Carleton Forehoe *Carle/ Karletuna: King's land, in the custody of Godric; Count Alan; Abbot of Holme.* Green; pond; moated site.

Carleton Rode *Carletuna: King's land, in the custody of Godric; Count Alan; William de Warenne; Roger Bigot; Eudo FitzSpirwic. 2 churches.* Scattered.

BINHAM: *The nave of the Benedictine priory is now the parish church; the excavated site is nearby.*

Carleton St Peter *Carletuna/Karlentona: Roger Bigot of the King's livery; Godric the steward; Reynald FitzIvo; Nigel from Ralph Baynard. Church. Horse at the hall.* Scattered.

Castle Rising *Risinga:* see page 182.

Caston *Caste(s)tuna: King's land, also in the custody of Godric; William de Warenne.* Restored medieval cross on the green.

Catfield *Cate(s)felda: Count Alan; Roger Bigot. Church.* Catfield Hall. The poet Cowper often stayed here as a child, with his cousins, the Donnes, whose father was rector.

Catton (near Norwich) *Cat(e)tuna: King's land, in the custody of Godric and in the charge of William de Noyers.* Suburb of Norwich. The late Georgian hall has grounds by Repton.

Catton (in Postwick) *Cai/Ca(t)/tuna:* Lost.

Cawston *Calvestune/Castona/tune/Cauestuna/Caupstuna/Caustituna/Caustona/tuna/Gaustuna: King's land, in the custody of Godric; William de Warenne, formerly Harold. 2 mills, 1000 pigs, 4 cobs, 20 cattle, 50 goats.* Small town.

Chedgrave *Scatagrava: Einbold and Geoffrey from Ralph Baynard. Mill.* Some of the church window glass is said to have come from Rouen Cathedral during the French Revolution.

Claxton *Clakestona/Clarestuna: Robert de Vaux from Roger Bigot; Godric the steward. Church. 200 sheep.* Broadland.

Clenchwarton *Ecleuuartuna: Richard and Wulfwy from William d'Ecouis.* Fenland.

Clipstone *Clipestuna: William de Warenne. Church (with Little Snoring and Kettlestone).* Now Lower Clipstone; Clipstone House.

Cockley Cley *Claia/Cleia: King's land, in the custody of Godric; William de Warenne. 2 mills, beehive.*

Cockthorpe *Torp: Bishop William and William de Noyers from him.*

Colby *Colebei: King's land. Mill.* Scattered.

Colkirk *Colechirca/Cole/kirka: Bishop William. Church. 160 goats.* Church with a circular Norman font.

Colney *Coleneia/eii: Warenger from Roger Bigot; Walter from Godric the steward; Robert de Vaux from William d'Ecouis. 2½ mills.* Church with a Saxon tower.

Coltishall *Cokereshala/Coketeshala/Colceteshala: Thorold from William de Warenne. Church.* Church with a thatched roof, 2 circular Saxon windows and a Norman font.

Colton *Coletuna: William de Warenne.*

Colveston *Covestuna: William de Warenne. Fishery, 2 mills.* Colveston Manor Farm.

Congham *Concham,/Congheham/Congreham: William de Warenne; Berner the Crossbowman. Mill, ½ salt-house, church.* Home of Sir Henry Spelman, 17th-century antiquarian.

Corpusty *Corpestig/stih/Corpsty: William de Warenne; Bishop William; William d'Ecouis. ¾ church.* Divided from Saxthorpe by the River Bure.

CLEY NEXT THE SEA: *Windmill, 1713, on the marshes between the village and the sea.*

Cley next the Sea *Claia: King's land.* Small town on the coastal salt marshes. Knucklebone House has cornice and panelling made from sheep's vertebrae.

Cleythorpe *Cleietorpe:* Lost.

Clippesby *Clipesby/Clipestuna/Clepe(s)be(i): King's land, and in the custody of Godric; Roger Bigot, of the King's gift, and Stanard from him; Bishop William; Abbot of Holme. Salt-house.* Near the Broads.

Costessy *Costesei(a)/Coteseia: Count Alan. 2 mills, park for beasts of chase. 14 cattle.* On the outskirts of Norwich.

Crackford *Crachefort/Crakeforda:* Lost.

Cranwich *Cranwisse: William de Warenne. Mill, fishery, 7 beehives. 4 cattle.* Near the River Wissey; Church with interlacing stonework in the Saxon tower, a thatched roof and a circular churchyard.

DENVER: *Windmills are an important part of the Norfolk skyline.*

Cranworth *Cranaworda/Craneworda: King's land, in the custody of Godric. Mill. 20 goats.* Moated site nearby; stocks at the church gate.

Creake *Crehic/Creic(h)/Kreic(h)/Suthcreich: King's land; William de Warenne; Thurstan FitzGuy from Roger Bigot; Thurstan from William d'Ecouis; Hugh de Montfort. Church, mill. 264 sheep.* Now 2 villages, North and South Creake.

Crimplesham *Crep(e)lesham: Reynald FitzIvo and Thorkell from him, formerly a free woman. 1½ fisheries. 300 sheep.* Fenland; moated site.

Cringleford *Cringaforda/Kiningaforda/Kringeforda: Roger Bigot; Roger Bigot and Holverston from Bishop of Bayeux; Roger Bigot from Count Alan. 1¾ mills, ⅛ of another.* Suburb of Norwich; church with a Saxon nave and chancel.

Crostwick *Crostueit/Crotwit: Ralph de Beaufour; Roger de Poitou.* Large village green.

Crostwight *Crostwit: Geoffrey from Ralph Baynard.*

Crownthorpe *Congrethorp/Cronkethor: King's land, in the custody of Godric; Ralph de Beaufour. Mill.*

Croxton (near Fakenham) *Crokestona: William de Warenne. Church.*

Croxton (near Thetford) *Crokestuna: King's land, in the charge of William de Noyers. 215 sheep, 50 goats.* In the Breckland woods; Croxton Heath. The church has a Norman tower.

Custthorpe *Culestorpa:* Lost.

Denton *Dentuna: King's land, in the charge of William de Noyers; Eudo FitzSpirwic. ½ mill.* Broadland.

Denver *Danefaela-fella: William de Warenne and Hugh from him. 2 fisheries.* Fenland; Denver Sluice, the key to the drainage system of the South Fenlands.

Deopham *D(i)epham: William de Warenne; Ralph de Beaufour. 17 pigs, 32 goats.*

Dersingham *Dersincham: Ricwold from Eudo FitzSpirwic; Peter de Valognes and Anand from him. Mill, 2 salt-houses, fishery. 646 sheep.* Small town near the coast and Sandringham Estate.

Dickleburgh *Dicclesburc: St Edmund's who held before and after 1066. Church.* Imposing perpendicular church; birthplace of the watercolourist George Cattermole (1800–68).

Didlington *Dudelingatuna: William de Warenne; Ralph de Limésy. Mill, fishery.* On the River Wissey; weir; Watermill Farm.

Dilham *Dilham/Dillam: Count Alan; Robert Malet; Roger Bigot; Abbot of Holme.* Near Broad Fen.

Diss *Dice: Roger Bigot from the king. Church. 5 goats.* Attractive market town built around a mere. The Poet Laureate John Skelton, tutor to Henry VIII, was rector here (1504–29).

Ditchingham *Dicingaham: King's land, in the charge of William de Noyers. 2 mills. 55 goats.* Early 18th-century hall with a garden by Capability Brown.

Docking *Doching(h)e: Bishop of Bayeux; Ricwold from Eudo FitzSpirwic. Cow, 17 pigs.* The Roman Catholic martyr, Henry Walpole was baptized here c.1588.

Downham Market *Dun(e)ham: William de Warenne; Roger Bigot; Abbot of Ely.* Town with a market reputedly established before the Conquest; remains of a Roman road.

Drayton *Draituna: Ralph de Beaufour. Church.* Town adjoining Norwich.

Dunham *Dumham/Dunham: King's land, in the charge of William de Noyers; Ralph de Tosny; Reynold the priest with the daughter of Payne from Edmund FitzPayne. ½ market, mill, 3 beehives. 19 cattle, 17 pigs.* Now 2 villages, Little Dunham, and Great Dunham village with a flint, mainly Saxon, church.

Dunston *Dunestun(a)/Dustuna: Count Alan; Roger Bigot; Godric the steward; Ralph de Beaufour. 1⅓ mills.* Queen Anne manor house.

Dunton *Dontuna: King's land. Mill.*

Dykebeck *Hidichetorp/Idikethorp: Ralph Baynard. ¼ church. 22 pigs.* Dyke Beck; and Dykebeck Hall.

Earlham *Erlham: Wulfgeat from the king, in the custody of Godric; Count Alan. Mill.* Part of Norwich on the River Yare; part of the University of East Anglia.

Earsham *Ersam/Hersam: King's land, in the charge of William de Noyers. 2 mills, 3 horses at the hall.* Mill.

East Beckham *Beccheham/Bech(e)am: King's land, in the custody of Godric; Roger Bigot; Bishop William. Church.*

East Carleton *Carletuna/Karletuna: Walter and Ulf from Roger Bigot; Ralph de Beaufour; Ranulf Peverel and Waring from him. 2 churches.* Hall, a Cheshire Home.

East Dereham *Derham: Abbot of Ely before and after 1066; Oder from Ralph de Beaufour. 4 mills.* Town with some industry on a tributary of the River Wensum.

Easton (near Norwich) *Estuna: Count Alan.* On the River Tud; site of the Royal Norwich Showground.

Easton (in Scottow) *Estuna:* Lost.

East Ruston *Ristuna: Geoffrey from Ralph Baynard. 51 goats. Mill.* Birthplace of the famous academic Richard Porson, in 1759.

East Tuddenham *Easttudenham/Todeneham/Toddenham/Tudenham: Count Alan; Hermer de Ferrers; Ralph de Beaufour. ½ mill, church. 160 sheep.* Church with many 13th-century and early features.

East Walton *Waltuna: Count Alan; Robert de Vaux from Roger Bigot; Ralph de Tosny. Mill, Church.* Church with a Norman tower.

EAST TUDDENHAM: *The parish pump, a feature of many villages until the 1900s.*

East Winch *Estuuininc/ Eastwninc/Estuunic/Estwnic: King's land, in the custody of Godric, also Bordin from Annex: of Hermer; Roger Bigot, and Robert de Vaux from him; Ralph de Tosny. Fishery, 1 ½ salt-houses, ½ church.* Ruins of the moated manor of Sir William Howard, of the family which became dukes of Norfolk in 1483; church with Norman features.

Eaton *Aietona/tuna/Etona/ Ettuna/ttune: King's land, in the custody of Godric. Mill, church.* Part of Norwich near the River Yare; tumuli; golf course.

Eccles (near Attleborough) *Eccles: Bishop William. Mill.* Now Eccles Road.

Eccles (in Hempstead) *Eccles/ Heccles: Abbot of Holme before and after 1066; Aelmer FitzGodwin.* Also called Eccles on Sea; ruined church on the beach.

Edgefield *Edisfelda: Peter de Valognes; Humphrey from Ranulf brother of Ilger. Mill, 2 beehives.* Near the River Geet. Richard Lubbock, author of *Fauna in Norfolk* was rector here for 40 years in the 19th century.

Egmere *Edgamere/Egemere/ Estgamera: King's land; Frederic from William de Warenne; Morel from Bishop William.*

Ellingham (near Loddon) *Elincham: King's land, in the charge of William de Noyers. Church.* Clock tower (1855) with living accommodation at its base.

Elsing *Helsinga: Wymer from William de Warenne. 2 mills, church, 12 beehives. 10 cattle.* Mill at Mill Street nearby. The Tudor moated manor was held by descendants of Wymer until 1958.

Erpingham *Erpincham/ Herpincham: Roger Bigot; Abbot of Holme; Drogo de Beuvrière; Humphrey from Ranulf brother of Ilger. Church.* Church with a brass memorial to Sir Thomas Erpingham, companion of Henry V at Agincourt. His family is said to have arrived with King William.

Fakenham *Fac(h)enham/ Fagan(a)ham/Fagenham/ Fangeham/Phacham: King's land. 3 mills, ½ salt-house, flour mill. 200 sheep.* Pretty market town on the River Wensum. John of Gaunt was Lord of the Manor here in the 14th century.

Felbrigg *Felebruge: Roger Bigot and Metton from him.* Felbrigg Hall, 1620, with a fine park probably landscaped by Repton.

Felmingham *Felmi(n)cham: Asford from the king; Roger Bigot; Abbot of Holme before and after 1066. Mill, church.*

Felthorpe *Faltorp/Felethor(p)/ torp: King's land; Count Alan; Richard from Ralph de Beaufour; Walter Giffard.*

Feltwell *Fatwella/Feltwella: King's land, in the charge of William de Noyers; William de Warenne; Abbot of Ely before and after 1066. 2 churches, mill, 2 fisheries.* Fenland; 2 churches, one with Norman side walls and arch.

Fersfield *Ferseuella/Feru(ess)ella: Alsi, King Edward's thane, from the king, in the custody of Godric.* Church with an effigy of Sir Robert de Bois, Lord of the Manor in 1285.

Field Dalling *Dalli(n)ga: King's land; Count Alan; Roger Bigot; Robert de Verly.* Straggling; Manor House Farm.

Filby *Filebey/Phileb(e)y: Thorold from William de Warenne; Stanard from Roger Bigot; Abbot of Holme before and after 1066; William d'Ecouis; Rabel the engineer. 10½ salt-houses.* On Filby Broad; Churchyard with a tombstone to a couple whose combined age was 200.

Fincham *F. . ham/P(h)incham: William de Warenne and Hugh and William Brant from him; Hermer de Ferrers; St Edmund's; Abbot of Ely before and after 1066; Reynald FitzIvo; Ralph Baynard, formerly Aethelgyrth, a free woman. ¼ church. 4 cattle, 175 sheep.* On a Roman road; Moat House with a square moated island, possibly a medieval cattle enclosure.

Fishley *Fiscele: King's land, in the custody of Godric; Abbot of Holme; William d'Ecouis.* Church with a pre-Conquest tower and Norman doorway.

Flitcham *Flicham/Phlicham/ Plic(e)ham: Bishop of Bayeux; William de Warenne; Robert and Ranulf Fitz Walter from Roger Bigot. 4 mills, church 3 oxen.* Remains of Flitcham Abbey; Church with Norman arcading.

Flockthorpe *Floc(he)thor(p)/ Flokethorp:* Lost.

Flordon *Florenduna: Roger Bigot from Bishop of Bayeux; Count Alan; Roger Bigot; Godric the steward.* Church with Saxon windows.

Fodderstone *Fo(r)testhorp/ Photestorp: Abbot of Ely before and after 1066; Ranulf from Reynald FitzIvo.* Now Fodderstone Gap.

Fordham *Ford(e)ham/Forham/ Phor(d)ham: Abbot of Ely; St Benedict's of Ramsey; Ralph Baynard.* Fenland; on the River Great Ouse cut-off Channel.

Forncett *Foneseta/Forne(s)/seta: Roger Bigot; Bishop Osbern.* Now 2 villages, Forncett St Mary and St Peter. Dorothy Wordsworth lived at St Peter, with her uncle the rector, for 3 years.

Foulden *Fugalduna/Fulenduna: Ribald from Count Alan; William from William de Warenne; Walter Giffard. 2 mills, 2 fisheries.* Common.

Foulsham *Folsa(m)/Folsham: King's land before and after 1066 and Walter Giffard from the king in the custody of Godric. 2 churches, mill. 12 cattle, 400 pigs, 50 goats, 13 sesters of honey.* Small town; moated site.

Foxley *Foxle: Godric from Count Alan. 7 beehives.* Manor Farm, moated site.

FRAMINGHAM: *Church with a Saxon chancel.*

Framingham *Fram(m)ingaham: King's land and 2 Burgesses of Norwich from the king; Roger Bigot from Bishop of Bayeux; Roger Bigot. Godric the steward. Church.* Now 2 villages, Framingham Earl, whose church has a Saxon chancel and windows, and a Norman tower, and Framingham Pigot, where the church retains a Norman piscina.

Fransham *Frande(s)ham/ Frouuesham: Gilbert from William de Warenne; Ralph de Tosny. 3 mills.* Now 2 villages, Great and Little Fransham.

Freethorpe *Frietorp/Torp: King's land, in the custody of Godric; Bishop William; Rabel the engineer.* Remote; Broadland. The church has a Squires' pew with a fireplace.

Frenze *Frense/Frisa: Hubert from Robert Malet; St Edmund's. Mill.* One of the country's smallest churches.

Frettenham *Fret(h)an: Roger de Poitou. 24 pigs.*

Fring *Frainghe/Frenga/e: Count Eustace; William de Warenne; Bishop William.*

Fritton *Fred/Fridetuna/ Frie(s)tuna/Frithtuna: Robert Malet and Warin Cook from him; Roger Bigot and Ranulf from him; Robert de Vaux from St Edmund's; Gifard from Robert FitzCourbucion.* Green; church has a Saxon/Norman tower.

Fulmodeston *Fulmotestuna: Walter from William de Warenne. Church, beehive.* Ruined church.

Fundenhall *Fundahala/ehala: Roger Bigot from Earl Hugh; Roger Bigot and Osbert from him. 9 cattle, 48 goats.*

Garboldisham *Berboldesham: King's land, in the custody of Godric.* Some houses built of clay lump, large blocks of unfired clay once common in South Norfolk; sections of the Devil's Dyke nearby.

Garveston *Gerolfestuna/ Giro(l)festuna: Hermer de Ferrers.* Moated site.

Gasthorpe *Gadesthorp/ Gatesthor(p): King's land, in the custody of Godric; a certain Englishman from St Edmund's.*

Gateley *Catelea: Bishop William; Hugh de Montfort; Ralph from Peter de Valognes.* Church with some Saxon work.

Gayton *Gaituna: William de Warenne and Ralph from him, formerly a free woman, Aelfava; St Stephen de Caen; Wulfwy from William d'Ecouis; Roger from Hugh de Montfort. ½ mill.* Lake.

Gayton Thorpe *T(h)orp: Bishop of Bayeux; Robert from Roger Bigot; Ralph de Tosny. ½ church.* Church with an 11th-century tower and Saxon splayed windows.

Gaywood *Gaiuude: Bishop William. Mill, 21 salt-houses. 100 sheep.* Part of King's Lynn on the Gaywood River.

Gillingham *Kildincham/ Gillingaham: King's land, in the charge of William de Noyers. Church.* By Gillingham Marshes.

Gimingham *Giming(e)ham/ Gimingeham: William de Warenne. Church, 4 mills, 30 goats, 7 wild mares.* Church with a watching window over the porch.

Gissing *Gersinga/Gessinga: King's land, in the custody of Godric; William from Robert Malet; Roger Bigot; St Edmund's and Fulcher from it.* Moated sites; church with a Saxon tower.

Glandford *Glamforda/ Glanforda: King's land; Walter Giffard.* Model village built c.1900 by Sir Alfred Jodrell.

Glosthorpe *Glorestorp:* Lost.

Gnatingdon *Nettinghetuna:* Lost.

Godwick *Goduic: Ralph de Tosny.* Ancient village site nearby; a barn; ruined church tower.

Gooderstone *Godestuna: Godric the steward. 5 mills, fishery.*

Gorleston *Gorlestuna: King's land. 3 salt-houses. 300 sheep.* Suburb of Great Yarmouth and a seaside resort, also known as Gorleston-on-Sea, with a church on the site of a small wooden church built by Felix, Bishop of Dunwich, in the 7th century.

Great Bircham *Brecham: William d'Ecouis and Roger d'Evreux from him; Ralph de Beaufour. Church.* Line of Bronze Age Wessex barrows nearby.

Great Cressingham *Cresincghaham/Cressingaham: Count Alan; Bishop William and Ralph from him; Ralph de Tosny. 4 mills, 3 fisheries, 3 churches.* Ruins of an ancient priory, built in 1545, at Priory Farm.

Great Ellingham *Elincham/ Helincham/Helingham: Warenbold from Hermer de Ferrers. Church. 6 mares with foals, 8 cattle.* Common; moated sites; decorated church.

Great Hockham *Hocham: Roger Bigot. 220 sheep.* Now Great Hockham.

Great Melton *In Duabus Meltunis, Meltuna(na): Godric the steward; Waring from Ranulf Peverel.* All Saints Church has Saxon walling in the chancel and nave, and the Saxon tower of another church stands in the same churchyard.

Great Moulton *Muletuna: Count Alan; Roger Bigot and Mauger from him. Church.* Windmill; church with some Norman features.

Great Ryburgh *Reieborh/ Reienburh: William de Warenne and Peter from him; Ralph the Fat from Peter de Valognes. Mill.*

Great Snarehill *Snareshella/hul: Roger Bigot; Fulcher the Breton from St Edmund's. ½ fishery.* Great Snarehill Hill.

Great Snoring *Snaringa: King's land, in the custody of Godric. 2 mills. 180 sheep.* Rectory, 1525, formerly the manor house.

Grensvill *Grenesvill:* Lost.

Gresham *Gersam/Cressam: William de Warenne; Roger Bigot. Mill.* Foundations of Gresham Castle, a fortified manor house and moat, ancestral home of John Gresham, founder of the Royal Exchange in 1566.

Gressenhall *Gressenhala: Wymer from William de Warenne. 3 mills. 11 cattle, 30 goats.* Rural life museum, built in 1777 and once a workhouse.

Grimston *Erimestuna/ Grimestuna: Bishop of Bayeux; William de Warenne; Robert de Vaux from Roger Bigot; Berner the Crossbowman. 3 mills, ½ salt-house.* Common; moated site; a Roman villa site.

Griston *Gres-Gristuna: King's land, also in the custody of Godric, formerly a free woman; William de Warenne; Roger Bigot; Ralph Baynard; Osbert from John nephew of Waleran. Church, 10 beehives. 30 pigs, 10 cattle.* The Elizabethan Hall, now a farmhouse, is said to have been the home of the Babes in the Wood, murdered in nearby Wayland, or Wailing Wood. The story dates from Stuart days.

Guestwick *Geg(h)estueit: Bishop William; Hagni.* Partly Saxon, partly Norman church tower.

Guist *G(r)egeseta/sete: Bishop William; Walter Giffard.* Model village, laid out this century by the family of Thomas Cook and Son.

Lynford *Lineforda: Stanard from Roger Bigot; Walter Giffard.* Lynford Hall and Farm in a military training area.

Lyng *Ling: Count Alan. Mill.* Formercorn and paper mill.

Lynn *Lena/Lun: Ralph de Tosny; Ralph Baynard. 9½ salt-houses.* North and West Lynn, part of King's Lynn, an ancient port on the Great Ouse, with many canals and waterways, now heavily redeveloped.

Mangreen *Mangrena: Roger Bigot.* Mangreen Hall; Hall Farm; cottages near Norwich.

Mannington *Mani(n)ctuna: King's land, in the custody of Godric; William de Warenne. 2 mills. 40 goats.* 18th-century Mannington Hall, part restored by the author Horatio Walpole.

Manson *Mantatestuna: King's land, in the custody of Godric the steward.* Now Manson Green.

Marham *Mar(e)ham/Marsam: Ralph from William de Warenne; Hermer de Ferrers; Abbot of Ely before and after 1066; Hugh de Montfort. Mill. 4 cobs, 6 cows, 300 sheep.* Formerly Cherry Marham because of its many cherry trees.

Markshall *Markeshalla/ Merkeshala/essal(l)e: Ralph de Beaufour. Church, 2½ mills.*

Marlingford *Marthingheforda/ Merlingeforda: Count Alan.* Scattered; church with an hour glass for timing sermons.

Marsham *Marsham: King's land, formerly Harold; Bishop William. 6 beehives.* Titus Oates father was rector here in the early 17th century.

Martham *Marcham/Martham: King's land, also in the custody of Godric; Count Alan; Bishop William; Abbot of Holme. 2 churches, 2 salt-houses.* Broadland. In its huge church, an inscription (1730), by Christopher Burraway, the illegitimate child of an incestuous union, to his wife Alice reads, 'in this life my sister, my mistress, my mother and my wife'.

Massingham *Marsincham/ Marsingharc/Masincham// Masing(h)eham/icham: King's land, formerly Harold; Guy d'Anjou from Count Eustace; William de Warenne, formerly Alflaed, a free woman; Ralph FitzHerlwin from William d'Écouis; Roger Bigot; Ralph from Reynald FitzIvo; Berold from Eudo FitzSpirwic. ¼ salt-house. 260 sheep.* Now 2 villages, Great Massingham, with a pond and green, and Little Massingham.

Matlask *Matelasc/lesc/ Matingeles: King's land, also in the custody of Godric the steward; Count Alan and Ribald from him.*

Mattishall *Mateshala: William de Warenne; Abbot of Ely; Ralph de Beaufour.* Small market town. The church's 18th-century barrel organ is still in use.

Mautby *Maltebei/bey/by: King's land, in the custody of Godric; Hugh from William d'Écouis. 18½ salt-houses, ½ mill.*

Mayton *Maidestuna: Albert from Roger de Poitou. Mill.* Mayton Hall; moated site.

Melton Constable *Maeltuna: Roger Longsword, Ansketel the Reeve and Roger from Bishop William. Church, 8 cattle.* Church with a Norman tower and possible Reubens triptych; Hall and park which was enclosed by one of the earliest charters in England, c.1290.

Mendham *Men(da)ham: William de Noyers; Bishop William; Frodo from St Edmund's.* Birthplace of artist, Sir Alfred Munnings (1878–1959), son of John, the miller.

Merton *Meretuna: Ralph Baynard. 24 pigs.* Church with a Saxon wall and north tower; hall. Edward Fitzgerald, translator of *The Rubaiyat of Omar Khayyam*, died here (1883).

Methwold *Matelwalde/ Methelwalde: King's land, in the charge of William de Noyers; William de Warenne and Simon and Walter from him. 2½ mills, 7 fisheries, 27 beehives. 800 sheep, 12 cattle.* Bordering the fenlands. The 14th-century peasant rising started at Methwold Hythe, a nearby hamlet.

Metton *Hametuna/Metune: Roger Bigot. Mill.* Moated site.

Middleton (in Forncett) *Mildeltuna:* Lost.

Middleton (near King's Lynn) *Mid(d)eltuna/Mildetuna: Ribald from Count Alan; Richard from St Edmund's; William d'Ecouis; Aethelwold from Hugh de Montfort. 2 mills, 18 salt-houses, 2 fisheries.* Middleton Tower, a moated brick house with a gate tower.

Mileham *Mele(ha)m/Milham/ Mulcham/Mul(e)ham/Mullam: King's land, in the custody of Godric, and a widow from the King, also in the charge of William de Noyers; Count Alan; Bishop William. 2 mills, salt-house, woodland for 1140 pigs.* Straggling; remains of Mileham Castle nearby; church with 14th-century glass.

Mintlyn *Meltinga: Bishop William.* Mintlyn Wood.

Moor *Mora:* Lost.

Morley St Botolph *Morlea: William de Warenne; Hugh from Ralph de Beaufour.*

Morningthorpe *Maringatorp/ Torp: Count Alan; St Edmund's and Robert de Vaux from it. Church, mill.* Scattered; church with a Saxon tower and arch, and a 6–7th-century cemetery.

Morston *Marstuna/Merstona: King's land, also in the custody of Godric; Thorold from Roger Bigot.* Marshland; tumuli nearby.

Mortoft *Mortofst:* Lost.

Moulton St Mary *Modetuna/ Mothetuna: King's land, also in the custody of Godric.* Several moated sites.

Mulbarton *Molkeber(tes)tuna: Roger Bigot, formerly a free woman; Richard from Ralph de Beaufour.* One of Norfolk's biggest greens.

Mundesley *Muleslai: William de Warenne. Church.* Small seaside town.

Mundford *Mondefort/ Mundeforda: William de Warenne; Roger Bigot; Abbot of Ely. ½ mill.*

Mundham *Mundaham/ Mundhala: King's land, in the custody of Godric; also in the charge of William de Noyers; Thorold, Ulfketel and Robert de Vaux from Roger Bigot; Jocelyn from St Edmund's; Nigel and Ansger from Robert FitzCorbucion; Isaac; Roger FitzRainard; Ralph FitzHagni. ½ church. Horse at the hall.* Scattered; one ruined church and another with a Norman doorway.

Narborough *Nereburh: Roger Bigot. 3 mills.* Ancient settlement site nearby; Tudor manor.

Narford *Nereforda: Phanceon from Count Alan. 1½ mills, 5 beehives, fishery.* Narford Hall; cottages; saw mill.

Nayland *Eilanda/Neilanda:* Lost.

Neatishead *Snateshirda: Abbot of Holme before and after 1066. 100 pigs.* Broadland; by a nature reserve.

Necton *Ketuna/Noche/ Naketune/Neche/Neketuna: Ralph de Tosny, formerly Harold. Church, mill, salt-house. 19 cattle.* Church with a carved, painted roof.

Ness *Nessa:* Lost.

Newton (near Castle Acre) *Nieutuna: King's land, in the custody of Godric; Odo from Ivo Tailbois. 2 mills, ½ salt-house.* Church with Saxon work including a tower.

Newton (near Norwich) *Newtona: King's land, in the custody of Godric, formerly a free woman.* Part of Norwich.

Newton Flotman *Niwe(s)tuna: Roger Bigot; Tovi. Mill.* Medieval bridge.

North Barningham *Berni(n)geham: Thorold, from William de Warenne; Roger Bigot and Osferth from him; William de Noyers from Bishop William; Walter Giffard; Drogo de Beuvriere.* 17th-century hall.

North Barsham *Norbarsam: William de Warenne.*

North Burlingham *Berlingaham/ingeham/ Berlungeham: King's land, in the custody of Godric; William de Noyers and Eli from Bishop William. William d'Ecouis and Hugh from him. 2 churches, ½ salt-house.* 2 churches, one a ruin.

North Elmham *Elmenham: Bishop William. 4 mills. 300 sheep.* Vineyards. The village was the seat of a Bishopric founded in 673, and there are traces of a Saxon cathedral and bishop's castle behind the present church.

North Runcton *Runghetuna/ Rynghetona: Hermer de Ferrers; William d'Ecouis. Church, 1½ mills.* Suburb of King's Lynn.

North Tuddenham *Dodenham/ Nordtudenham/Todden(c)ham/ Totdenham/Toteham: Abbot of Ely; Richard from Ralph de Beaufour; Starculf. 3mills, 2 churches.* Scattered; church with a red-tiled interior and stencilled decorations done by the rector in the late 19th century.

North Walsham *Walsam: William de Warenne; Abbot of Holme before and after 1066. Church, 2 mills. 16 pigs.* Small market town, with Norfolk's 2nd largest church and a Saxon church tower.

Northwold *Norhwalde/ Norfwalde: William de Warenne; William de Warenne from Abbot of Ely who held before and after 1066. Church, 2 mills, 2 fisheries. 11 cattle.* Some chalk-built cottages; church with an Easter Sepulchre.

Norton Subcourse *Norfen/ Nortuna: Roger Bigot; Godric the steward and Abbot of Holme from him; St Edmund's and Jocelyn from it; Ralph de Beaufour; Ralph Baynard; Robert Gernon; Jocelyn of Norwich, a freeman of the king.* Broadland.

Norwich *Noruic/Norwic: King's land; Earl Ralph; Reynold FitzIvo; approximately 665 English burgesses, 41 French burgesses. 2100 sheep. 1 goshawk.* Leading provincial city since the 11th century, with a Norman castle and a cathedral which was founded in 1096 by the first bishop of Norwich.

OXBOROUGH: *Oxburgh Hall's gatehouse rises out of the moat.*

Oby *Houby Oebei/Orbi/Othebe: Roger Bigot and Stanard from him; Abbot of Holme before and after 1066. 3 cobs.* Oby Mill, South Oby Dyke by the rivers Bure and Acle.

Ormesby *Orbeslei/Ormesbei/ bey/by/Osmesbei: King's land; Roger Bigot; Richard FitzAlan from Bishop William.* Now 2 villages, Ormesby St Margaret, home of some of the Pilgrim Fathers, and Ormesby St Michael.

Osmondiston *Osmundestuna: Roger Bigot and Hugh de Corbon from him; Ralph de Fougères, formerly Harold. Horse at the hall.* Now Scole, once an important staging post between Norwich and Ipswich; Roman road; Roman station remains, gabled coaching inn (c.1655).

Ottering Hithe *Otringheia/ Otrinkeehia:* Lost.

Oulton *Oulstuna: King's land and Abbot of Holme from the king.*

Outwell *Utwella/Wtwella: William de Warenne; St Benedict's of Ramsay.* Fenland.

Overstrand *Othestranda: Berner the crossbowman. Mill.* Seaside resort.

Oxborough *Oxenbur(c)h: Godric the steward; Ralph de Limésy. 2 mills, fishery. 180 sheep.* Fenland. Oxburgh Hall, a fine 15th-century moated mansion is still occupied by its founders, the Bedingfield family.

Oxnead *Oxenedes: Godwin Haldane. Mill, church, 6 beehives.*

Oxwick *Ossuic: Reynald FitzIvo from Abbot of Ely who held before and after 1066.* Moated site.

Palgrave *Pag(g)rava: King's land, in the custody of Godric; Count Alan; St Riquier from William de Warenne.* Palgrave Hall; some isolated houses.

Palling *Pal(l)inga: King's land, in the custody of Godric; Count Alan, annexed by Edric; Roger Bigot and Hugh de Houdain from him. 14 wild mares.* Now Sea Palling, a seaside resort.

Panworth *Pennewrde: Reynald FitzIvo, formerly Harold.* Panworth Hall.

Panxworth *Pancforda/ Pankesford(a): King's land, in the custody of Godric; Count Alan and Ralph the Constable from him; Hugh from William d'Ecouis. Church.* Broadland.

Paston *Pastuna: Thorold from William de Warenne; William d'Ecouis; Abbot of Ely before and after 1066. Church, mill.*

Pattesley *Patesleia: Roger from Peter de Valognes. ½ fishery.* Pattesley House.

Pensthorpe *Penestorpa: Ranulf from Reynald FitzIvo. Mill, 4 beehives. 60 pigs, 240 sheep.* Part of Fakenham; common, with destroyed Bronze Age barrows.

Pentney *Penteleia: Robert de Vaux from Roger Bigot. 3 mills, 7 beehives, ½ salt-house.* Scattered. A cross marks the way to the flint gatehouse and 12th-century Augustinian priory ruins.

Pickenham (Altera) *Pichenham/Pickeham/ Pickenha(m)/Pinkenham: King's land and the reeve of the Hundred through the King's Sheriffs, in the custody of Godric; Ribald from Count Alan; William de Warenne; Reynald FitzIvo; Ralph de Tosny; Berner the Crossbowman. 5 mills, fishery, church.* Now 2 villages, North Pickenham, with a manor farm and traces of a Roman road, and South Pickenham with a round-towered church.

Pirnhow *Pirenhou: King's land, in the custody of Godric. Mill. 2 horses at the hall.* Roman road; mill house.

Plumstead (near Holt) *Plumestede: Thorold from William de Warenne.*

Plumstead *Plum(m)esteda/stede: King's land, in the custody of Godric; Bishop William and Robert Blunt from him; Hugh from William d'Ecouis; Ralph de Beaufour; Ralph the Crossbowman.* Now 2 villages, Great and Little Plumstead. Little Plumstead church has a possibly Saxon/Norman tower.

Poringland *Porri(n)kelanda/ Porring/alanda/helanda/elanda: King's land, in the custody of Godric; Bishop of Bayeux; Roger Bigot; Godric the steward; Brooke from St Edmund's. Church.* New housing estates; aisleless church with a Norman tower.

Postwick *Possuic: Eudo the steward. Mill, church.*

Potter Heigham *Echam: Godric de Heigham, a freeman of the king.* Site of a Roman pottery.

Pudding Norton *Nortuna: King's land. Church.* Church ruins.

Pulham *Pul(la)ham: Abbot of Ely before and after 1066. 2 churches, mill. 3 cobs, 11 cattle, 40 goats.* Now 2 villages, Pulham Market and St Mary.

Quarles *Gueruelei/Huerueles: King's land; Thurston FitzGuy from Roger Bigot.* Quarles Farm.

Quidenham *Cuid/Guidenham: King's land, in the custody of Godric; Roger Bigot; Jocelyn from St Edmund's. Mill.* Church with a Saxon tower. Saxon's Mound nearby is said to be Boadicea's burial place.

Rackheath *Rechei(th)a: King's land, in the custody of Godric; Abbot of Holme; Ralph de Beaufour.* Scattered.

Rainthorpe *Rainestorp/ Rainiltorp: Warenger from Roger Bigot; William from Roger de Raismes. 2½ mills.* Rainthorpe Hall. The ghost of Amy Robsart, wife of Robert Dudley, Elizabeth I's favourite, is said to appear here annually.

Ranworth *Randuorda: King's land.* Broadland. Church, with fine painted rood screen.

Raveningham *Ravelincham/ nicham/erincham/ingham/ Ravincham/Ravingeham/ Ruverincham: King's land, in the custody of Godric; also in the charge of William de Noyers; Earl Hugh; Robert from Roger Bigot; Bishop William; Ralph de Beaufour; Ralph Baynard and Einbold from him; Roger FitzRainard. Mill, 2 churches. 200 sheep.* Raveningham Hall; church with a Norman tower.

Raynham *Rein(e)ham: King's land, in the custody of Godric; Roger Bigot; Reynald FitzIvo and Boteric from him; Hugh de Montfort. 3 mills, salt-house.* Now 2 villages, East Raynham, home of Charles 'Turnip' Townsend (1674–1738) who introduced the turnip to England and West Raynham.

Redenhall *Rada(na)halla/ Radenhala/Redanaha(lla): King's land and Agneli from the king, in the custody of Godric, also in the charge of William de Noyers.* Near ancient earthworks.

Reedham *Redaham/Redeham: King's land, in the custody of Godric; Abbot of Holme; Richard from William d'Ecouis. Church.* Broadland; on the River Yare; ferry.

Reepham *Refham: Ralph Baynard.* 2 adjacent churches, joined by a parsonage.

Repps (near Acle) *Repes: Count Alan; Roger Bigot; Abbot of Holme; William d'Ecouis; freemen in the charge of Aelmer.* Broadland.

Repps (Northrepps and Southrepps) *Nor(h)repes/Repes/ Sutrepes: William de Warenne; Abbot of Holme; Quintin from William d'Ecouis. In Northrepps, 2 mills, church; belonging to both, another church.* 2 villages near the coast. Southrepps has a stump cross.

Reymerston *Raimcrestuna: Under dispute.*

Riddlesworth *Redelefuuorda: Humphrey FitzAubrey.* Scattered; Riddlesworth Hall.

Ridlington *Ridlinketuna: Ranulf brother of Ilger.*

Ringland *Remingaland: Walter Giffard.* On the outskirts of Norwich.

Ringstead *Rinc(s)teda: Roger Bigot, and Ralph FitzHelwin Abbot of Holme, and Ralph de Tourleville from him; St Benedict's of Ramsey before and after 1066; Richard from Ralph de Beaufour; Roger from William d'Ecouis; John nephew of Waleran. 1⅛ mills.* Roman Peddars Way.

Rippon *Rippetuna: Walter Giffard.* Rippon Hall.

Rising (in Feltwell) *Risinga:* Lost.

Rockland *Rokelun(d)lunt: Simon from William de Warenne; Roger Bigot; Richard de Sackville from Eudo the steward; Roger FitzRainard. ⅛ mill.* Now Rockland All Saints; also a ruined church, all that remains of Rockland St Andrew.

Rockland St. Mary *Rokelonda/ lund(a): King's land, in the custody of Godric; Roger Bigot; William de Noyers from Bishop William; Godric the steward. Church.* Broadland.

Rockland St Peter *Tofftes: William de Warenne. Mill.*

Rollesby *Roluesb(e)/ Rothbfuesbei/Rotholfuesbei/bey/ Thoroluesby: King's land, in the custody of Godric; Bishop William; Abbot of Holme before and after 1066; 8½ freemen in the charge of Aelmer. ½ salt-house.* Broadland.

Roudham *Rudham: King's land, in the custody of Godric the steward; William de Warenne; Abbot of Ely; Eudo the steward and Ralph from him.* Roudham Hall.

Rougham *Ruhham: King's land, in the custody of Godric; William de Warenne; Fulbert, the pre-Conquest holder, from Hermer de Ferrers.*

Roughton *Rof/Ruftuna/ Rugutune: Count Mortain; Roger Bigot; Hugh de Montfort. Mill.* Near the coast; church with a Saxon tower; a prehistoric burial ground nearby.

Roxham *Rochesham: In dispute.* Roxham Farm on the Great Ouse cut-off channel in the Fens.

Roydon (near Diss) *Ragadona/ Rag(h)eduna/Regadona/ Regedona: Walter from Robert Malet; St Edmund's; Hugh from Ralph de Beaufour. 2 horses at the hall. 30 pigs.* Home of Sir Henry Bartle Frere (1815–84), who negotiated the suppression of the Zanzibar slave trade.

Roydon (near King's Lynn) *Reiduna: Bishop of Bayeux; St Edmund's. 3½ salt-houses.* Duckpond; on the edge of Roydon Common.

Rudham *Rudeham: Alfheah from Count Alan; William de Warenne and Ralph and Lambert from him; Peter de Valognes and Thorgils from him. 2 churches, 2 mills, salt-house. 22 wild mares, 180 sheep, 300 sheep, mule.* Now 2 villages, East and West Rudham.

SALL: *The school is a delightful example of Norfolk village vernacular building.*

Runcton *Runghetuna: St Edmund's. Mill, fish pond.* Now the village of Runcton Holme and South Runcton, a hamlet.

Runhall *Runhal(a): King's land, in the custody of Godric; Count Alan.*

Runham *Romham/Ronham: King's land, in the custody of Godric; Roger Bigot; Aelmer FitzGodwin, a freeman of the king. 18 salt-houses.* Broadland; on the Bure marshes.

Runton *Runetune: Roger Bigot; Ingulf from William d'Ecouis. Church.* Now East and West Runton, seaside resorts. A continuing medieval claim to common grazing rights, 'Half Year Rights', has prevented development on the cliff tops.

Rushall *Riuessal(l)a: King's land, in the charge of William de Noyers; Ranulf Peverel and Waring from him; Gunfrid from Robert FitzCorbucion. Beehive. 17 pigs.* Church with a possibly Saxon tower.

Rushford *Riseurda/ Rusceuuorda: John, nephew of Waleran from Abbot of Ely; Ulfketel. 52 goats.* A college for priests, founded in 1342 by Edmund Gonville, was destroyed during the Dissolution, but 2 sides of the quadrangle are now part of the rectory.

Ryston *Ristuna: Aelmer from Hermer de Ferrers. ½ fishery. 5 cows.* 17th-century Ryston Hall, remodelled by Sir John Soane.

Saham Toney *Saham: King's land and Reynald FitzIvo and Berner the Crossbowman from the king; Robert from Roger Bigot. 8 cattle, 40 goats, 3 cows.* Scattered; large mere.

Sall *Salla: King's land, in the custody of Godric; Oder from Ralph de Beaufour; Hagni; Ralph FitzHagni. ¾ mill.* Salle Park, home of the Boleyn's. Anne Boleyn's ghost is said to walk in Bullen's Lane.

Salthouse *Sal(t)hus: William de Warenne; William d'Ecouis. 40 goats.* Threatened by the sea; Bronze Age barrows nearby.

Sandringham *Santdesincham: Ranulf from Robert FitzCorbucion. Salt-house.* Royal Estate, bought by Queen Victoria for the Prince of Wales, later Edward VII, in 1861.

Santon *Santuna: William de Warenne; Walter.* Now Santon Downham; woodland; local Forestry Commission headquarters.

Saxlingham (near Holt) *Saxeling(h)(a)ham/Sexelingaham: Bishop William; Peter de Valognes and Theodoric from him. Church.*

SANDRINGHAM: *One of the royal family's favourite homes.*

Valognes. 7 mills, 7 beehives, 180 sheep. Now Little Walsingham, a place of pilgrimage on the River Stiffkey, and Great Walsingham, a small market town, with a market place and 15th-century Guildhall, now a museum.

Walsoken *Walsocam: St Benedict's of Ramsey before and after 1066. Fishery.* Part of Wisbech. Its name derives from the Roman sea wall.

Warham *Guarham/Warham: King's land; Bishop of Bayeux; Ribald from Count Alan; Bishop William; Walter Giffard.* Now 2 hamlets, Warham All Saints, and Warham St Mary with a magnificent fort, possibly built by the Iceni between 50 BC and AD 50.

Washingford *Wasingaford: Godric the steward. Mill.* Washingford House.

Waterden *Waterdenna: Lambert from William de Warenne.* Roman road nearby.

Watton *Wadetuna: Ranulf FitzWalter from Roger Bigot, formerly Aldreda, a free woman. Mill, church. 13 cattle.* Small town, once famous for its butter market; church with a Norman tower.

Waxham *Wacstanest/ Wacstenesham/Wactanesham: Count Alan; Roger Bigot; Abbot of Holme before and after 1066; Aelmer son of Godwin, a freeman of the king. 2 churches.* Seaside; ancient hall, now a farmhouse.

Weasenham *Wesenham: King's land, in the custody of Godric; Wymer from Roger Bigot.* Now 2 villages, Weasenham All Saints and St Peter.

Weeting *Wetinga/inge: King's land, in the charge of William de Noyers; William de Warenne and Wazelin and Osward from him. ½ fishery.* Breckland, Devil's Dyke, a Saxon defence system; Grimes Graves, perhaps the most important group of flint mines in Britain; moated site of William de Warenne's castle.

Welborne *Walebruna: William de Warenne.* Scattered.

Well *Wella: St Stephen de Caen. 2 mills.* Well Hall.

Wellingham *Walnccham: Ralph Baynard.*

Wells next the Sea *Etduuella/ Gu(u)ella/Guelle: King's land, also in the custody of Godric; Ribald from Count Alan; Bishop William; Peter de Valognes; Aldith. 1½ mills.* Picturesque seaside town.

Wendling *Wenlinga: Richard from St Edmund's. Mill.* Site of a 12th-century abbey.

Wereham *Wigreham: Reynald FitzIvo. ½ mill, fishery. 28 mares, 25 foals, 260 sheep.* Fenland; duck pond.

West Beckham *Becham: Walter Giffard.*

West Bilney *Benelai, Bilenei, Binelai: Hugh de Montfort. 3 mills, ½ salt-house. 200 pigs.*

WALSINGHAM: *Combination lock-up and beacon.*

West Briggs *Wesbruge: Hermer de Ferrers. Church, mill. 13 cattle.* Fenland.

West Carbrooke *Weskerebroc: Osbert from John nephew of Waleran. Church.* Earthworks of Norfolk's only house of the Knights Hospitallers. It was founded in the mid-12th century by the de Clare family, whose memorial slabs are in the church.

West Dereham *Der(e)ham: William de Warenne; Hugh from Roger Bigot; St Benedict's of Ramsey; Ralph Baynard and Lovel from him. Church, mill.* Church with a Norman tower; remains of an abbey, founded in 1198, at Abbey Farm.

Westfield *Westfelda: Phanceon from Count Alan. Mill.*

West Newton *Niuetuna: Bishop of Bayeux. 8 cobs, 2300 sheep, 16 cattle.* Part of the Sandringham Estate; houses built by Edward VII.

Weston Longville *Westuna: Bishop of Bayeux; Count Alan; William d'Ecouis; Hagni. Church.* The Diarist James Woodeforde was rector here for 29 years in the late 18th century; his portrait hangs in the church.

West Tofts *Stoffta: Richard and Eli from Bishop William.* Moated site; military training area.

West Walton *Waltuna: Abbot of St Peter and Paul, Cluny, from William de Warenne; Abbot of Ely before and after 1066; Oder from Ralph de Beaufour. ½ church, 38 salt-houses, fishery. 1100 sheep.* Fenland; orchards. One of Norfolk's finest Early English churches.

Westwick *Westwic: Roger de Poitou.* Church in the grounds of Georgian Westwick Hall.

West Winch *Eswinic/Weswenic/ winic: Godwin, the pre-Conquest holder, and Ranulf from Reynald FitzIvo. 2 salt-houses.*

Weybourne *Wabrune/brunna: Ranulf from Earl Hugh. 2 mills. 10 cattle, 36 goats.* On the coast; Saxon church tower. The deeply shelving beach was heavily defended from 1588 to 1939, for 'He that would old England win/ Must at Weybourne Hope begin.'

Wheatacre *Hwateaker/ Wateaker: Ralph Baynard and a Frenchman and Geoffrey from him. 2 churches. 176 sheep.* Church with a curious chequered flint and brick tower.

Whimpwell *Hwimpwella: Abbot of Holme before and after 1066.* Now Whimpwell Green.

Whinburgh *Wineberga: Hermer de Ferrers. Church, 2 mills. 8 cattle, 60 goats.* Moated site.

Whissonsett *Witcingkeseta: Ranulf FitzWalter from Roger Bigot. 7 beehives. ¼ fishery.* Ancient gravel pit, the source of rounded building flints. A celtic interlaced wheel cross was uncovered by the sexton in 1900.

Whitlingham *Wisinlingaham/ Wislingeham: King's land, in the custody of Godric; Robert from Roger Bigot, formerly Wulflet a free woman. Church.* Ruined church; sewage works.

Whitwell *Witewella: King's land; Reynald FitzIvo. 3 mills, ½ fishery.* Part of Reepham.

Wick *Wica: William de Warenne; Bishop Osbern; Hugh de Montfort. Mill.* Part of Garbolidsham.

Wickhampton *Wichamtuna/ Wichhamtun: King's land, in the custody of Godric.* Church with a tomb dated 1280.

Wicklewood *Wiclurde/ Wicklepuda: William de Warenne; Ralph Sturmy from Ralph Baynard. Mill. 4 beehives.* Remains of an ancient church.

Wickmere *Wicmare/mera: King's land; Tihel de Hellean from Bishop of Bayeux; William de Warenne; Robert de Courson from Roger Bigot; Abbot of Holme before and after 1066.* Early round-towered church with possible Saxon work.

Wiggenhall *Wignehala: Ralph Baynard. Fishery, ½ mill.* Now 4 villages: Wiggenhall St Germans, St Mary Magdalen (once famous for its eels), St Peter and St Mary the Virgin whose church has an eagle lectern given by Robert Barnard in 1518.

Wighton *Guistune/Wistune: King's land. 2 mills. 6½ sesters of honey.* On the River Stiffkey; Roman camp site nearby.

Wilby *Wilebey/Wilgeby/ Willebeih: Roger Bigot; William d'Ecouis; a soldier from Ralph Baynard. Church.*

Wilton *Wiltuna: William de Warenne. 6 fisheries. 200 sheep.* Now Hockwold cum Wilton.

Wimsbotsham *Winebotesham: William de Warenne; St Benedict's of Ramsey; Hermer de Ferrers.* Marshland.

Winfarthing *Wineferthinc: King's land, in the custody of Godric. 2 horses at the hall.* Famous for the Sword of Winfarthing, reputedly left by a thief who sheltered in the churchyard, and enshrined later in the church. It was said to help find lost objects, and lose unwanted husbands, although the sword was itself lost.

Winterton *Wintretona/tuna: King's land, also in the custody of Godric; Aelward of Felbrigg from Roger Bigot; Bishop William; Abbot of Holme before and after 1066; Hugh from William d'Ecouis; a freeman of the king; ½ salt-house.* Also known as Winterton-on-Sea; church with a Fisherman's Corner.

Witton (near North Walsham) *Widituna/Wi(t)tuna: King's land, in the custody of Godric; William de Warenne; Abbot of Holme. Church.* Now Witton Bridge; church with a Saxon quoin and round windows.

Witton (near Norwich) *Witona: King's land, in the custody of Godric; Bishop William; Ulfketel.*

Wiveton *Wiventona/Wivetuna: Reynald FitzIvo. 2 mills.* Medieval bridge over the River Glaven; flint house built by John Gifford of Gloucester in 1653.

Wolterton *Ultertuna/Ultretune: Thorold from William de Warenne; Abbot of Holme before and after 1066; Ralph de Beaufour. ½ church.* Wolterton Hall, built by Horace Walpole, brother of Sir Robert, contains some fine Gobelins tapestries.

Woodbastwick *Bastu(u)ic: King's land, also in the custody of Godric; Abbot of Holme before and after 1066; Ralph de Beaufour.* Broadland.

Wood Dalling *Dallinga: William de Warenne; Walter Giffard; Peter de Valognes.* 16th-century hall.

Wood Norton *Nortuna: Hugh from Bishop William; Reynald FitzIvo; Walter Giffard; Hagni. ⅓ church.* Ruined church; manor farm.

Wood Rising *Risinga: King's land; William de Warenne.* Moated site; church with a barrel organ.

Woodton *Uidetuna/Wdetuna/ Wodetone/tuna: King's land, in the custody of Godric; Earl Hugh; Robert Malet and Walter from him; Roger Bigot; Eudo FitzSpirwic; Isaac. Church.* Scattered; church with a Norman font.

Wootton *Wdetuna: King's land, in the custody of Godric the steward.* Now South Wootton, a suburb of King's Lynn, and the village of North Wootton.

Wormegay *Wermegai: Hermer de Ferrers. Church, 3 fisheries, ¼ mill.* Farmland; ancient cross; motte and bailey castle remains.

Worstead *Ordesteda/Urdestada/ Wrdesteda: Count Alan; Abbot of Holme before and after 1066; Reynald FitzIvo. Mill. 16 pigs.* Once a weaving centre, it gave its name to worsted cloth.

Wramplingham *Waranpli(n)cham/ Wranplincham: Count Alan; Ralph from Godric the steward. 1½ mills.*

Wreningham *Urnincham: Roger Bigot; Wagen from Hermer de Ferrers. Church.* Expanding.

Wretham Alia *Wer(e)tham/ Wretham: Ralph de Tosny, formerly Harold. Mill. 21 pigs.* Now 2 villages, East and West Wretham.

Wroxham *Grossa(ha)m/ Uroc(he)sham/Urocsham/ Wrossham: King's land, in the custody of Godric; Abbot of Holme; Ralph de Beaufour. 2 churches.* Broadland holiday town. The church has a Norman doorway.

Wymondham *Widmundha(m)/ Wimund(e)ham:* See page 185.

Yarmouth *Gernemutha/ Gernemwa/Iernesmua: King's land. Hawk.* Now Great Yarmouth, a seaside resort and port. St Nicholas' is the biggest parish church in England.

Yaxham *Iachesham/Lakesham: Count Alan; Ranulf FitzWalter from Roger Bigot; Hermer de Ferrers; Abbot of Ely; Reynald FitzIvo.* Saxon church tower.

Yelverton *Ailuertuna/ Ailunituna/Aluertuna/Aluntuna: King's land, in the custody of Godric, with Aitard, Roger Bigot's man, holding part; Bishop of Bayeux; William de Warenne; Roger Bigot and Ulfketel from him; Godric the steward. Church.*

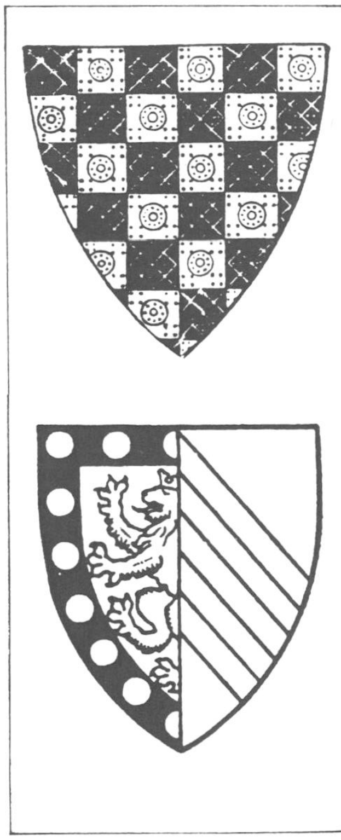

HERALDRY: *Shields often carried simple but brilliantly coloured patterns to identify a family name. The chequered diaper of gold and azure blue for the de Warenne family was known throughout Norfolk. Divided shields were used when 2 families were united in marriage. The de Clare family (see* **West Carbrooke***) chevrons were joined to the lion of Cornwall when Richard de Clare's daughter married the Earl of Cornwall.*

Northamptonshire

Domesday Northamptonshire was somewhat larger than the modern county, for it included the Soke of Peterborough and the Wapentake of Witchley which later became part of Rutland. Other smaller portions have also been lost to neighbouring counties. Although over 300 Domesday place names correspond to today's, a few, – Brime and Hantone for example – have disappeared, and many present-day villages are not mentioned despite being recorded in medieval documents of only slightly later dates.

There are Northamptonshire peculiarities in the survey, the result of the county's having been half English and half Danish. Either a decimal or a duodecimal assessment of ploughland was used, depending on whether the fields belonged to an English or to a Danish part of the county. The Danish measurements, carucates and bovates, are also found, the latter mixed with English measurements. Woodland was invariably quantified in leagues, furlongs and perches, in contrast with neighbouring Bedfordshire and Buckinghamshire, where it was not measured at all. The Northamptonshire survey also records a striking amount of 'waste' – mainly the result of the devastating march of Morcar, Earl of Northumbria, through the shire a year before the Conquest.

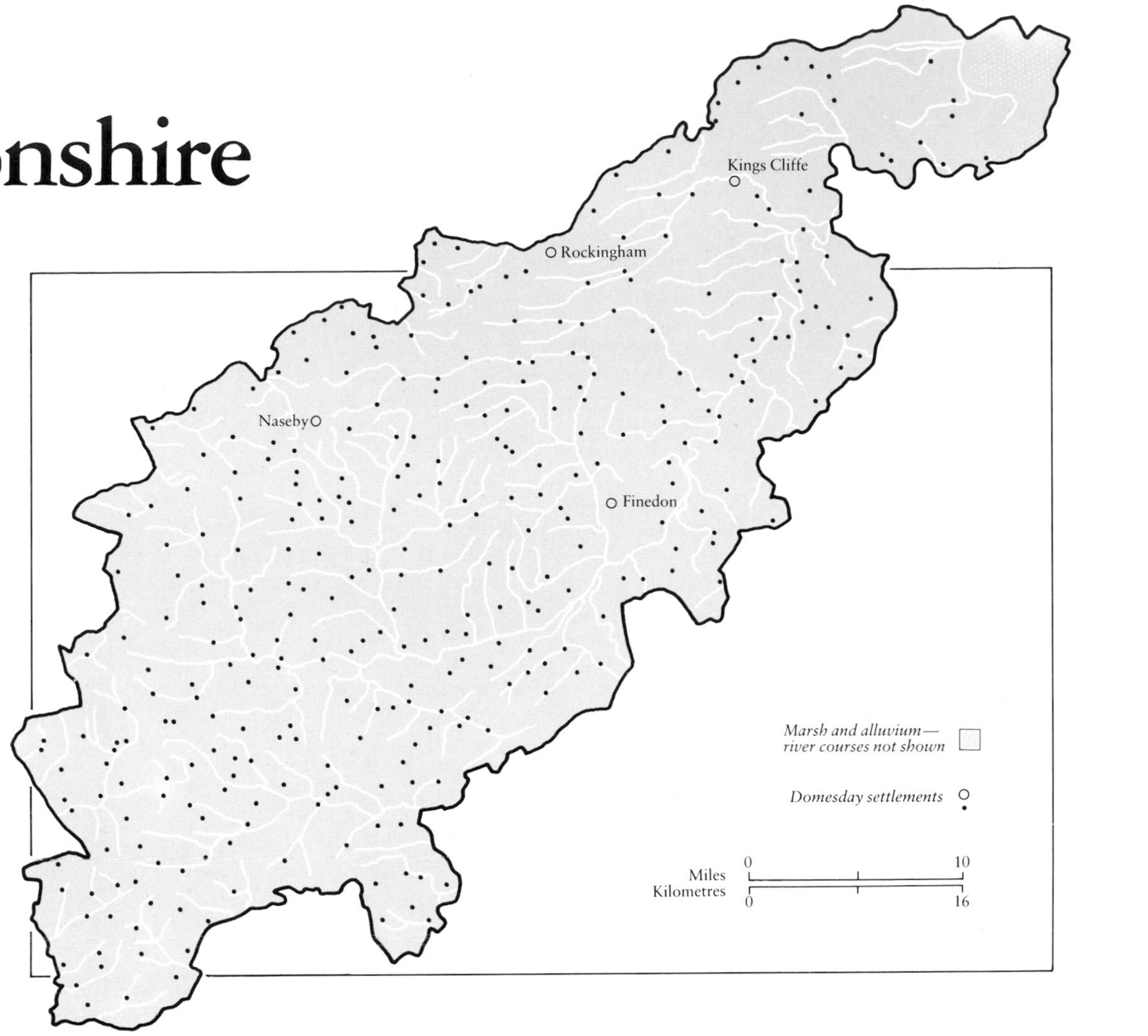

Finedon

The King holds FINEDON *TINGDENE*. Queen Edith held it. 27 hides with its dependencies. Land for 54 ploughs. In lordship 3 hides; 4 ploughs there; 7 slaves; 30 villagers and 15 smallholders with 11 ploughs; 50 Freemen with 24 ploughs. 2 mills at 18s and a third at 16s. Meadow, 50 acres; woodland 1 league long and 1/2 league wide. It paid £20 at face value before 1066; now £40 by weight at 20 (pence) to the *ora*. The 50 Freemen pay £8 and 10d a year for the jurisdiction.

This large village lying at a busy cross-roads in prime ironstone country has one of *Domesday*'s more interesting entries. In the reign of Edward the Confessor the locally governed 'soke' of Finedon contained 27 hides dispersed among six 'Hundreds' and was held by Queen Edith. After the Conquest it became the King's land, and although it retained its status as a soke, its fifty freemen were made to pay for the "jurisdiction", *i.e.* the right to try cases and keep the fines.

Finedon Manor itself contained only nine and a half hides, later expanded to ten, but *Domesday* also mentions half a hide of Finedon land outside the manor, held by a man called Richard, a sub-tenant of the Bishop of Coutances. This, together with other holdings of Richard's, eventually found its way into the hands of a 16th-century lord of Finedon via the Abbot of Croxton. The expression of the manor's value in *oras*, although interesting, is not unusual. The *ora* was an ounce of silver which in this case was taken to equal 20 pence. In areas where Danish influence was strong the rate was 16d to the ounce.

In 1200 King John granted Finedon to his clerk. Thereafter the different parts of the manor had a number of different holders. Late in the thirteenth century a market was established, and the tenants, who were given the use of a free fishery, also gained the right to administer punishment, sentencing the guilty to the gallows, pillory and tumbril. To match the villager's new prosperity a splendid church was built with local ironstone.

In the mid-sixteenth century the Mulsho family, who had held a part of Finedon Manor for generations, gained control of the whole. In the late seventeenth century Anne Mulsho married Gilbert Dolben, son of the Archbishop of Canterbury, and Gilbert, after buying out a second Mulsho heiress, became the new lord. He was an Irish judge from 1701 and was made a baronet in 1704. But his greatest distinction came from his presentation to the poet John Dryden (born in nearby Aldwincle) of 'all the several editions of Virgil, and all the commentaries of these editions in Latin'.

Gilbert's brother John was more colourful. After wasting most of his inheritance on loose living he fled to the West Indies, where he married. In time he was elected to Parliament and headed the impeachment proceedings against the 'seditious' Henry Sacheverell.

In the next century Frances Dolben married William Mackworth, who added Dolben to his name, and, on becoming lord of the manor in 1837, altered the Elizabethan hall in line with his taste for extravagant, theatrical high Gothicism. A number of buildings in and around Finedon bear his mark – the Bell Inn, for instance, and Thingden Cottage. William Dolben's son Digby was born in 1848 and was an Eton friend of Robert Bridges, the poet, who was related to the family. Like his father, Digby was a man of strong convictions. While still in his teens he became a convert to Roman Catholicism, and poems he wrote in those years reflect his spiritual preoccupations. On 28 June 1867 he drowned while bathing in the River Welland near South Luffenham Rectory, where he was staying before going up to Oxford. No one has ever been sure whether it was an accident or suicide.

Finedon is somewhat swollen with twentieth-century housing, but in the old village centred on the hall and church, the vicarage dated 1688 has survived, as have the sixteenth-century boys' school, and the girls' school of 1712. There is also Mulsho Square to remind us of Finedon's early lords of the manor.

Naseby

William [Peverel] also holds 7 hides in NASEBY *NAVESBERIE*. Land for 14 ploughs. In lordship 2. 8 villagers with a priest, 2 Freemen and 11 smallholders have 3 ploughs. Meadow, 8 acres. The value was 20s; now 60s.

The village lies 600 feet up on a ridge which stretches nearly the whole western length of the county. Naseby was included in the lands held by Gytha – she was the wife of Earl Ralph of Hereford, Edward the Confessor's nephew – which passed to William Peverel, the sheriff of Nottinghamshire and Derbyshire. Land at neighbouring Thornby to the south, and Clipston to the north, also came under the manor's jurisdiction.

After the Peverels' rule ended, the manor passed through many families, but little is known of its descent. In 1855 it was bought by the Clifdens, who still owned it 25 years later when the power of such local landowners came under attack from the Naseby branch of the national farm labourers' union. The occasion was the anniversary of the Battle of Naseby during the Civil War in 1645, when the Royalists had been severely trounced. The result was a radical movement for agricultural reform that culminated in petitions to Parliament advocating the abolition of primogeniture and entail, and the repeal of the Game Laws.

The decisive battle that inspired the demonstrators had been fought after Charles I took Leicester and began to move towards the Royalist stronghold of Newark. The Roundheads under General Fairfax, rushed to meet him. The confrontation opened with the Royalists on Dust Hill, and the Cromwellians just south of the present Broadmoor Farm. Although Charles's men were heavily outnumbered they routed 2700 Parliamentarians with their first charge, and captured artillery. But the Parliamentarians soon outflanked them and they panicked. In the words of Clarendon, the Royalist historian, 'they all run near a quarter of a mile without stopping'. The king lost all his foot, his artillery, and 100 cavalry officers and 'gentlemen'.

The dip where the battle was fought can still be seen, and a monument stands on the hillside, though unfortunately not in the correct position.

Rockingham

The King holds ROCKINGHAM *ROCHINGEHA*. 1 hide. Land for 3 ploughs. 5 villagers and 6 smallholders with 3 ploughs. Bovi held this land with full jurisdiction before 1066. It was waste when King William ordered a castle to be built there. Value now 26s.

The village and castle of Rockingham stands on a hillside near the Leicestershire border, close to sprawling Corby New Town. According to *Domesday* when William chose this site for a castle the land was 'waste' – one of four Northamptonshire places so described. The *Anglo-Saxon Chronicle* reveals that in 1065 the county had been devastated by marauding hordes from the north who 'slew men and burned houses and corn, and took all the cattle'. The Northamptonshire Geld Roll corroborates this report. Recent excavations have found evidence of Roman and pre-Roman occupation, as well as of Saxon fortifications. King William built his castle on a site long renowned as a vantage point, commanding magnificent views over the Welland Valley.

The Norman castle consisted of motte, double bailey, curtain walls, a gatehouse, great hall and chapel. Subsequent monarchs used it regularly, and King John stayed here early in the thirteenth century, the night before he lost his baggage in the Wash. At the end of the same century, Edward I undertook major reconstructions which included adding domestic buildings. In the middle of the sixteenth century the castle passed into the hands of the Watson family and became a private residence. Lewis Watson, the owner during the Civil War, was a lukewarm Royalist and when his militarily strategic home was too easily captured by the Roundheads in 1642 he was himself seized by the Royalists for failing to hold it. He was eventually forgiven and was created Baron Rockingham. During the attack, however, Cromwell had entirely destroyed the castle's keep as well as a 30-feet-high outer wall.

'The dear old Rockingham days are always fresh in my heart,' Charles Dickens wrote in 1870. He was recalling his visits to the castle between 1847 and 1852, when the owner was a Richard Watson. The castle became the model for Chesney Wold in *Bleak House*, and in 1851 Dickens arranged elaborate farces here, inspired by his having met an amateur actress, Mary Boyle.

Rockingham Castle today is open to the public, who may wander about its Tilting Lawn, peer into a strange dell where a twentieth-century vicar of Rockingham advised the Watson family to dig for King John's lost treasure, or look out across the many miles of countryside which King William's formidable stronghold once commanded.

ROCKINGHAM: *The vista from the terrace of the castle.*

King's Cliffe

The King holds (KING'S) CLIFFE *CLIVE*. 1 hide and 2 1/2 virgates. Earl Algar held it. Land for 14 ploughs. In lordship 2 ploughs, with 1 slave; 7 villagers with a priest and 6 smallholders who have 5 ploughs. A mill at 12d; meadow, 4 acres; woodland 1 league long and 1/2 league wide. It paid £7 before 1066; now £10.

The large stone-built village of King's Cliffe nestles in the valley of the Willow Brook on the edge of the ancient Rockingham Forest. It and has the air of a small town, and it was once a thriving centre of the wood-turning industry. The manor had been held by Algar, son of Earl Leofric of Mercia, until his death in 1062. After the Conquest King William made it a royal manor and so it remained until early in the nineteenth century, often being given as part of a marriage settlement to a new queen of England.

The comparatively small amount of cultivated land recorded in *Domesday* contrasts tellingly with the large tract of woodland listed – over a square mile. Since transforming woods into arable land was forbidden in royal forests, this suggests that the manor had been afforested long before the first reference to a hunting lodge, the King's House, in Henry II's time. A few years later, deer were kept in the hunting park and granted to various lords. In the thirteenth

KING'S CLIFFE: *Warm honey-coloured stone is used for almost all the village houses.*

century village tenants had difficulty in enforcing their common rights in the forest. The land remained unfenced until late in the next century, and it was only after the manor passed into private hands that serious cultivation began.

By early in the fourteenth century the royal seat of 'Clive', as it was called, was one of the district's most flourishing towns. It had a market and Henry III had granted it a three-day fair where a popular article was the excellent turned wood for which the area became renowned. During the fairs, a bizarre custom prevailed: placing a bough of wood on the doorstep of a private home instantly transformed it into a licensed ale-house!

The church was no longer the simple barn-like structure in which the *Domesday* priest had held his services. A central tower had been added around 1100 and this was topped just over a century later by a handsome broach spire, a sure sign of prosperity. A north transept was added in about 1260, and in the fifteenth century, the Norman chancel was rebuilt. By then, two mills were in operation on the Willow Brook, in contrast to the distinctly modest Domesday affair worth 12 shillings. It was probably the same two which were grinding corn in 1650, one of which still survives.

In the mid-fifteenth century King's Cliffe went through a depression, chiefly because the king himself no longer came, but also because of serious fires. One of the worst occurred in 1462 when 100 houses were destroyed, including the Manor House where Kings Edward I and II had stayed. Many of the destroyed buildings had already become derelict. A document of about 1439 reveals that numerous houses were 'waste' – returning no revenue to the king. The town's decline was severe enough for the authorities to suspend the market and fair. These were not reinstated until 1604.

King's Cliffe boasts one genuine hero, Michael Hudson, who was first a fellow of Queen's College, Oxford, and then Rector of King's Cliffe. At the outbreak of the Civil War he became ostensibly a royal chaplain, but actually undertook dangerous courier work for the king. In 1646 he was captured three times by Cromwell's men. He was released once and escaped twice, the second time in disguise with a basket of apples on his head. In 1648, while returning from a successful recruiting drive in East Anglia, he and his force occupied Woodcroft Castle, near Stamford. Parliamentarian troops stormed the stronghold, forced Hudson up to the battlements and flung him over the edge into the moat beneath. Half drowned, he was clubbed on the head with a musket until he was dead. His tongue was cut out and carried about as a trophy.

Although considered a small town at least until Victorian times, King's Cliffe today is no more than a large village. Its population is now slowly expanding, but it has never truly recovered from its late medieval decline.

Northamptonshire Gazetteer Each entry starts with the modern place name in **bold** type. The *Domesday* information that follows is in *italic* type, beginning with the name or names by which the place was known in 1086. The main landholders and undertenants are next, separated with semi-colons if a place was divided into more than one holding. A number of holdings were granted by the king to his thanes; these normally come at the end of the list of landholders and are described as holding land 'from the king'. More general information completes the *Domesday* part of the entry, including examples of dues such as eels rendered by tenants. The modern or post-Domesday section is in normal type. represents a village, a small village or hamlet.

Abington *Abintone: Richard. Mill.* Suburb of Northampton.

Achurch *Asechirce: Azelin and 2 Englishmen from Peterborough Abbey.* Riverside. Also known as Thorpe Achurch.

Adstone *A/Etenestone: King's land; Leofwin the priest from the king; Alfred from Count of Mortain. 2 mills.*

Ailsworth *Eglesworde: Peterborough Abbey; 3 of the abbot's men-at-arms. 2 mills.*

Alderton *Aldritone: Count of Mortain and a thane from him.* Attractive; limestone; castle ringwork.

Aldwincle (All Saints and St Peter) *Aldevincle/Eldewincle: Peterborough Abbey; Picto, Landric and Oger from Guy de Raimbeaucourt. Mill.* 2 medieval churches. Birthplace of the poet John Dryden (1631–1700).

Althorp *Olletorp: Count of Mortain; William Peverel.* Althorp Park, a Tudor house transformed by Henry Holland, is ancestral home of the Spencer family, to which the Princess of Wales belongs.

Apethorpe *Patorp: King's land. Mill.* 15th-century hall.

Armston *Mermeston: Peterborough Abbey, and 5 men-at-arms from the Abbey.*

Arthingworth *Arninguorde/Arniworde/Erniwade/Narninworde: King's land; St Edmund's Abbey; Humphrey from Count of Mortain.*

Ashby St Ledgers *Ascebi: Hugh de Grandmesnil.* The Gunpowder Plot is said to have been planned in house of Catesbys here.

Ashley *Asce/Ascele(i): Gunfrid, Walkelin and Wibert from Robert de Tosny; Walter from Robert de Bucy; 3 freemen from Countess Judith. Mill.* Remodelled by Richard Pulteney, a 19th-century squarson.

Ashton (near Oundle) *Ascetone: Peterborough Abbey and Ivo from the Abbey. 2 mills (325 eels).* Model village re-created in 1900 by Charles Rothschild.

Ashton (near Roade) *Asce: Dodin and Bondi from Winemar.* Sprawling.

Astcote *Aviescote: Gelder from Walter the Fleming.*

Aston le Walls *Estone: Maugar from Geoffrey de Mandeville.* Traces of a wall; 18th-century manor house.

Astwell *Estwelle: Geoffrey and Robert from Giles brother of Ansculf. Mill.* Astwell Castle.

Aynho *Aienho: Geoffrey de Mandeville. Mill.* Aynho Park, extensively altered by John Soane, 1800–1805.

Badby *Badebi: Crowland Abbey. Mill.* Pretty; ironstone. Prehistoric earthworks.

Barby *Berchebi: Payne from William Peverel.*

Barford *Bereford(e): Oslac White with 2 freemen from the king. Mill.*

Barnack *Bernac: Odbert from William FitzAnsculf.* Barnack Rag, quarried here from Roman times to the 18th century, was used to build cathedrals, abbeys and the local Saxon church; Saxon tower.

Barnwell *Bernewelle: King's land; Ramsey Abbey. 2 mills.* Remains of 13th-century castle in the grounds of Tudor Barnwell Castle.

Barton Seagrave *Bertone: Robert from Bishop of Coutances. 2 mills.* Expanding; Queen Anne rectory; Georgian hall.

Benefield *Benefeld: Richard the Artificer.* Medieval castle site.

Billing *Bel(l)inge/Bellica: Count of Mortain; Gunfrid de Chocques; Gilbert Cook. 2 mills.* District of Bellinge, containing former villages of Great and Little Billing, now lost among housing estates. Great Billing church was reconsecrated in 1759 because it was thought the Devil had destroyed its spire.

Blakesley *Baculveslea/Blachesleuue/Blaculveslea/Blaculveslei: King's land; Saegrim from Count of Mortain; Earl Hugh; Walter from William Peverel. Mill.* The poet John Dryden lived here.

Blatherwycke *Blarewiche: Norman from Robert de Bucy. Mill.* Lake.

Blisworth *Blideswordc: William Peverel. Mill.* Grand Union Canal.

Boddington *Botendone: Leofwin from Count of Mortain; Robert from Earl Hugh.* Now 2 hamlets, Lower and Upper Boddington.

Boughton *Bochetone/Buchedone/Buchetone/Buchenho: Godwin the priest from the king; Robert from Robert de Bucy; Countess Judith and Gerard from her.* On the edge of suburban Northampton.

Boughton (in Weekley) *Boctone: St Edmund's Abbey Gunfrid de Chocques. Mill.* 17th-century Boughton House; grounds by Le Notre.

Bozeat *Bosieta/Bosiete: Lancelin from William Peverel; Thurstan and Winemar from Countess Judith.* Ironstone.

Brackley *Brachelai: King's land. Church, mill.* Market town.

Bradden *Bradene: William from Robert de Bucy; David.* Manor house.

Brafield on the Green *Brache(s)feld/Bragefelde: William from Bishop of Bayeux; Countess Judith and Winemar from her.*

Brampton *Brantone: Wulfmer from the Count of Mortain. Mill.* 2 adjoining hamlets, Chapel and Church Brampton.

Brampton Ash *Brantone: Hildwin from Robert de Tosny; Hugh from Robert de Bucy; Countess Judith.* Sarah, Duchess of Marlborough, is said to have won the manor while gambling with a member of the Norwich family, who had held it since 1427.

Braunston *Brandestone: William from Bishop of Bayeux; Walter d'Aincourt. Mill.* Canalside.

Braybrooke *Badebroc/Baiebroc/Bradebroc: St Edmund's Abbey; Grestain Abbey; Robert de Vessey; Hugh from Robert de Bucy.* Medieval castle earthworks.

Brigstock *Bricstoc: King's land. Mill.* Saxon church tower; medieval manor; market cross.

Brington *Brin(in)tone: Count of Mortain; William Peverel.* Now 2 villages, Little Brington, with a Roman road, and Great Brington.

Brixworth *Bricleswordc: King's land; 2 mills, priest.* Large; Saxon church, probably the finest surviving 7th-century building north of the Alps.

Brockhall *Brocole: Count of Mortain.* Jacobean manor house; Elizabethan hall.

Broughton *Burtone: King's land; Countess Judith.* Large; industrial.

Bugbrooke *Buchebroc(h): Count of Mortain. 2 mills.* Mill; manor house.

Burghley *Burglea: Geoffrey from Peterborough Abbey.* Elizabethan Burghley House, home of the Cecil family since c.1520.

Burton Latimer *Burtone: Walkelin and Richard from Bishop of Coutances; Guy de Raimbeaucourt. 2 mills.* Small industrial town; mill.

Byfield *Bifelde/Bivelde: Ivo from Hugh de Grandmesnil; Robert from Earl Hugh.* Manor house.

Caldecott *Caldecote: William Peverel.*

Canons Ashby *Ascebi: Hugh from Walter the Fleming.* Bronze Age barrow nearby. House built by John Dryden, an ancestor of the poet.

Castle Ashby *Asebi: Hugh from Countess Judith. Mill.* House with screen by Inigo Jones; grounds by Capability Brown.

Castor *Castre: Peterborough Abbey. Mill.* Roman remains excavated here; farmhouse with Saxon window.

Catesby *Catesbi: William Peverel. 2 mills.* Now 2 hamlets, Upper Catesby and Lower Catesby which has the fishponds of a 12th-century Benedictine nunnery.

Chacombe *Cewecumbe: Godfrey from Bishop of Lincoln. 3 mills.*

Chadstone *Cedestone: Drogo de Beuvrière.*

Charlton *Cerlintone: Adam from Bishop of Bayeux; Ralph from Count of Mortain.* Iron Age Rainsborough Camp with Roman dry-stone walling.

Charwelton *Celverton/Cerveltone/Cerweltone: Baldwin from Thorne Abbey; Ralph and William from Count of Mortain; Walter from Hugh of Grandmesnil. Mill.*

Chelveston *Celuestone: William Peverel.*

Chilcotes *Cildecote:* Lost.

Clipston *Clipestone/tune: King's land; Walkelin from Bishop of Coutances; St Edmund's Abbey; William Peverel.*

CASTOR: *The site of a Roman camp; the 12th-c. church has this 9th-c. carving.*

Clopton *Clotone/Dotone: Navisford; Eustace and Aelmer from Peterborough Abbey; Alfred from Eustace of Huntingdon.* Was also known as Clapton.

Cogenhoe *Cugenho: Norigot from Guy de Raimbeaucourt; Norgiold from Countess Judith. Mill.* Mill.

Cold Ashby *Essibi: Coventry Abbey; Count of Mortain; William Peverel; Geoffrey de La Guerche.*

Cold Higham *Hecham: Count of Mortain; Godwin from Walter the Fleming.* Windswept.

Collingtree *Colentreu: Geoffrey Alselin.*

Collyweston *Westone: Herlwin from Ralph de Limesy. Mill.* Church with possible Saxon fabric; manor house with locally quarried roof tiles.

Corby *Corb(e)i: King's land. Iron workings before 1066.* New Town, formerly a steel town.

Cosgrove *Covesgrave: Count of Mortain; Winemar. Mill.* Roman bath house.

Coton *Cota/Cote: William Peverel. Mill.*

Cotterstock *Codestoche: 2 men-at-arms from Peterborough Abbey.* Medieval hall.

Cottesbrooke *Codesbroc/Cotesbroc: Walter the Fleming; Dodin from the king. Mill.* The Hall possibly the model for Jane Austen's Mansfield Park.

Cottingham *Cotingeham: Peterborough Abbey. Mill.* Roman road.

Courteenhall *Alio Cortenhalo/Cortenhale/halo: William Peverel and Thurstan from him.* Hall in park.

Cranford *Craneford: Robert from Bishop of Coutances; Robert and Godric from Peterborough Abbey; Odelin from Guy de Raimbeaucourt. Mill.* Now 2 villages, Cranford St John, with a manor house, and Cranford St Andrew.

ALTHORP: *James I's wife was a guest here and watched a masque by Ben Jonson.*

Cransley *Craneslea/leg: King's land; Gunfrid de Chocques; Countess Judith.* Now Great Cransley, a village, and Little Cransley, some houses.

Creaton *Craptone/Cre(p)tone: Count of Mortain; Robert from Robert de Bucy; Countess Judith.* Also Little Creaton, a hamlet with a motte.

Crick *Crec: Geoffrey de La Guerche.* Vyntner's Manor with medieval vaulted cellars. William Laud, later Archbishop of Canterbury, was rector here, 1622–4.

Croughton *Cliwetone/Creveltone/Criweltone: Aelfric from the Bishop of Coutances; Count of Mortain; Osbern and Sweetman from Geoffrey de Mandeville. Mill.* Limestone.

Culworth *Culeorde: Osbern from Geoffrey de Mandeville. Mill.*

Dallington *Dailintone: Richard from Peterborough Abbey. Mill.* Absorbed by Northampton; 17th-century almshouses.

Daventry *Daventrei: Countess Judith.* Market town with Georgian houses. Charles I camped here before the battle of Naseby.

Deene *Dene: Westminster Abbey before and after 1066. Mill.* Deene Park, mainly Tudor and Georgian, owned by the Brudenell family, who bought the estate in 1514. Lord Cardigan of the Light Brigade debacle lived here.

Denford *Deneford. Bishop of Coutances. 2 mills (250 eels).*

Denton *Dodintone: Ramsey Abbey; Countess Judith and Winemar from her. Mill.* The coal store of the church may have been an anchoress's cell.

Desborough *De(i)sburg/Dereburg: King's land; Alan from Count of Mortain; Robert de Tosny; Ambrose from William Peverel. Mill.* Footwear industry; Saxon church graves.

Dingley *Dingle(i)/Tinglea: Count of Mortain; Hildwin from Robert de Tosny; Robert de Bucy; Countess Judith.* Tudor Dingley Hall nearby.

Dodford *Dodeforde: Count of Mortain. 2 mills.* Scattered; Dodford Mill.

Draughton *Bracstone/Dractone: King's land; Countess Judith.*

Duddington *Dodintone: King's land. Mill.* Manor house, 1633; 14th-century bridge; 17th-century watermill nearby.

Duston *Dustone: William Peverel. Mill.* Absorbed into Northampton; Iron Age and Roman settlement; mill.

Earls Barton *Burtone: Countess Judith. 3 mills.* Shoe-manufacturing town with a fine Saxon tower adjoining an early Norman Castle motte.

East Carlton *Carlintone: Humphrey from Count of Mortain. Mill.* Quiet, in park.

East Farndon *Faredone/Ferendone: St Edmund's Abbey; Count of Mortain; Oslac from the king.* Charles I's despatches were sent here for safety after his defeat at Naseby.

DUDDINGTON: *The bridge and the quiet river make a pleasant scene.*

East Haddon *E(d)done/Hadone: Ralph and Alric from Count of Mortain. Mill.* Ironstone; park.

Easton Maudit *Estone: William Peverel; Dodin from Countess Judith.*

Easton Neston *Adestanestone/Estanestone: Count of Mortain; Bondi, the pre-Conquest holder, from Gunfrid de Chocque. Mill.* Magnificent house, Nicholas Hawksmoor's work.

Easton on the Hill *Estone: Roland from Eudo FitzHubert, Gilbert of Ghent and Saint-Pierre-Sur-Dives from him. Mill.* Rare, pre-Reformation rectory.

Ecton *Echentone: Ralph from Henry de Ferrers. 2 mills.* Manor house. Ancestors of Benjamin Franklin were blacksmiths and farmers here.

Edgcote *Hocecote: Walkelin from Bishop of Coutances. Mill.* Pretty manor house; rectory.

Elkington *Eltetone/Etendone: Count of Mortain; Thorkell from Guy de Raimbeaucourt; Geoffrey de La Guerche.* Manor farm.

Elmington *Elmintone: Crowland Abbey.*

Evenley *Avelai/Evelai: Count of Mortain; Gilbert and Odbert from Walter the Fleming. 3 mill.* 17th-century manor house.

Everdon *Everdone: William from Bishop of Bayeux.* Manor house; also nearby Little Everdon.

Eydon *Egedone: Hugh from Hugh de Grandmesnil. Mill.* Largely destroyed by fire in 1651; stone cottages.

Farthinghoe *Ferningeho: King's land. Mill.* Manor farm.

Farthingstone *Fordinestone: Count of Mortain and Ingelrann from him.* Medieval earthworks.

Fawsley *Falelau/Falewesle(i)(ie)/Feleslewe(sleie)/Felveslea: King's land; Godwin the priest from the king.* 17th-century hall.

Faxton *Fextone:* Lost.

Finedon *Tingdene:* See page 197.

Flore *Flora/Flore: Count of Mortain; William de Keynes; William Peverel; Baldwin from Geoffrey de Mandeville; Wulfbald from Gunfrid de Chocques. 2 mills.* Old manor.

FOTHERINGAY: *The ornate gateway to Garden Farm.*

Fotheringhay *Fodringeia: Countess Judith. Woodland for hunting game. Mill.* Castle, near a grassy mound, where Richard III was born (1452) and Mary Queen of Scots executed (1587).

Foxley *Foxeslea: Count of Mortain.*

Furtho *Forho: Count of Mortain, and William from him.* Manor farm; dovecote.

Geddington *Gadintone/Geitentone: King's land; St Edmund's Abbey.* Body of Eleanor of Castile, Edward I's Queen, rested here on its way to Westminster Abbey in 1290. The Eleanor Cross in the square is one of 3 of the original 12 to have survived. 13th-century bridge; part-Saxon church; priory.

Glassthorpehill *Clachestorp: Count of Mortain; William Peverel.* Isolated; in army 'danger area'.

Glendon *Clen(e)done: King's land; de Grestain Abbey.* Glendon Hall.

Glinton *Glintone: Peterborough Abbey. 2 mills.* Stone; Jacobean manor house.

Grafton Regis *Grastone: William from Count of Mortain.* Manor house, partly 15th century. Elizabeth Woodville, whose family held the manor, became Edward IV's queen and mother of the ill-fated princes in the Tower.

Grafton Underwood *Grastone: Roger from Robert Blunt; Agemund from Eustace of Huntingdon.*

Great Addington *Edintone: Hugh from Bishop of Coutances; Peterborough Abbey. 3 mills (200 eels).* Scene of 17th-century riot between peasants and gentry; Roman graves on nearby Shooters Hill.

Great Doddington *Dodintone: Countess Judith.* Manor House, now the vicarage.

Great Harrowden *Hargedone/Hargindone/Harginintone: Walkelin from Bishop of Coutenaces; Norigot from Guy de Raimbeaucourt. 2 mills.*

Greatworth *Grentevorde: William from Bishop of Bayeux.*

Greens Norton *Nortone: King's land, woodland stocked with game, 2 mills. Honey.* Part-Saxon church.

Grendon *Gre(n)done: Countess Judith. 3 mills.* Large; Manor farm house.

Gretton *Gretone: King's land. Mill.* Manor house; iron-workings.

Guilsborough *Gisleburg: Count of Mortain; Alfred from William Peverel. Church, mill site.* The poet William Wordsworth often stayed at the vicarage.

Hackleton *Bachelinton/Hachelintone: Winemar from Bishop of Coutances; Countess Judith.* Modern housing.

Halefield *Hala: Ramsey Abbey.* Halefield Lodge.

Halse *Hasou: King's land.*

EARL'S BARTON: *Characteristic strip and pilaster work on a small Anglo-Saxon tower.*

Hanging Houghton *Hohtone: St Edmund's Abbey; Ralph from Count of Mortain; Dodin from Walter the Fleming; Hugh from Countess Judith.* Modern housing.

Hannington *Hani(n)tone: William from Count of Mortain; Countess Judith.* Double-naved church, possibly 13th-century monastic origin.

Hardingstone *Hardingestone/ Hardingestorp: King's land; William Peverel and Gunfrid de Chocques from the king; Countess Judith. 2 mills.* Queen Eleanor's funeral cortège halted here; an Eleanor cross stands in the grounds of Delapré Abbey.

Hardwick *Hardewiche/ Herdewiche: Alan from Countess Judith.* 14th-century manor house.

Hargrave *Haregrave/ (H)eregrave: Eustace from William Peverel.*

Harlestone *Erlestone/ Herolvestone/Herolvestune: King's land; Count of Mortain; William Peverel. Mill.* Scattered; in parkland; Roman villa.

Harpole *Horpol: Bishop from William Peverel.* Suburb of Northampton; Roman remains nearby.

Harrington *Arintone: Grestain Abbey. 4 mills.* Manorial earth works, possibly Elizabethan, nearby.

Harringworth *Haringeworde: Countess Judith. Mill.* Manor house; farm.

Hartwell *Hertewell: William from Bishop of Bayeux. Mill.* Expanding; on the edge of ancient Salcey Forest.

Haselbech *Esbece: Count of Mortain.* Wind-blown.

Helmdon *Elmedene: Count of Mortain. Mill.* Fine local stone.

Hemington *Hemintone/ Hinintone: 3 men-at-arms from Peterborough Abbey, Ramsey Abbey.* Jacobean manor house.

Higham Ferrers *Hecham: William Peverel. Market, mill.* Market town; earthworks of William Peverel's castle.

Hinton (in Woodford Halse) *Hintone: Wihtbert from Geoffrey de Mandeville. Mill.* Manor house.

Hinton-in-the-Hedges *Hintone: Arnold from Geoffrey de Mandeville. Mill.* Secluded.

Holcot *Holecote: King's land; Hugh from Countess Judith.*

Holdenby *Aldenesbi/ Aldenestone: Ralph and Ordmer from Count of Mortain. Mill.* Mill. Charles I was held prisoner in 1647 at Holdenby House.

Hollowell *Holewelle: Bishop of Lincoln; Count of Mortain; William Peverel; Gilbert Cook.*

Horton *Hortone: Thorbern from Bishop of Coutances; Odbert from Walter the Fleming; Countess Judith and Thorbern from her. Mill.* Birth place of Charles Montagu (1661–1715) 1st Earl of Halifax, the Restoration poet and politician.

Hothorpe *Udetorp: St Edmund's Abbey.*

Houghton *Hohtone: William from Bishop of Bayeux; Robert from William Peverel; Winemar from Countess Judith. Mill.* Now 2 villages, Great and Little Houghton.

Hulcote *Halecote/Hulecote: William Peverel from Bishop of Bayeux; Theobald from Gunfrid de Chocques. Mill.* On the edge of Easton Neston park; manor farm.

Irchester *Hirecestre/Irencestre: Count of Mortain; William Peverel. Mill.* Housing estates; a Roman town and Saxon graveyard were unearthed here.

Irthlinborough *Erdi(n)burne: Peterborough Abbey and 4 men-at-arms from the Abbey. 2 mills.* Small industrial town; 14th-century bridge.

Isham *Hisham/Isham: Walkelin from Bishop of Coutances; Ralph from Guy de Raimbeaucourt; Eustace of Huntingdon. 2 mills, 3 gardens.* Manor farm.

Islip *Islep/Slepe: King's land; Algar from Bishop of Coutances.*

Kelmarsh *Cailmarc/Keilmerse: King's land; William Peverel.* Hall by James Wyatt.

Kettering *Cateringe: Peterborough Abbey. 2 mills.* Market town, a centre of the boot and shoe industry; Georgian manor house; remains of Roman industrial centre.

Kilsby *Chidesbi: Coventry Abbey.* Lords of manor once had the power to execute felons at nearby Gallows bank.

King's Cliffe *Clive:* See page 199.

King's Sutton *Su(d)tone: King's land; Godwin the priest and Wulfwin from the king; William from Count of Mortain; Hugh from Hugh of Grandmesnil. 3 mills, market place.* Large; 14th-century church spire; manor house; Mill House farm.

Kingsthorpe (in Northampton) *Torp: King's land. 3 mills.* Absorbed by Northampton; green with ancient spring.

Kingsthorpe (in Polebrook) *Chingestrop: 5 men-at-arms from Peterborough Abbey.* Part of Northampton; remains of medieval moat.

Kirby *Chercheberie: Richard.* Ruins of hall begun in 1570 and added to by Inigo Jones.

Kislingbury *Ceselingeberie/ Cifelingeberie: Count of Mortain; Geoffrey from Gilbert de Ghent. 2 mills.*

Knuston *Cnutestone: William Peverel; Winemar from Gunfrid de Chocques. 2 mills.*

Lamport *Langeport: St Edmund's Abbey; Fulchere from Walter the Fleming; Countess Judith. Ash wood.* Lamport Hall, seat of the Ishams, manor residents since 1560.

Laxton *Lastone: William from the king.* Rebuilt in the late 18th century.

Lilbourne *Lilleburne/Lineburn: Count of Mortain; Ralph from the king.* Roman earthworks nearby.

Lilford *Lilleforde: Walter from Countess Judith. Mill.* Parkland; Jacobean hall.

Litchborough *Liceberge: Evesham Abbey.* Ironstone; manor house.

Little Addington *Alia Edintone: Osmund from Bishop of Coutances.*

Little Harrowden *Alia Hargindone: Walkelin from Bishop of Coutances.* Larger than Great Harrowden, despite its name.

Little Weldon *Parva Weledone: Hugh d'Ivry.* Weldon Lodge.

Loddington *Lodintone: King's land.* Jacobean hall.

Long Buckby *Buchebi: Alfred from Count of Mortain.* Small town.

Lowick *Ludewic/Luhwic: Edwin and Algar from Bishop of Coutances; Sibold from the king. Mill.* Drayton House, nearby, has a 13th-century crypt.

Luddington in the Brook *Lullintone/Lolinctune: Walter from Peterborough Abbey.* Secluded.

Lutton *Lidintone/Ludintone/ Lodintune: William from Peterborough Abbey; Ramsey Abbey.* Quiet; manor house.

Maidford *Merdeford: Hugh from Hugh de Grandmesnil.* Remains of manor house moat; manor farm.

KIRBY: *The ruins of Kirby Hall from the south.*

Maidwell *Medewelle: St Edmund's Abbey; Ansger the Chaplain from the king; Berener from Mainou le Breton.* Site of manorial fishpond.

Marston St Lawrence *Merestone: Earl Hugh. Mill.* Manor house. Charles Chauncy, 17th-century vicar, became President of Harvard University in the US.

Marston Trussell *Mersitone: Hugh from Hugh de Grandmesnil.* After their Naseby defeat, many Royalists fled here and were massacred.

Mears Ashby *Asbi: Countess Judith.* Church with Saxon carving; manor house.

Middleton Cheney *Mideltone: Ralph from Count of Mortain; Earl Hugh; Hugh from Hugh de Grandmesnil.* Civil War battle was fought here in 1643.

Milton (in Castor) *Meletone: Roger from Peterborough Abbey.* 2 standing stones, Little John and Robin Hood.

Milton Malsor *Mideltone/ Mildetone: William from Geoffrey Alselin. Mill.* Scattered; manor house.

Moreton Pinkney *Mortone: Geoffrey from Giles brother of Ansculf.* Pretty; scattered homesteads; manor farm.

Moulton *Moltone/Mul(e)tone: King's land; William from Robert de Bucy; Grimbald, Bishop and Hugh from Countess Judith. Mill.* Part of suburban Northampton, Moulton Park was once a Carthusian Monastery.

Muscott *Misecote: Count of Mortain.*

Naseby *Navesberie:* See page 197.

Nassington *Nassintone: King's land. 2 mills.* Stone; in Rockingham Forest; 13th-century prebendal house; 15th-century manor house; church with Saxon nave.

Nether Heyford *Hai/Heiford(e): William from Bishop of Bayeux; Count of Mortain and Ralph from him; Sasgar from Gilbert de Ghent. Mill.* Large; manor house; roman building in Horestone Meadow.

Newbottle (near Brackley) *Niwebotle: Ivo from Hugh de Grandmesnil.* Manor house; church; cottages.

Newbottle (in Harrington) *Neubote: Grestain Abbey. Mill.* 17th-century bridge.

Newton (near Geddington) *Neutone/Newentone: Gunfrid de Chocques; Thorgar and Lancelin from Countess Judith. 2 mills.* Peaceful. Also called Newton-in-the-Willows; Elizabethan dovecote.

Newton Bromswold *Neuuentone: William from Bishop of Coutances.* Manor farm.

Nobottle *Neubote: William Peverel. Mill; woodland.* On Roman road; Nobottle Wood; Nobottle House.

Northampton *Hantone/ Northantone: King's land; 14 derelict burgess's residences out of a total of 61.* Boot and shoe manufacturing town. Norman churches; traces of castle; medieval market place, rebuilt after 17th-century fire.

Nortoft *Nortot: Count of Mortain; William Peverel. Mill.* Nortoft Grange, part of Guilsborough Village.

Norton (near Daventry) *Nortone: Count of Meulan. Mill.* Roman site at Whilton Lodge.

Oakley *Achelau: Lancelin from Countess Judith.* Now 2 villages of Great and Little Oakley, facing each other across quarries.

Old Walda *King's land.* Also known as Wold.

Orlingbury *Ordinbaro: Count of Mortain.* Queen Anne hall.

Orton *Overtone: King's land. 2 mills (with Rockwell).* Manor farm.

Oundle *Undel(e): Peterborough Abbey. Mill (250 eels), market.* Market town with a public school founded in 1556 by William Laxton, a grocer who became Lord Mayor of London.

Oxendon *Ocedone/Oxe(n)done: King's land; Count of Mortain, Ulf from Countess Judith.* Near the village of Great Oxenden and hamlet of Little Oxendon, the latter on the site of a medieval village.

Passenham *Pas(s)eham/ Passonham: King's land and Reginald from the king. Mill.* 17th-century manor house and rectory.

Pattishall *Pascelle: Walter the Fleming. 2 mills, church.* Partly Saxon church; Roman Watling Street. Simon de Pattishall supported the barons against King John.

Paulerspury *Pirie: Robert from William Peverel. Mill.* Scattered.

PETERBOROUGH: *The abbey was a Saxon monastery (650).*

Peterborough *Burg: Peterborough Abbey. Mill.* City, a brickmaking centre, with a fine Norman cathedral begun in 1118.

Piddington *Pidentone: Gilbert from Countess Judith.* Manor farm.

Pilsgate *Pillesgete: Peterborough Abbey. Mill.* Pilsgate Grange.

Pilton *Pilchetone: Roger from Peterborough Abbey.*

Pipewell *Pipewelle: Humphrey from Count of Mortain; Roger from Robert de Tosny; Dodin from Walter the Fleming.*

Pitsford *Pidesford/Pitesford: Count of Mortain, Fulchere from Walter the Fleming. 2 mills.* Scattered; Long Barrow nearby.

Plumpton *Pluntune: Leofnoth from Walter the Fleming.* Jacobean manor house.

Polebrook *Pochebroc: Eustace and Geoffrey from Peterborough Abbey; Alfred from Eustace of Huntingdon.* Jacobean hall, early Norman church, probably built by the masons of Peterborough Cathedral.

Potterspury *Perie/Pirie: Henry de Ferrers; William Peverel from Countess Judith. Mill.* Expanding; on Roman Watling Street.

Preston *Prestetone: Count of Mortain and Ralph and Nigel from him.* Now Preston Capes; remains of 11th-century castle. Nearby, hamlet of Little Preston.

Preston Deanery *Prestone: Winemar from Bishop of Coutances and Countess Judith.* Scattered.

Purston *Pres(te)tone: Count of Mortain; Robert D'Oilly.* Now 2 hamlets, Great and Little Purston.

Puxley *Pocheslai/lei: King's land; William from Bishop of Bayeux.*

Pytchley *Picteslei/Pi(h)teslea: Azo from Peterborough Abbey; Count of Mortain; William from the king. Mill.* Jacobean manor house. Lords of Manor were obliged by ancient tradition to keep hounds here to destroy vermin. The famous pack of hounds was formally established in the mid-18th century.

Quinton *Quintone: Countess Judith and Winemar from her.* Manor farm.

Radstone *Rodestone: Earl Hugh.*

Raunds *Rande: Bishop of Coutances; William Peverel. 2 mills (100 eels).* Town, a centre of the footwear industry; Roman earthworks at Mallows Cotton.

Ravensthorpe *Ravenestorp: Count of Mortain; Drogo from William Peverel; Gilbert Cook.*

Roade *Rode: King's land; Dodin from Gunfrid de Chocques.* Large; developing.

Rockingham *Rochingeha:* See page 198.

Rothersthorpe *Torp: Winemar from Geoffrey Alselin; Gunfrid de Chocques. Mill.* 17th-century manor house.

Rothwell *Rodewelle: King's land. 2 mills. (Surveyed with Orton).* Town with a magnificent medieval church. The annual Charter Fair dates from 1204.

Rushden *Ris(e)dene: William Peverel. Mill.* Footwear manufacturing town; red-brick Victorian terraces.

Rushton *Ricsdone/Rise(e)tone: King's land; Grestain Abbey; Hugh from Robert de Tosny; William from Robert de Bucy; Eustace from Countess Judith. 2 mills.* 16th-century Triangular Lodge was built by Sir Thomas Tresham as a manifestation of his Roman Catholic faith.

Scaldwell *Scalde(s)welle: Aubrey from Bishop of Coutance; St Edmund's Abbey (gift from King William for the soul of Queen Matilda); also Hugh from Countess Judith.*

Seawell *Sewelle: Robert de Tosny. Mill.* Isolated.

Sibbertoft *Sibertod: Count of Mortain.* Castle Yard, a large motte and bailey nearby.

Silverstone *Sel/Silvestone: Count of Mortain, Godwin from Giles brother of Ansculf; Arnold from Geoffrey de Mandeville.*

Slapton *Slaptone: Jocelyn from Earl Hugh.* Secluded; manor farm.

Slipton *Sliptone: Peterborough Abbey.*

Snorscomb *Snochescumbe: Count of Mortain, and Alric from him.* Isolated; mill.

Southorpe *Sudtorp: Geoffry and 2 other men-at-arms from Peterborough Abbey. 2 ½ mills.* String of houses. Mill Farm.

Spratton *Spretone/Sprotone: William and Durand from Count of Mortain; Ralph from Robert de Bucy; Rohais from Countess Judith. 2 mills.* Hall.

Stanford on Avon *Stanford: Abbot Benedict of Selby from Guy de Raimbeaucourt.*

Stanion *Stanere: King's land; Edwin from Bishop of Countances. Mill.* In Rockingham Forest.

Stanwick *Stanewiga/wige: Peterborough Abbey. Mill.* Manor house.

Staverton *Stavertone: Count of Mortain; Hugh de Grandmesnil.* Stone-built, manor house.

Steane *Stane: Giles brother of Ansculf. Mill.* 17th-century chapel and manor house. The site of the medieval village wiped out by the Black Death is still visible.

Stoke Albany *Stoche: Robert de Tosny. Mill.* Manor house, mainly 17th century.

Stoke Bruerne *Stoche: Swein from the king. Mill.* Canalside; pavilions designed by Inigo Jones nearby.

Stoke Doyle *Stoche: Peterborough Abbey.*

Stowe *Stowe: Gilbert de Ghent. Mill.* Now Church Stowe, also known as Stowe Nine Churches because there were 8 fruitless attempts to build the church, with its mainly Saxon tower, elsewhere.

Stuchbury *Stoteberie: Hugh and Landric from Giles brother of Ansculf.* Isolated; manor farm; hall.

SULGRAVE: *The manor is a place of pilgrimage for patriotic Americans.*

Sudborough *Sutburg: Westminster Abbey. Mill.* Riverside; in Rockingham Forest. 'Money Holes' are the remains of a medieval monastery.

Sulby *Solebi: Walter from Guy de Raimbeaucourt; Geoffrey de La Guerche.* Large area of lonely farmsteads, including Sulby Grange.

Sulgrave *Sulgrave: Hugh, Landric and Odbert from Giles brother of Ansculf.* The manor was owned by George Washington's family from 1540 to 1659; Church with Saxon doorway.

Sutton Bassett *Sutone: Robert de Bucy; Countess Judith.*

Syresham *Sigre(s)ham: Ralph from Count of Mortain; King's land, Geoffrey from Giles brother of Ansculf.* Sprawling; Kingshill Farm; Earl's Wood.

STOWE: *Monument to Lady Danvers by Nicolas Stone.*

Sywell *Snewelle: Count of Mortain.* On the edge of Northampton, Elizabethan hall.

Tansor *Tanesovre: King's land. Mill.*

Teeton *Teche: William Peverel.*

Thenford *Taneford/Teworde: Roger from Robert d'Oilly; Mainou le Breton. Mill.* Peaceful; in woodland setting; Roman site nearby.

Thornby *Torneberie: William Peverel and Robert from him.*

Thorpe (in Peterborough) *Torp: Peterborough Abbey.* Suburb of Peterborough. Longthorpe Hall is by Peter Mills a contemporary of Christopher Wren.

Thorpe Lubenham *Torp: Hugh from Hugh de Grandmesnil.* Hall, parkland with remains of medieval moat.

Thorpe Malsor *Alidetorp: Fulchere from Count of Mortain.* Hall.

Thorpe Mandeville *Torp: Ingelrann from Giles, brother of Ansculf.* The site of the ancient manor house is still visible.

Thrapston *Trapestone: Odelin from Bishop of Coutances; Oger Breton. Mill.* Small market town with a 13th-century bridge.

Thrupp Grounds *Torp: Alfred from the Count of Mortain; Hugh de Grandmesnil; Gunfrid de Chocques, Leofric the pre-Conquest holder, from Countess Judith.* Handful of houses on Roman Watling Street.

Thurning *Terninge/Torninge: Peterborough Abbey.* Peaceful.

Tiffield *Tifelde: Ralph and William from Count of Mortain.* Straggling.

Titchmarsh *Ticemerse/Tircemesse: Azelin from Peterborough Abbey; Saswalo from Henry de Ferrers. Mill.* Castle remains.

Towcester *Touecestre: King's land. Mill.* Town that grew up along Roman Watling Street. In the 13th century Benedetto Gaetano, who later became Pope, held the living. The Saracen's Head Inn was immortalised by Charles Dickens in *The Pickwick Papers*.

Trafford *Trapeford: Robert from Earl Hugh. Mill.* Isolated. Georgian Trafford bridge carries the ancient 'Welsh Road' across the River Cherwell.

Twywell *Teowelle/Tuiwella: Thorney Abbey; Countess Judith. 2 mills.* Elizabethan manor house.

Upper Heyford *altera Haiford: Count of Mortain.*

Upton (near Northampton) *Optone: King's land. Mill.* 18th-century hall. Mill.

Wadenhoe *Wadenho: Aubrey from Bishop of Coutances; Roger from Peterborough Abbey. 2 mills (65 eels).* Pretty; manor house; mill.

Wakefield *Wacafeld: Ralph the Steward from Count Alan.* In ancient Whittlewood Forest.

Wakerley *Wacherlei: Eudo FitzHubert. Mill.* On the edge of Rockingham Forest.

Walgrave *Waldgrave/ Wold(e)grave: King's land; Robert from Count of Mortain; Fulchere from Countess Judith.* Jacobean hall.

Walton Grounds *Wal(e)tone: William from Bishop of Bayeux; Ralph from Count of Mortain. Mill.* Lonely; Mill House Farm.

Wappenham *Wapeham: Giles brother of Ansculf. Mill.*

Warkton *Werchintone: St Edmund's Abbey; formerly Countess Aelfeve mother of Earl Morcar. Mill.* Estate village.

Warmington *War/ Werminstone: Peterborough Abbey, and 2 men-at-arms from the Abbey. Mill (325 eels).* Pretty; stone-built manor house; mill.

Watford *Wat/Wadford: Gilbert Cook. Mill.* In parkland.

Weedon Bec(k) *Wedone: Count of Mortain; Hugh de Grandmesnil, in exchange for Watford. 2 mills.* Expanding.

Weedon Lois *Wedone: Giles brother of Ansculf. Mill.* Remains of fishponds. The poet Edith Sitwell was buried here in 1964.

Weekley *Wiclei: King's land. Mill.*

Weldon *Wale(s)done/Weledene/ Weledone: Robert de Bucy; Olaf from the king.* Roman villa nearby; the Romans were the first to work the much-valued local stone.

Welford *Wellesford: Alfred from Geoffrey de La Guerche.* Brick-built, manor house.

Wellingborough *Wedlingeberie/Wendle(s)berie: Norigot from Bishop of Coutances; Crowland Abbey; Hugh and Gilbert from Countess Judith. 3 mills.* Victorian brick-built town, a centre of footwear and clothing industries. Earlier buildings include the largely Jacobean Croyland Abbey. Mills.

Welton *Waletone/Weletone/ Welintone: Wulfmer the pre-Conquest holder from Count of Mortain; Osbern from Hugh de Grandmesnil; Leofric, the pre-Conquest holder; from Countess Judith. Mill.* Georgian manor house.

Werrington *Widerintone: Peterborough Abbey and 4 of the Abbot's men-at-arms from the Abbey.* Suburb of Peterborough; Georgian hall.

West Farndon *Ferendon(e): Ralph from Count of Mortain; Hugh de Grandmesnil.*

West Haddon *Ecdone/E(d)done: Coventry Abbey; William Peverel; Gunfrid de Chocques.* Hall.

Weston by Welland *Westone: Robert de Bucy; Countess Judith.*

Weston Favell *Westone: King's land; Grestain Abbey; Count of Mortain and Walter from him; John from Gunfrid de Chocques.* Part of Northampton.

Whilton *Woltone: Count of Mortain. Mill.* Quiet.

Whiston *Wice(n)tone: Ramsey Abbey; Countess Judith. Mill.* Quiet. King John may have used the Moat House, which has remains of a bailey.

Whitfield *Witefelle: King's land.* Unspoilt.

Wicken *Wicha/Wiche: Roger from Robert d'Oilly; Mainou le Breton.*

Wilbarston *Wilberdestone/ Wilbertestone: King's land; Robert de Tosny.* Ironstone.

Wilby *Wilebi: Countess Judith.*

Winwick *Winewic(he): Coventry Abbey; William Peverel.* Elizabethan manor house. Sir Thomas Malory author of the *Morte d'Arthur* (1469–70), was Lord of Winwick Manor.

Wittering *Wit(h)eringham: Ansketel from Peterborough Abbey. Mills.* Swamped by housing estates; RAF station; Saxon church.

Wollaston *Wilavestone: Gunfrid de Chocques; Countess Judith and Corbelin from her. 2 mills.* Large; industrial.

TOWCASTER: *Entrance to the chantry courtyard, in the local stonework. The town was fortified and protected by Edward the Elder and his sister Ethelfleda, c. 910–921.*

WELLINGBOROUGH: *The nave ceiling of St Mary's church, begun 1908.*

Woodford (near Denford) *Wodeford: Ralph from Bishop of Coutances; Roger, Hugh and Siward from Peterborough Abbey. Mill.* Rectory Farm, formerly the manor house. General Charles Arbuthnot and his diarist wife, friends of the Duke of Wellington, lived at Woodford House in the early 19th century.

Woodford Halse *Wodeford: Richard from Hugh de Grandmesnil. Mill.* Transformed by the arrival of railway, now quiet again.

Woodnewton *Niwetone: Reginald from Eustace of Huntingdon. Mill.* Pretty; limestone.

Wootton *Witone: Winemar from Walter the Fleming and Countess Judith.* Dormitory.

Wothorpe *Wri(d)torp: Alwin from Peterborough Abbey; Crowland Abbey; Robert from Countess Judith. Mill.* Towers, the remains of a small house built in the early 17th century for Thomas Cecil, son of Lord Burghley.

Wythemail *Widmale: Fulchere from Walter the Fleming.* Wythemail Park Farm with part of a moat was perhaps the old manor house.

Yardley Hastings *Gerdelai: Countess Judith.* Attractive; 14th-century manor house; Ancient Yardley Chase to the south.

Yelvertoft *Celvrecot/Gelvrecote/ Givertost: Count of Mortain; Earl Hugh.*

Nottinghamshire

Nottinghamshire, as the vocabulary used for its holdings and measurements reveals, was in the Northern Danelaw.

In 1068, it had revolted under the Earls Edwin and Morcar, but when William I marched into Nottingham the town seems to have surrendered quickly. The county's Norman settlement probably began immediately afterwards. William's men on the spot were Domesday's *two great tenants-in-chief, Roger de Bully and William Peverel.*

Geographically, the county's main feature was the great expanse of infertile sandy soil which stretched north from Nottingham for 25 miles, and not long afterwards became Sherwood Forest. The forest is first mentioned 68 years later, when William Peverel, grandson of Domesday's *Peverel, controlled it for the king; but the survey shows that William I had large holdings here and he had probably already afforested the area.*

Blyth

[Land of Roger de Bully . . .] In BLYTH *BLIDE* 1 bovate of land and the fourth part of 1 bovate taxable. Land for 1 plough. 4 villagers and 4 smallholders have 1 plough. Meadow 1 acre.

'There is nothing like Blyth', wrote Nikolaus Pevsner, the architectural historian, 'to get a feeling for early Norman grimness.' He was referring specifically to the church, which was begun two years after *Domesday* when Roger de Bully gave Blyth to Benedictine monks so that they could found a priory here. The priory's charter, one of the earliest to survive, presents a vivid picture of the work which the people of a manor owed their overlord.

Blyth's four village householders and four smallholders had to plough, fetch and carry, mow, reap, pay marriage dues and repair the mill pool. The charter does not, unfortunately, specify how often and for how long these duties had to be performed, but it is safe to assume that the agricultural tasks would have had their natural seasons, and that repairing the millpool would have been winter work.

So little is known about Roger de Bully, Nottinghamshire's leading tenant-in-chief, that he has been described as 'famous in *Domesday* but nowhere else'. He probably came from Busli near Rouen in Normandy. He does not seem to have been one of William's regular advisers, for his name appears only occasionally on the king's writs and charters, yet his large holdings prove that William trusted him. He also had many in Yorkshire and Derbyshire, and he was almost certainly granted all these northern lands between 1068 and 1070, after risings which resulted in the loss of everything by the previous English holders during William's infamous 'Harrying of the North'.

Blyth was, at first, the centre of de Bully's northern estates, which were known as the Honour of Blyth, a name they kept even after he built a castle at Tickhill, four miles to the north-west. Remnants of this castle survive, but the one that he is believed to have built earlier at Blyth, is lost. Roger's son inherited his lands but he died without issue and they reverted to the king. By then Blyth already had a special place in the rituals of medieval England. In 1194 Richard I ruled that only five places in the country could be licensed for tournaments, one of which was '*Blie et Tykehill*'. Blyth's tournament field had been lost for centuries, but it has now been pinpointed as slightly north of the village, near the hamlet of Styrrup.

Here, a field known as Terminings Meadow (from 'tourneyings') and another known as Raker Field (from 'wrecker', or 'combatant') lie close to a point where five separate roads converged, an indication that the place must have been important. Nearby was a small enclosure called Gallant Steads ('stand' or 'steading' for the knights); and the name Styrrup itself has a significantly equine flavour. Just to the north is a convenient low ridge for spectators. Whenever the king chose to cancel a tournament he would send a message to the knights by way of the Prior of Blyth.

The style of the priory's church is older than that of any other surviving Norman church in England. It was probably copied from the Abbey of Jumièges in Normandy, which was built 40 years earlier. Only the Norman north aisle and the nave survived the destruction during the Dissolution. They are 'massive, rough . . . bare and cold to the eye, but majestic and enduring'.

The priory land was eventually bought by the Mellish family, and in 1703 Edward Mellish, who had spent 20 prosperous years as a merchant in Portugal, built a new house on the site – a site now occupied by a housing estate. Edward's tomb is in the church, where he lies, a short stout gentleman wearing a full wig, on his side supported by one elbow.

There might still be Mellishes at Blyth but for the notorious Colonel Henry Mellish, who inherited the hall at the end of the eighteenth century and dissipated the family fortune. Horses and gambling were his weaknesses. By 1807, when he had to abandon his racing career, he had '39 racers in training, 17 carriage horses, 12 hunters in Leicestershire, 4 chargers in Brighton and hacks past all counting'. He bet obsessively – and never less than 500 guineas!

At Doncaster, close to Blyth, he won the St Leger both in 1804 and in 1805, but in 1806, when a million guineas are said to have been laid on the race and he hoped to recover his gambling debts, his horse was beaten. The Prince Regent and the Duke of Clarence visited him at Blyth Hall on their way back from this disastrous race meeting, and he lost £40,000 to them on a single throw of the dice. He had already lost £97,000 in one gaming session at Brooks in London.

He was a soldier by profession and went to fight in the Peninsular War, but he was so bad an influence on his fellow officers that the Duke of Wellington sent him home. He then fought a duel near York, calling out to his who had hit him in the elbow, 'Hang it! You've winged me, but give me your hand.'

He was at last forced to sell Blyth, and in the nineteenth century, parts of the ruined priory church which had lain in the gardens were used

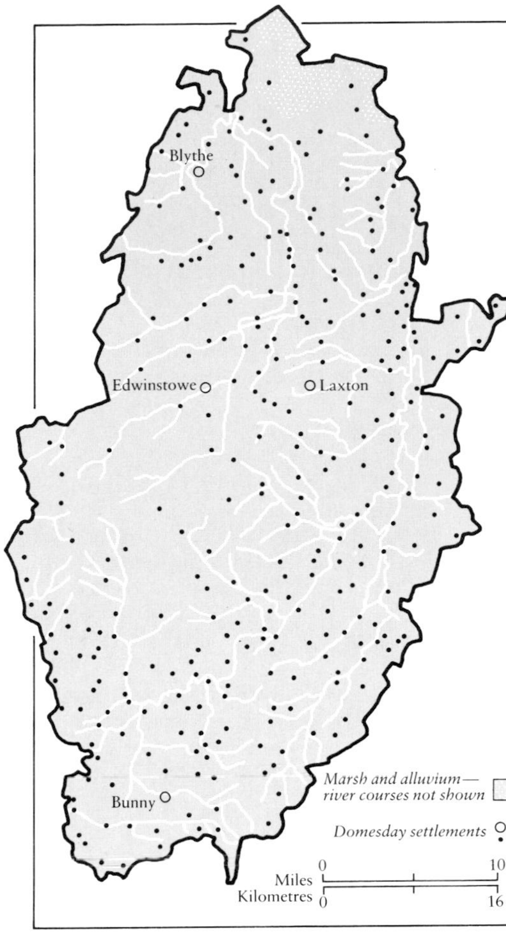

to enclose an aviary. But the hall's real decline dated from World War II when the army occupied it. Nothing remains today.

The village itself declined when it became a bottleneck on the Great North Road. It has, however, now been by-passed, and it can be seen again for the pleasant small town it is. Old red brick cottages border a long green on which stand the rebuilt remains of a twelfth-century hospital. The Angel Inn which faces the church claims to date from 1274. 650 years ago it was used by knights and their retinues, gathering for tournaments. By the monks of the priory, too, it seems. A tunnel, now blocked, ran under the road from the priory to the Angel's cellars.

Bunny

[Land of Ralph FitzHubert . . .] In BUNNY *BONEI* Leofnoth had 2 c. of land taxable. Land for 6 ploughs. Ralph has in lordship 2 ploughs and 18 villagers, 7 Freemen and 2 smallholders who have 7 ploughs. A church and a priest; 1 mill, 12d; meadow, 160 acres; underwood 10 furlongs long and 1 wide. Value before 1066 £4; now 60s.

The village of Bunny lies six miles south of Nottingham, on the Fairham Brook, a small stream that flows through low-lying fields at the foot of the Derbyshire Wolds. Today it is an odd mixture of the new and ugly with the old and crazy.

In 1086 it was a prosperous manor, assessed at two carucates, with another bovate three miles away at Widnerpool. Ralph FitzHubert, its tenant-in-chief, was not one of Nottinghamshire's great landholders, but he had a group of some dozen holdings, mainly in the west of the county. In Derbyshire he had over twice as many. He farmed part of Bunny himself; 27 families shared the rest. It had sizeable areas of meadow, and of woodland (unusual in these parts), a mill, a priest and a church.

St Mary's church at Bunny contains the tomb of the village's strangest resident, Sir Thomas Parkyns, (1663–1741), the Wrestling Baronet. He is said to have carved it himself. Although some of the workmanship suggests that this might be true, the upright figure was probably the work of a professional. There Sir Thomas stands, life-size, knees slightly bent, hands forward, palms open, alert for a wrestling bout. Alongside and much smaller, he lies on his back beside a grotesque winged Father Time, who had just defeated him. The inscription reads,

'That Time at LENGTH did throw him it is plain
WHO liv'd in hope that he should RISE again.'

Not only did Sir Thomas himself wrestle and publish a book on wrestling, *The Cornish Hugg*, but he also promoted an annual wrestling competition at Bunny with a gold-laced hat as the prize.

He also obsessively decorated the village with Latin texts. This was perhaps part of his campaign to educate the villagers, for he built them a grammar school (now a men's club) and published a Latin grammar. Stone coffins also interested him. He would supply them for his friends.

His house, which dominates the village, is almost as astonishing a memorial as his tomb. He designed it himself, with a massive tower, four brick corner battlements and an enormous crest. There are many more of his buildings in the village, mainly in red brick. Most charming are the decaying barns and stables near the hall. Most expensive, after the hall itself, was the £5000 wall with which he encircled his gardens. Part of it remains, near the Fairham Brook.

It was the brook which powered Bunny's mill in 1086. And although its church, sometimes called the Cathedral of the Wolds, dates mostly from the fourteenth century, it undoubtedly stands where the *Domesday* church once stood.

Laxton

[Land of Geoffrey Alselin...] In LAXTON *LAXINTVNE* Toki had 2 c. of land taxable. Land for 6 ploughs. Walter, Geoffrey Alselin's man, has 1 plough and 22 villagers and 7 smallholders who have 5 ploughs; 5 male slaves, 1 female slave; meadow, 40 acres; woodland pasture 1 league long and 1/2 wide. Value before 1066 £9; now £6.

The secluded village of Laxton lies down narrow lanes six miles south-east of Thoresby Hall, the great ducal house. For many years Laxton was part of the Thoresby estate. Its twelfth-century church, still impressive despite a disastrous 1860 restoration, together with what is left of its once formidable Norman castle and its three huge hedgeless fields combine to connect Laxton more closely with medieval England than any other village in the country.

The castle, a typical motte-and-bailey construction, had a large mound, 816 feet in circumference at the base, surmounted by a smaller one, 145 feet in circumference. Today they are no more than a double hill, topped with an old beech or two and surrounded by hawthorn scrub. Overgrown too are the banks and ditches of the vast open courtyard which lay closer to the village. The entire great fortification, the best of its type in the county, dates from at latest Henry I's reign (1100–35), and the site might well have been fortified in Geoffrey Alselin's time, for in 1086 Laxton, with its 29 families, was his principal manor.

Laxton's hedgeless fields are the remains of an agricultural system several centuries older. The system survives today in modified form, making the village into a living medieval museum and telling us much about how such early rotation farming was carried out.

Each open field is divided into a number of strips which vary in size from one-half to 10 acres: they used to be much smaller. The Ministry of Agriculture which has been their landlord since 1951, lets these strips to 16 farmers each of whom has some in every field. Every year all the strips in one field must grow winter wheat. In the second field they may grow various crops but these, like the wheat, must be harvested by a certain date because both fields are then thrown open for common grazing. A third field lies fallow.

Two other features of a typical *Domesday* village survive at Laxton, although less perfectly: its common meadowland, and its pasture. The meadows, once also divided into strips for hay, were enclosed in the eighteenth century, but remnants survive as the 'sykes', or low-lying parts of the open fields which cannot be ploughed; these are still cropped for hay. Its pasture land, in addition to the fallow fields and the cultivated fields after harvest, consisted of two commons. Cocking Moor, the larger, was ploughed up during World War II but certain farmers may still graze a cow on the smaller East Moor.

There are complex rules governing who may grow what in the open fields of Laxton, when to sow and when to harvest; what animals may graze and when; who shall maintain common hedges, ditches, gates and roadways, and so on. These are controlled by the Court Leet of the Manor, which swears in a Field Jury to administer the system.

All in all, Laxton suggests that even when farmers owed service as well as rent to the manor, a village community was less like a company commanded by a tough sergeant than a co-operative in which everyone knew the rules and it was in everyone's interest to keep them.

A map of 1635 shows how Laxton's main street was lined on both sides with the houses of its farmers. Behind each was a small paddock with farm buildings. There seems little doubt that these houses stood where the huts of their ancestors had stood in 1086. Their successors still occupy most of these same sites today.

BUNNY: *Sir Thomas Parkyns' nickname, The Wrestling Baronet, came from his absolute passion for the sport. He established an annual competition at Bunny Hall which lasted until 1810.*

Edwinstowe

[Land of the King . . .] In EDWINSTOWE *EDENESTOU* 1 c. of land taxable. Land for 2 ploughs. A church and a priest and 4 smallholders have 1 plough. Woodland pasture 1/2 league long and 1/2 wide.

The only part of Sherwood Forest which Robin Hood might recognize lies slightly to the north of Edwinstowe. Here some 450 acres known as the Hay of Birklands are wooded with groves of silver birch and astonishing ancient oaks. This, together with the neighbouring Hay of Billhagh (now a tip for Thoresby Colliery) probably made up the woodland pasture which belonged to Edwinstowe in 1086.

It was a berewick of the royal manor of Mansfield, and one of William I's many holdings in this sandy infertile part of Nottinghamshire, so it would have been convenient for him – or perhaps for his immediate successors – to afforest Sherwood.

Even when Sherwood Forest was far larger, the Robin Hood legend collected around Edwinstowe and its neighbouring hays. Here, till a few years ago, stood a massive oak known as 'Robin Hood's larder', from the branches of which he was supposed to have hung his venison. Spectacular as they are, the oaks of the Hay of Birklands, reckoning from the rings of some that have fallen, are no more than 450 years old. In Edwinstowe church Robin is said to have married Maid Marion. In fact, if he existed at all he probably operated farther north, in the Barnsdale area of Yorkshire.

Edwinstowe church has a curiosity of another kind: set in a wall is a stone eighteen inches long which is said to have been the standard measure for a 'forest foot'; 30 of these made a perch.

EDWINSTOWE: *The legend of Robin Hood and Sherwood forest is so much a part of local history that individual trees have been named – this is one of the candidates for 'Robin's Larder'.*

In 1672 the church spire was 'beaten down by thunder'. Seven years later the parishioners humbly petitioned Charles II for 200 trees out of Birkland and Billhagh because 'the whole Body of the Church is shaken and in a very ruinous condition'. This may explain why the present steeple is an irregular polygon.

Today the village of Edwinstowe receives more than its share of tourists, on their way to the Sherwood Forest Visitors Centre. And its outskirts have grown dismayingly since large-scale coal mining began here in the 1920s. Best to close your eyes to such housing developments as Maid Marion Drive and find the heart of the original village which still has old houses and a besieged charm.

Nottinghamshire Gazetteer Each entry starts with the modern place name in **bold** type. The *Domesday* information that follows is in *italic* type, beginning with the name or names by which the place was known in 1086. The main landholders and under-tenants are next, separated with semi-colons if a place was divided into more than one holding. A number of holdings were granted by the king to his thanes; these holders, always the last in a list, are described as holding land 'from the king'. More general information completes the *Domesday* part of the entry, including examples of dues such as eels rendered by tenants. The modern or post-Domesday section is in normal type. represents a village, a small village or hamlet.

Adbolton *Alboltune: William Peverel. Church.* Part of West Bridgford.

Alverton *Alvretun/Alvriton: Mauger from Walter d'Aincourt; Ilbert de Lacy.*

Annesley *Aneslei: Richard from Ralph FitzHubert.* Ruined 14th-century church; motte and bailey; Annesley Forest. Annesley Hall, home of Mary Chaworth, Lord Byron's boyhood love is nearby.

Arnold *Ernehale: King's land. 6 sesters of honey.* Urban district of Nottingham. Ernehale means 'place frequented by eagles', and eagles are incorporated into the Council Coat of Arms. Birthplace of the painter Richard Bonington (1801–28).

Askham *Ascam: Archbishop of York. Church, 2 fisheries, mill.*

Aslockton *Haslachestone/Aslache(s)tone/tune: King's land; Wakelin from Walter d'Aincourt; Gilbert de Ghent; Wulfric from Ilbert de Lacy; Wulfric from the king.* Ancient earthworks; the county's only 3 mud cottages. Birthplace (1489) of Thomas Cranmer, Archbishop of Canterbury.

Averham *Aigrun: Gilbert Tison. Church, 2 mills.* Church with Norman, possibly Saxon, masonry. The Robin Hood Theatre, built in 1913, was the scene of Sir Donald Wolfit's first stage appearance in 1917.

Awsworth *Elde(s)u(e)de/Eldeurde: Alwin from William Peverel; Haldane from the king.*

Babworth *Baburde: King's land; Geoffrey from Roger de Bully.* Some villagers sailed to America in the *Mayflower*.

Balderton *Baldretone/tune: Bishop of Lincoln, formerly Countess Godiva.* On the outskirts of Newark; named after the Saxon god Balder. Birthplace of Sir Donald Wolfit.

Barnby in the Willows *Barnebi: Bishop of Lincoln; Losoard from Bishop of Bayeux. Church, mill.* Early 14th-century church.

Barnby Moor *Barnebi: King's land; Roger de Bully.*

Barnstone *Bernestune: William Peverel; Walter d'Aincourt.* In the Vale of Belvoir.

Barton in Fabis *Bartone: William Peverel; Ralph FitzHubert; Salwin from the king. ½ church with Chilwell.* Otherwise called Barton in the Beans due to large crops of this staple food. Site of British and Roman fortifications.

Basford *Baseford: Payne and Saxfrid from William Peverel; Aelfric, the pre-Conquest holder, and Aswulf from the king. 5 mills.* A district of Nottingham since 1877, on the River Leen. One part called Old Basford.

Bassingfield *Basin(g)felt: Roger de Bully; William Peverel.* By the disused Grantham Canal and Nottingham Airport.

Beckingham *Beching(e)ham: 2 men at arms from Archbishop of York; Geoffrey from Roger de Bully.*

Beeston *Bestune: William Peverel.* Industrial town. Home of Jesse Boot the founder of Boots the Chemist.

Besthorpe (in Caunton) *Bestorp: King's land; Geoffrey Alselin.* Besthorpe Hall near Caunton.

Bilborough *Bileburch/burg: King's land; Ambrose from William Peverel.* Part of Nottingham.

Bilby *Billebi: Ingran from Roger de Bully.*

Bilsthorpe *Bildestorp: Gilbert de Ghent.* Near Sherwood Forest.

Bingham *Bingheham: Roger de Bully.* Large; a church floorstone commemorates Sir Thomas Ramston who helped Henry Tudor defeat Richard II. He appears as John Ramston in Shakespeare's *Richard II*.

Blidworth *Blidworde: Archbishop of York before and after 1066.* Large; in Sherwood Forest. Maid Marion is said to have lived here, and Will Scarlet to be buried in the churchyard.

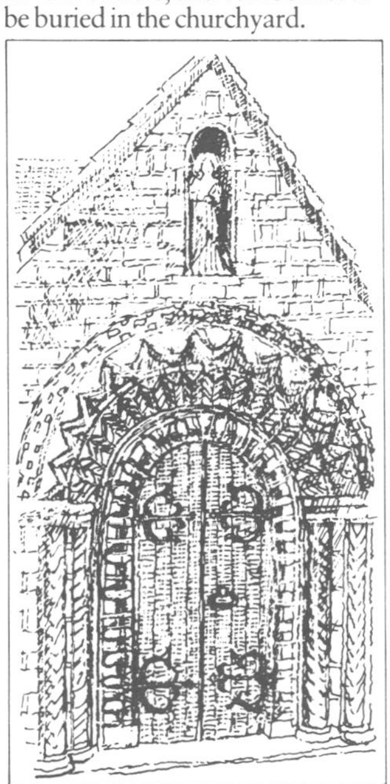

BALDERTON: *Decorated Norman doorway to the porch.*

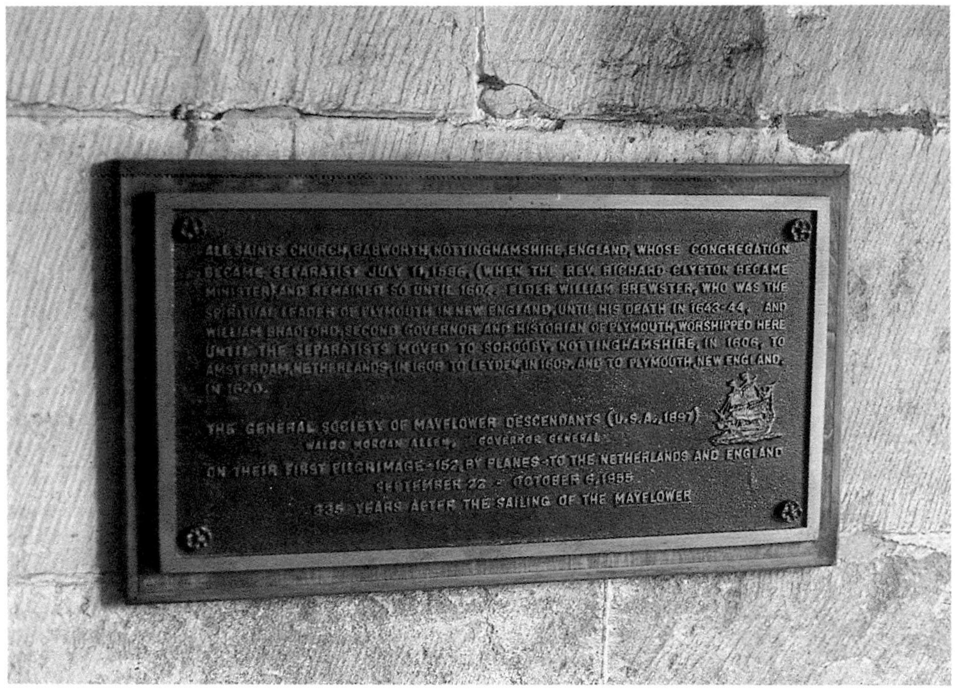

BABWORTH: *Plaque in the church, dedicated to the Pilgrim Fathers.*

Blyth *Blide:* See page 205.

Bole *Bolun: 2 men-at-arms from Archbishop of York; Geoffrey from Roger de Bully. ¼ church, 2 mills.* Site of old fishpond; church with a Norman font.

Bothamsall *Bodmescel(d): King's land; Roger de Bully. Mill.* Quiet; overlooking the Meden and Maun rivers; site of an ancient camp or fortification; mining museum nearby.

Boughton *Buchetone/tun: Roger de Bully; Gilbert de Ghent.* Part of Ollerton.

Bradmore *Brademere: Robert Malet.*

Bramcote *Broncote/Brun(e)cote: King's land; William Peverel; William the Usher.* Beautiful views; 15th-century manor.

Brinsley *Brunesleia: Alric from William Peverel.* Brinsley Hall.

Broadholme *Brodeholm: Roger de Bully; Berengar de Tosny and William de Percy.*

Broxtow *Brochelestou: King's land; William Peverel; Robert FitzWilliam.* Part of Nottingham; evidence of early British settlement. Thomas Helwys of Broxtowe Hall built the first Baptist church in England, at Spitalfields, London, in 1611.

Budby *Butebi: King's land.* Tiny; in Sherwood Forest; built by the 1st Earl Manvers in 1807; castle site.

Bulcote *Bulecote: Walter d'Aincourt.*

Bulwell *Bul(e)uuelle: William Peverel.* District of Nottingham since 1877; known for Bulwell rockery stone.

Bunny *Bonei:* See page 205.

Burton Joyce *Bertune: Roger de Bully; Geoffrey Alselin. Church.* Owned by the Jortz de Bertun family. The 13th-century tomb of Robert de Jortz de Bertun is in the church.

Calverton *Calvretone: Archbishop of York; Roger de Poitou; Aelfric, the pre-Conquest holder, from the king. Church.* Large; mining; Norman carved stones in the church. Probably the birthplace of William Lee, inventor of the stocking frame which began the Nottinghamshire hosiery industry in the 17th century; stocking knitters' cottages and museum.

Carburton *Carbertone: King's land.* In Sherwood Forest.

Car Colston *Colestone/tune: King's land; Roger from Roger de Bully; Walkelin from Walter d'Aincourt.* 17th-century hall; prettiest village in the county.

Carlton (near Nottingham) *Carentune: Geoffrey Alselin.* Urban district adjoining Nottingham.

Carlton in Lindrick *Careltune/Caretone: King's land; Turold from Roger de Bully. Church, 2 mills.* Hall and lake; church with a Saxon tower and 12th-century chapel.

Carlton-on-Trent *Carentune/Carleton(e)/Carle(n)tun(e): King's land; William from Count Alan; Archbishop of York; Roger de Bully; Geoffrey Alselin; Haldane from the king. Mill.* Quiet; by the River Trent.

Caunton *Calnestone/tune: Archbishop of York; Geoffrey Alselin. Mill.* On The Beck stream; 15th-century manor and windmill.

Chilwell *Chideuuelle/Ciduuelle/Cilleuuelle: William Peverel; Walter from Geoffrey Alselin.* Part of Beeston by Nottingham; nature reserve and lake.

Clarborough *Claueburgh/Claureburg: Archbishop of York; Fulk and Ulfkell from Roger de Bully; Ernwin, the pre-Conquest holder, and Wulfmer from the king.* By Chesterfield Canal; hall and ancient yew tree.

Clayworth *Clauorde: King's land; Fulk from Roger de Bully.* On Chesterfield Canal; manor house.

Clifton *Cliftun(e): William Peverel, formerly Countess Gytha; Ulfkell from the king. Church and mill.* Now part of Nottingham; green. The church contains relics of the Clifton family, after whom the village was named.

Clifton *Cliftone/Cliftune/Cli(s)tone: Bishop of Lincoln; Siwat, Agemund and Ralph from him; Roger from Roger de Bully. ¼ church.* Now 2 small villages, North and South Clifton.

Clipston *Clipestune: Roger de Bully.* Clipston Wolds.

Clipstone *Clipestune: Roger de Bully. Mill.* On the River Maun by Sherwood Forest; remains of King John's Palace, possibly built by the kings of Northumbria. Edward I held a parliament here in 1290. It was also a Tudor hunting lodge.

Clown *Clune: King's land.* Clown Hill Plantation by Great Lake in Welbeck Park.

Clumber *Clumbre/Clunbre: King's land; Fulk and Ulfkell from Roger de Bully. Mill.* Clumber Bridge and Weir on the River Poulter; Clumber Park.

Coddington *Cotintone/tun: Bothild from Bishop of Lincoln; Losoard and Oudkell from Bishop of Bayeux.* Old dovecote; ruined windmill.

Coldcoates *Caldecotes:* Lost.

Collingham *Collingeham: Peterborough Abbey before and after 1066; Ralph de Limesy. 2 churches, 2 mills.* Now 2 villages, North and South Collingham, near the Roman town of Crococalana; remains of a Roman bridge by Cromwell Lock and Weir on River Trent. 2 churches are possibly 7th century, but were rebuilt in Norman times.

Colwick *Colui/euul: Waland from William Peverel; Aelfric and Bugg from the king. Church, mill, ½ fishery.* Part of Nottingham; old church; racecourse and country park.

Cossall *Coteshale: William Peverel; Ralph FitzHubert.* The first coal was dug here 7 centuries ago.

Costock *Cortingestoche(s)/Cotingestoche: Roger de Bully; Godwin from William Peverel; William from Ralph de Buron.* Church with a fragment of Saxon preaching cross.

Cotgrave *Godegrave: Ralph de Buron and Jocelyn and Warner from him; Roger de Poitou. ½ church.* Large; colliery. The remains of Roman soldiers were found in graves nearby.

Cotham *Cotes/Cotun(e): Bishop of Lincoln; Wazelin from Bishop of Bayeux; Walter d'Aincourt. Church.* Cotham Grange.

Cottam *Cotune: Fulk from Roger de Bully.*

Cromwell *Crunuuelle: Gilbert Tison; Haldane from the king. Church, mill, fishery.* On the River Trent; lock and weir; ruins of house said to be that of Ralph Lord Cromwell, Treasurer to Henry VI; 13th-century restored church on old foundations.

Cropwell Bishop *Crophelle/hille: Archbishop of York.* Originally called Crophill Bishop.

Cropwell Butler *Crophelle/hille: Walter d'Aincourt; Roger de Poitou; Ilbert de Lacy.* Agricultural.

Cuckney *Chuchenai: Geoffrey from Roger de Bully; Richard from Hugh FitzBaldric. Church, 2 mills.* In Sherwood Forest, on the River Poulter. In 1950 a number of skeletons, possibly of men killed in battle in the 12th century, were found buried under the nave.

Dallington *Dallintune:* Lost.

Danethorpe *Dordentorp: Ralph de Limesy. Church.* Danethorpe Hill; Thorpe Field Farm.

Darlton *Derluuetun: King's land.* Ancient earthworks.

Dunham *Dune/ham: King's land. Mill, fishery.* On the River Trent; designated recreational area.

Eakring *Ec(he)ringhe: King's land; Geoffrey Alselin; Erchenbrand and William from Gilbert de Ghent. Church.* In Sherwood Forest; church.

East Bridgford *Brugeford: Roger de Bully. Church.* On the River Trent; bridge. A Saxon cross and foundation were discovered under the present church, rebuilt in the 12th century.

East Chilwell *Estrecille(u)elle/Cum duabus Ciluellis: Ralph FitzHubert; Ernwin from the king. ½ church, willow beds (with Chilwell).* Part of Beeston; nature reserve with a lake.

East Drayton *Draitone/tun: King's land.*

COTHAM: *1601 monument to Anne Markham, in the church.*

East Markham *Marcham, Markham: King's land; Ulfkell, Geoffrey and Turold from Roger de Bully. 2 churches, mill.* Church; hall; home of the 18th-century historical writer 'Mrs Markham'.

East Stoke *Stochas/chas: Bishop of Lincoln; Osbert from Walter d'Aincourt; Manfred from Ilbert de Lacy.* Stoke Hall was the home of Lord Pauncefote, the first British Ambassador to the United States.

Eastwood *Estewic: William Peverel.* Mining town; birthplace of D. H. Lawrence (1885–1930), whose house is now a museum.

Eaton *Aettune/Ettone/Etun(a)e: Archbishop of York; Fulk from Roger de Bully. 2 mills, a garden in Gameston.* On the River Idle. Redwald of East Anglia slew Ethelfrith of Northumbria at the Battle of the Idle here, in 617.

Edwalton *Edwoltone/tun: Roger de Poitou; Hugh de Grandmesnil.* Part of West Bridgford.

Edwinstowe *Edenestou:* See page 207.

Egmanton *Agemuntone: Roger de Bully. 2 mills.* On a stream; remains of a Norman castle.

Elkesley *Elchesleie/leig/lie: King's land; Claron from Roger de Bully; Ernwin the Priest from the king. Church, mill.* On the River Poulter; church.

Elston *Eluestun(e): Bishop of Lincoln; Ravensward and Arngrim from him. Norman the priest from Roger de Bully; Arngrim from Ilbert de Lacy.* Hall.

Elton *Ailetone: Ralph from Roger de Bully. Church.* Church with a Norman arch.

Epperstone *Ep(re)stone: Roger de Bully; Ralph de Limesy. Mill and 4 mills (with woodborough), church.* By Dover Beck; church with a Norman font; paper mill until 1723; old dovecote.

Everton *Evretone: Archbishop of York; Roger de Bully.* Fenland. Church with a Saxon tympanum.

Farndon *Farendune: Bishop of Lincoln, formerly Countess Godiva.*

EASTWOOD: *The town was used by Lawrence as 'Bestwood' in* Sons and Lovers*; this is his birthplace.*

Farnsfield *Farnesfeld/Franesfeld: King's land; Walter d'Aincourt.* Traces of a Roman Camp nearby; birthplace of A. C. Gregory, who explored Australia in the mid-19th century.

Fenton *Fentone/tune: King's land; Roger de Bully, formerly Sparrowhawk.*

Finningley *Feniglei: Gilbert Tison.* Fenland; manor owned by Sir Martin Frobisher, Elizabethan navigator.

Fiskerton *Fiscartune: Walter d'Aincourt. 2 mills, fishery.* On the River Trent; mill.

Flawborough *Flodberga/berge: Robert from Roger de Bully; Walter d'Aincourt and Mauger from him. Church, mill site.* Famed for the longevity of its inhabitants; church with a Norman doorway and font.

Fledborough *Fladeburg: Nigel from Bishop of Lincoln, formerly Countess Godiva. Church, mill.* A port in the 13th century and second Gretna Green in the 18th under Rector Sweetapple; church.

HAWKSWORTH: *In the church, the Norman tympanum with an awkwardly balanced inscription.*

Flintham *Flint(e)ham: King's land; Roger and Ernwin the priest from Roger de Bully; Reginald from Walter D'Aincourt. Church.* 13th-century church.

Gamston (near Eaton) *Gamesletun(e): Roger de Bully; Roger de Poitou and Ketelbern, the pre-Conquest holder, from him. 2 mills. 2 gardens.* On the River Idle.

Gamston (in West Bridgford) *Gamelestune: William Peverel.* On the outskirts of West Bridgford.

Gedling *Ghellinge: Roger de Bully; Geoffrey Alselin. Church.* District on the outskirts of Carlton, Nottingham; church; Gedling Wood Farm.

Gibsmere *Gipesmare: Ralph FitzHubert.* Fenland.

Girton *Gretone: Bishop of Lincoln.*

Gleadthorpe *Gletorp: Roger de Bully.* Gleadthorpe Grange; Gleadthorpe Breck Plantation; a few houses.

Gonalston *Gunnulfstone/Gunnuluestone/Gunnuluestune: William Peverel; Ralph de Limesy. 2 mills (with Milton).* On Dover Beck; 2 water mills in 1179. A mill towards Lowdham worked on child labour into the 19th century.

Gotham *Gatham: Count Robert from Count of Mortain; Saewin from the king.*

Granby *Gran/Grenebi: Walter d'Aincourt; Robert d'Oilly from Osbern FitzRichard. 2 churches, 3 mills.* 13th-century church.

Grassthorpe *Grestorp: Roger from Roger de Bully. 3 mills.* On the River Trent.

Greasley *Griseleia: Alric from William Peverel. Church.* Moorland. The church has a list of parish priests from 1254.

Grimston *Grimestone/tune: King's land.* Grimston Hill, overlooking Sherwood Forest.

Gringley on the Hill *Gringeleia: Roger from Roger de Bully. Church, fishery (1000 eels).* Hillside; views over Chesterfield Canal; church with a possibly Norman arch.

Grove *Grave: Robert from Roger de Bully. Church.* Church.

Gunthorpe *Gulne/Gunnetorp: Roger de Bully. 2 fisheries.* On the River Trent; once owned by Simon de Montfort.

Harby *Herd(r)ebi: Bishop of Lincoln.* Queen Eleanor of Castile died here in 1290 on a visit to Sherwood Forest.

Harwell *Hereuuelle: Roger de Bully.*

Harworth *Hareworde: Fulk from Roger de Bully. Church.* Colliery; church with Norman fragments and 2 sedilia.

Haughton *Hoctun: Roger de Poitou.* In Sherwood Forest; motte and bailey; home of Denzil Holles, Lord Mayor of London, and Speaker of the House of Commons in 1599.

Hawksworth *Hoches(u)uorde: Walter d'Aincourt; Gilbert de Ghent.* Fenland; site of a Wars of the Roses battlefield.

Hawton *Holtone/Houtune: Bishop of Lincoln; Walter d'Aincourt; Alfred from Ralph de Limesy. 2 churches, mill.* Earthworks; fine 14th-century church.

NOTTINGHAM: *In 868–70 Nottingham was part of a major power struggle between the Danes and the Mercians; St Edmund was captured and killed.*

Headon *Hedune: King's land; William from Roger de Bully.*

Hempshill *Hamessel: William Peverel.* Hempshill Vale, part of Nottingham.

Hickling *(H)Echelinge/ Hegelinge: Archbishop of York; Gilbert de Lacy. Mill.* On the Grantham Canal and River Smite.

High Marnham *Marneham: Fulk from Roger de Bully.* On the River Trent.

Hockerton *Hocretone/-tune/ Ocretone: Archbishop of York; Roger de Bully; Walter d'Aincourt. Church.* Church with a Norman chancel, rch and window.

Hodsock *Odesach: Turold from Roger de Bully. 2 mills.* Ancient gatehouse and priory.

Holme Pierrepont *Holmo: Thored from Roger de Bully. Mill.* Early 17th-century Hall; Holme Pierrepont Country Park nearby.

Horsepool *Horspol:* Lost.

Hoveringham *Horingeham: Walter d'Aincourt. Church, 2 mills, 2 fisheries.* Farming; Still-medieval; church with a Norman font.

Hucknall Torkard *Hochehale/ enale: William Peverel; Osmund from Ralph de Buron.* Mining town; church with 8th-century Saxon work. The Torkards were landowners in the 12th century. Lord Byron is buried here in the family vault.

Inkersall *Wirchenefeld: Gilbert de Ghent.* Inkersall Farm and Inkersall Grange Farm in Sherwood Forest. Formerly Winkerfield.

Kelham *Calun: Turold from Roger de Bully; Walter d'Aincourt; William from Ralph de Burson; Haldane from the king; William Tison.* 19th-century hall by Gilbert Scott; theological college.

Kersall *Cherueshale: Gilbert de Ghent.*

Keyworth *Cau(u)orde: Alfred from Count Mortain; Roger de Bully; William Peverel; Ralph FitzHubert.* Large; views of the Wolds.

Kilvington *Chelvinctune/ Chelvintone/Chelvintun: Bishop of Lincoln; Ilbert de Lacy; Ansger from Hugh FitzBaldric.* Hilltop; fine views.

Kimberley *Chinemarel(e)ie: Grimketel from William Peverel.* Town near Nottingham, part owned in the 19th century by Viscount Melbourne.

Kingston on Soar *Chinestan: a freeman from Earl Hugh; Saewin from the king; Godric. Mill-site.* On Kingston Brook, near the River Soar. Home of Antony Babington, page and follower of Mary Queen of Scots, who was the figurehead in the plot to murder Queen Elizabeth in 1586. He was caught and executed, aged 25.

Kinoulton *Chineltone/tune: Walter d'Aincourt; Azor's son from the king.* On the Grantham Canal, fine views, cricket ground.

Kirkby in Ashfield *Chirchebi: Ralph FitzHubert; Aelfric, the pre-Conquest holder, from the king. Church, 2 mills.* Coal mining town in Sherwood Forest; church; source of 3 rivers; Erewash, Leen and Maun.

Kirklington *Cherlinton: Gilbert de Ghent; mill.* On the River Greet; millpool.

Kirton *Schidri(n)ctune/ Schidrnton/tune/Schitrintone: King's land; Roger de Bully; Geoffrey Alselin.* Sherwood Forest.

Knapthorpe *Chena(pe)torp: Walter d'Aincourt; Geoffrey Alselin; Haldane from the king.*

Kneesall *Cheneshale: Gilbert de Ghent.* Part of a Saxon cross in the church.

Kneeton *Cheniueton(e): King's land; Count Alan; Roger de Bully. ½ church, mill.* Hilltop. The church register dates from 1592.

Lambley *Lambeleia: Haldane from the king. 2 mills.* On Lambley Dumble (a small gorge) and Cocker Beck; birthplace of Ralph, Lord Cromwell c.1394, High Treasurer of England.

Lamcote *Lambecotes/Lanbecote: Roger de Bully; Osmund from Ralph de Buron; Haldane from the king.* Lamcote Field near Radcliffe on Trent.

Laneham *Lanun: Archbishop of York. Church, mill.* 2 villages, Laneham and Church Laneham which has a church with Norman features and font.

Langar *Langare: William Peverel; Walter d'Aincourt. 2 mills, ½ church.* In Belvoir Vale; church called the 'cathedral of the Vale'.

Langford *Landeforde: Ranulf from Geoffrey de La Guerche. Church, 2 mills, fishery.* Church; Tudor manor house.

Laxton *Laxintune:* See page 202.

Leake *Lec(c)he: Count of Mortain; Ernulf from Roger de Bully; Henry de Ferrers. Church, Mill.* Now 2 villages, East and West Leake. Church with Norman or Saxon masonry, and a tin trumpet 8ft long, used until 1855 to make 'a joyful noise'.

Lenton *Lentone/tune: King's land; William Peverel. 2 mills.* District in central Nottingham; White Hart Inn contains remnants of old Peverel Jail founded in 1113 for debtors.

Leverton *Cledretone/Legretone: 22 freemen from the king; Roger de Bully; Count Alan; 2 men-at-arms from Archbishop of York. ½ church.* Now 2 villages, North and South Leverton.

Linby *Lidebi: William Peverel. Mill.* Mining; stream and converted Castle Mill with water wheel. Stone crosses nearby are thought to mark the ancient boundaries of Sherwood Forest.

Littleborough *Litelburg: King's land.* On the River Trent; remnants of a Roman ford; the smallest Norman church in the county.

Little Gringley *Grenelei(g)/ Grenleige: King's land; Archbishop of York.*

Lound *Lund: Archbishop of York; Roger de Bully.*

Lowdham *Lud(e)ham: Archbishop of York; Roger de Bully. Mill.* Near Dover Beck and Broughton Hall.

Low Marnham *Alia Marneham: Roger de Bully. Mill, fishery.*

Mansfield *Mamesfeld/ Memmesfed: King's land. Mill, fishery, 2 churches.* Important industrial town with cliff cave dwellings at Rock Hill. It was the home of the Mercian Kings and a royal hunting resort in Sherwood Forest; Norman church.

Manton *Mennetune: William Peverel.* Part of Worksop.

Maplebeck *Mapelbec/berg: King's land; Gilbert de Ghent.* Smallest pub in Nottinghamshire.

LINBY: *Castle Mill, scene of James Watt's first steam-engine installation for cotton spinning.*

Markham Clinton *Westmarcham: Roger de Bully from Claron and 6 Frenchmen from him.* Church with Saxon masonry (mud floors until 1949); formerly West or Little Markham.

Martin *Martune: Roger de Bully.* Martin Grange; ancient moat; Martin Common Farm.

Mattersey *Madressei: King's land; Roger de Bully.* Old bridge; remains of Mattersy Priory, a small Gilbertine monastery founded in 1185.

Meering *Meringe: King's land.* Between Sutton on Trent and Carlton on Trent.

Milton *Miletune: William Peverel. 2 mills (with Milton).* On the River Maun.

Misson *Misna/ne: Roger de Bully; Ernwin from the king.*

Misterton *Ministrone: King's land; Roger de Bully; church.* Straggling; fenland; church.

Morton (in Babworth) *Mortune: King's land.*

Morton (in Fiskerton) *Mortun(e): Walter d'Aincourt; Ralph FitzHubert.* Old dovecote.

Morton (in Lenton) *Mortune: William Peverel.* Part of central Nottingham.

Newark *Newerc(h)e: Bishop of Lincoln, formerly Countess Godiva. 10 churches, mill, fishery.* Important market town on a Roman road, called 'the Key of the North' in Anglo-Saxon times.

Newbold *Neubold.* Lost.

Newbound *Neubold: William Peverel.* Newbound Farm; Newbound Cottage; Newbound Lane.

Newthorpe *Neutorp: Count of Mortain; William Peverel.* Part of Eastwood.

Newton *Neutone/Niuuetune: Roger de Bully; Geoffrey Alselin.* RAF station.

Normanton *Normantun/menton: Gilbert de Ghent.* Hall opposite Southwell on the River Greet.

Normanton by Clumber *Normentone: King's land.* In Sherwood Forest.

Normanton on Soar *Normanton(e)/tune: Earl Hugh; Roger de Bully; Haldane from Count Mortain; Raven from the king.* On the River Soar.

Normanton on Trent *Normentone/tune: Bishop of Lincoln; Roger from Roger de Bully.*

Normanton on the Wolds *Normantone/tun: Roger de Bully; William Peverel.*

North Muskham *Nordmuscham: Peterborough Abbey; Geoffrey Alselin; Bishop of York; Siward, the pre-Conquest holder, from the king. 2 churches, 6 mills.* Church with Norman fragments.

Norwell *Nortwelle: Archbishop of York. Church, mill, fishery.* Church with a Norman doorway and coffin stone; old moat; Watermill Farm. Previously Northwell.

Nottingham *Snoting(e)ham/quin: King's land; Hugh FitzBaldric; the Sheriff; Roger de Bully; William Peverel; Ralph de Buron; Wulfbert; Ralph FitzHubert; Geoffrey Alselin; Richard Frail. Church.* Thriving, modern county town, traditionally renowned for its lace. Its imposing castle, now a museum, is on a post-Conquest site.

Nuthall *Nutehale: William Peverel; Aelfric from the king.* Small town north of Nottingham.

'Odsthorpe' *Odestorp:* Lost.

Ollerton *Alretun: Roger de Bully. Mill.* Coal mining town; old mill; Ollerton Hall.

Ompton *Almentun(e)/Almuntone: King's land; Geoffrey Alselin.*

Ordsall *Ordeshale: Roger de Bully; Ernwy from the king.* Part of East Retford. During the Commonwealth the vicar was turned out for playing cards with his wife.

Orston *Oschintone: King's land. Church.* Church with Norman transitional font. A hoard of Civil War coins was discovered nearby in 1952.

Osberton *Osbernestune: Swein and Wulfgate from the king. Church.* Osberton Hall built by Wyatt in 1806 has a church in its grounds.

Osmanthorpe *Osuuitorp: Archbishop of York.* Osmanthorpe Manor.

OSSINGTON: *The Denison monument to Robert, d. 1785.*

Ossington *Oschintone: Ralph de Buron.* Secluded; seat of the Denison family since 1768; hall demolished in 1963.

Owthorpe *Obetorp/Oretorp: William from Roger de Bully; Geoffrey Alselin; Durand Malet.* Home of John Hutchinson, Puritan Governor of Nottingham and signatory to Charles I's death warrant. He died in prison after the Restoration, and is buried in the churchyard. The gardens of his Hall remain.

Oxton *Ostone/tune: Archbishop of York; Roger de Bully; Walter d'Aincourt. Mill.* In Sherwood Forest. Robert and Marie Scothorn sailed from here to America in 1684 to join William Penn.

Papplewick *Papleuuic: William Peverel.* Cave, said to be Robin Hood's stable. Papplewick Hall, designed by the Adam brothers, was owned by John Walter, proprietor of *The Times*. The first English steam-powered mill was built here in 1785.

Perlethorpe *Torp: King's land; Richard from Roger de Bully.*

Plumtree *Pluntre: Roger de Bully; church.* Church with 9th-century Saxon work, and a Norman arch.

Radcliffe on Trent *Radeclive: Fredegis and Wulfgeat from William Peverel; Walter d'Aincourt; ½ fishery, ⅓ fishery.* Town opposite Nottingham on the River Trent. Henry VII heard mass here before leading his army to defeat his enemies at East Stoke in 1487.

Radford *Redeford: William Peverel; Wulfnoth from the king. 4 mills, ½ fishery.* Part of central Nottingham. The River Leen runs, partly underground, through it.

Ragnall *Ragenehil: King's land.* Near the River Trent; ponds.

Rampton *Rametone: Roger de Bully. Church 3½ fisheries.* Church with possible Saxon features and a Norman font.

Ranby *Rane(s)bi: King's land; Roger de Bully.* In Sherwood Forest; Ranby House.

Ranskill *Raveschel: Archbishop of York.* On the Great North Road.

Ratcliffe on Soar *Radeclive: Saewin from the king. Church, mill.* Church with a 12th-century tower; old manor house, now a farm.

Rayton *Reneton/Rouuetone: King's land.* Rayton Farm and Rayton Angle Wood, on the outskirts of Worksop.

Rempstone *Rampestone/Rampestune/Repestone: Roger de Bully; William Peverel; Ralph de Buron.*

Retford *Redford(e): Archbishop of York; Roger de Bully. Mill, ¼ mill.* Market town of East and West Retford, divided by the River Idle.

Rolleston *Roldestun/Rollestone/Rollestune: Archbishop of York; Bishop of Bayeux; Walter d'Aincourt. Mill, church.* On the River Greet; church with Saxon masonry and fragments of a Saxon cross; manorial earthworks; racecourse.

Roolton *Rolvetune:* Lost.

Ruddington *Roddington(e)/Rodintone/Rodintun: Count Alan; Roger de Bully; Gilbert de Ghent; Robert Malet.* Small town on the outskirts of Nottingham. Henry VII's army camped here before the battle of East Stoke in 1487.

Rufford *Rugforde: Gilbert de Ghent.* Ruined Abbey founded in 1148 by Gilbert de Ghent; Elizabethan manor, now a country park.

Salterford *Saltreford: Osbern FitzRichard.* Salterford Farm.

Saundby *Sandebi:* King's land; Archbishop of York.

Saxondale *Saxeden: Roger de Bully. Church.*

Scaftworth *Scafteorde: Archbishop of York.* On the River Idle.

Scarrington *Scarintone: King's land.* Quiet; ancient dovecote, now a garage.

Scofton *Scotebi: King's land.* Tiny, in Sherwood Forest.

Screveton *Escreventone/Screvetone/Screvintone: King's land; Hugh the nephew of Herbert from Bishop of Bayeux; Roger de Bully.* Church with an Anglo-Saxon cross.

Scrooby *Scrobi: Archbishop of York.* Brewster Cottage, said to be the home of William Brewster, Pilgrim Father and founder of Plymouth, New England; site of a moated archbishop's palace, visited by Henry VII and Cardinal Wolsey.

Selston *Salestune: William Peverel. Church.* Now 2 villages, Selston and Selston Green; church with Norman arches and pillars.

Serlby *Serlebi: Roger de Bully.* Roman bank and earthworks nearby.

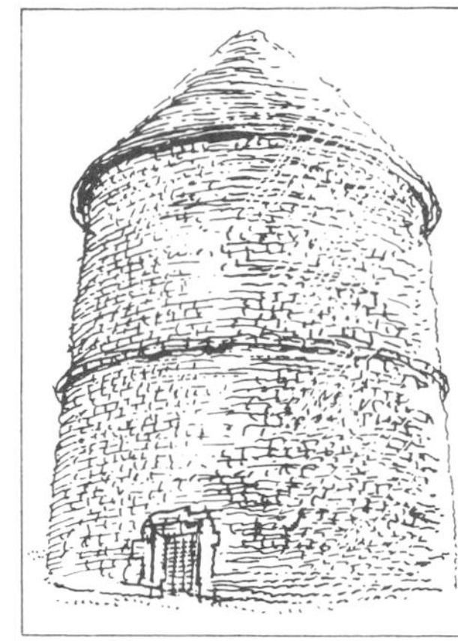

SIBTHORPE: *Medieval dovecote with 1260 nesting places in 28 tiers.*

Shelford *Scelford: Roger de Bully, Geoffrey Alselin. Church.* Site of 12th-century priory; church with the remains of an Anglo-Saxon cross with Virgin and Child. A Royalist stronghold during the Civil War, the manor house was burned by the Roundheads.

Shelton *Sceltun(e): Robert from Roger de Bully; Ralph de Limesy; Ilbert de Lacy. Church (with Flawborough); mill site.* By the River Devon.

Sibthorpe *Sibetorp: Fredegis from Count Alan; Robert from William Peverel; Arngrim from Ilbert de Lacy. Church, 1¼ mills.* Easter Sepulchre in church; 20 Irish yew trees in graveyard, said to be 1000 years old; old manor house; traces of a moat; medieval dovecote, 98ft in circumference.

Skegby (in Marnham) *Scachebi: Roger de Bully.* Near the Lincolnshire border.

SCROOBY: *Brewster's Cottage; William kept the post office at Scrooby 1594–1600.*

Skegby (in Sutton in Ashfield) *Schegebi: King's land. Fishery, 2 churches.* Church.

Sneinton *Notintone: King's land.* Part of Nottingham; birthplace of William Booth (1829–1912), founder of the Salvation Army.

South Muskham *Muscham: Archbishop of York; Seric from the king.* Near the River Trent.

South Ordsall *Suderdeshale: King's land.* Part of Ordsall.

South Scarle *Scornelei: Bishop of Lincoln.* Views of Lincoln Cathedral; dovecote with a pyramidical roof.

Southwell *Sudeuuelle/Sudwelle: Archbishop of York. 3 mills, fishpond, ferry.* Town. Southwell Minster, the mother church of Nottinghamshire, was begun in 1108 under the Archbishop of York and retains all 3 Norman towers. Charles I spent his last night of freedom at the 17th-century Saracen's Head.

Spalford *Spaldesforde: Bishop of Lincoln; Roger de Bully.* On the Lincolnshire border.

Stanford on Soar *Stanford: Roger de Bully; Robert FitzWilliam. Mill, mill site.*

Stanton on the Wolds *Stantun(e): Alfred from Count of Mortain; Roger de Bully; William Peverel; Robert FitzWilliam.* Nearly deserted.

Stapleford *Stapleford: Robert from William Peverel. Church.* Town on the outskirts of Nottingham. St Helen's Church is 13th century with a 10ft-high Saxon Cross.

Staunton *Stantun: King's land; Walter d'Aincourt. Church, mill.* Now Staunton in the Vale; church with a Norman font. Sir Walter Scott stayed with the Staunton family and used the 16th-century Hall as 'Willingham' in *The Heart of Midlothian*, 1818.

Staythorpe *Startorp: Gilbert Tison. Mill.* On Pingley Dyke.

Stoke Bardolph *Stoches: Geoffrey Alselin. Church, fishery, 2 mills.* Chapel.

Stokeham *Estoches: Nigel from Bishop of Lincoln, formerly Lady Godiva.*

Strelley *Straelie/Straleia: Godwin the priest and Ambrose from William Peverel; Wulfsi and Godwin from the king.* Unspoilt. Owned by 2 families since the 12th century: the Strelleys until the 17th century, the Edges until today.

Sturton le Steeple *Estretone: King's land; Roger de Bully.*

Styrrup *Estirape: Bernard from Roger de Bully.* The 'Hanging Field' in this parish might have been the gallows site for Blythe and the surrounding area.

Sutton *Sudtone: Archbishop of York.* Near East Retford.

Sutton Bonington *Su(d)tone: Robert FitzWilliam from Earl Hugh; Count of Mortain; Henry de Ferrers; Siward and Coleman from the king. Mill.* 17th-century houses.

Sutton in Ashfield *Sutone: King's land. Mill, fishery (with Mansfield and Skegby).* Mining town; lake.

Sutton on Trent *Sudtone: Hervey from Count Alan; Roger de Bully. Church, 3 fisheries.* Church with Saxon foundations.

Sutton Passeys *Sudtune/Sutone.* Lost.

Swanston *Suanesterne:* Lost.

Syerston *Sirestun(e): King's land; Robert from Count Alan; Bishop of Lincoln; Godwin from Berengar de Tosny.*

Teversal *Tevreshalt: Ralph FitzHubert. Mill.* Colliery; manor house.

Thoresby *Turesbi: King's land.* In Sherwood Forest; Thoresby Park, with lake and medieval oaks. Thoresby Hall was rebuilt on the site of the home of Lady Mary Wortley Montagu, the great English letter-writer.

Thorney *Torneshaie: Bishop of Lincoln.*

Thoroton *Toruentun/ertune: King's land; Ilbert de Lacy.* Gave its name to Robert Thoroton, author of *Antiquities of Nottinghamshire* (1677).

Thorpe by Neward *Torp: Manfred from Ralph de Limesy.*

Thorpe in the Glebe *Torp: King's land. Roger de Bully.* Ancient site on the Leicestershire border.

Thrumpton *Turmodestun: Roger de Bully; William Peverel; Hugh de Grandmesnil.* Prehistoric trackway nearby.

Thurgarton *Turgarstune: Walter d'Aincourt.* Walter's son Ralph founded the Augustinian Priory. Parts remain in the rebuilt church and the undercroft of an adjoining house.

Tiln *Tille/Tilne: King's land; Archbishop of York. 2 mills, 2 mills (with Clarborough).* On the River Idle.

Tithby *Tiedebi: Fredegis from William Peverel; Walter d'Aincourt.* Tythby Grange.

Tollerton *Troclavestune: Roger de Bully. 2 mills, church.* Near Polser Brook; church; airport.

Torworth *Turdeworde: Azor the priest from Roger de Bully.*

Toton *Toluestone/Touetune: Warner from William Peverel; Ralph FitzHubert. ½ church, 2 mills, small willow bed.* Part of Beeston, Nottingham; near the marshes and lakes of a nature reserve.

Treswell *Tireswelle: Robert de Moutiers from Count Alan; Roger from Roger de Bully.*

Trowell *Torwalle/Trouualle: William the Usher; Aelfric, the pre-Conquest holder, Haldane and Ernwin from the king. ½ church.* Within a few miles of the exact centre of England.

WOLLATON: *The Hall, splendid architecture by Robert Smythson, 1580s.*

Tuxford *Tuxfarne: Roger de Bully. Mill.* Small market town. Its charter for a weekly market and annual fair was granted by Henry III in 1218.

Upper Broughton *Brotone: King's land. Mill.* Also called Broughton Sulney; known for its healing spring waters.

Upton *Uptone/tun(e): King's land; Roger de Bully.* Within village of Headon; birthplace of James Tennant (1808–81) who superintended the cutting of the Koh-i-noor diamond for Queen Victoria's crown.

WHATTON: *In St John's, a late 13th-c. bracket with a carving of King David.*

Walesby *Walesbi: King's land; Roger de Bully; Geoffrey Alselin; Roger de Poitou.*

Walkeringham *Wachering(e)ham: King's land; Roger from Roger de Bully.* Between the Chesterfield Canal and the River Trent.

Wansley *Wanddeslei: Ralph FitzHubert. ½ church.* Wansley Hall; Wansley Hall Farm.

Warborough *Wareberg:* Lost.

Warsop *Wares(h)ope/Warsope: King's land and a blind man from the king; Roger de Bully. Church, mill, ½ mill-site.* Mining town divided by the River Meden; mainly Norman church.

Watnall *Watenot: Grim, Aelmer, Jocelyn and Grimkell from William Peverel.* On the outskirts of Nottingham.

Welham *Wellon/Wellun: King's land; Archbishop of York.* Welham Hall.

Wellow *Creilege: Gilbert de Ghent.* Wellow Park; ducking stool.

West Bridgford *Brigeforde: William Peverel.* Town adjoining Nottingham, mentioned in *The Anglo-Saxon Chronicles* for the year 920, when Edward the Elder ordered a bridge across the Trent, and a borough to be built on the south side of the river.

West Burton *Burtone: 2 men-at-arms from Archbishop of York.* Site of Burton Round, now fenland; new power station nearby.

West Drayton *Draitone: Roger de Bully. 3 mills.* Between the Maun and Idle rivers.

Weston *Westone: Fulk, Robert and Turold from Roger de Bully. Church, mill.* Church; moat.

Whatton *Watone: Robert from Gilbert de Ghent. Mill, millstone quarry.* Ancient fish pond.

Wheatley *Watelaie: King's land; 2 men-at-arms from Archbishop of York; Roger de Bully.* Now 2 villagers, North and South Wheatley, on a Roman road.

Widmerpool *Wimarspol(d): Ralph FitzHubert; Haldane from the king.* Among the Wolds.

Wigsley *Wigesleie: Bishop of Lincoln.* Near the Lincolnshire border.

Wilford *Wilesforde: William Peverel. ½ fishery.* District of Clifton, Nottingham. The ashes of the 19th-century poet Henry Kirke White are in the churchyard.

Willoughby *Wilgebi: Archbishop of York; Geoffrey Alselin. ½ mill.* Willoughby Farm, near Norwell.

Willoughby *Wilgebi: King's land; Geoffrey Alselin; Roger de Poitou.* Near Walesby.

Willoughby-on-the-Wolds *Wigebi/Willebi: Roger de Bully; William Peverel; Roger de Poitou; Henry de Ferrers; Algar; Alwin and Ernwin from the king.* Home of the Willoughby family from 13th century to 1924; Site of one of Nottinghamshire's 5 Roman stations.

Wimpton *Wimentun: King's land.* Whimpton Moor, near Dunham.

Winkburn *Wicheburne: Gilbert Tison. Church.* Secluded; owned, with the mainly Norman church, by the Knights Hospitalers in the 12th century.

Winthorpe *Wimuntorp: Bishop of Lincoln.*

Wiseton *Wisetone: King's land.* Unspoilt.

Wiverton *Wivretone: William Peverel; Walter d'Aincourt.* 15th-century gatehouse.

Wollaton *Waletone/Ol(l)avestone: King's land; Warner from William Peverel.* Part of Nottingham; Elizabethan Wollaton Hall, now a Natural History museum.

Woodborough *Ude(s)burg: Archbishop of York; Roger de Bully; Ralph de Limesy; Haldane, Ulfkell, the pre-Conquest holder, and Aelfric from the king. Mill with Epperstone, 4 mills, church.* Large; Iron Age hill fort discernible; Norman church rebuilt in 14th century; once a centre for stocking knitting.

Worksop *Werchesope: Roger de Bully.* Market town on the edge of Sherwood Forest. Remains of Anglo-Saxon and Norman residences, and an Ancient British earthwork, are on Castle Hill.

Wysall *Wisoc: Roger from Roger de Bully. Church.* In the Wolds; church with the county's oldest pulpit, c.1400.

Oxfordshire

With the exception of forested areas on the Chilterns and between Wychwood and Shotover, Oxfordshire seems to have been fairly evenly settled in 1086. The most cultivated parts were on the Redland-Cotswold uplands, where villages were strung out along the numerous river valleys, and on the Gault Clays between Oxford itself and the Chilterns. The land is particularly fertile along the loamy shelf that runs along the foot of the Chilterns (the Icknield Way follows it), and settlement here was centred on the spring-line villages between Chinnor and Goring.

Odo, Bishop of Bayeux, had large holdings in Oxfordshire, as did Roger d'Ivry and Robert d'Oilly (who were 'sworn brothers' and had some joint holdings). Besides the king and Odo, the Bishop of Lincoln (Oxfordshire was in the diocese of Lincoln until 1836) was the other big landholder. His holdings at Dorchester, Thame and Banbury account for no less than 210 hides, although the details are largely unknown because these are blanket entries, not broken down at all.

At the start of Oxfordshire's Domesday *the city of Oxford is given a long entry which details the owners of the 243 houses that paid tax. Another 478 were so derelict that they paid none. It was a time when Wallingford was becoming as prosperous as Oxford and many Oxford tenants (for example, Walter Giffard, Roger d'Ivry, Robert d'Oilly and the Abbot of Abingdon) had taken the precaution of having holdings in both places.*

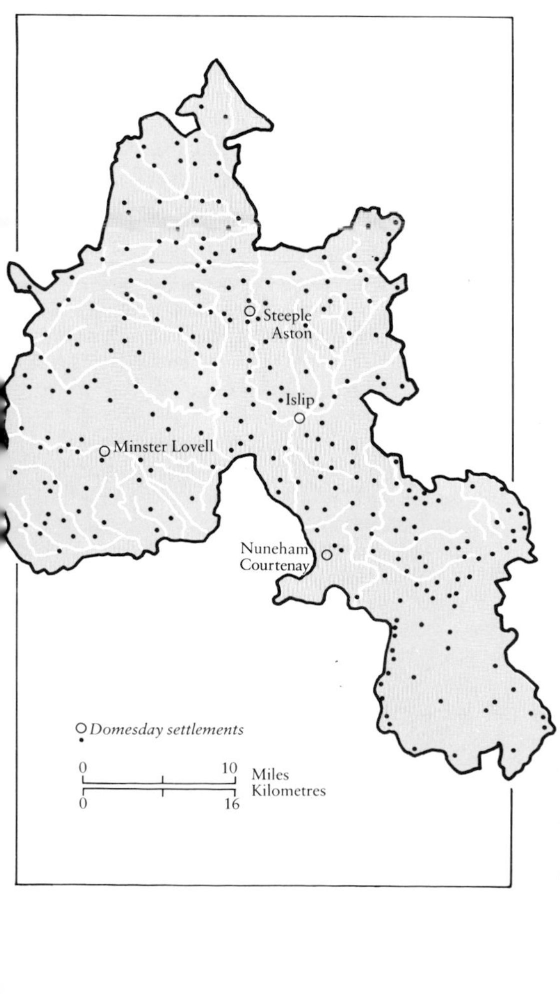

Minster Lovell

[Earl Aubrey] also held 7 hides in MINSTER (LOVELL) *MINSTRE.* Land for 10 ploughs. Now in lordship 6 ploughs; 2 slaves. 17 villagers with 10 smallholders have 7 ploughs. 2 mills at 20s; meadow, 78 acres; woodland 1 league long and 4 furlongs wide. The value was £10; now £7.

Minster Lovell lies on the north bank of the River Windrush not far from the last remnants of Wychwood Forest. Upstream is Little Minster, and to the south the Victorian settlement of Charterville. At its centre, The Street runs north-east from The Olde Swan, between well-groomed and cosy limestone cottages, today much sought after. Only periodic bursts of aerial activity by the RAF base at Brize Norton disturb this little upland valley.

Domesday states that Earl Aubrey held it; the use of the past tense (*tenuit*) indicates that he did so no longer. He had been deprived and sent back to Normandy for being 'of little use in difficult circumstances'. Radway in Warwickshire, another of his holdings, was also in the king's hands by 1086.

The name Minster Lovell derives from the minster church that lay on the pilgrim route to Winchcombe – to the shrine of St Kenelm, a Mercian prince murdered in 819. 'Lovell' was added late in the thirteenth century, after the family to whom Henry I had granted the land in 1124. William, the seventh Baron Lovell, rebuilt the manor and the church in about 1450 after service in the French wars had ruined his health. Extensive estates in four counties made him a rich man and what remains of the courtyard and the west wing shows how elegantly a fifteenth-century nobleman could ensconce himself. Permission to empark some of the king's forest gave the Lovells free chase and, later, virtual control of Wychwood Forest.

Francis Lovell, the ninth baron, was initially a Lancastrian, but changed allegiance and became Chamberlain of the Household to Richard III. He chose the wrong side again when he joined Lambert Simnell's rebellion against Henry VII in 1487 and if he did not die swimming the Trent after the Battle of Stoke, as some believe, he may have starved to death in an underground vault at Minster Lovell, where a skeleton seated at a table was found during alterations to a chimney in 1708.

The settlement on the ridge to the south comprises twin lines of single-storey houses originally of identical design (the pattern has been somewhat upset in recent years), built by Feargus O'Connor's National Land Company in 1847. The development was an attempt to turn Chartist political failure into social action. Settlers from the cities held two to four acres from the company and did modestly well until depression hit the Oxford potato market. The original houses are readily identified by their bold symmetry and by the ornamental tile over each front door.

The company's 'Three acres and a cow' for every worker was, in its way, a re-creation of the sort of eleventh-century community, with its seven ploughs shared between 27 village families. The two landlords seem to have been equally unpopular with the authorities. Just as Aubrey lost his estates to the Crown, so, in 1851, the National Land Company was dissolved by Parliament. Both were declared incompetent.

Steeple Aston

[Land of the Bishop of Bayeux . . .] Humphrey holds 5 hides in (STEEPLE) ASTON *ESTONE* from Adam FitzHubert. Land for 9 ploughs. Now in lordship 4 ploughs; 6 slaves. 12 villagers with 2 smallholders have 6 ploughs. Meadow, 29 acres. The value was £10; now £14.

Steeple Aston, together with Middle Aston (4 hides and $3^{1}/_{2}$ virgates) and North Aston (9 hides) are Cherwell villages. Their eastern lands lie alongside the river, and their western rise on the oolitic strata up to 300 feet. Meadowland for pasture and haymaking, and ploughland on the higher ground was their classic pattern. Middle Aston's unusual hidage is possibly explained by the transfer to it, from North Aston, of the 'lost' village of Nidrecote.

In a county which today is left with only 3000 agricultural workers and which has one of Britain's fastest growing populations, this village typifies all those that have lost their roots in the land. Unlike some, however, the people of Steeple Aston are no strangers to demographic change. This was set in motion by a resident of Middle Aston, Sir Francis Page (1661–1741). Son of the vicar of Bloxham, he was a 'hanging' judge in King's Bench, lampooned by the poet Alexander Pope:

> Slander or poison dread from Delia's rage
> Hard words and hanging if your judge be. . . .

Pope left the judge – or the public – to fill in the blank.

Sir Francis applied for, and got, a faculty to remove several graves in the church to make way for a baroque memorial of heroic proportions for himself and his wife. But he moved things about on a far more devastating scale in the land of the living.

Although his house in Middle Aston was demolished, a private Act of Parliament allowed him to exchange lands in Steeple Aston for the glebe and the tithes in Middle Aston. By the time of his death he had acquired almost complete dominion in the village.

The man who bought his property, Sir Clement Cottrell Dormer, was thus in a position to turn Middle Aston into a 'closed' village in which no further houses could be built. Indeed, in order to reduce the poor rate, some were pulled down. Steeple Aston, without such protection became an 'open' village, and something of a dumping ground for the homeless. Its population catapulted – from 441 in 1831 to 749 in 1871 – with the Methodist chapel helping to sustain the newcomers. So great were the pressures that the vestry offered £3 to anyone who would emigrate to the colonies.

Steeple Aston had by then already endured a long stormy period. At the time of the French Revolution the parson, the Reverend R. Lamley Kenning, preached support for it from the pulpit. During the disturbances of the 1830s, when agricultural labourers revolted against their extreme poverty and the tyrannical treatment they received from the parish overseers, one man was hanged, and in 1831 the villagers were so terrified by the Captain Swing rick-burning riots that they clubbed together with seven other parishes to purchase a fire engine.

The coming of the commuter has smoothed out the social differences between the Astons, and the superiority of Middle Aston is of a different sort since it was bought by Spillers Limited. None of the villages – North, Middle or Steeple – will be unaffected if the National Coal Board decides to pursue its interest in what lies beneath them.

Nuneham Courtenay

Richard de Courcy holds NUNEHAM (COURTENAY) *NEUHAM* from the King. 16 hides. Land for 10 ploughs. Besides the *inland* he has 2 hides and 1 virgate of villagers' land. Now in lordship 3 ploughs. 35 villagers with 3 fishermen have 14 ploughs; they pay 30s. 7 slaves; a mill at 20s; meadow, 40 acres; pasture, 10 acres; copse 2 furlongs long and 1 furlong wide. Value before 1066, later and now £13. Hakon held it.

There are two Nunehams: Nuneham-on-the Road, through which the traffic streams constantly, and Nuneham-by-the-River, which Horace Walpole described as one of the most beautiful landscapes in the world. The first was built along the new (1736) Oxford–London turnpike, for those who had had to make way for the splendid 'villa with a view' being built by Leadbetter for the first Earl Harcourt. It consists of 'Two rows of low, neat houses, built close to each other and as regular and as uniform as a London street.' Provision was made for an inn, a forge and a house for the curate. Even so, the curate protested. By demolishing the old church, he said, Lord Harcourt had done everything except cut his throat. The second (Nuneham-by-the-River) is dominated by the Palladian villa, approached down twin carriage drives which meet in a crescent-shaped forecourt, and by the domed church, which crowns the bluff above the Thames.

Nuneham is one of those *Domesday* places which can be identified with certainty only by reference to another part of the folios. 'Richard de Courcy withdrew from himself (the Jurisdiction) of 16 hides', we read under Headington. It was at Nuneham that he held 16 hides (from the king) although, according to the Abingdon Chronicle, he secured them only after their purchase by the Abbot of Abingdon from Leofwin of Nuneham had been invalidated. The sale had taken place while William was abroad and Odo of Bayeux was governing the country. When Odo was disgraced for practising extortion during the king's absence, all such deals that he had confirmed were cancelled.

Nuneham had many owners between 1086 and the eighteenth century. Its poorish soils on the Lower Greensand produced a woodland that became attractive only to the landscapers. When the Harcourts decided to transplant themselves from the dull vale of the Upper Thames they had no difficulty in making a cheap buy. Lord Harcourt was rich enough not to have to wait for the Duke of Marlborough to finish his new mansion, which was keeping the Headington quarries fully occupied. He had the stones of the house at Stanton Harcourt shipped down the Thames in barges. The former village green was planted with trees and its pond transformed into a curving lake with water pumped up from the Thames. Twenty years later the second Earl of Harcourt (the first had been drowned in a well, rescuing his dog) employed Capability Brown, who, in one of his last commissions, 'broke the whole prospect enjoyed from the house and the walks into a series of vistas with hanging woods, featuring the windings of the river [and] the spire of

NUNEHAM COURTENAY: *A tranquil Thames-side scene; Horace Walpole believed it was one of the world's most beautiful landscapes.*

Abingdon Church...' It delighted the poet William Whitehead, who made Brown address Nature thus:

> The ridges are melted, the boundaries are gone:
> Observe all these changes, and candidly own
> I have cloath'd you when naked, and when
> o'erdrest
> I have stripped you again to your bodice and
> vest.

Through the munificence of an American marriage in 1899, Nuneham, like Blenheim, was able to prolong the life of a great house into the twentieth century. Today it is owned by Oxford University and is used as a business conference centre. A miniature golf course now renders cute what was once grand. Brown's Claude Lorraine-like landscape, although still identifiable, looks somewhat plucked. The chapel is closed and part of the park has been sold to the Admiralty for their Air Station at Culham. Lock Cottage has fallen down and the seventeenth-century Old Barn Farmhouse was destroyed by troops encamped in the park before D-Day.

Despite all this, a certain magic still lingers in the first earl's new church which combines remoteness, austerity and the grandeur of a royal court.

Islip

Roger d'Ivry's wife holds 5 hides in ISLIP *LETELAPE* from the King. Three of these hides never paid tax. Land for 15 ploughs. Now in lordship 3 ploughs; 2 slaves. 10 villagers with 5 smallholders have 3 ploughs. A mill at 20s; meadow, 30 acres; pasture 3 furlongs long and 2 wide; woodland 1 league long and 1/2 league wide. The value was £7 before 1066; when acquired £8; now £10. Godric and Alwin held it freely.

Islip straddles a hill undercut by the River Ray, shortly before it flows into the River Cherwell. The heart of the village is a nicely proportioned cluster of warm Oxford ironstone houses. Its angular streets make a welcome contrast to the dreariness of Otmoor to the east, and the dull country to the west – where a huge cement factory dominates the horizon.

The village was once a place of considerable strategic importance, because in floodtime, and with Oxford held by an enemy, Islip Bridge lay on the only dry route between the north and the south. It was because raiders were bound to use this route (and live off the land as they went) that Islip suffered so badly when the Northumbrians rebelled against Earl Tosti in 1065. Charles I installed a garrison here during the Civil War, knowing that with the bridge safe the route between London and Worcester was secure. Today the road through Islip still provides a pleasing route around Oxford, for those coming from London who want to avoid the hassle of the Oxford ringroad, though less pleasing to the inhabitants of this otherwise secluded village.

There is a remarkable continuity about Islip's history. Edward the Confessor, who was born here and is said to have been baptized in the font (moved to Middleton Stony in 1780), gave the holding to his favourite foundation of St Peters, Westminster (Westminster Abbey). While it is not clear how Godric and Alwin (who *Domesday* declares held it freely) got their hands on it, the fact that Roger d'Ivry's wife, Azelina, held it (and land in Oddington) in commendation from the king suggests that by 1086 some controversy surrounded it. The likelihood is that the abbey was still trying to get it back. By the time Azelina died, it may have been successful. By 1302 it unquestionably was, for an Exchequer inquiry in that year credits it with Islip. The abbey continued to hold the manor until the twentieth century, when the Ecclesiastical Commissioners finally took over from the Dean and Chapter.

North of the river, ridge and furrow identify the arable land of Islip. To the south, forest land made arable may have reverted from time to time, for example after the Northumbrian raid. The fields closest to the river, however, seem to have changed hardly at all. The mill is where it was in 1086 , and Cow Meadow and Holme Common are shown on the 1806 enclosure map to be identical in size to the *Domesday* meadowland; neither has ever been ploughed.

ISLIP: *Once the site of a fierce Saxon battle, Islip's quiet history of Church ownership was broken only during the Civil War.*

Oxfordshire Gazetteer
Each entry starts with the modern place name in **bold** type. The *Domesday* information that follows is in *italic* type, beginning with the name or names by which the place was known in 1086. The main landholders and under tenants are next, separated with semi-colons if a place was divided into more than one holding. A number of holdings were granted by the king to his officers; these are normally at the end of the list of landholders and are described as holding land 'from the king'. More general information completes the *Domesday* part of the entry, including examples of dues such as eels rendered by tenants. The modern or post-Domesday section is in normal type. represents a village, a small village or hamlet.

Adderbury *Edburgberie: King's land; Bishop of Winchester; Robert from Robert of Stafford. 8 mills. Wool and cheese.* Now 2 adjoining villages, East and West Adderbury. Adderbury House was the home of the poet John Wilmot, 2nd Earl of Rochester, in the 17th century.

Adwell *Aduelle: William from Miles Crispin. Mill.* Adwell House.

Albury *Al/Eldeberie: Reginald from Earl William.* Some houses.

Alkerton *Alcrintone: Ralph from Bishop of Bayeux; Richard from Miles Crispin.* Jacobean rectory built by Thomas Lydiat, cosmographer, and tutor to Henry, Prince of Wales, in the early 17th century.

Alvescot *Elfegescote: Saeric from the king.*

Ambrosden *Ambresdone: Hugh d'Ivry.* Said to be the site of the camp of Ambrosius Aurelianus, summoned by the Britons to drive back the invading Saxons.

Ardley *Ardulueslie: Robert from Earl Hugh and Robert from him.* A castle was built and destroyed by the Normans.

Arncott *(Alia) Ernicote: Robert d'Oilly and Roger d'Ivry from Abingdon Abbey; William son of Manai from the king.* Now 2 villages, Lower and Upper Arncott.

Ascott d'Oyley *Est(h)cote: Roger from Robert d'Oilly. Mill.* Area adjoining Ascott-under-Wychwood.

Ascott Earl *Est(h)cote: Ilbert from Bishop of Bayeux.* Area adjoining Ascott-under-Wychwood.

Asthall *Esthale: Roger d'Ivry. 2 mills.* Asthall Manor House; Saxon Asthall Barrow.

Aston Rowant *Estone: Miles Crispin.* Aston House.

Astrop *Estrope: Roger from Earl William.* St Rumbald's Well, a mineral spring.

Badgemore *Begeurde: Ralph from Henry de Ferrers.*

Bainton *Baditone: Erchenbald from Giles brother of Ansculf.*

Balscott(cote) *Berescote: Wadard from Bishop of Bayeux.* Pond in a dell.

Bampton *Bentone: King's land; Bishop Robert from Bishop of Exeter; Ilbert from Bishop of Bayeux; Roger from Robert d'Oilly. 4 mills, 2 fisheries, market, salt-houses.* Market town, noted for morris dancing.

Banbury *Banesberie: Bishop of Lincoln. 4 mills.* Town famed for its cakes since 1608. Banbury Cross, built in 1859, replaced the original, which was destroyed by Puritans in 1602.

Barford St John *Bereford: Robert d'Oilly from Bishop of Bayeux.*

Barford St Michael *Bereford: Roger from Abingdon Abbey and Wadard's son from him; Ilbod. Mill.*

Barton Ede *Bertone: Wadard and Adam from Bishop of Bayeux. Mill.* Now Bartongate, scattered houses.

Beckley *Bechelie: Roger d'Ivry.* Traces of a Roman road; Saxon and Norman church; Beckley Park, a moated Tudor manor house.

Begbroke *Bechebroc: Ralph from Roger de Lacy.*

Benson (Bensington) *Besintone/Besentone: William from the king; Theodoric the Goldsmith from the king. 2 mills, fisheries.* The lock on the River Thames is where Romans crossed the ford and where Offa of Mercia won a victory over the Saxons in 777.

Berrick Salome *Berewiche: Ordgar from Miles Crispin.*

Bicester *Bernecestre: Robert d'Oilly. 2 mills.* Market town.

Bix *Bixa: Hugh from Walter Giffard; Hervey from the king.* Grim's Ditch.

Black Bourton *Borburtone: Wimund from Arnulf de Hesdin; Roger d'Ivry and Ansketel from Earl William and Payne from Roger d'Ivry. 2 mills.*

Bladon *Blade: Adam from Bishop of Bayeux. 2 mills.* Earthwork of Round Castle. Lord Randolph Churchill (1847–95) and Sir Winston are both buried here.

Bletchingdon/ton *Blecesdone/Blicestone: Gilbert from Robert d'Oilly; Alfwy the Sheriff. Mill.* The original house in Bletchingdon Park, fortified for Charles I during the Civil War, was captured by Cromwell.

Bloxham *Blochesham: King's land. 6 mills. Wool and cheese, a year's corn.*

Bodicote *Bodicote: Count of Evreux; Hugh from Walter Giffard; Berengar de Tosny from Robert his father.* Bodicote Grange; Bodicote House.

Bolney *Bollehede: Gilbert de Bretteville from Earl William.*

Brighthampton *Bristelmestone: Wadard from Bishop of Bayeux; Ansketel from Earl William. Mill.*

BANBURY: *The famous Banbury spiced currant cakes are sold in the market near this Victorian cross.*

Brightwell Baldwin *Brete/Britewelle: Hervey from Bishop of Bayeux; Roger from the king. Mill.*

Britwell Salome *Brutuelle: Amaline and William from Miles Crispin.*

Brize Norton *Nortone: Fulk from Roger d'Ivry; Theodoric the Goldsmith and Godwin from the king.* RAF base.

Broadwell *Bradewelle: Christina. 2 mills, fishery.* Broadwell Grove.

Bromscott *Bumerescote: Gosbert from Robert of Stafford.*

Brookhampton *Hantone: Reginald from Roger d'Ivry.* Some houses.

Broughton (near Banbury) *Brohtune: Robert, Reginald and Gilbert from Berengar de Tosny. 2 mills.* Broughton Castle.

Broughton Poggs *Brotone: Robert FitzMurdoch. 2 mills.*

Bucknell *Buchehelle: Gilbert from Robert d'Oilly.* Bucknell House.

Burford *Bureford: Bishop of Bayeux. 2 mills.* Small Cotswold town, a wool centre in the 16th century and horse-racing centre in the 17th–19th centuries.

Cadwell *Cadewelle: Brown the priest, the pre-Conquest holder.*

Cassington *Cersetone/Cersitone/Chersitone: Wadard and Ilbert from Bishop of Bayeux. Mill, fishery (175 eels).*

Caversfield *Castrefelle: Bryant from William de Warenne. Fishpond.* Caversfield House; Norman church with an early 13th-century bell, the county's oldest.

Chadlington *Cedelintone: Reginald the Archer and Siward Hunter from the king.* Chadlington Manor House; prehistoric remains on Chadlington downs; trackway, enclosure, standing stone ('The Hawk Stone') and barrows.

Chalford *Celford: Robert from Henry de Ferrers. Mill.* Now 2 hamlets, Chalford Green and Old Chalford.

Chalgrove *Celgraue: Miles Crispin. 5 mills.* On Chalgrove Field (1643) a skirmish was fought between Royalists and Parliamentarians in which John Hampden was mortally wounded.

Charlton on Otmoor *Cerlentone: Roger d'Ivry from Hugh de Grandmesnil.* White-clad village girls bring the 'May Cross' of flowers in procession to the church every May Day.

Chastleton *Cestitone: Urse, Ilbert, Ralph and Ansketel from Bishop of Bayeux; Henry de Ferrers from Winchcombe Abbey; Aelfric from the king. Mill.* Chastleton House.

Checkendon *Cecadene: Alfred nephew of Wigot.* Traditionally, the tenure of Wyfold Court is held on condition its owner presents a rose to the king if he passes that way on May Day.

Chesterton *Cestretone: William from Miles Crispin. Mill.* Roman Akerman Street; remains of the Roman town of Alchester.

Chilworth *Celelorde: Hugh from Roger d'Ivry; Hascoit Musard.*

Chinnor *Chenore: Leofwin.*

Chipping Norton *Nortone: Arnulf de Hesdin. 3 mills.* Cotswold town.

Chippinghurst *Cibbaherste: Count of Evreux.*

Churchill *Cercelle: Walter from Earl Hugh, formerly Earl Harold. 2 mills.* Birthplace of Warren Hastings (1731–1818).

Clanfield *Chenefelde: Payne from Roger d'Ivry.*

Cogges *Coges: Wadard from Bishop of Bayeux. Mill.* Some houses.

Combe *Cumbe: Bishop of Bayeux. Mill.* Church, rebuilt c.1400 by the monks of Eynsham, to whom it had belonged since Norman times.

Cornbury *Corneberie: Reginald. Forests.* Cornbury Park House.

Cornwell *Cornewelle: Ansketel from Earl William. Mill.* Cornwell House.

Cottisford *Cotesforde: Roger d'Ivry from Hugh de Grandmesnil.* Cottisford House.

Cowley *Covelie: Roger from Bishop of Bayeux; Roger from Count Eustace; Toli from Miles Crispin; Leofwin from the king. 2 mills, 2 fisheries.* Adjoining Oxford; motor works.

Cropredy *Cropelie: Ansgered, Gilbert, Theodoric, Richard, Edward and 2 Roberts from Bishop of Lincoln. 5 mills.* Charles I won the Battle of Cropredy Bridge (1646).

Crowell *Clawelle: William Peverel.*

CROWMARSH GIFFORD: *Antique shop with an unusual sign.*

Crowmarsh Gifford *Craumares: Hugh from Walter Giffard, formerly Earl Harold. 2 mills.* Norman church, once a leper hospital.

Cuddesdon *Codesdone: Abingdon Abbey. Mill, 2 fisheries.* Bishop of Oxford's palace; theological college.

Cutteslowe *Codesdlam/lane: Siward from the canons of Oxford; Alfred the clerk from Roger d'Ivry.*

Cuxham *Cuchesham: Alfred from Miles Crispin. 3 mills.*

Dean *Dene: Robert from Henry de Ferrers. 2 mills.*

Deddington *Dadintone: Bishop of Bayeux. 3 mills.* Small market town. In its church are wooden crosses from Flanders with the mud of the battlefield clinging to them.

Dorchester *Dorchestre/Dorkecestre: Bricteva from Bishop of Lincoln. 5 mills. 51* *sticks of eels.* Originally an Iron Age settlement, later a Roman camp (Dorocine), then a Saxon cathedral city.

Draycot *Draicote: Richard from Miles Crispin.*

Drayton (near Wroxton) *Draiton: Robert d'Oilly; Thorkell; Thurstan from William FitzAnsculf. 3 mills.*

Ducklington *Dochelintone: Roger from Robert d'Oilly; Robert from Earl William. Mill.*

Duns Tew *Teowe/Tewa/Twam: Wadard from Bishop of Bayeux; Bishop of Lisieux; Everwin from Robert of Stafford; Everwin from Robert d'Oilly.* Duns Tew Manor House.

Dunsden *Dunesdene: Bishop of Salisbury.*

Dunthrop *Dunetorp: Bishop of Lisieux; Count of Evreux.*

Foscot *Foxcote: Richard de Courcy.*

Fringford *Feringeford: Wadard from Bishop of Bayeux. 2 mills.* Fringford Hall.

Fritwell *Fert(e)welle: Reginald Wadard from Bishop of Bayeux; Reginald from Earl William.*

Fulbrook *Fulebroc: Roger d'Ivry. Mill.*

Fulwell *Fulewelle: Gilbert from Robert d'Oilly. Mill.*

Gangsdown *Ganguluesdene: Ordgar, the pre-Conquest holder, from Miles Crispin.* Gangsdown Hill, near Nuffield.

Garsington *Gersedune: Gilbert and Sweeting from Abingdon Abbey; Toli from Miles Crispin.* Garsington Manor House.

Gatehampton *Gadintone/Gratentun: Brian from William de Warenne; Miles Crispin. Mill.*

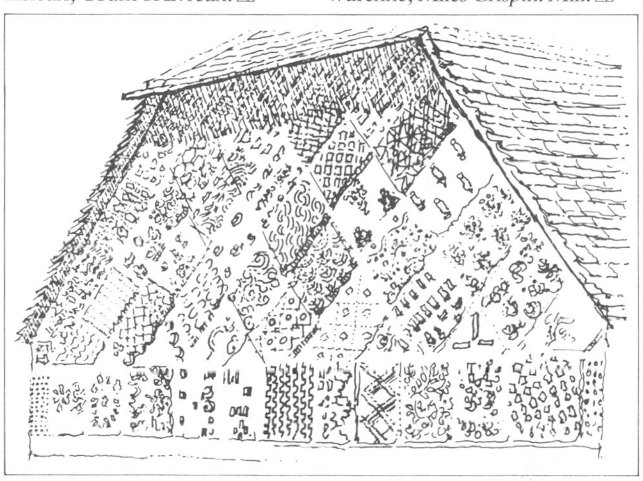

HARPSDEN: *An extraordinary barn, faced with old blocks for printing calico wallpaper designs.*

Easington *Esidone: Robert FitzRalph from the king.* Some houses.

Elsfield *Esefelde: Thurstan from Robert d'Oilly.* John Buchan (1875–1940) lived at the manor house before he was made Lord Tweedsmuir, and his ashes lie in the churchyard.

Emmington *Amintone: William Peverel.*

Enstone *Henestan: Winchcombe Abbey. 4 mills.* The Hoar Stone, 9ft high, marks a burial chamber.

Ewelme *Lau(u)elme/Auuilma/-ilme: Hugh from Walter Giffard; Ranulf Peverel; Robert from Gilbert de Ghent; Robert FitzRalph from the king.* Jerome K. Jerome (1859–1927) is buried here.

Eynsham *Eglesham: Columban from Bishop of Lincoln. Mill.* Eynsham Hall.

Fifield *Fifhide: Henry de Ferrers.* Fifield Manor House.

Finmere *Finemere: Robert from Bishop of Bayeux; Robert from Bishop of Coutances. Mill.*

Forest Hill *Fostel: Roger from Bishop of Bayeux.* The poet John Milton was married here to his first wife, Mary Powell, in 1643.

Glympton *Glintone: William from Bishop of Coutances. Mill.* Glympton Park.

Godington *Godendone: William from Richard Poynant. Mill.* Old Moat Farm.

Goring *Garinges: Robert d'Oilly. Mill.*

Grafton *Graptone: Count of Evreux.*

Great Haseley *Haselie: Miles Crispin.*

Great Milton *Mid(d)eltone: Bishop of London. 2 mills.* Milton House; Milton Priory. Little Milton, a village, is close by. John Milton's family may have derived their name from it.

Great Rollright *Rolle(a)ndri (majore): Robert of Stafford; Robert FitzThurstan and William from the king.*

Great Tew *Tewa: Bishop of Bayeux.* Transformed when Loudon, the 19th-century landscape gardener, surrounded it with evergreens.

Grimsbury *Grimberie: Gunfrid de Choques. Mill.* Part of Banbury.

Hampton *Hamtone/Hantone: Reginald from Roger d'Ivry; Gernio from the king. Mill.* Now the village of Hampton Poyle and hamlet of Hampton Gay.

Hanborough *Haneberge: Robert from Gilbert de Ghent. Mill.*

Hanwell *Hanewege: Leofwin from the king, formerly Earl Harold.* Tudor house, home of the Cope family. Sir Anthony, a Puritan leader, was imprisoned by Elizabeth I for presenting a revised Prayer Book to the Speaker.

Hardwick (near Stoke Lyne) *Hardewich: Drogo from Robert d'Oilly.*

Harpsden *Harpendene: Alfred from Miles Crispin.* Harpsden Court.

Headington *Hedintone: King's land; Richard de Courcy. 2 mills, 5 fisheries. A year's corn.* Headington House; Headington Hill Hall. Stone from Headington Quarry was used to build much of old Oxford.

Hempton *Hentone: Ralph from Walter Giffard; Edward of Salisbury. Mill.*

Hensington *Hansitone: Ansger from Bishop of Bayeux; William from Roger d'Ivry; Robert from Earl William and Peter from him. Mill.* Now 2 villages, Hensington Within and Without.

Henton *Hentone: William from Miles Crispin.*

Hethe (Heath) *Hedham: Roger from Bishop of Coutances.* Farmhouse given by Rahere (Henry I's jester) to St Bartholomew's Hospital, which he founded.

Heyford *Haiforde/Hegford/Egforde: Roger from Robert d'Oilly; Ralph from Miles Crispin; Robert from Bishop of Coutances. 3 mills, 2 fisheries (900 eels).* Now 2 villages, Lower Heyford (Heyford at Bridge), and Upper Heyford (Heyford Warren) with Heyford House. Ares Ditch is a mile-long, possibly Roman, earthen wall.

BLADON: *Lord Randolph and Sir Winston Churchill are buried in St Mary's churchyard.*

Heythrop *Edrope: Hascoit Musard. Mill.* Birthplace of Jane Dormer (1538–1612), Mary Tudor's closest friend.

Holton *Eltone: Godfrey from Roger d'Ivry.* Cromwell's daughter, Bridget, married Henry Ireton in the manor house (1646).

Holywell *Haliwelle: St Peter's Church, Oxford, from Robert d'Oilly.*

Hook Norton *Hochenartone: Robert d'Oilly. 2 mills.* Site of a Danish massacre.

Horley *Hornelie: Ralph from Count of Mortain; monks of St Peter's from Count of Mortain; Richard from Robert of Stafford; Ralph from Berengar de Tosny. 2 mills.*

Horspath *Horspadan: Gilbert from Roger d'Ivry.*

Idbury *Ideberie: Odelard from Ralph de Mortimer.* Burial place of Sir Benjamin Baker (1840–1907), the civil engineer who built the Forth Bridge, the London Underground and the Aswan dam.

Iffley *Givetelie: King's land. Fishery.*

Ilbury *Galoberie: Gadio from Robert of Stafford.* Ilbury Farm.

Ingham *Adingeham: Robert from Earl William.*

Ipsden *Yppesdene: Reginald the Archer from the king.* Roman Icknield Road; Ipsden Wood with a Roman well, nearby.

DORCHESTER: *The Jesse window in the chancel of the abbey.*

STANTON HARCOURT: *The original site of the Harcourt seat which was demolished and replaced by Nuneham Courtnay.*

Islip *Letelape.* See page 211.

Kencot *Chenetone: Roger from Robert d'Oilly.* Kencot Manor House.

Kiddington *Chidintone: Mainou from Hascoit Musard; Roger de Lacy from Earl William and Ralph from him.* Some houses.

Kidlington *Chedelintone: Robert d'Oilly. Mill.*

Kingham *Caningeham: Geoffrey de Mandeville. Mill.*

Kingston Blount *Chingestone: Miles Crispin.*

Kirtlington *Chertelintone/ Cherielintone/Cortelintone: King's land and Osmund the priest from the king; Herbert from Robert d'Oilly; Robert from Earl William. 2 mills.* Kirtlington Park.

Langford *Langefort: King's land. 2 mills.* Saxon church.

Lashbrook *Lachebroc:* Lost.

Launton *Lantone: St Peter's of Westminster and Baldwin, 'godson' to King Edward, who gave it to them.*

Ledwell *Ledewelle: King's land.*

Lew *Lewa: Hugh from Walter Giffard; Aretius from the king.* Lew House.

Lewknor *Levec(h)anole: Abingdon Abbey; Peter from Robert d'Oilly.*

Little Baldon *Baldendone: Isward and Bricteva from Bishop of Lincoln.*

Little Haseley *Haselie: Hervey from Bishop of Bayeux.* Haseley Court. John Leland, antiquarian to Henry VIII, was rector for 10 years.

Little Rollright *Parva Rollandri: Columban from Bishop of Lincoln.* Druidical Rollright Stones on the edge of the Cotswolds. The King's Stone, a monolith, is a few hundred yards away.

Littlestoke *Stoch: Alfred nephew of Wigot. Mill.* Manor house.

Little Tew *Tewe/Teowe/ Teova/Tewa: Wadard, Humphrey and Ilbert from Bishop of Bayeux; Rotroc from Bishop of Lisieux.*

Ludwell *Ludewelle: Wadard from Bishop of Bayeux; Reginald from Robert d'Oilly; Osmund from Arnulf de Hesdin; Thurstan's son from the king and Osmund from him; Ranulf from the king.* Ludwell Farm.

Lyneham *Lineham: Ilbert from Bishop of Bayeux. Mill.*

Mapledurham *Malpedreham/ Mapeldreham: William de Warenne; Miles Crispin. Mill.* The best mill on the River Thames. Mapledurham House was fortified for Charles I during the Civil War.

Marsh Baldon *Baldedone: Geoffrey from Miles Crispin.*

Merton *Meretone: Countess Judith.*

Middle Aston *Estone: Gosbert and Gilbert from Robert of Stafford; Sacric from the king.* With North Aston and Steeple Aston (see page 213).

Middleton Stoney *Mideltone: Richard Poynant.* Traces of a Norman castle in Middleton Park.

Milcombe *Midelcombe: Count of Evreux; Aelfric from the king. Mill.* Milcombe Hall, now a farmhouse.

Milton-under-Wychwood *Mideltone: Ranulf Flambard; Roger from Earl William and Alfwy from him.*

Minster Lovell *Minstre:* See page 213.

Mixbury *Misseberie: Roger d'Ivry. 2 mills.*

Mollington *Molliton/Molitone: Count of Evreux; William from Osbern FitzRichard.*

Mongewell *Mongewel: Roger de Lacy. 2 mills.* Mongewell Park House.

Nethercote (in Lewknor) *Altera Cote: Miles Crispin and Tovi from him. Mill.*

Nethercott (in Tackley) *Hidrecote: Hugh from Bishop of Bayeux.*

Newington *Neutone: Archbishop of Canterbury.* Newington House.

Newnham Murren *Niweham/ Neuueham: Miles Crispin.* Newnham Manor.

Noke *Ac(ham): Robert, Roger and Reginald from Earl William.* Church built by William I's daughter, Gundrada.

North Aston *Estone: Edward of Salisbury. Mill, fishery.* With Middle Aston and Steeple Aston (see page 213).

North Leigh *Lege: Godfrey from Roger d'Ivry. Mill.* Windmill; Saxon church; remains of a Roman villa nearby.

North Stoke *Stoches: Miles Crispin.*

Northbrook *Nor(t)broc: Reginald from Robert of Stafford; Reginald from Roger d'Ivry.*

Nuneham Courtnay *Neuham:* See page 214.

Oddington *Otendone: Roger d'Ivry's wife.* Joseph's Stone, possibly a Roman milestone, near the Roman road from Alchester to Dorchester.

Oxford *Oxeneford/juxta Oxeneford/juxta murum/ Oxineford: King's land (royal borough), also various landholders and burgesses holding 243 dwellings.* University city, allegedly founded as a nunnery by Frideswide (d. 735). The first college, University College, dates from 1249. The city was the Royalist headquarters during the Civil War.

Pemscott *Pismanescote: Gosbert from Robert of Stafford.*

Piddington *Petintone: Countess Judith.*

Preston Crowmarsh *Crem: Battle Abbey.*

Pyrton *Peritone/Piritune: William from Earl Hugh. Mill.* John Hampden, leader of the Long Parliament (1640), married Elizabeth Symeon in the Norman church.

Radford *Radeford: Ansketel of Graye from Earl William. Mill.*

Rofford *Ropeford: Saewold from the king (Robert d'Oilly by pledge).*

Rotherfield Greys *Redrefeld: Ansketel from Earl William.*

Rotherfield Peppard *Redrefeld: Miles Crispin. Mill.*

Rousham *Rou(u)esham: Reginald from Robert d'Oilly; William from Roger d'Ivry. Miles.* Rousham House.

Rycote *Reicote/Rocote: Hugh de Bolbec; Saswalo from Geoffrey de Mandeville; Alfsi from the king.*

Salford *Salford/Salwood: Roger de Lacy from Earl William. Part of mill.*

Sandford-on-Thames *Sanford: Wenric, Robert and Roger from Abingdon Abbey. 2 fisheries.* Paper mill.

Sandford St Martin *Sanford: Adam from Bishop of Bayeux. Mill.* Sandford Park.

Sarsden *Secendene: Richard de Courcy. 3 mills.*

NORTH LEIGH: *Windmill, possibly on its original* Domesday *site.*

Shelswell *Scildeswelle: Herlwin from Bishop of Coutances.*

Shenington *Senendone: Robert d'Oilly. Mill.*

Shifford *Scipford: Columban from Bishop of Lincoln. Fishery (250 eels).* Saxon ford and earthworks. Alfred held one of the earliest parliaments on Court Close near the church, in the late 9th century.

Shipton-on-Cherwell *Sciptone/ Sciptune: Ilbert from Bishop of Bayeux; Hugh de Grandmesnil. Mill.* Shipton House.

Shipton-under-Wychwood *Sciptone: King's land, formerly Earl Harold, and Alfsi of Faringdon from the king; Geoffrey and Alfsi from the king. 6 mills.* Shipton Court; Shipton Lodge.

Shirburn *Scir(e)burne/Sireburne: Drogo from Robert d'Oilly; Ralph from Roger d'Ivry.* Shirburn Castle; Shirburn Lodge.

Shotover *Scotorne: Reginald. Forests.* Shotover House.

Showell *Seve/Sivewelle: Wimund, Godric and Count of Evreux from Bishop of Bayeux.*

Sibford Ferris *Sibeford: Rolf from Henry de Ferrers.*

Sibford Gower *Sibeford: Aba from Hugh de Grandmesnil; William FitzCorbucion from William FitzAnsculf and Ralph from him. 2 mills.*

Somerton *Sumertone: Reginald Wadard from Bishop of Bayeux; Reginald from Miles Crispin. Mill (400 eels).* William Juxon, rector of Somerton became Archbishop of Canterbury to Charles II (1660–63).

South Newington *Niwetone: Adam and Wadard from Bishop of Bayeux; Ansketel from Earl William and Robert from him. 2½ mills.*

South Stoke *Stoch: Bishop of Lincoln.*

South Weston *Westone/ Westune: Robert from Earl Hugh. Mill.*

Spelsbury *Spelesberie: Urso from Bishop of Winchester. Mill.* Three earls of Rochester, including John the notorious 17th-century poet, are buried in the Norman church.

Stanton Harcourt *Stantone: Bishop of Bayeux. 3 mills, 2 fisheries.* Standing stones and circles.

Stanton St John *Stantone: Ilbert from Bishop of Bayeux.*

Steeple Aston *Estone:* See page 213.

Steeple Barton *Bartone: William from Roger d'Ivry.* Adjoining Bartongate.

Stockley *Stochelie: King's land.* Stockley Copse.

Stoke Lyne *Stoches: Hugh and Thorold from Walter Giffard; Hugh from Roger d'Ivry.*

Stonesfield *Stuntesfeld: Aelfric from Robert of Stafford.* The Romans worked the sandstone quarries under the grass hilltop.

Stowford *Stauuorde: Reginald from the king. Forest.*

Stratton Audley *Stratone: Alfward from Robert d'Oilly.* Stratton Audley Park. James Audley, one of the original Knights of the Garter (1344) built a moated castle here.

Swerford *Surford: Robert from Earl William.* Mill.

Swinbrook *Suinbroc: Geoffrey.*

Swyncombe *Suinecombe: Monks of Bec from Miles Crispin.*

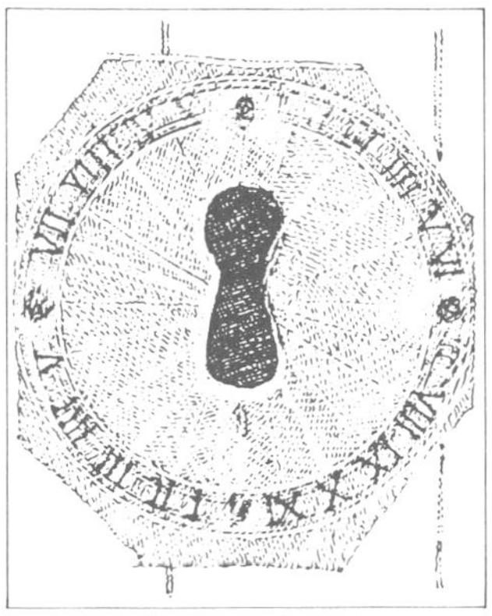

SYDENHAM: *Brass sundial, now a keyhole plate on the church door.*

Sydenham *Sidreham: Gilbert de Bretteville from Earl William.*

Tackley *Tachelie: Robert from Earl Hugh. Mill.* Tackley Park.

Tadmarton *Tademertone: Abingdon Abbey and a man-at-arms from the abbey. 2 mills.*

Taynton *Teigtone/Tentone: St Denis' Church, Paris. 2 mills, quarries. Eels.* Celebrated Taynton stone quarries.

Thame *Tame: Bishop of Lincoln. Mill.* Market town with the remains of a 12th-century abbey.

Thomley *Tobelie/Tumbeleia: Hervey from Bishop of Bayeux; Roger from Miles Crispin.*

Thrupp *Trop: Wadard's son from Roger d'Ivry. Mill (125 eels).*

Tiddington *Titendone: Saewold from the king.*

Toot Baldon *Baldentone: Robert d'Oilly and Roger from Bishop of Bayeux; Count of Evreux; Swein the Sheriff from the king.*

Tusmore *Toresmere: Thorold from Walter Giffard.* Tusmore House. Pope's *Rape of the Lock* (1712) was based on Lord Petre, a 20-year-old peer, who cut off one of the curls of a Tusmore belle, Arabella Fermor.

Wainhill *Winchel(l)e: Reginald from Miles Crispin; Reginald from Earl William.*

Walton *Waltone: Roger d'Ivry. Fishery.* Walton Manor.

Warpsgrove *Werplesgrave: Hervey from Bishop of Bayeux.*

Watcombe *Watecumbe: Geoffrey from Miles Crispin; Robert from Earl William.* Watcombe Manor near Pyrton.

Water Eaton *Etone: Robert d'Oilly. Mill, 3 fisheries.*

Waterperry *Pereiun/Perie: Robert from Robert d'Oilly.* Waterperry House.

Waterstock *Stoch: Saewold from Bishop of Lincoln. Mill.*

Watlington *Watelintone/tune: Preaux Abbey; Robert d'Oilly; Robert from Earl William. 2 mills.* Market town near the old Icknield Way.

Weald *Welde: Theodoric the Goldsmith.* Now Bampton, some houses.

Wendlebury *Wandesberie: Saswalo from Geoffrey de Mandeville.* By the site of Roman Alchester, now fields.

Westcott Barton *Bertone: Rotric from Bishop of Lisieux.* Adjoining Bartongate.

Weston-on-the-Green *Westone: Gilbert from Robert d'Oilly. 2 mills.* Weston House.

Westwell *Westwelle: Walter Poyntz.* Westwell Manor.

Wheatfield *Witefelle: Peter from Robert d'Oilly.* Wheatfield Park.

Whitchurch *Witecerce: Miles Crispin. Mill.* Also Whitchurch Lock and Hall. Sir John Soane, founder of the Soane Museum, was born John Swan here (1753).

Whitehill *Wistelle: Roger from Bishop of Bayeux; Godfrey from Roger d'Ivry. Mill.*

Widford *Widiforde: Archbishop Thomas; St Oswald's of Gloucester. Mill.* Norman church with a Roman floor.

Wigginton *Wigentone: Guy d'Oilly. Mill.* Extensive Roman remains.

Wilcote *Widelicote: Wadard from Bishop of Bayeux.* Wilcote Manor House.

Witney *Witenie: Bishop of Winchester. 2 mills.* Market town. Blankets have been made here since the 14th century.

Wolvercote *Ulfgarcote: Godfrey from Roger.*

Wood Eaton *Etone: Fulk from Roger d'Ivry.* Wood Eaton Hall. Roman remains including a coin of Cunebelinus, Shakespeare's Cymbeline; Roman or Saxon well.

Woodleys *Widelie: Ansketel of Graye from Earl William.*

Woodperry *Peregie: Roger from Bishop of Bayeux.*

Woodstock *Wodestoch: King's land. Forest.* Market town, known for manufacturing gloves. Blenheim Palace, given to the Duke of Marlborough, and designed by Vanbrugh, is one of England's greatest houses.

WITNEY: *South of the green, the 17th-c. butter cross stands on its 13 legs; a fine church is nearby.*

Wootton *Optone/Oitone: King's land; William and Ilger from Bishop of Coutances. 2 mills.*

Worton (in Cassington) *Wrtone: Roger from Earl William and Robert from him.*

Worton *Hortone: Adam from Bishop of Bayeux; Alfwy from the king; Thurstan from Bishop of Coutances; 2 mills.* Now 2 hamlets, Nether and Over Worton.

Wroxton *Werochestan: Ingelrann from his father Guy de Raimbeaucourt. Mill.* Burial place of the banker Thomas Coutts (1735–1822).

Wychwood *Hucheuuode: King's land. Forest.*

Wykham *Wicham: Robert from Bishop of Lincoln. Mill.*

Yarnton *Hardintone: Roger d'Ivry from Bishop of Lincoln; Roger from Bishop of Bayeux. Church, fishery.*

Yelford *Aieleforde: Walter Poyntz.* Family home of Warren Hastings, governor-general of India (1773–85).

WOODSTOCK: *Street scene in one of Oxfordshire's most attractive market towns.*

Rutland

The origin of Rutland is uncertain, but according to a recent reconstruction, the area was the home of an Anglian tribe during and after Roman times. After it was absorbed into the kingdom of Mercia it retained its integrity as the dower of the successive queens of Mercia, and later of Saxon England. When the Danish armies overran the rest of eastern England in the ninth century, Alfred obtained an agreement from them not to settle it. Instead it was partitioned between the Danish administrations based at Nottingham and Northampton, and later between the counties that emerged out of the areas occupied by those administrations.

By the time of Domesday *the section administered from Northampton had been absorbed as the 'hundred' or 'wapentake' of Witchley. But the rest of the land (the 'wapentakes' of Martinsley and Alstoe) which had no common border with Nottinghamshire, was listed separately under* Roteland *as an appendix to the Nottinghamshire section. In the following century the entire area was reconstituted as a separate county. (Today Rutland no longer exists, swept away by the Local Government Reorganization of 1974.)*

This account clarifies many of the peculiarities of the Rutland entries, and it also explains William's subsequent decision to retain most of that part of Rutland that was still in royal hands as an inheritance for the successive queens of England.

Great Casterton

The King holds CASTERTON *CASTRETONE.* Earl Morcar held it. 3½ hides. Land for 9 ploughs. In lordship 1. 24 villagers, 2 Freemen and 2 smallholders with a priest and 2 slaves have 7 ploughs. A mill at 16s; meadow, 16 acres; spinney 3 furlongs long and 2 furlongs wide. The value was £6; now £10. Hugh FitzBaldric holds it from the King at a revenue.

Great Casterton is a stone village just outside Stamford on the Great North Road. It has recently been bypassed, and the main road now runs a few hundred yards away across fields. The change must be a relief for the inhabitants, but the main street, now unnecessarily wide, gives the village a slightly hollow feel.

The village of Great Casterton and the nearby hamlet of Little Casterton, are indistinguishable in *Domesday*. Casterton, as it was then called, had been a thriving Roman town between the second and the fifth centuries. But by 1086 it had long been overtaken by Stamford, and there is nothing in *Domesday* to indicate that it was in any way distinctive, aside from the fact that it fell into Witchley Wapentake, the only area north of the Welland River to be assessed in hides. It is possible that the 'number of ploughs for which there is land' was an artificial figure. Rather than being a genuine estimate of the amount of land available for cultivation, it seems to have been the record of an old geld assessment, which was later revised.

Casterton's 'mill at 16s' was probably the

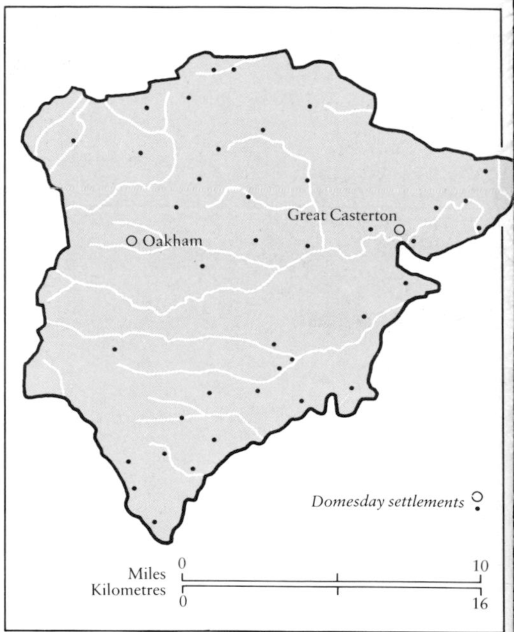

GREAT CASTERTON: *Although the mill itself has vanished, the mill pond is still peaceful and deep.*

GREAT CASTERTON: *The Church of St Peter and St Paul; built in the 13th c., with a later tower, it contains traces of wall paintings and a Norman font, still in use. An earlier church is mentioned in the* Domesday *entry.*

predecessor of a watermill mentioned in 1540 and again in 1598. It is still possible to find traces of the mill where the old Great North Road leads out of the village towards Stamford. Here, on a large wooded embankment, a footpath winds down past a little graveyard onto a meadow beside the River Gwash, where grinding stones were found in the nineteenth century. A mill-stream running parallel to the river is still easy to make out, with recognizable pieces of cut stone hidden in the undergrowth – a direct link with the mill at Casterton in 1086.

Oakham

[Land of the King] In OAKHAM *OCHEHAM*, with 5 outliers, Church jurisdiction, Queen Edith had 4 carucates of land taxable. Land for 16 ploughs. The King has 2 ploughs at the hall; however, another 4 ploughs possible. 138 villagers and 19 smallholders who have 37 ploughs. Meadow, 80 acres. A priest and a church to which 4 bovates of this land belong; woodland pasture 1 league long and 1/2 league wide. Value before 1066 £40.

Oakham was the capital of Rutland when it was still a county, but guidebooks tend to attribute to it the same isolated rural sleepiness that they do to the entire area. For its size, it is an active town. Its main street is filled with shoppers, and juggernauts roar through between Peterborough and Nottingham.

Its *Domesday* figures make it look like a large settlement, but this is misleading; they are a consolidated total for Oakham plus five outliers, whose names are not given. All of Martinsley Wapentake – about one third of Rutland – is grouped into three enormous manors, each formerly held by Queen Edith (Edward the Confessor's wife), and before her by at least two previous Saxon queens. Edward the Confessor ended this tradition by decreeing that the entire estate was to go to Westminster Abbey after Edith's death. However, William I allowed Edith to keep her lands until she died in 1076, then took them into his own hands. All three manors have the words 'church jurisdiction' in their *Domesday* entries; this probably refers to dues that William allowed Westminster Abbey to collect by way of compensation for not getting what it had been promised.

The evidence of Danish influence in Oakham and the two other manors of Martinsley is contradictory. Although the area is assessed in carucates, 'free peasants', the other standard sign of Danish influence, are entirely missing. This has led to the conjecture that the Danes may have refrained from colonizing Rutland because of Saxon pressure, even though they controlled the region politically in the ninth century.

Another oddity of the Oakham entry is that although it states that there is 'land for 16 ploughs', there are 39 ploughs working, and 'another 4 ploughs possible'! The most likely explanation is that the figure of 16 is artificial, the record of a former geld assessment which had since been reduced.

The 'hall' mentioned in *Domesday* was probably of timber, but it was succeeded only a century later by the Great Hall of Oakham Castle, a large stone structure which still stands in a wide stretch of greensward surrounded by old fortifications. Inside, its clean whitewashed walls are decorated with a display that has a tantalizing connection with *Domesday* – a collection of more than 230 horseshoes, donated, according to tradition, by every king, queen and peer of the kingdom who has visited Oakham.

The custom was already long established by the end of the fifteenth century; it is believed to have begun when the bailiffs started to demand from any aristocratic visitor a shoe from his horse as a guarantee that he would not leave without paying his bills. It seems more than a coincidence that the custom grew up at the hall built by Walkelin de Ferrers, whose surname in French means 'to bind with iron' or 'to shoe a horse'. His great-grandfather Henry de Ferrers was a *Domesday* Commissioner as well as a great landholder. He had come with William from Normandy, where he was the lord of Ferrières, known for its iron-working industry. The Ferrers coat-of-arms was six black horseshoes on a silver ground. Oakham continued to be described as 'of the inheritance of Lord Ferrers' long after the family lost possession in 1252, and the horseshoe tradition may have grown up around their memory even if it did not begin in their time. If so it provides an odd memorial to one of the men who helped create *Domesday*.

OAKHAM: *The castle's Great Hall was built in the 12th c. and its fortifications still stand. The* Domesday *hall was probably timber.*

Rutland Gazetteer
Each entry starts with the modern place name in **bold** type. The *Domesday* information that follows is in *italic* type, beginning with the name or names by which the place was known in 1086. The main landholders and under-tenants are next, separated with semi-colons if a place was divided into more than one holding. More general information completes the *Domesday* part of the entry, including examples of dues (eels, etc.) rendered by tenants. The modern or post-Domesday section is in normal type. [village symbol] represents a village, [hamlet symbol] a small village or hamlet.

Ashwell *Ex(e)welle: Earl Hugh and Jocelyn from him, formerly Earl Harold.* [village symbol] Attractive.

Barrowden *Berchedone: King's land; Robert de Tosny.* [village symbol]

Belmesthorpe *Belmestorp: Countess Judith. Mill.* [hamlet symbol]

Bisbrooke *Bitlesbroch: King's land. Robert from Countess Judith.* [hamlet symbol]

Burley *Burgelai: Gilbert de Ghent and Geoffrey from him.* [village symbol] Burley House, home of the 1st Duke of Buckingham in the 15th century.

Caldecott *Caldecote: Walter from Bishop of Lincoln.* [village symbol] Roman site by the river; Norman church, partly built with Roman tiles.

Casterton *Castretone:* See Great Casterton, page 220.

Cottesmore *Cotesmore: King's land.* [hamlet symbol] Site of Bronze Age, Roman and Saxon settlements.

Empingham *Epingeham: Sasfrid from William Peverel; Gilbert de Ghent. 11½ mills.* [village symbol] Mill Farm.

Essendine *Esindone: Walter from Bishop of Lincoln. Mill.* [hamlet symbol] Ruined castle, once the home of the Cecil family.

Exton *Exentune: Countess Judith. 2 mills.* [village symbol] Pretty; green.

Glaston *Gladestone: King's land; William from Countess Judith.* [hamlet symbol] Saxon cemetery; hall.

Greetham *Gretham: King's land. Mill.* [village symbol] A stream runs through the village.

Hambleton *Hameldun(e)/ Hemeldune: King's land. Albert. 3 churches. Mill.* [village symbol] Hilltop; Norman church.

Hardwick *Hardvic:* [village symbol] Deserted.

Horn *Horne: Bishop of Durham; Grimbald from Countess Judith. 4 mills.* [hamlet symbol] Lakeside.

Ketton *Chetene: King's land. Mill.* [village symbol] Well known for its stone and cement works.

Luffenham *Lufenham: King's land and Hugh de Port from the king. 2 mills.* Now 2 villages, North Luffenham, site of a Saxon settlement, 450–650, and South Luffenham.

Lyddington *Lidentone: Walter from Bishop of Lincoln. 2 mills.* [village symbol] Ironstone; fishponds nearby.

Market Overton *Overtune/ Ovretone: Countess Judith and Earl Waltheof from her.* [village symbol] Green; whipping post; site of a Saxon village, *c.* 600. The tower arch of the village church is late Saxon.

Morcott *Morcote: King's land.* [village symbol] Attractive.

Oakham *Ocheham:* See page 221.

Ridlington *Redlinctune: King's land. Church jurisdiction. 3 churches, 2 mill sites.* [village symbol] Church with a Norman tympanum.

Ryhall *Riehale: Countess Judith. 2 mills.* [village symbol] During the 7th century St Tibba, patron saint of falconers, is said to have lived in a cell on the site where the church now stands.

Scolthorpe *Sculthorp:* Lost.

Seaton *Segentone/gestone/ Seieton(e): King's land; Countess Judith; Robert de Tosny.* [hamlet symbol]

Snelston *Smelistone:* Lost.

Stoke Dry *Stoche: Walter from Bishop of Lincoln; Peterborough Abbey.* [village symbol] Isolated; seat of the Digbys, who produced Everard, the Gunpowder Plotter.

Stretton *Stratone/-tune/Stratone: Countess Judith and Earl Waltheof from her.*

Teigh *Tie: Robert Malet. Mill.* [hamlet symbol] Limestone. Anthony Jenkinson, the first Englishman to enter central Asia (in the 1550s), is buried here.

Thistleton *Tistertune/Tisteltune/ Tisteltone: Hugh from Countess Judith; Alfred of Lincoln and Gleu from him; Gleu from Godfrey de Cambrai.* [village symbol] Peaceful.

Thorpe-by-Water *Torp: King's land. William from Countess Judith.* [hamlet symbol] Riverside.

Tickencote *Tichecote: Grimbald from Countess Judith. Mill.* [hamlet symbol] 2 carved heads in the chancel arch of the church possibly represent Robert Grimbold and his wife.

Tinwell *Tedinwelle: Peterborough Abbey. 2 mills.* [village symbol]

Tixover *Tichesovre: King's land. Mill.* Early 12th-century church, now alone in the fields, which once served a riverside community who were probably wiped out by the Black Death. The present village is ¼ mile away.

Tolethorpe *Toltorp: William FitzAnsculf and Robert from him. 4 mills.* Tolethorpe Hall where Robert Brown, the Puritan and founder of the Brownist sect was born in 1549; medieval gatehouse.

Whissendine *Wichingedene: Hugh de Hotot from Countess Judith.* [village symbol] Large; earthworks of a medieval manor house.

Whitwell *Witewell: Countess Judith and Herbert from her. Church, mill.* [hamlet symbol] 13th-century church. Much of the parish was flooded when the Rutland Water reservoir was constructed in the early 1970s.

Shropshire

Only parts of Shropshire were open to settlement in 1086. To the west the barren moorlands rise to 1700 feet, and to the north intractable glacial clays lay between meres and peatbogs awaiting modern drainage. To the east, the great forests of the Midland Triangle were not easy to clear. In the Severn valley alone (between Welshpool and Ironbridge) the population may have been as high as six per square mile. It was in the centre of this region that Shrewsbury emerged, within a loop of the River Severn that leaves a gap of only 300 yards to defend.

In 1086 Roger of Montgomery, Earl of Shrewsbury, was incomparably the most important figure in the county. He built castles at Montgomery and Shrewsbury which, together with those at Oswestry, Clun and Ludlow, were to be the focus of the Marcher lordships.

West Shropshire was ravaged by the Welsh in 1077 (and again in 1088). Domesday *references to waste are numerous, suggesting the straits to which some areas had been reduced. Possibly no more than half the ploughlands were cultivated (e.g.* Myddle *– in the north-west – had only one team on 20 ploughlands).*

A number of places that are now in Wales were in Shropshire at the time of Domesday*. These are listed at the end of the gazetteer.*

ACTON BURNELL: *The castle was a protected home rather than a fortress. The church nearby has memorials to the Lee family, General Robert E. Lee of the US Confederate Army.*

Acton Burnell

Roger [FitzCorbet] also holds ACTON (BURNELL) *ACTUNE* [from Earl Roger] and a certain Roger from him. Godric held it; he was a free man. 3½ hides which pay tax. In lordship 1 plough; 2 slaves; 1 villager, 4 smallholders and 1 rider with 1½ ploughs. Value before 1066, 30s; later 15s; now 20s. 1 more plough would be possible there.

Acton Burnell is a neat, precisely tailored village half-way between the Stretton hills and Shrewsbury. It could easily be taken for an estate village because both its timber frame and stone cottages have been covered with stucco, and uniform hood porches have been added to give a rustic effect. Between the village and the park, a high-walled farm complex with a square corner tower bears a distinct resemblance to the thirteenth-century castle, which still stands here.

Roger FitzCorbet was an under-tenant of Earl Roger. He belonged to the family that built Caus Castle to guard the valley which runs south-east from Shrewsbury under Long Mountain, naming it after Caux in Normandy, from which they came. The Burnells acquired the manor of Acton from the Corbets – it reverted temporarily after a Burnell committed murder – and Robert Burnell, Edward I's Chancellor for 18 years from 1274, made it famous. Born in the village, he was a thrusting cleric out to found a dynasty. Pope Nicholas III thought him unfit to be Bishop of Winchester and the monks of Canterbury turned a deaf ear to Edward's frantic demands that they should elect his protégé archbishop. Burnell had to be content with becoming Bishop of Bath and Wells which he did much to enhance and adorn. He was too successful to be popular, but he gave Edward's administration a competence it lacked after he was gone. He died at Berwick on Tweed in 1292.

The visitor today approaches the castle through a rhododendron grove, which gives way to meticulously mown lawns. A giant cedar enhances the south-eastern of the four corner towers. The building is of red sandstone with something of the Italian villa about it. Agreeably un-military, it is the earliest of the only nominally fortified country houses. Beyond, and across the tennis courts of Acton Burnell Hall, two huge stone gables face each other, one graced by two tall lancet windows. Tradition has it that in this building, now called Parliament Barn, Burnell entertained not only the king but parliament as well. Given the peripatetic nature of medieval monarchy, it is not unlikely that parliament sat here; there was indeed a Statute of Acton Burnell. Whether the Commons then sat with the Lords for the first time is more open to doubt. Oddly enough, Burnell's best claim to be remembered is that he anchored the Court of Chancery in London, where it has since remained.

Despite his efforts to make Acton Burnell a town, it remains a village, and a fairly remote one. As for the Burnell family, the peerage had died out by the end of the fourteenth century: the Corbets of *Domesday*, on the other hand, still turn up all over this part of Shropshire.

MUCH WENLOCK: *The priory was a Cluniac abbey from the 10th c. until the Dissolution.*

Much Wenlock

The Church [of St Milburga] itself holds (Much) WENLOCK *WENLOCH* it held it before 1066. 20 hides; 4 of them were exempt from tax in King Canute's time, the others paid tax. In lordship 9½ ploughs; 9 villagers, 3 riders and 46 smallholders; between them they have 17 ploughs; another 17 would be possible there. 15 slaves. 2 mills which serve the monks. 1 fishery; woodland for fattening 300 pigs; 2 hedged enclosures. Value before 1066 £15; now £12.

Hidden away in a muddle of small wooded hills at the northern end of Corvedale lies Much Wenlock, Shropshire's 'Sleepy Hollow'. Inside the old borough town, like a cocoon in a wall cranny, lies concealed possibly the finest medieval domestic house in Britain – once the infirmary and prior's house of the Cluniac abbey. This was the church which *Domesday* records that Roger of Montgomery had turned into an abbey. The foundation had been started by St Milburga, the granddaughter of Penda, King of Mercia.

Domesday's information about Much Wenlock (then the manor of Wenlock) is of peculiar interest, for it shows not only the indulgence the church had been given in getting relief from tax before the Conquest, but it also lists (following the above entry) all of the land of St Milburga's church. The eighth-century Testament of St Milburga (included in the Life of St Milburga, now in the British Museum) contains the same list. The accuracy of the testament, which has stood up well to the analysis of modern scholars, goes a long way towards substantiating the claim that this estate was amongst the most ancient to be dispersed at the Dissolution. Had it been kept together, St Milburga might have been hailed as the patron saint of the Industrial Revolution, which was cradled on the lands she had acquired for her church.

A mile or two from the abbey, the Severn valley cuts through seams of ironstone and coal. In 1322 Walter de Caldebrook paid six shillings to the abbey to 'dig for seacoal in Le Brocholes' (still identifiable between Ironbridge and Madeley). St Milburga's had its own coal mines at Little Wenlock, across the Severn, and at Broseley; and its own iron foundries in Shirlett Forest. Sir Basil Brooke, who in 1638 built the first blast furnace at Coalbrookdale, owned Madeley Court, which had formerly been the grange. After 1709 this became the home of Abraham Darby, the first man to use coke to smelt iron – vital to the industry, because Crown authority was then required to fell a tree within ten miles of the Severn. Little Wenlock, busy in 1086 raising swine and eagles, had become so important by 1750 that wagon-ways were planned to bring coal down to the river. Today the churchyard at Little Wenlock has not only iron tombstones but iron urns and plinths as well.

Darby's concentration of a previously dispersed iron industry – furnace, forge and engineering works close together and connected by railway – brought about the astounding growth of the steel industry early in the nineteenth century. People came from all over Europe to see what was going on. It is no exaggeration to say that the forge hammer which was to be heard around the world first began to strike on iron smelted with coke amidst the woodlands of the ancient lands of St Milburga. But this left Much Wenlock pretty much as it is today. It is probably better known that its Olympic Games, founded by Dr William Penny Brook, helped to trigger the revival in 1896 of the international Olympic Games.

Clun

[Picot holds] CLUN *CLUNE* [from Earl Roger]. Edric held it; he held it as a free man. 15 hides which pay tax. Land for 60 ploughs. In lordship 2; 5 slaves; 10 villagers and 4 smallholders with 5 ploughs. A mill which serves the court; 4 Welshmen pay 2s 4d. Of this land Walter holds 2 hides from Picot; Picot, a man-at-arms, 3 hides; Gislold 2 hides. They have 3 ploughs and 2 slaves; 2 ploughmen; 8 villagers, 4 smallholders and 2 Welshmen with 2 ploughs between them. 2 riders pay 2 cattle in dues. Value of the whole manor before 1066 £25; later £3; now, of what Picot has, £6 5s; of what the men-at-arms (have), £4 less 5s.

Clunton, and Clunbury, Clungunford and Clun
Are the quietest places under the sun.
Anon

Clun, the most westerly ancient English settlement in Shropshire, lies a couple of miles to the east of Offa's Dyke, which rises over Spoad Hill like some giant mole-tunnel. A towering Norman keep tops this steep man-made mound, an outlying part of which is now the village's bowling green – a feature that softens the martial profile of the castle walls. With its half-timbered church tower on the south side of the river, a seventeenth-century almshouse quadrangle on the north side, and a narrow old saddleback bridge in between, Clun has a simple easy-going charm.

Whatever its origins – its status as a mother church for a host of medieval chapels suggests that it was well established before the Conquest – it was selected, like nearby Richards Castle and Bishops Castle, to be a base from which to subdue the Welsh. '4 Welshmen pay 2s 4d' reveals, however, that this was a hybrid area: 'Welshmens' Meadow' may have been named long before the Normans arrived. It is likely that animals as well as consignments of bronze axe-heads were already being moved along Clun Trackway, which follows the high ground south of Clun before dropping down to the river at Clungunford.

Picot de Say, who gave his name to Stokesay Castle near Craven Arms, held Clun from Earl Roger, who had been given palatine authority in the Northern March. Later Clun became the stronghold of the FitzAlans of Oswestry, forebears of the Earls of Arundel. It was a member of this family, Henry Howard, who in 1614 founded the hospital for decayed tradesmen, the almshouses by the river.

Clun was a borough settlement planted by the Normans, and like the others, had a precarious existence: Clun itself was reduced to ashes by Prince Rhys in 1195; Bishops Castle was nearly wiped out in 1263, and Richards Castle, which had been started before the Conquest by Richard le Scrob, shrank to the hamlet it is today. Clun survived, although the castle was said to be in acute need of repair by 1272. That it had an important place in the administration of justice is implied in the record of one Willam Kempe, who held his land by virtue of conveying the heads of those executed at Clun to Shrewsbury, presumably for counting and display.

But Clun seems never to have lived up to expectations. 'Land for 60 ploughs' reads like a house agent's blurb: in reality there must have been less – the nineteenth-century enclosure of 27,000 acres hardly suggests much arable land. If Clun Castle is really the Garde Doloreuse of Sir Walter Scott's *The Betrothed*, as some believe, the author's imaginative flight is impressive, for the historical half-life of this obscure border borough gave him little to build on.

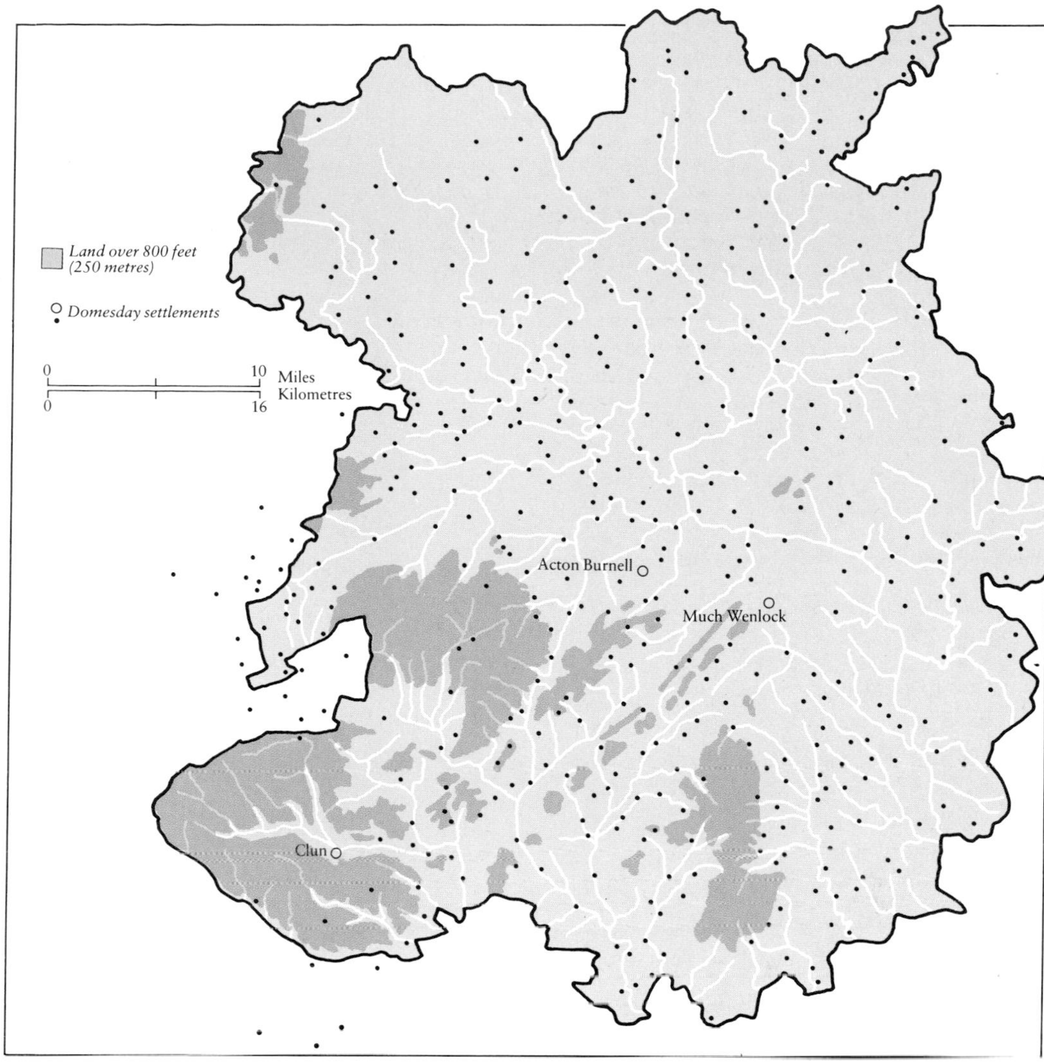

MUCH WENLOCK: *A Romanesque carved lavabo, c. 1180, in the priory.*

Shropshire Gazetteer
Each entry starts with the modern place name in **bold** type. The *Domesday* information that follows is in *italic* type, beginning with the name or names by which the place was known in 1086. The main landholders and under-tenants are next, separated with semi-colons if a place was divided into more than one holding. More general information completes the *Domesday* part of the entry, including examples of dues such as eels, rendered by tenants. The modern or post-Domesday section is in normal type. represents a village, a small village or hamlet.
Places now in Wales are listed at the end of the gazetteer.

Abdon *Abetune: Rainald the Sheriff from Earl Roger.* Manor house; Iron Age forts nearby.

Acton Burnell *A(e)ctune:* See page 224.

Acton Pigott *Aectune: Rainald the Sheriff from Earl Roger.*

Acton Reynold *Achetone: Rainald the Sheriff from Earl Roger.* Victorian mansion incorporating 17th-century work.

Acton Round *Achetune: Rainald the Sheriff from Earl Roger. Mill.* Queen Anne manor house.

Acton Scott *Actune: Eldred from Earl Roger.* Pretty; late Elizabethan manor house; Roman site.

Adderley *Eldredelei: Nigel from Earl Roger.* Edward II granted a Thursday market here to his favourite, Bartholomew de Badlesmere.

Alberbury *Alberberie: Earl Roger and Roger FitzCorbet from him.* Quiet; on Welsh border; 13th-century castle ruins.

Albright Hussey *Abretone/ Etbretone: Rainald the Sheriff from Earl Roger.* Timber-framed house, 1524.

Albrightlee *Etbretelie: Church of St Almund before and after 1066; Earl Roger.* Farmhouse. St. Almund's Church, Shrewsbury, was pulled down soon after 1788.

Albrighton (near Shifnal) *Albricstone: Norman from Earl Roger.* Large; a thriving market town from the 14th to the 19th century.

Albrighton (near Shrewsbury) *Etbritone: Rainald the Sheriff from Earl Roger.* Hall.

Alcaston *Aelmundestune: Helgot from Earl Roger.* Picturesque manor farm; moated site nearby.

Aldon *Alledone: Roger de Lacy and Richard and Aeldred from him. Mill, church.* Aldon Court.

Alkington *Alchetune: William Pantulf from Earl Roger. Mill.* Alkington Hall, 1592.

Alveley *Alvidelege: Earl Roger.* Pool Hall with the remains of a moat in its grounds.

Amaston *Enbaldestune: Elmund, the pre-Conquest holder, and Alward his son from Earl Roger.* Isolated Heath Farm.

Ashford *Esseford: Osbern FitzRichard. Mill.* Now 2 small villages, Ashford Bowdler and Ashford Carbonel, facing each other across the River Teme.

Astley *Hesleie: Church of St Mary.* Norman church, much altered.

Aston (in Munslow) *Estune: Rainald the Sheriff from Earl Roger. Mill.* Hall.

Aston (in Oswestry) *Estone: Robert the Butler from Earl Roger.* Aston Hall, 1780; 1742 chapel in parkland; remains of a motte.

Aston (in Wem) *Estune: William Pantulf from Earl Roger.* Timber-framed hall.

Aston Botterell *Estone: Rainald the Sheriff from Earl Roger.* Manor farm with a 13th-century hall.

Aston Eyre *Estone: Rainald the Sheriff from Earl Roger. Mill.* Overlooking Mor Brook. Hall Farm dates from the 13th century and may have been a fortified manor house.

Atcham *Atingeham: Church of St Almund before and after 1066 and Godebold from the church.* Severnside; Roman stones probably from nearby Wroxeter. Ordericus Vitalis, author of *Historia Ecclesiastica*, 1141, was baptized here.

Badger *Beghesovre: Osbern FitzRichard from Earl Roger.* Surrounded by trees; Georgian Hall, recently demolished.

Barlow *Berlie: Picot from Earl Roger.* Isolated farmhouse.

Baschurch *Bascherche: Earl Roger; Church of St Peter. Church, 3 fisheries.* On the River Perry; late 12th-century church; Iron Age earthworks.

ATCHAM: *Attingham House with a picture gallery by Nash.*

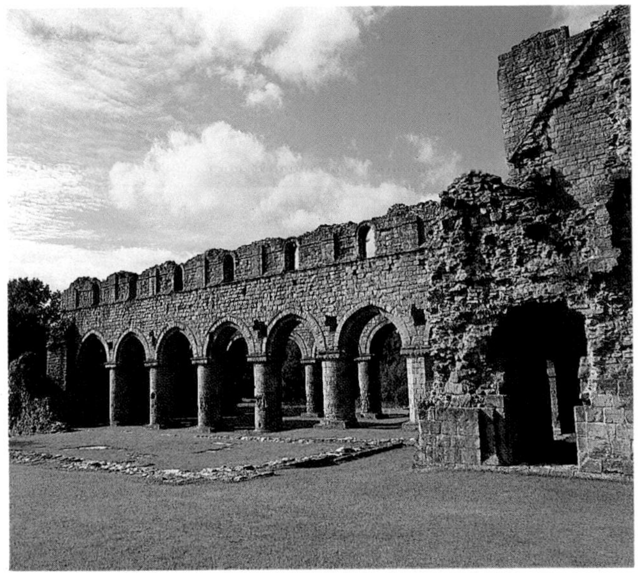

BUILDWAS: *Remains of the abbey church.*

Baveney *Barbingi: Ralph de Mortimer from Earl Roger.* Scattered community on the edge of Wyre Forest; site of a Roman fort.

Bayston *Begestan: William Pantulf from Earl Roger; Edric from Bishop of Hereford.* Baystonhill, a dormitory village outside Shrewsbury; village green; ancient earthworks.

Bearstone *Bardestune: Turold from Earl Roger. Mill.* Moated site; Bearstone Mill nearby.

Beckbury *Becheberie: Roger Venator from Earl Roger.* Elizabethan hall.

Bedstone *Betietetune: Picot from Earl Roger.* Quiet; Castle Ditches on Bedstone Hill; manor farm.

Belswardine *Belleurdine: Helgot from Earl Roger.* Hall, 1542.

Benthall *Benehale: Alward son of Elmund from Earl Roger.* Part of Greater Telford.

Berrington *Beritune: Rainald the Sheriff from Earl Roger; Church of St Peter. Church.* Norman church; manor house, 1658.

Berwick (in Atcham) *Berewic: Rainald the Sheriff from Earl Roger.* Attingham Park nearby was owned by Lord Berwick in the 19th century.

Berwick (in Shrewsbury) *Berewic: Earl Roger.* Also known as Great Berwick; Georgian Berwick House.

Besford *Betford: Gerard from Earl Roger.*

Beslow *Beteslauue: William Pantulf from Earl Roger.* Isolated farmhouse.

Betton (in Berrington) *Betune: Bishop of Chester before and after 1066.* Betton Strange and Betton Alkmere, 2 large houses.

Betton (in Norton in Hales) *Baitune: Gerard from Earl Roger. Mill.* On the River Tern; Betton Hall.

Bicton *Bichetone: Wiger from the Church of St Chad.* Quiet; manor house.

Bishton *Bispetone: Norman from Earl Roger.* Bishton Manor House.

Bitterley *Buterlie: Roger de Lacy from Earl Roger. Church.* Pretty; church with a Norman font.

Boreton *Burtune: Church of St Peter before and after 1066.* Quiet.

Bouldon *Bolledone: Helgot from Earl Roger.* Quiet.

Bourton *Burtune: Church of St Peter before and after 1066.* Manor house by Norman Shaw, 1870s.

Bratton *Brochetone: William Pantulf from Earl Roger.*

Brockton (in Longford) *Brochetone: Richard from Earl Roger.* Adjoining Lilleshall.

Brockton (in Sheriff Hales) *Brotone:* Lost.

Brockton (in Stanton Long) *Broctune: Rainald the Sheriff from Earl Roger.* At crossroads; Norman castle mound.

Brockton (in Sutton Maddock) *Broctone: Osbern FitzRichard from Earl Roger.* Overlooking industrial Telford.

Brogyntyn *Burtone: Madoc from Earl Roger.* Norman castle mound in the grounds of an early Georgian house.

Bromfield *Brunfelde: Church of St Mary before and after 1066; Robert son of Wimarch, the pre-Conquest holder, from Earl Roger.* Church.

Brompton (in Berrington) *Brantune: Robert FitzCorbet and Picot from Earl Roger.* Quiet; on the Severn.

Broom *Bruma: Rainald the Sheriff from Earl Roger and Alfred from him.* Broom Farm near Hordley.

Broome *Brame: Earl Roger and Rainald the Sheriff from him.*

Broseley *Bosle: Helgot from Earl Roger.* Decayed manufacturing town best known for its clay pipes. Matthew Boulton and James Watt erected the first steam engine here in 1776.

Broughton *Burtone/tune: Church of St Mary; Church of St Chad.* Scattered community; ruins of an old church in a field.

Bucknell (near Clun) *Buchehalle: Ralph de Mortimer and Helgot from him.* Norman motte; ancient earthworks in woods.

Buildwas *Beldewas: Bishop of Chester before and after 1066. Mill.* In 1135 Roger de Clinton, Bishop of Lichfield and Coventry, founded an abbey here; remains date from 1147.

Burford *Bureford: Osbern FitzRichard, the pre-Conquest holder, from Earl Roger. 2 mills, church.* On the Teme; church with some Norman work.

Burwarton *Burertone: Ralph de Mortimer from Earl Roger.* Hall.

Buttery *Buterel: William Pantulf from Earl Roger.* Buttery Farm.

Calverhall *Cavrahalle: Nigel from Earl Roger.* Also called Cloverley and Corra; medieval moated sites nearby.

Cantlop *Cantelop: Norman from Earl Roger. Mill.* Quiet; on Cound Brook.

Cardestone *Cartistune: Roger FitzCorbet from Earl Roger.*

Cardington *Cardintune: Rainald the Sheriff from Earl Roger.* Pretty; on a hillside.

Catsley *Cateschesleie: Ralph de Mortimer from Earl Roger.* Catsley Farm.

Cause *Alretone: Earl Roger and Roger FitzCorbet from him.* Earthworks of castle founded by Roger FitzCorbet. A Royalist garrison during the Civil War, it was besieged for 12 days by Parliamentary forces and then destroyed.

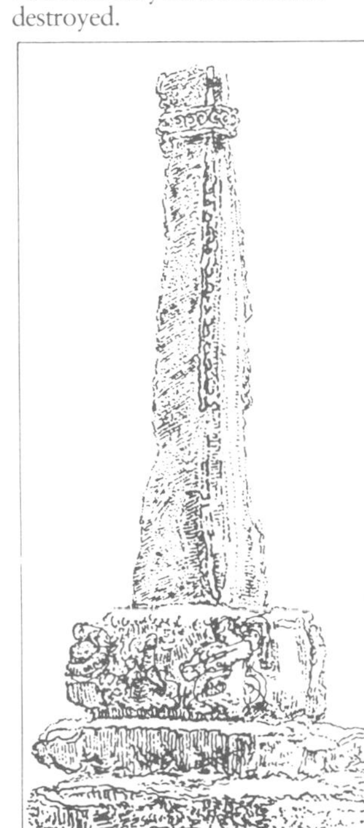

CAYNHAM: *A headless cross in the churchyard.*

Caynham *Caiham: Ralph de Mortimer from Earl Roger. Hill.* On Ledwyche Brook; Caynham Camp, an Iron Age hill-fort.

Charlcotte *Cerlecote: Helgot from Earl Roger.* Quiet; small manor house.

Charlton *Cerletone/itone:* Lost.

Chelmarsh *Celmeres: Ralph de Mortimer from Earl Roger.* Scattered; 13th-century hall. Hugh de Mortimer built the chancel of the present church in c.1345.

Chelmick *Elmundewic: Hugh son of Turgis from Earl Roger.* Isolated.

Cheney Longville *Languefelle: Siward, the pre-Conquest holder, from Earl Roger.* Farming; moated manor house.

Cherrington *Cerlintone: Gerard from Earl Roger.* Scattered. The half-timbered moated manor house, dated 1635, is supposed to be the original 'House that Jack built'.

Chesthill *Cesdille/Cestulle:* Lost.

Cheswardine *Ciseworde: Robert de Stratford and Gilbert from him.* Moated site.

Chetton *Catinton: Earl Roger. New mill.* Beautifully situated; mill downstream.

Chetwynd *Catewinde: Turold from Earl Roger. Mill, 2 fisheries (64 sticks of eels).* Chetwynd mansion and park, haunted by the ghost of Mrs Pigott (one of the family), who was killed in childbirth.

Child's Ercall *Arcalun: Rainald the Sheriff from Earl Roger.* Built up.

Chipnall *Ceppecanole: Robert de Stratford and Gilbert from him.* Large; includes Cheswardine Hall.

Chirbury *Cireberie: Earl Roger. 2 churches.* Compact; castle mound; nave and aisle of an Augustinian priory.

Choulton *Cautune: Robert FitzCorbet from Earl Roger.* On a hillside, overlooking the River Onny.

Church Preen *Prene: Helgot from Earl Roger.* Quiet; Preen Manor, built by Norman Shaw 1870–71 as an extension of an existing building.

Church Pulverbatch *Polrebec: Roger Venator from Earl Roger.* Motte of a Norman castle at Castle Pulverbatch nearby.

Claverley *Claverlege: Earl Roger. Mill.* Large; sprawling. The original fabric of a church built by Earl Roger is still visible.

Clee St Margaret *Cleie: Helgot from Earl Roger. Mill.* On a hill; Clee Brook.

Cleestanton *Clee: Church of St Milburga.*

Cleobury Mortimer *Claiberie/Cleberie: Ralph de Mortimer, formerly Queen Edith. Mill (2 horseloads of corn).* Town with a fortress destroyed by Henry II c.1154 and rebuilt by the Mortimers; part of the castle remains.

Cleobury North *Claiberie/Cleberie: Roger de Lacy and Ulward from him. Mill.* Mill Farm.

Clun *Clune: See page 221.*

Clunbury *Cluneberie: Picot from Earl Roger.* Quiet; on the River Clun.

Clungunford *Clone: Rainald the Sheriff and Picot from Earl Roger, formerly Gunward. 2 mills.* On the River Clun. The latter part of its name is a corruption of Gunward.

Clunton *Clutune: Picot from Earl Roger.*

Cold Hatton *Hatune: Gerard from Earl Roger.* 2 clusters of houses, Cold Hatton and Cold Hatton Heath.

Colemere *Colesmere: Norman from Earl Roger.* The mere from which it takes its name is part of a country park; rich agricultural land.

Condover *Conendovre: Earl Roger and Roger Venator, Osbern and Elward from him.* Large; late Norman church. The hall is the best Elizabethan house in Shropshire.

Coreley *Cornelie: Ralph de Mortimer.* Name of a large parish with many hill farms.

Corfham *Corfan: Earl Roger, formerly King Edward, with Church of St Peter holding the church.* Castle remains.

Corfton *Cortune: Roger de Lacy from Earl Roger. Enclosed hunting wood.* Remains of a medieval chapel; Elsich, a stone Elizabethan house.

Cosford *Costeford: Ralph de Mortimer from Earl Roger.* Airfield; museum; waterworks; wooded setting.

Coston *Cozetune: Picot from Earl Roger.* Coston Manor House.

Cothercott *Cotardictoe: Avenel from Earl Roger.* Hillside.

Coton (in Wem) *Cote: William Pantulf from Earl Roger.* Scattered community; hall in parkland.

Coton upon Tern *Ludecote: Ralph the Cook and Thochi from Earl Roger.* Cotton Farm.

Cound *Cuneet: Rainald the Sheriff from Earl Roger. 2 mills.* On Cound Brook; hall, 1704, built for Edward Cressett (later Bishop of Llandaff).

Cressage *Cristesache: Ranulf Peverel from Earl Roger. Fishery.* Large; Severnside. St Augustine of Canterbury is said to have found the district already Christian in c. 600.

Cross Hill(s) *Corselle: William Pantulf from Earl Roger.*

Crudgington *Crugetone: Robert Pincerna from Earl Roger. 4 fisheries.* On crossroads; by confluence of the rivers Strine and Tern.

Culmington *Comintone: Earl Roger.* Quiet; Culmington Manor School nearby.

Dawley *Dalelie: William Pantulf from Earl Roger.* Part of Telford; originally a small medieval village.

Detton *Dodintone: Rainald the Sheriff from Earl Roger.* Detton Hall.

Deuxhill *Dehocsele: Church of St Milburga before and after 1066.*

Dinthill *Duntune: Church of St Almund before and after 1066.* Early Georgian Dinthill Hall.

Ditton Priors *Doden/Dodintone: Earl Roger and Roger de Lacy from him.* Stone-quarrying.

Doddington *Dodetune: Roger de Curcelle from Earl Roger.* Part of southern Whitchurch.

Donington *Donitone: Earl Roger. Mill (5 horseloads of corn).* Adjoining Albrighton; St Cuthbert's Well, whose water is said to cure eye complaints; ancient pool nearby.

Dorrington *Derintune: William Malbedeng from Earl Roger.* Birthplace of John Boydell (1719–1804), publisher and Lord Mayor of London.

Dudston *Dudestune: Earl Roger.* Farmhouse; traces of a castle mound and ponds.

Eardington *Ardintone: Earl Roger. Mill.* Daniel's mill nearby. From 1281 a descendant of Earl Roger yielded annually to the king a pair of knives as part of his tenancy agreement. Today a billhook and hatchet are paid each year to the Crown by the tenants of Moor Ridding Farm on what was the earl's land.

Earls Ditton *Dodentone: Ralph de Mortimer.* Isolated.

Easthope *Stope: Rainald the Sheriff from Earl Roger.* On Wenlock Edge; Elizabethan manor house.

Eaton Constantine *Etune: Rainald the Sheriff from Earl Roger. Fishery in Severn.* Baxter's Cottage, where Richard Baxter, a puritan preacher, spent his boyhood in the early 17th century.

Eaton Mascott *Etune: Rainald the Sheriff from Earl Roger. Mill.* Tiny. Named after the Marscotts; the first tenant of this name was recorded in 1166.

Edenhope *Etenehop: Earl Roger.* Now Lower Edenhope; Edenhope Hill.

Edg(e)bold *Edbaldinesham: Ralph de Mortimer, formerly Queen Edith.* Now 2 hamlets, Lower and Upper Edgebold.

Edgeley *Edeslai: Roger de Curcelle.*

Edgmond *Edmendune: Earl Roger. Mill, fishery.* Large; 14th-century Old Rectory.

Edgton *Egedune: Picot from Earl Roger.* Superb scenery.

Edstastone *Stanestune: William Pantulf from Earl Roger.*

EASTHOPE: *Replica of an hour glass in an iron grille, in St Peter's Church.*

Ellerdine *Elleurdine: Gerard from Earl Roger.*

Ellesmere *Ellesmeles: Earl Roger and Mundret and Rainald from him. Mill.* Town with Georgian houses. The site of the castle is now a bowling green.

Emstrey *Eiminstre: Church of St Peter.*

English Frankton *Franchetone: Rainald the Sheriff from Earl Roger.*

Eudon Burnell *Eldone: Rainald the Sheriff from Earl Roger.*

Eudon George *Eldone: Ralph de Mortimer from Earl Roger.* Facing Eudon Burnell across the Borle Brook; timbered houses.

Eyton (in Alberbury) *Etune: Roger FitzCorbet and Elric from Earl Roger.* Farming.

Eyton (in Baschurch) *Hestone: Robert Pincerna from Earl Roger.*

Eyton-on-Severn *Aitone: Church of St Peter. 2 fisheries.* Birthplace of the philosopher Edward Herbert, 1st Lord Cherbury (1583–1648).

Eyton-upon-the-Weald-Moors *Etone: William Pantulf from Earl Roger.* On the edge of well-watered lowland; Eyton Hall.

Faintree *Faventrei: Walchelin from Earl Roger.* Now Lower Faintree; hall.

Farley *Fernelege: Roger FitzCorbet from Earl Roger.* Low-lying; remains of a moat at Lower Newton farm.

Farlow *Ferlau: King's land; Widard from Earl Roger. Assessed with Leominster, Herefordshire.* Quiet; hillside.

Felton Butler *Feltone: Helgot from Earl Roger.*

Fenemere *Finemer: Earl Roger.* Small lake.

Fitz *Witesot: Picot from Earl Roger.* Severnside.

Ford *Forde: Earl Roger. Mill, fishery.* Large.

Forton *Fordune: Roger de Lacy from Earl Roger.* Also Forton Heath.

DITTON PRIORS: *The nearby landscape shows 2 faces of Shropshire; deep clay soils and stone quarried hills.*

Frodesley *Frodeslege: Siward, the pre-Conquest holder, from Earl Roger. 3 enclosed hunting woods.* Quiet. Parts of the Georgian stone boundary walls that enclosed the park remain.

Fulwardine *Fuloordie:* Lost.

Glazeley *Gleslei: Rainald the Sheriff from Earl Roger. Mill.*

Golding *Goldene: Rainald the Sheriff from Earl Roger.*

Gravenhunger *Gravehungre: William Malbedeng from Earl Roger. Enclosed hunting wood.* Quiet.

Greater Poston *Possetorna: Church of St Michael from Earl Roger.* Farm.

Great Hanwood *Hanewde: Roger FitzCorbet from Earl Roger.* Moated sites nearby.

Great Wytheford *Wicford: Rainald the Sheriff and William Pantulf from Earl Roger, and Alcher from Rainbald. Mill.* On the River Roden; remains of a fortified manor house.

Gretton *Grotintune: Rainald the Sheriff and Robert from Earl Roger.*

Grinshill *Grivelesul: Walchelin from Earl Roger.* Pretty; source of the 'white' stone used by the Romans to build *Viriconium*; Stone Grange, built or bought by Shrewsbury School as a refuge from the plague *c.*1617.

Hadley *Hatlege: Rainald the Sheriff from Earl Roger. Mill.* Industrial area.

Hadnall *Hadehelle: Rainald the Sheriff from Earl Roger.* Remains of moat.

Halston *Halstune/Haustune: Rainald the Sheriff from Earl Roger.* Late 17th-century Halston Hall; rare timber-framed hall.

Harcourt (in Stanton upon Hine Heath) *Harpecote: William Pantulf from Earl Roger.*

Harcourt (in Stottesdon) *Havretescote: Alcher from Earl Roger.* Upper Harcourt, a farmhouse.

Harley *Harlege: Helgot from Earl Roger. Mill.* There is a private house on the site of the watermill.

Hatton (in Shifnal) *Etone: Gerard from Earl Roger.* Hatton Grange, 1748, in parkland.

Haughton *Haustone: Roger Venator from Earl Roger.* Quiet; well watered; ancient earthworks at Ebury Hill.

Hawk(e)sley *Avochelie:* Lost.

Henley (in Bitterley) *Haneleu: Rainald the Sheriff from Earl Roger. Mill.* Henleyhill, a farmhouse.

Higford *Huchefor: Roger de Lacy from Earl Roger. Mill.* Pretty; on the River Worfe.

High Hatton *Hetune: Rainald the Sheriff from Earl Roger.* High Hatton Hall.

High Ercall *Archelou: Earl Roger. 2 mills, fishery (1502 large eels). By custom whenever the countess visited the manor 18 ounces of pence were brought to her.* Remains of moat. The hall was the last Shropshire garrison, except Ludlow, to hold out for the Royalists during the Civil Wars.

Highley *Hugelei: Ralph de Mortimer from Earl Roger.* Coal mining; in the Severn valley.

Hinstock *Stoche: William Pantulf from Earl Roger.*

Hockleton *Elchitun: Earl Roger.* Tiny; site of a motte and bailey castle.

Hodnet *Odenet: Earl Roger with the Church of St Peter holding the church.* Pretty; church with a Norman door; mound of a medieval castle nearby.

Hope Bendrid *Edretehope:* Lost.

Hope Bowdler *Fordritishope: Helgot from Earl Roger.* Stone built; hall.

Hopesay *Hope: Picot from Earl Roger. 2 enclosed hunting woods.* In cleft; hill-forts on Wart Hill and The Burrow.

Hopton (in Hodnet) *Hotune: Roger de Lacy from Earl Roger.* Hopton Farm.

Hopton Castle *Opetune: Picot from Earl Roger.* Ruined keep of a Norman castle; remains of an earlier fort nearby.

Hopton Wafers *Hoptone: Roger de Lacy.* Late Georgian manor house.

Hordley *Hordelei: Odo from Earl Roger.* Former seat of Kynaston family; Tudor brick barns.

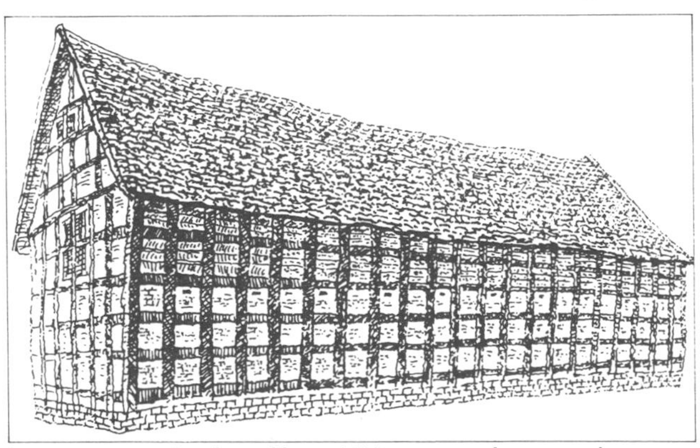

HODNET: *Fine timber-framed barn, 1619; water gardens at nearby Hodnet Hall cover 60 acres.*

Horton (in Hadley) *Hortune: William Pantulf from Earl Roger. Enclosed hunting wood.*

Horton (in Wem) *Hortune: William Pantulf from Earl Roger.* Horton Hall.

Howle *Hugle: Turold from Earl Roger. Mill.* Wooded; on the River Meese; New Caynton mill; manor house.

Huntington *Hantenetune: Ralph de Mortimer from Earl Roger. Mill (400 eels).* Scatter of buildings in an orchard.

Ightfield *Istefelt: Gerard from Earl Roger.* In landscape pock-marked with ponds. Tudor moated Ightfield Hall was the home of Arthur Cainwaring, an early 18th-century poet.

Ingardine *Ingurdine:* Lost.

Isle Farm *Aitone: Rainald the Sheriff from Earl Roger. Mill.* 17th-century Isle House; remains of medieval fishponds. The loop of the River Severn nearly forms an island.

Isombridge *Asnebruge: Ralph de Mortimer from Earl Roger. Mill.*

Kemberton *Chenbritone: Robert FitzTetbald from Earl Roger.* Large.

Kempton *Chenpitune: Picot from Earl Roger. 3 enclosed hunting woods.* Farming; on the River Kemp; facing Walcot Park.

Kenley *Chenelie: Rainald the Sheriff from Earl Roger.* Straggling.

Kingsnordley *Nordlege: Earl Roger. Mill.* Farmhouse with ponds; on the Staffordshire border.

Kinlet *Chinlete: Ralph de Mortimer and Richard from him.* Norman church in the grounds of 18th-century Kinlet Hall.

Kinnerley *Chenardelei: Ernucion from Earl Roger.* Belan Bank, the remains of a Norman motte and bailey castle built to preserve the border with Wales, nearby.

Kinnersley *Chinardeseie: Gerard from Earl Roger.* On the Weald Moors; large hill-fort at Wall.

Kynaston *Chimerestun: Rainald the Sheriff from Earl Roger.*

Lack *Lach:* Lost.

Lacon *Lach: Ranulf Peverel from Earl Roger.* Now 2 hamlets, Lower and Upper Lacon, in moorland.

Langley *Languelege: Toret from Earl Roger.* The seat of the Lee family; Sir Richard Lee was a Royalist commander. Only a timber-framed gate-house remains of their home.

Lawley *Lauelei/lie: William Pantulf; Turold from Earl Roger.* Industrial; on the edge of Telford.

Leaton *Letone: Anschitil from Earl Roger.* Severnside; in a wooded setting.

Ledwyche *Ledewic: William Pantulf from Earl Roger.* Now Upper Ledwyche; on the Ledwyche Brook.

Lee (in Leebotwood) *Lege:* Lost.

Le(e)botwood *Botewde: Auti, the pre-Conquest holder, from Earl Roger.* Castle Hill earthworks nearby. The name means 'clearing in the Forest of Botwood'.

Lee Brockhurst *Lege: Norman from Earl Roger. Mill.* In hunting country.

Leegomery *Lega: Rainald the Sheriff from Earl Roger.* Industrial; Leegomery House.

Leighton *Lestone: Rainald the Sheriff from Earl Roger. Mill.* Hall of the Leighton and Kynnersley families, who dominated the area from the 13th to the 19th century; Kynnersley Arms Inn, formerly a mill.

Lesser Poston *Possetorne: Helgot from Earl Roger.* Isolated farm.

Lilleshall *Linleshelle: Church of St Almund and Godebold the priest from the church. Mill.* Large; abbey church.

Little Drayton *Draitune: Turold from Earl Roger.* Suburb of Market Drayton.

Little Dawley *Dalelie: Rainald the Sheriff from Earl Roger.* Area near Great Dawley.

Little Ness *Nesse: Rainald the Sheriff from Earl Roger. Mill (600 eels).* Pretty; castle motte; watermill near Adcote House.

Little Sutton *Sudtone: William Pantulf from Earl Roger.* Farming.

Little Wenlock *Wenloch: Church of St Milburga before and after 1066. 2 enclosed hunting woods, eyrie of falcons.* Compact; under the Wrekin; densely wooded.

Little Wytheford *Wideford: Roger de Lacy and Fulco from Earl Roger.*

Llanvair Waterdine *Watredene: Ralph de Mortimer.* Sheep-farming; on the River Teme, at the Welsh border.

Longden *Langedune: Robert FitzCorbet from Earl Roger.* Straggling.

Longdon-upon-Tern *Languedune: Church of St Almund.* One street; hall, a fragment of an impressive Tudor mansion.

Longford *Langeford: Turold from Earl Roger. Mill.* By the Strine Brook; Hall (1794–97) by the Italian architect Joseph Bonomi.

Longner *Languenare: Bishop of Chester and Wigot from him.* Hall by John Nash. Edward Burton, a Protestant zealot, who died from joy on learning that Elizabeth I had acceded to the throne, is buried in its garden.

Longslow *Walanceslau: Gerard from Earl Roger.*

Loppington *Lopitone: Earl Roger.* Queen Anne hall. The church was attacked and set alight in 1643 by Royalist forces determined to capture an enemy garrison within.

Loton *Luchetune: Roger FitzCorbet from Earl Roger. Enclosed hunting wood.* Loton Park; deer park, developed from the hunting wood.

The Low(e) (in Wem) *Lai: Roger de Lacy from Earl Roger.* Lowe Hill farm.

Lowe (in Stottesdon) *Lau: Ralph de Mortimer and Richard from him.* Lowe Farm.

Ludford *Ludeford: Osbern FitzRichard. Mill.* Connected to Ludlow by a 15th-century bridge; mill.

Lutwyche *Loteis: Rainald the Sheriff from Earl Roger and Richard from him.* Lutwyche Hall, a late 16th-century brick mansion, now a school.

Lydbury North *Lideberie: Bishop of Hereford before and after 1066. Church, mill supplying the manor house.* Huddled; late Norman church; Walcot Hall, built after 1763 for Clive of India.

Lydham *Lidum: Earl Roger. Mill.* Manor house nearby.

Lydley Heys *Litlega:* Lost.

Madeley *Madelie: Church of St Milburga before and after 1066.* Town with a grange built by the priors of Much Wenlock, probably in the 13th century. It was a thriving iron-manufacturing centre in the 19th century, and home of the industrialist Abraham Darby from 1709 until his death in 1717.

Maesbrook *Meresbroc: Rainald the Sheriff from Earl Roger.* Area with many Welsh place names.

Maesbury *Meresberie: Earl Roger and Rainald the Sheriff from him. Oswestry castle (built by Rainald), church.* Scattered communities.

Market Drayton *Draitune: William Pantulf from Earl Roger.* Town with fine 18th-century buildings; well known for the manufacture of horse-hair for chairs in the 19th century.

Marchamley *Marcemeslei: Rainald the Sheriff from Earl Roger. Mill.* Overlooking wooded Hawkstone Park.

Marrington *Meritune: Robert FitzCorbet.* Isolated; on the River Camlad; Marrington Hall.

Marton *Mertune: Edward from Church of St Chad, who held it before and after 1066.* Close to the Welsh border. Thomas Bray, who was instrumental in founding the Society for Promoting Christian Knowledge, was born at Marton Crest, 1656.

Mawley *Melela: Ralph de Mortimer.* Mawley Hall c.1730, set in parkland; Mawleytown Farm.

Meadowley *Madolea: Helgot from Earl Roger.*

Melverley *Melevrlei: Rainald the Sheriff from Earl Roger.* On the River Vyrnwy at the Welsh border.

Meole Brace *Melam/Mela: Ralph de Mortimer and Church of St Mary from him. Mill.* Suburb of Shrewsbury.

Merrington *Gellidone: Picot from Earl Roger.* Medieval shape; large green; ponds.

Middlehope *Mildehope: Roger de Lacy from Earl Roger.* On Wenlock Edge; remains of a large motte and bailey castle.

Middleton (in Bitterley) *Middeltone: William Pantulf from Earl Roger. Mill.* Norman church.

Middleton (in Chirbury) *Mildetune: Robert FitzCorbet and Ertein, the pre-Conquest holder, from Earl Roger.* Isolated on a hilltop; many prehistoric standing stones.

Middleton *Scriven Middeltone: Rainald the Sheriff from Earl Roger.*

Millichope *Melicope: Helgot from Earl Roger.* Upper Millichope Farm, a 14th-century stone-built tower house, was probably the manor house.

Milson *Mulstone: Osbern FitzRichard.* Orchards; Norman church; manor farm.

Minsterley *Menistrelie: Earl Roger and Roger FitzCorbet from him.* Busy.

Minton *Munetune: Picot from Earl Roger. Enclosed hunting wood.* The arrangement of cottages and gardens around a green suggests a Saxon settlement; Saxon castle mound.

Montford *Maneford: Roger from Earl Roger. ½ fishery.* Quiet; Severnside.

MORETON CORBET: *House incorporating castle ruins.*

Moreton Corbet *Mortone: Turold from Earl Roger.* Ruins of an Elizabethan house, in corporating parts of an earlier castle.

Moreton Say *Mortune: Roger de Lacy from Earl Roger.* Clive of India (1725–74) was born at nearby Styche Hall.

Morton (in Oswestry) *Mortune: Rainald the Sheriff from Earl Roger.* Straggling.

Morville *Membrefelde: Earl Roger with Church of St Peter, Shrewsbury holding the church and Richard the Butler and the earl's chaplains from Earl Roger. Mill.* Elizabethan Morville Hall; church with many Norman features including a font and door ironwork.

Moston *Mostune: Roger Venator from Earl Roger.*

Much Wenlock *Wenloch:* See page 220.

Myddle *Mulleht: Rainald the Sheriff from Earl Roger.* Circular stair turret of castle. Richard Gough's *History of Myddle* is a graphic chronicle of the village in the 17th century.

Myndtown *Munete: Picot from Earl Roger.* Under the Long Mynd cliffs; many tumuli.

Mytton *Mutone: Church of St Mary and Picot from the church.* On the Severn.

Neen Savage *Neen: Ralph de Mortimer and Ingelrann from him. Mill.* Papermaking was once a flourishing local industry.

Neen Sol(l)ars *Nene: Osbern FitzRichard and Siward, the pre-Conquest holder, from him. Mill.* Between the Mill Brook and River Rea; weir.

Neenton *Newentone: Ralph de Mortimer from Earl Roger.* On the River Rea.

Netley *Netelie: Earl Roger.* Netley Hall in parkland; Netley Old Hall, a country house; Higher, Side and Lower Netley Farms; earthwork.

Norton (in Aston Botterell) *Nortone: Rainald the Sheriff from Earl Roger.* Farmhouse.

Norton (in Condover) *Nortune: William Pantulf from Earl Roger.* Norton Farm.

Norton in Hales *Nortune: Helgot from Earl Roger.* Large; on the Staffordshire border.

Oaks *Hach: Robert FitzCorbet from Earl Roger.*

Obley *Obelie: Picot from Earl Roger.* Isolated; sheep-farming country.

Oldbury *Aldeberie: Rainald the Sheriff from Earl Roger. Mill.* Growing; Daniel's Mill; castle mound.

Onibury *Aneberie: Bishop of Hereford before and after 1066 and Roger de Lacy from him.* Norman church.

Onneley *Anelege: William Malbedeng from Earl Roger.*

Onslow *Andreslaue:* Lost.

Onslow (near Ford) *Andrelau: Church of St Chad before and after 1066.* Hall, 1820.

Osbaston *Sbernestune: Rainald the Sheriff from Earl Roger.*

PRESTON GUBBALS: *Looking across to Long Mountain with its ancient camp*

Oswestry *Luure: Earl Roger and Rainald the Sheriff from him. Castle, church.* Town with the mound of the castle built by Rainald, and Old Oswestry, a huge Iron Age hill-fort. Canon Spooner was educated at the Grammar School about 450 years after its foundation in 1407.

Overs *Ovre: Siward, the pre-Conquest holder, from Earl Roger.*

Overton *Ovretone: Ralph de Mortimer from Earl Roger.* Quiet.

Oxenbold *Oxibola: Helgot from Earl Roger.* Great and Little Oxenbold, farmhouses.

Patton *Patintune: Roger de Lacy from Earl Roger.*

Peplow *Papelau: Ralph de Mortimer from Earl Roger.* Georgian Peplow Hall, home of the eccentric millionaire philanthropist Francis Stanier (d. 1900).

Petton *Pectone: Robert Pincerna from Earl Roger.* Medieval castle mound; moat nearby.

Pickthorn *Pichetorne:* Lost.

Pitchford *Piceforde: Turold from Earl Roger.* 16th-century hall, possibly Britain's finest black and white house, is on the site of an earlier manor house.

Plaish *Plesham: Roger de Lacy from Earl Roger.* Pla(i)sh Hall, built c.1540.

Polmere *Pole: Alward son of Elmund from Earl Roger.*

Pontesbury *Pantesberie: Roger FitzCorbet from Earl Roger. Mill (corn-rent).* Small town since the 16th century; prehistoric hill-forts on Pontesbury Hill; castle mounds.

Poynton *Peventone: Ulviet, the pre-Conquest holder, from Earl Roger.* The wall of a medieval chapel is incorporated into a farm outbuilding.

Prees *Pres: Bishop of Chester before and after 1066 and Anschitil and Fulcher from him.* Large, spread-out; manor house.

Preston Brockhurst *Preston(e): Turold; Gerard from Earl Roger.* Green.

Preston Gubbals *Prestone: Church of St Almund before and after 1066 and Godebold from the church.* Named after Godebold the priest, one of Earl Roger's men.

Preston Montford *Prestone/tune: Church of St Almund before and after 1066; Roger FitzCorbet from Earl Roger.* Severnside; early 18th-century hall.

Preston upon the Weald Moors *Prestune: Ralph de Mortimer from Earl Roger.* Flat country.

Priest Weston *Westune: Robert FitzCorbet from Earl Roger.* In moorland; on the Welsh border; many cairns and standing stones.

Pulestone *Plivesdon: Turold from Earl Roger.* Chetwynd Park.

Pulley *Polelie: Teodulf from Earl Roger; Ralph de Mortimer.* Near Bayston Hill.

Purslow *Posselau: Picot from Earl Roger.* On a crossroads; hall.

Quatford *Quatford: Earl Roger.* Large; Norman church, founded by Earl Roger at the request of his 2nd wife, the Countess Adeliza; castle mound nearby. The Danish ford from which the village takes its name still survives.

Quatt *Quatone: Outi, the pre-Conquest holder, from Earl Roger. Mill.* Early 18th-century Dower House.

Ratlinghope *Roetelingehope: Robert FitzCorbet from Earl Roger.* Isolated; in wild country; hill-forts; manor house.

Rhiston *Ristune: Elward from Earl Roger.* Near Offa's Dyke.

Rodington *Rodintone: Rainald the Sheriff from Earl Roger. Church, mill.* On the River Roden; church, 1851.

Romsley *Rameslege: Walter from Earl Roger.* On the Staffordshire/Worcestershire border.

Rorrington *Roritune: Roger and Robert, sons of Corbet, from Earl Roger.* Hillside; castle mound.

Rossall *Rosela: Church of St Chad.* Rossal Grange, 1677, overlooking the Severn.

Rowton (in Alberbury) *Rutune: Alward son of Elmund from Earl Roger.* Gothicized Queen Anne mansion (1809–12) on the site of a medieval castle.

Rowton (in Ercall Magna) *Routone: Eddiet from Earl Roger.* Birthplace of Dr Richard Baxter (1615–91), the eminent divine.

Rudge *Rigge: Ralph from Earl Roger.* Rudge Hall; on the Staffordshire border.

Rushbury *Riseberie: Roger de Lacy from Earl Roger. Mill, falcon's eyrie.* Attractive; Norman church with material from a nearby Roman station; timber-framed manor house.

Ruthall *Rohalle: Gerard from Earl Roger.* Secluded.

Ruyton-of-the-Eleven-Towns *Ruitone: Odo from Earl Roger. 5 fisheries.* Castle ruins.

Ryton *Ruitone: Osbern FitzRichard from Earl Roger. Mill.* Pretty.

Sambrook *Semebre: Turold from Earl Roger. Mill.* Quiet; mill.

Sandford *Sandord: Gerard. Enclosed hunting wood.* Compact; early 18th-century hall; ponds; castle mound.

RUSHBURY: *An example of vernacular architecture.*

Shavington *Savintune: Nigel from Earl Roger.* Hall, 1685, in vast grounds on the Cheshire border; moated site.

Shawbury *Sawesberie: Gerard from Earl Roger. Church, mill.* Large; adjoining airfield; late Norman church nearby.

Sheet *Setham: Ralph de Mortimer and Ingelrann from him.*

Sheinton *Sc(h)entune: Ralph de Mortimer from Earl Roger. Mill.* In the Severn valley.

Shelton *Saltone: Bishop of Chester and Church of St Chad from him.* On the outskirts of Shrewsbury.

Sheriff Hales *Halam/Halas: Rainald the Sheriff from Earl Roger. Mill.* Pond near the site of the medieval manor house.

Shifnall *Iteshale: Robert FitzTetbald from Earl Roger.* Small town, once a Georgian coaching town.

Shipley *Sciplei: Ralph from Earl Roger.*

Shipton *Scipetune: Church of St Milburga before and after 1066.* Tiny; hall, 1587.

Shrawardine *Saleurdine: Rainald the Sheriff from Earl Roger.* Masonry from a medieval keep dismantled by the Roundheads in 1645.

Shrewsbury *Ciropesberie: Earl Roger.* County town, an important military centre until the Civil War and a leading trading centre for wool and cloth. The medieval street plan remains; many timber-framed buildings.

Sibdon Carwood *Sibetune: Picot from Earl Roger.* Isolated; 17th-century castle.

Sidbury *Sudberie: Ralph de Mortimer from Earl Roger.*

Siefton *Sireton: Earl Roger.* Orchards; ponds.

Sleapa *Eslepe: William Pantulf from Earl Roger.* Farmhouse on the edge of an airfield.

Smethcott *Smerecote: Edmund, the pre-Conquest holder, from Earl Roger.* Castle mound.

STOKESAY: *The fortified manor house.*

Soulton *Suletune: Church of St Michael.* Soulton Hall, 1668.

Spoonley *Sponelege: Nigel from Earl Roger.*

Stanton Lacy *Stantone: Roger de Lacy and Richard, Azelin, Roger and Auti from him; Church of St Peter. Church, 3 mills.* Mainly Saxon church.

Stanton *Stantune: Roger de Lacy from Earl Roger and Herbert from him; Helgot from Earl Roger. Castle, church.* Now 2 villages: Holdgate which has a castle mound, the remains of a castle built by Helgot; and Stanton Long, which has developed since the 13th century.

Stanton upon Hine Heath *Stantune: Rainald the Sheriff from Earl Roger and Richard from him. Church, mill. Smith.* Early Norman church; 2 mills; Forge coppice across the River Roden.

Stanwardine in the Fields *Staurdine: Robert Pincerna from Earl Roger.*

Stanway *Staneweie: Rainald the Sheriff from Earl Roger.* Late Victorian Stanway Manor House.

Stapleton *Hundeslit: Roger FitzCorbet and Alward from Earl Roger.* Norman castle mound; Tudor house on a medieval stone plinth.

Steel *Stile: Roger de Curcelle from Earl Roger.* Steel Heath.

Stepple *Steple: Ralph de Mortimer and Goisfrid from him.* Stepple Hall.

Steventon *Scevintone: Helgot from Earl Roger.* Jacobean manor house.

Stockton *Stochetone: Gerard from Earl Roger.*

Stoke St Milborough *Godestoch: Church of St Milburga from Earl Roger.* Church; ancient well; named after the Saxon saint, Milburga.

Stokesay *Stoches: Roger de Lacy. Mill.* Fortified manor house built by Laurence de Ludlow, a wealthy clothier, in 1290. Undamaged by the Civil War, it is one of the finest examples of its kind in Britain.

Stoke upon Tern *Stoche(s): Roger de Lacy from Earl Roger. Church, mill.* Victorian church; manor house with earthworks and ponds.

Stottesdon *Stodesdone: Earl Roger. Mill.* Quiet; church with a Saxon doorway and early Norman tower and font.

Strefford *Straford: Rainald the Sheriff from Earl Roger.* Strefford Hall.

Stretton *Stratun(e): Earl Roger. Church, mill, 5 enclosed hunting woods.* Now All Stretton, a village, Little Stretton, a hamlet and Church Stretton.

Sutton (near Shrewsbury) *Sudtone: Church of St Milburga before and after 1066.* Outer suburb of Shrewsbury, spring dispensing metallic-tasting water.

Sutton Maddock *Sudtone: Gerard from Earl Roger.* Quiet; Severnside.

Sutton upon Tern *Sudtone: Roger de Curcelle from Earl Roger. Mill.*

Tets(t)ill *Tedenesolle: Osbern FitzRichard.*

The Marsh *Me(r)sse: Roger and Robert, sons of Corbet, from Earl Roger.* Timber-framed manor house, 1604.

Tibberton *Tetbristone: Roger de Curcelle from Earl Roger.* Long; manor house.

Ticklerton *Tichelevorde: Church of St Milburga before and after 1066.* Secluded.

Tittenley *Titesle: William Malbank from Earl Hugh.* Tittenley Farm.

Tong *Tuange Earl Roger.*

TONG: *The church is filled with monuments, like this one to the Vernon family, 16th c.*

Tugford *Dodefort: Church of St Peter (given by Rainald the Sheriff for the soul of Warin, his predecessor) Rainald the Sheriff from Earl Hugh and Rayner from him. Mill.* Norman church.

Uckington *Uchintune: Church of St Almund and Godebold from it.* Farming.

Uffington *Ofitone: Helgot from Earl Roger.* Severnside.

Uppington *Opetone: Gerard from Earl Roger.* Church with a Saxon tympanum and a Roman alter in the north wall.

Upton Cresset *Ultone: Rainald the Sheriff from Earl Roger.* .

Upton Magna *Uptune: Rainald the Sheriff from Earl Roger. Mill, fishery.* Homestead moat in a wood nearby.

Walcot *Walecote: Earl Roger.*

Walford *Waleford: Robert Pincerna from Earl Roger.*

Walltown *Walle: Ralph de Mortimer from Earl Roger.* On the site of a Roman fort.

Walton *Waltone: Ralph de Mortimer from Earl Roger.* Farmhouse.

Waters Upton *Uptone: Roger de Lacy from Earl Roger. Mill.* Named after an early lord of the manor, Walter FitzJohn.

Wattlesborough *Wetesburg: Roger FitzCorbet from Earl Roger.* Georgian Hall with farm buildings and a Norman keep, one of the chain of defences against the Welsh.

Welbatch *Huelbec: Roger FitzCorbet from Earl Roger. Mill.* 17th-century Seveon's Mill, now derelict.

Wellington *Walitone: Earl Roger. Mill, 2 fisheries.* Industrial town, a manufacturing centre for glass and nails during the 19th century.

Welshampton *Hantone: Rainald the Sheriff from Earl Roger and Albert from him.* On the Welsh border; Hampton House.

Wem *Weme: William Pantulf from Earl Roger. Falcon's eyrie, enclosed hunting wood.* Small market town. The notorious Judge Jeffreys was sold the barony of Wem, 1685.

Wentnor *Wantenoure: Roger FitzCorbet from Earl Roger.* Stone built under Long Mynd. Robury Ring is a rectangular camp.

Westbury *Wesberie: Roger FitzCorbet from Earl Roger..*

West Felton *Feltone: Rainald the Sheriff from Earl Roger.* Castle moat and mound.

Westhope *Weshone: Picot from Earl Roger.* In Hope Dale; moated site; manor house, 1901.

Weston Cot(t)on *Westune: Rainald the Sheriff from Earl Roger.* Ancient Wat's Dyke nearby.

Weston Rhyn *Westone: Rainald the Sheriff from Earl Roger.*

Weston under Redcastle *Westune: Ranulf Peverel from Earl Roger.* Pretty; parkland scenery; 13th-century Red Castle, now ruined; Bury Walls, an Iron Age fort.

Wheathill *Waltham: Roger de Lacy from Earl Roger.*

Whitchurch *Westune/tone: William de Warenne from Earl Roger, formerly Earl Harold. 3 enclosed hunting woods.* Town with Georgian buildings; birthplace of Edward German the composer (1862–1936).

Whittingslow *Witecheslaw: Earl Roger.*

Whittington *Wititone: Earl Roger. Mill.* Gatehouse of a 13th-century castle.

Whitton *Wibetune: Roger FitzCorbet from Earl Roger.* Whitton Hall; Whitton Grange; Whitton Farm.

Whixall *Witehala: Ranulf Peverel from Earl Roger.* Near the Welsh border; moated site.

Wigmore *Wigemore.* Lost.

Wigwig *Wigewic: Turold from Earl Roger.* Moated site.

WROXETER: *Roman remains from the settlement of* Viroconium.

Wilderley *Wildredelega: Hugh son of Turgis from Earl Roger.* Remains of motte and bailey castle.

Willey *Wilit: Turold from Earl Roger.* The old village was removed in c.1815 to provide privacy for the Forrester family.

Winsley *Wineslei: Roger FitzCorbet from Earl Roger.* Winsley Hall.

Wistanstow *Wistanestou: Nigel the Doctor.* Moated site, well on the River Onny.

Withington *Wientone: Fulco from Earl Roger.* Flat country.

Wollaston *Willavestune: Roger FitzCorbet from Earl Roger.* Motte and bailey castle site.

Wollerton *Uluretone: Gerard from Earl Roger. Mill.* On the River Tern.

Wolverley *Ulwardelege: William Pantulf from Earl Roger.* Isolated; Wolverley Hall.

Womerton *Umbruntune: Robert FitzCorbet from Earl Roger.*

Woodcote (in Bicton) *Udecote: Robert FitzCorbet from Earl Roger.* Pond.

Woodcote (near Newport) *Udecote: Robert FitzTetbald from Earl Roger.* Woodcote Hall.

Woolstaston *Ulestanestune: Robert FitzCorbet from Earl Roger.* Quiet; Castle Bank, the probable site of a pre-1292 manor house.

Woolston (in West Felton) *Osuluestune: Rainald the Sheriff from Earl Roger.* St Winifred's well marks spot where the saint's body rested on its way from Holywell to Shrewsbury.

Woolston (in Wistanstow) *Wistanestune: Picot from Earl Roger.*

Woore *Waure: William Malbedeng from Earl Roger.* Large; hall; moated site at Syllenhurst Farm.

Wootton *Udetone: Rainald the Sheriff from Earl Roger.*

Worfield *Gurulede/Wrfeld: Hugh de Montgumeri. 3 mills, fishery.* Timber-framed buildings.

Worthen *Wrdine: Roger FitzCorbet from Earl Roger. 2 mills, enclosed hunting woods.* Large; on Rea Brook.

Wotherton *Udevertune: Alward son of Elmund, the pre-Conquest holder, from Earl Roger. Mill.* Castle mound.

Wrentnall *Werentenehale: Roger Venator from Earl Roger. Enclosed hunting wood.*

Wrockwardine *Recordine: Earl Roger with the Church of St Peter holding the church.* Norman church; Jacobean Hall.

Wroxeter *Rochecestre: Rainald the Sheriff from Earl Roger. Church.* The Roman city of *Viriconium*. Saxon church.

Wykey *Wiche: Odo from Earl Roger. Fishery.*

Yagdon *Iagedone:* Lost.

Yockleton *Iochehuile: Roger FitzCorbet from Earl Roger. Mill (1 horseload of malt).* Castle mound.

Yorton *Iartune: Church of St Chad before and after 1066.*

Wales Gazetteer

Ackhill *Achel: Osbern FitzRichard.* Wood; Ackhill Lodge.

Ackley *Achelai: Elward from Earl Roger.* Ackley Farm.

Aston *Esto(u)ne: Earl Roger.* Aston Hall; near a hill-fort.

Bausley *Beleslei: Earl Roger and Roger FitzCorbet from him.* Area with Bausley House, Bausley Hill and Iron Age fort remains.

Castlewright *Cestelop:* Lost.

Churchstoke *Cirestoc: Earl Roger and Elward from him.*

Edderton *Edritune: Roger Corbet from Earl Roger.* Edderton Hall.

Forden *Furtune: Roger Corbet from Earl Roger.* Scattered; near Offa's Dyke, an ancient system of earthworks that stretched 120 miles.

Hem *Heme: Roger Corbet from Earl Roger.* Some houses.

Hopton *Hoptune: Roger Corbet from Earl Roger.* Scattered; areas of Hopton Uchaf and Hopton Isaf nearby.

Hyssington *Stantune: Roger Corbet from Earl Roger.*

Knighton *Chenistetune: Hugh Lasne. A great wood.* Industrial town with forestry and saw-mills; motte and bailey.

Leighton *Lestune: Earl Roger and Roger Corbet from him.* Leighton Hall.

Mellington *Muletune/Mulitune: Roger Corbet and Elward from Earl Roger.* Now Lower Mellington.

Montgomery *Montgomeri/Muntgumeri: Earl Roger built the castle; Roger Corbet.* Site of an ancient British camp. The motte and bailey probably marks the site of Earl Roger's castle; the present castle ruins date from the 13th century.

Norton *Nortune: Hugh de Lasne. A great wood.* Norton Manor in parkland; motte and bailey; wood.

Stanage *Stanege: Osbern FitzRichard.* A few houses at Lower Stanage on the River Teme; Stanage Park.

Thornbury *Torneberie: Roger Corbet from Earl Roger.* Area near a Roman road; Romn fort.

Weston *Westune: Roger Corbet from Earl Roger.* Little and Great Weston farms in Weston Madoc.

Wolston Mynd *Ulestanesmude:* Lost.

Woodluston *Wadelestun:* Lost.

Wropton *Urbetune:* Lost.

Somerset

There are approximately one million acres of Somerset, and its topography is extremely varied, from the high wastes of Exmoor in the north-west to the flat boggy lands beneath the River Severn. The climate is remarkably mild: a few places such as Glastonbury were able to cultivate vineyards at the time of Domesday; *the industry has begun again in a small way today.*

Somerset was known to the Saxons as Somer Shire, and its inhabitants were called Sumersetas. Its areas of bleak hills and unproductive bog were thinly populated in early times, but there was much valuable pasture and cultivated land elsewhere in the county. After the Conquest, the king either retained these holdings himself, or allocated them to his Norman barons – in particular to Robert, Count of Mortain, who ruled over 86 manors with a greedy and iron hand from his castle at Montacute.

Another set of returns, known as the Exeter (Exon)Domesday, *covered the three western counties of Somerset, Devon and Cornwall, as well as part of Dorset and one holding in Wiltshire, and included details about animals, names and jobs, omitted from the so-called Exchequer version. These details are included in the translations of the entries used here.*

Nether Stowey

Alfred [d'Epaignes] holds (NETHER) STOWEY *STALWEI* himself. Earl Harold held it before 1066; it paid tax for 3 hides. Land for 5 ploughs. In lordship 1 plough; 5 slaves; 2 hides. 8 villagers and 4 smallholders with 2 ploughs. A mill which pays 4d; meadow, 7 acres; pasture, 100 acres; woodland, 1 1/2 leagues in both length and width. 9 cattle; 7 pigs; 100 sheep, less 10. Value £10; when he acquired it, £8.

Osward and Alfward hold (Nether) Stowey from Alfred. They held it themselves before 1066; it paid tax for 2 hides. Land for 4 ploughs. In lordship 1 1/2 ploughs & the whole of that land, with 1 slave; 4 villagers and 3 smallholders with 1 plough & 1/2 virgate. Meadow, 3 acres; woodland, 1 league. 8 pigs; 20 sheep. Value always 20s. This land has been added to Alfwy's land which Alfred holds.

Alfred held twenty-four manors in Somerset, six of which he kept for himself. Among them was one of the two manors that made up Stowey; it was by far his most valuable property lying on the edge of the Quantock hills and thus ideally placed for sheep farming.

Nether Stowey is an exceptionally pretty, unspoiled village, with rows of plastered and pantiled houses crowding its few narrow streets. One, at the end of Lime Street, was the home of Samuel Taylor Coleridge between 1797 and 1800. He wrote much of his finest verse here, including *Christabel* and *The Ancient Mariner*. He rented his little cottage for eight guineas a year from his friend, the wealthy tanner Tom Poole, a native of the village. Coleridge was twenty-four when he arrived, and blissfully contented with his young wife Sara and his infant son:

'From seven till half past eight I work in my garden, from breakfast till twelve I read and compose, then read again, feed the pigs, poultry, etc. till two o'clock; after dinner work again till tea; from tea till supper, *review*. So jogs the day, and I am happy . . . my little David Hartley grows a sweet boy and has high health . . . You would smile to see my eye rolling up to the ceiling in a lyric fury, and on my knee a diaper pinned to warm . . .'

The cottage was dark and dingy, with two little beamed parlours downstairs and three small, draughty bedrooms upstairs. Coleridge later recalled Sara's forcing him out of bed on cold winter mornings in his nightshirt to light the fire before she would get up and dress the baby. She was less enamoured of their poor life than he, a prime cause in the eventual break-up of their marriage.

William and Dorothy Wordsworth lived nearby at Alfoxden, and it was during a walk with William, along the coast near Minehead, that Coleridge conceived the idea for *The Ancient Mariner*. He began to use the drug laudanum (tincture of opium) at Nether Stowey as a pain-killer and if he realized its dangers, he was none the less enchanted by its effects: 'An illness . . . originated in the stump of a tooth over which some matter had formed; this affected my eye, my eye my stomach, my stomach my head, and the consequence was a general fever, and the sum of pain was considerably increased by the vain attempt of our surgeon to extract the offending member. Laudanum gave me repose, not sleep; but you, I believe, know how divine that repose is, what a spot of enchantment, a green spot of fountain and flowers and trees in the very heart of a waste of sands! . . .'

The country surrounding Nether Stowey that Coleridge loved so much is little changed, although the inn facing his cottage is now called The Ancient Mariner. The hills where Alfred's sheep once grazed are now rich pasture dotted with small dairy farms, as they were in the poet's time when he fell in love with the landscape's gentle beauty.

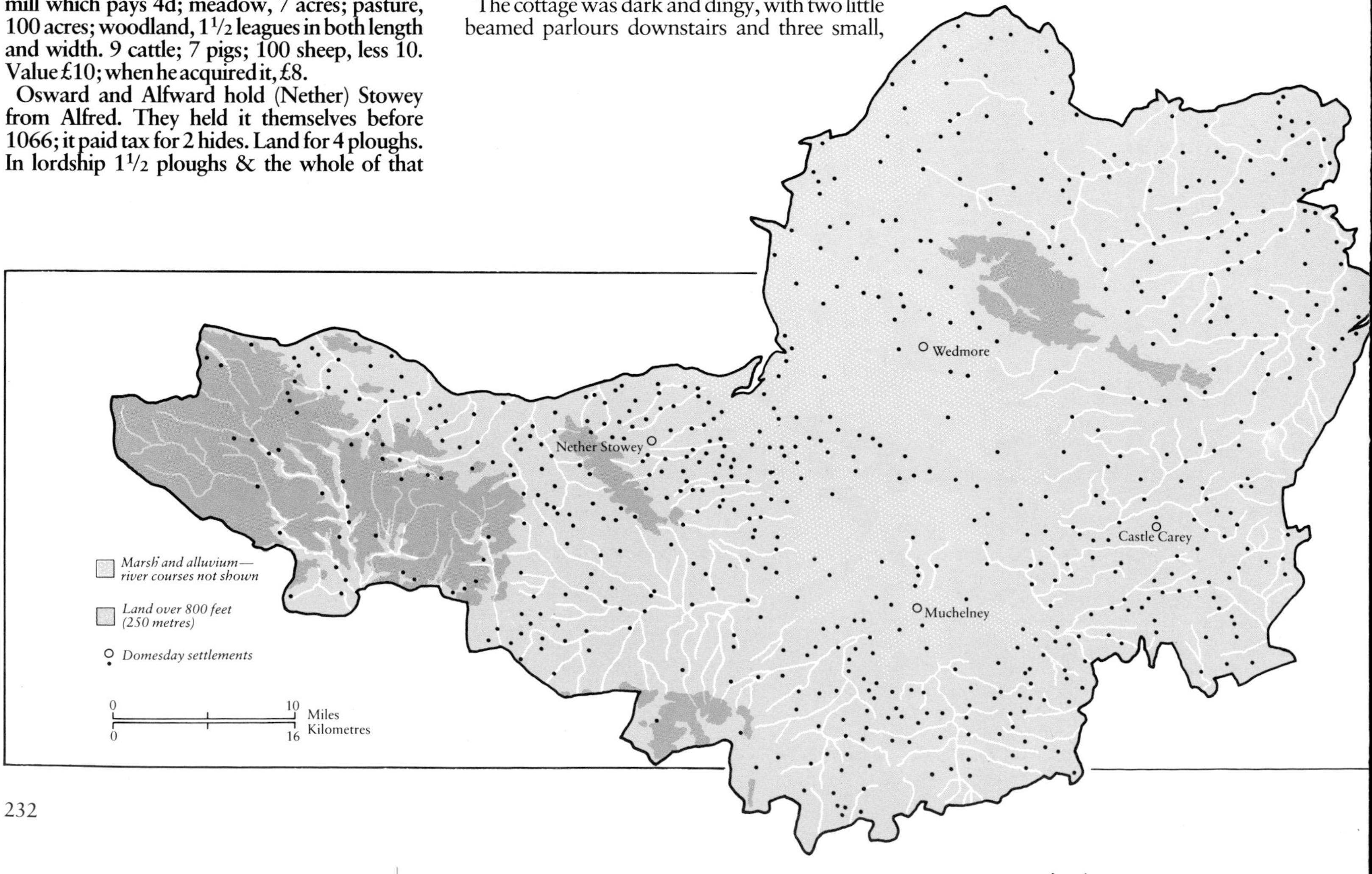

CASTLE CARY: *Earthworks on the site of the 12th-c. castle.*

Muchelney

St Peter's Church, Muchelney, has 4 carucates of land which have never paid tax in these 3 islands: MUCHELNEY *MICHELENIE*, MIDELNEY and THORNEY. In lordship 2 ploughs; vineyard, 1 *arpent*. 4 slaves. 3 villagers and 18 smallholders with 2 ploughs. 2 fisheries which pay 6000 eels; meadow, 25 acres; woodland, 12 acres, pasture, 100 acres. 1 cob; 21 cattle; 6 pigs; 30 goats. The value was and is £3.

The 'little monastery' of Muchelney, as King Ethelred referred to it in 995, lies on the edge of the wet, peaty land of Sedgemoor, which had consisted of islands and watercourses until systematic drainage and land reclamation began in the thirteenth century. The *Domesday* entry credits Muchelney with a few pigs, goats and cattle, but even when these are combined with its vineyard and fisheries, they add up to a very few assets for a religious foundation.

According to tradition, King Athelstan founded the abbey in 933, to atone for his part in the murder of his brother Edwin, whom he had sent out to sea in a small open boat during a storm. But the foundation is older than that: there were Benedictines here in the eighth century. Although the monastery was small, its inhabitants were more than comfortable. In 1335 the abbot was reprimanded for the luxury in which his monks lived. They slept in private rooms instead of dormitories, ate in private if they chose – and from costly plate, not simple utensils – and came and went as they pleased. The public, it seems, wandered in and out of the cloisters just as freely.

The abbey was dissolved in 1538, and then, too, the lack of authority aroused comment: 'I found the abbot negligent and of doubtful character; and ten brethren which all war ignorant and unlernyd and in manor no servauntes maynteynyd or hospialite kept', an official visitor complained.

In the late Middle Ages a church was founded next door to serve the needs of the villagers. It was not under the monastery's authority, but its vicar received a large loaf daily 'and two pitchers of the best conventual ale, and from the abbey kitchen twice a week . . . a dish of meat; but the rest of the week only a dish of eggs or fish, at the pleasure of the kitchen steward'. The church's most notable feature is the wooden 'waggon' roof over the nave, painted with a flock of angels, many bare-breasted and bearing words of advice. 'Com up hether', one beckons; 'Flye to mercy', another counsels.

Only traces of the abbey's Norman church remain, although its crypt is clearly visible. The abbot's house is in fine condition, but other domestic parts of the monastery are now farm buildings. The waste-land that surrounded the 'Great island' of Muchelney in the time of *Domesday* is now rich pasture. An air of peace and seclusion still hangs over the abbey ruins, keeping them, as an eighteenth-century visitor observed, 'a place well adapted to retirement and religious contemplation'.

Castle Cary

Walter holds (CASTLE) CARY *CARI*. Alfsi held it before 1066; it paid tax for 15 hides. Land for 20 ploughs, of which 8 hides are in lordship; 6 ploughs there; 6 slaves; 23 villagers and 20 smallholders with 17 ploughs & 7 hides. 3 mills which pay 34s; meadow, 100 acres; woodland 1 league long and 1/2 league wide. 2 cobs; 16 cattle; 20 pigs. 8 pigmen who pay 50 pigs. 117 sheep. A burgess in Ilchester and another in Bruton pay 16 1/2d to this manor. Value when he acquired it, £16; now £15.

The prosperous manor of Cary was in the hands of Walter (probably Walter of Bainton), who held it from the Norman Walter de Douai. The latter was tenant-in-chief of 37 manors in the county, of which Cary was the most valuable. An abundance of meadow and woodland made it ideal for cattle and pig farming, and its mills, powered by the little River Cary, must have been flourishing, to be worth an annual rent of thirty-four shillings.

The castle that provides the prefix to the town's modern name is heard of first in 1138, and last, less than twenty years later. It had been besieged by the Norman King Stephen in his fight against his cousin Maud for the English throne. Its site, excavated in the nineteenth century, showed it to have been a fairly massive fortification.

Until the Industrial Revolution, the town was famous for a tough woollen cloth known as Cary, which was mentioned in William Langland's fourteenth-century epic, *The Vision of Piers the Plowman*. When mechanization eventually settled the wool industry in the north of England there was much unemployment and unrest here. It was then that a little windowless circular lock-up – now a tourist attraction – was built, to chastise the unruly.

Sociologically, the most important legacy left by Castle Cary was that bequeathed by James Woodforde (1740–1802), for eight years its curate. From his nineteenth year until his death, he kept a meticulous diary, recording all the minutiae of his daily round – pleasures, vexations, conversations, meals. Nothing else in English letters so accurately encapsulates the domestic life of middle-class England at this period:

'. . . Mrs. Carr, Miss Chambers, Mr. Hindley, Mr. Carr, and Sister Jane dined, supped and spent the evening with me, and we were very merry. I gave them for dinner a dish of fine Tench which I caught out of my brother's Pond in Pond Close this morning, Ham, and 3 fowls boiled, a Plumb Pudding; a couple of Ducks rosted, a roasted neck of Pork, a Plumb Tart and an Apple Tart, Pears, Apples and Nutts after dinner; White Wine and red, Beer and Cyder. Coffee and Tea in the evening at six o'clock. Hashed Fowl and Duck and Eggs and Potatoes etc. for supper. We did not dine until four o'clock – nor supped till ten. Mr. Rice, a Welshman who is lately come to Cary and plays very well on the Triple Harp, played to us after coffee for an hour or two . . . the Company did not go away till near twelve o'clock . . .'

Grieving a death, he wrote:

'We were sorry to see on this Days Paper from Bath that our very valuable and worthy friend the Revd. Mr. DuQuesne of Tuddenham was no more. It is a very great Loss to us, but I hope to him, Gain. Pray God he may be eternally happy. Dinner today boiled Leg of Mutton & a rosted Rabbit . . .'

He faced even the sternest of his duties with heartening equanimity:

'. . . One Sarah Gore, came to me this morning and brought me an instrument from the Court of Wells, to perform publick Pennance next Sunday at C. Cary Church for having a child, which I am to administer to her publickly next Sunday after Divine Service . . .

. . . I married Tom Burge of Ansford to Charity Andrews of C. Cary by License this morning. The Parish of Cary made him marry her, and he came handbolted to Church for fear of running away, and the Parish of Cary was at all the expense of bringing of them to, I rec^{d} of Mr. Andrew Russ the overseer of the Poor of Cary for it 0.10.6 . . .'

Local dramas he likewise took in his stride:

'I read Prayers and preached at Cary Church and whilst I was preaching one Thos Speed of Gallhampton came into the Church quite drunk and crazy and made a noise in the Church, called the Singers a Pack of Whoresbirds and gave me a nod or two in the pulpit. The Constable Roger

Coles Sen[r] took took him into custody after and will have him before a Magistrate to-morrow...'

There is in the Diary above all an impression of tranquillity, of the basic pattern of life having been the same for hundreds of years with only superficial change. If the social structure still had echoes of feudalism – recalling the distant days of *Domesday* – it was on the whole benevolent.

Wedmore

The Bishop [of Wells] also holds WEDMORE *WEDMORE*. He held it himself before 1066. It paid tax for 10 hides; however there are 11 hides there. Land for 36 ploughs, of which 5 hides, less 1 virgate, are in lordship; 4 ploughs there; 4 slaves; 13 villagers and 14 smallholders with 9 ploughs & 5 hides & 1 virgate. 18 cottages. Meadow, 70 acres; 2 fisheries which pay 10s; woodland, 50 acres; pasture, 1 league jein both length and width. Moors which pay nothing. 6 unbroken mares; 17 cattle; 3 pigs. The value was £20; now £17.

Wedmore was one of 19 holdings of the Bishop of Wells. As *Domesday* shows, it was among his most valuable, together with Wells itself, Chard, Wellington and Combe St Nicholas. One of the largest villages in the county, Wedmore sits on a rocky eminence above the surrounding marshland and was already important in Saxon times. This area had been much harassed by the Danes during the ninth century; at Wedmore Alfred the Great baptized the Danish king Guthrun into the Christian faith soon after overwhelming his forces at the Battle of Edington. It was a brilliant political move. The Peace of Wedmore lasted for fifteen years, giving Alfred time to fortify vulnerable burghs, build ships and reinforce his army.

'The writer of English history may be pardoned if he lingers too fondly over the King in whose court, at whose impulse, it may be in whose very words, English History begins', commented John Green in his *Short History of the English People* (1874).

In one of the village's many lovely stone dwellings, Porch House, there lived in the seventeenth century a remarkable man, Dr John Westover. He built in his grounds an extraordinary stone outhouse where he opened what was probably England's first private lunatic asylum. Sufferers came from all over the West of England, to be treated with compassion; Westover realized the value of life's smaller pleasures, and his patients could obtain such luxuries as tobacco, playing-cards and hair-powder.

He was also a prosperous doctor in general practice, and kept a detailed journal in which 'we set down all the ailments, agues, distempers, distractions, dislocations, fractures, fevers, jaundices, melancholies, pains, swellings, stitches, itches etc., which the people of this parish and neighbourhood suffered during 15 years; all the cordials, carminatives, decoctions, electuaries, dyet drinks, juleps, marmalades, opiates, pills, potions, sudorifics, cephallicals, pectorals and stomachicals which they swallowed; all the blisters, plasters, poultices and cataplasms which were applied to them, and all the teeth and all the fees which were extracted from them.' The fees did not seem to matter to him too much; he was willing to accept goods instead of cash:

'Richard Champion of Blackford sent his brother Edward to desier me to visit him, whond had a fracture of the major and minor foott juent, and redused it. Rec[d] one gd fether bedd of fiftey pounds weight in part of pay.'

There is evidence that Westover was brave enough to treat some of the wounded of the Duke of Monmouth's fugitive army. A few pages are missing from his diary for dates following the Battle of Sedgemoor, as if they had been ripped out. The doctor may have done this hastily to coincide with the visit to Wedmore of the ubiquitous hanging Judge Jeffreys, who put the village's pretty stone cross to use as a gibbet.

Wedmore is a quieter place today. Quiet it also seems to have been in 1086, as well as prosperous. But there is evidence that there had been recent trouble. A pot was dug up in the churchyard last century that had been hidden there in about 1040. It contained more than 200 silver coins from the reigns of Ethelred, Canute and Harold I. Whoever hid it as he fled may not have lived to retrieve it.

NETHER STOWEY: *The Quantock Hills near the village.*

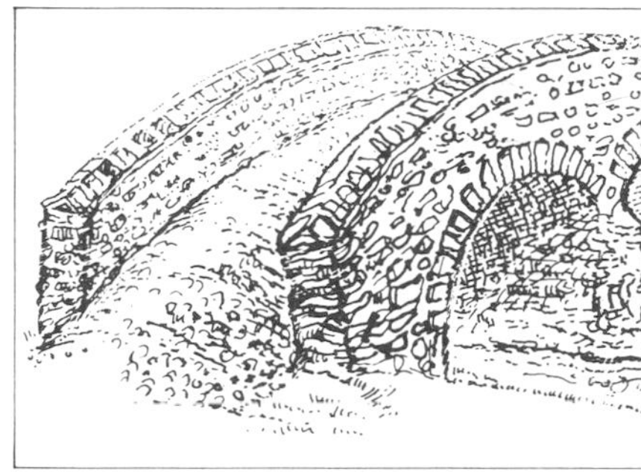

ALLERFORD: *The cobbled pack-horse bridge.*

Somerset Gazetteer
Each entry starts with the modern place name in **bold** type. The *Domesday* information that follows is in *italic* type, beginning with the name or names by which the place was known in 1086. The main landholders and undertenants are next, separated with semi-colons if a place was divided into more than one holding. A number of holdings were granted by the king to his thanes; these normally come at the end of the list of landholders and are described as holding land 'from the king'. More general information completes the *Domesday* part of the entry, including examples of dues such as eels rendered by tenants, and animals given in the *Domesday* entries when the totals reach or exceed: 3 cobs, 7 cows, 150 sheep, 20 pigs, 50 goats, 10 cattle, 5 unbroken mares, 2 oxen, 100 wethers and 6 wild mares. All brood mares, asses and mares are listed. The modern or post-Domesday section is in normal type. ▣ represents a village, ⌂ a small village or hamlet.

Abbas Combe *Cumbe: Shaftesbury Church. 7 cows.* ▣

Abbot's Leigh *Lege/Lega: Thurstan, formerly his father.* ▣ Near Avon Gorge Nature Reserve; manor house.

Adsborough *Tetesberge/berga/ Tegesberia: Hugh from William de Mohun, formerly 6 thanes.* ⌂

Aisholt *terra Olta: Robert from Roger de Courseulles.* ⌂ Aisholt Wood.

Alcombe *Aucome/coma: William de Mohun. 200 sheep.* Part of Minehead.

Aldwick *Alduic/uica: Walter from Serlo de Burcy. Mill.* Farm; manor house.

Aley *Ailgi/Aili: Warmund from William de Mohun.* ⌂

Alford *Aldedeford: Ansger from Robert de Mortain. Mill.* ⌂ Farm.

Alfoxton *Alfagestone/tona: Ranulf from Alfred d'Epaignes.* Alfoxton Park, an 18th-century house, now a hotel.

Alhampton *Alentone/tona: Ralph Crooked Hands from Glastonbury Church.* 3 mills (with Hornblotton and Lamyatt).

Aller (in Carhampton) *Alre/ Alra: Ogis from Roger de Courseulles.* Farm, below Aller Hill.

Aller (near Langport) *Alre/ Alra: Ralph de Limesy.* ▣ Farm. The Danish king Guthrun was converted to Christianity on Aller Moor.

Aller (in Sampford Brett) *Alre/ Alra:*. Lost.

Allercott *Alurenecote/ Alueronecota: Durand from William de Mohun.* ▣

Allerford *Alresford/forda: Ralph de Limesy. Mill.* ▣ Attractive; pack-horse bridge.

Allerton *Alwarditone: Ralph de Contev ille from Walter de Douai.* Now 2 hamlets, Chapel and Stone Allerton.

Almsworthy *Edmundesworde/ worda:* Lost.

Alstone *Alsistune/Alesistuna: Rademar from Walter de Douai.* ▣ Adjoining Highbridge.

Alston Sutton *Alnodestone/ tona/tuna: Hubert from Walter de Douai.* ⌂

Alwin's Land: Lost.

Andersey *Ederesige: Godwin from Glastonbury Church.* ⌂ Now Nyland.

Ansford *Almundesford/ Almondesford: Wulfric from Walter de Douai. Mill.* ▣ Near Castle Cary.

Appley *Ape/Appelie/Ape/ Appeleia: Bretel from Count of Mortain; Drogo from Baldwin of Exeter.* ⌂ Cothay Manor nearby.

Ashbrittle *Aisse/Aissa: Bretel and Ansger from Count of Mortain. 2 mills.* ⌂ On the Somerset/Devon border.

Ashcombe *Aisecome/coma: Herlwin from Bishop of Coutances. 60 goats.* Ashcombe Park in Weston-super-Mare.

Ashcott *Aissecote/cota: Walter de Douai and Roger de Courseulles from Glastonbury Church.* ⌂

Ashill *Aiselle/Aisselle: Mauger from Count of Mortain. 70 pigs.* ▣ Partly Norman church.

Ashington *Essentone/tona: Vitalis from Roger de Courseulles.* ⌂ 16th-century manor house.

Ash Priors *Aissa: Roger Arundel.* ▣ Ash Priors Common.

Ashway *Ascwei: Hugh from Roger de Courseulles.* ⌂ On the River Barle.

Ashwick *Escewiche/Escwica: Bath Church.* ⌂ Burial urns in nearby Beacon Hill Barrows.

Athelney *Adelingi/Adeliniensis: Count of Mortain, Roger de Courseulles and Ralph de Limesy from Athelney Church.* Formerly an island that was a stronghold of King Alfred but now rises above drained moors. Burrow Mump, site of a 12th-century fortification.

Avill *Avena: Ralph from William de Mohun. Mill.* Farm; on the River Avill.

Axbridge *Aissebrige/Axebruge/ Alsebruge: King's land.* Market town with timbered and Georgian houses.

Babcary *Babacha/Babakari/ Babecari/Babbacari: Robert FitzIvo from Count of Mortain; Humphrey the Chamberlain.* ▣

Babington *Babingtone/Babbig/ Babbingtona: Azelin from Bishop of Coutances. Mill. 200 sheep.* 18th-century Babington House and church.

BATH: *The great Roman baths with Bath Abbey in the background.*

Backwell *Bacoile/Bacoila: Fulcran and Nigel from Bishop of Coutances. Mill.* Manor house; Backwell Quarries.

Badgworth *Bagewerre/werra: Fulcwin from Walter de Douai.* Manor house.

Bagborough *Bageberge/berga/ Bagaberga/Baweberga/ Bagueberga: William de Mohun; Ralph from Ralph Pagnell.* Now the village of West Bagborough and hamlet of East Bagborough; church in the grounds of Bagborough House.

Bagley (in Stoke Pero) *Bagelie:* Deserted site.

Baltonsborough *Baltunesberge/ berga: Glastonbury Church. Mill.* Birthplace of St Dunstan (924–88).

Banwell *Banwelle/Banuela: Bishop of Wells and Serlo de Burcy, Ralph Crooked Hands, Roghard, Fastrad, Bofa and Alfry from him, formerly Earl Harold. 3 mills.* 19th-century '*cottage orné*' and park, 'The Caves'. Remains of prehistoric mammals were found in Bone Caves on nearby Banwell Hill.

Barrington *Barintone/tona: Roger de Courseulles.* Thatched cottages; 16th-century manor house.

Barrow (near Castle Cary) *Berrowene: Bretel from Count of Mortain; Ralph from Walter de Douai.* Now 2 villages, North and South Barrow.

Barrow Gurney *Berue/Berua: Nigel de Gournai-en-Brai from Bishop of Wells. Mill.* Named after its Domesday holder; 16th-century manor house.

Barton St David *Bertone/tuna/ tona: Norman from Roger de Courseulles; Edmund FitzPayne from the king. 2 mills.* Overlooking Glastonbury Tor.

Batcombe *Batecumba/comba: Roger de Courseulles and Azelin from Glastonbury Church, formerly Alfhild, the Abbot's mother. Mill. 150 sheep.* The 'raging Batcombeites', Puritans who fought in the Civil War, are commemorated in Bruton parish register.

Bath *Bada/Bade: King's land; Bath Church. Mint, 6 derelict royal houses, 1 house held by Hugh the Interpreter, mill.* City, originally called Aquae Sulis by the Romans, after its mineral springs. The See of Wells was transferred here in 1088; fine 18th-century architecture.

Bathampton *Hantone/ Hamtona: Hugh the Interpreter and Colgrim, an Englishman from Bath Church.* Close to Bath. The quarries on Bathampton Downs provided stone for many houses in Bath.

Bathealton *Badeheltone/tona: Nigel from William de Mohun. 50 goats.* Partly 17th-century farm.

Batheaston *Estone/tona: King's land; Walter Hussey from Bath Church; Hugolin the Interpreter. 2 mills. 150 sheep.* Suburb of Bath.

Bathford *Forde/Forda: Bath Church'. Mill.* On the outskirts of Bath, by the River Avon.

Bathwick *Wiche/Wica: Bishop of Wells. Mill. 250 sheep.* Part of Bath.

Bawdrip *Bagetrepe/Bagatrepa: Rainward from Walter de Douai. Mill. 20 pigs.* Ruins of a 19th-century 'castle'.

Beckington *Bechintone/tona: Roger Arundel. Mill. 50 goats.* 16th-century houses; Birthplace of Thomas Beckington (1390–1465), Bishop of Bath and Wells and secretary to Henry VI.

Beercrocombe *Bere/Bera: Reginald de Vautortes from Count of Mortain.*

Beere *Bera: Leofa, the pre-Conquest holder. Mill.* Manor farm.

Belluton *Beletone/Belgetone/ tona: Alfred from Count Eustace. Mill.* Adjoining Pensford on the River Chew.

Berkley *Berchelei/lec: Robert from Roger Arundel. Mill.* 17th-century manor house; Georgian church.

Bickenhall *Bichehalle/halda: William de Lestre from Count of Mortain.* Farm.

Bickham *Bichecome/comma/ cumma: Richard from William de Mohun.* On the River Avill.

Bishop's Lydeard *Lediart/ Liediart/Lidegar: William de Mohun. Mill.*

Bishopsworth *Bicheurde/ Bischeurda/Biscopewrde/wrda: Herlwin and Azelin from Bishop of Coutances.* Church with a Poussin painting of the Madonna.

Blackford (near Wincanton) *Blacheford/Blachafort: Alwaker from Glastonbury Church; Alfward from Thurstan FitzRolf.* Thatched cottages; medieval dovecote.

Blackmore *Blachemore/ Blachamora: Ansketel from Roger de Courseulles.* Farm.

Blagdon *Blachedone/dona: Serlo de Burcy. 2 mills.* Near Blagdon Lake Reservoir.

Blaxhold *Blachesale/ssala:* Lost.

Bleadon *Bledone/dona: Bishop of Winchester. 250 sheep.* Near beautiful Bleadon Hill.

Bossington *Bosintone/tuna/ tona: Ralph de Limesey.* Coastal; Bossington Hill.

Bradford (on Tone) *Bradeforde/forda: Alfred the Butler from Count of Mortain. Mill.* On the River Tone; 2 originally 14th-century bridges.

Bradney *Bredenie/neia: Rainward from Walter de Douai.*

Bradon *Brede/Bredde/Bredene/ Brade: Mauger and Drogo from Count of Mortain; Harding from the king.* Now North Bradon; South Bradon farm.

Bratton (in Minehead) *Bratone/ tona: Roger from William de Mohun. 12 cattle, 60 goats.* On the outskirts of Minehead.

Bratton Seymour *Broctune/ tuna: Gerard from Walter de Douai.* Bratton Hill.

Brean *Brien: Walter de Douai.* Holiday resort. Brean Sands were noted for shipwrecks.

Brewham *Briweham: William de Mohun. 2 mills, 300 sheep, 22 wild mares.* Now 2 villages, North and South Brewham; Brewham House.

Bridgwater *Brugie: Walter de Douai. Mill.* Industrial town, port in the Middle Ages.

Broadway *Bradewei: Mauger from Count of Mortain.* Called after the road leading to the medieval forest of Neroche.

Broadwood *Bradewrde/euda: William de Mohun.* Farm.

Brockley *Brochelie/leia: Aldred, the pre-Conquest holder.* Brockley Court manor house, with a farm. A nature trail leads through Brockley Combe.

Broford *Broford/Brofort: William from Roger de Courseulles.* Farm.

Brompton Ralph *Burnetone/ tuna/tona: Thorgils from William de Mohun. Mill.* On the edge of the Brendon Hills; Elworthy Barrows an Iron Age hillfort.

Brompton Regis *Brunetone/ tona: Count of Mortain from the king and Hugh de Vautortes from him, formerly Countess Gytha. 2 mills.* King's Brompton Forest nearby.

BISHOP'S LYDEARD: *Carved bench ends.*

Broomfield *Brunfelle/fella: William de Mohun. 155 sheep.* Fyne Court is part of Somerset Trust for Nature Conservation.

Brown *Brune: Durand from William de Mohun. 190 sheep, 44 goats.* Court Farms on the *Domesday* site.

Brushford *Brigeford/fort/ Bricefort/Brucheford: Mauger from Count of Mortain. Mill.* 17th-century hospital.

Bruton *Brauetone/Briuetona/ Briutona/Briweton/tone/tona/ Brumetone: King's land, formerly King Edward. 6 mills.* Small town on the River Brue.

Brympton *Brunetone/tona: Herbert from Roger de Courseulles.* Mainly 16th century, Brympton House, with a church and a dower house.

Buckland Dinham *Bochelande/ land/landa: Dunn, the pre-Conquest holder, from the king. Mill.*

Buckland St Mary *Bocheland/ lande/landa: Brictric, Wulfward and Harding from the king.* In the Black Down Hills.

Burnett *Bernet: Wife of Wulfward from the king.* Manor house; gabled farm.

Burnham on Sea *Burneham: Walter de Douai.* Holiday resort. The church contains the remains of an alterpiece carved by Grinling Gibbons for Whitehall Palace.

Butcombe *Budicombe/comba: Fulcran from Bishop of Coutances. Mill.* Farm near Blagdon Lake.

Butleigh *Bodechelie/Bodecaleia/ Boduchelei/Boduccheleia: Roger de Courseulles from Glastonbury Church; Count of Mortain; formerly Winegot the Priest.* Butleigh Court; monument on nearby Windmill Hill to Admiral Sir Samuel Hood (1724–1816).

Cameley *Camelei/leia: Geoffrey de Mowbray. Mill. 150 sheep.* Partly 11th-century church with a Georgian interior.

Camerton *Camelertone/tona: Glastonbury Church. 2 mills. 154 sheep.* Coal-mining in the 18th century; pyramid of spoil and remains of a colliery.

Cannington *Candetone/tona/ Cantocton/tona/Cantetone/tona: Erchenger the Priest from the king; Robert from John the Usher. 2 mills. 350 sheep (with Carhampton and Williton).* Large; Cannington Park, an Iron Age hill-fort, nearby. Cannington Priory was founded c.1138 by Robert de Courcy; the present house is Elizabethan.

Capland *Capilande/landa: Harding from the king and Ceolric from him.*

Capton *Capintone/tona: King's land, formerly Earl Harold.*

Carhampton *Carentone/ Caretone/Carentona/tuna: King's land. Assessed with Cannington, etc.* Surrounded by orchards. The ceremony of wassailing is still practised here.

Carlingcott *Credelincote/cota:* Lost.

Castle Cary *Cari:* See page 233.

Cary Fitzpaine *Cari: Robert from Roger Arundel. 10 cattle.*

Catcott *Caldecote/Cadicota: Roger de Courseulles from Glastonbury Church.* Catcott Heath; 13th-century church.

Cathanger *Cathangre/hangra: Muchelney Church; Ingulf.* Cathanger Farm.

Chaffcombe *Caffecome/coma/ Cafecoma: Ralph Rufus from Bishop of Coutances. 24 pigs.* Farm.

Chard *Cerdre: Giso of Wells, the pre-Conquest holder. 300 sheep.* Town, a cloth-making centre until the 19th century, with flint and thatched houses; manor farm.

Charlcombe *Cerlecume/ Cerlacuma: William Hussey from Bath Church. 200 sheep.* On the outskirts of Bath.

Charlinch *Cerdesling: Roger de Courseulles. Mill.* Now Little Charlynch; view of the Quantocks.

Charlton (in Shepton Mallet) *Cerletone/tona:* Lost.

Charlton Adam *Cerletone: Reginald de Vautortes from Count of Mortain, formerly 3 thanes and a clerk.* A square; pretty cottages.

Charlton Mackrell *Cerletune: Roger Arundel.* 2 Roman sites nearby.

Charlton Musgrove *Cerletone: Jocelyn from Robert FitzGerald. Mill.* 15th-century church with medieval roodloft and gargoyles.

Cheddar *Ceder/Cedre/Ceadra/ Ceddra/Cedra: King's land; formerly King Edward. 2 mills, 3 fisheries.* The ruins of a Saxon chapel and the outlines of the royal palace to which it belonged are marked out in the grounds of the Kings of Wessex School. Cheddar Gorge contains over 400 caves with stalactites and stalagmites. There are Stone Age tools, weapons and a skeleton c.12,000 years old in the Gough Cave Museum.

Cheddon Fitzpaine *Cedre/ Cedra/Succedene/dena: Roger Arundel.*

Chelvey *Caluiche/uica/Celuia: Rumold from Matthew de Mortagne, formerly Thorkell the Dane.* Partly Norman church; rectory; old barn.

Chelwood *Celeworde/worda/ Cellewert: Alfred from Count Eustace; Nicholas from Alfred of Marlborough.* 13th-century church.

Cheriton *Cherintone/tona/ Ciretune/Eiretone: Warmund from William de Mohun; Bernard from William FitzGuy; Robert from Thurstan FitzRolph.* Now 2 villages, North and South Cheriton.

Chew Magna *Chiwe/Chiu: Giso of Wells, the pre-Conquest holder. 3 mills.* Chew Valley Lake, the site of a Roman villa.

Chew Stoke *Stoche/Stocca/Stoca: Serlo de Burcy; Aldwin, the pre-Conquest holder, from the king. Mill. 13 cattle.* Well known for its 18th-century bell-founders, the Bilbies.

Chewton Mendip *Ciwetune/ tuna: King's land with the Abbot of Jumièges holding the church. 5 mills. 800 sheep.* In a pre-Roman lead-mining area. Burial urns were found in nearby Ashen Hill barrows.

Chilcompton *Contone-tune-tona/Comtuna/Cumtona: Walter Tirrell from Bishop of Salisbury; Ralph from Walter de Douai. 2 mills. 220 sheep, 70 goats.* On Wellow Brook, Chilcompton Wood.

Chillyhill *Cilele/ela:* Lost.

Chilthorne *Cilterne/terna: Alfred and Alfred the Butler from Count of Mortain. 48 pigs, 179 sheep.* Now Chilthorne Domer; near the Roman road to Ilchester.

Chilton Cantelo *Citerne/erna: Warner form William d'Eu; formerly Alstan Boscombe, a thane of King Edward.* On the River Yeo.

Chilton Polden *Ceptone/tona: Roger de Courseulles from Glastonbury Church.* On the Roman road across the Polden Hills; 19th-century tower built of stone from all over the county.

Chilton Trinity *Cildetone/tona: Ansketel from Roger de Courseulles; Ansger Fower.* 13th-century church; manor farm.

Chilton Trivett *Cildetone/tona: Ansketel from Roger de Courseulles. 6 unbroken mares, 16 cattle.*

Chinnock *Cinioch/ioc: Count of Mortain and Mauger and Alfred from him. 2 mills, 122 sheep.* Now 2 villages, East and West Chinnock.

Chipstable *Cipestaple/apula: Muchelney Abbey.* In the Brendon Hills; named after a Saxon boundary mark, Cippa's Post.

Chiselborough *Ceolseberge/ Ceoselbergon/Ceselberia: Alfred from Count of Mortain. Mill.* Fair, manor farm.

Chubworthy *Cibewrde/wrda: Manfred and Robert from William de Mohun.* Farm.

Clapton (in Cucklington) *Clopetone/Cloppetona: Mauger de Carteret from Count of Mortain.* Farm.

Clapton (in Maperton) *Cloptone/Clopptona: Bernard Pancevolt from Thurstan FitzRolph.* Farm.

Clapton in Gordano *Clotune/ tuna: Herlwin from Bishop of Coutances. 40 pigs, 50 goats.* Church with a Norman doorway and tympanum; Clapton Court, partly late medieval.

Clatworthy *Clateurde/eurda: Ogis from William de Mohun, formerly Alfgeat, a woman. Mill.* In the Brendon Hills.

Claverham *Cliveham/Claveham: Fulcran from Bishop of Coutances, formerly Gunhilda.*

Claverton *Claftertone/tona: Hugolin the Interpreter from Humphrey the Chamberlain. Mill.* American Folk Museum at Claverton Manor.

Clayhill *Claihelle/hella: Ansketel from Roger de Courseulles.* Clayhill House.

Clevedon *Clivedone/dona: Hildebert from Matthew de Mortagne, formerly John the Dane. 22 cattle.* Seaside resort, developed in the 19th century, with 14th-century Clevedon Court and Walton Castle, a 16th-century folly.

Clewer *Cliveware/wara: Fulcran and Nigel from Bishop of Coutances.*

Cloford *Claford/forda/ Cladforda: Alfred from Count of Mortain. Mill. 38 unbroken mares, 150 sheep.* Cloford House, common.

Closworth *Clovewrde/eswrda: Count of Mortain. Mill. 100 goats.* Manor farm.

Clutton *Clutone/tona: William from Bishop of Coutances. Mill. 176 sheep.*

Coker *Cocre/Cochra: King's land, formerly Countess Gytha. Mill. 150 sheep.* Now 2 villages, West Coker (closest to the Domesday site) and East Coker, where T.S. Eliot (1888–1965) is buried.

Coleford *Coleford/Colforde/ forda: Alric, the pre-Conquest holder, from Roger de Courseulles; Dodman from William de Mohun.* Farm.

Colgrim's land *Terracolgrin:* Lost.

Combe (in Withycombe) *Cumbe/Comba: Roger de Courseulles.* Farm.

Combe Hay *Cume/Cuma: Agelric from the king; formerly Queen Edith. Mill.* 18th-century manor house. On nearby Somerset Coal Canal are 22 locks to carry the canal up-hill.

Combe St Nicholas *Cumbe/ Cumba: Bishop of Wells. 315 sheep.* Bronze Age barrows on nearby Combe Beacon.

Combe Sydenham *Come/ Comma: Thorgils from William de Mohun. Mill.* 16th-century manor, home of Elizabeth Sydenham, who married Sir Francis Drake.

CLAPTON IN GORDANO: *14th-c. manor house.*

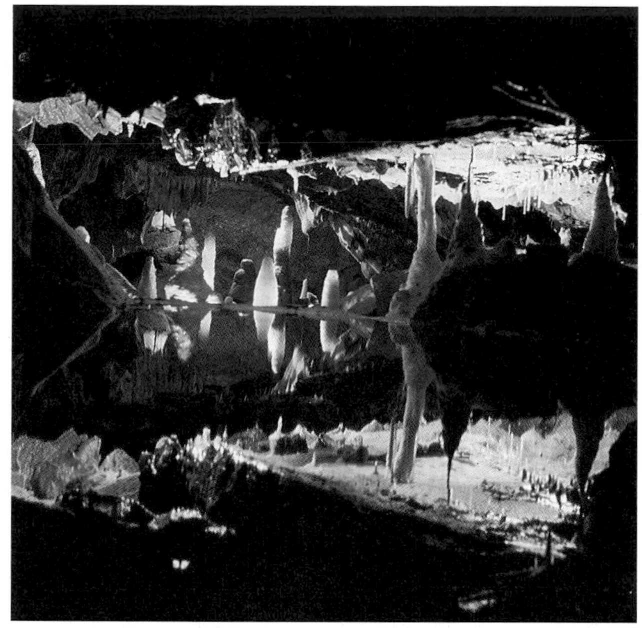

CHEDDAR: *Natural marvels in Gough's Cave.*

Combwich *Comich/Commiz/ Commit: Alfred of Marlborough from Count Eustace; Walter Bowman from Ralph de Limesy.* Small port on the River Parrett, with a new wharf for Hinkley Point nuclear power station.

Compton Dando *Contone/ Comtuna: Bishop of Coutances. 2 mills.* Roman sculpture from Bath built into the church wall.

Compton Dundon *Contone/ tona: Roger de Courseulles from Glastonbury Church.* Now 2 villages, Compton and Dundon; Iron Age hill-fort with well-preserved ramparts in the latter.

Compton Durville *Contone/ tona/Cumtona/Contune/ Comtuna: Mathilda from Count Eustace; Mauger from Count of Mortain. Mill. 182 sheep.*

Compton Martin *Contone/ Comtona: Serlo de Burcy.* Fine Norman church.

Compton Pauncefoot *Contitone/tona: Geoffrey from Thurstan FitzRolph. Mill.* 19th-century Gothic Compton Castle, with lake and parkland.

Congresbury *Con/ Cungresberie/Con/Cungresberia: King's land; formerly Earl Harold; 3 thanes, the pre-Conquest holders. 20 cattle, 200 sheep.* 15th-century priest's house. King Alfred gave a monastery here to his tutor Asser.

Corston *Corstune/tuna: Bath Church. Mill.* On the River Avon.

Corton Denham *Corfetone/ tona: King's land, formerly Wulfward White, a thane of Queen Edith. 150 sheep.*

Cossington *Consintone/tona: Walter de Douai from Glastonbury Church. 26 pigs.* Pretty; in the Polden Hills; manor house; 13th-century church.

Crandon *Grenedone/dona: Aldred, the pre-Conquest holder, from Humphrey the Chamberlain. Mill.* Now Crandon Bridge.

Creech St Michael *Crice: King's land, formerly Earl Godwin's daughter, Gunhilda. Mill, fishery.* On the River Tone and the Bridgwater and Taunton Canal.

Crewkerne *Cruche/Chruca/ Cruca/Crucca/Crucche: King's land, formerly Edeva. 4 mills. 400 sheep.* Market town, a centre of cloth-making and associated trades.

Cricket Malherbie *Cruchet: Drogo from Count of Mortain.* Cricket Court.

Cricket St Thomas *Cruche/ Cruca: Thurstan from Count of Mortain. Mill. 14 cattle.* Wild-life park in the grounds of Cricket House.

Crook *Cruce: Rademar from Walter de Douai.* Great and Little Crook fields, in Bawdrip.

Croscombe *Coristone/ Coriscoma: Roger de Courseulles from Glastonbury Church. 2 mills (with Shepton Mallet).* Weaving industry; 2 manor houses; church with rare 17th-century wood carving.

Crowcombe *Crawecumbe/ coma: Robert the Constable from Count of Mortain. 26 cattle.* Church house, 1515; 18th-century Crowcombe Court.

Cucklington *Concintone/tona/ Cucintona: Bretel from Count of Mortain.* Near the Dorset border.

Cudworth *Cudeworde/worda/ Cudeorda: Odo from Roger Arundel.*

Culbone *Chetenore/nora: Drogo from Bishop of Coutances.* England's smallest complete parish church, probably Saxon, with a 12th-century nave.

Curry Mallet *Curi: Roger de Courseulles.* Called after the Norman Mallet family, whose arms are on the manor house.

Currypool *Curiepol: Roger de Courseulles.* Farm.

Curry Rivel *Churi/Curi/Chori: King's land, formerly King*

GLASTONBURY: *The Tor.*

Edward. Burton Pynsent column, designed by Capability Brown and erected by William Pitt the Elder in memory of his benefactor.

Cutcombe *Udecome/coma: William de Mohun and 3 men-at-arms from him. Mill. 36 brood mares, 250 sheep.* In Somerset's highest parish, near Dunkery Beacon, built 1707.

Deadman's Well *Denesmodeswelle/suella/ Denemodeswella:* Lost.

Dinnington *Dinnitone/tona/ Duintone/tona: Siward from Glastonbury Church; Siward Falconer from the king. Mill.* Near Hinton House, where Roman pavements were found.

Discove *Dinescove/Digenescova: Harding from the king. 28 pigs.*

Ditcheat *Dicesget: Glastonbury Church. Mill.* Below Ditcheat Hill.

Dodington *Stawe: Doda from the king. Mill.* Dodington Hall.

Dodisham *Dudesha:* Lost.

Donyatt *Doniet/Donieht: Drogo from Count of Mortain. Mill. 12 brood mares.* Once 'Dunna's Gate', marking the boundary of Neroche Forest.

Doulting *Doltin: Glastonbury Church, Roger de Courseulles. Mill. 340 sheep.* Famous for quarries which provided stone for Glastonbury and Wells.

Doverhay *Dovri/Doveri: Alric from Roger de Courseulles, formerly Edeva.* Adjoinint Porlock.

Dowlish *Doules/Douelis/ Duuelis: Bishop of Coutances and William de Monceaux from him.* Now Dowlish Wake.

Downhead *Dunehefde: Erneis from Glastonbury Church, formerly Wulfgar, a monk.* Manor farm.

Downscombe *Donescumbe/ cumba: Aeleva from Roger de Courseulles.* On Exmoor.

Draycott (in Limington) *Draicote/Draecota/Dreicote/ Dregecota: Count of Mortain from the king and William de Courseulles from him. Mill.*

Draycott (in Rodney Stoke) *Draicote: Godwin the Englishman from the king with his mother the pre-Conquest holder. 2 oxen.*

Drayton *Draitune/tunna/ Draintuna: Muchelney Abbey and Ceolric and Wulfward from the Abbey.*

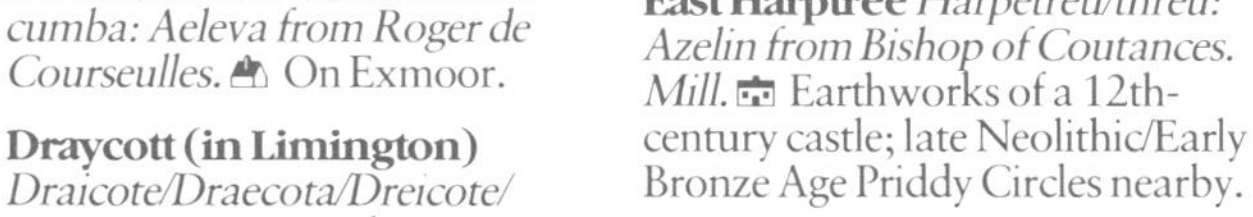

DOWLISH: *17th-c. stone farmhouse with fine lintels.*

Dulverton *Dolvertone/tune/Dol/ Dulvertona: King's land, formerly Earl Harold.* Small market town.

Dunkerton *Duncretone/tona/ tun: Bernard Pancevolt from Thurstan FitzRolph. Mill. 212 sheep.* On Cam Brook.

Dunster *Torre/Torra: William de Mohun. 2 mills.* Market town. Dunster Castle was rebuilt in stone in 12th century; 16th-century hotel, the Luttrell Arms; Georgian town centre. De Mohun founded the priory here in 1095.

Dunwear *Doneham: Walter de Douai.* Dunwear House on the outskirts of Bridgwater.

Durborough *Dereberge/berga: Roger de Courseulles from Glastonbury Church.* Farm.

Durleigh *Durlege/lega: Ansger.* Durleigh Reservoir.

Durston *Destona/Derstona: Richard from Roger Arundel.* Buckland Farm nearby was built with stone from a priory of the Knights of St John.

Dyche *Leding/Ledich: Ranulf from Alfred d'Epaignes.*

Earnshill *Erneshel/Erneshele/ helt: Wulfward from Roger de Courseulles; Gerard, the king's servant.* Earnshill House.

East Bower *Bur/Burh: Rademar from Walter de Douai; Alfred d'Epaignes. 16 cattle, 23 pigs.* On the outskirts of Bridgwater.

East Brent *Brentemerse: Glastonbury Church.* Below Brent Knoll, an Iron Age hillfort occupied by the Romans.

East Cranmore *Crenemelle/ Crenemella: Harding, the pre-Conquest holder, from Glastonbury Church. Mill.* Saxon cross over the church's vestry door.

East Harptree *Harpetreu/threu: Azelin from Bishop of Coutances. Mill.* Earthworks of a 12th-century castle; late Neolithic/Early Bronze Age Priddy Circles nearby.

East Lydeard *Lidiard: William de Mohun.*

East Lydford *Lideford/forda: Roger de Courseulles from Glastonbury Church. Mill. 160 sheep.*

East Quantoxhead *Cantocheheve/tocheve/heva: Ralph de Reuilly from Ralph Pagnell. Mill.* 16th-century farm near Quantock's Head Point.

Easthams *Estham/Esteha/ham: Thurstan from Count of Mortain, formerly Godwin, the king's reeve.* Farm.

Easton in Gordano *Estone/tona: Roger FitzRalph from Bishop of Coutances. Mill. 12 cattle, 200 sheep.* Adjoining Pill on the River Avon.

Eastrip *Estrope/ropa/Storpe: Ripe from Thurstan; Guard from the king.* Eastrip field near Bruton.

Eckweek *Ecewiche/Eccewica: Alfred from Count of Mortain; Walter de Douai.* Eckweek House.

Edington *Edwinetone/tona: Roger de Courseulles from Glastonbury Church.* Holy well, said to be the site of Aethandune, King Alfred's victory over the Danes.

Edingworth *Lodenwrde/ Lodenawirda: Walter de Douai from Glastonbury Church. 15 cattle.* Manor farm.

Edstock *Ichetoche/tocha:* Lost.

Elborough *Eleberie/Elleberia/ Lilebere/Illebera: Azelin from Count of Mowbray. 200 sheep.*

Eleigh *Illege/lega: William de Daumeray from Roger de Courseulles.* Eleighwater House.

Elm *Telwe: Osbern Giffard. 2 mills. 250 sheep.* Now Great Elm.

Elworthy *Elwrda/wrda: Dodman from William de Mohun. Mill.*

Emble *Imele/Imela: Alric from Roger de Courseulles.* Embelle Farm.

Emborough *Amelberge/berga/ beria: Robert from Bishop of Coutances. 25 pigs, 158 wethers.* Emborough Ponds; Emborough Grove.

Englishcombe *Engliscome/ Ingleliscuma: Nigel de Gournai from Bishop of Coutances. 2 mills. 137 sheep.* Near the Saxon Wansdyke; traces of Gournay Castle; tithe barn of Bath Abbey.

Enmore *Animere/mera: Geoffrey from Roger de Courseulles.* Church; park; remains of Enmore Castle; an 18th-century Gothic building.

Evercreech *Evrecriz/Evercriz: Bishop of Wells, the pre-Conquest holder, and Erneis, Maghere and Hildebert from him. 200 sheep.* Attractive; Old cottages; almshouses; Iron Age hill-fort on nearby Small Down.

Eversy *Eveshe:* Lost.

Exford *Aisseford/forde/forda: Roger de Courseulles and Ednoth and William from him; William de Mohun.* Kennels of the Devon and Somerset stag-hounds.

Exton *Essetune/tuna/Essatuna: Drogo from Bishop of Coutances.* On Exmoor.

Fairoak *Ecferdintone/ Hecferdintona:* Lost.

Farleigh Hungerford *Ferlege/ lega: Aelmer from Roger de Courseulles.* Ruins of Farleigh Castle, built by Sir Thomas Hungerford, Speaker of the House of Commons, in 14th century; Farleigh House nearby.

Farmborough *Ferenberge/ berga/beria: William from Bishop of Coutances. 215 sheep.* Farmborough Common.

Farrington Gurney *Ferentone/ tona: Azelin from Bishop of Coutances.*

Fiddington *Fitintone/tona: Hugh from Roger Arundel. 2 mills. 12 cattle.*

Fivehead *Fifhide/Fihida: Bertram from Roger de Courseulles.* John Wesley preached one of his first sermons at nearby Cathanger Farm.

Foddington *Fedintone/ Fodintona/Fodindone: Hugh de Vautortes from Count of Mortain; Hugh de Vautortes and Azelin from Humphrey the Chamberlain.*

Ford *Aeford/Eford/Laford/Iafort: Alfred from Count of Mortain.* On the River Tone.

Foxcote *Fuscote/cota: William de Monceaux from Bishop of Coutances. Mill, 20 cattle, 177 sheep.* On Wellow Brook.

Freshford *Firford/forda: Roger Whiting from Bishop of Coutances, formerly Tovi, Sheriff of Somerset.* On the Avon Canal.

Frome *Frome/Froma: King's land, formerly King Edward; Reinbald of St John's Church. 4 mills, market. 228 sheep.* Market town, formerly a cloth centre, with narrow, old streets and 18th-century almshouses.

Gilcott *Gildenecote:* Lost.

Glastonbury *Glastingberie/ Glaestingeberia: Glastonbury Church. Vineyard. 5 cobs, 58 cattle, 20 pigs, 50 goats.* Town, famous for the Glastonbury legends and the site of the country's earliest Christian shrine, also Avalon in Arthurian legend; abbey ruins. Glastonbury Tor has a 13th-century tower, and was first occupied in the Dark Ages; mounds in the valley were a pre-Roman lake village.

Goathurst *Gahers: Walter and Ansger Fower from Alfred of Spain.* Tudor Halswell Park.

Gothelney *Godelege/lega: Geoffrey from Roger de Courseulles. Share of a mill.* Now Gothelney Green; Gothelney Hall.

Greenham *Grindeham: Bretel from Count of Mortain. Mill.* On the River Tone, 14th-century manor house.

Greinton *Graintone/tona: Gerard Ditcher from Glastonbury Church.*

Hadworthy *Hateware/wara:* Lost.

Hallatrow *Helgetrau/ Helegetriueia: Roger from Bishop of Coutances.*

Halse *Halsa/Halse: Roger Arundel. Mill.* Attractive; on Halse Water.

Halsway *Halsweie/weia: Alric, the pre-Conquest holder, from Roger de Courseulles.* Halsway Manor.

Halswell *Hasewelle/willa: Guy from Roger Arundel.* 17th-century Halswell Park, with a small temple in its park.

Ham *Hame: Glastonbury Church and Robert d'Auberville, Serlo de Burcy and Gerard Ditcher from the abbot. 150 sheep.* Village of High Ham overlooking Sedgemoor.

Hamp *Hame-Hamet: Athelney Church.* Hamp House in Bridgwater.

Hardington (near Frome) *Hardintone/Hardingtona/ Hardintona: Ralph Rufus from Bishop of Coutances. 28 pigs, 2 asses.*

Hardington Mandeville *Hardintone/tona: King's land, formerly Gunhilda, Earl Godwin's daughter.*

Hartrow *Haretreu: Roger from William de Mohun. Mill.* Hartrow House.

Haselbury Plucknett *Halberge/ berga: Brictmer the Englishman, the pre-Conquest holder, from the king. Mill.* Manor farm; St Wulfric's cell under the church.

Hatch Beauchamp *Hache/ Hachia/Bachia: Robert the Constable from Count of Mortain. 58 goats.* Church in the grounds of Hatch Court.

Havyat *Atigete/Attigetta: Brungar the Englishman from Bishop of Coutances.* Farm.

Hawkwell *Hauechewelle/ Hauekewell: Ulf, the pre-Conquest holder, from the king.* Now Hawkwell Cross; farm.

Hay Street *Haia:* Lost.

Heathfield *Hafella/Herfeld/felt: Ralph from William de Mohun. Mill.* Heathfield Lodge.

Hele (in Bradford) *Hela/Hele/ Bela: Alfred from Count of Mortain. Mill.* Manor house.

Hemington *Hamintone/ Hamitone/Hamintona/ Hammingtona: Baldwin of Exeter, Sheriff of Devon. 245 sheep.*

Henstridge *Hengesterich/ Hesterige: King's land, formerly Earl Harold; St Severus Church from Hugh d'Avranches. 438 wethers.*

High Littleton *Liteltone/tona: Ralph Rufus from Bishop of Coutances. Mill.*

Hill *Hille/Hilla: Roger de Courseulles.* Farm.

Hillfarrance *Hilla/Hille/Billa: Walter from Alfred d'Epaignes. Mill.* On Hillfarrance Brook; cottages round a green.

Hinton Blewett *Hantone/tona: Ralph Blewitt from William d'Eu. Mill. 150 sheep.*

Hinton Charterhouse *Hantone/ tona: Edward of Salisbury. 2 mills. 200 sheep.* Ruins of Hinton Priory, founded by the Countess of Salisbury in 1232.

HASELBURY PLUCKNETT: *Mill and millhouse, in handsome Ham stone.*

Hinton St George *Hantone/ tona: William d'Eu; 2 mills. 200 sheep.* Attractive; Hinton House.

Hiscombe *Hasecumbe/Hasce/ Hassecomba/Hetsecome/coma:* Lost.

Holcombe *Holearbe:* Lost.

Holford (near Lydeard St Lawrence) *Holeford/fort: William and Alric from Roger de Courseulles.* Now 2 hamlets, Treble and Rich's Holford.

Holford St Mary *Holeford/ Hulofort: Hugh from William de Mohun. Mill. 64 goats.* Now Holford.

Holne *Holme:* Lost.

Holnicote *Hunecote/cota/ Hunnecota: 2 nuns, as a royal grant; William from Roger de Courseulles.*

Holton *Altone/Haltona: Aelfric from Humphrey the Chamberlain.* 13th-century church.

Honibere *Herdeneberie/ Herderneberia: Ansketel.* Farm.

Hornblotton *Horblawetone/ tona: Serlo de Burcy from Glastonbury Church. Assessed with Alhampton, etc.* Near the Roman Fosse Way; cottages round a green.

Horsey *Hursi: Rademar from Walter de Douai. 20 pigs.* Manor farm nearby.

Horsey Pignes *Pignes/Peghenes:* Lost.

Horsington *Horstenetone/ Horsstenetona: William FitzGuy. Mill.*

Houndstone *Hundestone/tona: Ansger from Count of Mortain.* Near Yeovil Aerodrome.

Huish (in Burnham on Sea) *Hiwis:* Lost.

Huish (in Nettlecombe) *Hewis: Bertram from Roger de Courseulles; Ralph de Reuilly from Ralph Pagnell. Mill.* Now Huish Barton; on Exmoor.

Huish Champflower *Hiwis/ Hiwys: Roger Arundel. Mill.* Attractive.

Huntspill *Honspil: Walter de Douai. 14 mares, 6 wild mares.* On Huntspill River, recently re-channelled to prevent flooding.

Hunstile *Hustille/illa: John the Usher.*

Huntworth *Hunteworde/ euorda: Richard de Merri from Alfred d'Epaignes.*

Hutton *Hotune/tuna/Hoctona/ Hutune/tona: Azelin from Bishop of Coutances.* Hutton Court.

Idson *Edeuestone/tona: Ansketel from Roger de Courseulles.* Farm.

Ilchester *Giuelcestre/ Giuelecestre/Giuel/Giulecestra/ Ciulecestra/Ecclesia S Andreae: Bishop Maurice of London holding St Andrew's Church and some land. Mill.* Town, once a Roman settlement, on the Fosse Way; birthplace of Roger Bacon (1214–94).

Ilminster *Ileminstre/monstre: Muchelney Abbey. 3 mills, market.* Busy market town with 18th-century houses.

Ilton *Atiltone/tona/Hiltona: Athelney Church. Mill.* 17th-century almshouses.

Isle Abbots *Ile/Ila: Muchelney Church. Mill.* Marshland. The north aisle of the church was added by Margaret Beaufort, Henry VIII's mother.

Isle Brewers *Ile/Isle/Ila/Isla: Ansger le Breton from Count of Mortain; Richard de Merri from Alfred d'Epaignes. 2 mills, 150 sheep, 60 goats.* Called after the Norman de Briwere family.

Keinton Mandeville *Chintone/ tune/tona/tuna/Chigtona: Mauger from Count of Mortain.* Birthplace of Sir Henry Irving (1838–1905).

Kenn *Chen/Chent: Bishop of Coutances.* On the River Kenn; manor farm on Kenn Moor.

Kewstoke *Chiwestoch/stoc: Osbern from Gilbert FitzThorold. 5 unbroken mares, 18 cattle.* Adjoining Weston-super-Mare. The Becket Cup in Taunton Museum is purportedly a relic containing the blood of Thomas à Becket.

Keyford *Caivel/Chaivert/ Kaivert: Nigel from Bishop of Coutances. Norman from Thurston FitzRolf. Mill.* Now Little Keyford.

Keynsham *Cainesham/essam: King's land and Bishop of Coutances, Wulfward's wife and Aelfric from the king. 6 mills, 700 sheep.* Commuter area for Bristol; modern shopping centre.

Kilmersdon *Chenemeresdone/ Chinemeresdone: King's land.*

Kilton *Chilvetune/tun/Diuetona: William de Mohun and Ralph, a man-at-arms, from him.* Coastal.

Kilve *Clive/Cliva: Roger de Courseulles. Mill. 50 goats.* Ruins of a 14th-century chantry.

Kingsbury Episcopi *Chingesberie/Kingesberia: Bishop of Wells and 3 men-at-arms and a clerk from him. 2 mills.* On the River Parrett.

Kingstone *Chingestone/stana: Hubert de St Clair from Count of Mortain.*

Kingston Seymour *Cingestone/ tona: William de Monceaux from Bishop of Coutances.* Marshland.

Kingweston *Chinwardestune/ Kinuardestuna: Ida of Boulogne, formerly Wulfeva.* Kingweston House.

Kittisford *Chedesford/forda: William from Roger Arundel. Mill.*

Knowle (in Timberscombe) *Ernole: Roger from William de Mohun. 7 wild mares, 20 cattle.* Knowle Hill.

Knowle Park *Chenolle/nolla: Drogo de Montacute. 26 pigs.* Knowlepark Farm.

Knowle St Giles *Chenolle/nolla: William de Daumeray from Roger de Courseulles.*

Lamyatt *Lamieta/Lamigeta: Nigel the Doctor from Glastonbury Church. Assessed with Alhampton, etc.* 15th-century church in a farmyard; Lamyatt Lodge.

Langford Budville *Langeford/ forda: King's land, formerly Godwin FitzHarold. Mill.*

KINGSBURY EPISCOPI: *Octagonal lock-up.*

Langham *Langeham/Langaham: 3 men-at-arms from William de Mohun. Mill.* Farm.

Langport *Langeport/Langporth/ Lanport/Lanporth/Lanporda/ Lantporta: King's land; Count of Mortain (a garden). 500 sheep.* On the River Parrett.

Langridge *Lancheris: Azelin from Bishop of Coutances. Mill. 200 sheep.* Old farm-house; Langridge House.

Lattiford *Lodreford/forda/ Lodereforda: Humphrey the Chamberlain.* Mill; Lattiford House.

Laverton *Lavretone/tona: Herbert from William d'Eu.* On Henhambridge Brook.

Leigh (in Old Cleeve) *Lege: Hugh from Alfred d'Epaignes.* Now Leigh Barton.

Leigh (in Lydeard St Lawrence) *Lega: Bishop of Winchester.* Now Chapel Leigh.

Leigh (in Milverton) *Lege/Lega: Manfred from William de Mohun.* Farm.

LANGRIDGE: *Drystone walls.*

Leigh (in Winsham) *Lege/Lega: Robert from William de Mohun.* Leigh House.

Lexworthy *Lecheswrde/surda: Evrard from Count Eustace; Geoffrey from Roger de Courseulles. 2 mills.*

Lilstock *Lulestoch/stoc: Ansger Cook. 25 pigs.* Coastal.

Limington *Limingtone/Limintone/Limigtona/Limintona: Roger de Courseulles. Mill.* On the River Yeo.

Litnes *Litelande/Littlelaneia: Bishop of Wells before and after 1066.* Litnes field.

Littleton (in Compton Dundon) *Liteltone/tona: Norman from Roger de Courseulles.* Between 2 Roman sites.

Litton *Litune/tuna: Canons of St Andrews from Bishop of Wells before and after 1066. 3 mills.*

Long Ashton *Estune/Esttuna: Bishop of Coutances and Roger the Bursar and Guy the Priest from him. Mill.* On the outskirts of Bristol; Ashton Court, 16–17th-century with later additions.

Long Sutton *Sutone/tune/Sutona/tuna/Suttona: Athelney Church; Roger de Courseulles.* Medieval Load Bridge; manor farm. Oliver Cromwell described his victory at Langport as the 'Long Sutton Mercy'.

Lopen *Lopen(e)/Loptone/Lopena: Gerard from Count of Mortain; Gerard Ditcher from Roger de Courseulles; Harding FitzAlnoth from the king.* On Lopen Brook, beside the Roman Fosse Way.

Lovington *Lovintune/tona: Serlo de Burcy. Mill.*

Loxton *Lochestone/tona: Count Eustace. Mill.* Church with fine stone pulpit, typical of the Mendip area.

Luccombe *Locumbe/cumba: Ralph de Limesy, formerly Queen Edith; Vitalis from Odo FitzGamelin.* Pretty; thatched cottages.

Luckington *Lochintone/tona: Alfred d'Epaignes. Mill.* Now Luckington Cross; farm.

Lufton *Lochetone/Locutona: Ansger from Count of Mortain.* Manor house.

Lullington *Loligtone/tona: Bishop of Coutances formerly Earl Harold. Mill. 220 sheep.* Norman church.

Luxborough *Lolochesberie/beria: Ranulf and Nigel from William de Mohun.* In the Brendon Hills, a Roman iron-working area; a lead-mining community in the 19th century.

Lyde *Eslide/lida: Azelin from Roger Arundel.* Now Great Lyde Farm and Little Lyde in Yeovil.

Lydeard St Lawrence *Lidiard/Lediart/Lidiarda: Bishop of Winchester.*

Lyncombe *Lincume/cuma: Bath Church. 2 mills. 180 sheep.* South Lyncombe, part of Bath.

LYTES CARY: *Gateway to the medieval manor of the Lyte family, restored in 1948. The great chamber has a coved and ribbed plaster ceiling, 1533.*

Lyng *Lege/Lega: Athelney Church.* Once fortified; traces of earthworks. King Alfred built a causeway joining it to Athelney.

Lytes Cary *Curi/Kari: Humphrey the Chamberlain. 12 cattle.* Lytes Cary manor house.

Maidenbrook *Maidenbroche/broca: Bishop of Winchester.* Farm.

Manworthy *Maneworde/Maneurda:* Lost.

Maperton *Malpertone/Malperettona: Geoffrey from Thurstan FitzRolf. 2 mills. 17 cattle.*

Marksbury *Mercesberie/beria: Glastonbury Church. 29 pigs.* 18th-century manor house.

Marsh Mills *Mulselle/sella: Hugh from Alfred d'Epaignes.*

Marston Bigot *Mersitone/tona: Roger Arundel. Mill.* 17–18th century Marston House.

Marston Magna *Merstone/tona: Count of Mortain and Robert from him.* Once made cider.

Martock *M(a)ertoch/tocha/Mar/Mertocha/Maertoc/toca: King's land, formerly Queen Edith. 2 mills, fishery. 300 sheep.* House with a 13th-century hall.

Meare *Mere/Mera: Glastonbury Church. 3 fisheries, vineyard.* Iron Age lake village, now on its own 'island' above the moors; 14th-century Fish House; manor house, once the summer retreat of the Abbots of Glastonbury.

Melcombe *Melecome/coma: Robert d'Auberville. Mill.*

Mells *Mulle/Mulla: Glastonbury Church and Bishop of Coutances and Godiva, whose husband was the pre-Conquest holder, from the church. Mill.* Beautiful Tudor manor house, seat of the Horne family, one of whom was 'little Jack Horner' of the nursery rhyme. 4 prehistoric camps nearby: Wadbury, Tedbury, Newbury and Kingsdown.

Merridge *Malrige: Ranulf from Alfred d'Epaignes. Mill.* Also Lower Merridge hamlet.

Merriott *Meriet: Dodman from Count of Mortain; Harding from the king. 4 mills. 10 cattle.* Once a centre for flax and canvas.

Middlecote *Millescote:* Lost.

Middlezoy *Sowi: Glastonbury Church. 17 cattle.* Above marshes once crossed only by causeways.

Midelney *Midelenie/neia: Muchelney Church. Vineyard, 2 fisheries (6000 eels), 21 cattle, 30 goats (with Muchelney and Thorney).* Elizabethan manor; mews for falcons.

Midgell *Megele/gela: Leofwin from Bishop of Coutances.* Farm.

Milborne Port *Meleburne/borna/burna/Milburne/borna/Meleburne: King's land, with Reinbald holding the church. 6 mills, market. 22 pigs, 153 sheep.* Market town.

Milton (in Skilgate) *Mildetune/tuna:* Lost.

Milton (in Weston-super-Mare) *Middeltone/Mildeltuna/Mideltone/tona: Richard from Walter de Douai; Alfward from Ansketel.* Part of Weston-super-Mare.

Milton Clevedon *Mideltune/tuna: Hildebert from Matthew de Mortagne. Mill. 10 cattle, 60 sheep, 40 goats.* Manor farm.

Milverton *Milvertone/tune/tona/tuna/Melvertona: King's land, with Stephen the Chaplain holding the church. Mill, market.* Large. Archbishop Thomas Cranmer was an incumbent of the 15th-century parsonage.

Minehead *Maneheue/heua: William de Mohun. Mill. 16 cattle, 300 sheep.* Seaside resort. Its oldest part, Quay Town, has a 17th-century harbour.

Monksilver *Selve/vere/vre/Selva/vera/vra: Aldred and Alric from Roger de Courseulles. Richard from Alfred d'Epaignes. Mill. 2 oxen.*

Monkton Combe *Cume/Cuma: Bath Church'. 2 mills.* Large; on Midford Brook.

Montacute *Montagud/gut: Count of Mortain (his castle).* Montacute House, built of Ham Hill stone.

Moortown *Lamore: Ogis from Roger de Courseulles.* Farm.

Moreton *Mortone/Morthona: Serlo de Burcy. Mill.* Flooded by the Chew Valley Reservoir.

Muchelney *Michelenie/neia:* See page 233.

Mudford *Mudiford/forda/Mundiford/forda/Modiforda: King's lands, Warmund from Wulfward White, an English thane; Dodman from Count of Mortain; Reginald from Serlo de Burcy. Mill. 23 pigs.* On the River Yeo.

Mudford Sock *Soche: Vitalis from Roger de Courseulles.*

Myne *Mene:* Lost.

Nether Stowey *Stalwei/Estalweia/Stawe:* See page 232.

Nettlecombe *Netecumbe/coba/comba/Netelcumbe/comba: King's land, formerly Godwin FitzHarold.* On Exmoor; Nettlecombe Court, home of the Raleigh family.

Newhall *Neuhalle/Newiahalla:* Lost.

Newton (in Bicknoller) *Niwetune/Niuetuna: William de Mohun. Mill.*

Newton (in North Petherton) *Newentone/tona/Newetone/tune/Niwetone/tona: Alfred of Marlborough from Count Eustace; Robert from Roger de Courseulles; Ralph from Roger Arundel; Stable from John the Usher. Mill.* On the Bridgwater and Taunton Canal.

MONTACUTE: *Gable of the house built by Ed. Phelips, with riotous ornamentation.*

Newton St Loe *Niwetone/Newe/Niwetona: Bishop of Coutances. Mill. 12 cattle.* Newton Park, now a teacher-training college.

North Cadbury *Cadeberie/beria: Thurstan FitzRolf. 2 mills. 31 cattle, 60 pigs.* Attractive. Tudor manor house.

North Curry *Nortcuri/Nordchori/Nortchori: King's land, formerly Earl Harold, with Bishop Maurice holding the church; Ansger le Breton from Count of Mortain. Fishery, vineyard. 20 cattle, 20 pigs, 100 sheep.*

North Perrott *Peret/Peredt: Bretel from Count of Mortain. 2 mills.* Manor house and park.

North Petherton *Nordperet/pereth/Nortperret/Petreta/Pedret/Peretune/tuna: King's land, formerly King Edward. Mill.* Large.

North Wootton *Utone/Utona: Edred from Glastonbury Church.*

Norton Fitzwarren *Nortone/tona: Alfred from Count of Mortain. 2 mills.* Attractive; 14th-century church.

Norton Malreward *Nortone/tona: Wulfeva from Bishop of Coutances. Mill.* Hauteville's Quoit, a single stone forming part of a Bronze Age complex, nearby.

Norton St Philip *Nortune/tuna: Edward of Salisbury, Sheriff of Wiltshire. Mill. 20 cattle, 28 pigs, 240 sheep.* Partly 14th-century George Inn.

Norton sub Hamdon *Nortone/tona: St Mary's Church, Grestain from Count of Mortain. 2 mills. 10 cattle.*

Nunney *Noiun/Nonin: Thorgils from William de Mohun. ½ mill. 20 pigs.* Attractive; Ruins of a 14th-century moated castle.

Nynehead *Nichehede/Nichebede: Bishop of Winchester.* Nynehead Court.

Oake *Acha/Ache/Acca: Geoffrey de Vautortes from Roger de Courseulles. Mill.* Farm house; tithe barn.

Oakley *Accheleia/Achelai/Achelaia: King's land.* Oakley House; Oakley Farms.

Oaktrow *Wochetreu: Durand from William de Mohun.* Oaktrow Wood.

Oare *Are/Ar: Ralph de Pomeroy. 20 cattle.* Remote; features in *Lorna Doone* by R.D. Blackmore.

Odcombe *Udecome/Odecoma: Ansger le Breton from Count of Mortain. Mill. 126 sheep.* Birthplace of Thomas Coryate (1577–1617), whose *Crudities*, about his travels in Europe, was published in 1611.

Old Cleeve *Clive/Cliva: King's land, formerly Earl Harold. 2 mills. 300 wethers, 50 goats.* Cleeve Abbey, founded in 1138, an unusual example of Cistercian domestic architecture.

Old Stowey *Staweit/Estaweit: Durand from William de Mohun.* In the Brendon Hills.

Orchardleigh *Horcerlei/Hordcerleia/Orcerleia: Bishop of Coutances. Mill. 3 cobs.* 19th-century Elizabethan-style house; church where the poet Sir Henry Newbolt (1862–1938) is buried.

Otterhampton *Otramestone/tona/Otremetone/Otrammetona/Oterammatona: Robert from Roger de Courseulles; Herbert from Alfred d'Epaignes, Osmer, whose father was the pre-Conquest holder, from the king.* Hill House, near the mouth of the River Parrett.

Overleigh *Lega: Glastonbury Church. 20 pigs.* Part of Street.

Over Stratton *Stratone: King's land.*

Panborough *Wadeneberie/Padenaberia: Glastonbury Church. Island, vineyard.* Locality near Wedmore.

Pardlestone *Plestone/tona: Roger de Courseulles.* Farms; Pardlestone Hill.

Pawlett *Pauelet/Paulet: Rademar from Walter de Douai.* Church with a fine Norman doorway; owned by John of Gaunt in the 14th century.

Pedwell *Pedewelle/willa: Walter de Douai from Glastonbury Church.*

Pendomer *Penne/Penna: Alfred from Count of Mortain. 12 cattle, 35 pigs, 250 sheep.* Remote; 16th-century manor house.

Pennard *Pennarminstre/ministra: Glastonbury Church and Serlo de Burcy from the church. 42 cattle, 25 pigs.* Now East Pennard; Pennard House.

Penselwood *Penne/Penna: William Gerald from Roger Arundel. Mill.* Site of a Saxon victory in 658.

Perry *Peri/Pedri: William and Geoffrey de Vautortes from Roger de Courseulles; Ralph from Roger Arundel; John the Usher.* Farm.

Petherham *Perredham: Ansketel from Roger de Courseulles.* Farm.

Pightley *Puchelege/lega: Geoffrey de Vautortes from Roger de Courseulles. ½ mill.*

Pillock's Orchard *Pilloch/Pilloc: Ansketel from Roger de Courseulles.* Field in Cannington.

Pilton *Piltone/tona: Glastonbury Church and Ralph Crooked Hands from the church. 2 mills, 4 cobs, 35 cattle, 56 pigs, 500 sheep, 42 goats.*

Pitcombe *Pidecome/coma: Thurstan FitzRolf. 2 mills. 6 unbroken mares, 12 cattle, 60 pigs.* Godminster Farm, mainly 15th century, nearby.

Pitcott *Picote/cota/Piccota: Edmund FitzPayne; William Hussey from Geoffrey of Mowbray. Mill.*

Pitminster *Pipeminstre/Pinpeministra: Bishop of Winchester. Mill. 2 pigs.* 16th-century houses, Poundisford Park and Poundisford Lodge, nearby.

Pitney *Petenie/neia: King's land, formerly Wulfward White.* Pitney House.

Pixton *Potesdone/dona: Roger de Courseulles.* Pixton Park; remains of a 12th-century priory at nearby Barlinch.

Plainsfield *Planesfelle/fella: Hugh from Alfred d'Epaignes.* On the edge of Quantock Forest.

Podimore *Mideltone/Middeltona: Glastonbury Church.*

Poleshill *Pouselle/ella: Dodman from William de Mohun.*

Ponteside *Panteshede: Roger de Courseulles.* Possibly the valley where Towerhead Brook rises.

Porlock *Portloc: Drogo from Baldwin of Exeter.* Coastal; tourist centre.

Portbury *Porberie/beria: Bishop of Coutances. 2 mills. 14 unbroken mares, 15 cattle, 216 sheep.* Portbury Dock at the mouth of the Avon.

Portishead *Porteshe/heue: William de Monceaux from Bishop of Coutances. Mill. 60 goats.* Part of the Severnside Industrial Area; resort in the 19th century.

Preston (in Milverton) *Prestetone/tune/Prestitone: Robert FitzIvo from Count of Mortain, formerly Earl Harold; Hugh from Alfred d'Epaignes. 2 mills. 13 cattle.* Now Preston Bowyer.

Preston Plucknett *Prestetone: Ansger of Montacute.* On the outskirts of Yeovil; fine medieval tithe barn.

Priston *Prisctone/tona: Bath Church. Mill.* Remote.

Puckington *Pochintune/Pokintuna/Pochingtona: William from Roger de Courseulles.*

Puriton *Peritone/tona: The only holding of St Peter's, Rome, a reward for the Pope's encouragement of the Conquest.* Town, site of the Royal Ordnance Factory.

Pylle *Pille/Pilla: Serlo de Burcy from Glastonbury Church.* Manor house.

Quantock *Cantoche/toca:* Lost.

Quarme *Carme/Carma: Manfred from William de Mohun, Godbold. 15 cattle.* Now 2 hamlets, North and South Quarme.

Queen Camel *Camel: King's land, formerly Countess Gytha. 2 mills. 12 cattle, 20 pigs, 300 sheep.* Hazelgrove Park, a Tudor house rebuilt in the 18th century.

Raddington *Radingetune/tuna/Radinghetona: Robert from Roger Arundel. Mill for the hall.*

Radlet *Radeflot/Ratdeflot/Radeflote/flota: Robert from Roger de Courseulles; Herbert from Alfred d'Epaignes. Mill.* Farm; Radlet Common.

Radstock *Stoche/Estoca: Roger from Bishop of Coutances. Mill. 22 pigs, 210 sheep.* Large; on the Roman Fosse Way. Coal-mining began here in the 18th century.

REXWORTHY: *Moated farmhouse; 'worthy' was the Saxon term for an isolated farm.*

Rapps *Epse/Eppsa: Ralph de Limesy.*

Redlynch *Retlis/Redlisc/Roliz/Reliz: Bretel from Count of Mortain. 20 pigs.* 18th-century church; Redlynch House.

Rexworthy *Rachedeworde/worda: Robert from Roger de Courseulles.* Farm.

Ridgehill *Ragiol: Guntard from Serlo de Burcy; Godwin, the pre-Conquest holder, from the king. 15 cattle.*

Rimpton *Rintone/tona: Bishop of Winchester. 20 cattle, 24 pigs.*

Rodden *Reddene/dena: Ingelrann from Arnulf de Hesdin. 2 mills. 20 cattle, 50 pigs, 300 sheep.* Farm with a 17th-century Gothic chapel.

Rode *Rode/Roda: Bishop of Coutances and Robert, Moses, Robert, Roger, Sherwold and Richard the Interpreter from him. Mill.* On the River Fro.

Rodhuish *Radehewis: Hugh from Alfred d'Epaignes.* On the edge of Exmoor.

Rodney Stoke *Stoches/Stocca: Bishop of Coutances. Mill. 20 mares, 20 pigs, 68 goats.* On the edge of the Mendips; church with some 17th-century woodwork.

Runnington *Runetone/tona: Dodman from William de Mohun. Mill. 23 pigs.* On the River Tone.

St Michael Church *Michaeliscerce/Michelescerca: Ansger Fower.* Small church and a few buildings.

Saltford *Sanford/fort: Roger Whiting from Bishop of Coutances. Mill.* Large; partly Norman house with traces of 14th-century frescoes.

Sampford Arundel *Sanford/forda: Ogis from Roger de Courseulles. Mill. 11 cattle.*

Sampford Brett *Sanford/forda: William from Hugh d'Avranches. Mill.*

Sandford (in Wembdon) *Sanford/Santfort: Ralph from Roger Arundel. 11 cattle, 23 pigs.* Farm.

Seaberton *Sedtamtone:* Lost.

Seavington *Seouenamentone: Athelney Church; Mauger from Count of Mortain. Siward from the king. Mill.* Now Seavington St Mary; Seavington St Michael nearby.

Selworthy *Seleurde: Ralph de Limesy, formerly Queen Edith. Mill.* Attractive. Thatched cottages. Bury Castle, near Selworthy Beacon, is an Iron Age camp.

Shapwick *Sapeswich/Sapaeswica: Glastonbury Church and Roger de Courseulles, Alfred d'Epaignes and Warmund from the church.* 17th-century Shapwick House.

Shearston *Siredestone/tona: Robert Herecom from Roger de Courseulles.*

Shepton Beauchamp *Sceptone/tona: Count of Mortain.* 19th-century Beauchamp Manor; traces of a medieval field system.

Shepton Mallet *Sepetone/tona: Roger de Courseulles from Glastonbury Church. 2 mills (with Croscombe).* Town, prosperous in the 18th century. *Domesday Book* and other public records were kept here for safety during World War II.

Shepton Montague *Sceptone/Sheptuna/Septona: Drogo from Count of Mortain. 2 mills. 23 pigs, 210 sheep.*

Shipham *Sipcham: Robert from Roger de Courseulles.* Calamine for the Bristol brass and zinc industries mined here in the 18th century.

Shopnoller *Scobindare/Scobinalre: Bishop of Winchester.*

Shortmansford *Sordemaneforde: Brictric from William de Mohun. 11 goats.* Lost.

Shovel *Siwoldestone/tona: Ansger.* Shovel House.

Skilgate *Scheligate/Schiligata: Robert of Gatemore from Roger Arundel. Mill. 10 cattle, 150 sheep.* Skilgate Wood.

Sock Dennis *Soche/Socca: Robert FitzIvo from Count of Mortain. 35 pigs.* On Bearley Brook.

Somerton *Sumer/Summertone/Sumertona: King's land, fisheries. 500 sheep.* Market town; the county centre from 1278–1371, with a 17th-century town hall and a market cross.

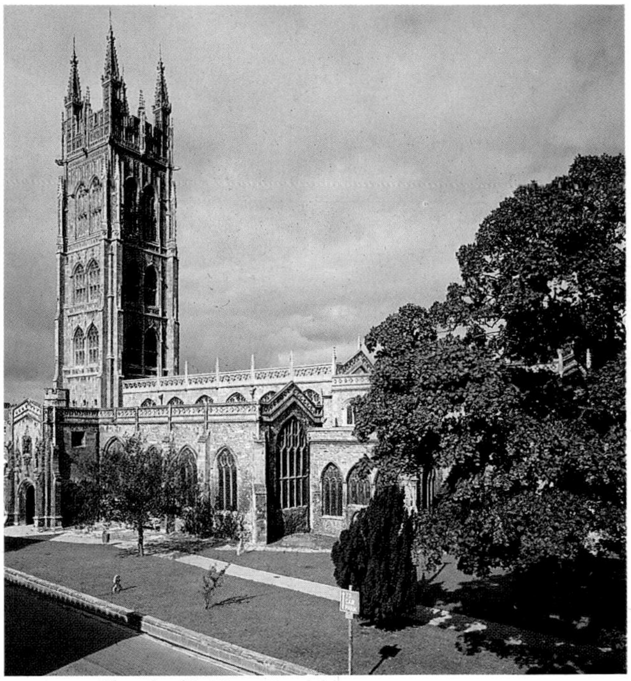

TAUNTON: *Church of St Mary Magdalena.*

South Cadbury *Sudcadeberie/ Sutcadaberia/deberia: Bernard from Thurstan FitzRolf; Bernard Pancevolt, a clerk and an Englishman.* Below Cadbury Castle, one of England's finest Iron Age hill-forts; believed to have been King Arthur's Camelot.

South Petherton *Sudperet/ Sutpedret/perret/petret/ Sudperetone/Sutperettona: King's land, formerly King Edmund; Alfgeat the Priest from the king. Mill.* Attractive; King Ina's Palace, a 14th-century house, restored in the 19th century.

Sparkford *Spercheford/ Sparkeforde: Fulcwin from Walter de Douai. Mill.* Sparkford Hill.

Spaxton *Spachestone/ Espachestona: Alfred d'Epaignes.* Cloth fulling centre; Church with a 15th-century bench-end carving of a fuller.

Standerwick *Stalrewich/ Estalrewicca: Robert from Roger de Courseulles.* Farm; manor house.

Stanton Drew *Stantone/ Estantona: King's land and Roger from the king. Mill.* On the River Chew; 3 prehistoric stone circles nearby.

Stanton Prior *Stantone/tona: Bath Church.*

Staple Fitzpaine *Staple/Estapla: Count of Mortain. Mill. 100 goats.* 17th-century cottages round the church. Hestercombe House, headquarters of the Somerset Fire Brigade, garden designed by Lutyens and Gertrude Jekyll.

Staunton *Stantune/Estantone/ tuna: William de Mohun.* Staunton Plantation.

Stawell *Stawelle/Estawella: Godescal from Glastonbury Church. 200 sheep.*

Stawley *Stawei/weia: Robert and Herbert from Alfred d'Epaignes.* Farm.

Steart *Esturt: 2 porters from Montacute from Count of Mortain.* Farm.

Stockland *Stocheland(e): Ansketel from Roger de Courseulles; William de Mohun; Ralph de Reuilly from Ralph Pagnell. Mill.* Close to Bristol; manor house; manor farm.

Stocklinch *Stoche: Roger from William de Mohun; formerly Queen Edith; Alfward and his brothers, the pre-Conquest tenants, from the king.*

Stogumber *Warverdinestoch/ stoc: Richere de Les Andelys. Church.* Large.

Stogursey *Stoche/Estocha: William de Falaise. Mill. 250 sheep.* Ruins of a castle, probably 12th century, belonging to the de Curci family.

Stoke Pero *Stoche/Esthoca: Roger de Courseulles.* Remote.

Stoke St Mary *Stocha/Stoche/ Estoca/Stoca: Bishop of Winchester.* Stoke House.

Stoke sub Hamdon *Stoca/ Stoche/Stochet/Estocha/Estochet: William de Mohun; Mauger from Count of Mortain. Mill.* Now 2 villages, East and West Stoke; below Ham Hill, with one of Britain's largest hill-forts, traces of a Roman villa, and stone quarries.

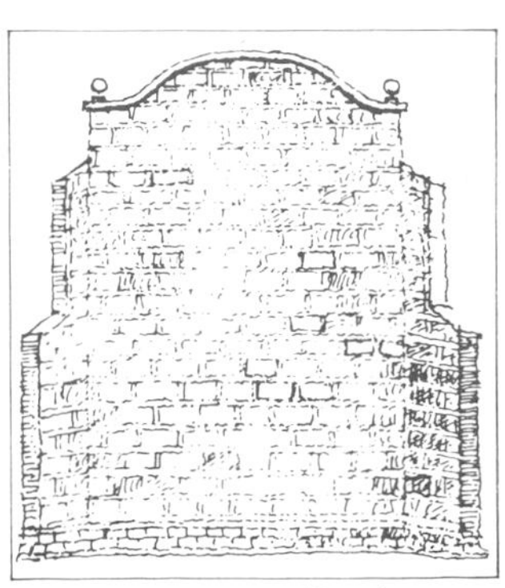

STOKE SUB HAMDON: *'Fives' stone wall, c. 1780.*

Stoke Trister *Stoche/Stoca: Bretel from Count of Mortain. Mill. 70 goats, 8 unbroken mares.*

Stone (in Exford) *Estone/ Estana: Roger de Courseulles.* Near Exford.

Stone (in Mudford) *Stane/ Stana: Reginald from Serlo de Burcy.* Farm.

Ston Easton *Estone/tona: Azelin from Bishop of Coutances; Gilbert FitzThorold; Manasseh Cook's wife. Mill.* Georgian Ston Easton Park.

Stoney Stoke *Stoche/Stocca/ Estoca: Drogo from Count of Mortain.*

Stony Littleton *Liteltone/tona: Osmund from Bishop of Coutances. Mill. 200 sheep.* On Wellow Brook.

Stowell *Stanwelle/Estanwella: Azelin from Bishop of Coutances.*

Stowey (in Oare) *Stawei/ Estaweia:* Lost.

Stratton on the Fosse *Stratone/ Stretone/Stratona/Stretona: William de Monceaux from Bishop of Coutances. Mill. 27 unbroken mares.* On the Roman Fosse Way; Downside public school.

Street (in Winsham) *Strate/ Estrat/Estrart: Roger from William de Mohun. 4 oxen.*

Stretcholt *Stragelle/Estragella: Rainward from Walter de Douai. 43 pigs.* Near the mouth of the River Parrett.

Stringston *Strenegestone/ Strengestune/Strengestona/tuna: William from Roger de Courseulles; Ranulf from Alfred d'Epaignes. 200 sheep.*

Sutton Bingham *Sutone/tona: Roger Bushell from Roger Arundel. Mill.* Fine Norman church with wall-paintings, c.1300; Sutton Bingham Reservoir nearby.

Sutton Mallet *Sutone/tona: Roger de Courseulles from Glastonbury Church.*

Sutton Montis *Sutone/tuna: Drogo from Count of Mortain. Mill.* Sutton Farm below Cadbury Hill.

Swainswick *Wiche/Wica: Nigel de Gournai from Bishop of Coutances; Alfred, the pre-Conquest holder from the king. Mill.* Lower Swainswick, part of Bath; Upper Swainswick village.

Swang *Suindune/duna: Ranulf from Roger de Courseulles. Mill.* Farm.

Swell *Sewelle/ella: Bretel from Count of Mortain.*

Sydenham *Sideham: William from Roger Arundel.* Tudor manor in Bridgwater.

Syndercombe *Sindercome: Hugh from Thurstan FitzRolf.* Lost. Flooded by Clatworthy Reservoir.

Tadwick *Tatewiche/wica: William Hussey; Ralph of Berkeley. 189 sheep.*

Tarnock *Ternoc: Ludo and Richard from Walter de Douai. 17 unbroken mares.*

Taunton *Tantone/tona: Bishop of Winchester. 3 mills, market.* County town and commercial centre; 12th-century castle keep, with later additions. The Bloody Assizes were held here after Monmouth's Rebellion in 1685. 17th-century alms-houses.

Tellisford *Tablesford/forda: Moses from Bishop of Coutances. ½ mill.*

Temple Combe *Come: Samson the Chaplain from Bishop of Bayeux.* Called after the Knights Templars, and said to have been owned by them.

Tetton *Tedintone/tona: William from Hugh d'Avranches.* Tetton House; farm.

Theodoric's Land *Terra Teodrici:* Lost.

Thorent *Tornie/Turnie/ Turnietta:* Lost.

Thorne *Torne/Torna: Drogo and Ralph the Priest from Count of Mortain.*

Thorne St Margaret *Torne/ Torna/Tornet: Alric from Roger de Courseulles. Mill.*

Thorney *Torleie/leia: Muchelney Church. Assessed with Midelney, etc.* On the River Parrett; Thorney Moor.

Thornfalcon *Torne/Torna: Ansger from Count of Mortain.*

Thurlbear *Torlaberie/beria: Drogo from Count of Mortain.*

Tickenham *Ticheham/Ticaham: William d'Eu.*

Timberscombe *Timbrecumbe/ racumba: Drogo from Roger Arundel.*

Timsbury *Temesbare/bara/ Themesbera/Timesberie/berua: William from Bishop of Coutances. Part of a mill.* 19th-century church chancel by Gilberto Scott.

Tintinhull *Tintehalle/ehella/ Tutenelle/Tintenelle/Tuttehella: Count of Mortain. Mill.* Dower House, 1687; 2 17–18th-century houses, Tintinhull Court and Tintinhull House, the latter with beautiful formal gardens.

Tolland *Talanda/Talham/ Talam: William FitzRoger from Roger de Courseulles.* 17th-century Gaulden Manor nearby.

Torweston *Turvestone/tona: Hugh from William de Mohun. Mill. 14 cattle.*

Treborough *Traberge/berga: Ralph de Limesy.* In the Brendon Hills; remains of 19th-century iron and copper mines.

Tuxwell *Tocheswelle-willa: Hugh from Roger Arundel; Brictric.* Farm.

Twerton *Twertone/tona: Nigel de Gournai and Geoffrey Malregard from Bishop of Coutances. 4 mills. 4 cobs, 17 cattle, 35 pigs, 400 sheep.* Part of Bath. Yarn was produced here in the early 18th century.

Ubley *Tumbeli: Walter from Gilbert FitzThorold. Mill.* Trout hatchery near the Chew Valley and Bladgon lakes.

Uphill *Opopille/illa: 4 men-at-arms from Serlo de Burcy. 25 pigs.* Large; probably a port in Roman times; traces of a Roman camp.

Upper Cheddon *Opecedre/ cedra/Ubcedene/dena: Roger Arundel. Mill.*

Upton Noble *Opetone/tona: Ralph Rufus from Bishop of Coutances. 21 pigs.*

Vexford *Fescheforde/forda: Alric and Robert from Roger de Courseulles.* Now Lower Vexford.

Waldron *Ulveronetone/tona/ Ulvererona:* Lost.

Walpole *Wallepille/pilla: Rademar from Walter de Douai.* Area near the River Parrett.

Walton (near Glastonbury) *Waltone/tona: Glastonbury Church. 10 cattle.* Thatched 15th-century rectory. Novelist Henry Fielding was born at nearby Sharpham Park in 1707.

Walton (in Kilmersdon) *Waltune/tuna: Edmund FitzPayne.* Farm.

Walton in Gordano *Waltone/ tona: Richard de Barre from Ralph de Mortimer, formerly Gunni the Dane.* On the outskirts of Clevedon; ruins of 17th-century Walton Castle.

Wanstrow *Wandestreu: Bishop of Wells and the Canons of St Andrew's from him before and after 1066.*

Warleigh *Herlei/Heorleia: Hugolin the Interpreter. 100 sheep.* Regency and late Gothic Warleigh Manor.

Watchet *Wacet: Dodman from William de Mohun. Mill.* Small port, a paper-making centre since the 17th century. Coleridge's 'ancient mariner' set sail from here.

Weacombe *Waicome/ Waiecoma: Geoffrey and William from Roger de Courseulles.* Below Weacombe Hill.

Weare *Werre/Werra: Walter de Douai. 2 mills. 18 cattle.* Also Lower Weare village; near the River Axe.

Wearne *Warne/Warna: Robert d'Auberville.*

Wedmore *Wedmore/Wedmor/ mora/Wetmore/mora:* See page 235.

Wellington *Walintone/tona/ Wellintona: Bishop of Wells and John the Usher from him. 2 mills. 17 cattle.* Town, a centre of the wool industry. The Duke of Wellington took his title from here and his monument is on the nearby Black Down hills.

Wellisford *Wilesford/ Welesforda: Robert d'Auberville. 18 cattle.* 17th-century Wellisford Manor.

Wells *Welle/Wella: Bishop of Wells before and after 1066, and Canons of St Andrew's, Fastrad,*

Richard, Erneis, Ralph, Alfward Croc and Edric from him; Manasseh's wife. 9 mills. 22 cattle, 150 sheep. Cathedral city, the county's largest urban centre in the 14th century. The cathedral dates from the 12th century; moated Bishop's Palace; 14th-century Vicar's Close.

Wembdon *Wadmendune/duna: Ludo from Walter de Douai. 18 cattle, 20 pigs.* On the outskirts of Bridgwater.

Wemberham *Waimore/ Weimorham: Bishop of Wells. Pasture.* Cottage and lane.

West Bower *Bur/Bure:* Lost.

Westbury sub Mendip *Westberie/beria: Bishop of Wells before and after 1066. 10 cattle, 200 sheep.*

West Camel *Camelle/ella: Muchelney Church and Dodman from the church. Mill.* On the River Camel; fragment of a Saxon cross in the church.

Westcombe *Westcumbe/ Westecomba: Azelin from Glastonbury Church, formerly Alfhild, the abbot's mother. 2 mills.* Westcombe House.

West Cranmore *Crenemelle/ mella: Harding, the pre-Conquest holder, from Glastonbury Church. Mill.* On the former East Somerset railway line.

West Harptree *Har/Herpetreu: Azelin from Bishop of Coutances. Mill.* Jacobean manor house beside the church.

West Lydford *Lideford: Aelfric from the king, formerly Brictric, his father. Mill. 20 cattle, 25 pigs.* Remote, on the River Brue.

West Monkton *Monechetone/ Morchetona: Glastonbury Church and Bishop of Winchester, Roger de Courseulles and Serlo de Burcy from the church.* Almshouse, once a leper hospital, rebuilt by the Abbot of Glastonbury 1510–1515.

Weston (near Bath) *Westone/ tona: Bath Church; Arnulf de Hesdin. 2 mills. 7 cobs, 450 sheep.* Part of Bath.

Weston Bampfylde *Westone/ tona: Alfred from Count of Mortain; Richard and Alwin from Thurstan FitzRolf. Mill. 3 cobs.* Church; Norman font.

Weston in Gordano *Westone/ tona: Azelin and William from Bishop of Coutances. 167 sheep.* Church with 15th-century tombs of the Percevals, originally a Norman family.

Westowe *Waistou/Westou: King's land; William from Roger de Courseulles.*

West Quantoxhead *Cantocheve: William de Mohun. 200 sheep.* Farm.

Whatley (near Frome) *Watelei/ leia: Walter Hussey and John the Usher from Glastonbury Church. Mill.* Also Lower Whatley hamlet.

Whatley (in Winsham) *Watelege/lega: William d'Eu.*

Wheathill *Watehelle/hella: Serlo de Burcy and Geoffrey from him.*

Whitcomb *Witecumbe/cumba: King's land.*

Whitelackington *Wislagetone/ Wyslagentona: Roger Arundel. Mill.* Dillington House, home of the 19th-century explorer, John Hanning Speke.

White Ox Mead *Witochesmede/ meda: Robert Gernon from Roger de Courseulles. Ass.*

Whitestaunton *Stantune/tuna: Ansger le Breton from Count of Mortain. Mill.* Ruins of a Roman villa beside a 15th-century manor house.

Wigborough *Wincheberie/ Winchinberia: John the Usher.* Manor house.

Willett *Willet: Dodman from William de Mohun. Mill.* Willett House.

Williton *Welletone/tune/ Willetone/Wile/Willetona: King's land. Assessed with Cannington, etc.* Birthplace of Reginald Fitzurse, one of Thomas à Becket's murderers.

Wilmersham *Winemeresham: Drogo from Bishop of Coutances.* On Exmoor.

Wilmington *Wimedone/ Wimmadona: Walter Hussey from Bath Church. 300 sheep.*

Wincanton *Wincaletone/ Wincalletonna: Rainward from Walter de Douai. Mill.* Small town with 18th-century houses built by clothmakers; racecourse.

Winford *Wenfre/fro/frod: Bishop of Coutances and Roger Whiting, Fulcran and Colswein from him. Mill.*

Winscombe *Winesome/coma/ cuma: Glastonbury Church and Roger de Courseulles, Ralph Crooked Hands and Pipe from the church; Bishop of Coutances. Mill. 8 cows.* Commuter, for Bristol; Sidcot School, at nearby Shipham, founded by 17th-century Quakers.

Winsford *Winesford-forda: King's land. Mill.* Thatched inn; pack-horse bridge.

Winsham *Winesham: Osmund from Bishop of Wells. 2 mills. 13 cattle, 270 sheep.*

Winterhead *Wintreth/tret: Herlwin from Bishop of Coutances. 8 cows.* Below Winterhead Hill.

Witham Friary *Witeham: William from Roger de Courseulles.* Ruins of England's first Carthusian monastery, founded by Henry II in penance for Becket's murder, near Witham Farm Hall. The church, c.1200, was restored in the 19th century.

Withiel (in Cannington) *Widiete/ieta: William from Roger de Courseulles. Mill.* Farm.

Withycombe *Widicumbe/ comba: Edmer from Bishop of Coutances.* Attractive.

Withypool *Widepolle/polla: Robert d'Auberville.* On Exmoor; prehistoric Stone Circle on Withypool Hill.

Wiveliscombe *Wivelescome/ coma: Bishop of Wells before and after 1066, and 3 men-at-arms from him. Mill.* 14th-century archway leading to Palace Green, all that remains of a medieval house belonging to Bishop of Bath and Wells.

Woodborough *Udeberge/berga: Osbern Giffard. 150 sheep.* Farm.

Woodspring *Worsprinc-princa: William de Falaise (given to him by Serlo de Burcy when he married Serlo's daughter).* Woodspring Priory, founded c.1200 by the grandson of Reginald Fitzurse, one of Thomas à Becket's murderers; recently restored.

Woodwick *Undewiche:* Lost.

WELLS: *One of the loveliest cathedral towns.*

Woolavington *Hunlavintone/ tona: Alfred d'Epaignes from Glastonbury Church. 11 cattle, 13 horses, 33 pigs, 151 sheep.* Woolavington Level.

Woolley *Wilege/Wlega/Wllega: Bishop of Coutances. 2 mills.* Remote.

Woolmersdon *Ulmerestone/ tona: Walter from Alfred d'Epaignes.*

Woolston (in Bicknoller) *Ulvretune/Ulfertuna: William de Mohun.* On Doniford Stream.

Woolston (in South Cadbury) *Ufetone/tona/tuna: Drogo from Count of Mortain; Leofgeat from Thurstan FitzRolf. Mill.* Manor farm.

Woolston (in Stogursey) *Ulwordestone: Robert from Roger de Courseulles.* Farm.

Wootton Courtenay *Otone/ Ottona: William de Falaise. Mill. 13 cattle, 150 sheep.*

Worle *Worle/Worla: Walter de Douai. 24 cattle.* Part of Weston-super-Mare.

Worth *Worde:* Lost.

Wraxall *Werocasale/ Worocosala/Worochesela: Bishop of Coutances and a man-at-arms from him. 2 mills. 24 cattle, 170 sheep.* Tyntesfield, a Victorian Gothic house, nearby.

Wrington *Weritone/tona: Glastonbury Church and Roger de Courseulles and Saewulf, the pre-Conquest holder, from the church. 3 mills. 46 cattle, 30 pigs, 278 sheep.* Birthplace of the philosopher John Locke (1632–1704).

Writhlington *Writelinctone/ tuna: Brictward from the king.*

Yarlington *Gerlintune/ Gerlincgetuna: Count of Mortain. Mill.* Yarlington House.

Yatton *Iatune/tuna/Eatona: Bishop of Wells and Fastrad, Hildebert and Benzelin the Archdeacon (holding the church) from him. 11 cattle, 15 pigs.* Near the marshlands of the River Yeo and subject to flooding.

Yeovil *Givele/Givela/Ivle/Ivla: Count of Mortain and Amund from him; Hugh from William d'Eu. 2 mills.* Market town, known for glove-making since the 18th century; industries now include helicopter manufacture.

Yeovilton *Geveltone/tona/ Giveltona: Ralph Blewitt from William d'Eu. 2 mills. 12 cattle.* On the River Yeo; Royal Naval Air Station; Fleet Air Arm Museum.

WEST HARPTREE: *Tilley manor built 1659, 18th-c. facade.*

Staffordshire

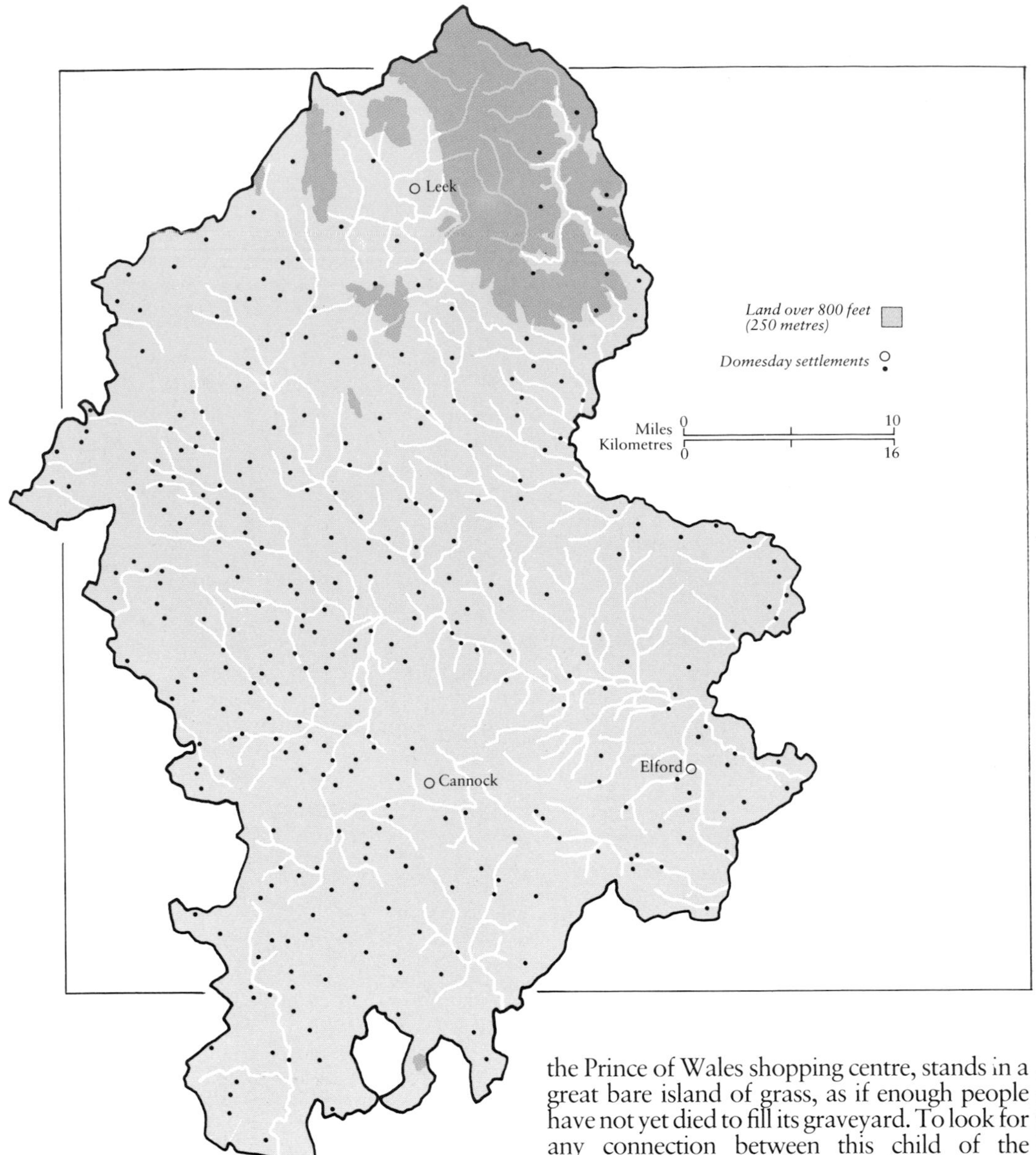

Domesday *surveyors were interested in statistics, not history. When they came across a community that was no longer tilling the land, they would often write merely* wasta est *('it is wasted') and move on. These grim little words figure large in the returns for Staffordshire, about one-fifth of which was waste in 1086. One possible cause was William's brutal suppression of a northern rebellion in 1069. Twice he and his army 'visited' the county. Little is known of what actually happened on these campaigns, but more than fifteen years later Staffordshire was a poor county.*

The relatively populous central and south-eastern areas rarely averaged more than five inhabitants to the square mile. The hilly northern region bordering the Pennines was barren and almost completely unpopulated. There are fewer entries for Staffordshire than for any other Domesday *county, excepting the much smaller Rutland and Middlesex, and more than half of these settlements were valued at less than £2. Stafford, which with Tutbury and Tamworth included burgesses among its inhabitants, was by far the largest 'city', although its population was probably under 1000. Add to this wasted and empty scene a substantial covering of forest, and* Domesday *Staffordshire appears more welcoming to deer, boar and wolves than to its struggling men and women.*

Elford

[The King holds...] ELFORD *ELEFORD*. Earl Algar held it. 3 hides. Land for 11 ploughs. In lordship 3; 24 villagers and 8 smallholders with 8 ploughs. Meadow, 24 acres; 2 mills at 20s. Value before 1066 £11; now [£]12.

Four miles north of Tamworth, on the banks of the River Tame, is the village of Elford, only slightly larger now than it was in 1086. The great families who once dominated Elford's (and sometimes England's) history – the Ardernes, Stanleys, Nevilles and Pagets – no longer live here; the great hall was demolished in 1964. But the church and its grounds have a manorial feel of their own. A long avenue of lime trees leads to the gate, where two imposing cedars stand guard. The churchyard is painstakingly maintained to create that combination of bowling green and botanical garden with gravestones which is so 'typically English' but rarely exists except in the minds of film directors.

In Norman times, when the first church was built, Elford was one of the most prosperous communities in an impoverished county. Like several other villages in south-eastern Staffordshire, it benefited from a river which provided not only rich soil for growing grain but power for grinding it into flour. Elford's two water mills were relatively productive, if *Domesday* assessments can be believed. The 20s at which they were valued is far more than that for most Staffordshire mills. (Both were still working in the eighteenth century.) There was substantial meadowland and enough ploughs to keep all the available arable land under cultivation. While much of Staffordshire was still devastated by William's punitive expeditions, Elford had increased in value from £11 to £12.

Robin Hood and Henry VII are both reputed to have visited Elford, but most of the local who-was-who keep company in the church, where their effigies lie in the chantry. Best known of these memorials is that of an otherwise undistinguished child, John Stanley, who was killed while playing tennis in about 1460. In his left hand is a tennis ball; his right is raised to his temple. *'Ubi dolor, ibi digitus'* ('where the hurt, there the hand'), says the inscription, as if after 500 years the boy is still pathetically hoping that the pain will go away.

Cannock

[The King holds...] CANNOCK *CHENET*. Earl Algar held it. 1 hide, with its dependencies. Land for 15 ploughs. 8 villagers and 3 smallholders with 3 ploughs. Woodland (b) 4 leagues wide and (a) 6 leagues long. Before 1066 it paid nothing; value now 20s.

Cannock is on the northern fringe of one of the most populous and heavily industrialized areas of England, the vast urban complex of the West Midlands. It is a town that appears to have forgotten its distant past. A few old houses look uncomfortably small amid modern shops and wide streets. The church of St Luke, dwarfed by the Prince of Wales shopping centre, stands in a great bare island of grass, as if enough people have not yet died to fill its graveyard. To look for any connection between this child of the industrial revolution and the depressed and underpopulated Cannock of 1086 at first seems ludicrous.

Chenet, as the settlement was known to the *Domesdays* surveyors, was possibly a victim of William's army, which 'pacified' large areas of Staffordshire in 1069 and 1070. At any rate, the eleven householders who occupied this king's holding could muster among them only three ploughs in 1086. (Aelfric, one of the king's thanes, had land for one plough.) Arable land for twelve ploughs apparently went to seed, with neither oxen nor people enough to cultivate it. But *Domesday* Cannock was rich in woodland, and this link has survived armies and industry for 900 years. The word 'forest' does not appear in the entry, but the Norman kings reserved much of the neighbouring land, including the town of Lichfield and half of Wolverhampton, as a vast hunting retreat. The King's Forest of Cannock became Cannock Chase when it was bought by the Bishop of Lichfield in 1189, but it remained for centuries a pleasure ground for the rich. Those who lived within the forest boundaries were allowed to look but rarely to touch. Landholders had to obtain a licence to fell their own trees and cultivate their land, while he who trapped a rabbit or cut a sapling without authorization could bring down upon himself the complex machinery of forest law.

Cannock Chase had beneath it the seeds of its own destruction. As early as 1298 coal was mined from shallow pits in the forest. In the sixteenth century many of the great oaks were felled to fuel a thriving iron industry. By the early years of this century Cannock pits employed 20,000 coal miners. Miraculously, a herd of fallow deer still roam on what remains of Cannock Chase. A Country Park of 3000 acres provides a valuable day out for the overpopulated district. Another 6000 acres are woodland once again, although the stark conifers of the Forestry Commission are an unsatisfactory replacement for the oak and ash of 1086.

Leek

[The King holds . .] LEEK *LEC*. Earl Algar held it. 1 hide with its dependencies. Land for 12 ploughs. 15 villagers and 13 smallholders with 6 ploughs. Meadow, 3 acres; woodland 4 leagues long and as wide. Value before 1066 £4; now 100s.

Early visitors to Leek found little to write home about. 'An old church but a poor town,' remarked Samuel Johnson in a letter to Mrs Thrale. Fifty years later, in 1828, Walter Scott spent the night in Leek. 'I did not come from Scotland to see rocks, I trow,' he concluded uncharitably. These travellers cannot have given the place a chance (Sir Walter left before breakfast), for among local people Leek has been thought of with affection. 'Geen Leek ite th'nise', meaning 'Going to Leek out of the noise', was once a popular colloquialism, a compliment to the town's relative tranquillity among the roaring mills and potteries of North Staffordshire.

It is not particularly quiet today. 'The metropolis of the moorlands', as a nineteenth-century historian called it, Leek is a thriving market town of more than 20,000 inhabitants. The sloping main streets are crowded with shoppers, and the self-important little buildings, many dating from the silk-rich eighteenth and nineteenth centuries, exude an air of confidence and prosperity. This small pond was once swarming with big fish and, as if to keep them all happy, there is a large number of public houses. In the centre is the market place, an attractive cobbled square where bull-baiting was popular until the middle of the last century. And at the top of the town is the sooty red church of St Edward the Confessor, its neat graveyard overlooked by the hills, a reminder that Leek still lies amid moorland.

It is believed that there was a church here in Saxon days, but *Domesday* makes no mention of one. Its *Domesday* name, Lec, may derive from the Welsh word *lech*, meaning stone. In common with other Staffordshire entries, the changes that occurred here between the Conquest and the survey are unrecorded; but it may be inferred that much of the arable land fell out of use (probably as a result of William's northern campaign), for in 1086 there were only half the number of ploughs needed for the available land. *Domesday* measurements are notoriously open to different interpretations, but Leek's woodland was substantial. One local historian calculated that the four-league-square forest recorded represented 23,040 acres. The trees have mostly disappeared, but the eponymous stone remains, especially in the walls that criss-cross the grazing land above the town.

Soon after the survey, Leek was given to the Earls of Chester as part of their huge domain. It is likely that conditions deteriorated under the rule of Hugh Lupus, the first earl. He was William the Conqueror's nephew, known as Hugh the Fat, and, according to the Norman historian Ordericus Vitalis, was 'profusely prodigal', eventually growing 'so fat that he could scarce crawl'. A century later Leek took a great leap forward under Randle, the sixth earl. 'I will that my burgesses may be as free as the most free burgesses of any borough of Staffordshire,' he wrote in a charter of about 1209. Under his liberal regime each burgess was assured an acre of farmland and half an acre by his house. He could use the earl's forest for timber and firewood, and was guaranteed the right of grazing his animals on one of the largest commons in England. Citizens of Leek were allowed to let their pigs forage free of charge and, throughout the county, were exempt from a water tax. All of this cost them twelve pence in tax a year.

Such a rosy picture of medieval life must be qualified by the usual plagues, petty rebellions and local misfortunes of the time, but compared to many English cities Leek has over the centuries benefited from a relatively undramatic history. Failing to amuse Dr Johnson or Sir Walter Scott is a small price to pay for remaining safely 'ite th'nise'.

ELFORD: *Church of St Peter with its original 16th-c. tower. The peaceful churchyard is beautifully kept and contains many local monuments.*

LEEK: *Drystone walls are a reminder that the town's Churnet valley is surrounded by moors and mountains.*

Staffordshire Gazetteer
Each entry starts with the modern place name in **bold** type. The *Domesday* information that follows is in *italic* type, beginning with the name or names by which the place was known in 1086. The main landholders and undertenants are next, separated with semi-colons if a place was divided into more than one holding. A number of holdings were granted by the king to his thanes; these holders, always the last in a list, are described as holding land 'from the king'. More general information completes the *Domesday* part of the entry, including examples of dues (eels, etc.) rendered by tenants. The modern or post-Domesday section is in normal type. represents a village, a small village or hamlet.

Abbey Hulton *Heltone: Wulfgeat, the pre-Conquest holder, from Robert of Stafford.* Suburb of Stoke-on-Trent.

Abbot's Bromley *Brunlege: Burton Abbey.* Traditional horn dance is celebrated in autumn.

Acton Trussell *Actone: Robert from Bishop of Chester. Mill.*

Adbaston *Edboldestone: Fran and Fragrin from Bishop of Chester.*

Agardsley *Edgareslege: Henry de Ferrers.* Isolated area; Agardsley Park Manor.

Aldridge *Alrewic: Robert from William, FitzAnsculf.* Industrial town. Stone Age flint has been found here.

Almington *Almentone: William from Earl Roger.* Hall. Site of a battle during the Wars of the Roses (1459).

Alrewas *Alrewas: King's land. Eel fishery.* Town. Lady Godiva reputedly worshipped in a Saxon church here; now disappeared.

Alstone *Aluerdestone: Robert of Stafford and a man-at-arms.* Alstone Farm; Alstone Hall Farm.

Alstonefield *Ænestanefelt: William from Earl Roger.* Saxon cross. Six barrows house the dead from the Bronze Age. Poet Charles Cotton entertained Izaak Walton here 300 years ago.

Alton *Elvetone:* Conservation area. Alton Towers, set in parkland by the River Churnet, was once a Gothic nunnery.

Amblecote *Elmelecote: Payne from William FitzAnsculf.* Birmingham suburb.

Amerton *Mersetone: Wulfric and Gosbert from Earl Roger.*

Apeton *Abetone: Robert of Stafford.*

Ashley *Esselie: Geoffrey from Earl Roger.* Scholar John Lightfoot was rector until 1642.

Ashwood *Haswic: Canons of Wolverhampton.*

Aspely *Haspeleia: Bishop of Chester.*

Aston by Stafford *Estone: 2 Frenchmen and a thane from Bishop of Chester.* Hall.

Aston (in Stone) *Estone: King's land; Cadio and Algot from Robert of Stafford, formerly Godiva.* Moated hall.

Audley *Aldidelege: Gamel, the king's thane.* Coal mines nearby. Ryknield Street is Roman-built.

ALTON: *Decorated chapel roof in Alton Towers.*

Baden Hall *Badehale: Leofnoth from Bishop of Chester.* Only the house remains.

Balterley *Baltredelege: Wulfwin and Gamel from the king.*

Barlaston *Bernulvestone: Helgot from Robert of Stafford.* Pottery museum; Josiah Wedgwood's factory on the Trent and Mersey Canal. The Wedgwood family lived in Barlaston Hall in the 1850s.

Barton (in Bradley) *Bernertone: Robert of Stafford.*

Barton-under-Needwood *Bertone: King's land. Mill.* Barton Park and moat nearby.

Basford *Bechesword: William from Earl Roger.*

Baswich *Bercheswic: Bishop of Chester.* Stafford suburb with the remains of a 12th-century Augustinian priory, now a farm called St Thomas's.

Bednall *Bedehala: Bishop of Chester.*

Beffcote *Beficote: King's land.* Windmill near what used to be a Roman road.

Beighterton *Bertone: King's land and Reginald de Balliol from the king.*

Bescot *Bresmundescote: King's land.* Industrial area.

Betley *Betelege: Wulfwin from the king.* Once a market town.

Bickford *Bigeford: Alric, the pre-Conquest holder, from the king.*

Biddulph *Bidolf: King's land.* Large town with coal and iron mines and a burial chamber dating from 2000 BC. Bidolf means 'place by the mine' implying mining before the Conquest. Biddulph Hall was ruined by cannon-fire in the war of 1642.

Bilbrook *Bilrebroch: Priests of Tettenhall.* Industrial area.

Billington *Belintone: Robert of Stafford.* 7-acre prehistoric earthwork, Berry Ring.

Bilston *Billestune: King's land.* Large suburb with a museum and iron foundries, originally a market town. In 1832 a cholera epidemic wiped out 742 inhabitants in 6 weeks. Sir Henry Newbolt, who wrote the song *Drake's Drum*, was born here in 1862.

Bishops Offley *Offeleia: Leofnoth from Bishop of Chester.*

Bishton *Bipestone: Aelmer, the king's thane.* Hall.

Blithfield *Blidevelt: Roger from Earl Roger.* Blithfield Hall; reservoir.

Blore *Blora: Edric from Robert of Stafford.* Scenic; hall and chapel parklands. Henry VI was captured at Blore Heath in 1459.

Bloxwich *Blocheswic:* Lost.

Blymhill *Brumhelle: Warin from Robert of Stafford.* Pretty; moat.

Bobbington *Bubintone: Helgot from Robert of Stafford.* Airport nearby.

Bradeley *Bradelie: Tanio from Robert of Stafford.* Suburb of Stoke-on-Trent.

Bradley (in Bilston) *Bradeleg: Walbert from William FitzAnsculf.* Suburb of Bilston.

Bradley (near Stafford) *Bradelia/lie: Robert of Stafford. Mill.* Bradley Hall.

Bradley-in-the-Moors *Bretlei: Ralph FitzHubert from the king and Robert de Bucy from him.*

Bramshall *Branselle: Bagot from Robert of Stafford.*

Branston *Brantestone: Burton Abbey, formerly Countess Godiva.* Gravel and cement works; nature reserve. Sinai Park belongs to Burton Abbey.

Brewood *Breude: Bishop of Chester. Mill.* Burial place of William Carlos, who hid in the oak tree with Charles II. Black Ladies House was a Norman convent (the nuns wore black habits). The woods were once part of a royal forest.

Bridgeford *Brigeford: 2 Frenchmen and a thane from Bishop of Chester.* Mill; Worston Hall.

Brineton *Brunitone: Warin from Robert of Stafford.*

Brockhurst *Ruscote: Warin from Robert of Stafford.* Remains of a moat nearby.

Brockton (in Eccleshall) *Broctonne: Leofnoth from Bishop of Chester.*

Brocton (nr Stafford) *Broctone: Bishop of Chester.* Booden Farm.

Brough Hall *Bughale: Houghton from Robert of Stafford.* Hall.

Broughton *Hereborgestone: Bishop of Chester.* During the Civil War a Royalist refugee, Colonel Blagg, hid with one crown jewel at Broughton Hall (now a nunnery) after the battle of Worcester. He escaped leaving the jewel with Izaak Walton, who returned it to Charles I.

Bucknall *Buchenole: King's land.* Absorbed into Stoke-on-Trent.

Burslem *Bacardeslim: Robert of Stafford.* Birthplace of Josiah Wedgwood (1730–95).

Burton (in Castle Church) *Burtone: Robert of Stafford.* Probably absorbed into Stafford.

Burweston *Borouestone:* Lost.

Bushbury *Biscopesberie: Canons of Wolverhampton; Robert from William FitzAnsculf.* District of Wolverhampton.

Cannock *Chenet:* See page 244.

Cauldon *Caldone: Robert of Stafford, formerly Countess Godiva.* Stone Age remains and a moat nearby.

Caverswall *Cavreswelle: Arnulf de Hesdin from Robert of Stafford.* The castle became a convent and is now privately owned.

Chapel Chorlton *Cerletone: Leofnoth from Bishop of Chester.*

Charnes *Ceruernest: Leofnoth from Bishop of Chester.* Charnes Old Hall; moat.

Chartley *Certelie: King's land.* Chartley Castle with a cattle and deer park; Chartley Hall, where Mary, Queen of Scots, was imprisoned in 1585.

Chasepool *Catspelle: William FitzAnsculf.* Chasepool Farm.

Chatcul *Ceterville: Leofnoth from Bishop of Chester.* Hall; ford.

Cheadle *Cedla/Celle: King's land; Robert of Stafford, formerly Countess Godiva. Mill.* Market town with a coal and textile industry; nature reserve.

Chebsey *Cebbesio: Humphrey from Henry de Ferrers. Castle.* Saxon cross in the churchyard.

Checkley *Cedla: Otto, from the king.* Pretty; 6 Saxon crosses in the churchyard, with figures of the bishops slain in a battle between Saxons and Danes.

Cheddleton *Celtetone: William from Earl Roger.* County's only working flint mill; museum of ceramic milling industry; paper mills.

Chillington *Cillentone: William FitzCorbucion.* Chillington Hall, on the site of a castle where the Giffards (who came to England with William I) lived for over 800 years. The park was laid out by Capability Brown in 1730.

BUSHBURY: *Moseley Old Hall; Charles II slept here.*

Church Eaton *Eitone: Godric from Robert of Stafford.*

Clayton *Claitone: Nigel from Richard Forester.* Suburb of Newcastle-under-Lyme.

Clifton Campville *Cliftone/ Clistone: King's land. 2 mills.*

Codsall *Codeshale: Kenwin, the pre-Conquest holder, from the king.* RAF station during World War II.

Cold Meece *Mess: Leofnoth from Bishop of Chester.*

Coley *Scoteslei: Nigel from Bishop of Chester.* Building near Great and Little Haywood remains.

Colton *Coltone/une: Ascelin from Earl Roger.* Colton House.

Compton *Contone: King's land.* Absorbed into Wolverhampton.

Congreve *Comegrave: King's land.*

Consall *Cuneshala: King's land.* Consall forge.

Cooksland *Cuchesland:* Lost.

Coppenhall *Copehale: Burgred from Robert of Staffrd.* Moat nearby.

Cotes *Cota: Leofnoth from Bishop of Chester.*

Coton Clanford *Cote: 2 Frenchmen and a thane from Bishop of Chester.* Coton House.

Coton (in Milwich) *Cote: King's land.*

Coton (nr Stafford) *Cote: Ascelin from Earl Roger.* Lost.

Cotwalton *Codeuualle/ Cotewoldestune: King's land; William from Earl Roger, formerly Countess Godiva.*

Coven *Cove: Burgred from Robert of Stafford.* Industrial.

Cowley *Covelau: King's land.* On the Shropshire Union Canal.

Crakemarsh *Crachemers: King's land. Mill.* Wooded; by a lake.

Creswell *Cressvale: William Pandolf from Earl Roger. Mill.*

Crockington *Cocortone/ Cocretone:* Lost.

Croxall *Crocheshalle: Roger from Henry de Ferrers. 2 mills.* Saxon mound nearby.

Croxden *Crochesdene: Alfwold, the pre-Conquest holder, from the king.* The Abbey, the best-preserved monastic ruin in England, was founded for Cistercian monks by Bertram de Verdun in 1176. King John died near here in 1216, ministered to by the monks of Croxden.

Croxton *Crochestone: Bishop of Chester.*

Cubbington *Cobintone:* Lost.

Darlaston *Derlavestone: Burton Abbey.* Darlaston Grange.

Denstone *Denestone: King's land.* Pretty.

BARLASTON: *The church in its pleasant setting. The Wedgwood Museum is nearby.*

Derrington *Dodintone: William from Earl Roger.*

Dilhorne *Dulverne: Walbert from Robert of Stafford.* Pretty.

Dimsdale *Dulmesdene: Richard Forester.* Suburb of Newcastle-under-Lyme.

Dorsley *Doriueslau:* Lost.

Doxey *Dochesig: 2 Frenchmen and a thane from Bishop of Chester.* On the outskirts of Stafford.

Draycott (in the Clay) *Draicote: Henry de Ferrers.* Draycott House.

Drayton Bassett *Draitone: King's land. 2 mills.* A Lower Palaeolithic handaxe dating back to 30,000 BC was found here.

Drayton (in Penkridge) *Draitone: King's land.* Lower Drayton; Lower Drayton Farm.

Drointon *Dregetone: Nigel from Bishop of Chester.*

Dunston *Dunestone: King's land.*

Eccleshall *Eches(h)elle: Bishop of Chester, formerly St. Chad's. 2 mills.* Market town. The church has Saxon stones in the tower. The castle was the home of the Bishops of Lichfield for centuries, and has Saxon and Norman remains.

Edingale *Edunghal(l)e: Henry de Ferrers; Algar, from the king.*

Elford *Eleford:* See page 244.

Ellastone *E(de)lachestone: Bishop of Chester.* Augustinian Abbey, founded in Norman times. George Eliot (Mary Ann Evans) made this village the scene of many incidents in *Adam Bede*; her grandfather lived and is buried here.

Ellenhall *Linehalle: Fran and Fragrin from Bishop of Chester.* Pretty; manor house.

Endon *Enedun: King's land.* Well-dressing ceremony in May.

Enson *Hentone: King's land.*

Enville *Efnefeld: Gilbert from William FitzAnsculf.* 2 fragments of Saxon work in the church. Enville Hall has belonged to the Grey family for 500 years; its grounds were designed by the poet William Shenstone in the 18th century.

ENVILLE: *A summerhouse, now a museum for Enville Hall.*

Ettingshall *Etinghale: Robert from William FitzAnsculf.* Industrial area.

Farley *Fernelege: King's land.* Hall; prison nearby.

Fauld *Felede: Hubert and Robert from Henry de Ferrers.* Mine; Fauld Hall.

Featherstone *Ferdestone: Canons of Wolverhampton.* Disused mine.

Fenton *Fentone: Alfward, the king's thane.* Suburb of Stoke-on-Trent, a pottery centre where Whieldon ware was first made.

Flashbrook *Fletesbroc:* Lost.

Forsbrook *Fotesbroc: King's land.*

Fradswell *Frodeswelle: Alfhelm from Bishop of Chester.* Pretty.

Freeford *Fraiforde: Ranulf from Bishop of Chester.* Freeford Manor.

Fulford *Fuleford: King's land.*

Gailey *Gragelie: Hervey from Robert of Stafford.*

Gayton *Gaitone: Wulfric and Gosbert from Earl Roger.* Ford.

Gerrard's Bromley *Bramelie: Fran and Fragrin from Bishop of Chester.* Lake; mill; ford.

Gnosall *Geneshale: Canons of Wolverhampton. Mill.*

Gratwich *Crotewiche: Wulfheah from Robert of Stafford. Mill.*

Great Barr *Barra/e: Robert and Drogo from William FitzAnsculf.* On the outskirts of Birmingham.

Great Haywood *Haiwoda/e: Bishop of Chester. Mill.* Mill; farm museum. Essex Bridge, the longest pack-horse bridge in England, was built by the 17th-century Earls of Essex as a short-cut to Cannock Chase.

Great Madeley (in Checkley) *Madelie: Wulfgeat from Robert of Stafford.* Wharf; brick works.

Great Saredon *Sardone: Hervey from Robert of Stafford.*

Grindon *Grendone: Robert of Stafford.* Isolated; Grindon Moor nearby.

Hammerwich (Over and Nether) *Duae Humerwich: Bishop of Chester before and after 1066.* Hall; windmill.

Hamstall Ridware *Rid(e)ware/ Ridvare: Godric from St Remy's Church, Rheims; Walter from Earl Roger; Herman from Robert of Stafford. Mill.* Hamstall Hall; Elizabethan Manor house. Ridware comes from an old word for 'river folk'.

Hanchurch *Hancese: Richard Forester.*

Handsacre *Hadesacre: Robert from Bishop of Chester.* Handsacre Hall was largely demolished by vandals in 1972.

Hanford *Heneford: Nigel from Richard Forester.* Suburb of Newcastle-under-Lyme.

Harlaston *Horuluestone: King's land. Mill.*

Hatherton *Hargedone: Samson from the king and the Canons of Wolverhampton from him.* Parkland; lake; hall.

Hatton *Hetone: King's land.* Now 2 hamlets, Upper and Lower Hatton.

Haughton *Hal(s)tone: Robert of Stafford and Urfer from him.*

Heighley *Heolla: King's land.* Remains of 13th-century Heighley Castle.

High Offley *Offelie: Urfer from Robert of Stafford.*

High Onn *Anne: St Evroul's Church from Earl Roger.* Near St Edith's Well.

Hilcote *Helcote: King's land.* Hilcote Hall.

Hilderstone *Helduluestone/ Hilduluestune: King's land; Vitalis from Robert of Stafford.* Straggling.

Hill Chorlton *Cerueledone: Leofnoth from Bishop of Chester.*

Hilton (in Shenstone) *Iltone: Canons of Wolverhampton.*

Hilton (near Wolverhampton) *Haltone: Canons of Wolverhampton.* Hilton Park; lake; moat.

Himley *Himelei: Arni and Gilbert from William FitzAnsculf.* Near Himley Hall, once the home of the Earls of Dudley; now a teacher training college.

Hints *Hintes: Oswald from Bishop of Chester.* The name is Welsh for 'road', and it lies on Watling Street. A lead pig with Roman inscription was found here.

Hixon *Hustedone: Picot from Bishop of Chester, and Nigel from him.* Industrial.

Hopton *Hotone: Gilbert from Robert of Stafford.*

Hopwas *Opewas: King's land. Mill.*

Horton *Hortone:* Lost in Fisherwick.

Huntingdon *Estendone: Richard Forester.* Industrial; mining; 1876 pumping station.

Ingestre *Gestreon: Hugh from Robert of Stafford. Part of a mill.* Hall with a Wren-built church, and a Nash front, where Edward VII spent his holidays,damaged by fire in 1882.

King's Bromley *Bromelei: King's land, formerly Earl Harold.* Named after the Mercian kings.

Kingsley *Chingeslei/a: Robert de Bucy from Ralph FitzHubert; Nigel from the king.* Industrial; ruined moat nearby.

Kingswinford *Suinesford: King's land. Mill.* Small town.

Kinvaston *Chenwardestone: Canons of Wolverhampton before and after 1066. Mill.* Kinvaston Hall Farm.

Kinver *Chenevare/fare: King's land. 2 mills.* An Iron Age promontory fort stands on the summit of Kinveredge.

Knightley *Chenistelei: Reginald from Earl Roger.*

Knighton (in Adbaston) *Chnitestone: Fran and Fragrin from Bishop of Chester.* Wooded; on the Shropshire Union Canal.

Knighton (in Mucklestone) *Chenistetone: Dunning, the king's thane, the pre-Conquest holder.*

Knutton *Clotone: Richard Forester.* Industrial suburb of Newcastle-under-Lyme.

Lapley *Lepelie: St Remy's Church, Rheims before and after 1066.* On a Roman road. Lapley Hall was originally a Saxon Benedictine priory, founded 1063.

Leek *Lec:* See page 245.

Leigh *Lege: Burton Abbey.* Now Church Leigh.

Levedale *Levehale: Bryant and Drogo from Robert of Stafford.*

Lichfield *Lece/Licefelle: Bishop of Chester before and after 1066. 2 mills.* City. Birth place of Samuel Johnson (1709–84). Its name comes from 'Lych Field', meaning 'field of the dead': thousands of Christians were martyred here by the Roman Emperor Diocletian in the 3rd century.

Littlehay *Colt: Ascelin from Earl Roger.* Lost in Colton.

Littywood *Lutiude/dae: Robert of Stafford.* Manor house within a double moat; held by the de Staffords in the Middle Ages, it may once have been a castle.

Little Onn *Otne: Richard, from the king.* Hall; on the Shropshire Union canal.

Little Sandon *Parva Sandone:* Lost.

Little Saredon *Seresdone: Udi from the king.* Windmill.

Longnor (in Lapley) *Longenalre: Robert of Stafford.* Market.

INGESTRE: *The Royal Arms in the church; dated 1676.*

Lower Penn *Pennae: Gilbert from William FitzAnsculf, formerly Countess Godiva.*

Loxley *Locheslei/Locheslei: Ascelin from Earl Roger.* Now 2 hamlets, Loxley Green and Lower Loxley.

Loynton *Levintone: Gilbert from Robert of Stafford.* Loynton Hall.

Madeley Holme *Madelie: Wulfheah from Robert of Stafford.* Madeley Park.

Maer *Mere: Wulfgeat from Robert of Stafford.* Tudor hall, once the home of the Wedgwood family.

Marchington *Merchametone: Henry de Ferrers.* On the outskirts of Needwood Forest.

Marston (by Stafford) *Mer(se)tone: St Evroul's Abbey from Earl Roger.*

Marston *Mersetone: St Remy's Church, Rheims.* Scattered houses.

Mavesyn Ridware *Rid(e)ware/ Ridvare: Ascelin from Earl Roger.* Named after the Mavesyn family, called Mal-voisins (bad neighbours) in Norman times.

Mayfield *Medevelde: King's land.* 2 mills; weir; hanging bridge. Saxon cross in the churchyard.

Meaford *Mep-/Metford: Nawen from St Remy's Church; Rheims; Helgot from Earl Roger.*

Mere town *Mera: King's land. Mill (4000 eels).* On the course of an old canal; mere; deer park.

Mill Meece *Mess: King's land.* Pumping station.

Milwich *Melewich/Mulewiche: King's land; Osbern from Robert of Stafford.* The church bell, dated 1409, is the county's oldest and rang for Agincourt.

Mitton *Mutone: Robert of Stafford.*

Moddershall *Modredeshale: William from Earl Roger.* Wooded; built by the Wedgwood family in 1903.

Moreton (in Colwich) *Mortone: Nigel from Bishop of Chester.* Now Upper Moreton; Moreton House.

Moreton (in Gnosall) *Mortone: Benedict from Earl Roger. Mill.*

Moreton (in Hanbury) *Mortune: Alchere from Henry de Ferrers.*

Morfe *Morve: William FitzAnsculf.* Morfe House Farm; Morfe Hall Farm.

Moseley *Moleslei: Roger from William FitzAnsculf, formerly Countess Godiva.* Charles II stayed in hiding in Moseley Old Hall in 1651, after his cause was lost at Worcester.

Mucklestone *Moclestone: Leofing, from the king.* 2 stones nearby, Devil's Ring and Devil's Finger, were both pierced in prehistoric days. Queen Margaret of Anjou reputedly watched the rout of 10,000 Lancastrians in the Battle of the Roses at Blore from the church tower.

Musden *Musedene: King's land.* Musden Grange and Musden Wood.

Newton (in Blithfield) *Niwetone: Reginald de Balliol. Mill.* Nearby is the River Blithe.

Newton (in Draycott-in-the-Moors) *Niwetone: King's land.*

Norbury *Northerie: Roger from Earl Roger.* Records date back to Saxon times.

Normacot *Normanescote: Aelmer and Wulfric from Richard Forester.* Part of Stoke-on-Trent.

Norton Canes *Nortone: Bishop of Chester before and after 1066.* Coal-mining; Watling Street nearby.

Norton-in-the-Moors *Nortone: Robert of Stafford.* Built-up, on the outskirts of Stoke-on-Trent.

Oaken *Ache: Hugh from Robert of Stafford.*

Oakley (in Croxall) *Acle: Helio from Robert of Stafford.* Oakley Farm.

Oakley (in Mucklestone) *Aclei: King's land.* Oakley Hall.

Ogley Hay *Hocintune:* Lost.

Okeover *Acoure: Burton Abbey. Mill.* Okeover Hall. The Okeover family have held land here for 800 years.

Orton *Overtone: Walbert from William FitzAnsculf.*

Otherton *Orretone: Clodoen from Robert of Stafford.* Moat nearby.

Oxley *Oxelie:* Lost.

Packington *Pad-/Pagintone: Bishop of Chester before and after 1066.* Packington Hall.

Patshull *Pecleshella: Hugh from Robert of Stafford. Mill.* Patshull Hall, now a hospital.

Pattingham *Patingham: King's land.* Church with an 800-year-old font. A 1200-year-old gold collar was found here.

Paynsley *Lufamesles: King's land.* Paynsley Hall.

Pelsall *Peleshale: Canons of Wolverhampton.* Town outside Walsall.

Pendeford *Pendeford: Aelmer from William FitzAnsculf.* Now Upper Pendeford, an industrial hamlet.

Penkhull *Pinchetel: King's land.* A road in Stoke-on-Trent.

Penkridge *Pancriz: King's land; Canons of Wolverhampton. Mill.* Town.

Perton *Pertone: Westminster Abbey.* Outside Wolverhampton.

Pillaton *Beddintone: Burton Abbey.* Pillatone Hall has been the home of the Littleton family for 400 years.

Pipe Ridware *Rid(e)ware/ Ridvare: Alric from Bishop of Chester.*

Podmore *Podemore: Fran and Fragrin from Bishop of Chester.*

Ranton *Rantone: Godric from Robert of Stafford.* Ranton Hall; modern abbey and the remains of an 12th-century Augustinian priory.

Rickerscote *Ricardescote: Robert from Robert of Stafford.* Suburb of Stafford.

Rocester *Rowecetre: King's land. Mill.* Reputedly the site of a Roman camp; mill; weirs; Augustinian priory. Sir Richard Arkwright built the cotton mill, the first in Stafford, in 1782.

Rodbaston *Redbaldestone: Richard Forester.*

Rolleston *Rolvestune: Henry de Ferrers. Mill.* Head of a Saxon cross on the church tower. The hall, once the home of Oswald Moseley's family, was pulled down in the 1920s.

Rowley *Rouueleia: Bishop of Chester before and after 1066.* Now Rowley Elms.

Rownall *Rugehala: King's land.* Rownall Hall.

Rudyard *Rudierd: King's land.* The architect, J.L. Kipling, got engaged here and named his son Rudyard after the spot.

Rugeley *Rugelie: King's land. Mill.* Industrial town, home of William Palmer, The Rugeley Poisoner, a 19th-century doctor who turned to murder to pay his gambling debts.

Rushall *Rischale: Thorkell from William FitzAnsculf. Mill.* Suburb of Walsall. In 1643 Prince Rupert attacked Rushall Hall and made it a Royalist headquarters.

Rushton Grange *Risctone: Wulfgeat from Robert of Stafford.* Lost in Stoke-on-Trent.

Rushton (in Leek) *Risetone: King's land.* Rushton Hall.

Salt *Selte: Gilbert from Robert of Stafford. Mill.* The name comes from ancient salt pits.

Sandon *Scandone: King's land.* Sandon Park, a hall set in wooded parkland with a church and moat, was the home of the 1st Earl of Harrowby, Foreign Secretary during Pitt the Younger's time as Prime Minister; Pitt Column in the park is a memorial.

Sedgley *Segeslei: William FitzAnsculf from the king, and Geoffrey from him.* Industrial town.

Seighford *Cesteforde: 2 Frenchmen and a thane from Bishop of Chester.* Church with Saxon foundations.

Seisdon *Seisdone: Walbert from William FitzAnsculf.*

Shareshill *Servesed: Hervey from Robert of Stafford.* Hilton Park Hall, the guest house of a Roman Catholic convent.

Sheen *Sceon: King's land.*

Shelfield *Scelfeld: King's land.* Suburb of Walsall.

Shelton-under-Harley *Scelfitone: King's land.*

Shenstone *Seneste: Robert d'Oilly from Earl Roger. Mill.*

Shushions *Sceotestan: Leofhild from the king.* Shushions manor house.

Silkmore *Selchemore:* Lost.

Slindon *Slindone: Leofnoth from Bishop of Chester.*

Smethwick *Smedeuuich: William from Bishop of Chester.* Industrialized area on the outskirts of Birmingham.

Stafford *Stad-/Statford: King's land; Bishop of Chester; Burton Abbey; Earl Roger and Hugh from him; Robert of Stafford; William FitzAnsculf; Henry de Ferrers. Mill.* City on the site of a hermitage built by St Bertelin 1200 years ago. Birthplace of Izaak Walton (1593–1683). Richard Sheridan, the dramatist, was MP for Stafford for 26 years from 1780.

Standon *Stantone: Bryant from Robert of Stafford. Mill.*

Stanshope *Stanesope: King's land.*

Stanton *Stantone: King's land.* Birthplace of Gilbert Sheldon (1598–1677), Archbishop of Canterbury, who built the Sheldonian Theatre in Oxford at his own expense.

Stappenhill *Staenhille: Burton Abbey before and after 1066.* Suburb of Burton-on-Trent. 30 Saxon skeletons were found here.

Stoke-by-Stone *Stoca: Cadio from Robert of Stafford.* On the outskirts of Stone.

Stramshall *Stagrigesholle: Alric, the pre-Conquest holder, from the king.* Suburban.

Stretton (near Penkridge) *Estretone: Hervey from Robert of Stafford. Mill.* Roman road nearby.

Stretton (nr Burton-on-Trent) *Stratone: Burton Abbey.* Industrial suburb of Burton-on-Trent, with clay mills, near the Roman Ryknild or Rykniеld Street.

Stychbrook *Tichebroc: Bishop of Chester before and after 1066.* A single building.

Sugnall *Sotehelle: Fran and Fragrin from Bishop of Chester.* Hall and Park.

Swinchurch *Suesneshed: Fran and Fragrin from Bishop of Chester.* Swinchurch Farm.

Swynnerton *Sulvertone: Aslen from Robert of Stafford.*

Syerscote *Fricescote: Thorkell from Robert of Stafford.* Syerscote Manor and Barn.

Talke *Talc: Gamel, the king's thane.* Suburban; Talke pits nearby.

SHENSTONE: *The Hall with an 18th-c. porch.*

Tamhorn *Tamahore: Nigel from Bishop of Chester.* Tamhorn House Bridge on the Birmingham and Fazeley canal.

Tamworth *Tamuuorde: King's land.* Market town where Offa, King of Mercia, built a palace which was desrtoyed by the Danes in AD 874. It was rebuilt by Alfred's daughter Ethelfleda who died here AD 918. Tamworth Castle has Saxon and Norman remains. The mint, built in Offa's time, went on working until the 12th century.

Tean *Tene: Robert of Stafford.* Now 2 hamlets, Upper and Lower Tean.

Tettenhall *Totenhale/Totehala: King's land. Canons of Wolverhampton.* Suburb of Wolverhampton. The wood nearby was the site of a battle between Danes and Saxons 1000 years ago when Alfred's son-in-law, Ethelred, defeated the invaders. Tettenhall Church is on the site of a 10th-century church built by King Edgar.

The Rudge *Rigge:* Lost.

Thorpe Constantine *Torp: Nigel.* Thorpe Hall.

Thursfield *Turvoldesfeld: Richard Forester and Nigel from him.* Thursfield Lodge.

Tillington *Tillintone: Robert of Stafford.* Lost in Stafford.

Tipton *Tibintone: William from Bishop of Chester.* Industrial.

Tittensor *Titesoure: Stenulf from Robert of Stafford. Mill.*

Tixall *Ticheshale: Hugh from Robert of Stafford.* Obelisk; ruined roofless gatehouse where Mary, Queen of Scots, was detained for 2 weeks. Queen's Low and King's Low, on the heath nearby, are burial places of great antiquity.

Trentham *Trenham: King's land.* Suburb of Newcastle-under-Lyme.

Trescott *Cote: Canons of Wolverhampton.*

Trysull *Treslei: Baldwin from William FitzAnsculf. Mill.*

Tunstall (in Adbaston) *Tunestal: Fran and Fragrin from Bishop of Chester.* Hall.

Tutbury *Toteberie: Henry de Ferrers. Market.* Norman church, once part of a Benedictine priory built by Henry de Ferrers. The castle dates back to William I's reign.

Tymmore *Timmor:* Lost.

Tyrley *Tirelire: Lost.*

Upper Penn *Penne: William FitzAnsculf and Robert from him. Mill.* Base ofa preaching cross, reputedly set up by Lady Godiva in 1050.

Uttoxeter *Wotocheshede: King's land.* Large town with agricultural machinery works. Birthplace of the philosopher Thomas Allen (1542–1632).

Walton Grange *Waltone: Roger from Earl Roger.* The grange, near the course of an old Roman road.

WESTON-UNDER-LIZARD: *The Temple of Diana by James Paine.*

Walton (in Eccleshall) *Waletone: Bishop of Chester.*

Walton (in Stone) *Waletone: Arnold from Robert of Stafford.* Walton Hill House, just outside Stone.

Walton-on-the-Hill *Waletone: Bishop of Chester.* On the outskirts of Stafford.

Warslow *Wereslei: Earl Roger.* Georgian manor, Warslow Hall.

Water Eaton *Etone: Hervey from Robert of Stafford. Mill.* Mill nearby.

Wednesbury *Wadnesberie: King's land. Mill.* Industrial town surrounded by rivers and canals. St Bartholomew's Church on the hilltop was once the site of a heathen temple to Woden. A battle is said to have been fought there between Britons and Saxons, in AD 592.

Wednesfield *Wodnesfelde: Canons of Wolverhampton.* Industrial town. 1000 years ago the Danes were heavily defeated in a battle here with Alfred's son, Edward.

Weeford *Weforde: Ralph from Bishop of Chester. Mill.* Birthplace of John Wyatt (1700–66) who invented and used the first spinning machine in a cotton mill here.

West Bromwich *Bromwic: Ralph from William FitzAnsculf.* City. Mining (coal, firestone) is its main industry.

Weston Coyney *Westone: Arnulf de Hesdin from Robert of Stafford.* Suburb of Longdon.

Weston (in Standon) *Westone: Bryant from Robert of Stafford.* Weston Hall; Weston House Farm.

Weston-under-Lizard *Westone: Reginald de Balliol.* By Watling Street. Hall. The park was landscaped by Capability Brown in the 18th century.

Weston-upon-Trent *Westone: Aelfric, the king's thane.* Weston Hall.

Wetmore *Witmere: Burton Abbey.* Suburb of Burton-on-Trent; Wetmoor Hall Farm.

Whiston *Witestone: Nawen from Burton Abbey.*

Whitmore *Witemore: Nigel from Richard Forester.*

Wigginton *Wigetone: King's land.* Near Wigginton Fields.

Wightwick *Wisteuuic: King's land.* Wightwick Manor.

Wilbrighton *Wilbrestone: Lawrence from Robert of Stafford.* Wilbrighton Hall.

Willenhall *Winehala/ Winenhale: King's land; Canons of Wolverhampton.* Market town. Charles II hid at Bentley Hall nearby.

Winnington *Wennitone: Leofing, from the king.*

Winshill *Wineshalle: Burton Abbey before and after 1066. Mill.* Part of Burton-on-Trent; mill.

Wolgarston *Turgarestone: King's land.*

Wolseley *Ulselei: Nigel from Bishop of Chester.*

Wolstanton *Wlstanetone: King's land.* Suburb of Newcastle-under-Lyme, on the site of a Saxon settlement.

Wolverhampton *Hantone: Canons of Wolverhampton from Samson the Clerk.* City, a centre of the wool industry in the Middle Ages. Danes cross dates from the 9th century. St Peter's Church stands on a hill where Christians have worshipped for 10 centuries.

Wombourn *Wamburne: Ralph from William FitzAnsculf. 2 mills.* Town. A church is dedicated to St Benedict Biscop (b. AD 628), said to have introduced glass windows to England.

Woolaston *Ullavestone: Robert of Stafford.*

Wootton (in Eccleshall) *Wodestone: Bishop of Chester.*

Wootton (nr Uttoxeter) *Wodetone: King's land.* Wootton deer park. Wootton Lodge, badly damaged in the Civil War in 1643.

Wrottesley *Wrotolei: Clodoen from Robert of Stafford..* Wrottesley Lodge Farm; Old Park.

Wychnor *Wicenor: Robert from Robert of Stafford. Mill.* Moat and park nearby.

Wyrley *Wereleia: Bishop of Chester.* Now Little Wyrley. Hall; common; woods.

Yarlet *Erlide: Robert from Earl Roger.* Yarlet Hall, now a school.

Yoxall *Loches/Iocheshale: Rafwin and Alwin from Bishop of Chester.*

Suffolk

Suffolk, with Norfolk and Essex, is included in a separate volume known as the Little Domesday Book. *This is a misleading description, since its entries are considerably more detailed than those of* Domesday *itself. Unfortunately, the additional information does not always enhance or clarify what is known about Norman Britain. Indeed, it sometimes adds to the confusion.*

The system of gelding, for instance, which appears to have been used only in Suffolk and Norfolk, is totally unexplained. It is believed that each of the 24 Suffolk hundreds was divided into units called leets, which figured significantly in apportioning the payment of the geld, or tax. But scholarly head-scratching has failed to determine precisely what this entailed.

Nevertheless, a clear picture of Suffolk does emerge. It was a county predominantly of villages and freemen, rather than of manors and feudal vassals. Its population was fairly evenly distributed. Only in the north-west, where sandy, barren breckland gave way to the fens, were there large uninhabited areas. Forest covered much of the central and north-eastern uplands; the sandy eastern shore was crumbling then as it is now. None of the seven principal towns, which included Ipswich, Bury St Edmunds and Dunwich, had more than 3000 inhabitants.

One of the curious pleasures of Little Domesday *is its meticulous census of livestock. In Suffolk it records 4343 goats, but only two lonely donkeys.*

Dunwich

Edric of Laxfield held DUNWICH *DUNEUUIC* before 1066 as one manor; now Robert Malet holds it; then 2 carucates of land, now 1, the sea carried off the other (carucate). Always 1 plough in lordship. Then 12 smallholders, now 2. 24 Frenchmen with 40 acres of land. They pay every customary due to this manor. Then 120 burgesses, now 236; poor men, 180 less 2. Then 1 church, now 3; they pay £4 10s. In total, value £50 and 60,000 herrings as a gift; before 1066 it paid £10. Also Robert de Vaux holds 1 acre of land. Value 8d. Norman holds 1 acre. Value 2s. 8d. Godric (holds) 1 acre. Value 8d. He holds this from Robert Malet. Gilbert Blunt holds 80 men. He pays £4 and 8,000 herrings. [He holds them] from the same Robert.

'I defy anyone at desolate exquisite Dunwich to be disappointed in anything,' wrote the Anglo-American novelist Henry James at the turn of the century. At first sight Dunwich is, however, disappointing – a mere straggle of cottages along a quiet street, with a nineteenth-century church at the landward end, and an old public house at the other. Beyond stretch the monotonous strand and the low sandy cliffs.

It takes a little exploration to discover what it was that so delighted James. In the churchyard stand the elegant ruins of a Norman chapel and, startlingly alone, a buttress supporting nothing at all. At the top of the cliff near the sea, tucked away among cabbages in a field, are the remains of a Franciscan friary. And near the edge of the crumbling cliff is the most poignant monument of all, a mossy tombstone in a rabbit-cropped patch of grass. 'Sacred to the memory of John Brinkley Easey,' the inscription reads, 'who died September 2 1826 aged 23 years.' Alone above the grey sea, this grave is the last fragment of All Saints churchyard. All of John Brinkley Easey's companions have plunged down the cliff to join a city beneath the waves. Of the church itself only that single buttress remains. It was removed stone by stone from the perilous cliff and rebuilt in its present safe position in the modern graveyard.

Dunwich is the English Atlantis – once the prosperous capital of East Anglia – overwhelmed by the ocean. Its long history of struggle and decline has made it irresistible to historians and poets. 'Dunwich, in ancient time,' wrote John Stow in his sixteenth-century *Chronicle*, 'had brazen gates, fifty-two churches, chapels, religious houses, and hospitals; a king's palace, a bishop's seat, a mayor's mansion, and a mint.' He was safe enough in making these extravagant claims, for by the time he was writing only a quarter or so of Dunwich remained, and no one could be sure exactly how many buildings had slid into the sea.

At the time of *Domesday* Dunwich was still a thriving city, but the survey appears to have been inaccurate. While Ipswich had 11 churches in 1086, Dunwich apparently had only three and had had only one in 1066. Yet in the seventh century Dunwich had already been a centre of Saxon Christianity, the seat of St Felix, Bishop of East Anglia. It is possible that the *Domesday* commissioners did not keep a careful count of Suffolk churches; this seems likely since the population of Dunwich in 1086 has been estimated at around 3000, about the same as Bury St Edmunds and nearly twice that of Ipswich. The *Domesday* entry also records that the number of burgesses had almost doubled since the Conquest, indicating economic growth, yet there was still a worrying number of poor men. A clearer indication of prosperity lay in the fishing industry: Dunwich paid an annual 'gift' of 68,000 herring, more than any other Suffolk port.

If Dunwich took its wealth from the sea, it gave up its land in return. There is an ominous portent – as well as a report – of disaster in the terse *Domesday* description: 'Then 2 carucates of land, now 1. The sea carried away the other.' The town had lost half its farmland in 20 years! Farming, however, was of minor interest to the burgesses. They had a fine harbour for trade and fishing, and for 200 years after *Domesday* Dunwich prospered. It became Suffolk's major port, with a daily market, eight or nine churches and a fleet of some 80 ships. It carried on a thriving trade with France and was able to send ships to fight for Henry III in the thirteenth century. Strongly walled, Dunwich remained

DUNWICH: *Little is left of the Friary; parts of the cloister walk and refectory.*

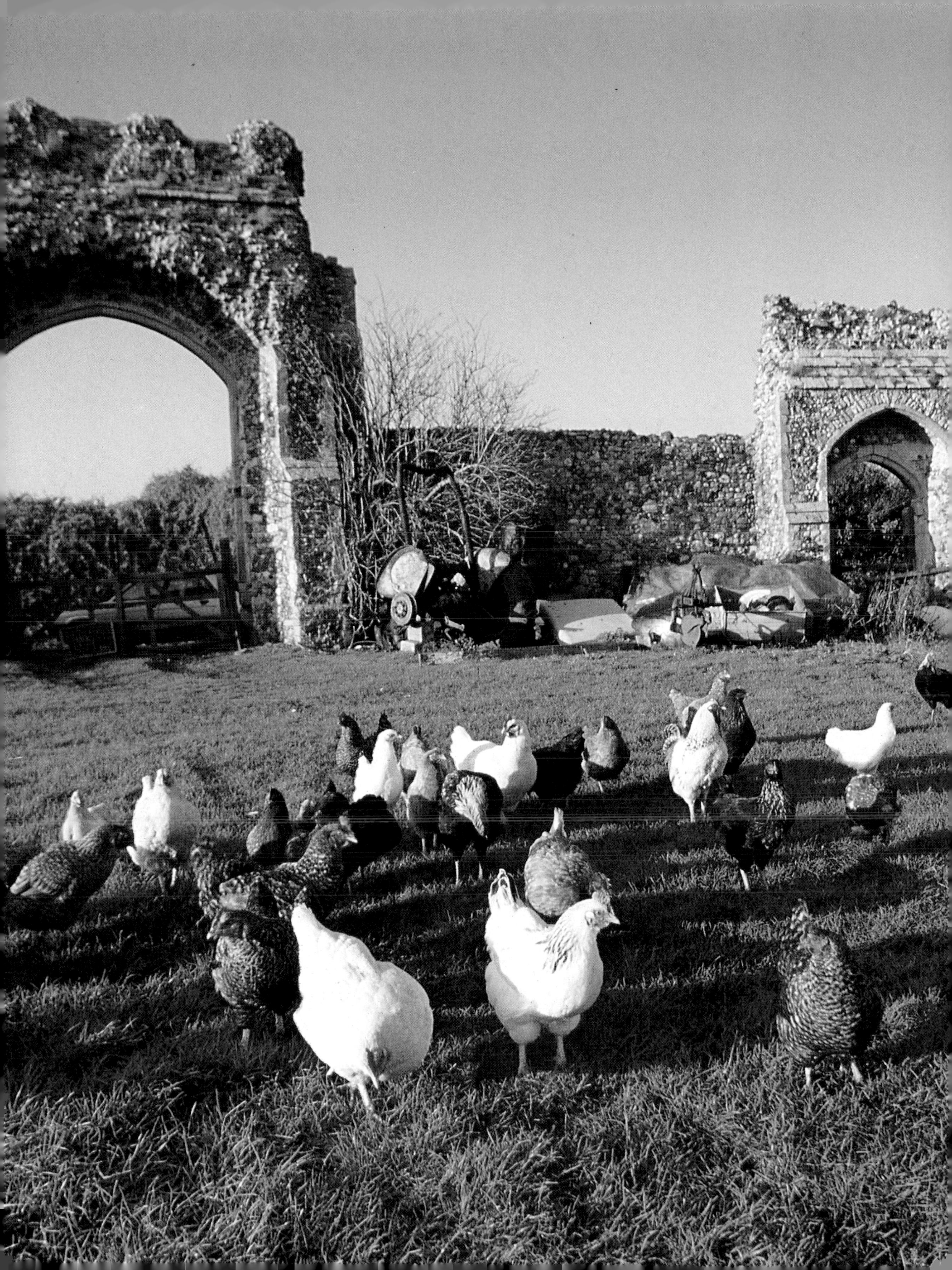

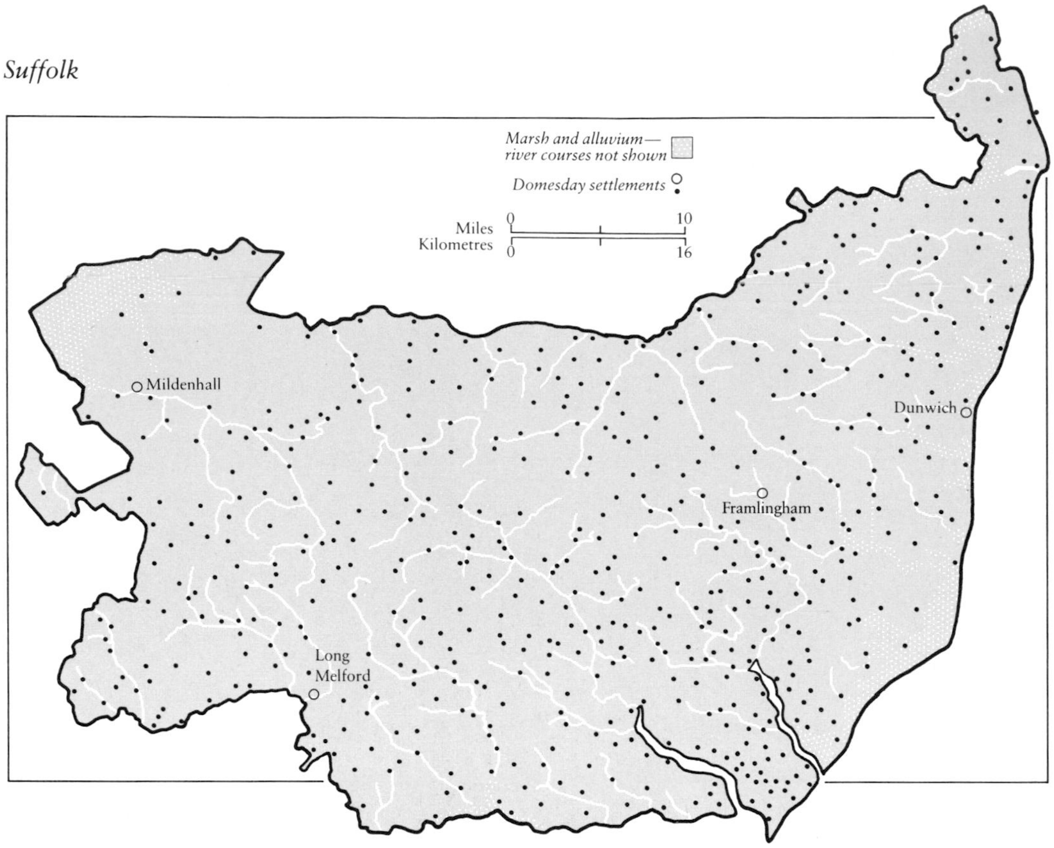

wealthy and impregnable during the early Middle Ages.

But already during Henry III's reign the ocean had renewed its campaign against the city. The shifting sands of the Suffolk coast could silt up a harbour overnight, and these uncertain conditions began to affect the local merchants. The king was obliged to give Dunwich £47 10s 'to remove and repair their port'. The effect of the shoring up was only temporary. In 1328 the old port was abandoned after a huge storm had blocked it off from the sea. The ocean then began its direct assault on the city. A single storm in the fourteenth century destroyed 400 houses, as well as shops and windmills. From then on Dunwich suffered increasingly. Excerpts from a history written in 1754 by Thomas Gardner give a grim catalogue of the destruction:

> In the fourteenth century the churches of St Martin and St Nicholas were overthrown by the waves of the sea.
> 1608 – the High Road was eaten away.
> 1677 – the sea reached the market place, when the townsmen sold the lead of the cross.

By Gardner's time only 35 houses and All Saints Church remained standing. 'And yet,' he wrote, 'the inhabitants entertain reviving hopes of becoming once more a flourishing town.' These hopes proved vain. In 1778 All Saints finally ceased to offer services. Submerged Dunwich's only link with its glorious past was still to have two Members of Parliament, as it had done since 1297, and was to continue to do until the Reform Bill of 1832.

Swinburne wrote in *By the North Sea*:

> Miles on miles on miles of desolation!
> Leagues on leagues on leagues without a change!
> Graves where hope and prayer and sorrow brooded
> Gape and slide and perish ranks on ranks.

Edward Thomas, Jerome K. Jerome, Edward Fitzgerald, Thomas Carlyle and M.R. James (who used Dunwich as a setting for a ghost story) also felt the lure of the spot.

'A month in the place,' wrote Henry James, 'is a real education to the patient, the inner vision.' Essential to this inner vision was an awareness of the prosperous eleventh-century borough now lying on the sea bed, where romantics claim they can hear the bells of its churches still being rung.

Mildenhall

[Lands of the king...] King Edward gave MILDENHALL *MITDENHALLA* to St Edmund's; later Stigand held (it) in King Edward's lifetime under St Edmund's as a manor; 12 carucates of land. Then and later 30 villagers, now 33; then 8 smallholders, later and now 15; always 16 slaves. Always 6 ploughs in lordship; 8 men's ploughs. Meadow, 20 acres. A church, 40 acres. 1 mill; 3½ fisheries. 31 wild mares, 37 cattle, 60 pigs, 1,000 sheep. 8 Freemen; 30 acres. Always ½ plough. 1 outlier, ICKLINGHAM, belongs to this...

A nineteenth-century historian, writing about Mildenhall, remarked that it was unusual to find a town of only 2000 inhabitants prosperous enough to support two jeweller's shops. One of the jewellers, he added in surprise, had a steam-powered revolving display case in its window.

There are still surprises for the window shopper in Mildenhall. It must be one of the few market towns in Britain where you can find ceramic raccoons, bald eagles and hedgehogs for sale in the High Street. The local tradesmen are not being capricious. They are catering to the whims of the American airmen who crowd into the town from their base nearby.

Mildenhall's prosperity is nothing new. In 1043, King Edward, worried because the monks of Bury St Edmunds were so poor that they had only barley-flour bread to eat, asked the abbot how he could help. 'Give us the Manor of Mildenhall and all its land,' was the reply. Stigand, the English Archbishop of Canterbury, subsequently became the monks' under-tenant, but when he lost his lands in 1070, Mildenhall among others was taken by the king and given to William de Noyers to manage.

It continued to prosper as a royal manor, showing no sign of the decline which affected many new Norman properties. By the time of *Domesday* the population had increased and the number of working ploughs had remained the same. *Domesday*, alas, does not make clear how different eleventh-century Mildenhall and its surroundings were from what they are today. Only the unusual number of fisheries shows that it was then a coastal settlement. It stood on the shores of the fenland, the shallow sea that covered much of Cambridgeshire and flooded this north-west corner of Suffolk. To the south and east of Mildenhall was the sandy breckland. Both fen and breckland have long been under the plough and modern Mildenhall lies on a fertile, populous plain with Forestry Commission conifer plantations as a backcloth.

Had it not been for the aeroplane, Mildenhall would now be no more than a bustling market town with a stately parish church. A new era began with the opening of an airfield in 1934, celebrated by its serving as the starting point for an air race to Melbourne, Australia. The winners, C.W.A. Scott and T. Campbell Black, established a speed record of 71 hours. The new airfield, however, soon turned to grimmer duties. On Sunday, 3 September, 1939, three planes set out from here for the German naval base at Wilmenshaven in the first British bombing mission of World War II. With the onset of the cold war in the early 1950s it began to bustle not only with ordinary military hardware, but also with nuclear weapons. Mildenhall, which made a modestly prosperous contribution to 1086's *Domesday*, may thus be contributing less happily to doomsday itself.

Long Melford

St Edmund's held (LONG) MELFORD *MELAFORDA* as a manor before 1066; 12 carucates of land. Of this land, Walter holds 40 acres from the Abbot. Always 37 villagers. Then 25 smallholders, now 10. Then 8 ploughs in lordship, now 6; then 20 men's ploughs, now 13. Always 16 slaves. Meadow, 50 acres; woodland, 60 pigs; 2 mills. Now 3 cobs; always 30 cattle. Now 300 sheep; always 140 pigs. Now 12 [bee] hives; now 40 wild horses. 2 Freemen with 80 acres of land. The same Walter holds 1 with 40 acres from the Abbot. Always 2 ploughs. Over these (Freemen), St (Edmund's) has patronage and full jurisdiction and every customary due. They could not ever grant or sell their lands without the Abbot's full assent. A church with 2 carucates of land. 4 villagers; 9 smallholders. Always 2 ploughs belonging to the church; always 2 men's ploughs. Value of this manor then £20; now [£]30. It has 18 furlongs in length and 1 league in width; 20½d in tax, whoever holds there.

Most of Long Melford is visible from its very long High Street, which forms part of the main route from Sudbury to Bury St Edmunds. Handsome houses face each other across the wide main road, becoming grander as they approach the top of the village. At the head stand two great Elizabethan mansions: Kentwell, which looks proprietorially down its long avenue of limes, and Melford Hall, opposite the huge village green, its pepperpot turrets like props from a comic opera. Everything about this

FRAMLINGHAM: *Bigod's castle, c. 1190, had advanced defences behind a new curtain wall.*

end of Long Melford is oversized, including Holy Trinity, a vast and elegant Tudor barn of a church, which shelters the remains of the Cloptons, the Martyns and other great families who long presided over the village.

At the time of *Domesday*, Suffolk was not yet in the grip of a strict feudal hierarchy. In most of the region, especially in the north, villages populated by freemen outnumbered manors in which lords held control over the lives and belongings of their subjects. In southern Suffolk, however, the manor, with its pecking order of villagers (*villani*), smallholders (*bordarii*), cottagers (*cotarii*) and serfs had begun to predominate. Melford was one of the largest of these feudal estates. The Abbot of Bury St Edmunds, Suffolk's greatest tenant-in-chief, seems to have created a particularly subservient village community. The manor had a relatively large number of serfs, and the two sokemen, who on another estate might have enjoyed considerable freedom, were here little more than well-to-do vassals, with no rights to dispose of their landholdings.

The *Domesday* description of Long Melford, then Melford, includes one particularly interesting detail. 300 sheep may not seem a great number (there were nearly 40,000 recorded in the county), but it was 300 more than there had been at the time of the Conquest. And the wealth of medieval Suffolk depended upon the wool trade. In the fifteenth century, with the help of Flemish immigrant weavers, Suffolk grew fat on the export of cloth to the Continent. Long Melford became one of the country's richest wool towns, and Holy Trinity, a great wool church. Although the two rows of fine houses on the High Street are by no means medieval, they may be said to have their origins in a flock of *Domesday* sheep.

Framlingham

Aelmer, a thane, held FRAMLINGHAM *FRAMELINGHAM.* Now R(oger) Bigot holds (it) [from Earl Hugh]; 9 carucates of land as a manor. Then 24 villagers, now 32; then 16 smallholders, now 28. Then 5 ploughs in lordship, now 3; then 20 men's ploughs, now 16. Woodland, 100 pigs; meadow, 16 acres. Then 2 cobs, now 3; then 4 cattle, now 7; then 40 pigs, now 10; then 20 sheep, now 40; always 60 goats; now 3 beehives. Value then £16; now £36.

In the same (Framlingham) Munulf held, half under the patronage of Aelmer and half under (that) of Malet's predecessor; 1 carucate of land and 40 acres as a manor. Always 4 villagers; 12 smallholders; 2 ploughs in lordship; 2½ men's ploughs. Woodland, 100 pigs; meadow, 6 acres. 8 cattle, 20 pigs, 60 sheep, 40 goats, 4 beehives. Value always 40s. William Malet was in possession. Under him, 6 whole free men and 4 half (free) men; 30 acres of land. Always 1 plough. Meadow, 1 acre. They are in the assessment of 40s. In the same (Framlingham) 1 free man under patronage; 40 acres. 1 villager who dwells in *Ethereg*; 3 smallholders. Meadow, 1 acre. 1 plough. Woodland, 4 pigs. Value 8s. In the same (Framlingham) 3 free men under patronage; 56 acres. Always 3 ploughs. Meadow, 2 acres; woodland, 4 pigs. Value 17s. 1 church, 60 acres. 1 villager; 4 smallholders. 2 ploughs. Value 15s. In length 14 furlongs, and 12 in width; 20d in tax. [St.] Etheldreda's (had) the jurisdiction but (Earl) Hugh's predecessor had it from it.

Heir of Antiquity – fair castled Town,
Rare spot of beauty, grandeur and renown.

A modern visitor to Framlingham will have difficulty recognizing the subject of this ecstatic couplet, by the Suffolk poet, James Bird. It is a charming little town lying between Saxmundham and Stowmarket, but its neat streets, prosperous houses and sloping market place suggest security rather than grandeur. From the outside the Tudor church of St Michael is as tranquil as its surroundings. The chancel tells another story. It is crowded with the sixteenth-century tombs of the Howards, Dukes of Norfolk, a mausoleum of vanity and bloodshed.

Only a quarter of a mile from the church is Framlingham Castle, a tall, irregular circle of grey stone. A castle stood here in Saxon times, perhaps as early as the sixth century. King Edmund, it is said, sought protection within its walls from the Danes, but was driven forth and murdered (or martyred, as the Saxons soon claimed) in the forests which covered much of this region – far more forest than there were swine to feed in it at the time of *Domesday*. John Evelyn in his *Discourse of Forest Trees* (1664) praised Framlingham for its magnificent oaks, the finest 'perhaps in the world'. And the seventeenth-century warship *Royal Sovereign*, the flagship of King Charles II's navy, was built of Framlingham oak.

In 1086 it was divided into several manors and freemen's holdings. Earl Hugh of Chester was the tenant-in-chief of the largest of these with Roger Bigot holding from him. Roger's manor had grown substantially since the Conquest. His total of 19 ploughs indicates that a large area had been cleared for crops. Together with the smaller holdings of other men, which included two mills and a church, Bigot's land formed a prosperous community. Framlingham, it appears, suffered less in the transition from Saxon to Norman rule than many neighbouring settlements. About 300 men, women and children can be assumed to have lived on Roger Bigot's land. But why there were so many goats – well above the local average – is one of the many minor curiosities of *Domesday*.

The Bigot family (especially Roger's son, the scheming and ruthless Hugh) became warlords of Suffolk, taunting successive kings from the refortified Saxon castle. Subsequent castle owners continued to fall foul of royalty. The Howards, Dukes of Norfolk, who took possession late in the fifteenth century, had a disastrous history, from the first duke, who backed the losing side in the Battle of Bosworth, to the fifth, beheaded for plotting to free Mary Queen of Scots.

Yet despite such vicious feuding, the Howards and Framlingham Castle remained a powerful magnet to royalty. Edward VI held his first court here, and his sister Mary (later Bloody Mary) proclaimed herself queen in the castle while rallying her forces against the armies of Lady Jane Grey. There is a legend that, during her stay, she 'gave birth to a monster, which ... she instantly destroyed'. The stone upon which she is said to have smashed this creature was pointed out to eighteenth-century travellers. By then Framlingham had ceased to have any political or military importance. The inside of the castle was gutted and a workhouse, which still stands, was built within the walls. This picturesque shell of the Norman castle and the proud tombs of its later owners are all that remain of grandeur in Framlingham.

Suffolk Gazetteer
Each entry starts with the modern place name in **bold** type. The *Domesday* information that follows is in *italic* type, beginning with the name or names by which the place was known in 1086. The tenants-in-chief and main undertenants are next, separated with semi-colons if a place was divided into more than one holding. More general information completes the *Domesday* part of the entry, including examples of dues such as herrings rendered by tenants and animals when the totals reach or exceed 20 pigs, 7 beasts, 20 goats, 100 sheep, 3 horses, 1 cow, 3 oxen and 2 donkeys. The modern or post-Domesday section is in normal type. ▦ represents a village, ⌂ a small village or hamlet.

Acton *Achetuna/Aketona/Aratona: Ranulf Peverel. Church, 2 mills, 7 beehives. 11 horses, 31 beasts, 160 pigs, 423 sheep.* Church with one of the finest military brasses in existence (1302).

Akenham *Acheham/Achre(h)am/Acreham: King's land, kept by William de Noyers; Roger de Poitou; Roger de Raismes's daughter from him; Turstin, Bernhard and Roger from Walter the Deacon. Church.* ⌂ Partly Norman church.

Akethorpe *Aketorp:* Lost.

Aldeborough *Aldeburc: Robert Malet's mother; Abbot of Ely and Norman from him. 2 churches.* Seaside town. Ship auctions were held in the church. Benjamin Britten and Peter Pears founded the famous music festival here in 1948.

Alderton *Al(r)etuna: Robert Malet's mother and Walter de Caen from her; Abbot of Ely. Church.* ▦ Marshland; near the sea; Martello tower; signs of early settlements; remains of an ancient moated hall.

Aldham *Aldeham/Ealdham/Ialelham: Abbot of St Edmund's and Berard from him; Aubrey de Vere. Church, 2 mills.* ⌂ Priory remains.

Aldringham *Alrincham: Robert Malet.* ▦ Expanding; Bronze Age barrows.

Alnesbourn *Alvesbrunna: Roger de Poitou and Albert from him.* Remains of a priory near Ipswich.

Alston *Alteinestuna:* Lost.

Ampton *Hametuna: Abbot of St Edmund's and Robert from him. Church.* ▦ Wooded. The hall, now rebuilt, was the birthplace of the meteorologist Vice-Admiral FitzRoy, who commanded the *Beagle* (1828–36).

Ash *Esce: Robert Malet's mother and Norman the Sheriff from her.* ⌂ Probably Ash Abbey, on the River Deben; remains of priory; mill.

Ashbocking *Ass(i)a/Essa/Hassa: King's land, kept by Godric; Osbern de Wancey from Richard FitzGilbert; Abbot of Ely.* ▦ Roman road; Iron Age and Roman remains.

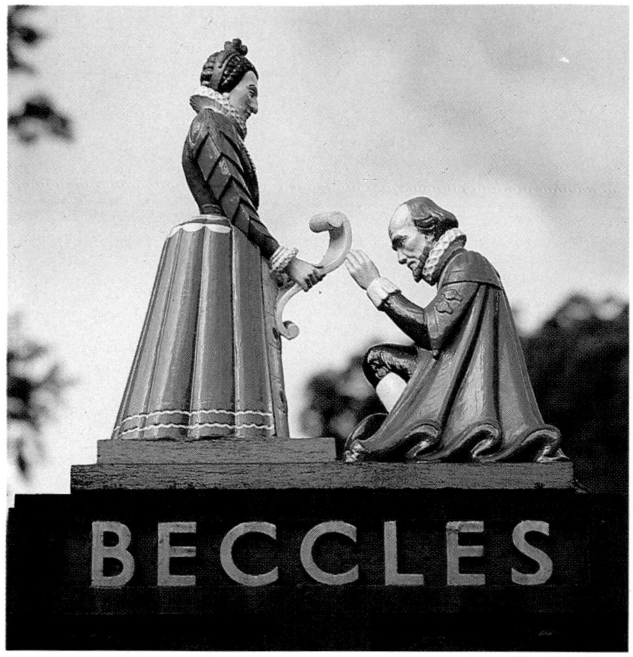

BECCLES: *A town sign; 16th and 17th-c. fires destroyed many houses.*

Ash Street *Asce: Count of Mortain.* ⌂

Ashfield *Asfelda/Assafelda/Assefelda: Count Alan; Earl Hugh; Gilbert from Robert Malet; Bishop of Bayeux; Humphrey the Chamberlain; Ranulf from Hervey de Bourges; Abbot of Ely. Church (with Thorpe in Ashfield).* ▦ Roman road nearby.

Great Ashfield *Eascefelda: Robert Blunt and William from him. Church, 10 beehives.* ⌂ 2 moated sites; Castle Hill.

Aspall *Aspala/-pella/Espala/-palle: Robert Malet's mother; Bishop of Bayeux and Roger Bigot and Ralph de Savigny from him; Ranulph Peverel. ⅓ church; ⅓ fair.* ⌂ Jacobean Hall with moats converted into watergardens and an ancient Cider House.

Assington *Asetona: Ranulph Peverel. Church, mill, 14 beehives. 5 horses, 23 beasts, 60 pigs.* ⌂ Mill Farm.

Aveley *Aluenelega: Swein of Essex. Mill. 49 pigs, 4 beasts.* Aveley Hall near Assington.

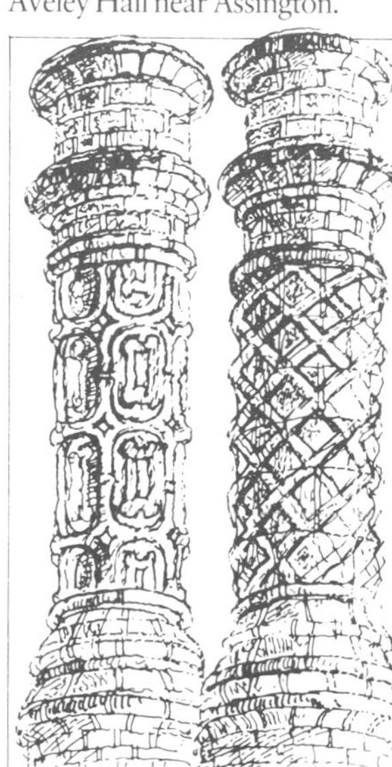

ALDEBURGH: *Chimney stacks on Moot Hall.*

Bacton *Bachetuna: Walter the Deacon. Church. 100 sheep, 36 goats.* ▦ Manor House Farm, c.1715, owned by the Pretymans since 1568; church with glass by William Morris and Sir Edward Burne-Jones.

Badingham *Badincham/Hadincham: Robert Malet's mother and Walter, Loernic and Robert from her. Church, beehive. 60 goats, 32 pigs.* ▦ Partly Norman church; Okenhill Hall, 1552.

Badley *Badele(i)a: King's land, kept by Godric; Richard FitzGilbert; Abbot of Ely. Church, ½ mill.* ⌂ Ancient Lady Well.

Badmondisfield *Bademondes/Bademundesfelda: King's land, kept by Picot. Church.* ⌂ Moated hall.

Ballingdon *Belindune: Ralph the Haunted from Peter de Valognes. 33 cattle, 28 pigs.* Some houses.

Bardwell *Bardewella:* Lost.

Bardwell *Beordewella/Berdeuuella: Abbot of St Edmunds and Peter de Valognes from him. Church, 2 parts of mill.* ▦ Elizabethan hall.

Barham *Bercham: William Gulaffra from Robert Malet; Roger de Poitou and Gosbert from him; Roger d'Auberville, the pre-Conquest holder, from Abbot of Ely. Church, mill.* ⌂ 6 Roman roads converged here; Shrubland Hall, 1850–2, now a health farm.

Barkestone *Barchestuna:* Lost.

Barking *Berchingas/-ingis/Berkinges: Abbot of Ely before and after 1066. 2 churches, weir, vineyard 23 beasts, 30 pigs, 100 sheep, 48 goats.* ▦ Home of Sir Nicholas Bacon, brother of Francis and High Sheriff of Suffolk, 1581; Iron Age farm with storage pits.

Barnby *Barnebei/-by: King's land, kept by Roger Bigot; Hugh FitzNorman from Earl Hugh. Church.* ▦ Thatched church.

Barnham *Ber(n)ham: Earl Hugh; Roger Bigot; Abbot of St Edmund's and Fulchard from him; Hugh FitzGold from William de Warenne; Hugh de Montfort. 3 mills. 12 forest mares, 25 pigs, 420 sheep.* ▦ Anglo-Saxon coffin lid in a cottage wall.

Barningham *Berni(n)cham/Berningham: Henry de Ferrers; Abbot of St Edmund's; Peter de Valognes. Church.* ▦ Surrounded by ponds.

Barrow *Barro: King's land, kept by Picot. Church. 40 swine, 100 sheep, 60 goats.* ▦ Large green; church with a Norman window; Wolf Hall, a Tudor farmhouse.

Barsham *Barsham/Bersham: Warin son of Brunwin from Robert Malet's mother; Roger Bigot and Robert de Vals from him; Bishop of Thetford. ½ church, ½ mill.* ▦ Thatched, partly Norman church.

Barton Mills *Bertona/-tunna: Richard FitzGilbert, formerly Godeva a free woman; William de Watteville. 2 fisheries.* ▦ Named after a large corn-mill on the River Lark; Bronze Age barrow.

Battisford *Beteforda/Betes-/Botes-/fort: Count of Mortain; Roger Bigot and William de Brunoville from him; Roger de Cando from Hugh de Montfort; Eudo FitzSpirwic and Jarnagot from him; Siward from the Vavassors. 2 churches.* ▦ Moated site. Sir Thomas Gresham, founder of the Royal Exchange (1564), had estates here.

Bawdsey *Balde(re)seia: Robert Malet's mother; Ralph de Beaufour; Abbot of Ely. Church.* ▦ Martello tower built as a defence against Napoleon.

Baylham *Bel(e)ham: Roger Bigot and William de Burnoville, Ulmar and Waranger from him. ½ church, 2 mills. 8 beasts, 40 pigs, 105 sheep.* ▦ Ancient mill house; watermill; moated 16th-century farmhouse.

Beccles *Becles: King's land, kept by Roger Bigot; Abbot of St Edmund's before and after 1066. Church, market, manor (60,000 herrings).* Ancient town. On the sea in 1086, it now looks over marshes and the River Waveney.

Bedfield *Berdefelda: Robert Malet's mother and Humphrey from her.* ▦

Bedingfield *Badinga/Bedingafelda/Bading(h)efelda/gelelda-/Bating-/Bedingefelda: Robert Malet; Robert Malet's mother; Abbot of St Edmund's; Bishop of Thetford; Roger de Candos from Hugh de Montfort; Ralph de Limesy; a freeman. ¼ church.* ⌂ Named after the family who lived almost continuously at Fleming's Hall from c.1309.

Belstead *Bel(e)steda: Robert Malet; Bishop of Bayeux; Aubrey de Vere; Countess of Albemarle; Robert de Stratford. Church, mill.* ▦

Belton *Beletuna: King's land, kept by Roger Bigot. 160 sheep.* ▦ Belton marshes; dormitory development for Yarmouth.

Benacre *Benagra: Abbot of St Edmund's.* ⌂ By marshes and sea.

Benhall *Benehal(l)a/Benenhala: Count Alan; Robert Malet and Robert de Glanville and Hubert from him; Roger Bigot and Norman from him.* ⌂ Now Benhall Street. The lord of the manor married Geoffrey Chaucer's daughter here.

Bentley *Benetleia: King's land, kept by Aluric Wanz; Furic and Aluric from Count Alan. Church, mill, ½ park.* ▦ Straggling; near a Roman road; church with Norman traces.

Beversham *Beuresham:* Lost.

Beyton *Begatona: Hugh de Montfort, formerly Edith the Rich.* ▦ Adjoins Beyton Green village.

Bildeston *Bilestuna: Walter the Deacon, formerly Queen Edith. Church.* Small town which once had an important market and was famous for its cloth.

Bing *Benga/ges: Walter de Caen from Robert Malet's mother.* Byng Hall near Ufford.

Bixley *Bichelea: Count Alan; Abbot of Ely; Hugh de Montfort.* Bixley Farm by Ipswich suburbs.

Blakenham *Blac(he)ham: King's land, kept by Roger Bigot and Godric; Roger de Poitou and Albert from him; William d'Ecouis and Brunard from him; Roger d'Auberville. Church, 2 mills.* Now 2 villages, Great and Little Blakenham; mill at Little Blakenham.

Blaxhall *Bla(c)cheshala/-essala/Blactheshala: Hamo de Valenis from Count Alan; Gilbert, William de Smalavilla and Ranulph from Robert Malet; Roger Bigot and Norman from him; Roger de Poitou; Ralph de Langhetot from Walter Giffard; Abbot of Ely.* ▦ Heathland; tumuli nearby.

Blundeston *Dun(e)stuna: Count Alan; Roger Bigot and Robert de Vals from him.* ▦ Near coast; said to be the Blunderstone of Dickens's *David Copperfield.*

Blyford *Blideforda: Godric the Steward. Church, mill.* ▦ Church with a Norman doorway.

Blythburgh *Blede-/Blieburc/Blideburc/-burgh/-buro: Osbern Masculus from the king, held by Roger Bigot; Robert Malet's mother. Church. 3000 herrings, a days provision of honey. 3 oxen.* ▦ Flourishing Roman and Saxon port. Its church, among the finest in Suffolk, is on a 7th-century church site.

Bosmere *Besemera: Abbot of Ely.* Bosmere Hall near Needham Market.

Boulge *Bulges: Count Alan; Robert Malet's mother and Robert de Glanville from her; Roger de Poitou; William de Warenne and Robert from him; Geoffrey de Mandeville; Ralph brother of Ilger; Countess of Albemarle; Hervey de Bourges. Church.* ⌂ Family home and burial place of Edward FitzGerald (1809–93), translator of Omar Khayyám.

Boxted *Boesteda: Roger de Poitou.* The Poley family home since c.1400.

Boynton *Boituna: Count Alan and Ulesan from him; Robert de Stratford.* Boynton Hall near Capel St Mary.

Boyton (near Alderton) *Bohtuna/Boituna: Walter son of Grip, Humphrey FitzRobert and William Gulafa from Robert Malet's mother. 3 churches, mill.* In marshland. It was once a coastal village; the remains of a jetty are below Dock Farm.

Boyton (in Stoke-by-Clare) *Alia Boituna: Robert FitzGilbert and Ralph and W. Peret from him.* Now Boyton End.

Bradfield *Bradefelda/fella: Count of Mortain; Abbot of St Edmund's before and after 1066 and Roric and Falk from him. Church. 80 goats.* Now 3 villages, Bradfield Combust, St Clare and Bradfield St George, which has a partly Norman church.

Bradley *Bradeleia: Abbot of St Edmund's; Richard FitzGilbert and 4 freemen from him; Robert de Tosny. Church, beehive. 53 pigs.* Now 2 villages, Great and Little Bradley. There is an aisle-less, 11th-century church in Little Bradley.

Braiseworth *Briseuolda/ Briseworde/wrda: Robert Malet's mother. Church, mill.* Church with a Norman doorway.

BRAMFIELD: *Bramfield Hall boasts a serpentine garden wall for protecting crops.*

Bramfield *Bru(n)felda: Count Alan. 24 pigs, 30 goats.* Ancient Castle Yard; Tudor hall with a Georgian front.

Bramford *Bran/Brunfort: King's land, kept by Roger Bigot. Church. 12 sheep, 20 pigs, 24 beasts.* Now a suburb of Ipswich; 16th- and 17th-century cottages.

Brampton *Bramtuna/Brantuna: King's land, kept by William de Noyers; Ralph Baynard; Robert de Curcan from Roger Bigot. Church.* Manor farm.

Brandeston (near Framlingham) *Brandes/ Brantestuna: Abbot of Ely and Hervey de Bituricensis from him; William d'Arcis. Church, mill, 3 beehives. 20 pigs.* Weir; working forge. John Lowes, a 16th-century vicar, was condemned to death for witchcraft; he confessed under torture to employing imps to sink ships.

Brandeston (in Waldingfield) *Brantestona: Ralph de Courbépine from Bishop of Bayeux. 23 pigs, 2 horses, 100 sheep.* Brandeston Hall near a Roman road.

Brandon *Brandona/Brantona: Abbot of Ely; Eudo the Steward. Church, fishery. 2 donkeys. 200 sheep.* Town, once a flint-knapping centre.

Brantham *Brantestuna/ Branham/Brantham: Godinc from Count Alan; Hubert from Robert Malet; Bishop of Bayeux; William d'Alno from Robert Gernon, formerly Tela a free woman; Roger from Ralph brother of Ilger. Mill, salt-pan.* Large, industrial.

Bredfield *Berdefelda/Berdesfella/ Bradefelda/-fella/Bredefeld(a)/-fella: Count Alan; Robert Malet's mother and Walter de Caen and Norman from her; Roger Bigot; Abbot of Ely and Robert Malet and Hervey de Berruarius from him; Richard FitzGilbert; Robert de Glanville from William de Warenne; Hervey de Bourges and Peter from him. Church. 3 oxen.* Moated site known as Bradfield Castle; birthplace of Edward FitzGerald (1809–83).

Brettenham *Bretenhama/ Bretham/Brettham: Count of Mortain; Abbot of St Edmund's and Arnulf from him; Richard FitzGilbert. Church.* Roman camp.

Bricett *Brieseta: Richard FitzGilbert and Roger de Orbec and Ranulph Peverel from him; Gilbert from Roger d'Auberville; William, brother of Roger d'Auberville and Fulcho from him; Anschetill from Roger de Raismes. Church. 15 beasts, 50 pigs, 140 sheep.* Now the village of Great Bricett with a partly Norman church, and Little Bricett, a hamlet with a moated site.

Bridge *Briges/Bringas: Roger Bigot and Robert de Curcun from him. 2 mills, salt-pan. 20 goats.* Bridge Farm by Dunwich River and the sea.

Brightwell *Brihtewella: Abbot of Ely. 2 mills, church.* Heathland.

Brockford *Brocfort: Abbot of St Edmund's before and after 1066.* Now Brockford Street; Brockford House near a Roman road; moated site.

Brockley (near Whepstead) *Brocle(ga): Roger de Poitou; Richard from Robert FitzCorbucion; Abbot of St Edmund's. Church.* 2 moated sites; ancient hall site.

Brockley (in Kedington) *Brochola: Robert FitzGilbert.* Now Brockley Green near Kedington.

Brome *Brom/Brum: King's land, kept by Roger Bigot; Robert Malet and William Scutet and Warin from him; Roger Bigot and Hugh de Corbon from him; Ralph de Beaufour; Abbot of St Edmund's; Bishop of Thetford. ½ church.* Moated site; church with a Norman doorway.

BURY ST EDMUNDS: *Scattered stones of the Benedictine abbey.*

Bromeswelle *Bram(m)eswella/ Bromeswella/Brumesuelle/-swella, Brumfella: Count Alan; Robert Malet's mother and Hubert de Monchensey and Gilbert de Colville from her; Abbot of Ely and Robert Malet from him. 2 churches.* Large; partly Norman church.

Browston *Brockestuna: King's land, kept by Roger Bigot.* Now Browston Green.

Bruisyard *Buresiart: Hamo de Valenis from Count Alan; Roger Bigot and Ralph de Turlaville from him. 24 pigs.* Hall, c.1610, on the site of a 14th-century chantry college, later a nunnery of Poor Clares.

Brundon *Branduna: Ralph de Limesy.* Brundon Hall on the River Stour near Sudbury.

Bucklesham *Buclesham/ Bukelesham: Count of Mortain; Abbot of Ely. Church.* Hall on a prehistoric settlement and burial site.

Bulcamp *Bulecampa/campe: Roger Bigot from the king and Robert de Vals from him. Godric the Steward. 40 goats.* Bulcamp House, built 1765–6 as a workhouse by Thomas Fulcher, who received 15 guineas for his drawings and attendances; now an old people's 'hospital'.

Bungay *Bongeia, Bung-/Burghea: King's land, kept by William de Noyers; Earl Hugh and William from him. 4 churches, 2½ mills. 60 goats, 100 sheep.* Town, mainly 18th century. Its 12th-century castle, built by Earl Hugh Bigod, was restored in 1965. St Mary's was originally the church of the Benedictine nunnery founded by Gundreda, wife of Roger de Glanville. There is a Butter Cross in the market place.

Bures *Bura/Bure: Abbot of St Edmund's before and after 1066; Richard Fitz Gilbert; Roger de Raismes; John FitzWaleran, formerly King Edward. Church, mill. 50 pigs, 100 sheep.* Mill. St Edmund was crowned here, Christmas Day, 855. St Stephen's Chapel, 1218, contains the tombs of 3 Earls of Oxford. 2 16th-century houses.

Burgate (near Eye) *Burgata: Adelm from Aubrey de Vere. Churches. 12 horses, 80 pigs, 176 sheep, 57 goats.* Name means 'burial gate'. King Edmund the Martyr's body lay for a night here on its journey from Hoxne to Bury St Edmunds. Traces of Iron Age occupation; Saxon earthwork.

Burgate (in Walton) *Buregata: Roger Bigot and Wihtmar from him.* Part of Felixstowe.

Burgh (in Walton) *Burch/Burg: Ralph brother of Ilger.* Part of Felixstowe.

Burgh (near Woodbridge) *Burc(g)/Burg/Burch/Burh(c): Count Alan; Earl Hugh; Roger de Poitou and Ernolf from him; Abbot of Ely; Roger de Glanville from William de Warenne; Hugh de Montfort; Geoffrey de Mandeville; Countess of Albemarle; Humphrey the Chamberlain.* Roman villa site above an important Belgic Iron Age site containing pottery.

Burgh Castle *Burch: Ralph the Crossbowman. 3 salt-pans. 160 sheep.* Marshes. The castle is a Roman fort, *Garianonum*, probably built c.AD 290; 3 massive walls remaining.

Burstall *Burgestala/Burghestala: Bishop of Bayeux and Ralph de Savigny and Roger Bigot from him; Richard FitzGilbert and Ulmar from him; Ranulph Peverel. Church, ½ mill.*

Bury St Edmunds *Villa Sancti Eadmundi: Abbot of St Edmund's. 2 mills, monastery, 2 fishponds. 30 priests, deacons and clerks, 28 nuns and poor persons, 75 bakers, ale brewers, tailors, washerwomen, shoemakers, robe makers, porters, cooks and agents, 34 knights, French and English, 342 houses, 118 monks.* Town on the River Lark. Industries include brewing as well as agriculture. The ruins of the medieval abbey are in Abbey Gardens.

Butley *Butelai/lea: Count Alan; Robert Malet's mother and Walter FitzAubrey from her; Roger de Poitou.* Coastal; marshland; remains of Augustinian priory, founded 1171 by Ranulph de Glanville. 14th-century gatehouse; late Neolithic 'Beaker' settlement nearby.

Buxhall *Bukeshala/-ssalla/ Buressalla: Count Eustace; Roger Bigot; Roger de Poitou; Frodo the Abbot's brother; Abbot of Ely; William de Warenne and Humphrey from him. Church, ½ mill.* Copinger family manor, 1428–1948. Sir William (b. 1512) was Lord Mayor of London.

Caldecott (in Fritton) *Caldecotan: Ralph the Crossbowman.* Caldecott Hall; tumulus nearby.

Campsea Ash *Campese(i)a/ Capeseia: Count Alan; Robert Malet's mother; Bishop of Evreaux; Hervey de Bourges. 2 mills, 3 beehives.* 16th-century mill; huge fishpond. Part of the 12th-century priory for Augustinian canonesses, a fine 14th-century timbered hall, survives in Ash Abbey house.

CLARE: *The Ancient House, c. 1473, once the priest's home.*

Candlet *Candelenta: Bigot.* Group of cottages; Candlets Farm in Trimley St Mary.

Capel St Andrew *Capeles: Count Alan; Robert Malet's mother and Walter FitzAubrey from her; Roger Bigot and Norman from him; Abbot of Ely and Robert Malet from him. Church.* Wooded.

Carlton (in Kelsale) *Carletuna: Hamo from Count Alan; Robert Malet. ½ fishery.*

Carlton Colville *Carletuna/ Karletuna: Earl Hugh; Hugh de Montfort. 300 herrings. 100 sheep.* Dormitory village for Lowestoft.

Cavendish *Kanauadis(c)/ Kauanadis(c): Roger de St Germains from Richard FitzGilbert; Ralph de Limesy. Church, mill. 24 beasts, 110 sheep, 50 pigs.* Water mill; picturesque cottages.

Cavenham *Canauatham/ Kanauaham: Richard FitzGilbert; Eudo the Steward. Church, 4 mills.* Near the Icknield Way; ancient Black Ditches.

Chadacre *Scerdatra: Countess of Albemarle.* Chadacre Hall, an agricultural college.

Chamberlain's Hall *Coclesworda:* Lost.

Charsfield *Caresfelda/-fella/ Carsfelda/Cere(s)felda/ Cer(es)fella/Cerresfella/ Keresfelda: Robert Malet's mother; Roger Bigot and Turstan son of Witdo from him; Bishop of Bayeux and Ralph de Savigny from him; Abbot of Ely; Hugh de Montfort; Geoffrey de Mandeville; Countess of Albemarle.* Ronald Blythe based *Akenfield* on it.

Chattisham *Cetessam: King's land, kept by Aluric Wanz.*

Chedburgh *Cedebena: Frodo from Abbot of Ely.* Large.

Chediston *Cedestan/ Cidesan(es)/Sedetana: Count Alan; Roger Bigot and Robert de Vals, Anant, Edric and Urf from him; Gilbert the Crossbowman and Osketel and Godric from him. Church.* Partly Norman church.

Chelsworth *Cerleswrda: Abbot of St Edmund's before and after 1066. Church, mill. 9 beasts, 20 pigs.*

Chevington *Ceventuna: Abbot of St Edmund's before and after 1066. Church, 3 beehives. 22 beasts, 30 pigs, 140 sheep, 40 goats.* Pond; moated site of an ancient house of the monks of Bury.

Chickering *Ciccheli(n)ga/ Cikelinga/Citiringa: Robert Malet's mother and Walter from her; Roger de Poitou; Bishop of Thetford. Church (with Wilby).* Moated site.

Chilbourne *Cileburna:* Lost.

Chillesford *Cesefortda: Count Alan. Church.*

CHILTON HALL: *Moat and gable of the manor house.*

Chilton (in Stowmarket) *Ciltuna: Abbot of Ely; Hugh de Montfort. Church.* Chilton Hall, part of Stowmarket.

Chilton (near Sudbury) *Ciltona: Walter FitzAubrey from Robert Malet.* On the outskirts of Sudbury; Tudor hall; moat.

Chippenhall *Cebbenhala/Cibbe- /Cipben-/hala/Cybenhalla: Robert Malet's mother and Walter, Humphrey and Walter son of Grip from her; Abbot of St Edmund's before and after 1066; Hervey de Bourges. 1½ churches.* Now Chippenhall Green.

Clare *Clara: Richard FitzGilbert. Church, market, mill, vineyard, 12 beehives.* Small town, an important borough in the 13th century, with a prehistoric earthwork, and the remains of a Norman castle containing traces of Gilbert de Clare's 1090 priory.

Claydon *Calinduna/dune: Aluric from the Vavassors.* 17th-century Hall; moated site.

Clopton (-in-Wickhambrook) *Cleptuna/Cloptuna/Copletuna: Abbot of Ely; Richard FitzGilbert and William Pecche from him; Hugh from William de Warenne.* Now Clopton Green.

Clopton (near Woodbridge) *Cleopetona/Clopetona/-tuna/ Cloptuna: Hugh de Montfort; Thorold from Ranulph Peverel; Countess of Albemarle and Ulwin the priest from her; William d'Arcis and Bernard de Sancto Audoeno from him; Humphrey the Chamberlain and Amund from him; Robert Malet's mother and Tiger and Gilbert de Colville from her; Roger de Poitou and Roger FitzErnald from him. Church. 30 pigs.*

Cockfield *Cothefelda: Abbot of St Edmund's before and after 1066, and Berard, James and Coleman from him. Winter mill, 12 beehives. 37 pigs.* 15th-century cottage.

Coddenham (in Boxford) *Kode(n)ham: Ralph de Limesy. 1½ mills.* Coddenham Hall.

Coddenham (near Needham Market) *Cadenham/ Code(n)ham: King's land, kept by Godric; Count Alan; Roger de Poitou and Raymond Giralt from him; Bishop of Bayeux; Humphrey FitzAubrey from Ranulph Peverel; Roger de Raismes and Milo from him; Eudo FitzSpirwic; Abbot of Ely; the Vavassors and Friebarn a priest from them. 2 churches.* Church with Norman work. The post office is a former inn, c.1500.

Colston *Colestuna: Warner from Hervey de Bourges.* Colston Hall near Roman road.

Combs *Cambas: Count of Mortain; Hugh de Montfort. 3½ mills. 2 horses, 24 beasts, 101 sheep, 60 goats.*

Coney Weston *Cunegestuna: Abbot of St Edmund's before and after 1066. Church.*

Cookley *Cokel(e)i: Robert de Vals from Roger Bigot; William d'Ecouis.* Agricultural.

Cornard *Corn(i)erda: King's land, kept by William the Chamberlain and Otto the Goldsmith; Abbot of St Edmund's before and after 1066; Richard FitzGilbert; Ralph de Limesy. Church, mill. 4 horses, 18 beasts, 80 pigs, 473 sheep.* Now Great Cornard, a suburb of Sudbury, and the hamlet of Little Cornard.

Corton *Caretuna/Karetuna: King's land, kept by Roger Bigot.* Seaside caravan site.

Cotton *Codetuna/Cotetuna/ Coti(n)tuna/Cottuna/Kodetun: King's land, kept by Godric; Robert Malet; Abbot of St Edmund's; Walter the Deacon from Richard FitzGilbert; Hugh de Montfort. Church.* Extensive moats.

Covehithe (formerly North Hales) *Nordhalla/Norhals/ Norhhala/Northala/-hals: Roger Bigot, the pre-Conquest holder, and Norman from him; William de Warenne; William de Boeville from Geoffrey de Mandeville.* Seaside.

Cowlinge *Culinge: Count Alan. Church. 7 beasts, 40 pigs, 40 goats.* Scattered; 2 moated sites; prison.

Cranley *Cranlea: Ralph de Limesy.* Scattered; manor house; moated site.

Cransford *Craneforda/-fort/ Cranesfod/-forda/Crenefort: Count Alan; Robert and Walter from Robert Malet; Gilbert from Robert Malet's mother; Roger Bigot and Norman from him. Hervey de Bourges.*

Cratfield *Cratafelda: William Baynard from his uncle Ralph Baynard. Church.* 2 greens; church with a clock-bell, c.1400.

Creeting *Cratinga(s)-ingis/ Gratingis: Abbot of Bernai; Robert Malet and Walter de Caen and Robert Glanville from him; Roger de Poitou; Roger Bigot and Garenger from Bishop of Bayeux; Count of Mortain; Humfrid from William de Warenne; Walter de St Valery. Church, mill.* Now Creeting St Mary; partly Norman church.

Creeting St Peter *Cratina/-ingis/ Gratinga: Robert de Glanville from Robert Malet; Bishop of Bayeux and William de Boeville from him; William de Boeville from Geoffrey de Mandeville; Abbot of Bernai; Walter de St Valery; St Mary of Gerstein from Count Mortain. Church, 2 mills. 7 beasts.* Church with a Norman doorway and nave walls.

Cretingham *Gratingeham/ Gretingaham/-ingeham: Count Alan; Earl Hugh; Bishop of Bayeux and Ralph de Savigny from him; Abbot of Ely; Roger de Candos from Hugh de Montfort; Humphrey the Chamberlain and Amund from him. Church, mill.* Iron Age earthworks.

Crowfield *Crofelda: Bishop of Bayeux and Roger Bigot from him; Roger de Raismes.* Long; built along 'Stone Street', a Roman road.

Culford *Culeforda: Abbot of St Edmund's before and after 1066 and Peter from him.* Mill.

Culpho *Culfol(a)/fole: Roger de Poitou. Church.* Abbey Farm with a moat on the Culpho Abbey site.

Dagworth *Dagawarda/worda: Hugh de Montfort and Roger and William FitzGross from him; Walter the Deacon. 2 churches, mill. 10 beasts, 40 goats.* Wooded.

Dalham *Dalham: Richard FitzGilbert and William Pecche from him. Church. 50 goats.* Church with a bust of Sir Martin Stuteville, who 'saw the new world with Francis Drake'.

Dallinghoo *Dal(l)ingahou/ Dalingehou/Delingahou: Count Alan; William and Robert de Glanville from Robert Malet's mother; Roger de Poitou; Abbot of Ely; Hervey de Bourges. Church.*

Darmsden *Dermodesduna: King's land, kept by Godric; Count Alan; Hugh de Montfort; Roger Bigot from Abbot of Ely. Mill.*

Darsham *Ders(h)am/Diresham: King's land, kept by Roger Bigot; Count Alan; Robert Malet's mother and Walter FitzRichere and Fulcred from her; many freemen and Robert de Vals from Roger Bigot. ½ church.* Church with Saxon work, some Roman tiles and a Norman doorway.

Debach *De(ben)beis/Depebecs/- bek/-bes: Count Alan; Roger Bigot and Sturstan son of Widdow and Roger de Poitou from him; Bishop of Bayeux; William de Warenne; Geoffrey de Mandeville; Ranulph Peverel.* Airfield, once a US base and now a mushroom factory.

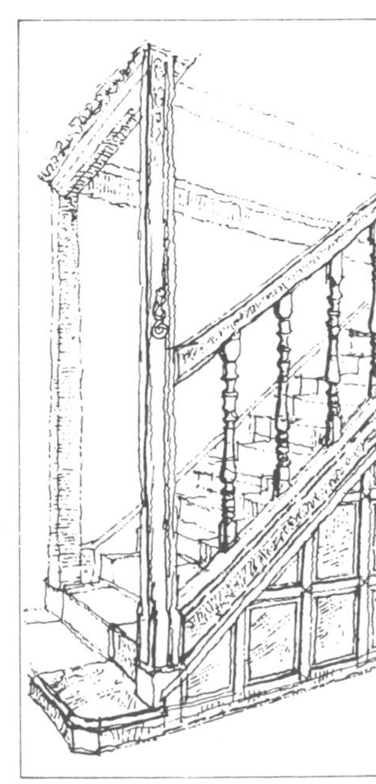

CREETING ST PETER: *Steps and balustrade worked in solid oak at Roydon Hall.*

Debenham *Depbe(n)ham/Deph(e)am/Dephenham/Depleham: William Gulafra from Robert Malet and his mother from him; Bishop of Bayeux; Ralph de Savigny from Ranulph Peverel; Abbot of Ely. 2 churches, St Mary and St Andrew. 20 pigs, 28 goats.* Small town. St Mary's church has Saxon and Norman work in the tower and porch. Crows Hall is a fine moated house, c.1508.

Denham (near Bury St Edmunds) *Denham: Richard FitzGilbert and W. Hurrant from him. Church.* Orchards; Denham Castle, motte and bailey earthworks, nearby.

Denham (near Eye) *De(l)ham: King's land, kept by William de Noyers; Robert Malet; Roger Bigot and Aitard from him; Bishop of Thetford. Church. 2 horses, 20 goats.* Scattered; church may have been a college connected with Hoxne priory; moated College Farm.

Dennington *Binneuetuna/Dingifetuna/Dingiuetona/-tuna/Dinguiet': Robert Malet's mother. Church, park, 5 beehives. 40 pigs, 30 goats.* Church with rich furnishings. Home of Bardolph, who fought at Agincourt (1415) and was Henry V's Treasurer. His tomb is in the church; his home now a farm.

Denston *Damar-/Danar-/Danerdestuna: Richard FitzGilbert and Robert from him; Gerald the Marshal.* Green.

Depden *Depdana: Richard FitzGilbert and Frodo and Osbern from him; Hugh de Wancey from William de Warenne. Church, 13 beehives. 17 beasts, 72 pigs, 112 sheep.* Highest point in Suffolk; church with a Norman doorway.

Desning *Deselinga/Dsilinges: Richard FitzGilbert. 2 churches, 4 mills, 9 beehives.* Desning Hall; moated site.

Dodnash *Todenes: Count Alan. Mill, church.* Dodnash Priory Farm and wood near Bentley.

Drinkstone *Drences/Rengestuna/Drincestona: Count of Mortain; Abbot of St Edmund's; Abbot of Ely. Church. 2 horses, 32 pigs.* 17th-century windmill.

Dunningworth *Duniworda: Roger Bigot.* Dunningworth Hall.

Dunwich *Duneuuic:* See page 250.

East Bergholt *Bercolt: King's land, in the charge of Aluric Wanz; Aubrey de Vere from Aluric. Mill.* Birthplace of the painter John Constable (1776–1837). His father was a miller who owned 16th-century Flatford Mill, the manor house and Willy Lotts cottage.

Easton *Estuna: Robert Malet's mother; Roger de Poitou; Milo from Roger de Raismes; Gilbert the Crossbowman from the king.* Moated sites.

Easton Bavants *Estuna: King's land, kept by Roger Bigot.* Seaside.

Edwardstone *Eduardestuna: Hubert from Robert Malet. Church, winter mill.* On the River Box, on the site of a Norman monastery.

Eleigh *Ilelega/Illeleia/Lelega: Archbishop Lanfranc; Abbot of St Edmund's before and after 1066 and Arnulf from him; Tihell de Herion; Bishop of Bayeux; Richard FitzGilbert. Church, 3 mills. 20 pigs, 160 sheep.* Now 2 villages, Monks and Brent Eleigh.

Ellough *Elga: Roger Bigot and Robert de Vals from him.* Name is Old Norse for heathen temple.

Elmsett *Elmeseta: Roger d'Auberville. Church.*

Elmswell *Elmeswella: Abbot of St Edmund's before and after 1066. 48 goats.* Large; mill. Almshouses, c.1614; Romano-British kiln with pottery, discovered 1964.

Elveden *Eluedena/Haluedona/Heluedana/-dona: Count Eustace; Abbot of St Edmund's before and after 1066; Richard FitzGilbert; Nicholas from William de Warenne. 4 churches, fishery. 410 sheep, 94 goats.* Forest; Roman finds; church with a Norman window. Thetford Hall was transformed by the Maharaja Duleep Singh, in the 1860s, into an oriental extravaganza.

Eriswell *Hereswella: Eudo the Steward. Church, 2½ mills, 2 fisheries. 800 sheep.* Heathland.

Erwarton *Alwartuna/Eurewardestuna: Richard FitzGilbert and Roger from him. ⅓ fishery. 8 beasts, 26 pigs.* Elizabethan hall.

Euston *Eu(e)stuna: Abbot of St Edmund's and Adelund from him. 2 mills.* Weir; hall, seat of the Earl of Arlington and later the Dukes of Grafton; gardens and temple by William Kent.

Exning *Essel: King's land, formerly Edeva the Fair; Wymarc from Count Alan. 3 mills (7000 eels), mill, fishery (1200 eels).*

Eye *Eia/Heia: Robert Malet's mother and Walter the Crossbowman and Walter de Caen from her. Church, market, fishery park, 2 mills. 60 pigs.* Small market town. William Malet built a motte and bailey castle on the site of a Saxon fortress; remains of a priory, founded c.1100 by Malet's son. The 101ft tall church steeple is one of the wonders of Suffolk.

Falkenham *Faltenham: Roger Bigot and Ralph de Turlaville from him; Ralph, brother of Ilger.*

Farley *Farleia: Richard FitzGilbert.* Now Farley Green, near Cowlinge.

Farnham *Faraham/Ferneham/Farnham: Robert from Robert Malet's mother and Norman from him; Roger Bigot. 2 mills.*

EAST BERGHOLT: *Colour-washed cottages in simple East Anglian style.*

Felsham *Fealsham: Abbot of St Edmund's and Adelelund from him. Church.* Old farmhouse; moat site. Remains of the mausoleum of John Reynolds, sheriff 1735, who 'thought differently from all men while he lived'.

Fenstead *Finesteda: Ralph de Limesy.* Now Fenstead End; moated site.

Finborough *Fineberga: King's land, kept by Godric; Count Eustace; Abbot of Ely and Roger d'Auberville from him. Church, mill.* Now 2 villages, Great and Little Finborough.

Finningham *Felincham/Finingaham: Robert Malet's mother; Abbot of St Edmund's; Robert Blunt. Church.*

Flempton *Flemingtuna: Abbot of St Edmund's and Ulward from him. Church.* Barrows nearby.

Flixton (near Bungay) *Flixtuna: Bishop of Thetford and William de Noyrs from him; Eudo FitzSpirwic and Geoffrey from him. Church, ½ mill. 160 sheep.* Church, rebuilt 1835; remains of a priory.

Flixton (near Lowestoft) *Flixtuna: King's land, kept by Roger Bigot.* Ruins of a church, destroyed in 1730 by a hurricane; Flixton House, on the outskirts of Lowestoft.

Flowton *Flochetuna: Roger Bigot and Hugh de Hosdenc from him; Germond from Richard FitzGilbert; Roger d'Auberville.*

Fordley *Forle(a)/lei: Robert Malet's mother; Gilbert from Robert Malet; Roger Bigot. Mill.* Fordley Hall on a tributary of the River Minsmere.

Fornham All Saints *Fornham: Abbot of St Edmund's before and after 1066. Church, mill.* Church with a Norman doorway.

Fornham St Genevieve *Genonefae Forham: Abbot of St Edmund's before and after 1066 and Peter and Ralph from him. Church, 3 mills.* Weir; ruins of a church; site of a demolished hall.

Fornham St Martin *Fornham: Abbot of St Edmund's before and after 1066. Church. 100 sheep.*

Foxhall *Foxehola: Abbot of Ely.* Parish near Ipswich.

Framlingham *Fram(a)lingaham/Frameeling(a)ham/Framincham:* See page 253.

Framsden *Framesdena: Earl Hugh. Church, mill. 31 goats, 50 sheep.* Hall, originally a medieval hall-house.

Freckenham *Frakenaham: Bishop of Rochester. Church, mill, 2 fisheries, 6 beehives. 3 horses, 13 beasts, 40 pigs, 230 sheep.* Overlooking fens; remains of a small motte and bailey castle.

Fressingfield *Fessefelda: Robert Malet's mother.* Large. The initials of Alice de la Pole, Chaucer's granddaughter, are on a church bench.

Freston *Frese/Frisetuna: Roger de Arbernum from Richard FitzGilbert; Ernulf from Swein of Essex. Church, mill. 101 sheep.*

Fritton *Fridetuna: King's land, kept by Roger Bigot. 3 beehives, salt-pan. 160 sheep.* Partly Norman church with Saxon tracings and early wall paintings.

Frostenden *Froxedena: Ranulf from Ralph Baynard. 2 churches, sea fort, 2 beehives. 24 goats.* Now some miles from the sea; Church with Norman work.

Gapton *Gabba/Gabbetuna: King's land, kept by Roger Bigot.* Gapton Marshes adjoining Great Yarmouth.

Gedding *Ge(l)dinga: Abbot of St Edmund's; William de Warenne. Church.* Church, once moated, with some Norman windows. The gatehouse of the hall is early 16th century.

Gedgrave *Gata/Gategrava: Count Alan; Robert Malet's mother and Gilbert de Wisant from her; Roger Bigot.* Some houses; on marshes.

Gisleham *Gisleham: Earl Hugh; Robert Malet's mother and Lewin, son of Ringulf, from her; Hugh de Montfort; Aubrey de Vere.* Moated site.

Gislingham *Gildincham, Gis(i)lincham/Gislinga-/Gislingeham/Gissilincham: King's land, kept by Godric; Abbot of St Edmund's; Robert Blunt; Gilbert the Crossbowman.* Old guildhall; manor house.

Glemsford *Clamesford(a): Abbot of Ely; Garin from Ranulph Peverel. Church, mill. 3 horses, 8 beasts, 200 sheep, 32 pigs.* Large; long history of cloth making; early 19th-century silk mill.

Glevering *Glerevinges: Odo from Hervey de Bourges.* 18th-century Glevering Hall, with fine orangery.

Great Ashfield *Eascefelda/Escefella: Abbot of St Edmund's and Odar from him. Church.* 3 moated houses; motte at Castle Hill.

Great Barton *Bertuna: Abbot of St Edmund's before and after 1066. Church.* Growing.

Great Bealings *Belinges: Robert Malet's mother; Hervey de Bourges.*

Great Fakenham *Fachenham: Abbot of St Edmund's and Peter from him; Peter de Valognes. 2 churches, mill. 16 forest mares.* Heath; Honington airfield; church with some Saxon and Norman work.

GEDDING: *The gatehouse of Gedding Hall; originally Tudor, the drawbridge still exists. Restored.*

Great Livermere *Liuel-/Liuermera/Litla-/Liuermera: Abbot of St Edmund's and Fulcher, Frodo and Walter from him; Abbot of Ely; Hugh de Beuerda.* Divided from Little Livermere by a mere.

Great Glemham *Clieham/Cliemham/Glaim-/Gl(i)emham: Hamo from Count Alan; Walter from Robert Malet; Norman from Roger Bigot; Roger de Poitou; Pirot from Eudo the Steward; Walter Giffard. 1½ churches, mill.*

Grimston (Hall) *Grimestuna: Udo from Count of Mortain; Roger Bigot and Ralph de Turlaville from him.* Grimston Hall near Felixstowe.

Groton *Grotena: King's land, kept by William the Chamberlain and Otto the Goldsmith; Abbot of St Edmund's before and after 1066; Richard FitzGilbert.* Home of John Winthrop, who organized local migration to America and became governor of Massachusetts, 1660–76. A church window, in his memory, was donated by New England Winthrops.

Grundisburgh *Grundesbur/burc(h)/burg(h)/burg: Earl Hugh; Humphrey from Robert Malet's mother; Roger de Poitou and Roger from him; Abbot of Ely and Hervey de Beruari and Algar from him; Geoffrey de Mandeville and Eilric from him; Hervey de Bourges. 3 beehives.* Large; central green; stream. A house rebuilt in 1515 by Thomas Awall, a salter, has a salt-cellar.

Gulpher *Gulpelea: Roger Bigot.* On the outskirts of Felixstowe.

Gusford *Gutthuluesforda:* Lost.

Hacheston *Hacestuna/Hece(s)tuna/Hetcetuna: King's land, kept by Godric; Count Alan; Robert Malet's mother and Gilbert from her; Abbot of St Edmund's.*

Hadleigh *Hetlega: Archbishop Lanfranc. Church, 3 mills. 120 sheep, 20 pigs.* Ancient market town with late medieval buildings and a half-timbered Town Hall. A Romano-British building was found here in 1954.

Halesworth *Halesuuorda/-eurda/Healesuuorda: Count Alan; Bigot de Loges from Earl Hugh; Roger Bigot and Robert de Vals from him. Mill.* Busy town.

Hanchet *Haningehest: Richard FitzGilbert.* Now Hanchet End; Hanchet Hall.

Hargrave *Haragrava: William de Watteville. Church. 40 pigs.* Straggling.

Harkstead *Herchesteda: King's land, kept by Peter de Valognes; Robert Gernon; Countess of Albemarle, formerly Edith the Fair. 2 churches, mill.* Church with Norman windows and a blocked Norman doorway.

Harleston *Heroluestuna: Abbot of St Edmund's before and after 1066 and Aelons and Peter from him. Church.* Thatched church with a Norman nave and doorway.

Harpole *Holap-/Horap-/Horpola/Horepola/-polo:* Lost.

Hartest *Herte(r)st: Abbot of Ely before and after 1066 and Berner the Crossbowman from him; Richard FitzGilbert. Church. 4 horses, 20 beasts, 25 pigs.* Green.

Hasketon *Hasc(h)etuna/Hashetuna: Robert Malet's mother; Roger de Poitou and Roger son of Ernolf from him; Abbot of Ely; Geoffrey de Mandeville.* The medieval Hundred met by what is now the village post office.

Haspley *Haspelega/Hespelea:* Lost.

Haughley *Hagala: Hugh de Montfort. Church. 6 horses, 18 beasts, 46 sheep, 80 goats.* Farming; remains of a motte and bailey castle destroyed by Flemings, 1173.

Haverhill *Hauerha/Hauerhella/-hol: Abbot of St Edmund's; Bishop of Bayeux and Tihell from him; Richard Fitz Gilbert and Pagan from him; Tihell de Herion. Church.* Expanding town, with new estates.

Hawkedon *Auokeduna/Hauokeduna/Hauochenduna: Roger de Poitou; Richard FitzGilbert and Gislebert and Folkered from him. ½ church.* Quiet; 2 timber-framed houses.

Hawstead *Haldsteda/Hersteda: Abbot of St Edmund's and Odo, Albold, Peter, clerics and Agenetus from him; Richard FitzGilbert.*

Helmingham *Elming-/H(el)mingheham/Helmincham/(Hmingheham): Count of Mortain; Earl Hugh; Roger de Poitou; Bishop of Bayeux; Richard FitzGilbert; Roger de Raismes; Humphrey the Chamberlain and Amund from him. 2 churches, 2 beehives.* The hall, the Tollemache family home from the 16th century, is partly Tudor with alterations by Nash and Repton.

Hemingsone *Hami(n)-/Hauungestuna/Haminghelanda: King's land, kept by Roger Bigot; Count Alan; Robert Malet and his mother from him; Garengar from Roger Bigot; Roger de Poitou and Almar the king's reeve and Isaac from him; Rainald from Hervey de Bourges; the Vavassors; William d'Ecouis from Abbot of Ely. 1½ churches.* Straggling; church with Saxon work.

Hemley *Almelega/Halmelega/-leia/Helmele(a): Roger Bigot; Roger de Poitou; William de Nomore from Ralph brother of Ilger; Countess of Albemarle; William d'Arcis.*

Hengrave *Hemegretham: Abbot of St Edmund's before and after 1066. Church, mill. 12 beasts, 20 pigs.* Church with an early Norman tower.

Henham *Henham: Robert of Blythburgh from Ralph Baynard. Mill.* Henham Park, designed by Humphrey Repton.

Henley *Henle(i)a/leie: Humphrey from Robert Malet; Roger de Poitou; Roger d'Auberville and Eudo the Steward from him; Walter the Deacon; Isaac; Abbot of Ely. 2 churches.* Tithe barn.

Henstead *Henestede: William de Warenne and Godfrey de Petro Ponte from him.*

Hepworth *Hepworda: Abbot of St Edmund's and Fulcher and Peter de Valognes from him; Robert Blunt. Church.* Church with traces of Norman work.

Herringfleet *Heringaflet: King's land, kept by Roger Bigot.* Seaside resort; marshes; remains of a 13th- and 14th-century Austen priory.

Herringswell *Herni(n)gawella/Hyrningwella: Abbot of St Edmund's before and after 1066; Richard FitzGilbert; William de Warenne and Roger and Nicholas from him. Church, 2 mills.* Icenian tumuli nearby; remains of a church, possibly Norman.

Hessett *Eteseta/Heteseta: Frodo the Abbot's brother; Abbot of St Edmund's and Berard from him. Church.* 3 moat sites; late medieval church.

Hestley *Hastelea: Ralph de Limesy.* Hestley Hall; moat site.

Heveningham *Evelincham/Heveniggeham: Roger Bigot and Anskettle from him.* Palladian hall, 1778, with a park landscaped by Capability Brown, and an orangery by James Wyatt.

Higham (near Brantham) *Hecham/Hei(h)ham: Ralph de Marci from Count Eustace; Bishop of Bayeux; Osbern from Richard FitzGilbert; Garenger from Roger de Raismes; Gondwin. Mill, 1¼ churches.*

Hinderclay *Hilderclea: Abbot of St Edmund's before and after 1066. Church.* Early Iron Age settlement nearby.

Hintlesham *Hintlesham: King's land, kept by William de Noyers; Ralph from Count Alan. 1½ churches, mill, salt-pan. 30 pigs, 200 sheep.* Elizabethan and Palladian hall restored by restaurateur Robert Carrier, 1972.

Hinton *Hinetuna: Roger Bigot and Robert of Blythburgh from him. Church.* Scattered; Hinton Hall; Hinton Springs.

Hitcham *Hecham/Hetcham: Abbot of Ely and Roger Bigot from him; Richard FitzGilbert and Ailward son of Bell from him. Church.* Romano-British settlement site nearby. John Henslow, who influenced Darwin and secured his appointment to the *Beagle*, was rector here from 1837.

Holbrook *Holebroc: Odo from Count Alan.* Royal Hospital School for sons of naval officers.

Hollesley *Holeslea: Robert Malet's mother and Robert de Glanville from her. Church, fishery. 30 pigs, 100 sheep.* Heathland; near the sea.

Holton (near Halesworth) *Holetuna: Robert Malet's mother; Godric the Steward; Robert de Curcun from Roger Bigot.* Church with a Norman tower.

Holton St Mary *Holetuna: Geoffrey de Mandeville. Church.*

Homersfield *Humbresfelda: Bishop of Thetford before and after 1066. 2 churches, mill. 26 pigs, 200 sheep.* Romano-British pottery kilns, excavated 1959.

Honington *Hunegetuna: Abbot of St Edmund's. Church.* Marshland; church with a Norman doorway.

Hoo (near Kettleburgh) *Hou: Abbot of Ely before and after 1066 and William de Buville from him. Church, mill. 24 pigs, 40 goats.* Moated site; 17th-century farmhouse.

Hoo (in Sutton) *Hoi/Hou: Robert Malet's mother; Abbot of Ely.* Now Sutton Hoo; Saxon royal burial ground which has yielded a vast amount of archaeological treasure.

Hopton (near Fakenham) *Hopetuna: Abbot of St Edmund's and Fulcher from him. Mill.* On the Little Ouse.

Hopton (near Lowestoft) *Hotuna: King's land, kept by Roger Bigot. 3 beehives.* Holiday camp near sandy cliffs.

Horham *Horam/Horan(t): Robert Malet's mother and Robert de Glanville, Walter son of Grip and Walter de Caen from her; Abbot of St Edmund's; Bishop of Thetford; Roger de Candos from Hugh de Montfort; Juhichell the Priest; a freeman. Church, 3 beehives. 30 goats, 24 pigs.* Tiny church, with a Norman doorway.

Horringer *Horningeserda/eswordа: Abbot of St Edmund's before and after 1066; Richard FitzGilbert. Church. 14 beasts, 30 pigs.* Round a green; formerly Horningsheath.

Horswold *Horswalda:* Lost.

Houghton *Hoketona:* Lost.

Hoxne *Hox(a)/Hox-/Hoxna/Oxa: Bishop of Thetford. Church, market. 12 beasts, 80 pigs, 40 goats.* Attractive; round a green.

Hundon *Hune(n)dana: Richard FitzGilbert and Hamo from him. Church, mill, 12 beehives.* Quiet; hillside; overlooking a tributary of the River Stour; 15th-century timber-framed house.

Hunston *Hunterstuna: King's land, kept by Godric; Abbot of St Edmund's and Bucard from him.* Many old cottages; 2 moated sites.

HADLEIGH: *The 15th-c. Guildhall has 2 overhanging storeys.*

IPSWICH: *Christchurch Mansion, 16th c., on the site of an Augustinian priory.*

Huntingfield *Huntingafelda/felde: Walter FitzAubrey from Robert Malet's mother. Church. 6 beehives.* Once part of the estate given to Anne of Cleves by Henry VIII; church with Norman work.

Icklingham *Ecclingaham: King's land, kept by William de Noyers; Ranulph Peverel; Moruant from Eudo FitzSpirwic. Church, 2 mills.* 2 parish churches; site of a Roman villa.

Ickworth *Ikewortha: Abbot of St Edmund's before and after 1066. Church, mill.* Home of the Hervey family since the 15th century; church with traces of Norman work.

Ilketshall *Elcheteshala/Ilchet(el)eshala: Earl Hugh; Godric the Steward. Church, ½ mill.* Now 4 villages, Ilketshall St Andrew, St John and St Margaret, all with churches with Norman traces, and Ilketshall St Lawrence, which stands within a Roman earthwork.

Ingham *Incham/Ingham: Roger de Poitou; Abbot of St Edmund's before and after 1066. Church, mill. 30 pigs, 520 sheep.*

Instead *Isteda: A freeman. ¼ mill.* Instead Manor House by the River Waveney.

Ipswich *Gepesuiz/-wic/Gopeswic/wiz/Gipewid/-wiz/Gypeswiz: King's land, kept by William de Noyers; Count Alan; Robert Malet; Lefflett a free woman; Bishop of Bayeux and Roger Bigot from him; Richard FitzGilbert; Hugh de Montfort; Geoffrey de Mandeville; Roger de Raismes; Ralph brother of Ilger; Walter the Deacon; Norman. 6 churches, 1⅓ mills, grange, 130 burgesses, 100 poor burgesses.* Thriving port and market town, the county's administrative centre. Settled since Paleolithic times it was a walled town in the Middle Ages, but retained its Anglo-Saxon street pattern. 12 medieval churches still stand; St Mary at the Elms contains Norman work.

Isleton *Isleuestuna.* Lost.

Ixworth *Giswortha/Icse-/Ixewrda: Abbot of St Edmund's and Robert Blunt from him; a freeman. Church, mill, park, vineyard.* Ancient; on the Roman Peddar's Way; 13th-century Abbey House.

Ixworth Thorpe *Torp(a): William d'Ecouis; Peter de Valognes, formerly Queen Edith; Abbot of St Edmund's and Robert Blunt from him; Sasselin; a freeman. Church (with Market Weston), mill.* Manor house.

Kalweton *Caluwetuna:* Lost.

Kedington *Kidituna: Abbot of St Edmund's; Richard FitzGilbert; Ralph Baynard. Church, mill.* Suburb of Haverhill; church with a Roman building under the floor and a Saxon cross, c. 900.

Kelsale *Cara-/Kereshalla/Cheres(s)ala/Chylesheala/Keles-/Kireshala: Robert Malet; Roger Bigot. Church. 100 sheep, 30 pigs.* Guildhall, c.1500, now a school; church with a Norman doorway.

Kembroke *Kele-/Kenebroc/Kinebroh: Roger Bigot and William de Burnoville from him; Abbot of Ely; Kenold from Hervey de Bourges. 2 mills.* Kembroke Hall; cottages by Mill River.

Kenton *Chenetuna/Kenetona/-tuna: Robert Malet's mother and Tiger and William Gulafra from her; Abbot of St Edmund's and Dorand from him; Roger Bigot and Ralph de Savigny from Bishop of Bayeux. Church, 6 beehives. 16 beasts, 40 pigs, 25 goats.*

Kentwell *Kanewella: Frodo the Abbot's brother. 40 pigs.* Kentwell Downs, an ancient hall near a Roman road.

Kersey *Cereseia: Chatteris Abbey; Richard FitzGilbert. Church, mill.* Centre for manufacturing Kersey cloth in the Middle Ages. The main street runs down both sides of a valley to a water-splash.

Kesgrave *Gressegrava: Robert Malet's mother. ½ church.* Suburb of Ipswich.

Kessingland *Kessingalanda/gelanda: King's land, kept by Roger Bigot; Earl Hugh and Hugh FitzNorman from him; Hugh de Montfort. Mill (100 herrings). 43 pigs.* Seaside town.

Kettlebaston *Kitelbeomastuna: Abbot of St Edmund's and Gamas and Humphrey from him.* Remote; moated site.

Kettleburgh *Cetelbirig/Chetel-/Ketelbiria/Chettlebiriga/Ketdesbirig/Ketlebere/KettlebergaCount Alan; Robert Malet's mother and Humphrey from her; Roger de Poitou. Church.*

Kingsland *Kingeslanda:* Lost.

Kingston *Kyngestuna: Abbot of Ely before and after 1066.* Adjoining Woodbridge.

Kirkley *Kirkelea: King's land, kept by Roger Bigot; Hugh de Montfort.* Part of Lowestoft.

Kirkton (in Shotley) *Cherchetuna: Richard FitzGilbert.* Now Shotley.

Kirton *Kirketuna: Roger Bigot and Wihtmar from him; Roger de Raismes. Church.*

Knettishall *Ghenetessala/Gnedassala/-eshalla/Gnateshala: King's land; Abbot of St Edmund's and Fulcher from him. Church, mill, ½ mill.* Barrows nearby.

Knoddishall *Chenotessala/Cnotesheala/-heale: Roger Bigot and Ranulf FitzWalter from him.*

Lackford *Leacforda: Abbot of St Edmund's before and after 1066. Church, 2 mills. 9 beasts, 160 sheep.* On the Roman Icknield Way; church with Norman work.

Lakenheath *Lakingaheda/-hethe/Laringahetha/-geheta: Abbot of Ely before and after 1066; Richard FitzGilbert; Eudo the Steward. Church, mill, 8 fisheries, fishing boat. 100 sheep.* Overlooking fenland; church with a Norman chancel arch; Neolithic to Roman settlements; one of the largest US airbases in Britain.

Langer *Langestuna: Roger Bigot and Ralph de Turlaville from him.* Landguard Common and Point, near Felixstowe Port.

Langham *Langham: Abbot of St Edmund's; Robert Blunt. Church.*

Lavenham *Lauen(ham): Frodo the Abbot's brother from the king; Aubrey de Vere. Mill, vineyard.* Small agricultural and weaving town famous for its beauty; 15th- and 16th-century timber-framed houses, including a Wool Hall and Guildhall. The cloth trade flourished here from the 14th to 16th century.

Lawshall *Lawesscla: Abbot of Ramsey. Church.* Linear earthworks.

Laxfield *Laxefelda: Robert Malet's mother and Walter from her. Church, 7 beehives. 392 sheep, 20 beasts, 37 pigs, 23 goats.* Guildhall (c.1519) now a museum. Birthplace of William Dowsing (c.1596), Hammer of the Puritans; who smashed his way through 150 churches in 50 days.

Layham *Lafham/Latham/Leiham: King's land, kept by William de Noyers; Abbot of St Edmund's and Berard from him; Eudo the Steward; William de Alno from Robert Gernon; Hugo de Grandemesnil; Ralph Pinel. Church, mill.* Watermill.

Leiston *Le(d)estuna/Len-/Leis-/Leestuna: Robert Malet's mother and Gilbert and Fulcred from her. 3 churches, mill.* Coastal town. In the early 19th century, the Leiston Iron Works produced a famous portable steam engine and threshing machine.

Letheringham *Letheringaham/Ledringaham: Roger de Poitou; Abbot of Ely; Geoffrey de Mandeville. Church, mill, 5 beehives. 30 pigs, 80 goats.* Watermill.

Levington *Leventona/Levetuna: William de Burnoville from Roger Bigot; Hugh de Montfort. Church.*

Lidgate *Litgata: Walter de Vatteville; Rainald le Breton.* Motte and bailey castle; birthplace (c.1370) of the poet John Lydgate, also known as the Monk of Bury.

Linburne *Linburna:* Lost.

Lindsey *Balesheia/Blalsega: Abbot of St Edmund's before and after 1066; Richard FitzGilbert. Church.* Motte and bailey castle site.

Linstead *Linesteda/stede: Walter from Robert Malet's mother. 20 pigs, 20 goats.* Now the hamlet of Linstead Magna with moated sites, and the village of Linstead Parva.

Little Bealings *Parva Belinges: Roger Bigot from Bishop of Bayeux; Abbot of Ely; Hugh de Montfort; Hervey de Bourges and Geoffrey from him. Mill.*

Little Charsfield *Parva Ceresfella: Count Alan.* Now Charsfield.

Littlecross *Litelcross:* Lost on the Deben estuary.

Little Fakenham *Litla Fachenham: Abbot of St Edmund's and Peter from him. 12 beasts, 20 pigs, 300 sheep.*

ICKLINGHAM: *Unique wrought-iron chest in the church.*

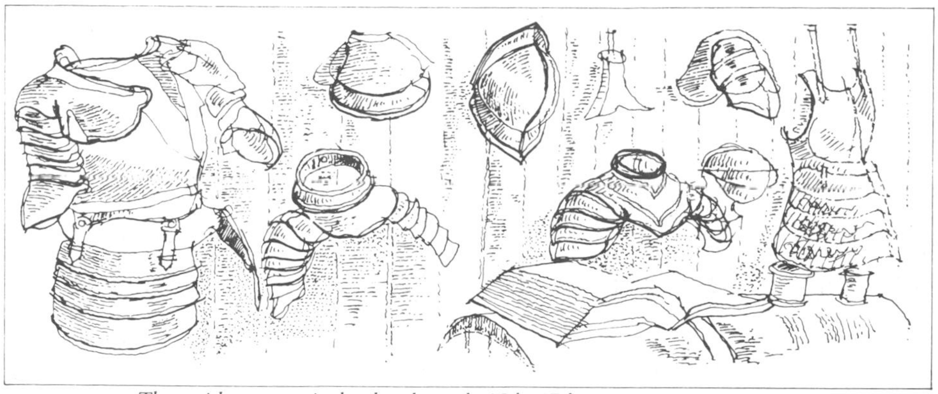

MENDLESHAM: *The parish armoury in the church porch; 15th–17th c.*

Little Glemham *Thieue Gliemham: Count Alan.*

Little Livermere *Litla Livermera: Abbot of St Edmund's. Church.*

Long Melford *Melaforda:* See page 252.

Loose *Losa: Leustan, the pre-Conquest holder, from Ranulph Peverel, formerly King Edward.* Loose Hall, near Wattisham.

Loudham *Lud(e)hum: Count Alan; Robert Malet's mother and Walter FitzAubrey and Walter de Caen from her; Roger Bigot; Abbot of Ely; Bishop of Evreux; Hervey de Bourges. Church, mill.* Loudham Hall, near the River Deben and Wickham Market.

Lound *Lunda: King's land, kept by Roger Bigot. 2 beehives.* Duckpond.

Lowestoft *Lothuwistoft: King's land, kept by Roger Bigot. 160 sheep.* Large holiday resort, fishing port and industrial town.

Malton *Meltuna: Count Alan; Robert Malet's mother and Humphrey from her; Roger de Poitou and Roger FitzArnold from him; Abbot of Ely; William son of Sahuala from Geoffrey de Mandeville. Mill.* Suburb of Woodbridge; mill house on the River Deben.

Manston *Manestuna: Abbot of St Edmund's and Garin from him; Richard FitzGilbert; Swein of Essex.* Manston Hall, near Whepstead.

Manton *Manetuna:* Lost.

Market Weston *Westuna: William d'Ecouis and Huard de Vernon from him. Church (with Ixworth Thorpe).* Moated site; Romano-British kiln, excavated 1965.

Marlesford *Marl/Merlesforda: King's land, kept by Godric; Count Alan; Robert Malet's mother; Abbot of St Edmund's before and after 1066. Church, mill, 3 beehives.*

Martlesham *Merlesham: Ralph brother of Ilger. Church, mill, 12 beehives. 20 beasts, 212 sheep.* Large; tumuli and signs of early settlements; large airfield.

Martley *Martelaialle/Mertlega: Count Alan; Robert Malet's mother and William Gulafra from her; Roger de Poitou; Hervey de Bourges. Church.* Martley Hall.

Mellis *Melle(l)s/Metles: Abbot of St Edmund's; Aubrey de Vere and Adelm from him.* Enormous green bounded by huge ditches; moated site; ancient manor house.

Mells *Mealla: Robert de Tosny. Church.* Remains of a Norman chapel.

Mendham *Men(d)ham/Menneham: Robert Malet's mother and Humphrey from her; Roger de Poitou; Godric the Steward; Abbot of St Edmund's and Frodo from him; Bishop of Thetford. 2 churches, 2 mills. 41 pigs, 36 goats.* Marshland.

Mendlesham *Melde(s)ham/Melnesham/-ssam/Menlessam/Mun(d)lesham: King's land, kept by Godric. Church.* Large; moated site.

Mettingham *Metingaham: Warin from Earl Hugh. Church.* Gatehouse and ruins of castle, 1344; church with a Norman doorway.

Mickfield *Mucelfelda/Mulcelfel: Abbot of St Edmund's before and after 1066 and Berengar from him; Ralph de Savigny from Ranulph Peverel. Church. 21 goats.* Moated farmsteads.

Middleton *Middeltuna/Mi(l)detuna: Count Alan; Roger Bigot from Earl Hugh; Gilbert Blunt from Robert Malet; Ranulf the nephew from William de Warenne. Church.* The parish was united with Fordley in 1620 'because the bells and people of one church disturbed those of the other'; church with Norman work.

Milden *Mellinga: Abbot of St Edmund's; Walter the Deacon. Church, mill. 22 pigs.* Motte.

Mildenhall *Mitden/Mudenehe/halla:* See page 252.

Minsmere *Menesmara/Milsemere: Robert Malet's mother and Leuric Coc from her; Roger Bigot.* Area by the sea; Minsmere Level at the mouth of the River Minsmere.

Monewdon *Munge-/Mangedena/Mun(e)gadena: Humphrey from Robert Malet's mother; Roger de Poitou; Abbot of Ely; Countess of Albemarle. Church.* Straggling; 3 Elizabethan farms; church with Norman windows.

Morston *Morestuna/-tona/Mot(h)estuna: Count of Mortain; Roger Bigot and William de Silva from him; Robert Malet from Abbot of Ely; Ralph brother of Ilger.* Morston Hall.

Moulton *Muletuna: Archbishop Lanfranc. 4 beehives.* Large; medieval packhorse bridge over the River Kennet.

Mutford *Mutford: King's land, kept by Roger Bigot. 2 churches, 2 beehives. 7 beasts, 30 pigs, 160 sheep, 50 goats.* Church with Norman work.

Nacton *Nachetuna/Nechetuna: Hugh de Montfort.* Wooded; 13 barrows nearby.

Nayland *Eilanda: Swein of Essex, formerly Robert his father. Mill.* Small market town. Court Knoll, an island field nearby, was the Norman centre of the 1086 lordship.

Nedging *Niedinga: Abbot of Ely before and after 1066. Church, mill. 14 beasts, 120 pigs.* Church with 2 Norman doorways; mill.

Nettlestead *Nede/Netlesteda: Count Alan. 2 churches, mill. 27 pigs.*

Newbourn *Nebrunna/Neubrumna/-brunna: Roger de Poitou and Albert 'Crematus' from him; Roger Bigot from Abbot of St Edmund's.* Timber-framed hall, c. 1500.

Newton (near Bury St Edmunds) *Neutuna: Abbot of St Edmund's. Church, mill.* Now Nowton, on the River Lark; church with 2 Norman doorways.

Newton (near Sudbury) *Newetona/Niwetuna: Ralph de Limesy. 1½ churches, 9 beehives. 20 pigs, 102 sheep.* Green; church with a Norman doorway.

Newton (near Lowestoft) *Neutuna: King's land, kept by Roger Bigot.* The village was destroyed by the sea.

Newton (in Swilland) *Neutuna/Niwetuna: Roger de Raismes and Ernald and Ralph from him.* Newton Hall; cottages.

Norton (near Bury St Edmunds) *Nocturna/Nortu(r)na: King's land, kept by Godric. Church. 150 pigs, 30 goats.* Scattered Tudor farmhouses.

Norton (in Trimley) *Nortuna:* Lost.

Oakley *Acle: William Gulafra from Robert Malet; Abbot of St Edmund's and Gotselin from him; Bishop of Thetford and Drogo from him. Church (with Stuston), part of another church, 2 mills.*

Occold *Acolt: King's land, kept by Godric; Robert Malet's mother; Abbot of St Edmund's; Hugh de Montfort and Roger de Candos from him; Ralph de Limesy. 3 churches. 8 beasts, 60 pigs, 21 goats.* Quiet; church with a Norman doorway.

Offton *Offetuna: King's land, kept by Godric; Hugh de Hosdenc, Blacsun and Aldwyn from Roger Bigot; William from Roger d'Auberville; Isaac. 2 churches.* Green mound where an 11th-century castle once stood; church with a Norman doorway.

Olden *Uledana/Wledana:* Lost.

Old Newton *Neutuna/Newetuna/-tona/Niue-/Niwetuna: Bishop of Bayeux and Roger Bigot and Warenger from him; Abbot of Bernai; Hugh de Montfort. Part of a church, 2 mills.* Large; moated site.

Onehouse *Ane(h)us/An(u)hus: Count of Mortain; Abbot of St Edmund's before and after 1066; Ranulph Peverel and Osbert Masculus from him; Humphrey FitzAubrey. Church. 30 pigs, 22 goats.* Large 18th-century House of Industry; church with a Norman round tower.

Otley *Atelega/leia: Andrew from Roger de Poitou; Milo de Belefol from Roger de Raismes; Walter the Deacon; Humphrey the Chamberlain and Mund from him, formerly Queen Edith. Church, 6 beehives.* Large; earthworks of a Norman castle beside a Roman road.

Ousden *Uuesdana: Count Eustace; Stanard FitzAlwi. Church. 30 pigs.* Church with many Norman features.

Pakefield *Pagafella/Paggefella: King's land, kept by Roger Bigot; Earl Hugh. ½ church.* Seaside suburb of Lowestoft; 2 churches in one building.

Pakenham *Pachenham: Abbot of St Edmund's before and after 1066. Church, 2 mills, 8 beehives.* On Pakenham Fen; fort, villa and kilns; church with many Norman features.

Palgrave *Palegrava: Abbot of St Edmund's before and after 1066. 2 churches.* Green; church with a Norman font.

Pannington *Painetuna: Aluric the priest from Count Alan; Algar from Swein of Essex. Salt-pan. 8 beasts, 20 pigs, 28 goats.* Pannington Hall on the outskirts of Ipswich.

Parham *Per(re)ham: King's land, kept by Godric; Roger Bigot from Earl Hugh; Hamo de Valenis from Count Alan; Robert Malet and Walter FitzAubrey from him. Church. 58 goats.* Moat Hall, a 16th-century timber-framed house with a moat.

Peasenhall *Pesehal(l)a/-healle/-nhala/Pisehalla: Fulchred, Walter de Caen and Gilbert from Robert Malet's mother; Roger Bigot and Ranulph FitzWalter and Norman, the pre-Conquest holder, from him.* Small agricultural town.

Pettaugh *Pet(t)ehaga: Bishop of Bayeux and Garenger from him; Hervey de Bourges; Abbot of Ely. Church.* Moated hall; church with Norman traces.

Peyton *Peituna: Swein of Essex. Mill.* Peyton Hall near the Deben estuary.

Playford *Plegeforda: Humphrey FitzRobert from Robert Malet's mother. Church, beehive.* Moated hall; barrows.

Polstead *Polesteda: Swein of Essex, formerly Robert his father. Mill. 8 horses, 28 beasts, 40 pigs, 150 sheep.* Pond; known for its cherries and the murder of Maria Marten (the 'red barn' murder) in 1827.

Poslingford *Poslindewrda/Polingeorda/-ewrda: Abbot of St Edmund's; Richard FitzGilbert and Loher from him; Ralph Baynard and Noriolt, Walter and Richard from him. Church.* Church with a Norman doorway.

Potsford *Potesforda:* Lost.

Preston (near Lavenham) *Prestetona/tune: Roger de Poitou; Abbot of St Edmund's before and after 1066 and Ernulf from him. Church.* Church with an early Norman font.

Preston (in Martlesham) *Prestetuna: Ralph brother of Ilger.* Lost.

Ramsholt *Ram(m)esholt: Robert Malet's mother and Ralph from her; Ralph de Beaufour.* Area on the Deben estuary.

Rattlesden *Rasted/Rathsted/Ratlesdena/Ratesdana/-dane: Heltret from Count Eustace; Count of Mortain; Abbot of Ely and William de Warenne and Count of Mortain from him; Richard FitzGilbert; William de Warenne and Humphrey son of Rodric from him. Church. 40 pigs.*

Raydon *Reinduna/-dune/Rienduna: Count Eustace; Bishop of Bayeux and Roger Bigot from him; Richard FitzGilbert; Osbern from Eudo the Steward; Geoffrey de Mandeville and Gilbert the priest and Alured from him; Ralph Pinel. ½ church.*

Rede *Re(o)da/Riete: Abbot of St Edmund's and Henry and Berard from him; Abbot of Ely; Richard FitzGilbert; Swein of Essex..* Church, possibly with Norman work.

Redgrave *Regrava: Abbot of St Edmund's before and after 1066. Church. 12 beasts, 30 pigs, 30 goats.* Large.

Redisham *Redesham: Roger Bigot and Robert de Curcun from him.* Castle mound.

Redlingfield *Radinghefelda: William de Arches from Robert Malet's mother. Church. 34 goats.* Remains of a 12th-century nunnery in the barn.

Rendham *Rimdham/Rindram/-d(e)ham/-ham: Count Alan; Robert from Robert Malet; Roger Bigot and Norman and Ralph from him.* Straggling; manor farm.

Rendlesham *Remle/Ren(d)le/Renne/Renslesham: Count Alan; Gilbert de Colville and Gilbert de Wishant from Robert Malet's mother; Roger Bigot; Abbot of Ely; Bernard de Alencun from Harvey de Bourges. Church, mill.* Large. Thirstly Belt, a ring of trees, may mark the seat of the Saxon Wuffingas dynasty.

Reydon *Rienduna: Ralph Baynard. 2 churches. 30 pigs, 110 sheep.* Charming almshouses.

Rickinghall Inferior *Richingehalla/Rikinchala: Abbot of St Edmund's before and after 1066. Church, winter mill. 20 pigs.* Church with a Norman round tower and, probably, Saxon foundations.

Rickinghall Superior *Richinge/Richingahala: Robert Malet's mother and Hubert from her; Abbot of St Edmund's; Aubrey de Vere. Part of a church.* On the Norwich coaching road.

Ringsfield *Ringesfelda/fella: King's land, kept by Roger Bigot; Warin FitzBurnwin from Earl Hugh. Church, ½ mill. 30 sheep, 16 goats.* Circular henge monument.

Ringshall *Riges/-Ringeshala/Ringhesehla/-shala: Count of Mortain; Roger Bigot and William de Burnoville from him; William d'Auberville and Fulcho from him. 1 ½ churches. 18 beasts, 40 pigs, 100 sheep, 72 goats.* Church with a Norman tower.

Risby *Resebi/Risebi/-by: Roger de Poitou; Abbot of St Edmund's before and after 1066 and Norman from him. Church, ½ mill. 12 beasts, 20 pigs, 32 goats.* Church with a Norman tower.

Rishangles *Risangra: Robert Malet's mother. Church. 30 goats.* Named after the rushes growing in nearby streams.

Rougham *Ruhham: Abbot of St Edmund's before and after 1066. Church.* Roman burial chambers nearby.

Rumburgh *Ramburc/Romburc/-borc/-boro: Count Alan.*

Rushbrooke (near Bury St Edmunds) *Rycebroc: Abbot of St Edmund's.* Rebuilt by Lord Rothschild, 1955–63.

Rushbrooke (in Thorpe Morieux) *Rescebroc/Risebroc: Abbot of St Edmund's before and after 1066 and Arnulf from him; Richard FitzGilbert.*

Rushford *Riseurda: Peter de Valognes. 4 beehives.*

Rushmere (in Friston) *Riscemara: Robert Malet's mother and William from her.* Rushmere Lodge Farm.

Rushmere (near Lowestoft) *Riscemare/Ryscemara: Earl Hugh.* Scattered near Lowestoft.

Rushmere St Andrew *Ris(c)emara/Ris(h)emara/Rissemera/Ryscemara: Count Alan; Humphrey from Robert Malet's mother; Roger de Poitou and Hunebot from him; Abbot of Ely; Hugh de Montfort; Hervey de Bourges. 1 ¼ churches.* Suburb of Ipswich.

Santon Downham *Dunham: Abbot of St Edmund's and Frodo from him; Abbot of Ely. Church, fishery. 900 sheep.* Wooded; church with traces of Saxon and Norman work.

Sapiston *Sapestuna: Abbot of St Edmund's; Peter de Valognes; Sasselin; Robert Blunt, formerly King Edward. ⅔ church, 3 mills.* Church with a Norman font and doorway.

Saxham *Sax(h)am/Sexham: King's land, kept by Godric. Abbot of St Edmund's before and after 1066 and Albert and Fulcher from him; Richard FitzGilbert. ⅔ church, ½ mill.* Now the locality of Great Saxham with Great Saxham Hall, and the village of Little Saxham whose church has a spectacular Norman tower.

Saxmundham *Samundeham/Sasmunde(s)ham/Saxmondeham: Roger Bigot and Norman, the pre-Conquest holder, from him. 3 churches.* Small market town.

Saxtead *Saxteda: Earl Hugh.* Windmill on the green; suburban development.

Seckford *Sekeforda: Bishop of Bayeux and Aluric and Roger Bigot from him. Mill.* 16th-century Seckford Hall on the outskirts of Woodbridge.

Semer *Seamera: Abbot of St Edmund's before and after 1066. Church, mill. 16 beasts, 24 pigs.* Mill at Ash Street.

Shadingfield *Scadona(fella): King's land, kept by William de Noyers, Roger Bigot and Godwin son of Tuka, the pre-Conquest holder, from him; Geoffrey de Mandeville; Ralph Baynard. 2 beehives.* Farmland.

Sharpstone *Escarletuna/-uestuna/Scarverstuna/-ve(s)tune:* Lost.

Shelland *Sellanda: Richard FitzGilbert.* Extensive moats.

Shelley *Sceueliea: King's land, kept by Aluric Wanz. Mill.* Dispersed; mill farm.

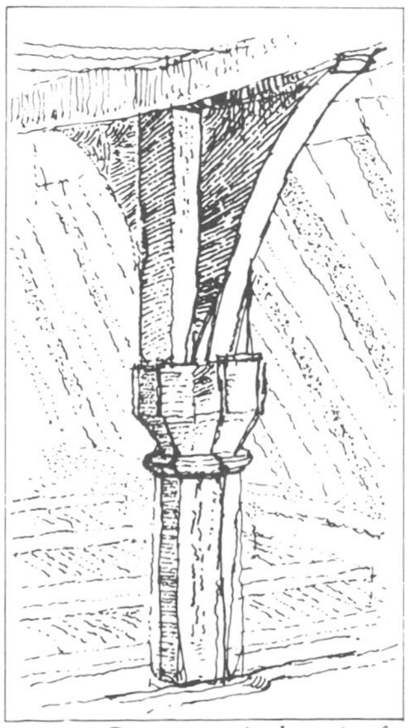

SAXTED: *Crown post in the attic of Manor Farm, 1450.*

SOUTHWOLD: *Shell wall mural in this delightful seaside town.*

Shimpling *Simplinga: Ralph Baynard; Countess of Albemarle. 2 churches. 24 pigs, 100 sheep.*

Shipmeadow *Scipmedu/metdua: Earl Hugh; Roger Bigot and Godwin son of Tura from him.* 18th-century workhouse, later a poultry farm.

Shotley *Scoteleia: King's land, kept by Aluric Wanz; Roger from Richard FitzGilbert. 2 churches.* Naval training vessel HMS *Ganges* and naval school nearby. 'Shotley church, without a steeple. Drunken parson, wicked people', was an old sailor's view.

Shottisham *Scotesham: Robert Malet's mother and Walter the Crossbowman from her; Abbot of Ely. Church.* On Shottisham Creek.

Sibton *Sib(b)etuna: Count Alan; Walter de Caen from Robert Malet's mother. 2 churches, 5 beehives. 20 beasts, 60 pigs, 51 goats.* Abbey; overgrown walls and Norman arch of a Cistercian abbey, c. 1150.

Snape *Snapes: Robert Malet's mother and Walter and Gilbert Blunt from her. Church, mill.* Now 6 miles from the sea. In 1862 a 48 ft Saxon boat was discovered, contemporary to that of Sutton Hoo. Maltings (industrial buildings) was converted into a concert hall for Aldeburgh Festival in the 1960s. Benjamin Britten lived in a converted windmill, where he wrote *Peter Grimes* (1st produced in 1945).

Sogenhoe *Suggenhou:* Lost.

Soham *Saham: Count Alan; Walter de Risbon from Robert Malet's mother; Abbot of St Edmund's before and after 1066; Abbot of Ely; Roger de Candos from Hugh de Montfort. Church. 81 goats, 30 pigs.* Now 2 villages, Earl and Monk Soham.

Somerleyton *Sumerlede(s)tuna: King's land, kept by Roger Bigot; Ralph the Crossbowman. Church.* Built by Samuel M. Peto, a rich railway contractor in the mid-19th century; ornamental cottages.

Somersham *Sumers(h)am: King's land, kept by Roger Bigot, and William de Burnoville from him; Roger d'Auberville; Isaac. ¼ church.* New development in the Glem valley.

Somerton *Somerledetone/-tuna/Sumerledetuna: Abbot of St Edmund's before and after 1066 and Frodo from him; Roger from Robert FitzCorbucion.*

Sotherton *Sudretuna: Franc from Drogo de Beuvriere. Church. 24 pigs.* Scattered.

Sotterley *Soterlega: Mundet from Earl Hugh. Church. 3 oxen, 31 pigs, 120 sheep, 30 goats.*

South Cove *Cova: Count Alan; Robert Malet's mother.*

South Elmham *Almaham/-eham/El-/Malmeham: Count Alan; Robert Malet's mother; Godric the Steward; Bishop of Thetford and William from him. 5 churches, part of a mill. 7 beasts, 30 pigs, 30 goats.* Now the 3 hamlets of All Saints, St Michael and St Nicholas South Elmham, and 3 villages of St Cross, St James and St Margaret South Elmham.

Southwold *Sudholda/Sudwolda: Abbot of St Edmund's. Moiety of sea weir, 25,000 herrings.* Little picturesque town on a cliff top with marshes behind, a prosperous fishing town until the sea began to close the harbour mouth in the late 16th century.

Stanningfield *Stanesfelda/Stanfella: Count of Mortain; Abbot of St Edmund's and Gaurinc from him; Ralph Baynard. Church, mill.* Church with a Norman nave.

Stansfield *Stanesfelda/Stenesfelda: Abbot of St Edmund's; Richard FitzGilbert and Roger, Gilbert and Robert from him; Church. 25 pigs.* Late 13th-century aisled hall in a nearby farm.

Stanstead *Stanesteda: Hugh de Montfort. Church, mill. 4 horses.*

Stanton *Sta(n)tuna: Robert Malet's mother and Walter de Caen from her; Abbot of St Edmund's before and after 1066. 2 churches. 28 pigs, 30 goats.* 2 parish churches, 1 abandoned; Roman villa nearby.

Staverton *Stauer-/Stauretuna/Strauretuna: Robert Malet's mother and Hubert de Monchensey from her. Church, mill, 4 beehives. 20 goats.* Staverton Park near Butley and the Butley River.

Sternfield *Sternefella/Sternesfelda/-fella: Count Alan; Robert Malet's mother and William from her; Roger Bigot and Norman from him.*

Stickingland *Stichinghel-/Stigkingalanda/Stikelande/Stikingalande/Stykelande:* Lost.

Stoke (in Ipswich) *Stoches: Abbot of Ely before and after 1066. Church, mill. 12 beasts, 20 pigs.* Part of Ipswich.

Stoke Ash *S(t)oches/Stota(s): King's land, kept by Godric; Robert Malet's mother; Abbot of St Edmund's. 20 goats.*

Stoke by Clare *Stoches: Richard FitzGilbert. Church.* Green; college incorporates small parts of the Benedictine priory, c.1090.

Stoke by Nayland *Stokes: Swein of Essex and Robert from him. Church, 2 mills. 3 horses, 8 beasts, 20 pigs.* Painted by Constable.

Stokerland *Stokerlanda:* Lost.

Stone Street (in Hadleigh): *Richard FitzGilbert.*

Stone Street (in Rumburgh) *Ston: Count Alan.* On a Roman, now a major, road.

Stonham *Sta/Stal/Stan(a)ham: King's land, kept by Godric and Roger Bigot; Count Alan and Garanger from him; Robert Malet; Roger de Poitou; Abbot of St Edmund's and Ailbold the priest from him; Bishop of Bayeux; Richard FitzGilbert; Ranulph Peverel; Juhichell the Priest. 3 churches.* Now 2 adjoining hamlets, Earl and Little Stonham.

Stonham Aspel *Estena/tuna: Milo from Roger de Raismes. Mill, church. 36 pigs.* Romano-British bath house.

Stoven *Stou(o)ne: Roger Bigot; Hugh de Montfort. 100 herrings.* Remote.

Stowlangtoft *Stou(a): Abbot of St Edmund's. Church, mill.* Moated farms.

Stowmarket *Stou: Robert Blunt from Richard FitzGilbert.* Small market town, with industrial architecture; regional museum with agricultural machinery; 1340s farmhouse; water mill.

Stradbroke *Statebroc/Stetebroc: Robert Malet's mother; Roger de Poitou.* Large.

Stradishall *Stratesella: Richard FitzGilbert. Church.* Orchards; maximum security prison.

Stratford St Andrew *Straffort: Robert Malet; Ralph de Langhetot from Walter Giffard. Mill.* Straggling.

Stratford St Mary *Stratfort: Robert from Swein of Essex. Church, mill.*

Stratton *Strattuna: Bernard of London from Robert Malet's mother; Roger Bigot and William de Burnoville from him. Church, mill.* Stratton Hall Farm by the River Orwell. The church site is still visible from the air.

Stuston *Estutestuna/Stutestuna: Abbot of St Edmund's; Ralph de Felgeris. Church (with Oakley).* Moated site; church with a Norman round tower.

Stutton *Stot(t)una/Stuttuna: Count Alan. 2 beehives.*

Sudbourne *Sudburnham/Sutburna/-burne: Walter de Caen and Gilbert de Wiscand from Robert Malet's mother; Abbot of Ely. 2 churches, mill, fishpond, salt-pan. 30 pigs.* In Sudbourne Marshes; church with a blocked Norman doorway.

Sudbury *Sudberia/Sutberie(a): William the Chamberlain and Otto the Goldsmith, in the king's hand; Richard FitzGilbert. Church of St Gregory, mill, market. 2 horses, 24 pigs, 120 sheep.* Ancient clothing and market town, with 3 churches; St Gregory's, the mother church, was founded by St Felix in the 7th century.

Sutton *Stituna/Suthtuna/Suttuna: Count Alan; Robert Malet's mother and Walter de Caen, Hubert and Gilbert Blunt from her; Abbot of Ely; Rainelm from Geoffrey de Mandeville; William d'Alno from Robert Gernon; Arcenbald from Hervey de Bourges. 1 ½ churches, mill.* Heathland.

Swefling *Sueflinga/Sueftlingan/-gua: Count Alan; Robert de Claville and Robert son of Fulchered from Robert Malet; Ralph from Roger Bigot. Church.* Church with a Norman doorway.

Swilland *Suinlanda: Walter the Deacon, formerly Queen Edith. Church. 100 sheep.* Mill, now a studio.

TATTINGSTONE: *Curious disguise for a farmhouse, with a church 'tower' front and lancet windows.*

Syleham *Seilah/Seilanda: Bishop of Thetford; Robert de Tosny. Church, mill, beehive. 44 pigs.* On marshes by the River Waveney. The church, with Norman and Saxon work, is accessible only by a causeway.

Tannington *Tatintuna: Richard and Garin from Robert Malet's mother. Church, 3 beehives. 20 goats.* Scattered; church with a Norman doorway.

Tattingstone *Tati(s)tuna: Bishop of Bayeux and Roger Bigot from him; Robert Gernon.*

Theberton *Thewardetuna: Hubert from Robert Malet's mother.* Coastal; memorial to Germans brought down in a Zeppelin, 1917.

Thelnetham *Teluetteham/Teolftham/Thelueteham: Robert Malet's mother; Frodo the Abbot's brother; Abbot of St Edmund's and Fulcher from him. Church, mill, 3 beehives. 25 pigs.* Part of an ancient preaching cross at a crossroads.

Thistleton *Thisteldena:* Lost.

Thorington (in Stoke by Nayland) *Torintuna: Robert FitzCorbucion and Giffard from him. Church. 40 pigs, 120 sheep.* Thorington Hall.

Thorington (near Dunwich) *Torentuna/Tor(n)intuna/Turintuna: Count Alan; Geoffrey de Mandeville and William de Boeville from him; Roger Bigot and Norman from him; Godfrey de Petro Ponte from William de Warenne. 2 churches, mill (with Wenhaston) another mill, 8 beehives.* Tiny, partly Norman church, with possibly some late Saxon work.

Thorndon *Torentuna/Torn(e)duna: Robert Malet's mother; Abbot of St Edmund's. Church, mill. 31 pigs.* Expanding.

Thorney *Tornai/Tornei(a):* Lost.

Thornham Magna *Marthorham/Martonham/Thor(n)ham/Tor(n)ham: King's land, kept by Godric; Robert Malet's mother; Abbot of St Edmund's; Aubrey de Vere; Isaac. 27 goats.* Scattered.

Thornham Parva *Parva Thornham: Robert Malet's mother. Church.* Scattering of houses among fields; thatched church with a circular Saxon window.

Thorpe (in Aldringham) *Torp:* Lost.

Thorpe (in Ashfield) *Torp: Earl Hugh; Walter and Gilbert from Robert Malet; Abbot of St Edmund's; Abbot of Ely. Church (with Ashfield).* Thorpe Hall.

Thorpe (in Dallinghoo) *Torp: Geoffrey de Mandeville.* Lost.

Thorpe (in Trimley) *Torp(a): Count of Mortain; Hugh de Hosden and William de Silva from Roger Bigot.* Off Thorpe Common.

Thorpe Morieux *Torp(a): Roger de Poitou; Abbot of St Edmund's and Arnulf from him. Church.* Moated site.

Thrandeston *Fran-/Frondestuna/Stran-/Thran-/Thrun-/Thraudestuna: Godman, William de Caen and Hugh from Robert Malet; Roger de Poitou; Abbot of St Edmund's and Anselm from him; Ralph de Felgeris; Aubrey de Vere. 2 churches. 12 pigs.*

Thurlow *Thrillauura/Tridlauua/Tritlawa: King's land, kept by Godric; Abbot of St Edmund's; Richard FitzGilbert and Widard from him. Church. 33 goats.* Now 2 adjoining villages, Great Thurlow, and Little Thurlow, which has a church with a Norman font.

Thurlston *Torolues/Turoues/Turles/Turolu(u)es/Turuestuna: King's land, kept by Roger Bigot; Aluric the priest from Count Alan; Roger de Poitou and Gosbert from him; William d'Ecouis; Richard FitzGilbert; Walter the Deacon; Aluric from the Vavassors. 6 churches.* Thurleston Lodge on the outskirts of Ipswich.

Thurston (near Bury St Edmunds) *Thurs/Torstuna: Godric from the king; Abbot of St Edmund's before and after 1066 and Richard from him. 32 pigs.*

Thurston (in Hawkendon) *Thurstanestuna: Roger de Poitou. ½ church, 6 beehives.*

Timworth *Timeworda/Timwrtha: Abbot of St Edmund's and John from him; Richard FitzGilbert. Church.*

Toppesfield *Topesfelda:* Lost.

Tostock *Totestoc/Totstocha: King's land, kept by Godric; Abbot St Edmund's before and after 1066 and Frodo from him. Church.* Water meadows.

Trimley St Martin *Tremelaia/Tremlega: Ralph brother of Ilger.* On the outskirts of Felixstowe.

Trimley St Mary *Tremlega: Roger Bigot and Wihtmar from him; Abbot of St Edmund's. Church.* Adjoining Felixstowe.

Troston *Trostuna: Abbot of St Edmund's and Frodo from him.* Elizabethan hall.

Tuddenham (near Ipswich) *Tod(d)-/Totdenham/Tude(n)ham: Count Alan; Roger de Poitou; Robert Malet's mother; Roger de Raismes and Gerold from him; Bernard de Alencun from Hervey de Bourges. Church.* Church with a Norman doorway.

Tuddenham (near Mildenhall) *Tode(n)/Totenham: Richard FitzGilbert; Eudo the Steward; Frodo the Abbot's brother. Church, mill. 10 horses, 40 pigs, 11 beasts.* Old houses round a green.

Tunstall *Tonestala:* Lost.

Tunstall (near Wickham Market) *Tunestal: Gilbert from Robert Malet.* Tumuli.

Ubbeston *Upbestuna: Ralph Baynard. Church.*

Ufford *Offeworda/Ufforda/Uffeford/Uffeworda/Usforda: Robert Malet's mother and Gilbert de Witshant from her; Roger Bigot; Abbot of St Edmund's; Abbot of Ely before and after 1066. 2 mills.* 3 fords.

Uggleshall *Ugg/-acehala/-hecala/-iceheala/Ulkesala/Wggessala: Robert de Curcun from Earl Hugh; Roger Bigot and Robert Grun from him; Abbot of St Edmund's; Gilbert the Crossbowman. Church, salt-pan.* Church with a Normana nave.

Ulverston *Oluestuna/Uluestuna/-tune: Bishop of Bayeux and Roger Bigot, Ralph de Savigny and Garenger from him; Ranulph Peverel and Robert Malet's mother from him. 2 cows.* Ulverston Hall near Debenham.

Undley *Lundale: Abbot of Ely before and after 1066. Church, 2 fisheries. 24 beasts.* Fenland; earthwork.

Wadgate *Wadgata: Roger Bigot and Wihtmar and freemen from him.* Part of Felixstowe.

Waldingfield *Altera Walingafella/Waldingafella/-gefelda/Walingafella: Roger de Poitou; Abbot of St Edmunds before and after 1066; Richard FitzGilbert and Elinant from him; Ranulph Peverel; Aubrey de Vere; Ralph brother of Ilger. 1 ⅓ churches. 100 sheep.* Now 2 adjoining villages, Great and Little Waldingfield.

Waldringfield *Minima Waldringafelda/Wald(r)ingafelda: Robert Malet's mother; Abbot of St Edmund's before and after 1066; Ralph brother of Ilger. Mill. 100 sheep.* Small quay on the Deben estuary, used by small sailing boats; barrow on the nearby heath.

Walpole *Walepola: Count Alan. Church.* Church with a Norman doorway.

Walsham le Willow(s) *Wal(e)sam/Washam: Hubert from Robert Malet's mother; Abbot of St Edmund's and Robert Blunt from him; Robert Blunt. ½ church.* Attractive, with a stream running through its centre.

Walton *Waletuna: Roger Bigot and Norman, the pre-Conquest holder, from him; Abbot of Ely and Hervey Beruarius from him; Hugh de Montfort. Church, mill. 146 sheep.* Merged with Felixstowe in 1895; submerged ruins of a Roman fortress. It may be the site of St Felix's See of Dommoc.

Wangford (near Brandon) *Wamforda: Abbot of St Edmund's before and after 1066; Richard FitzGilbert. Church, 7 beehives. 17 beasts, 26 pigs, 413 sheep.*

Wangford (near Southwold) *Wankeforda: Ralph Baynard. Mill.*

Wantisden *Wantesdana/-dena/Wantesdena: Count Alan and Hubert, Gilbert, Gilbert de Wiscant and William de Malavilla from him; Robert Malet; Norman from Roger Bigot; Roger de Poitou; Morwin, the pre-Conquest holder, from Abbot of Ely. Church.* Area on the edge of an air-base; partly Norman church; hall, c.1550.

Wattisfield *Wate(s)felda/Watlesfelda: Earl Hugh; Abbot of St Edmund's and Rork from him; Roger d'Auberville; Hugh de Montfort; Ranulph Peverel; Berard from Robert FitzCorbucion. Church.* Attractive; pottery. The clay here has attracted potters since Roman days; 25 Roman kilns were found nearby.

Wattisham *Wecesham: Richard FitzGilbert; Jarnacot from Eudo, FitzSpirwic.* Near airfield; moated hall.

Welnetham *Huelfiham/Telueteham: King's land, in the charge of Picot; Abbot of St Edmund's and Ernulf and Robert from him. 2 churches.* Now 2 districts, Great and Little Welnetham, near a Roman road.

Wenham *Wenham: Ermiot from Count Alan; Bishop of Bayeux and Roger Bigot from him; Robert FitzCorbution and Girard from him. Church, mill. 75 pigs.* Now 2 villages, Great and Little Wenham. Little Wenham Hall, c.1270–80, is one of the earliest brick-built houses.

Wenhaston *Wenadestuna: Count Alan. Mill (with Thorrington).* Expanding.

Westerfield *Westrefelda: Norman from Count Alan; Humphrey from Robert Malet; Roger de Poitou; Hugh de Montfort; William from Geoffrey de Mandeville; Roger de Raismes and Girold and Ernold from him; Walter the Deacon; the Vavassors; Hervey, the pre-Conquest holder, from Abbot of Ely. ½ church. 100 sheep.*

Westhorpe *Westor(p)/Westtorp/Westurp: Hubert from Robert Malet; Abbot of St Edmund's; Peter de Valognes; Geoffrey from Eudo FitzSpirwic; Robert Blunt. 5 beehives.* Moat from the old hall (demolished 1764), spanned by a 3-arched medieval bridge.

Westleton *Wesletuna/Westledestuna/-lentuna: Robert Malet's mother and Gilbert Blunt and Fucred from her; Robert Blunt. 2 churches, 2 beehives. 20 pigs, 24 goats.* Duckpond; near the coast; surrounded by heath.

Westley *Westlea: Abbot of St Edmund's and Peter from him; Richard FitzGilbert. 2 churches, ⅔ mill.*

Weston *Westuna: King's land before and after 1066, kept by Roger Bigot and William de Noyers; Robert de Vals from Roger Bigot; Hugh de Montfort; Geoffrey de Mandeville; Robert de Verli. 2 churches, mill. 400 herrings.* Church with a Norman window.

West Stow *Stowa: Abbot of St Edmund's. Church.* Heathland; church with a Norman doorway. A pagan Saxon village, recently excavated, was established c. AD 400–650 on an island in the marsh; partly Norman church.

Wetherden *Watdena/Wederdena: Abbot of St Edmund's before and after 1066 and Ralph and Ernulf from him; Hugh de Montfort; Walter the Deacon. Church.* Farming; moated site.

Wetheringsett *Wederingaseta/Weringheseta: King's land, kept by Godric; Abbot of St Edmund's and Godwin from him; Ranulph Peverel and Ralph de Savigny from Abbot of Ely. Church. 107 sheep.* Attractive. Its 16th-century rector, Richard Hakluyt, edited and wrote *Navigation, Voyages, Traffiques and Discoveries of the English Nation* (1589).

Weybread *Wcibrada/Weibrada/-brede: Godric from the king; Robert Malet's mother and Humphrey and Walter from her; Roger de Poitou; Abbot of St Edmund's; Bishop of Thetford. ½ church, 4 mills, 4 beehives. 30 pigs.* On a Roman road; church with a Norman round tower.

Whatfield *Watefelda/-fella/Watesfelda: Count of Mortain; Hugh de Hosdene from Roger Bigot; Abbot of St Edmund's before and after 1066 and Berard from him; Richard FitzGilbert; Robert Blunt.* 2 ancient moated houses.

Whepstead *Huepestede: Abbot of St Edmund's before and after 1066 and Ralph from him. Church. 18 beasts, 30 pigs, 100 sheep.* Late 15th-century Manston Hall; late 15th-century church with traces of Norman work.

Wherstead *Weruest(ed)a: Furic and Alvaric the priest from Count Alan; Swein of Essex. Salt-pan.* On the outskirts of Ipswich.

Whittingham *Wettingaham: Roger de Poitou. Beehive. 40 goats.* Now Whittingham Green; on a Roman road.

Whitton *Widituna: The Vavassors. Church.* Suburb of Ipswich.

Wickhambrook *Wicham: Richard FitzGilbert.*

Wickham Market *Wik(h)am: Count Alan; Robert Malet's mother; Norman from Roger Bigot; Bishop of Bayeux and Ralph de Savigny from him; Geoffrey de Mandeville; Ranulph from Hervey de Bourges.* Small town, originally a settlement beside a Roman road.

Wickham Skeith *Wic(c)ham/Wik(h)am: King's land, kept by Godric; Robert Malet's mother; Roger de Poitou; Orger the Abbot's reeve and Alvric from the Abbot of St Edmund's. Church.*

WICKHAM MARKET: *The mill was working until 60 years ago.*

WOODBRIDGE: *The only example of a tide-mill in Suffolk.*

Wilby *Wilebey/bi: Loernic from Robert Malet's mother; Bishop of Thetford. Church (with Chickering).* 15th-century Wilby Hall surrounded by a moat.

Wilford *Wileford(a): Robert Malet's mother and Aedi from her; Norman from Roger Bigot.* Wilford Bridge on the outskirts of Woodbridge.

Willingham *Well/Willingaham: Roger Bigot; Hugh de Montfort. Church. 20 goats.*

Willisham *Willaluesham: Albert from Roger de Poitou. Church.* A few houses; small church.

Wingfield *Wighefelda/Wineberga: Walter son of Grip, Robert de Glanville and Loernic from Robert Malet's mother; Bishop of Thetford; Abbot of Ely and Roger Bigot from him. Church.* Church built by Sir Thomas Wingfield for his college of priests in the 14th century.

Winston *Winestuna: Earl Hugh; William Gulafra from Robert Malet; Bishop of Bayeux; Abbot of Ely. Church. 25 pigs.*

Wisset *Wis(s)eta: Count Alan. 2 churches, one with a monk's chapel under it.* Church with a Norman tower and window. Wissett Lodge was rented by Duncan Grant, who entertained members of the Bloomsbury group there.

Withermarsh *Withermers:* Lost.

Witherdale *Weresdel: Robert Malet's mother.* Withersdale Street on the Waveney marshes.

Withersfield *Vrdresfelda/Wedresfelda: Richard FitzGilbert and Pagan, Goddard and Wilard from him; Wimer, the pre-Conquest holder, from William de Warenne. 6 beehives. 45 pigs, 20 beasts, 123 sheep, 57 goats.* Moated site.

Witnesham *Witdesham: Walter the Deacon. 7 beehives. 8 beasts, 68 pigs, 80 sheep.*

Wixoe *Witeskeou: Ralph Baynard. Church, mill.* Church with Norman work.

Woodbridge *Udebriga/-brige/-bryge/Wdebride/-brige/Wudebrige/-bryge: Count Alan; Humphrey and Gilbert from Robert Malet's mother; Roger Bigot and William de Nemore from him; Roger de Poitou; Robert Malet from Abbot of Ely; William son of Sahuala from Geoffrey de Mandeville; Roger de Raismes. Church.* Attractive small town, a yachting centre with a weatherboarded tide-mill and a market place.

Woolpit *Wlfpeta: Abbot of St Edmund's before and after 1066. Church.* Large; on a Roman road; many fine old buildings.

Woolverstone *Hulferestuna/Uluerestuna: Aluric the priest from Count Alan; Robert Gernon. Church. 12 beasts, 30 pigs, 100 sheep, 36 goats.* Church rebuilt by Sir Gilbert Scott in the 19th century.

Wordwell *Wridewella: Abbot of St Edmund's. Church, mill.* Hall in Kings Forest; church with Norman features.

Worlingham *Wer/Warlingaham: King's land, kept by Roger Bigot with Roger de Vallibus holding ½ church from the king; Earl Hugh; Abbot of St Edmund's; Hugh de Montfort. ½ church.*

Worlington *Wirilintona: Frodo the Abbot's brother. Church, mill, 2 fisheries.* Large; overlooking the fens.

Worlingworth *Wyrlingwortha: Abbot of St Edmund's before and after 1066. Church. 2 horses, 8 beasts, 24 pigs, 33 goats.*

Wortham *Word(h)am/Wortham: Robert Malet's mother; Ralph de Beaufour and Richard de St Clair from him; Abbot of St Edmund's; Aubrey de Vere. 2 churches. 20 goats.* Church with England's largest Norman round tower, partly ruined. The Dick Inn commemorates the fall of Tumble-down-Dick, Cromwell's son.

Wratting *Vratinga/Wratinga/Waratinge: Abbot of St Edmund's; Richard FitzGilbert and Ulmar and Pagan from him. 2 churches, 2 mills, 6 beehives. 13 beasts, 48 pigs, 100 sheep.* Now 2 hamlets, Great Wratting, and Little Wratting with what may be a late Saxon church.

Wrentham *Uuereteham/Wretham: Robert de Petro Ponte and William FitzRainard from William de Warenne. 2 churches, 5 beehives. 13 beasts, 113 sheep, 20 goats.* Large; home of the Brewsters, who made this an important centre of Puritanism.

Wyken *Wica: Peter de Valognes; Robert Blunt. ¼ mill. 100 sheep.* Wyken Hall; Wyken Wood.

Wyverstone *Wiverdestuna/-t(h)estuna/Wluerthestuna: King's land, kept by Godric; Hubert from Robert Malet; Abbot of St Edmund's; Hervey from Hugh de Montfort; Richard from Hubert de Monchensey; R. Ovethel from Robert Blunt. Church.* Scattered; 2 moated sites.

Yaxley *Iachele(i)a/Iacheslea: Hubert from Robert Malet's mother; Bishop of Thetford and Othem from him.* On a Roman road.

Yoxford *Gokesford/Iokesfort: Roger Bigot and Ayleward the king's reeve from him; Roger de Tosny.* Called 'the garden of Suffolk'. The village street was once a Roman road.

Surrey

In 1086 large parts of Surrey were still wild country. To the south lay the great Sussex forest of Andredeswald, an area so remote that the border of the two counties was uncertain. To the west beyond Guildford, stretches of heath and woodland formed part of the forest of Windsor. London, across the river to the north, was becoming an increasingly important influence on Surrey, suggesting a time ahead when the county would be largely suburban. Southwark was already its most important town, and Guildford never became a provincial centre in the way other county towns did.

Although Domesday *shows that many Norman barons held land in Surrey, none had their seats here, and the largest tenants-in-chief (apart from the abbots of religious houses and such bishops as Canterbury and Wichester) were Odo, Bishop of Bayeux and Richard Fitz-Gilbert. Odo was virtual Earl of Kent, with special responsibility for Dover, and Richard had his castle at Tonbridge, Kent. It seems clear that Surrey was treated as something of an appendage to Kent, and that the Surrey lands of Odo and Richard were meant to increase their ability to defend the approaches to London.*

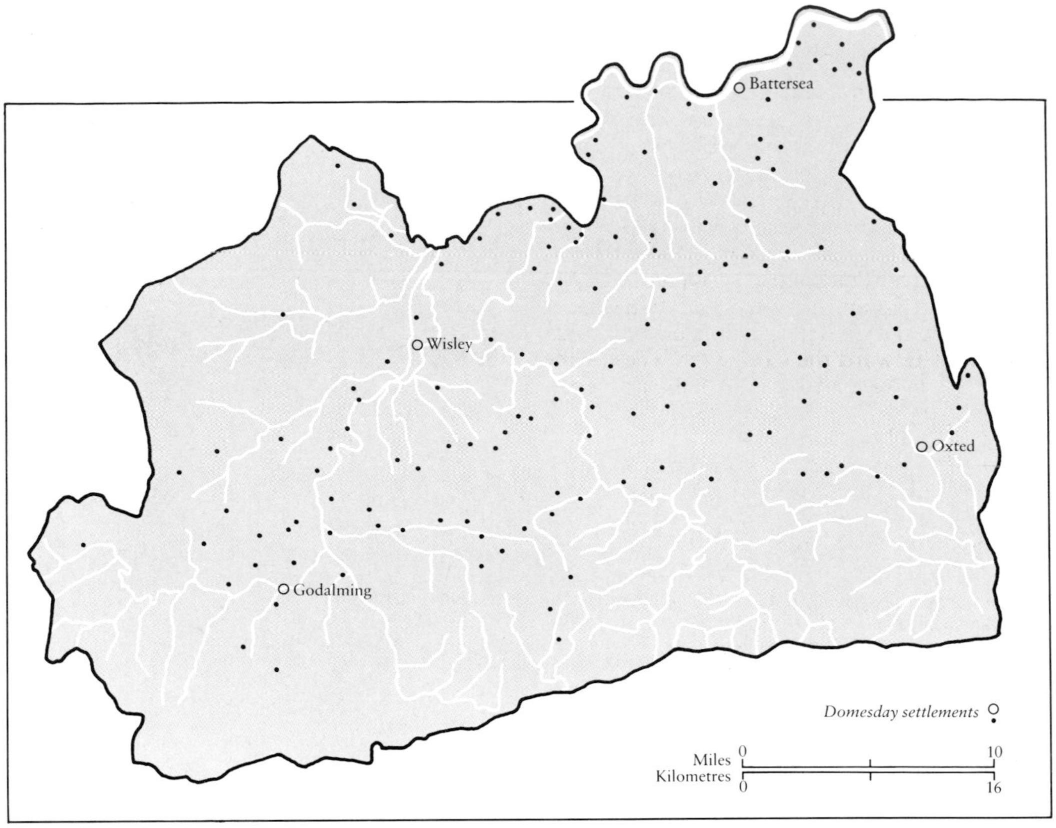

Oxted

Count Eustace holds OXTED *ACSTEDE*. Cytha, Harold's mother, held it before 1066. Then it answered for 20 hides; now for 5 hides. Land for 20 poughs. In lordship 2 ploughs; 34 villagers with 18 ploughs. 2 mills at 12s 6d; meadow, 4 acres; woodland, 100 pigs from pasturage; in Southwark, 1 dwelling at 2d; 6 slaves; 9 smallholders; a church. Value before 1066 £16; when acquired £10; now £14.

Today Oxted is a hybrid – half town, half village – victim of a north–south railway line, and of roads running east–west along the foot of the Downs. One of these splits Old Oxted, with its little hill of timber-framed houses and inns, from the modern town of Oxted, with its elaborate shopping-parade Tudor which grew up around the railway station. To add to the sense of division, the new town has the old church, which stands almost two miles from the earlier settlement.

Looking northward from the churchyard, you can still get something of the flavour of *Domesday* Oxted. The view is across more or less unspoiled country to the wooded escarpment of the North Downs. Twenty-two years before the survey, the manor had belonged to King Harold's mother, one of many Surrey manors that the King and his relatives held. Immediately after the Battle of Hastings, William's armies had passed through on their way to London, pillaging, burning and drastically reducing the land's value here, as in many other manors along his route. By 1086 Oxted was growing prosperous again and had chosen this low green hill as the site for its church.

For centuries it remained a rural community, cut off from London by the Downs, but its timber-framed buildings show that it was modestly prosperous. And if it was cut off to the north, its concerns were not entirely parochial. In 1726 the church wardens voted relief of 4 shillings to 46 seamen who had been slaves in Turkey (probably Algiers), some of them 'burned in a barbarous manner'.

The tunnelling of the North Downs in 1877 brought the railway, which began to transform Oxted. By the 1930s the process had gone so far that a local historian forecast that in 50 years it would be as merged into London's sprawl as Islington, Chelsea or Streatham. Fortunately he has been proved at least half wrong.

The Church of St Mary's, to which the people of Oxted made a four-day pilgrimage from Winchester in 1985 to celebrate its nine hundredth anniversary, is not exactly the one that was first mentioned in 1085. That was 'burned downe by thunder and lightening' in 1719, but the present church has a 12th-century tower, and ministers to a settlement which is still recognizably the same old place.

Battersea

St Peter's of Westminster holds BATTERSEA *PATRICESY*. Earl Harold held it. Then it answered for 72 hides, now for 18 hides. Land for . . . In lordship 3 ploughs; 45 villagers and 16 smallholders with 14 ploughs. 8 slaves. 7 mills at £42 9s 8d, or corn of the same price; meadow, 82 acres; woodland at 50 pigs from pasturage. In Southwark 1 smallholder at 12d; from the tolls of Wandsworth, £6; from a villager who has 10 pigs, 1 pig; if less, he pays nothing. 1 man-at-arms holds 4 hides of the land of this manor; his stock is accounted above with the rest. Total value before 1066 £80; later £30; now £75 9s 8d. King William gave this manor to St Peter's in exchange for Windsor. The Count of Mortain holds 1½ hides of the land of this manor; they were there before 1066 and for some time after. Gilbert the priest holds 3 hides; they were there in the same way. The Bishop of Lisieux, 2 hides of which the church had possession after 1066; but the Bishop of Bayeux dispossessed it later. The Abbot of Chertsey holds 1 hide, which the reeve of this village took from the manor because of a feud, and put in Chertsey.

The large and (apart from its park and church) unlovely modern London parish of Battersea had by 1086 already been a valuable manor for 400 years. A charter of 693 shows that it lay in the gift of the West Saxon king, Caedwalla. It included not only a low-lying area south of the Thames, reaching from today's Battersea Bridge to beyond Chelsea Bridge, but, to the south-west, much of modern Wandsworth as far as the River Wandle, and, to the south, the high land beginning at Lavender Hill and extending to take in half of today's Clapham Common.

This high ground of heath and woodland cut Battersea off to the south. The actual settlement lay at the western end of its riverside lowlands (where the Thames runs north, then turns east), and it was therefore surrounded both to the west and to the north by the river. To the east lay an extensive marsh, part of which is now Battersea Park. So it was virtually an island, and it is possible to understand why, as documentary evidence indicates, it was first named Badric's Island, and then, for a time, Peter's Island – hence 'Patricesy' in *Domesday*.

Its value had fallen dramatically by the time William I granted it to St Peter's Church (Westminster Abbey). This fall was very likely connected with events immediately following the Battle of Hastings, when William marched via Dover and Canterbury to London, destroying crops and manors as he went. He camped at Battersea long enough to burn Southwark before turning west and ravaging as far as Winchester. *Domesday* shows that a string of Surrey manors – not only Battersea, but Mortlake, Combe, Malden, Ditton, Shalford and Godalming – had all suffered similar falls in value; they almost certainly mark the route of the Conqueror.

Domesday's entry for Battersea is interesting in other ways. By describing Harold as an earl (the word *com* is inserted above his name), it

BATTERSEA: *For many Londoners on the north side of the Thames, the power station is still one of the best-known landmarks on the opposite bank. Corn and vegetables, including asparagus, were once grown on Battersea's low lands.*

confirms that although he had been elected by the Witan the Normans never admitted that he was king. And the survey was almost certainly wrong about the terms on which Westminster Abbey obtained Battersea. Although it records that the king gave it to the church in exchange for Windsor, the original grant of 1066 states that the abbey gave Windsor to the king in exchange for lands in Essex, not here. For Battersea it surrendered the crown, royal regalia and royal insignia of Edward the Confessor. These symbols then had real value, and William's gratitude is suggested by the great reduction of Battersea's tax liability – from 72 hides to 18.

Battersea's seven mills were probably on the River Wandle, now largely underground, which then formed the manor's western boundary; the toll valued at £6 would have been for a ferry. Battersea's 500 pigs were fattened in woodland on the higher ground towards Clapham. The villager who paid one pig in ten was probably paying for pannage (the right to the autumn fall of acorns and beech nuts). This is one of only a few places where *Domesday* gives a definite, and no doubt typical, rate for pigs.

The Bishop of Bayeux, who had grabbed land assessed at two hides, was William I's greedy brother, Odo. He had also usurped property in other Surrey boroughs and manors – Southwark, Guildford, Bramley and Comshall. This particular holding, which he had passed on to the Bishop of Lisieux, was at Peckham, and is mentioned in another *Domesday* entry.

There is no physical evidence for a church at Battersea in 1086, but Gilbert the priest's holding strongly suggests one. Today's brick building with green copper spire dates only from 1777. A little to the north, a flour mill stands where the manor stood. Nearby on the river front was Battersea's thirteenth-century landing stage, or *porta*. Although *Domesday* makes no reference to fishing, this was almost certainly a local industry and fish would have been landed at this spot.

During the following centuries the marshes to the east of the village, probably where the *Domesday* meadows had been, played their part in local prosperity. Their fertile if swampy soil was protected by a river wall, first built by the Romans. An order of 1591, in the reign of Elizabeth I, required the people of Battersea to make this 'higher above the high water marke', and many market gardens flourished here, supplying vegetables to London. They were started in the late sixteenth century by Huguenot refugees who were famous for their asparagus, the first to be grown in England.

By 1830 Battersea Fields, as these low lands were called, were growing corn (there was a prominent windmill here) and supporting an enormous herd of cows. But it was a dangerous area, with Sunday fairs attended by 'the roughest and most vicious characters in the neighbourhood'. It was remote enough to be a good place for duels, and here on 21 March 1829, the Duke of Wellington fought the Earl of Winchelsea.

When Winchelsea had taken up his position the Duke told his own second, 'Now then Hardinge, look sharp and step out the ground. I have no time to waste. Dame it! Don't stick him up so near the ditch. If I hit him he will tumble in.' He fired wide and Winchelsea fired in the air.

Battersea Park was never a deer park, but was created on the Fields between 1844 and 1855, largely through the efforts of Thomas Cubitt, the builder of so many London squares and terraces. Despite this civilizing development, the novelist Walter Besant was less than enthusiastic. Writing of the same period, he remembered 'old Battersea Fields perfectly well; they were low, flat, damp, and, I believe treeless; they were crossed . . . by paths raised above the level . . . As a boy I have walked across the fields in order to get to the embankment or river wall from which one commanded a view of the Thames, with its barges and lighters going up and down . . . a mere shadow of the ancient glory when the pleasure barges and the state barges swept majestically up the river with the hautboys and the trumpets in the bows.'

Today it is only around the church that *Domesday* Battersea can be imagined with any ease. Here two ancient sailing barges are moored, their gangways thrust through the churchyard rails, their letter boxes nailed to its trees.

Wisley

Oswald holds WISLEY *WISELEI* himself. He held it himself from Earl Harold. Then it answered for $3\frac{1}{2}$ hides, now for $1\frac{1}{2}$ hides. Land for 2 ploughs. In lordship 1; 4 villagers and 4 smallholders with 2 ploughs. A church; 2 slaves. A mill at 10s; meadow, 6 acres; a fishery at 5d; woodland at 6 pigs. Value before 1066, 40s; now 60s.

The small village of Wisley on the River Wey is today, at least to gardeners, one of the best known in the country. It owes its fame to the Royal Horticultural Society's gardens, established here when the Society left its Chiswick gardens in 1904.

Wisley's *Domesday* entry is of interest, chiefly because Oswald was one of the few English tenants-in-chief left in the country. In most places by 1086, the land was in Norman hands. Besides Wisley, Oswald held three other nearby manors directly from the king; Fetcham, Wotton and 'Pitchingworth'; the last has disappeared but may have been at Picket's Hole near Effingham. At Effingham he also held land as under-tenant of his brother Wulfwold, Abbot of Chertsey, and from Richard FitzGilbert. Before the Conquest Oswald had held Worth, which the same Richard now held from the king. Oswald and Richard appear to have come to an agreement by which Oswald gave up Worth in exchange for a holding in Effingham. The Victoria County History, commenting on his prosperity under the Normans, describes him as 'a prudent man rather than a patriot'.

For 800 years this quiet low-lying village remained undistinguished. Then in 1878, George F. Wilson, treasurer of the Royal Horticultural Society, began not only to plant his small estate but, more significantly, to establish a woodland garden beside the River Wey in an oak wood whose sandy acid soil was ideal for the exotic rhododendrons, magnolias and camelias then being sent to England by adventurous botanists. He had still, however, developed only six acres of garden when Thomas Hanbury bought the estate in 1903 and gave it to the RHS. Today the Society gardens 240 acres and owns another 60, including Wisley itself.

Sadly the modern village is a straggle of bungalows, with a prominent sewage farm. But at the opposite end from the gardens the tiny church stands on a low green mound, still surrounded by a picturesque cluster of red brick farm buildings. It is not the 1086 church – most of what survives was built in the next century – but it almost certainly stands on the *Domesday* site. The nearby reaches of the Wey, where it runs between green water meadows, would have been those once fished by Wisley's villagers and smallholders.

Godalming

[Land of the King] GODALMING *GODELMINGE* in lordship. King Edward held it. Then 24 hides; they never paid tax. Land for 30 ploughs. In lordship 3 ploughs; 50 villagers and 29 smallholders with 19 ploughs. 2 slaves. 3 mills at 41s 8d; meadow, 25 acres; woodland, 100 pigs. Value before 1066 £25; later £20; now £30 at face value; however, it pays £30, weighed and assayed. Ranulf Flambard holds the church of this manor, to which 3 hides belong. Wulfmer held it from King Edward; it never paid tax. Land for 2 ploughs. In lordship 1; 5 villagers and 12 cottagers with 2 ploughs. Meadow, 15 acres; woodland at 3 pigs. Ranulf also holds a second church there, which pays 12s a year. Value of these 3 hides before 1066 and now £4; when acquired £3.

In 1086 Godalming was unusually well supplied with resources. Its woodland was sufficient for 700 to 1000 pigs, roughly ten per family. There were two churches, one on the site of the present Church of St Peter and St Paul – two blocked Saxon windows were found here in 1890 – the other at Tuesley, where its foundations were discovered in 1860.

The Ranulf who held both churches was a much disliked political adventurer who was prominent during the next two reigns. In William Rufus's time he survived a sea abduction by bribing the crew while his kidnappers discussed how to kill him. Henry I imprisoned him in the Tower of London, from which he escaped by a rope. He was later pardoned and recovered his Godalming lands as tenant of the Bishop of Salisbury.

Godalming also had three corn mills, either on the Wey or on the smaller Ock. In medieval times they became fulling mills, vital for its chief industry, cloth manufacture, fuller's earth being employed to absorb the wool's oils. Godalming specialized in blue cloth known as Hampshire Kersies, which, according to the seventeenth-century antiquary John Aubrey, was unequalled for colour by any in England and was exported to the Canaries.

In coaching times Godalming was well known for its inns; in 1698 Czar Peter the Great stayed at the King's Arms on his way from Portsmouth, ate lustily and failed to pay. He and his party went on to stay with the diarist John Evelyn, whose bailiff described them as 'right nasty'.

General James Oglethorpe is Godalming's best-remembered citizen. In 1732 he sailed to America, where he founded the state of Georgia. On a return visit he astonished the town by bringing with him ten Yamacraw Indians. He later fought at Culloden, where he was accused of treasonable indolence in pursuing the Jacobites, but he was acquitted.

Central in Godalming today and adding oddity to its narrow streets of timber-framed houses, is the old Town Hall, known as the Pepperbox. It dates only from 1814, but it stands on the site of far older predecessors. By 1086 the court of Godalming Hundred was already meeting here, and here *Domesday's* returns for the 'hundred' would have been collected.

GODALMING: *The delightful and tiny town hall houses a museum of local antiquities; the site has been in use for over 1000 years.*

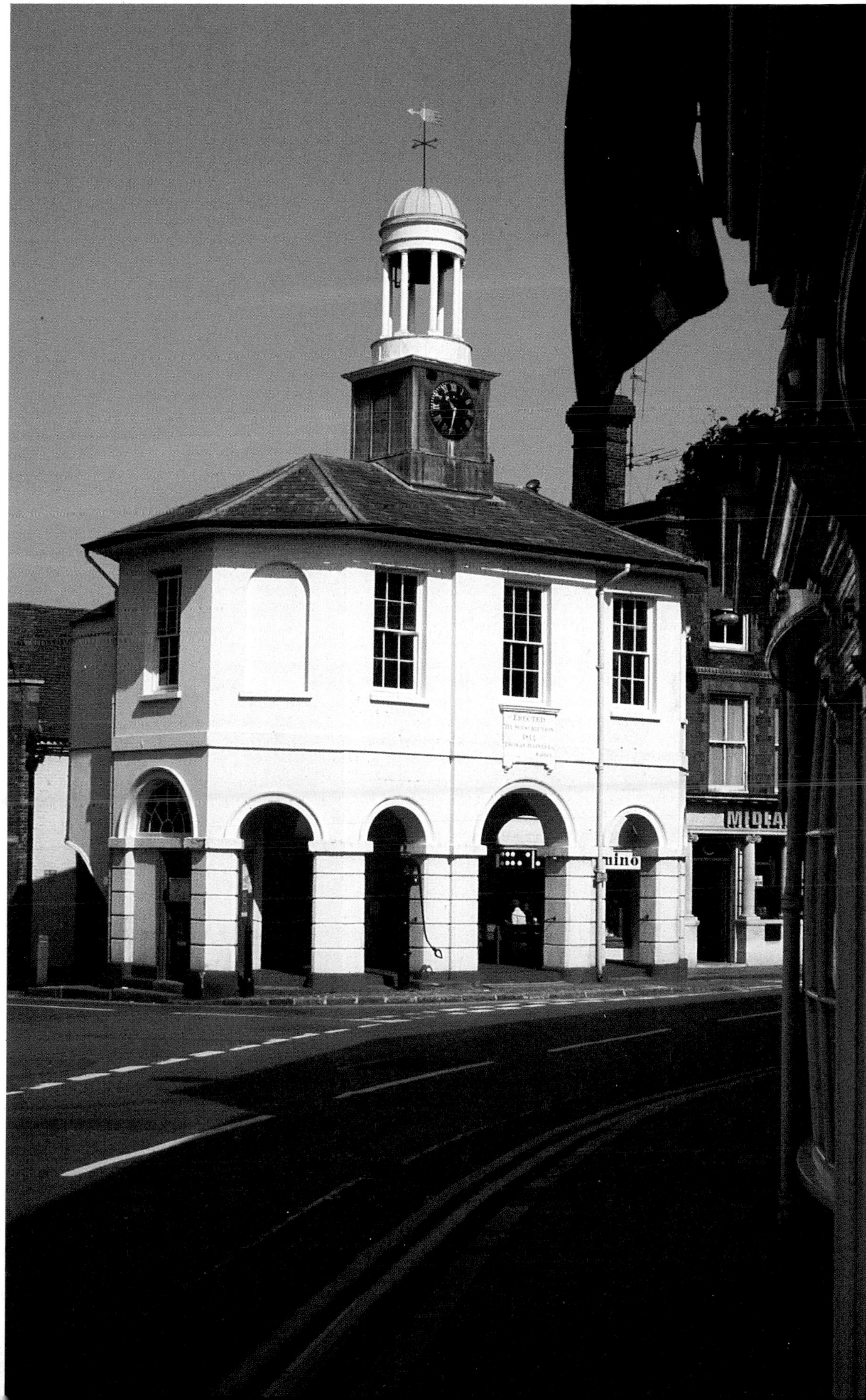

WISLEY: *One of the loveliest sites in England, the village has been the home of the Royal Horticultural Society since 1903 and is a source of inspiration to every gardener in the world.*

Surrey Gazetteer
Each entry starts with the modern place name in **bold** type. The *Domesday* information that follows is in *italic* type, beginning with the name or names by which the place was known in 1086. The main landholders and undertenants are next, separated with semi-colons if a place was divided into more than one holding. A number of holdings were granted by the king to his thanes; these holders, always the last in a list, are described as holding land 'from the king.' More general information completes the *Domesday* part of the entry, including examples of dues (eels, etc.) rendered by tenants. The modern or post-Domesday section is in normal type. ▦ represents a village, ⌂ a small village or hamlet.

Abinger *Abinceborne: William FitzAnsculf. Mill.* Now 2 villages, Abinger Hammer, and Abinger Common.

Addington *Ed(d)intone: Albert the Clerk; Tesselin Cook from the king.* ▦ 18th-century Addington Palace was the home of the Archbishops of Canterbury from 1808–96.

Albury *Eldeberie: Roger from Richard FitzGilbert. Mill.* ⌂

Anstie *Hanstega: Baldwin from William FitzAnsculf.* Anstie Grange. Anstiebury Hill was an Iron Age fort.

Apps *Ebsa:* Lost.

Ashstead *Stede: the Canons from Bishop of Bayeux.* Large residential area; 18th-century Ashstead Park, now the City of London Freemen's School.

Balham *Belgeham: Geoffrey Orletaile without the King's gift or warrant.* Part of London.

Banstead *Benestede: Richard from Bishop of Bayeux and Geoffrey, Ralph and Wulfsi from him. Church, mill.* Large suburban area. A 12th-century house was excavated on Banstead Downs in 1952.

Barnes *Berne: St Pauls London.* Part of London.

Battersea *Patricesy* See page 264.

Beddington *Beddinton(e): Robert de Watteville from Richard FitzGilbert; William FitzThorold from Miles Crispin. 4 mills, church.* Suburb of London and Croydon; 14th-century church.

Bermondsey *Bermundsey(e): King's land, formerly Earl Harold, and Count of Mortain from the king. A new and beautiful church.* Part of London.

Betchworth *Beceswordе: Richard FitzGilbert. Mill, church.* ⌂ Church with 11th-century fragments; 16th-century Old Mill Cottage.

Bletchingley *Blachingelei: Richard FitzGilbert.* ▦ Site of Roman building nearby.

Bramley *Bronlei/Brolege/ Brunlege: Bishop of Bayeux. 3 churches, 5 mills.* ▦

Buckland *Bochelant: John from Richard FitzGilbert. Church, mill.* ⌂ Church with a medieval belfry.

Burgh *Berge: Hugh de Port from Bishop of Bayeux.* Great Burgh, a suburb of Banstead and Tadworth.

Burpham *Borham: Thorold from Earl Roger. Mill.* Suburb of Guildford.

Byfleet *Biflet: Wulfwin from Church of Chertsey. Church, mill, 1½ fisheries.* Suburban district. St Mary's Church has a 13th-century nave, chancel and belfry.

Camberwell *Cambrewelle: Hamo the Sheriff. Church.* Part of south London.

Carshalton *Aultone: Geoffrey de Mandeville and Wesman from Geoffrey FitzEustace. Church, mill.* Outer London suburb; part-medieval church.

Chaldon *Calvedone: Ralph from Bishop of Bayeux. Church.* ⌂ 12th- and 13th-century church with a unique 'Doom' wall-painting, c. 1200.

Cheam *Ceiham: Archbishop of Canterbury. Church.* Large suburb. St Dunstan's Church was rebuilt in 1864, but the medieval chancel stands as Lumley Chapel, in the churchyard.

Chelsham *C(h)elesham: Robert de Watteville from Richard FitzGilbert. Church.* ▦ Scattered. St Leonard's Church is of medieval flint.

Chertsey *Certesi: Church of Chertsey; Richard Reckless from the king. Mill at the hall, smithy.* Small town once famous for its huge Benedictine Abbey founded in 666, dissolved in 1538.

Chessington *Cisedune/ndone: Robert from Richard FitzGilbert; Miles Crispin. ½ mill.* Inter-war and post-war housing; Burnt Stub Zoo.

Chilworth *Celeorde: Bishop of Bayeux. Mill.* ▦

Chipstead *Tepestede: Church of Chertsey; William nephew of Bishop Walkelin from Richard FitzGilbert. Mill.* Scattered development.

Chivington *Civentone:* Lost.

Chobham *Cebeham: Church of Chertsey and Odin and Corbelin from the church. Church, chapel.* ▦ St Lawrence Church.

BETCHWORTH: *Elaborate gateway to the church.*

Clapham *Clopeham: Geoffrey de Mandeville.* Part of London.

Claygate *Claigate: Westminster Abbey.* Large suburban area; Semaphore House on Telegraph Hill, built in 1822.

Cobham *Covenham: Church of Chertsey. 3 mills.* Now 2 villages, Church Cobham and Street Cobham; early 19th-century mill.

Compton *Contone: Walter FitzOthere. Church.* ⌂ St Nicholas's Church, with many 11th-century parts and some pre-Conquest details.

Coombe *Cumbe: Humphrey the Chamberlain; Ansgot the Interpreter.* Wooded suburb. Coombe Hill supplied the water for Hampton Court in Tudor times.

Coulsdon *Colesdone: Church of Chertsey. Church.* Suburban area; mainly 13th-century church.

Croydon *Croindene: Archbishop of Canterbury. Mill, church.* Surrey's largest town and a prominent shopping, office and cultural centre. It was the seat of the Archbishops of Canterbury from the 11th to 19th century and a large medieval market town. The Church of St John the Baptist, founded in the 10th century, was rebuilt in the 19th.

Cuddington *Codintone: Ilbert from Bishop of Bayeux. Mill.* Suburb between Ewell and Cheam.

Dirtham *Driteham:* Lost.

Dorking *Dorchinges: King's land. 3 mills, church.* Dormitory town once famous for its medieval poultry market. 2 mills: Pixham and Castle Mills.

East Clandon *Clanedun: Church of Chertsey.* ▦ Mainly the farming estate of Hatchlands, an 18th-century house.

East Horsley *Horslei/Orslei: Archbishop of Canterbury.* ▦ Surburban.

East Molesey *Molesham: John from Richard FitzGilbert.* ▦ Suburban.

Effingham *Epingeham: Oswald from Church of Chertsey; Oswald and Azor from Richard FitzGilbert.* ▦

Egham *Egeham: Church of Chertsey and Jocelyn from the church.* Town by historic Runnymede field where King John signed the Magna Carta in 1215.

Epsom *Evesham: Church of Chertsey. 2 churches, 2 mills.* Dormitory town famous for Epsom Salts and the Derby horse-race.

Esher *Aissela/ele: Hugh de Port from Bishop of Bayeux; William de Watteville and Reginald from Church of Chertsey; St Leufroy; Odard the Gunner.* Small town with Sandown Park racecourse. Esher Place estate, now expensive Surrey housing, was bought in 1816 for Princess Charlotte and King Leopold. It was acquired by Queen Victoria in 1882 and broken up in the 1920s.

Ewell *Etwelle: King's land. 2 mills.* Small town surrounded by suburbs; early 18th-century mill.

Farleigh *Ferlega: Robert de Watteville from Richard FitzGilbert.* Farleigh Court farm.

Farncombe *Fernecome: Bishop of Bayeux.* Suburb of Godalming; Wyatt almshouses, built 1622.

Farnham *Ferneham: Bishop of Winchester before and after 1066 and Ralph, William and Wace from him. 6 mills.* Town which once had the county's most important corn market. Prehistoric and Roman remains have been discovered here. A castle, built in Norman times, is now partly a conference centre.

Fetcham *Feceham: King's land, formerly Queen Edith; Richard from Bishop of Bayeux; Oswald from the king. 4 mills.* ▦ Medieval, surrounded by a sprawling suburb.

Gatton *Gatone: Herfrid from Bishop of Bayeux. Church.* Church; Gatton Hall and Park.

Godalming *Godelminge:* See page 267.

Gomshall *Gomeselle: King's land, formerly Earl Harold; Bishop of Bayeux. Mill.* ▦ Old tannery; 16th-century packhorse bridge.

Great Bookham *Bocheham: Church of Chertsey. Church, mill.* Suburb of Leatherhead; partly 12th-century church.

Guildford *Gelde/Gildeford: King's land and Ranulf Clerk, Ranulf the Sheriff, Bishop of Bayeux, Odbert and Robert de Watteville from the king.* Town with a Norman castle, the site of a Saxon cemetery, a modern cathedral (built 1932) and university (started 1966) and the Yvonne Arnaud Theatre.

Ham (Croydon) *Estreham: Count of Mortain.* Part of Croydon.

Ham (Richmond) *Estreham: Hamo the Sheriff from Church of Chertsey.* Residential area. 17th-century Ham House, was owned by the descendants of the Duchess of Lauderdale until 1948.

Hambledon *Hameledone: Ranulf from Edward of Salisbury. Mill.* ▦ Scattered.

Hartshurst *Arseste: Richard FitzGilbert.* Hartshurst Farm.

Hatcham *Hacheham: Bishop of Lisieux from Bishop of Bayeux.* Part of London.

Headley *Hallega: Ralph de Feugeres.* ▦ Headley Heath.

Henley *Henlei: Church of Chertsey. Church.* Henley Park and farm, now on Ministry of Defence land.

Hurtmore *Hormera: Tesselin from Walter FitzOthere. Mill.* ▦ Almost a suburb of Godalming.

Immerworth *Limevrde: Picot from Richard FitzGilbert.* Part of Esher.

Kennington *Chenintune: Theodoric the Goldsmith from the king.* Part of London.

Kingston *Chingestone/tune: King's land. Church, 5 mills, 3 fisheries.* Within Greater London, but the county town of Surrey. It was a Saxon capital and the site of the Saxon church remains next to the part 13th-century All Saints Church. The aqueduct built by Wolsey to carry water from Coombe to Hampton Court Palace passes under the river.

Lambeth *Lanchei: Lambeth Church; Count of Mortain. Church.* Part of London. 15th-century Lambeth Palace is the London residence of the Archbishops of Canterbury.

Leatherhead *Leret: Osbern d'Eu from the king. Church.* Town; part 12th-century church.

Limpsfield *Limenesfeld: Battle Church, formerly Harold. Mill, fishery, church, 2 stone quarries, 3 hawk's nests.* ▦ Scattered; part 12th- and 13th-century church.

Little Bookham *Bocheham: Halsard from William de Braose.* Partly a suburb of Leatherhead, partly rural.

Littleton *Liteltone: Wulfwy Hunter.* ⌂

Lollesworth *Lodesorde: Ketel Hunter from the king. Mill.* Lollesworth Farm in Horsley.

Long Ditton *Ditone/une: Picot from Richard FitzGilbert. Church, mill. 500 herrings.* Suburb of Surbiton.

Loseley *Losele: Thorold from Earl Roger.* Loseley House, built in 1562 for Sir William More, one of Elizabeth I's counsellors.

Malden *Meldone: William de Watteville from church of Chertsey; Robert de Watteville from Richard FitzGilbert. Chapel, mill.* Now 2 villages, Old and New Malden.

Merstham *Merstan: Archbishop of Canterbury. Church, mill.* ▦ Part medieval St John's Church.

HAM: *Walnut panelling on the staircase of 17th-c. Ham House.*

Merton *Meretone: King's land, formerly Earl Harold. Church, 2 mills.* Part of London, famous for its silk weaving works on the River Wandle in the 17th century; church with a Norman nave.

Mickleham *Michelham/ Micleham: Nigel from Bishop of Bayeux; Oswald from Richard FitzGilbert. Church.* Church with Norman foundations.

Milton *Mildetone: Baldwin from William FitzAnsculf. Mill.* Milton Court.

Mitcham *Michelham: Canons of Bayeux from Bishop of Bayeux; William FitzAnsculf. ½ mill.* Part of London, once famous for its lavender fields.

Morden *Mordone: Westminster Abbey. Mill.* Part of London, it was a tiny village until the 20th century. Morden Hall park has 2 18th-century snuff mills on the River Wandle.

Mortlake *Mortelaga/age: Archbishop of Canterbury; St Pauls, London. Church, 2 mills.* London suburb, the finish of the Oxford and Cambridge boat race. Mortlake tapestry works was founded in 1619.

Nutfield *Notfelle: Countess of Boulogne. Church, mill.* Largely 13th-century church.

Ockham *Bocheham: Richard FitzGilbert. Church, 2 fisheries.* Part 13th-century church; orangery and stables of Ockham Park, built by Hawksmoor in 1725 and burnt down in 1948.

Ockley *Hochlei: Richard FitzGilbert and Ralph from him.* Scattered; site of a 12th-century castle.

Oxted *Aestede:* See page 264.

Pachevesham *Pachesham: Hugh from Bishop of Bayeux. 2½ mills.*

Paddington *Padendene: William FitzAnsculf. Mill, hall.* Paddington Farm.

Peckham *Pecheham: Bishop of Lisieux from Bishop of Bayeux.* Part of London.

Peper Harow *Pipereherge: Gerard from Walter FitzOthere. Mill.* 18th-century house with a dovecote; church; farm.

Petersham *Patricesham: Church of Chertsey. Church, fishery. 1000 eels, 1000 lampreys.* Residential area.

Pitchingworth *Pechingeorde:* Lost.

Pyrford *Peliforde: Westminster Abbey, formerly Harold. 2 mills.* Now Old Pyrford.

Reigate *Cherchefelle: King's land.* Town with a motte and bailey, the remains of Reigate Castle. 2 18th-century windmills: a postmill, now a chapel, and a tower mill.

Rodsall *Reddesolham/ Redessolham: Bishop of Bayeux.* Rodsall Manor.

Sanderstead *Sandestede: St Peter's of Winchester.* Suburb of Purley; 16th-century White House.

Send *Sande: Reginald from Alfred of Marlborough. Mills, church, 5 fisheries.* Scattered; part 13th-century church.

Shalford *Scaldefor: Robert from Richard FitzGilbert. Church, 3 mills.* Mill on the Tillingbourne; 17th-century mill house.

Shere *Essira/Essire: King's land. Church, mills.* 13th-century church.

Southwark *Sudwerc(h)a/werche: King's land; Bishop of Bayeux. Monastery, tidal waterway.* Part of London; 13th-century cathedral.

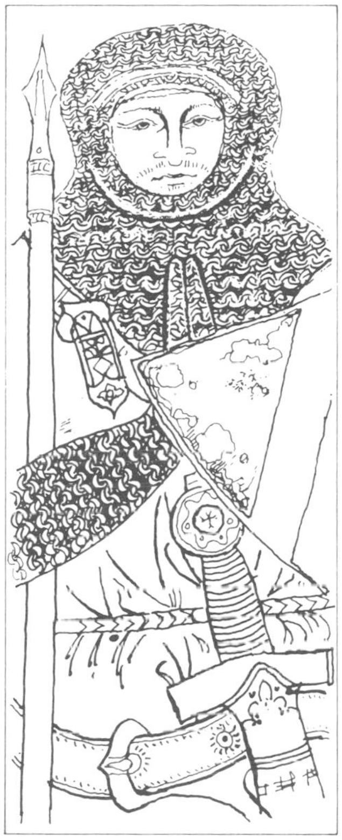

STOKE D'ABERNON: *Church brass, dated 1277.*

Stoke d'Abernon *Stoche: Richard FitzGilbert. Church, mill.* Large; church with 7th-century foundations, famous for its brasses.

Stoke (Guildford) *Stochae: King's land. Church, mills.* Part of Guildford.

Streatham *Estreham: Ansgot from Bishop of Bayeux.* Part of London.

Sutton (Cheam) *Sudtone: Church of Chertsey. 2 churches.* London suburb.

Sutton (Guildford) *Sudtune: Robert Malet. Mill.*

Sutton (Shere) *Sudtone: Bishop of Bayeux.*

Tadworth *Tadeorde: Ralph from Bishop of Bayeux.* Town.

Tandridge *Tenrige: Salie's wife from Richard FitzGilbert. Mill.* 12th-century church.

Tatsfield *Tatelefelle: Ansketel de Rots from Bishop of Bayeux.* Part of Biggin Hill; 13th-century church.

Thames Ditton *Ditone/une: Wadard from Bishop of Bayeux. Part of a mill.* Suburb.

Thorncroft *Tornecrosta:* Lost.

Thorpe *Torp: Church of Chertsey.* Growing town; 12th-century church.

Tillingdown *Tellingedone: Salie's wife from Richard FitzGilbert. Church.* Part of Caterham.

Titsey *Ticesei: Hamo the Sheriff. Church.* A Roman villa and temple were excavated in 1969.

Tolworth *Taleorde: Oswald from Richard FitzGilbert. Mill.* Part of London.

Tooting *Totinges: Westminster Abbey.* Part of London.

Tooting Bec *Totinges: St Mary's of Bec as a gift from Richard FitzGilbert.* Part of London.

Tuesley *Tiwesle: Ranulf from the king.*

Tyting *Tetinges: Bishop of Osbern.*

Waddington *Watendone:* Lost.

Walkingstead *Wachelestede:* Lost.

Wallington *Waletone: King's land.* Large town, part of Sutton.

Walton-on-Thames *Waletone: Richard FitzGilbert. Church, mill, fishery.* Large town; 13th-century church.

Walton-on-the-Hill *Waltone: John from Richard FitzGilbert.* 14th-century manor house, the home of Anne of Cleves in the 16th century.

Walworth *Waleorde: Baynard from Archbishop of Canterbury. Church.* Part of London.

Wanborough *Weneberge: Geoffrey de Mandeville. Church.* 13th-century church.

Wandsworth *Wand(el)/ Wendelesorde: St Wandrille's through the monk Ingulf; William FitzAnsculf.* Part of London.

GUILDFORD: *The castle, now overshadowed by the town.*

West Clandon *Clanedun: Hugh from Edward of Salisbury. Mill, church.* Straggling. Church of St Peter and St Paul with 13th-century nave walls.

West Horsley *Horslei/Orslei: Walter FitzOthere. Church.* Formerly Horsley Green; mainly 13th-century church.

Westcott *Wescote: Ralph de Feugeres. Mill.*

West Molesey *Molesham: Odard the Gunner. Church.* Suburban; church with a 15th-century tower.

Weston *Westone: Barking Church.* Part of London.

Weybridge *Webrige/bruge: Herfrid from Bishop of Bayeux.* Part of London; site of a palace for Henry VIII.

Whitford *Witford: Canons from Bishop of Bayeux.* Part of Outer London.

Wisley *Wiselei:* See page 265.

Witley *Witlei: Gilbert FitzRichere. Church.* Saxon church, extended by the Normans.

Woking *Wochinges: King's land. Church, mill.* Large town with a Norman church.

Woldingham *Wallingeham: John from Richard FitzGilbert.* Surrey's smallest church.

Woodmansterne *Odemerestor: Richard FitzGilbert. Church, mill.* Part of Coulsdon.

Worplesdon *Werpesdune: Thorold from Earl Roger. Mill.* 2 timber fronted 17th-century farmhouses.

Wotton *Odetone: Oswald from the king, formerly Harold. Mill.* Pre-Conquest church.

Wyke *Wucha: Godric from Earl Roger. Manor.*

PEPER HAROW: *Rich Surrey countryside at Oxenford Farm.*

Sussex

Domesday's account of Sussex is unique in that it subdivides the county into 'rapes', a term used nowhere else. There were five rapes, running in parallel strips from the coast to the county's northern border. Whether or not they were based on a Saxon division is uncertain; if they were, the Normans made them more systematic. Saxon settlements had often held outlying lands elsewhere; William I transferred such holdings to manors of the rapes in which they lay geographically.

Each rape was given its lord, a powerful Norman baron, who, as the king's tenant-in-chief, held all its lands except for ecclesiastical property and royal manors. They ruled from their respective castles at Hastings, Pevensey, Lewes, Bramber and Arundel. These fortresses suggest that the Conqueror took advantage of – or created – the rapes because Sussex was dangerously vulnerable to continental invasion. He himself had landed at Pevensey. He obviously intended his tenants-in-chief to defend their separate approaches in depth, for all their castles were supported by such inland mottes as Verdley, Pulborough, Knepp, Channelbrook, Caburn and Burglow.

Ditchling

William [de Warenne] holds DITCHLING *DICELINGES* himself in lordship. King Edward held it. It never paid tax. Before 1066 it answered for 46 hides; when acquired only 42 hides; the others were in the Count of Mortain's Rape, and 6 woods which belonged to the head of the manor. Now it answers for 33 hides. Land for 60 ploughs. In lordship 8 ploughs. 108 villagers and 40 smallholders have 81 ploughs. A church; 1 mill at 30d; meadow, 130 acres; woodland, 80 pigs; 11 dwellings in Lewes at 12s. Gilbert holds 1½ hides of this land; Hugh 2 hides; Alfward 3 hides; Warin 3 hides; Richard 1 hide. In lordship they have 7½ ploughs, with 29 smallholders, 3 villagers and 10 slaves with 3 ploughs. 6 burgesses in Lewes at 43d. Value of the whole manor before 1066 £80 and 66d; later £25; now, William's lordship £60; his men's £12 10s.

Ditchling, at the foot of the Sussex Downs, is a self-consciously picturesque small town. Its narrow High Street, which impedes a main route to Brighton, is lined with timber-framed and Georgian houses, several converted to antique shops or art galleries. It was a royal manor long before *Domesday*, in King Alfred's day. Later it was Edward the Confessor's, but William I gave it away to his tenant-in-chief of the Rape of Lewes, William de Warenne.

Four of its hides lay in the neighbouring Rape of Pevensey. It was almost certainly these hides to which *Domesday* refers in an entry for the Hundred of (East) Grinstead, where Ansfrid is said to hold land which was once Ditchling Manor's. On this stood Sussex's only recorded iron works.

The Romans had smelted iron extensively in what is now Ashdown Forest. They left behind seven acres of slag near Fairwarp, which stayed there until it was used for road building in the last century. Ansfrid's iron works may have been nearby. Evidence that the Saxons had worked iron in the vicinity was provided in 1980 when a Saxon bloomery smelter was found some three miles north-west of Fairwarp near Millbrook Bottom.

Certainly Ditchling's lands stretched north into the thickly wooded Weald and it would have been here that its pigs were kept. The 80 mentioned were the number paid annually as dues – probably one in seven if the pigs were grazed, but perhaps only one in ten if they were turned out for the autumn acorn and beech-mast pannage. The figure indicates that Ditchling's 148 families kept between 580 and 800 pigs, showing how important the animals were to such Sussex settlements.

For 300 years after the Conquest the de Warenne family dominated Ditchling. They were violent and authoritarian, but also sometimes pious – or at least repentant. The first William de Warenne founded the Cluniac priory at Lewes, and his son gave it Ditchling church and land to the north which became Ditchling Garden Manor.

In the present century Ditchling was the home of the sculptor and engraver Eric Gill. Here he formed the Ditchling Community, a community of craftsmen and artists, in 1915 and although he only finished the Gill Sans typeface for which he is best remembered in 1928, after he had left, the community printed books on its own press.

South of Ditchling there are two roads, one running through the old park to cross the Downs near Clayton, the other climbing steeply to Ditchling Beacon, the Downs' highest point in East Sussex. Almost 2000 years ago the Romans built a fort here. Today hang-gliders use its thermal currents. The splendid view north shows 15 miles of cultivated fields and meadows – once the woodlands in which Ditchling's pigs roamed. Even further north, where the land rises to the High Weald, lies Ashdown Forest where Ansfrid's smeltery probably stood.

Alciston

The Abbot of St Martin's of Battle holds ALCISTON *ALSISTONE* from the King. Young Alnoth held it from King Edward. Then it answered for 50 hides; now for 44½ hides. Land for 28 ploughs. 3½ of these hides lie in the Rape of Hastings; and 2 hides in the Rape of Lewes; 7 burgesses. The Abbot has 4 ploughs in lordship. 65 villagers with 7 smallholders have 21½ ploughs. 12 slaves; meadow 50 acres; woodland, 4 pigs from pasturage; 6 pigs from grazing. Of the said 5 hides, Robert holds 1 hide and 3 virgates from the Abbot; Reinbert 5 virgates; Geoffrey ½ hide; Alfred 3 virgates. In lordship they have 4 ploughs. 5 villagers and 1 smallholder with 1½ ploughs. Value of the whole manor before 1066 £48; later £30; now, what the Abbot holds £36; what his men hold £4 5s.

Although a tributary of the Cuckmere River rises near the small village of Alciston, its position on the northern slopes of the Downs gives it no strategic importance, unlike that of its neighbour Alfriston, two and a half miles to the

DITCHLING: *Just outside the town lies some of the most evocative scenery in southern England, the Sussex downs.*

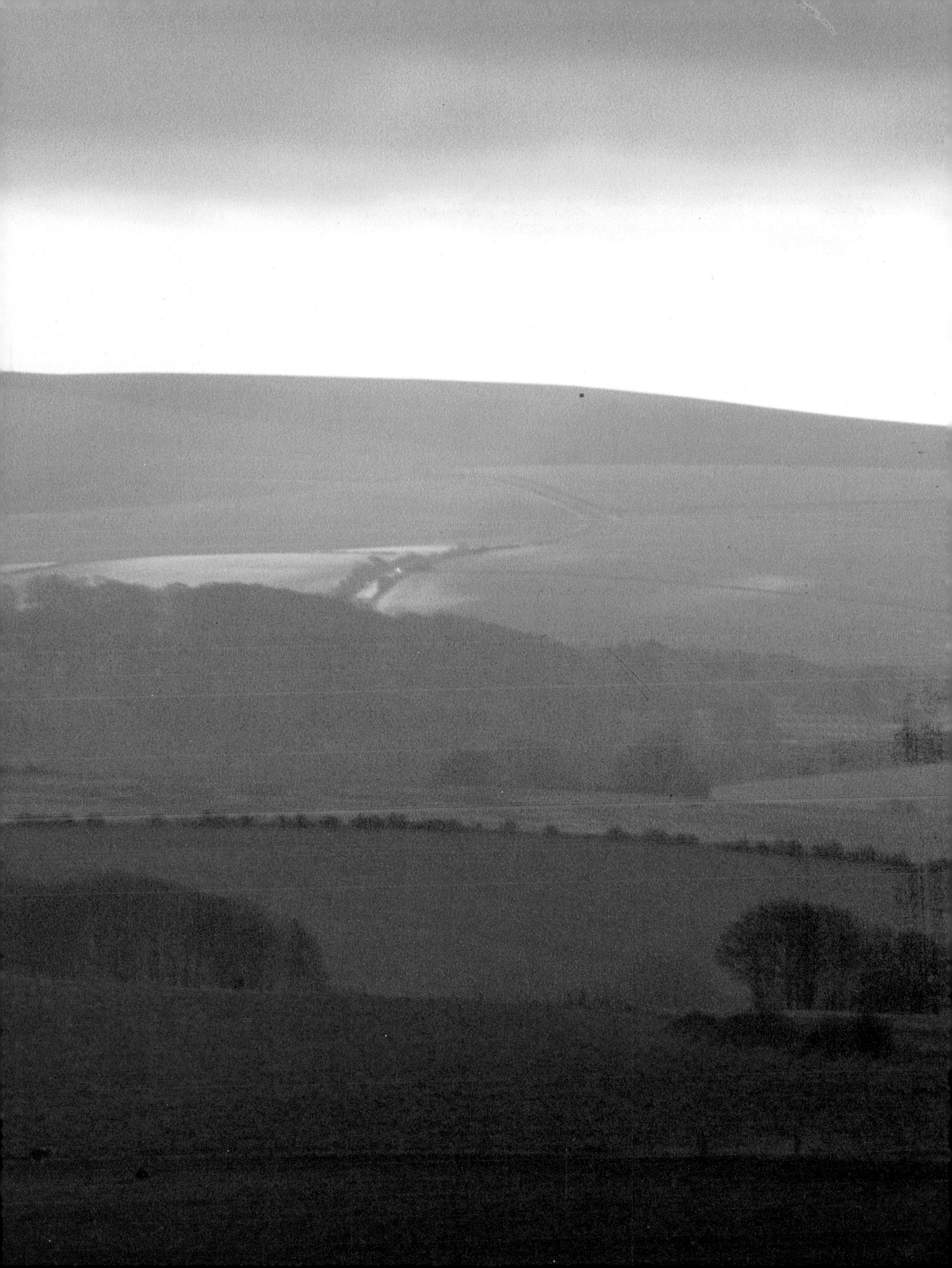

south-east, which guards the Cuckmere Gap. But it was once a large settlement and is mentioned in six *Domesday* entries. Five of these, held by the Count of Eu, are assessed in total at a mere one and a half hides; the sixth (above) was by far the largest. Its tenant-in-chief was the Abbot of Battle (Battle Abbey).

Battle Abbey had been founded by William I soon after 1066 at the place where Harold fell, and named to commemorate the battle because there was no nearby village after which to call it. William gave the abbot all the land within one and a half miles of the abbey as well as other lands throughout the country. Although most of its 16 Sussex holdings were near to Battle, Alciston lay 17 miles to the west. Sheep are not mentioned in the surveys, but shepherding was already important on the Downs – at Patcham, north of Brighton, there were ten shepherds – and for many centuries sheep farming was the village's chief business.

By the nineteenth century the parish had dwindled so that it shared a vicar with the nearby, equally small parish of Selmeston. For 41 years he was William Parish, who compiled from his daily experience a dictionary of the Sussex language, first published in 1875. His humble parishioners, he believed, used British, Roman, Saxon and Norman words which had been abandoned by better-educated people.

Rye

The Abbot of Fécamp holds RYE *RAMESLIE* from the King, and held it from King Edward. Then it answered for 20 hides; now for 17½ hides. Land for 35 ploughs. In lordship 1 plough. 100 villagers, less 1, have 43 ploughs. 5 churches which pay 64s; 100 salt-houses at £8 15s; meadow, 7 acres; woodland, 2 pigs from pasturage. In this manor is a new Borough; 64 Burgesses pay £8 less 2s; in Hastings 4 burgesses and 14 smallholders pay 63s. Robert of Hastings holds 2½ hides of this manor from the Abbot; Herewulf ½ hide. They have 4 villagers, 4 cottagers and 2 ploughs. Value of the whole manor before 1066 £34, now, the Abbot's lordship £50; the men's 44s.

The small town of Rye stands on a hilltop, now two miles from the English Channel. Its narrow cobbled streets have probably a greater concentration of old houses and more of the atmosphere of a sixteenth-century town than any others in the country. This quaintness makes it hard to believe that Rye was once important; yet it was a thriving port from Norman times onwards and, as late as the mid-nineteenth century, employed hundreds of men in its shipyards.

The *Domesday* entry is confusing. The name Rye, used in the above translation, reads 'Rameslie' in the original. Most historians agree, however, that the 'new Borough' with its 64 burgesses must be the original of today's town. At that time Rye seems to have had no name and to have been a new settlement. This is not surprising since it was an island surrounded by sea and marshes. It was part of the manors of Rameslie and Brede, which, in about 1030, had been given to the Abbot of Fécamp in Normandy by Cnut; some time during the next 50 years the abbey had presumably established a branch in this inhospitable but potentially valuable corner.

The Norman kings confirmed the abbey's grant. This seemed harmless enough, so long as England and Normandy remained under one rule. But when John lost Normandy in 1204, a foreign settlement at such a strategically significant place became less than satisfactory. Rye was, indeed, among the ports captured in 1216 by Louis of France when he invaded England to support the barons against John. Sixteen years later Henry III took Rye from the abbey, giving it in exchange the manor of Cheltenham and other places in Gloucestershire and Lincolnshire. He also ordered the constable of the Cinque Ports to build a fortress for Rye's defence. Ypres Castle, the town's oldest building, now a museum, was the result. Its name comes from John d'Ypres, who bought it in 1430 when it was no longer considered useful for defence.

Long before this, Rye, together with its neighbour, Winchelsea, had been added to the original five Cinque Ports. It was required to provide five ships to serve the king for 15 days a year; at other times they fished. Rye was an important supplier of fish to London and its 'rippiers' had the right to sell fish to whom they wanted.

Salt was another of Rye's products. Its recreation ground, which lies below its walls beside the River Rother, is still known as the Town Salts. Although salt was also produced at other places along the coast, it is fair to assume that some at least of the 100 salt-houses mentioned in *Domesday* stood here.

Despite its new defences, Rye continued to be vulnerable. It was sacked by the French in 1339, in 1365 and most thoroughly in 1377, when the complete peal of bells from St Mary's, the church on the hilltop which dominates the town, was taken away. The next year the men of Rye and Winchelsea made a counter-raid and recovered them.

Meanwhile weather and sea were creating their own havoc. A great storm in 1277 destroyed Old Winchelsea, and diverted the full flow of the River Rother into its outlet at Rye. This may have brought some benefit by adding to the inland waterways to which the town was connected. But turbulent seas periodically swept sections of Rye away. The original Augustine Friary which stood at the west end of the town was lost in this way. As late as 1823, the Town Salts were still flooded at high tide.

But by the mid-fifteenth century all had begun to change. The sea was rapidly receding. By 1562 the River Rother's channel had been reduced to between 16 and 25 feet and the eastward drift of shingle along the English Channel had filled its estuary with low-lying marshes.

This transformation provided perfect conditions for smuggling, for which the people of Rye soon became famous. Boats now had to pass up two miles of narrow channel with marshes alongside onto which contraband could easily be unloaded. Charles Wesley, brother of John, the founder of Methodism, reported in 1773 that he encountered 'abundance of people willing to hear the good word, at Rye in particular. And they do many things gladly, but they will not part with the accursed thing, smuggling'.

Smuggling here went through two phases. The first had begun in the fourteenth century, soon after Edward I established a customs system, and even before the sea's retreat. Woolen goods were the main contraband as they were three centuries later when the writer and traveller Daniel Defoe watched the smugglers, known as 'owlers', being pursued by mounted dragoons 'as if they were huntsmen beating up their game'. They would fight back, he was told, and Revenue Officers had been 'attack'd in the night, with such numbers, that they dare not resist, or if they do, they are wounded and beaten, and

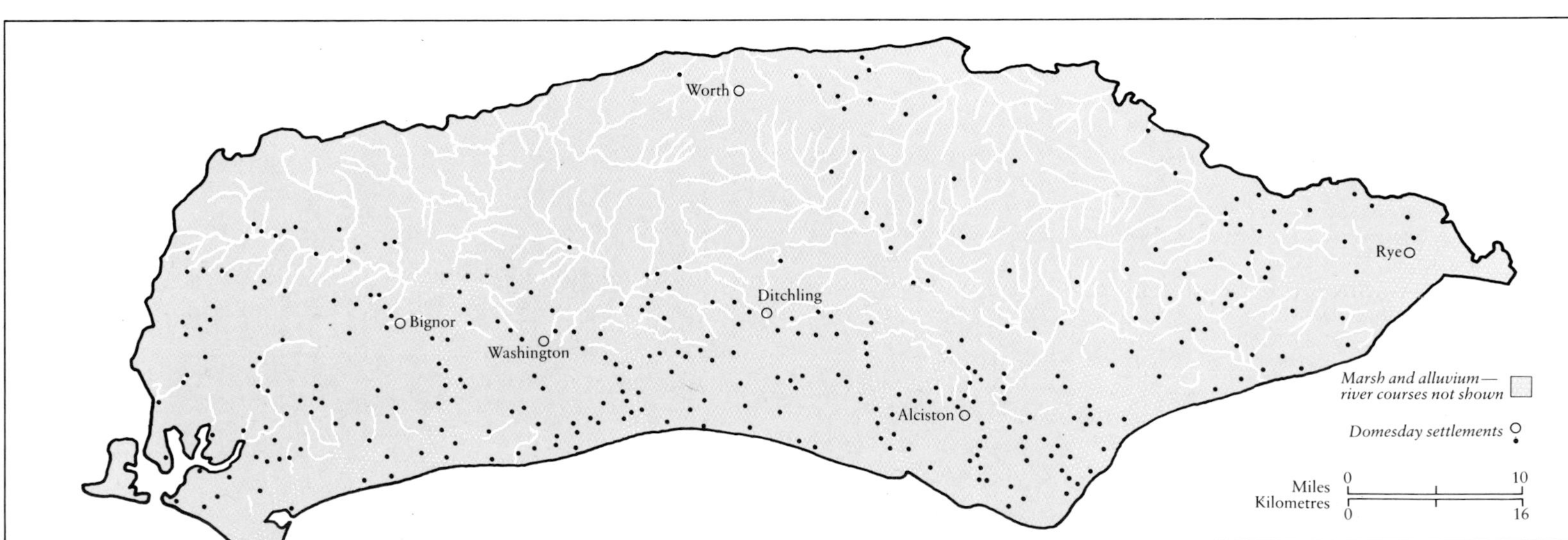

sometimes kill'd; and at other times are oblig'd ... to ... see the wool carry'd off before their faces, not daring to meddle'.

Later, brandy, Dutch gin, rum, tea and lace became the goods most smuggled. Then the notorious Hawkhurst gang of about 600 terrorised the town. At Rye they used the Mermaid Inn – it survives little changed – as their meeting place. One habitué remembered 'when the Hawkhurst gang of smugglers were at the height of their pride and insolence, to have seen them (after having successfully run a cargo of goods on the sea shore) seated at the windows of this house carousing and smoking their pipes, with loaded pistols on the table before them, no magistrate daring to interfere with them'.

Today in summer Rye is a pullulating mass of tourists. But it is different from other resorts not only because it has no beach (even the single-track railway which connected it with Halfway House and Camber Sands has gone), but because nautical matters are still a part of its life. Several boat yards are now at work again, and across the Town Salts 20 or 30 fishing boats are moored. Genuine sea-booted sailors walk Rye's streets, and interspersed with its galleries and craft shops are genuine ships' chandlers.

Important as these changes are, Rye today is a backwater, even if a more hospitable one than 950 years ago, when the monks of Fecamp were making it Sussex's seventh borough.

Washington

William de Braose holds... WASHINGTON *WASINGETUNE*. Earl Gyrth held it before 1066. Then it answered for 59 hides; now it does not give tax. Bramber Castle is situated in one of these hides. Land for 34 ploughs. In lordship 5 ploughs; 120 villagers and 25 smallholders with 34 ploughs. 5 salt-houses at 110 ambers of salt or 9s 2d; meadow, 4 acres. From woodland pasturage 60 pigs; 6 slaves. Gilbert holds 1/2 hide of this land, Ralph 1 hide, William 3 virgates, Leofwin 1/2 hide; he could withdraw his land. He gave tax to his lord and his lord gave nothing. These have 4 villagers and 2 smallholders with 2 1/2 ploughs. Meadow, 7 acres; woodland at 10 pigs. Value of the whole manor before 1066 £50; later £50; now William's lordship £50 5s, his men-at-arms 50s and 12d. However this manor was at a revenue at £100.

The village of Washington lies close below Chanctonbury Ring, the hilltop clump which is a conspicuous landmark throughout western Sussex. At the time of *Domesday* some 157 families were attached to the manor; Washington parish today has scarcely more. In 1086, Steyning, its neighbour four miles to the south-east, was already a borough with a port. So it is strange to find that Bramber Castle, a mile even further to the south-east, stood on Washington Manor's lands.

Bramber is now a ruin owned by the National Trust, with only one massive piece of the gatehouse wall standing. Here William de Broase built the castle soon after 1066, when William I carved out Bramber Rape for him from the Rape of Arundel to the west and the Rape of Lewes to the east. Since its hilltop commands the River Adur it was a natural site to choose.

The lands of the manor reached down to the Adur itself, where its five salt-houses must have stood, the river being still tidal at this point. The salt production figures for Washington are of particular interest, for they show that salt was assessed at a penny per amber and so make it possible to calculate production at the many manors throughout the country, where only a value is given.

The entry for Washington makes another revealing point. It confirms that hides credited to manors were nominal (Washington could not physically have lost 59) and were the number for which it 'defended itself', *ie* paid tax. These tax hides were reduced in Sussex between the times of Edward the Confessor and *Domesday*, but the reduction was not similar for the different rapes, nor spread evenly inside them. Often, as at Washington, tenants-in-chief made large reductions in the assessments of their own demesne manors but left others little changed.

The last de Broase to hold Bramber died in 1325, and it has since become a separate parish, and Steyning a town. Washington has remained a quiet agricultural village, its only distinguished inhabitant the twentieth-century composer, John Ireland. The parish now includes the smaller manor of Chancton (only four hides in *Domesday*), where a remarkable discovery was made in 1866 when a ploughman at Upper Chancton Farm unearthed a crock containing a huge collection of Saxon coins.

'A general scramble took place amongst the labourers on the spot, and twelve pieces of 'old Tin' were for a day or two the common price for a quart of beer at the Washington Inn [now the Frankland Arms]. Indeed, half a pint of the coins were offered for a quart of 'double X'.'

A treasure trove of 1720 coins was recovered. They are now displayed at the British Museum, where they more than doubled its Edward-the-Confessor collection. Many had been minted at Steyning, where, until this find, it had not been known that a mint had existed. Some were of Harold's brief reign, buried, no doubt, during the last months before the Battle of Hastings. Until 1066, Chancton had been held by an Englishman, Essocher. Perhaps, like Harold's brother, Earl Gyrth, who held Washington, he was killed at Hastings and the secret of his hoard died with him.

BIGNOR: *The Normans may have taken some of the Roman stones for this church; they certainly benefited from the fertile soil as the local farms do now.*

Bignor

Robert holds BIGNOR *BIGENEURE* from the Earl [Roger], and Ralph from him. 3 free men held it before 1066. Then and now it answered for 4 hides. Land for 3 ploughs. In lordship 2 ploughs; 9 villagers and 5 cottagers with 2 ploughs. A church; 2 mills at 28s; 1 millstone quarry at 4s. 2 slaves; meadow, 2 acres; woodland at 3 pigs. Value before 1066 £3; later 40s; now £4.

The small village of Bignor, which lies in West Sussex, just north of the Downs, has a few pleasant stone and timber-framed houses but nothing to compare with its imposing Roman villa, one of the largest in the country. Bignor was tiny in 1086, as its rating of 4 hides shows. It lay in Arundel Rape, whose tenant-in-chief was Earl Roger of Montgomery.

Its church, although much restored, preserves an early Norman chancel arch and south doorway which may be those of a *Domesday* building. Its two mills no doubt stood on the small tributary of the Arun which runs north of the village, one probably on the site of today's abandoned mid-nineteenth-century mill. The millstone quarry, one of only four Sussex quarries mentioned in *Domesday* and the only one which supplied millstones, would have been in the Upper Greensand which outcrops nearby. Since 87 Sussex settlements had mills, this quarry must have been kept busy.

Also to the north is Bignor Park, which was enclosed at the latest in the thirteenth century, during Henry III's reign. It was a private park, but it lay close to the royal Forest of Arundel, the only one of Sussex's six forests not on the Weald, and its deer came from the forest.

The Roman villa, which was found in 1811, had a vast inner courtyard measuring 200 feet by 114, with fine mosaics. Its living rooms were centrally heated and it had a walled farmyard of four and a half acres, all indicating great prosperity. It was connected by its own road to Stane Street, the Roman road which ran from London to Chichester and crossed the Downs just south of Bignor.

When the villa was discovered, more than six centuries had passed since the *Domesday* assessors had been there. By that time it was undoubtedly buried, for it had already been abandoned for over seven centuries.

Worth

Siward holds WORTH *ORDE* from Richard [FitzGilbert]. Oswald held it from King Edward. It answered for ½ hide, then and now. 1 villager with ½ plough. Value before 1066, 30s; later 2s; now 20s.

Worth lies in the modern county of West Sussex, but it was considered by *Domesday* to be in Surrey. The border of the two counties was at this time so wild that the exact boundary was uncertain. To the south lay the Wealden forest of Andredeswald, which was inaccessible in the eighth century, according to the great monk, the 'venerable' Bede, and even at the time of *Domesday* it was sparsely inhabited.

By then the Normans had divided the vast forest into five, of which Worth Forest was second from the west. The area included the modern parishes of Ardingly, Balcombe, Crawley and Slaugham. When, soon after *Domesday*, Worth Manor was given to the de Warenne family, the lords of the Rape of Lewes, Worth Forest became the forest of the rape.

Surprisingly the *Domesday* entry for Worth includes no assessment for pigs. As so often with the survey, it is impossible to know whether this was an oversight, or whether it truly recorded the remarkable fact that no pigs were kept in this rich forest. Equally surprisingly, no church is mentioned, because Worth already had a fine one some 60 or 80 years old. It is today considered one of the country's most splendid Saxon churches.

In the chancel, among other sections, an irregular rubble of ironstone was used for the walls. It was this local ironstone, together with the forest, that made Worth prosperous in the sixteenth and seventeenth centuries. The forest was cropped for wood for charcoal to provide fuel for the furnaces and forges of the Sussex iron industry. Huge quantities were needed, after 1493, when the first English blast furnace began to operate ten miles to the east at Hartfield. Sixty years later, after the first English cannon was cast in a single piece at Buxted 14 miles to the south-east, the whole area became an arsenal. In Worth Forest in the years 1547 and 1548, Lord Admiral Seymour's iron works alone produced 56 tons of cannon and 52 tons of shot, his furnaces and forges using a total of 8625½ cords of wood (a cord was 128 cubic feet).

The fine houses of many of these wealthy ironmasters survive. Crabbet Manor, the best known, passed to the poet, anti-imperialist politician and romantic philanderer, Wilfrid Scawen Blunt (1840–1922), in the nineteenth century. He imported into England the horses which formed the famous Crabbet Arabian Stud. In the 1870s he and his wife (the poet Lord Byron's only granddaughter) travelled the deserts of the Middle East, dressed in local costume, searching for suitable animals. In 1884, in the remote Nedj, the emir gave them his choicest brood mares, from which the stud at Crabbet grew.

Politically Blunt was less successful. In Ireland he was imprisoned for two months for trying to rabble-rouse the tenants of the Marquess of Clanricarde into resisting eviction. At Crabbet he formed a club for distinguished politicians and men of letters which flourished until his own political diatribes 'so shocked and disconcerted the company' that they ceased to come.

Today Worth struggles to retain its village identity within the engulfing suburbs of Crawley New Town. The grounds of Crabbet Manor are bisected by a motorway but the house itself survives, as does Worth's remarkable Saxon church.

WORTH: *The Saxon church of St Nicholas, of cruciform design; tower added in 1871 when the church was restored; 13th-c. font and fine woodwork, including a 16th-c. pulpit and a 17th-c. gallery.*

Sussex Gazetteer
Each entry starts with the modern place name in **bold** type. The *Domesday* information that follows is in *italic* type, beginning with the name or names by which the place was known in 1086. The main landholders under-tenants are next, separated with semi-colons if a place was divided into more than one holding. More general information completes the *Domesday* part of the entry, including examples of dues such as eels and herrings rendered by tenants. The modern or post-Domesday section is in normal type. represents a village, a small village or hamlet.

Alchin *Alsihorne:* Lost.

Alciston *Alsi(s)tone:* See page 270.

Aldingbourne *Aldingeborne: Bishop of Chichester and Robert, Hugh and Alfward from him. Church.* Norman church with carving by cathedral masons.

Aldrington *Eldretune: Godfrey from William de Braose. Hall.* Mid-Victorian suburb.

ALFRISTON: *Ship's dragon figurehead outside the Star Inn.*

Alfriston *Alvricestone: Gilbert and Ranulf from Count of Mortain.* Once a medieval market-town; timber-framed buildings; Saxon cemetery by South Downs Way.

Allington *Alintune/Alitone: Ralph, Hugh and Nigel from William de Warenne.* Allington Farm.

Amberley *Ambrelie: Bishop of Chichester and William the Cleric, Aldred the Priest, Baldwin, Ralph, Theodoric and Guard from him.* Picturesque. Manor house built by a bishop 1150–60 was converted into a castle by Bishop Rede, c. 1380.

Angmering *Angemare, Langemare: Warin and Geoffrey from Earl Roger and William de Braose.* Expanding; Roman villa; early Neolithic flint mines at Harrow Hill.

Annington *Haningedune: William de Braose. Church.* Now Botolphs; Saxon church; Annington Hill; Annington Farm.

Applesham *Aplesham: William from William de Braose. Mill, 2 salt-houses.* Adjoining Lancing College; situated on estuarial Adur, hence the ancient salt-houses.

Arlington *Herlintone: Count of Eu.* Quiet.

Arundel *Harundel: Earl Roger. Fishery, castle, mill (10 measures of wheat, 10 measures of rough corn).* Hilltop town with a Roman Catholic cathedral and famous cricket ground. Roger, Earl of Shrewsbury's castle, built soon after the Conquest, was later enlarged and is now the home of the Duke of Norfolk.

Ashburnham *Esseborne: Robert de Criel from Count of Eu. Church, 3 salt-houses.* Name of a parish with many hamlets in wooded country, church with monuments to the Ashburnhams, a pre-Conquest family.

Ashcombe *Acescome: William FitzReginald from William de Warenne.* Georgian Ashcombe House.

Ashington *Essingetune: Robert from William de Braose.* Large; much ribbon development.

Balmer *Berge/Burgemere: Gozo from William de Warenne. Small church.* St Mary's Farm nearby.

Barcombe *Bercham. William de Watteville from William de Warenne. Church, 3 ½ mills.* Scattered, 3 mills in mid-Victorian times, none remains, Norman church.

Barkham *Bercheham: Gilbert and Warner from Count of Mortain.* Barkham Manor House.

Barlavington *Berleventone: Robert from Earl Roger. 2 mills.* Downland.

Barnham *Berneham: William from Earl Roger. Church, mill.* Norman church; Jacobean manor house.

Bathurst *Wasingate: Battle Church from Reinbert.* Wooded.

Battle *La Batailge: Battle Abbey.* Small town around the abbey, built by William after the battle of Hastings on the spot where Harold died, and consecrated in 1094.

Bechington *Bechingetone:* Lost.

Beddingham *Bed(d)ingham/Beling(e)ham: Count of Eu; Count of Mortain and Godfrey, Gilbert and Abbot of Grestain from him. 4 salt-houses, mill.* On the Ouse marshes; Iron and Bronze Age settlements nearby.

Beech (in Battle) *Bece: Abbot of Battle and Osbern from Count of Eu.* Isolated; Beech Farm.

Bellhurst *Bellest: William from Count of Eu.* Isolated; Bellhurst Farms.

Benefeld *Benefelle:* Lost.

Bepton *Babintone: Geoffrey from Earl Roger. Church.* Scattered; 13th-century church.

Berth *Berts:* Lost.

Berwick *Berewice/Bervice: Reinbert from Count of Eu. Mill, 2 fisheries.* Quiet.

Bevendean *Bevedene: Walter from William de Warenne.* Downland; part of surburban Brighton.

Beverington *Bevringetone:* Lost.

Bexhill *Bexelei: Count of Eu and Osbern, Venning, William de Sept-Meules, Robert St Leger, Reinbert, Ansketel, Robert of Criel and Geoffrey and Roger from him. 2 churches.* Late-Victorian seaside resort; originally Saxon church; 14th-century manor house.

Bignor *Bigeneure:* See page 273.

Bilsham *Bilesham: Hugh from Earl Roger.* Secluded.

Binderton *Bertredtone: Earl Roger. Church.* Roadside; ruined late 17th-century chapel.

Binsted *Benestede: Osmelin from Earl Roger.*

Birchgrove *Bontegraue: William from Count of Mortain.* Wooded.

Birdham *Brideham: William from Earl Roger. Mill, 2 fisheries.* Expanding; on Chichester harbour.

Bishopstone *Biscopestone: Bishop of Chichester and Geoffrey, Harold and Richard from him.* Saxon church with a sundial bearing the name BADRIC.

Bodiam *Bodeham; Osbern from Count of Eu. Hall.* Edward Dalyngrydge's castle, now National Trust-owned, built during the Hundred Years War in 1385; moat from his manor house.

Bosham *Boseham: King's land with Bishop Osbern of Exeter holding the church. 11 mills, 2 fisheries, salt-house.* Church, with many Saxon features, that appeared on the Bayeux tapestry; manor house. In 1064 Harold sailed from here to Normandy.

Bowley Bogelie: *Lost.:*

Boxgrove *Bosgrave: William from Earl Roger.* Priory church from the Benedictine monastery founded in 1117.

Bramber *Brembre: William de Braose. Castle.* Joined by new housing to Steyning; once a medieval port. De Braose's keep dates from soon after the Conquest.

Brambletye *Branbertei: Ralph from Count of Mortain. Mill.*

Brightling *Brislinga: Robert from Count of Eu. Church. Woodland.* Surrounded by woodlands. 'Mad Jack' Fuller, a Regency eccentric, lived at Brightling Park.

Brighton *Bristelme(s)tune: Ralph, Widard and William de Watteville from William de Warenne. 4000 herrings, church.*

BATTLE: *The remains of the Benedictine Abbey on Battle Hill, built on the spot where Harold died.*

Major seaside resort, a small fishing village until the mid-18th century, when Richard Russell promoted the medicinal uses of sea-water; the Pavilion was built for the Prince Regent by Henry Holland, 1787.

Broadwater *Bradewatre: Robert from William de Braose. Church, mill.* Suburb of Worthing.

Brockhurst *Biochest: Ansfrid from Count of Mortain.*

Broomham *Brunham: Venning the priest from Count of Eu.*

Broughton *Bortone:* Lost.

Buddington *Botintone: Robert from Earl Roger.* Buddington Farm.

Bullington *Bol(l)lintun:* Lost.

Buncton *Bongetune: Robert from William de Braose. Mill.* Under Chanctonbury Ring; church, c. 1070.

Burgham *Burgeham: Reinbert from Count of Eu.* Isolated; on the River Limden.

Burleigh *Berchelie: William from Count of Mortain.* Burleigh House Farm.

Burpham *Bercheham: Roger from Earl Roger. Church.* Early Norman church.

Burton *Botechitone: Robert from Earl Roger. Mill, fishery (260 eels).* Idyllic setting; Burton Mill pond, surrounded by woods.

Bury *Berie: Abbot of Fecamp. Church, fishery.* Early Norman church.

Catsfield *Cedesfeld/felle: Waring from Battle Abbey and Count of Eu. Small church, mill which serves the Hall.* Church and manor house.

Chalvington *Calvintone, Caveltone: Count of Eu and Reinbert from him; Count of Mortain and Ansfrid from him.*

Chancton *Cengeltune: Richard and Theodbert from William de Braose.* Area near the Iron Age Chanctonbury Ring, a hill-fort containing the sites of two Roman buildings.

Charleston *Cerlocestone: Durand and Hubert from Count of Mortain.* Charleston Farm, an isolated homestead; Iron Age and Roman settlements.

Charlston *Cerletone: Ralph from Count of Mortain. 3 salt-houses.* Manor house with a late Norman window; medieval dovecote; salt marshes nearby.

CHICHESTER: *A very fine market cross, given to the city in 1501 by the Bishop.*

Chichester *Cicestre: Earl Roger. City, church, mill.* Cathedral city. The medieval town was built over the Roman city, part of whose walls survive. The ancient street plan and a few medieval buildings remain.

Chiddingley *Cetelingei: Ralph and Godwin from Count of Mortain. Mill.* Tudor mansion.

Chithurst *Titeherste: Morin from Earl Roger. Small church, mill (100 eels).* Riverside.

Chollington *Clotintone: Heming from Count of Mortain.* Suburb of Eastbourne.

Clapham *Clopeham: Gilbert from William de Braose.* Quiet.

Claverham *Clave(s)ham/Clavreham: Reinbert and William from Count of Eu; Count of Mortain and Alfred, Morin and Hugh from him.* Lower Claverham Farm; medieval moat, probably the site of the manor house.

Clayton *Claitune: William de Watteville's wife from William de Warenne. Church.* Mainly Saxon church with wall paintings of *c.* 1140; house called 'The Warenne'.

Climping *Clepinges: Almenesches Abbey and St Martin's of Sees from Earl Roger in alms. Church.* Coastal; church (*c.* 1170).

Cocking *Cochinges: Robert from Earl Roger. Church, 5 mills.* On a stream in the South Downs; church, *c.* 1080.

Cokeham *Cocheham: Ralph and Ralph FitzTheodoric from William de Braose, formerly Earl Harold. Salt-house.* In coastal suburbs of Lancing.

Compton (near Harting) *Contone: Geoffrey from Earl Roger. Church.* Pretty; Norman church; Neolithic long barrow.

Compton (in West Firle) *Contone:* Lost.

Coombes *Cumbe: William FitzNorman from William de Braose. Church, salt-houses.* Tiny church, *c.* 1080; salt marshes.

Cootham *Codeham: Robert from Earl Roger.*

Crowhurst *Crohe(r)st: Walter and Walter FitzLambert from Count of Eu, formerly Earl Harold.* Scattered; remains of a manor house built *c.* 1360 by the Earl of Richmond.

Dallington *Dalintone: Count of Eu and William from him.* Wooded.

Dankton *Dentune:* Lost.

Ditchling *Dicelinges:* See page 270.

Donnington *Cloninctune: Winchester Abbey before and after 1066.* Straggling; Donnington Manor.

Duncton *Donechitone: Robert from Earl Roger. Church, 4 mills, 2 fisheries (360 eels).* Church; Duncton Mill, Duncton Manor Farm.

Durrington *Derentune: Robert from William de Braose, formerly Earl Harold. Church.* An outer suburb of Worthing.

Eastbourne *Borne/Burne: Count of Mortain and Reinbert from him. Mill, fishery, 16 salt-houses.* Sea-side resort, expanded *c.* 1851 on the initiative of the 7th Duke of Devonshire of Compton Place.

East Chiltington *Childe(l)tune: Robert and Godfrey from William de Warenne. ½ mill.* Quiet; Old Mill House.

East Dean *Esdene: Wibert and Walter from Count of Eu.* Expanding; church with a Saxon tower and 11th-century nave.

Eastergate *Gate: St Martin's of Sees from Earl Roger, formerly Earl Harold. Church.* Straggling; isolated Norman church; Elizabethan manor farm.

Easthall *Eshalle: Walter and Ralph FitzGunfrid from Count of Mortain.* Absorbed in Eastbourne.

East Hampnet *Antone: William from Earl Roger.*

East Lavington *Levitone: Richard from Bishop Osbern of Exeter. Church.* Under the Downs; Early English church.

East Preston *Prestetune: Robert from Earl Roger. 3 salt-houses.* Now coastal suburbia.

Eaton(s) *Etune: William FitzBonnard from William de Braose.* Eatons Farm.

Eckington *Achiltone/Achintone/Alchitone/Echentone/Eschintone/Hechestone: Count of Eu and Osbern, Walter and Reinbert from him; Count of Mortain and William from him.* Eckington Manor; Eckington Lodge; Eckington Corner.

Elsted *Halestede: Bishop Osbern of Exeter, before and after 1066. Mill, church.* Compact; partly 11th-century church.

Erringham *Eringeham: William de Braose.* Old Erringham Farm.

Etchingwood *Achingeworde: Osbern from Count of Eu.*

Ewhurst *Werste: Count of Eu.* Dispersed.

Exceat *Essete: Walter and Heming, the pre-Conquest holder, from Count of Mortain.* Farm.

Eyelid *Ellede/Eslede: Count of Eu and Hugh from him.* Eyelids Farm.

Fairlight (near East Grinstead) *Ferlega: Count of Mortain.* Fairlight Farm.

Falmer *Falemere: St Pancras from William de Warenne. Church.* Victorian church.

Felpham *Falcheham: St Edward's Abbey, Shaftesbury before and after 1066. Church, fishery.* Cottage, home of the poet and painter William Blake for 3 years from 1800.

Ferring *Feringes: Bishop of Chichester and Ansfrid from him.* Swallowed up by seaside housing.

Filsham *Pilesham/Wilesham: Count of Eu and Abbot of Battle, Geoffrey, Robert, William, Hugh Bowman, Ingelrann, Robert Cook, Walter, Sasward, Venning the priest, Osward and Roger Daniel from him, with Wulfward the priest holding the church.* Filsham Farm.

Findon *Findune/Fintune: William from William de Braose. Church.* Surrounded by new housing. The Iron Age hill-fort at Cissbury was refortified by the Romans.

Fishbourne *Fiseborne: St Martin's Church, Sees, from Earl Roger. 2 mills.* Expanding; Roman Villa site.

Fletching *Flescinge(s): Ansfrid, Morin and Hugh from Count of Mortain.* Burial place of the historian Edward Gibbon (1737–94).

Folkington *Fochintone: William from Count of Mortain.* Secluded; early Victorian Manor House.

Footland *Fodilant: Ansketel from Count of Eu.* Footland Wood; Footland Farm.

Frankwell *Francwelle.* Lost.

HERSTMONCEUX: *Restored in 1933, now the Royal Observatory.*

Frog Firle *Ferle(s): Abbot of Grestain and Alan from Count of Mortain.* Cluster of houses.

Fulking *Fochinges: Tesselin from William de Warenne.* Downland; motte and bailey castle on Edburton Hill.

Glatting *Clotinga: Robert from Earl Roger.* Glatting Farm; isolated.

Glossams *Glesham: 3 men, the pre-Conquest holders, from Count of Eu.* Glass Eye Farm.

Goring *Garinges: Robert from Earl Roger.* Absorbed by seaside housing.

Graffham *Grafham: 4 Frenchmen, Robert, Roland and Arnold from Earl Roger. Church.* Pretty; Norman church rebuilt by George Street in the 19th century; Bronze Age barrows on Graffham Down.

Greatham *Gretham: Ernucion from Earl Roger. 4 fisheries.* Tiny. On the Arun; mainly Jacobean manor house.

Grittenham *Greteham: Robert from Earl Roger. Mill, quarry.* Grittenham Farm.

Guestling *Gestelinges: Geoffrey de Flocques from Count of Eu.* A 'Guestling' was a Parliament that represented the interests of the Cinque Ports.

Hailsham *Hamelesham: William from Count of Mortain. 2 salt-houses.* Town.

Halnaker *Helnache/neche: William from Earl Roger.* On Roman Stane Street; ruins of Halnaker House, 14th century.

Hamsey *Hame: Ralph from William de Warenne. Church.* Scattered; church on a hill above the Ouse.

Hangleton *Hangetone: William de Watteville from William de Warenne.* Modern housing; Church with Saxon walling.

Hankham *Henecham: Count of Mortain and Ansgot and William from him.* Large, sprawling.

Hardham *Heriedeham: Robert from Earl Roger. 3 fisheries.* Church with 12th-century wall paintings. The rivers Arun and Rother meet near here.

Harpingden *Herbertinges:* Lost.

Hartfield *Hertevel: Walter from Count of Mortain. Mill (350 eels).* Pleasant.

Harting *Hertinges: Earl Roger and clergy of St Nicholas, Arundel, from him. 9 mills.* Now 3 adjoining villages, East and West Harting, and South Harting with a possibly pre-Conquest church.

Hastings *Hastinges: Count of Eu and Robert from him. Castle, church.* Town with the ruins of a castle and church (one of whose Deans was Thomas à Becket) built by the Count of Eu.

Hawkridge *Haingurge: Count of Mortain.* Westenden Wood; Sandbrook.

Hazelden *Halseeldene: Ansfrid from Count of Mortain.* Hazelden Farm.

HAMSEY: *Medieval church; traces of 15th c. paintings.*

Hazelhurst *Haslesse: Walter FitzLambert from Count of Eu. Church.*

Heene *Hene: Ralph from William de Braose.* Engulfed by Worthing.

Henfield *Hamfelde: Bishop of Chichester and William, a man-at-arms, from him. Church.* Small town with a mainly Perpendicular and Victorian church.

Herstmonceux *Herste: Wibert from Count of Eu. Church.* Castle built by Roger Fiennes, *c.* 1440; Norman church.

Higham *Hiham: Count of Eu.* Absorbed in Northiam village; Higham Farm.

Hoe *How: William FitzBonnard from William de Braose.* Hoe Court Farm; Anglo-Saxon burial ground nearby.

Hollington *Holintun/Horintone: Count of Eu and Abbot of Battle, Reinbert, William, Hugh and Wulfward from him.* Residential suburb of Hastings.

Hooe *Hou: Count of Eu and Abbot of Battle from him. Small church, mill, 30 salt-houses.* Scattered; church raised above salt marshes.

Hooe Level *Hou: Count of Mortain.* Hooe Level Nature Reserve.

Horns *Orne: Ansfrid and Ranulf from Count of Mortain.*

Horsey *Horselie: Roger from St Michael's, Eastbourne, in alms.* Suburb of Eastbourne.

Horsted Keynes *Horstede: William from Count of Mortain. Mill.* Large.

Hunston *Hunestan: William from Earl Roger. Mill, 2 salt-houses.* Manor house.

Hurst *Herste: Ednoth from Count of Eu.* Hurst House; Hurst Wood.

Hurstpierpoint *Herst: Robert from William de Warenne. Church, 3 mills.* Large; church; some Georgian houses.

Iden *Idene: Geoffrey and Leofwin from Count of Eu.* On the Kent border.

Ifield *Ifelt: William FitzRanulf from William de Braose.* Part of Crawley New Town; moats at Ifield Court.

Iford *Niworde: William de Warenne and monks of St Pancras, Lewes, Hugh and Tosard from him. Church, 2 mills.* ⛫ Norman church.

Iping *Epinges: Aldred. Mill, quarry.* ⛫ Tiny; mill.

Itchenor *Icenore: Warin from Earl Roger.* ⛫ Fishing; sometimes called West Itchenor.

Itford *Litelforde: William from Count of Mortain.* Itford Hill; Itford Farm.

Jevington *Lov(r)ingetone: Hugh from Count of Eu, Ralph from Count of Mortain. Mill.* ⛫ Neolithic causeway camp on Combe Hill; Bronze Age barrow nearby; church with a Saxon tower.

Keymer *Chemere: William de Watteville from William de Warenne. Church, 2 mills.* Part of modern Hassocks; church rebuilt in 1866.

Kingston-by-Sea (Kingston Buci) *Chingestone/tune: Ralph and William FitzRanulf from William de Braose. Church, 9 salt-houses (10 ambers of salt).* ⛫ Swamped by seaside housing; church with a Saxon nave.

Kitchenham *Checeham: Rainer from Count of Eu.* Isolated farmhouse on the Kent border.

Lancing *Lancinges: Robert and Ralph from William de Braose. Mill, 23 salt-houses.* ⛫ Overwhelmed by new suburban housing; Old Salts and New Salts Farms on the Adur marshes.

Langney *Langelie: Ranulf and William from Count of Mortain.* Outer suburb of Eastbourne.

Laughton *Lestone/tun: Count of Eu and Osbern FitzGeoffrey and Wibert from him; Count of Mortain. 16 salt-houses.* ⛫ The Pelham family, lords of the manor from the mid-14th century until recently, carved their symbol, a buckle, on local churches and on the manor house, now in ruins.

Lavant *Loventone/Lovintune: Archbishop Lanfranc and Ralph from him; Ivo from Earl Roger. 2 mills.* Now 2 villages, East and Mid Lavant.

Lewes *Lewes/Lau(u)es: King's land; Archbishop of Canterbury; William de Warenne. 4000 herrings.* Market and county town with a castle built by William de Warenne.

Lidham *Luet: William de Sept-Meules and William from Count of Eu.* Now 2 hamlets, Lidham Hill and Upper Lidham Hill.

Linch (near Bepton) *Lince: Robert from Earl Roger. Church.* Huddle of buildings; Linch Farm.

Littlehampton *Hantone: William from Earl Roger.* Seaside resort, originally a small fishing town.

Little Horsted *Horstede: Ranulf from Count of Mortain. Mill.* ⛫ Church dating from 1080.

Lodsworth *Lodesorde: Ketel Hunter. Mill.* ⛫ Large. The manor house dates from the 13th century.

Lordine *Lordistret: Wibert from Count of Eu.* Lordine Court, isolated.

Lordington *Harditone: William from Earl Roger. Mill.* ⛫ Quiet; on a stream.

Lyminster *Lolinminstre: Earl Roger and Robert from him. Church, mill, 2 salt-houses.* ⛫ Near Arun salt-marshes, church with a Saxon nave, part of a Benedictine nunnery established after the Conquest.

Marden *Meredone: Robert, Engelhere, Azor and Alwin from Earl Roger.* Now 2 villages, East and West Marden, and North Marden, a hamlet. Magnificent settings.

Mayfield *Mesewelle: Count of Mortain and William de Warenne from him; mill.* ⛫ Swept by fire in 1389. The palace, built for the Archbishops of Canterbury and now a school, was saved.

Merston *Mersitone: Osmelin from Earl Roger. 3 mills.* ⛫ By a stream.

Middleton-on-Sea *Middeltone:: William from Earl Roger. Church.* Seaside housing. The medieval church was swept out to sea as a result of erosion and replaced in 1849.

Morley *Morleia: William FitzRanulf from William de Braose.* Morley Farm.

Moulstone *Moulstan: Jocelyn from William de Warenne.* Absorbed in Sussex University.

Mountfield *Montifelle: Reinbert from Count of Eu.* ⛫ Woodland.

Mundham *Mundreham: Alchere from Earl Roger. Church, 1½ mills.* Now 2 villages, North and South Mundham.

Muntham *Moham: Morin from William de Braose.* Muntham Farm.

Netherfield *Nedrefelle/Nirefeld: Abbot of Battle and Herewulf from Count of Eu. 8 salt-houses.* ⛫ Straggling.

Newtimber *Niuembre: Ralph from William de Warenne. Mill.* Moated Newtimber Place, 16th-century seat of the Buxton family.

Ninfield *Nerewelle: Count of Eu and Robert Cook from him. Church.* ⛫ Large; Norman church. William the Conqueror was erroneously thought to have planted his flag here on Standard Hill.

North Stoke *Stoches: Reginald from Earl Roger. Church, 2 fisheries.* ⛫ Riverside; Norman church; manor farm.

Nutbourne *Nordborne: Robert from Earl Roger. 2 mills.* ⛫ By a stream; Heath Mill.

Nyetimber *Nitinbreham: Roger from Earl Roger.* ⛫ Nyetimber Farm.

Offham *Offham: Azor from Earl Roger. 2 mills, fishery.* ⛫ On the River Arun; close to marshland.

Offington *Offintune: William FitzNorman from William de Braose.* Absorbed in Worthing; name survives in Offington Avenue, Drive and Lane.

PENHURST: *Church Farm has both a 17th c. house and a church dated 1340–1500.*

Ovingdean *Hoingesdene/Hovingedene: Godfrey from William de Warenne. Small church.* ⛫ New estates; Norman church's 13th-century aisle was destroyed by pirates in 1377.

Pagham *Pageham: Archbishop of Canterbury and Osmelin from him. Mill, church.* ⛫ Holiday resort; dried-up harbour; Norman church.

Pangdean *Pinhedene/Pinwedene: William FitzReginald from William de Warenne.* Pangdean Farm.

Parham *Perham: Abbot of Westminster before and after 1066; Robert from Earl Roger. Mill.* Tudor Parham House.

Parrock *Apedroc: Count of Mortain, formerly Earl Harold. Hall.* Now Little Parrock.

Patcham *Piceham: William de Warenne and Richard from him. Church.* ⛫ On the edge of Brighton; 12th-century church; Court Farm, formerly the manor house.

Patching *Petchinges: Archbishop of Canterbury. Church.* ⛫ Neolithic flint mines nearby.

Pawthorne *Paveorne:* Lost.

Peelings *Palinges/Pellinges: Godfrey the cleric, Godfrey, Alan, Ansfrid and Roger from Count of Mortain.* Peelings farmhouse.

Penhurst *Penehest: Abbot of Battle from Osbern.* 17th-century manor house.

Perching *Berchinges/Percinges: Osward the pre-Conquest holder, Tesselin and William de Watteville from William de Warenne. Mill, hall.* Georgian Perching Manor Farm, beneath Perching Hill, now in Fulking village.

Petworth *Peteorde: Robert from Earl Roger. Church; mill (189 eels).* Town with a 17th-century mansion, originally a manor house converted into a castle by the Percy family c. 1309.

Pevensey *Pevenesel: Count of Mortain. Mint, mill.* ⛫ Former Saxon borough with the remains of a moated castle, built by the count within the walls of the Roman Anderida.

Playden *Pleidena: Count of Eu and Ednoth, Walter, Remir, Geoffrey, Theobald the priest from him. Church.* ⛫ Church, c. 1190.

Plumpton *Pluntune: Hugh FitzRanulf from William de Warenne. Church, 2 mills.* ⛫ Norman church; Plumpton Place c. 1568.

Portslade *Porteslage/lamhe: Osward, the pre-Conquest holder, and Albert from William de Warenne.* ⛫ On the medieval pilgrim's route to Canterbury.

Poynings *Poninges: William FitzReginald from William de Warenne. Church, 2 mills.* ⛫ 14th-century church.

Preston (in Beddingham) *Prestetone: Osbern from Count of Eu; Ralph from Count of Mortain.* Preston Court; Preston House.

Preston (in Binderton) *Presteton: Durand from Bishop Osbern of Exeter.* Preston Farm.

Preston (in Brighton) *Prestetone: Bishop of Chichester and Lovell from him. Church, mill.* Now Preston Park, a Brighton suburb; 13th-century church; 14th-century manor house.

Pulborough *Poleberge: Robert from Earl Roger. 2 mills, 2 fisheries, 2 churches.* Small town on the River Arun with a 13th-century church.

Racton *Rachetone: Ivo from Earl Roger.* Cottages; church.

Ratton *Radetone/Radintone/Ratendone: Wibert, Reinbert and Eustace the cleric from Count of Eu; Jocelyn, Ralph, Morin, Hugh and Azelin from Count of Mortain. Mill, salt-house.* Part of Eastbourne; Ratton Farm, an 18th-century manor house; and 15th-century gatehouse.

Ripe *Ripe: Count of Eu and Alwin, his man, Reinbert, and Walter FitzLambert from him; Count of Mortain; Formerly Earl Harold. 8 salt-houses.* ⛫ 15th-century manor house.

Rodmell *Ramelle/Redmelle: William de Warenne, formerly Earl Harold. 11 salt-houses, church. 4000 herrings.* ⛫ South of marshy brooks; Norman church; remains of Rodmell Place.

Rotherfield *Reredfelle: King's land. Park.* ⛫ Large, manor house.

Rottingdean *Rotingedene: Hugh from William de Warenne.* ⛫ Many seaside villas. Sir Edward Burne-Jones lived at North End House.

Rumboldswhyke *Wiche: Hugh from Earl Roger.* Suburb of Chichester.

Runcton *Rochintone: Troarn Abbey from Earl Roger. 2 mills, fishery.* ⛫

Rye *Rameslie:* See page 272.

Saddlescombe *Salescome: Ralph from William de Warenne. Salt.* ⛫ Early 16th-century manor house.

Sakeham *Sacheham: William from William de Braose.* Sakeham Farm; isolated.

Salehurst *Salhert: Reinbert from Count of Eu. Church.* ⛫ Late 13th-century church.

Sedlescombe *Sales/Selescome: Walter FitzLambert from Count of Eu. Small church.* ⛫ Pretty; mainly 15th-century church.

Selham *Seleham: Robert from Earl Roger. Mill (100 eels).* ⛫ Isolated manor farm.

Selmeston *S(i)elemestone: Reinbert from Count of Eu, William from Count of Mortain. Church.* ⛫ 14th-century church rebuilt in 1867.

Selsey *Seleisie: Bishop of Chichester and Geoffrey and William from him.* Holiday resort, once an important Saxon town.

Sessingham *Sasingham/Sesingeham: Count of Eu; Gerald from Count of Mortain. Mill (500 eels).* Sessingham Farm; isolated.

Sheffield *Sifelle: Count of Mortain. Mill (500 eels).* Now Sheffield Park, originally Tudor and Gothicized by James Wyatt in the 18th century; grounds laid out by Capability Brown and Humphrey Repton.

Shermanbury *Salmonesberi: Ralph from William de Braose. Small church.* On the road; medieval church adjoining Shermanbury Place in parkland.

Sherrington *Esserintone/Serin-/Sirintone: Count of Eu and Walter from him; William and Heming, the pre-Conquest holder, from Count of Mortain.* Sherrington Manor House.

SHIPLEY: *Octagonal smock mill with a gallery.*

Shipley *Sepelei: William de Braose.* Many farms.

Shoreham *Sore(s)ham: William de Braose. Church.* Now the district of Old Shoreham, and Shoreham-by-the-Sea, a port. The Saxon church at Old Shoreham and New Shoreham's early Norman church were bequeathed to the abbey of Saumur.

Shovelstrode *Calvrestot/Celrestuis: Ansfrid from Count of Mortain.* Shovelstrode Manor; Shovelstrode Farm.

Sidlesham *Filleicham: Bishop of Chichester and Gilbert, Rozelin and Ulf from him.* Many glass-houses.

Singleton *Silletone: Earl Roger and Payne, Geoffrey, William and a monk of St Evroul's from him. 3 mills, church.* Wooded; church with a Saxon tower.

Slindon *Eslindone: Hugh from Earl Roger. Church.* Church with an 11th-century nave.

Somerley *Summerlege: Reginald from Earl Roger.*

Sompting *S(t)ultinges: Ralph, another Ralph and Robert from William de Braose. Church, mill, 9 salt-houses.* On the edge of seaside suburbia; Saxon church tower with Britain's only gabled pyramidal cap.

Southease *Suesse: Winchester Abbey; Church. 38,500 herrings, porpoises.* Compact; above the Ouse marshes; Saxon church.

South Heighton *Estone/Hectone: William from Count of Mortain.* Suburb of Newhaven; manor house.

South Malling *Mellinges: Archbishop of Canterbury. 5 mills (2000 eels).* Large; new housing; 11th-century walling, part of the archbishop's manor house, remains.

South Stoke *Stoches: Arnold from Earl Roger. Church.* Norman church.

Standen *Standene: Count of Mortain.* Standen House.

Stanmer *Stanmere: Canons of Malling from Archbishop of Canterbury.* Mansion.

Stedham *Stedeham: Robert from Earl Roger. Church, 3 mills, quarry.* Victorian church; sand-pit nearby.

Steyning *Staninges: Fecamp church; William de Braose. 2 churches, 5 mills, 3 salt-houses.* Littletown with a Norman church and 15th-century buildings.

Stopham *Stopeham: Robert from Earl Roger. 3 fisheries.* 16th-century manor house.

Storrington *Estorchetone/Storgetune: Robert from Earl Roger. Church, 3 mills.* Small town with a partly 11th-century church.

Stoughton *Estone: Earl Roger. Church.* Norman church dating from just after the Conquest; Neolithic long barrows and flint mines on the Downs.

Streat *Estrat: Ralph from William de Warenne. 2 small churches.* 12th-century church.

Strettington *Stratone:: William, Augustine and Arnold from Earl Roger.*

Sullington *Semlintun/Sillintone: Robert from Earl Roger; William de Braose. Mill.* Isolated.

Sutton *Sudtone: Robert from Earl Roger. 3 mills.* 11th-century church.

Tangmere *Tangemere: Archbishop of Canterbury. Church.* Old RAF station; 12th-century church with Saxon carved fragment.

Tarring Neville *Toringes: Count of Mortain.*

Thakeham *Taceham: Morin from William de Braose. Church, mill.* Partly Norman church.

Tillington *Tolintone: Robert from Earl Roger. Mill (120 eels).* Adjoining Petworth Park; Jacobean manor house.

Tilton *Telentone/Tilitone: Count of Eu, formerly Earl Harold. William of Keynes and Osbern from Count of Mortain.* Tilton Farm; cottages.

Toddington *Totintone: Robert from Earl Roger.* Built up.

Todham *Tadeham: William from Earl Roger. Mill.* Great Todham Farm.

Tortington *Tortinton: Ernucion from Earl Roger. Park.* Wooded common; remains of pre-1180 Augustinian priory.

Tottington *Totintune: William de Braose and William from him.* Cluster of houses.

Treyford *Treverde: Robert FitzTheobald from Earl Roger and Bishop of Chichester. Mill.* Scattered; late 17th-century manor house.

Trotton *Traitone: Earl Roger. Church, mill.* 13th-century church; its brasses include one of Lady Camoys (d. 1310), the earliest existing female brass.

Truleigh *Trailgi: William, a man-at-arms from William de Braose. 2 mills.* Truleigh Manor Farm.

Uckham *Bocheham: Battle Abbey.* Now Uckham Lane Gardens.

Udimore *Dodimere: Reinbert from Count of Eu. Church.* Quiet; church with a Norman nave. Edward I and Edward III stayed at Court Lodge when it belonged to the Echynghams.

Upper Beeding *Bed(d)inges: Hugh from William de Warenne; William de Braose. 2 churches.* Residential; church, c. 1300, belonging to a Benedictine priory founded by William de Braose in 1075.

Up Waltham *Waltham: Earl Roger and Arnold, Troarn Abbey and Geoffrey from him. Park.* Downland; encircled by woodland; barrows on Waltham Down.

Walberton *Walburgetone: William from Earl Roger; Roland and Acard the priest. Church, park.* Church, probably of Saxon origin, but badly restored in 1903.

Waldron *Waldere/Waldrene: Osbern from Count of Eu; Ansfrid from Count of Mortain.*

Wannock *Walnoch: William from Count of Mortain.* Housing estates.

Wantley *Wantelei: William FitzRanulf from William de Braose.* Wantley Hill Estate and Wantley Manor Farm.

Wappingthorn *Wapingetorne: William FitzMann from William de Braose. Salt.* Manor house, 1609.

Warbleton *Warborgetone: Wibert from Count of Eu.* Quiet.

Warningcamp *Garnecampo/Warnecham: Nigel from Earl Roger. 2 fisheries.* Facing Arundel across the river.

Warningore *Venningore/Waningore: Hugh from William de Warenne.* Warningore House; Warningore Farm.

Wartling *Werlinges: William from Count of Eu. 3 salt-houses.* On highish ground overlooking Pevensey Levels.

Washington *Wasingetune:* See page 273.

Wellhead *Waliland: 5 men from Count of Eu.* Part of Wellhead Wood.

Wepham *Wepeham: Picot from Earl Roger. Mill, 2 fisheries.* Adjoining Burpham. Wepham Wood nearby.

Westbourne *Borne/Burne: Earl Roger. 4 mills, fishery.* Large; former small market town on the Hampshire border.

Westburton *Westbortone:* Lost.

West Chiltington *Cilletone/tune: Robert from Earl Roger; Ralph from William de Braose. Church.* 11th-century church; pleasant cottages.

West Dean *Dene: Osbern and Ralph from Count of Mortain. 4 salt-houses.* Secluded. King Alfred had a palace here, probably on the site of the manor house, now in ruins.

Westfield *Westewelle: Wibert from Count of Eu.* Large.

West Firle *Ferla/Ferle: Count of Eu and Osbern, Walter and the monks of Treport from him; Count of Mortain and the clergy of St Pancras, Lewes, Jocelyn, William, Gilbert and the Castle Wardens from him. 3 mills.* Iron Age and Roman settlements; Neolithic long barrow.

Westhampnett *Hentone: William from Earl Roger. Mill, church.* On Roman Stane Street; 11th-century church.

West Itchenor *Icenore: Warin from Earl Roger.* Fishing; on Chichester harbour.

Westmeston *Westmestun: Robert from William de Warenne.* Middleton Manor House.

West Tarring *Terringes: Archbishop of Canterbury; William de Braose. 2 churches.* Part of Worthing; some old buildings. Thomas à Becket is said to have introduced the fig into his garden here.

West Thorney *Tornei: Mauger from Bishop Osbern of Exeter.* On an island in Chichester Harbour.

Whatlington *Watlingetone: Reinbert from Count of Eu, formerly Earl Harold.*

Whalesbeach *Waslebie:* Lost.

Wickham *Wicham: William de Watteville's wife from William de Warenne and Alwin from her.* Now Hurst Wickham, a built-up adjunct of Hurstpierpoint.

Willingdon *Wilendone/Wille(n)done: Count of Eu and Reinbert, Osbern FitzGeoffrey, and Hugh from him; Count of Mortain and Osbern, William, Jocelyn, Gilbert, Alwin, Ansgot, Godfrey the priest and Ansfrid from him. 11 salt-houses.* Suburb of Eastbourne.

Wilmington *Wilminte/Wineltone: Abbots of Battle and Grestain from Count of Mortain.* Long barrows and flint mines nearby.

Wilting *Wiltingham/Witinges: Ingelrann from Count of Eu; the Abbot of Battle from Ingelrann. Park.* Lower and Upper Wilting Farms.

Winterbourne *Wintreburne: Aldith from William de Warenne* Lost in Kingston village.

Winton *Wigentone: Reinbert from Count of Eu.*

Wiston *Wistanestun: Ralph from William de Braose. Church.* Under the Downs; 11th-century church.

Wittering *Westringes: Bishop of Chichester and Ralph and Herbert from him; Robert from Earl Roger and Ralph from him. Mill.* Now East Wittering, a coastal resort with bungalows and holiday chalets, and West Wittering village with an 11th-century church.

Woodmancote *Odemanscote: William FitzRanulf from William de Braose. Church.* Church, largely rebuilt in 1868.

Woolbeding *Welbedlinge: Odo of Winchester from the king. Mill, church.* Pretty; on the River Rother; Saxon church.

Woolfly *Ovelie: Ralph from William de Braose.* Woolfly Wood.

Wootton (in East Chiltington) *Odetone/Odintune: Archbishop of Canterbury; Nigel from William de Warenne. Mill.* Wootton Farm, probably the ancient manor house.

Wootton (in Folkington) *Lodintone/Lodiutone: Count of Mortain. Mill, 5 salt-houses.* Wootton Manor, a Jacobean house.

Worth (near Little Horsted) *Gorde: Ralph from Count of Mortain. Mill.* Worth Farm.

Worthing *Mordinges/Ordinges: Robert and Ralph from William de Braose.* Seaside resort, a fishing hamlet until the 19th century.

Yeverington *Lovringetone: William de Keynes from Count of Mortain.* Housing estates; near Eastbourne.

WILMINGTON: *Chalk romano-British figure, The Long Man.*

Warwickshire

Warwickshire in 1086 consisted of two quite dissimilar sections: Arden (in the north and west), with isolated farms and hamlets, and settlers still moving into the forest; and Feldon (in the south and east), with compact villages supported by extensive cultivation on open lands from which dense oak woods had been cleared.

The holdings of Thorkell of Warwick, and of Robert Beaumont, Count of Meulan, comprised three-quarters of the non-ecclesiastical property. Thorkell, son of Alwin, the sheriff under Edward the Confessor, was one of the only two Englishmen in the county still holding a baronial estate from the king after the Conquest; his descendants perpetuate the name of Arden today.

Robert Beaumont, having distinguished himself at the Battle of Senlac, was rewarded on William's march into the Midlands in 1068 with vast estates. He later became Earl of Leicester, and, by a ruse, acquired land in Leicestershire as well. He survived every shift of power and died in 1118, one of the last of the Conquest generation. His brother Henry was invested with all the Thorkell lands when he became the first Earl of Warwick, a title which descended by marriage first to the Beauchamps and then to the Nevilles.

BRAILES: *The tower of the church of St George rises far above the rich countryside; the 13th c. church was restored in the 19th c.*

Brailes

[The King holds] BRAILES *BRAILES*. Earl Edwin held it. 46 hides. Land for 60 ploughs. In lordship 6; 12 male and 3 female slaves; 100 villagers and 30 smallholders with 46 ploughs. A mill at 10s; meadow, 100 acres; woodland 3 leagues long and 2 leagues wide. Before 1066 it paid £17 10s; value now £55 and 20 packloads of salt.

With land for 60 ploughs, Brailes, called the capital of Feldon, 700 feet up on the Cotswold scarp, was the largest holding in Warwickshire; Tysoe, Long Compton and Ettington were its nearest rivals. Its working population of 130 households must have enabled the manor to keep many thousands – perhaps 5000 – acres under cultivation.

The castle earthworks, now barely discernible, recall the battle to seize it for King William from Earl Edwin of Mercia; this probably took place between the Conquest and *Domesday*. From the king it passed to Henry Beaumont, Earl of Warwick, and on to his successors, first the Beauchamps, then the Nevilles. Twice the size of any other manor in the Earl of Warwick's estates, Brailes was valued in 1315 at only a few shillings less than the manor of Warwick and its magnificent castle combined.

The community suffered a steep decline starting in the fifteenth century, when sheep began, in Thomas More's phrase, to eat up men. From 1485 onwards enclosure was conducted relentlessly until all the arable land was gone; hedges and ditches partitioned the ground, messuages were turned into cottages and there was wholesale depopulation. In 1630, the rapidly rising Sheldon family (from Weston Park in Long Compton) acquired Brailes, except for Tanworth-in-Arden, which went to the Throckmortons of Coughton. The day of the baronial magnates was over; the Earl of Warwick had possessed 27 manors in Worcestershire and Warwickshire during the reign of Henry VI (1422–61); by the end of the fifteenth century he had none.

The Sheldons acquired their wealth chiefly through judicious purchase at the Dissolution – in particular at Studley Priory and at Pershore Abbey. They were Protestants, but Ralph Sheldon (1537–1613) married a member of the fiery Catholic Throckmorton family and became a convert. He and his descendants suffered both from reverting to the Old Faith and from loyalty to Charles I. Their devotion did not falter, however, and they returned to the Church of England only in the nineteenth century.

The last of the family, Henry James Sheldon who claimed to be seventeenth in direct descent from Edward III, died at Brailes House in 1901. He is buried in the huge church, known as the cathedral of Feldon, which is out of all proportion to the size of the present settlement. The fourth bell, recast in 1688, has an apposite inscription:

Ime not the bell I was, but quite another.
Ime now as rite as Merry George, my brother.

It might speak for Brailes today: no match for its mighty predecessor.

Bidford on Avon

[The King holds] BIDFORD (-ON-AVON) *BEDEFORD*. King Edward held it. 5 hides. Land for . . . In lordship 5 ploughs; 8 male and 5 female slaves; 28 villagers and 13 smallholders with 16 ploughs. 4 mills at 43s 4d; meadow, 150 acres; woodland 4 leagues long and 1 league wide.

With its fifteenth-century bridge crowded with trippers and with the famous Falcon Inn converted into flats and up for sale, Bidford is like some beached galleon. Cars meander along the High Street (it is the Evesham–Stratford road) where modern structures of fierce red brick and plate glass crowd out the old timber-frame houses. The church upsets the chiselled symmetry of the new buildings with a tower of surprising narrowness and a nave of unusual width.

King Edward held Bidford, thus making it 'ancient demesne', which meant for its inhabitants a number of privileges, including protection from any attempt by a new lord to exact increased services. This *Domesday* statement won a court case for Bidford in 1567, when it was confirmed that the manor was still entitled to freedom from toll throughout the kingdom; exemption from jury service, and from contributing to the expenses of knights of the shire. The town enjoyed something of the status of a borough and was governed in the seventeenth century by the bailiffs, one of whom signed himself 'His Maieste's Bailiffe of the Burrow of Bidford'. A gilt-brass bailiff's mace engraved with the Tudor royal arms is preserved in the church.

Bidford's history became distinctly secular from the moment the land-grasping and worldly Odo of Bayeux seized the Evesham Abbey lands there

For a short time Robert Burnell (Bishop of Bath and Wells in Edward I's reign) regained Bidford and its manors, but the church went down to final defeat at the Dissolution, when the abbot was refused permission to go on living in Bidford Grange.

The town has been nicknamed 'Drunken Bidford' and no one knows why or when. It was infamous in the nineteenth century for the drinking bouts of German huntsmen at the Falcon Inn, but the tag is much older than that, perhaps dating as far back as the days when William Shakespeare is said to have been a Falcon habitué. The association is commemorated at the poet's Birthplace Museum in Stratford-upon-Avon which houses both the Inn's furniture and its old sign.

Domesday records four mills at Bidford. The one at the Grange was carried off in the great Avon flood of 1588, but a later paper mill remained standing here until the nineteenth century. Nearby on the River Arrow the corn mill at Great Alne is working again.

Coughton

William holds 4 hides in COUGHTON *COCTUNE* [from Thorkell of Warwick]. Land for 6 ploughs. 2 free men, 7 smallholders and 4 slaves with 3 ploughs. A mill at 32d; in Warwick 1 house which pays 8d; meadow, 10 acres; woodland 6 furlongs long and 4 furlongs wide; pastureland, 50 pigs. The value was 40s; later 20s; now 50s. Untan held it freely.

Most of Coughton lies on the west side of the busy Alcester–Birmingham road, part of the Roman Ryknild Street, as it strikes south to cross the Avon at Bidford. To the east, Warwick Lane drops down to a ford over the Arrow; to the west, the land climbs to the Ridgeway, the border between Warwickshire and Worcestershire. Coughton Park, a nearby woodland, still has trees surviving from the ancient Forest of Feckenham. Medieval travellers successfully emerging from the forest wilderness are said to have offered prayers on their deliverance at the cross near the entrance to the manor house, Coughton Court. The Court today comprises a massive gatehouse (Gothicized in the 1830s) dominating elegantly remodelled wings (1780s) with elongated ogee windows.

William Bonvallet, who held Coughton from Thorkell, with under-tenants in neighbouring Spernall and Studley, also had a house in Warwick. Eleven other manors in Warwickshire held houses in Warwick and therefore had responsibilities for its defence. Its first castle had been built by King Alfred's daughter in 914; this gave way in 1068 to a motte and bailey which William the Conqueror threw up, destroying four houses to do so.

After 1086 Coughton's connection with Warwick became even closer when Henry of Newburgh, constable of William's castle, acquired it along with Thorkell's other Warwickshire holdings.

The Throckmorton family, originally of Worcestershire, owned the manor from 1472, and might have been justifiably famous because a member of the Northamptonshire branch, Sir Nicholas (1515–71) was Elizabeth I's ambassador to France. But instead they became notorious for their fanatical Catholicism in the face of persecution.

In 1584 Francis Throckmorton was hanged at

Tyburn. His cousins Muriel and Anne were the mothers, respectively, of Francis Tresham and Robert Catesby, the Gunpowder conspirators. Francis died before the hangman could get him, and Robert was blown to bits in the last-ditch stand at Holbeach House in Staffordshire. Their uncle, Sir Thomas Throckmorton, was spared because he was travelling abroad. He had let the Coughton gatehouse to Sir Everard Digby, where Lady Digby and the Throckmorton sisters are believed to have waited for news from London. Ironically, it was Tresham who wrecked the enterprise by warning his cousin Lord Monteagle to keep out of the Parliament house that fateful day.

A siege, much damage in the Civil War and a fearsome riot in 1688 when a Protestant mob from Alcester set fire to the house, gave Coughton little peace in the succeeding decades. Now, with the moat filled in and the Long Hall transformed into National Trust tearooms, tranquillity has returned.

HAMPTON IN ARDEN: *The packhorse bridge; low parapets meant the packs would clear them on either side of the animal; modern rails have been added for safety.*

Hampton-in-Arden

[Geoffrey de La Guerche holds] HAMPTON (-IN-ARDEN), *HANTONE.* 10 hides. Land for 22 ploughs. In lordship 2; 2 male and 2 female slaves. 50 villagers with a priest and 16 smallholders have 13 ploughs. A mill at 40d; meadow, 10 acres; woodland 3 leagues long and 3 wide. The value was and is 100s.

'Ay now am I in Arden; the more fool I; when I was at home, I was in a better place: but travellers must be content.' Touchstone, *As You Like It*.

Hampton-in-Arden retains a certain rural ambience despite being sandwiched between the conurbations of Birmingham and Coventry, bisected by the railway carrying the Inter-City to London and less than two miles from the runways of Elmdon Airport. Were it not for the busy road from Solihull to Meriden – literally the heart of England – which swings round the church at a dangerous angle, the village would be tranquil. Its houses are a polyglot of styles, with here and there a glimpse of sixteenth-century timber or classic Georgian lines. Hampton's character, however, comes not from its architecture, but from the way it straggles down a hillside, sloping eastward to the River Blythe.

Geoffrey de La Guerche, a follower of the Duke of Brittany, scooped up Hampton together with a dozen other Warwickshire manors from its Saxon owners, and taxed all the Hampton lands for the benefit of his monastery of St Nicholas at Angers. *Domesday* makes no mention of Balsall or Knowle, both part of Hampton until the nineteenth century and important in its history.

For an entry in the Forest of Arden a woodland reference is predictable; the loam derived from the local rock supports considerable amounts of wood. The settlement probably spread up the Blythe basin from the north, which was less populated than the south of the country. The *Domesday* verdict that there was more land that could be ploughed perhaps took too little account of how poorly drained this river basin is; cattle would always do better.

Arden was the high ground of Warwickshire, reaching south as far as Henley. Hampton is an appropriate name for a place on a hill; in Old English it is Hean Tun, which means 'high tun'. A defensible site, it was once part of Coventry's vital salt route. Until its church steeple was struck by lightning in 1643 it was 'a noted mark to a great part of the woodland'.

The River Blythe, which surrounds Hampton on three sides, was at times a serious obstacle to travellers. The King's Commissioners who wanted to rifle the chapel at Knowle in 1547 stated that the people could not reach their 'poche churche' – at Hampton – because of 'the greate and dangerowse water wch in winter at every Raine so Rageth and overfloweth all the Cuntry thereabout that neyther man nor beaste can pass without ymmynent daunger of perysh-ing'. To the east of the village, too, accidents were frequent during crossings of the ford at Bradnock's Marsh. Salters' Lane leads into the village from the west, the route taken by the salt carriers on their way from Droitwich to Coventry. The elegant little packhorse bridge, with five bays, still presents its wedge-shaped feet to the treacherous River Blythe.

The lordship of the manor of Hampton was frequently held either *in absentia* or by the Crown. It was part of the dowry of Queen Henrietta Maria. Roger Mowbray, the son of Geoffrey de La Guerche's successor, granted Balsall, south of Hampton village, to the Knights Templar, which meant that for 350 years – until the Dissolution – the land in the loop of the Blythe was carefully regulated and some impressive buildings were put up. Perhaps prompted by these, Lady Katherine Leveson, a grand-daughter of Robert Dudley, Earl of Leicester (to whom Balsall came via the attainted Lord Protector Somerset), founded a hospital here for poor women in 1678. Their graves, with small Celtic crosses, are set in rows beneath the cedars of the chapel. Until quite recently the pensioners wore grey gowns embroidered with 'K.L.'

Sir Hugh Arden – the old Turchill family of Warwick took the name of Arden – secured a weekly market and an annual fair for Hampton in 1250, which seems never to have been seriously disrupted. This area of North Arden weathered the agrarian difficulties of the early modern period better than most; there were no depopulating enclosures and although the radical Diggers ploughed up Hampton Field in 1607, there was nothing to indicate any malaise in Hampton itself.

Prime Minister Sir Robert Peel bought the lordship of Hampton for his second son Frederick, who made his home here from 1852 until his death in 1906. A successful lawyer who held office under both Lord John Russell and Lord Palmerston, he was not content to have his architect, W. Eden Nesfield merely build him a new manor house; he must also rebuild the church and much of the village. Tudoresque in style, his manor is rather dull except for a spectacular clock tower surmounted by a pyramid and the signs of the Zodiac. In the village he brought half-timbered cottages tumbling down to be replaced by houses of contrived rusticity. John Hannett in his travels in the Forest of Arden (1863) was well pleased with the result: 'Although so close upon large seats of manufacturing industry Hampton's peculiarly rustic features have been preserved almost intact.' To the modern eye the rusticity is distinctly artificial.

Frederick Peel was conscious of his own importance and it is said that he refused to allow anyone to precede him on the pathways leading to his house. He wanted the trains to stop at his village, and being a railway commissioner, he made sure that they did. It is from his station that today's commuter departs in order to arrive in Birmingham in ten minutes.

Successive restrictions on development, culminating in the Conservation Order of 1969, have ensured that Hampton-in-Arden remains a dormitory village. It retains some of its past, however; the church still rises above the trees, and there are working farms nearby. It recorded a priest in *Domesday*, relatively unusual in these parts – a reminder that the Anglo-Saxon church was not entirely swept away in the Norman revolution.

Warwickshire Gazetteer
Each entry starts with the modern place name in **bold** type. The *Domesday* information that follows is in *italic* type, beginning with the name or names by which the place was known in 1086. The main landholders and under-tenants are next, separated with semi-colons if a place was divided into more than one holding. A number of holdings were granted by the king to his thanes; these normally come at the end of the list of landholders and are described as holding land 'from the king'. More general information completes the *Domesday* part of the entry, including examples of dues such as eels rendered by tenants. The modern or post-Domesday section is in normal type. represents a village, a small village or hamlet.

Abbots Salford *Salford: Evesham Abbey. Mill (20 sticks of eels).*

Admington *Edelmintone: Winchcombe Abbey.* Admington Hall.

Ailstone *Alnodestone: Nicholas the Gunner.*

Alderminster *Sture: St Mary's of Pershore. 2 mills.* Tithe Farm.

Alspath *Ailespede: Countess Godiva.*

Alveston *Alvestone: Bishop of Worcester. 3 mills (1012 sticks of eels).*

Amington *Ermendone: Robert from William FitzCorbucion.* Amington Hall.

Arley *Arlei: Christina.* Formerly mining; Arley Hall.

Arrow *Arue: Stephen from Bishop of Bayeux. Mill.* Arrow mill was grinding corn until the 1960s; now a restaurant.

Ashow *Asceshot: Ermenfrid from Thorkell of Warwick, the pre-Conquest holder. 2 mills.* On the River Avon.

Astley *Estein: Godric from Count of Meulan.* Anstey Castle, the seat of Lady Jane Gray's family.

Aston (in Birmingham) *Estone: Godmund from William FitzAnsculf. 2 mills.* Part of Birmingham. Charles I was entertained at Aston Hall before the Battle of Edge Hill.

Aston Cantlow *Estone: Osbern FitzRichard.* Aston Hall; Aston Lodge.

Atherstone *Aderestone: Nicholas from Countess Godiva. 10 sticks of eels.* Market town on the Roman Watling Street, Atherstone Hall.

Atherstone on Stour *Edricestone: Corbin from Bishop of Bayeux. Mill.*

Austrey *Aldulvestren: Burton Abbey; Nigel from Henry de Ferrers; Nigel d'Aubigny.* Austrey House.

Avon Dassett *Derceto: Count of Meulan.*

Baddesley Ensor *Bedeslei: William from Thorkell of Warwick.* Thomas

ANSLEY: *Norman carving on the chancel arch of St. Lawrence church.*

Ansley *Hanslei: Nicholas from Countess Godiva.* The family of Captain Mark Phillips, husband of Princess Anne, originally came from this mining district.

Ansty *Anestie: Nicholas from Countess Godiva.* Ansty Hall built in the 17th century for Richard Taylor, a Roundhead leader.

Ardens Grafton *Graston: Leofric and Aelfeva, the pre-Conquest holders, from William FitzCorbucion.*

Arlescote *Orlavescote: St Peter's of Preaux from Count of Meulan.* Below Iron Age Nadbury Camp. Charles I's sons lodged at Arlescote Manor House with their tutor William Harvey, who discovered the circulation of the blood. Harvey became warden of Merton College, Oxford, 1645.

d'Ednesoure gave the ground for the original Norman church.

Baginton *Badechintone: Alwin from Thorkell of Warwick. Mill.* Once a Bronze Age and Roman settlement; military buildings, 3 granaries and a gateway were discovered at The Lunt.

Barcheston *Berricestone/tune: Johais from William FitzCorbucion; Aelfric from the king. Mill.* Richard Hicks established his famous manufacture of arras fabric here in the 16th century.

Barford *Bereford(e): William FitzCorbucion Hugh from Osbern FitzRichard. Mill.*

Barnacle *Bernhangre: Hereward, the pre-Conquest holder, from Count of Meulan.* The original hall was burnt down by Parliamentary troops during the Civil War.

CHARLECOTE: *The gatehouse, 1558; the house was re-built later.*

Barston *Bercestone/ Bertanestone: Robert d'Oilly from Thorkell of Warwick; Robert the Bursar; Robert from the king. Mill.*

Bartley Green *Berchelai: Wibert from William FitzAnsculf.* District of Birmingham.

Barton on the Heath *Bertone: Grim from Robert of Stafford.* Barton House 4 Shire Stone nearby marks the meeting point between Warwickshire, Gloucestershire, Oxfordshire and Worcestershire.

Bearley *Burlei: Alric, the pre-Conquest holder, from Robert of Stafford; William FitzCorbucion.* Charles II avoided a troop of horse near Bearley Cross when fleeing after the Battle of Worcester.

Beausale *Beoshalle: Wadard from Bishop of Bayeux.* Beausale House.

Bedworth *Bedeword: Ulfketel from Count of Meulan.* Mining town. Fleeing French Protestants sought refuge here and set up looms to weave silk ribbons.

Bentley *Benechelie: Ansgot the priest from Geoffrey de La Guerche.*

Bericote *Bericote: Tonni from Thorkell of Warwick. Mill.*

Berkswell *Berchewelle: Count of Meulan and Walter from him.* Name derives from the Anglo-Saxon Bercol, who owned a well in the Forest of Arden, where Lichfield monks baptized the king of the Mercians.

Bevington *Buintun: Evesham Abbey.*

Bickenhill *Bichehelle: Thorkell of Warwick.*

Bidford on Avon *Bedeford:* See page 280.

Biggin *Holme: Wulfric, the pre-Conquest holder; Ralph from Thorkell of Warwick.* Now Biggin Mills, previously Holme.

Billesley *Billeslei: Osbern from Hugh de Grandmesnil.*

Bilton *Beltone/Bentone: William from Earl Roger; Gilbert from Thorkell of Warwick.* Bilton Manor House; Bilton Hall.

Binley *Bilnei/Bilueie: Coventry Abbey; formerly Aldith wife of Gruffydd; Adolf, the pre-Conquest holder, from Thorkell of Warwick. Mill.*

Binton *Beninton(e)/Benitone: William from William FitzCorbucion; Gerin; Urso d'Abetot; Hugh from Osbern FitzRichard. 3½ mills (4 packloads of corn, 8 sticks of eels).* Scott of the Antarctic married the rector's daughter in 1908.

Birdingbury *Berdingeberie/ Derbingerie: Coventry Abbey; Jocelyn from Thorkell of Warwick.*

Birmingham *Bermingeham: Richard from William FitzAnsculf.* City. Its Bull Ring Centre, on the site of the original village green, used for tethering cattle.

Bishop's Itchington *Icetone: Coventry Abbey.*

Bishops Tachbrook *Taschebroc: Bishop of Chester. 2 mills.*

Blackwell *Blachewelle: Worcester Church.*

Bourton on Dunsmore *Bortone: Ingenwulf from Count of Meulan.*

Brailes *Brailes:* See page 280.

Bramcote *Brancote: Earl Aubrey; Robert Hunter from Robert of Stafford; Richard the Forester from the king.*

Brandon *Brandune: Wulfsi from Thorkell of Warwick, the pre-Conquest holder. Mill.* Brandon Hall, formerly the Salisbury family seat.

Broom *Brome: Stephen from Bishop of Bayeux.*

Brownsover *Gaura: Brown from Geoffrey de La Guerche.* A few houses on the outskirts of Rugby.

Bubbenhall *Bubenhalle: Aelfric, the pre-Conquest holder, from Robert of Stafford. Mill.*

Budbrooke *Budebroc: Ralph de Limesy. Mill.*

Bulkington *Bochintone: Salo from Count of Meulan.* Richard Hayward, the sculptor who created North America's oldest public statue, was born here in 1789.

Burmington *Burdintone: Robert of Stafford. Mill.*

Burton Dassett *Dercetone: Harold son of Earl Ralph.*

Burton Hastings *Bortone: Ralph from Henry de Ferrers. 2 mills.*

Butlers Marston *Mersetone: Hugh de Grandmesnil. 2 mills.* Butlers Marston House.

Calcutt *Caldecote: Ermenfrid, Richard and Ordwic, the pre-Conquest holder, from Thorkell of Warwick.*

Caldecote *Caldecote: Bishop of Chester. Mill.* Caldecote Hall.

Cawston *Calvestone: Aelmer and Ulf from Thorkell of Warwick.* Cawston Grange Farm; Cawston Old Farm.

Cestersover *Wara: Robert from Geoffrey de La Guerche. Mill.* Some houses.

Chadshunt *Cedelehunte: Coventry Abbey.*

Charlecote *Cerlecote: Count of Meulan. 2 mills.* Charlecote Park, seat of the Lucy family. Shallow in *Merry Wives of Windsor* is a portrait of Sir Thomas Lucy.

Chesterton *Cestedone/ Cestreton(e): Coventry Abbey; Abingdon from Thorkell of Warwick; Wazelin from Henry de Ferrers; Richard Hunter from the king.* Remains of a Roman camp.

Chilvers Coton *Celverdestoche: Harold son of Earl Ralph.* District of Nuneaton. George Eliot, as Mary Ann Evans, lived at Griff House from 1820–41.

Church Lawford *Leileforde: Reginald from Earl Roger. Mill.* The River Avon crosses the Roman Fosse Way here.

Churchover *Wara/Wavre: Robert from the king. Mill.*

Claverdon *Clavendone: Count of Meulan.* Claverdon Hall; Cloverdown, home of Sir Francis Galton, founder of eugenics.

Clifford Chambers *Clifort: King's land. Mill.* Clifford Chambers Mill, occupied by Tibor Reich, fabric manufacturers.

Clifton upon Dunsmore *Cliptone: Coventry Abbey before and after 1066; Earl Aubrey. 2 mills.* Clifton Court.

Clopton (in Quinton) *Cloptune: King's land; William Goizenboded.*

Clopton (in Stratford-upon-Avon) *Clotone: William from Robert of Stafford.*

Coleshill *Coleshelle: King's land. Mill.* Market town.

Compton Scorpion *Parva Contone: Alwin from Robert of Stafford.*

Compton Verney *Contone: Count of Meulan; Alwin from Thorkell of Warwick.*

Corley *Cornelie: Godwin, the pre-Conquest holder, from the king.* Corley Ash and Corley Moor hamlets; prehistoric fort above Corley Rocks. Corley Hall Farm is described by George Eliot in *Adam Bede* (1859) as the Poysers' farmhouse.

Coten *Cotes: King's land. 2 mills.* Coten End, a suburb of Warwick.

Coughton *Coctune:* See page 280.

Coundon *Condelme/Condone: Coventry Abbey; Roger from William FitzCorbucion.* Coundon Court; Coundon Hall; Coundon House.

Coventry *Coventreu: Nicholas from Countess Godiva. Mill.* Industrial city with a modern cathedral (1954–62) beside the ruins of its medieval predecessor. A Saxon nunnery was destroyed by Canute and converted into a Benedictine Priory by Leofric, Earl of Chester, and Countess Godiva.

Cubbington *Cobintone/Cubi(n)tone: Coventry Abbey; Bosker from Count of Meulan; Roger d'Ivry.*

Curdworth *Credeworde: Thorkell of Warwick.* Named after Crida, 1st King of the Mercians (583); said to be the oldest English settlement in the Midlands and the exact centre of England.

Dorsington *Dorsitone/Dorsintune: Stephen; Robert from Roger de Beaumont.*

Dosthill *Dercelai: Robert d'Oilly from Thorkell of Warwick. Mill.* Dosthill House.

Dunchurch *Donecerce: William from Osbern FitzRichard.* Guy Fawkes House, formerly the Lion Inn, where the Gunpowder Plot conspirators met.

Edgbaston *Celboldestone: Drogo from William FitzAnsculf.* District of Birmingham; famous for its cricket ground.

Edstone *Edricestone: Robert of Stafford.* Edstone Hall.

Elmdon *Elmedone: Roger from Thorkell of Warwick.* Near Birmingham's commercial airport.

COLESHILL: *Norman font, 1150, carved with the Evangelists and a cruxifiction scene.*

Erdington *Hardintone: Peter from William FitzAnsculf. Mill.* Area in Birmingham.

Ettington *Ete(n)done: Ermenfrid from Thorkell of Warwick; Robert from Hugh de Grandmesnil; Saswalo from Henry de Ferrers; Ordric from the king. Mill.* Now 2 hamlets, Lower and Upper Ettington. Ettington Park is the most impressive High Victorian house in the country.

Exhall (near Alcester) *Ecleshelle: Thorkell from William FitzCorbucion.* By the Icknield Way.

Farnborough *Ferneberge: Bishop of Chester.*

Fenny Compton *Contone: Gilbert from Count of Meulan; Aelmer and Roger from Thorkell of Warwick.*

Fillongley *Fel-/Filingelei/Filungelei/Filunger: Bishop of Coutances; Coventry Abbey; Robert the Bursar; Alfsi, the pre-Conquest holder, from the king.* Ruins and moats of 2 castles, allegedly demolished by Cromwell.

Flecknoe *Flechenho/Flechenoc: Leofwin from Bishop of Worcester; Oslac and Alric from Thorkell of Warwick; Leofwin from the king.*

Foleshill *Focheshelle: Nicholas from Countess Godiva.* Part of Coventry.

Frankton *Franchetone: Earl Roger; Ranulf from Count of Meulan.* Henry Holyrake, 1st memorable headmaster of Rugby School, was rector here from 1712.

Fulbrook *Fulebroc: Count of Meulan. Mill.*

Ful(l)ready *Fulrei: Ermenfrid from Thorkell of Warwick.*

Grandborough *Graneberge/Greneberge: Coventry Abbey; Richard the Forester from the king. Mill.*

Great Alne *Alne: Winchcombe Abbey. Mill.* Great Alne Hall.

Grendon *Grendone: Thurstan from Henry de Ferrers. Mill.* Grendon Hall; Croft House, built in 1781 above the old mill race.

Hampton in Arden *Hantone:* See page 281.

Hampton Lucy *Hantone: Bishop of Worcester. Mill.*

Handsworth *Honesworde: Drogo from William FitzAansculf. Mill.* Matthew Boulton and James Watts set up the 1st steam engine in the Midlands here.

Harborne *Horeborne: Robert from Bishop of Chester.* District of Birmingham.

Harborough *Herdeberge: Richard the Forester and Ansegis from the king. Mill.*

Harbury *Erdburberie/Erbur(ge)berie: Coventry Abbey; Count of Meulan; William from Thorkell of Warwick; Wazelin from Henry de Ferrers; William Bonvallet.*

Hartshill *Ardreshille: Nicholas from Countess Godiva.* Stone quaries including the Blue Hole; birthplace of the poet Michael Drayton (1563–1631).

Haseley *Haseleia: Humphrey from Hascoit Musard. Mill.* Haseley Hall; Haseley Manor.

Haselor *Haseloue: Nicholas the Gunner. Mill, salt-house.* Late Georgian watermill.

Hatton *Altone: Nigel d'Aubigny.*

Hill *Hille: Warin from Abingdon Abbey.*

Hillborough *Hildebereurde/Hildeborde: Urso d'Abetot; Hugh from Osbern FitzRichard. Mill, salt-house.* Ghosts, including that of Shakespeare's White Lady, Anne Whateley, are reputed to haunt Hillborough Manor.

Hillmorton *Mortone: Waltheof and Merwin from Count of Meulan; Hugh de Grandmesnil; Richard the Forester from the king.* James Petiver, 16th to 17th-century botanist and entomologist, lived here.

Hodnell *Hoden(h)elle: Gilbert from Count of Meulan; Harding and Godwin from Thorkell of Warwick; Roger from William FitzCorbucion.*

Honington *Hunitone: Coventry Abbey. 4 mills.* Honington Hall.

Hopsford *Apleford: Wulfric from Geoffrey de La Guerche.* Hopsford Hall.

Hunningham *Huningeham: Osmund and Ketel from William FitzCorbucion.*

Idlicote *Etelincote: Robert of Stafford.* Idlicote House.

Ilmington *Edelmitone/Ilmedone: Count of Meulan and Odard from him; Alric, the pre-Conquest holder, from Robert of Stafford.*

Kenilworth *Chinewrde: Richard the Forester from the king.* Market town with the ruins of 12th-century Kenilworth Castle.

Kineton *Quintone: King's land.* Market town. Charles I met his bride, Henrietta Maria, here.

Kineton Green *Cintone: Aelmer from William FitzCorbucion.*

Kingsbury *Chinesberie: Nicholas from Countess Godiva.* Said to be the site of the palace of the kings of Mercia. Kingsbury Mill made guns for the Napoleonic wars.

King's Norton *Nortune: King's land.* Area in Birmingham; early 15th-century Old Grammar School, originally a priest's house.

Kington *Cintone: Count of Meulan.*

Kinwarton *Chenevertone: Ranulf from Evesham Abbey. Mill.*

Ladbroke *Lodbroc(h): William from Count of Meulan; Ermenfrid, Aelmer, William, a priest, and Gilbert from Thorkell of Warwick; William from Hugh de Grandmesnil. Mill.*

KENILWORTH: *Begun in 1122, owned by Henry II, enriched for Elizabeth I's visits; the castle is an impressive ruin.*

Langley *Longelei: Ludichael from Robert of Stafford.*

Lapworth *Lapeforde: Hugh de Grandmesnil.*

Lark Stoke *Stoche: St Mary's of Evesham.*

Lea Green *Lea:* Lost.

Lea Marston *Leth Merstone: Robert d'Oilly and Robert Hunter from Thorkell of Warwick; Robert the Bursar. Mill.* Home of Lord Norton (1814–1905), who pioneered selfgovernment for territories in the British Empire.

Leamington Hastings *Lunnitone: Hascoit Musard. Mill.* Attractive; by the River Leam.

Leamington Spa *Lamistone: Earl Roger. 2 mills.* Town, a fashionable Regency spa. Napoleon III lived here after the collapse of the 2nd Empire in 1871.

Lighthorne *Listecorne: William Bonvallet.*

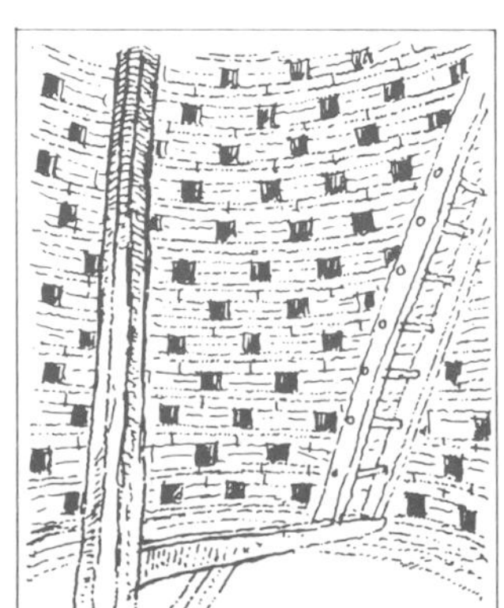

KINWARTON: *Revolving inspection ladder in a circular 14th c. dovecote.*

Lillington *Ulintone/Lillintone: Warin and Roger from Count of Meulan; Robert d'Oilly from Thorkell of Warwick. Mill.*

Lindsworth *Lindeorde: King's land.* Lindsworth Road and Approach, in King's Norton.

Little Compton *Contone: Warin from Robert of Stafford; St Denis' Church of Paris.* In a valley it was once known as 'Compton in the flowers'.

Little Lawford *Lilleford: Leofeva from Thorkell of Warwick. Mill.*

Long Compton *Cuntone: Geoffrey de Mandeville. Mill.* Rollright Stones and King Stone nearby.

Longdon (in Solihull) *Langedone: Aelmer from Thorkell of Warwick.*

Longdon (in Tredington) *Longedun: Gilbert FitzThorold from Worcester Church.* Longdon Manor.

Long Itchington *Icentone: Christina. 2 mills.* Birthplace of St Wulfstan, Bishop of Worcester (c.1012–95). Dudley, Earl of Leicester, entertained Elizabeth I here.

Long Lawford *Lelleford: Geoffrey de La Guerche. Mill.*

Long Marston *Merestone: St Mary's, Coventry.*

Loxley *Lochesham/Locheslei: Bishop of Worcester; Hugh from Count of Meulan; Hugh FitzConstantine from Hugh de Grandmesnil.* Loxley Hall. The church stands on one of the country's oldest foundations: a site given by Offa, King of Mercia, to the Cathedral Church of Worcester in 760.

Luddington *Luditone: 4 men-at-arms from Count of Meulan.* Shakespeare allegedly married Anne Hathaway here, in the chapel (replaced in the 19th century).

Mackadown *Machitone: Alnoth from Thorkell of Warwick.*

Map(p)eborough *Mapelberg: Geoffrey from William FitzCorbucion.* Mapleborough Green.

Marston Green *Merstone: Roger from Thorkell of Warwick.*

Marston Jabbett *Merstone: Hereward, the pre-Conquest holder, from Count of Meulan.*

Meon *Mene: King's land.* Meon Hill; ancient camp.

Middle Bickenhill *Alia Bichehelle: Thorkell of Warwick.*

Middleton *Mideltone/ Mildentone: Hugh de Grandmesnil and Adelaide his wife. Mill.* Middleton Hall.

Milcote *Melecote: Stephen.*

Milverton *Malvertone: Count of Meulan. Mill.* Now 2 villages, New and Old Milverton.

Minworth *Meneworde: Thorkell of Warwick.* Area near Sutton Coldfield.

Monks Kirby *Chircheberie: Geoffrey de La Guerche.*

Moreton Morrell *Mortone: Count of Meulan.* Former home of the Randolph family; Jane was the mother of Thomas Jefferson, 3rd President of USA.

Morton Bagot *Mortone: Hugh from Robert of Stafford.*

Moseley *Museleie: King's land.*

Myton *Moi/Muitone: Count of Meulan; Count of Meulan, St Mary's Church and Algar from Thorkell of Warwick.*

Napton on the Hill *Eptone/Neptone: Robert from Count of Meulan; Robert and Ulfketel, the pre-Conquest holder, from Thorkell of Warwick.*

Nether Whitacre *Witecore: Robert de Vessey; Edwin from Thorkell of Warwick.* Whitacre House.

Newbold Comyn *Niwebold: Malmesbury Abbey before and after 1066; Gilbert from Count of Meulan. Mill.*

Newbold on Avon *Newebold: Geoffrey de La Guerche.* Newbold Grange; Newbold House.

Newbold Pacey *Niwebold: Humphrey from Hascoit Musard.* Newbold Pacey Hall.

Newbold Revel *Feniniwebold: Geoffrey de La Guerche.* Home Office building, once a country house.

Newnham (in Aston Cantlow) *Neweham: Coventry Abbey.*

Newnham Paddox *Niweham: Ansegis from Geoffrey de La Guerche. Mill.* Home of Earl of Denbigh.

Newton (near Rugby) *Niwetone: Godric, Aldith and Ralph from Thorkell of Warwick.*

Northfield *Nordfeld: Alfwold from William FitzAnsculf.* District of Birmingham.

Norton Lindsay *Mortone(sic): Hervey from Robert of Stafford.*

Nuneaton *Etone: Earl Aubrey; Robert d'Oilly from Thorkell of Warwick. Mill.* Market town, once a Saxon settlement at the edge of the Forest of Arden. 'Nun' was added in 1290 when a Benedictine nunnery was established.

Offord *Offeworde: Robert of Stafford and Leofing from him. Mill.*

Oldberrow *Oleberge: Evesham Abbey.*

Oversley *Oveslei: Fulk from Count of Meulan. Mill.* Area near Alcester.

Over Whitacre *Witacre: Walter from Hugh de Grandmesnil.*

Oxhill *Octeselve: Hugh de Grandmesnil. Mill.* In 1183 Robert of Stafford granted the Bordesley monks land 'on the torrent of Oxhill where my oxherds dwell'.

Packington *Patitone: Godmund from Thorkell of Warwick. 2 mills.* Now 2 villages, Great and Little Packington.

RATLEY: *A richly-tiled sanctuary floor in the church of St. Peter and Vincula.*

Perry Barr *Pirio: Drogo from William FitzAnsculf. Mill.* Suburb of Birmingham. The Romans built a bridge here to carry the Icknield Way over the River Tame.

Pillerton Hersey *Pilardetone: Hugh de Grandmesnil. Mill.*

Pillerton Priors *Pilardetune: Waleran from Earl Hugh; St Evoul's Abbey from Hugh de Grandmesnil.*

Preston Bagot *Prestetone: Count of Meulan and Hugh from him.* Preston Bagot House.

RADWAY: *The honey-toned stone of Radway Grange, typical of many Warwickshire villages.*

Preston on Stour *Preston: Church of St Denis, Paris.* 17th-century Alscot House.

Priors Hardwick *Herdewicke: Coventry Abbey.*

Quinton *Quenintune: Hugh de Grandmesnil and Roger from him; Hugh de Lacy.* Now 2 villages, Upper and Lower Quinton.

Radbourn *Redborne: Aelmer from Thorkell of Warwick.* Radbourne Manor Farm and Upper Radbourne Farm.

Radford Semele *Redeford: Ermenfrid from Thorkell of Warwick. Mill.* Radford House.

Radway *Radwei(a)/Rodewei: Ermenfrid from Coventry Abbey; Earl Aubrey; Richard the Forester from the king and Ermenfrid from him.* Radway Grange, where Henry Fielding read *Tom Jones* (1749) in manuscript to the Earl of Chatham.

Ratley *Rotelei: Aelmer from Thorkell of Warwick.*

Rednal *Weredeshale: King's land.* Part of Birmingham.

Round(s)hill(s) *Rincele: Count of Meulan.*

Rowington *Rochintone: Roger from Hugh de Grandmesnil.* An early clearing in the Forest of Arden; Shakespeare Hall, home of the Shakespeare family, to whom, allegedly, the playwright was related.

Rugby *Rocheberie: Edwulf from Thorkell of Warwick. Mill.* Market town; home of Rugby School.

Ruin Clifford *Cliforde: Hugh from Robert of Stafford.*

Ryton on Dunsmore *Rietone: Thorkell of Warwick, formerly his father. Mill.* Ryton House.

Salford Priors *Salford: Leofeva the nun, formerly Godiva, Earl Leofric's wife. Mill.* Given with Abbots Salford by Kenred, King of Mercia, to the Abbey of Evesham in 708.

Sambourn(e) *Sandburne: Evesham Abbey.*

Sawbridge *Salwebrige: Thorkell from Thorney Church.* Some houses near Daventry.

Seckington *Sec(h)intone: Ingenwulf and Arnulf from Count of Meulan; Iudhael from William FitzCorbucion.* Set on a rock where Saxon nobles murdered King Ethelbald in 757.

Selly Oak *Escelie: Wilbert and Robert from William FitzAnsculf.* District of Birmingham; ruins of medieval Weoley Castle, on the site of a pre-Norman settlement.

Sherbo(u)rne *Seireburne: Count of Meulan.*

Shilton *Seelftone: Waltheof, the pre-Conquest holder, from Count of Meulan.* Shilton House.

Shipston *Scepwestun: Worcester Church. Mill.* Wool town; rope-making; Georgian houses.

Shrewley *Seruelei: Hugh de Grandmesnil.*

Shuckburgh *Socheberge: Herlwin from Count of Meulan; Alwin from Thorkell of Warwick; Richard the Forester from the king.* Now 2 villages, Lower and Upper Shuckburgh. Shuckburgh Park, home of the Shuckburgh family since the 12th century.

Shustoke *Scotescote: Soti from Geoffrey de La Guerche.* Shustoke House; birthplace of the historian William Dugdale (1605–86), who became Garter king-of-arms.

Shuttington *Cetitone: Leofwin and Godric, the pre-Conquest holder, from Count of Meulan. Mill.*

Smeeton *Smitham: Earl Aubrey.*

Smercote *Smerecote: Godric from Count of Meulan.*

Snitterfield *Snitefeld: Count of Meulan.* Originally Neolithic; ancient Marroway road, along which the men of Mercia marched to attack to Wessex warriors. Richard Shakespeare, grandfather of William, farmed here.

Sole End *Soulege: Godric from Count of Meulan.* Mrs Ann Garner, one of the Dodson sisters in George Eliot's *The Mill on the Floss*, lived at Sole End Farm.

Southam *Sucham: Coventry Abbey. 2 mills.* Market town.

Spernall *Spernore: William from William Bonvallet.*

Stoneleigh *Stanlei: King's land. 2 mills.* Stoneleigh Abbey, seat of Lord Leigh (Jane Austen's mother was a Leigh). Fulling was carried out at 6 mills here.

Stoneton *Stantone: Hugh from Robert of Stafford.* Some houses.

Stratford-upon-Avon *Stradforde: Bishop of Worcester. Mill (1000 eels).* Market town, the birhplace of William Shakespeare (1564–1616) and home of the Royal Shakespeare Theatre.

Stretton Baskerville *Stratone: Roger from Ralph de Mortimer; Walter from Gilbert FitzThorold.*

Stretton-on-Dunsmore *Stratone: Reginald from Earl Roger.* Stretton Manor House.

Stretton-on-Fosse *Stratone: Walter from Osbert FitzRichard.*

Studley *Stodlei: William FitzCorbucion. Mill, salt-house.* Studley Castle. James Pardow, who first used steam for needle-making, established a mill here in 1800.

Sutton Coldfield *Sutone: King's land.* 'Royal town' by charter of Henry VIII; now, a residential suburb of Birmingham.

Sutton-under-Brailes *Sudtune: Westminster Abbey.*

Tachbrook Mallory *Tacesbroc: Roger from Count of Meulan. 2 mills.*

Temple Grafton *Grastone: Gilbert from Osbern FitzRichard.*

Tessall *Thessale: King's land.* Tessall Lane in King's Norton.

Thurlaston *Torlavestone: Robert from Count of Meulan; Hubert from Hugh de Grandmesnil.* Thurlaston Grange.

Tidmington *Tidelmintun: St Mary's Church, Worcester.*

Tredington *Tredinctun: St Mary's Church, Worcester. 3 mills.* At the crossing of the Roman Fosse Way and the Oxford–Stratford road; brick mill.

Tysoe *Tiheshoche: Robert of Stafford.* Now 3 villages; Middle, Upper and Lower Tysoe in the Vale of the Red Horse, named from the figure of a horse cut into a red hill and dedicated to the Saxon horse god, Tui.

Ufton *Ulchetone: Coventry Abbey.*

Ullenhall *Holehale: Robert of Stafford.* Barrells Hall, the centre of a literary coterie in the 18th century.

Ulverley *Ulverlei: Christina.* In the Solihull urban district.

Upton *Optone: King's land; Albert the Clerk from the king; Roger from William Bonvallet.* Upton House, on Edge Hill.

Walcot(e) *Walecote: Ordric, the pre-Conquest holder, from Thorkell of Warwick.*

Walsgrave on Sowe *Sowa: Coventry Abbey; Richard Hunter from the king. Mill.* Traces of Neolithic settlement; coal mining since the late 16th century.

Walton *Waltone: Count of Meulan. 3 mills.*

Wappenbury *Wapeberie: Geoffrey de La Guerche. Mill.* Wappenbury Hall.

Warmington *Warmintone: Count of Meulan and a man-at-arms from him.*

Warwick *Waru(u)ic: King's land and various landholders and burgesses holding dwellings. 24 sesters of honey.* County town with partly Norman Warwick Castle.

Wasperton *Wasmertone: Coventry Abbey. Mill (4 packloads of salt, 1000 eels).*

WARWICK: *The castle, a medieval fortress, is still lived-in; the curtain wall and towers are intact.*

Weddington *Wattune: Hereward from Count of Meulan.*

Weethley *Wilelei: Evesham Abbey.*

Welford-on-Avon *Welleford: St Denis Church, Paris.*

Wellesbourne *Waleborne: King's land.* Now 2 villages, Wellesbourne Hastings and Mountford. Wellesbourne Hall was the home of the Granville family; Mary Granville, 18th-century collagiste, was a favourite of George III.

Weston in Arden *Westone: Fulk from Count of Meulan.* 16th-century hall, home of the 11th Baron la Zouche, sole dissenter at the trial of Mary, Queen of Scots.

Weston-on-Avon *Westone/tune: Evesham Abbey; Roger from Hugh de Grandmesnil. Mill.*

Weston under Wetherley *Westone: Robert from Count of Meulan; Robert from Thorkell of Warwick; Johais from William FitzCorbucion.*

Whatcote *...atercote: Roger from Hugh de Grandmesnil.*

Whichford *Wicford: Robert from Gilbert de Ghent. 2 mills.*

Whitchurch *Witecerce: Count of Meulan and Walter from him. 2 mills.*

Whitley *Witeleia: Drogo from Robert of Stafford.* Whitley Abbey; Whitley Bridge on the River Avon.

Whitnash *Witenas: Humphrey from Hascoit Musard.*

Wibtoft *Wibetot: Fulk and Robert from Count of Meulan.* Site of the 1st to 2nd-century Roman settlement of Venonae, now vanished.

Wiggins Hill *Winchicelle: Browning, the pre-Conquest holder, from Thorkell of Warwick.* Wiggins Hill Farm.

Willey *Welei: Fulk and Robert from Count of Meulan.*

Willicote *Wilcote: Hugh's clerk from Hugh de Grandmesnil.* Small, scattered.

Willington *Ullavintone: Ewein from Robert of Stafford; Fulbric from Gilbert de Ghent. Mill.*

Willoughby *Wilebec/bei/bene/bere: Wulfric, Ordric, Leofgeat and Godwin, all pre-Conquest holders, from Thorkell of Warwick; Hugh de Grandmesnil.* Warwick House.

Wilmcote *Wilmecote: Urso from Osbern FitzRichard.* Mary Arden's House.

Wilnecote *Wilmundecote: Ingenwulf and Arnulf from Count of Meulan.* Castle Liberty; Wilnecote Hall.

Wincot *Wenecote: William the Chamberlain; Reginald the Chaplain from the king.* A farm.

Wishaw *Witscaga: Ordric, the pre-Conquest holder, from William FitzCorbucion.*

Witton *Witone: Stanketel, the pre-Conquest holder, from William FitzAnsculf.*

Wixford *Witeleavesford: Evesham Abbey. Mill (20 sticks of eels).*

Wolfham(p)cote *Ulfelmescote/Wlfemescot: Thorkell of Warwick and 4 brothers, the pre-Conquest holders, from him.*

Wolford *Ulwarda/Ulware/Volwarde/Worwade: Wadard from Bishop of Bayeux and Gerald from him; Ralph from Count of Meulan; Robert of Stafford and Ordwy and Alwin, the pre-Conquest holders, from him. Mill.* Now 2 villages, Great and Little Wolford.

WILMCOTE: *Mary Arden's home as a girl.*

Wolston *Ulvestone/Ulvricetone: Reginald from Earl Roger. Mill.* Wolston Grange; Manor house; earthworks of 13th-century Brandon Castle, destroyed in 1266 probably by Simon de Montfort.

Wolverton *Ulwarditone: Urfer from Robert of Strafford; William FitzCorbucion.*

Wolvey *Ulveia: Robert of Vessey.* Also the hamlet of Wolvey Heath. The Rev. Hugh Hughes, a non-resident vicar here, was George Eliot's Mr Crew in *Scenes of Clerical Life*.

Woodcote *Widecote: Count of Meulan and Gilbert from him.* County Police Headquarters.

Wootton Wawen *Wotone: Robert of Stafford. 2 mills.*

Wormleighton *Wimeles/Wimenes/Wimerestone: Gilbert from Count of Meulan; Warin from Thorkell of Warwick; William from Geoffrey de Mandeville.* Extensive earthworks of the medieval village, depopulated in 1498.

Yardley *Gerlei: St Mary's of Pershore.* Area in Birmingham.

Westmorland

The Domesday *surveyors, so expansive with their statistics about pigs, bees and plough-teams in the southern counties, became almost speechless in the north. About Westmorland they were characteristically tight-lipped. Its 24 holdings were taxed at a total of 68 carucates of land. Most of these were owned by the king; Roger de Poitou held the others. All were entered as a part of Yorkshire, for Westmorland was still not a county in 1086. Like neighbouring Cumberland, its territory was divided between the new Norman rulers and the Scottish Kingdom of the Clyde. Nervously the Normans kept to low ground in Westmorland. No holding was at an altitude of more than 800 feet; and all were in the southern part of the county, near the rivers Lune and Kent.*

Little else is known for certain about Domesday *Westmorland, but the inferences are tragic. In 1069, says the* Anglo-Saxon Chronicle *with terrible simplicity, the king 'laid waste all the shires'. The number of deserted villages recorded elsewhere in the north indicate that this was no extravagant claim. 'The outstanding fact about the human geography of the northern counties,' wrote H. C. Darby in* The Domesday Geography of Northern England, *'was the devastated condition of the countryside.' It seems unlikely that Westmorland would have been an exception.*

Kendal

[Land of the King . . .] In Strickland, Mint, KIRKBY (KENDAL) *CHERCHEBI*, Helsington, Stainton, 'Bothelford', (Old) Hutton, Burton, Dalton, Patton. Gillemichael had them. There are 20c., of land taxable in them.

Kendal calls itself the 'Gateway to the Lakes', a claim which is unfortunately true. On weekends in July and August its streets are jammed with weary families in overheated cars, whose only aim is to pass through to the lakes or mountains just beyond. But those who stop here find that Kendal is more than a mere gateway.

It was Westmorland's principal city before that county became engulfed by Cumbria – a gracious, busy town with a stimulating mix of industry and antiquity. Behind the Kendal rock, the mint cake and the Lake District tea towels, it has a thriving life of its own. All it lacks is colour; houses, churches, factories and mills are a uniform limestone grey.

It might well have been grey in 1086. The only certainty is that there was a church, for Kendal was known to the *Domesday* surveyors as Cherchebi (Kirkby), which can be translated literally as churchtown. Later it became Kirkby Kendal, taking this name from the dale of the River Kent in which it nestled. Otherwise *Domesday* reveals little. It belonged to the king and, like all the other holdings listed above, was included as a part of the West Riding of Yorkshire.

It was possibly one of the many towns savaged by William's army in the campaigns of 1069–70. With the Scots so close on the one hand and the Normans on the other, it is unlikely that it was a thriving community in 1086.

The recorded history of Norman Kendal begins only with the reign of William Rufus, the Conqueror's successor. In 1092 he drove the Scots from the north-west and established his barons in the wild lands of the Lake District. Kendal he gave to Ivo de Taillbois, whose descendants maintained an interest in the town until the nineteenth century. The Scots were not good losers, and they harried the borders for centuries, seizing and then losing land in a series of bloody wars. As a result, all the Lakeland communities were militarized. Men from 16 to 60, equipped at their own expense, were required to respond immediately when called to arms by beacon fires. In 1584 Westmorland could muster 4142 armed men, 1400 of them longbowmen. Among these archers, the men of Kendal, dressed in the heavy wool cloth known as Kendal Green, became the romantic heroes of this cruel era.

Kendal Castle, on a low hill looking west across the River Kent, was the birthplace of Katherine Parr, Henry VIII's last wife. She was a cultivated, strong-minded woman, who very nearly lost her head for being both more tolerant and more Protestant than her husband. In her day the castle was already falling into disrepair. By 1586, according to the historian William Camden, it was 'ready to drop down with age'. Now it is a charming ruin, refreshingly free of turnstiles or signs warning one off the walls. Below is a grand view of the 'auld grey town', still the industrial centre of the Lake District. And just on the west side of the river is Holy Trinity Church, a vast building considerably wider (103 feet) than it is high (about 80 feet). This substantial monument is believed to stand on the same site as the tiny Saxon 'cherche', which gave its name to *Domesday* Kendal.

Levens

[Land of Roger de Poitou . . .] In Beetham [Westmorland] Earl Tosti had 6c. taxable. Now Roger de Poitou has them, and Ernwin the priest under him. In Yealand 4c., Farleton [W] 4c., Preston [W] 3c., Borwick 2c., Hincaster [W] 2c., Heversham [W] 2c., LEVENS *LEFUENES* [W] 2c.

South of Kendal the River Kent widens and relaxes a little as it flows towards Morecambe Bay. Both the Britons and the Romans fortified this precious stretch of fertile, low-lying ground, and the Normans obtained one of their first toeholds in the north-west when they took over the Saxon holdings here. Beetham, Hincaster, Heversham and Levens, tiny communities still, are among the Norman properties that took advantge of the fertile soil and easy access to the sea. They were possibly only partly inhabited at the time of *Domesday*, victims of King William's revenge against the rebellious north. They would have been easy plunder.

Levens is a grey little village on a hillside, its streets flanked by high stone walls. In the valley below, four and a half miles south of Kendal, is Levens Hall, one of Westmorland's great houses. It dates from the thirteenth and fourteenth centuries, when a rich man's home in these parts was literally his castle. The modern building is mainly Elizabethan, but it is built around a medieval pele tower, a short, thick fortress characteristic of the north-west, made to offer protection both to the lord and to his villagers.

For all its Elizabethan panelling and Restoration furniture, the true riches of Levens Hall are in the garden. At the end of the seventeenth century Colonel James Grahme brought to Levens (which he is said to have won from his cousin Alan Bellingham over a game of cards – the Ace of Hearts) Monsieur Beaumont, the royal gardener, who had lost his job when James II fled abroad. Beaumont, a designer of genius, devoted one corner of the grounds to topiary. Amazingly, not only his overall design but his shapes for individual bushes have been scrupulously maintained for nearly 300 years. Here are pyramids, parapets, birds, spirals, obelisks, blocks and grottoes. Colourful ghosts, all quite benign, haunt Levens Hall. There are the Grey Lady, the Pink Lady and the woolly Black Dog that several times this century has dashed under the feet of house guests, before disappearing to some unheard whistle from the other side.

LEVENS: *The topiary gardens of Levens Hall are a remarkable sight. First laid out in 1689–92, they have been maintained with care and attention. The steam engine collection also on show at the hall provides a contrast.*

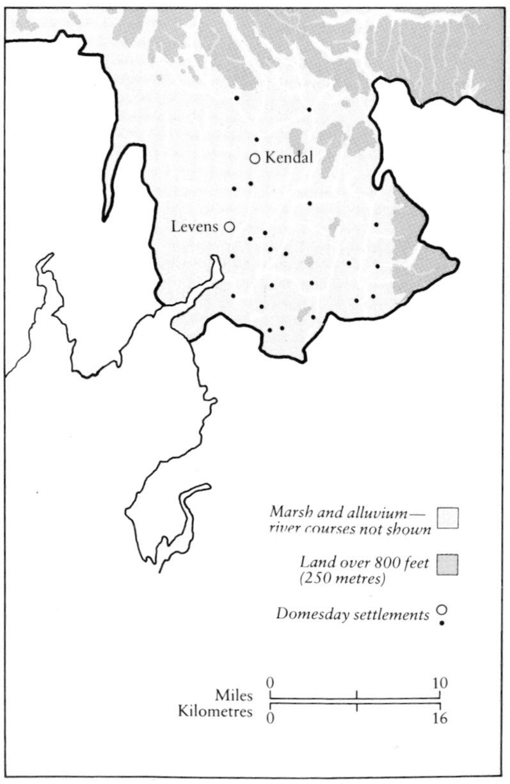

Westmorland Gazetteer
Each entry starts with the modern place name in **bold** type. The *Domesday* information that follows is in *italic* type, beginning with the name or names by which the place was known in 1086. The main landholder and undertenants are next. The modern or post-Domesday section is in normal type. represents a village, a small village or hamlet.

Barbon *Berebrune: King's land.* Barbon Manor; below Calf Top Peak.

Beetham *Biedun: Ernwin the priest from Roger de Poitou.* On the River Beta; the hall was originally a pele tower and then a castle.

Bothelforde *Bodelforde:* Lost in Helsington.

Burton *Bortun: King's land.* Now Burton-in-Kendal.

Casterton *Castretune: King's land.* Its school was probably the model for Lowood in *Jane Eyre*; High Casterton hamlet nearby.

Dalton *Daltun: King's land.* Dalton Hall; Dalton Old Hall Farm.

Farleton *Fareltun: Ernwin the priest from Roger de Poitou.*

Helsington *Helsingetune: King's land.* Helsington Laithes; Helsington Barrows.

Heversham *Eureshaim: Ernwin the priest from Roger de Poitou.* Attractive; hall.

Hincaster *Hennecastre: Ernwin the priest from Roger de Poitou.*

Holme *Holme: King's land.* Limestone; Holme Mills.

Hutton Roof *Hotun: King's land.* Hutton Roof Crags; Hutton Roof Park.

Kendal *Cherchebi:* See page 286.

Kirkby Lonsdale *Cherchebi: King's land.* Attractive town on the River Lune.

Levens *Lefuenes:* See page 286.

Lupton *Lupetun: King's land.* Also the hamlets of Lupton Tower and Lupton High; Lupton Hall.

Mansergh *Manzserge: King's land.* Mansergh Hall.

Middleton *Middeltun: King's land.* 15th-century Middleton Hall. A milestone from the Roman way to Carlisle was discovered here in the 19th century.

Mint *Mimet: King's land.* Mint House; Mint Bridge over the River Mint.

Old Hutton *Hotun: King's land.*

Patton *Patun: King's land.* Now Patton Bridge on the River Mint; Patton Hall Farm.

Preston *Prestun: King's land; Ernwin the priest from Roger de Poitou.* Now Preston Patrick Hall and the area of Preston Richard.

Stainton *Steintun: King's land.* On Stainton Beck.

Strickland *Stercaland: King's land.* Now Strickland Roger.

Wiltshire

Today's open downs and tidily hedged fields give little idea of the Wiltshire countryside at the time of Domesday. *Then it was largely unenclosed, and within 70 years vast stretches had been legally afforested. By the mid-thirteenth century unbroken royal forest stretched from Marlborough south to the New Forest in Hampshire, while in the north there was Blaydon Forest, in the west Chippenham Forest, in the centre Melksham Forest and in the south-west Selwood Forest.*

Although settlements existed within them they were on the whole sparsely populated, as were parts of Salisbury Plain. In contrast, the valley of the Bristol Avon, which flows west out of the county, and of the Salisbury Avon, which leaves it to the south, were well populated with ten or more people per square mile. Here were most of Wiltshire's meadows and mills.

Of the 335 settlements which Domesday *names, ten were boroughs, but these did not all have the same status. Malmesbury was so far the most important that it was given a separate entry preceding even the list of the county's landowners.*

First of these landowners, as usual, comes the king. 18 religious establishments of different sorts follow. Of the bishops, Winchester and Salisbury had the greatest holdings, of the abbeys Malmesbury and Wilton. 46 lay tenants-in-chief come next, many of them familiar as the great Norman barons who held estates in other counties. Finally come groups described as the king's servants, his thanes (the Englishmen who still held land directly from the king) and his officers.

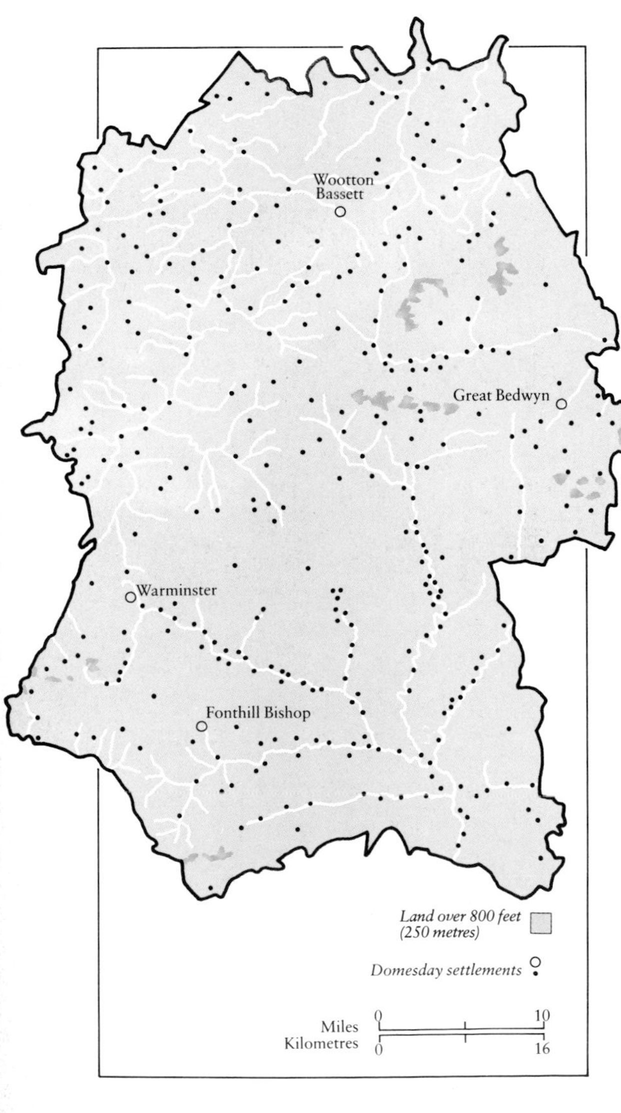

Warminster

[The King holds] WARMINSTER *GUERMINSTRE*. King Edward held it. It did not pay tax and was not assessed in hides. Land for 40 ploughs. In lordship 6 ploughs; 24 slaves; 13 pigmen. 15 villagers, 8 Cottagers and 14 freedmen with 36 ploughs. 7 mills at £4; meadow, 80 acres; pasture 1 league long and 1/2 league wide; woodland 2 leagues long and 2 wide. 30 burgesses. This manor pays one night's revenue, with all its customary dues.

The small town of Warminster, which lies at the north-west corner of Salisbury Plain, takes its name from the minster which was founded here on the River Were, at the latest early in the tenth century. The fact that *Domesday* fails to mention a church is not surprising since it also omits other Saxon churches in Wiltshire, for example the fine one at Bradford-on-Avon.

In the reign of Ethelred the Unready (979–1016) moneyers were already working at Warminster, proving that it was a borough, since minting was forbidden elsewhere. At least from the time of his son, Edward the Confessor, it was a royal manor; here, as at Wiltshire's five other royal manors, the old system of paying the king by providing him with an annual night's lodging survived. *Domesday* confirms that it had 30 burgesses, but this does not mean that it was a town in today's terms. Probably they were craftsmen who provided the goods and services needed by so large a manor.

In the middle ages Warminster grew prosperous, partly because of its cloth-making and malting, but more because of its market. Corn especially was sold here and the sixteenth-century historian William Camden describes the vast quantities brought to the market as 'scarcely credible'. As late as 1798 this was said to be the largest inland corn market in England. In 1855, when railways had forced it to compete with towns like Devizes, Melksham, Chippenham and Salisbury, the Marquess of Bath, whose family had bought the manor in 1611, tried to save it by building a new market with a central courtyard and cast-iron-supported arcades; despite his efforts it was 'almost dead' by the end of the century. Warminster's other industries had also declined and by 1860 the town was in a 'lukewarm, stagnant, bankrupt state'. It recovered only in 1937 when the army established an infantry school here, and it thrives today because it remains a garrison town.

Although Warminster's history seems in the main peacefully provincial, it has been the scene of fierce religious controversies. In 1585 the vicar, Lewis Evans, a one-time papist turned enthusiastic Anglican, was accused of churching harlots. Sixty years later there was violent opposition to William Woodward, the vicar appointed by the Parliamentarian Committee of Plundered Ministers. But the most notorious dispute, known as the Warminster Pew Case, occurred less than 100 years ago. When the high church vicar, Sir James Erasmus Philipps, rebuilt the church he removed several pews to which certain citizens claimed rights. One of these, J. E. Halliday, a dissenter, brought an action which he eventually won in the House of Lords. The seat was not replaced until friends of Halliday wished to use it six years later. It was at once removed by night, smashed and partly burned. After it was repaired, it was returned to the church under police escort and secured to the floor by a blacksmith.

Nonconformism was always strong in Warminster, and ministers of non-Anglican sects also had their problems. In the first half of the nineteenth century the congregation of the Methodist, William Daniell, threw stones and rotten fruit at him when he preached. As a result he devoted himself to the shanty town on the edge of Warminster Common, where over a thousand poor lived in squalor. By the time he died in 1860 he was known as the Bishop of Warminster Common.

During the last 20 years Warminster has become known for another reason: its inhabitants have seen many and various Unidentified Flying Objects, from glowing cigar-shaped cylinders to flaming crimson balls. In 1967 a local journalist, Arthur Shuttlewood, published *The Warminster Mystery*, which presented the evidence to date.

There is nothing to be seen today of *Domesday's* Warminster. Even when Philipps rebuilt the church in 1887–89 only one small eleventh-century window survived. But it stands where the original minster stood, and the same low ridge at the western end of the town was the site of the *Domesday* manor. It has now been built over. Further south, the Enwell Cross, which once marked the junction of Silver Street and Church Street, has also gone. This, if early nineteenth-century tradition is right, was the centre of the first settlement, and the 30 burgesses of *Domesday's* royal manor would have had their workshops nearby.

Wootton Bassett

Miles Crispin holds WOOTTON (BASSETT) *WODETONE* from the King. Leofnoth held it before 1066; it paid tax for 12 hides. Land for 12 ploughs, of which 6 hides are in lordship; 3 ploughs there; 5 slaves; 11 villagers and 14 smallholders with 6 ploughs. A mill which pays 30d; meadow, 24 acres; pasture, 33 acres; woodland 2 leagues long and 1 league wide; in Malmesbury 1 house which pays 13d. The value was £10; now £9.

The small town of Wootton Bassett lies in the north of Wiltshire, five miles west of Swindon, and consists essentially of a long wide main street across which stone-tiled early Georgian houses face each other. In 1086 it was the largest of the 13 Wiltshire manors held by the powerful Norman tenant-in-chief Miles Crispin. Crispin also had extensive holdings in Oxfordshire, Buckinghamshire and Berkshire, including Wallingford Castle; his entire fief came to be known as the Honour of Wallingford.

A hundred years later it was said that he had acquired his lands by marrying the daughter of the first Norman holder. Certainly in Wiltshire's *Domesday* there are indications that he was acquisitive: at Swindon he held 2 hides which Odin, the manor's tenant, also claimed, and one of his men-at-arms claimed a disputed virgate of land at Ashley.

Wootton Bassett gets its modern name from the Basset family, who, early in the thirteenth century, built the great fortified house of Vastern to the south-west of the village, surrounding it with a deer park. Vastern became the parish's chief manor, with Wootton a subsidiary, and Vastern Park continued to expand until the beginning of the fifteenth century, encompassing most of the west and north of Wootton Parish as well as land in neighbouring parishes. It was still important at the start of the nineteenth century. In 1801, when the Wilts and Berks Canal arrived from the west, it was given its own wharf for the delivery of coal and the export of local produce. But the house itself was already much reduced and today includes only part of the medieval gatehouse.

Meanwhile Wootton has grown and much of the parish to the north has become a dormitory suburb for Swindon. At the centre of the main street stands a reminder of the past, the Town Hall, a small early eighteenth-century building set on 15 stone columns. The *Domesday* manor house may have stood in this area, but it was more probably on the site of Vastern, which lies in still unspoiled hilly countryside.

Great Bedwyn

[The King holds] BEDWYN *BEDVINDE*. King Edward held it. It never paid tax and was not assessed in hides. Land for 80 ploughs less one. In lordship 12 ploughs; 18 slaves. 80 villagers, 60 cottagers and 14 freedmen with 67 ploughs. 8 mills which pay 100s; two woodlands which have 2 leagues length and 1 league width. Meadow, 200 acres; pasture, 12 furlongs long and 6 furlongs wide. To this manor belong 25 burgesses. This village pays one night's revenue, with all customary dues. In this manor before 1066 there was a wood which had 1/2 league length and 3 furlongs width and was in the King's lordship; now Henry de Ferrers holds it.

Bedwyn (today's Great Bedwyn) was one of the six royal manors in Wiltshire in which the old system of paying the king with an annual night's lodging still survived. This service had been valuable when the court moved continually around the country, but it was already being superseded by money payments; at two of these manors the equivalents are given: Tilstead (£100) and Chippenham (£110). Such sums were big for the time and suggest that receiving the king and his court must have been a doubtful privilege.

Of the six, Bedwyn, with a higher total of families than any of the others, was probably the largest, so its good fortune in remaining a village instead of growing into a town seems suprising. The explanation may lie in its two large woodlands, which became part of the great Forest of Savernake; indeed the whole manor was soon included in the forest and therefore subject to the economic restrictions imposed by forest law.

Savernake Forest survives today although it has frequently changed in size and nature. Every royal forest had its own warden and the one constant feature at Savernake has been the family which supplies this officer. Today's Marquess of Ailesbury is a direct descendant (three times through a female line) of the Richard Sturmy who is found in *Domesday* holding seven Wiltshire manors, five (Huish, Burbage, Grafton, Harding and Shalborne) in the Bedwyn area.

Although Richard Sturmy – unlike his son Henry Esturmit – is never specifically called Warden of Savernake, he is listed among the tenants who were servants of the king, and he took over four of his holdings from an Englishman, Aelfric, who at one point is called Aelfric Hunter. Aelfric's name and the fact that the Sturmy family succeeded him strongly suggest that there was already a forest at Savernake and that Richard Sturmy had charge of it.

For many centuries the family residence was Wolf Hall, two and a half miles to the south-west of Great Bedwyn, in the modern parish of Grafton. In Tudor times, the family – by now called Seymour – became involved in the affairs of the nation when Henry VIII took Jane Seymour for his third wife. When her son became Edward VI, her brother, the Duke of Somerset, made himself Protector of the Realm, and planned a house vast enough to match his new stature, to be built in Great Bedwyn parish, in the forest's Le Broyle bailiwick. The site, near the road which connects East Grafton with Hungerford, can still be identified by a long conduit intended to supply the house's fresh water. But the Protector fell from power as quickly as he had risen; 2,000,000 bricks, made at the nearby Dodsdown brickworks, had to be carried away unused.

When the Protector's son returned to royal favour he turned another building in Bedwyn Parish, the old forest lodge of Tottenham, into a fine mansion. This was probably burned down a hundred years later, but by the 1730s his great-great-great granddaughter was living in a new house on the same site, complete with follies in the grounds.

She was married to the second Earl of Ailesbury; her only son died young and her nephew, Thomas Bruce Brudenell, who became next warden, brought Capability Brown, then at the height of his fame, to redesign not only the gardens but the forest itself. Under Brown's instructions, a three-and-a-half-mile Grand Avenue of beech and oak trees was completed, and the gaps between the medieval coppices were planted with oak to make it, in Brown's words a 'great whole'.

Late in the nineteenth century the forest almost passed out of the family's hands when the fourth Marquess of Ailesbury, a young man addicted to 'drink and bad company', accumulated vast gambling debts. To pay off the first £175,000 the family estates in Yorkshire were sold, but only on condition that the marquess (known to the family as 'dear Willie') agreed to Savernake's being entailed, to prevent him from selling this too when he inherited it. But after he had accumulated another £230,000 debt he brought an action against the trustees to force them to let him sell. After five years and four law suits dear Willie won his case but by then his purchaser had lost interest. He died soon after, aged 29.

GREAT BEDWYN: *Grand Avenue.*

Most of Great Bedwyn parish had ceased to be part of Savernake during Elizabeth's reign when the forest was deprived of the Le Broyle bailiwick – probably because of the Protector's plans to build here. But the family still owned much of the village's land and many of its buildings, including its burgage houses, which carried with them parliamentary votes. This was a valuable asset since Great Bedwyn returned two members to parliament. Unfortunately Stokke Manor, also in the village, belonged to the Verney family, who supported the opposite party.

In the early eighteenth century the second Earl of Ailesbury went to great expense to have his candidates elected. In urging the electors to vote for himself alone, he paid them £200 to be divided among 100 of them. When he wanted them to vote for a Mr Millington as well, they raised their price to £5 each. His nephew, Thomas Bruce Brudenell (he married the daughter of the banker Henry Hoare, creator of the magnificent gardens at Stourhead), bought out Lord Verney to relieve them both of such election expenses. Great Bedwyn did not lose its parliamentary seats until the great Reform Bill of 1832.

Rotten boroughs were anathema to the radical politician William Cobbett, and in his book *Rural Rides* he several times picked out Bedwyn as an example of the poverty they produced. When he came here in November 1821 he found

FONTHILL BISHOP: *18th-c. fake of an 11th-c. abbey; fragments of the cloister remain.*

the labourers more wretched even than the hop pickers of Farnham. Bedwyn's early nineteenth-century poverty is all the more surprising since the Kennet and Avon Canal already ran past the village and the Great Western's main line to the West Country soon arrived.

Despite canal and railway, and the absence of any very old buildings – many were destroyed in a fire in 1716 – the Great Bedwyn of *Domesday*, set in its upland valley beside its little chalk stream, the River Dun, is more easily imagined than almost any other Wiltshire manor of its size.

Fonthill Bishop

The Bishop [of Winchester] also holds FONTHILL (BISHOP) *FONTEL*. Before 1066 it paid tax for 10 hides. Land for 7 ploughs. In lordship 5 hides of this land; 2 ploughs there; 5 slaves. 8 villagers and 5 smallholders with 3 ploughs. A mill at 5s; meadow, 8 acres; pasture 1/2 league long and 3 furlongs wide; woodland, as much. The value was £10; now £14.

The scatter of stone cottages which make up the tiny village of Fonthill Bishop lies in the wooded southern part of the county. It might be 100 miles from the bare chalk downs of Salisbury Plain although in fact the plain begins only five miles to the north. Fonthill Bishop had been the Bishop of Winchester's before 1066 and *Domesday* shows that, like so many bishops and abbots, he had been allowed to keep his holding. Just as typically, the English lay holder at the nearby tiny village of Fonthill Giffard had been replaced by a Norman, Berengar Giffard.

Fonthill Bishop was a small manor, its mill on the River Nadder its only special asset. But over the generations a succession of distinguished houses was built here, and in the eighteenth century one of these, Fonthill Splendens, standing near a lake created by damming the river, was considered the finest in the south-west of England. It was then owned by William Beckford, a phenomenally rich West Indian sugar merchant, and here his son, also William, was born.

William, the son, suffered from a powerful mother, and although he married and produced two daughters, he undoubtedly had homosexual inclinations. In 1786 he was accused of misbehaviour with a young man, William Courtenay, and forced to live abroad. When he returned after ten years he first built a twelve-foot-high, seven-mile-long wall to keep the local hunt off his land, then set about creating the country's most famous folly, Fonthill Abbey.

Although he destroyed the older house for its material, the abbey was 'run up with a speed suggestive of the scene-shifter rather than the builder'. Its great 225-foot octagonal tower, made of wood and 'compo-cement', was blown down during its construction and had to be rebuilt in heavier material. Eventually Beckford was forced, as a result of neglecting his business affairs, to sell the abbey. Soon afterwards he was called to the deathbed of his clerk of works, who admitted that the tower's foundations had never been reinforced to take the new weight.

Beckford at once informed John Farquhar, the septuagenarian who had bought the abbey, but Farquhar was unconcerned, saying that it would last his time. He was wrong. On 21 December 1825 the tower collapsed with such force that one man was shot along a passage 'as if he had been in an air-gun, to the distance of 30 ft, among dust so thick as to be felt'.

Only a fragment of the abbey survives, but its wooded situation high above the lake is still delightful. It is easy to imagine Nelson, Lady Hamilton and other guests wending their way uphill for the three-day and three-night celebration which Beckford organized for them in 1800, outclassing in expense and ostentation all other English house parties. Nothing remains from the eleventh century in either Fonthill, but their names continue to remind us that in 1086 one was held by the Bishop of Winchester and the other by Baron Giffard.

AVEBURY: *The standing stones enclose over 28 acres; Avebury Manor nearby is Saxon.*

Wiltshire Gazetteer
Each entry starts with the modern place name in **bold** type. The *Domesday* information that follows in is *italic* type, beginning with the name or names by which the place was known in 1086. The main landholders and under-tenants are next, separated with semi-colons if a place was divided into more than one holding. A number of holdings were granted by the king to his thanes; these normally come towards the end of the list of landholders and are described as holding land 'from the king'. More general information completes the *Domesday* part of the entry including examples of dues such as timber rendered by tenants. The modern or post-Domesday section is in normal type. ▣ represents a village, ⌂ a small village or hamlet.

Ablington *Alboldintone: King's land.* ⌂ On the River Avon.

Addeston *Wintreburne: Winchester Abbey.* Addestone Farm on the River Till.

Aldbourne *Aldeborne: King's land formerly Countess Gytha, mother of Earl Harold. 4 mills, church.* ▣ Bronze Age relics unearthed nearby; church with a Norman doorway and nave.

Alderbury *Alwar(es)berie: Osbern the priest from the king; Engenwulf from Waleran Hunter; Edward, from the king. Church.* ▣ Large; on the River Avon by the site of Clarendon Palace, where the Normans built the first known tile kiln. Ivy Church is based on the remains of an Augustinian priory founded by King Stephen in the 12th century.

Alderstone *Ferstesfeld: Aldred, the pre-Conquest holder, from the king.* Alderstone Farm.

Alderton *Aldri(n)tone: Richard from Ralph de Mortimer; Walter; Hugh from Drogo FitzPoyntz. Mill, part of another mill.* ▣

All Cannings *Caninge: St Mary of Winchester before and after 1066. Mill.* ▣ All Cannings Cross Farm on an Iron Age settlement site; Rybury Camp on a nearby hill, also Iron Age.

Allington *Adelingtone: Alfred of Marlborough; 2 men-at-arms.* ⌂ Many ancient barrows.

Allington (near Amesbury) *Al(l)entone: King's land, formerly Earl Aubrey; Amesbury Church before and after 1066. Town with a mill.* ▣ On the site of an old Roman road, by the River Bourne.

Alton (in Figheldean) *Eltone: John the Usher; Thurstan and Frawin.* ⌂ On the River Avon.

Alton Barnes *Aultone: Edward of Salisbury. Mill.* ▣ On the path of a Saxon ridgeway; Adam's Grave, a prehistoric barrow.

Alton Priors *Awltone: Bishop of Winchester and William Shield from him. 2 mills.* ▣ Knap Hill, the site of a Stone Age camp.

Amesbury *Ambles/ Ambresberie: King's land; 3 thanes, the pre-Conquest holders; Osmund from Edward of Salisbury. 8 mills.* Town on the River Avon; Stonehenge and Woodhenge, both c.1500 BC. In AD 980, Queen Elfrida founded a nunnery here.

Ansty *Anestige: Walter from Waleran Hunter; Aldred from the king. 2 mills.* ⌂ Sprawling.

Ashton *Aistone: St Mary of Romsey; Edward, William and Englishmen. 3 mills.* ▣ Now Steeple Ashton; possibly 11th-century cross on the green; Ashton village nearby.

Ashton Gifford *Schetone:* Lost.

Ashton Keynes *Essitone: Cranborne Abbey before and after 1066. Mill.* ▣ Sprawling; Ashton Mill on Swill Brook.

Avebury *Avreberie: King's land. Reinbald the priest. Church.* ▣ Surrounded by a megalithic stone circle, older even than Stonehenge. Silbury Hill, nearby, is the largest man-made hill in Europe, and dates from the same period.

Badbury *Badeberie: Glastonbury Abbey. Mill.* ⌂

Bagshot *Bechesgete: Henry de Ferrers; Earl Roger. Churches, mill.* Some houses.

Barford (in Downton) *Bereford: Engenold from Waleran Hunter.* Barford Park; Barford Park Farm, Barford Down Farm, Barford Down.

Barford St Martin *Berford: Berengar Giffard, formerly Earl Harold; John the Usher and Wado, the pre-Conquest holder, from the king.* ▣ On the River Nadder; by the Hamshill Ditches, ancient earthworks.

Barley *Berrelege: Azor from the king.* Lost in South Wraxall.

Bathampton *Wili/Wilrenone: Humphrey de L'Isle. 2 mills.* Bathampton House.

Baverstock *Babestoche: Abbess of Wilton.* ⌂

Baycliff *Ballochelie: Aethelhelm from Edward of Salisbury.* Baycliff Farm.

Beckhampton *Bachentune: Ansfrid from Gilbert de Breteuil.* ▣ Near Harepit Way, an ancient earthwork.

Beechingstoke *Bichenestoch: Abbess of Shaftesbury and Thurstan from her. Mill.* ⌂ Mill.

Bemerton *Berment/Bimertone: Aiulf the Sheriff; Aldred from the king.* Suburb of Salisbury; on the River Nadder. The poet George Herbert was rector from 1630 to 1633.

Beversbrook *B(r)evresbroc: William Delamare from William d'Eu; Nigel the Doctor.* ⌂ Tiny.

Biddesden *Bedesdene: Robert FitzGerald.* Biddesden House.

Biddestone *Bedestone: Thorketel from Humphrey de L'Isle.* ▣

Bincknoll *Bechenhalle: Gilbert de Breteuil.* Ruins of Bincknoll Castle; Bincknoll Farm; Bincknoll Wood.

Bishop's Cannings *Bishop of Salisbury and a priest, Ebrard, Herman, Quintin, Walter, Brictward, Alfward and the Reeve's wife from him. 6 mills.* ▣ Many ancient earthworks, including the Wansdyke, a Saxon camp site.

Bishopstrow *Biscopestreu: Edward of Salisbury. Mill.* ▣ On the site of a Roman villa.

Blunsdon *Bluntes/Blontesdon: Robert from Edward of Salisbury; Ilbert from Humphrey de L'Isle; Edward the Sheriff in the king's hand. Mill.* Now the village of Broad Blunsdon with an Iron Age fort nearby, and the neighbouring village of Blunsdon St Andrew with Blunsdon Abbey.

BRADFORD ON AVON: *The magnificent 14th-c. tithe barn; its roof spans over 10,000 sq. ft.*

Boscombe *Boscumbe: Amesbury Church before and after 1066; Edward from William d'Eu.* On the River Bourne; the theologian Richard Hooker was rector in the 16th century.

Boyton *Boientone: Edward of Salisbury. Mill.* On the River Wylye. The Giffard family home until 14th century, the church has an effigy of Alexander Giffard (d. 1265), a crusading Knight and brother of Walter Giffard, Lord Chancellor of England.

Bradenstoke *Bradenestoch(e): Edward of Salisbury, William FitzAnsculf and Croc from him. Mill.* Bradenstoke Augustinian Priory, founded 1142; ancient earthworks on Clack Hill.

Bradfield *Bradefelde:* Lost.

Bradford-on-Avon *Bradeford: Abbess of Shaftesbury. 2 mills, market, vineyard. 1 sester of honey.* Milling town on the River Avon with England's most complete Saxon church, founded in the 11th century.

Bremhill *Breme: Malmesbury Abbey. 3 mills.*

Brigmerston *Brismartone: Robert from Robert FitzGerald, formerly Brictmer. Mill.* On the River Avon; named after its 1066 holder.

Brinkworth *Brecheorde/ Brenchewrde: Malmesbury Abbey and a man-at-arms from the abbey; Humphrey from Miles Crispin.* On Brinkworth Brook.

Britford *Bred/Bretford: King's land; Osbern the Priest; Edmund Fitz Aiulf, Wulfric and Osward from the king. Church, 2 mills.* Anglo-Saxon remains; Roman tiles.

Brixton Deverill *Devrel: St Mary of Bec (given by Queen Matilda) formerly Brictric. Mill, church.* On the River Wylye; formerly 'Ecbryghts-stane', where Alfred and Grtea collected an army together before the Battle of Bratton Down (878).

Broad Hinton *Han/Hentone: Gilbert de Breteuil.* Monument to Colonel Glanville, who was killed in 1645 during the Civil War, fighting for the King at Bridgewater.

Brokenborough *Brochen(e)berge: Malmesbury Abbey and Robert, William, an English woman and 2 men-at-arms from the abbey. 8 mills.* Near the course of a Roman road.

Bromham *Bromham: King's land, formerly Earl Harold. 2 mills.* Near a Roman villa site; Wans House, in the Park, on a Roman station site; burial place of the Irish poet Thomas Moore (1779–1852).

Broughton Gifford *Broctone/ tune: Humphrey de L'Isle; Saeward from the king. 2 mills.* Near Broughton Common; Broughton House and Gifford Hall, both 17th century.

Budbury *Bodeberie: Ulf from the king.* Lost in Bradford-on-Avon.

Bulford *Boltintone: Amesbury Church before and after 1066; Alfward from the king. 2 mills.* On the River Avon; military camp.

Burbage *Buberge/Burbed/ Burbetc(e): King's land with Vitalis the priest holding the church; Blackman from Humphrey de L'Isle; William from Richard Sturmy; Ralph of Hauville. Church.* On the downs near Wolf Hall.

Burcombe *Bredecumbe: Abbess of Wilton, the pre-Conquest holder; Haimo from Earl Hugh. Mill.* On the River Nadder; Roman settlement site; church with a Saxon chancel and arch.

Bushton *Clive: Bishop of Winchester.* Georgian farmhouse.

Buttermere *Butremare/mere: Arnulf de Hesdin; Azelin from Waleran Hunter; Ansketel.*

Cadenham *Cadeham: William from Earl Hugh.* Manor house.

Calcutt *Colecote: Odo of Winchester from the king.* On the River Thames.

Calne *Calne/Caunalne: King's land with Nigel holding the church. 9 mills.* Town on the River Marden with the site of a Roman building. Joseph Priestley experimented here and discovered oxygen (1774).

Calstone Wellington *Calestone: Edric's wife from Arnulf le Hesdin, formerly Edric; Gunfrid Mawditt and Richard Poynant from the king. 4 mills.* By Calstone Down near the course of a Roman road.

Castle Combe *Come: Humphrey de L'Isle. 3 mills.* Once a cloth-weaving centre; remains of a 13th-century castle built by Walter de Dunstanville.

Castle Eaton *Ettone: Earl Roger; Herman de Dreux. Mill.*

Chalfield *Caldefelle: Arnulf de Hesdin. ½ mill.* Now 2 hamlets, Great and Little Chalfield; manor house and moat built by Thomas Tropenell, 1480.

Chalke *Chelche: Abbess of Wilton. 5 mills.* Now 2 villages, Bower Chalke with many watercress beds, and Broad Chalk, which was given by a Saxon king to the abbess of a convent 1000 years ago.

Charlton (near Malmesbury) *Cerletone: Malmesbury Abbey and Ranulf Flambard and Ralph from the abbey. Mill.* Large; near the River Avon. The poet John Dryden sought refuge in Charlton House (believed to have been built by Inigo Jones in 1607) during the Great Plague of 1665.

Charnage *Chedelwich: Bishop of Salisbury and Hugh from him.*

Chedglow *Cheses/Cheieslaue/ Chegeslei/Chigelei: Arnulf de Hesdin and a thane from him; Edward from Alfred of Marlborough; Siward from Miles Crispin; Edwin, the pre-Conquest holder, from the king.*

Chelworth (in Cricklade) *Celewrde: Warin Bowman.* Moat.

Chelworth (in Crudwell) *Celeorde: Tovi, William and Ansketel from Malmesbury Abbey. Mill.*

Cheverell *Chevrel: Lethelin from Arnulf de Hesdin. ½ mill.* Now 2 villages, Great and Little Cheverell.

Chilmark *Chilmerc: Abbess of Wilton. Mill.* Chilmark stone, quarried since Roman times, was used in Salisbury Cathedral.

Chilton Foliat *Cilleton: Reginald from Miles Crispin. 2 mills.* On River Kennet.

Chippenham *Chipe-/ Chepeham: King's land with Bishop Osbern holding the church; Roger of Berkeley; Reginald Canute. Church. 12 mills.* Industrial town, originally a Saxon market town.

Chirton *Ceritone: Durand of Gloucester. Mill.* Manor house.

Chisbury *Cheseberie: Gilbert de Breteuil; 2 mills.* Chisbury Camp, an ancient British earthwork.

Chisenbury *Chesigeberie: Nigel the Doctor. Mill.*

Chisledon *Chiseldene: Winchester Abbey before and after 1066. Mill.* Chisledon Camp, a modern army base.

Chitterne *Che(l)tre: Edward of Salisbury and Robert from him.* 2 ancient burial mounds.

Cholderton *Celdre/Celdrintone: Arnulf de Hesdin and Godric and Wulfward from Arnulf; Bernard from William d'Eu.*

Choulston *Chelestanestone: Amesbury Abbey and Alfward from the Abbey.* Lost near Fittleton.

Christian Malford *Cristemeleford(e): Glastonbury Abbey and Robert and Edward from the abbey. 2 mills.* On the River Avon.

Clatford *Clatford: Ralph de Mortimer. Mill.* Clarendon House with Sarcen stones in its walls; built on the site of one of King John's hunting lodges.

Clevancy *Clive: Roger from Alfred of Marlborough.*

Clyffe Pypard *Clive: Count of Mortain and Gilbert from him; Robert from Arnulf de Hesdin and Alfred of Marlborough; Humphrey de L'Isle; Miles Crispin and Humphrey from him; Gilbert de Breteuil and William FitzAnsculf and Ansfrid from him Henry de Ferrers; Hugh de Lasne; Thurstan the Chamberlain; Wilbert; Wulfric Waula from the king. 3 mills.*

Codford *Coteford: Bernard from William d'Eu; Waleran Hunter; Osbern Giffard. 1½ mills.* Now 2 villages, Codford St Mary and Codford St Peter; by the Codford Circle, an ancient ring of stones.

Colerne *Colerne: Humphrey de L'Isle. Mill.* Near Roman village site; church with fragments of Saxon carvings. Sir Walter Raleigh (1552–1618) was born at Euridge Farm nearby.

Collingbourne Ducis *Colingeburne: King's land, formerly Earl Harold, with Gerald, priest of Wilton holding the derelict church.* On the River Bourne; church, rebuilt 700 years ago, still stands.

Collingbourne Kingston *Coleburne: Winchester Abbey, before and after 1066, and Croc and Fulcred from the abbey.* Dame Pile met Charles Stuart and gave him a lapful of gold on the rise in the village called King's Hill.

Compton (in Enford) *Contone: King's land, formerly Earl Aubrey. Mill.*

Compton Bassett *Contone: Payne from Humphrey de L'Isle; William from William d'Eu; Thorkell, the pre-Conquest holder, from the king. 2 mills.* Compton House.

Compton Chamberlayne *Contone: King's land, formerly Earl Harold. Mill.* Wooded; on the River Nadder; home of the Penruddock family for 400 years.

Conock *Cowic: Count of Mortain and St Mary's of Grestain from him.* 18th-century manor house.

Coombe Bissett *Cumbe: King's land, with Leofric the priest holding the Church. 2 mills.* Church with Norman work.

Corsham *Cosseham: King's land, with St Stephen's of Caen holding the church. 2 mills, 2 churches.* Small town with Norman remains in the church. Corsham Court was seat of the Methuen family for over 200 years; alterations on the house were carried out by Capability Brown and Nash.

Corsley *Corselie: Azor from the king. Mill.* Corsley Heath, also a village.

Corston *Corstone: Ranulf Flambard.* On Gauze Brook.

Corton *Cortitone: William from Hugh de Lasne. Mill.* Pretty.

Coulston *Covelestone: Brictric from the king. Mill.* Now East Coulston with a Georgian Coulston House.

Cowesfield *Colesfeld: Richard Sturmy; Brictric and his brother Alfwy from the king.* Cowesfield Green.

Cricklade *Crichelade: Westminster Abbey. Church.* On a Roman building site; Alfred the Great is said to have built a fortification here.

Crofton *Crostone: Hugh from Alfred of Marlborough. Mill.* On the course of a Roman road; Victorian pumping station by the Kennet and Avon Canal.

Crudwell *Credvelle: Malmesbury Abbey before and after 1066.* Crudwell Court, a Georgian manor house.

Cumberwell *Cumbrewelle: Payne from Humphrey de L'Isle.* Great Cumberwell.

Dauntsey *Dantesie: Malmesbury Abbey before and after 1066, and Robert from the abbey. Mill.*

Deptford *Depeford: Azelin from Edward of Salisbury. Mill.* On the River Wylye.

Deverill *Devrel: Irso from Arnulf de Hesdin; Edgar the priest from the king; Aubrey the Chamberlain. 2 mills.* Name given to a cluster of villages on the River Wylye.

Dinton *Domnitone: Abbess of Shaftesbury before and after 1066. 2 mills.* By the site of an ancient British fort; birthplace of Edward Hyde (1609–74), the first Lord Clarendon.

Ditchampton *Dechementune/ Dicehantone: Bishop of Bayeux and Robert from him; Abbess of Wilton. 4 mills.* By the River Nadder.

Ditteridge *Digeric: Warner from William d'Eu. ½ mill.* Church by a Roman villa site.

Donhead *Duneheve: Abbess of Shaftesbury before and after 1066. 8 mills.* Now 2 villages on either side of the River Nadder, Donhead St Mary and Donhead St Andrew; ancient camp of Castle Rings.

Downton *Duntone: Bishop of Winchester before and after 1066 and William de Braose, Waleran, Ralph and the king (in the forest) from him. 7 mills.* On a Roman village site, later a British defence and a Saxon meeting place; Cleobury Ring, a prehistoric earthwork.

Draycot Cerne *Draicote: Geoffrey Marshall. Mill.*

Draycot Fitzpayne *Draicote: Bishop of Coutances and Roger from him.* Oare House.

Draycot Foliat *Dracote: Reginald from Miles Crispin.* On the outskirts of Chiseldon Camp, a military base.

Durnford *D(i)arneforde: Abbess of Wilton before and after 1066 and Edward from her; William d'Eu. 4 mills.* Ogbury Camp, an ancient earthwork.

Durrington *Derintone: King's land, formerly Earl Aubrey.* On the River Avon; near Woodhenge, c.2000BC.

Earlscourt *Ardescote: Stephen Carpenter.* Earlscourt and Upper Earlscourt Farms.

Easton Grey *Estone: Roger de Berkeley. Mill.* Mainly stone-built; on a Romano-British settlement site.

Easton Piercy *Estone: Arnulf de Hesdin.*

East Overton *Overtone:* Lost.

Ebbesborne Wake *Eblesborne: Robert from Robert FitzGerald.*

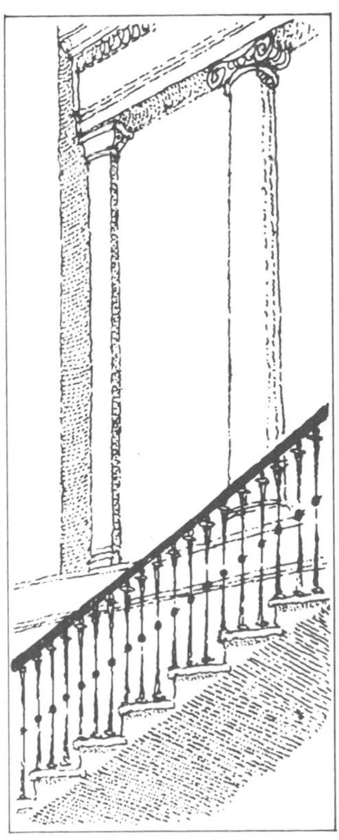

DINTON: *The staircase hall of Philipps House, 1817.*

Edington *Edentone: St Mary of Romsey before and after 1066; Hervey of Wilton. 2 mills.* Priory and church founded 1351 by the Bishop of Winchester, William of Edington.

Elcombe *Elecome: King's land, formerly Earl Aubrey.* Elcombe Hall.

Elston *Wintreburne: Osbern Giffard.* Elston House, Elston Farm.

Enford *Enedforde: Bishop of Winchester before and after 1066; 2 mills.* On the River Avon; Enford Farm.

Etchilhampton *Ec(h)esatingetone: Edward of Salisbury; Edric's wife from Arnulf de Hesdin, formerly Edric; Erlechin from the king.* Rural.

Eysey *Aisi: Reinbald the Priest. 2 mills (with Latton).*

Fifield Bavant *Fifhide: Alfred of Marlborough, and Ralph and Wulfmer, the pre-Conquest holder, from him.* On the River Ebble; Norman church, one of the smallest in Wiltshire.

Figheldean *Figheldean Fisgledene: King's land, formerly Earl Aubrey; Harding the pre-Conquest holder, from the king. Mill.* Near a Roman building site; Old Mill.

Fisherton Anger *Fiscartone: Haimo from Earl Hugh. Mill.* Old mill.

Fisherton de la Mere *Fisertone: Roger de Courseulles. Mill.* On the River Wylye.

Fittleton *Viteletone: Rainer from Robert FitzGerald. Mill.* On the River Avon.

Fonthill Bishop *Fontel.* See page 291.

Fonthill Gifford *Fontel: Berengar Giffard. Mill.* Wooded; Fonthill House and a deer park.

Fosbury *Fistesberie: Rainer from Robert FitzGerald.* Fosbury Manor.

Fovant *Febefonte: Abbess of Wilton. 2 mills.* Norman church; World War I army training area with regimental badges cut into the hillsides.

Foxley *Foxelege: Roger de Berkeley. Mill.* Foxley Manor; Foxley Green.

Frustfield *Ferst-/Fristesfeld/ Cristesfeld/Fistesferie:* Lost.

Fyfield *Fifhide: Edward from Bishop of Winchester.*

Garsdon *Gardone: Malmesbury Abbey. 2 mills.* Tudor manor house, home of George Washington's ancestors; Garsdon Wood.

Gore *Gare: Robert Marshall.* St Joan à Gore's Cross and Farm.

Grafton *Graf/Grastone: Hugh from William d'Eu; Richard Sturmy; Robert FitzRalph; Ralph de Hauville.* Now 2 villages, East and West Grafton; Grafton Downs.

Great Bedwyn *Beduin(d)e:* See page 289.

Grimstead *Gram/Gremestede: Herbert from Waleran Hunter; Cola and Aiulf's son from the king. Mill.* Now 2 villages, East and West Grimstead.

Grittleton *Gretelintone: Glastonbury Abbey, Bishop of Coutances; Urso.* Near Fosse Way, a Roman road.

Groundwell *Grendewelle: Hugh and Gerald from Humphrey de L'Isle.* Groundwell Farm.

Grovely (Wood) *Grauelinges: the King's Foresters from the king.* Huge wood; Grovely earthworks, an ancient settlement, nearby, ruined Grovely Castle.

Ham *Hame: Bishop of Winchester before and after 1066 and William from him.* Georgian manor house.

Hampton *Hantone: Ranulf from Humphrey de L'Isle; Robert FitzRolf.*

Hannington *Hanindone/dine: Glastonbury Abbey and Robert from the abbey. 2 mills.* Hannington Hall, built 1653.

Hardenhuish *Hardenehus: Thorkell from Arnulf de Hesdin.* Now a suburb of Chippenham.

Harding *Haredone: Richard Sturmy and Robert from him.* Harding Farm.

Hartham *He(o)rtham: Edward from Earl Hugh; Thorketel from Edward of Salisbury; Hugh from Humphrey de L'Isle; Godric and Alfhild from the king. Small wood.* Hartham Park, a Georgian house designed by James Wyatt.

Hazelbury *Haseberie: Reginald from Miles Crispin; Nigel the Doctor; Chipping, the pre-Conquest holder, from the king. Church.* Well-restored Tudor manor house.

Heddington *Edintone: Edward of Salisbury, formerly Earl Harold.*

Heytesbury *Hestebe: King's land with Alfward the Priest holding the church.* Empress Maud, Henry II's mother, is said to have had a palace here.

Highway *Hiw(e)i: Malmesbury Abbey; Ralph de Mortimer.*

Highworth *Wrde: King's land; Ralph the priest. Church.* Town. A battle in 1645 left its mark on the church, where a Cromwellian cannonball is preserved.

Hill Deverill *Devrel: Edward of Salisbury and Aethelhelm from him; Osbern Giffard. Mill.* Formerly a village.

Hilmarton *Adhelmertone/ Helmerin/Helmertune: Robert from Arnulf de Hesdin, Ralph from William d'Eu; Aelfric Small from the king. 2 mills.* On Cowage Brook; Hilmarton House.

Hilperton *Helperintone/-itune/ Helprintone: Ansger Cook; William Cornelian; Godwin Clack, and Ealdhild, from the king.* Large, by Hilperton Marsh on the outskirts of Trowbridge.

LACOCK: *The Abbey; 15th-c. cloisters were the inspiration for the 18th-c. re-building.*

Homington *Humi(n)tone: Osbern the Priest.* On the River Ebble; Homington House on Homington Downs.

Horningsham *Horning(es)ham: Agenwulf, formerly his father, from the canons of Lisieux; Osmund from Alfred of Marlborough. Mill.* Mill Farm on a stream. The Meeting House, probably the oldest dissenting chapel in England, was built by Sir John Thynne in 1566, for Scottish Presbyterian workers who were building Longleat at the time.

Huish *Iwis: Richard Sturmy.* By Huish Hill where a prehistoric village was built.

Hullavington *Hunlavintone: Ralph de Mortimer, formerly Earl Harold.* Disused airfield.

Hurdcott (in Barford St Martin) *Hardicote: Humphrey de L'Isle. Mill.* Hurdcott House and Upper Hurdcott Farm on the River Nadder.

Hurdcott (in Winterbourne Earls) *Herdicote: Waleran Hunter. ½ mill.* Tiny; on the River Bourne.

Idmiston *Eunestetone: Glastonbury Abbey before and after 1066.* On the River Bourne.

Imber *Immerie: Ralph de Mortimer.* Desolate; within an army battle training area; long barrow nearby.

Keevil *Chivele: Arnulf de Hesdine. 2 mills.* Pretty; Keevil Manor, built 1580, where Ann Beach was imprisoned by her father for 2 years for falling in love with a curate.

Kennett *Chenet(e): Nicholas. Thurstan. Wulfgeat, Leofric and Wulfmer from Alfred of Marlborough; Richard from Waleran Hunter; St Mary of Winchester from Hugh de Lasne. Mill.* Now the village of East Kennett, where Stone Age skeletons and Bronze Age pottery have been found, and West Kennett, a hamlet by West Kennett Long Barrow.

Kilmington *Chelmetone/ Cilemetone: Serlo de Burcy.*

Kingston Deverill *Devrel: Canons of Lisieux.* Sarcen stones mark the spot where Alfred met the forces from Hampshire, Somerset and Wiltshire on his march against the Danes in 878.

Kington Langley *Langhelei: Glastonbury Abbey, before and after 1066.* Langley Gate Farm.

Kington St Michael *Chintone: Roger from Ralph de Mortimer. Mill.* Large; Priory Farm, with the remains of a Benedictine priory, founded 1155.

Knighton *Wenistetone: Harding, the pre-Conquest holder, from the king. Mill.* Knighton Down long barrow.

Knook *Cunuche: Alfward Colling and Leofgeat (a woman who makes and made the king and queen's gold fringe) from the king. 2 mills.* On the River Wylye; Knook Mill Farm.

Knoyle *Chenvel: King's land; Abbess of Wilton.* Now 2 villages, West Knoyle and East Knoyle, birthplace of Sir Christopher Wren (1632–1723).

Lackham *Lacham: Ralph from William d'Eu. 2 mills.* Lackham College of Agriculture.

Lacock *Lacoc(h): Edward of Salisbury; Alfred of Marlborough. 2 mills, vineyard.* One of England's most beautiful abbeys, founded as an Augustinian nunnery, 1229. W.H. Fox Talbot, father of photography, carried out his experiments here, in 1839.

Landford *Langeford: Otho, formerly his father, from the king. Mill.* 16th-century Landford Manor.

Langford *Langforde: Glastonbury Abbey; Edward of Salisbury and Leidhard from him, Abbess of Wilton; Count of Mortain; Waleran Hunter and Ernburgis from him. 3 mills.* Now 2 villages, Little and Steeple Langford, and a hamlet, Hanging Langford with an Iron Age camp.

Langley Burrell *Langefel: Burghelm from Edward of Salisbury; Wulfwy, the pre-Conquest holder.* On the outskirts of Chippenham.

Latton *Latone: Reinbald the Priest. 2 mills (with Eysey).*

Laverstock *Lauvrecestohes/ Lavertestoche: Abbess of Wilton; Saeric from the king. Mill.* Suburb of Salisbury.

Lavington *Laventone: Robert Marshall; Robert Blunt. 3 mills.* Now 2 villages, Market Lavington, once a market town, and West Lavington.

Liddington *Ledentone: Abbess of Shaftesbury. 2 mills.* Iron Age earthworks, Liddington Castle; Elizabethan manor house.

Littlecott *Litlecote: Thorketel from Miles Crispin.* On Cowage Brook.

Littleton Drew *Liteltone: Robert from Bishop of Coutances. Mill.*

Littleton Pannell *Liteltone: William d'Audrieu from William d'Eu.* 2 houses, à Beckett's, and the 18th century manor house.

Lockeridge *Locherige: Durand of Gloucester.* On the River Kennet, Lockeridge House, Georgian.

Longbridge Deverill *Devrel: Glastonbury Abbey. 4 mills.* Now 2 villages, Monkton and Longbridge Deverill. In 1665 Sir James Thynne of Longleat founded the Thynne almhouses at Longbridge Deverill; the church at Monkton Deverill is dedicated to 'Alfred, King of the West Saxons', who 'camped the night in the Deverill valley before giving the Danes a sound beating at the great Battle of Ethandune' in 878.

Longford *Langeford: Wulfgeat Hunter from the king. Mill.* Longford Castle in Longford Park, built in the late 1500s by Sir Thomas Gorges. Capability Brown laid out the park and gardens.

Luckington *Lochintone: Herman from Durand of Gloucester, formerly Earl Harold; Edward from Ralph de Mortimer.* Luckington Court, once called Peach House, was one of King John's hunting boxes.

Ludgershall *Litlegarsele: Edward of Salisbury.* Ruined keep of a castle built by the Normans on the site of a Saxon stronghold. Queen Maud sought shelter here when fleeing from King Stephen.

Lus Hill *Rusteselle: Edward of Salisbury and Howard from him; Gunter from Humphrey de L'Isle. 2 mills.*

Lydiard Millicent *Lidiarde: King's land. Mill.* Quiet.

Lydiard Tregoze *Lediar: Alfred of Marlborough.* Lydiard Park, home of the St John family for 4 centuries, now open to the public.

Maddington *Wintreburne: Amesbury Church; Matthew de Mortagne.* A nunnery once stood at Maddington Farm.

Maiden Bradley *Bradelie: Walter Giffard from the king. 2 mills.* Priory Farm on the site of a 12th-century leper hospital, later an Augustinian priory.

Malmesbury *Ma(l)mesberie: King's land, Malmesbury Abbey; Glastonbury Abbey and various landholders. Mill.* Town, a weaving centre until the 18th century. King Athelstan, who founded the hospital, was buried here 1000 years ago; the Normans built Malmesbury Abbey on the spot.

Manningford *Maniford/ Maneforde: Winchester Abbey; Almaric of Dreux; Grimbald Goldsmith from the king. 2 mills.* Now 3 villages, Manningford Abbots, Bohune and Bruce, on the River Avon.

Manton *Manetune: Reginald from Miles Crispin.* Pretty; on the River Kennet.

Marden *Meresdene: Hugh FitzBaldric and Walter, his son-in-law, from him. Mill.* Marden Circle, a Stone Age earthwork; mill.

Marlborough *Merleberge: King's land; William Beaufour. Church.* Town called after 'Maerl's Barrow,' an ancient burial place in the grounds of Marlborough College. St Mary's church is Norman; Cardinal Wolsey was ordained in the other church, St Peter's, in 1498.

Marten *Mar/Mertone: Odolina from the king; Ralph and Thorbert. Vines.*

Melksham *Melchesham: King's land, formerly Earl Harold, with Rumold the priest holding the church; Liseman from the king. 8 mills.* Industrial. St Michael's Church has Norman features.

Mere *Mera/Mere: Godric Hunter, Wulfric and Wulfnoth from the king.* Castle Hill, site of a medieval fortress. Its terraces were supposedly built by the Romans for vines.

Middleton (Lilbourne) *Mideltone:* Lost.

Mildenhall *Milenhalle: Edward from Glastonbury Abbey. Mill.* On the River Kennet.

Milford *Meleford: Jocelyn from Humphrey de L'Isle (half in the king's forest); Wulfgeat from the king.* Now a suburb of Salisbury; medieval double bridge over the River Bourne.

Milston *Mildestone: Earl Roger and Thorold from him; Robert from Robert FitzGerald. Mill.* On the River Avon, birthplace of the politician and writer Joseph Addison (1672–1719).

Monkton Farleigh *Farlege: Brictric, his brother from him and Aelfric from the king..* Tudor manor house on the site of an ancient priory.

Moredon *Mordone/tune: Albert from Alfred of Marborough; Thurstan from Gilbert de Breteuil; Robert FitzRolf.* District of Swindon.

Netheravon *Nigra Avra/ Nigravre: King's land, formerly Earl Harold, with Nigel the Doctor holding the church; Durand from Nigel the Doctor; Hervey. Derelict church with damaged roof, 3 mills.* On a Roman building site; All Saints Church, originally Saxon.

Nettleton *Niteltone: Glastonbury Abbey. 3 mills.* A Roman temple was built on top of Nettleton Tumulus, a long green mound with 3 stones.

Newton Tony *Newentone: Alfred of Marlborough. Mill.* On the River Bourne; named after the de Tosny family, 13th-century lords of the manor.

North Newnton *Newetone: Abbess of Wilton before and after 1066. Mill.* On the River Avon.

North Tidworth *Todew(o)rde/ Todowrde: Bishop of Bayeux and Odo from him; Edward of Salisbury; Croc.* Town near Sidbury Hill, an ancient fort. Now dominated by military barracks.

North Wraxall *Werochesalle: Godfrey from Edward of Salisbury. 2 mills.* Pretty; in woods.

Norton *Nortone: Malmesbury Abbey. Mill.* Manor house.

Norton Bavant *Nortone: Alfred of Marlborough. 2 mills.* By the River Wylye, on a Roman villa site. Scratchbury Camp, a fort built *c.*100BC is nearby, with traces of a smaller camp (*c.*2000 BC) within it.

Oaksey *Wochesie: Brictric from the king. Mill.* Norwood Castle, a group of earthworks; Oaksey Moor Farm.

Odstock *Odestoche: Brictric from the king. Mill.* 17th-century manor house on the River Ebble.

Ogbourne *Ocheburne/borne: King's land; Miles Crispin, formerly Earl Harold; Harding; the pre-Conquest holder and Thorkell from the king. Mill.* Now 2 villages, Ogbourne St Andrew and St George on the River Og; many ancient earthworks.

Orcheston *Orc(h)estone: Hugh and William from Edward of Salisbury; Osbern Giffard.* Named for its abundance of Orcheston grass.

Pertwood *Perteworde: Osbert from Bishop of Coutances.* Split into Higher and Lower Pertwood by a Roman road.

Pewsey *Pevesei/sie: King's land with Reinbald the priest holding the church; Westminster Abbey before and after 1066; Arnulf de Hesdin; and Edric from the king. Church, 7 mills.* Town. Its church stands on Sarcen stones laid by the Saxons.

Pomeroy *Ponberie: Osmund.* Pomeroy Farm; Pomeroy Wood.

Porton *Po(e)rtone: Peter from Edward of Salisbury; Wulfric, formerly his father, from the king. Mill.* On the River Bourne.

Potterne *Poterne: Bishop of Salisbury before and after 1066; Arnulf of Hesdin and Robert from him; Alfward from the king. 7 mills.* Near Potterne Wood; manor house; Blounts Court.

Poulshot *Paueshou: King's land with Edgar holding the church. Corsham church.* Quiet; ancient water mill.

Poulton *Poltone: Humphrey de L'Isle. Mill.* Poulton House, outside Marlborough.

Purton *Piritone: Glastonbury Abbey. Mill.* Straggling; Purton Common; manor house, *c.*1600.

Ramsbury *Ramesberie: Bishop of Salisbury. 10 mills.* On the River Kennet; water mill at Axford Farm.

Ratfyn *Rotefeld(e): Edward of Salisbury, formerly Earl Harold, and Hervey from him.* Ratfyn Barrow nearby.

Rockley *Rochelie: Edward of Salisbury; Alfred of Marlborough.* Manton Down Burial Chamber.

Rodbourne Cheney *Redborne: Reginald from Miles Crispin.* On the outskirts of Swindon.

Rowde *Rode: William, Gilbert and Wulfgeat from Alfred of Marlborough. 2 mills.* Many modern developments; Bronze Age barrow on Roundway Down.

Rushall *Rusteselve: King's land, with St Wandrille's holding the church. 5 mills.* On the River Avon; church with a Norman font.

Salisbury *Sarisberie: King's land; Bishop of Salisbury. 10 mills.* City on the River Avon. Originally Old Sarum (*Sorbiodunum*), an ancient British hill-fort, it was then Roman, and Saxon. The cathedral was built in 1220.

Salthrop *Salteharpe: Humphrey de L'Isle.* Salthrop House.

Seagry *Segrete/grie: Durand of Gloucester and 2 men-at-arms from him.* By the River Avon; Seagry Wood.

Sevington *Sevementone: William from William d'Eu.* Stonebuilt.

Shalbourne *Saldeborne/ Scaldeburne: Hugh de Lasne and William from him; Wulfric and Osgot from the king. Mill.*

Shaw (in Chute) *Scage:* Lost.

Shaw (in West Overton) *Essage: William de Braose and Robert from him.* Georgian Shaw House.

POTTERNE: *15th c. Porch House.*

Sherrington *Scarentone: Osbern Giffard. Mill.* On the River Wylye; nearby, mound on which a castle belonging to the Gifford family once stood.

Sherston *Sorestone/Sorstain: King's land with St Wandrille's holding the church.* On Avon; church with a Norman tower, and a chest containing armour worn by John Rattlebone during a victorious battle with the Danes, 1016.

Shipley *Scepeleia: Bishop of Salisbury.* Shipley Bottom.

Shrewton *Wintreburne: Edward of Salisbury and Godfrey and Theobald from him. Mill.* Bridge over the River Till. At the Blind House, shaped like a beehive, people were imprisoned before execution.

Smallbrook *Smalebroc: Aubrey the Chamberlain.* Part of Warminster.

Smithcot *Smitecote: Albert from Humphrey de L'Isle. Mill.* Cotsmiths Farm.

Somerford *Sumre/Somreford(e): Gunfrid from Malmesbury Abbey; Theodoric from Edward of Salisbury; Siward from Alfred of Marlborough; Humphrey de L'Isle; Alwin, Alfwy, Edward and Saeva from the king. 3 mills.* Now 2 villages, Great and Little Somerford. 16th-century Mount Farmhouse stands on the site of a motte and bailey castle in Great Somerford.

Sopworth *Sopeworde: Hugh from William d'Eu.* Georgian manor house.

South Newton *Neweton(e): Abbess of Wilton. 2 mills. In Melchet Forest 80 cartloads of timber.* In the Wylye valley.

Standen *Standone: Benzelin from Arnulf de Hesdin. Mill.* Standen House, in Chute, a late 18th-century mansion with thatched boundary walls.

Standlynch *Staninges: William de Falaise from the king and Alfward from him; Waleran Hunter; Alfwy son of Thurber from the king.* Standlynch Farm and Down. Trafalgar House, given to Nelson's brother as an act of national gratitude, houses a large collection of the Admiral's possessions.

Stanley *Stanlege: Azelin from Waleran Hunter.* Stanley Abbey Farm.

Stanmore *Stamere:* Lost.

Stanton Fitzwarren *Stantone: Grimbald Goldsmith from the king.* By the site of a Roman building; church with Saxon remains, in the park surrounding Stanton House.

Stanton St Bernard *Stantone: Abbess of Wilton. 2 mills.* Between All Cannings Bridge and Stanton Bridge on the Kennet and Avon Canal.

Stanton St Quintin *Stantone: Glastonbury Abbey and Osbern Giffard from the abbey.*

Stapleford *Stapleford: Swein, formerly his father, from the king.*

Charming; on the site of Stapleford Castle, once owned by Waleran Hunter, the Conqueror's huntsman.

Staverton *Stavretone: Brictric, formerly his father, from the king. Mill.* On the River Avon; once a minor weaving centre.

Stert *Sterte: Humphrey de L'Isle, 2 mills.* Pretty.

Stitchcombe *Stotecome: Goda, a woman, from the king. Mill.* On the River Kennet.

Stockton *Stottune: Bishop of Winchester before and after 1066. Mill.* Stockton House, built by John Topp, an Elizabethan cloth merchant.

Stourton *Stortone: Ralph from Walscin de Douai. 2 mills.* Stourhead, in beautiful gardens, the Stourton family home from Saxon times until the 18th century. Alfred's Tower marks the spot where Alfred set up his standard against the Danes in 879.

Stratford Tony *Stradford: King's land, formerly Earl Aubrey. 2 mills.* Near the River Ebble; named after Ralph Toni, William the Conqueror's standard-bearer at the Battle of Hastings, who was granted this land for his services.

Stratton St Margaret *Stratone: Nigel the Doctor. Mill.* Suburb of Swindon.

Surrendell *Sirendone: Richard from Ralph de Mortimer.* Surrendell Farm.

Suton Mandeville *Sudtone: Richard FitzGilbert and Berengar from him. Mill.* Near the River Nadder.

Sutton Veny *Su(d)tone: William de Mohun and Walter from him; William FitzGuy; Nigel the Doctor and St Mary of Montebourg from him. 2 mills.* Sutton Veny House.

Swallowcliff *Svaloclive: Abbess of Wilton; Brictric and Alfward from the king.* Manor house by Swallowcliff Wood.

Swindon *Suindone/dune: Bishop of Bayeux and Wadard from him; Alfred of Marlborough; Wulfric and Wulfward, the king's purveyor from the king; Odin the Chamberlain. 2 mills.* Now the large, industry-based New Town and the Old Town with a market-place and the ruins of the ancient Holy Rood Church in the grounds of the Goddard family house.

Teffont Evias *Tefonte: Alfred of Marlborough. Mill.* Pretty; Teffont Mill. Sir James Ley, Lord Chief Justice and friend of John Milton, lived at Teffont Manor in the 17th century.

Thickwood *Ticoode: Gilbert from Edward of Salisbury.* By the site of a Roman building.

Thornhill *Torn(v)elle: Ansfrid from Gilbert de Breteuil; William FitzAnsculf. Mill.*

Tidcombe *Titicome: Wenesi's wife, formerly her husband, from the king. Mill.* Near the course of a Roman road.

Tilshead *Theodulveside/ Tidulfhide: King's land; Alfward, Aelfric Small, Alstan and Aelmer from the king. 9 mills.* Large; on Salisbury Plain; Bronze Age ditch nearby.

Tisbury *Tisseberie: Abbess of Shaftesbury. 4 mills.* Burial place of Rudyard Kipling (1865–1936); 2 castles, ruined (14th-century) Wardour Castle and an 18th-century castle of the same name, now Cranbourne Chase girls' school.

Tockenham *Tocheham: Roger from Durand of Gloucester; Odilard from Ralph of Mortimer; Aelfric Small, Alric and Algar from the king. Mill.* Church with a Roman god in a wall niche.

Tollard Royal *Tollard: Aiulf from Edward of Salisbury; William d'Eu. Vineyard.* Burial place of Lieutenant-General Pitt-Rivers (1827–1900). His museum at Oxford holds weapons and relics from the Stone Age onwards.

Trow *Troi: Richard Poynant.* Trow Farm and Down.

Trowbridge *Straburg: Brictric, formerly his father, from the king. Mill.* Town on the River Kennet, the administrative capital of Wiltshire and an industrial and weaving centre. The poet George Crabbe was rector, 1814–32.

Trowle *Trole: Brictric from the king.* Now Trowle Common; bridge over the River Biss.

Tytherington *Tedrintone: King's land, formerly Earl Aubrey. ½ mill.* St James's Church, founded in 1083 by Queen Maud, mother of Henry II.

Tytherton Kellaways *Terintone: Osbern Giffard.* Now known as Kellaways.

Uffcott *U(l)fecote: Roger from Durand of Gloucester; Wulfric, formerly his father, from the king.* By an ancient ridgeway; Barbury Castle, a prehistoric hill-fort where the West Saxons beat the Britons in the Battle of Beranburh, AD 556.

Ugford *Ocheforde/Ogeford: Abbess of Wilton; Gundwin from Osbern Giffard. 2 mills.* On the outskirts of Wilton.

Upavon *Oppavrene: King's land with St Wandrilles holding the church.* Quiet; Casterley Camp, Wiltshire's biggest prehistoric fortesss; church originally Norman.

Upton Lovell *Uptone: Gerald of Wilton from the king. Mill.* On the River Wylye.

Upton Scudamore *Opetone: Reinbald from Arnulf de Hesdin; Ralph from Alfred of Marlborough; Ansfrid from William d'Eu. 2 mills.*

Urchfont *Ierchesfonte: St Mary of Winchester before and after 1066. 3 mills.* Upton Manor, 1688, now a college.

Walcot *Walecote: Reginald from Miles Crispin.* Suburb of Swindon.

Wanborough *Wemberge: Bishop of Winchester before and after 1066. Mill.* By the Key of Wessex, where 3 Roman roads met and 2 Saxon battles were fought.

Wardour *Werdore: Abbess of Wilton and Brictmer from her.* 3 buildings: 14th-century Wardour Castle, where the aged Lady Arundell held out for 5 days with only a handful of servants against Cromwell's soldiers during the Civil War; 17th-century Old Wardour House, and Georgian New Wardour Cast.

Warminster *Guerminstre:* See page 288.

Washern *Waisel: Abbess of Wilton. In Melchet Forest 80 cartloads of timber.* 17th-century Washern Grange.

Westbury *Wes(t)berie: King's land, formerly Queen Edith with a minor clerk holding the church; William Shield. Potters, 8 mills.* Small industrial town where Judge James Ley, 1st Earl of Marlborough (1550–1629) is buried; late Georgian cloth mills.

West Dean *Duene: Waleran Hunter. 1½ mills.* Near the site of a Roman villa; remains of a motte and bailey castle.

Westlecott *Wichelestote:* Lost.

West Overton *Ovretone: Abbess of Wilton. Mill.* On the River Kennet; near the course of a Roman road.

West Tytherton *Tedelintone/ Terintone: Burghelm from Edward of Salisbury; William Hard from Alfred of Marlborough. 4 parts of a mill, 2 parts of a mill.* Scott's Mill Farm.

Westwood *Westwode: Bishop of Winchester before and after 1066. Mill.* Now 2 villages, Westwood and Upper Westwood.

Whaddon (in Alderbury) *Watedene: Engenwulf and 2 men-at-arms from Waleran Hunter.* On the outskirts of Alderbury.

Whaddon (in Semington) *Wadone: Aelfric of Melksham, the pre-Conquest holder, from the king. Mill.*

Whitecliff *Witeclive: Gundwin the Keeper of the granaries.* Whitecliff Farm on the River Wylye.

Whitley *Witelie: Gunfrid Mawditt.*

Widhill *Wi(l)dehille: Gunfrid from Alfred of Marlborough; Theobald the doctor; Humphrey the cook. Mill.* Widhill Farm.

Wilcot *Wilcote: Edward of Salisbury. New church, very good house, good vineyard.* Wilcot Manor and its vineyards were originally 11th century; church with a Norman chancel arch.

Wilsford (near Amesbury) *Wiflesford(e): Haimo from Earl Hugh; Hugh from Robert FitzGerald. Mill.* On the River Avon; Elizabethan manor house.

Wilsford (near Pewsey) *Wivlesford: Aelfric of Melksham from the king; Edward in pledge.*

WILTON: *Inigo Jones' great house.*

Wilton *Wiltone/tune: Hervey of Wilton; William d'Eu; Hugh FitzBaldric.* Town. Wilton House and Park, seat of the Earls of Pembroke was built in 1545, on the site of a 9th-century nunnery founded by Alfred the Great. It was famous in the Middle Ages for its many religious houses (12 parish churches). Carpets were first made here in the 17th century.

Wingfield *Winefel: Bishop of Coutances and Roger from him. Mill.* Midway House, once the home of General Shrapnel, who invented the shrapnel shell early in the 19th century.

Winterbourne *Wintreburne: Bishop of Coutances; Glastonbury Abbey; Waleran Hunter; Godescal, Aldred and Saeric from the king. 2 mills, ½ mill, parts of 2 mills.* Area along the River Bourne comprising 6 or 7 villages; Figsbury Ring, made up of Sarcen stones.

Winterbourne Bassett *Wintreburne: Amesbury Church; Humphrey de L'Isle.*

Winterbourne Earls *Wintreburne: Edward of Salisbury. Mill.* On the River Bourne.

Winterbourne Monkton *Wintreborne: Glastonbury Abbey.* Sprawling; Middle Farm built of Sarcen stones; Neolithic camp nearby.

Winterbourne Stoke *Wintreburne-(stoch): King's land, formerly Queen Edith; with the Abbot of Jumièges holding the church; Edward of Salisbury and Walter from him; Alfwy's wife from the king. Mill.* Pretty; Yarnbury Castle, a huge Iron Age earthwork; church with 2 Norman doorways.

Winterslow *Wintreslei/leu: King's land, formerly Earl Aubrey; Count of Mortain; Wulfric, 4 countrymen and Wulfward from the king. Mill.* On the site of a Roman building, Bronze Age flint mines. The essayist William Hazlitt lived here, 1808–1823.

Wishford *Wicheford/Witford: Abbess of Wilton before and after 1066; Robert from Waleran Hunter; William Cornelian from the king. 3 mills.* Now the village of Great Wishford, where Sir Richard Grobham founded the almshouses in 1628, and the hamlet of Little Wishford.

Witcomb *Widecome: Robert from Arnulf de Hesdin.* Witcomb Farm.

Witherington *Widetone: Edward, formerly his father, from the king. Mill.* Witherington Farm; Witherington Ring.

Wittenham *Withenham: Bishop of Coutances and Roger from him. Mill.* Lost in Wingfield.

Wolf Hall *Ulfela: Ralph de Hauville. Mill.* House where Jane Seymour was born (c.1509).

Woodborough *Witeberge: Robert FitzGerald and Jocelyn from him. Mill.* Sprawling.

Woodhill *Wadhulle: Bishop of Bayeux and Odo from him.* Woodhill Park Farm.

Wootton Bassett *Wodetone:* See page 288.

Wootton Rivers *Otone: King's land, formerly Queen Edith, with Mont St Michel holding the 2 churches.* On the Kennet and Avon Canal. The church clock was made out of old prams and bedsteads by Mr Jack Spratt, to commemorate George V's Coronation (1911).

Wroughton *Wertune/ Wervetone: Bishop of Winchester before and after 1066; Robert from Humphrey de L'Isle; Aldred from the king. 7 mills.* Large, almost swallowed up by Swindon.

Wylye *Wilgi: Abbess of Wilton. Mill.* On the River Wylye.

Yarnfield *Gernefelle: William from Walter Giffard.* Deserted medieval village.

Yatesbury *Etesberie: Alfred d'Epaignes.* The church rests on Sarcen stones.

Yatton Keynell *Etone/Etune/ Getone: Thurstan from Bishop of Lisieux; Judicael from Arnulf de Hesdin; an Englishman from William d'Eu. Mill.* Motor-racing circuit.

Zeals *Sela/Sele: Jocelyn Rivers; Alfgeat from the king. 2 mills.* Charles II hid in Zeals House when fleeing Cromwell's men in 1651.

Worcestershire

North of the Avon (Feckenham Forest) and west of the Severn (Malvern Chase) Worcestershire was heavily forested. By contrast, the terraces of the Avon have light, well-drained soils that have always made the Vale of Evesham with its gentle relief and its early springs favoured agricultural land. The great Benedictine houses of Pershore, Evesham and Worcester and, after Edward the Confessor's benefactions, St Peter's, Westminster, held the dominating position in the county. The Abbey of Pershore had, in fact, been deprived of half its lands to advance King Edward's aspirations for his new foundation.

The Conquest brought less disturbance to this county than to others, for Aethelwig, the Abbot of Evesham, and Wulfstan, the Bishop of Worcester, both found exceptional favour with William I. They helped to suppress the rising of the three earls in 1075, and Aethelwig went on to receive important commissions from William to act as justiciar in seven counties.

Droitwich had an importance in 1086 that it has lost today, for a stratum of rock salt in the Keuper Marls here produces plentiful brine springs; according to Domesday, *there were widespread interests in the local salt pans, spreading across many manors and counties. King William held an even bigger share of this wealth than had King Edward.*

Cleeve Prior

[Worcester Church] itself holds CLEEVE (PRIOR) *CLIVE* with (ATCH) LENCH. 10½ hides. In lordship 2 ploughs; A priest who has 1 hide and 2 ploughs; 9 villagers and 5 smallholders with 4 ploughs. A mill which pays 1 sester of honey. 4 male and 4 female slaves; meadow, 20 acres. The value was £7; now £6. 2 hides, less 1 virgate, of this land are waste.

Cleeve Prior, with its limestone houses, gives the first hint of the Cotswolds on a journey south from the Avon. Surrounded to the doorsteps by orchards and with access to extensive meadows, it must have been a choice manor in 1086. It remains a mystery why one-fifth of it should have been waste. The half hide (out of the ten and a half) combines with the four and a half hides recorded for Atch Lench, three miles away across the Avon, one of the Abbot of Evesham's manors, to total 15; hide assessments in multiples of five are familiar in *Domesday.*

In the politics of the thirteenth century Cleeve Prior seems to have served as a compensation package for losers. It was made over to the bishop's candidate for Prior of Worcester when the monks refused him in 1224; and it had to put up with the infamous William de Ledbury (he was said to have had 20 mistresses), when he was evicted from Great Malvern in 1284 after a conflict that dragged in the Bishop of London, King Edward I and the Pope. The king devised this face-saver for him, even though he had by then renounced the faith.

Cleeve Prior's most famous son was Thomas Bushell (1594–1674), lessee of the king's mines in Wales and founder of the mint in Aberystwyth. During the Civil War he procured arms abroad for the Royalists and led the final defence of Lundy Island. With the Roundhead's victory, he went to ground in his manor house, but soon emerged to reopen both mines and mint for Cromwell. He died in debt and obscurity, but achieved renown with his aquatic gardens at Enstone and his new techniques of adit mining—entering horizontally, rather than through a vertical shaft. His preoccupation with refining precious metals makes the discovery of a Roman gold hoard at Cleeve Prior in 1811 a puzzling coincidence.

The mill at Cleeve Prior, demolished only in 1940, was almost certainly the one mentioned in *Domesday.* It was unique in that it 'rendered' honey. It also provides an example of the decay of the feudal system of payment in kind: at the beginning of the thirteenth century it rendered three marks and 40 stitches of eels (1000 eels). By 1237 the render was in cash: four marks.

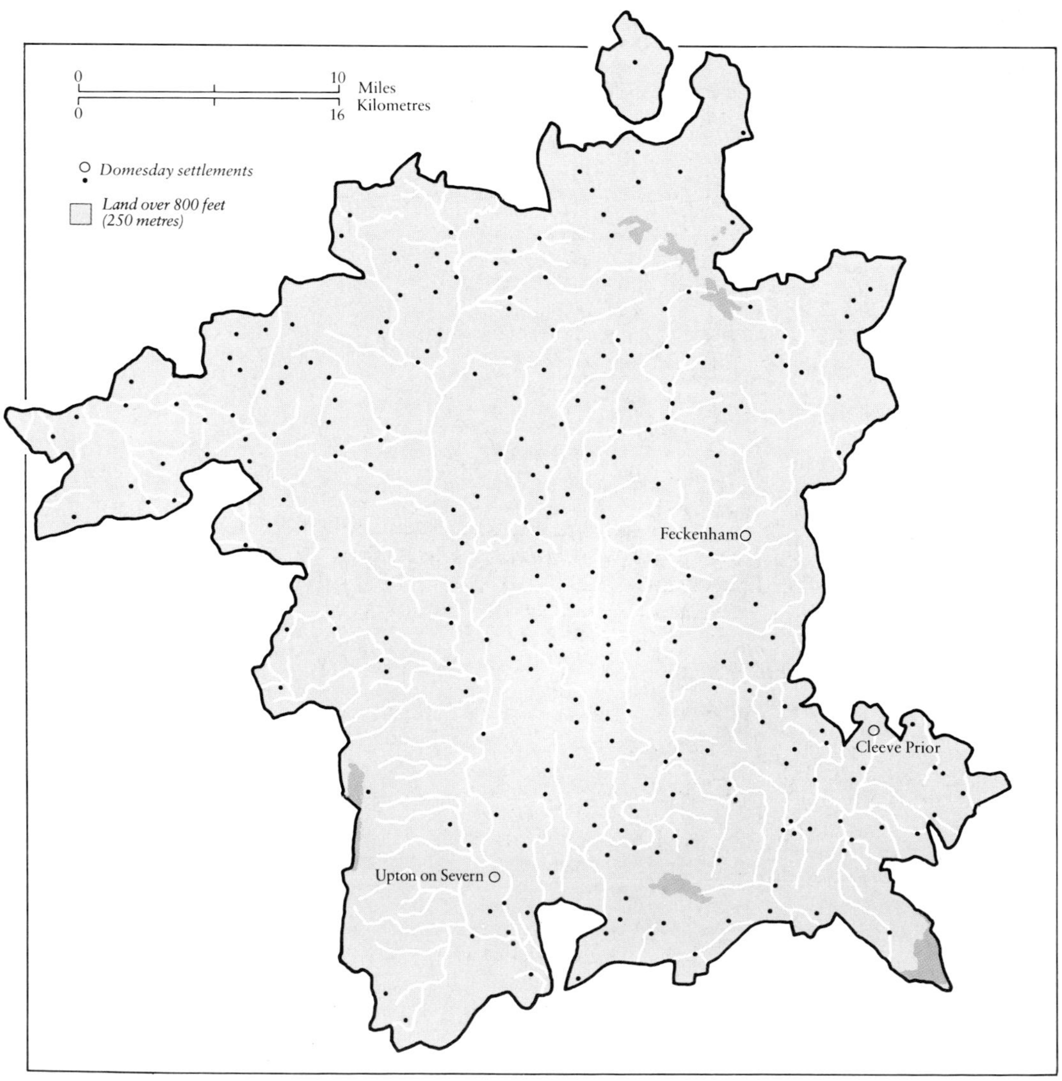

Feckenham

The King holds FECKENHAM *FECHEHA.* Five thanes held it from Earl Edwin; they could go where they wished with the land. Under them they had 4 men-at-arms, as free as they were themselves; between them there were 13 ploughs. 10 hides. In lordship 6 ploughs; 30 villagers, 11 smallholders, a reeve, a beadle, a miller and a smith; between them there were 18 ploughs. 12 male and 5 female slaves. A rider holds ½ hide, 2 parts of ½ hide and 1 croft; he has 1 plough. A mill at 2s. In Droitwich 4 salt-houses; the woodland of this manor has been put outside into the king's woodland, and ½ hide of land which Earl William gave to Jocelyn Hunter. Earl William gave to St Mary's Church [in Normandy] this manor's tithe and church with a priest and 2 virgates of land with 1 villager. Walter de Lacy gave 1 hide out of the lordship land to one Hubert; he has ½ plough.

Feckenham lies on the saltway that runs from Droitwich to Alcester, a mile or so before it starts its climb up the western slope of the Ridgeway. Only the giant pylons leading from an Alcatraz-like electricity sub-station hint at the nearness of modern Redditch, grown by overspill from Birmingham into an urban warren. The village seems relieved that with its water-powered needle mill shut down, it no longer hums with cottage industries.

That a royal manor deep in Worcestershire should appear in the Herefordshire folios (*'scriptae sunt in brevi de Hereford'* reads the Worcestershire entry) reveals how desperate things had become in the western marshes. William FitzOsbern, palatine earl of Hereford and confidant of William I, had transferred it to Herefordshire, together with other manors in the county and in Gloucestershire, to shore up the revenues he needed to police this chaotic area. The incursions of Edric the Wild left tracts of Herefordshire still waste in 1086. Even so, FitzOsbern diverted some of the Feckenham resources to his monastic foundation at La Vieille Lyre, where St Mary's was the abbey church. Such were the customary priorities of the age.

The *Domesday* entry suggests that Feckenham was well established before 1066; it had been in the hands of the Mercian royal family and 'a reeve, a beadle, a miller and a smith and 4 salt-houses in Droitwich' puts it in a different class from other villages in the region. What St Briavels was to the Forest of Dean, Feckenham was to the Forest of Feckenham: the centre of administration. Only an earthwork beside the church familiarly known as Bennett's Bower – it was a tobacco plantation in the 18th century – marks the site of the special prison for all forest offenders south of the Trent.

At its largest, Feckenham Forest reached south to the Avon and south-west to the gates of Worcester. Not even its usefulness as a source of fuel for the Droitwich salt industry, however, could prevent its being whittled away when the king, starting in the fourteenth century, allowed the gradual disafforestation of his hunting reserves, and assarting – ploughing up woodland – became legal.

Conflicts of jurisdiction fill every page of the forest's history, and one wonders what travail it brought to Geoffrey Chaucer, its Clerk of Works and Keeper of the Lodge in 1389. As in so many royal forests, commoners and landowners often fought physically; in 1558 the house of Sir John Throckmorton, then lord of the manor, was torn down by an angry crowd, and he was forced to 'wander up and down like an Egyptian in other men's houses for want of a house of my own'. Feckenham was finally disafforested in 1629, but not enclosed until 1819 and then only after the sheriff had been unhorsed by rioting freemen.

South-west of Feckenham it is still possible to pick out the core of the ancient forest by the network of bridle paths and by the absence of Norman churches.

Upton on Severn

. . . the Bishop [of Worcester] also holds RIPPLE with 1 member UPTON (ON SEVERN) *UPTUN*. 25 hides which pay tax. Of these 13 are in lordship; 4 ploughs there; 2 priests who have 1½ hides with 2 ploughs; 40 villagers and 16 smallholders with 36 ploughs. 8 male slaves, 1 female. A mill; meadow, 30 acres; woodland ½ league long and 3 furlongs wide, in MALVERN (CHASE) (MALFERNA). From this he had honey and hunting and whatever came from there and 10s in addition. Now it is in the Forest. The Bishop receives from it pasture dues, firewood and (timber) for repairing houses. The value was and is £10.

If it were not for the pubs and the teashops and the exquisite Georgian police station, Upton could be some foreign resort. The slender church tower with its baroque copper dome has an un-English look, as do the little tiled pagoda huts that have been built around the yacht marina.

Upton in 1086, with 25 hides all paying tax, must have been a thriving place. The reduction in the bishop's share of Malvern Chase after 1066 had been caused by the expansion of the king's forest, a phenomenon that began with

FECKENHAM: *This massive tree and its surrounding woodland are reminders of the days when the area, then called Feckenham Forest, was one of the King's hunting reserves.*

UPTON ON SEVERN: *No more lovely scene could be imagined than this distant view of the village, its 'oriental' church tower and dome silhouetted against the Malvern Hills and the Worcestershire Beacon.*

the Conqueror and continued throughout Henry I's reign. It is surprising that there is no *Domesday* reference to the river, which was probably already transporting timber, salt, wine and cider, as well as tiles and pottery made at nearby Hanley Castle.

The symbol of Upton's prosperity might well be the two-masted trow that employed sail – and, below Gloucester, the tide – to travel this once vital waterway. Along many stretches of the river the trows had to be hauled by gangs of 'bow halliers', which may explain the town's former rowdy reputation. In 1832, Scots Greys from Worcester were called out to disperse a crowd of them when they rioted in protest at horses being used on the towpath. Court records abound with references to river pirates and to the casting of gigantic nets by Upton men to haul in so many salmon that communities upstream were in uproar.

Upton had become an inland port by the seventeenth century, and rulings of 1690 reflect stupefying squalor: 'We do order yt no Cowes Bellys be emptied in the streets by ye buchers', and '. . . no person within the Berrow shall suffer any Mixon (dungheap) to lye above the space of 16 days.' With sawpits in the main street, pigsties on the bridge, and an overflowing gumstool (ducking pond) at the bottom of New Street, it is not surprising that Upton was swept by epidemics: plague in 1665, recurrent small-pox, and a cholera outbreak in 1832 which, at its height, killed 50 people in a month.

The decay of the river traffic altered everything. Once the railway arrived, the barge quays emptied and, as if to signal the end of an era, Upton Old Bridge fell down in the floods of 1852. Its replacements have been progressively uglier and the present one, a green steel trough with high walls, denies both motorists and pedestrians a view of anything at all. Except for summer holiday makers and the occasional flood, Upton hardly knows any more that it is on the Severn. The absence of any mention of the river in *Domesday* was perhaps a premonition.

Worcestershire Gazetteer
Each entry starts with the modern place name in **bold** type. The *Domesday* information that follows is in *italic* type, beginning with the name or names by which the place was known in 1086. The main landholders and under-tenants are next, separated with semi-colons if a place was divided into more than one holding. More general information completes the *Domesday* part of the entry, including examples of dues such as eels and corn rendered by tenants. The modern or post-Domesday section is in normal type. ▣ represents a village, ⌂ a small village or hamlet.

Abberley *Edboldelege: Ralph de Tosny.* ▣ Abberley Hall.

Abberton *Edbretitune: Pershore Church before and after 1066.* ▣ Hall.

Ab Lench *Abeleng: Urso from Worcester Church.* ⌂ Also known as Abbot's Lench, probably Hob's Lench originally.

Abbots Morton *Mortune: Ranulf from Evesham Church.* ▣ Black and white timbered houses; once a refuge from outlaw raiders from Feckenham Forest.

Aldington *Aldintone: Evesham Church. Mill.* ▣

Alton *Alvintune: Ralph de Tosny.* Alton Lodge; Alton Villa.

Alvechurch *Alvievecherche: Worcester Church.* ▣ Half-timbered houses; traces of a moat and fishponds; remains of an episcopal palace.

Ashborough *Asseberga:* Lost.

Ashton under Hill *Es(se)tone: King's land.* ▣

Astley *Eslei: St Taurin's Church from Ralph de Tosny. Church, 4 mills.* ▣ Astley Hall; church with Norman carvings.

Aston Fields *Estone: Worcester Church. 2 mills.* Part of Bromsgrove.

Aston Somerville *Estune: King's land.* ⌂ Manor farm.

Atch Lench *Achelenz: Worcester Church; Evesham Church. Mill. Honey.* ⌂

Baddington *Bedindone: Worcester Church.* Bant (originally Baddington) Mill.

Badsey *Badesei: Evesham Church.* ▣

Barley *Burgelege: Worcester Church, in the king's hands.* Barley House; Barley Cottage.

Bastwood *Bestewde:* Lost.

Bayton *Betune: Rayner from Ralph de Tosny. Mill.* ▣

Beckford *Beceford: King's land.*

Bellbroughton *Brotune: Urso d'Abetot, formerly Countess Godiva. Church.* ▣ Known for scythe-making.

Bell Hall *Bellem: Robert from William FitzAnsculf. Salt-house.* Bell Hall; Bell Hall Farm.

Bellington *Belintones: William FitzAnsculf.* Bellington Farm; Bellington Mill.

Bengeworth *Beningeorde/Bennicworte: Abbot of Evesham and Urso the Sheriff from Worcester Church; Evesham Church.* Part of Evesham.

Bentley *Beneslei: William from Urso d'Abetot.* ▣ Now Upper Bentley; Bentley House; Upper Bentley Farm.

Beoley *Beolege: Pershore Church.* Beoley Hall.

Berrington *Beritune: Osbern FitzRichard, formerly his father. Mill.* Now 2 hamlets, Berrington and Berrington Green.

Besford *Beford: William the priest from Westminster Church and Urso and Walter Ponther from him.* ▣ Besford Hall.

Bickmarsh *Bichemerse: King's land.* Bickmarsh Hall.

Birlingham *Berlingeham: Westminster Church and Urso from the church. Fishery.* ▣

Bishampton *Bisantune: Worcester Church, Roger de Lacy from the church and 2 Frenchmen from him. Mill.* ▣ Orchards.

Bockleton *Boclintun: Bishop of Hereford.* Bockleton Farm.

Bradley Green *Bradelege: Archdeacon Alric from Worcester Church.* ▣ Scattered; on the Roman road to Droitwich.

Bransford *Bradnesforde: Urso from Pershore Church. Mill.* ⌂ Bransford Court.

Bredicot *Bradecote: Walter Ponther from Worcester Church. Woodland in the king's forest.* ⌂ Roman coins were found here.

Bredon *Breodun: Worcester Church. Mill.* ▣ Bredon Hill with Iron Age fortifications and a view of 14 counties.

Bredons Norton *Nortune: Durand from Worcester Church.* ▣ Norton Park, home of Thomas Copley, Raleigh's companion on the voyage to America in the late 16th century.

Bretforton *Bratfortune: Evesham Church. Mill.* ▣ Timbered cottages.

BREDON: *The 14th-c. tithe barn has an unusual bailiff's room reached by steps.*

Bricklehampton *Bricstelmestune: Westminster Church.* ▣ Hall.

Broad Marston *Merestune: King's land.* ▣ Marston Grange.

Broadwas *Bradewesham: Worcester Church. 2 mills, fishery (with Hallow).* ▣ Black and white houses; Broadwas Court. Edward Elgar (1857–1934) was born at Broadheath nearby.

Broadway *Bradeweia: Pershore Church.* ▣ Stone-built; Cotswold.

Bromsgrove *Bremesgrave: King's land. 3 mills; 4 hawks' eyries; 6 lead vats for boiling the brine (with Wythall, Wythwood, Houndsfield, Lea Green, Comble, Burcot, Ashborough, Tutnall, Tynsall, Fockbury, Shurvenhill, Woodcote Green, Timberhanger, Moseley. Kings Norton, Lindsworth, Tessall, and Rednall which is now in Warwickshire).* Market town.

Broughton Hackett *Broctune: The Sheriff from Westminster Church and Aiulf from him.* ▣

Burcot *Bericote: King's land. Assessed with Bromsgrove, etc.* ⌂

Bushley *Biselege/Biselie: King's land. Cowman, dairymaid. Worcester Church, in the king's hands.* ▣ Bushley Park; Bushley Green.

Carton *Carletune: Odo from Osbern FitzRichard.* Carton Farm.

Chaddesley Corbett *Cedeslai: Aldeva, a woman, the pre-Conquest holder. 3 mills (12 packloads of corn).* ▣ Half-timbered house. Harvington Hall nearby is Tudor with wall-paintings and secret passages.

Chadwich *Celdu(u)ic: King's land.* Chadwich Manor; Chadwich Grange Farm. The estate was given to the National Trust by the Cadbury family.

Chawson *Celvestune: William from William Goizenboded; Earl Roger.* ▣ On the outskirts of Droitwich.

Childswickham *Wicuene: King's land.* ▣ Thatched cottages; a medieval wayside cross.

Chevington *Civintone: Pershore Church.* ⌂

Church Honeybourne *Uniburne: Evesham Church.* Part of Honeybourne. Separated from Cow Honeybourne by the Roman Rycknield Street.

Churchill (Kidderminster) *Corcehalle: Walter from William FitzAnsculf.* ▣ An old yew in the churchyard.

Churchill (Worcester) *Circehille: Walter from Worcester Church. Mill.* ⌂

Church Lench *Circelenz: Evesham Church.* ▣ Orchards.

Cleeve Prior *Clive:* See page 292.

Clent *Clent: King's land.* ▣ Celebrates the restoration of Charles II on Oak Apple Day.

Clifton upon Teme *Clistune: Osbern FitzRichard and Abbot of Cormeilles from the king; Robert d'Oilly from Osbern FitzRichard.* ▣ Red brick and black and white houses.

DROITWICH: *Worcestershire is well known for its many well-preserved timber houses.*

Clopton *Cloptune:* Lost.

Cofton Hackett *Costone: Worcester Church; Thorold and Walter from Urso d'Abetot. Mill.* ▣ Cofton Hall; Longbridge Motors nearby.

Comberton *Cumbrintune/Cumbritone: Gilbert FitzThorold and Urso from Westminster Church; Pershore Church. Mill.* Now 2 villages, Great and Little Comberton.

Comble *Comble:* Lost.

Conningswick *Colingvic: Ralph de Mortimer.* Conningswick Farm.

Cookhill *Cochehi: Erlebald from Urso d'Abetot.* ▣

Cooksey Green *Cochesei/sie: King's land; Herbrand and William from Urso d'Abetot.* ⌂

Cotheridge *Codrie: Osbern FitzRichard from Worcester Church. Mill.* ▣ Timber-framed Cotheridge Court.

Cow Honeybourne *Heniberge: King's land.* Part of Honeybourne, on the Roman Rycknield Street.

Cradley *Cradeleie: Payne from William FitzAnsculf.* On the outskirts of Stourbridge which was famous for gunsmiths.

Croome d'Abitot *Crumbe: Siward from Worcester Church.* Croome Court and gardens, designed by Capability Brown, with work by Adam and Chippendale.

Cropthorne *Cropetorn: Worcester Church, Mill. 20 sticks of eels.* ▣ Church with a Saxon cross.

Crowle *Croelai/Crohlea: Roger de Lacy from Worcester Church and Odo from him; Urso from Osbern FitzRichard. Mill, 2 salt-houses.* ▣ Red brick and half-timbered cottages; orchards.

Cudley *Cudelei: Urso from Worcester Church, formerly Alfeva 'on the terms she could beg'.* Cudleigh Court Farm.

Defford *Depeforde: Westminster Church and 2 Frenchmen from the church.* ▣

Doddenham *Dodeham: Gilbert FitzThorold. Mill.* ⌂

Dormston *Dormestun: William FitzCorbucion from Westminster Church and Albert from him.* ▣ Dormston Manor.

Doverdale *Lunvredele: William from Urso d'Abetot. Church, mill.* ⌂ Doverdale Manor; traces of the old manor house moat.

Drake's Broughton *Broctune: Pershore Church and Urso from the church.* ▣ Orchards.

Droitwich *Wic/Wich: King's land; Worcester Church; St Denis' Church; Coventry Church; Westminster Church; Pershore Church; Evesham Church; St Guthlac's Church; Ralph de Tosny; Roger de Lacy; Osbern FitzRichard; Harold FitzRalph; Urso d'Abetot; Hugh de Lasne; Aldeval. All holding and/or receiving revenue from brine pits, lead vats, leadworks, 4 furnaces and many salt-houses.* Market town with timber-framed houses, once the Roman site of *Salinae* and a Saxon centre of salt production. 'Droit' indicates the right, given by Edward III, to manufacture salt; previously the settlement was only 'Wich'.

Dudley *Dudelei: William FitzAnsculf, whose castle is there.* Industrial town with a partly Norman castle. Coal was first used here for smelting iron in the 17th century.

Dunclent *Dunclent: Nigel the Doctor from St Guthlac's Church and Urso from him.* Dunclent Farm.

Eardiston *Ardolvestone: St Mary's from Worcester Church, for the monks' supplies. Mill, fishery (with Knighton).* ▣

KNIGHTON ON TEME: *The church stands by the river.*

Earls Croome *Crumbe: Ordric from Worcester Church.*

Eastbury *Eresbyrie: Walter of 'Burgh' from Worcester Church.* Now Little Eastbury, on the outskirts of Worcester.

Eastham *Estham: Herbert from Ralph de Tosny. Mill.* Eastham Grange.

Eckington *Aichintune: Westminster Church and Urso and Thurstan FitzRolf from the church.* One of the oldest bridges over the River Avon.

Eldersfield *Edresfelle: King's land, formerly Reinbald the Chancellor, and Ansgot and Wulfgeat from the king. Mill.* Largely Norman church with the arms of Dick Whittington's family.

Elmbridge *Elmerige: Osbern FitzRichard. Salt-house.* Purshall Court, nearby, was used by the Gunpowder Plot conspirators.

Elmley Lovett *Aelmeleia: Walter from Ralph de Tosny, formerly Queen Edith. 3 mills, 4 salt-houses.*

Evesham *Evesham: Evesham Church. Abbey, mill.* Town in the centre of the Vale of Evesham orchards with the ruins of an 8th-century Benedictine abbey.

Feckenham *Fe(c)cheham:* See page 292.

Fladbury *Fledebirie: Worcester Church. Mill. 20 sticks of eels.* Partly Norman church.

Fockbury *Focheberie: King's land. Assessed with Bromsgrove, etc.* Fockbury Farm.

Franche Alia *Frenesse/Frenesse: King's land. Assessed with Kidderminster, etc.* Part of Kidderminster.

Frankley *Franchelie: Baldwin from William FitzAnsculf.* Frankley Lodge Farm and Frankley Beeches, with a view of 7 counties. The reservoirs supply Birmingham with water.

Glasshampton *Glese: Drogo FitzPoyntz. Mill.* Glasshampton Monastery.

Grafton (near Bromsgrove) *Grastone: King's land.* Grafton Manor House.

Grafton Flyford *Garstune: Urso and Walter from Westminster Church.*

Greenhill *Gremanhil: Urso from Worcester Church and Godfrey from him.* Greenhill Farm.

Grimley *Grimanleh: Worcester Church. Mill, ½ fishery (sticks of eels).* Napoleon's brother, Lucien, lived here after he was captured by the British in 1810.

Habberley *Harburgelei: King's land. Assessed with Kidderminster, etc.* Now High and Low Habberley, on the outskirts of Kidderminster.

Hadzor *Hadesore: Walter from his father-in-law Gilbert FitzThorold. 7 salt-houses (111 measures of salt).* Hadzor Hall.

Hagley *Hageleia: Roger from William FitzAnsculf.* Hagley Hall, a Palladian mansion with 18th-century paintings and furniture.

Halesowen *Hala: Earl Roger and Roger Hunter from him. Church.* Industrial town with a part Norman church on a Saxon site.

Hallow *Halhegan: Worcester Church. 2 mills, fishery (with Broadwas).* Hallow Park.

Hampton (near Evesham) *Hantun(e): Abbot of Evesham from Worcester Church; Evesham Church. Vines, 2 mills.* Part of Evesham.

Hampton Lovett *Hamtune: Robert from Urso d'Abetot. 8 salt-houses, mill.* Hampton Farm; on the outskirts of Evesham.

Hanbury *Hambyrie: Worcester Church and Urso from the church and Ralph from him.* Hanbury Hall. Nearby is a small village of the same name.

Hanley (near Stockton on Teme) *Hanlege: Roger and Hugh from Gilbert FitzThorold.* Now Hanley William; Hanley Court; Hanley Childe nearby.

Hanley Castle *Hanlege/Hanlie: King's land. Mill, woodland with a hedged enclosure.* Traces of the castle moat.

Hartlebury *Huerteberie: Worcester Church. 2 mills (10 packloads of corn).* County museum. The castle belonged to the Bishops of Worcester from the 13th century.

Harvington *Herferthun: Worcester Church. Mill.* Black and white thatched cottages.

Helpridge *Helperic:* Lost.

Hill *Hylle: Robert the Bursar from Worcester Church.* Now 2 hamlets, Hill and Hill Furze.

Hill Croome *Hilcrumbe: Roger de Lacy from Worcester Church.*

Himbleton *Himeltun: Roger de Lacy from Worcester Church.*

Hindlip *Hindelep: Urso from Worcester Church and Godfrey from him, formerly Edric the Steersman, commander of a ship.* Hindlip Park. Meetings to plan the Babbington Plot to put Mary Stuart on the throne, and later the Gunpowder Plot, were held here; the present house is 19th century.

Hinton on the Green *Hinetune: King's land.*

Holdfast *Holefest: Urso from Worcester Church.* Holdfast Hall.

Hollin *Holim: Drogo FitzPoyntz.* Hollin Farms.

Hollow Court *Holowei/Haloede: King's land. Park for wild animals, put outside the manor.*

Holt *Holte: Urso the Sheriff from Worcester Church. Fishery, salt-house, hedged enclosure.*

Homme Castle *Hamme: Osbern FitzRichard. Fishery, mill (16 packloads of corn).* Castle motte and bailey.

Horton *Hortune: Robert from Urso d'Abetot. Salt-house, small wood.* Horton Farms.

Houndsfield *Hundesfelde: King's land. Assessed with Bromsgrove, etc.* Lower Houndsfield Farm.

Huddington *Hudintune: Archdeacon Alric from Worcester Church. Mill.* Huddington Court, the headquarters of the Gunpowder Plot.

Hurcott *Worcote: King's land. Assessed with Kidderminster, etc.* Hurcott Manor Cottages; Hurcott Wood; on the edge of Kidderminster.

Inkberrow *Interberga/berge: Bishop of Hereford from Worcester Church; Bishop of Hereford, formerly Earl Harold, wrongfully. Salt-house.* Charles I spent the night here, before the Battle of Naseby (1645), and left a book of maps behind.

Ipsley *Epeslei: King's land.* Part of Redditch; Ipsley Court.

Kemerton *Caneberton/Chenemertone/-tune/Chinemertune: King's land.* Limestone houses.

Kempsey *Chemesege: Worcester Church.* Simon de Montfort and his prisoner, Henry III, heard mass here, before the Battle of Evesham in 1265. Samuel Butler is said to have written part of *Hudibras*, published 1663–78, at the Ketch Inn.

Kenswick *Checinwiche: Urso from Worcester Church and Walter from him.* Kenswick Manor.

Kidderminster *Chideminstre: King's land. 2 mills, 2 salt-houses, fishery (with Franche, Habberley, Hurcott, Mitton, Oldington, Ribbeford, Sutton, Trimpley, Wannerton, Wribbenhall and 4 unidentified settlements).* Town, famous for its carpet-making industry, developed in the 18th century.

Kington *Chintune: 2 men-at-arms from Roger de Lacy. Hedged enclosure for catching wild animals.*

Knighton on Teme *Cnistetone: St Mary's from Worcester Church for the monks' supplies. Mill, fishery (with Eardiston).*

Knightwick *Cnihtewic: Robert the Bursar from Worcester Church, formerly Edith, a nun.* Knightwick Manor.

Kyre *Chure: Urso from Bishop of Hereford; Osbern FitzRichard and Herbert from him. Mill (10 packloads of grain).* Now Kyre Green; Kyre Park House, mainly 18th century, with gardens by Capability Brown.

Laugherne *Laure: Urso and Robert the Bursar from Worcester Church. Mill, 12 oaks.* Temple Laugherne, a house in a large orchard.

Lea Green *Lea: King's land. Assessed with Bromsgrove, etc.*

Leigh *Lege: Pershore Church and Urso the Sheriff from the church. 3 mills.* Leigh Court.

Lenchwick *Lenchewic: Evesham Church.* Orchards.

Lindon *Linde:* Lost.

Littleton *Liteltune: Evesham Church.* Now 2 villages, Middle Littleton, with a 14th-century tithe barn built by Abbot Ombersley of Evesham, and South Littleton.

Little Witley *Witlege: Urso from Worcester Church and Walter from him. 1 sester of honey.* Ruins of Witley Court.

Longdon (near Upton on Severn) *Langedune/Longedune: Westminster Church.* Longdon Hall. Maritime plants can still be found in Longdon Marsh, once covered by the tidal River Severn.

Lower Sapey *Sapie: Osbern FitzRichard. Mill (6 packloads of corn).*

Lutley *Ludeleia: The clergy of Wolverhampton before and after 1066.* On the edge of Halesowen.

Lyppard *Lappewrte: Hugh de Grandmesnil from Worcester Church and Baldwin from him.* Lyppard Grange; on the outskirts of Worcester.

Malvern Chase *Malferna: Worcester Church. Woodland in Dean Forest paying dues in pasture, firewood and timber.* Little Malvern, at the foot of the Malvern Hills; the ruins of a 12th-century priory; Little Malvern Court. Malvern Chase was a large area of forest and marshland.

Mamble *Mamele: Ralph de Mortimer.* A Roman brick kiln was found here.

Martin Hussingtree *Husentre: Westminster Church.* Stone Court House.

Martley *Merlie/Mertelai: King's land; Roger de Lacy; Drogo FitzPoyntz. Mill, 2 weirs (2500 eels and 5 sticks).*

Middlewich *Midelwic:* Lost.

Mitton (in Bredon) *Mitune: Worcester Church, for the monks' supplies.* Part of Tewkesbury. Mitton Lodge.

Mitton (in Stourport on Severn) *Mettune: King's land. Assessed with Kidderminster, etc.* Now Lower Mytton, absorbed by Stourport on Severn. Upper Mitton remains as part of the town.

Moor (near Pershore) *More: Robert the Bursar from Worcester Church.* Now 2 villages, Upper and Lower Moor.

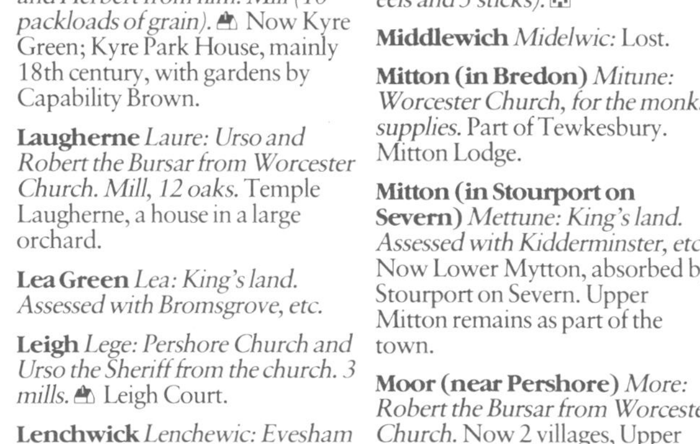

KIDDERMINSTER: *The 14th-c. Church of St Mary, on a hill above the Stour, was restored in the 19th c.*

Morton Underhill *Mortune: Arnold from Robert of Stafford. Salt-house.* Morton Hall.

Mucknell *Mucenhil: Urso the Sheriff from Worcester Church.* Mucknell Farm.

Nafford *Nadford: Westminster Church; Robert Parler from Gilbert FitzThorold.* Nafford Lock.

Naunton Beauchamp *Newentune: Urso from Westminster Church and Herbraund from him.* Naunton Court, a half-timbered, Elizabethan house.

Netherton *Neotheretune: Worcester Church. Mill. 20 sticks of eels.*

North Piddle *Pidelet: Urso the Sheriff from Westminster Church.* Traces of a moat, marking the site of the old manor house.

Northwick *Norwiche: Worcester Church. 3 mills, fishery.* Part of Worcester.

Norton (near Evesham) *Nortune: Evesham Church. 2 mills. 2000 eels.* A 12th-century marble lectern in the church was found near the site of Evesham Abbey.

Oddingley *Oddunclei: Ordric from Worcester Church. Salt-house.*

Offenham *Offenham: Evesham Church.* 7 thatched cottages under one roof; modern development.

Offerton *Alcrintun: Urso from Worcester Church and Godfrey from him, formerly Edric the Steersman.* Offerton Farm.

Oldington *Aldintune: King's land. Assessed with Kidderminster, etc.* Oldington Farm.

Old Swinford *Suineforde: Acard from William FitzAnsculf. Mill.* The original centre of Stourbridge.

Ombersley *Ambreslege: Evesham Church. 1½ fisheries (2000 eels), 2 mills.* Half-timbered houses.

Orleton *Alretune: Hugh from Gilbert FitzThorold. 2 fisheries (40 sticks of eels).* Orleton Court.

Osmerley *Osmerlei:* Lost.

Overbury *Ovreberie: Worcester Church.* Stone built.

Pebworth *Pebeworde: King's land.* On Buckle Street, originally a Celtic highway; moated site.

Pedmore *Pevemore: Acard from William FitzAnsculf.* Part of Stourbridge; earthworks of a prehistoric camp on Wychbury Hill.

Pendock *Pe(o)nedoc: Worcester Church and Urso from the church.*

Pensham *Pendesham: Westminster Church.* Pensham Fields Farm.

Peopleton *Piplintune: Westminster Church and Walter Ponther and Urso the Sheriff from the church.* Timbered, part 13th-century church.

Perry *Pirian:* Lost.

Pershore *Persore: Westminster Church, given by King Edward, and a Frenchman from the church; Pershore Church. Church; 4½ mills.* Town of 7th-century origin. Parts of a Norman Benedictine monastery are now the parish church.

Phepson *Fepsetenatun: Worcester Church and Walter Ponther from the church.*

Pirton *Peritune: Walter Ponther from Westminster Church.*

Powick *Poiwic: Westminster Church. Mill for the hall. 3 sesters of honey.* Royalists won the first engagement of the Civil War at Powick Bridge in 1642.

Pull Court *Lapule: King's land and a man of the monks of Lyre from the king.* Bredon School.

Queenhill *Cunhille: Worcester Church, in the king's hands.*

Radley *Rodeleah:* Lost.

Redmarley (in Great Witley) *Ridmerlege/Redmerleie: Ralph, a man-at-arms, from Ralph de Tosny; Ralph from Gilbert FitzThorold.* Redmarley House.

Ribbesford *Alia Ribeford/ Ribeford: King's land. Assessed with Kidderminster, etc.* Ribbesford House.

Ripple *Ripel: Worcester Church. Mill.* Norman church on a Saxon site.

Rochford *Recesford: King's land.* Now Lower Rochford. Nearby are Upper Rochford and Rochford Mount.

Rockmoor *Moor: Ralph de Tosny.* Rockmoor Farm near the village of Rock.

Rous Lench *Biscopesleng: Urso from Worcester Church and Alfred from him. Mill.* Half-timbered Court with a topiary garden.

Rushock *Russococ: Hunwulf from Urso d'Abetot. Salt-house.*

Salwarpe *Salewarpe: Urso from Coventry Church and Earl Roger. Mill, 5 salt-houses.* Half-timbered Salwarpe Court and Old Mill House.

Sedgeberrow *Seggesbarue: Doda from Worcester Church, for the monks' supplies. 2 mills.* First granted to Worcester Church in 777. The manor house is on a site which belonged to the Worcester monks.

Severn Stoke *Stoche: Alfred of Marlborough from Westminster Church.*

Shell *Scelves: Herman from Roger de Lacy. 4 salt-houses, enclosed woodland.*

Shelsley *Caldeslei/Celdeslai: Walter from Ralph de Tosny; Osbern FitzRichard. 2 fisheries (16 sticks of eels).* Now 2 villages, Shelsley Walsh, whose part Norman church is limestone quarried from Southstone Rock, and Shelsley Beauchamp.

Sheriffs Lench *Lenche: Urso the Sheriff from Bishop of Bayeux, who seized the land from Evesham Church.* Sheriffs Lench Farm.

Shurvenhill *Suruehel:* Lost.

Sodington *Sudtune: A man-at-arms from Ralph de Mortimer.* Sodington Hall, near a moated site.

Spetchley *Speclea: Roger de Lacy from Worcester Church.* Spetchley Park.

Stanford on Teme *Stanford: Hugh from Roger de Lacy; Osbern FitzRichard.* Stanford Court, now a factory.

Stildon *Stilledune: Drogo FitzPoyntz.* Stildon Manor.

Stockton on Teme *Stotune: Roger de Lacy. Mill.*

Stoke Bliss *Heref Stoch: King's land.*

Stoke Prior *Stoche: Worcester Church. 2 mills.* 19th-century salt trade centre; salt works, built by John Corbett, the 'salt king'.

Stone *Stanes: Erlebald from Urso d'Abetot. Mill.*

Stoulton *Stoltun: Urso the Sheriff from Worcester Church.*

Suckley *Suchelei/Suchelie: King's land. Mill, 12 beehives, fishery.* Suckley Court.

Sutton *Sudtone: King's land. Assessed with Kidderminster, etc.* Part of Kidderminster; Sutton Farm.

Tardebigge *Terde(s)berie: King's land. 2 lead vats.*

Tenbury Wells *Tame(t)deberie: Cormeilles Church; Osbern FitzRichard, formerly his father.* Market town, a saline spa in the 19th century.

Thickenappletree *Tichenapletreu:* Lost.

Tibberton *Tidbertun: Worcester Church. 3 mills.*

Timberhanger *Timbrehangre: King's land. Assessed with Bromsgrove, etc.*

Tonge *Tonge:* Lost.

Trimpley *Trinpelei: King's land. Assessed with Kidderminster, etc.* Scattered.

Tutnall *Tothehel: King's land. Assessed with Bromsgrove, etc.*

Tynsall *Tuneslega:* Lost.

Ullington *Wenitone: King's land.*

Upper Arley *Ernlege: King's land.* Arley Park.

Upton Snodsbury *Snodesbyrie: Westminster Church and Urso from the church.* Black and white cottages.

Upton on Severn *Uptun:* See page 293.

Upton Warren *Uptune: Erlebald from Urso d'Abetot. Mill.* 17th-century Badger Court.

Upwich *Upeuuic:* Lost.

Wadborough *Wadberge: Pershore Church and Robert the Bursar and Urso from the church. Pasturage for the monks' cows.*

Wannerton *Wenuertun: King's land. Assessed with Kidderminster, etc.* Wannerton Farm.

Warley *Werwelie: Alfhelm from William FitzAnsculf.* Warley Woods in Birmingham.

Warndon *Wermedun: Urso from Worcester Church and Robert from him.* Suburb of Worcester.

Wast Hills *Warstelle: Worcester Church.* Hill and playing fields on the outskirts of Birmingham.

Westmancote *Westmonecote: Urso from Worcester Church.* Now 2 villages, at the foot of Bredon Hill.

White Ladies Aston *Estun: Urso from Worcester Church and Robert from him.* Named after a 13th-century Cistercian nunnery.

Whittington *Windintun: Walter Ponther from Worcester Church. Fishery.* Suburb of Worcester.

Wick (near Pershore) *Wicha/ Wiche: Westminster Church and Urso and Gilbert from the church; Pershore Church. Fishery.* Half-timbered cottages.

Wick Episcopi *Wiche: Worcester Church. 2 mills, 2 fisheries.* Part of Worcester.

Wickhamford *Wiquene: King's land; Evesham Church. Mill.* Timbered manor house; arms of George Washington's family in the church.

Willingwick *Welingewiche/ Willingewic:* Lost.

Witton in Droitwich *Witone/ tune: William FitzCorbucion; Gunfrid from Urso d'Abetot. 3 salt-houses (60 measures of salt), part of a salt-house (10 measures of salt).* Part of Droitwich.

Wolverley *Ulwardelei: Worcester Church. Mill.* Wolverley Court; birthplace of the printer John Baskerville (1706–75).

Wolverton *Ulfrintun: Urso the Sheriff and Worcester Church; Roger de Lacy from Worcester Church, and Aiulf from Roger.* Now 2 hamlets.

Woodcote Green *Udecote: King's land. Assessed with Bromsgrove, etc. Erlebald from Urso d'Abetot.* Woodcote Manor, 2 farms and a lodge.

WORCESTER: *The gateway to the cathedral green.*

Worcester *Wirecestre: Worcester Church, and Urso, Osbern FitzRichard, Walter Ponther and Robert the Bursar from the church; Evesham Church.* City on the River Severn. The cathedral, rebuilt by Bishop Wulfstan, c. 1080, has an 11th-century crypt, Norman cloisters and a Norman chapter house.

Worsley *Wermeslai: Ralph de Tosny.* Worsley Farm.

Wribbenhall *Gurbehale: King's land. Assessed with Kidderminster, etc.* Nature reserve.

Wychbold *Wicelbold: Osbern FitzRichard. 5 mills, 26 salt-houses.* Hall.

Wyre Piddle *Pidele: Robert the Bursar from Worcester Church.*

Wythall *Warthuil: King's land. Assessed with Bromsgrove, etc.* Commuter suburb of Birmingham.

RIPPLE: *15th-c. misericords in Ripple church. 16 stalls of the 15th c.*

Yorkshire

The vast and varied area of Yorkshire and the grave disturbances that it had suffered during the previous 20 years presented special problems to the Domesday *Commissioners. Inevitably, therefore, Yorkshire's is among the least satisfactory of county texts.* Domesday *records 1830 place names in its three Ridings – the administrative districts into which it was divided. For so large an area there are surprisingly few tenants-in-chief – only 28 plus the king's thanes. Of these eight are major landholders: the king, the Archbishop of York, Robert Count of Mortain, Count Alan of Brittany, Ilbert de Lacy, Hugh FitzBaldric, William de Percy, and Drogo de Beuvriere.*

Although there is waste in most counties the amount in Yorkshire is proportionately enormous; waste is mentioned on every page. Half the vills in the North Riding and about a third in the East and West were wholly or partly affected. The blame is usually placed on the devastation wrought by William's 'harrying of the North' in the winter of 1069–70, but this is probably only part of the explanation; there had also been attacks by the Vikings and the Scots.

*The longest and most informative entry is that for the city of York, where there were about 800 inhabited houses and a population of between 4000 and 5000. Villagers (*villani*) constituted 66 per cent of the rural population and smallholders (*bordarii*) 24 per cent. Slaves are not mentioned. Industry is represented only by watermills in 92 places and by six iron-workers at Hessle in the West Riding.*

The summary of Yorkshire landholdings known as the recapitulation which concludes the section is unique; there is no similar document for any other county.

WHARRAM PERCY: *The original settlement in this quiet dip of the Yorkshire hills was established a long time ago; there are neolithic barrows nearby, and clear evidence of trade with the Lake district.*

Saxon finds include wattles from 650–750, fragments of a cross and stone grave slabs, 950–1040, near the church. There are also two Romano-British manor sites, and new houses were built later on the same foundations. Very gradually, in the 13th and 14th centuries, the village filled in along the line of the cleft, with gardens and farming strips running up the hillside. Ridges still mark some of the medieval boundaries, themselves laid out on Romano-British and Saxon divisions.

The church expanded with the village at the end of the 13th century and contracted again around 1500 when the local population had almost vanished. However, neighbouring parishes continued to use the smaller building until the end of the 19th century; and the last service was held c. 1945. Only then, when the roof was stripped of lead, did the church gradually deteriorate to its present condition.

Wharram Percy is remarkable for many of its finds; it has increased our understanding of the very varied and lively history to be found under the surface. The Domesday *settlement may not have looked very different from the landscape we see today, and within those 900 years, a community lived and died.*

East Riding

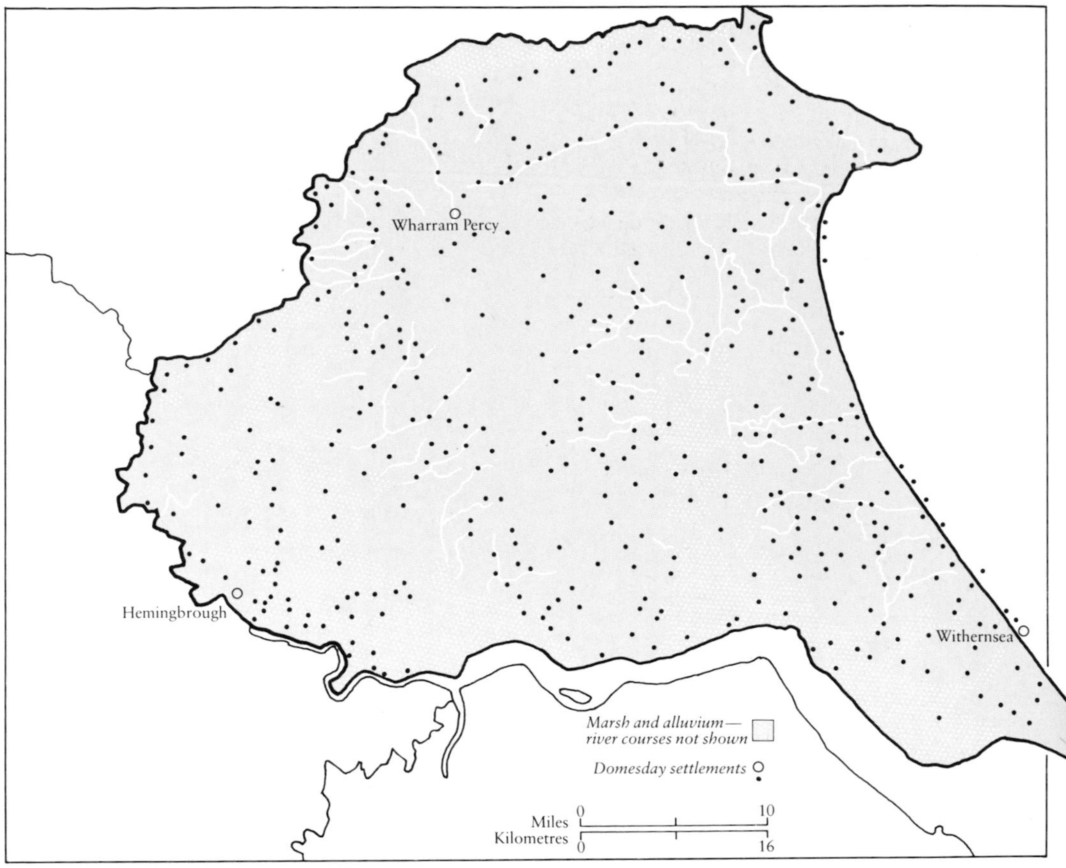

Wharram Percy

[Land of the King] In WHARRAM (PERCY) *WARHAM*, Lagmann and Karli, 8 carucates taxable. Land for 4 ploughs. 60s. Land of the king's thanes. In Warran Gilbert has 1 carucate of land of the king which renders 10s. Land for half a plough.

Wharram Percy, which lies hidden and virtually inaccessible in an isolated valley six miles south-east of Malton, consists today of nothing more than a cottage, a ruined church and the remarkably clear earthworks of the deserted village. In 1952 Wharram was chosen by the newly formed Deserted Medieval Village Research Group as its main project, and for over 30 years an intensive annual summer excavation has been going on there. These excavations have meant that more is known about the origins and medieval development of Wharram Percy than of any other village in Britain.

Although the all too brief entries in *Domesday* are the first documentary references to Wharram Percy, excavations have shown that the site had already been occupied for at least 500 years. It would appear that before the Conquest the estate was divided among three Saxon owners: Lagmann, Karli and Gilbert. The last retained his small estate in 1086, while the king held the greater part of Wharram as two manors denoted by the prefix '2M'. Although no population is mentioned the reference to four ploughlands and the reasonable valuation suggests a thriving community, unlike neighbouring settlements, which are described as 'waste'. Percy was added to the place name in the fourteenth century in deference to the then owners of the manor.

By the middle of the sixteenth century, Wharram had been depopulated, a phenomenon which took place in at least three phases. In the late thirteenth century, the village still had as many active arable units as in 1086, but by 1323 there were many waste tenements, the two water-mills were derelict, and the population had been severely reduced. Then the Black Death struck: the vicar, Peter Lyelff, died in September 1349, and in the same month the non-resident Lord of the Manor was carried off. The village revived later in the fourteenth century (some 30 houses, a rectory, manor house and water-mill are recorded) but this was reversed in the fifteenth century, when agriculture gave way to sheep farming, with the resultant destruction of houses and the enclosure of ploughlands. By the end of the seventeenth century, only two houses are recorded.

Although *Domesday* has no reference to a church at Wharram, the tower of the present ruined building is of the eleventh century, and excavations have revealed a short Anglo-Saxon nave and a Norman chancel and apse. Among other structures that have been uncovered are peasant long-houses and a fine twelfth-century stone building associated with a Norman manor house.

The village site is in the care of the Department of the Environment and is open to visitors. Signposts on nearby roads show the way.

Withernsea

In WITHERNESEA *WITFORNES* Morcar had 18 carucates and 6 bovates of land taxable, where 15 ploughs are possible. Now Drogo has there 1 plough and 4 villagers and 5 smallholders and 2 priests. These (have) altogether 2 ploughs and 100 acres of meadow. To this manor belongs this jurisdiction: *ANDREBI*, 2 c.; BURTON (Pidsea), 7 c.; DANTHORPE, 2 c. and 6 bovates; FITLING, 6 c.; SPROATLEY, 5 bovates; GRIMSTON, 4 c.; WAXHOLME, 6 bovates; TUNSTALL, 1 c; (OW)THORNE, 5 bovates; HOLLYM, 1 c.; REDMERE, 3 bovates. Together 32 carucates of land taxable, where 25 ploughs are possible. Now Drogo has there 10 Freemen, 10 villagers and 2 smallholders, who have 7 ploughs. Value before 1066 £56; now £6.

Although Withernsea, situated on the East Yorkshire coast 16 miles east of Hull, once had pretensions to becoming both a thriving port and a seaside resort, it is today chiefly a residential town with a little holiday trade and some light industry. At the time of *Domesday*, however, it had 11 subsidiary settlements within its soke, and was one of the valuable manors that made up the large compact estate of Holderness, which the king had granted in 1071 to the Fleming, Drogo de la Beuvriere.

Drogo had come to England with the Conqueror and was married to one of his relatives. But soon after the compilation of *Domesday* he accidentally killed his wife, and fearing William's anger, he fled overseas. His estates were confiscated and in 1087 were granted to Count Odo, the husband of the king's sister Adelaide. Odo's descendants became Counts of Aumale and Lords of Holderness.

With two priests recorded in *Domesday* at Withernsea, the manor must obviously have included at least one church, and possibly also the so-called 'sister kirk' at neighbouring Owthorne. Both these churches were later devastated by the violent seas of the East Yorkshire coast. Part of Withernsea's churchyard, high on a cliff top, was destroyed in a storm in 1444, after which the parishioners were granted permission to build a new church on a safer site much further inland. But in 1609 this church was unroofed in a violent gale and fell into ruins. As for Owthorne's church, it was consumed by the sea early in the nineteenth century.

In 1854, an impressive 40-bedroom hotel was built beside the ruined shell of Withernsea church. This was part of an ambitious scheme to turn Withernsea and Owthorne, which then consisted of some 30 to 40 houses, into a premier resort. In that year a railway line was opened from Hull to Withernsea and the railway company bought land and made plans for a large development of classical terraces and semi-detached villas. Although visitors came to the new resort, the only houses that were built were homes for artisans far removed from the company's land. Other ambitious projects were outlined, including tree-lined crescents of detached villas, but nothing was completed except for a 1196-foot pier, wrecked in 1880 when a ship crashed through it in a storm.

Early holidaymakers found Withernsea 'somewhat dreary and depressing', but by Edwardian times it had developed into 'Hull by the sea' with thousands of day trippers and a considerable resident population of Hull professional and businessmen. Today it caters to a far wider public, and its Sunday markets attract thousands of visitors. Coastal erosion, however, remains a serious problem, and over the last nine centuries much of the land recorded at Withernsea by *Domesday* has been lost to the sea.

Hemingbrough

In HEMINGBROUGH *HAMIBURG* there are 3 carucates taxable which 2 ploughs can plough. Tosti held this as one manor. Now the King has there 5 villagers and 3 smallholders with 2 ploughs. A priest is there and a church. Meadow, 7 acres; woodland pasture, 1/2 league long and as wide. In all, 1 league long and 1/2 wide. Value before 1066, 40s; now 16s.

Hemingbrough, on the River Ouse near Selby, was a natural site for a Viking stronghold. It may take its name from Jarl Hemingr, who captained the northern detachment of King Sweyn's troops. According to the *Knytlinga Saga*, 'Hemingaborg' was captured, some years later, by Sweyn's son, King Canute. Before the Conquest, Hemingbrough had been owned by Tosti, Earl of Northumbria, King Harold's brother and the son of Canute's supporter, Earl Godwin. In 1066 Tosti joined with the Norwegian Harold Hardrada to invade England. The attackers probably stopped at Hemingbrough before marching on to Stamford Bridge, where on 25 September King Harold's forces defeated them, killing Tosti.

By 1086, as *Domesday* shows, Hemingbrough had been greatly reduced in value. It was taxed for three carucates of land (300 to 400 acres), which was worked by a modest community of five villagers, each of whom would have held land for which they owed services and dues to the lord, plus three smallholders with less land, or none at all, who probably not only gave service but also hired out their labour. Much of the manor was taken up by woodland, a comparative rarity at that time in East Yorkshire.

Domesday records a priest and a church, and after nine centuries, the parish church, which has a spectacular spire, is still the village's most striking building. Although the king held Hemingbrough at the time of *Domesday*, he soon granted the manor, which covered almost 11,000 acres, to the Bishop of Durham. The bishop in turn assigned it to Durham Priory, which was responsible for today's splendid church.

Although the present building dates in part from the eleventh century, its most notable architectural features – the large Perpendicular windows in the transepts and chancel and remarkable, 126-foot spire – were all added after the church had been made collegiate in 1427. The slender spire, the inspiration of the Prior of Durham, John of Wessington, stands oddly on the squat 63-foot tower, whose top was rebuilt at the same time and on which was carved just below its battlements a series of washing tuns or tubs, a punning memorial to Wessington.

All the college buildings have long disappeared and only the church survives from the middle ages. Its size and its limestone material contrast markedly with the eighteenth- and nineteenth-century brick-and-pantile farmhouses and cottages which form the older part of the present village. Hemingbrough has become increasingly residential over the generations, but its economy is still firmly based, as it was in 1086, on agriculture. Only tanneries during the seventeenth and eighteenth centuries and a modest brick and tile works which still produced drainage tiles in the 1970s provided non-agricultural work for the villagers.

East Riding Gazetteer
Each entry starts with the modern place-name in **bold** type. The *Domesday* information is in *italic* type, beginning with the name or names by which the place was known in 1086. The main landholders and under-tenants follow, separated with semi-colons if a place was divided into more than one holding. A number of holdings were granted by the king to his thanes; these holders are described, at the end of a list of landholders, as holding land 'from the king'. More general information completes the *Domesday* part of the entry. The modern or post-Domesday section is in normal type. represents a village, a small village or hamlet.

Acklam *Aclun: King's land; Count of Mortain. Church.* Early Bronze Age round barrows.

Aike *Ach: Archbishop of York; Earl Hugh and Nigel from him; Count of Mortain.*

Aldborough *Aldenburg: Drogo de Beuvriere, formerly Ulf.* Saxon sundial in the church inscribed with: 'Ulf ordered this church to be built for his own and Gunware's souls.'

Allerthorpe *Aluuarestorp: King's land.* Allerthorpe Common; manor farm.

Anlaby *Umlouebi/Unlouebi: King's land; Count of Mortain; Ralph de Mortimer; Torchil from the king.* Suburb of Hull.

Argam *Ergone: King's land; Count of Mortain.* Medieval village earthworks; prehistoric Argam Dykes.

Arram *Argun: Rayner from Drogo de Beuvriere.* Arram Hall.

Asselby *Aschilebi: Bishop of Durham; Count of Mortain and Nigel from him. 5 fisheries.*

Auburn *Eleburne: King's land.*

Aughton *Actun: Count of Mortain and Nigel Fossard from him.* Motte of Nigel Fossard's castle.

Babthorpe *Babetorp: Bishop of Durham.* Moated site, the position of the medieval village.

Bainton *Bagenton(e): Count of Mortain and Nigel Fossard from him; Hugh FitzBaldric and William from him.*

Barlby *Bardulbi: King's land; Bishop of Durham; Ralph Pagnell.*

Barmby on the Marsh *Barnebi: Bishop of Durham.*

Barmby on the Moor *King's land; Archbishop of York.*

Barmston *Benestone/tun: Drogo de Beuvriere.* Remains of manor house; late Bronze Age settlement site.

Barnhill *Berneheld/helt: Bishop of Durham.* Moated Barnhill Hall.

Barthorpe *Barche(r)torp: Count of Mortain; Odo the Crossbowman.*

Beeford *Biuuorde: Drogo de Beuvriere. Church.* Church, rebuilt in the late 14th century.

Belby *Ballebi/Bellebi: King's land.* Belby Hall.

Belthorpe *Balchetorp: Archbishop of York.* Now 2 hamlets, High Belthorpe, with a moated site, and Low Belthorpe.

Bempton *Bentone: Count of Mortain.*

Benningholme *Beni(n)col: Drogo de Beuvriere.*

Bentley *Benedlage: Archbishop of York; Count of Mortain.*

Bessingby *Basing(h)ebi: King's land.* Romano-British site.

Beswick *Baseuuic/ewic: King's land and Nigel Fossard from the king; Count of Mortain. Mill.* Beswick Hall.

Beverley *Beureli: Archbishop of York and St John's church, Beverley, from him. 3 mills, fishery (7000 eels).* Prosperous mid-12th-century trading centre for wool and cloth. An encompassing 13th-century defensive ditch determined the street pattern of the town.

Bewholme *Begun: Manbodo from Drogo de Beuvriere.*

Bewick *Biuinch/Biuuich: Drogo de Beuvriere.* Bewick Hall, a farmhouse; moated site.

Bielby *Belebi: King's land.*

Bilton *Bileton(e)/Billetone: Franco from Drogo de Beuvriere; Archbishop of York.* Moated site.

Binnington *Bigneton/Binneton: Count of Mortain.*

Birdsall *Brideshala/Briteshala/-hale: King's land; Archbishop of York; Nigel Fossard from Count of Mortain; Ulchil, the pre-Conquest holder, from the king.*

Bishop Burton *Burtone: Archbishop of York and Canons of St John's church, Beverley, from him.* 13th-century church with a Norman carved figure; an earlier, 8th-century church was founded by Puch, an Anglican chief.

Bishop Wilton *Widton/Wilton(e): Archbishop of York. Church.* Norman church; moated site; round barrows on Callis Wold.

Bolton *Bodelton: King's land; Archbishop of York. Carle from the king.* Moated site.

Bowthorpe *Boletorp: Bishop of Durham.* Bowthorpe Hall.

Boynton *Bouinton(e)/Bouintorp/Alia Bouintone: King's land; Count of Mortain.* Boynton Hall; fishponds.

Boythorpe *Buitorp: King's land.*

Bracken *Brachen: Erneis de Buron.*

Brackenholme *Brachene(l)holm: Bishop of Durham; Gilbert de Tison.*

Brandesburton *Bortun/Brantisburtone/-tune/Branzbortune/Burtun: Archbishop of York; Drogo de Beuvriere; William Malet, according to the men of Holderness.* Manor house; medieval village cross.

Brantingham *Bre(n)dingham/Brenting(e)ham/Bretingham: Bishop of Durham; Nigel Fossard from Count of Mortain; Robert Malet.* Hall; pond.

Brantingham Thorpe *(Alia) Bretingham/Brentingham: Bishop of Durham.* Adjoining Brantingham.

Breighton *Bricstune/Briston(e)/tun: Ralph de Mortimer.* Moated site.

Bridlington *Bredinton/Bretlinton: King's land; Count of Mortain. Church.* Town with the church of the Augustinian Priory founded c.1115.

Brigham *Bringeham: King's land; Count of Mortain.* Manor house; moated site.

Bubwith *Bubuid: Ralph de Mortimer; Gilbert de Tison and Richard from him.*

Buckton *Bocheton(e): King's land; Earl Hugh; Count of Mortain; Berengar de Tosny; Hugh FitzBaldric. 2 mills, church.* Adjoining Bempton; formerly Buckton Holms.

Bugthorpe *Buchetorp/Bug(h)etorp: Archbishop of York; Odo the Crossbowman.* Green.

BURTON AGNES: *The Hall, 1601–10, with its early bow windows.*

FLAMBOROUGH: *Dane's Dyke runs across the headland coast to coast.*

Burdale *Bred(d)ale/Bredhalle: King's land; Hugh FitzBaldric.*

Burland *Birland: Bishop of Durham; Gilbert de Tison.* Burland Hall; moat.

Burnby *Brunebi: King's land; Archbishop of York and Geoffrey from him; Robert Malet; William de Percy; Archbishop held the manor before 1066.*

Burstwick *Bro(c)stewic: Drogo de Beuvriere.* North Park and South Park show where the Earl of Aumale had his game parks in the mid-13th century.

Burton Agnes *Bortona/ Burton(e): King's land.* The Old Hall, built by Robert de Stuteville, (c.1170–75), has a vaulted undercroft with piers and carved water-leaf capitals. Romano-British settlement site nearby.

Burton Constable *Santriburtone: Archbishop of York.* Late 16th century manor house.

Burton Pidsea *Bortun(e): Drogo de Beuvriere.* Manor house.

Burythorpe *Berg(u)etorp: King's land; Berengar de Tosny.* Neolithic round barrow.

Butterwick *Butruid: Count of Mortain.*

Camerton *Camerinton: Drogo de Beuvriere.*

Carnaby *Cherendebi: King's land.*

Catfoss *Catefos(s): Drogo de Beuviere and Franco from him; William Malet formerly Cnut, according to the men of Holderness.* Manor Farm.

Catton *Caton/Cattune: Earl Hugh and William from him, formerly Earl Harold. Mill.* Now the village of Low Catton and the hamlet of High Catton; Catton Park; some mills.

Catwick *Catin(ge)uuic/ Cotingeuuic: Archbishop of York; Drogo de Beuvriere; William Malet, according to the men of Holderness. Church, mill.* Church, partly rebuilt in 1862–63, a Norman figure in chancel.

Cavil *Cheuede: Bishop of Durham.*

Caythorpe *Caretorp: King's land; Archbishop of York; Count of Mortain.* Medieval village, Thorpe Hall.

Cherry Burton *Burton(e): King's land; Archbishop of York and St John's church, Beverley, from him; Count of Mortain.*

Cleaving *Cleuinde/inge: King's land.* Cleaving Grange, with moated site.

Cleeton *Cleton/tun(e): Drogo de Beuvriere.* Remains of Drogo's castle.

Cliffe (near Hemingborough) *Clive: Count of Mortain; Nigel Fossard.* Now Long Cliffe.

Coniston *Co(i)ningesbi: Drogo de Beuvriere.*

Cotness *Cotes: Bishop of Durham.* Moated site and hall.

Cottam *Cottun: St Peter's church, York, from Archbishop of York.* Cottam House; Medieval village earthworks.

Cottingham *Coting(e)ham: Hugh FitzBaldric. 5 fisheries (8000 eels), mill.* Dormitory suburb for Hull; Snuff Mill House.

Cowlam *Coletun/Colnun: King's land with Archbishop of York holding the church; Berengar de Tosny.* Medieval village site adjoining the manor house; Victorian church with a Norman font.

Cranswick *Cransuuic/Cranzuic: King's land; Count of Mortain and Nigel Fossard from him; Hugh FitzBaldric.* Adjoining Hutton; 2 moated sites.

Croom *Cogrun/Crogun: King's land; Archbishop of York; FitzBaldric.* Deserted medieval village site; Croome House.

Danthorpe *Danetorp: King's land; Archbishop of York; Drogo de Beuvriere.* Hall.

Deighton *Diston(e): Count Alan.* Hall.

Dimlington *Dimeltun: Drogo de Beuvriere.* On the coast. The medieval village, lost to the sea.

Dowthorpe *Duuetorp: Drogo de Beuvriere.* Dowthorpe Hall.

Drewton *Drouueton(e): Robert Malet.* Manor house.

Dringhoe *Dringolme: Drogo de Beuvriere.* Moated site of a grange belonging to Meaux Abbey.

Drypool *Dridpol/Dripold/ Dritpol: Archbishop of York; Drogo de Beuvriere.* Part of Hull.

Duggleby *Difgelibi/Dighelibi: King's land; Berengar de Tosny.* Howe Hill, a late Neolithic burial mound.

Dunnington (in Bewholme) *Dodintone: Drogo de Beuvriere.* Manor house; grange.

Dunnington (near York) *Domniton/Do'niton: Canons of St Peter from Archbishop of York; Geoffrey from William de Percy.*

Easington *Esintone/Hesinton(e): Drogo de Beuvriere.* Rare 15th century tithe barn built by Meaux Abbey.

Eastburn *Au(gu)stburne: King's land.*

East Cottingwith *Coteuuid: Count of Mortain and Nigel Fossard from him.*

East Heslerton *Eslerton/ Esrelton/Heslerton(e)/Haselinton: Count of Mortain; Berengar de Tosny; Hugh FitzBaldric.*

Easthorpe *Est(t)orp: Nigel Fossard from the Count of Mortain; Geoffrey from William de Percy. 2 mills.* Medieval village site in the centre of Londesborough Park.

East Newton *Niuuetone/tun: Drogo de Beuvriere.*

Easton *Eston(e): King's land.*

Eastrington *Estrin(c)ton: Bishop of Durham.* Moated site; by railway.

Eddlethorpe *Eduardestorp/Ged- /Gudwalestorp: King's land.* Medieval village site.

Ellerby *Aluuardehi/Alverdebi: Drogo de Beuvriere and Tedbald from him; William Malet, according to the men of Holderness.* Now Old Ellerby; moated site, near Wood Hall.

Ellerker *Alrecher: Bishop of Durham.* Pond.

Ellerton *Elreton(e): King's land.*

Elloughton *Elgendon: Archbishop of York and Godwin from him. Church (with Wauldby).* Church with Saxon carving in the chancel.

Elmswell *Elmesuuelle/ Helmesuuelle: King's land; Norman, the pre-Conquest holder, from the king.* Romano-British settlement site with tumuli.

Elstronwick *Asteneuuic: Drogo de Beuvriere.*

Elvington *Aluuinton(e): Alulf from William de Percy. Church, 2 fisheries.* Manor House Farm; late Victorian church.

Escrick *Ascri: Count Alan.*

Eske *Asch: Archbishop of York.* Earthworks and ridge-and-furrow on a medieval village site.

Etherdwick *Redeuuic/uuince: Drogo de Beuvriere.*

Etton *Eton/Etton(e): St John's church, Beverley, from Archbishop of York before and after 1066; Nigel Fossard from Count of Mortain; Hugh FitzBaldric and Hugh from him.* Traces of a 13th-century deer park.

Everingham *Euringham: Archbishop of York. 2 mills.*

Everthorpe *Euertorp: Count of Mortain.* Manor house.

Fangfoss *Frangefos: King's land.* Green.

Filey *Fiuelac: King's land.* Seaside resort, originally a fishing village.

Firby *Friebia: King's land.* Hall.

Fitling *Fidlinge/Fitlinge: Drogo de Beuvriere.* Remains of a moat around Moat Farm.

Flamborough *Flaneburc/burg: Earl Hugh and Hugh FitzNorman from him; Clibert, the pre-Conquest holder, from the king.* Traces of Constable family's 14th-century fortified manor house. Danes Dyke, probably Iron Age; Mesolithic Beacon Hill.

Flinton *Flentun/Flintone: Archbishop of York; Drogo de Beuvriere.*

Flixton *Fleuston(e): King's land.*

Flotmanby *Flotemanebi: Clerks of Beverley from Archbishop of York; Gilbert de Ghent.* Now West Flotmanby.

Foggathorpe *Fulcartorp: Nigel Fossard from Count of Mortain; Ralph de Mortimer; Gilbert de Tison.* Moated Manor Farm.

Folkton *Fulcheton: King's land.* Manor house; church with Saxon carving; round barrows.

Fordon *Fordun: King's land.*

Fosham *Fos(s)ham: Drogo de Beuvriere.* Now Low Fosham.

Foston-on-the-Wolds *Fodstone: Hugh from William de Percy. Church, mill.* Norman church; windmill.

Foxholes *Foxele/Foxhole/ Foxohole: King's land.* Manor house.

Fraisthorpe *Frestintorp: King's land; Count of Mortain; Hugh FitzBaldric; Uctred from the king.* Manor Farm; marshland enclosed with a dyke (c.1307).

Fridaythorpe *Fridag(s)torp/ Frida(r)storp: King's land; Archbishop of York; Count of Mortain; Odo the Crossbowman.*

Ganstead *Gagenestad: Drogo de Beuvriere and Albert from him.* Old Hall Farm, with the remains of a moat.

Ganton *Galmeton: King's land.* Hall.

Gardham *Gerdene: Bishop of Durham.*

Garrowby *Geruezbi/Gheruenzbi: King's land; Game, the pre-Conquest holder, from the king; Count of Mortain.* Hall; medieval village site.

Garton (near Aldbrough) *Garton/tun: Count of Mortain; Drogo de Beuvriere. Church.* 13th-century church.

Garton-on-the-Wolds *Garton/ tune: St John's church, Beverley, from Archbishop of York before and after 1066; Count of Mortain. Church.* Church, established by Kirkham Priory in 1132; evidence of continuous settlement since Neolithic times.

Gate Fulford *Foleforde/ Fuleford(e): Count Alan.* Suburb of York; also known as Fulford.

Gembling *Chemelinge/ Ghemelinge: St John's church, Beverley, from Archbishop of York.*

Goodmanham *Gudmundham: King's land; Archbishop of York; Nigel Fossard from Count of Mortain; William de Colevil from William de Percy; Gilbert de Tison.* Tumuli; Norman church built over a pagan temple destroyed in 627 after King Edwin had been converted.

Gowthorpe *G(he)uetorp: Archbishop of York.*

Goxhill *Golse: Drogo de Beuvriere.* Manor Farm.

Gransmoor *Grentesmor(a)/ Grenzmore: King's land.* Medieval village earthworks.

Great Cowden *Coledun: Archbishop of York.* Manor Farm.

Great Driffield *Drifeld/felt: King's land; Count of Mortain.* Market town with the motte of a small medieval castle.

Great Givendale *Geuedale/ Ghiuedale: King's land.*

Great Hatfield *Haiefelt/Haifeld/ -felt: Drogo de Beuvriere and Walter from him.*

Great Kelk *Chelc(he): St John's church, Beverley, from Archbishop of York.*

Greenwick *Greneuuic: Archbishop of York.* Greenwick Farm.

Gribthorpe *Gripetorp: Ralph de Mortimer; Gilbert de Tison.* Moated site.

Grimston (in Dunnington) *Grimeston(e): Nigel Fossard from Count of Mortain (claimed by William de Percy and Ernuin the priest).*

Grimston Garth (in Garton) *Grimeston(e)/tun: Archbishop of York; Drogo de Beuvriere.* Moated farmhouse; ponds; remains of the medieval village.

Grimthorpe *Grimtorp/Grintorp: King's land.* Grimthorpe manor house; ancient hill-fort.

Grindale *G(e)rendele: King's land; Archbishop of York.* Roman building site.

Gunby *Bonnebi: Count of Mortain; Gilbert de Tison.*

Hagthorpe *Achetorp: Bishop of Durham; Gilbert de Tison.* Moated Hagthorpe Hall.

Haisthorpe *Aschel/Aschiltorp: King's land; St John's church, Beverley, from Archbishop of York before and after 1066.* Moated site.

Halsham *Halsam/-sem/ Halsham: Archbishop of York, before and after 1066 and 2 knights from him; Gumar from Drogo de Beuvriere.* Monuments to the Constables, descended from one of the knights, are in the church and mausoleum.

HOWSHAM: *The Hall, 1619.*

Hanging Grimston *Grimeston(e): St Mary's church, York (given by Odo the Crossbowman); Osward and Rodmund from the king.*

Harpham *Arpen/Harpein: King's land.* Manor house earthworks.

Harswell *Erseuuelle: King's land.* Manor house; moated site.

Hawold *Holde: King's land; Archbishop of York.* Haywold Farm.

Hayton *Haiton(e): King's land; William de Percy.* Roman fort site.

Helperthorpe *Elpetorp: Archbishop of York.* Manor house; long barrow.

Hemingbrough *Hamiburg:* See page 305.

Heslington *Eslinton/Haslinton: Archbishop of York; Count Alan; Hugh FitzBaldric.* Victorianized hall, the centre of York University.

Hessle *Hase: Ralph de Mortimer; Gilbert de Tison. Church.* Outer suburb of Hull; late 13th-century church. Hull was a chapelry of Hessle until 1661.

Hilderthorpe *Hilgertorp/ Hilgretorp: King's land; Count of Mortain; Clibert, the pre-Conquest holder, from the king.* Suburb of Bridlington. Medieval village earthworks.

Hilston *Heldeuueston/ Heldouestun: Drogo de Beuvriere.*

Hive *Hidon: Bishop of Durham.* Adjoining Sandholme; moated site.

Hollym *Holam/Holun: Drogo de Beuvriere.*

Holme-on-the-Wolds *Hougon: Bishop of Durham and Nigel Fossard from him.*

Holme-upon-Spalding-Moor *Holme: Gilbert de Tison and Geoffrey from him. Church.* 13th-century church with Norman masonry and a pre-Conquest carved stone.

Holmpton *Holmetone/-tune/ Ulmetun: Walter from Drogo de Beuvriere.* Hall.

Hornsea *Hornesse(i): Drogo de Beuvriere and Wizo from him; Church.* 13th-century church.

Hornsea Burton *Bortun/ Burtune: Drogo de Beuvriere.* Suburb of Hornsea. The medieval village was washed away by the sea.

Hotham *Hode/Hodhu': King's land; Bishop of Durham; Count of Mortain and Nigel Fossard from him; Robert Malet. Mill.* Manor Farm.

Houghton *Houeton(e)/-tun/ Oueton: King's land; Robert Malet; Hunfrid from Gilbert de Tison.* Houghton Hall; manor farm.

Howden *Houed'/Houeden(e): Bishop of Durham. Church.* Town with the remains of an episcopal manor house and church.

Howsham *Huson: Count of Mortain. Mill.* Water-mill, now derelict.

KIRKHAM: *Priory doorway.*

Huggate *Hughete: King's land; Ernuin the priest from the king.* Tumuli; pond may be Anglo-Danish in origin.

Humbleton *Humeltone/ Umeltun: Drogo de Beuvriere.* Manor house.

Hunmanby *Hundemanebi: Gilbert de Ghent; Church.* Norman church; Low Hall, formerly the manor house.

Hunsley *Hund(r)eslege: Bishop of Durham; Hugh FitzBaldric.* The area of High Hunsley; Low Hunsley Farm.

Hutton *Hotone/Hot(t)une: Nigel Fossard from Count of Mortain; Hugh FitzBaldric.* Adjoining Cranswick.

Kelfield *Chelchefeld/felt: Count Alan; Hugh FitzBaldric.*

Kelleythorpe *Calgestorp: King's land; St John's church, Beverley, from Archbishop of York. Mill.*

Kendale *Cheldal(e): King's land.* Great and Little Kendale Farms.

Kennythorpe *Cheretorp: Hugh FitzBaldric and Geoffrey from him.*

Kettlethorpe *Torp: Robert Malet.* Kettlethorpe Farm.

Keyingham *C(h)aingeham: Drogo de Beuvriere; William Malet, according to the men of Holderness. Church.* Populous; Keyingham Grange; late 13th-century church.

Kilham *Chillon/Chillun: King's land; Odo the Crossbowman; Ernuin the priest, the pre-Conquest holder.* Evidence of continuous settlement since Neolithic times; medieval street plan.

Kilnsea *Chilnesse: Drogo de Beuvriere.*

Kilnwick *Chileuuid/uuit: King's land; Nigel Fossard from Count of Mortain.*

Kilnwick Percy *Chelingewic/ Chileuuic/Chilleuuinc: King's land. Hall.* 18th-century hall.

Kilpin *Chelpin: Bishop of Durham.* Hall.

Kiplingcotes *Climbi/Clinbicote: St John's church, Beverley, from Archbishop of York before and after 1066; Richard Surdeval from Count of Mortain (in dispute); William de Percy.* Kipling House on the site of a medieval village.

Kirby Grindalythe *Chirchebi: King's land; Count of Mortain and Nigel Fossard from him.*

Kirby Underdale *Cherchebi/ Chirchebi: King's land; Hernegrim the monk and Seward, the pre-Conquest holders, from the king.* Manor house; late 11th-century church.

Kirkburn *Burnous/Westburne: King's land.* Manor house.

Kirk Ella *Aluengi: Count of Mortain and Nigel Fossard from him; Ralph de Mortimer; Gilbert de Tison; Hugh FitzBaldric. Church.* Suburb of Hull.

Kirkham *Chercan: Count of Mortain. Mill, church.* The Priory, founded c.1125, was centred on the *Domesday* church, which was replaced c.1150; finely preserved gatehouse.

Knapton *Cnateton(e): Ralph de Mortimer.* Hall. Near Staple Howe, one of the earliest Iron Age settlements in Britain.

Knedlington *Cledinton: Bishop of Durham.*

Langthorpe *La'be/Lambe/ Lanbetorp: Drogo de Beuvriere; William Malet, according to the men of Holderness.* Langthorpe Hall.

Langtoft *Lang(h)etou: King's land; St Peter's church, York, from Archbishop of York.*

Langton *Lanton: Hugh FitzBaldric and Geoffrey from him.* Roman villa site nearby. The triple dykes on Langton Wold are late Iron Age.

Langwith *Languelt: Count Alan; Hugh FitzBaldric.* Langwith Lodge; mound of a former hunting-lodge.

Laxton *Laxinton: Bishop of Durham.* Manor house.

Laytham *Ladon(e): Count of Mortain and Nigel Fossard from him; Gilbert de Tison.*

Leavening *Alia Ledlinge/ Ledling(h)e: Count of Mortain; 2 of the king's thanes.*

Leconfield *Lachinfeld/felt: St John's church, Beverley, from Archbishop of York; Count of Mortain and Nigel Fossard from him; William de Percy. 11 fisheries.* Remains of the moat of the Percy family castle.

Lelley Dyke *Dic(he): Drogo de Beuvriere.* Lelley Dyke Farm.

Leppington *Lepinton: Count of Mortain.* Norman castle mound.

Leven *Leuene: Archbishop of York. Church.* Early Victorian church with Saxon sculpture.

Linton *Linton: Ralph de Mortimer.* Linton Farm; site of a medieval village.

Lissett *Lessete: Drogo de Beuvriere.* Church with part of a Saxon tombstone.

Little Cowden *Coldun: Drogo de Beuvriere.*

Little Driffield *Drigelinghe: King's land.* Church with a fragment of a Saxon cross. Aldfrith, king of Northumbria (d. AD705) is reputedly buried here.

Little Givendale *Alia Geuedale: King's land; Archbishop of York.* Little Givendale Farm; house sites, remains of a village deserted in the 15th century.

Little Hatfield *Hei(e)feld: Drogo de Beuvriere and Rayner from him.* Manor farm.

Little Kelk *Alia Chelch/Chelche: King's land.*

Little Weighton *Wideton(e): Hugh FitzBaldric. 2 mills.* Expanded.

Lockington *Lecheton/Locheton: St John's church, Beverley, from Archbishop of York; Count of Mortain and Nigel Fossard from him. Mill.* Remains of the Fossard family castle.

Londesborough *Lodenesburg: Archbishop of York.* Park; church with an Anglo-Danish 11th-century cross-head.

Long Riston *Riston/tun(e): Drogo de Beuvriere and Gerbodo from him.* Manor house.

Lowthorpe *Langetorp/ Log(h)ctorp: King's land; St John's church, Beverley, from Archbishop of York before and after 1066; Game from the king. Church.* Church with an Anglo-Saxon cross-head.

Lund (near Beverley) *Lont: Bishop of Durham.*

Lund (in Bubwith) *Lont: Ralph de Mortimer; Gilbert de Tison.*

Lutton *Ludton: Archbishop of York.* Now East Lutton, a hamlet, and the village of West Lutton.

Mappleton *Mapletone: Drogo de Beuvriere. 100 acres of meadow.* On the coast; much meadow land.

Marfleet *Mereflet/flot: Drogo de Beuvriere's men from him; Archbishop of York before and after 1066.* Suburb of Hull.

Market Weighton *Wicstun: King's land.* Town. Its church retains some 11th-century work; Iron Age Barrow cemetery at Arras.

Marton (in Bridlington) *Marton(e)/tun: King's land; St Peter's church, York, from Archbishop of York before and after 1066; Count of Mortain; Clibert, the pre-Conquest holder, from the king.* Marton Hall, formerly the manor house.

Marton (in Burton Constable) *Meretone/tune: Drogo de Beuvriere and Franco from him.*

Meaux *Melse: Drogo de Beuvriere.* Moats and earthworks of a Cistercian house, founded 1150.

Melbourne *Middelburne/ Midelborne: Ralph de Mortimer.*

Meltonby *Metelbi: King's land.* Hall.

Menethorpe *Mennistorp: King's land; Berengar de Tosny. Mill.*

Middleton-on-the-Wolds *Middeltun(e): St John's church, Beverley, from Archbishop of York; Nigel Fossard from Count of Mortain and Richard Surdeval from him. Church.* Church with a late Norman doorway.

Millington *Mileton/Milleton(a): King's land; Archbishop of York.*

Molescroft *Molescroft: Archbishop of York and St John's church, Beverley, from him.* Suburb of Beverley; manor farm.

Monkwick *Mon(n)euuic: Archbishop of York.* Also known as Monkwith. The medieval village was washed away by the sea.

Moreby *Morebi: Count Alan; Hugh FitzBaldric.* Moreby Hall; site of a medieval village.

Mowthorpe *Mele/Muletorp: Archbishop of York; Nigel Fossard from Count of Mortain.* Now 2 hamlets, Low Mowthorpe, on a medieval village site and High Mowthorpe.

Muston *Muston(e): King's land; Gilbert de Ghent.* Hall.

Myton *Mitun(e): Ralph de Mortimer.* Part of Hull.

Naburn *Naborne: King's land; Robert de Tosny.*

Nafferton *Nadfartone: King's land; William de Percy. Mill.* Water-powered mill by the pond.

Neswick *Nesseuuic/Nessuinc: Nigel Fossard from Count of Mortain.* Neswick Farm.

Newbald *Niuuebold/Niwebolt: Archbishop of York and the canons of St Peter's church, York, from him. 4 mills, church.* Now 2 villages, North and South Newbald, known as Newbald; Lower Mill Farm; church, c.1120, the finest of its date in the Riding.

Newsholme *Nesse/Neuhusa: Ralph de Mortimer.* Newsholme Parks; site of a 16th-century deer park.

Newsome *Neuhuson/Niuuehusu': Drogo de Beuvriere.* Great Newsome Farm.

Newton (in Cherry Burton) *Neuton(e): Lost.*

Newton (in Wintringham) *Neuton/Neuutone: Ralph Pagnell.* Place Newton, a mansion, c.1837; medieval village site.

Newton Garth *Nichuetun/Niuueton: Drogo de Beuvriere.* Farmhouse; medieval village site.

North Burton (or Burton Fleming) *Burton(e): King's land.* Manor house.

North Cave *Alia Caue/Caue: Canons of St Peter's church, York, from Archbishop of York; Nigel Fossard from Count of Mortain; Robert Malet; Hugh FitzBaldric. 2 mills.* Large, residential.

North Cliffe *Clive: King's land.* Manor House Farm.

North Dalton *Dalton(e): Nigel Fossard from Count of Mortain; Robert de Tosny and Berengar from him; Autbert, the pre-Conquest holder, from the king. Church.* Manor house; Norman church; tumuli.

North Duffield *Dufeld/-felt/Nordufelt: Count of Mortain; Gilbert de Tison.* Triangular market place-cum-green.

North Ferriby *Ferebi: Nigel Fossard from Count of Mortain; Ralph de Mortimer. Church.* Large, residential; Victorian church.

North Frodingham *F(r)otingham: Drogo de Beuvriere. Church, 3 fisheries.* Church with a Saxon cross-head.

North Grimston *Grimestona/ton(e): King's land; Archbishop of York; Hugh FitzBaldric.*

Northorpe *Torp: Walter from Drogo de Beuvriere; William Malet, according to the men of Holderness.* The medieval village was washed away by the sea.

North Skirlaugh *Schire(s)lai/Scirlai: Archbishop of York; Drogo de Beuvriere.*

Norton *Norton(e): King's land; Ralph de Mortimer; Hugh FitzBaldric. Church, mill.* Town. Its church has a Norman font; disused water-mill.

NUNBURNHOLME: *Cross in 2 fragments.*

Nunburnholme *Brunham: King's land; Forne FitzSigulf from the king.* Norman church with an Anglo-Saxon cross, c.1000; Manor named after a nunnery, founded c.1150.

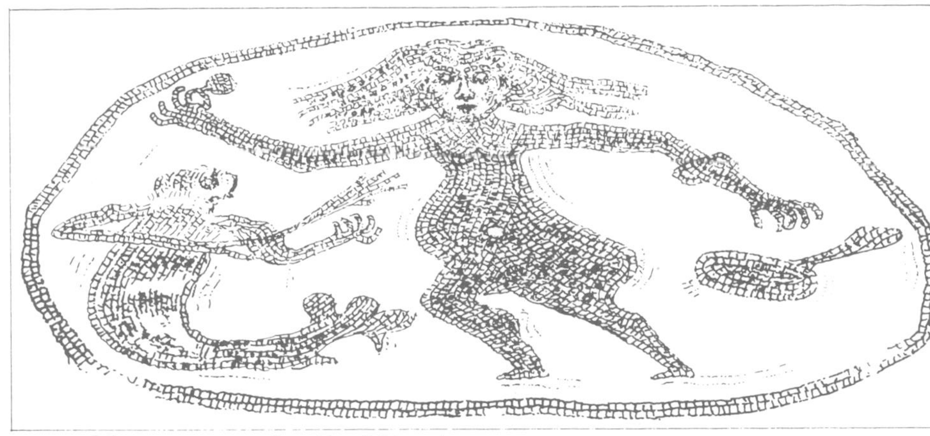

RUDSTON: *Roman pavement, found in a field nearby.*

Nunkeeling *Chelinge/Chiling(h)e: Baldwin from Drogo de Beuvriere.* Remains of a buttress from a house of Benedictine nuns, founded 1152, after which the hamlet was named.

Nuthill *Not(h)ele: Drogo de Beuvriere.* Nuttles Hall Farm.

Octon *Ocheton: King's land; Count of Mortain.* Manor house; medieval village site.

Osgodby *Ansgote(s)bi: Nigel Fossard from Count of Mortain.*

Ottringham *Otrege/Otrengham/Otringeham: Archbishop of York; Drogo de Beuvriere. Church.* Church with a Norman tower arch.

Oubrough *Ule(n)burg: Frumold from Drogo de Beuvriere.*

Ousethorpe *Torp: King's land.* Medieval village site; moat.

Out Newton *Niuueton(e): Drogo de Beuvriere.* Much of it washed away by sea.

Owsthorpe *Duuestorp: Bishop of Durham.* Manor farm.

Owstwick *Hosteuuic/Osteuuic: Drogo de Beuvriere.* Hall and grange.

Owthorne *T(h)orne: Drogo de Beuvriere.* Part of Withernsea.

Painsthorpe *Thorf/Torfe: King's land; Arnegrim, the pre-Conquest holder.* Tumuli.

Patrington *Patrictone: Archbishop of York before and after 1066.*

Paull *Pagele/Paghel: Drogo de Beuvriere.*

Paull Holme *Holm(e): Drogo de Beuvriere.* Remains of a manor house.

Pillwoods *Pileford: Hugh FitzBaldric.* Pillwood Farm.

Pocklington *Poclinton: King's land. 2 mills.* Town with a Norman church; Devonshire Mill.

Pockthorpe *Pochetorp: Count of Mortain; William de Percy.* Hall, site of a medieval village.

Portington *Portiton: Bishop of Durham.* Manor house, surrounded by a water-filled moat.

Potter Brompton *Bruneton(e): King's land.*

Preston *Preston(e)/tune: Drogo de Beuvriere and Baldwin from him. Church.* Large, sprawling; mainly 13th-century church.

Raisthorpe *Redrestorp: King's land; Hugh FitzBaldric; Odo the Crossbowman.* Raisthorpe manor house; medieval village; earthworks and pond nearby.

Raventhorpe *Rag(h)eneltorp: Archbishop of York and St John's church, Beverley from him before and after 1066; Count of Mortain and Nigel Fossard from him.* Medieval village site.

Redmere *Redmaere/Redmar(e)/Rotmare: Lost.*

Reighton *Ricton(e): King's land; St John's church, Beverley, from Archbishop of York.*

Riccall *Richale: Archbishop of York and the canons of St Peter's church, York, from him; Bishop of Durham.* Expanded.

Rillington *Redlinton(e)/Renliton: King's land; Count of Mortain; Berengar de Tosny.* Manor house.

Rimswell *Rimesuuelle: Baldwin and Guntard from Drogo de Beuvriere.* Manor farm.

Ringbrough *Rigeborch/Righeborg/Ringeborg/-burg/Ringheborg/-burg: Drogo de Beuvriere and Baldwin from him.*

Riplingham *Ripingham: Ralph de Mortimer.* Manor farm.

Risby *Rasbi/Risbi: Archbishop of York.* Ponds near a medieval village site; Fishpond Wood.

Rise *Rison/Risun: Archbishop of York; Franco from Drogo de Beuvriere; William Malet, according to the men of Holderness.* Mote Hill, probably a medieval hunting lodge site.

Roos *Rosse: Drogo de Beuvriere and Fulco from him. Church.* 13th-century church; moated site.

Rotsea *Rotesse: Count of Mortain.* Medieval village site.

Routh *Rute/Rutha: Archbishop of York; Drogo de Beuvriere.* Manor house farm.

Rowlston *Roluestun/Roolfestone: Drogo de Beuvriere.* Hall.

Rowton *Rug(h)eton: Drogo de Beuvriere.* Adjoining South Skirlaugh; medieval village site.

Rudston *Rodesta(i)n/stein: Richard Surdeval from Count of Mortain; Ralph de Mortimer; Uctred from the king.* Roman villa; round barrow.

Ruston Parva *Roreston: King's land; St John's church, Beverley, from Archbishop of York before and after 1066.*

Rysome Garth *Rison/Utrisun: Drogo de Beuvriere; William Malet, according to the men of Holderness.* Moated farmhouse.

Saltmarshe *Saltemersc: Bishop of Durham.*

Sancton *Santun(e): Robert Malet; Gilbert de Tison.* Anglo-Saxon burial ground.

Scagglethorpe *Scachetorp: Count of Mortain; Berengar de Tosny.*

Scampston *Scameston(a) King's land; Ralph de Mortimer.* Hall.

Scorborough *Scogerbud: Bishop of Durham and William de Percy from him. Mill.* Motte and bailey; on the site of a medieval village.

Scoreby *Scornesbi: Osbern from William de Percy.* Scoreby Manor House.

Scrayingham *Escr(a)ingham/Screngham: Walo from Hugh FitzBaldric. Mill.*

Seaton *Settun: Drogo de Beuvriere.* Manor farm.

Seaton Ross *Seton/Setton(e): King's land; Nigel Fossard from Count of Mortain.* Seaton Old and New Halls.

Settrington *Sendriton: Berengar de Tosny.*

Sewerby *Siuuar(d)bi: Earl Hugh; Richard Surdeval from Count of Mortain; Clibert, the pre-Conquest holder, from the king.* Adjoining Bridlington.

Sherburn *Schiresbur(ne)/Scriesburne: Archbishop of York; Count of Mortain; Hugh FitzBaldric.* Church with Saxon carvings.

Shipton *Epton: King's land.* Now Shiptonthorpe; manor farm.

Sigglesthorne *Siglesto(r)ne: Archbishop of York. Church.* 13th-century church.

Skeckling *Scachelinge: Lost.*

Skelton *Sc(h)ilton: Bishop of Durham.*

Skerne *Schirne: King's land; Hugh FitzBaldric.* Skerne Grange, once owned by Meaux Abbey.

Skidby *Schitebi: Canons of St John's church, Beverley, from Archbishop of York.* Dormitory for Hull.

Skipwith *Schipewic: Hugh FitzBaldric. Church.* Church with a Saxon tower; Skipwith Common.

Skirlington *Schereltun(e): Drogo de Beuvriere.* Now 2 hamlets, High and Low Skirlington; medieval village site.

Skirpenbeck *Scarpenbec/ Scarpinberg: Count of Mortain; Odo the Crossbowman. Mill.* Manor house; Haybridge Mill Farm.

Sledmere *Slidemare: Nigel Fossard from Count of Mortain; Gospatric.* Estate village; site of a medieval village near the church.

Southburn *Sudburne: King's land.*

South Cave *Caue: Robert Malet; Nigel Fossard. Church, 2 mills.* Church; Mill Beck; market hall.

South Cliffe *Clive: Bishop of Durham.*

Southcoates *Sotecote(s). Archbishop of York; Drogo de Beuvriere.* Suburb of Hull.

South Dalton *Delton: Archbishop of York and St John's church, Beverley, from him.* Estate village.

South Duffield *Suddufel(d)/-felt: Count of Mortain and Nigel Fossard from him.* Hall.

Southorpe *Torp: Drogo de Beuvriere.* Medieval village site.

South Skirlaugh *Scherle/ Sc(h)ire/-lai/Schirle: Drogo de Beuvriere.* Adjoining North Skirlaugh.

Spaldington *Spellinton: Count of Mortain; Gilbert de Tison.* Moated site.

Speeton *Specton/Spetton/ Spretone: King's land; Count of Mortain.* Manor house.

Sproatley *Sprotelai/l(i)e: Archbishop of York before and after 1066; Drogo de Beuvriere and Roger from him; William Malet, according to the men of Holderness.* Grange.

WRESSLE: *Percy's castle with 'manor house' windows.*

Staxton *Stactone/Staxtun: King's land.* Iron Age, Romano-British and Anglian excavations.

Stillingfleet *Steflinflet/ Steflingefled: King's land; Count Alan; Hugh FitzBaldric; Erneis de Buron and Hunfrid from him.*

Storkhill *Estorch: St John's church, Beverley, from Archbishop of York.* Stork Hill Farm; deserted medieval village site.

Sunderlandwick *Sundre(s)lanuuic. King's land, Gospatric.* Medieval village site.

Sutton (in Norton) *Sudton(e)/ Suton: King's land; Archbishop of York; Count of Mortain; Ralph de Mortimer; Ulchil, the pre-Conquest holder, from the king.* Absorbed into Norton. Grange.

Sutton-on-Hull *Su(d)tone: Archbishop of York; Drogo de Beuvriere and Lanbert from him.* Suburb of Hull.

Sutton-upon-Derwent *Sudton(e): Count of Mortain and Nigel Fossard from him; William de Percy and Picot from him. 3 fisheries.* Lock; water-mill.

Swaythorpe *Suauetorp: Odo the Crossbowman.* Medieval village site.

Swine *Su(u)ine: Archbishop of York before and after 1066.*

Tansterne *Tansterne: Drogo de Beuvriere.* Medieval village site.

Tharlesthorpe *Toruelestorp: Lost.*

Thirkleby *Alia Turgislebi/ Turgi(s)lebi: Nigel Fossard from Count of Mortain; Ralph de Mortimer; Archbishop of York.* Thirkleby manor house, on the site of a deserted medieval village.

Thirtleby *Torchilebi: Drogo de Beuvriere.*

Thixendale *Sixte(n)dale/ Xixtendale: Count of Mortain; Odo the Crossbowman.* Ancient barrows and earthworks.

Thoralby *Turalzbi: Game, the pre-Conquest holder, from the king.* Thoralby Hall, on the site of a medieval village.

Thorganby *Turgisbi: Ralph Pagnell. 8 fisheries.* Lock.

Thorngumbald *Torn(e): Drogo de Beuvriere.* Dormitory for Hull.

Thornholme *Thirnon/Tirnu': King's land.* Adjoining Burton Agnes.

Thornthorpe *Torgrimestorp: King's land.* Thornthorpe House; site of a medieval village.

Thornton *Tornetun/Tortetun: Ralph de Mortimer.*

Thorpe (in Rudston) *Torp: Count of Mortain.* Thorpe Hall, on the site of a medieval village.

Thorpe Bassett *Torp: King's land; Count of Mortain.*

Thorpe le Street *Rud(e)torp: King's land; Gilbert de Tison.* Manor farm; medieval village site.

Thorpe Lidget *Torp: Bishop of Durham.* Thorpe Hall and Common.

Thwing *Tu(u)enc: King's land.* Willy Howe, a late Neolithic round barrow.

Tibthorpe *Tibetorp/Tipetorp: Game, the pre-Conquest holder, from the king.* Manor farm.

Tickton *Tichetone: Archbishop of York.* Hall and Grange.

Totleys *Totele: Drogo de Beuvriere.* Totleys Farm marks the site of a medieval village.

Towthorpe (in Fimber) *Touetorp: King's land; Count of Mortain.*

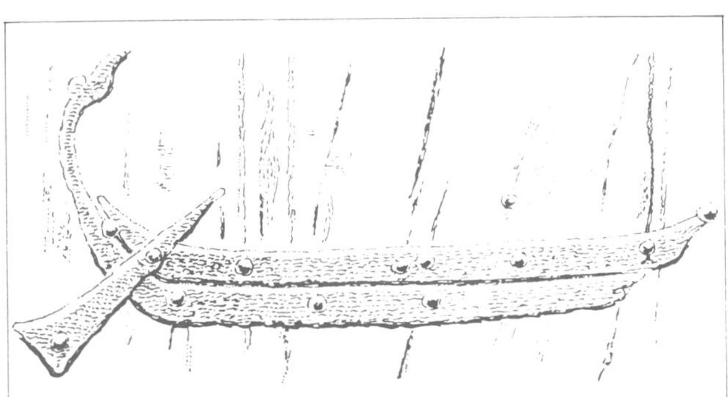

STILLING FLEET: *12th c. church door, Viking boat.*

Towthorpe (in Londesborough) *Toletorp: Archbishop of York.* Medieval village site.

Tunstall *Tunestal(e): Drogo de Beuvriere.*

Ulrome *Ulfram/Ulreham: Erenbald from Drogo de Beuvriere.* Prehistoric 'lake village' site.

Uncleby *Unchel(f)sbi/Unglesbi: King's land; Berengar de Tosny.*

Upton *Uptun: Drogo de Beuvriere.*

Walkington *Walcheton/ Walchinton(e): Canons of St Peter's church, York, from Archbishop of York; Bishop of Durham; Gamel, the pre-Conquest holder, from the king.* Recently expanded; manor farm.

Waplington *Waplinton: King's land.* Waplington Hall; manor farm; fish-pond.

Warter *Warte/Wartre: King's land; Geoffrey from William de Percy. Church, mill.* Mid-Victorian church. Warter Priory grounds with Augustinian priory earthworks.

Wassand *Wadsande: Drogo de Beuvriere and Turstin from him.* Wassand Hall.

Water Fulford *Fuleforde/ Fuletorp: Archbishop of York; Count Alan; Erneis de Buron.* In outer York.

Watton *Waton/Wattune/Watun: Count of Mortain and Nigel Fossard from him; Tored, the pre-Conquest holder, from the king.* Ruins of a Gilbertian house, founded c.1150. In the 8th century there was a nunnery here.

Wauldby *Walbi: Archbishop of York and Godwin from him; Ralph de Mortimer. Church (with Elloughton).* Manor farm; hall; chapel.

Wawne *Wag(h)ene: Archbishop of York; Drogo de Beuvriere.*

Waxholme *Was(s)ham/ Wassum/Waxham: Drogo de Beuvriere and Alelm from him; William Malet, according to the men of Holderness.*

Weaverthorpe *Wifretorp: Archbishop of York.* Manor house.

Weel *Uela/Wela: Archbishop of York.*

Weeton *Wideton: Archbishop of York.* Manor farm.

Welham *Wellon/Wellun: Ralph de Mortimer; Hugh FitzBaldric.* Welham Hall Farm.

Welton *Wellet'/Welleton(e): Bishop of Durham. 3 mills.* Dormitory for Hull; manor house; Welton Mill. Dick Turpin was arrested at an inn here in 1739.

Welwick *Weluuic: Archbishop of York. Church.* 13th-century church.

Welwick Thorpe *Torp: Lost.*

West Carlton *Carle(n)tun: Drogo de Beuvriere and Radulph from him.*

West Cottingwith *(Alia) Coteuuid/Cotinuui: Count of Mortain and Nigel Fossard from him; Ralph Pagnell; Erneis de Buron.*

West Heslerton *Alia Eslerton/ Alia Heslertone/Haselintonis: Count of Mortain; Osward, the pre-Conquest holder, from the king.*

West Newton *Neutone: Archbishop of York.*

Wetwang *Wetwangham: Archbishop of York.*

Wharram-le-Street *Warham/ Warran: Nigel Fossard from Count of Mortain.* Saxon Church.

Wharram Percy *Warran/ Warron:* See page 304.

Wheldrake *Coldrid: William Colevile from William de Percy. 3 fisheries, church.* Hall; 13th-century church, rebuilt in 1779.

Willerby (near Hull) *Wilgardi: King's land.* Dormitory for Hull.

Willerby (near Hunmanby) *Widlafeston/Widlaueston: King's land.* Medieval village site with the earthworks of Bridlington Priory's grange.

Willitoft *Wilgetot: King's land; Count of Mortian and Nigel Fossard from him; Ralph de Mortimer; Gilbert de Tison.* Moated hall.

Wilsthorpe *Wiflestorp/ Wiulestorp: King's land; Drogo de Beuvriere.* Much was washed away by the sea.

Winestead *Wifestad/-stede/ Wistede/Wiuestad: Archbishop of York.* Moated site.

Winkton *Wincheton(e): Drogo de Beuvriere and his priest from him.* Swept away by sea.

Wintringham *Wentrig(e)ham: Ralph de Mortimer.*

Withernsea *Widfornessei/ Witfornes:* See page 304.

Withernwick *Widforneuui(n)c/ Wit(h)forneuuinc: Archbishop of York; Drogo de Beuvriere and Wazelin from him.*

Wold Newton *Neuton(e): King's land; Gilbert de Ghent.* Anglian settlement with a monument to a 56 1lb meteorite which fell here in 1795.

Wolfreton *Ulfardun/Uluardune: Ralph de Mortimer.* Medieval village site.

Wressle *Weresa: Ralph de Mortimer; Gilbert de Tison. Church.* Late Georgian church; ruins of a castle built about 1380.

Wyton *Widetun(e): Drogo de Beuvriere.* Hall.

Yapham *Iapun: King's land.*

Yokefleet (in Blacktoft) *Iucufled/Iugufled: Bishop of Durham.* Victorian Hall.

Yokefleet (in Gilberdyke) *Iugufled: Bishop of Durham; Robert Malet.* Yokefleet Grange, Yokefleet Lodge.

Youlthorpe *Aiul(f)torp: Archbishop of York; Odo the Crossbowman.*

West Riding

Wath upon Dearne Wentworth

In WATH (UPON DEARNE) *WADE* Reitharr had 6 carucates of land taxable where 3 ploughs are possible. Roger [de Bully] now has there 1 plough; and 4 villagers and 8 smallholders with 1 plough. Value before 1066, 40s; now 10s. To this manor belongs jurisdiction in SWINTON and WENTWORTH *WINTREVUORDE* 2 carucates and 2 bovates of land taxable. This land is waste. Woodland pasture, 14 furlongs long and 5 wide.

Wath upon Dearne is a South Yorkshire industrial town nine miles north-east of Sheffield. The name means 'ford on the River Dearne'. The settlement was the centre for two manors in *Domesday*, one held by the Saxon thane Ulsi and the other by the Norman, Roger de Bully, from Bully near Neuchatel. De Bully was granted a large estate consisting of 54 manors in South Yorkshire and 163 in north Nottinghamshire, centred on the castle at Tickhill. Both Wath manors had declined in value and had far fewer ploughs than before the Conquest, but only the holdings at Swinton and Wentworth were described as waste. Wentworth, a neighbouring village, which was in the soke of de Bully's manor and was a berewick of Ulsi's, was probably largely woodland; by 1303, however, some land here had been cleared and a farm called Wentworth Woodhouse established.

Wentworth Woodhouse is the name given today to one of the grandest of English stately homes. The house, which has two contrasting fronts, was built between 1725 and 1750 for Thomas Wentworth, the first Marquis of Rockingham. The ambitious 600-foot east façade designed by Henry Flitcroft is the longest in England. There was an earlier house on the site built about 1630 by Thomas Wentworth, the first Earl of Strafford, Charles I's chief adviser, who was executed in 1641. From the mid-eighteenth century to the early nineteenth, the great fortune and ability of the Wentworths and their successors, the Fitzwilliams, enabled them to control the political life of Yorkshire and to some extent that of the country. Charles, the second Marquis of Rockingham, was twice prime minister and he and his father erected various 'follies' on the estate expressing their Whig political views. These include the pyramidal Hoober Stand commemorating the defeat of the Jacobites in 1745; the Needle's Eye, and Keppel's Column celebrating the acquittal of Rockingham's friend, Admiral Keppel, at his court-martial in 1779. Sadly, however, these land mark's, as well as the Rockingham mausoleum of 1788, are threatened by neglect and subsidence caused by nearby mining.

Coal-mining, a major source of the Wentworth/Fitzwilliam fortune, had begun at Wentworth by the late fourteenth century, but the greatest development came later in the nineteenth century with the sinking of the 'Main' collieries, which still have considerable reserves of coal. Wath upon Dearne, although it received a market charter in 1312, remained largely an agricultural village until the opening of the Dearne and Dove Canal in 1797, which led to extensive coal mining here too. The rural landscape portrayed by the *Domesday* entries for the Wath manors, with ploughlands, woodland and meadow, is today predominantly industrial.

Ilkley

In OTLEY with these outliers: STUBHAM; MIDDLETON; DENTON; CLIFTON; *BICHERTUN*; FARNLEY; (Nether) TIMBLE; *ECTONE*; POOL; GUISLEY; HAWKSWORTH; another ('Little') HAWKSWORTH; BAILDON; MENSTON; BURLEY (in Wharfedale); ILKLEY *ILLICLEIA*. Between them all, 60 carucates and 6 bovates taxable, in which 35 ploughs are possible. Archbishop Aldred had this as 1 manor. Now Archbishop Thomas has in lordship 2 ploughs; and 6 villagers and 10 smallholders who have 5 ploughs. There are there 5 Freemen who have 4 villagers and 9 smallholders with 5 ploughs. A church and a priest with 1 villager and 1 plough. Meadow, 4 acres; woodland pasture, 2 leagues, 3 furlongs long and as wide; underwood, 9 leagues long and as wide; arable land, 2 leagues long and 2 wide; moor, 2 leagues long and 1 wide. The largest part of this manor is waste. Value before 1066 £10; now £3.

Ilkley is a popular residential town and holiday centre some ten miles north of Bradford and 15 miles north-west of Leeds, attractively situated below extensive moorland in Lower Wharfedale. In 1086 the manor was held by William de Percy (whose land is described as waste) as well as by Archbishop Thomas of York, whose holding was largely waste. A priest is common to both entries. There are no architectural remains of the church he served, but the present All Saints' Church, begun in the thirteenth century, was no doubt built on its site. The Roman fort of Olicana once stood here, and in the church are three fine ninth-century Anglo-Saxon crosses. Nearby is a collection of Bronze Age carvings on rocks and boulders which have been brought from the surrounding moorland.

Present day Ilkley is largely a creation of the past 150 years. Early in the eighteenth century, it was said to be 'a very mean place – equally dirty and insignificant, and chiefly famous for a cold well, which has done very remarkable cures in scrofulous cases by bathing, and drinking of it'. The curative properties of the waters were attracting considerable numbers by the end of the century, but the town's potential as a spa was not fully realized until after the building in 1846 of the extensive Ben Rhydding Hydropathic Establishment. Other large hydros and hotels followed, and with the opening of the railway in 1864–65 Ilkley became one of the major health resorts of Victorian England. The population rose from 778 in 1841 to about 7455 in 1901. There were that number again of resident visitors, and, in addition, some 200,000 day trippers a year.

Ilkley is no longer primarily a resort, but its attractive Victorian character and austere moorland scenery have made it an affluent residential town with an important annual literature festival. A considerable area of the parish is still 'wasteland', as in *Domesday*, but its thousands of acres of unproductive moorland are now much valued by hiking holidaymakers. They also give Yorkshire its unofficial 'national' anthem: *On Ilkla Moor baht'at'*.

Pontefract
(Tanshelf in Pontefract)

In TANSHELF *TATESHALLA* there are 16 carucates of land without tax where 9 ploughs are possible. The King had this manor. Now Ilbert has there 4 ploughs; and 60 petty burgesses, 16 cottagers, 16 villagers and 8 smallholders who have 18 ploughs. A church is there and a priest. 1 fishery; 3 mills which pay 42s; meadow, 3 acres; woodland pasture, 1 league long and 1/2 wide. The whole manor, 1 1/2 leagues long and 1/2 wide. Value before 1066 £20; now £15. Within this boundary are contained alms of the poor. To the same manor appertains this jurisdiction: MINSTHORPE, 2 c.; BARNBY (Hall) 2 c.; and SILKSTONE, 1 1/2 c. Together 5 1/2 carucates of land taxable where 5 ploughs can be. These are there 9 villagers and 3 smallholders who have 4 ploughs.

Although the town of Pontefract, which lies ten miles east of Wakefield, is rich in historical associations, it remains one of the least known and least appreciated in Yorkshire. The manor of Tateshall recorded in *Domesday* is represented today by Pontefract's north-western suburb of Tanshelf. The name Pontefract – 'broken bridge' – does not appear until early in the twelfth century.

Domesday's entry for Pontefract, with its reference to 60 petty burgesses, is one of the most interesting in Yorkshire, clearly indicating that Tanshelf was already something of a town. Except for York, burgesses are recorded at only three other places in Yorkshire: Bridlington, Pockington and Dadsley on the outskirts of Tickhill; and they all have considerably fewer than Tanshelf. The town's population may have been between 400 and 500, including 16 cottagers (*cotarii*), the only time these are mentioned in Yorkshire's *Domesday*. The reference to alms of the poor is also unusual; presumably it describes land where the income was used to care for the poor of the town.

The sites of the mills and fishery are uncertain, but the latter was probably on the River Aire. The 1086 church would have been on the site of the present All Saints' Church, a large, impressive, partly ruined building which stands close to the castle, in the history of which it played a dramatic part.

Little survives of Pontefract Castle, which Ilbert de Lacy began to build on a prominent rock outcrop to the east of the town in 1082. Both town and castle remained the property of the de Lacy family for some 240 years, before passing by marriage to Thomas, Earl of Lancaster. Once in the hands of a member of the royal family the castle became nationally significant, and, over the next four centuries, it was the scene of numerous major events. Here in 1322 Thomas, Earl of Lancaster, was sentenced to death. He was beheaded on a nearby hill where the locals

ILKLEY: *Roman garrisons may well have looked towards the moor with apprehension. The Elizabethans built a manor house on the Roman site (now a museum) but today it is the moor itself which draws visitors from all over Britain.*

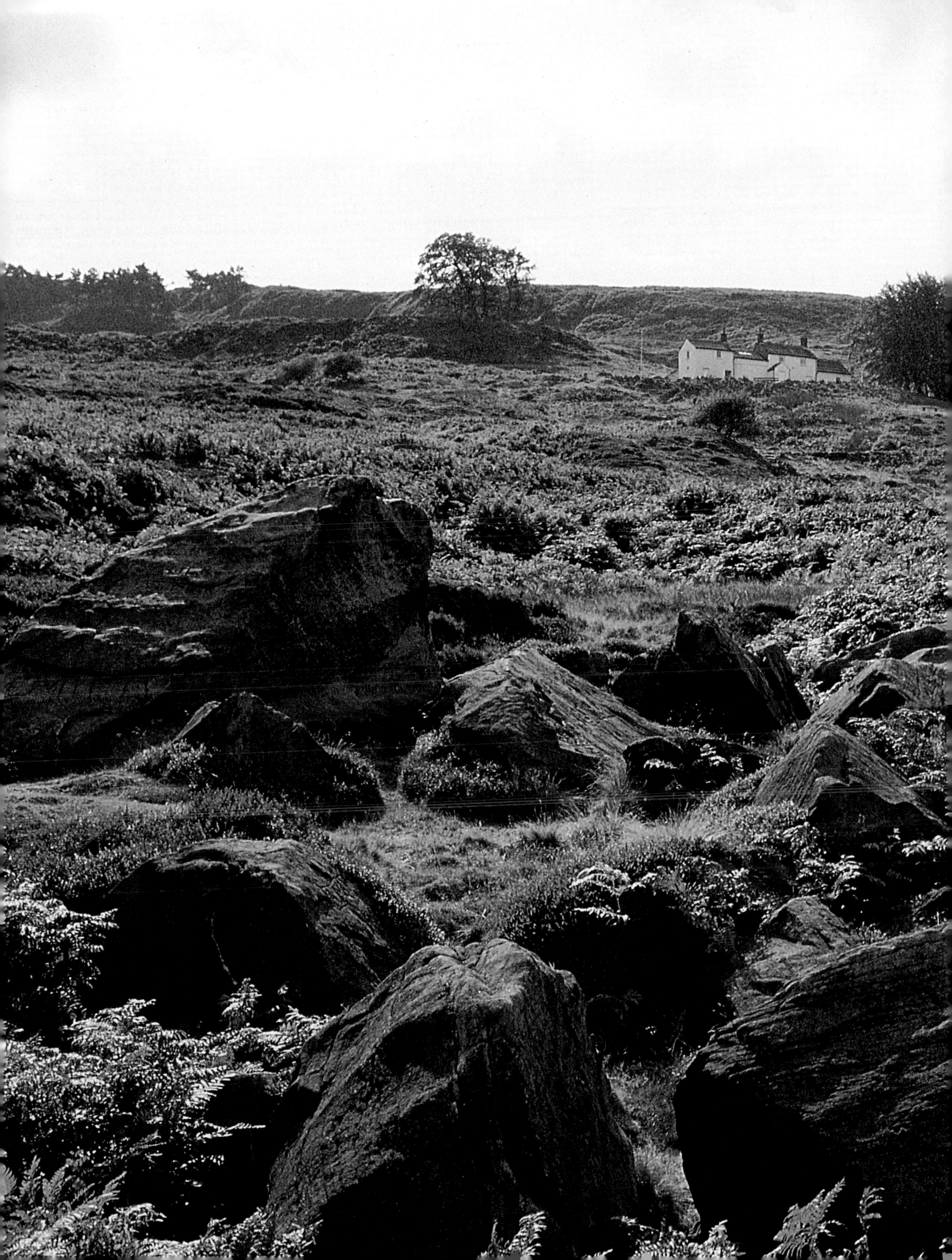

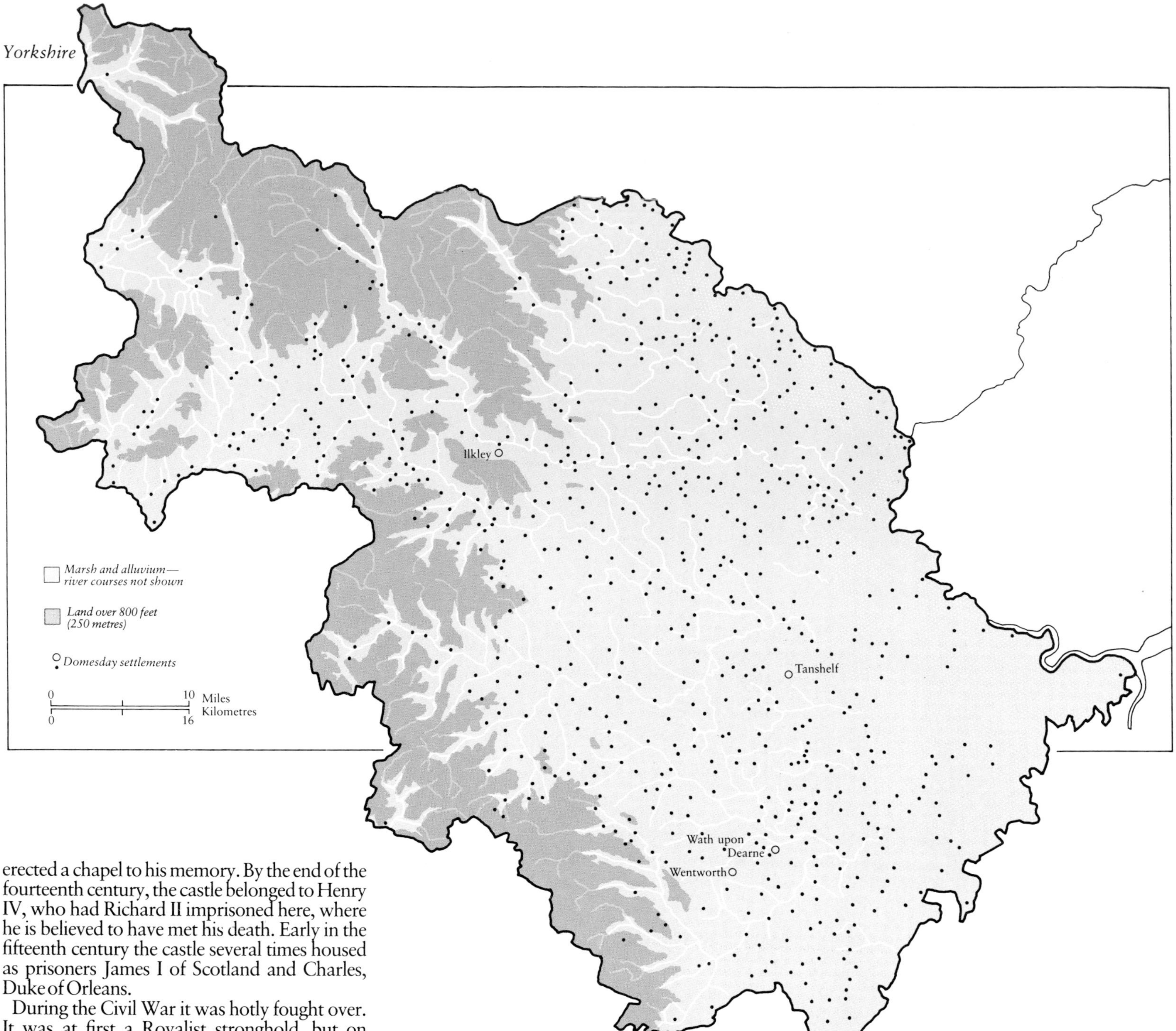

erected a chapel to his memory. By the end of the fourteenth century, the castle belonged to Henry IV, who had Richard II imprisoned here, where he is believed to have met his death. Early in the fifteenth century the castle several times housed as prisoners James I of Scotland and Charles, Duke of Orleans.

During the Civil War it was hotly fought over. It was at first a Royalist stronghold, but on Christmas Day, 1644, the Parliamentary forces began a seven-month siege during which 99 Cavaliers and 470 Roundheads were killed. All Saints' Church was a key stronghold, held at various times by each side and suffering much at the hands of the Parliamentarians. In July 1645, the Royalists, by now entirely without fresh provisions and with no possibility of relief, surrendered.

On 3 June, 1646, John Morris, a Royalist Colonel, succeeded in retaking the castle, a move which marked the beginning of a second siege which continued for almost three years, by which time Charles I was dead. On 2 February, 1649, Morris proclaimed Charles II king and struck new coinage marked with the motto *Post mortem patris pro filio* (After the death of the father we are for the son). The next day the Parliamentarians began a heavy bombardment of the castle, and by the end of the month the garrison had been so reduced that Morris had no choice but to surrender. He himself escaped, but was later captured and hung, drawn and quartered at York.

As soon as the battle was over, the inhabitants of Pontefract called for the castle to be 'wholly razed down and demolished' because of the devastation it had brought to the town. This was agreed by Westminster, and in April 1649 the formal order for its demolition was issued. It is said that it was pulled down in 10 weeks. Little remains now except for one large chunk of wall and some lengths of the curtain wall. The precincts were for a time used as a field for growing liquorice.

The town's liquorice confectionery has brought it almost as much fame as its castle. The deep sandy local soils are ideal for the long roots of the liquorice plant cultivated at Pontefract since at least the seventeenth century and possibly since medieval times. The distinctive Pontefract cakes are mentioned as early as 1614, although it was not until the nineteenth century that the manufacture of liquorice sweets was diversified and became a major source of employment.

Pontefract was an active commerical town even before the advent of its liquorice industry. Its street names – Shoemarket, Salter Row, Cornmarket, Beastfair, Ropergate, Woolmarket, Baxtergate, Tanners Row and The Booths – reflect its early trades. A market developed to meet the needs of the castle, and St Giles Church was built in 1105. Now rebuilt, it remains the focal point of the market place. In 1194 the burgesses received various privileges by charter which culminated in 1484 in the establishment of a mayor and corporation. During most of the four centuries Pontefract was a cloth-making centre, and, until the decline of the cloth industry in the fifteenth century, the largest town in the West Riding.

Although it then became again only a market town and a minor social centre, it remained modestly prosperous. Near St Giles Church stands a fine eighteenth-century buttercross, and many of the surrounding buildings are also Georgian, including the town hall and the Red Lion Inn, which has a façade designed by Robert Adam. Starting in 1620, it returned two Members of Parliament, and in 1872 it became the first constituency in the United Kingdom to elect an MP by secret ballot.

Pontefract is today chiefly a marketing and shopping centre with various light industries, including the manufacture of sweets, made from imported liquorice, and coal-mining. The race course laid out in the park early in the eighteenth century regularly brings the town to the notice of the rest of the country with news of a very different sort from that which it made when its castle earned it the name of 'bloody Pomfret'.

West Riding Gazetteer
Each entry starts with the modern place-name in **bold** type. The *Domesday* information is in *italic* type, beginning with the name or names by which the place was known in 1086. The main landholders and under-tenants follow, separated with semi-colons if a place was divided into more than one holding. A number of holdings were granted by the king to his thanes; these holders are described at the end of a list of landholders, as holding land 'from the king'. More general information completes the *Domesday* part of the entry. The modern or post-Domesday section is in normal type. ▦ represents a village. ⌂ a small village or hamlet.

Acaster Malbis *Acastra/tre: Robert Malet.* ▦ On the River Ouse.

Acaster Selby *Acastra/-tra/Alia Acastra/Altera Acastre: King's land; Count Alan; Robert Malet; Ulric from Erneis de Buron; Landric from the king; William de Percy.* ▦ Acaster Hall, formerly the manor house.

Ackton *Aitone/Attone: William from Ilbert de Lacy.* ▦

Ackworth *Aceuurde: Hunfrid from Ilbert de Lacy. Church, mill.* ▦ Now divided into High, Low, and Ackworth Moor Top. Church with a 15th-century tower; medieval village cross. Georgian house, now Quaker school.

Acomb *Ac(h)um/Acun: Archbishop of York and St Peter's Church from him; Ulchel from the king.* ▦ Suburb of York.

Addingham *Edi(d)ham/Odingeham/-hen: King's land.* ▦ Church with a late Saxon cross.

Addlethorpe *A(r)dulfestorp/Arduluestorp: King's land; Gospatric.* ⌂

Adel *Adele: Count of Mortain and Richard from him.* ▦ On the outskirts of Leeds; Roman camp; medieval village site. Norman church with many fine carvings of exceptional detail

Adlingfleet *Adelingesfluet: Geoffrey de La Guerche; church. Mill.* ▦ Church with a picturesque, essentially 13th-century interior; manor farm.

Adwick-le-Street *Adeuui(n)c: Count of Mortain, Nigel Fossard from him; Roger de Bully and Fulk from him.* ▦ Moated site nearby.

Adwick-upon-Dearne *Adeuuic/Hadeuuic: Roger de Bully. Mill.* ▦ Watermill.

Airton *Airtone: Roger le Poitevin.* ▦ Pleasant green; manor house, now an inn.

Aismunderby *Asmundrebi: Archbishop of York; Bernulf from William de Percy.* ⌂ Site of a medieval village.

Aldborough *Burc/Burg: King's land, formerly King Edward.* ▦ Georgian manor house with Roman pavements beneath. Nearby is the site of *Isurium*, a once important Roman city. A prosperous *Domesday* village, Aldborough, was the 'old borough'.

Aldfield *Aldefeld/felt: King's land; Archbishop of York; Gospatric.* ▦

Allerton (in Bradford) *Alreton/tune: Ilbert de Lacy.* ▦ Suburb of Bradford; 17th-century farmhouses; Georgian hall.

Allerton Bywater *Alretun(e): Ilbert de Lacy.* ▦ On the River Aire.

Allerton Mauleverer *Aluertone/Alureton(a)/-tone: King's land; Gospatric; Ulchil, the pre-Conquest holder, from the king.* ▦ Home of Lord Mowbray, descendant of the Earl of Northumberland, one of the Conqueror's henchmen. The Mauleverer family were landowners since the 12th century.

Almondbury *Almaneberie: Leusin from Ilbert de Lacy.* ▦ Large; outside Huddersfield; Castle Hill, an Iron Age camp.

Alwoodley *Aluuoldelei: King's land.* ▦ Outer Leeds suburb. 17th-century hall.

Anley *Anele/Anlei(e): King's land; Roger le Poitevin.* ⌂

Appleton Roebuck *Apeltone/Apelton(e): Osbern d'Arcis.* ▦ Thomas, Lord Fairfax, the Parliamentary general, retired to Nun Appleton Hall where he entertained Andrew Marvell, who wrote of the place in several poems.

Appletreewick *Apletreuuic: Dolfin from the king.* ▦ Monk's Hall was probably a medieval monastic grange.

Arkendale *Archedene/Arghendene: King's land; Gamel from Erneis de Buron.* ▦

Arksey *Archesei(a): Roger de Bully.* ▦ Oasis in a coal-mining area; 17th-century almhouses and grammar school.

Armley *Ermelai: Ilbert de Lacy.* Suburb of Leeds, also known as West Armley.

Armthorpe *Einuluestorp/Ernulfestorp: Erniun the priest from the king.* ▦ Large, industrial.

Arncliffe *Arneclif: Roger le Poitevin.* ⌂ Victorian house on the site of the manor house; Celtic field system.

Arnford *Erneforde: Roger le Poitevin.* ⌂ Arnford Farmhouse, 1690–1700.

Arthington *Ardinton/Hardinctone: Richard de Surdeval from Count of Mortain.* ▦ The nunnery of 1585 was probably built on a 12th-century site.

Askam Bryan *Asc(h)am: Count Alan.* ⌂

Askham Richard *Asc(h)am: Osbern d'Ancis, formerly Ulf the deacon.* ▦

Askwith *Ascuid: Berengar de Tosny; William de Percy; Gospatric.* ▦ In Wharfedale.

Aston *Estone: Count of Mortain and Richard de Surdeval from him. Church.* ▦ Large; among coal-pits; 12th-century church.

Attercliffe *Ateclive: Roger de Bully; Countess Judith.* Suburb of Sheffield.

Auckley *Alceslei/Alchelie/Alcheslei: Nigel Fossard from Count of Mortain.* ▦

Aughton *Actone/Hac(s)tone: Count of Mortain and Richard de Surdeval from him; William de Warenne.* ▦ Coal-mining adjoining Aston.

Austerfield *Oustrefeld: Nigel Fossard from Count of Mortain.* ▦ Birthplace of William Bradford (1590–1657), who sailed in the *Mayflower* and became governor of Plymouth, Massachusetts.

Austhorpe *Ossetorp: Ilbert de Lacy.* ▦ On the outskirts of Leeds. Hall begun in 1694.

Austonley *Alstaneslei(e): King's land.* ▦ Large; part of Holmfirth.

Austwick *Ousteuuic: King's land.* ▦ Manor house at nearby Wharfe.

Azerley *Aserla/As(s)erle/Haserlai: Gospatric; Orm from the king.* ⌂ Secluded; medieval village site.

Badsworth *Badesuu(o)rde: Ilbert de Lacy. Church (with Rogerthorpe and Upton).* ▦ Norman church.

Baildon *Beldone/dun(e): Archbishop of York; Erneis de Buron. Church.* ▦ Industrial suburb.

Balby *Balle(s)bi: Nigel from Count of Mortain; Roger de Bully.* ▦ Outer suburb of Doncaster.

Bank Newton *Neutone/tune: Berengar de Tosny.* ⌂ 17th-century Newton Hall.

Bardsey *Berdesei/Bereleseie: King's land.* ▦ Church with Saxon tower; Norman castle mound. Birthplace of Restoration dramatist William Congreve (1690–1729).

Barge Ford *Bogeuurde: Roger le Poitevin, formerly Earl Tosti.* ⌂ In Newton-in-Craven.

Harkston *Barchestun: Ilbert de Lacy.* ▦ Large fishpond.

Barlow *Berlai: Ralph Pagnell. Church (with Drax, Little Airmyn and Camblesforth).* ▦ Hall, recently enlarged.

Barnbrough *Barneburg/Berneborc/-burg: Roger de Bully; William de Warenne. Mill.* ▦ The hall was the seat of the Cresacres, one of whom was said to have been killed by a wild cat in the church porch.

Barnby (in Cawthorne) *Barnebi: King's land; Ilbert de Lacy.* Barnby Hall.

Barnby Dun *Barnebi: Count of Mortain; Roger de Bully; Malger from William de Percy; 3 waste fisheries; church.* ▦ On the River Don; also called Barnby-on-the-Don; 14th-century church.

ADEL: *A monster swallowing a man's head; rare bronze knocker on the door of St John the Baptist.*

Barnoldswick (in Burton in Lonsdale) *Bernulfesuuic: King's land.* ⌂ Also known as Barlawick.

Barnoldswick (near Gisburn) *Bernulfesuuic: Roger le Poitevin, formerly Berengar de Tosny.* Cotton-manufacturing town that grew from a village in the 19th century. Roman road nearby.

Barnsley *Berneslai: Ilbert de Lacy.* Town. In the 18th century linen-weaving, flax-spinning, wire-drawing, and coal mining were the chief industries.

Barrowby *Berghebi: William de Percy; Erneis de Buron.* ⌂ Barrowby Grange.

Barugh *Berg: Gerneber, the pre-Conquest holder, from Ilbert de Lacy.* ⌂ Now Barugh Green a dormitory for Barnsley.

Barwick-in-Elmet *Bereuuit(h): Ilbert de Lacy. 3 churches, 3 mills.* ▦ Dormitory for Leeds; church with a Saxon cross; impressive motte and bailey site.

Bashall *Baschelf: Roger le Poitevin.* ⌂ Also known as Bashall Town; Georgian hall.

Batley *Bateleia/Bathelie: Ilbert de Lacy. Church.* Woollen town with a 14th-century church.

Battersby *Badresbi:* Lost.

Beal *Begale: Ilbert de Lacy and a certain thane from him.* ▦ On the River Aire.

Beamsley *Bedmeslei(a)/Bemeslai/Bomeslai: King's land; Gilbert de Tison; Erneis de Buron.* ▦ Stone cottages; Hall.

Beckwith *Becui: Gilbert de Tison.* ⌂ Isolated.

Beeston *Bestone: Ilbert de Lacy.* Suburb of Leeds.

Bentham *Benetain: King's land.* ▦ Now 2 villages, High and Lower Bentham.

Bentley *Benedleia/Benelei/Beneslaie/-lei: Count of Mortain; Roger de Bully.* Town, a coal-mining centre; moated sites.

Bewerley *Beurelie: Erneis de Buron.* ▦ Old hall c.1600.

Bickerton *Bic(h)retone: Gospatric.* ▦

Bierley *Birle: Ilbert de Lacy.* Suburb of Bradford.

Bilbrough *Mileburg: Christ's Church from Richard son of Erfast.* ▦

Bilham *Bilam/Bilan/Bil(e)ham: Count of Mortain, and Richard de Surdeval from him; Roger de Bully; William de Warenne.* Bilham House Farm; ponds of a medieval village nearby.

Billingley *Bilingelei(a)/lie/Bingelie: Roger de Bully; Arton, the pre-Conquest holder, from the king.*

Bilton (in Harrogate) *Biletone/Billeton(e): Gilbert de Tison; Archil, the pre-Conquest holder, from the king.* Suburb of Harrogate; church with 3 Saxon carved stones.

Bilton (near Wetherby) *Biletone: Osbern d'Arcis.* ▦ Church with Saxon sculpture; manor farm.

Bingley *Bingelei/Bingheleia: Erneis de Buron.* Small town with an ancient market cross and Georgian market hall. Church with an early Norman font and fragments of a Saxon cross; Bronze Age round barrows.

Birkby *Bretebi: King's land.* Suburb of Huddersfield.

Birkin *Berchi(n)ge/Berchine: Gamel from Ilbert de Lacy. Mill.* ▦ On Old Eye stream.

Birstwith *Beristade: King's land; Gospatric.* ▦ Hall.

BEAMSLEY: *Hospital for women founded by the Clifford family of Skipton.*

Bishop Monkton *Monucheton(e): Archbishop of York.*

Bishop Thornton *Torentone/tune: Archbishop of York.*

Bishopthorpe *Badetorp(es): King's land and Landri from the king; Archbishop of York.* Dormitory for York. Chapel built by Archbishop Grey to serve the manor house he bought in 1241; little of the house survives.

Bolton *Bodeltone: Ilbert de Lacy.* Suburb of Bradford; medieval village site at Bolton Woods.

Bolton Abbey *Bodeltone: King's land.* Bolton Priory is a magnificent ruin. Founded in 1154 by Alicia de Romilly, Bolton Hall incorporates 14th century Priory Gatehouse.

Bolton by Bowland *Bodeltone: William de Percy.* Pretty; 2 greens; 17th-century houses.

Bolton Percy *Badetone/Bode(l)tone/-tune: Rozelin from William de Percy. Church.* Church, consecrated in 1424.

Bolton upon Dearne *Bode(l)tone: Roger de Bully; Picot from William de Percy. Mill, church.* Small colliery town with a late Norman church.

Bordley *Borelaie: Roger le Poitevin.* Isolated in moorland; Bordley Hall.

Bowling *Bollinc: Ilbert de Lacy.* District of Bradford; 14th-century Bolling Hall, remodelled in Jacobean times and now the local history museum.

Bracewell *Braisuelle: Roger le Poitevin.* Hall, Henry V's refuge after the Battle of Hexham in 1464.

Bradford *Bradeford: Ilbert de Lacy.* City. Its wealth derives from wool-sorting and weaving in the Middle Ages; later, from the cotton and silk industry; more recently, from engineering. The church, mainly 15th century with Saxon sculpture, was designated a cathedral in 1919.

Bradley (in Huddersfield) *Bradeleia/lie: Chetel from Ilbert de Lacy.* Large, industrial; Neolithic long barrow on nearby Black Hill.

Bradley *Bradelei: King's land.* Now 2 villages, High Bradley with its Old Hall dated 1672, and Low Bradley.

Braithwell *Bradeuuelle: William de Warenne; Malger from William de Percy. Church.* Norman church; partially medieval Moat Hall.

Bramham *Brameham/Bra(m)ham: Count of Mortain and Nigel Fossard from him. Mill. church.* Large, recently expanded; Church, part Norman, part 13th century; Georgian Bramham Park and gardens.

Bramhope *Bra(m)hop: Ulchil, the pre-Conquest holder, from Gilbert de Tison.* Dormitory of Leeds; Old Bramhope hamlet nearby.

Bramley (in Grewelthorpe) *Brameleia/lie: Gospatric.* Now 2 hamlets, High and Low Bramley; lonely, on moorland.

Bramley (in Leeds) *Bramelei(a): Ilbert de Lacy; William de Warenne.* District of Leeds.

Bramley (near Rotherham) *Bramelei: William de Warenne.* Residential, outside Rotherham.

Brampton *Bierlow/Brantone: Artor the priest, the pre-Conquest holder, from the king.* Large, industrial.

Brampton-en-le-Morthen *Brantone: Richard de Surdeval from Count of Mortain.* In a mining district.

Branton (in Cantley) *Brantone: Geoffrey Alselin. Church.* Grange.

Branton Green *Brantona/Brantun(e): King's land; Erneis de Buron; Gospatric and Turbern, the pre-Conquest holders, from the king.* Near Great Ouseburn.

Brayton *Bretone/Brettan: Ilbert de Lacy. Church.* Norman church with 14th-century additions.

BRAMHAM: *Queen Anne mansion with fine collections of art.*

Brearton *B(r)aretone: King's land.* Secluded.

Bridge Hewick *Hadeuuic: Archbishop of York.*

Brierley *Breselai/lie: Elric from Ilbert de Lacy.* Mining, manor house with medieval fabric.

Brimham *Birnebeham: Gilbert de Tison; Erneis de Buron; Gospatric.* Brimham Hall incorporates the remains of an early Tudor chapel built for Abbot Huby of Fountains Abbey.

Brinsworth *Brinesford: Roger de Bully; Rozelin from William de Percy.* Houses, near Rotherham.

Brodsworth *Brochesuuorde/Brodesuu(o)rde: Count of Mortain and Nigel Fossard from him; Roger de Bully. Church.* Unspoiled; Norman church; hall, 1850.

Broughton *Broctune: Berengar de Tosny; Roger le Poitevin.* In the parkland of an Elizabethan hall.

Burden *Burg(h)edurun: Count of Mortain and Richard de Surdeval from him.* Burden Head Farm.

Burghwallis *Burg: William from Ilbert de Lacy.* In the ancient Barnsdale Forest, haunt of the legendary Robin Hood. Norman church; rare rood screen.

Burley In Wharfedale *Burgelei/Burghelai: Archbishop of York. Church..* Large, semi-industrial.

Burnsall *Brin(e)shale: Osbern d'Arcis; Hardulf, the pre-Conquest holder, from the king.* Attractive, church with a possibly 11th-century font and fragments of Saxon sculpture.

Burton (in Gateforth) *Burtone/tun: Ilbert de Lacy.* Burton Hall.

Burton in Lonsdale *Borctune: King's land.* Silk and wool-weaving. Behind the green is the mound of the Mowbrays' Castle.

Burton Leonard *Burton(e): King's land.*

Cadeby *Catebi: Roger de Bully; Aubrey de Coucy.* Small, in a mining area.

Calton *Caltun: Roger le Poitevin, formerly Erneis de Buron.* Hall, now a farmhouse.

Calverley *Caverlei(a): Ilbert de Lacy.* Dormitory for Leeds and Bradford; seat of the Calverleys for centuries. Walter Calverley (d.1605) was the subject of *A Yorkshire Tragedy*, a drama published in 1608, possibly the work of William Shakespeare. He murdered two sons and was pressed to death at York.

Camblesforth *Camelesford(e)/Canbesford/Gamesford: Ralph Pagnell; Ernuin the priest from the king. Church.* Hall, c.1700.

Campsall *Cansale: Ilbert de Lacy.* In ancient Barnsdale Forest, early Norman church; 15th-century manor house, now the vicarage.

Cantley *Canteleia/lie/Cathalai: Geoffrey Alselin. Church.* Norman church, swamped by housing estates; Roman sites.

Carlesmoor *Carlesmor(e): Gospatric.* On the edge of moorland. In 1850, the well-preserved body of a Romano-British man was dug out of the peat here.

Carleton (near Skipton) *Carlentone: Roger le Poitevin.* Also called Carl(e)ton-in-Craven; manor farm nearby.

Carlton (in Barnsley) *Carlentone/Carleton: Gamel and Elric from Ilbert de Lacy.*

Carlton (in Lofthouse) *Carlentone: Ilbert de Lacy. Mill. 4 halls before 1066.*

Carlton (near Otley) *Carletun(e): Robert Malet.* Now the village of East Carlton and hamlet of West Carlton, with a manor house lying between them.

Carlton (near Snaith) *Carletone/tun: Ulchil from the king.* Large, also known as Carlton-in-Balne.

Cartworth *Cheteruurde/Cheteuuorde: King's land.* Picturesque.

Castley *Castelai: King's land.* Severed by railway.

Cattal *Catale/Cattala: Osbern d'Arcis.*

Catterton *Cadretone/tune: Osbern d'Arcis and Fulk from him.* Moated site.

Cawthorne *Caltorn(e): King's land.* Attractive old cottages; church with an 11th-century font and Saxon carvings.

Cayton *Chettone/Chetune: King's land.* Scattered; site of a medieval village near High Cayton Hall.

Chapel Allerton *Alretun: Ilbert de Lacy.* District of Leeds, 19th-century Gledhow Grange.

Chellow *Celeslau: Ilbert de Lacy.* District of Bradford; large reservoir.

Chevet *Ceuet: Ilbert de Lacy.* Site of a medieval village in Chevet Park. Village pond remains.

Church Fenton *Fentun: Archbishop of York before and after 1066.* Medieval moated site, 13th-century church.

Clapham *Clapeham: King's land.* Picturesque, beneath Ingleborough; manor house, 1705.

Clareton *Clareton(e): King's land; Gospatric.* Medieval village site.

Clayton (near Bradford) *Claiton(e): Ilbert de Lacy.* Suburb of Bradford.

Clayton (near Thurnscoe) *Claitone: Count of Mortain and Richard de Surdeval from him.* Also known as Clayton-in-the-Clay.

Clayton West *Claitone: Ilbert de Lacy.* Large, residential.

Cleckheaton *Hetone/tun: Ilbert de Lacy.* Industrial town with Roman iron workings at nearby West Brierley.

Clifford *Cliford: Nigel Fossard from Count of Mortain. Mill.* On a tributary of the River Wharfe.

Clifton (in Brighouse) *Cliftone: Ilbert de Lacy.*

Clifton (in Conisbrough) *Clifton(e)/tune: William de Warenne.* On the edge of Conisbrough Parks.

Clifton (with Newhall) *Cliftun: Archbishop of York; Count Alan. Church.* Suburb of Otley.

Clifton (with Norwood) *Cliftone: King's land.* Part of Norwood hamlet.

Clotherholme *Cludun: William de Percy.* Isolated.

Coldcotes *Caldecotes: Ilbert de Lacy.* Near Ingleborough.

Cold Hiendley *Hindelei(a): Ilbert de Lacy.* Large reservoir.

Colton (near Leeds) *Col(l)etun: Ilbert de Lacy.* On the edge of Temple Newsam Park.

Colton (near York) *Coletone/tune: Osbern d'Arcis.* Colton Lodge.

Compton *Contone: Possibly Richard de Surdeval.*

Conisbrough *Coningesborc/burg/Cuningesburg: William de Warenne, formerly Earl Harold. Church, 2 mills.* Picturesque town with steep streets and a famous castle, featured in Sir Walter Scott's *Ivanhoe*. The church has Saxon long-and-short work and a Saxon cross.

Coniston Cold *Coneghestone/Coningeston/Cuningestone: King's land, William de Percy; formerly Roger le Poitevin.* Earthwork on Coniston Moor.

Conistone *Cunestune: Gospatric; Chetel from the king.* Old field systems are still visible on either side of the River Wharfe.

Cononley *Cutnelai: King's land.* Hall.

Cookridge *Cucheric: Richard de Surdeval from Count of Mortain.* Outer suburb of Leeds.

Copgrove *Copegraue: Erneis de Buron and Turstin from him. Church.* In the parkland of the mid-18th century hall; Norman church, probably 11th century.

Copmanthorpe *Copemantorp: Erneis de Buron; Earl (?)William.* Dormitory for York. The Knights Templar held land here in the Middle Ages.

Copt Hewick *Hauui(n)c: Archbishop of York.* Hall.

Cottingley *Cotingelai/lei: Erneis de Buron.* Residential.

Cowling *Collinghe: Roger le Poitevin.* 17th-century houses.

Cowthorpe *Coletorp: Godefrid from William de Percy. Church.* Secluded; church built in 1450. Cowthorpe Oak was centuries old when John Evelyn's *Sylva* mentioned it (1664).

CONISBROUGH: *The castle keep, with six massive buttresses*

Cowthwaite *Cu(d)ford: Ilbert de Lacy.* Cowthwaite Plantation; near Cufforth House on Becca Banks, an Iron Age earthwork.

Crigglestone *Crigest'/Crigeston(e): King's land.*

Crofton *Scroftune/Scrotone: Gerbodo from Ilbert de Lacy.* 14th-century church with fragments of Saxon crosses.

Crooks *Croche(s): William de Percy; Roger le Poitevin.* Crooks House, earthwork.

Cullingworth *Colingauuorde: Erneis de Buron.* Large, residential; hall.

Cusworth *Cuzeuuorde: Roger de Bully; William de Warenne.* Outer suburb of Doncaster; hall, 1740.

Dacre *Dacre: Erneis de Buron.* Low Hall, said to have been built of stones from Fountains Abbey.

Dadsley *Dadeslei(a): Roger de Bully, 3 mills, church.* De Bully's castle became the market town of Tickhill; Dadsley Farm.

Dalton (near Huddersfield) *Dalton(e): Swen from Ilbert de Lacy.* District of East Huddersfield.

Dalton (near Rotherham) *Dalton(e): Rozelin from William de Percy.* Dalton Magna and Parva, a suburb of Rotherham.

Darfield *Dereuueld/uuelle: Alsi from the king.* Coal-mining town. Norman church tower with Perpendicular top; carved pews and alabaster effigies.

Darrington *Darni(n)tone: Ilbert de Lacy. Church, mill.* 12th-century church.

Darton *Dertone/tun(e): King's land.* Coal-mining town; Jacobean hall.

Deightonby *Dictenebi:* Lost.

Denaby *Degenebi/Denegebi: Roger de Bully. Mill.* In Old Denaby; remains of a 15th-century manor house.

Denby (near Penistone) *Denebi: Elric from Ilbert de Lacy.* Now Upper and Lower Denby; near Denby Dale, a small industrial town; Iron Age hill-fort.

Denby (in Upper Whitley) *Denebi: Ilbert de Lacy.* Denby Hall.

Denton *Dentun(e): Archbishop of York. Church.* Georgian church.

Dewsbury *Deusberia/berie: King's land, formerly King Edward. Church.* Large manufacturing and engineering town; church with fine Saxon cross fragments; 13th-century Moot Hall.

Dinnington *Domnitone/Dunintone/Dunnitone: Roger de Bully; William de Warenne.* Coal-mining town.

Dodworth *Dodesuu(o)rde: Swan, the pre-Conquest holder, from Ilbert de Lacy.* Coal-mining town.

Doncaster *Donecastre: Nigel Fossard from Count of Mortain; William de Percy and Malger from him.* Famous for its railway workshops, race course, and butterscotch. The Roman fort of *Danum* stood here. Mansion house by James Paine, 1745–8, with fine ballroom.

Draughton *Dractone: King's land.* Manor house.

Drax *Drac: Ralph Pagnell. Church.* Norman church tower; perpendicular clerestory, 13th-century chancel.

Drebley *Drebelaie: Osbern d'Arcis.*

Drighlington *Dreslin(g)tone: Ilbert de Lacy.* Industrial; scene of a Civil War battle in 1643.

Dunkeswick *Chesuic: Ulchil, the pre-Conquest holder, and his wife from the king.*

Dunsforth *Doneforde/Dunesford/Dunesforde: Rannulf; Turbern the pre-Conquest holder, from the king.* Now the village of Lower Dunsforth and hamlet of Upper Dunsforth.

Earby *Alia Eurebi/Eurebi: Roger le Poitevin.* Cotton town.

Earlsheaton *Et(t)one: King's land.* District of East Dewsbury.

Easington *Esintune: Roger le Poitevin.* In the Forest of Bowland.

East Ardsley *Erdeslau(ue): Ilbert de Lacy and Swen from him.* Jacobean hall.

Eastburn *Esebrune/Estbrune: King's land; Gilbert de Tison.* Adjoining Steeton.

East Halton *Altone/Haltone: King's land.* 17th-century Halton Hall.

East Keswick *Chesinc/ing: King's land.* Large.

East Stainley *Estanlai/Stanlai.* Lost.

Eastwick *Estuinc/Estuuic:* Lost.

Eavestone *Euestone: Archbishop of York.* Isolated; medieval village site.

Ecclesfield *Eclesfeld/felt: Roger de Bully.* Suburb of Sheffield, church with 11th-century cross fragments; chapel of about 1300; moated site.

Eccleshill *Egleshil: King's land.* District of Bradford.

Eccup *Echope: Count of Mortain and Richard de Surdeval from him.* Reservoir.

Edenthorpe *Scires/Stirestorp: William de Warenne, formerly Earl Harold.* Suburb of Doncaster; formerly known as Streetthorpe.

Edlington *Eilin/Ellintone: Malger from William de Percy.* Nearby is New Edlington, a large mining village.

Eggborough *Acheburg/Eburg/Eg(e)burg: Baret from Ilbert de Lacy. Mill.* Now 2 villages, Low and High Eggborough. Mill at the former.

Eldwick *Helguic/Heluuic: Erneis de Buron.* Eldwick Hall.

Elland *Elant/Elont: Ilbert de Lacy.* Tudor Old Hall.

Ellenthorpe *Eluuinetorp/Haluuidetorp: William de Percy; Roger le Poitevin.* Hall and lodge. The Battle of Boroughbridge was fought here in 1322.

Elslack *Eleslac: Roger le Poitevin.* Remains of a Roman road and a fort known as Burwen's Castle, medieval Elslack Hall.

Elsworth *Eleuuorde: King's land.* Farmhouse.

DRAX: *Charming carved figure, 15th c, in the Norman church of St Peter and St Paul.*

Elwicks *Eleuuic: King's land.* Farmhouse.

Embsay *Embesie: King's land.* Embsay Hall, 1652.

Emley *Amelai/leie: King's land.* Remains of a market cross, centre of the medieval iron industry.

Eshton *Estune: Roger le Poitevin.* Eshton Hall; medieval St Helen's Well.

Fairburn *Fareburne: Ilbert de Lacy and Ligulf, the pre-Conquest holder, from him.* Coal-mining.

Farnham *Farneham: King's land, formerly King Edward; Gospatric. Church.* Hall; Norman church.

Farnhill *Fernehil: King's land.* 14th-century Farnhill House.

Farnley (in Leeds) *Fernelei: King's land; Ilbert de Lacy.* Suburb of Leeds.

Farnley (near Otley) *Fernelai/lie: Archbishop of York. Church.* J. M. W. Turner painted at the hall while a guest of Walter Fawkes from 1810 until 1825.

Farnley Tyas *Fereleia/Ferlei: Ilbert de Lacy.*

Farsley *Fersellei(a): Ilbert de Lacy.* Residential district adjoining Pudsey.

Featherstone *Ferestane/Fredestan: Ilbert de Lacy and Ralph and Ernulf from him. 2 churches.* Coal-mining town.

Felliscliffe *Felgesclif: King's land.*

Ferrensby *Feresbi: King's land, formerly King Edward.*

Ferrybridge *Fereia/Ferie: Hamelin from Ilbert de Lacy.* Site of a Norman ford; one of Britain's most interesting round barrows.

Fewston *Fostun(e): King's land, formerly King Edward.* Part of the village was lost to its two reservoirs.

FISHLAKE: *Decorated Norman church doorway.*

Fishlake *Fiscelac/Fixcale: William de Warenne.* Moated site in the fens.

Fixby *Fechesbi: King's land.* On the edge of Huddersfield.

Flasby *Flatebi: Roger le Poitevin.* Flasby Hall.

Flaxby *Flatesbi: Erneis de Buron.*

Flockton *Flocheton(e): Ilbert de Lacy.* Manor house. Medieval open field system.

Frickley *Fricelei(a)/Frichelie/ Frichehale: Ilbert de Lacy; Roger de Bully and Fulk from him. Church and mill.* Norman church with an organ from the hall, presented in 1937 by lord of the manor; medieval village site.

Fryston *Fristone: Gerbodo from Ilbert de Lacy. Church.* Now Water Fryston. Ferry Fryston was on the site of the present power station.

Fulstone *Fugelestun: King's land.*

Garforth *Gereford(e): Ilbert de Lacy and William and Warin from him. Church.* Coal-mining town. The church, 1844, contains fragments of a Saxon cross.

Gargrave *G(h)eregraue: King's land; Berengar de Tosny; Roger le Poitevin.* Victorian church with fragments of Saxon crosses; Roman villa; prehistoric camp.

Giggleswick *Ghigelesuuic: Roger le Poitevin.* Stocks; village cross; tithe barn.

Gipton *Chipertun/C(h)ipetun: Ilbert de Lacy.* District of Leeds.

Gisburn *Ghiseburne: William de Percy; Roger le Poitevin.* Compact; almost a small town; Bronze Age barrows nearby; Gisburn Forest, once a hunting ground.

Givendale *Gherindale: Archbishop of York.* Medieval village site; mound of the medieval manor house.

Glass Houghton *Hoctun: Ilbert de Lacy.* Part of Castleford.

Glusburn *Glusebrun: William de Percy; Gilbert de Tison.* Glusburn Old Hall.

Golcar *Gudlagesarc/argo: Dunstan from Ilbert de Lacy.* On the outskirts of Huddersfield.

Goldsborough *God(en)esburg: Ralph Pagnell and Hubert from him. ½ fishery.* Hall, c.1620. A Viking silver hoard was unearthed here.

Goldthorpe *Go(l)detorp/ Guldetorp: King's land; Roger de Bully.* Mining.

Gomersal *Gome(r)shale: Ilbert de Lacy.* Mills and factories; Tudor manor house; Red House, featured in Charlotte Brontë's *Shirley* (1849).

Grafton *Graftona/tone/tune: King's land; Canons from Archbishop of York; Erneis de Buron; Torbern, the pre-Conquest holder, from the king.* Grafton Grange.

Grantley *Grentelai(a): Archbishop of York.* Now the village of High Grantley, and Low Grantley hamlet.

Grassington *Chersintone/ Ghersintone: King's land; Gilbert de Tison.* 13th-century manor house, part of the 19th-century hall; many Iron Age remains nearby.

Greasbrough *Gersebroc/ Gres(s)eburg: Roger de Bully; William de Warenne.* Roman Ridge, an ancient earthwork.

Great Braham *Michelbram/ Bran: William de Percy and Godefrid from him; Gilbert de Tison; Erneis de Buron.* Braham Hall.

Great Houghton *Haltun(e): King's land; Count of Mortain and Richard de Surdeval from him.* The old hall, now an inn, is probably Elizabethan.

Great Mitton *Mitune: Roger le Poitevin.* Former manor house, now the hall with a 14th-century doorway.

Great Ouseburn *Usebruna/ Useburne: King's land.* One-street only.

Great Timble *Timble: King's land.* Quiet, secluded.

Green Hammerton *Alia Ambretone/Altera Hanbretone: Osbern d'Arcis.* Green surrounded by houses.

Greetland *Greland: King's land.* Possibly the site of the Roman station *Cambodunum.*

Grewelthorpe *Torp: Gospatric.* Straggling; green; duckpond.

Grimston *Grimeston/tun: Ilbert de Lacy. 2 churches, 2 mills.* Grimston Park mansion, built in 1840.

Grindleton *Gretlintone: Roger le Poitevin.* Sheepfarming.

Guiseley *Gisele: Archbishop of York. Church.* Town with a village cross and stocks in its market place; timber-framed wall in the rectory is believed to be Saxon.

Hainworth *Hageneuuorde: Erneis de Buron.*

Hallam *Hallun: Roger de Bully from Countess Judith.* Hallam Head, a district of Sheffield.

Halton *Halletun(e): Ilbert de Lacy.* District of Leeds.

Hambleton *Hameltun: Ilbert de Lacy and Ernulf from him.* Large, sprawling.

Hammerton *Hamereton: Roger le Poitevin.* Elizabethan hall marking the site of a medieval village.

Hamphall Stubbs *Hanepol: Ansgot and Robert from Ilbert de Lacy. Mill.* Stubbs Hall nearby.

Hampole *Honepol: Roger de Bully. ½ mill.* Castle mound. Richard Rolle (*d.*1349), the mystical writer, lived as a hermit here and is buried in the church of the now vanished Cistercian nunnery.

Handsworth *Handesuuord/ uurde: Count of Mortain and Richard de Surdeval from him.* District of Sheffield; coal-mining.

Hanging Heaton *Etun: King's land.* Suburb of Dewsbury.

Hanlith *Hangelif: King's land.* Hall.

Harewood *Hareuuode: King's land.* Ruins of a 12th-century castle. Harewood House, magnificent 18th century home of the Earl, has grounds by Capability Brown.

Harthill *Hertil: William de Warenne.* Church, said to have been founded by William de Warenne; manor farm.

Hartlington *Herlintone/tun: Dolfin from the king.* Hall.

Hartshead *Hortes(h)eue: Elsi from Ilbert de Lacy.* Walton Cross, an Anglo-Saxon carved stone, in a field near the church.

Hatfield *Hedfeld: William de Warenne. Church.* Large; rows of miners' houses. Medieval manor house; Norman church.

Hathelton *Hatelton/tun:* Lost.

Hawkswick *Hochesuuic: Roger le Poitevin.* On the River Skirfare.

Hawksworth *Hauocesorde/ Henochesuurde: Archbishop of York. Church.* Jacobean hall.

Hawksworth Mill *Alia Hauochesord/Alia Henochesuurde: Archbishop of York.* Watermill nearby.

Hazelwood *Eseleuuode/ Heseleuuode: Malger from William de Percy.* Chapel, 1286, of the medieval castle built by William Vavasour; medieval village site.

Headingley *Hedingelei(a): Ilbert de Lacy.* District of Leeds.

Healaugh *Hailaga/Helage: Geoffrey Alselin.* The manor farm near the village incorporates the remains of a priory founded in 1190; moated.

Heathfield *Higrefeld/felt: Berengar de Tosny.* In moorland.

Hebden *Hebedene: Osbern d'Arcis.* Hall farm.

Hellaby *Elgebi/Helgebi: Roger de Bully. 3 mills, church.* Hellaby Hall, 1700.

Hellifield *Haelgefled/Helgefeld/ felt: King's land; William de Percy; Roger le Poitevin.* Peel Castle, now ruined, with a medieval foundation.

Hemsworth *Hamelesuurde/ Hilmeuuord: Gamel from Ilbert de Lacy.* Town Hall, now a school.

Hensall *Edeshale: King's land.*

Heptonstall *Crumbetonestun: King's land, formerly King Edward. 2 churches.* Old hand-weaving centre; steep streets; weavers' cottages.

Hepworth *Heppeuuord: King's land.* Steep streets.

Herleshow *Erleshold/holt: Archbishop of York.* Earth works and ponds, the site of a medieval village.

Hessay *Esdesai/Hesdesai: Richard son of Erfast; Osbern d'Arcis and Eldred from him.* On the edge of Marston Moor.

Hessle *Asele/Hasele: Malger from Ilbert de Lacy; 6 iron workers.* Remains of bell-pits, used for ironstone extraction. This is one of *Domesday's* few allusions to Yorkshire iron making. The monasteries later took up the industry.

Hetton *Hetune: Roger le Poitevin.* On the moors.

Hexthorpe *Egescop/Estorp/ Hestorp: Count of Mortain and Nigel Fossard from him. Church, 2 mills.* District of Doncaster.

Hickleton *Chicheltone/ Icheltone: Aubrey de Coucy.* Picturesque; Georgian Hickleton Hall.

High Hoyland *Holand/Holant: Osulf, the pre-Conquest holder, from Ilbert de Lacy.* Church with Saxon cross fragments.

High Melton *Medeltone/ Middeltun: Roger de Bully; Swen, the pre-Conquest holder, from the king.* Georgian hall with a supposedly medieval tower.

Hilton *Hilton(e):* Lost.

Hipperholme *Huperun: King's land.* Outside Brighouse.

Holdworth *Aldeuuorde/ Haldeuurde: Roger de Bully.* Secluded.

Holme (near Gargrave) *Holme: King's land.* Holme House.

HEPTONSTALL: *18th-c. carving on a cottage wall.*

Holme (near Holmfirth) *In duabus Holne/Holne: King's land.* On the edge of moors.

Honley *Hanlei(a): Ilbert de Lacy.* Town; an old weaving centre.

Hooton Levitt *Hotone: Count of Mortain. Mill.* Adjoins Maltby.

Hooton Pagnell *Hotone: Count of Mortain and Richard de Surdeval from him. Mill.* Stone houses on a hillside. Norman church, possibly 11th century, hall with a 14th-century gatehouse.

Hooton Roberts *Hotun: Roger de Bully. Mill.* On a tributary of the River Don.

Hopperton *Hom(p)tone/ Hopretone: King's land; Erneis de Buron; Chetel from the king.*

Horbury *Horberie/Orberie: King's land.* Small, industrial town.

Hornington *Hornictune/ Horni(n)tone: Godefrid from William de Percy; Osbern d'Arcis.* Manor house.

Horsforth *Horseford(e)/ Hoseforde: King's land.* Suburb of Leeds.

Horton (near Bracewell) *Hortone/tun: William de Percy; Roger le Poitevin.* 17th-century hall.

Horton-in-Ribblesdale *Hortune: Roger le Poitevin.* Limestone cottages; hall.

Hoyland Nether *Ho(i)land: Roger de Bully; William de Warenne.* Sprawling industrial town.

Hoyland Swaine *Holan(de)/ Holant: Ilbert de Lacy; Swen, the pre-Conquest holder, from the king.* Probably named after Swen.

Hubberholme *Huburgheham: Roger le Poitevin.* In Upper Wharfedale.

Huddersfield *Oderesfelt/ Odresfeld: Godwin from Ilbert de Lacy.* Town. Industries include textiles, engineering and chemicals.

Hunshelf *Hunescelf: Alric, the pre-Conquest holder, from Ilbert de Lacy.* Hall.

Hunsingore *Hol/Hulsingoure/ Ulsigouere: Count of Mortain and Richard de Surdeval from him; Erneis de Buron.*

Hunslet *Hunslet: Ilbert de Lacy.* District of Leeds.

Hutton Wandesley *Wandeslage: Elwin, the pre-Conquest holder, from Osbern d'Arcis.* Hall with the remains of a medieval moat.

Ilkley: See page 310.

Ingbirchworth *Berceuuorde: Ilbert de Lacy.*

Ingleton *Inglestune: King's land.* Manor house.

Ingmanthorpe *Gemunstorp/ Germundstorp: Count of Mortain; Erneis de Buron.* Secluded; Ingmanthorpe Hall.

Ingthorpe *Ucnetorp: Roger le Poitevin.* Ingthorpe Grange.

Kearby *Cherebi: William de Percy.* Also called Kearby Town End.

Keighley *Chichelai: King's land.* Manufacturing town. The medieval church, with a possible Saxon cross-fragment, was rebuilt in the 19th century.

Kelbrook *Chelbroc/Cheuebroc: William de Percy; Roger le Poitevin.*

Kellington *Chel(l)inctone/ Chelintune/Ghelintune: Elric from Ilbert de Lacy.* Sherwood Hall, once the manor house.

Keresforth *Creusford:* Lost.

Kettlewell *Cheteleuuelle: Roger le Poitevin.* Once a market town.

Kexbrough *Cezeburg/ Chizeburg: Swen from Ilbert de Lacy.* Coal-mining.

Kex Moor *Chetesmor/ Cotesmore: Gospatric.* Near the source of the Kex Brook.

Kiddal *Chidal(e): Ilbert de Lacy.* Also known as Kiddal Lane End.

Kildwick *Childeuuic: King's land. Church before 1066.* Saxon church, rebuilt after the Conquest and again in the 14th century; Saxon cross fragments. Bolton Abbey built the fine bridge over the Aire about 1305.

Killinghall *Chenehall/ Chenihalle/Chilingale/Kilingala: King's land, formerly King Edward; Archbishop of York.* Outside Harrogate.

Kilnsey *Chileseie: Ulf from the king.* 17th-century Old Hall; ancient field systems.

Kimberworth *Chiberewoorde: Roger de Bully.* District of Rotherham; manor house; Norman motte and bailey castle.

Kinsley *Chineslai/lei: Gamel from Ilbert de Lacy.* Moated site.

Kippax *Chipesch: Ilbert de Lacy; 3 churches, 3 mills.* Large, residential; Norman church with a Saxon cross-shaft; traces of an early stronghold on Manor Garth Hill.

Kirby Hall *Chirchebi: Osbern d'Arcis.* Grounds of an 18th-century hall; medieval village site.

Kirk Bramwith *Branuuat/-uuet/ Branuuit(h)e/Branuuode: Roger de Bully.* On the River Don; hall.

Kirk Deighton *Distone: Ralph Pagnell; Erneis de Buron. Church.*

Kirkburton *Bertone: King's land.* Small industrial town. The Norman church has Saxon cross fragments.

Kirkby Malham *Chirchebi: Roger le Poitevin.* Picturesque; inspired Charles Kingsley's *The Water Babies* (1863).

Kirkby Malzeard *Chirchebi: Gospatric.* Street of stone houses. Site of a Norman castle owned by the Mowbrays; Mowbray House.

Kirkby Overblow *Cherchebi/ Chirchebi: William de Percy.* Rebuilt medieval church with possibly Saxon door; Tudor Low Hall.

Kirkby Wharfe *Chirchebi: Archbishop of York; Ilbert de Lacy.* Secluded; on the edge of parkland; Norman church with Saxon cross fragments; Roman villa site.

Kirk Hammerton *Ambretone/ Hanbretone: Osbern d'Arcis and John from him. Church, mill, fishery.* Among the meadows of the River Nidd; Saxon church with additions, 1891; hall with a pond; mill farm.

KNARESBOROUGH: *Cliff carving of a Knight Templar at the entrance to St Robert's Cave chapel.*

Kirkheaton *Heptone: Ilbert de Lacy and Gamel from him.* Church with Saxon cross fragments and a stone with a runic inscription.

Kirk Sandall *Sandale/Sandalia/ -lie: Count of Mortain; William de Warenne. Church.* Suburban; large glass works; Norman church with a possibly Saxon wall.

Kirk Smeaton *Smedetone: Robert from Ilbert de Lacy. Church, mill.* Now 2 villages, Kirk and Little Smeaton. Kirk Smeaton church has a Norman font.

Kiveton *Ciuetone: William de Warenne.* Facing Kiveton Park.

Knapton *Cnapetone: Richard son of Erfast; Aelwin from Osbern d'Arcis.* On the outskirts of York.

Knaresborough *Chenaresburg: King's land, formerly King Edward.* Town; picturesquely sited, on a sandstone cliff above the River Nidd; steep streets; caves; remains of a Norman castle; partly 14th-century court house.

Knaresford *Chenaresford/ Keenaresforde/Neresford(e):* Lost.

Knottingley *Notingelai/leia: Rannulf from Ilbert de Lacy.* Industrial town with Bronze Age round barrows nearby.

Lacock *Lacoc: King's land.* Also spelt Laycock.

Langcliffe *Lanclif: Roger le Poitevin.* Jacobean hall.

Langthwaite *Langetouet: Count of Mortain.* Possibly near Hangthwaite, with a motte and bailey site and nearby moat.

Laughton-en-le-Morthen *Lastone: Roger de Bully.* Norman church with a Saxon doorway; castle mound.

Laverton *Lauretona/ Laureton(e): King's land; Gospatric; Ulohil and Uluric, the pre-Conquest holders, from the king.* On the River Laver.

Lead *Led(e)/Lied: Ilbert de Lacy, William from him, formerly William Malet.* Lead Hall Farm, site of the medieval manor house and village.

Leathley *Ledelai: King's land; Ebrard from William de Percy; Gilbert de Tison. Mill.* Pretty, riverside; water-mill; possibly 11th-century church; hall.

Ledsham *Ledesham: Ilbert de Lacy.* Saxon church with marble effigies. 17th-century manor farm.

Ledston *Ledestun(e): Ilbert de Lacy; 3 churches, 3 mills.* Hall with a 13th-century chapel undercroft, built by the monks of Pontefract Priory.

Leeds *Ledes: Ilbert de Lacy. Church, mill.* City, Yorkshire's second largest city, an important textile centre from the late 14th century. The Industrial Revolution brought new industries and expansion. The Victorian church contains a Saxon cross fragment.

Lepton *Leptone: Ilbert de Lacy.* Here is also Little Lepton.

Lindley *Lillai(a): Ulchel from Ilbert de Lacy. Church.* District of Huddersfield.

Linton (near Hebden) *Lipton: Gilbert de Tison.* Green with maypole; hall.

Linton (near Wetherby) *Lintone: Ebrard from William de Percy. Mill.* On the River Wharfe.

Little Airmyn *Ermenia/nie: Ralph Pagnell. Church.* At the mouth of the River Aire. Henry I gave it to St Mary's, York.

Little Fenton *Fentun: Osbern, the pre-Conquest holder, from Ilbert de Lacy.*

Little Houghton *Haltone: Roger de Bully.*

Little Newton *Neutone: Roger le Poitevin.* Some houses.

Little Ouseburn *Usebruna/ Useburne/Alia Useburne: King's land and Malcolm from the king.* Norman church; Moat Hall, said to be on the site of a Roman house.

Little Smeaton (near Pontefract) *Smedeton(e): Robert with Ilbert de Lacy. Church, mill.*

Littlethorpe *Torp: Archbishop of York before and after 1066.*

Little Timble *Timbe: Archbishop of York before and after 1066. Church.*

Littleworth *Sciteleswordel/ Scitesleswordе: Nigel from Count of Mortain.* Some houses adjoining Rossington; formerly Shuttleworth.

Litton *Litone: Roger le Poitevin.* In Littondale, the Vendale of Charles Kingsley's *The Water Babies* (1863).

Liversedge *Liuresech/Livresec: Ralph from Ilbert de Lacy.* Wool town. There were Luddite riots at Rawfolds Mill in 1812, when weavers attacked Edmund Cartwright, inventor of the power loom; Charlotte Brontë described these events in *Shirley* (1849).

Lofthouse (in Harewood) *Locthusum/Lofthuse: King's land.* Farm.

Lofthouse (near Wakefield) *Locthuse/Loftose: Ilbert de Lacy. Mill.* Coal-mining.

Loftus *Locthusun/Lotes/Lothuse: Gamel, the pre-Conquest holder, from Erneis de Buron; 3 thanes, the pre-Conquest holders, from the king.* Some houses at Loftus Hill.

Longfield *Langefelt: King's land. 2 churches.* Moorland area.

Long Holme *Holme: William de Percy.* Some houses at Long Holme Row.

Long Marston *Mersetone: 2 of Osbern's men from Osbern d'Arcis.* Marston Moor, site of a Parliamentary victory in the Civil War (1644) is nearby; Cromwell said, 'God made them as stubble to our swords.'

Long Preston *Prestune: Roger le Poitevin. Church.* Site of a Roman fort nearby; church with a Saxon tombstone and a Norman font.

Long Sandall *Sandala(e)/-ie/ Sandela: Nigel from Count of Mortain.* Some houses.

Lothersdale *Lodresdene: Roger le Poitevin.* Mammoth bones found nearby; a safe refuge for the Quakers in the reign of Charles II; Stone Gappe, the house called Gateshead by Charlotte Brontë in *Jane Eyre* (1847); old silk mill, still working, retains its water-wheel.

Loversall *Geureshale/ Luvreshale: Nigel from Count of Mortain.*

Lower Cumberworth *Combreworde/Cumbreworde: Ilbert de Lacy.*

MALHAM: *Monks Bridge, once used by monastic flocks of sheep.*

Malham *Malgon/gun: King's land; William de Percy.* Popular walking and climbing centre on the Pennine Way; impressive limestone rock-faces at Gordale Scar and Malham Cove; Malham Tarn, a bird sanctuary. Charles Kingsley wrote *The Water Babies* (1863) at Malham Tarn House.

Malkton *Malchetone:* Lost.

Maltby (near Tickhill) *Maltebi: Roger de Bully.* Town. Industries include coal-mining, brick manufacture and engineering; inhabited since 1500 BC. Roche Abbey, founded by Richard de Bully in 1147, is nearby; grounds were landscaped by Capability Brown.

Manston *Mainestune/Manestun: Ilbert de Lacy.* Part of the Seacroft district of Leeds.

Markenfield *Merchefeld: Bernulf from William de Percy.* Markenfield Hall, a fortified 14th-century manor house, now a farmhouse.

Markington *Merchinton(e): Archbishop of York before and after 1066.* Home of the slavery abolitionist, Wiliam Wilberforce (1759–1833).

Marley *Mardelei/Merdelei: Erneis de Buron.* Some houses.

Marr *Marle/Marra: Count of Mortain.* Traces of Roman and prehistoric settlements. Christopher Booker, a printer of the Bible in Elizabethan times, was born in the vicarage.

Marton (near Boroughbridge) *Martone: Gospatric, the pre-Conquest holder.* Now Marton-with-Grafton; church with Saxon pillars, window and cross.

Marton *Martun: Roger le Poitevin.* Now 2 villages, East Marton with a fragment of a Saxon cross in the church, and West Marton.

Meltham *Meltham: Ilbert de Lacy.* Town. Industries include textiles and engineering; fort, probably Iron Age, nearby.

Menston *Mersintone: Archbishop of York before and after 1066. Church.* Fairfax Hall, the home of Charles Fairfax, whose son Thomas planned the Battle of Marston Moor here with Cromwell (1644).

Methley *Medelai: Ilbert de Lacy. Church.* Coal-mining. Church with a 14th-century nave and fine family tombs; medieval stone carvings inspired the sculptor Henry Moore, as a boy.

Mexborough *Mechesburg: Roger de Bully. Mill.* Town. Industries include coal-mining, steel, engineering and brick-manufacture. A prehistoric earthwork, partly built over, stretches from here to Sheffield.

Micklethwaite *Muceltuit/tuoit: Erneis de Buron.* Some houses.

Middlethorpe *Torp: Robert Malet; Richard, son of Erfast.* Some houses on outskirts of York.

Middleton (near Ilkley) *Middeltune/Mideltun: Archbishop of York before and after 1066. Church.* Packhorse bridge; Elizabethan Middleton Lodge, now a retreat of the Passionist Fathers.

Middleton (in Leeds) *Mildentone/Mildetone: Ilbert de Lacy. Mill.* District of Leeds; Middleton Colliery railway was the first to be authorized by Act of Parliament (1758).

Middop *Mithope: William de Percy.* Scattered houses.

Midgeley *Micleie: King's land. 2 churches.*

Minskip *Minescip: King's land.*

Minsthorpe *Manestorp: Ilbert de Lacy.* Some houses.

Mirfield *Mirefeld/felt: 3 Englishmen from Ilbert de Lacy.* Town. Industries include textiles, chemicals, and malting. Robin Hood is said to have died at nearby Kirklees. Roe Head, the school attended by the Brontë sisters, is now a Roman Catholic seminary.

Monk Bretton *Breton/ttone: Ilbert de Lacy.* Coal-mining district; remains of priory dating from 1154 nearby.

Monkton *Monecheton/ Monuchetone:* Lost.

Moor Monkton *Monechtone/ tune: Richard, son of Erfast.* Quiet; 12th-century church. Charles II stayed at the Red House, now a school, with Sir Henry Slingsby, who was later beheaded for Royalist activities.

Moorthorpe *Torp: Ilbert de Lacy. Church, onset of a mill.* Now a district of South Elmsall.

Morley *Morelege/lei/leia: Ilbert de Lacy. Church.* Town. Industries include textiles, coal-mining and engineering. Home of Prime Minister Herbert Asquith.

Morton (near Keighley) *Mortun(e): King's land.* Now East Morton; also the district of West Morton on the outskirts of Keighley.

Nappa *Napars: William de Percy.* Some houses.

Nesfield *Nacefeld: William de Percy.*

Nether Poppleton *Alia-/Altera Popletone/In duabus Popletunis/ Popletun: Herm(en)frid from Osbern d'Arcis.* Quiet; on the River Ouse. Norman church with 17th-century wall monuments.

Newhall *Neuhalle/Neuue-/ Newehalla: Roger de Bully. Church.* Some houses at Newhall Grange.

Newhill *Neuhalle/Niwehalla: Roger de Bully.* District of Wath upon Dearne.

Newsham *Neuhuse/-um.* Lost.

Newsholme (near Gisburn) *Neuhuse: William de Percy; Roger le Poitevin.* Some houses.

Newsholme (in Keighley) *Neuhuse: King's land.*

Newsome *Neusone: John from Erneis de Buron.* Farm.

Newton (in Ledsham) *Niuueton/-tun/Niweton/-tun: Hunfrid from Ilbert de Lacy.* Farm.

Newton Kyme *Neuton(e)/Niwe- /Niuueton/Newe-/Neuueton: Count of Mortain; Fulk from Osbern d'Arcis. Onset of a mill.* Newton Hall, home of the pro-Cromwellian family, the Fairfaxes.

Newton on Hodder *Neutone: Roger le Poitevin.* Pleasant; Browsholme Hall (1507) nearby.

Nidd *Nit(h): Archbishop of York before and after 1066.* A great church council is said to have met here over 1000 years ago.

Normanton *Normatone/atune/ etune: King's land. Church.* Town. Industries include coal-mining, railway engineering and textiles. The church contains a 15th-century Pieta and 13th-century arcade.

North Anston *Anestan: Roger de Bully.*

North Crosland *Crosland/ Croisland/Altera Crosland: King's land; Ilbert de Lacy.* District of Huddersfield.

North Deighton *Distone: Erneis de Buron.* Manor house; remains of a castle mound.

North Elmsall *Ermeshala(e): Elric from Ilbert de Lacy.* Coal-mining town.

North Milford *Mileford(e): Tursten from Ilbert de Lacy.* North Milford Hall near Ulleskelf.

Northowrun *Oure/Overe: King's land; Ilbert de Lacy.* NE suburb of Halifax.

North Stainley *Nordstanlai(a)/ Estanlai/Stanlei/Staneleia: Archbishop of York before and after 1066; Count of Mortain.* Traces of a Roman house and an ancient moated encampment.

Norton (near Doncaster) *Nortone: Elsi and Orm from Ilbert de Lacy.* Church with a fine Norman tower.

Norton (near Sheffield) *Nortun(e): King's land; Ingran from Roger de Bully.* District of Sheffield. Home of Sir Francis Chantrey (1781-1841), who began as a donkey boy and left a fortune as the Chantrey Bequest to purchase pictures for the nation.

Nostell *Osle/Osele: Ralph and Ernulf from Ilbert de Lacy. 2 churches.* Now Nostell Priory, an 18th-century mansion with work by Robert Adam and Thomas Chippendale. Ilbert's son, Robert, gave the land to the Augustinians, whose 12th-century priory was on the site of a Saxon hermitage; canons of Nostell worked the coal seams.

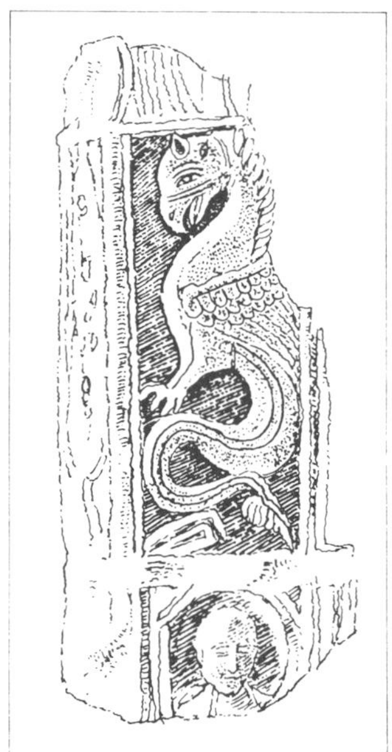

OTLEY: *In the church, a fragment of Saxon carving from 9th-c. cross.*

Notton *Norton/Notone: Ilbert de Lacy.* Straggling; modern housing.

Nun Monkton *Monech/ Monuchetone: Hugh from Osbern d'Arcis. ½ fishery.* At the confluence of the Nidd and Ouse rivers. The old church (with William Morris glass) is a fragment of the 12th-century nunnery founded by William de Arches, a descendant of Osbern, and given after its suppression to John Neville, whose widow, Catherine Parr, was the last wife of Henry VIII.

Nunwick *Nonnewic/Nonewica: Rainald from Archbishop of York before and after 1066.* Some houses.

Oakworth *Acurde: Gilbert de Tison.* In hills near Keighley. Home of Isaac Holden (1807–97), inventor of the lucifer match.

Oglethorpe *Oceles/Oglestorp: Nigel from Count of Mortain; Fulk from Osbern d'Arcis.* Oglethorpe Hall Farm.

Old Lindley *Linlei/leie: King's land.* Some houses on the outskirts of Huddersfield.

Old Thornville *Catala/-le/ Cathale: Erneis de Buron.* Some houses near Cattal; previously known as Little Cattal.

Onesacre *Anesacre: King's land.* Some houses near Sheffield.

Orgreave *Nortgrave: Roger de Bully.* Coal-mining district near Sheffield. Iron and coal were mined here by the Romans; the name means 'pit from which ore was dug'.

Ossett *Osleset: King's land.* Town. Industries include textiles, engineering and coal-mining.

Otley *Otelai/Othelai: Archbishop of York before and after 1066. Church.* Wool town for 1000 years; other industries include engineering and tanning. Bull Stone nearby is prehistoric. The Norman church has fragments of 8th-century crosses. Birthplace of Thomas Chippendale (1718–79).

Otterburn *Otreburne: King's land; Roger le Poitevin.* On the edge of the Yorkshire Dales National Park.

Ouston *Ulsitone/Wlsintone: William de Percy.* Farm.

Owston *Austhun/Austun/ Austhu': Alured from Ilbert de Lacy.*

Oxspring *Osprinc/pring: Ilbert de Lacy.*

Oxton *Ositone/Ossetone/ Oxetone: Osbern d'Arcis; Nigel Fossard from Count of Mortain.*

Painley *Padehale/Paghenale: William de Percy.* Some houses at Little Painley.

Pallathorpe *Torp: Nigel from Count of Mortain; Fulk from William de Percy; Osbern d'Arcis.* Farm; remains of a moat.

Parlington *Perlinctune/lintun/ tilintun/tilinctum: Ilbert de Lacy.* Some houses.

Paythorne *Pathorme/Pathorp: William de Percy.*

MALHAM: *Grykes; bare, limestone pavements, the fissures enlarged by rain water, leaving a flat plateau of stone.*

SLAIDBURN: *The valley of the River Hodder cuts through the Bowland fells.*

Penistone *Pangeston/ Pengeston(e): King's land; Elric, the pre-Conquest holder, from Ilbert de Lacy.* Town on the River Don. Industries include engineering, steel; church, with a Saxon cross.

Pickburn *Picheburn(e): Nigel from Count of Mortain.* Some houses adjoining Brodsworth.

Pilley *Pillei: Richard from Count of Mortain.*

Plompton *Plontone: Eldred from William de Percy; Gilbert de Tison.* Some houses near Knaresborough Park.

Pontefract (Tanshelf in Pontefract) *Tateshalla:* See page 310.

Pool *Pouele: Archbishop of York before and after 1066. Church.* Handsome; on the River Wharfe.

Potterton *Potertun: Ilbert de Lacy.* Hall; some houses.

Preston *Prestun(e)/Preston: Ilbert de Lacy.* Now the village of Great Preston, in a coal-mining area, and some houses at Little Preston, adjoining Swillington.

Pudsey *Podechesai(e): Ilbert de Lacy.* Town. Industries include textiles, engineering and tanning; birthplace of the cricketers Len Hutton and Herbert Sutcliffe.

Purston Jaglin *Preston(e): Ralf and Ernulf from Ilbert de Lacy. 2 churches.*

Quarmby *Cornebi/elbi: Ilbert de Lacy.* District of Huddersfield.

Quick *Thoac/Tohac: King's land.* Now Quick Edge, some houses near Mossley.

Radholme Laund *Radun: Roger le Poitevin.* Some houses.

Rastrick *Rastric: King's land.* Now a district adjoining Brighouse; Saxon cross in the churchyard. Brighouse and Rastrick is a famous brass band.

Rathmell *Rodemare/mele: Roger le Poitevin.* The first Nonconformist College in England was founded here by Richard Franklin in 1670; it is now a row of cottages.

Ravenfield *Rauenesfeld: Roger de Bully; William de Warenne, formerly Earl Harold.*

Rawdon *Rodum/Roudun: King's land.* District of Yeadon.

Rawmarsh *Rodemesc: Walter d'Aincourt. Mill.* Town. Industries include coal-mining, steel and chemicals.

Raygill *Raghil: William de Percy.* Some houses.

Ribston *Ripestain/sten/stan: King's land; Godefrid from William de Percy; Ralph Pagnell; Erneis de Buron.* Now the village of Little Ribston and the site of a medieval village at Great Ribston.

Riddlesden *Redelsden(e): King's land.* East and West Riddlesden Halls are 17th century. The last three Murgatroyds, owners of the East Hall, ended up in York Debtor's Prison in the reign of Charles II; fine timbered barn.

Rigton (near Bardsey) *Riston/ Ritone/-tun: Ligulf from the king.* Now the village of East Rigton.

Rigton (near Harrogate) *Riston(e): Gilbert de Tison; Archil, the pre-Conquest holder, from the king.* Now North Rigton.

Rimington *Renitone: William de Percy.* Quiet.

Ripley *Ripeleia/leie/lie: Ralph Pagnell; Ramechil and Archil, the pre-Conquest holders, from the king.* 18th-century estate village, remodelled in 1827 in Alsace-Lorraine style; the Hotel de Ville dates from 1854. The castle is the home of the Ingilby family, who have been here for 700 years; Sir Thomas Ingilby saved Edward III from a boar in Knaresborough Forest.

Ripon *Ripun/Ripum: Archbishop of York before and after 1066. Church, mill, fishery.* Market town with some light industry. Cathedral is 12th to 15th century, but there have been monasteries on the site since the 7th century. The Saxon crypt (AD 670) has a narrow passage called St Wilfrid's Needle, the ability to pass through it being a mark of chastity. 13th-century Wakeman's House; Wakeman's Horn still blown at 9.00 pm.

Riston *Riston(e): Ligulf from Ilbert de Lacy.* Part of Leeds.

Roall *Ruhale: Baret, the pre-Conquest holder, from Ilbert de Lacy. Mill (with Egborough).* Farm; hall; waterworks.

Rogerthorpe *Rogar/Rugartorp: Ilbert de Lacy. Church.* Rogerthorpe Manor.

Rossett *Rosert(e): King's land; Gilbert de Tison.* Rossett Green, a district of Harrogate.

Rotherham *Rodreham: Nigel from Count of Mortain. Church.* Town. Industries are coal-mining, iron, steel, and glass. The fort at nearby Scholeswood is probably prehistoric. The boys of the Grammar School unsuccessfully helped to defend the bridge against Royalist troops in 1643.

Rothwell *Rodeuuelle/-ouuelle/ Rodewelle/-owelle: Ilbert de Lacy. Mill.* Town. Coal-mining and chemicals. John Blenkinsop (1783–1831), the railway pioneer, is buried here.

Roughbirchworth *Berceuuorde/Bercewrde/-worde: Ilbert de Lacy.* Some houses near Oxspring; field patterns preserve outlines of medieval strip-farming.

Rowden *Rodun: King's land.* Some houses.

Royston *Rorestone/un: Ulchel from Ilbert de Lacy.* Town in coal-mining area; railway engineering.

Rudfarlington *Rofellinton(e)/ Rofellnton: Eldred from William de Percy; Gilbert de Tison.* Farm.

Rufforth *Ruford(e)/fort: Osbern d'Arcis and his man from him.* Rufforth Hall nearby.

Ryhill *Rihella/helle: Ilbert de Lacy.* Coal-mining area near Royston.

Rylstone *Rilestun/istune: Dolfin and Rauenchil, the pre-Conquest holder, from the king.* The Norton family lived here at Norton Tower and suffered for their part in the Rising of the North (1569); Wordsworth wrote of this in *The White Doe of Rylstone* (1807).

Ryther *Ridre/Rie: Hugh from Ilbert de Lacy. Church.* Church with a possibly Saxon chancel arch.

Sandal Magna *Sandala/dale: King's land. 2 churches).* District of Wakefield; castle besieged and destroyed in the Civil War; church with a partly Norman tower.

Santon *Sactun/Santone:* Lost.

Sawley *Sallai(a): Archbishop of York before and after 1066.*

Saxton *Saxtun: Ilbert de Lacy. Church, 3 parts of 1 church, 2 mills.* Ancient graves and Roman entrenchments nearby; church with a Saxon cross; communal grave for Lancastrians defeated at the Battle of Towton.

Scagglethorpe *Scachertorp/ Scarchetorp: Erm(en)frid from Osbern d'Arcis.*

Scawsby *Scalchebi: Roger de Bully.* Scawsby Hall and the district of Scawsby near Doncaster; Roman road nearby.

Scosthrop *Scotorp: King's land; Roger le Poitevin.* Some houses.

Scotton *Scotona/tone: Gilbert de Tison; Ramechil, the pre-Conquest holder.* Guy Fawkes may have lived at the Old Hall.

Scotton Thorpe *Torp:* Lost.

Scriven *Scrauinge/inghe: King's land.* On the edge of Knaresborough.

Seacroft *Sacroft/roff: Robert from Ilbert de Lacy.* District of Leeds.

Sedbergh *Sedbergt: King's land.* Small town on the slopes of the Rawther valley with a 17th-century Friends' Meeting House where George Fox preached; boys' boarding school, begun about 1525.

Selby *Salebi: Abbot of Selby from the Archbishop of York.* Ship-building port on the River Ouse with flour and mustard mills. It is believed to be the birthplace of Henry I (1068–1135), the Conqueror's only English-born son. The abbey church (built for the Benedictines established here in 1097) has fine Norman doorways. Selby coalfield is nearby.

Selside *Selesat: Roger le Poitevin.*

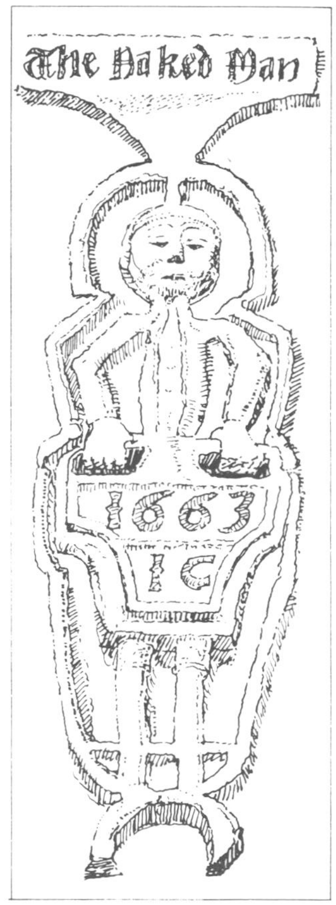

SETTLE: *A "green" man, the traditional naked figure which identified an inn.*

Settle *Setel: Roger le Poitevin.* Charming town on the River Ribble; museum with bones and artefacts from Victoria Cave nearby, some dating from the Iron Age.

Shadwell *Scadeuuelle/welle: King's land.* Some houses on the outskirts of Leeds.

Shafton *Sceptone/tun: Richard from Count of Mortain.*

Sheffield *Escafeld/Scafeld: Roger de Bully.* Industrial city, a centre of the steel industry since the 14th century. The Cutlers' Company

STUDLEY ROYAL: *The vaulting of the refectory at Fountains Abbey.*

was founded here in 1624, and the first Bessemer steel works built here in 1859. There is a historic hill-fort at nearby Wincobank. Mary, Queen of Scots was imprisoned at Sheffield Manor; University.

Shelf *Scelf: King's land.* District of Bradford.

Shelley *Scelneleie/Sciuelei/Scelueleie: King's land.*

Shepley *Scipelai/Seppeleie: King's land.*

Sherburn-in-Elmet *Sciretburne: Archbishop of York before and after 1066. 2 churches, mill.* Given to York by Athelstan in thanksgiving for driving out the Danes; partly Norman church.

Shipley *Scipelei/leia: Ilbert de Lacy.* Industrial town on the River Aire and the Leeds and Liverpool Canal; textiles, engineering.

Shippen *Scipene: Rannulf from Ilbert de Lacy.* Farm, cottages.

Sicklinghall *Sidingal(e): King's land.*

Silkstone *Silchestone/Silcston: Ilbert de Lacy.* Now 2 villages, Silkstone and Silkstone Common. 26 children drowned in the mines here in 1838.

Silsden *Siglesdene: Osbern d'Arcis.* Textile town in Airedale.

Sitlington *Scellintone/Schelintone: King's land.* District near Horbury.

Skelbrooke *Scalebre/Bro: Hervey from Ilbert de Lacy.* 18th-century hall.

Skellow *Scanhalla/-halle/Scauhalla: William from Ilbert de Lacy.* Some houses; Cromwell's Batteries nearby.

Skelmanthorpe *Scelmertorp/Scemeltorp: Ilbert de Lacy.* Town, once a Danish settlement.

Skelton (near Boroughbridge) *Scheldone/tone: Archbishop of York before and after 1066; Gospatric.* Newby Hall nearby contains Gobelins tapestries designed by Francis Boucher.

Skelton (in Leeds) *Sceltun(e): Ilbert de Lacy.* Cottages and power station at Skelton Grange.

Skibeden *Schibeden/Scipeden: King's land.* Some houses at Far, High and Low Skibeden.

Skinthorpe *Scinestorp:* Lost.

Skipton *Scipton(e): King's land.* Market town. The castle dates from the 11th century and was held by the Cliffords for 300 years. 'Butcher' Clifford was a leading Lancastrian in the Wars of the Roses, his son, the Shepherd Lord, led the men of Craven at Flodden (1513). The castle was besieged for 3 years during the Civil War.

Slade Hooton *Hotone: Roger de Bully.*

Slaidburn *Slateborne: Roger le Poitevin.* Attractive, Grammar School building, c.1717.

Sleningford *Scleneforde/Sclenneford: Archbishop of York before and after 1066.* Site of a former village.

Snaygill *Snachehale: King's land.* Some houses at High and Low Snaygill.

Snydale *Snitehala/hale: Hunfrid from Ilbert de Lacy.* Some houses at Old Snydale.

South Anston *Litelanstan/astone: Roger de Bully.*

South Bramwith *Alia Branuuat/wat: Roger de Bully.*

South Crosland *Crosland/Croisland/Altera Crosland: King's land; Ilbert de Lacy.* District of Huddersfield.

South Elmsall *Ermeshale: Ilbert de Lacy. Church, onset of a mill.* Coal-mining town.

South Hiendley *Hindeleia/Indelie: Elric from Ilbert de Lacy.* Coal-mining.

South Kirkby *Cherchebi/Chirchebi: Ilbert de Lacy. Church, onset of a mill.* Town in a coal-mining area adjoining South Elmsall, with a prehistoric fort nearby. The church is partly 13th-century.

Southowrum *Oure/Overe/Ufron: King's land; Ilbert de Lacy.* SE suburb of Halifax; Shibden Hall, partly 15th-century, houses a folk museum.

South Stainley *Stanlai/lei(e): King's land; Archbishop of York before and after 1066.* Sir Solomon Swale of nearby Swale Hall received his baronetcy for moving the resolution for the restoration of Charles II (1660) in the House of Commons.

Sowerby *Sorebi: King's land. 2 churches.* Branwell Brontë was a railway booking clerk at nearby Sowerby Bridge.

Spofforth *Spoford: Wiliam de Percy.* Spofforth Castle, home of the Percys for 300 years, now a ruined 14th-century house; reputedly the birthplace of Henry Percy (Hotspur) (1367–1413).

Sprotbrough *Sproteburg: King's land; Roger de Bully.* Sir Walter Scott is said to have lived here, gathering local colour for *Ivanhoe* (1819).

Stackhouse *Stacuse: Roger le Poitevin.* Some houses.

Stainborough *Stainburg/Stanburg: Ilbert de Lacy.* Stainborough Castle, the remains of an 18th-century folly, in the grounds of Wentworth Castle. Birthplace of James Bramah (1749–1814), inventor of the hydraulic press.

Stainburn *Sta(i)nburne: King's land.* Moorland.

Stainforth (near Settle) *Stain/Stranforde: Roger le Poitevin.* Packhorse bridge above the waterfall at Stainforth Force.

Stainforth (near Thorne) *Ste(i)nforde: William de Warenne.* Coal-mining town.

Stainland *Stanland: King's land.* Large, moorland.

Stainton (in Bank Newton) *Stainton(e): King's land; Roger le Poitevin. 3 mills, church.* Some houses at Stainton Hall and Stainton Cotes.

Stainton (near Tickhill) *Stainton(e)/Stantone: Roger de Bully. Church, 3 mills.* Norman church; Roman camp nearby.

Stancil *Steineshale: Roger de Bully.* Farm; Roman villa nearby.

Stanley *Stanlei(e): King's land.* Coal-mining and brick-making area near Wakefield. A Bronze Age canoe was found at Stanley Ferry.

Stansfield *Stanesfelt: King's land. 2 churches.* Scattered moorland houses.

Stapleton *Stapleton(e): Gislebert from Ilbert de Lacy.* Stapleton Park and Hall.

Starbotton *Stamphotne: Roger le Poitevin.* Most houses were built after 1686, when a great flood of the River Wharfe destroyed the village.

Staveley *Stanlei(a): Gospatric.* Church with a Saxon cross.

Steeton (near Keighley) *Stieutone/tune: Gilbert de Tison.*

Steeton (near York) *Stiueton(e)/-tune: Osbern d'Arcis; Nigel Fossard from Count of Mortain; Ernuin.* Some houses; partly 14th-century hall.

Stock *Stoche: Roger le Poitevin.* Some houses; earthworks nearby.

Stockton *Stochetun: King's land.* Farm.

Stotfold *Stod-/Stofald/Stotfalde: Richard from Count of Mortain; Fulk from Roger de Bully.* Scattered farms.

Stubham *Stube: Archbishop of York before and after 1066; Church.* Stubham Wood, with some houses nearby.

Stub House *Stubus(h)un: King's land.* Some houses.

Studley Roger *Estollaia/Stollai: Archbishop of York, before and after 1066.*

Studley Royal *Stollai/lleia: Archil from William de Percy; Gospatric; Esnerbern, the pre-Conquest holder, from the king.* Deer-park, outstanding 18th-century gardens, leading to the impressive ruins of Fountains Abbey, a 12th-century Cistercian foundation. Fountains Hall nearby dates from 1611.

Sturton Grange *Stretun(e): Rannulf and Ralph Pagenell from Ilbert de Lacy.* Some houses.

Stutton *Stanton/-tun/Stouetun/Stutone/-tun(e): Ilbert de Lacy; Malger from William de Percy; 2 of Osbern's men from Osbern d'Arcis. Mill.*

Susacres *Sosacra/-acre/Sotesac: Osbern d'Arcis.* Susacres Farms.

Sutton (near Keighley) *Sutun: King's land.* Some houses at Sutton-in-Craven.

Sutton (in Norton) *Sutone: Ilbert de Lacy. Mill.* Some houses; earthworks nearby.

Sutton Grange *Sudton/tunen: Archbishop of York before and after 1066.*

Swetton *Sualun/Suatun(e): Gospatric.* Some houses; earthworks nearby.

Swillington *Suillictun/intun/igtune: Ilbert de Lacy. Church.* Church with a curious black tower.

Swinden *Suindene: William de Percy.* Some houses.

Swinton *Sinitun/Suintone: Roger de Bully; Gilbert de Tison.* Town in a coal-mining area; also steel, iron and electrical goods.

Tadcaster *Tatecastre: William de Percy. 2 mills, fishery.* Busy, market town, an important centre settled by Brigantes, Saxons and Danes; site of the Roman *Calcaria*. Stone for York and its minsiter was quarried here.

Tankersley *Tancreslei/leia: Richard from Count of Mortain. Church.* 14th-century church; medieval hunting park; manor-house moat; site of a Civil War battle (1643). Custom of Embracing the Church involves the villagers dancing round it hand-in-hand to music.

Tanshelf *Tateshalla/-hal(l)e/Tatessella:* See Pontefract, page 310.

TEMPLE NEWSHAM: *The house is now a museum with fine silver, furniture and art.*

Temple Newsham *Neuhusum: Ansfrid from Ilbert de Lacy.* Magnificent Tudor and Jacobean house in a Leeds park. Darnley, husband of Mary, Queen of Scots, is said to have been born here; 4 ghosts.

Thorlby *Torederebi/Toreilderebi: King's land.* On the edge of the Yorkshire Dales National Park.

Thornborough *Torn(e)burne: Gospatric.* Farm.

Thorne *Torne: William de Warenne.* Town. Built on marshes drained by the Dutch. Rare large heath butterfly and bog rosemary found nearby.

Thorner *Torneure/oure: Ilbert de Lacy.* Farming.

Thornhill *Torni/nil: Gerneber from Ilbert de Lacy. Church.* District of Dewsbury; mainly 15th-century church, with fine glass; ruins of the 15th-century home of the Saviles, destroyed by the Roundheads.

Thornton (near Bradford) *Torenton(e)/tune: Ilbert de Lacy.* District of Bradford. The Rev Patrick Brontë was the parson here and his 4 children were born at 74 Market Street (1816–20).

Thornton in Craven *Torentun(e): William de Percy.* Almshouses c. 1815.

Thornton in Lonsdale *Tornetun: King's land.* Yorda's Cave nearby.

Thorp Arch *Torp: Osbern d'Arcis. Church, onset of a mill.* Traditional, with a green; mill; partly Norman church with some Saxon carving; Rudgate Roman road nearby.

Thorpe (near Hebden) *Torp: Osbern d'Arcis.* Navvy Noddle Hole, a nearby cave where human bones c. 100 BC were found.

Thorpe Audlin *Torp: Radulf from Ilbert de Lacy. Onset of a mill.*

Thorpe Hesley *Tor/Torp: Swen from the king.*

Thorpe Hill *Torp: Gospatric.* Farm.

Thorpe on the Hill *Torp: Ilbert de Lacy. Mill.* Coal-mining and quarrying area.

Thorpe Salvin *Torp: Roger de Bully.* Manor house remains.

Thorpe *Stapleton Torp: Gislebert from Ilbert de Lacy.* Site of Thorpe Hall; farm called Temple Thorpe.

Thorpe Underwood *Tuadestorp: Ralph Pagnell.* Anne and Branwell Brontë were governess and tutor at the hall.

Thorpe Willoughby *Torp: Ilbert de Lacy. Church.*

Threshfield *Freschfelt: King's land; Gilbert de Tison.* 17th-century school.

Throapham *Trapu'/pun/pum: Roger de Bully.* Some houses. 2000 Roman coins found here.

Thrybergh *Triberga/berge: Rozelin from William de Percy.* Church with a Saxon cross.

Thurgoland *Turgesland: Ilbert de Lacy.*

Thurlstone *Turoluestonl/ Turulfestune: Ilbert de Lacy.*

Thurnscoe *Dermescop/Ternusc/-usch(e): Richard from Count of Mortain; Roger de Bully; William de Percy.* Colliery town.

Thurstonland *Tostenland: King's land.*

Tidover *Todoure: William de Percy.* Lost in Kirkby Overblow.

Previous page STUDLEY ROYAL: *Fountains Abbey.*

Tinsley *Tin-/Tirneslauue/Tin-/Tirneslawe: Roger de Bully. Onset of a mill.* District of Sheffield.

Tockwith *Tocri: 2 of Osbern's men from Osbern d'Arcis.* Small house, said to have sheltered Cromwell during the Battle of Marston Moor (1644), after a bullet grazed his neck.

Todwick *Tateuuic/wic: Richard from Count of Mortain. Church.* Church with Norman doorways.

Tong *Tuinc: Ilbert de Lacy.* Hall (1702) with carvings by Grinling Gibbons; 18th-century church with a 3-decker pulpit.

Totley *Totingelei: King's land.* District of Sheffield, including Totley Bents, Totley Brook, Totley Rise and New Totley.

Toulston *Oglestun/Togleston/-tun: Nigel from Count of Mortain.* Some houses.

Towton *Touetun: Ilbert de Lacy.* The Battle of Towton nearby (1461) was a great Yorkist victory during the Wars of the Roses.

Treeton *Tre(c)tone: Richard from Count of Mortain. Church, ½ mill, onsets of 2 mills.* Coal-mining, 12th-century church.

Tudworth *Tudeforde/ Tudeworde/-euuorde: William de Warenne. 20 fisheries (20,000 eels).* The early village declined after the river was diverted into the 'Dutch River' in 1627.

Ughill *Ughil: Roger de Bully.* Hall; some houses.

Ulleskelf *Oleschel/slec: Archbishop of York before and after 1066, and William de Verli from him. Church.* On the River Wharfe.

Ulley *Ollei(e): Richard from Count of Mortain.* Farming.

Upper Cumberworth *Cumbreuu(o)rde/ Cumbrew(o)rde: King's land.*

Upper Hopton *Hoptone/tun: Alric from Ilbert de Lacy.*

Upper Poppleton *Popletone/-tune/In daubus Popletunis: Archbishop of York before and after 1066; Osbern d'Arcis.*

Upton *Ultone/Uptone: Ilbert de Lacy. Church.*

Utley *Utelai: King's land.* District of Keighley.

Waddington *Widitun: Roger le Poitevin.* Henry VI was hidden in a secret room in the Old Hall in 1464, but was betrayed by a monk and captured by the Yorkists. He was taken back to London tied backwards onto a horse.

Wadsley *Wadelai/Wadesleia: Roger de Bully.* Wadsley and Wadsley Bridge, districts of Sheffield.

Wadsworth *Wadesuurde/wrde: King's land. 2 churches.* Moorland area with scattered houses. An isolated building at Top Withins is said to be the setting for Emily Brontë's *Wuthering Heights* (1847).

Wadworth *Wadeuuorde/wrde: Roger de Bully.* Romano-British sites were nearby.

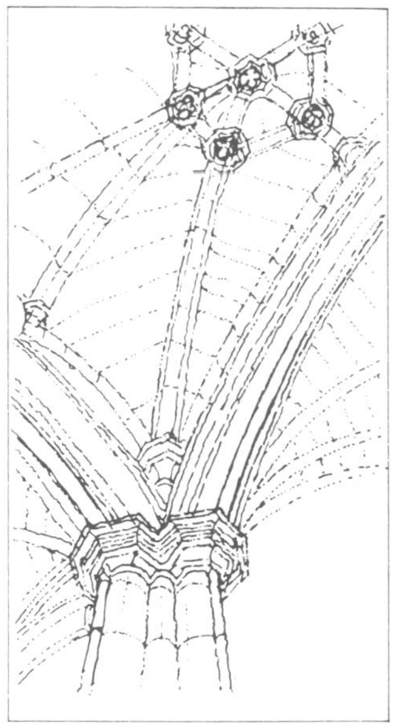

WAKEFIELD: *Cathedral extension, 1905.*

Wakefield *Wachefeld/-felt/ Wach'f': King's land. 2 churches.* County town and cathedral city. Industries include coal-mining, textiles, brewing, and engineering. Its cathedral has Norman traces and the tallest crocketed spire in Yorkshire (247 ft.); famous cycle of Mystery Plays.

Walden Stubbs *Eistop/Istop: Robert from Ilbert de Lacy.*

Waldershelfe *Sceuelt: King's land.* Lost.

Wales *Wales/Walis(e): Richard from Count of Mortain; Roger de Bully.*

Walkingham *Walching(e)ham: King's land.* Some houses at Walkingham Hill.

Walton (in Kirkby Overblow) *Waltone: William de Percy.* Farm at Walton Head.

Walton (near Wakefield) *Waleton: King's land.* Old village overwhelmed by new housing. Charles Waterton, the naturalist (1782–1865), established Britain's first bird sanctuary in the park of Walton Hall.

Walton (near Wetherby) *Waletone/tune/itone: Osbern d'Arcis and one of his men from him.* Roman road nearby.

Warley *Werla(feslei): King's land. 2 churches.* Warley Town, a district of Halifax.

Warmfield *Warnesfeld: Archbishop of York before and after 1066; Peter, the pre-Conquest holder, from Ilbert de Lacy.*

Warmsworth *Wernesford(e)/ Wermesford/Wirmeswerthe: Nigel from Count of Mortain.* Attractive. Its bell-tower announced services at the isolated church ½ mile away.

Warsill *Wifleshale/Wiueshale: Archbishop of York before and after 1066.* Some houses at Warsill Hall.

Wath upon Dearne *Wade/ Wat(e):* See page 310.

Weardley *Warda(m)/Wartle: King's land; Gospatric.*

Weeton *Widetone/-tun(e)/ Widitun: King's land and Ulchil from the king; Gospatric.*

Wentworth *Wintreuuord(e)/ -word(e)/Winteuuord(e)/-word(e):* See Wath upon Dearne page 310.

West Ardsley *Erdeslau(ue): King's land.*

West Bradford *Bradeforde: Roger le Poitevin.* On the River Ribble.

West Bretton *Bretone: King's land.* Bretton Hall nearby, an 18th-century house, now a training college, specializing in music and drama.

Westerbi *Westrebi:* Lost.

West Hardwick *Arduwic/ Harduic: Ralf and Ernulf from Ilbert de Lacy. 2 churches.*

West Melton *Medeltone/ Merelton(e)/Middeltun/ Mideltone: Roger de Bully; Walter d'Aincourt; Tor, Swen and Artor the priest, pre-Conquest holders, from the king.* A residential district near Wath upon Dearne.

Weston *Westone: Berengar de Tosny. Church.* Partly Norman church; Elizabethan hall.

Westwick *Westu(u)ic: Archbishop of York before and after 1066.* Some houses.

Wetherby *Wedrebi: William, a knight, from William de Percy; Erneis de Buron.* Small market town with a racecourse. Roman relics were unearthed here.

Wheatcroft *Watecroft:* Lost.

Wheatley *Watelag(e): Count of Mortain.* Wheatley Hills, a district of Doncaster; a settlement in the 3rd century.

Wheldale *Queldale/Weldale: Gerbodo from Ilbert de Lacy. Church (with Fryston).* Some houses.

Whipley *Wipelei(e)/lie: King's land and Archil from the king; Erneis de Buron.* Some houses at Whipley Hall.

Whiston *Widest(h)an/Witestan: Richard from Count of Mortain; William de Warenne, formerly Earl Harold.* Suburb of Rotherham, hamlet of Upper Whiston nearby; medieval long barn; Roman road nearby; Viking assembly and court nearby.

Whitley *Witelai(e): Elric from the king.* Whitley Hall.

Whitley Lower *Witelaia/lei: Gamel and Elric from Ilbert de Lacy.*

Whitwood *Whitewde: Ilbert de Lacy and Roger from him.* District near Castleford.

Whixley *Crucheslaga/ Cucheslage/Cuselade: Godefrid from William de Percy; Osbern d'Arcis. 2 churches.* Large 14th-century church.

Wibsey *Wibetese: Ilbert de Lacy.* District of Bradford.

Wickersley *Wicresleia/ Wincreslei: Roger de Bully.* Suburb of Rotherham.

Widdington *Widetona/tone: Alured, the pre-Conquest holder, from the king.* Houses and farms at Widdington Manor, Widdington Grange and Widdington Hall Farm.

Wigglesworth *Winchelesuu(o)rde/-wrde/ Wiclesforde: Roger le Poitevin.*

Wighill and Wighill Park *In daubus Wicheles: Geoffrey Alselin.* Church with a magnificent Norman doorway; traces of a moated house near Wighill Park.

Wike *Wic(h): King's land.*

Wildthorpe *Widuntorp: Roger de Bully.* Lost in Cadeby.

Wilsden *Wilsedene: King's land.*

Wilsic *Wilseuuice/-wice/ Wiseleuuinc/-winc: William de Warenne.* Some houses at Wilsic Lodge.

Wilstrop *Wi(u)lestorp: 2 of Osbern's men from Osbern d'Arcis.* Houses at Wilstrop Hall and Grange.

Winksley *Wichingeslei/ Wincheslaie: Gospatric.*

Winterburn *Witreburne: Roger le Poitevin.*

Wombwell *Wanbella/buelle: Roger de Bully; Walter d'Aincourt; Tor, the pre-Conquest holder; from the king.* Coal-mining, iron-founding and engineering town with Iron Age earthworks nearby.

Womersley *Wilmereslege/ Wlmeresleia: Ilbert de Lacy. Church.* Partly 13th-century church, moated farm; Elizabethan hall.

Wooldale *Uluedel: King's land.* District adjoining Holmfirth.

Woolley *Wiluelai/Wivelai: King's land.* Unspoilt; Woolley Hall, home of the Wentworths, is now a college of adult education.

Worrall *Wihala/hale: King's land.*

Worsbrough *Wircesburg: Gamel and Chetelber from Ilbert de Lacy. Mill.* Coal-mining district adjoining Barnsley; includes Worsbrough Bridge and Worsbrough Dale.

Wortley *Wirlei/Wirtleie/Wrleia: Richard from Count of Mortain; Elric from the king.* The Romans mined iron here, and the opening scene of *Ivanhoe* (1819) is set here.

Wothersome *Wodehuse/husum: King's land.* Farm.

Wyke *Wich(e): Ilbert de Lacy.* Now Wyke and Lower Wyke, districts adjoining Bradford; 18th-century Moravian chapel.

Yateholme *Altera Holne/In duabus Holne: King's land.* Yateholme Reservoir near Holmfirth.

Yeadon *Iadon/dun: King's land.* Town with Leeds and Bradford Airport nearby.

North Riding

Coxwold

Before 1066 these had full jurisdiction, market rights and all customary dues: Earl Harold, Merlesveinn, Ulfr Fenise, Thorgautr Lagr, Toki son of Ottarr, Edwin and Morcar over Ingjaldr's land only, Gamall son of Osbert over COTTINGHAM only, Kofsi over COXWOLD *CUCUALT* only, and Knutr. Of these men, anyone incurred a forfeit (for doing wrong) made amends (by fine) to no one, unless to the King and the Earl.

Coxwold lies at the western end of a small valley between the Hambleton and Howardian Hills 16 miles north of York. In 1086 it was the centre of a well-populated manor with considerable woodland. Before the Conquest Kofsi had had the rare privilege of having full jurisdiction, market rights and all customs here. The estate passed eventually to the Mowbray family and they and their under-tenants the Colvills became great benefactors of the two monastic houses, the Cistercian Abbey of Byland and the Augustinian Priory of Newburgh, which were established in the parish in the mid-twelfth century.

At the Dissolution, Newburgh Priory was granted to the Belasyse family, who converted it into a country house. Thomas Belasyse, the second Viscount Fauconberg, married Oliver Cromwell's daughter Mary and it is alleged that the Protector's body lies in the present house – rebuilt first in Jacobean and again in early Georgian days. The Belasyses are commemorated by elaborate monuments in the fine fifteenth century church.

In the churchyard are the supposed remains of the novelist Laurence Sterne – a burial ground in London's Paddington also claimed him – who was vicar of Coxwold 1760–68 and lived in nearby Shandy Hall. Sterne wrote *Sentimental Journey* and *The Journal to Eliza* in 'sweet retirement' here. In June 1767 he commented, 'I am happy as a prince at Coxwold . . . I am in high spirits; care never enters this cottage.'

The village has changed little in appearance since Sterne's day. Its wide grass-verged street, where markets were held in the Middle Ages, as well as a number of handsome seventeenth-century buildings, including the Fauconberg Hospital and the old grammar school, indicate that this was once a place of some standing.

Fylingdales

In FYLING (OLD HALL) *FIGCLINGE* Merewine had 1 carucate of land taxable, which ½ plough can plough. William [de Percy] has (it). Waste. Value before 1066, 5s 4d.

Today the principal settlements in Fylingdales are the village of Fyling Thorpe and the picturesque fishing village of Robin Hood's Bay, on the coast some five miles south-east of Whitby. *Domesday* records that two vills, Fyling (one carucate) and North Fyling (five carucates), were part of the soke of Whitby and held by William de Percy from Earl Hugh. The entry above, however, relates to a carucate at Fyling which William held as tenant-in-chief and which was claimed by Earl Hugh. No matter whose claim was just, all the land at Fyling seems to have been waste in 1086, and the vills uninhabited. All eventually passed to Whitby Abbey.

No mention of Robin Hood's Bay has been found before that recorded in about 1538 by John Leland, who described it as 'a fischer tounlet of 20 bootes caullid Robyn Huddes Bay, a dok or bosom of a mile yn lenghth'. The village is built in a ravine with sandstone and tiled houses and cottages, set one above another. Many, precariously perched on their rocky ledges, are linked by a maze of narrow passages and steep steps. Fishing, once the village's main occupation, has all but disappeared, and its business today is tourism, its residents and artists and holiday-makers.

Above the bay near Fylingdales stands the parish church of St Stephens, built in 1822, which contains galleries, box pews and a three-decker pulpit. But the greater part of Fylingdales remains what it was in 1086, barren moorland. Set here surrealistically since 1961–62, are the three gigantic 'golf balls' of Fylingdales' Early Warning Station, a sensitive radar system designed to detect any impending nuclear attack.

Guisborough

[Land of the King . . .] In GUISBOROUGH *CHIGESBURG*, Ulfketill [had] 1 carucate of land taxable. Land for ½ plough.

Guisborough is a small town on the northern edge of the North Yorkshire moors about eight miles south-east of Middlesbrough. At the time of *Domesday* it was divided among four land holders: the king, Robert, Count of Mortain, Robert Malet and Earl Hugh of Chester. This division of the landholdings, as well as the grouping together of the Count of Mortain's holding with his holdings at Hutton and Middleton, make it difficult to be certain of either the population or the degree of prosperity in Guisborough. The value had decreased since 1066, and part of the area was described as

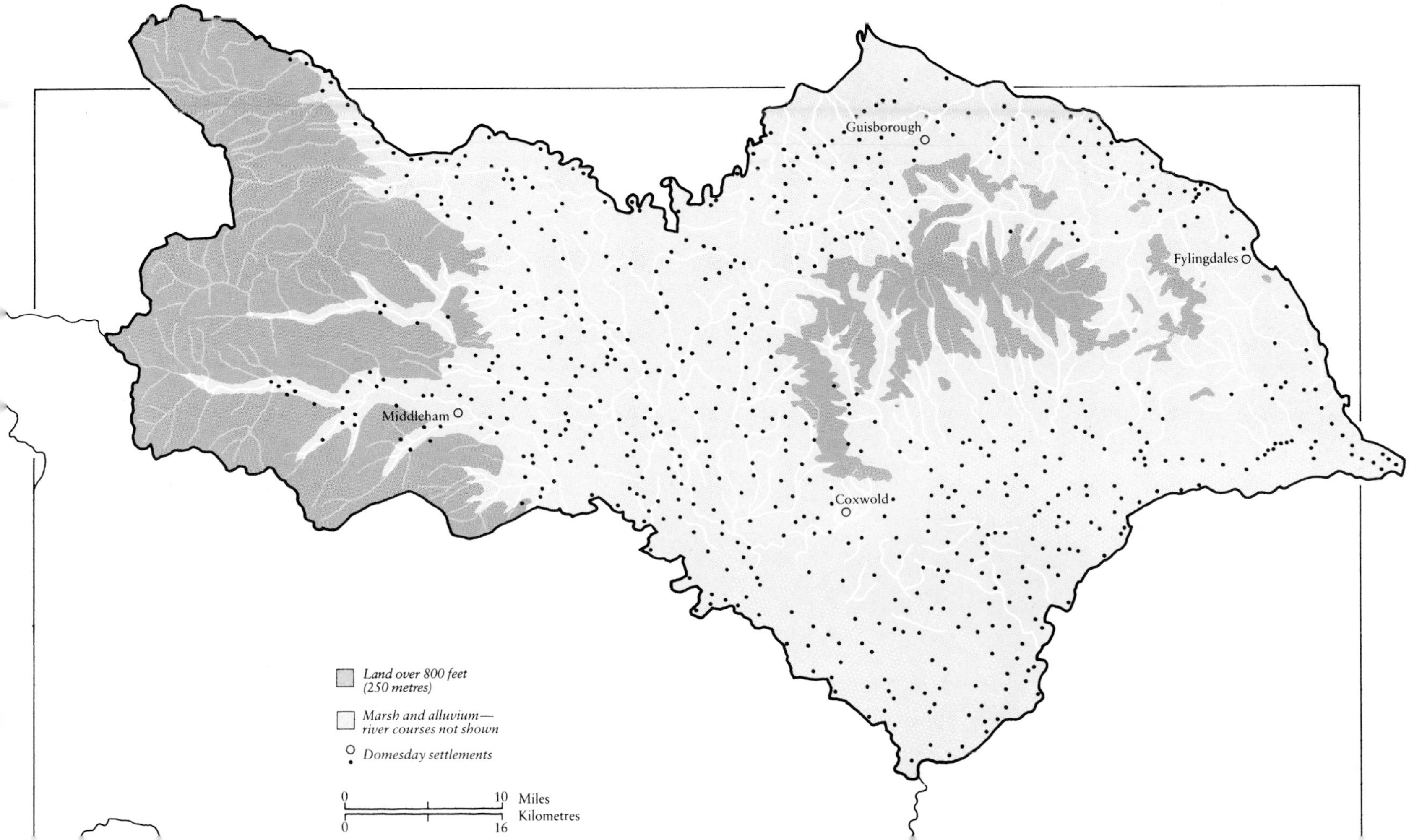

'waste'; there were possibly 13 villagers and seven ploughs.

Soon after the survey, the king's land was granted to Robert de Bruis, ancestor of the Bruces, the kings of Ireland and Scotland. Within a few years he had secured all the property in Guisborough, which, in 1120, he gave to the newly founded Augustinian priory. By 1535 this had become the fourth wealthiest in Yorkshire. Although its ancient church is now a ruin, its one-time splendour can still be discerned. It was ravaged by fire in 1289, but obviously rebuilt shortly afterwards with the east end of the magnificent chancel containing a window 56 feet high and 23 feet wide.

The last prior of Guisborough, Richard Pursglove, who was also suffragan bishop of Hull, surrendered the priory to Henry VIII in 1539 in return for a handsome pension. The priory and the estate were sold in 1550 to Sir Thomas Chaloner, later ambassador to the Spanish Netherlands and Spain, whose family still owned it in the twentieth century. The second Sir Thomas Chaloner discovered alum-stone at Guisborough, late in the sixteenth century and in 1607 he and others were granted the monopoly of alum manufacture. The mineral salt was important to the cloth, leather, fur and paper trades. Alum-making came to an end at the beginning of the nineteenth century, but before the century was out, ironstone mines were opened in the district, bringing new prosperity which continued until the 1920s. In more recent years, chemical and other Teesside industries have been the town's main employers.

The parish church, rebuilt late in the fifteenth century, contains the Bruce Cenotaph, a memorial erected in about 1520, which displays the resplendent figures of ten knights. It commemorates the Bruces of Skelton and Annadale, an imperious reminder of the family who acquired land at Guisborough just as the *Domesday* survey was being completed.

Middleham

[Land of Count Alan...] In MIDDLEHAM *MEDELAI* 5 carucates taxable; 3 ploughs possible. Gillepatric had a manor there. Now Ribald has (it). Waste. The whole, 1 league long and 1 wide. Value before 1066, 20s.

Middleham is picturesquely situated in Wensleydale, nine miles south of Richmond, between the rivers Ure and Cover, whose streams converge just beyond the parish. The small town of stone and slate buildings, which centres on the market place, is dominated by the great keep of the ruined, Norman castle. The castle was built in about 1170 by Ralph, the son of the *Domesday* under-tenant, Ribald, who was Count Alan's younger brother. His estate was described as 'waste'. It had been worth 20 shillings before the Conquest, when it was held by a Dane, Ghilepatric.

Late in the thirteenth century the manor passed by marriage to the Nevilles, Earls of Westmor-

MIDDLEHAM: *Although the 11th-c. castle was built as a defensive bastion, it is domestic and comfortable. It was the favourite home of Richard III and his family.*

land and Warwick. Middleham Castle was a favourite residence of 'Warwick the Kingmaker' and it was here, under his guardianship, that Richard, the eleventh child of Richard, Duke of York, trained as a knight, starting in 1462. This ill-fated boy, who was eventually to become Richard III, was joined at the castle in 1465 by his brother, Edward IV, who came as a prisoner. Six years later, after Warwick was killed during the Yorkist victory at the Battle of Barnet, Richard, who had supported him, was granted Middleham. He married Anne Neville, Warwick's younger daughter and made the castle his home, but when he was killed at Bosworth Field in 1485, after only a two-year reign as Richard III, the estate was forfeited to the new king, Henry VII.

The manor, held by kings and barons in the Middle Ages, is today held by Middleham Parish Council in trust for every 'inhabitant householder'. Middleham's economy depends partly on the tourist trade and partly on the dozen racing stables in the neighbourhood. Some 400 racehorses are exercised daily on the Low and High Moors above the town.

North Riding Gazetteer
Each entry starts with the modern placename in **bold** type. The *Domesday* information is in *italic* type, beginning with the name or names by which the place was known in 1086. The main landholders and under-tenants follow, separated with semi-colons if a place was divided into more than one holding. A number of holdings were granted by the king to his thanes; these holders are described, at the end of a list of landholders, as holding land 'from the king'. More general information completes the *Domesday* part of the entry. The modern or post-Domesday section is in normal type. ⌂ represents a village, ▲ a small village or hamlet.

Agglethorpe *Aculestorp: Torchil from Count Alan.* ▲

Ainderby Miers *Endrebi: Landric from Count Alan.* Lost.

Ainderby *Quernbow A(ie)ndrebi: Count Alan.* ⌂

Ainderby Steeple *Andrebi/ Eindrebi: King's land; Count Alan.* ⌂

Airy Holme *Ergun: King's land.* Now part of Great Ayton.

Aiskew *Echescol: Count Alan.* ⌂ Adjoining Bedale.

Aislaby (near Pickering) *Aslache(s)bi: Turgis de Radeham; King's land.* ▲

Aislaby (near Whitby) *Asuluebi/esby: Richard Surdeval from Count Alan; Count of Mortain.* ⌂

Aldborough *Borch/Burg: King's land.* ⌂ On the site of the Roman town of *Isurium*. The Battle Cross may commemorate the Battle of Boroughbridge, 1322.

Aldbrough *Aldeburne: Enisan from Count Alan. Mill, church.* ⌂ Church retains a Saxon sundial.

Aldwark *Aldeuuerca/erc: Count of Mortain.* ⌂ Toll bridge over the River Ouse.

Allerston *Aluestun(e)/ Alurestu(i)n: King's land.* ⌂ Scanridge Dikes are Stone Age burial mounds.

Allerthorpe *Erleuestorp/ Herleuestorp: Ribald from Count Alan.* Area near Leeming.

Alne *Alne: Archbishop of York.* ⌂

Amotherby *Aimundrebi/ Andebi/Edmundrebia/Eindebi: King's land; Hugh FitzBaldric.* ⌂

Ampleforth *Ambre/ Ampreforde: King's land; Archbishop of York; Hugh FitzBaldric.* ⌂ Studfold ring is an ancient encampment.

Appleton-le-Moors *Apeltun: Abbot of York from the king.* ⌂

Appleton-le-Street *Apeltun/ Apletun: King's land; Count of Mortain.* ⌂ Church has a pre-Conquest tower.

Appleton Wiske *Apeltona/ Apletun(e): King's land.* ⌂

Arden *Ardene: Hugh FitzBaldric.*

Arncliffe *Erneclive/Gerneclif/ Eerneclif: Roger le Poitevin.* ⌂ Pretty, in Litondale.

BARDEN: *Barden Tower, originally one of six lodges for the keepers of the Forest of Barden.*

Asenby *Aestanesbi: William de Percy. Church, mill.* ⌂

Askrigg *Ascric: Gospatric from Count Alan.* Small town. In Wensleydale, once noted for its clockmakers. Nappa Hall is 15th century; Coleby Hall, 1655, is now a farmhouse.

Aysgarth *Echescard: Goisfrid from Count Alan.* ⌂ In Wensleydale with Ayesgarth Force, waterfalls. Yore Mill, 1539, rebuilt in the 19th century, is now a coinage museum.

Bagby *Bag(h)ebi: Hugh FitzBaldric.* ⌂

Baldersby *Baldrebi: Count Alan.* ⌂

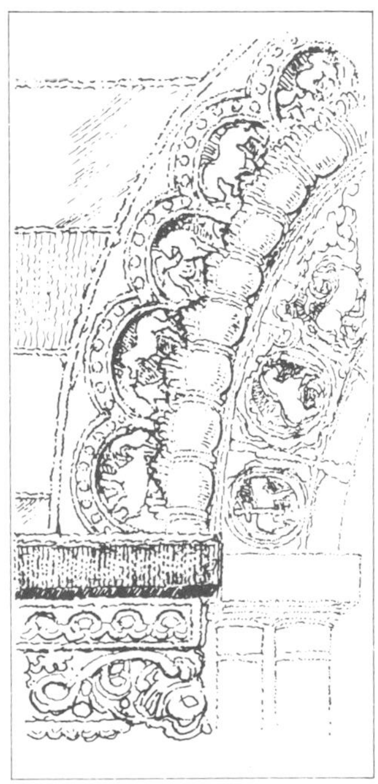

ALNE: *St. Mary's church; Norman doorway to the nave.*

Barden *Bernedan: Count Alan.* Moorland area. Barden Bridge is 17th century; Barden Tower is the remains of a house, c.1485.

Barforth *Bereford: Count Alan.* Houses at Barforth Hall and Barforth Grange.

Barnaby *Bernodebi: Richard from Count of Mortain.* Houses at Barnaby Grange, Barnaby Side and High Barnaby Farm.

Barnby (in Bossall) *Barnebi: Hugh FitzBaldric. Church.* Barnaby House.

Barnby (near Whitby) *Barnebi: King's land; Count of Mortain.* Now two villages, East and West Barnby.

Barningham *Berningham: Count Alan.* ⌂ An 8ft-high monument commemorates the shooting of 190 grouse in 25 minutes in 1872.

Barton (near Aldbrough) *Barton: Count Alan.* ⌂

Barton le Street *Bartone/tun(e): King's land; Richard from Count of Mortain. Church.* ⌂ Norman church.

Barton le Willows *Barton: Count of Mortain.* ⌂

Barwick *Bereuuic/Englebi: Hugh FitzNorman from Earl Hugh. Church.* Part of Teesside.

Battersby *Badresbi: King's land.* ⌂

Baxby *Bachesbi/Basche(s)bi: Archbishop of York; Hugh FitzBaldric.* Lost.

Beadlam *Bodlum/lun: Count of Mortain.* ▲ Adjoining Nawton.

Bedale *Bedale: Bodin from Count Alan. Church, mill.* Small market town with an old cross and old inns. The church is 13th–14th century with Saxon parts. The hall is 18th century.

Bellerby *Belgebi: Count Alan.* ⌂ Moorland.

Beningbrough *Benniburg: Ralph, Hugh FitzBaldric's man.* Hall in large park, is 18th century.

Birkby *Bretebi: King's land.*

Blansby *Blandebi: King's land.* Church has fragment of a Saxon cross.

Blaten Carr *Blatun: Count of Mortain.* Lost near Great Busby.

Boltby *Bolteby: Girard, Hugh's man, from Hugh FitzBaldric.*

Bolton on Swale *Boletone: Enisan from Count Alan.*

Bordelby *Bordalebi/Bordelbia: King's land.* Mount Grace Priory, the remains of a 14th-century Carthusian priory, open to the public.

Borrowby (near Loftus) *Berge(s)bi: Nigel from Count of Mortain.*

Borrowby (near Northallerton) *Bergebi: King's land.*

Bossall *Boscele/iale: Hugh FitzBaldric. Church.* Part 12th-century church.

Brafferton *Bradfortone/tune/ Bratfortune: King's land; Count of Mortain; Gospatric. Church.* Part 15th-century church.

Brampton *Bran(s)tone: King's land; Count of Mortain.* Now Brampton Hall near Boroughbridge.

Brandsby *Branzbi: Hugh FitzBaldric. Church.* Church 1770.

Brawby *Bragebi: Archbishop of York.*

Breck *Brecca/Breche: William de Perci from Earl Hugh.*

Breckenbrough *Bracheberc: Count of Mortain.* Location south of Kirby Wiske.

Brignall *Bring(en)hale: Count Alan.* A ruined church here was painted by both Turner and Scott. The new church has an altar from a Roman temple.

Brompton (near Northallerton) *Brinton/ Bruntone/tun(e): King's land; Bishop of Durham.* Suburb. Nearby is the site of the Battle of the Standard, 1138, where King Stephen of England defeated King David of Scotland. Church has Saxon hogbacks and crosses.

Brompton (near Scarborough) *Brunetone/ Bruntun(e): King's land; Berengar de Tosni. Church, mill.* Church is 14th and 15th century. William and Mary Wordsworth were married here.

Brompton on Swale *Brunton: Count Alan. Mill.*

Brotton *Bro(c)tune: Richard from Count of Mortain.* Small town.

Brough *Borc/Burg: Enisan.* Brough Hall is Elizabethan, with fragments of Roman columns in the grounds.

Broughton (near Malton) *Broctun(e): King's land; Berengar de Tosni; 2 of Hugh FitzBaldric's men.*

Bulmer *Boleber/Bolemere: Nigel from Count of Mortain. Church, mill.* Church is part Norman and has the wheel-head of a Saxon cross. Traces of a 6-acre Roman camp have been found here.

Burneston *Benningston: Robert, the Count's man, from Count Alan.* 17th-century almshouses.

Burniston *Brinitun/Brinnistun: King's land.*

Burrill *Borel: Count Alan.*

Burton Dale *Bertune/Bortun: King's land.* Part of Scarborough.

Buttercrambe *Butecram(e): Hugh FitzBaldric. Church, mill.* Aldby Park on a Roman, then Saxon, site. Church is part 13th century.

Butterwick *Butruic: Hugh FitzBaldric.*

Caldbergh *Caldeber:* Lost.

Caldwell (near Barforth) *Caldeuuelle: Enisan from Count Alan.*

Carlton (near Middleham) *Carleton: Bernulf from Count Alan.*

Carlton (in Stanwick) *Cartun/ Cattune: Count Alan.*

Carlton (in Stockton on the Forest) *Careltone/tun: Archbishop of York.*

Carlton (near Stokesley) *Carletun: Richard from Count of Mortain.*

Carlton Husthwaite *Carleton/ tun: Archbishop of York.* Several fine old houses.

Carlton Minniott *Carleton/tun: King's land; Hugh FitzBaldric.*

Carperby *Chirprebi: Enisan.* 17th-century cross.

Carthorpe *Caretorp: Gospatric from Count Alan.*

Castle Bolton *Bodelton: Count Alan.* Ruins of 14th-century castle; Mary Queen of Scots imprisoned here in 1568.

Castle Leavington *Alia Lentun(e)/Alia Leuetona: King's land.* Remains of motte and bailey castle.

Catterick *Catrice: Count Alan. Church.* On the site of a Roman town, *Cataractonium.* Racecourse at Catterick Bridge; airfield and army camp. Church part 13th century.

Catton *Catune: William de Percy.*

Cawthorn *Calthorn(a)torne: King's land.* Site of Roman camp.

Cawton *Calvetone/tun: Count of Mortain; Hugh FitzBaldric.*

Cayton *Caimtona/Caitun(e): King's land.*

Claxton *Claxthorp: King's land; Nigel from Count of Mortain.*

Cleasby *Clesbi: Enisan.* Vicarage is 17th century; several fine old houses.

Cliffe *Cliue: Count Alan.*

CASTLE BOLTON: *Built by Richard Scrope; crenellated c. 1379.*

Clifton (near York) *Cliftun(e): Archbishop of York; Count Alan.* Part of York.

Clifton upon Ure *Clifton:* Lost.

Cloughton *Cloctone/une: King's land; Count of Mortain; Richard from William de Percy.* Roman burial grounds; Cober Hill, now a guesthouse in 100 acres of grounds.

Colburn *Corburne: Gospatric from Count Alan.*

Cold Kirby *Carebi: King's land.* Bleak.

Coneysthorpe *Coningestorp/ Coung: Count of Mortain.* Estate of Castle Howard, which was designed by Sir John Vanbrugh (1664–1726) and completed in 1714.

Constable Burton *Ber/Bortone: Enisan from Count Alan.* Burton Hall, a fine colonnaded house designed by John Carr, is the home of the Wyvills, whose ancestor fought for the Conqueror.

Corburn *Coteborne/burun:* Lost.

Cornbrough *Corlebroc:* Lost.

Cotherston *Codreston/tune: Count Alan.* Remains of a Norman castle; the Butter Stone, where people brought and sold in the time of the Great Plague.

Coulby *Colebi: Earl Hugh.* Now Collesby.

Coulton *Coletun/Coletun(e): King's land; Archbishop of York.*

Coverham *Covreham: Count Alan.* Remains of 13th-century abbey, now incorporated into Coverham Abbey.

Cowesby *Cahosbi/Cole(s)bi: King's land; Girard, Hugh's man, from Hugh FitzBaldric.*

Cowling *Torneton: Robert.*

Coxwold *Cucualt:* See page 321.

Crakehill *Crecala: William de Percy.* Area near Topcliffe.

Crambe *Crambom/-bun/ Cranbon(e): King's land; Count of Mortain. Church.* Part Norman church.

Crathorne *Cratorn(a)/-torne/ Gratorne: King's land; Count of Mortain.* Part Saxon church.

Crayke *Creic: Bishop of Durham. Church.* Remains of 15th-century castle, part incorporated into 19th-century house; Great Chamber, 15th-century tower house, remains of a 15th-century house, New Tower; 15th-century church. Dean Inge was born here.

Croft *Crof(s)t: Enisan from Count Alan.* Famous for its wells. Clervaux Castle, 17th century; church contains the famous Millbanke pew (the Millbanke family lived at Hanlaby Hall, now gone). Lewis Carroll grew up here.

Crooksby *Croc(he)sbi: Bernulf from Count Alan.* Now Newbiggin.

Cropton *Croptun(e): King's land.* Site of an 11th-century castle; nearby are the Roman Cawthorn Camps.

Crosby *Crox(e)bi: King's land.*

Crunkly Gill *Crunbeclif/cliva/ clive:* Lost.

Cundall *Cundel/Goindel: Alured from Count of Mortain.*

Dalby *Dalbi:* Lost.

Dalby (near Whenby) *Dalbi: Abbot of York from Berengar de Tosni. Mill.*

Dale Town *Dal:* Lost.

Dalton (near Ravensworth) *Alia Dalton/Alia Daltun/Dalton/ -tun: Bodin; Count Alan.*

Dalton (near Topcliffe) *Deltune: William de Percy. Church, mill.* Church.

Danby (near Moorsholm) *Danebi(a): Hugh FitzBaldric.* Scattered, moorland; remains of 14th-century Danby Castle.

Danby (in Thornton Steward) *Danebi: Gamel's son from Count Alan.* Part of Thornton Steward. Danby Hall is partly 14th century.

Danby Wiske *Danebi: Landric, the Count's man, from Count Alan.* Lazenby Hall, now a farmhouse; moated rectory.

Deepdale *Depedale: King's land.* A few houses.

Deighton *Dictune: Bishop of Durham.*

Didderston *Dird(r)eston:* Lost.

Dishforth *Disforde: William de Percy.* Airfield.

Downholme *Dune: Gospatric from Count Alan.* Small. Walburn Hall, Elizabethan, was garrisoned for Charles in the Civil War. It is now a farmhouse.

Dromonby *Dragmalebi:* Lost.

Dunsley *Dunesla/le: King's land; Berengar de Tosny.*

Earswick *Edresuuic/Edrezuic: Archbishop of York.* Adjoining York. New Earswick is a suburb of York.

Easby (near Ingelby Greenhow) *Esebi: King's land.* Captain Cook's monument, an obelisk on Easby Moor commemorating the 18th-century explorer.

Easby (near Richmond) *Asebi: Enisan; Count Alan.* Remains of a 13th–14th-century abbey. The abbey church has fine 13th-century wall paintings.

EASBY: *The Abbey's ruined 13th c. refectory.*

Easington *Esingeton/tun: Earl Hugh. Church.* Grinkle Park, in 200 acres. Church has Norman and Saxon stones incorporated.

Easingwold *Eisicewalt/Eisincewald: King's land. Church.* Small market town with a bull-ring and old houses. The church is mostly 14th century.

East Appleton *Apelton/Apleton: Count Alan.*

East Ayton *Atun(e): Berenger de Tosny; William de Percy. Mill.* Pretty.

East Cowton *Corketune/Cottune/Cotun(e): King's land; Landric from Count Alan.*

East Harlsey *Alia Herlesege/Induabus Erleseie: King's land.* Remains of medieval Harsley Castle to the south.

East Hauxwell *Hauoc(he)swelle: Ribald; Game.*

Easthorpe *Estorp: King's land.* District near Malton.

East Layton *Latone/Latton: Bodin from Count Alan.*

East Lilling *Lilinga/inge:* Lost.

East Newton *Neutone/tun: King's land; Archbishop of York; Hugh FitzBaldric.* District near Oswaldkirk.

East Rounton *Rantune/Tontun: King's land.* The Grange in a spacious park is the home of a famous northern family, the Bells.

East Tanfield *Danefeld/telt/Tanefeld: Count of Mortain; Gospatric.* Lost near West Tanfield.

East Witton *Witone/tun: Count Alan.* Attractive, with old houses; Cistercian Abbey of Jervaulx, founded in 1145 and moved to its present site in 1156, nearby. Monks were famous for their Wensleydale cheese. Sedburgh, the last Abbot, was executed at Tyburn for his unwilling part in the Pilgrimage of Grace (1536).

Ebberston *Edbriztun(e): King's land.* Ebberston Hall, 18th century. North of the village are ancient burial mounds and Ilfrid's Cave, where King Aldfrith of Northumbria is said to have sheltered after fighting Oswin.

Egglestone *Eghiston/tun: Count Alan.* Remains of 12th-century abbey, dissolved by Henry VIII.

Egton *Egetune: Nigel from Count of Mortain.* Many bronze and jet ornaments found in ancient graves here.

Ellenthorpe *Adelingestorp: William de Percy; Roger Poitevin.* District near Boroughbridge.

Ellerbeck *Alre/Elrebec: King's land; Girard, Hugh FitzBaldric's man.*

Ellerburn *Elrebrune/burne: King's land.* Church with Saxon crosses.

Ellerby *Alwardebi/Elwordebi: Nigel from Count of Mortain.*

Ellerton Abbey *Elreton: Count Alan.* One house and the remains of a Cistercian nunnery.

Ellerton on Swale *Alreton: Gospatric from Count Alan. Mill.*

Ellington *Ellintone: Gospatric from Count Alan.* Now a hamlet, Low Ellington, and a village, High Ellington.

Eppleby *Apelbi: Count Alan.*

Eryholme *Argun: Count Alan.* Hall.

Eshingtons *Ecinton:* Lost.

Eston *Astun(e): Richard from Count of Mortain.* Part of Teesside.

Everley *Evrelag/lai: William de Percy.* District near Scarborough.

Exelby *Aschilebi: Robert, the Count's man, from Count Alan.*

Faceby *Fe(i)zbi/Foitesbi: King's land.* Roman finds here. Charity loaves are still given away here after a will of 1634.

Fadmoor *Fademore/more: Count of Mortain.*

Falsgrave *Wal(l)esgrif/grip: King's land.* District of Scarborough.

Farlington *Far/Ferlintun: Nigel from Count of Mortain.*

Farmanby *Farmanesbi:* Lost.

Fearby *Fedebi: Gospatric from Count Alan.*

Fingall *Finegal(a): Count Alan.* Church has Saxon fragments.

Firby *Fredebi: Count Alan.*

Flaxton *Flastun/Flaxtun(e): King's land; Archbishop of York; Hugh FitzBaldric. Mill.*

Flowergate *Flore/Florun: William de Percy from Earl Hugh.* Now part of Whitby.

Forcett *Forsed/et: Count Alan.* Part of an ancient entrenchment can be seen in the 200-acre park.

Fors Abbey *Fors:* Lost.

Foston *Fostun: Count Alan.*

Foxton (in Crathorne) *Fostun/Foxtun: King's land; Richard from Count of Mortain.*

Foxton (in Thimbelby) *Fo(u)stune: Bishop of Durham.*

Fremington *Fremin(g)ton: Count Alan.* Now two hamlets, High and Low Fremington.

Fryton *Frideton/Fritun: Count of Mortain; Hugh FitzBaldric.* Lost.

Fyling Old Hall *Figclinge/Fig(e)linge:* See Fylingdales page 321.

Fyling Thorpe *Nortfigelinge: William de Percy from Earl Hugh.*

Ganthorpe *Galmetona/Gameltorp: King's land; Nigel from Count of Mortain.*

Garriston *Gerdeston(e): Goisfrid.* West Garriston Beck.

Gate Helmsley *Alia Hamelsech/sec: Archbishop of York.*

Gatenby *Chenetesbi/Ghetenesbi: Robert, the Count's man, from Count Alan.*

Gillamoor *Gedlingesmore: Hugh FitzBaldric.*

GILLING EAST: *Gilling Castle, 1575–85.*

Gilling *Gellinges/Ghelling(h)es: Count Alan. Church.* Built on the site of a Saxon town. Church tower base is Norman, the rest 14th and 15th century.

Gilling East *G(h)ellinge: Ralph de Mortimer; Hugh FitzBaldric.* Gilling Castle, a 14th–18th-century house, is now a prep school for Ampleforth College.

Girlington *Gerlinton:* Lost.

Girsby *Grisebi: Bishop of Durham.*

Gnipe Howe *Ghinipe: Earl Hugh.* Now High and Low Hawsker. Old sail-less windmill.

Goldsborough *Golborg/Goldeburg: Nigel from Count of Mortain.*

Goulton *Goltona/Go(u)tun: King's land; Count of Mortain.* Lost.

Great Ayton *Alia Atun: King's land; Nigel from Count of Mortain; Robert Malet. Church.* Captain Cook grew up here. Now two churches: All Saints, Norman, with Saxon fragments and Christ Church.

Great Barugh *Berch/Berg: King's land; Archbishop of York; Hugh FitzBaldric.*

Great Broughton *Alia Broctun/Broctun/Magna Broctun: King's land; Nigel from Count of Mortain; Hugh FitzBaldric.*

Great Busby *Buschebi/Indaubus Buschebi: Land of the King's thanes; Robert Malet.*

Great Crakehall *Crachele: 2 knights from Count Alan; William de Percy. Church, mill.* Large green; 19th-century church.

Great Edstone *Micheledestun: Berengar de Tosny.* Church has a Saxon sundial over the door.

Great Fencote *In duabus Fencotes/Fencotes: Odo from Count Alan.*

Great Langton *Langeton: Count Alan.*

Great Smeaton *Smet(t)on/Smidetun(e): King's land; Count Alan.* Manor; church is the only one in England to be dedicated to St Eloy, the blacksmith's saint.

Griff *Grif: King's land; Count of Mortain.* Farm. Nearby are the ruins of Rievaulx Abbey, founded in 1131, the first Cistercian house in Yorkshire.

Grimston *Grimeston: Two of Hugh's men from Hugh FitzBaldric.* Lost.

Grinton *Grinton: Bodin from Count Alan.* Maiden Castle, ancient barrows.

Gristhorpe *Grisetorp: King's land.* Hall is now a guest house. An Ancient Briton in a tumulus grave was found here, now in Scarborough Museum.

Guisborough *Chigesburg/Ghisgesborg/burg:* See page 321.

Habton, Great and Little *Ab(b)etune/Habetun: King's land; Count of Mortain.* Now a village, Great Habton, and a hamlet, Little Habton.

Hackforth *Acheford(e): Goisfrid and Odo from Count Alan.*

Hackness *Hagenesse: William de Percy.* Hackness Hall; church is part 13th century, with a Saxon arch to the nave.

Hangton and Hangton Hill *In daubus Hanechetonis:* Lost.

Harmby *Ernebi/Hernebi: Wihomarc from Count Alan.*

Harome *Harem/Harum/un: King's land; Count of Mortain; Berengar de Tosny; Hugh FitzBaldric.*

Hartforth *Herford/fort: Godric the Steward from Count Alan.*

Harton *Heretun(e): King's land.*

Hawnby *Halm(e)bi: King's land; Robert Malet.* Arden Hall, seat of the Earl of Mexborough, mostly 17th century, with a Tudor wing.

Haxby *Haxebi: Archbishop of York before and after 1066.*

Helmsley *Almeslai/Elmeslac: King's land; Count of Mortain. Church.* Small market town with cobbled market square and many old houses, including Tudor Canon Garth. Remains of 12th-century castle; part 18th-century Duncombe Park, now a girls' school, built by Sir John Vanbrugh.

Helperby *Hel/Hilprebi/Ilprebi: Archbishop of York.*

Hemlington *Himeligetun/Himelintun: Earl Hugh.*

Henderskelfe *Hildreschelf/Ilderschelf:* Lost.

Hesselton *Eslinton/Heslintone:* Lost.

Heworth *Hewarde/worde: Hugh FitzBaldric; Count Alan.* District of York.

High Burton *Burton(e):* Lost.

High Stakesby *Staxebi: William de Percy from Earl Hugh.* District of Whitby.

High Sutton *Sudton(e)/Sutone: Count Alan.*

High Worsall *In daubus Wirceshel/Wercesel: King's land.*

Hildenley *Hildingeslei/Ildingeslei: King's land.* District near Malton.

Hill Grips *Hildegrip/Ildegrip: William de Percy.*

Hilton *Hiltone/tun(e): King's land; Count of Mortain.*

Hinderwell *Hildrewelle/Ildrewelle: Earl Hugh; William de Percy.* Stump of an old windmill; a well which St Hilda of Whitby is said to have blessed in the 8th century.

Hipswell *Hiplewelle: Enisan from Count Alan.* Old houses and hall; birthplace of John Wycliffe.

Holme (near Thirsk) *Hulme: Robert from the Bishop of Durham.*

Holtby (near Kirkby Fleetham) *Heltebi/Eltebi: Gospatric from Count Alan.* Now Little Holtby.

Holtby (near York) *Boltebi/Holtebi: King's land.*

Hornby (near Hackforth) *Hornebi: Gospatric from Count Alan. Church in Middleton.* Castle dating partly from the 14th century.

Hoveton *Houetune:* Lost.

Hovingham *Hovingham: Hugh FitzBaldric. Church.* Hovingham Hall, 18th-century seat of the Worsley family, built on the site of a Roman villa, where an annual cricket and music festival is held. Church tower is Saxon. There is a Spa House with 3 springs on the road to Cawton.

Howe *Hou: Robert from Count Alan.*

Howgrave *Hogram/Hogrem/Hograve:* Lost.

Howthorpe *Holtorp:* Lost.

Huby *Hobi: King's land; the king's thanes.*

Hudswell *Hudreswelle/Udreswelle: Enisan from Count Alan.* Woods are National Trust.

Humberton *Burton(e)/tun: Gospatric.* District across River Ure from Boroughbridge.

Hunderthwaite *Hundredestoit(h): Bodin from Count Alan.*

Hundulfthorpe *Hundulftorp:* Lost.

Huntington *Huntindune: King's land; Nigel from Count of Mortain; Count Alan.* Suburb of York.

Hunton *Hunton(e): Gospatric and Bodin from Count Alan.*

Hutton Bonville *Hotune: King's land.* District near Northallerton.

Hutton Buscel *Hotun(e): King's land.*

Hutton Conyers *Hoton(e)/Hottone: Archbishop of York.*

Hutton Hang *Hotun(e): Landric from Count Alan.* District near Constable Burton.

Hutton-le-Hole *Hotun: Hugh FitzBaldric.* 17th- and 18th-century houses; Ryedale Folk Museum nearby; Farndale, now a protected daffodil reserve.

Hutton Lowcross *Hotun: Count of Mortain. Church, mill.* Hutton Hall, 19th-century, built on the site of an earlier house, has a park famous for its rhododendrons. A Cistercian nunnery was found here.

Hutton Magna *Hottun/Hotune: Tor from Count Alan.*

Hutton Mulgrave *Hotune/tune: Nigel from Count of Mortain.* Some houses.

Hutton Rudby *Hotun: Count of Mortain. Church.* Church is chiefly 14th century and there are some Saxon stone fragments.

Ilton *Hilchetun/Ilcheton: Gospatric from Count Alan.*

Ingleby Arncliffe *Englebi(a): King's land.* Hall, 18th century, with moat left from earlier house.

Ingleby Greenhow *Englebi: The king's thanes.* Ingleby Manor, 17th century.

Ingleby Hill *Englebi:* Lost.

Inglethwaite *Inguluestuet:* Lost.

Irby *Irebi:* Lost.

Irton (near Scarborough) *Iretune: William de Percy.*

Irton (in Thornton on the Hill) *Iretone:* Lost.

Islebeck *Iselbec: Hugh FitzBaldric.*

Kelsit *Chelesterd/Chelestuit:* Lost.

Kepwick *Capiuc/Chipuic: King's land; Hugh FitzBaldric.*

Kettlethorpe *Chetelestorp:* Lost.

Kilburn *Chileburne: Hugh FitzBaldric.* Kilburn White Horse cut in chalk on the hillside in 1857; hall part Tudor; home of 'mouse' artist Robert Thompson; High Kilburn adjoining hamlet.

Kildale *Childala/dale: Orme from the king. Church.* Viking bones were unearthed here when the church was rebuilt in the 19th century.

Killerby (near Catterick) *Chiluordebi: Count Alan.* Killerby Hall and farm.

Killerby (in Cayton) *Chelverte(s)bi: William de Percy.* Killerby Halls and Killerby Grange.

Kilton *Chilton/tun: King's land; Count of Mortain.*

Kilton Thorpe *Torp: King's land; Count of Mortain.*

Kingthorpe *Chinetorp: King's land.* Districts of High and Low Kingthorpe, near Pickering.

HOVINGHAM: *Built by Thomas Worsley, the Hall contains a gift of George III.*

Kiplin *Chipeling: Enisan from Count Alan.* Kiplin Hall, 17th century, with large park.

Kirby (in Kirby Misperton) *Alia Cherchebi/Alia Chirchebi/Cherchebi/Chirchebi: King's land and Haregrin and Siward, the pre-Conquest holders, from the king.* Part of Kirby Misperton.

Kirby (in Stokesley) *Chirchebi: King's land and Haregrin and Siward, the pre-Conquest holders, from the king.*

Kirby Hill *Chirchebi: Gospatric.* Windmill and part Saxon church.

Kirby Wiske *Cherchebi/Chirchebi/Kirkebi: King's land; Picot from Count Alan.* Home of Roger Ascham, tutor to Elizabeth I; site of Breckenbrough Castle; Tudor Breckenbrough Hall and park.

Kirkby (in Kirkby Fleetham) *Cherch/Chirchebi: Eldred, the pre-Conquest holder, from Count Alan.* Some houses and a church, containing a Norman font, at Kirkby Hall.

Kirkby Fleetham *Fleteham: Odo, the Count's man, from Count Alan. Church.* Traces of a dry moat.

Kirkby Knowle *Chirchebi: Hugh FitzBaldric.* Moorland; New Building enlarged in the 17th century.

Kirkby Moorside *Chirchebi: Hugh FitzBaldric.* Small market town, home of George Villiers; headquarters of the Sinnington Hunt, said to be the country's oldest; traces of medieval castle; many old houses; Slingsby glider works and two glider centres on moors.

Kirkleatham *Weslide/Westlid(um)/-lidun/Westude: King's land; Earl Hugh; Count of Mortain; William de Percy.* The great house is demolished; its stables form patt of Kirkleatham Hall and ESN school. There are 17th-century almshouses, built by Sir William Turner, a Lord Mayor of London, with a museum and chapel.

Kirk Leavington *Lentune/Leuetona: King's land.* Remains of Norman castle on Castle Hill; old houses; church has Saxon fragments.

Kirklington *Cherdinton: Robert, the Count's man, from Count Alan.* Hall part 16th century.

Knayton *Cheneuetone/Cheniueton/-tune/Chennieton/Keneueton: King's land; Bishop of Durham before and after 1066.* Several large houses.

Kneeton *Naton:* Lost.

Lackenby *Lach(en)ebi: Earl Hugh; Nigel from Count of Mortain.* District near Middlesbrough.

Landmoth *Landemot: King's land.* Landmoth Hall and wood.

Langthorne *Langetorp: Odo from Count Alan.*

Langthorpe *Torp: Gospatric.*

Lartington *Lertinton: Bodin from Count Alan.* Hall dates from Stuart times.

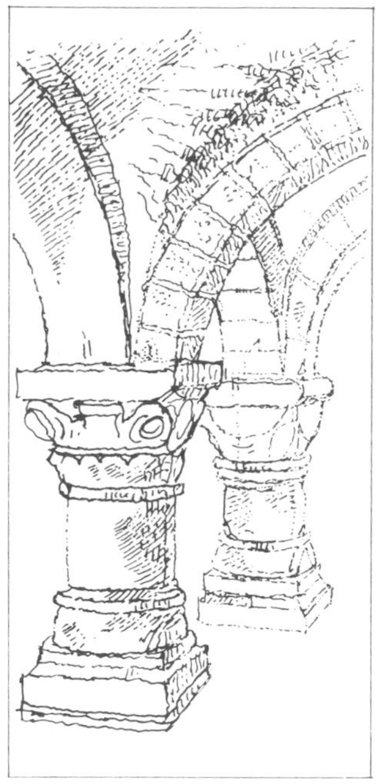

LASTINGHAM: *The Norman crypt (1075–85) has low heavy columns.*

Lastingham *Lesting(e)ham: King's land; Abbot of York from Berengar de Tosny.* Roman and Saxon remains found here; late Norman church incorporates part of an 11th-century abbey.

Laysthorpe *Lechestorp:* Lost.

Lazenby (near Guisborough) *Laisinbia/Leisingebi/Lesighebi/Lesingebi: King's land; Earl Hugh.*

Lazenby (near Northallerton) *Leisenchi/Leisenghi: King's land.* Now Lazenby Hall in Danby Wiske and Lazenby Grange.

Leake *Lec(h)e: King's land; Count of Mortain.* A few scattered houses and a church. Leake Hall, now a farmhouse, is 17th century.

Lealholme *Laclum/Lelun: Hugh FitzBaldric.* With what is said to be the largest rock gardens in England, along the Esk.

Lebberston *Ledbestun/Ledbeztun: King's land.*

Leckby *Ledebi: Alured from Count of Mortain.* Leckby Grange and two farms.

Levisham *Leu(u)ecen: King's land.* Tumuli and earthworks.

Leyburn *Leborne: Wihomarc from Count Alan.* Small market town; tradition has it that Mary Queen of Scots was captured on the limestone terrace, Leyburn Shawl, after escaping from Bolton Castle.

Linton upon Ouse *Luctone: Count of Mortain.* Airfield.

Little Ayton *Atun: King's land; Robert Malet.*

Little Barugh *Alia Berg: King's land; Archbishop of York; Hugh FitzBaldric.*

Little Broughton *Broctun(e):* Lost.

Little Busby *Alia Buschebi/Buschebia/In duabus Buschebi: King's land; Robert Malet; the kings thanes.* Busby Hall.

Little Edstone *Alia Edestun/Parva Edestun: Berengar de Tosny.* District near Great Edstone.

Little Fencote *In daubus Fencotes/Fencotes: Odo from Count Alan.*

Little Langton *Langeton: Count Alan.* Little Langton Grange.

Little Marish *Parva Merse: Berengar de Tosny.* Hamlet now Marishes.

Little Moorsholm *Alia Morehusum: Richard from Count of Mortain.* Lost, near Moorsholm.

Little Smeaton *Smidetun(e)/Smitune: King's land.* District near Great Smeaton.

Liverton *Liureton: Earl Hugh.* Waterwheel Inn has an old wheel outside; Liverton iron ore mines.

Lockton *Lochetun: King's land.*

Loft Marishes *Loctemares/mersc: King's land; Count of Mortain.* Now Marishes.

Loftus *Alia Loctehusum/Loctusum: King's land; Earl Hugh.* Iron ore mining town.

Lonton *Lontone/tune:* Lost.

Low Haile *Hale:* Lost.

Low Hutton *Hotun: King's land.* Now Huttons Ambo. High and Low Hutton joined. Traces of a Roman camp.

Low Worsall *Alia Wercesel/In duabus Wirceshel/Wercheshala: King's land.*

Lythe *Lid: Nigel from Count of Mortain.* Part Saxon church.

Maltby *Maltebi: Earl Hugh.*

Manfield *Manefeld/Mannefelt: Count Alan. Church, fishery.* Grave of a woman who was harvesting at the age of 106.

Mardeby *Martrebi:* Lost.

Marrick *Mange: Gospatric from Count Alan.* Remains of 12th-century Benedictine Priory, now a religious retreat for young people.

Marske (near Saltburn) *Mersc/Mersch(e): Count of Mortain; William de Percy.* Now the small town of Marske-by-the-Sea. Marske Hall is now a Cheshire Home.

Marton (near Middlesbrough) *Martona/tun(e): King's land; Robert Malet; Archil from the king.* Birthplace of Captain Cook; Marton Hall, rebuilt last century, has a museum.

Marton (near Pickering) *Martone/tun: Berenger de Tosny.* Hugh FitzBaldric.

Marton-in-the-Forest *Martun: Nigel from Count of Mortain. Church.* Now just a mostly 15th-century church; site of Marton Priory, only fragments remaining in farmhouse, Marton Abbey.

Masham *Massan: Ernegis from Count Alan.* Small market town; remains of large Saxon cross; 19th-century almshouses; Swinton Park, now a Conservative College.

Maunby *Manne(s)bi: King's land; Picot from Count Alan.*

Melmerby (near Hutton Conyers) *Malmerbi: Count Alan.*

Melmerby (near Middleham) *Melmerbi: Eldred from Count Alan.*

Melsonby *Malsenebi: Bodin from Count Alan. Church.* Church is part 1200, some Saxon fragments; fragment of a 12th-century nunnery near the rectory.

Mickleby *Michelbi: Nigel from Count of Mortain.*

Mickleton *Micleton: Bodin from Count Alan.*

Middleham (near Leyburn) *Medelai: Ribald from Count Alan.* Small town; 2 market-places; remains of 12th–15th-century castle; old bull ring; Saxon Well of St Alkelda; Braithwaite Hall, 17th-century farmhouse, now National Trust.

Middleton (in Appleton Wiske) *Middletun: Nigel and Richard from Count of Mortain; Gospatric. Church.* Now Hornby.

Middleton (near Guisborough) *Middletone/Mideltune: Count of Mortain. Church, mill (with Guisborough, etc.).* Now the village of Middleton St George and the adjoining hamlet of Middleton One Row.

Middleton (near Pickering) *Mid(d)eltun: King's land.* Saxon church tower.

Middleton Quernhow *Mideltune: Enisan from Count Alan.*

Middleton Tyas *Midletun/Midelton: Uctred from Count Alan.* Middleton Lodge.

MASHAM: *The Druid's Circle of 'standing stones', a strange Victorian folly.*

MORTHAM: *The Tower, with windows at the top.*

Middleton upon Leven *Middelton/-tun/Mideltun(e): Count of Mortain.* Some houses.

Milby *Mildebi: King's land.*

Misperton (in Kirby Misperton) *Mispeton: Hugh FitzBaldric.* Lost in Kirby Misperton.

Moorsholm *Morehusum/-husun/Morhusum: King's land; Richard from Count of Mortain.*

Mortham *Mortham: Count Alan.* Mortham Tower, part 14th-century house.

Morton (in East Harlsey) *Mortona/tune:* Lost.

Morton (near Guisborough) *Mortona/tun: King's land.* Suburb of Middlesbrough.

Morton (in Skelton) *Mortun: Archbishop of York.* Lost.

Morton-upon-Swale *Mortun(e): Gospatric from Count Alan and Walter from him. Onset of a fishery.*

Mortun (in Sutton on the Forest) *Mortun(e): King's land; Archbishop of York.* Lost.

Moulton *Molton: Count Alan.* Manor house and hall, 17th century.

Mowthorpe *Muletorp: Count of Mortain.* A few farms, no village.

Moxby *Molscebi/Molzbi: King's land.* A few farms; remains of a priory and earthworks.

Mulgrave *Grif: Nigel from Count of Mortain.* In Mulgrave Woods are an 18th-century castle and the ruins of one dating from 1200, garrisoned for Charles I.

Murton (near Cold Kirby) *Mortun: Robert Malet.*

Murton (near York) *Mortun(e): King's land; Archbishop of York.*

Myton-on-Swale *Mitune: King's land; Archbishop of York; Count of Mortain.* Hall, home of the Stapletons since Charles I's time with a beautiful park.

Nawton *Nageltone/-tune/Naghelton/Nagletune: Archbishop of York; Berengar de Tosny; Hugh FitzBaldric.* Nawton Tower, home of the Earls of Feversham.

Ness Hall *Ne(i)sse: Ralph Pagenel; 2 of Hugh's men from Hugh FitzBaldric. Church, mill.* Now two hamlets, East and West Ness.

Nether Silton *Alia Silftune: Count of Mortain.* Hall, farm with mullioned windows.

Newham *Neuham/Neweham/Niu(u)eham:* Lost.

Newholme *Neu(e)ham: William de Percy from Earl Hugh.*

Newsham (in Amotherby) *Neuhuse/Newe-/Niehusum:* Lost.

Newsham (in Brompton) *Neuhuse: King's land.* Lost.

Newsham (near Hutton Magna) *Neuhuson: Count Alan.*

Newsham (near Kirby Wiske) *King's land; Hugh FitzBaldric; king's thanes.*

Newton (near Guisborough) *Newetun/Nietona: King's land.* Under famous hill, Roseberry Topping, 1057 feet above sea level.

Newton (near Levisham) *Neuton/Newetun(e): King's land; Berengar de Tosny.*

Newton (in West Ayton) *Newetone/tun: King's land.* Lost.

Newton-le-Willows *Neuton: 2 knights from Count Alan.* Coal mining town, railway works.

Newton Morrell *Neuton: Godric the Steward from Count Alan.*

Newton Mulgrave *Newtone/Newetune: Count of Mortain.* A few houses.

Newton Picto *Neutone:* Lost.

Newton-upon-Ouse *Neuton/Newetone: Ralph Pagenel.* Beningbrough Park is National Trust.

Normanby (near Eston) *Normanebi: Count of Mortain; Robert Malet; William de Percy.* Suburb of Middlesbrough.

Normanby (in Fylingdales) *King's land.* Lost.

Normanby (near Thornton Risborough) *Normanebi: King's land; Hugh FitzBaldric.*

Northallerton *Aluerton/tune/Aluretune: King's land; Picot from Count Alan.* Town. The Romans had a settlement here; market place; Maison Dieu almshouse has a 15th-century foundation; the old grammar school dates from c.14th century.

North Cowton *Alia Cudton(e): Godric the Steward from Count Alan.*

Northfield *Nordfeld/Norfel: King's land.* Northfield Farm in Suffield.

North Holme *Holm(e): King's land; Berengar de Tosny.* A couple of farms.

North Kilvington *Chelvinctune/Chelvintun: King's land.*

North Otterington *Otrinctun/Otrintune: King's land.* Church has some Saxon stones.

Norton Conyers *Norton(e): Robert from Bishop of Durham.* House dating from c.16th century.

Norton-le-Clay *Nortone: Alured from Count of Mortain.*

Nunnington *Noningtune/Nonnin(c)tune/Nunnigetune: King's land; Count of Mortain; Ralph Pagenel.* Hall is 16th–17th century and stands on the site of a nunnery; buildings founded as almshouses and a school in the 17th century.

Nunthorpe *Torp: King's land.* District of York.

Old Boulby *Bol(l)ebi: King's land; Earl Hugh.* A few houses.

Old Byland *Begeland: Robert Malet. Wooden church.* Tiny part Norman church with oak roof.

Old Malton *Maltun(e): King's land; Archbishop of York; Count of Mortain.* Adjoining Malton. Church has part of a 12th-century Gilbertine priory; Abbey House.

Ormesby *Ormesbi(a): Orme, a king's thane. Church.* Suburb of Middlesbrough. Hall is 18th century; restored church with some Saxon carving.

Osbaldwick *Osboldewic: Archbishop of York.* Suburb of York.

Osgodby *Asgozbi: King's land.*

Osgoodby *Angsotebi: Hugh FitzBaldric.* A few houses; Osgoodby Hall is 17th century.

Osmotherley *Asmundrelac: King's land.* Stone houses; a mile north is the start of Lyke Wake Walk across 40 miles of the North York moors.

Oswaldkirk *Oswaldescherca/cherce: Count of Mortain;.* Berengar de Tosny. Malt Shovel Inn c.18th century.

Oulston *Uluestone/tun: King's land; Gospatric.*

Over Dinsdale *Di(g)neshale/Dirneshala/-hale: King's land; Count Alan.*

Over Silton *Silftune/Siluetune: King's land.*

Overton *Overtun(e)/Ovretun: Count Alan.*

Ovington *Ulfeton: Count Alan.*

Patrick Brompton *Brunton(e): Three knights from Count Alan. Mill.* No mill but a house called Mill Close.

Pickering *Picheringa/inge: King's land.* Market town; remains of Norman castle; Pickering Vale Museum and Arts Centre.

Pickill *Picala/le: Count Alan.*

Pinchingthorpe *Oustorp/Torp: King's land; Robert Malet.* A few houses.

Pockley *Pochelac/laf: Archbishop of York; Count of Mortain.*

Prestby *Prestebi:* Lost.

Preston (in Hutton Buscel) *Presteton/tune: King's land.* Lost.

Preston-upon-Scar *Preston/tun: Bodin from Count Alan.* Quarries.

Rainton *Painingewat/Rainewat/Reineton: Count Alan.*

Raskelf *Raschel: King's land.* Nearby moorland well known for rare orchids.

Ravensthorpe *Ravene(s)torp: King's land; Hugh FitzBaldric.* Ravensthorpe Manor.

Ravensworth *Ravenesu(u)et: Bodin from Count Alan. Church.* Remains of medieval castle featured in Walter Scott's *Rokeby*.

Rawcliff Banks *Roudclive/Roudeclif:* Lost.

Rawcliffe *Roudclif/Roudeclif(e): King's land; Archbishop of York.* Suburb of York.

Redmire *Ridemare: Ribald from Count Alan.* Redmire Force nearby.

Reeth *Rie: Bodin from Count Alan.* Large; old lead mines.

Riccall *Ricalf: King's land.*

Richmond *Hindrelag(he)/Indrelag(e): Enisan; Count Alan. Church, fishery.* Town, capital of Swaledale. Remains of 12th-century St Martin's Priory; market place; Georgian theatre; St Mary's church; imposing castle dating from the 11th century.

Rokeby *Rochebi: Count Alan.* Rokeby Hall, 18th century, is associated with Sir Walter Scott and his novel *Rokeby* and was painted by Turner.

Romaldkirk *Rumoldesc(h)erce: Bodin from Count Alan.* Fragments of the old stocks; an old pound for livestock.

Romanby *Romund(r)ebi: King's land.* Suburb adjoining Northallerton.

Rookwith *Rocuid: Count Alan.*

Roskelthorpe *Roscheltorp:* Lost.

Roxby (near Loftus) *Roscebi/Rozebi: King's land; Nigel from Count of Mortain.* Roxby Castle.

Roxby (in Thornton Dale) *Rozebi: King's land.*

Rudby *Rodebi: Count of Mortain.*

Ruston *Rostun(e): King's land.*

Ruswick *Risewic: Count Alan.* Ruswick Manor.

Ryton *Ritone/tun: King's land; Hugh FitzBaldric.* Ryton Grange.

Salton *Saletun: Archbishop of York. Mill.*

Sandburn *Sambura/bure:* Lost.

Sand Hutton (near Thirsk) *Hot(t)une: King's land.*

Sand Hutton (near York) *Hotone/Hotun(e)/Hottune: Gulbert, Hugh FitzBaldric's man; Nigel Fossard unjustly claimed land but gave it up to the king.*

Scackleton *Eschalchedene/Scachelden(e): King's land; Count of Mortain; 2 of Hugh's men from Hugh FitzBaldric.*

Scalby *Scal(l)ebi: King's land.* Small town, suburb of Scarborough.

Scargill *Scracreghil/Seacreghil: Count Alan.* Remains of medieval castle with a 15th-century gatehouse.

Scawthorpe *Scage(s)torp:* Lost.

Scawton *Scaltun(e): Count of Mortain; Robert Malet.* The Hare Inn was supposed to be the smallest inn in England before living quarters were added.

Scorton *Scortone: Bodin from Count Alan.* Large village green with old houses around.

Scotton *Scot(t)une: Gospatric before and after 1066 and Bodin from Count Alan.* Near Catterick Camp.

Scruton *Scurueton(e): Picot, Count Alan's man, from Count Alan.*

Seamer (near Scarborough) *Semaer/Semer: William de Percy. Church.* Site of Mesolithic settlement; part Norman church.

Seamer (near Stokesley) *Semer(s): Richard from Count of Mortain.*

PICKERING: *15th-c. painting of St George.*

Seaton *Scetun(e):* Lost.

Sessay *Sezai: Bishop of Durham.*

Sheriff Hutton *Hotone/Tun(e): King's land; Nigel from Count of Mortain.* Remains of 14th-century castle; home of poet John Skelton; Warwick the Kingmaker lived in the castle.

Shipton *Hipton: Count Alan.*

Sigston *Sig(h)estun: King's land.*

Sinderby *Senerebi: Count Alan.*

Sinnington *Sevenictun/Sivenintun/Siverinctun/-intune: Berengar de Tosny.* Barn with 13th-century walls and windows; church has many Saxon stones.

Skeeby *Schirebi: Enisan from Count Alan.*

SKELTON: *13th-c. church carvings, probably by masons who built York Minster.*

Skelton (near Saltburn) *Sc(h)eltun: Richard from Count of Mortain.* Castle, 1794, built on the site of a Norman one; remains of old well and cross.

Skelton (near York) *Sc(h)eltun: King's land; Archbishop of York before and after 1066; Count Alan.* Manor; Skelton Hall.

Skewsby *Scoxebi: Count of Mortain.*

Skipton-on-Swale *Schipetune: William de Percy. Church, mill.* Church.

Skutterskelfe *Codeschelf/Codresche(l)f: King's land; Count of Mortain; king's thanes.* Skutterskelfe Hall.

Slingsby *Eslingesbi/Selungesbi: Count of Mortain; Hugh FitzBaldric.* Remains of Slingsby Castle, 17th century.

Snainton *Snechintone/tun(e): King's land; Berengar de Tosny; Fulk from William de Percy; Gospatric.* Earthworks of Scamridge Dikes.

Sneaton *Sneton/tune: William de Percy from Earl Hugh.* Rigg Mill and waterwheel.

Solberge *Solberge: Count Alan; Picot.* Solberge Hall and site of old village.

South Cowton *Cudton(e): Godric the Steward from Count Alan.* 15th-century tower house, called Cowton Castle.

South Holme *Holm(e): Ralph Pagenel; Hugh FitzBaldric. Church, mill.*

South Loftus *Loctehusum/Loctushum: King's land; Earl Hugh.* Part of the town of Loftus.

South Otterington *Ostrinctune/Otrintona/-tune: King's land.*

Sowerby (near Thirsk) *Sorebi: King's land.* Adjoining Thirsk.

Sowerby (in Whitby) *Sourebi: King's land.* Lost.

Sowerby (under Cotcliffe) *Sourebi: King's land.* Lost.

Spaunton *Spantun(e): King's land; Abbot from Berenger de Tosny.*

Spennithorne *Speningetorp: Ribald from Count Alan. Church.* Spennithorne Hall dates partly from the 16th century; part Norman church.

Sproxton *Sprostune: King's land.*

Stainsby *Steinesbi: Earl Hugh.* Part of Stockton on Tees.

Stainton (in Stanghow) *Esteintone/Steintun: King's land; Earl Hugh; Richard from Count of Mortain; Robert Malet.*

Stainton (near Thornaby) *Steintun: King's land.*

Stainton Dales *Steintun: King's land.*

Stanwick *Alia Stenweghe/In daubus Steinueges/Ste(i)nwege/Stenweghes: Count Alan.* Stanwick Camp, extensive military earthworks from 1st century.

Stapleton *Staple(n)dun: Enisan from Count Alan.*

Startforth *Stradford: Enisan and Bodin from Count Alan. Church.* Church, 19th century; hall.

Stearsby *Estiresbi/Stirsbi: Count of Mortain; Hugh FitzBaldric. Church.*

Stillington *Stivelinctun: Archbishop of York. Mill.*

Stiltons *Tilstun(e): King's land; Count of Mortain.* Stiltons Farm.

Stittenham *Stidnum/nun: Nigel from Count of Mortain, Church, mill (with Bulmer).* Now High Stittenham.

Stockton on the Forest *Stochetun/Stochthun: Archbishop of York; Count Alan.*

Stokesley *Stocheslag(e): Uctred, a king's thane. Church, mill.* Small town; market place; part medieval church.

Stonegrave *Sta(i)ne/Steingrif: Archbishop of York; Ralph Pagenel. Church, mill.* Saxon or Norman church tower.

Strensall *Strenshale: Archbishop of York.* Army camp.

Suffield *Sudfeld/felt: William de Percy. 3 churches.* No church.

Sutton Howgrave *Sudton(e)/Sutone: Archbishop of York; Robert from the Bishop of Durham; Count Alan.*

Sutton on the Forerst *Su(d)tune/Suton: King's land.* Birthplace of Laurence Sterne (1713–68), author of *Tristram Shandy*.

Sutton under Whitestone Cliff *Sudtune: Girard, Hugh's man, from Hugh FitzBaldric. Mill.*

Swainby *Suanebi: Ribald from Count Alan.* Location.

Swarthorpe *Siwartorp:* Lost.

Swinton (near Malton) *Suintun(e): King's land.*

Swinton (near Masham) *Suinton: Count Alan.* Swinton Park, 19th century, with a copy of Stonehenge in the grounds.

Tanton *Tametona/tun: King's land; Richard from Count of Mortain; king's thanes.*

Terrington *Teurinctun(e)/Teurinton(e)/-tune: Count of Mortain; Count Alan; Berenger de Tosny.* Hall is now a school.

Theakston *Eston: Robert, Count Alan's man.*

Thimbleby *Timbelbi/belli: King's land.*

Thirkleby *Turchilebi: Hugh FitzBaldric.* Now two villages, High and Low Thirkelby; hall.

Thirley Cotes *Tonelai/Torneslag: King's land.* Thirley Cote Farm.

Thirn *Thirne: Bernult, the pre-Conquest holder, from Count Alan.*

Thirsk *Tresc/Tresch(e): King's land; Hugh FitzBaldric.* Town; racecourse; site of a Norman castle built by Roger de Mowbray and destroyed after he rebelled against Henry II.

Tholthorpe *Turoluestorp/Turulfestorp: Archbishop of York before and after 1066.*

THIRSK: *St Mary's, c. 1430–80.*

Thoralby *Turo(l)desbi: Bernulf from Count Alan.*

Thoraldby *Tor/Turoldesbi: King's land and the king's thanes from him.* Farm.

Thoresby (near Castle Bolton) *Toresbi: Gospatric from Count Alan.* Farms at High and Low Thoresby.

Thormanby *Tor/Turmozbi: King's land; Robert Malet.* Hill-top; partly Norman church.

Thornaby (on Tees) *Tormozbi(a)/Turmozbi: King's land; Earl Hugh; Robert Malet.* Urban district, now part of Stockton on Tees and the Tees-side conurbation; St Peter's church is partly Norman.

Thornton (near Thornaby on Tees) *Torentun: Earl Hugh; Robert Malet.*

Thornton (in Thornton Watlass) *Torreton/tun: Ribald from Count Alan.* Now combined with Watlass as a single village; spacious green; late 16th-century hall, remodelled in 1727; the Dodsworth family kept the Scropes' horses here when Catholics were forbidden to keep them; tumulus nearby.

Thornton Bridge *Torenton(e): Gospatric.* Thornton Manor and other houses at a crossing of the River Swale.

Thornton Dale *Torentona/tun(e): King's land; Berengar de Tosny.* Attractive, with Georgian mansions and Tudor thatched cottages; almshouses date from 1656.

Thornton Fields *Tornetun: King's land.* Some houses.

Thornton le Beans *Gri(s)torenun: King's land.* Roman road nearby.

Thornton le Clay *Torentun(e): Nigel from Count of Mortain; Count Alan; Robert Malet.* Sydney Smith (1771–1845) lived nearby when the Residence Bill compelled him to attend to his parish at Foston.

Thornton le Moor *Torentone/tune: Robert Malet.* Every house in the village was destroyed when the Scots invaded Yorkshire in 1318.

Thornton le Street *Torentun: King's land.* On site of a Roman settlement; stud farm.

Thornton Riseborough *Tornitun/entun: King's land.* Farms at Low Riseborough and Riseborough Hagg.

Thornton Rust *Tore(n)ton: Count Alan.* House called St Restitutus, from whom the hamlet takes its name.

Thornton Steward *Torenton(e)/tune: Gospatric from Count Alan. Church.* Church, although repaired by the Normans, still has Saxon traces and contains an Anglo-Danish crosshead. Cistercian Abbey 1145, nearby.

Thorpe (in Sutton on the Forest) *Torp: King's land.* Lost.

Thorpe (near Wycliffe) *Torp: Count Alan.* Houses and farms at Thorpe Hall, West Thorpe, South Thorpe and Thorpe Farm; Roman fort nearby.

Thorpefield (near Scarborough) *Torp: William de Percy.* Lost.

Thorpefield (near Thirsk) *Torp: Hugh FitzBaldric.* Some houses.

Thorpe Hill *Torp: Hugh FitzBaldric.* Farm.

Thorpe le Willows *Torp: King's land; Gospatric.* Houses at Thorpe Hall and Thorpe Grange.

Thorpe Perrow *Torp: Count Alan.* Mansion in landscaped grounds.

Thrintoft *Tirnecoste/etoste: Count Alan.* Remains of a medieval chapel, now part of a farm.

Tocketts *Tocstune/Toscutun: Richard from Count of Mortain.* Farm and mill.

Tollerton *Tolentun/Tolletune: Archbishop of York before and after 1066.* Near the River Kyle with a small green and a large windmill, on the edge of the vanished Forest of Galtres, which is mentioned in Shakespeare's *Henry IV*.

Tollesby *Tol(l)esbi: King's land; Robert Malet; king's thanes.* Suburb of Middlesbrough.

Topcliffe *Topeclive: William de Percy. Church, mill.* On the River Swale; mills; airfield nearby; only a few fragments of the 14th-century church, but there is magnificent 14th-century brass; William de Percy built a timber castle on the ancient earthworks at Maiden Bower and the Percys' medieval manor house was also nearby.

Towthorpe *Touetorp: Archbishop of York before and after 1066; Count of Mortain.* Near Strensall army camp; remains of a moat are next to the River Foss nearby.

Troutsdale *Truzstal: King's land.* House at Troutsdale Low Hall with scattered houses in Troutsdale and on Troutsdale Moor; extensive earthworks in the area.

Tunstall (near Catterick) *Tunestale: Count Alan.*

Tunstall (near Stokesley) *Ton(n)estale: King's land.* High Tunstall Farm.

Twislebrook *Tuislebroc: Count Alan.* Lost near Masham.

Ugglebarnby *Ugle/Ulgeberdesbi: Earl Hugh and William de Percy from him.* Hillside; the Lord of Ugglebarnby led the hunters whose murder of a hermit for protecting a boar about 1160 led to the yearly penance of 'Planting the Penny Hedge' in Whitby.

Ugthorpe *Ug(h)etorp: King's land.* Moorland; canoe coffin dating from 1700 BC and bronze age artefacts were found in a nearby barrow.

Upleatham *Upelider: Earl Hugh.* Hillside above a deep wooded valley; church has a Norman font.

Upper Helmsley *Hamelsec(h): Nigel from Count of Mortain.* Hall.

Upsall (near Eston) *Upes(h)ale: King's land; king's thanes.* Houses at Upsall Hall and East Upsall Farm.

Upsall (near Kirkby Knowle) *Upsale: Count of Mortain and Richard from him.* Remains of a 19th-century castle which was originally 14th century and a home of the Scropes.

Upsland *Opsala/Upsale: Count Alan.* Farm.

Walton *Waleton/tun(e): Berengar de Tosny; Hugh FitzBaldric.* Lost near Wombleton.

Warlaby *Warlavesbi/-lauesbi/Wergelesbi/-legesbi: King's land; Herveus from Count Alan.* Some houses.

Warthill *Wardhilla/Ward(h)ille: Archbishop of York before and after 1066; Count of Mortain.* Moat.

Wath (near East Tanfield) *Wat: Count Alan.* Brass effigies of the Norton family in the church; hump-backed bridge believed to have been originally built by the monks of Fountains Abbey.

Wath (near Hovingham) *Wad: 2 of Hugh's men from Hugh FitzBaldric.* Some houses.

Watlass (in Thornton Watlass) *Wadles: Ribald from Count Alan.* Now joined with Thornton in one village.

Welburn (near Bulmer) *Wellebrune: Nigel from Count of Mortain.* On the edge of the estate of Castle Howard; tumulus nearby.

Welburn (near Kirkby Moorside) *Wellebrune: King's land; Berengar de Tosny; Hugh FitzBaldric.*

Welbury *Welberga/Welleberg(e): King's land.* Roman road nearby.

WHITBY: *Probably the most spectacular cliff-top monastic site in Britain.*

Well *Welle: Bernulf from Count Alana. Church.* Church contains many references to the great Neville family and a section of floor mosaic from the nearby Roman villa; Ralph Neville rebuilt the Norman church (1320–50) and endowed the adjoining Hospital of St Michael for the poor.

Wensley *(Alia) Wendreslaga/In daubus Wendreslage: Count Alan.* Scattered; on the River Ure; the leading market town of Wensleydale until struck by the plague in 1563, when most people fled to Leyburn; Holy Trinity church was built in 1245 on Saxon foundations; Bolton Hall is 17th century.

WENSLEY: *Delightful font in Holy Trinity with carved date and pineapple-topped cover.*

West Acklam *Aclun/-lum/ Achelum: King's land; Earl Hugh and Hugh, son of Norman, from him; Count of Mortain; Robert Malet. Church.* Now a district of Middlesbrough; church has been made new; moat nearby.

West Ayton *(Alia) Atune: King's land.* On the west bank of the River Derwent; Ayton Castle is a ruined 14th-century tower house.

West Bolton *Alia Bodelton: Count Alan.* Farm.

West Burton *Burton: Goisfrid from Count Alan.* The large hillside green has a cross like a church spire on a flight of steps; waterfall nearby where Walden Beck falls into the River Ure.

West Harlsey *Herelsaie/ Herlessege/Herselaige/In daubus Erleseie: King's land.* Remains of the medieval Harlsey Castle.

West Hauxwell *Alia Hauoc(he)swelle: Ribald from Count Alan.* Isolated church and Hall.

Westhouse *Westhuse: King's land.* Lost near Yafforth.

West Layton *Laston/tun: Count Alan.* Roman road nearby.

West Lilling *Lilinga/inge: King's land; Nigel from Count of Mortain.* Moat.

West Newton *Neu/Newetune: King's land.* West Newton Grange, birthplace of the antiquarian Roger Dodsworth (1585–1654).

West Rounton *Runtune: King's land.* On the River Wiske; green; Norman traces in the church.

West Scrafton *Scalf/Scraftun: Ribald from Count Alan.*

West Tanfield *Alia Tanefeld: Count Alan.* Attractive; on the River Ure; 15th-century Marmion gateway is all that remains of the castle of the Marmion family; henges and barrows nearby.

West Witton *Witun: Count Alan.* In Wensleydale, on the northern slope of Penhill; custom of 'Burning Owd Bartle' in effigy on the Saturday after St Bartholomew's Day is thought to commemorate the fate of a local thief.

Whenby *Quennebi: King's land.* Isolated collection of farms and cottages; 15th-century church.

Whitby *Witebi/Streanaeshalch: Earl Hugh and William de Percy from him.* Town, resort and small port; fishing and boat-building. The boyhood home of Captain Cook (1728–79) is preserved; remains of the 13th-century abbey are on the site of the abbey of 657, which was destroyed by the Danes in 867.

Whitwell on the Hill *Witeuella/ uuelle/welle: One of Count Robert's men from Count of Mortain.*

Whorlton *Wirueltun(e): Count of Mortain.* Remains of a motte and bailey castle which was originally Norman and built by Robert de Meynell; gatehouse dates from 1400.

Wide Open *Wibedstune/ Wipestune: Archbishop of York before and after 1066.* Farm.

Wiganthorpe *Wichinga(s)torp: King's land; Count of Mortain; Berengar de Tosny.* Some houses; tumulus nearby.

Wigginton *Wichintun/istun: Archbishop of York.*

YORK: *An old wall safe in All Saint's church.*

Wildon *Wilema: Hugh FitzBaldric.* Houses at Wildon Grange and Wildon Hill Farm.

Wilton (near Eston) *Wid/ Wiltune: Nigel from Count of Mortain; Maldred from the king.* Early 19th-century castle is part of the administrative block for the nearby chemical works.

Wilton (near Pickering) *Wiltune: King's land.* Stone-built houses and farms.

Winton *Winetun(e): Bishop of Durham before and after 1066.* Some houses.

Wombleton *Wilbetun/ Winbeltun: Archbishop of York.*

Worton *Werton: Bodin from Count Alan.* In Wensleydale.

Wrelton *Wereltun: King's land.*

Wycliffe *Witclive/clive: Count Alan.* On the south bank of the River Tees; Wycliffe Hall was the home of the Wycliffe family, whose most famous member was John Wycliffe (c.1320–84), the religious reformer and translator of the Bible; church has a 13th-century nave and chancel, a hogback tomb and fragments of Saxon crosses; earthwork at Wycliffe Wood.

Wykeham (in Malton) *Wich/ Wicum: King's land.* Some houses.

Wykeham (near Scarborough) *Wic(h)am: King's land.* Wykeham Abbey nearby was a house of Cistercian nuns founded in the 12th century by Paganus de Wykeham.

Wykeham Hill (in Malton) *Wichum/Alia Wich(e): King's land; Archbishop of York before and after 1066; Ralph Pagnell. Church, mill.* Farm.

Yafforth *Eiford/Iaforbe/ Ia(i)forde: King's land; Count Alan.* Motte nearby.

Yarm *Geron/Iarun: King's land.* Town in a loop of the River Tees; almost an island, which makes it liable to flooding; many Georgian buildings; a meeting at the George and Dragon Inn in 1820 planned the first public railway – from Stockton to Darlington.

Yarnwick *Gernuie: Robert from Count Alan.* Lost near Sinderby.

Yearsley *Eureslage: Hugh FitzBaldric.* Tumulus nearby.

York *Eboracum/juxta civitatem (Eboraci)/juxta urbem: King's land; Archbishop of York before and after 1066; numerous other holders and burgesses. Churches, castle, many dwellings.* City and archiepiscopal see. University; racecourse; industries include chocolate (established by the Quaker families of Rowntree and Terry. The medieval city walls are largely intact and the Shambles is possibly the finest medieval street in Europe. St Peter's School, which claims to be the oldest in Britain, forbids bonfires as Guy Fawkes was a pupil.

Youlton *Ioletun(e)/Loletune: Archbishop of York before and after 1066.* James I is said to have slept at Youlton Hall.

YORK: *The Minster.*

Glossary

This brief glossary has been designed to give some of the most common words used in the Domesday entries, and in comments on the period. Some of the definitions are still a matter of disagreement between scholars, others have been more or less universally accepted.

Acre *acra, agra, ager* Measurement of land used in *Domesday* mainly for pasture, meadowland and woodland, which varied from region to region.

Arpent *arpent* Measurement of land originally a hundred square perches; used in *Domesday* for vineyards; about one modern acre.

Assart To clear land, to turn woodland into arable or pastureland.

B Marginal abbreviation in *Domesday* used to mean a berewic, or outlying part of a manor.

Before 1066 *(TRE)* In the time of King Edward the Confessor.

Berewic See B, above, and **Outlier.**

Bodyguard *Heuuard* The obligation to provide a lord with a bodyguard, or the king with one, during a visit.

Boor *borus* a peasant or a villager.

Bovate *bovata* An eighth of a carucate. Used in *Domesday* like carucate, for tax purposes.

Burgess *burgus* Holder of land or a house in a borough.

Cartage *avera* The obligation to provide mules or draught horses for the king's use.

Carucate *carucata, carrucata* Measurement of land in Danish counties, the equivalent of a hide. Used in *Domesday* for tax purposes.

Commote Welsh area or district.

Cottager *cotarius, coscat* A peasant of a lower class, probably with a cottage but often no, or very little, land.

Customary due *consuetudo* A regular fixed rent or service, or percentage of a tax.

Defence obligation *wara* The obligation for military service or for payment in substitution of personal service.

d Denarius The English silver penny, the only coin in circulation in 1086.

Dreng Free peasant especially used in Northumbria; he held lands in return for military service. Recorded in Yorkshire and Lancashire.

Escort *inward* The obligation to provide the king with a mounted man for his service or protection.

Exon *Exeter Domesday* An early draft of *Domesday* covering Cornwall, Devon, Somerset, parts of Dorset and one holding in Wiltshire.

Fief See Holding.

Forest *foras* Not necessarily woodland, but land reserved for the King's hunting; usually under Forest Law controlled by the Forester instead of the sheriff. Forests are never mentioned by name in *Domesday* except for the New Forest.

Freedman *colibertus, quolibertus* a former slave, now of similar status to the lower class of peasant.

Freeman *liber homo and sochemann* The two Latin terms have similar meanings; a villager of higher class than a villanus, with more land and obligations; a soke man, for example, was liable to attend the court of his soke.

Frenchman *Francus homo, francigena* A French settler, usually a Norman, of similar standing to a freeman.

Furlong *ferlinus, ferdinus, fertinus* A quarter of a virgate, or a measure of length, originally Roman; commonly 220 yards, similar to the modern furlong used in horse racing.

Geld See Tax.

Hide *hida* 120 acres, although this could vary, and sometimes was apparently around 240 acres. *Domesday* hide values were not real measurements of land, but figures on which tax (geld) was based.

Holding *feudum* Often translated as a fief; the land of a tenant-in-chief, or an under-tenant.

Honour *honor* A holding, or more often a group of holdings forming a large estate. Honor and feudum seem to be used interchangably in *Domesday.*

Housecarl Equivalent to a thane, or thegn, in Scandinavian parts of the country.

Hundred *Hundredum* Subdivision of a county, with its own assembly of notables and village representatives.

Go where he will Landholder free to place himself under the protection of a lord of his own choosing.

Inland *inland* Equivalent to 'in lordship'; such land was often exempt from tax.

Jurisdiction *saca et soca* The right to administer justice, and keep the resulting fines. Soca also meant the area over which an individual or manor had jurisdiction.

Landholder See tenant-in-chief.

Lease for three lives A term of a lease, usually for the life of the leasor, his son or wife and the grandson.

Leet Subdivision of Kent, similar to a Sussex rape.

Livery To be given rights or ownership of land as a gift from the king.

Lordship *dominium* Land held and farmed by the tenant-in-chief himself, or by the under-tenant himself (or herself).

M Marginal abbreviation in *Domesday* use to mean manor.

Man *homo* To be someone's man, to owe obligations to, usually in the form of labour or service. A woman could also be someone's man in this sense.

Man-at-arms *miles* A soldier holding his land specifically in return for military service.

Manor *manerium, mansio* Equivalent to a single holding, with its own court and probably its own hall, but not necessarily a manor house as we think of it. The manor was the basic unit of *Domesday*.

Mark *marka* Money of accounting purposes. A silver mark was worth 13s 4d, a gold mark was worth £6.

Mill A watermill. There were no windmills in England for another 100 years.

Moneyer Coiners; a person licensed to strike coins, receiving the dies from the government, and keeping 6 silver pennies in the pound.

Ora *ora* Money of accounting purposes worth 16d or 20d.

Outlier *berewica* Outlying part of a manor; a holding separate from a manor, taxed as if it were part of that manor rather than as a separate holding.

Packload *summa* A dry measure, used mainly for salt, corn or sometimes for fish.

Pannage *pannequion* Mast, or autumn feed for pigs, which were allowed to graze freely on the acorns and beechnuts on the woodland floor. The right to pannage is still part of some forest laws.

Plough *caruca, carruca* In *Domesday* the word implies a plough team with its eight oxen and the plough itself. The measure of a carucate was originally the amount of land which such a team could plough in one day.

Predecessor *antecessor* Previous land holder or holder of an office. Using the term implied that the succession has been legally made, and the powers have passed rightfully to the present holder.

Presentations *presentationes* A payment for fishing rights.

Rape One of five, later six, subdivisions of Sussex, each with its lord and castle.

Reeve *praepositus, praefectus* A royal official. Also a manor official, appointed by the lord, or sometimes elected by the peasants.

Relief *heriot* Money or kind paid to a lord by relatives after a man's death in order for them to inherit.

Revenue *firma* The provision which a manor owed the king, for example one night's keep for his court. In *Domesday* this is often translated into a money equivalent as cash replaced the barter economy.

Rider, Riding-man *radman, radcaitt* Riding escorts for a lord, chiefly recorded in the Welsh Marches.

Seat *caput* The principal manor of a lord. Still used today.

Sester *sextarium* Measure of volume, commonly used for honey, when it amounted to about 32 ounces.

Sheriff The royal officer of a shire, managing its judicial and financial affairs.

Shilling *solidus* Money for accounting purposes (there was no actual coin) worth 12 pennies.

Slave A man or woman who owed personal service to another, and who was un-free, and unable to move home or work or change allegiance, to buy or to sell, without permission.

Smallholder *bordariums* Middle class of peasant, usually with more land than a cottager but less than a villager.

Sokeman See Freeman.

Steersman Commander of a ship.

Sulong Measurement of land in Kent, usually 2 hides; used in *Domesday* for tax purposes.

Tax *Geldum* Periodic tax, first raised for the Danish wars, at a number of pence per hide, carucate or sulung.

Tenant-in-chief *Dominus* Lord (or institution, such as a church) holding land directly from the king; also called the 'landholder'.

Thane *tainus, teignus* Originally a military companion of the king, later one of his administrative officials. In *Domesday* most thanes were Anglo-Saxons, who had retained some of their land. Now known to most people through *Macbeth*, the thane of Cawdor.

Third Penny The local earl's share of fines in shire or hundred courts, often allocated afterwards to a particular manor or church as a regular income.

TRE *tempora regis Edwardis* In the time of King Edward the Confessor; by implication, when all in the realm was legally correct and ownership would have been rightfully secured.

Under-tenant Tenant holding land from a main landholder or tenant-in-chief.

Village *villa* Village; but the same Latin word was sometimes used for a larger village or a town.

Villager *villanus* Member of the peasant class with most land.

Virgate *virgata, virga* A quarter of a hide. Used in *Domesday* for tax purposes.

Yoke Measurement of land in Kent, a quarter of a sulung. Used in *Domesday* for tax purposes.

Wapentake *wapentac* Same as a hundred, in the Danish counties of England.

Warland Land which was liable for tax, in contrast to inland.

Waste Land which was either unusable or uncultivated, and in any case not taxed. Although sometimes waste was the result of William's wars in the North, it could also simply mean land not fit for agricultural use.

Major Domesday Landholders

Although many of the landholders listed in the Domesday Book are well-known to historians, others have vanished into obscurity, and we know little or nothing about them.

This, then, is not a complete list of all the names which have appeared in the previous pages, but it includes almost 200 brief biographical notes of the most important names together with a few other people who are known for some other aspect of their lives.

d'Abetot, Urso Also called Urso of Worcester. From Abbetot, Seine-Maritime. Brother of Robert the Bursar. Sheriff of Worcestershire. Helped crush revolt of Roger of Hereford, 1075. Took much land from Worcester church and Odo of Bayeux after his disgrace. Large holdings in Worcester. Also Glos., Herefords., Warwicks.

d'Aincourt, Walter Holdings in six midland and northern counties.

Aiulf the Chamberlain Brother of Humphrey the Chamberlain. Sheriff of Dorset and later (1091) Somerset. Large holdings in Dorset. Also in Berks. and Wilts.

Alan, Count See Brittany.

Albert the Clerk See Albert de Lorraine.

Alfred the Butler Butler to William I's half-brother, the Count of Mortain.

Alselin, Geoffrey Holdings in seven northern and midland counties, mostly taken from an Englishman, Toki.

Arden also called Thorkell of Warwick Descendant of the Danish earl, who retained lands in Warwickshire.

Aubrey, Earl See Northumbria.

d'Aubigny, Nigel From St Martin d'Aubigny, near Coutances. Eldest son took name of Mowbray, ancestor of Dukes of Norfolk. Large holdings in Beds. Also Bucks., Leics., Warwicks.

Baldwin, Abbot of Bury St Edmunds Abbot 1065–1097/8. Edward the Confessor's doctor. Abbey holdings in seven southern counties.

Bayeux, Odo, Bishop of Also Earl of Kent (1067–1082). Half-brother to William I, son of Robert of Normandy and Herleva his mistress. Regent in William I's absence. Arrested 1082, in prison at Rouen in 1086, pardoned by William I on his death-bed; rebelled against William Rufus in 1088, defeated; fled to Normandy, died 1097 on the First Crusade. Holdings in 22 counties, some still under his name, some not.

Beauchamp, Hugh de Ancestor of Beauchamp family; large holdings in Beds. Also in Herts. and Bucks.

Beaumont, Robert of Also called Count of Meulan which he became through his mother. Brother of Henry, son of Roger. Earl of Leicester from 1107; d.1118. Robert became close advisor of Henry I. His twin children, Robert who inherited the title, and Walerun, Count Meulan and later Earl of Worcester were a great influence on King Stephen. Gilbert de Clare was a brother-in-law; their half-brother William de Warenne became second Earl of Surrey. Holdings in Leics., Northants., and Warwicks.

Beaumont, Roger of Probably from Beaumont-le-Roger, Eure. Father of Henry and Robert. Old in 1086. Entered monastery of St Pierre, Preaux, 1094–95. Holdings in Dorset and Glos.

Bello Fargo, William of, Bishop of Thetford From Beaufour, Calvados. Nominated Bishop of Thetford, Dec. 1085; d.1091. Holdings in Norfolk and Suffolk. Church holdings in the same counties.

Berkeley, Roger de Became a monk of Gloucester in 1091. Large holdings in Glos. Also in Wilts. Brother, Ralph, had holdings in Glos. and was under-tenant in Somerset.

Bernay, Ralph de From Bernay, Eure. Sheriff of Herefordshire under Earl William FitzOsbern. Imprisoned by William I.

Beuvriere, Drogo de A Fleming who came to England with William I. Holdings in six counties in East Anglia, Midlands and North.

Bigot, Roger Also called Roger the Sheriff. From Les Loges, Calvados. Daughter married Robert of Stafford. Sheriff of Norfolk and Suffolk in 1086. Ancestor of Bigot family, the earls of Norfolk. Large holdings in Essex, Norfolk and Suffolk.

Blunt, Robert Also called *Albus, Blancardus* (white), *Flavus* (fair), *Blundus* (blonde). Holdings in Essex, Middx. and Suffolk.

Bolbec, Hugh of Heirs became Earls of Oxford. Large holdings in Bucks. Also in Berks., Hunts. and Oxon.

Boulogne, Eustace, Count of Son of Eustace, Count of Boulogne. Lands became Honour of Boulogne. Large holdings in Essex. Also in 11 other counties.

Braose, William de From Braose, near Falaise. Lord of the Sussex rape of Bramber, with castle there. Holdings in five other southern counties.

Breteuil, Earl Roger de Son of William FitzOsbern. Earl of Hereford, 1071, till 1075–76, when he rebelled with Earl Ralph of East Anglia and his lands were forfeited.

Brittany, Count Alan of Married William I's daughter, Constance. Also called Earl of Richmond. Head of Bretons in England. Large holdings in Yorks. Also in 12 other counties throughout the country.

Bully, Roger de Perhaps from Bully-en-Brai, Seine-Maritime. Described as 'famous in *Domesday* but nowhere else'. Founded priory at Blythe in 1088. Castle at Tikhill, Yorks. Holdings in six counties, mainly in the north but also in Devon.

Burcy, Serlo de Daughter married William de Falaise. Large holdings in Somerset. Also in Dorset.

Canterbury, Lanfranc, Archbishop of Norman archbishop, 1070–89. Won famous case against Odo of Bayeux at Penenden, 1072, for taking church lands. Holdings in Berks., Bucks., Kent and Suffolk. Abbey holdings in these and six other southern counties.

Canterbury, Stigand, Archbishop of Saxon Archbishop of Canterbury, from 1052–70, then deprived of lands. Died 1072.

Chester, Hugh, Earl of Also Earl of Avaranches. Also called Hugh Lupus (wolf) and Hugh the Fat. Nephew of William I, sister married Count William d'Eu; daughter, Matilda, married Count Robert of Mortain. Virtual sovereign of Cheshire. Captured Anglesea from the Welsh, 1098; became so fat he could barely crawl; d.1101. Holdings in 20 counties.

Chester, Peter, Bishop of Moved the diocese from Lichfield to Chester in 1075. Succeeded in 1085 by Robert de Limésy.

Chester, Roger, Bishop of Nominated 1085; moved see to Coventry 1102. Holdings in Herts. Church holdings in six other midland counties.

Chocques, Gunfrid de From Chocques, Pas-de-Calais. Holdings in Beds., Bucks., Leics., Lincs., Northants.

Chocques, Sigar de From Chocques, Pas de Calais. Holdings in Beds., Glos., Herts., Northants.

Christiana Princess of West Saxon house. Holdings in Oxon. and Warwicks.

de Clare, Richard see Tonbridge, Richard.

de Clare, Gilbert Son of Richard; conquered lands in Wales, to become Earl of Pembroke. Gilbert held Tonbridge Castle against Rufus in 1088 after William's death, but was reconciled later and also served Henry I. Died 1115.

Clifford, Walter Domesday commissioner.

Courbépine, Ralph de Holdings in Kent.

Courseulles, Roger de Also called Roger Whiting. From Coursellles-sur-Mer, Calvados. Large holdings in Somerset. Also in Dorset and Wilts.

Coutances, Geoffrey, Bishop of Also called Bishop of Lô. Bishop of Coutances from 1048; William I's trusted friend. A chief justice. Presided at Penenden, Kent, at case brought by

Lanfranc against Odo of Bayeux; rebelled with Odo and others against William Rufus, 1088; d.1093. Church holdings in 13 southern and midland counties.

Crispin, Miles Related to Gilbert Crispin, Abbot of Westminster. Married Maud, daughter of Roger d'Oilly. Castle at Wallingford. Lands became Honour of Wallingford. Holdings in Berks., Surrey and five other neighbouring counties.

Curcy, William de Married William I's daughter Emma.

Donkey, Hugh Probably served under Earl William FitzOsbern defending West against the Welsh. Lands later formed the Honour of Snodhill. Holdings in Glos., Hereford., Shrops., Wilts., Worcs.

Douai, Walter de Also called Walscin, a nickname. From Douai, Nord. Holdings in Devon, Essex, Somerset, Surrey, Wilts.

Drogo, Count See Mantes.

Drogo, FitzByntz see FitzPoyntz.

Durham, William, Bishop of Bishop of Durham, 1082–96. Chief justice and *Domesday* commissioner; driven from see by William Rufus. Abbey holdings in nine counties from Yorks. south to Beds.

East Anglia, Algar, Earl of Also Earl of Mercia 1057–62. Son of Countess Godiva and Earl Leofric. Married Countess Aelfeva. Father of rebel earls Edwin and Morcar. Earl of East Anglia 1051–52 and 1053–57; outlawed 1055 and 1058, but pardoned each time.

East Anglia, Ralph, Earl of Also called Ralph Waher and Ralph Guader. Rebelled with Earl Roger of Breteuil and Hereford, 1075. Married Emma, daughter of Earl William FitzOsbern.

Edeva the fair Possibly King Harold's mistress or sometimes identified with his first wife, Edith Swanneck.

Edith, Queen Daughter of Earl Godwin. Edward the Confessor's queen (d.1075). She rebuilt Wilton Abbey church for the Benedictine nuns.

Edric Sheriff of Wilts. before Edward of Salisbury.

Edward, King King Edward the Confessor, June 1042–5th Jan 1066.

Edwin, Earl See Mercia.

Essex, Swein of Son of Robert FitzWymarc. Probably once Sheriff of Essex; Castle at Rayleigh; greatest sheepmaster in Essex. Holdings in Essex and Hunts.

d'Eu, William, Count of Eu From Eu, port of Seine-Maritime. Second son of Count Robert. Second wife, Hugh of Chester's sister. Lord of Sussex rape of Hastings. Rebelled 1088 and 1094; blinded, castrated and executed, 1096. Holdings in nine southern and western counties.

Eudo, Count Father of Count Alan of Brittany.

Eudo the Steward See FitzHubert.

Eustace Sheriff of Hunts. Holdings in Hunts.

Eustace, Count see Boulogne.

Evreux, William, Count of Married to daughter of Walter de Lacy. Fought with his father, Richard, at Hastings. Holdings in Berks., Hants. and Oxon.

Exeter, Osbern, Bishop of Brother of Earl William FitzOsbern. Before the Conquest a Norman chaplain of Edward the Confessor. Favourite and chaplain of William I. Bishop of Exeter 1072/4–1103. Holdings in six southern counties. Church holdings in three more.

Fafiton, Robert Holdings in Beds., Cambs., Hunts., Middx.

Falaise, William de From Falaise, Calvados. Married daughter of Serlo de Burcy. Holdings in Devon, Dorset, Somerset, Wilts.

Ferrers, Henry de From Ferriers-St Hilaire, Eure. Lord of Longueville, Normandy; castle at Tutbury, Staffs.; *Domesday* commissioner. Ancestor of Earls of Derby. Large holdings in Derby. Also in 14 other counties.

FitzAnsculf, William Also called William of Pinkeni. From Picquigny, Somme. Son of Sheriff of Buckinghamshire. Castle at Dudley, Worcs. Holdings in 12 midland and western counties.

FitzAzor, Henry Holdings in Beds.

FitzAzor, Jocelyn Large holdings in IOW.

FitzAzor, William Large holdings in IOW. Probably brother of Jocelyn.

FitzBaderon, William Lord of Monmouth. Holdings in Hants., Herefords., Glos.

FitzBaldric, Hugh Sheriff of Nottinghamshire and Derbyshire. Holdings in Berks., Hants., Lincoln., Notts., Wilts. and Yorks.

FitzBohun, Humphrey From Bohun, La Manche. Ancestor of Earls of Hereford. Holdings in Norfolk.

FitzCorbucion, William Became sheriff of Warwicks. soon after 1086. Holdings in Berks., Staffs., Warwicks., Worcs.

FitzHubert, Eudo Also called Eudo the Steward. Youngest of four sons of Hubert of Ryes; married daughter of Richard FitzGilbert of Tonbridge; sister married Peter de Valognes. William I's steward, succeeding William FitzOsbern. Founded Abbey of St John's at Colchester. Castle at Préaux in Normandy. D. 1120. Large holdings in Cambridgeshire. Also in Beds., Essex, Herts. and Norfolk.

FitzHubert, Ralph Holdings in Derbys., Leics., Lincolns., Notts. and Staffs.

FitzNigel, William Constable of Earl Hugh of Chester. Ancestor of Lacy earls of Lincoln.

FitzOsbern, Earl William Also Earl of Hereford. Son of Osbern Sieward of Normandy; brother of Osbern, Bishop of Exeter. Married Adeline, sister of Ralph de Tosny. Large estates in west and Isle of Wight, broken up when his son, Roger, rebelled. Regent, with Odo of Bayeux, 1067.

FitzPoyntz, Drogo Son of William of Poyntz. Holdings in Glos., Herefords., Wilts., Worcs. Also 73 holdings in Devon as under-tenant of Bishop of Coutances.

FitzRalph, Harold Son of Earl Ralph the Timid. In 1086 held castle of Ewyas Harold in Worcs., named after him. Holdings in Glos., Warwicks. and Worcs.

FitzRolf, Thurstan Perhaps standard bearer at Hastings. Holdings in eight southern and western counties.

FitzStur, William From Tourville, near Cherbourg. Holdings in Hants. and IOW.

FitzThorold, Gilbert Follower of Earl William FitzOsbern, said to have collected gold for the king. Holdings in Cambridge., Essex, Glos., Herefords., Somerset and Warwicks.

FitzWymark, Robert Sheriff of Essex, succeeded by his son, Swein of Essex.

Flambard, Ranulf One time chief justice. Bishop of Durham, 1099–1128. Imprisoned by Henry I. Holdings in Hants. and Oxon.

Flanders, Walter of Perhaps the same as Walter Bec. Large holdings in Beds. Also in Bucks., Herts., Northants.

Fougères, Ralph de Holdings in Bucks., Devon, Norfolk, Suffolk, Surrey.

Gernon, Robert Name from *grenon, gernon*, meaning moustache. Ancestor of Cavendish family. Holdings in Bucks., Cambs., Herefords., Herts., Middx.

Ghent, Gilbert de Abbot from 1076. Came from French monastery of Marmoutie. Abbey holdings in southern counties. One of few to escape Danish siege of York in 1067; died 1094. Holdings in 15 counties from Berks northwards.

Giffard, Walter Son of Osbern of Bolbec. *Domesday* commissioner; keeper of Windsor Castle; Earl of Buckingham (1100); d.1103. Holdings in 10 counties.

Giffard, Osbern Holdings in Northamptonshire and five southern counties.

Gilbert Grus Bishop of Evreux. Made bishop in 1071; d.1118. Holdings in Suffolk.

Giles, brother of Ansculf Holdings in Berks., Bucks., Northants., Oxon.

Gloucester, Durand of Constable of Gloucester Castle. Sheriff of Gloucestershire 1086, succeeding his brother, Roger. Holdings in Hants. Wilts.

Goda, Countess Sister of Edward the Confessor, wife of Drogo of Mantes, then first wife of Count Eustace of Boulogne; d.1056.

Godiva, Countess Wife of Earl Leofric of Mercia, sister of Thorold, sheriff of Lincs., grandmother of rebel earls Edwin and Morcar. Famous for her naked bareback ride on a horse at Chester; founded Stow Priory near Lincoln. Holdings not yet re-granted, in Leics., Notts. and Warwicks.

Godwin, Earl Father of King Harold. Father-in-law of King Edward the Confessor, who married his daughter, Edith. Earl of the West Saxons; d.1053.

Grandmesnil, Hugh de From Grandmesnil, Calvados. Daughter married Roger of d'Ivry. Sheriff of Leicestershire, constable of Leicester Castle. Went into St Evroul's Monastery in Normandy and died there, 1094. Holdings in eight southern and Midlands counties. Wife's holdings listed separately, in Beds., Herts., Leics., Warwicks.

La Guerche, Geoffrey de Holdings in Leics., Lincs., Northants., Notts. and Warwicks.

Gytha, Countess Wife of Earl Godwin, mother of King Harold and Earl Leofwin.

Gytha, Countess Wife of Earl Ralph of Hereford (Ralph the Timid).

Hamo the Steward Also called Hamo the Sheriff. Sheriff of Kent; a judge at Penenden in case between Lanfranc and Odo of Bayeux. Holdings in Essex, Kent and Surrey.

Harold, King King of England, Jan–Oct 1066; usually called Earl Harold in *Domesday* since the Normans did not admit his claim to the throne.

Hereford, Earl Ralph of Also called Ralph the Timid. Son of Count Drogo of Mantes and Goda, Edward the Confessor's sister. Earl of Hereford *c.*1053–57; disgraced in 1055 for cowardice against the Welsh.

Hereford, Robert, Bishop of Bishop of Hereford 1079–95. Church holdings in Essex, Glos., Herefords., Oxon., Shrops., Worcs.

Hereford, Walter, Bishop of Bishop of Hereford, 1061–79. Chaplain to Edward the Confessor's Queen Edith.

Hesdin, Arnulf de From Hesdin, Pas-de-Calais. Large holdings in Wilts. Also in 10 other southern counties.

Hugh, Earl See Chester.

Hugh, son of Grip Also called Hugh of Warham. Sheriff of Dorset before Aiulf the Chamberlain; wife held his lands. Exon *Domesday* comments on his lack of land. Wife remarried Alfred of Lincoln.

Humphrey the Chamberlain Brother of Aiulf, Sheriff of Dorset; in service of Queen Matilda. Holdings in nine counties from Leics. south.

Huntingdon, Earl Waltheof of Son of Earl Siward, husband of Countess Judith. Earl of Northumbria. 1072–75; executed 1076.

Ilbert Sheriff of Hertfordshire.

Ivry, Roger d' Also called 'Butler'. From Ivry la Bataille, Eure. Married to Adeline, daughter of Hugh de Grandmesnil. Sworn brother-in-arms of Robert d'Oilly. Held several estates jointly. Perhaps Sheriff of Gloucestershire at one time. Holdings in Beds., Bucks., Glos., Hunts., Oxon., Warwicks.

Ivry, Hugh d' Butler in Norman household before 1066. Probably brother of Roger d'Ivry. Holdings in Oxon.

Jocelyn le Breton Holdings in Beds., Bucks., Glos.

Judith, Countess Niece of William I, daughter of his half-sister Adelaide and Lambert, Count of Lens. Widow of Earl Waltheof of Huntingdon and Northumbria, whom she betrayed. Holdings in 10 counties in Midlands and East Anglia.

Kent, Leofwin, Earl of Son of Countess Gytha and Earl Godwin, younger brother of King Harold. Earl of Kent and the home counties.

Keynes, William of Sheriff of Northants.

Kent, Odo, Earl of See Bayeux.

Lacy, Roger de Son of Walter de Lacy, succeeded him, 1085. Rebelled 1088 and 1094. Banished 1096; d. after 1106. Head of his fief at Weobley. Became Abbot of St Peters, Glos. Holdings in Berks., Glos., Herefords., Shrops., Worcs.

Lacy, Walter de From Lassy, Calvados. Western lands made him important defender against Welsh. Helped crush rebellion of Earl William FitzOsbern's son, Roger; d.1085. Succeeded by son Roger.

Leofwin, Earl See Kent.

Limesy, Ralph de From Limésy, Seine-Maritime. King William's sister's son, probably brother of Robert of Limesy. Holdings in 10 counties in East, West and Midlands.

Limesy, Roger de Probably brother of Ralph de Limesy. See Chester.

Lincoln, Remigius, Bishop of Provided William I with ships for invasion of 1066; moved see from Dorchester, Oxon., to Lincoln between 1072 and 1086; *Domesday* commissioner. Holdings in Beds., Berks., Bucks., Lincs. Church holdings in five other counties.

Lisieux, Gilbert, Bishop of Bishop of Lisieux, Calvados, 1077–1101. William I's doctor. Holdings in Yorks. Church holdings in Dorset, Herts., Glos., Oxon., Wilts.

London, Maurice, Bishop of Bishop of London, April 1086– 1107. Chancellor after Bishop Osmund of Salisbury. Holdings in Somerset. Church holdings in Dorset, Essex, Herts., and Middx.

London, William, Bishop of Bishop of London, 1051–1075. Church holdings in Dorset, Essex, Herts., and Middx.

Lorraine, Albert de A clerk or chaplain favoured by Edward the Confessor and William I. Holdings in Beds., Herefords., Rutland and Surrey.

Malet, Robert From Graville-Ste-Honorine, Seine-Inf. Son of William Malet. King William's great chamberlain; stronghold in Suffolk; probably Sheriff of Suffolk. Holdings in 10 counties from Essex and Surrey to Yorks.

Mandeville, Geoffrey de Perhaps from Mandeville, Eure. Ancestor of Earls of Essex. Lord of Pleshey. Holdings in 11 Home and Midlands counties.

Mantes, Count Drogo of Married Edward the Confessor's sister, Countess Goda. Father of Ralph the Timid, Earl of Hereford.

Marlborough, Alfred of Lord of Ewyas Harold Castle, Herefordshire. Holdings in Devon, Hants, Herefords., Somerset, Surrey and Wilts.

Matilda, Queen Matilda of Flanders. William I's queen; d.1083. Holdings still listed as hers in Bucks., Corn., Glos.

Mercia, Edwin, Earl of Son of Earl Algar of East Anglia. Rebellious earl, killed by his own men, 1071.

Mercia, Leofric, Earl of Married to Countess Godiva. Grandfather of rebel earls Edwin and Morcar.

Merleswein Sheriff of Lincolnshire.

Meulan, Count of See Beaumont, Robert.

Moeles, Baldwin of Also called Baldwin of Exeter, Baldwin de Brion, and Baldwin de Sap. From Meulles, Calvados. Son of Gilbert of Brion, brother of Richard FitzGilbert of Tonbridge. Sheriff of Devon. Castle at Okehampton. Custody of castle at Exeter. Large holdings in Devon. Also in Dorset and Somerset.

Mohun, William de From Moyon, La Manche. Head of Fief at Dunster, where he founded the priory, 1095. Holdings in Devon, Dorset, Somerset and Wilts.

Montfort, Hugh de Also called Hugh Beard. From Montfort-sur-Risle, Eure. Regent with Odo of Bayeux and Earl William FitzOsbern in 1067. Castle at Saltwood, with extensive Kent holdings to defend coast. Also holdings in Essex, Norfolk and Suffolk.

Montgomery, Count Roger of See Shrewsbury.

Morcar, Earl See Northumbria.

Mortagne, Matthew de From Mortagne, La Manche. Holdings in Berks., Dorset, Essex, Glos., Somerset, Wilts.

Mortain, Robert, Count of Half-brother of William I; younger brother of Odo of Bayeux; Married Earl Hugh of Chester's daughter. Lord of the Sussex rape of Pevensey, with castle there; Virtual earl of Cornwall; fief included Honour of Berkhamsted with castle there. Rebelled 1088; pardoned; d. 1091. Largest land holder in the country after the king. Holdings in 19 counties.

Mortimer, Ralph de From Mortemer, Seine-Maritime. Son of Roger. Lord of Wigmore Castle. Received lands which had been Earl Roger of Hereford's after his rebellion, 1075. Land in 13 counties all over the country.

Musard, Hascoit Named perhaps from *muscardus*, lazy or stupid. A Breton. Holdings in Berks., Bucks., Glos., Oxon., Warwicks.

Nigel the Doctor One of William I's doctors and perhaps also of Roger of Shrewsbury. Holdings in Hants, Herefords., Shrops. and Wilts.

Northumbria, Aubrey, Earl of Also called Aubrey of Coucy. Made Earl of Northumbria, 1080, but sent back in 1086 as incompetent. Holdings still listed as his in seven counties from Bucks. and Wilts. to Yorks.

Northumbria, Morcar, Earl of Son of Earl Algar of East Anglia. Chosen earl by Northumbrians in 1065 when they deposed Tosti, Harold's brother. Rebelled with his brother Edwin in 1071. In prison in 1086.

Northumbria, Tosti, Earl of Brother of King Harold. Became earl, 1055, deposed 1065 in favour of Morcar. Killed at Stamford Bridge, 25 Sept 1066.

Noyers, William de Probably from Noyers, Calvados. Had charge of many Norfolk and Suffolk manors for the king which had been Archbishop Stigand's.

Odo, Bishop see Bayeux.

d'Oilly, Robert Probably from Ouilly-de-Gasset, near Falaise. Probably married daughter of Wigot of Wallingford; daughter married Miles Crispin. Sworn brother-in-arms of Roger d'Ivry; held some estates jointly with him. Sheriff of Warwickshire in 1080s; also of Oxon. and perhaps of Berks.; Constable of Oxford Castle. Lands, with those of Miles Crispin became Honour of Wallingford. Holdings in eight Midland and Home counties.

Otto the Goldsmith Maker of William I's ornate tomb at Caen. His descendants were engravers for the king's mint. Holdings in Essex.

Pagnell, Ralph Sheriff of Yorkshire. Holdings in five other counties.

Percy, William de Holdings in Hunts, Lincs., Notts., Yorks.

Peverel, William Perhaps illegitimate son of William I by his mistress; took name of Peverel from stepfather, who married her. Large holdings in Notts. and Derbys. Also in six other counties.

Peverel, Ranulf Married former mistress of William I. Holdings in Berks., Norfolk, Oxon. and Suffolk.

Picot of Cambridge Sheriff of Cambs.; described as 'a roving wolf, a crafty fox, a greedy hog, a shameless dog, who feared not God'. Holdings in Cambs.

Poitou, Roger de Third son of Roger of Montgomery. In 1086 already had his holdings confiscated, perhaps for supporting William I's son, Robert of Normandy; later got most of them back. Holdings in Essex, Lincs., Suffolk and Yorks. shown as his; in Norfolk as *once* his; in Derbys., Lancs. and Notts. as in the king's hands.

Port, Hugh de From Port-en-Bessin, near Bayeux. Sheriff of Hants, 1070–96 and of Notts. and Derbys., 1081–1087; vassal of Odo of Bayeux; founded Sherborne Priory. Large holdings in Hants. Also in Berks., Cambs., and Dorset.

Ralph, Earl See Hereford. See East Anglia.

Ranulf, brother of Ilger Holdings in eight East Anglian and Home counties.

Reinbald the priest Also called Rainbald the Chancellor and Reinbald of Chichester. Appointed first chancellor of England by Edward the Confessor in 1042. Holdings in Bucks. and probably several other counties.

Ribald Brother of Count Alan of Brittany, probably an illegitimate son of Count Eudo.

Rhuddlan, Robert cousin and lieutenant of Count Hugh of Chester. Extended his territory into Wales.

Robert the Bursar Brother of Urso d'Abetot, who was Sheriff of Worcestershire; castle at Tamworth, Staffs. Holdings in Glos., Leics., Lincs., Warwicks.

Robert, son of Fafiton Holdings in Beds., Cambs., Hunts., Middx.

Robert, son of Gerald Holdings in Berks., Dorset, Hants, Somerset and Wilts.

Rochester, Gundulf, Bishop of Church holdings in Kent and 16 other southern and midland counties.

Roger, Earl See Shrewsbury. See Breteuil.

Ryes, Hubert de Father of Adam de Ryes and of Eudo the Steward. William I's ambassador to Edward the Confessor; persuaded the king to appoint William as his successor to English throne.

Salisbury, Edward of Also called Edward the Sheriff. Possibly an Englishman. Daughter married the second Humphrey de Bohun. Sheriff of Wiltshire; ancestor of Earls of Salisbury. Holdings in nine southern counties.

Salisbury, Osmund, Bishop of Earl of Seez, Normandy. Bishop of Salisbury, 1078–99; Memberof Privy Council, chancellor, 1073/8–1082; probably Earl of Dorset and Somerset. Canonised 1457. Holdings in Berks. and Lincs.; Church holdings also in Dorset, Oxon., Surrey and Wilts.

Samson, the Chaplain Chaplain to William I; Bishop of Worcester, 1096–1112. Possibly the *Domesday* scribe.

Scrope, Richard A Norman who settled in Herefordshire before the Conquest. Castle there.

Serlo, Abbot of St Peter's, Gloucester Abbot 1072– 1104. Abbey holdings in Herefords., Hants, Worcs.

Shrewsbury, Roger, Earl of Also Roger of Montgomery. From St Germain de Montgomery, near Lisieux. Lord of Sussex rape of Arundel, with castle there; Earl of Shrewsbury from 1071–74 to death in 1094. Holdings in 12 counties in south, east and west.

Siward, Earl Also called Siward bairn, (the warrior). Joined Edwin and Morcar in rebellion of 1071. Holdings in Notts.

Siward, Earl Digera (the strong) Father of Waltheof; d. 1056.

Spain, Alfred of From Espaignes, Eure. Large holdings in Somerset. Also in five other western and south-western counties.

Stafford, Robert of Son of Roger de Tosny, brother of Ralph; married Roger Bigot's daughter. Large holdings in Staffs. Also in five other western and Home counties.

Sturmy, Richard Probably Forester of Savernake, and ancestor of all subsequent Wardens of Savernake. Holdings in Hants. and Wilts.

Swein Son of Robert FitzWymark. Sheriff of Essex for a period between 1066 and 1086; built Rayleigh Castle. Holdings in Essex.

Tallboys, Ivo Also called 'cut-bush'. Married Lucy. In charge of siege of Hereward the Wake at Ely, 1069. Steward to William II. Holdings in Lincs. and Norfolk.

Tirrell, Walter Suspected murderer of William Rufus. Under-tenant in Somerset.

Tonbridge, Richard of Also called Richard de Clare, and Richard, FitzGilbert. Son of Count Gilbert of Brion, brother of Baldwin of Exeter. Lord of Clare, Suffolk, Lord of Lowry of Tonbridge and Tonbridge Castle. Holdings in eight counties from Suffolk to Devon.

Tosny, Berenger de Second son of Robert de Tosny. Holdings in Lincs., Notts., Oxon., Yorks.

Tosny, Ralph de Also called Ralph of Conches. From Tosny, Eure. Son of Roger de Tosny; older brother of Robert of Stafford; sister, Adeline, married Earl William FitzOsbern. Seat at Flamstead, Herts.; Lord of Clifford Castle, Herefordshire. Holdings in seven southern, East Anglian and Home counties.

Tosny, Robert de Founder of Belvoir Castle. Holdings in 13 counties from Herts. north.

Tosti, Earl See Northumbria.

Totnes, Iudhael of Large holdings in Devon. Also in Cornwall.

Valognes, Peter de Nephew of William I; married Albreda, sister of Eudo the Steward. Sheriff of Essex and Herts in 1086. Founded

Binham Priory, Norfolk. Holdings in six counties in the East.

Vere, Aubrey de Perhaps from Ver, La Manche, or Ver, Calvados. Ancestor of De Vere earls of Oxford. Large holdings in Hunts. Also in Cambs., Essex, Middx. and Suffolk.

Vessey, Robert of Holdings in Leics., Lincs., Northants and Warwicks.

Wader, Earl Ralph See East Anglia.

Walter, son of FitzOther Founder of the House of Windsor; keeper of the Forests of Berkshire and Constable of Windsor Castle; ancestor of FitzGeralds of Ireland. Large holdings in Bucks. Also in Berks., Hants, Middx. and Surrey.

Walter, Abbot of St Mary's of Evesham Abbot 1077–1104. Abbey holdings in Glos., Northants, Warwicks. and Worcs.

Wallingford, Wigot of Related to Edward the Confessor. His Butler. Sheriff of Oxon. Made peace with William I. By 1086 his lands had gone to Miles Crispin and Robert d'Oilly.

Waltheof, Earl See Huntingdon.

Warenne, William de From Varenne, near Bellencombre, Seine-Inf. Lord of the Sussex rape of Lewes, with castle there; created Earl of Surrey, 1088; died same year. Holdings in 13 counties all over the country.

William, (the) King William the Conquerer. Duke of Normandy 1035–1087. King William I of England 1066–87.

William, Count See Eu.

William the Chamberlain Son called 'William the Chamberlain of London'. Holdings in Beds., Bucks. and Glos.

Winchester, Walkelin, Bishop of Bishop of Winchester 1070–98; builder of the cathedral. Church holdings in nine southern counties, including Cambs. and Oxon.

Worcester, Wulfstan, Bishop of English Bishop of Worcester, 1061–95, only English bishop to be retained by William; simple and saintly man. Holdings in Glos., Warwicks., Worcs.

Wulfwold, Abbot of Chertsey Holdings in Berks., Hants. and Surrey.

York, Thomas, Archbishop Thomas of Bayeux. Brother of Samson, Bishop of Worcester. Archbishop of York, 1070–1100. Holdings in Glos., Hants. and Lincs. Church holdings in Leics., Lincs., Notts. and Yorks.

Bibliography

A.A. Book of British Towns Drive Publications Ltd. 1982

A.A. Book of British Villages Reader's Digest Association with Drive Publications Ltd. 1980

A.A. Book of Town Plans Automobile Association

A.A. Illustrated Guide to Britain Drive Publications Ltd. 1984

A.A. Road Book of England and Wales Automobile Association

A.A. Stately Homes, Museums, Castles and gardens in Britain Automobile Association 1982

A.A. Treasures of Britain Drive Publications Ltd. 1968 (revised 1977)

Anglo-Saxon Chronicles Transl. and coll. Anne Savage, Phillips/Heinemann 1982

The Anglo-Saxons Ed. James Campbell, Phaidon Press Ltd. 1982

Armstrong, J.R. **A History of Sussex** Phillimore & Co. Ltd. 1961

Aspden, J.P. **Warrington Hundred** 1947

Bagley, J.J. **A History of Lancashire** Phillimore & Co. Ltd. 1976

Bailey, Brian J. **Portrait of Leicestershire** Robert Hale Ltd.

Bailey, Francis A. **A History of Southport** Angus Downie. 1955

Baker, Timothy **Medieval London** Cassell Ltd. 1970

Ballard, C. **The Domesday Inquest** London* 1906

Banks, F.R. **English Villages** B.T. Batsford Ltd. 1963

Banks, F.R. **The Peak District** Robert Hale Ltd. 1975

Baring-Gould, Sabine **Further Reminiscences** The Bodley Head Ltd. 1925

Barker, Malcolm **Yorkshire, The North Riding** B.T. Batsford Ltd. 1977

Barley, M.W. **Lincolnshire and the Fens** E.P. Publishing Ltd. 1952

Barman, R.J. **The Parish Church of Melbourne, Derbyshire** Royden Green 1980

Barnard, E. **The Sheldons** Cambridge 1936

Bartholomew Gazetteer of Britain Comp. Oliver Mason, John Bartholomew & Son Ltd. 1977

Batey, M. **Nuneham Courtney** Oxford University Press 1970

Bayne, A.D. **Royal Illustrated History of Eastern England** James Macdonald & Co Ltd. c1875

Beckinsale, R. and M. **The English Heartland** Gerald Duckworth & Co. Ltd. 1981

Bellamy, Rex **The Peak District Companion** David & Charles Ltd. 1981

Bennett, Charles R. **The Story of Knutsford** The Knutsford Society 1975

Bentwich, Helen C. **History of Sandwich** The author 1975

Beresford, Maurice and Hurst, John G. **Deserted Medieval Villages** Lutterworth Press 1971

Besant, Walter **South London** Chatto and Windus 1898

Betjeman, John **Pocket Guide to Parish Churches** Wm. Collins PLC. 1975

Bettey, J.H. **Dorset** David & Charles Ltd. 1974

Bignell, Alan **Kent Villages** Robert Hale Ltd. 1975

Bird, James **Dunwich; A Tale of the Splendid City** Baldwin & Craddock 1828

Bird, James **Framlingham, A Narrative of the Castle** Baldwin & Craddock 1836

Bird, Vivian **Staffordshire** B.T. Batsford Ltd. 1974

Blue Guides to England Benn Bros. Ltd. 1972

Blue Guide to Wales and the Marches Ed. John Tomes, Benn Bros. Ltd.

Bond, C. **The Estates of Evesham Abbey** Vale of Evesham Historical Society (Vol. 4) 1973

Brach, Alan **The Wirral** B.T. Batsford Ltd. 1980

Bradfer-Lawrence, H.L. **Castle Rising** 1932

Branigan, Keith **Roman Britain** Reader's Digest Association Ltd. 1980

Brentwall, Margaret **The Cinque Ports and Romney Marsh** John Gifford 1980

Brett, Peter **Bonchurch** Bonchurch P.C.C.

Bricknell, D.C. **Guide to Wisley Gardens** The Royal Horticultural Society 1983

Brookes, C. **History of Steeple and Middle Aston** Oxford University Press 1929

Brooks, Peter **Have You Heard About Blakeney?** Poppeyland Publications 1981

Bryson, Emrys **Portrait of Nottingham** Robert Hale Ltd. 1974

Bulpot, Rev. W.T. **Notes on Southport and District** Privately 1908

Burke, John **Suffolk** B.T. Batsford Ltd. 1971

Burton, I.E. **The Royal Forest of the Peak** The Peak Park Planning Board 1966

Butterworth, G. **Deerhurst** Tewkesbury* 1890

Bygone Derbyshire Ed. William Andrews, Privately

Bygone Lincolnshire Ed. William Andrews, Privately 1891

Bygott, John **Lincolnshire** 1952

Byne, J. and Sutton, G.J. **High Peak** Martin Secker & Warburg Ltd. 1966

Cameron K. **The Place-Names of Derbyshire** Cambridge University Press 1959

Camp, Robert **Portrait of Buckinghamshire** Robert Hale Ltd. 1972

Carter, George A. **A History of Warrington to 1847** Warrington* 1947

Castles of England Charles Letts & Co. Ltd.

Chambers Biographical Dictionary W.R. Chambers Ltd. 1975

Cheal, Henry **The History of Ditchling** Lewes and South Counties Press 1901

Christian, Roy **Nottinghamshire** B.T. Batsford Ltd. 1974

Church, Richard **Kent** Robert Hale Ltd. Rep. 1972

Clark, Alan C. **Saltwood Castle** English Life 1975

Clarke, W.G. **In Breckland Wilds** Robert Scott 1925

Colbeck, Maurice **Yorkshire** B.T. Batsford Ltd. 1976

Colbeck, Maurice **Yorkshire, The Dales** B.T. Batsford Ltd. 1979

Coleridge at Nether Stowey Ed. Ursula Codrington, National Trust 1972

Concise Dictionary of National Biography Oxford University Press 1953

Cook, Olive **Breckland** Robert Hale Ltd. 1956

Copinger, W.A. **The Manors of Suffolk** Taylor, Garnett, Evans & Co. 1902

Cox, C. Carew **The Church of St. Michael the Archangel, Lyme Regis** Lyme Regis Parochial Church Council 1979

The Crabbet Arabian Stud Rosemary Archer and others Alexander Heriot 1978

Crouch, Marcus **Essex** B.T. Batsford Ltd. 1969

Crouch, Marcus **Kent** B.T. Batsford Ltd. 1966

Crowe, Austin M. **Warrington, Ancient and Modern** J.H. Teare & Son 1947

Dallaway, James **A History of the Western Division of the County of Sussex** T. Bensley 1815–30

Darby, H.C. **Domesday England** Cambridge University Press 1977

Darby, H.C. and Versey, G.R. **Domesday Gazetteer** Cambridge University Press 1975

Darson, William and White, William **A History, Directory and Gazetteer of Cumberland and Westmorland** 1829 (re-pub. Michael Moon 1976)

Davidson, Robin **Cornwall** B.T. Batsford Ltd. 1978

Davies, C. Stella **History of Macclesfield** Manchester University Press 1961

Defoe, Daniel **A Tour through the Whole Island of Great Britain** Penguin Books Ltd. 1971

Dent, Robert K. and Hill, Joseph **Historic Staffordshire** E.P. Publishing Ltd. 1975

Dicks, Brian **The Isle of Wight** David & Charles Ltd. 1979

Dictionary of National Biography Oxford University Press.

Domesday Book (History from the Sources) Ed. John Morris, Phillimore & Co. Ltd. 1975

The Domesday Geography of Eastern England Ed. H.C. Darby, Cambridge University Press 1952 and 1971

The Domesday Geography of Midland England Ed. H.C. Darby and I.B. Terrett, Cambridge University Press 1971

The Domesday Geography of Northern England Ed. H.C. Darby and I.S. Maxwell, Cambridge Univeristy Press 1962

Dorman, Bernard E. **Norfolk** B.T. Batsford Ltd. 1972

Drabble, Margaret **A Writer's Britain** Thames & Hudson Ltd. 1979

Dunning, Robert **A History of Somerset** Phillimore and Co. Ltd. 1983

Dyer, James **Prehistoric England and Wales** Allen Lane 1981

Eames, Elizabeth **English Medieval Tiles** Harvard University Press 1985

Early Cambridgeshire Alison Taylor and others The Oleander Press 1977

Earwater, J.P. **The History of the Ancient Parish of Sandbach** 1890

Edwards, Dudley George Cary **Castles, Mansions and Manors of Western Sussex** Longman & Co. 1876

Ellis, Sir Henry **A General Introduction to the Domesday Book** The Public Record Office 1833

English Romanesque Art 1066–1200 Arts Council of Great Britain with Weidenfeld & Nicolson 1984

Explore the New Forest Ed. Don Small, H.M.S.O. 1975

Eyton, R. **Antiquities of Shropshire** Russell Smith 1861

Fairburn, Neil **A Traveller's Guide to the Battlefields of Britain** 1983

Farrer, William **A History of the Parish of North Meols** Henry Young & Sons 1903

Fellows, Arnold **England and Wales; A Traveller's Companion** Clarendon Press 1964

Finberg, H.P.R. **The Early Charters of the West Midlands** Leicester University Press 1961

Finberg, H.P.R. **Gloucestershire (The Making of the English Landscape)** Leicester University Press 1975

Finberg, H.P.R. **Gloucestershire Studies** Leicester University Press 1957

Finn, R. Welldon **The Domesday Book, A Guide** Phillimore & Co. Ltd. with Rowman & Littlefield 1973

Finn, R. Welldon **Domesday Studies: The Eastern Counties** Longman Group Ltd. 1967

Firth, J.B. **Highways and Byways into Derbyshire**

Fletcher, H.L.V. **Herefordshire** Robert Hale Ltd. 1948

Fletcher, H.L.V. **Portrait of the Wye Valley** Robert Hale Ltd. 1968

Fodor's 1980 Guide to Great Britain Ed. Richard Moore, Hodder & Stoughton Ltd. 1980

Ford, Harry **Steyning** Steyning Society 1980

Ford, Trevor D. and Rienwerts, J.H. **Lead Mining in the Peak District** Peak Park Planning Board 1983

Forde-Johnston, James L. **Hillforts of the Iron Age in England and Wales** Liverpool University Press 1976

Foster, C.W. and Longley, T. **The Lincolnshire Domesday and the Lindsey Survey** 1924 (rep. 1976)

Fowles, John **A Brief History of Lyme** Friends of the Museum, Lyme Regis 1981

Fraser, Maxwell **Companion into Lakeland** Spurbooks 1973

Freeman, Edward A. **The History of the Norman Conquest of England** 1869–79 (Rep. University of Chicago Press 1974)

Freeman, Edward A. **The Reign of William Rufus** Oxford University Press 1882

Galpin, Francis W. **Hatfield Broad Oak** (from Essex Review, Oct. 1934 and April 1935)

Gant, Roland **Dorset Villages** Robert Hale Ltd. 1980

Gardner, Thomas **An Historical Account of Dunwich, etc** 1754

Garratt, Thomas **Original Poems** London* 1818

Gaunt, Arthur **History, People and Places in Yorkshire** Spurbooks 1975

Gay, Norman **Glorious Dunwich** Suffolk Press 1946

Gethyn-Jones, J. **Dymock down the Ages** A.E. Smith 1951

Gibbons, Thomas **An Account of a Most Terrible Fire that happened on Friday, the Eighth of September, 1727 at a Barn at Burwell** 1769

Green, John Richard **The Conquest of Britain** Date and publisher unknown.

Green, R. **The History, Topography and Antiquities of Framlingham and Saxsted** Whittaker, Treacher & Co. 1834

Gunn, Peter **The Yorkshire Dales. Landscape with Figures** Century 1984

Hadfield, John **The Shell Book of English Villages** Michael Joseph Ltd. 1980

Handpicked Tours in Britain Ed. Joe Burling, Reader's Digest Association Ltd.

Harrison, David **Along the South Downs** Cassell Ltd. 1958

Harrod, Wilhelmina **Norfolk** Faber & Faber Ltd. 1966

Haslam, Richard **The Buildings of England: Powys** Penguin Books Ltd. 1979

Haslewood, Francis **The Parish of Benenden, Kent** Privately 1889

Hatfield Forest National Trust Booklet 1978

Hey, David **The Making of South Yorkshire** Moorland Publishing Co. 1979

Higham, Roger **Berkshire** B.T. Batsford Ltd. 1977

Hill, M.H. **Bunny and Bradmore**

Hillaby, J. **The Book of Ledbury** Barracuda Books Ltd. 1982

Hilton, R. **A Medieval Society: the West Midlands at the End of the Thirteenth Century** Weidenfeld & Nicolson 1967

Hinde, Thomas **Forests of Britain** Victor Gollancz Ltd. 1985

Hogarth, F. Whewell **A History of Heysham** Morecambe*

Hogg, Garry **History, People and Places in Dorset** Spurbooks Ltd. 1976

Holder, Christopher **Wales, An Archaeological Guide**

Hoskins, W.G. **Essays in Leicestershire History** 1950

Hoskins, W.G. **Old Devon** David & Charles Ltd. 1966

Hoskins, W.G. **The Shell Guide to Leicestershire** Faber & Faber Ltd. 1970

Humphreys, J. **Studies in Worestershire History** Cornish 1938

Humphreys, J. **The Forest of Feckenham** Transactions of the Birmingham Archaeological Society (Vol. 45) 1919

Hunt, A. Leigh **The Capital of the Ancient Kingdom of East Anglia** A.G. Dennant 1870

Hurle. P. Upton. **A Portrait of a Severnside Town** Phillimore & Co. Ltd. 1979

Igglesdon, Charles **A Saunter through Kent with Pen and Pencil** Kentish Express 1928

Ingulph's Chronicle of the Abbey of Croyland Transl. Henry T. Riley 1854

James, Henry **English Hours** William Heinemann Ltd. 1905

Janaway, John **The Story of Godalming** Local Heritage Books 1983

Jennett, Sean **Cambridgeshire and the Isle of Ely** Darton, Longman & Todd Ltd. 1972

Jessup, Frank W. **A History of Kent** Phillimore & Co. Ltd. 1974

Jessup, Frank W. **Kent History Illustrated** Kent Education Committee 1966

Johnson, Derek **Essex Curiosities** Spurbooks 1973

Johnson, J. **Stow on the Wold** Alan Sutton Publishing Ltd. 1980

Johnstone, Clive and Weston, Winifred **The Which Heritage Guide** Consumers' Association and Hodder & Stoughton 1981

Jones, Charles A. **A History of Dedham** Wiles & Son 1907

Jowitt, D. and R. **Hampshire** Spurbooks 1975

Keates, Jonathan **The Companion Guide to the Shakespeare Country** Collins 1979

Kennet, David H. **Norfolk Villages** Robert Hale Ltd. 1980

Kent, Charles **The Land of the Babes in the Wood** Jarrold & Sons 1909

Kerr, Lord John **Melbourne Hall** Derbyshire Countryside 1979

Kerr, Nigel and Mary **A Guide to the Anglo-Saxon Sites** Granada 1982

Kerry, Charles **The History and Antiquities of the Hundred of Bray** Savill & Edwards 1861

Laing, Lloyd and Jennifer **A Guide to the Dark Age Remains in Britain** Constable & Co. Ltd. 1979

Leicester and Its Region Ed. N. Pye, Leicester University Press 1972

The Letters of Rupert Brooke Ed. Geoffrey Keynes, Faber & Faber Ltd. 1968

Lloyd, Michael **Portrait of Linconshire** Robert Hale Ltd. 1983

Lofthouse, Jessica **Portrait of Lancashire** Robert Hale Ltd. 1977

The London Encyclopaedia Ed. Ben Weinreb and Christopher Hibbert, Book Club Associates with Macmillan Ltd. 1983

Manning, S.A. **Portrait of Cambridgeshire** Robert Hale Ltd. 1978

Mannix and Whellan **History, Gazetteer and Directory of Cumberland** 1847 (Repub. Michael Moon 1974)

Marrat, W. **The History of Lincolnshire, Topographical, Historical and Descriptive** 1814

Maxwell, Herbert **The Life of Wellington** Sampson Low, Marston & Co. 1899

Maycock, A.L. **The Story of Little Gidding** Pamphlet 1980

Mee, Arthur **The King's England** Hodder & Stoughton Ltd.

Melbourne John Blunt and others, Derbyshire Countryside 1980

Memorials of Old Leicestershire Ed. Alice Dryden 1911

Memorials of Old Lincolnshire 1911

Midmer, Roy **English Medieval Monasteries, 1066–1540** William Heinemann Ltd. 1979

Millward, R. and Robinson, A. **The Welsh Borders** Eyre Methuen 1978

Muir, Richard **The Lost Villages of Britain** Michael Joseph Ltd. 1982

Muir, Richard **A Traveller's History of Britain and Ireland** Michael Joseph Ltd. 1983

Muir, Richard and Welfare, Humphrey **The National Trust Guide to Prehistoric and Roman Britain** G. Philip/National Trust 1983

Mumford, W. **Wenlock in the Middle Ages** Wildings 1977

The National Trust Guide (Revised Edition). Ed. Robin Fedden and Rosemary Joekes, Jonathan Cape Ltd. 1973

Nelson, L. **The Normans in South Wales (1070–1171)** University of Texas Press 1966

Neubecker, Ottfried **Heraldry. Sources, Symbols and Meaning** Macdonald & Co. Ltd. 1977

Nicholson, Cornelius **The Annals of Kendal** Whitaker & Co. 1861

Nicholson, Joseph and Burn, Richard **The History and Antiquities of the Counties of Westmorland and Cumberland** Repub. E.P. Publishing 1976

Nicolson, Nigel **The National Trust Book of Great Houses of Britain** The National Trust and Weidenfeld & Nicolson 1978

Old Blakeney Blakeney Preservation Society, Pamphlet

Ordnance Survey Maps 1:50.000 Landranger Series and 6″ Series

Oxted and Limpsfield Ed. Lewis G. Fry, W. & G. Godwin 1932

Paget, Rev. Francis E. **Some Account of Elford Church** Lichfield* 1870

Parker, John **Cumbria** John Bartholomew & Son Ltd. 1977

Parker, Sir William **The History of Long Melford** Wyman & Sons 1873

The Past All Around Us Ed. Noel Buchanan, Reader's Digest Association Ltd. 1979

Perks, J.C. **Chepstow Castle** H.M.S.O. 1978

Pevsner, Nikolaus **The Buildings of England** Penguin Books Ltd. 1951 onwards

Phil, David H. **Yorkshire, The West Riding** B.T. Batsford Ltd. 1977

A. Phillips **A Look Round the Monasteries of North-East Yorkshire** H.M.S.O. 1962

Phillips, Robert **Faringdon – A Short History of a Wessex Town** Privately

Porter, Lindsey **A Visitor's Guide to the Peak District** Moorland Publishing Co. 1985

Porteous, Chrichton **Derbyshire** Derbyshire Countryside 1970

Poucher, W.A. **The Peak and the Pennines** Constable & Co. Ltd. 1966

Proctor, Alan **A Visitor's Guide to Somerset and Dorset** Moorland Publishing Co. 1983

R.A.C. Great Britain Road Atlas 1977

R.A.C. Guide and Handbook 1983

Rackham, Oliver **Trees and Woodlands in the British Landscape** J.M. Dent & Sons Ltd. 1976

Raistrick, Arthur **West Riding of Yorkshire** Hodder & Stoughton Ltd. 1970

Rees, H.G. St. Michael **A Short history of the Paris and Church of Mildenhall**

Rendall, Gerald H. **Dedham in History** Benham & Co. 1937

Reynolds, Susan **An Introduction to the History of English Medieval Towns.**

Rhea, Nicholas **Portrait of the North York Moors** Robert Hale Ltd. 1985

Rice, H.A.L. **Lake Country Towns** Robert Hale Ltd. 1974

Rogers, P.G. **Battle in Bossendon Wood** Privately

Rowley, T. **The Shropshire Landscape** Hodder & Stoughton Ltd. 1972

Rowley, Trevor **The Norman Heritage 1055–1206** Routledge Kegan Paul plc. 1983

Rowse, A.L. **Ralegh and the Throckmortons** MacMillan Ltd. 1962

Sayles, G.O. **The Medieval Foundations of England** Methuen & Co. Ltd. 1948

Scarfe, Norman **Essex**, Faber & Faber Ltd. 1968

Scarfe, Norman **Suffolk** Faber & Faber Ltd. 1960

Scarfe, Norman **The Suffolk Landscape** Hodder & Stoughton Ltd. 1972

Scott, W.S. **Selborne** B.B. Patton 1977

Seymour, John **The Companion Guide to East Anglia** William Collins plc. 1970

Shaw, Stebbing **The History and Antiquities of Staffordshire** E.P. Publishing 1976

The Shell County Guides Ed. John Betjeman and John Piper, Faber & Faber Ltd.

The Shell Guide to Britain and Northern Ireland, Ed. Geoffrey Boumphrey, Ebury Press with George Rainbird 1967

The Shell Guide to Country Museums Comp. Kenneth Hudson, William Heinemann Ltd. 1980

Simmons, Jack **Leicester Past and Present** Methuen & Co. Ltd. 1974

Skillington, S.H. **A History of Leicester** 1923

Skipp, V. **The Central Midlands** Eyre Methuen 1978

Slack, Margaret **Portrait of West Yorkshire** Robert Hale Ltd. 1984

Smith, Tom C. and Shortt, Rev. Jonathan **The History of the Parish of Ribchester** Bemrose & Sons 1890

The South Saxons Ed. Peter Brandon, Phillimore & Co. Ltd. 1978

Stapleton, Michael **The Cambridge Guide to English Literature** Cambridge University Press and Newnes Books 1983

Steinberg, S.H. **Historical Tables 58 BC. – AD. 1965** Papermac 1966

Stenton, Sir Frank Merry **The First Century of English Feudalism: 1066–1166** Oxford University Press 1932

Stenton, Sir Frank Merry **The Free Peasantry of the Northern Danelaw** Oxford University Press 1969

Steward, A.V. **A Suffolk Bibliography** Suffolk Records Society 1979

Stokes, J. and A.E. **Just Rutland** 1953

Stories of Old Blyth in Nottinghamshire S.D.A. Widdowson and others, Ratcliff & Roper 1977

Sturges, George W. **Edmonton Past and Present** The Montagu School Press 1941

Suffolk, The County of, The British Publishing Co. Ltd.

Sulley, Phillip **The Hundred of Wirral** Birkenhead* 1889

Swinburne, A.C. **Studies in Song** Chatto & Windus 1880

Sylvester, D. **Rural Landscape of the Welsh Borderland** The MacMillan Press Ltd. 1969

Taylor, A. **Minster Lovell Hall** H.M.S.O. 1955

Taylor, John George **Our Lady of Battersea** George White 1925

Taylor, William **The Pictorial Guide to Castle Rising** Norfolk 1858

Tease, Geoffrey **London** Thames & Hudson Ltd. 1975

Tonkin, J.W. **Herefordshire** B.T. Batsford Ltd. 1977

Toy, Sidney **The Castles of Great Britain** Heinemann Educational Books Ltd. 1966

A Translation of that Portion of the Domesday Book which Relates to Lincolnshire and Rutlandshire Charles G. Smith 1870

Veysey, A. Geoffrey **Mr. Gladstone and Hawarden** Clwyd Record Office

The Victoria History of the Counties of England Archibald Constable & Co. Ltd./W.H. Smith/ Oxford University Press for the University of London 1900

Wagner, Sir Anthony **Heralds and Ancestors** British Museum Publications Ltd. 1978

Wales: A New Study Ed. David Thomas

Warren, W. Lewis **Henry II** Eyre Methuen 1973

Warriner, Frank **The Millom District** 1932 (repub. Michael Moon 1974)

Warriner, Frank **Millom People and Places** Michael Moon 1974

Webb, William **Kent's Historic Buildings** Robert Hale Ltd. 1977

Wedderspoon, John **Historic Sites of Suffolk** J.M. Burton 1841

White, Joan **Boughton-Under-Blean** Faversham Society 1983

Whitlock, Ralph **Wiltshire** B.T. Batsford Ltd. 1976

Wiches, Michael **A History of the Parish of Great Gidding, Steeple Gidding and Little Gidding** Pamphlet 1979

Widnall, S.P. **A History of Grantchester** The author 1875

Wightman, W. **The Lacy Family in England and Normandy 1066–1194** Oxford University Press 1966

Williams, Moelwyn **The Making of the Welsh Landscape: South Wales** Hodder & Stoughton Ltd. 1975

Wilson, Derek **A Short History of Suffolk** B.T. Batsford Ltd. 1977

Wood, G. Bernard **Yorkshire** B.T. Batsford Ltd. 1967

Woodruffe, Brian J. **Wiltshire Villages** Robert Hale Ltd. 1982

Wright, Christopher John **A Guide to the Pilgrim's Way and the North Downs Way** Constable & Co. Ltd. 1971

Wright, Christopher **Kent through the Years** B.T. Batsford Ltd. 1975

Wright, Geoffrey N. **View of Wessex** Robert Hale Ltd. 1978

Wright, Geoffrey N. **The Yorkshire Dales** David & Charles Ltd. 1977

Wright, J. **History of Ludlow** Jones

Yarrow, Ian **Berkshire** Robert Hale Ltd. 1974

Yaxley, David **Portrait of Norfolk** Robert Hale Ltd. 1977

*Denotes place of publication, where publisher is not known.

Index to Main Text and Major Entries

Acknowledgements

We would especially like to thank the following libraries and organisations: The Telegraph Information Service; Kensington Reference Library; The London Library; Ordnance Survey; Victoria County history; Historical Association; British Museum Map Library; Abingdon Library, Oxford; The Cornwall Local Studies Library and the County Planning Department, Cornwall County Council.

We are also grateful to: Colchester Central Library, Local Studies; English Place Names Society; Chester Library; Hereford and Worcester County Libraries; Clwyd Library and Museum Service; Westcountry Studies Library; Leicestershire Record Office; Hertfordshire Local Studies Collection; Surrey County Library, Local Studies; Staffordshire County Library; Hillingdon Borough Libraries; East Sussex County Libraries; The Local Studies Collection, Kendal Library; Somerset Local History Library; Lincolnshire Recreational Services, Libraries and Archives; Local Studies Department, Shropshire Libraries; Wiltshire Library and Museum Service; Warwickshire County Library.

Picture acknowledgments
Marianne Majerus pp 6–7, 22–3, 26–7, 28, 31, 33, 34, 38–9, 46, 57, 58, 63, 66, 67, 73, 74, 75, 90, 91, 98, 99, 107, 108, 110–11, 117, 118, 119, 121, 127, 128, 135, 142–3, 145, 151, 152, 154, 158, 159, 166, 167, 179, 180, 182–3, 193, 198, 199, 206, 207, 214, 215, 220, 221, 222, 223, 224, 225, 233, 234, 245, 246, 250–1, 253, 265, 270–1, 273, 274, 279, 281, 289, 290, 297, 298, 302, 315, 326–7.
Public Records Office pp 14–15, 21
Anthony Short p 122
Stephen Beer p 174
Phillimore Ltd p 19
The Pierpoint Morgan Library p 206
The British Tourist Authority for all remaining photographs.